Contents

Introduction

In December 2005 the Qualifications and Curriculum Authority (QCA) issued its 2004/5 Annual Report on the teaching of History in secondary schools, based on investigation of curriculum, assessment, and qualifications issues. The QCA (a public body sponsored by the Department of Education and Skills, and governed by a board appointed by the Secretary of State for Education and Skills) drew on a wide range of evidence provided by individual teachers and learners, as well as by national agencies, including the Universities and Colleges Admission Service and the Office for Standards in Education. Additional evidence was gathered through conferences, seminars, focus groups, and other less formal communications. The report received immediate and widespread coverage in the media, which, unexpectedly, focused on the QCA's concern over black history. For the first time in British educational history, an official body had pronounced explicitly on the need for recognition of the black presence in Britain.

> Too little attention is given to the black and multi-ethnic aspects of British history. The teaching of black history is often confined to topics about slavery and post-war immigration or to Black History Month. The effect, if inadvertent, is to undervalue the overall contribution of black and minority ethnic people to Britain's past and to ignore their cultural, scientific and many other achievements. (*History 2004/5 Annual Report on Curriculum and Assessment*, QCA/05/2169, 2005)

The Oxford Companion to Black British History (*OCBBH*) aims to fulfil the QCA's call for greater recognition of black British history. It is a text that can be used in educational establishments as well as by the general public. It incorporates and builds upon the pioneering scholarship of Paul Edwards, Christopher Fyfe, Gretchen Gerzina, C. L. R. James, Kenneth Little, Edward Scobie, F. O. Shyllon, James Walvin, and Eric Williams, among others (see the Select Bibliography).

The September 1981 International Conference on the History of Blacks in Britain, organized by the universities of Edinburgh (Ian Duffield) and London (Jagdish Gundara), was a milestone in the study of black British history, bringing together new and established scholars from around the globe and giving unusual prominence to the subject (*History Today*, a journal with the specific aim of bringing important historical issues to a wide readership, devoted a whole issue to the subject, to coincide with the Conference). In his address to the Conference, James Walvin declared that, until the 1970s, black history was not even peripheral to the mainstream of British historiography, 'the basic texts lacking all but a passing reference to the history of Blacks in this country' ('The Emergence of British Black Historical Studies', unpublished paper presented to the 1981 International Conference on the History of Blacks in Britain). Walvin argued that three factors contributed crucially to the emergence of the discipline. Firstly, the flowering of social history in the 1960s, with the publication of E. P. Thompson's *The Making of the English Working Class* (1963). The study of the history of the common people—lost, forgotten, or neglected people—eventually encouraged scholarship that made British Blacks visible, using unconventional sources like local authority records, rates books, trade pamphlets, court records, private papers, baptismal records, gravestones, oral testimonies, etc. Secondly, the growth of African Studies following the rise of African nationalism and the movement for independence (exemplified by the scholarship of Walter Rodney, Philip Curtin, and others). Thirdly, the explosion of African-American studies, resulting from the Civil Rights Movement in the United States from the 1960s onwards (exemplified in the scholarship of Eugene Genovese, Michael Craton, and others).

To this list must be added the spectacular pioneering efforts of educationists and activists such as Gus John and Len Garrison, who since the 1970s had pushed for the incorporation of black history into the school curriculum. Garrison initiated the pioneering Afro-Caribbean Education Resource Centre in 1977, and, in 1981, the Black Cultural Archives in Brixton, initiatives intended to foster the development of black history within schools, and to bring together a wealth of materials suitable for young people of different age groups.

For decades, black parents, at the forefront of efforts to support their children within an educational system that undervalued their educational ability, have mobilized within and outside formal education systems to support the teaching of black history to their children. In Saturday and supplementary schools up and down the country, black parents and teachers have, since the 1960s, gathered to impart their knowledge of black history and culture to their children. These early initiatives were important in preserving the subjugated knowledge of black peoples, and in fostering mainstream initiatives and debates about the importance of black history as an academic subject in schools and higher educational institutions.

It is a measure of the success of scholars, grassroots educationists–activists, and parents that the teaching of black history is now widely accepted as necessary and integral to the curriculum. However, we are still at the beginning of this process. While African-Americans are currently engaged in debates about the content of Black History syllabuses within US institutions of higher education, the same debate is of little relevance in the United Kingdom, where in 2006 it remains impossible to pursue a degree in Black History.

The 1981 Conference ushered in a decade of landmark publications, which included Peter Fryer's *Staying Power: The History of Black People in Britain* (1984), Beverley Bryan, Stella Dadzie, and Suzanne Scafe's *Heart of the Race: Black Women's Lives in Britain* (1985), James Berry's edition of the first major anthology of black British poetry, *News for Babylon* (1984), and a new 1985 edition of Mary Seacole's *Wonderful Adventures* by Audrey Dewjee and Ziggy Alexander. The University of Warwick established its Centre for Caribbean Studies in 1984, with a view to promoting teaching and research on Caribbean and black British history and culture. It launched a prestigious and mainstream publication series with the publishers Macmillan. Hakim Adi, Stephen Bourne, Jeffrey Green, Roger Lambo, Howard Rye, Marika Sherwood, and others organized seminars and meetings that led eventually to the formation of the Association for the Study of African, Caribbean, and Asian Culture and History in Britain, and the launch of a newsletter in 1991. Black publishing houses such as Akira Press, Bogle-L'Ouverture, Hansib, Karia Press, Karnak House, and New Beacon Books produced a stream of literary and historical texts. Local history societies such as the Birmingham Black Oral History Project, the Black Cultural Archives (London), and the Butetown Oral History and Arts Project (Cardiff) made invaluable discoveries and contributions to black British historiography. Exhibitions, conferences, radio and television programmes, university courses, and a variety of other activities, such as guided tours, carnivals, poetry readings, and dramatic productions, from the 1980s to the present day have sustained the study and appreciation of black British history and culture. *OCBBH* is an attempt to consolidate the efforts of researchers, teachers, local activists, artists, and cultural practitioners by presenting in a single volume a scholarly and readable account of the black presence in Britain over the past 2,000 years.

Black people have lived in the British Isles since Roman times. There were so many of them in Shakespeare's London that the first Queen Elizabeth, in an ominous anticipation of 20th-century Powellite calls for repatriation, sought to have them all deported. Nevertheless, the increasingly complex and interdependent relations between Britain and its colonial possessions ensured that, since the later 16th century, black men and women have had a constant presence in these islands, as servants of the rich in country houses, as anonymous members of the London poor, but also as political campaigners, merchants, students, writers, musicians, soldiers, sailors, broadcasters, doctors, nurses, sporting personalities, and members of almost every imaginable occupation. The 18th-century writer Olaudah Equiano served in the Royal Navy on one of the earliest British voyages of exploration to the Arctic; nearly two centuries later the future Prime Minister of Barbados, Errol Barrow, like many other Caribbean people, served in the Royal Air Force during the Second World War. Not only great cities like London, Bristol, and Liverpool, but smaller ports such as Lancaster, were shaped by their trade with Africa and the Caribbean.

The arrival of the *Empire Windrush* in 1948, with some 450 immigrants from what were still the British colonies in the Caribbean, was new in scale and marked the beginning of the great post-war immigration that transformed British institutions like London Transport, the Post Office, and the National Health Service; but it should be seen only as a continuation of a process that is centuries old. At the same time, it must be emphasized that the black presence has been one not only of new arrivals but of settled communities, sometimes absorbed into their surroundings by intermarriage, like the descendants of Samuel Johnson's black servant Francis Barber: many apparently white British people of the present day have known or unknown black ancestors.

In 1998 the fiftieth anniversary of the arrival of the *Windrush* led to a number of celebrations, including radio and television programmes and print publications, which demonstrated the extent to which the black presence in Britain has come to be recognized as an integral part of the cultural landscape. Change continues in many ways: there is a greater visibility of black people in the political process, including in both Houses of Parliament, while at the same time new black communities, from places like Sudan or Somalia, have joined longer-established groups of Caribbean or West African origin or descent.

The *OCBBH* seeks to give coverage to nearly 2,000 years of black British history, from the presence of African soldiers defending Hadrian's Wall in the second century AD to contemporary issues relating to refugees and asylum-seekers.

Inevitably, there are important omissions. Paul Edwards has written briefly on black slaves in Ireland in AD 862, taken there after Viking raids in Moorish Spain and North Africa (*The Early African Presence in the British Isles*, Occasional Papers, no. 26, Centre of African Studies, Edinburgh University, 1990), but there has been no further research on the black presence in medieval Britain. Insufficient material prevents an entry on the 200 black attendants who accompanied William of Orange to Britain in 1688. Apart from Lucy MacKeith's discovery of a broadsheet account of William of Orange's arrival in Exeter on 17 October 1688, with 'two hundred Blacks, brought from the Plantations of the Neitherlands in America, Imbroyder'd Caps line'd with white Fur, and Plumes of white Feathers, to attend the Horse', no further documentation has come to light (*Local Black History: A Beginning in Devon*, 2003). Lack of data also prevented entries on individuals like John Blanke, the black trumpeter portrayed in the painted roll of the 1511 Westminster Tournament, held to celebrate the birth of a son to Catherine of Aragon. Apart from knowing that he was employed by both Henry VII and Henry VIII, at a rate of 8*d*. a day, and that the Court owed him 20*s*. in November 1507, no other biographical details have been found so far. Gravestones and church documents offer tantalizing glimpses of black people, but again, the records are too scanty for individual entries. Who, for instance, was Philip Scipio? He was buried on 10 September 1784 in Devon, the register of Werrington church stating that he was 'A black servant to Lady Lucy Morice'. The gravestone, now fixed to the exterior wall of the church, states:

Deposited Here
Are the Remains of Philip Scipio
Servant to the Duke of Wharton
Afterwards to Sir William Morice
An African
Whose Quality might have done Honour
To any Nation or Climate
And Give Us to See
That Virtue is Confined
To no Country or Complexion

Here Weep
Uncorrupted Fidelity
And Plain Honesty

In a pious regard to which virtue's approv'd
By a brother and husband

Who was the African baptized in 1642 in St Margaret's Church, King's Lynn, described as 'a black More of Mr Seth Hawleys . . . suppos'd about 11 or 12 years old'? His Christian name given to him at the font was Peter and he was surnamed Lynn after the town. In 1673 another black boy, 'Jeremiah, formerly call'd Andrew', was baptized in South Lynn church, and that is all that is known of him. Who was 'Mary Negro', baptized at St Stephen's Church, Exeter, on 16 February 1689? There are several hundred black people in 17th- and 18th-century records, but only their given Christian names testify to their existence. As James Walvin states, most black people in this period are consigned to the anonymous level of inanimate property, and are completely lost to history.

'Slavery is terrible for men; but it is far more terrible for women,' declared the formerly enslaved woman Harriet Jacobs in *Incidents in the Life of a Slave Girl* (1861), her autobiographical narrative. Harriet's searing indictment of the particular burdens exacted by the 'peculiar institution' of slavery on enslaved women has long been, and continues to be, a persistent refrain in anti-slavery literary writings. Yet, until recently, traditional historiographies of slavery paid scant attention to the specific experiences of women, black or white, free or unfree, within slave societies. If black people, as a group, have been largely written out of British colonial and imperial history, how much more so has been the case for black British women. With a few notable exceptions—the courageous nurse Mary Seacole, who made as much of a contribution to the development of her profession as Florence Nightingale, and Mary Prince, whose narrative of her experiences as an enslaved woman became a potent weapon in the armoury of the abolitionist movement—little is known about the historical experiences of the thousands of black women who for centuries resided, forcibly or voluntarily, in Britain. Why, for instance, do we not know the fate of Mary Prince after she won her struggle for freedom? Why do we not even know if Prince eventually returned to Bermuda to be reunited with her husband, Daniel James, or if she died in Britain? How is it possible that a woman who made such an impact on the struggle for the abolition of slavery simply disappears out of history?

African-American women have made great strides in the recovery of their histories, but similar progress has yet to be made by black women on this side of the Atlantic. The result is the almost total invisibility of black women in British history. A few glimpses are offered of ordinary individual women such as the infamous prostitute Black Harriot, but it is a measure of the disdain with which black women are held that Harriot has survived into historical memory because of her seedy occupation. What of the 80 West Indian nurses who went to Britain to nurse the wounded soldiers of the First World War? Rather more is known about the women of the Auxiliary Territorial Service who left the relative safety of the Caribbean to support the war effort in Britain, but what of ordinary black women who had lived for generations in Britain? Why do we know so little about those whose labour in raising, nurturing, and educating their children enabled the survival of their communities over so many centuries? That so many of the black women who appear in this volume are of African-American origin testifies to the neglect of black women's history in Britain. In this volume we have tried to ensure that as many black British women as possible are included, but we recognize that those who appear here are by no means the only ones to have made lasting contributions to the making of Britain. There is an urgency for more scholarship that would retrieve those others from their obscurity.

Another major omission is an entry on science and technology, simply because of the scarcity of information on black British contributions to the field. Documentation on African-American achievements is plentiful. Full biographies exist on engineers and scientists such as Elijah McCoy (1843–1929; the inventor of an automatic lubricator for machines) and Lewis Latimer (1848–1928; a member of Thomas Edison's research team and inventor of a process for making carbon filament for electric bulbs), but relatively little on black Britons such as John Edmonstone (who taught Charles Darwin taxidermy in the early 19th century) or the several 19th- and early 20th-century doctors who contributed to the development of British medicine.

This volume, nevertheless, is offered to the reader as an archive, incomplete as it is, of current knowledge of the black British presence, and in the expectation that its publication will not only provoke discussion and debate but will sustain ongoing research and encourage new scholarship, the results of which will, we hope, be included in any future editions of the *OCBBH*.

DD, JG, and CJ

Acknowledgements

For nearly two millennia people of African origin have contributed in diverse and significant ways to the creation of the rich multicultural society that is modern Britain. A few of those individuals are well known, but the majority remain anonymous. It has been a key objective of this *Companion* to uncover, name, and make known the achievements and struggles of the many thousands of black people who, over centuries, have helped to shape the social, political, and cultural landscape of Great Britain. This ambitious task has only been made possible by the involvement of a great many individuals. Happily, we are able to name and acknowledge the majority of the many people who contributed to the making of this volume.

Firstly, we would like to thank Michael Cox, Commissioning Editor at Oxford University Press, who conceived the idea for this *Companion*, and whose vision and encouragement was vastly inspiring to the writing of this historic project. We would also like to extend our thanks to our Advisory Editors, Vincent Carretta, Harry Goulbourne, David Killingray, James Walvin, and Lola Young, who proposed themes and contributors, and generally allowed us to plunder their vast collective knowledge. Their advice was highly instrumental in shaping the outline of the book. A multi-authored, interdisciplinary reference work such as this *Companion* necessarily relies greatly on the willingness of many individuals to share their expertise. We owe a tremendous debt of thanks to the many contributors (see the list of Editors and Contributors) whose diverse knowledge has been so crucial in enabling the rich history of the black British presence to be written. Certainly, as editors, reading and editing their essays has been a deeply enriching and fascinating learning experience for us also. Without doubt, the contributors are among the book's main assets. Our gratitude also goes to the doctoral students Jonathan Morley, Erin Somerville, and Shivani Sivagurunathan, who provided invaluable editorial and administrative assistance throughout. Many colleagues at the University of Warwick and elsewhere supported us in their own ways, offering encouragement, advice, and suggestions for inclusion. Pam Coote, Elizabeth Knowles, Jo Spillane, and the production team at Oxford University Press (especially the Production Editor, Sarah O'Connor, and copy-editor, Laurien Berkeley) deserve special praise for the patient professionalism they brought to the creation of this book. Their excellent advice and guidance on content and style was supplemented by their keen interest in black British history, and their collective dedication to the project's completion.

Finally, the editors wish to convey personal thanks and appreciation to their families and friends, many of whom were, inevitably, forced to give up part of their own lives in order to afford us the time and space to complete the project. David Dabydeen would like to thank Rachel Dabydeen. As always, John Gilmore would like to thank Marita and the children, Alex, Annabelle, and Giselle, whom he hopes will one day read the results. Cecily Jones offers praise and thanks to Ian Jones.

Editors and Contributors

General Editors

David Dabydeen is the former Director of the Centre for Caribbean Studies at the University of Warwick, and is now Professor of Literary Studies at the university. He is Guyana's Ambassador to the United Nations' Educational, Scientific, and Cultural Organization. His research interests are 18th-century black British writers and contemporary Caribbean literature.

John Gilmore is an Associate Professor at the Centre for Caribbean Studies and the Centre for Translation and Comparative Cultural Studies at the University of Warwick. Among his many publications are *Faces of the Caribbean* (2000) and *The Poetics of Empire: A Study of James Grainger's 'The Sugar Cane'* (2000). His research interests include 18th-century Latin poetry by Caribbean writers.

Cecily Jones is Director of the Centre for Caribbean Studies at the University of Warwick, where she also lectures in the Department of Sociology. Her research interests address the intersections of gender, 'race'-ethnicity, and class in New World slave-based plantation societies, enslaved children, and colonial slavery.

Advisory Editors

Vincent Carretta is a Professor at the University of Maryland. His books include *Equiano the African: Biography of a Self-Made Man* (2005) and editions of the works of Cugoano, Equiano, Sancho, and Wheatley.

Harry Goulbourne is Professor of Sociology at London South Bank University. His books include *Race Relations in Britain Since 1945* (1998) and *Caribbean Transnational Experience* (2002).

David Killingray is Emeritus Professor of History at Goldsmiths College, University of London. He has written books and articles on African, Caribbean, Imperial, and English local history, and also on the history of the black diaspora.

James Walvin is Professor Emeritus at the University of York. His books include *Black Ivory: Slavery in the British Empire* (2001) and *Atlas of Slavery* (2005).

Lola Young is a writer and broadcaster on culture. She is an arts and heritage consultant and sits as a cross-bench peer in the House of Lords.

Contributors

AFFR Anne Rainsbury is Curator at Chepstow Museum. Her interests cover all aspects of Chepstow's local history and historical links to the West Indies. Major exhibitions on Piercefield and Nathaniel Wells (2003) prompted extensive personal research, including at the St Kitts National Archives.

AJD Alison Donnell is a Reader in English and Postcolonial Literatures at Nottingham Trent University.

AM Annecka Marshall is a Lecturer in Gender and Development Studies at the Mona Campus of the University of the West Indies. Before working in Jamaica she taught sociology, and feminist and anti-racist courses in England.

AME Melinda Elder is an Associate Lecturer for the Open University.

AML Angela Leonard is an Assistant Professor in the Department of History, Loyola College, in Baltimore, Maryland.

AR Anthony Reddie is a Research Fellow at the Queen's Foundation for Ecumenical Theological Education in Birmingham, and is a consultant in Black Theological Studies for the British Methodist Church. He is also an Honorary Lecturer in the Theology and Education Departments of the University of Birmingham. In addition to being the author of several books, he is the editor of *Black Theology: An International Journal*.

ARF Ana Raquel Fernandes took her degree in Modern Languages and Literatures at Lisbon University. She received an MA in Comparative Literature. Since 2004 she has been a visiting student at the University of Warwick (where she is working on a Ph.D. in British Contemporary Literature) and lectured in the Department of Hispanic Studies at the University of Birmingham.

AS Annell Smith is the Programme Manager, London Probation Area.

ASS Amon Saba Sakaana is a writer and publisher.

ASW Amar Wahab is currently a postdoctoral Research Fellow at the University of Warwick. His research and teaching are in the areas of marginality and social exclusion, cultural studies, and Caribbean Studies.

AW Anne Walmsley is a former teacher and publisher in the Caribbean, and was herself an active member of the Caribbean Artists' Movement (CAM). She writes on the region's literature and visual arts. Publications include two school anthologies, a book on the artist Aubrey Williams, and a history of CAM.

BR Bob Ramdhanie has been involved in black performing arts in England since 1965. He has established professional performance companies and arts centres and completed a Ph.D. in 'African Dance in England'.

BW Brigid Wells is a retired teacher and former headmistress.

CA Cassandra Adjei did her MA at the Centre for Translation and Comparative Cultural Studies, University of Warwick.

CB Charlotte Breese studied at the Sorbonne and Bristol University, worked in publishing for many years, and is presently researching funerals. Her book *Hutch* was published in 1999 in hardback by Bloomsbury and the paperback version was launched at the University of the West Indies, Grenada, in 2001.

CF Christopher Fyfe taught African History at the University of Edinburgh from 1962 to 1991. His publications include *A History of Sierra Leone* (1962).

CFW Charlotte Williams is a Senior Lecturer in Social Policy in the Faculty of Humanities and Social Sciences at Keele University. She is co-editor of *A Tolerant Nation? Exploring Ethnic Diversity in Wales* (2003) and author of *Sugar and Slate* (2002).

CG Christabel Gurney is a freelance writer and editor.

CJ Cecily Jones. See 'General Editors' above.

CLI Lyn Innes is Emeritus Professor of Postcolonial Literature at Kent University, Canterbury. Her *History of Black and Asian Writing in Britain* was published in 2002.

CMC Christopher Campbell is a lecturer in Colonial and Post-Colonial Literatures, Queen Mary, University of London.

CN Charmaine Nelson is Assistant Professor of Art History, McGill University, Montreal.

DD David Dabydeen. See 'General Editors' above.

DEP Dianne Payne is a Ph.D. student at the University of Hertfordshire researching 'The Children of the Poor in London 1700–1780'.

DF Don Flynn is Policy Officer, Joint Council for the Welfare of Immigrants.

DHJ Douglas H. Johnson is Managing Director and Editorial Director of James Currey Publishers, a leading academic publisher of books on Africa.

DK David Killingray. See 'Advisory Editors' above.

DKP D. Keith Peacock is a Senior Lecturer in Drama at the University of Hull. His books include *Radical Stages, Harold Pinter and the New British Theatre* (1991) and *Thatcher's Theatre* (1999).

DL Dan Louw is a graduate of the University of Warwick. He has made documentaries for a variety of domestic and international broadcasters and has written for a number of music publications, including the *NME* and *Melody Maker*.

DO David Olusoga is a writer and television producer.

ECa Ellis Cashmore is Professor of Culture, Media, and Sport at Staffordshire University. His main area of research is contemporary culture, including sport and race and ethnic studies.

ECh Eddie Chambers is a curator and a writer of art criticism.

EDS Erin D. Somerville is a Ph.D. student at the University of Warwick working on Caribbean literature, environment, and culture. Her research focuses on the works of Sam Selvon.

GG Gretchen Gerzina is Professor of English at Dartmouth College in New Hampshire and an Honorary Fellow at

Exeter University. Her books include *Carrington: A Life* (1989); *Black England: Life Before Emancipation* (1995); *Black Victorians/Black Victoriana* (2003); and *Frances Hodgson Burnett: The Unpredictable Life of the Author of 'The Secret Garden'* (2004). She has appeared many times on British television and radio.

GH Glenford D. Howe is a graduate of the University of the West Indies and the University of London. He is currently employed at the Cave Hill (Barbados) campus of the University of the West Indies as a Senior Programme Officer, and has written extensively in the areas of history, education, and health.

HA Hakim Adi is a reader in the History of African Diaspora at Middlesex University. He is the author of *West Africans in Britain* (1998) and, with Marika Sherwood, *The 1945 Pan-African Congress Revisited* (1995) and *Pan-African History* (2003).

HB Hilary Beckles is Pro-Vice Chancellor and Principal of the Cave Hill (Barbados) campus of the University of the West Indies. He has published extensively on the history of Barbados and the Caribbean.

HG Harry Goulbourne. See 'Advisory Editors' above.

HR Howard Rye is co-author of *Blues and Gospel Records 1890–1943* (1997), principal researcher for *The New Dictionary of Jazz*, and a member of the editorial team of *Names and Numbers*.

HSM Heidi Safia Mirza is Professor of Racial Equality Studies at Middlesex University. She is known internationally for her work on ethnicity, gender, and identity in education.

IJ Ian Jones graduated from Queen Mary, University of London, with a degree in English Literature and has worked in the criminal justice system for many years.

IR Ismail Rashid is an Associate Professor in the History Department, Vassar College, Poughkeepsie, New York.

IvR Ingrid von Rosenberg has taught English Literature and British Cultural Studies at various German universities, most recently at the Technische Universität, Dresden. Her main areas of research are working-class culture, gender studies, and black and Asian British culture.

JAHE John Evans lectures at the Cardiff University Centre for Lifelong Learning on Industrial Archaeology of Communities in the South Wales valleys.

JC John W. Cairns is Professor of Legal History at the University of Edinburgh. His main interests lie in the 18th century.

JD Jenny Douglas is a Senior Lecturer in the Faculty of Health and Social Care at the Open University.

JG John Gilmore. See 'General Editors' above.

JHR Jane Robinson is a social historian and biographer.

JJGG James Graham is a Postgraduate Research Fellow at the University of Warwick. His primary research interests are in South African and Zimbabwean Literature.

JLMJ Jacqueline Jenkinson is a Lecturer in the History Department at the University of Sterling. She has researched and published extensively on the 1919 port riots in Britain, and also on health issues and health policy in 19th- and 20th-century Scotland.

JM Jonathan Morley is a Ph.D. student in Caribbean Literature and Modernism at the University of Warwick, the Editorial Director of the Heaventree Press, Coventry, and an Eric Gregory Award winning poet.

JPG Jeffrey Green is an independent historian who has published and lectured widely. He is especially interested in the period 1890–1930.

JPo Jane Poyner is a Lecturer in English at the University of Exeter, specializing in post-colonial literature and theory. She has written a monograph and edited and introduced a collection of essays on the South African novelist and intellectual J. M. Coetzee, and is now preparing her second monograph on the ethics of intellectual practice in post-apartheid literature.

JRP James Procter is Senior Lecturer at the University of Newcastle upon Tyne.

JW James Walvin. See 'Advisory Editors' above.

JWP John Picton is Emeritus Professor of African Art at the School of Oriental and African Studies, London University. He previously worked for the Nigerian government Department of Antiquities (1961–70) and the British Museum (1970–9).

JYD Jessica Dolcourt completed a Master's programme in Race and Ethnicity at the University of Warwick. Her areas of interest include the 'mixed-race' concept, comparative 'race'–ethnic structures, and the racialization of ethno-religious difference.

KAC Kathy Chater is a Ph.D. student at Goldsmiths College, University of London.

KHA Humayun Ansari is Director of the Centre for Ethnic Minority Studies, Royal Holloway, University of London.

KJ Kenny Jervis is a film-maker who was educated at Brunel University. His current work includes a documentary about Randolph Turpin entitled *A Forgotten Champion*.

KJC Karen Chouhan is a Visionary for the Joseph Rowntree Charitable Trust, and the 1990 Trust Board Member.

KJPL Kate Lowe is Professor of Renaissance History and Culture at Queen Mary, University of London. Her research interests include sub-Saharan Africans and people of African descent in Renaissance Europe.

KLG Kevin Le Gendre is a journalist and broadcaster with a special interest in black music and literature. He is the deputy editor of *Echoes* magazine and also contributes to the *Independent on Sunday*, *Jazzwise*, and BBC Radios 3 and 4.

KDO Kerstin D. Oloff is a Ph.D. student funded by the Arts and Humanities Research Council, and a Fellow in the Humanities Research Centre at the University of Warwick. Her research focuses on the works of three contemporary writers from the Caribbean and Latin America.

KO'B Karen O'Brien is Professor of English Literature at the University of Warwick

KS Kadija Sesay is a publisher of *SABLE LitMag*, series editor for the Inscribe imprint for Peepal Tree Press, and editor of several anthologies of work by writers of African descent.

LFK Leila Kamali is a Ph.D. student in the Department of English and Comparative Literary Studies at the University of Warwick. Her research concerns the ideal of Africa in contemporary African-American and black British fiction.

LG Letizia Gramaglia is a Ph.D. student in Caribbean Studies at the University of Warwick.

LKJ Linton Kwesi Johnson is a poet and recording artist.

LM Lynne Macedo is a Lecturer at the Centre for Caribbean Studies, University of Warwick.

LMacK Lucy MacKeith writes on black history and creates events for Black History Month in Devon. She works for the Devon Racial Equality Council.

LP Leslie Primo is a Lecturer at the National Gallery, London.

LET Laura Tabili is Associate Professor of Modern European History at the University of Arizona, and author of *'We Ask for British Justice': Workers and Racial Difference in Late Imperial Britain* (1994).

LW Leon Wainwright is a Lecturer in History of Art and Design at Manchester Metropolitan University. During 2004–5 he conducted fieldwork on visual and material culture in Trinidad and Guyana. His forthcoming book, *Diaspora Presence*, examines art of the African, Asian, and Caribbean diasporas in contemporary Britain.

LY Lola Young. See 'Advisory Editors' above.

MA Muhammad Anwar is Research Professor at the Centre for Research in Ethnic Relations, University of Warwick, where he was Director (1989–94). He was previously Head of Research at the Commission for Racial Equality (1981–9). He has written extensively on ethnic and race relations.

MGN Michael Niblett is a Ph.D. student working on Caribbean literature at the Centre for Translation and Comparative Cultural Studies, University of Warwick.

MJ Mike Jay is an author and historian. His books include *The Unfortunate Colonel Despard* (2004).

MJD Madge Dresser is Principal Lecturer in History at the University of the West of England. Author of *Slavery Obscured*, a study of the slave trade in Bristol, she is currently leading a Lottery-funded research project on 'Identity and the City: A History of Ethnic Minorities in Bristol *c.*1000–2001'.

MK Miranda Kaufmann is currently working on a Ph.D. entitled 'Africans in Early Modern Britain' at Christ Church, Oxford.

MSe Mark Sebba is Reader in Sociolinguistics and Language Contact in the Department of Linguistics and English Language at the University of Lancaster. In the 1980s he carried out research into the language of young African-Caribbeans in London, reported in his book *London Jamaican: Language Systems in Interaction* (1993). His interests include pidgin and Creole languages, bilingualism, and the sociolinguistics of spelling.

MSh Mimi Sheller is a Visiting Associate Professor in the Department of Sociology and Anthropology at Swarthmore College, and a Senior Research Fellow in the Centre for Mobility Research at the University of Lancaster. Her books include *Consuming the Caribbean* (2003), *Democracy After Slavery* (2000), and she co-edited *Uprooting/Regroundings* (2003).

NAA Nazneen Ahmed is studying for a D.Phil. in English Literature at Wadham College, University of Oxford. Her main areas of research are post-colonial literature and theory.

PAH Philip Herbert is a pianist, composer, and musicologist.

PBP Pathik Pathak is a Lecturer in Sociology at the University of Southampton.

PF Peter Fraser was formerly a Lecturer in History at Goldsmiths College, University of London.

PFW The Revd Paul F. Walker is minister of Highgate Baptist Church in Birmingham.

PK Philip Kaisary is a Ph.D. student in the Department of English and Comparative Literary Studies at the University of Warwick. His research focuses on the literary impact of the Haitian Revolution.

PM Parita Mukta is a Senior Lecturer in the Department of Sociology at the University of Warwick.

PNa Philip Nanton is Project Officer HIV/AIDS Response Program, University of the West Indies, Barbados.

PNu Paul Nugent is Professor of Comparative African History and Director of the Centre of African Studies at the University of Edinburgh. He has published *Big Men, Small Boys and Politics in Ghana* (1995); *Smugglers, Secessionists and Loyal Citizens on the Ghana–Togo Frontier* (2002), and *Africa Since Independence* (2004), and is the co-editor of four other books. He is also the Reviews Editor for *Africa: Journal of the International Africa Institute* and an elected member of the Council of the Royal African Society.

PR Peter Ratcliffe is Professor of Sociology and Director, UK National Focal Point for the European Monitoring Centre on Racism and Xenophobia.

PV Phil Vasili is a leading historian of British football. His books include *Colouring Over the White Line: The History of Black Footballers in Britain* (2000).

REL Rainer Lotz is a retired civil servant and lecturer in political science, and is an expert in jazz. He has compiled many anthologies of historic recordings, and is the recipient of an Association for Recorded Sound Collections Lifetime Achievement Award for excellence in recorded sound research.

RHC R. H. Costello was Education Adviser for Racial Equality, and is now an Educational Consultant specializing in the education of black children. He is the author of books on the history of Liverpool's black community.

RIL Richard I. Lawless is Emeritus Reader in Middle Eastern Studies at the University of Durham. His current research includes the history of the Yemeni diaspora and transnationalism in historical perspective.

RKPP Richard Pankhurst is the founder and first Director of the Institute of Ethiopian Studies at Addis Ababa University. He is the author of numerous works on Ethiopian history and culture.

RLT Robert Tignor is the Rosengarten Professor of Modern and Contemporary History at Princeton University. His books include *Worlds Together, Worlds Apart: A History of the Modern World* (2002).

RPB Richard Paul Benjamin is an archaeologist in the Department of Archaeology at the University of Liverpool. His chief interests are archaeological theory, community archaeology, and black British heritage.

RR Ron Ramdin is a member of the Mayor of London's Commission on African and Asian Heritage. His books include *The Making of the Black Working Class in Britain* (1987) and *Reimaging Britain: 500 Years of Black and Asian History* (1999).

RS Richard Smith teaches in the Department of Media and Communications at Goldsmiths College, London, where he researches race and masculinity during the First World War and Jamaica in the popular imagination 1900–62.

SB Stephen Bourne is the author of *Black in the British Frame: The Black Experience in British Film and Television* (2001) and *Speak of Me As I Am: The Black Presence in Southwark Since 1600* (2005).

SD Susan Dray is an Honorary Research Fellow at the University of Lancaster.

SGD Sharae Deckard is a Warwick Postgraduate Research Fellow in the Department of English and Comparative Literature at the University of Warwick. Her Ph.D. researches the uses of the paradise motif in post-colonial fiction.

SIM S. I. Martin is a writer and researcher working with London's museums, archives, schools, and borough councils. He is the founder of the 500 Years of Black London Walks and has published widely.

SM Sharon Meredith is a freelance ethnomusicologist specializing in Caribbean music, identity representation through music, and the revival of traditional music as popular culture in post-colonial contexts.

SS Shivani Sivagurunathan is a Ph.D. student at the Centre for Translation and Comparative Cultural Studies, University of Warwick.

SUM Sanjay Mistry is Communications Manager, Working Ventures UK.

SW Simon Woolley is Director of Operation Black Vote.

TL Tanuka Loha is a founding member of the Global Citizenship Foundation. She has been an anti-racist activist for eighteen years, working in the UK and internationally with communities, NGOs and governments for equality and justice. Her areas of interest are race, ethnicity, faith, gender, policing, citizenship, identity, and human rights. She is a (non-practising) barrister and has a Masters in Race and Ethnicity.

VC Vincent Carretta. See 'Advisory Editors' above.

VJP Victoria Perry is a practising architect, writer, and historian. Her latest work, *A Bitter-Sweet Heritage*, traces the links between sugar, slavery, and the development of British art, architecture, and landscape.

Thematic Contents List

All entries in the book are listed here according to broad subject areas. Many entries relate to more than one subject and accordingly appear under more than one heading.

Medicine and science

Music

Organizations

Politics, society, and economics

Religion

Slavery and abolition

Abbreviations

AAA	Amateur Athletics Association
AAM	Anti-Apartheid Movement
AFASS	American and Foreign Anti-Slavery Society
ANC	African National Congress
ATS	Auxiliary Territorial Service
AWS	African Writers Series
BBE	black British English
BDDT	Black Dance Development Trust
BFASS	British and Foreign Anti-Slavery Society
BFI	British Film Institute
bfm	*Black Filmmaker Magazine*
BMS	Baptist Missionary Society
BWIR	British West Indies Regiment
CAC	Carnival and Arts Committee
CAM	Caribbean Artistic Movement
CAO	Committee of African Organizations
CARD	Campaign Against Racial Discrimination
CARICOM	Caribbean Community
CASBAH	Caribbean Studies, Black and Asian History project
CAVE	Community and Village Entertainment
CES	Christian Evidence Society
CMS	Church Missionary Society
CPDA	Colonial People's Defence Association
CPGB	Communist Party of Great Britain
CRE	Commission for Racial Equality
CRER	Centre for Research in Ethnic Relations
EEC	European Economic Community
EIC	East India Company
ENSA	Entertainment National Service Association
ESN	educationally subnormal
FA	Football Association
FBI	Federal Bureau of Investigation
GCE	General Certificate of Education
GCSE	General Certificate of Secondary Education
GLC	Greater London Council
HCC	Handsworth Cultural Centre
IAI	International African Institute
IASB	International African Service Bureau
ICA	Institute of Contemporary Arts
ICS	Institute of Commonwealth Studies
ITN	Independent Television News
ITUCNW	International Trade Union Committee of Negro Workers
IWA	Indian Workers' Association
LEA	local education authority
LCP	League of Coloured Peoples
LMS	London Missionary Society
LPBS	Labour Party black sections
LSE	London School of Economics
MBE	Member of the Order of the British Empire
NCBWA	National Congress of British West Africa
NCO	non-commissioned officer
NHS	National Health Service
NIBMAR	No Independence Before Majority Rule
NWA	Negro Welfare Association
OCBBH	*The Oxford Companion to Black British History*
ODNB	*Oxford Dictionary of National Biography* (2004)
PAC	Pan-African Congress
PNM	People's National Movement
QC	Queen's Counsel
QCA	Qualifications and Curriculum Authority
RAAS	Racial Adjustment Action Society
RAF	Royal Air Force
RAS	Royal African Society
RCA	Royal College of Art
SANNC	South African Native National Congress
SATIS	Southern Africa the Imprisoned Society
SCM	Student Christian Movement
SPG	Society for the Propagation of the Gospel or Special Patrol Group
SSO	Southern Syncopated Orchestra
SWAPO	South West African People's Organization
TUC	Trades Union Congress
UCPA	Universal Coloured People's Association
UNIA	Universal Negro Improvement Association
WAAF	Women's Auxiliary Air Force
WASU	West African Students' Union
WISC	West Indian Standing Conference
WISU	West Indian Students' Union
YMCA	Young Men's Christian Association
YWCA	Young Women's Christian Association

Note to the Reader

This book is designed for ease of use but the following notes may be of help to the reader.

Alphabetical arrangement. Entries are arranged in word-by-word alphabetical order. 'St' is ordered as though spelt 'Saint' and 'Mc' is ordered as though spelt 'Mac'.

Bibliography. At the end of certain entries references provide guidance to further reading. In addition there is an extensive Select Bibliography at the back of the book (see pp. 553–9).

Chronology. A timeline of key events is given at the back of the book (see pp. 539–52). The year 2000 is the formal cut-off point for events, although there are general exceptions to this rule.

Coverage. The interpretation of the term 'black' follows the current definition established by the Commission for Racial Equality as pertaining to people of black African and African-Caribbean origin. No living persons are given individual entries, although they may be referred to in entries, and listed in the Index (see below).

Cross-references. These are denoted by asterisks preceding the entry form (in the body of an entry) and by small capitals at the end of an entry and sometimes in the body of an entry. They appear where reference is likely to amplify or increase understanding of the entry being read and they are not given merely to indicate that a separate entry can be found.

Index. A select index of names of persons mentioned in the text but who do not have their own entries appears at the back of the book (see pp. 000-0). In addition, a few references are given that lead the reader to specific information covered by a more general headword.

Thematic Contents List. The list of entries under major topics that appears at the front of the book (see pp. xix–xxiv) offers an alternative means of accessing the material in the *Companion*. It allows the reader to see at a glance the key headwords relating to a particular subject.

Abolition. The term can be applied either to the ending of *slavery, or to the ending of the *slave trade, but in British historical writing the former is more usually referred to as *emancipation.

While there are earlier examples of individuals who had doubts about the legality or morality of both the slave trade and slavery, serious public questioning of these institutions only began in Britain in the third quarter of the 18th century, with the attention focused on legal cases such as those of Jonathan *Strong and James Somerset (*see* SOMERSET CASE). The first group of people who collectively questioned the legitimacy of the slave trade were the Quakers, who formed a Committee on the Slave Trade in 1783 and were also prominent in the Committee for the Abolition of the Slave Trade (also referred to as the Society for the Abolition of the Slave Trade) established in 1787. From 1787 activists such as Thomas *Clarkson, Granville *Sharp, and William *Wilberforce gathered increasing popular support for the ending of the slave trade by legislation, aided by sympathetic writers such as William *Cowper, Hannah *More, and Ann *Yearsley.

Many abolitionists, as supporters of the movement were known, stated that their aim was the abolition of the slave trade, not slavery itself. This was essentially a practical measure; the legal and constitutional thought of the period set a very high value on property rights, and attacking slavery as such would have been seen as an attack on what were widely regarded as legally acquired rights of property (no matter how distasteful the idea of exercising rights of property over fellow human beings might be). The slave trade appeared to be an easier target, and many abolitionists also felt that if the slave trade were ended, the slave owners who were no longer able to bring fresh slaves from Africa would be forced to treat better the slaves they already had. A gradual improvement in the conditions of slaves in the British colonies would inevitably (or so it was hoped) lead to their emancipation in the long term.

The movement scored an early success with what was known as Dolben's Act, passed in 1788 and regulating the number of slaves who could be loaded on a ship in relation to its tonnage. However, this was to be the last significant achievement for a considerable time, although Wilberforce repeatedly brought motions relating to the slave trade before the House of Commons. One motion, in 1796, which appeared certain to succeed, was defeated because MPs among Wilberforce's supporters went to the opening of a comic opera instead, *I due gobi* (*The Two Hunchbacks*) on 15 March. Several other factors contributed to the length of time it took the abolitionist movement to achieve success. One was the structure of British politics in the period, which gave strength in the legislature to their main opponents, the *West India interest. Another was the reaction in Britain to the French Revolution of 1789, particularly after the execution of Louis XVI led to war between Britain and France in 1793. Any sort of social reform came to be seen by many as having the potential to cause revolutionary upheaval, and this attitude certainly damaged the abolitionist cause, even though many prominent abolitionists were socially and politically conservative. (This was not true of Clarkson, and there were other political activists who did see abolition as only one item on a much broader agenda of social and political reform.) Changes in British and international politics, particularly the collapse of the Peace of Amiens between Britain and France, made it possible to bring abolition back onto the British political programme in 1804. The fact that Napoleon was attempting to restore slavery in the French Caribbean colonies after it had been abolished by the earlier French republican government also allowed British activists to promote the abolitionist cause without appearing unpatriotic. The British Parliament finally passed a law in 1807 making it illegal for British ships to engage in the slave trade after 1 January 1808.

The reasons for the eventual success of abolition are complex. Few historians would now accept without reservation the argument of Eric *Williams that the slave trade was abolished because, and only when, it had ceased to be profitable. There is significant evidence that both the slave trade and slavery itself were still profitable in the early 19th century. The continuance of the transatlantic slave trade into at least the mid-1860s, long after it had been prohibited by all the European and American nations that had formerly regarded it as legal, suggests that illegal slave traders were prepared to run considerable risks (including, at some times and in some places, the possibility of the death penalty if caught) because they saw the trade as still significantly profitable. However, by the beginning of the 19th century, slave owners in some plantation colonies (such as Barbados) felt that their slave populations had reached adequate numbers; they were therefore prepared to acquiesce in the abolition of the slave trade, in the belief that this would give them an advantage over rival colonies. Another important factor was the growing fear of slave revolt, particularly after the success of the *Haitian Revolution (1791–1804), and the belief that slaves brought from Africa were more likely to revolt than those born in the colonies. Many abolitionists saw the slave trade not only as wrong in the eyes of God, but as a practical hindrance to the spread of Christianity in Africa and among the slaves in the colonies; the importance of this motive and its effectiveness in mobilizing popular support for the abolitionist cause in Britain should not be underestimated.

Denmark had abolished its slave trade in 1792, and the United States did so in 1807 (individual US states had done so earlier). After 1807 Britain devoted considerable energy to persuading other nations to give up the trade by diplomatic means, and for many years Royal Navy patrols in the Caribbean and off the coasts of Africa were used in attempts to suppress the illegal slave trade.

After the abolition of the slave trade, the expected improvements in the conditions of slaves in British colonies failed to materialize, and many abolitionists were involved in the later campaigns which eventually led to the passage of the Emancipation Act in 1833. JG

Blackburn, Robin, *The Overthrow of Colonial Slavery 1776–1848* (1988)

Brown, Ford K., *Fathers of the Victorians: The Age of Wilberforce* (1961)

Walvin, James (ed.), *Slavery and British Society 1776–1846* (1982)

See also ANTI-SLAVERY SOCIETY; CHRISTIANITY

Africa and British colonialism. In 1899 Mary Kingsley, the travel writer and advocate of self-determination in West Africa, wrote to the Liverpool merchant John Holt that the jingoist press 'do not care about West Africa *itself* but only about how it bears on politics . . . I fancy if I showed them I cared for W.A. quite apart from Imperialism they would think me a thundering fool & pay no more attention to me.' She pinpointed the way in which the reality of African societies faded, in the discourse of empire, into a vindication of how Africa was to be discussed. Elaborate, often inapplicable, ideological debates—the merits of different forms of colonialism, or of different forms of European government, or of the different political theories by which African wealth should be extracted from its indigenous owners—and prejudices—anti-Catholic in the first instances of slave trading, anti-Semitic in the left's reactions against capitalist expansionism in South Africa, white supremacist in almost every conceivable design for intervention—were what was being worked out. As Chinua Achebe has argued regarding Conrad's *Heart of Darkness*, Africa became nothing more than a way of framing the existential questions of the European mind.

1. 19th-century debates
2. The Egypt crisis
3. The Scramble for Africa
4. The First Boer War
5. The Second Boer War
6. 20th-century attitudes
7. Governing the Africans
8. Decolonization
9. Neocolonialism

1. 19th-century debates In the 19th century two schools of radical argument evolved regarding Britain's colonial possessions. The 'Liberal Tradition', epitomized first by Adam Smith, then by the 1830s parliamentary reformers Richard Cobden and John Bright, and ultimately by William Gladstone, was in this early period anti-imperialist, advocating self-government for the colonies: the 1865 Report of the Select Committee on Africa (Western Coast), for example, argued for British withdrawal from the region, except for government of the freed slaves in Sierra Leone (*see* SIERRA LEONE SETTLERS). The arguments were economic, highlighting the expense of governing the colonies. More pragmatic were the reformers, heirs of Edmund Burke, William Pitt, and William *Wilberforce, for whom the fates of Britain and her possessions were inextricably intertwined: here, commercial interests and moral argumentation dovetailed, as in Thomas Fowell Buxton's 1837 Report of the Select Committee on Aborigines (British Settlements) and *The Remedy; being a Sequel to the African Slave Trade* (1840), which contrasted the unprincipled nature of earlier colonialism with the opportunities to modernize Africa through introducing missions, schools, advanced industries, and agricultural techniques in the place of slavery. For John Stuart Mill, the Victorian equivalent of Smith, the promotion of representative government, Christian religious practices, a rationalist education, the efficient use of land, and trading links with Britain would increase colonial productivity, thus benefiting the 'heathen'. A handful of radicals—William Congreve, Robert Needham Cust—disputed the ethnocentric assumptions of the interventionists, though not to any significant effect. More common was the alliance between the reformist impulse and the urge towards opening up Africa for commerce, veiled in patronizing tones of racial superiority, evident in achievements such as the 1841 Niger expedition, Richard Burton's expedition to the Central African lakes in the early 1860s, or David Livingstone's travels across the Kalahari in 1849, along the Zambezi and across the African continent in 1853, and to the Victoria Falls in 1855. A new colonial ideology began to take hold, prompted by continental European realpolitik and the reportedly vast wealth that lay untapped in the African hinterlands.

In the two decades until the start of the 20th century, 10,000 African kingdoms would be transformed into 40 states, 36 of them under European control.

2. The Egypt crisis When Turkey went bankrupt in 1875, the result of her British-backed war with Russia in the Crimea, Egypt followed suit a year later. Like Turkey, the Egyptians had tried under Ishmail Pasha (Khedive from 1863 to 1879) to modernize, but the net result was that Disraeli bought the Khedive's shares in the Suez Canal for £4 million. The web of involvement between British bankers and politicians meant that financiers such as the Rothschilds could force the government's hand, demanding Ishmail's replacement by Tewfiq when, having spent the money, he opposed further losses of sovereignty. In 1881 Arabi Pasha led an uprising, but while France (owner of the rest of the Canal Company) pulled back, Britain intervened to set up a protectorate in 1882, bombing Alexandria in July and defeating Arabi's army at Tel-el-Kebir in September, before shipping him to Ceylon. Neighbouring Sudan demanded another intervention when an Islamist fanatic, the Mahdi, led a nationalist rebellion in 1884. The death of General Gordon on the steps of Khartoum (a few days before a relief force arrived) would result in the vilification of Gladstone, now Prime Minister, as a murderer.

3. The Scramble for Africa The renewed 'Scramble' for western and eastern Africa which ensued under the Unionist government of 1895 must be seen in the light of Britain's rivalry with other expansionist European powers, particularly France and the newly united Germany (which had seized Zanzibar, Togoland, Cameroon, and, by theft and genocide, the lands of the Herero and the Nama in south-west Africa, and established Belgian ownership of the Congo at the Berlin Conference of 1884–1885). French encroachments into eastern Sudan stopped when a French force under Jean-Baptiste Marchand was advised to back down in the face of Horatio Kitchener's British army at Fashoda in 1898 (the culmination of the campaign to quell the dervishes, in which 11,000 were massacred at the Battle of Omdurman and the Mahdi's bones exhumed and scattered). France had more successes against Britain in West Africa, spreading along the Senegambian coasts from Algeria and drawing strict boundaries around Sierra Leone and the Gambia; Britain negotiated Nigeria's immense territory in 1898, by which time the Royal Niger Company had pushed far upriver. Joseph Chamberlain, the powerful Colonial Secretary, bought out the Company on New Year's Day 1900.

A similar process occurred in Uganda, where the need to protect Egypt's source of water, the Upper Nile, influenced British policy: Frederick Lugard, agent of the East African Association, broke the ancient kingdoms of the Buganda and Bunyoro in the early 1890s by supporting different factions in a tribal and religious war, and Uganda was made a British protectorate when the government bought out the bankrupted Association (renamed the Imperial British East Africa Company) in order to block Germany (southern Sudan was also annexed, to enclose Belgium) in 1894. Lugard became Governor-General of Nigeria in 1912, to pioneer 'indirect rule': in his own definition the 'systematic use of the customary institutions of the people as agencies of local rule'. The Scramble was an untidy business, built on expediency and the urge to limit the spread of rivals. Important terms in the Entente Cordiale of 1904, for example, were mutual recognition of France in Morocco and Britain in Egypt. The most convincing moves on behalf of Britain in Africa came, in the form of laissez-faire capitalism, from the south: the diamond-rich lands of the Zulus and the Boer settlers.

4. The First Boer War Since the discovery of diamonds in the Orange Free State in the late 1860s, the British had attempted to weaken the Boers, seizing Basutoland, Griqualand West, and the Transvaal with the aim of creating a South African federation. The Ama-Zulu clan had two generations earlier expanded their territory to 100 times its size under colonial Africa's greatest leader, Shaka (*c.*1787–1828), who by military innovations such as a short, heavy stabbing assegai, new patterns of attack, and a disciplined army of fast, barefooted warriors had almost united Natal, Lesotho, and Swaziland by the time of his death. In 1879 the Zulus attacked under Cetewayo, ultimately losing but defeating the British at the Battle of Isandhlwana, where 1,600 troops were lost. In 1880 the Boers seized the opportunity to rebel, at the Battle of Majuba in 1881 forcing the return of the Transvaal to independence. They then expanded into Bechuanaland (to the west) and Zululand (in the east), seeking passage to the sea through alliances with Germany (in Namaqua-

Damaraland) and Portuguese Mozambique. To block them Britain annexed Bechuanaland in 1885; the gold discovered at Witwatersrand in 1886 came in the context of the gradual British encirclement of the Transvaal.

Cecil Rhodes and the Rothschilds amalgamated the competing diamond-mining companies into the De Beers Company in the mid-1880s, merging with the Bechuanaland Company to form the Central Search Association for Matabeleland (renamed the United Concessions Company in 1890, and granted gold and mineral rights in the region), effectively allowing Rhodes, the company director, commercial occupation of Matabeleland and Mashonaland in the north. A further charter was granted in 1889 to govern Rhodesia, as the British South Africa Company, the state being christened when Rhodes's Maxim guns mowed down the forces of Lobengala at the Battle of Shangani River in 1893. But the Afrikaners in the centre of this enterprise remained fiercely independent, their leader, Paul Kruger, encouraged in his defiance of the British by Bismarck, the German Chancellor.

5. The Second Boer War The megalomaniac Rhodes personified capitalism in southern Africa, and by extension in the entire process of colonization, because his advances opened a trading corridor north through the eastern-central continent. In 1890 he became Prime Minister of Cape Colony—both ruler of the colony and director of the company that monopolized most of its wealth (all spoils of the Kimberley diamond fields and much of the Transvaal's gold)—from there fuelling anti-British unrest in the Transvaal, which culminated in the Jameson Raid, led by his chief of police in Rhodesia, in the last days of 1895. This resulted in an uprising in Rhodesia (Dr Jameson's reign being so bloody that when his police force travelled to Pretoria, the Mashona rebelled, necessitating a war of reprisals in 1896). It also exacerbated Boer hostility to the British, whose own fervour for war was whipped up by Chamberlain and his High Commissioner, Alfred Milner. Milner was a half-German 'British race patriot' who visited South Africa in order to rally settlers around the British flag and scupper any chance of peace talks. In October 1899 the Boers declared war, amidst scenes of hysterical patriotism in England (the end of the Siege of Mafeking on 18 May 1900 is notorious), though this waned when the war, long and exhausting, dragged on until 1902. The victorious British pioneered techniques of repression such as concentration camps and the rewriting of history books for schools to diminish the significance of Afrikaner achievements.

6. 20th-century attitudes In 1906 the new Liberal government reversed the policies of the hawkish Unionists, ceding independent rule to the Boers in the Transvaal and Orange Free State. In 1910 these joined with Natal and the Cape in the South African Union, a Liberal achievement marred only by its enshrining of the apartheid system. It was during this period that two emblematic figures of 20th-century British history first appear in the textbooks: Winston Churchill, a veteran of the Boer War, was made Colonial Under-Secretary in the new Liberal administration; Gandhi (an ambulance corps organizer in the same conflict) rose to prominence as leader of the Natal Indian Congress, protesting against the colony's treatment of its Indian immigrants.

The germinal British left reacted fiercely against the excesses of capitalist imperialism. The Hobsonite Liberals and the Liverpool School supported indirect rule in West Africa, the latter group spearheading the public campaign against crimes in the Belgian Congo. The Fabians, however, were opportunistically imperialist, and their support of the Boer War was a factor in their schism with the Labour Party; under Keir Hardy, Labour was outspoken in condemning imperial atrocities (though socialist policies were advocated for the reason, voiced by Ramsay MacDonald among others, that African produce should be redistributed among workers of the world, rather than hogged by the Africans). At the other extreme of the political spectrum, the later heirs of Lord Rosebery, Chamberlain, and Milner were the press barons Alfred Northcliffe and Harold Rothermere, proprietors since the jingoistic 1890s of the *Daily Mail*. In 1934 the *Mail* campaigned for Germany's African territories, confiscated under the terms of Versailles, to be returned to the Hitler government since, wrote Rothermere, 'though this proposal may not be popular, I am convinced that it is wise . . . To deny this mighty nation, conspicuous for its organising ability and scientific achievements, a share in the work of developing backward regions of the world is preposterous.'

7. Governing the Africans In the 20th century, exploitation of Africa was commercially and racially motivated and upheld by violence: 2,000 Africans were killed during a rebellion in Sokoto, Nigeria, in 1906, thousands more during tribal uprisings in Kenya, and in 1915 the resistance to a nationalist rising in Nyasaland led by John Chilembwe was organized by German settlers, in which thousands of Blacks were slaughtered. As mining technologies developed in the early 20th century, the variety of African exports expanded, where previously plantation crops and ivory had dominated: gold and diamonds spilled from South Africa, iron ore and bauxite from Guinea and Sierra Leone, tin from Nigeria, gold and manganese from Ghana, phosphates, oil, lead, and zinc from North Africa, and copper, for electric wires, from Uganda and the Congo. East-central African copper ore supported the age of electricity just as slavery had built the foundations for the age of steam. The produce marketing boards, created after the 1937 'cocoa hold-up' in the Gold Coast, when farmers refused to sell at market price to the British, arranged for the state to purchase directly from the growers, rather than through intermediaries; however, the British government sold produce on at world price, its profits buffering the war economy. African surplus boosted the pound—and covered British scarcity: when Japan blockaded Britain in the Far East, East African sisal fibres could be used for ropes. The repayment of US loans after the Second World War was made in colonial goods.

8. Decolonization Given the contributions of Africans to the British war effort, it became necessary to award independence to the colonies. In Kenya, where trade unions and organizations such as the Young Kikuyu Association had been active since the 1920s, the Kenya-Africa Union, formed in 1945, was outlawed in 1950. In desperation, rebels killed 60 white settlers in 1952—the so-called Mau Mau uprising—in return for which 960 Kikuyu were tortured and executed. In the ensuing revolt, which lasted until 1957, 10,000 more peasants would die.

In Ghana the jailed Kwame Nkrumah was elected Prime Minister in 1957, declaring independence and proceeding to modernize the country, building schools, factories, and hydroelectric dams, funded by Russia and China. The former Secretary to the Pan-African Congresses in pre-war Manchester, and a Marxist who wrote that 'capitalism at home is domestic colonialism', Nkrumah campaigned for Pan-African solidarity, marrying the daughter of Gamal Abdel-Nasser, who had nationalized the Suez Canal in 1956 (prompting the British to attempt invading Egypt), and bankrolling Sékou Touré's government when Guinea-Conakry refused to become an overseas department of France. In 1958 he instigated at Accra the series of conferences and alliances that culminated in the founding of the Organization of African Unity in Addis Ababa in 1963. Asked to go to Indochina and negotiate a peace settlement to end the Vietnam War in 1967, Nkrumah was deposed in a CIA-backed coup. In Nigeria, which consists of over 350 ethnic groups, independence (1960) was soon followed by a series of military takeovers, then the secession of the oil-rich eastern region (Biafra) in

1967, which triggered a three-year civil war in which 2 million people may have died.

When the Federation of the Rhodesias and Nyasaland was broken up into Rhodesia, Zambia, and Malawi in 1964, the Rhodesian settlers rebelled, seeking to retain an apartheid system. Following African resistance, Ian Smith closed the borders in 1972, relying on alliances with South Africa and Mozambique (still governed by the fascist regime in Portugal). Not until the wars of decolonization in Guinea-Bissau, Angola, and Mozambique toppled the Salazar government in 1974 would Smith be weakened by civil war; a former prisoner and Marxist politician, Robert Mugabe, took control of Zimbabwe in 1980.

9. Neocolonialism Two recent examples must serve to illustrate this concept, which can be defined as the continuation of the colonial system in the period of globalization. In 1995 the show trial and execution of the Ogoni activist Ken Saro-Wiwa by the Nigerian government to protect the interests of Shell Oil drew international attention to the exploitation of small tribes in the Niger delta: the policies of multinationals in the region continue to encourage environmental degradation and the reign of warlords, destabilizing federal government. Throughout the 20th century and into the 21st the Congo has been a site of vicious exploitation: most recently the ore coltan (a compound of Niobium and Tantalite) has become a key export. Coltan is used to make capacitors, used in mobile phones and laptops, for which there is a voracious market in the developed world, with saturation advertising campaigns encouraging consumers to discard their current gadgets in favour of the latest 'mobile technologies' such as 'picture messaging'—in 2003 the United Nations estimated that 4 million Congolese had died as a result of the tribal wars over the coltan mines, with smuggling by militias in Burundi, Rwanda, Uganda, and Angola contributing to further civil wars. JM

Davidson, Basil, *Africa in History: Themes and Outlines* (2nd edn., 1974)
Porter, Bernard, *Critics of Empire: British Radical Attitudes to Colonialism in Africa 1895–1914* (1968)
Rodney, Walter, *How Europe Underdeveloped Africa* (rev. edn., 1988)
Walvin, James, *Making the Black Atlantic* (2000)

See also ETHIOPIA, ITALIAN INVASION OF; HEART OF DARKNESS; PAN-AFRICANISM

Africa and the World. Bulletin of the *International African Service Bureau (IASB). The IASB was founded in London in 1937 by the Trinidadian activists C. L. R. *James and George *Padmore, the Sierra Leonean I. T. A. Wallace-Johnson, the Kenyan Jomo Kenyatta, and the Guyanese radical Ras *Makonnen. All were leading figures within *Pan-Africanism, and their decision to establish the IASB was prompted in part by the Italian invasion of *Ethiopia.

The aim of the organization was to help enlighten the British public by distributing literature and holding talks on the issue of colonialism. *Africa and the World* was introduced in early 1937 to further these ends, the driving force behind it being the Marxist activist and trade unionist Wallace-Johnson, who became its editor as well as General Secretary of the IASB. By the autumn of 1937 the bulletin had developed into a journal, the *African Sentinel*, which published approximately four or five bimonthly issues until the spring of 1938. The journal adopted a resolutely Pan-African approach, seeking not only to raise black consciousness but also to help organize and unite various black movements around the world. In July 1938 the journal changed again to become *International African Opinion*. MGN

Macdonald, Roderick J., ' "The Wisers Who Are Far Away": The Role of London's Black Press in the 1930s and 1940s' in Jagdish S. Gundara and Ian Duffield (eds.), *Essays on the History of Blacks in Britain* (1992)

See also PUBLISHING

Africa Social and Technical Society. One of the major black associations in *Liverpool in the 1950s. It was established in September 1952 with a declared mission to advance the cause of Africans everywhere, and to bring 'honour and glory' to African peoples. The Society's aims and activities were diverse, and local and global in scope. Its primary objective was to promote employment opportunities for skilled black workers in the Gold Coast and elsewhere in Africa, to promote cultural, educational, and technical knowledge, and to encourage the greater participation of African people in the British and international civil services. It also aimed to provide financial aid and moral support to members.

The Society not only was concerned with the material welfare of Africans in Liverpool, but also sought to foster interest in, and international support for, Africa. To this end, it strove to build unity among the member states of the British Commonwealth.

Seeking to arouse the British public's consciousness of the rich cultural heritage of Africa, the Society advocated a broad cultural programme of African plays, dances, and exhibitions. Increasingly, however, its activities became 'mutual aid'-oriented.

Though the Society encouraged a multicultural membership, the majority of members were of African descent—the only white members being a dozen women. Internal dissent led eventually to the collapse of the Society. ARF

Ramdin, Ron, *The Making of the Black Working Class in Britain* (1987)

African art, British responses to.

1. Changing perceptions from the late 15th to the early 20th centuries
2. Modernism and 20th-century exhibitions

1. Changing perceptions from the late 15th to the early 20th centuries The direct engagement with African art in Britain, as in Europe generally, began with the ivory sculptures from Sierra Leone, Benin City (also known as Edo), and the kingdom of Kongo, carved in the late 15th and early 16th centuries for the Europeans who first opened up the coastal trade routes in the quest for direct access to gold from Mali and spices from India; and woven textiles in cotton and raffia. (It should not be forgotten that until the 'discovery' of the Americas the empire of Mali was the principal source of gold in Europe, and that the earliest gold coins in England were minted of Malian gold.)

In this initial phase, Europeans encountered civilizations of little material difference from Europe, and there is evidence of respect and admiration for these works of art. This was to change in the course of the 16th century with the advent of transatlantic slavery, and the origin of the ivories was quickly forgotten (and assumed to have been India), while the textiles were written off as mere curios along with the other African artefacts acquired sporadically. There were exceptions, notably the Roman and Islamic antiquities of North Africa and, especially, ancient Egypt and its Coptic Christian successor, including, also, Christian Ethiopia; but these were regarded as not really African, and Africa remained fractured in the imagination of 'the West', with sub-Saharan Africa seen as a region where little of note had happened, its technology merely primitive and curious, at best as evidence for earlier stages of human cultural evolution.

All this was to change gradually with the expanding direct European experience of Africa made possible by the mid-19th-century replacement of transatlantic slavery by colonial rule, and the acquisition of African art and material culture for public and private collections; and with the increasing archaeological interest in the continent. The 'stages of culture' hypothesis was discarded early in the 20th century as entirely untenable (it survives only within the perceptions of the misinformed), and there was a gradual perception of the antiquity and innovative character of African culture, including the recognition of ancient Egypt as a fundamentally African civilization, and, indeed, the recognition of Africa as the essential cradle of all humanity, and its art and civilization. However, problems still remain in regard to European (mis)perceptions of modernist developments in African art.

2. Modernism and 20th-century exhibitions In the early 20th century the national museums of Europe expanded their collections of African material largely on the basis of the colonial divisions of the continent, and in France these collections were dominated by the schematic forms typical especially of Mali and Gabon. These were the forms that excited the artists of Parisian modernism; and it was of this material, when shown in London, that Roger Fry wrote his celebrated essay of 1920 'Negro Sculpture', in which he asserted that African sculptors had discovered the three-dimensionality of sculpture in a way no other part of the world had done. Elsewhere sculpture had always emerged from a two-dimensional architectural frame. In an earlier essay of 1910 Fry had identified the southern African artists responsible for the rock art of the area as having independently discovered the visual trick of foreshortening. The problem with both essays was not that these opinions were faulty but that he was unable to move from his perceptions of African art to a revision of then current popular opinion of Africa as 'primitive' (a legacy of the untenable theory of 'stages of culture').

In Britain collections of African art had a different character, which may in part explain why the modernisms of Leon Underwood, Henry Moore, and Jacob Epstein take a rather different path from their continental colleagues. These differences were contingent upon, firstly, the acquisition by the British Museum in the course of the latter half of the 19th century of a substantial collection of those late 15th- and early 16th-century West African ivories, together with the assertion that they were indeed African; secondly, the arrival of several thousand works of art, especially in cast brass and ivory, looted from Benin City, in what is now Nigeria, in 1897 (though ironically the largest collection of this material ended up in Berlin, such was the tardiness of the relevant British authorities); and, thirdly, the collection of material commissioned by the British Museum from the Hungarian anthropologist Emil Torday from the Kuba peoples and surrounding areas of the Congo. All of this material was evidence of a high technical skill, easily recognizable as the equal of anything within European art history, and much of it was both highly decorative and tending towards a naturalism uncharacteristic of the material from French colonies. This in itself was sufficient to begin the process of deconstructing 'primitivist' notions of African art. Two kinds of display emerged: at the Pitt Rivers Museum, Oxford, African material was incorporated into a display of comparative technology, now preserved as an intellectual monument of its time; while at the British Museum the display of sub-Saharan material was organized according to region and 'tribe', but with the distinctive perceptions of African art reinforced by the decorative and naturalistic material from British colonies in West Africa, especially the growing collection of Yoruba sculpture from south-western Nigeria.

From 1939 until his retirement in 1974 the African collections of the British Museum were the responsibility of William Fagg, who is the pioneer of the systematic study of this art. Fagg's achievements were at least fourfold: firstly, he continued working on what he designated as the Afro-Portuguese ivories, establishing their points of origin in West Africa; secondly, he established a chronology for the art of Benin City; thirdly, through his art-historical study of Benin and his field study of Yoruba art he was able to demonstrate that art in Africa was as much the work of individual artists as anywhere else and that that individuality was evident in the works themselves; and, fourthly, he established the classification of forms based upon his concept of 'tribality', though by the end of his professional career the 'tribe' had become untenable within anthropological and historical research: while ethnicity matters in Africa, its relationship and relevance to art-making is by no means obvious, let alone clear-cut. Nevertheless, the idea of 'tribal art' continued to have an afterlife in ill-informed circles.

Fagg was also of the opinion that modernism in African art was really the intrusion of Europe via the education system that came with colonial rule, a perception that was hotly contested by African artists and others in the course of the period since the countries of Africa gained their independence, beginning with modern Ghana in 1957. For anyone working in countries such as Senegal, Ghana, Nigeria, Uganda, and South Africa, it was patently obvious that an art of international standing had emerged by turning the art technologies imported from Europe to the formation of distinctive national identities within the context of opposition to colonial rule, with specific local art movements such as *négritude* in Senegal and Natural Synthesis in Nigeria. In South Africa an art of overt resistance had also emerged. In the United Kingdom probably the one most significant event that moved this debate on towards the visual realities of modern Africa was 'Art from South Africa', the show at the Museum of Modern Art, Oxford, curated by David Elliot in 1989, which travelled through the United Kingdom the following year. (Unfortunately, in the same year the selection of African material for the Paris 'Magiciens de la terre' show by André Magnin and Jean-Hubert Martin had mischievously effected the bizarre invention of a neo-primitivism, as evident in Congo signage, Ghanaian fancy coffins, and so forth, completely writing out of consideration the modernist developments already referred to.)

The Royal Academy of Arts in London decided to put on a blockbuster African show. At first they imagined that it would be a 'tribal art' show, and in the early 1990s they asked the New York art historian and curator Susan Vogel to begin work on their proposal. By this time, however, scholarly perceptions of Africa had moved in three directions, well away from the 'tribal art' paradigm: firstly, the very notion of 'tribal art' was too simplistic a reckoning of the relationship between the histories of forms in art and evolving social identities; secondly, to make sense of Africa it was necessary to consider the whole continent, including ancient Egypt, and Coptic and Ethiopian art; and, thirdly, it was necessary to pay attention to the realities of African modernisms. This was all too much for the Royal Academy, and their invitation to Susan Vogel was withdrawn. The academician Tom Phillips took over the curating of the exhibition. However, in one respect Susan Vogel was successful in that the idea of exhibiting art from the whole continent was taken up, and palaeolithic tools, and ancient Egypt, Coptic, and Islamic North Africa were included, together with sub-Saharan sculpture, ceramics, and textiles, presented regionally and loosely according to current ethnic designations. This show, 'Africa: The Art of a Continent', opened in 1995, but all references to the modernist developments since the 1850s, beginning with photography as an African visual practice, were omitted. In this context, it was proposed that there should be an African festival, to be called 'africa95', that would permit other aspects of African art to receive due attention. These included: 'Seven Stories about Modern Art in Africa', at the Whitechapel Art Gallery, which focused upon the unique modernisms of Senegal, Nigeria, Sudan, Ethiopia, Uganda, and South Africa, curated by Clementine Deliss, and assisted by curators from each of the countries represented; 'The Art of African Textiles: Technology, Tradition and Lurex', curated by Carol Brown and John Picton at the Barbican Art Gallery, which looked at textile design history from the 18th century to the present; 'Play and Display', curated by Sokari Douglas Camp, looking at the relationship between her own sculpture and the British Museum's collections from her home region in Nigeria; metalwork curated by Magdalene Odundo at the Crafts Council Gallery; African and black British printmaking in the collection of the Victoria and Albert Museum, established by

Rosemary Miles (and at that time still the only national museum in the United Kingdom to have acquired modernist African art); and exhibitions and other events elsewhere in London and around the country.

Following 'africa95', Carol Brown curated the first substantial showing of African photography in the United Kingdom, in 1999 at the Barbican Art Gallery, in collaboration with *Revue Noire*, the Paris journal that, among other things, has pioneered research in this field. In 2001 the British Museum opened its new Africa Gallery, in which four contrasting ways of representing Africa are shown: thematic concerns with masquerade, and with the art of Benin City; a regional and ethnic display of sculpture; comparative technology, in particular metalwork, textiles, and ceramics; and the transformations of visual practice evident in local and diasporic modernisms. This last had been made possible by the very recent acquisition of contemporary work by artists from Nigeria, Kenya, Zimbabwe, Mozambique, South Africa, Egypt, and Tunisia, a development of the greatest importance for the public acceptance and recognition of the current art history of Africa. (In the British Museum show 'Collecting the 20th Century', ten years previously, the African element consisted almost entirely of ethnographic artefacts.) The next major events in the development of attitudes towards African art in the United Kingdom were the 'Black Style' show at the Victoria and Albert Museum in 2004, curated by Carol Tulloch and concerned with dress and fashion; and the 'Africa Remix' show at the Hayward Gallery, with Roger Malbert and David Elliot, which brought together artists from Africa working in internationally recognized ways. This, together with the still relatively new gallery at the British Museum, provided a focus for the Africa 2005 season of events dealing with many aspects of contemporary culture.

There are still those ill-informed critics who are disposed to write off developments in African visual practice, preferring to keep Africa in a mythic past of their own invention, and yet others who continue to espouse the neo-primitivist aesthetic of 'Magiciens de la terre'. Nevertheless, Africa 2005 represents real progress towards the public recognition of the continuing vitality in art on the continent of Africa. There has been informed progress on at least four counts: the clear recognition of innovation in antiquity, of photography as an African visual practice, of the complex relationships between forms in art and ethnicity together with all the other contexts of social identity, and of the variety of local African art modernisms. JWP

Deliss, C., and J. Havell (eds.), *Seven Stories About Modern Art in Africa* (1995)

Njami, S. (ed.), *Africa Remix: Contemporary Art of a Continent* (2005)

Oguibe, O., and Enwezor, O. (eds.), *Reading the Contemporary: African Art from Theory to the Marketplace* (2000)

Picton, J., *et al.*, *The Art of African Textiles: Technology, Tradition and Lurex* (1995)

Tulloch, C. (ed.), *Black Style* (2004)

See also CARIBBEAN ART, BRITISH RESPONSES TO

African Association. Also known as the Association for Promoting the Discovery of the Interior Parts of Africa, the African Association was founded in 1788 with the objective of sponsoring geographical expeditions to Africa, and in particular, to chart the course of the river Niger. A related aim was to open the African continent to British trade and influence. The founder member Sir Joseph Banks, a naturalist and a wealthy patron of science, was its president. The Association's first *Proceedings* were published in 1790, together with the account of Simon Lucas, one of the first explorers sent to Africa by the Association. However, Lucas's sensationalist travel memoirs were rapidly eclipsed by the publication of more accurate accounts produced by the celebrated explorers Mungo Park, the German Friedrich Hornemann, and the Swiss Jonathan Burckhardt, whose African expeditions were also sponsored by the Association.

With the assistance of Bryan Edwards, Secretary of the African Association, Park prepared his narrative *Travels in the Interior Districts of Africa Performed in 1795 and 1796 by Mungo Park*, published in 1799, which became a best-seller. James Rennell, an honorary member of the Association, also produced maps of Mungo Park's routes. ARF

Adi, Hakim, *West Africans in Britain: Nationalism, Pan-Africanism and Communism* (1998)

See also AFRICA AND BRITISH COLONIALISM

African Churches Mission. Mission to provide shelter to the black poor in *Liverpool. In the midst of economic depression, spreading poverty, and growing racism, the African Churches Mission was opened in Liverpool in 1931 by Pastor Daniels *Ekarte. Funded by the Church of Scotland, the Mission became a meeting point for many in need. Moreover, it became a refuge for Liverpool's black community in the face of worsening poverty and deprivation. It was the site from which Pastor Ekarte himself politicized around issues of racial inequality.

The Mission also provided shelter to those in need, including families affected by the air raids as well as stowaways and homeless people. Pastor Ekarte was heavily involved in raising funds to address humanitarian concerns. He was helped by many of the women, who provided secretarial and bookkeeping assistance and who also did the cooking and housekeeping. The Mission also played a critical role in providing a home for illegitimate coloured children, with Pastor Ekarte attempting to raise funds for a more permanent home for them, and becoming an advocate for increased attention to child welfare. However, he was unsuccessful, the money ran out, and the Mission home was closed down by inspectors from the Home Office in 1949. ASW

Ramdin, Ron, *The Making of the Black Working Class in Britain* (1987)

Sherwood, Marika, *Pastor Daniels Ekarte and the African Churches Mission* (1994)

See also CHRISTIANITY; CHURCHES

African Institution. Founded in 1807, in the wake of the abolition of the British slave trade, the African Institution replaced the Society for the Abolition of Slave Trade (1787) and had similar aims to the Sierra Leone Company (1791). Its purpose was to secure African freedom from British imperial rule, the 'civilization' of Africa through the dissemination of Christianity, and the establishment of profitable trade ventures that did not rely on slavery.

William *Wilberforce, who had led the parliamentary campaign for the abolition of the slave trade, was one of its vice-presidents. Other prominent abolitionists members of the Institution were Prince William Frederick, Duke of Gloucester (president of the Institution), James *Stephen, who served as one of its vice-presidents, Granville *Sharp, one of its first directors, Zachary *Macaulay, honorary secretary, Henry *Thornton, its treasurer, Edward Henry Columbine, who became a commissioner of the Institution, Sir Thomas Fowell *Buxton, and William Allen, among others. Some, including Wilberforce, Macaulay, and Buxton, also became members of the Anti-Slavery Society, founded in 1823.

The members of the Institution were motivated by strong religious convictions—most belonged to the group of evangelicals around Wilberforce—and for them the fundamental argument against slavery was rooted in a belief in the equality of humanity before God. Besides disseminating Christianity and 'civilization' in Africa, they also aimed to ameliorate the conditions of enslaved peoples in the West Indies, and prevent new slaves from being carried in foreign ships. ARF

Adi, Hakim, *West Africans in Britain: Nationalism, Pan-Africanism and Communism* (1998)

See also AFRICA AND BRITISH COLONIALISM

African Mail. Newspaper first published in Liverpool in April 1903 as the *West African Mail*. The paper was founded by Edmund Dene Morel (1873–1924). Born in Eastbourne, Sussex, Morel became a journalist and prominent campaigner against colonial abuses in Africa, and played a significant role in the movement against misrule in the Congo. After publishing a series of articles in 1900 on Belgian atrocities in the region, Morel was forced to resign from his job as a clerk in a shipping firm. He subsequently established his own illustrated weekly journal, through which, with total editorial control, he could continue his campaign.

Always insistent upon absolute veracity, Morel used his newspaper to publish the many letters and copies of documents sent to him by whistle-blowers, including damning official reports that revealed how Congolese women and children were being kidnapped and held hostage to compel their husbands to work without pay as rubber-harvesters. He also published photographs provided by missionaries, as well as numerous eyewitness accounts. As a result of Morel's disclosures, the British Parliament passed a resolution in 1903 committing the government to take a stand against the exploitation rife in the Congo. The newspaper (which became the *African Mail* in 1907) continued to appear until January 1917. By this time, Morel had helped found the pacifist political party, the Union of Democratic Control, in response to the *First World War. He was subsequently imprisoned for six months in 1917 for violation of the Defence of the Realm Act, forcing the closure of his publication. MGN

Cline, Catherine Ann, *E. D. Morel 1873–1924: The Strategies of Protest* (1980)

Hochschild, Adam, *King Leopold's Ghost: A Story of Greed, Terror, and Heroism in Colonial Africa* (1998)

See also PUBLISHING

African Progress Union. Black-rights group active in 1918–27, formed in London under the leadership of Liverpool-born John *Archer. From 1921 to 1924 the Trinidadian Dr John *Alcindor led it, then the Ghanaian Kwamina Tandoh. Its activities were broader than the reports in *West Africa* (London) and the *Sierra Leone Weekly News* (Freetown) suggest. It requested the government to include a black delegate at the post-war peace discussions in Versailles; it subsidized the lawyer Edward *Nelson, who defended Blacks on trial after the Liverpool riots of 1919; and it participated in the American-led Paris Pan-African Congress (1919) and the London congresses of 1921 and 1923. The Union sought justice when a Kenyan settler murdered a farmhand, alerted by an African-British Guianese barrister residing in that colony, and also provided practical help for students. Alcindor's committee included the merchant Robert *Broadhurst, the American composer Edmund *Jenkins, the lawyer W. E. S. Callender, Emma Smith, and the postmaster John *Barbour-James. Positive images were encouraged through concerts by the American tenor Roland Hayes. Visitors seeking justice were given guidance, including Sobhuza (from Swaziland), Oluwa (Nigeria), and Captain Cipriani (Trinidad).

Attempts were made to establish a branch in Cameroon, and contacts were developed with the Anti-Slavery Society, and with France and the United States. In New York in 1927 Tandoh (Chief Amoah III of Cape Coast), spoke of his plans to visit Cipriani. Reports of this panicked the Governor of Trinidad, who did not want an African chief visiting his colony. The Union's work at many levels has been revealed by newspaper reports and archive fragments, for few papers survive. JPG

Adi, Hakim, *West Africans in Britain: Nationalism, Pan-Africanism and Communism* (1998)

See also POLITICS

African Studies. Informed writing about Africa and its people dates back to the era of the *slave trade. However, most of these earlier accounts were written by travellers, traders, missionaries, and consular officials whose methods were random by contemporary standards and who often had an axe to grind. African Studies as a discipline—or rather as a crossroads between the disciplines of anthropology, history, politics, economics, religious studies, law, linguistics, literature, and sociology—really took off in the early 20th century. Within that brief history, it is possible to distinguish a formative period, up to roughly 1960, from the efflorescence which accompanied decolonization, when the shifting balance of power within Africa validated new approaches to study of the continent.

1. The heyday of anthropology
2. The travails of African Studies

1. The heyday of anthropology For more than half a century African Studies was dominated by the emerging discipline of anthropology, although the Royal African Society (RAS), founded in honour of the traveller Mary Kingsley in 1901, provided a forum for a much wider range of people with experience in Africa. Historians in Britain did not consider that sub-Saharan Africa had anything much that was worth studying, while colonies did not have politics in the accepted sense. Interestingly, the anthropological profession in Britain expended far more energy on Africa than on any other region. The first academic diploma in anthropology was offered at Oxford University in 1905, but it was only after the First World War that significant postgraduate studies began, with the London School of Economics (LSE) in the vanguard. In the 1930s anthropology reached its apogee.

Although it has been suggested that British anthropology thrived through its direct association with colonial rule, this has been disputed by Adam Kuper and Jack Goody. They point out that government anthropologists (such as R. S. Rattray in the Gold Coast) were few and far between, and that there was often considerable tension between colonial administrators and academic anthropologists. The former claimed a more long-standing engagement with their African wards and disputed the practical relevance of much anthropology. The anthropologists' riposte was that the district commissioners witnessed only a limited aspect of the everyday lives of the people, whereas they had more of an opportunity to study societies at close quarters. Despite the frequent backbiting, there were efforts to bridge the gaps. From his chair at the LSE, Bronisław Małinowski successfully championed the importance of extended periods of observation in the field, while accepting that anthropology could have a practical dimension.

The British government typically shared the scepticism of the field administrators and provided little in the way of financial encouragement. In fact, it was American philanthropy that helped to kick-start African anthropology in the inter-war years. From 1918 the Laura Spelman Rockefeller Memorial made substantial grants to British universities to establish academic posts, including a number of anthropology chairs. When the Memorial was absorbed into the Rockefeller Foundation in 1929, it became even more actively involved. In 1925 the International African Institute (IAI) was established, bringing together academic anthropologists, missionaries, administrators, educationists, and others with an Africa interest from right across the European continent. The Foundation approved a number of individual grants, and then, in 1931, it made a larger bequest, which provided the means for the IAI to support field research. Many landmark studies were carried out under the auspices of the IAI and published in its journal, *Africa*. Together with the RAS, and its journal *African Affairs*, the IAI was the primary vehicle of African Studies in Britain. The government subsequently gave some financial support when the Rhodes–Livingstone Institute was created in 1937. With its headquarters in Northern Rhodesia, the Institute was mandated to pursue research across Central Africa. Its experience tended to confirm the mutual suspicion that characterized relations between academic anthropologists on the one side and administrators and white settlers on the other.

One shared attribute between anthropologists and administrators was that they were white people observing African subjects, although (significantly perhaps) many were non-British—including Małinowski, who was Polish. But whereas the administrators were exclusively male, women such as Audrey Richards and Monica Wilson made singular academic contributions. In the 1930s the white female presence became more noticeable, while

Africans began to appear as researchers in their own right. Among the first-full time Fellows of the IAI was Z. K. Matthews, a black South African who went on to become Professor of Anthropology at Fort Hare University, and Jomo Kenyatta, the future President of Kenya. Both studied anthropology at the LSE and participated in Malinowski's seminars. Kenyatta himself wrote an acclaimed study of the Kikuyu, entitled *Facing Mount Kenya* (1938).

Later African Studies in Britain was in part a reaction against the dominance of social anthropology. One strand of thinking that was highly criticized by future generations was diffusionism, which held that Africa's past was a story of great migrations in which superior peoples established their dominance over lesser ones: hence the Bantu allegedly established their dominance over the Khoisan of southern Africa and the Twa of Central Africa, only to yield subsequently to the dominance of lighter-skinned cattle-keeping Hamites like the Tutsis. A classic statement was that of C. G. Seligman, Malinowski's mentor, whose *Races of Africa* (1930) adopted an explicitly racial framework of analysis in which anthropometry (the measuring of physical features) was married to linguistic evidence. By the 1950s, when racial theories were increasingly discredited by association with Nazism, such interpretations began to seem highly dubious—although Seligman's text was republished as late as 1957. The second target of criticism was structural functionalism, with which Malinowski and A. R. Radcliffe-Brown were associated. This approach tended to view cultures as made up of tightly interlocking systems in which each element supported every other.

In some respects, this insight mirrored that of the administrators who worried about rapid social change upsetting the delicate equilibrium. In the late 1940s colonial regimes began to take on board some of the liberal critiques, notably the charge that British rule was too conservative to benefit the colonized, and began to embrace the concept of development. At this point, anthropologists were invited to play a more active role by, for example, charting the social effects of urbanization. The irony is that, just as anthropology began to be valued in the creation of a new social contract between rulers and ruled, it drew flak for its association with colonialism. Anthropologists were criticized for presenting Africans as people without history and for doing the intellectual bidding of the colonial authorities. Whereas the new vogue for sociology gained some support in Africa, it is striking that the only African universities that established anthropology departments were in South Africa: elsewhere anthropology was a dirty word. Hence Kofi Busia, who wrote a doctorate in anthropology at Oxford (later published by the IAI), went home and was recruited by the University College of the Gold Coast in 1949. He objected to being part of a Department of African Studies, but when he was able to create a new unit he opted for sociology rather than anthropology.

2. The travails of African Studies One of the first things which newly independent African governments typically did, if it had not already been done, was to establish national universities. These were the cradles of African Studies in the 1960s. The new institutions were committed to research and teaching about African history and society, something which it was strongly felt had been suppressed during the colonial period. The sheer effervescence of African universities helped to build a momentum behind the study of Africa within Britain, where higher education was itself expanding very rapidly. Secondly, many young British scholars went to teach in African universities, often not knowing much before they arrived but then being converted to the cause. Institutions such as Makerere University in Uganda, the University of Ghana, and the University of Dar es Salaam in Tanganyika launched the careers of many of the Africanists who held sway in Britain until the new millennium. What was different was that it was no longer anthropology that dominated, but the study of African history. Given that Europeans had hitherto denied Africans a genuine history, the Africanist mission was to recapture the past, often using highly innovative methods such as oral tradition (which was copied by Europeanists). While some historians, like Basil Davidson, delved deeper into the pre-colonial past, others, like Terence Ranger and John Iliffe, sought to tease out the links between the nationalism of the 1950s and 1960s and earlier phases of opposition to European rule.

During the terminal phases of colonial rule, political contestation became more overt, and the study of African politics, especially that of political parties and voting patterns, became fashionable. Although British political science did not produce many big names to rival those of American universities, many new courses were established and much solid research was conducted. Political scientists and sociologists subjected trade unions, peasantries, traders, and so on to closer scrutiny, extending the insights of the anthropology of the 1950s. In universities like that of Kent, African literature courses were mounted, reflecting the growing reputation of writers like Chinua Achebe.

The course of African Studies was largely determined by the choices that were made in particular institutions, which in turn reflected their internal histories. Hence, while Oxford and Cambridge taught anthropology in the undergraduate curriculum, the highly conservative approach to the study of history in those institutions provided a blockage to the inclusion of African content except at the postgraduate level. However, a centre was established in Cambridge in 1965. In some of the newer universities, where there was not the same baggage, it was possible to launch African Studies teaching with much greater ease. The School of Oriental and African Studies, which was part of the University of London system, fell somewhere between these extremes: although it bore the legacies of the inter-war period, African history flourished, alongside the study of language, culture, politics, law, and of course anthropology.

Finally, the future direction of African Studies was determined by the Hayter Report of 1961, which recommended the funding of a handful of centres of African Studies. This led to the creation of cross-disciplinary centres being established at the universities of Birmingham, Edinburgh, Sussex, and York. Whereas Birmingham and York specialized on West Africa and southern Africa respectively, Edinburgh and Sussex assumed a continental remit. These Hayter Centres were fundamentally important in preventing African Studies from becoming the preserve of the 'golden triangle' of London, Oxford, and Cambridge—even if one might have thought that the strong black presence in Liverpool and Bristol would have made their universities natural candidates.

The dynamism of African Studies continued through the 1970s, when dependency theory struck a particular chord in African universities (especially Dar es Salaam) and led to a radical overhaul of the approaches that had dominated in Britain in the 1960s. The Guyanese historian of Africa Walter *Rodney was an influential exponent in London and East Africa alike. His polemic *How Europe Underdeveloped Africa* (1972) was widely read. However, in the early 1980s African Studies began to enter the doldrums. Some blamed dependency theory itself for having led Africanists up a conceptual blind alley. The introduction of hefty foreign-student fees in British universities by the government of Margaret Thatcher led to the drying-up of student recruits from African countries. At the same time, the excitement of studying Africa had waned for home students, who had come to associate the continent with perpetual crisis—the one crucial exception being South Africa, where research continued to thrive. The contrast with the expansion of the field in the United States is instructive: whereas African Studies thrived there by becoming attached to African-American Studies, the black community in Britain did not take African Studies to its bosom. Budgetary cuts led to a number of universities deleting African Studies altogether, notably at the universities of Aberdeen and York. Meanwhile, the generation that had cut its teeth after the war was coming up for retirement with apparently little prospect of being replaced. Finally, the engagement with Africa was not what it once had been. In 1986 one survey of Africanist scholars discovered that only 20 per cent were actively engaged in doing research in Africa. The author speculated that by the year 2000 African Studies would be represented by 'some elderly professors [and] . . . a handful of middle-level academics'.

In fact, the highly pessimistic prognoses did not come to pass, although African languages were a lasting casualty. At the start of the millennium African Studies bounced back. The Blair government sought to put Africa on the public agenda, as symbolized by the Commission for Africa (2005). This meant that greater value was placed on Africanist expertise. Those academics with a developmental focus were closely associated with consultancies funded by the Departmental for International Development, and this also helped in reconnecting British researchers with their African counterparts. While this did not exactly come at the expense of the humanities subjects like history and literature, it did tilt African Studies in a more developmental direction. Far from mass retirements killing off the profession, however, many new appointments were made, including at universities with no track record, like Durham. In London there were signs of rising recruitment levels among black students. In Edinburgh University postgraduate numbers rose to record levels, while Oxford University made a number of new appointments and founded its own Centre of African Studies in 2004. Moreover, European links provided a dimension that had been missing, particularly in the shape of the Africa–Europe Group for Interdisciplinary Study, which grew out of modest beginnings in 1991. Finally, the signs of a genuine recovery were also reflected in the volume and quality of research output, much of which was published inside Britain in the form of monographs (especially by James Currey and the university presses) and core journals like *Africa*, *African Affairs*, the *Journal of African History*, and the *Journal of Modern African Studies*. The crisis of reproducing African Studies had apparently passed, with the baton being successfully transferred to a younger generation.

PNu

Goody, Jack, *The Expansive Moment: The Rise of Social Anthropology in Britain and Africa 1918–1970* (1995)

Kuper, Adam, *Anthropologists and Anthropology: The British School 1922–1972* (1973)

Rodney, Walter, *How Europe Underdeveloped Africa* (1972)

See also CARIBBEAN STUDIES

African Telegraph. Newspaper founded in London in November 1914 by John Eldred Taylor, a Sierra Leonean businessman and journalist. In 1911 Taylor travelled to London, where he conceived the creation of a magazine to be concerned with West African issues. Three years later he had established the *African Telegraph*, with himself as editor. During the war, the paper remained loyal to British foreign policy. Once hostilities were over, however, it became a harsh and vocal critic, particularly as regards the treatment of Africa. Taylor formed the Society of Peoples of African Origin, which, with the *Telegraph* as its official news organ, called for an end to racial discrimination, the promotion of racial unity, and sociopolitical reforms in the colonies. In December 1918 it published an eyewitness account of the public flogging of two naked women in northern Nigeria. The officer who sanctioned the punishment, Captain Fitzpatrick, sued for libel. There followed a sensational court case in which Taylor used his position in the witness box to highlight flaws in the colonial legal system in Nigeria.

Towards the end of 1918, meanwhile, Taylor had granted editorship of the

Telegraph to the Trinidadian Felix *Hercules. Throughout 1919 the paper did much to expose racial tensions in Britain with its reports on the race riots in Cardiff and Liverpool. However, Taylor lost his libel case in November 1919 and incurred heavy damages, forcing the closure of the paper in December. MGN

Duffield, Ian, 'John Eldred Taylor and the West African Opposition to Indirect Rule in Nigeria', *African Affairs*, 70/280 (1971)

See also PUBLISHING

African Times and Orient Review. The first political journal produced by and for black people ever published in Britain. It was founded in London in July 1912 by the Egyptian-born Duse Mohamed *Ali in partnership with John Eldred Taylor. From 1883 to 1921 Ali lived mainly in Britain. Inspired by the ideas of Pan-Africanism, he began as a freelance writer, penning a series of anti-imperialist articles. Following the Universal Race Congress, held in London in 1911, Ali decided to launch his own, militant magazine. As he wrote in the journal's first issue, the Congress had shown the need for 'a Pan-Oriental, Pan-African journal at the seat of the British Empire which would lay the aims, desires, and intentions of the Black, Brown, and Yellow Races—within and without the Empire—at the throne of Caesar'.

Despite limited resources, Ali kept the journal alive. Aside from its exposure of various colonial injustices (for example, nude public floggings in Nigeria), the magazine carried the literary debuts of several important figures, including the Jamaican activist Marcus *Garvey and the Ghanaian philosopher and nationalist Kobina Sekyi. The paper's quality was high; it reached its intended readers and made a sizeable impact. Indeed, Duffield notes that 'it received the back-handed tribute of being disliked and rather feared by the Colonial Office, the Foreign Office and the Indian Office'. The final issue of *African Times and Orient Review* appeared in December 1920. MGN

Duffield, Ian, 'Dusé Mohamed Ali: His Purpose and His Public' in Alastair Niven (ed.), *The Commonwealth Writer Overseas* (1976)

See also PUBLISHING; PAN-AFRICANISM

African Training Institute. A school in Colwyn Bay, North Wales, *c.*1893–1912, whose students came from Africa and the diaspora. The Baptist missionary William Hughes developed the concept of a school in Britain where the education of Africans, including carpentry, printing, pharmacy, and tailoring, could be taught by local craftsmen. Five thousand copies of his *Dark Africa: And the Way Out* were printed in 1892, and distributed at Christian gatherings. Hughes went to Africa in 1893 to recruit, and there were a dozen students (from Angola to Sierra Leone) at the Institute (originally called the Colwyn Bay Institute) in 1895.

Later students included people from America, South Africa, Nigeria, and Zambia. Altogether, 100 students studied at Colwyn Bay (four are buried there), but Hughes was too busy to keep proper accounts. Financial support evaporated in 1912 and Hughes died in 1924. JPG

Hughes, William, *Dark Africa: And the Way Out* (1892)

King, H., 'Mojola Agbebi (1860–1917): Nigerian Church Leader' in Rainer E. Lotz and Ian Pegg (eds.), *Under the Imperial Carpet: Essays in Black History 1780–1950* (1986)

See also CHRISTIANITY; MISSIONARY SOCIETIES

African Writers Series. An imprint of Heinemann International Division publishing African literature, running from 1957 to 2003. In 1957 Van Milne at Heinemann received a manuscript of Chinua Achebe's *Things Fall Apart*, the seminal English-language African novel. He commissioned the work, together with its sequel, *No Longer At Ease*, Cyprian Ekwensi's *Burning Grass*, and a history book by Kenneth Kaunda, soon to be the democratic President of Zambia. The four books were published together in 1962, Achebe taking the editorship of the new series. *Things Fall Apart* would sell 8 million copies, translated into 32 languages.

Independent Africa's three Nobel

Laureates for Literature—Wole Soyinka (Nigeria), Naguib Mahfouz (Egypt), and Nadine Gordimer (South Africa)—were included, as were politicians such as Jomo Kenyatta (Kenya) and Nelson Mandela, whose collection of letters, speeches, articles, and trial transcripts, *No Easy Walk to Freedom*, was published in 1986, several years before the end of his 25-year period in jail. Other important novelists first published in the African Writers Series (AWS) included Doris Lessing (Rhodesia), Flora Nwapa, the first Nigerian woman writer to be published, Dennis Brutus and Bessie Head (South Africa), and Syl Cheney-Coker (Sierra Leone).

Foreign-language authors were translated into English, among them the Francophone Mongo Beti and Ferdinand Oyono (Cameroon), Soni Labou Tansi (Zaire), Veronique Tadjo (Côte d'Ivoire), Ousmane Sembène and Mariama Bâ (Senegal), and the Lusophone Lilia Momplé (Mozambique) and 'Pepetela' (Artur Carlos Mauricio Pestana, from Angola). The Sudanese Tayeb Salih's *Season of Migration to the North* was translated from the Arabic in 1969, and the Ugandan Okot p'Bitek's *Song of Lawino and Song of Ocol* (1966) brought the Acoli tradition of oral poetry onto the page for the first time.

Perhaps the biggest star of the imprint was Ngugi wa Thiong'o, whose successive works probing the myths surrounding the 'Mau Mau rebellion' of the 1950s brought him into conflict with the corrupt Kenyan administration of Daniel arap Moi. *I Will Marry When I Want* (1982), a play devised with Ngugi wa Mirii from peasant oral histories, resulted in the bulldozing of the Kamiriithu Cultural Centre, where rehearsals took place. *Devil on the Cross* (1987) marked Ngugi's conversion to writing in Kikuyu, his native language—it was drafted on toilet paper during a spell in prison. In 1989 Ngugi's new novel, *Matigari*, a fictional work concerning a veteran freedom fighter who wakes up in independent Kenya before going on a fruitless quest in search of truth and justice, provoked another crackdown: Moi issued orders for the arrest of Matigari before his mistake was realized and the novel was impounded.

This was the most extreme example, but it was representative of a broader editorial challenge to the corruption and backwardness of post-independence regimes. The trend—epitomized by Achebe's collection of essays *The Trouble with Nigeria* (1983), and by the posthumous writings of Steve Biko, which AWS published after his murder in a South African jail—was for African intellectuals to engage, directly and critically, with the failures of African leadership, regardless of 'Western' perspectives. Many of the early novels, such as Ngugi's *Petals of Blood* (1977), the South African Peter Abrahams's *Mine Boy* (1946), and the Ghanaian Ayi Kwei Armah's *The Beautyful Ones Are Not Yet Born* (1969), were symptomatic of the political disillusionment sweeping the continent, and have come to be studied from a Fanonian theoretical perspective as indicative of how the expectations for African independence deteriorated in the context of continuing neocolonial domination.

Other critical offshoots have grown from the AWS literature. Buchi Emecheta's *Second Class Citizen* (1974), set in London, appears on syllabuses for the British immigrant novel. Jack Mapanje's anthology *Gathering Seaweed: African Prison Writing* (2002) contributes to a growing body of scholarship on the literature of incarceration.

The series also promoted African writing at a regional level, encouraging the development of the Setswana-language Botswana Writers Series and creating regional offices in Nigeria, Kenya, and Zimbabwe, which supported democracy in those countries, since governments who closed down local publishers would be more nervous of tackling foreign investors.

Having ceased to be profitable, the series was closed down in 2003, though many key works are now available from other publishers. A collection of 59 works in typescript and manuscript form, with authorial emendations, is held at the School of Oriental and African Studies, London.

JM

<http://www.heinemann.co.uk>

See also POST-COLONIAL THEORY

Africanus, Scipio (1702–1720). African servant who served and died in Henbury, *Bristol. Africanus was the servant of Charles William, Earl of Suffolk and Bindon. The Earl married into the Astry family of Henbury House. Africanus, who was named after an ancient Roman general, was a symbol of their wealth. He, like other servants of African origin who worked in aristocratic homes, was a novelty who, besides doing domestic chores, also functioned as a showpiece for wealthy guests.

In the 18th century thousands of male and female slaves arrived in Britain to become servants of the rich minority. They mainly came from the New World, rather than directly from Africa. The common, erroneous belief was that Bristol slavers brought Africans back and kept them chained in the Redcliff caves before shipping them across the Atlantic. The truth was that most African slaves were part of the triangular trade, being transported from Africa to the New World and then to Britain.

It is not known how long Africanus served the Earl and his family. He died at the age of 18 in December 1720 and was buried in St Mary's churchyard, Henbury. Engraved on his gravestone are the words:

I who was born a pagan and a slave—
Now sweetly sleep a Christian in my grave.
What tho' my hue was dark! My Saviour's Sight
Shall change this darkness into radiant Light.
Such grace to me my Lord on earth hath given.
To recommend me to my Lord in Heaven,
Whose glorious Second Coming here I wait
With Saints and Angels Him to celebrate. DD/SS

ODNB

Shyllon, F., *Black Slaves in Britain* (1974)

See also SLAVE TRADE; SLAVERY

Aggrey, James Emmanuel Kwegyir (1875–1927). African educationist, variously called the Father of African education, the Booker T. Washington of Africa, and, in the title of Edwin W. Smith's 1929 biography, *Aggrey of Africa*. Born in Anomabo in the Gold Coast, the son of the chief linguist in the court of King Amona V, Aggrey was an able pupil and in 1898 travelled to America, where he joined Livingstone College in North Carolina. In 1903 he was ordained an elder of the African Methodist Episcopalian Zionist Church.

A compulsive learner, aside from his Master's degree (awarded in 1912), Aggrey also gained through correspondence courses a doctorate of Divinity from Hood Theological College and a doctorate of Osteopathy from the International College of Osteopathy, Illinois, before going to Columbia to undertake a Ph.D.

In 1920 the Phelps Stokes Fund sent Aggrey to Africa, the only black member of the Commission to investigate the state of education in the sub-Saharan colonies. He visited the Belgian Congo, where he was barred from travelling on trains, Angola, where he wept at Portuguese cruelty, and Nigeria, where at Lagos he gave the young Nnamdi Azikiwe, who would grow up to be the country's first President, a directory of American educational institutions. In 1921 he made 120 speeches in the South African colonies alone.

The second Phelps Stokes Commission, which visited the Gold Coast, Ethiopia, Kenya, Uganda, Tanganyika and Zanzibar, Nyasaland, and the Rhodesias, and returned to South Africa, departed from England in 1924. A photograph of Aggrey with Alexander Garden Fraser, taken in Surrey, is held in Cambridge University's Royal Commonwealth Society Library. The two men founded the Achimota Prince of Wales College in Ghana, where after completing his work for the Commission in 1927 Aggrey held the post of Vice-Principal, teaching among other children the young Kwame Nkrumah, the future first President of Ghana, and arranging speaking engagements in America for Hastings Kamuzu Banda, later to lead Malawi to independence.

The Phelps Stokes Report *Education in Africa* (1923), and the subsequent memorandum of the Advisory Committee on Native Education, *Education Policy in British Tropical*

Africa (1925), changed British policy on education in the African colonies. The focus became to develop the training of an elite generation to whom government could be handed. The mission schools were advised to work more closely with the 'higher type' leadership colleges to achieve this end. The use of vernacular languages in schools was encouraged, alongside the teaching of English as a second language. Skill-based agricultural training was recommended for inclusion in the curriculum, and the creation of departments of Native Education devolved the responsibility for schooling to individual colonies. Adult education was promoted, as well as that of children.

A great orator, Aggrey's sayings included, 'When you educate a woman, you educate a nation'; his philosophy of 'accommodation' between Blacks and Whites, which made him hostile to Garveyism, was summed up in his image of piano keys, each set capable of playing individual melodies, yet reaching their full potential in harmony. JM

Lewis, L. J. (ed.), *Phelps Stokes Reports on Education in Africa* (1962)

Akpabot, Samuel Ekpe (1932–2000). Nigerian composer, organist, and ethnomusicologist born in Uyo, Akwa Ibom state, Nigeria, in 1932. In his early education at King's College, Lagos, and as a chorister at Christchurch Cathedral, in that city, he was exposed to European classical music, Mendelssohn being his favourite composer. His musical outlook was eclectic, and he was involved in dance bands such as the Chocolate Dandies and the Akpabot Players (his own band), formed in 1949, as well as being organist at St Saviour's Anglican Church in Lagos.

Akpabot studied the trumpet and organ in London at the Royal College of Music in 1954, with teachers such as John Addison, Osborn Pisgow, and Herbert Howells. Study at the University of Chicago yielded a Master's degree in Musicology, and he also received a Ph.D. from Michigan State University. He was a broadcaster for the Nigerian Broadcasting Corporation (1959), a founder member of the academic staff at the University of Nigeria, Nsukka (1962), visiting lecturer in African Music at Michigan State University, and a Research Fellow at the University of Ife and Professor of Music at the University of Uyo in the 1990s.

Akpabot started to compose in 1959, with a style characterized by his use of the Hi Life music tradition, with his traditional Ibibio music, melded with elements of European approaches. Akpabot is the only Nigerian composer to write solely for the orchestra using African instruments. PAH

Omojola, Bode, *Nigerian Art Music* (1995)

See also BANKOLE, AYO

Alamayahu, Dajazmach (1861–1879). Son of Téwodros II, Emperor of Ethiopia. Alamayahu was orphaned when his father committed suicide during the British assault on Magdala in the war of 1868. He was brought to Britain in the care of Captain Tristram Speedy as a ward of the government. At Osborne, in the Isle of Wight, Alamayahu was introduced to Queen Victoria, who from then on took a distant interest in the young boy's welfare. While on the Isle of Wight, Alamayahu caused something of a sensation among the islanders, and he was photographed by Julia Margaret Cameron; her pictures show a listless and sad-looking boy. Speed took the young Ethiopian prince with him to India, but at the age of 10, and against his wishes and the advice of Queen Victoria, he was sent to boarding school in Britain. At the age of 17 Alamayahu entered the Royal Military Academy at Sandhurst, the idea being that he would become an officer in an Indian Army regiment. After a brief and unhappy year Alamayahu left Sandhurst; he was lonely, in poor health, and, suffering from what appears to have been paranoia, he refused to eat. He pined away and died. At Victoria's request, Alamayahu was buried in St George's Chapel, Windsor. Queen Victoria wrote: 'All alone in a strange country . . . his was no happy life, full of difficulties of every kind, and he was so sensitive, thinking that people stared at him because of his colour . . . Everybody is so sorry.' DK

Bates, Darrell, 'The Abyssinian Boy', *History Today*, 29 (1979)

—— *The Abyssinian Difficulty* (1979)

Marsh, Jan (ed.), *Black Victorians: Black People in British Art 1800–1900* (2005)

See also BONETTA, SARAH FORBES; GEORGIAN AND VICTORIAN BRITAIN

Albright, Arthur (1811–1900). Chemist and phosphorus manufacturer, well known for his philanthropic views, born on 3 March 1811 in Charlbury, Oxfordshire, into a Quaker family. He was the son of William Albright and Rachel Tanner. In 1842 he joined the firm of John and Edward Sturge, manufacturing chemists in Birmingham. He was responsible for the development of Anton Schrotter's (1802–75) method of producing red phosphorus, important for the use of safety matches. This interest grew out of a concern for the health of match workers. In 1854 Albright took over a phosphorus plant previously belonging to the Sturge brothers, in Oldbury, Worcestershire. In 1856 he went into partnership with J. W. Wilson. Their firm survived until the middle of the 20th century.

Throughout his life Albright travelled in Europe, Egypt, and the United States seeking new sources of raw materials and trying to expand his export trade. When the Civil War broke out in the United States (1861), he worked at getting financial and material support for emancipated slaves. In his life he was also concerned with alleviating the slave-like conditions of black people in the West Indies. Furthermore, following the Franco-Prussian War, he tried to alleviate distress in France. And he also became an active member of the Arbitration Society. Albright married in 1848 and died on 3 July 1900 at Cheyne Walk, Chelsea, London. He was buried at Witton, Birmingham. ARF

ODNB

See also ABOLITION

Alcindor, John (1873–1924). Born in Trinidad, John Alcindor was among the first black West Indians to practise medicine in Britain. Winning an Island Scholarship enabled him to study medicine at Edinburgh University, from where he graduated in 1899 with first-class honours in three subjects. He was among delegates from the Edinburgh-based Afro-West Indian Literary Society to the 1900 Pan-African Conference, where he met and developed friendships with Samuel *Coleridge-Taylor and W. E. B. DuBois. Moving to London, Alcindor practised his profession in the city's hospitals, and for several years played cricket for the Mill Hill Park club. His marriage to Minnie *Alcindor (née Martin) in 1911 produced three sons. In 1917 Alcindor established his own medical practice, and also worked as a Poor Law medical officer. He published three scholarly studies on his research.

Alcindor was a founder member of the African Progress Union, over which he was elected president in 1921. Under his leadership, the Union waged a series of political campaigns to publicize the oppressed conditions of black peoples throughout the world.

Alcindor was also a key figure in the London Pan-African congresses of 1921 and 1923. He died in London in 1924. JPG

ODNB

Patton, Adell, *Physicians, Colonial Racism and Diaspora in West Africa* (1996)

See also DOCTORS; MEDICINE

Alcindor, Minnie Martin (1879–*c*.1950). Manager of a hostel for Africans in London in the 1920s and wife of Dr John *Alcindor. Born in London of a French father, raised by her mother's family, she trained as a journalist. She was disowned by her family after her marriage in 1911 to John Alcindor, a Trinidadian.

While raising their three children, John (1912), Cyril (1914), and Roland (Bob, 1917), Alcindor also assisted her husband in his west London medical practice, often dealing with patients herself when the Harrow Road surgery was closed.

Along with her husband, Alcindor was active in the Pan-Africanist movement (*see* PAN-AFRICANISM), and during the early

1920s was one of only two white women to serve on the committee of the London-based *African Progress Union, over which her husband presided from 1921.

Her husband's death in 1924 left the family in straitened circumstances, and to make ends meet, Alcindor established Remi House, a hostel for African students in London. Although Remi House became a busy meeting place for lonely Africans, Alcindor was forced to close the hostel after it failed as a financial venture. The family later moved to the Essex coast. During the *Second World War, her sons joined the Allied struggle against fascism. Bob joined the RAF, Frank served in the engineers, and Cyril was an infantry commander. Alcindor died during the 1950s.

JPG

Green, Jeffrey, 'John Alcindor (1873–1924): A Migrant's Biography', *Immigrants and Minorities*, 6/2 (1987)

Rampersad, Arnold, *The Life of Langston Hughes*, i (1986)

See also MEDICINE

Aldridge, Amanda Ira (1866–1956). Composer, contralto, successful vocal coach, accompanist, and teacher. She was the eldest daughter of the famous African-American actor Ira *Aldridge, and born in Upper Norwood, London. Early on she was educated at a convent school in Belgium. At the age of 17 she was awarded a scholarship to study singing at the Royal College of Music. Her teachers included Jenny Lind and George Henschel for singing, along with Frederick Bridge and Frances Edward Gladstone for harmony and counterpoint.

Aldridge's career was successful and varied, as a contralto until an attack of laryngitis damaged her voice, an accompanist, vocal coach, and later a composer. She accompanied her brother Ira Frederick Aldridge on musical tours until his death in 1886. She also accompanied her sister Luranah in concerts at many well-known London venues at the turn of the 20th century.

Aldridge also played a seminal role in the life of London's black community. She helped Roland *Hayes settle in the United Kingdom, and Hayes went on to sing her songs in recitals. She also coached Marian *Anderson and Ida Shepley, as well as pupils from the upper classes. In addition, she provided elocution lessons for Paul *Robeson in 1930, before his first appearance in *Othello*.

In her thirties, Aldridge composed songs and instrumental music under the name Montague Ring, keeping composition separate from her other work. Her music is in the popular style of the day, with syncopated dance rhythms. She was also a frequent broadcaster on radio and television.

PAH

Fuller, Sophie, *The Pandora Guide to Women Composers: Britain and the United States, 1629–Present* (1994)

ODNB

See also MUSIC 2: EARLY POPULAR MUSIC; RADIO

Aldridge, Ira (1807–1867). African-American tragedian and Shakespearean actor who emigrated to England and performed extensively in Europe. Aldridge was born to Daniel and Lurona Aldridge on 24 July 1807 in West Broadway, New York. There has been some confusion concerning his genealogy. One suggestion of his lineage was that he was a descendant of a princely line of the Fulah tribe in Senegal. This version is probably a romantic tale fabricated to accentuate an exoticism that would have boosted his dramatic persona. What is known, however, is that Daniel Aldridge was a straw-vendor and a pastor, who might have been a slave. There are no records to verify that Daniel was indeed a slave, but the name Aldridge was most probably that of a slave master.

Although Daniel had intended his son to join the ministry, the young Aldridge was already passionate about the theatre. After his education at the African Free School, which provided free education for black children in New York, Aldridge joined the African Theatre, but as with most black actors of talent in the United States at the time, colour prejudice proved too trying and undermining. Thus, Aldridge left for England on a ship bound for Liverpool, where he worked as a steward and an attendant to James William Wallack and Henry Wallack, brothers who played a significant role in encouraging Aldridge as an actor.

Aldridge most probably arrived in England in 1824 and made his debut in *The Revolt of Surinam; or, A Slave's Revenge*, an adaptation of Thomas Southerne's **Oroonoko* (1696), at the Coburg Theatre, London. Aldridge found in London a less racially tense environment for the development of his craft. His next performances included Thomas Morton's *The Slave* (1816), in which he played Gambia. Despite the relative ease with which he found acceptance among English audiences, Aldridge was subjected to numerous racist reviews from the London press. References to his inability to pronounce words because of his 'Negro lips' were made, and such hostility drove Aldridge to the English provinces, where he performed in Sheffield, Halifax, Manchester, Newcastle, Edinburgh, Lancaster, Liverpool, and Sunderland, with his basic repertoire of Shakespeare's **Othello* (*c.*1604), Thomas Southerne's adaptation of Aphra Behn's *Oroonoko* (1688), Morton's *The Slave*, Matthew Gregory Lewis's *The Castle Spectre* (1797), and Isaac Bickerstaff's *The Padlock* (1815). The character *Mungo in *The Padlock* as well as Othello were the two roles, one comic, the other tragic, which he would always play and which gained him especial fame and success.

In his early years of acting Aldridge used the stage name Mr Keene, after the famous actor Edmund Kean. He later presented himself as 'the African Roscius', after the Roman actor Quintus Roscius Gallus. His fame as the African Roscius grew, and he became highly acclaimed not merely among his audiences, but among actors of high standing as well. He received his first honour from the government of Haiti, who hailed him as 'the first man of colour in the theatre'.

Aldridge initially only played black roles as there was a proliferation of black characters in the theatre of his time. They provided not merely a path for anti-slavery propaganda but a commercial advantage, owing to the exoticism associated with them. Productions such as James Cobb's musical *Paul and Virginia* (1800) carried abolitionist messages and were seen as relevant to the anti-slavery attitudes prevalent in Britain at the time. Although black roles were in abundance, Aldridge needed more challenging dramatic avenues to extend his art and his talent. Thus, he played his first non-black role in October 1827 as Rolla, the Peruvian hero in Richard Sheridan's *Pizarro* (1799), an adaptation of August von Kotzebue's *Die Spanier in Peru*. In August 1830 Aldridge proceeded to play his first white European part as Captain Dirk Hatteraick in Daniel Terry's adaptation of Walter Scott's novel *Guy Mannering* (1816). Subsequently, he attempted more white roles such as Bertram in the Revd R. C. Maturin's *Bertram; or, The Castle of St. Aldobrand* (1816), Shylock in *The Merchant of Venice* (1600), King Lear, Macbeth, and Richard III, all of which he first played in Hull. Marshall and Stock suggest the significance of Hull to Aldridge's career as 'the first Negro to play white roles', as it was the birthplace of the renowned abolitionist William *Wilberforce, 'and sympathy would be strong for the young Negro actor, especially in this period when Wilberforce was still leading the fight in the House of Commons for the abolition of slavery in the Colonies'.

Apart from England, Aldridge also toured Ireland, Europe, and Russia. In Russia he received, like Paul *Robeson almost 100 years later, an enthusiastic reception of his talents. Consequently, Aldridge spent much of his dramatic career there, creating a significant impact on Russian theatre. In 1833 he was back in London, set to replace Edmund Kean as Othello at the Theatre Royal, Covent Garden. This was an important moment for Aldridge as it offered him the opportunity to win the hearts of London society, something which he had never managed to achieve. History, however, was to repeat itself, and Aldridge only played for two days, receiving, as he had done almost ten years before, severe racist reviews from the London press. He returned to the provincial theatres, where he gained the respect of English audiences and the patronage of certain members of the English, Irish, and Scottish nobility.

While working in the provinces Aldridge added **Titus Andronicus* to his usual repertoire, but in order to make the play less horrific and more respectable, he altered the entire play, softening the characters and transforming Aaron, the Moor, from a villain into a hero. He made theatrical history as the play had not been performed in Britain for 128 years. In 1852 he went on his first tour of the Continent, where he received great acclaim and several honours and medals. In Germany he was awarded the Golden Order of Service by the Duke of Saxe-Meiningen and became Chevalier Ira Aldridge, Knight of Saxony. After years of waiting for an invitation to perform in London's West End, Aldridge was finally invited to play Othello at the Lyceum Theatre. Despite his attachments to Russia and Europe, he applied for and was granted British citizenship in 1863. He died on a tour in Łódź, Poland, on 7 August 1867, at the age of 59. DD/SS

Barthelemy, A., *Black Face, Maligned Race: The Representation of Blacks in English Drama from Shakespeare to Southerne* (1987)
Marshall, H., and Stock, M., *Ira Aldridge: The Negro Tragedian* (1958)
ODNB
Scobie, E., *Black Britannia* (1972)

See also LITERATURE 3: DRAMA

Ali, Duse Mohamed (1886/7–1945). African journalist and nationalist born in Egypt of Egyptian and Sudanese parentage. At the age of 9 or 10 Ali was sent to England to be educated. He never returned to Egypt and spent most of his time between 1883 and 1921 living in Britain. During this period, he was poverty-stricken, attempting to earn a living through his pen and tour acting. Ali published *Land of the Pharaohs* in 1911, an anti-imperialist book that became a significant contribution to the decolonization efforts in the United States and West Africa.

In 1912 Ali and John Eldred Taylor, a journalist from Sierra Leone, inaugurated the **African Times and Orient Review* (1912–20), a magazine that sought to deal with anti-colonial issues that not merely embraced Pan-African matters, but incorporated Pan-Oriental topics as well. The journal was inspired by the Universal Race Congress in London in 1911, which advocated unity among all colonized people. Among the contributors to the magazine was the black nationalist Marcus *Garvey, who often visited Ali's Fleet Street office.

Ali was always militant in his anti-imperial views, and his magazine was treated with hostility by the Colonial Office. He gave hope to many black people, intellectuals, and the general public alike, and continually predicted the collapse of the British Empire. He moved to Nigeria in 1931, where he launched the magazine *Comet*. It played a vital role in the nationalist movement there. Ali died in Lagos in 1945. DD/SS

Adi, Hakim, and Sherwood, Marika, *Pan-African History: Political Figures from Africa and the Diaspora Since 1787* (2003)
Fryer, Peter, *Staying Power: The History of Black People in Britain* (1984)

See also PAN-AFRICANISM; PUBLISHING

Anderson, Marian (1897–1993). African-American international contralto born in February 1897 in Philadelphia, Pennsylvania. She graduated from Southern High School, Philadelphia, and her talent was recognized and supported by the black community. Roland *Hayes mentored her development. Studies with the famous Giuseppe Boghetti enabled her to win first prize in a competition and gain confidence. Her first recital in New York's Town Hall revealed her unease with foreign languages, and nearly caused her to give up singing. Boghetti encouraged her to go on, but she was unable to forge a career in the United States.

Anderson moved to London in 1925 and stayed with John Payne. She studied with Amanda Aldridge, received coaching in German from Frederic Morena and in

French from Madame Pasquier, and met the composer Roger Quilter, who introduced her to fellow musicians. Her European tour was successful, winning the admiration of Jean Sibelius, Arturo Toscanini, and the Archbishop of Salzburg.

In 1935 she returned to the United States as a famous artiste, but was refused access to perform in Constitution Hall. Eleanor Roosevelt enabled her to perform to over 75,000 people on the steps of Lincoln Memorial Hall. At the age of 54 she was the first black singer to be invited to sing at the Metropolitan Opera, taking the role of Ulrica in *Un ballo in maschera*. She retired from singing in 1965 after an illustrious career, despite having suffered discrimination, having toured extensively and met kings, queens, and presidents. She died in April 1993 in Portland, Oregon. PAH

Vehanen, Kosh, *Marian Anderson: A Portrait* (1941)

See also MUSIC 1: CLASSICAL MUSIC

Anthropology. The study of mankind, linked with the scientific urge to classify discrete phenomena.

1. 'Scientific racism'
2. The Anthropological Society
3. Aboriginal Australians
4. Religion and mythology
5. Malinowski and Radcliffe-Brown
6. The dark-skinned 'other'

1. 'Scientific racism' As Peter Fryer has shown, the roots of 'scientific racism' lay in pre-modern beliefs about the inferiority and godlessness of the black world, and its rise in the 19th century was historically accompanied by the increase in popular racism, whose structures it used and legitimized, and by the encroachments of colonialism on the non-white world.

The first British scientific philosophers showed an anxiety concerning race. In 1690 John Locke (in the *Essay Concerning Human Understanding*) used the example of a white child being unable to identify a black man as human to illustrate the concept of empiricism, while David Hume added a footnote to *Of National Characters* (in the 1753 reprint) to assert his belief that 'Negroes' and other 'species' of men were inferior to Europeans. The ideas were incidental to the flow of each thinker's argument, and clearly responded to popular debates of the period, yet it is telling that in the logic of empiricism racial differences rather than mutual similarities were key ontological categories.

Continental science, meanwhile, was systematizing the classification of species. In 1735 the Swede Carl Linnaeus invented a system for identifying plants based on their reproductive parts, honing it for usage in successive publications. It became internationally accepted, with pupils of Linnaeus such as Daniel Solander, James Cook's naturalist, naming the flora of newly discovered continents according to Linnaeus' tripartite system of species, genus, and name. In 1760 Linnaeus produced a gradation of animals, which included six types of men, the 'mute, hairy' Wild Man, the coppery American, the 'fair, sanguine, brawny' European 'covered with close vestments', the 'sooty, melancholy, rigid' Asiatic, the Monster (to include giants, dwarfs, and eunuchs), and the African—'black, phlegmatic, relaxed . . . crafty, indolent, negligent'. Further down this modern chain of being were more bizarre specimens: troglodytes, satyrs, and pygmies. Earlier versions of such systems had been mooted in Britain, for instance by Edward Topsell in the *Historie of Four-Footed Beasts* (1607) and by Edward Tyson following his dissection of a chimpanzee in 1699—the collective result being that Africans blurred into apes, baboons, and Aegopitheci (goat-apes), and were alternatively conceived as a missing link between men and beasts, or a separate species of mankind, coming from different parents (the doctrine of polygeny). The Linnaean system, still used today to classify plants, formalized scientific enquiries into the differences between black and white.

From this trend grew the vogue for measuring, comparing, and drawing social conclusions from differences in human anatomy, particularly skulls, whose size and shape were assumed to denote intelligence. In the writings of

British phrenologists such as William Lawrence, George Combe, W. F. Edwards, and Robert Verity, the shapes of black people's skulls were claimed to denote their inferior character, more like monkeys than humans, and meant that they had no chance of constructing history or civilization, giving Europeans carte blanche to introduce these through colonization. Phrenology showed the same impulse to evaluate racial character according to anatomical distinctions that would later result in the misapplication of Charles Darwin's evolutionary theory to primitive societies, and would feed the proto-fascist theories of eugenicists such as Francis *Galton and Sidney Webb, who believed that criminality could be predicted from the size of one's head (the cure being enforced sterilization). During the same period, Fryer shows that racial theory was harnessed as a propaganda tool to justify slavery. For commentators such as Edward *Long in the *History of Jamaica* (1774), Charles White in *Account of the Regular Gradation in Man* (1799), and Robert Knox in *The Races of Men* (1850), the black race was savage, stupid, and fit only for slavery or, in the more chilling arguments of such prototype texts of anthropology, extinction.

A further aspect of the system of classification was that its usage shifted from the purely racial to the social, or class-based. In the Elizabethan period, for example, much of the discourse surrounding the colonization of Ireland had depicted its inhabitants as feral, if not actually savage, and this continued into later periods: Fryer notes the shock of a 19th-century visitor to Ireland on seeing the 'white monkeys' of the West Coast. The lascivious stereotypes applied to Blacks demanded, when small numbers of them began to live in England, the complementary belief in equally insatiable, or at least numerous, white participants: the 'loose women' of London whose degeneracy would result, in Long's analysis, in that horrifying prospect, a mixed-race Britain.

2. The Anthropological Society The Anthropological Society of London was founded by James Hunt in 1863, effectively removing the power of the former Ethnology Society (of which Hunt was secretary) from humanists such as Darwin, Thomas Hodgkin, and James Pritchard. Early speakers included Richard Burton on Dahomeyan circumcision rites (illustrated with male and female specimens), W. T. Pritchard on childbirth, menstruation, and defloration in the South Pacific, and Edward Sellon on phallus worship in India. Hunt himself spoke on 'The Negro's Place in Nature' (it was lowly), and at a moment of great crisis for the Society, British intellectuals including John Ruskin, Charles Dickens, Matthew Arnold, Charles Kingsley, and Alfred, Lord Tennyson, rallied behind its illustrious member Governor Eyre of Jamaica, whose punitive slaughter of 439 people following the *Morant Bay rebellion in 1865 resulted in a royal commission of inquiry. Eyre was exonerated, though this was not enough for the self-styled Eyre Defence Committee, who sought to get him a peerage; his opponents, who included Darwin, John Stuart Mill, Thomas Huxley, and Herbert Spencer, were called by Thomas *Carlyle 'Nigger-Philanthropists, barking furiously in the gutter'.

3. Aboriginal Australians By the time Darwin's evolutionary theory had been added to the mix, a new race of Blacks had been discovered, seemingly more primitive than Africans, with no written language, no concept of god, and, apparently, no social hierarchy—the aboriginal Australians, who were so primitive that even a Maori visitor to Sydney in 1800, Tipahee, was disgusted at their lack of sophistication. As well as supporting the doctrine of *terra nullius* (vacant land, or finders keepers), their bestial state excited social Darwinists: the swift demise of hundreds of thousands of Aborigines, hastened by smallpox, syphilis, warfare, and, in the case of Tasmania, genocide, seemed to prove the law of 'survival of the fittest'. Robert Hughes outlines the sad story of apartheid, grave-robbing, the mutilation and theft of corpses, all in the name of scientific enquiry, that followed the campaign to purge Tasmania of its Aboriginal population in the 1830s: there is today an ongoing battle to trace and have returned from British and European museums the ancestors of indigenous Tasmanians (a few of whom survived in mixed-race sealing settlements).

4. Religion and mythology In the early 20th century the workings of religious belief became a preoccupation of anthropology (aboriginal Australians were again the touchstone for much of the research). Researchers such as E. B. Tylor, Andrew Lang, Baldwin Spencer, and F. G. Gillen considered how the primitive mind conceived its world in mythological, rather than rational, structures; the most famous text is J. G. Frazer's immense catalogue of world religions, *The Golden Bough* (1911–15), which asserted the existence of a fertility myth of sacrifice and rebirth common to diverse world cultures. As James Clifford has noted, this twelve-volume compendium was the textual equivalent of jumbled storehouses of imperial relics such as the Pitt Rivers Museum in Oxford, the Museum of Archaeology and Anthropology in Cambridge, and London's Museum of Mankind, where vast arrays of artefacts are displayed thematically with little consideration of the divergence and historical variation between 'primitive' cultures.

5. Małinowski and Radcliffe-Brown Twentieth-century British anthropology adapted the ideas on fieldwork of Bronisław Małinowski, who was trapped on a small island near Papua New Guinea owing to Australian restrictions on central European residents during the First World War. These argued that immersion within a primitive culture was necessary to gain understanding of its individual perspectives, which were hidden to the outsider, but formed the rational basis of customary institutions; Małinowski trained a generation of eminent social anthropologists at the London School of Economics, including Raymond Firth, E. E. Evans-Pritchard, Isaac Schapera, Audrey Richards, Max Gluckman, and the future President of Kenya, Jomo Kenyatta. Opposed to this 'functionalist' model was A. R. Radcliffe-Brown, influenced by Émile Durkheim, who sought to understand the primitive world through the comparative study of its social structures, using fieldwork as a form of scientific data collection.

6. The dark-skinned 'other' In contemporary anthropology representations of non-white humanity as primitive beings continue to flourish, in the glossy close-up photos of black and brown faces, always decorated with dye, feathers, and beads, which adorn the majority of textbooks. These seem to belong to a tradition of exotica evident in ethnographic photograph albums such as the 19th-century Sturge Collection, held in Birmingham Central Library, where the display costumes of 'natives' symbolize their entire cultures, as if British subjects of the same period went around all the time in their 'Sunday best'. By this process the dark-skinned 'other' is laid out for white consumption. JM

Clifford, James, *The Predicament of Culture: Twentieth Century Ethnography, Literature and Art* (1988)

Fryer, Peter, *Staying Power: The History of Black People in Britain* (1984)

Hiatt, L. R., *Arguments About Aborigines: Australia and the Development of Social Anthropology* (1996)

Hughes, Robert, *The Fatal Shore: A History of the Transportation of Convicts to Australia, 1787–1868* (2003)

Monaghan, John, and Just, Peter, *Social and Cultural Anthropology: A Very Short Introduction* (2000)

Pratt, Mary Louise, *Imperial Eyes: Travel Writing and Transculturation* (1992)

See also EUGENICS; SKIN COLOUR AND RACE, THEORIES OF

Anti-Apartheid Movement. The Anti-Apartheid Movement (AAM) campaigned in Britain and internationally for the isolation of South Africa and for support for all those struggling against apartheid. From small beginnings in 1959, it became one of Britain's biggest ever international solidarity movements, campaigning against the Thatcher government's refusal to impose sanctions against South Africa in the 1980s and for the release of

Nelson Mandela. The AAM dissolved itself in 1995 after South Africa held its first free elections in April 1994.

1. 'A great cause'
2. Isolating South Africa
3. Campaigning for political prisoners
4. The unholy alliance
5. The Thatcher paradox
6. The black community in Britain

1. 'A great cause' On 26 June 1959 a group of South African exiles and their British supporters launched a campaign for a boycott of South African goods at a meeting in central London. They were responding to a call by the African National Congress (ANC) within South Africa for a boycott of products of Nationalist-controlled firms. The move to internationalize the ANC's appeal was endorsed by its President, Chief Lutuli, who stated that 'economic boycott is one way in which the world can bring home to the South African authorities that they must either mend their ways or suffer for them'. The Boycott Movement was part of a network which in the late 1950s campaigned against colonialism in Africa, for peace and nuclear disarmament, and against endemic racism in Britain. From the start it tried to appeal to a broad cross-section of British public opinion, asking people of all races, classes, religions, and political allegiances to 'unite in a great cause'. In March 1960 it organized a month of boycott action, which was supported by the Labour and Liberal parties and the TUC.

On 21 March 1960 the South African police shot dead 69 unarmed Pan-Africanist Congress (PAC) protesters at Sharpeville. The shootings attracted worldwide condemnation and were followed by the banning of the ANC and PAC. The British campaign, now renamed the Anti-Apartheid Movement, widened its demands to call for an international boycott of South Africa in every field—diplomatic, economic, military, sporting, cultural, and academic. Above all it campaigned for United Nations mandatory economic sanctions against South Africa under Chapter VII of the UN Charter, on the grounds that South Africa's racial policies were a threat to international peace.

2. Isolating South Africa The policies pursued by successive Conservative and Labour governments on South Africa from 1960 until the mid-1970s were essentially bipartisan. Governments condemned apartheid but were committed to safeguarding Britain's extensive economic interests in South Africa and the Cape sea route. The 1964–70 Labour government imposed an arms embargo, but this was so narrowly defined as to exclude almost everything except major weaponry. The 1970–4 Conservative government lifted the ban, but because of domestic and Commonwealth opposition only supplied South Africa with Wasp helicopters, which the Labour government had also supplied under the terms of its embargo. Neither government imposed any restrictions on investment or trade with South Africa. It was only in the late 1970s, when Britain's entry into the EEC and South Africa's own economic problems made it less important as an economic partner, that government ministers began to consider a change of policy. In November 1977 the Labour government voted for a mandatory arms embargo under Chapter VII of the UN Charter. Although the embargo was shot through with loopholes, it was a major step forward; in 1979 the AAM sponsored the World Campaign Against Military and Nuclear Collaboration with South Africa to monitor breaches of the embargo and campaign for its stricter enforcement.

In the 1970s, while the AAM bombarded the government with memos calling for a stricter arms ban and economic disengagement from South Africa, it put most of its energy into persuading individuals and organizations to boycott South African goods and disinvest from companies with South African interests. One of its most successful campaigns was against Barclays Bank, when campaigners pioneered the tactic of disrupting its annual general meeting in 1971 and students forced the closure of Barclays' campus branches. Britain's Afro-Caribbean community, many of whom banked with Barclays because of Barclays' presence in Britain's former colonies, withdrew their custom in their thousands. Barclays finally pulled out of South Africa in 1986, admitting accounts had haemorrhaged.

The AAM also campaigned for a sporting, cultural, and academic boycott of South Africa. In 1969 it mounted countrywide demonstrations against the Springboks rugby tour and called for the cancellation of the 1970 Springboks cricket tour. The cricket tour was called off because of widespread opposition within Britain and after Commonwealth countries threatened to withdraw from the 1970 Commonwealth Games. Britain's black community again played an important role, with the formation of the West Indian Campaign against Apartheid Cricket. In 1977 the British government endorsed the Commonwealth Gleneagles Agreement, which pledged governments to discourage sporting contacts with South Africa. In 1984 the Black British Standing Conference on Apartheid and Sport protested against the English rugby union tour of South Africa.

From 1957 the Musicians' Union, which had a history of combating race discrimination against musicians in Britain, prohibited its members from working in South Africa. The film technicians' union, the ACTT, also stopped its members from working there. In 1963 the AAM persuaded leading playwrights to stop their plays being performed in South Africa.

3. Campaigning for political prisoners In July 1963 the apartheid regime arrested Nelson Mandela and other leaders of the ANC's armed wing, Umkhonto we Sizwe, at their secret headquarters at Rivonia and charged them with planning guerrilla warfare. In response the AAM launched the World Campaign for the Release of South African Political Prisoners. Mandela and his comrades were convicted but, partly because of the campaign, they escaped the death penalty and were sentenced to life imprisonment.

For the next 30 years the AAM continued to work for the release of all southern African political prisoners. In 1973 it joined with the International Defence and Aid Fund and other organizations to set up the Southern Africa the Imprisoned Society (SATIS), which campaigned for freedom for all political prisoners and detainees, against torture, and to save the lives of those who, like the 20-year-old ANC militant Solomon Mahlangu, were condemned to death. Mahlangu was hanged in 1979, but in a series of high-profile cases in the 1980s the apartheid regime was forced by international protests to commute the death sentences imposed on political prisoners.

4. The unholy alliance As the rest of Africa won its independence, the AAM exposed the 'unholy alliance' of South Africa, Rhodesia, and Portugal, which fought a losing battle against the liberation movements in its colonies of Mozambique, Angola, and Guinea Bissau until 1975. After Ian Smith made his unilateral declaration of independence in Southern Rhodesia in 1965, the AAM campaigned for No Independence Before Majority Rule and for backing for the Zimbabwean liberation movements. In the late 1970s and throughout the 1980s the apartheid regime raided the front-line states and fomented civil war in Angola and Mozambique; the AAM worked to promote support for them within Britain and for international action in their defence. With the Namibia Support Committee it campaigned against de facto British backing for South Africa's illegal occupation of Namibia and in support of the South West African People's Organization (SWAPO), which won Namibia's first free election held in November 1989.

5. The Thatcher paradox The growth of above-ground opposition to apartheid within South Africa after the 1976 Soweto uprising and the township insurrections that began in 1984 led to growing international support for sanctions. Paradoxically, as the British Prime Minister, Margaret Thatcher, blocked the imposition of sanctions, her intransigence stimulated support for the AAM. In the 1980s the AAM drew together a unique alliance of opposition political parties, trade unions, local authorities, the churches, and hundreds of thousands of ordinary people of all races behind the demand for the isolation of South Africa. Beginning with a 50,000-strong demonstration against the South African Prime Minister, P. W. Botha's visit to Britain in June 1984, the AAM mounted some of the biggest demonstrations ever seen on the streets of London. Although Thatcher's obduracy stopped the imposition of significant economic measures against South Africa by Britain or the EEC, the AAM helped to put sanctions on the international agenda and to mobilize people in Britain to impose 'people's sanctions'.

From 1978, when Prime Minister James Callaghan called for Nelson Mandela's release on his 60th birthday, the campaign for freedom for Mandela mushroomed, culminating in the 1988 'Nelson Mandela: Freedom at 70' campaign. Seventy-two thousand people attended a birthday tribute concert at Wembley Stadium on 11 June 1988, which was televised in 63 countries and watched by millions of viewers all over the world. The day after the concert, a huge political rally in Scotland gave a send-off to 25 Mandela marchers, who set off on a five-week walk from Glasgow to London. The campaign climaxed on the eve of Mandela's 70th birthday on 18 July 1988, when a quarter of a million people gathered in London's Hyde Park. In June–July 1988 a Gallup Poll showed that a remarkable 77 per cent of people in Britain knew who Mandela was and that 70 per cent of them thought that he should be released.

6. The black community in Britain Britain's black community was prominent in the upsurge of anti-apartheid activity in the 1980s. The MP Bernie *Grant joined the AAM's Executive Committee and travelled to South Africa to greet Nelson Mandela on the day he was released from prison. The AAM's Black and Ethnic Minorities (later renamed Black Solidarity) Committee liaised with black organizations. The part played by black Britons was acknowledged by Mandela on his visit to Britain in 1990 and again in May 1993, a few weeks after the murder of Stephen *Lawrence, when he met Doreen and Neville Lawrence.

The AAM's campaigns contributed to pressure on the South African government, which led to the lifting of the bans on the ANC, PAC, and South African Communist Party, and Mandela's release in February 1990. Crucially, its consistent support for the ANC helped to confirm the ANC as the key organization in the negotiations with the National Party that led to the installation of Nelson Mandela as South Africa's first democratically elected President in May 1994.

The extent to which the AAM should support anti-racist struggles in Britain was an issue that recurred throughout its history. It spoke out against the Commonwealth Immigrants Act in 1968 and on high-profile deportation cases in the 1980s, but generally it was left to AAM local groups to take up local anti-racist campaigns. Implicit in this stance was the argument that British support for racism in southern Africa was a politically distinct issue from that of racism in Britain; but that the downfall of the world's most extreme racist regime and its replacement by a non-racial democracy would change the context of anti-racist struggles everywhere.

The AAM was unique as a British movement that saw its campaign to end British support for apartheid as part of a wider struggle in which the southern African liberation movements were the main protagonists. It thus eschewed the paternalism that underlay earlier movements such as the campaign for the abolition of the slave trade and which still informs much of Western attitudes to Africa today. CG

Archive of the Anti-Apartheid Movement, Bodleian Library of Commonwealth and African Studies, Rhodes House, Oxford

Fieldhouse, Roger, *Anti-Apartheid: A History of the Movement in Britain* (2005)

Guelke, Adrian, *Rethinking the Rise and Fall of Apartheid: South Africa and World Politics* (2004)

See also COMMUNISM; POLITICS

Anti-Slavery Society. Organization dedicated to securing the *emancipation of slaves in British colonies and elsewhere; the successor of earlier groups that campaigned for *abolition. The first formal organization in Britain dedicated to abolition was the Committee on the Slave Trade, established in 1783 by the London-based Quaker group the Meeting for Sufferings. The Committee for the Abolition of the Slave Trade (also referred to as the Society for the Abolition of the Slave Trade), which was established in 1787, included nine Quakers among its twelve members; the non-Quaker members included Thomas *Clarkson and Granville *Sharp. This committee was a major part of the campaign that eventually led to the ending of the British slave trade by Parliament in 1807, and it was also involved in the creation of the colony for freed slaves in Sierra Leone (*see* SIERRA LEONE SETTLERS). After 1807 the Committee's work was effectively done, and leading abolitionists transferred their efforts to the *African Institution founded the same year.

In 1823, however, a new organization was formed, called the Society for the Mitigation and Gradual Abolition of Slavery throughout the British Dominions, which was often called simply the Anti-Slavery Society. This included members of the older generation of abolitionists, such as William *Wilberforce, as well as newer activists such as Thomas Fowell *Buxton. The Society's purpose was explained by its longer title: the original expectation that ending the slave trade and thus new imports of slaves into the colonies would oblige slave owners to improve their treatment of the slaves they already possessed had turned out to be too sanguine, and it was planned to secure the passage of various legislative measures that would at once improve the position of the slaves in the present and prepare the way for their emancipation at some point in the future. The British Parliament did agree in 1823 to a series of measures for the amelioration of the condition of the slaves, and this in turn led to the passage of a range of similar measures by local legislatures in the colonies. These measures turned out to be of only limited effect, although they roused slave owners to greater determination to protect what they saw as their rights. The Society resolved in 1831 to campaign for immediate rather than gradual emancipation, and an Agency Committee was formed to carry a campaign for this throughout the country. In this they were seconded by local committees, which eventually numbered in the hundreds and presented thousands of petitions to Parliament. Even after the passage of the Emancipation Act in 1833, the Agency Committee continued to campaign against the apprenticeship system in the colonies, which continued to keep the former slaves in a state of semi-freedom, and this helped to secure the ending of apprenticeship in 1838, two years earlier than had originally been envisaged.

In 1839 Joseph *Sturge, who had been one of the leading members of the Agency Committee, joined with others to create a new group, the British and Foreign Anti-Slavery Society. This continued to campaign against slavery and the slave trade throughout the world. While a major focus in the 19th century was on the continuance of both slavery and the slave trade in Africa, the Society broadened its focus to draw attention to abuses of the indentured labour system which took workers from China and India to British colonies in the Caribbean, Mauritius, and Fiji. It also came to work increasingly closely with the Aborigines Protection Society, formed in 1837, and the two groups merged in 1909 to become the Anti-Slavery and Aborigines Protection Society. This still exists, though there was a further change of name, to Anti-Slavery International, in 1990. While formal slavery is no longer legally recognized anywhere in the world (though this only became true in the 1960s), conditions that are in practice indistinguishable remain widespread in many parts of the world. These include sex trafficking, types of child labour, and debt bondage, which, at the most conservative estimate, continued to affect the lives of millions at the beginning of the 21st century. JG

Anti-Slavery International, <http://www.antislavery.org>

Hurwitz, Edith F., *Politics and the Public Conscience: Slave Emancipation and the Abolitionist Movement in Britain* (1973)

See also GLADSTONE, JOHN; SLAVE TRADE; SLAVERY

Archer, John Richard (1863–1932). Pan-Africanist and the first black person to hold civic office in Britain. He was born in Liverpool, the son of a Barbadian, Richard Archer, and an Irishwoman, Mary Theresa Burns, but little is known of his early life, though he is believed to have lived in North America and the West Indies. Around 1898 he and his African-Canadian wife, Bertha, moved to Battersea, south London, where Archer established a photographic studio. His concern to eradicate social and racial injustices led to a lifelong career in local government and national and global politics. In 1906 he was elected as a Progressive (Liberal) councillor for the Latchmere ward, and in 1913 Archer became Mayor of Battersea, Britain's first black mayor. His interest in colonial politics led to his involvement in Pan-Africanism. In 1900 he joined the Pan-African Association, and he was a significant presence at the first Pan-African Congress (Paris, 1919). He chaired a session on colonial freedom at the second Pan-African Congress (London, 1921), where he introduced the Indian Shapurji Saklatvala, a member of both the Labour and the Communist parties in Great Britain. He served as president of the *African Progress Union (1918–21) and worked with many leading Pan-Africanists of the day. In 1925 Archer was elected an alderman, and at the time of his death in 1932 he was serving as Deputy Leader of Battersea Council. He had an extraordinary record of service to local and national politics and to black people worldwide. ARF

Fryer, Peter, *Staying Power: The History of Black People in Britain* (1984)

ODNB

See also PAN-AFRICANISM; POLITICS

Asa-Asa, Louis (fl. 1831). African slave who arrived in England and recorded his experiences in a narrative. Details of Asa-Asa's birth and death are unknown. He was captured from his home in Bycla, near Egie, West Africa, and was eventually placed aboard a French vessel called *The Pearl*. Owing to severe weather conditions, the ship landed in the port of St Ives, Cornwall. Subsequently, Asa-Asa and four other shipmates were taken to London. While in England, he wrote the 'Narrative of Louis Asa-Asa, a Captured African' (1831), which details his family background, the invasion of the 'Adinyes', or the African slave traders, who set fire to his village as they sought to kill, torture, or capture its inhabitants, and his experiences on the ships that eventually led him to England. Prior to his arrival, he was taken to various places and sold numerous times. After six months of journeying, he and his shipmates were bought by the French. They spent another six months on a large ship where they were brutally flogged and many slaves died following gross mistreatment. The narrative concludes with a rhetorical exaltation of England, a country, he stresses, that has brought him happiness and freedom. He insists on remaining in the country and appeals to the King of England, in whom he places faith, to cease the practice of slavery for the benefit of other Africans who have not attained the same comforts as he has. Unlike other slave narratives of the period, Asa-Asa's has been relatively under-explored. DD/SS

'Narrative of Louis Asa-Asa, a Captured African' in *The History of Mary Prince, a West Indian Slave as Related by Herself* (ed. Moira Ferguson, 1987)

Atwell, Winifred (1914–1983). Famous pianist in the United Kingdom during the 1950s, selling over 20 million records. She was born in Tunapuna, Trinidad, in February 1914. She studied the piano as a child and had a local following. It was hoped that she would eventually work for the family business, after her training in pharmacy.

To gain further musical training, Atwell moved to the United States in 1945, and then came to London in 1946, to the Royal Academy of Music, to become a concert pianist. To sustain her studies, she performed piano rags at hotels, theatres, and clubs in London. By 1950 she had attained national celebrity, and signed to record with Decca. She recorded such hits as *Let's Have a Ding-Dong*, *Poor People of Paris*, *Britannia Rag*, and many others. *The Black and White Rag* became the signature tune for the BBC's *Pot Black* snooker programme in the 1970s.

Atwell made numerous television appearances, concerts, and Royal Variety performances. The format for her concerts would include an opening classical work, played on a grand piano, followed by music played on a honky-tonk piano, purchased in a Battersea junk shop for the princely sum of £2 10s.

Atwell tried, unsuccessfully, to offset the decline of her popularity by playing more rock 'n' roll hits with her honky-tonk style. On emigration to Australia with her husband, Lew Levisohn, she concentrated on classical music, and toured with symphony orchestras. She continued to perform until her retirement in 1978. She died in February 1983.

PAH

Hardy, Phil, *The Faber Companion to Twentieth Century Popular Music* (2001)
ODNB

See also GRAMOPHONE RECORDINGS; MUSIC 1: CLASSICAL MUSIC

B

Baartman, Sarah. Also known as Sara or Saartjie, and as Bartman (1788?–1815/16), a member of the Khoisan people of southern Africa, exhibited as a 'freak' in 19th-century Britain. Her original name is unknown, but when she was employed by a Dutch farmer called Peter Cezar, she was given the Afrikaans name of Saartjie [Little Sarah] Baartman, and this was later Anglicized in various forms. In 1810 she was brought to Britain by Peter Cezar's brother Hendric [or Henrick], a Boer farmer at the Cape, and Alexander Dunlop, a British army surgeon. Dunlop soon sold his interest in the enterprise to Cezar, who made money by exhibiting Baartman in London and elsewhere in Britain under the name of 'the Hottentot Venus'. 'Hottentot' was a traditional derogatory term for Khoisan people, while 'Venus' appears intended to refer to the idea of 'the *Sable Venus', or more generally, to white assumptions about the sexuality of black people. While black people had been treated as exhibits in Britain before (*see* EXHIBITS, BLACK PEOPLE AS), this appears to be the first time in Britain, and possibly Europe, that a Khoisan person had been seen in this manner. It is clear from contemporary newspaper accounts that the main attraction for British curiosity-seekers was provided by Baartman's prominent buttocks. Although it is sometimes said that she was exhibited naked, contemporary accounts suggest that she was (at least usually) clothed, though in a dress that was both skimpy and deliberately of a colour as close to her skin as possible, so as to suggest nakedness. It is also clear that those who had paid to see her were allowed, or, indeed, invited by Cezar to poke and prod her as they saw fit.

While there seem to have been plenty of people willing to pay the not inconsiderable sum of 2*s*. to see Baartman in this manner, there were others who found the display distasteful, and letters of protest appeared in the newspapers. Cezar wrote to one paper in reply, denying accusations of cruelty, asserting that Baartman was not, as had been suggested, his slave, and claiming that she took part in the show of her own free will. Other (white) persons made, or had made, money by exhibiting themselves, he pointed out, asking whether Baartman had not the right to do the same thing.

Not everyone was satisfied, however, and in October 1810 Zachary *Macaulay and others sought to have a court of law order Baartman to be handed over to the *African Institution so that she could be returned to her homeland. Affidavits were given about her being mistreated by Cezar, and a museum proprietor stated that Dunlop had offered to sell the woman to him, which contradicted the claims that she was a free agent. When the case was brought before the Court of King's Bench in November 1810, so great was the public interest in the matter that the Attorney-General appeared on behalf of Baartman, and reports appeared in many London and provincial newspapers. By order of the court, Baartman was interviewed (in the absence of Cezar) by two interpreters, who spoke to her in Dutch, having satisfied themselves that this language was adequately understood by her. Their report (which is the nearest thing we have to a statement by Baartman herself, and which does provide a few personal details about her and her family) was that Baartman declared that she was employed by Cezar of her own free will, that she was to receive half of the money received for exhibiting herself, that she was 'perfectly happy', and that she had no desire to return to her own country. As a result, the case was dismissed. Whether her testimony was reliable, and whether she might still have felt pressured by Cezar even though he was not present during the interview, is something about which we can only speculate.

Baartman then seems to have continued to exhibit herself, or to have been exhibited, in London and elsewhere in Britain, for some considerable time. She was baptized in Manchester on 1 December 1811. In September 1814 she arrived in Paris, where she attracted enormous popular and scientific curiosity until her death at the end of 1815 or beginning of 1816. Both the exact date of her death and her age at the time are uncertain; statements by Baartman herself would place her date of birth around 1788, while later estimates suggested she was 10 years older.

After her death Baartman was dissected by Georges Cuvier (1769–1832), one of the leading naturalists of the day. A plaster cast was made of her body, and a wax cast of her genitals. Her skeleton was preserved and displayed together with the plaster cast until the 1980s at the Musée de l'Homme in Paris, which also kept her brain and her genitals. After a prolonged campaign by the South African government and others, her remains were finally returned to South Africa in 2002 and she was given an official funeral at Hankey in the Eastern Cape on 9 August 2002.

In the 19th century Baartman was the focus of considerable attention because the extent to which she differed from white anthropologists' ideas about 'normal' human anatomy was made to fit racial theories that interpreted difference from white 'norms' as evidence of inferiority. Her large buttocks and labia were also viewed as evidence that supported white prejudices about the alleged excessive sexuality of black people. More recently, she has been the subject of academic writings, journalistic essays, fiction, poetry, and films, which have seen her as a powerful symbol of racial, colonial, and sexual exploitation. Of Sarah Baartman as a human being we have only a few scattered hints, such as those in the account of her by Cuvier, published in 1824, which, although it described her physical appearance in a demeaning manner, called her personality 'sprightly', and noted that she could speak 'tolerably good Dutch' and a little English and French (as well as her native Khoi). JG

Edwards, Paul, and Walvin, James, *Black Personalities in the Era of the Slave Trade* (1983)

Gould, Steven Jay, *The Flamingo's Smile* (1985)

Lindfors, Bernth, 'Courting the Hottentot Venus' in Lindfors, *The Blind Men and the Elephant, and Other Essays in Biographical Criticism* (1987)

ODNB

See also GEORGIAN AND VICTORIAN BRITAIN

Ballets Nègres, Les. Black dance company, which presented its first season at the Twentieth Century Theatre in London on 30 April 1946 under their artistic director and choreographer Berto Pasuka. Pasuka, a Jamaican of mixed parentage, arrived in England in 1939. He obtained small parts in the films *Rain of the Pacific* and *Men of Two Worlds*, the latter providing the resources to establish Les Ballets Nègres. With Pasuka's close friend Richie Riley, this company laid the foundation for Caribbean and African theatrical dance in Britain.

A culturally diverse company of approximately 25 members (dancers, musicians, and other support staff), performers came from Jamaica, Liverpool, Ghana, Nigeria, England, and Trinidad. They presented four full-length ballets—*De Prophet*, *They Came*, *Aggrey*, and *Market Day*—generally receiving positive reviews. They toured extensively in the United Kingdom and Europe, and though they were very popular in post-war Britain, Pasuka's work was viewed as exotic and primitive. At the height of its fame, the company was excluded from the 1951 Festival of Britain.

Pasuka created work from a traditional African-Caribbean perspective and he reintroduced a close relationship between performers and audiences, something that was lost in British dance theatre. His work was about black life experiences was filled with rituals and symbolisms from Africa and the Caribbean. The company excited audiences for six years, but lack of funds forced it to close in 1953. Pasuka died in 1963 and Riley in 1997.

BR

Harpe, Bill, 'Steps into Black History', *The Guardian*, 15 Apr. 1997

See also BLACK DANCE

Banking, insurance, and the colonial trade. The triangular shipping route of the slave trade largely formed the banking industry in England. British goods such as textiles, arms, and iron were exchanged for slaves in Africa, which were then transported to the West Indies and traded for sugar, tobacco, cotton, spices, and rum. The triangular trade was a system of immense earnings, as every ship sailed with a profitable cargo. The wealth generated by the triangular trade brought increased affluence to the planters who cultivated the West Indian produce, the merchant capitalists who sold the slaves, and the industrial capitalists who produced the British goods, which in turn demanded new banking facilities and functions.

The first of these new requirements was insurance. Shipowners and slave merchants themselves insured early voyages travelling the triangular trade route. However, the increasing amount of bills drawn against West Indian merchants and accumulated wealth soon required large-scale insurance schemes, most often drawn by West Indian absentee landlords. Insurance covered both ships and cargo; this included African slaves, who were regarded as property of the shipowners and insured against 'perils of the sea' for as little as £30 each.

The insurance market is believed to have begun at Edward Lloyd's coffee house in London around 1688. Lloyd's began its association with the slave trade by providing up-to-date and reliable shipping news for sailors, shipowners, and merchants, who met to discuss private insurance agreements. Advertisements in the *London Gazette* also listed Lloyd's as a place where runaway slaves could be returned. While Lloyd's began to provide insurance against fires in the West Indies early in the slave trade, the first direct link between Lloyd's and slavery is a 1692 advertisement for the sale of three slave ships cleared for Barbados and Virginia. A 1720 record also links Lloyd's to trade to Barbary and Africa. Other insurance providers included the Phoenix, one of the first companies to open a branch in the West Indies, and the Liverpool Underwriters' Association, founded in 1802 and chaired by the prominent West Indian merchant John *Gladstone.

In addition to insuring ships and cargo, Lloyd's was also linked to the slave trade through its staff—illustrative of a widespread trend of slave trade merchants who had once offered private insurance on a smaller scale becoming involved in the new functions of banking. Joseph Marryat, one of Lloyd's most successful chairmen, was a West Indian planter who helped maintain the company's monopoly on marine insurance when he took on a rival business, also owned by a West Indian. Marryat was a slave-owner on a large scale; he received £15,000 compensation for 391 slaves in Trinidad and Jamaica in 1837.

Lloyd's was not the only financial organization to have its origins in the slave trade. David Barclay, influential London merchant and Jamaican plantation owner, is listed with his brother Alexander as Quaker slave traders in 1756. The brothers married into the banking families of Gurney and Freame to form Barclays Bank. The Bank of England shared a similar history; a report dated 1 January 1800 lists £581,000 of the bank's capital tied to sugar and slave merchants. Humphrey Morice, MP and director of the bank from 1716, owned six slave ships, while Sir Richard Neave, director of the bank for 48 years, was chairman of the Society of West India Merchants and the London

Dock Company. Sir Francis Baring, another prominent London banker, is thought to have started his career by trading slaves at the age of 16.

Bankers in port cities such as Manchester, *Bristol, and *Liverpool also benefited from the slave trade. William Miles chaired a committee to oppose abolition in 1789 in Bristol; six of the city's bankers served as members. Ten well-known slave merchants played a role in founding ten of Liverpool's fourteen major banks listed after 1750. Other local bankers, such as John Moss of Moss, Dale and Rogers, owned sugar plantations in the West Indies. The founders of Heywood Bank, established in 1773, are listed as merchants trading to Africa in 1752. The bank remained private until 1883, when the Bank of Liverpool bought it; the African interests of the Heywood founders survived until 1807. Other Liverpool families involved in both banking and the slave trade include the Bolds, Gregsons, and Staniforths. At their height, each of the Liverpool banks associated with the slave trade could claim assets between £200,000 and £300,000.

Foremost of these Liverpool bankers, however, is Thomas Leyland. One of the city's wealthiest and most active slave traders, Leyland became the senior partner in the banking firm of Charles and Roscoe in 1802 before launching his own bank with Richard Bullin, a slave trade merchant and shipowner, in 1807. The Leyland and Bullin Bank had assets of over £1 million within eight years.

The involvement of banks in the colonial trade did not stop with abolition. Barclays Bank and the Bank of British West Africa, financed by Lloyds Bank, the Westminster Bank, the Standard Bank, and the National Provincial Bank, were the dominant banks in Africa in the early 20th century. Barclays Bank was also involved in loaning money to British colonies. The bank's directors were members of a council established by the Colonial Secretary to allocate colonial development and welfare grants as a response to West Indian rioting in 1940, while the Barclays' Overseas Development Corporation helped fund African colonial governments.

Recent lawsuits against Lloyd's of London have sought reparations for descendants of African slaves insured by the company during transport. Most notable of these was a March 2004 class action lawsuit for $2 billion in compensation for Lloyd's of London's support of genocide, filed in New York by the American lawyer Edward Fagan. The ten plaintiffs argued that they continue to suffer the effects of slavery, and presented DNA evidence linking them to particular insured slaves.

EDS

Williams, Eric, *Capitalism and Slavery* (1944)

See also ZONG

Bankole, Ayo (1935–1976). Nigerian composer and ethnomusicologist born in Lagos. His early musical education included being a chorister at Christchurch, Lagos, and in 1945 he enrolled in the Baptist Academy in that city. In 1954 he met Fela *Sowande at the Nigerian Broadcasting Corporation, who gave him organ tuition. He found Sowande's nationalistic compositional style inspirational.

From 1957 onwards Bankole composed and studied music in England under a government scholarship. From the Guildhall School of Music and Drama he gained a graduate teaching diploma for studies in piano, organ, and composition. His brilliance at the organ was rewarded with a scholarship to Clare College, Cambridge, and he gained a Bachelor's degree in music in 1964, a Fellowship of the Royal College of Organists in the same year, and later a Master's degree. Through reading ethnomusicology at the University of California, his interest in the use of traditional African instruments and improvised composition grew. Between 1966 and 1976 he became senior music producer at the Nigerian Broadcasting Corporation, lectured at the University of Lagos (1969–76), and became involved in choral conducting.

Bankole's compositional style embraces eclectic influences, including Yoruba music melded with European tonality, modality, whole-tone scales, and chromaticism, to form a nationalistic style. *Three Yoruba Songs* (1959), three piano sonatas (1959–61), a cantata, *Baba Se Wa ni Omo Rere* ['Father Make Us Good Children'], for female choir and chamber orchestra (1958) are some his most popular works that exemplify his compositional style.

PAH

Omojola, Bode, *Nigerian Art Music* (1995)

See also MUSIC 1: CLASSICAL MUSIC

Barbary pirates. Privateers operating from the coasts of North Africa. 'Britons never will be slaves', proclaimed James Thomson's 'Rule Britannia' (1740), but between the early 17th and early 18th century up to 20,000 white, Christian 'Britons' experienced capture and servitude at the hands of Barbary corsairs. The corsairs were licensed by the Islamic governments of the Barbary powers, Morocco, Algiers, Tripoli, and Tunisia, to attack the shipping of Christian countries in the Mediterranean and also as far north as the British and Irish coasts. While the majority of attacks took place at sea, corsairs also ventured into British coastal waters, and nocturnal raids on sleepy fishing villages in south-west England and the south coast of Ireland were not unknown. In this way over 100 villagers from Baltimore, Ireland, were taken captive by Algerian pirates in 1631.

At one level, symptomatic of political tensions between the Islamic regencies of the Ottoman Empire and the expanding Christian empires of Europe, piracy and slaving also fulfilled a dual economic purpose. The majority of captives were used to row the corsairs in search of more plunder and slaves, and few of those taken inland spent their remaining days in the same household. Slaves would be resold and moved around North African cities. From the mid-17th century onwards, unlike the transatlantic slave experience, many were also ransomed and returned to their countries of origin.

This anxious and servile aspect of the early modern national imagination is often overlooked or rejected, as in Thompson's paean to Britain's seaborne imperial might. Contemporary writers provide more illuminating insights into the formative impact of the white slave experience on the early modern 'British' imagination. Before the shipwreck that sees him transform from castaway to proto-imperialist on Friday's island, Daniel Defoe's Robinson Crusoe (1719) is captured by Barbary corsairs and taken to be a slave in Morocco. Jonathan Swift's Gulliver (1726) is also taken captive and subjected to the political intrigues of other seaborne nations.

JJGG

Colley, Linda, *Captives, Britain, Empire and the World 1600–1850* (2002)

Davis, Robert C., *Christian Slaves, Muslim Masters: White Slavery in the Mediterranean, the Barbary Coast, and Italy, 1500–1800* (2004)

See also SLAVERY

Barber, Francis (*c*.1745–1801). Domestic servant to Samuel *Johnson. He was born a slave in Jamaica, but his date of birth and original name are unknown. He was brought to England by Richard Bathurst, formerly a planter in Jamaica, who had him baptized and who gave him the name by which he is known. Bathurst sent him for some time to a school at Barton in Teesdale in Yorkshire, and his will (dated 1754) left Barber his freedom and £12.

By this date, probably in 1752, Barber had entered the service of Samuel Johnson, who was a friend of Bathurst's son (also Richard). The exact date, and how old Barber was at the time, are uncertain, but he was probably still a young boy. In 1756 he ran away, and worked for about two years for a London apothecary, though he returned to visit Johnson regularly during this period. He returned to Johnson's household, but soon went off again, and he served in the Royal Navy from 1758 to 1760. Johnson made strenuous efforts to secure his release from the Navy, but it seems that Barber was quite happy there, and left with some reluctance. Nevertheless, he subsequently remained in Johnson's service until his master's death in 1784.

The fact that Johnson was one of the

most famous British literary figures of the later 18th century made Barber perhaps the best-known black domestic servant of the period (Olaudah *Equiano was also a domestic servant, but only for a small part of his life and this period is not recounted in any detail in his autobiography). However, Barber's experience was no doubt far from typical. Johnson seems to have treated him virtually as an equal rather than a servant, making a point, for example, of going out to buy food for the cat himself, so that (as a much quoted passage from Boswell's *Life of Johnson* puts it) Barber's 'delicacy be not hurt, at seeing himself employed for the convenience of a quadruped'. Johnson prayed with him, wrote affectionate letters when they were separated for any length of time, and paid for him to attend the grammar school at Bishop's Stortford for five years from 1767. Reportedly Johnson hoped to have Barber turned into a scholar of Latin and Greek like himself, in which case he was unsuccessful. How much schooling Barber had received at Barton is unclear, but by the time he was sent to Bishop's Stortford he would have been at least in his twenties. Nevertheless, Barber's surviving letters show that he could write English well and had, as a later Johnsonian scholar (A. L. Reade) put it, acquired 'a far better style of composition and address than would commonly have been found among white servants of his own standing'.

In 1773 Barber married a white Englishwoman (Elizabeth Ball, *c.*1755–1816), by whom he eventually had five children, one of whom (Samuel Barber, *c.*1785–1828) became well known in Staffordshire as a Primitive Methodist preacher. When Johnson died in 1784, Barber received an annuity of £70 and the residue of Johnson's estate. He moved with his family to Lichfield in Staffordshire, Johnson's birthplace. Although the annuity would have been a reasonable middle-class income by the standards of the time, Barber seems to have become poor, partly because of the cost of illnesses in the family, and perhaps because he was simply not good with money. For some time at the end of his life he kept a school at Burntwood, a village near Lichfield. Visitors to Lichfield in search of Johnsonian connections made a point of seeking him out, and Barber sometimes sold items he had acquired from Johnson to help make ends meet.

Contemporary reactions to Barber varied. One of Johnson's biographers, Sir John Hawkins (1719–89), thought that Johnson's generosity to Barber was foolish and excessive, and he allegedly tried to cheat Barber out of some items of Johnson's property that were rightfully part of his inheritance. Surviving letters of another friend and biographer of Johnson, James Boswell (1740–95), show him treating Barber with courtesy, if only because he was hoping to get information out of him. It is possible that another of Johnson's friends, the celebrated artist Sir Joshua Reynolds (1723–92), who himself employed a black servant, may have painted a portrait of Barber.

One of the most interesting aspects of Barber's life is the way in which it shows the extent to which a black presence was an everyday part of British life in the 18th and early 19th centuries, not only in fashionable London circles, but also in provincial towns and remote villages. JG

ODNB

Reade, A. L., 'Francis Barber: Some More Material for His Biography', *Johnsonian Gleanings*, 8 (1937)

—— *Johnsonian Gleanings*, ii: *Francis Barber: The Doctor's Negro Servant* (1912)

See also VISUAL ARTS 1: REPRESENTATIONS OF BLACKS

Barbour-James, John (1867–1954). Civil servant and author born in British Guiana (now Guyana). He became postmaster at Victoria-Belfield in the 1890s, where he organized a black self-help group with social and agricultural ambitions. He transferred to the Gold Coast (now Ghana) Post Office in 1902. With his wife, Caroline, and five children he settled in Acton, west London. Three more children were born, but five (and their mother) were dead by 1919, and in 1920, in London, he married Edith Goring (who was born in Barbados and had taught in the Gold Coast, 1906–20).

Barbour-James's *Agricultural and Industrial Possibilities of the Gold Coast* was published in London in 1911. In 1917 he retired from the colonial postal service, and he worked with the *African Progress Union from 1918 (his friend Kwamina Tandoh was president from 1924 to 1927), accompanied South African delegates to meet the Prime Minister in 1919, and arranged for the Acton boy scouts to attend the visit of Sobhuza of Swaziland in 1923. He was also the head of the Association of Coloured Peoples and worked on the Gold Coast pavilion at the *British Empire Exhibition. In 1938 he was vice-president of the *League of Coloured Peoples, whose founding Quaker meetings in 1931 he had attended.

He and Edith were in British Guiana when the Second World War broke out, and by the time the war ended he was too frail to return to Britain. He died in Georgetown. JPG

Barbour-James, John, *The Agricultural and Industrial Possibilities of the Gold Coast* (1911)
ODNB

See also PAN-AFRICANISM

Beauty, concepts of (*c*.1700–*c*.1800)

1. William Hogarth's analysis of beauty
2. Joseph Spence and Joshua Reynolds
3. William Hogarth's *Captain Lord George Graham in His Cabin*
4. Slavery

1. William Hogarth's analysis of beauty The black figure, apart from being found in innumerable drawings, prints, and paintings by European artists from the medieval period onwards, is also referred to constantly, and in a variety of ways, in the European art treatise, art essay, and related literature by theorists and practising painters. By far the most important reference is in connection with the definition of beauty. William *Hogarth, in his *Analysis of Beauty* manuscripts of the 1750s, in a section dealing with the difficulty of ascertaining what was beautiful, writes that the 'variety of contradictory opinions' about what constituted beauty have led some to '[discard] beauty as a reality, concluding it can only exist in Fancy, and Imagination'. Judgements about beauty are said to depend upon 'custom, Fashion, perswasion and delusion'. Hogarth further states that 'the most remarkable instance, that is given in support of this is, that the Negro who finds great beauty in the black Females of his own country, may find as much deformity in the european Beauty as we see in theirs'.

Already in the 17th century the point was being made that beauty was dependent upon national considerations, that it was impossible to judge of what was beautiful according to fixed, universally applicable criteria. 'For Beauty is determined by opinion,' Sir Thomas Browne writes in his *Enquiries* of 1646,

> and it seems to have no essence that holds one notion with all; that seeming beauteous onto one, which hath no favour with another; and that unto every one, according as custome hath made it natural, or sympathy and conformity of minds shall make it seem agreeable. Thus flat noses seem comely unto the Moor, and Aquiline or hawked onto the Persian, a large and prominent nose unto the Roman; but none of all these are acceptable in our opinion . . . Thus we that are of contrary complexions accuse the blackness of the Moors as ugly; But the Spouse in the *Canticles* excuseth this conceit, in that description of hers, *I am black, but comely*.

It was not, however, until the mid-18th century onwards, in the uncertainty arising partly from the increasing awareness of the sensory and psychological apparatus of man (the theories of David Hartley and David Hume being indicative of the mood of the age), and the consequent abandonment of the old classical absolutes, that the British began seriously and consistently to consider the black viewpoint.

2. Joseph Spence and Joshua Reynolds It is possible to compile a catalogue of quotations from a variety of writers to substantiate this claim, but to avoid repetition only Joseph Spence and Sir Joshua Reynolds will be cited since they voiced their opinions in the same decade which saw the publication of Hogarth's *Analysis of Beauty*. Spence and Reynolds in their writings on beauty give space to the black man's peculiar perceptions and judgements as evidence of the way national customs and tastes can radically contradict European conceptions of beauty and so throw definitions into disarray. Spence writes that 'every body may be beautiful in the Imagination of some one or other . . . some may delight themselves in a black Skin, and others in a white . . . the most opposite Things imaginable may each be looked upon as beautiful, in whole different Countries; or by different People, in the same Country.'

Spence cites the scarification of the faces of African people as an instance of the relativity of beauty:

> The greatest and most general Misleader of our Judgements, in relation to Beauty, is Custom, or the different national Tastes for Beauty; which turn chiefly on the Two lower Parts of it, Color and Form. . . . In some of the most military Nations of *Africa*, no Man is reckoned handsome that has not Five or Six Scars on his Face. This Custom might, possibly, at first, be introduced among them, to make them less afraid of Wounds in that Part, in Battle; but, however that was, it grew at last to have so great a Share in their Idea of Beauty, that they now cut and slash the Faces of their poor little Infants, in order to give them those Graces when they are grown up, which are so necessary to win the Hearts of their Mistresses; and which, with the Assistance of some Jewels, or Ingots of Gold, in their Noses, Ears and Lips, must certainly be irresistible to the Ladies of the Country.

He further recalls an amusing passage in a travel book on Africa which told of the absolute horror that greeted the arrival of the first white men at some remote Gambian villages: 'The Women ran frighten'd and screaming from them; on taking them to be Devils, merely on Account of the Whiteness of their Complexion.'

Reynolds, in an article written partly in opposition to Hogarth's 'line of beauty', argues that there is 'no criterion of form by which to determine our judgement' of what is beautiful, but that preference varies according to the 'pleasure' derived from viewing an object or else 'from some association of ideas' in the mind of the spectator: the influence of Hume (on feeling) and Hartley (on associationism) is apparent from Reynolds's choice of terms. As to colour, that too is subject to varying responses:

> Among the various reasons why we prefer one part of [Nature's] works to another, the most general, I believe, is habit and custom; custom makes, in a certain sense, white black, and black white; it is custom alone determines our preference of the colour of the *Europeans* to the Aethiopians, and they, for the same reason, prefer their own colour to ours. I suppose no body will doubt, if one of their Painters was to paint the Goddess of Beauty, but that he would represent her black, with thick lips, flat nose, woolly hair; and, it seems to me, he would act very unnaturally if he did not: For by what criterion will any one dispute the propriety of his idea? We, indeed, say that the form and colour of the *European* is preferable to that of the *Aethiopian*; but I know of no other reason we have for it, but that we are more accustomed to it. It is absurd to say, that beauty is possessed of attractive powers, which irresistibly seize the corresponding mind with love and admiration, since that argument is equally conclusive in favour of the white and the black philosopher.

There were, however, many who disputed the idea that black and white were equally beautiful. If Spence had evoked the story of black women's fright upon seeing white men as evidence of the relativity of beauty, Edmund Burke tells the story of a white boy's horror upon first seeing a 'Negress' to draw the contrary conclusion: that blackness is 'terrible in its own nature . . . independent of any association whatsoever'. Burke cites a Royal Society paper by the English surgeon William Cheselden, about a young gentleman who was born blind or was blinded very early in life but who later gained his sight: 'Cheselden tells us, that the first time the boy saw a black object, it gave him great uneasiness; and that some time after, upon accidentally seeing a negro woman, he was struck with great horror at the sight. The horror, in this case, can scarcely be supposed to arise from any association.'

Others disputed the belief in the relativity of beauty using different arguments. One writer in 1757, in discussing the opinion that 'Beauty is only a Relative to the human Taste', asserts that black is inferior to white according to the criterion of variety: the white woman has ruby lips, hazel eyes, brown or hyacinth hair and brows, and 'living Roses on the Cheek' when she blushes. By contrast, 'the sooty *African* seems to want the Pleasure resulting from so many Lights and Shades'. The point about the white person's ability to blush ('that charming suffusion in the human face, which can only take place where the skin is transparent') was also to be stressed by Uvedale Price. He quotes at length Reynolds's citation of the African viewpoint which he calls 'a lively and striking illustration' of the doctrine of the relativity of beauty, but he disagrees wholly with Reynolds. According to Price,

> Variety, gradation, and combination of tints, are among the highest pleasures of vision: black is absolute monotony. In the particular instance of the human countenance, and most of all in that of females, the changes which arise from the softer passions and sensations, are above all delightful; both from their outward effect in regard to colour, and from the connexion between that appearance and the inward feelings of the mind: but no Ethiopian poet could say of his mistress,
>
> . . . Her pure and eloquent blood
> Spoke in her cheeks, and so distinctly wrought,
> That you might almost say her body thought.

Price, however, admits that a contrary argument exists, 'an argument which had been made use of', namely that

> although we call the negro complexion black, from its being many degrees darker than that of the darkest European, yet it is far from being one of uniform blackness: and that its tint, though less varied, has a richness, which, in a painter's eye, may compensate its comparative monotony, and may, therefore, by him be called beautiful. It is true, that some of the greatest colourists have introduced negroes into their pictures, and seem to have painted them, as the Italians express it, *con amore*, and certainly with striking effect.

3. **William Hogarth's *Captain Lord George Graham in His Cabin*** Price is correct, for at least one artist, Hogarth, had recognized 'variety' in the black man, in terms of the texture of his skin, its absorption and reflection of light, and its shades of colour, this being evident from his extraordinary sensitive portrait of the black boy in his painting *Captain Lord George Graham in His Cabin* (*c.*1742). There, white and black features are carefully and consciously studied, the two figures of Lord George Graham and the black boy looking in opposite directions to present different profiles. They are deliberately paired off for comparison—both have pipes in their mouths, the red cloak of Lord George Graham connects with the red necktie of the black boy, and so on. The juxtaposition of Lord George Graham and the black servant may reveal the differences in social rank but on an aesthetic level it is the similarities between the two figures—the shape of their noses, the smooth, soft texture and round outline of their faces, and their youthful appearance—which emerge. The black colour of the boy throws into relief the fairness of Lord George Graham's face, and the fairness of the latter in turn enhances the darkness of the former: there is no question of superiority or inferiority, both are aesthetically equal though different. The black boy in his green livery flourished with gold buttons, his red scarf, and yellow waistcoat is as colourful and variegated a figure as Lord George Graham. The whiteness of his cap sets off the blackness of his hair, which qualifies the dark colour of his face, which is again qualified by his white collar. The glint on his forehead and nose connects with his gold buttons and yellow waistcoat. The light falling upon his skin varies the colour of it so that his forehead appears of a lighter hue in relation to the side of his face. Hogarth is revealing that colour is not uniform but that it is relieved or deepened by light or the absence of light.

Hogarth also recognizes in his *Analysis of Beauty* manuscripts that Blacks as are much conscious of the principle of variety as anyone else. He agrees that 'the Intricate dispos[it]ions of the gradating shades of colour makes the Beauty of complexion' and that monotony of colour is horrible, but interestingly enough, unlike Price *et al.*, he chooses the monotony of white instead of black flesh in presenting his argument: 'If this Intricate disposition of the tints is wanting in the general Hue of fair flesh the whole is of a doughy white or like drowned flesh the unnatural even colour of a waxwork hand or arm would be frigh[t]full sigh[t] alive.' In fact he goes on to write that the black man too may perceive monotony of colour as a deformity, thereby implying that the black man is not of an even colour: 'a black moor even colour'd as a cloath whole or velvet mask perhaps would shock the moors as much as one milkwhite'.

4. **Slavery** The question of the definition of beauty was more than an academic exercise. Adam Smith in his *Theory of Moral Sentiments* of 1759 writes that the customs of non-European nations in constricting the foot or forcefully shaping the skull to conform to their idea of beauty are no more ridiculous than the practice of European ladies in squeezing their bodies into tight-fitting corsets. He recognizes that Guinea Blacks in their preference for thick lips and flat noses have ideas of beauty that contradict the European criteria. Smith writes warmly of the stoicism, heroism, and magnanimity of Africans and he bitterly attacks the white slave traders, who lack all these qualities, for brutalizing them and destroying their lives. It would seem that in the case of Adam Smith recognition of the validity of the black man's concept of beauty is bound up with recognition of his status as a human being. Smith's essay is important at a time when slave traders were still classifying Blacks as belonging to the simian family, when Granville *Sharp in 1772 still had to urge Lord Mansfield that Blacks were human. Montesquieu had scornfully paraphrased the slave traders' justification of their commerce, their equation of the ugly with the non-human: 'These creatures [i.e. Africans] are all over black, and with such a flat nose, that they can scarcely be pitied. It is hardly to be believed that God, who is a wise Being, should place a soul, especially a good soul, in such a black ugly body.' DD

Bindman, David, *Ape to Othello: Aesthetics and the Idea of Race in the Eighteenth Century* (2002)
Burke, Edmund, *A Philosophical Enquiry into the Origin of Ideas of the Sublime and Beautiful* (ed. J. T. Boulton, 1958)
Dabydeen, David, *Hogarth's Blacks: Images of Blacks in Eighteenth Century English Art* (1985)

See also SKIN COLOUR AND RACE, THEORIES OF

Beckford, William (bap. 1709, d. 1770). Politician, born in Jamaica into a family of wealthy plantation owners. Sent to England in 1723, he was educated at Westminster School and Oxford. He later studied medicine at Leiden in Holland, but broke off his course there when the death of his father obliged him to return to Jamaica in 1735. When his elder brother died in 1737, he inherited most of the family properties and continued to add to them by inheritance and purchase over the next 30 years. At the time of his death he was sole owner of thirteen sugar plantations in Jamaica, together with other real estate and about 3,000 slaves.

In 1737 William Beckford became a member of the Jamaican House of Assembly, but by 1744 he had left Jamaica for Britain, where he settled in London as a West India merchant, selling the produce of his own estates and increasing his fortune by moneylending. His enormous wealth aroused suspicion and hostility in many quarters, and his Jamaican accent marked him as an outsider—Samuel *Johnson once enquired sarcastically where Beckford had learnt English. Nevertheless, Beckford was able to buy a large landed estate at Fonthill in Wiltshire, marry the granddaughter of an earl, and secure his entry into British politics. He was MP for Shaftesbury, 1747–54, and for London, 1754–70. He also became a London alderman, and was Lord Mayor of London for two terms, 1762–3 and 1769–70. In British politics Beckford counted as a radical reformer, and on one occasion not long before his death publicly rebuked King George III for unconstitutional behaviour. A monument erected to his memory, with part of his rebuke to the king in letters of gold on the pedestal, still stands in the Guildhall of the City of London.

Criticism of Beckford focused on his

wealth and ostentation, rather than on the source of it, and relatively few people at the time saw any incongruity in the fact that this defender of the liberties of the British subject owed his position to the ownership of the slaves who toiled to produce the sugar that made him rich. While Beckford was the outstanding example of colonial wealth being used to secure influence in Britain, he was far from the only one. His only legitimate son and heir was William Thomas *Beckford. JG

Boswell, James, *Life of Johnson* (ed. R. W. Chambers, introd. Pat Rogers, 1980)
ODNB

See also WEST INDIA INTEREST

Beckford, William Thomas (1760–1844). Writer, art collector, and owner of plantations in Jamaica. He was the son of William *Beckford, on whose death in 1770 he inherited an enormous fortune. This came under his control when he attained his majority in 1781 and for many years enabled him to travel extensively in Europe, and to fund his enthusiasm for building Fonthill Abbey in Wiltshire as a Gothic extravaganza to house himself and the books, pictures, and works of art that he collected on a prodigious scale. In the 1790s his income was estimated at well over £100,000 a year, and in 1809 the poet Lord Byron hailed him as 'England's wealthiest son'. From the 1820s the income from his Jamaican estates declined significantly, and he was forced to sell Fonthill and major parts of his collections. Beckford is remembered as the author of the novel *Vathek*, an Orientalist fantasy published in 1786, and although his collections have largely been dispersed, his role as a connoisseur and builder has received considerable attention from art historians in recent years. That it was all made possible by the labour of the slaves on the Jamaican plantations which Beckford never visited is seldom acknowledged in any detail, except by historians of the Caribbean, for whom Beckford and his father have long been proverbial examples of the absentee planter. JG

Fothergill, B., *Beckford of Fonthill* (1979)
Malcolm, J., *William Beckford: An English Fidalgo* (1992)

See also WEST INDIA INTEREST

Bethune, 'Blind Tom'. Alias of Thomas Wiggins (1849–1908), famous slave pianist, described by Mark Twain as a musical prodigy. He was born in May 1849 in Columbus, Georgia, being blind, and in today's terms an 'autistic savant'. The renowned lawyer James N. Bethune bought Wiggins's parents as slaves. Recognizing that Wiggins was a musical genius capable of imitating noises, improvising, and composing at 6, Bethune's daughter Mary taught him to play the piano.

In 1857 Bethune paraded Wiggins's talent across Georgia, meeting rapturous responses. Consequently, Bethune had tours organized by Perry Oliver (concert promoter) earning them $100,000 a year. Wiggins would play European classical music, improvisations, popular ballads, and his own compositions, examples of the last being 'The Rainstorm' (1865) and 'Cyclone Gallop' (1887).

The Bethune family forced him to tour the South, performing to raise funds during the Civil War for the confederacy and its army. Furthermore, Bethune enticed the parents of Wiggins to sign a contract relinquishing their guardianship, enabling Bethune to organize further tours. In 1865, via a court in Ohio, Bethune won a guardianship dispute with the promoter Tabbs Gross over Wiggins.

In 1866 Wiggins was sent on a tour to Great Britain. His performances drew crowds of admirers and earned much money for the Bethunes. He was closely listened to and examined by notable musicians like Sir Charles Hallé (German-English composer and President of the Royal College of Music in Manchester) and Ignaz Moscheles (London-based Czech composer and pianist), who wrote testimonial letters for Wiggins which the Bethunes seized upon as publicity material and published in pamphlet form (*The Marvellous Musical Prodigy, Blind Tom*, 1867). Hallé wrote that Wiggins's natural musical gifts seem to me quite marvellous, and the manner in which he repeated several pieces I played to him, which he had evidently never heard before, was most remarkable. Perhaps the most striking feature was the extraordinary quickness with which he named any notes struck by me on the piano, either single or simultaneously, however discordant they might be. I also named to him several notes, choosing the most difficult and perplexing intervals; these he instantly sang with perfect truth of intonation, although they might have puzzled a well-educated musician. Altogether 'Blind Tom' seems to be a most singular and inexplicable phenomenon.

Moscheles, who tested Wiggins's ability to analyse chords by asking him to play a complex passage from Moscheles's 'Recollections of Ireland', declared him to be 'marvellously gifted by nature'. Wiggins died in New Jersey in 1908. PAH

Southern, Eileen, *Biographical Dictionary of Afro-American and African Musicians* (1982)

See also MUSIC 1: CLASSICAL MUSIC

Birmingham. City with historic links to the slave trade. The first guns to be exported to Africa in 1698 were manufactured in Birmingham, renowned for its metalworking; this triggered a growth in the city's industries, and by 1766, 100,000 guns a year were shipped, as well as other tools of the slave trade: manacles, chains, branding irons, thumbscrews, pincers, muzzles, and instruments for prising open the mouths of recalcitrant slaves to make them eat. Cheaply made flintlock muskets, the guns were often dangerous to their users, and contributed to the militarization of the continent: it has been estimated that 20 million went to Africa by 1907.

The city's Lunar Society (a group of freethinkers and radicals) included members who were vehement abolitionists. Thomas *Day, from Lichfield, was co-author with Joseph Bicknell of the poem *The Dying Negro* (1773), a famous tract that spoke of a slave's suicide—by shooting himself in the head—in tones of heart-rending pity. The 'king of the potteries', Josiah *Wedgwood, manufactured the 'Am I not a man and a brother?' cameo medallion for the Society for the Abolition of the Slave Trade, purchased a Montserrat plantation in 1857, growing limes to produce acid for his chemical works and to demonstrate the viability of waged labour.

The Female Society for the Relief of British Negro Slaves was founded in 1825, and sent donations to black American educationists such as Amanda Smith and Booker T. *Washington, both of whom visited the city. In 1847 the Female American Serenaders, a group of 'coloured ladies', performed in Birmingham. A freed slave, the Revd Peter *Stanford, moved to Birmingham from America in 1887, setting up the Wilberforce Memorial Church (*see* WILLIAM WILBERFORCE) in 1889 and campaigning for funds to train black missionaries for Africa. CA/JM

Tait, Fiona, *Black History Sources in Birmingham City Archives* (2004)

See also AFRICA AND BRITISH COLONIALISM; MISSIONARY SOCIETIES

Black British English. A broad term covering a range of ways in which Caribbean Creole (commonly known as patois, or patwa) is combined with British varieties of English, resulting in one of the following:

(*a*) a Creole-influenced variety of British English;
(*b*) a variety of Creole influenced by local British varieties of English;
(*c*) a speech style involving mixing of English and Creole in conversation;
(*d*) a style of 'street language' or 'slang' associated with adolescents.

It is mostly spoken by black British people of Caribbean heritage (though not everyone in this category would use it), but in its sense of a 'street language' it has many users outside the black community, among adolescents of all ethnicities.

Black British English (BBE) is not confined to spoken language but can also be found in much informal written language, particularly among younger people, who draw on BBE forms in private communication such as letters, emails, Internet chat, and text messages. There is a growing body of published writing in BBE in Britain in a range of genres, such as (dub) poetry, lyrics (e.g. Jean Breeze, Linton Kwesi Johnson), and in the dialogue of novels. Like its spoken counterpart, written BBE shows a high degree of variability, in grammar and vocabulary, as well as in spelling.

1. Origins of black British English
2. The forms of black British English
3. Developments in black British English

1. Origins of black British English In most parts of the Caribbean that were formerly British colonies, a local vernacular language, of the language type called Creole by linguists, is spoken. Creole derives the majority of its vocabulary from a European language (the 'lexifier'), but has a grammar that is different in origin and in form. As a result it tends to be stigmatized as an inferior form of their lexifier languages; a popular view, held by both the educated elite and the mass of the population, has been that it is 'bad English'. Since the 1960s linguists have worked to dispel this view by showing how the grammatical and phonological structures of Creole are sufficiently different from the related standard to be considered a distinct linguistic system. Recently, Creole has become a marker of national pride in some countries and its status has improved somewhat.

In those parts of the Caribbean where an English-lexicon Creole vernacular coexists with Standard English as the official language and language of education, the majority of the population speak neither the one nor the other consistently. Instead, a wide range of intermediate varieties is found, linking the broadest Creole at one end of the scale with the local form of Standard English at the other end. This situation has been conceptualized as a dialect continuum.

In Britain cities such as *London, *Bristol, *Cardiff, and *Liverpool have long-established Caribbean communities dating back to the era of slavery. However, prior to the 1940s there is no record of any distinctively 'black' English in Britain. Contemporary BBE has emerged from within the present-day Caribbean communities in Britain, which date mainly from the period following the Second World War. Migrants to Britain came from all parts of the Caribbean region, bringing with them the distinctive Creole varieties of each territory. The first generation were thus linguistically diverse, in that they were speakers of different, though related, vernaculars. Most will have been speakers of intermediate varieties of Creole–English, and will have had some contact with Standard English at school, if not in the home.

This first generation came into contact with local varieties of British English, for example London English, in addition to Standard English, and the tendency was to alter their pronunciation in the direction of the local variety of English. They did, however, retain most of the linguistic characteristics of their native varieties while living in Britain.

Other migrant communities are known to pass their native language on, within the diaspora, for at least a generation or two. It might have been expected that the second generation would speak a range of Caribbean 'mother tongues'. What actually happened was that the Creole of Jamaica (Jamaican patois, or patwa) emerged as the 'heritage language' used among the second generation, even by those whose parents were *not* Jamaican Creole speakers. By the late 1970s a variety of Jamaican Creole was being used in British schools, by children of Caribbean heritage, although not necessarily Jamaican.

How can we account for the emergence of a single 'heritage language' based on Jamaican, given the diversity of backgrounds of the first generation of black migrants? According to Paul Gilroy, shared experiences of 'race' and social class in the first generation led to the territorial origins and previous social status of Caribbean immigrants becoming irrelevant: they were seen as 'West Indian' and working class by the white majority. The consciousness of this in the second generation gave rise to the new identity, self-consciously both British and black, lacking the strong links with specific

Caribbean places that the first generation had felt.

The adoption of Jamaican Creole as a unifying 'heritage language' for the second-generation Caribbean community could be seen as the linguistic equivalent of this social experience. The most likely reasons for adopting Jamaican for this purpose are that Jamaicans were the largest immigrant population from the Caribbean, and that they brought with them cultural forms in which Jamaican Creole was the predominant language: most importantly, *reggae music and *Rastafarianism, which were popular among Caribbean youth.

In the 1980s it became clear that, in London, Jamaican Creole had spread well beyond the boundaries of the Jamaican community and was being used as a symbol of group identity by black British children and adolescents generally—as well as by some white adolescents in friendship groups with black peers. This trend has continued, with forms of Creole (or related language) that are less and less close to the 'original' Jamaican patois being used by a wider and wider range of the general population. However, this use of patois outside its original speaker community (and even within it) is an age-graded phenomenon—an adolescent practice that rarely survives into adulthood.

2. The forms of black British English Jamaican Creole, while sharing much of its vocabulary with British English, is significantly different in certain aspects of its phonology (pronunciation), grammar (morphology and syntax), and lexicon (vocabulary). These differences have been well described for both the Caribbean variety of Jamaican Creole and its British variant. Some examples of salient distinguishing features would be:

Phonology:

- the pronunciation of <th> as in *think* as /t/ (/tink/), and <th> as in *them* as /d/ (/dem/);
- different pronunciations of the vowel sounds of *boy*, *gate*, *goat*, *hot*, *ball*, *cup*, and others.

Grammar:

- Personal pronouns have a wider range of functions than in Standard English, e.g. *me* (/mi/) functions as subject, object, and possessive (Standard *I*, *me*, and *my*). The second-person pronouns have different forms for singular (/yu/) and plural (/unu/).
- Verb forms do not have tense endings as in Standard English; past tense may be unmarked (*im sing* 'he sang'), and continuous forms are made by the addition of the particle *a* (*mi a go* 'I am going').
- No copula is used with adjectives (*dem bad* 'they are bad'), while there is a special copula *de* used with locations (*dem de a yaad* 'they are at home').
- The word order in Jamaican Creole of statements and questions is identical (see the next displayed example below).

Most Caribbeans of the first generation living in Britain are speakers of intermediate Creole varieties from their home territory, influenced to varying degrees by the English dialect of the place where they have settled. The degree of influence from British English will depend to some extent on their length of stay, as well as factors such as occupation and education. Thus their (British) English is likely to show some influences from Creole, while their Creole will have been affected somewhat by its long immersion in British varieties of English, which are also seen as more prestigious than Creole. Their use of Creole is likely to have become confined to family contexts.

In the second generation Mark Sebba noticed that although some second-generation Caribbeans spoke a local variety of English virtually identical to that of non-black neighbours, there were a few features of grammar (such as using *say* for Standard English *that* in 'I know say . . .') that could be attributed to influence from Creole. These speakers could then be regarded as speakers of British English influenced by Creole.

Second-generation speakers of BBE/ British Creole are bilinguals or multilinguals. They are users, from a very early age, of a local variety of British English, and will make contact with Standard English at school, if not earlier. For such individuals, British English is the dominant first language. Hence many BBE users in

Britain have less than native-speaker-like abilities in Creole, judged relatively to native speakers of Jamaican Creole *in Jamaica*. By this criterion, second-generation speakers vary greatly in their Creole 'fluency'. For some, their Creole has been described as that of second-language learners or second-*dialect* learners who have learned to transform their first (British English) dialect into a new one, making themselves 'sound Jamaican'.

This results in some linguistic forms that superficially resemble Jamaican Creole, but would sound very strange to a first-language speaker from Jamaica. For example, the following utterance was recorded from a second-generation speaker, and has Creole pronunciation, pronoun forms (*him*) and verb forms (*a look* for *looking*):

Did him give you what you a look for?
[Did he give you what you were looking for?]

However, a native speaker of Jamaican Creole would say

Him did give you . . . ? or *Him give you . . .* ?

as inversion of the subject and auxiliary in questions (*did he . . .* ?) is a grammar rule of English but is not part of the grammar of Jamaican Creole. The second-generation speaker's utterance is thus based on English rather than Creole sentence structure.

The language of the second and subsequent generations is characterized by the use of code-switching under appropriate social circumstances. When the participants in an interaction are able to use both Creole and English, where the speakers know each other, and where the setting is sufficiently informal or oriented towards a shared Caribbean culture, the speakers are likely to switch between Creole and English from time to time.

According to Sebba, second-generation Caribbeans in London in the 1980s used a very high proportion of London English in everyday informal conversation. Nevertheless, Creole was used in many conversations, often towards the end of a conversational sequence to highlight important points or a 'punchline'.

For the third generation, the use of Jamaican Creole may be mostly passive (i.e. they understand some Creole, but do not speak it fluently). Using Creole has to a large extent become a matter of vocabulary, the insertion of certain 'culturally loaded' terms into everyday (local English) speech. Adopting such speech styles shows symbolic association with certain subcultures (especially music) but seems to have little to do with ethnicity. At the same time, the linguistic resources on which such slang styles draw in their performance have broadened to include the African and Caribbean diaspora. Centres of particular influence appear to be the *hip hop culture originating in the United States and the equivalent British 'grime' or 'garage' culture originating in London.

3. Developments in black British English For individuals brought up as first-language users of British English, Creole has become in practice unnecessary for purely communicative functions. Its use is largely symbolic, and this symbolism, especially as a marker of group identity, is powerful. Creole serves this identity-marking function even for those speakers who have limited fluency in it. Such speakers may rely on the use of *token* Creole features as an indication that Creole is one of the codes in use. Using small amounts of stereotypically Creole vocabulary, pronunciation, and vocatives such as *man*, *raa(s)* ('arse'—an expletive), *nuff* ('a lot'), *vex* ('annoyed') may be enough to mark a conversation as a 'BBE/Creole event' or to have a particular utterance assigned to the 'BBE' code in contrast to the 'English' one. Seen in this way, BBE in the London context is a speech *style*, defined by the participants of an interaction in contrast with 'English', and marked by a selection of salient 'non-English' features. Put another way, BBE is a *performance*. This is different from the notion of Creole as a distinct language with its own norms of grammar, phonology, etc., which would be more appropriate to the Caribbean.

Linked to this symbolic use of Creole is the fact that adolescent speakers of BBE in the 1980s tended to draw on Creole forms that were maximally different from the corresponding Standard English ones, so where a Creole form could be realized in any of several ways, speakers tended to choose the one that is least English-like. This is to be expected if the main value of Creole is symbolic, as such choices maximize the distance from English and emphasize that the linguistic code in use is Creole.

A striking phenomenon in the period since the mid-1970s has been the adoption of BBE vocabulary and speech styles, and, to a lesser extent, Creole itself, by urban adolescents from outside the Caribbean community. In the 1980s a local multiracial vernacular was identified which drew on Creole language forms in what was essentially the London English speech of white, African, and South Asian adolescents living in an area highly populated by people of Caribbean origin. Ben Rampton described the use of Creole across ethnic boundaries for which he coined the term 'crossing'.

The popularization of Creole speech patterns through their association with cultural forms such as MCing (i.e. rapping) and hip hop has meant that they have become widely known outside the Caribbean community, and even outside urban areas. The popularity of BBE with adolescents of different heritages encourages use of particular areas of vocabulary to do with recreation, sex, and swearing, and in these areas there is a rapid turnover of slang vocabulary, some of which is also current in 'mainstream' British usage (recent examples are *bling* ('jewellery'), *big-up* ('praise'), and *punani* ('female genitals'). Around 2000 the notion of a 'non-Caribbean' Creole user was popularized and parodied by the comedian Sacha Baron Cohen through his character Ali G. in a series of television shows and films, leading to even wider public awareness of this language style.

BBE as spoken by the second and subsequent generations therefore continues to be influenced by Jamaican Creole, but over the three generations has developed in the ways in which Creole and English are combined. This is partly a result of the changing functions of BBE, which is now used more as a marker of style than as a first language of communication. In fact it may not be useful to talk about BBE in terms of its relation to Jamaican Creole for much longer, but rather to treat it as a British variety that is associated with a more international (transatlantic) youth culture and its associated forms of language.

Jamaican Creole has made its mark on the consciousness of speakers of British English—and not just in urban areas where Caribbeans and non-Caribbeans are most likely to mingle. This suggests that even if Creole is largely relinquished as a main medium of communication in the Caribbean community in succeeding generations, it will continue to exist as a language of youth and adolescence, well beyond the confines of its original ethnic roots. MSe/SD

Gilroy, Paul, *There Ain't No Black in the Union Jack* (1987)

Rampton, Ben, *Crossing: Language and Ethnicity Among Adolescents* (1995)

Sebba, Mark, *London Jamaican: Language Systems in Interaction* (1993)

Sutcliffe, David, *British Black English* (1982)

See also EMPIRE WINDRUSH; LITERATURE 2: FICTION AND POETRY

Black dance. Term used by African and Caribbean dancers to refer to dance forms utilizing vocabularies, rituals, and symbols from traditional African and Caribbean forms, combining music, movement, storytelling, and theatre. Adopted from North America, the term came into popular usage in the United Kingdom in the 1970s.

1. Phase 1: 1946–1974
2. Phase 2: 1975–1983
3. Phase 3: 1984–2005

1. Phase 1: 1946–1974 On 30 April 1946 Les *Ballets Nègres and its charismatic leader and choreographer Berto Pasuka (real name Wilbert Passley) opened for their first season at the Twentieth Century Theatre in London. Until then, resident, constituted black dance groups were non-existent, although solo performers (giggers) linked up with musicians and others (dance acts) to present dance displays. Pasuka laid the foundation for black theatrical dance. Following their opening night, *The Times* reported that 'Ballets Nègres presents works which impress us with their vitality and sincerity, and introduced to the English theatre a new dance drama . . . a novel venture which is a refreshing theatrical experience.' The company operated between 1946 and 1953, and after their demise, black dance remained visible through cabaret performances.

Individual freelance artistes continued to perform, and Evrol Puckerin, Geoffrey Holder, and Elroy Josephs, among others, were dancing in clubs and at social events. Allister Bain's Bee Wee Ballet reintroduced a degree of theatrical performance in 1958. Nonetheless, the 'gigging' format continued, and Ginger Johnson, Ambrose Campbell, Sheila Holder, Louis St Jules, Raymond McLean, and Dorothea Palmer, with others, continued the black dance tradition. In the 1960s and 1970s visiting artistes from the Caribbean and Africa joined with other UK-based performers to maintain a black dance profile. By then *reggae and *soul music were providing rhythms and lyrical content that resonated deeply within the black communities and new forms of black social dance emerged. Sacred and secular music combined to produce reggae, soul, blues, *jazz, and calypso dance styles.

Black dance provided entertainment that had accommodated and adapted to the new environment. Popular dance and music moved from the margins to the mainstream, and the first carnival ever in London was held on August Bank Holiday 1965. Black people raised a new voice and shifted their cultural emphasis from indoor to outdoor dance activities.

2. **Phase 2: 1975–1983** From the mid-1970s there was a gearshift in black dance development, moving away from the freelance dancer to organized group performances. Peter Blackman, Barry Anderson, Ben Baddoo, George Otoo, George Dzikunu, Carl Campbell, Chester Morrison, Julia Mathunjwa, Betty Boo, Tony Morgan, Kif Higgins, Bob Ramdhanie, and numerous other dancers and drummers were involved in taking dance to a new level.

Peter Blackman, Bravo Bravo, and many distinguished African dancers and drummers established Steel an' Skin. They supported the Ekome and Lanzel dance groups in Bristol and Wolverhampton. Black dance, however, was perceived not as an art form but as a community activity within the domains of social welfare, and Lanzel and Ekome established themselves as a full-time company, through financial support from the Manpower Services Commission work training programmes.

In 1977 Bob Ramdhanie founded the Kokuma Dance Company in Birmingham. Nationally, the majority of the practitioners were non-professionals, and Kokuma began to support a range of community dance groups including Kizzie (Leicester), Ajah (Derby), and Kantamanto (Manchester). Julia Mathunjwa and Betty Boo established Shikisha, and Elliot Ngubane formed Uthingo, both groups presenting traditional dances from South Africa. Mario Diekurroh (Dagarti Arts), Kwesi Owusu (African Dawn), Felix Cobbson (Aklowa), George Dzikunu (Adzido Pan-African Ensemble), Hermin McIntosh (Sankofa), George Otoo (Wantu Wanzuri), Kif Higgins (Delado), Beverley Glean (Irie! Dance Theatre), and H. Patten (Danse de l'Afrique) represented dance forms from Ghana and the Caribbean.

The establishment of the Handsworth Cultural Centre (HCC, 1980) and the Community and Village Entertainment (CAVE) Arts Centre (1985) in Birmingham signalled a new era in black dance development. These organizations regularly offered performances and training programmes. Both the HCC and the CAVE ensured that international professional artistes worked in the United Kingdom and dancers from Jamaica (Jackie Guy, Barry Moncrieffe, Sheila Barnett) and from Ghana (Francis Nii Yartey, Gideon Midawo, and others) came to England as tutors, prior and subsequent to the formation of the Black Dance Development Trust in Birmingham in 1986. Jackie Guy later returned to make Kokuma one of the most exciting professional companies. Most groups presented display dancing, i.e. a traditional dance, followed by a drumming and singing interlude and then dance again. Performances included social, ceremonial, and religious dances from Ghana with some improvised pieces from the Caribbean.

Culturally and politically, black dance was a public affirmation of 'self' and, to an extent, was an articulated voice from the more marginalized sections of society. Many young Blacks were making themselves visible through their positive commitment to black dance, and towards the middle of the 1980s the more established groups were seeking to move away from display dancing to more theatrical dance dramas.

3. Phase 3: 1984–2005 To underpin future developments and build a national infrastructure for black dance, representatives from the sector including Chester Morrison, Derek Anderson, Hermin McIntosh, George Dzikunu, Charles Washington, and Bob Ramdhanie worked together to establish the Black Dance Development Trust (BDDT). Dzikunu had established the Adzido Pan-African Dance Ensemble and, besides being the largest, building-based black dance company in England, its policy was to produce work for large-scale venues. Their productions included *In the Village of Africa*, *Coming Home*, *Under African Skies*, *Siye Goli*, *Akwaaba*, and *Thand' Abantwana*. In addition to Adzido, Peter Badejo (Badejo Arts) and Bode Lawal (Sakoba) from Nigeria established dance companies that offered new perspectives on West African dance forms. Both were highly skilled dancers, Badejo being a prolific artiste who was trained in Africa and North America before his arrival in the United Kingdom. This period also witnessed new dynamics in black dance development in England. Whereas in the first two phases the leading practitioners were mostly from the Caribbean, from 1984 continental Africans emerged in the forefront. Beverley Glean, a graduate dancer, had by then formed Irie! Dance Theatre to maintain the Caribbean input. The black dance movement peaked in the 1980s with formal and informal groups numbering over 40.

During the 1990s public awareness of and public subsidy to the sector was growing. Although black dancers were benefiting from the BDDT programmes, their groups remained under-resourced. Their productions were interesting though not artistically creative, as companies were essentially producing work for black community venues but then marketing their product to middle-scale and large white venues. The quality was variable and there was a perception by mainstream venues and promoters that all the companies were producing similar work. Black dance was at crossroads.

In 1996 the Arts Council of England produced its strategy for dance (*The Policy for Dance in the English Funding System*) and whereas in previous policy documents African, Caribbean, and Asian dance were noted for needing specific support, this was no longer the case. Culture-specific organizations for dance were not viewed as a necessity for the development of black dance in England. By then black international companies were having an impact on the dance scene in the United Kingdom as major dance venues imported contemporary and classically trained black companies. The black dance sector was under threat in terms of public subsidy and was losing its foothold. Black companies were being distanced to the margins of the cultural matrix. The United Kingdom's leading black dance companies, Kokuma and Adzido Pan-African Ensemble, based in Birmingham and London respectively, were stretched to the limits in terms of human and financial resources, and both were being nudged into new Western, contemporary-oriented dance directions.

There was a noticeable shift in emphasis from black dance practice to black people in dance. Black dancers, and racially mixed companies working across cultures and ethnicities, were becoming more visible as the members of traditional and contemporary dancers from Africa and the Caribbean were diminishing. By 2004 both the leading black dance companies in the United Kingdom (Kokuma and Adzido) had ceased to exist, leaving, once again, 'giggers' and 'dance acts', principally from the African continent, to continue the black dance tradition. At the time of writing, hybrid forms are indeed appearing, but if the nuances and core values are drawn primarily from Western dance practice, then it would be questionable to class current developments as 'black dance'. Black dance is once more at crossroads. BR

Race Today Collective, *The Arrivants* (1987)
Sunday Times, 5 May 1946

See also WILKINS, DAVE

Black History Month. Event observed every October throughout the United Kingdom to celebrate and recognize African and Caribbean contributions to British society. The foremost aims of the Month are to disseminate information on positive black contributions to British society, to heighten the confidence and awareness of black people in their cultural heritage, and to promote knowledge of black history and experiences. As well as a platform for black culture, it is part of an ongoing educational project to redress perceived distortions and omissions of Africa's global contribution to world civilization. The event's chosen symbol is the Sankofa bird, an Akan symbol showing a bird looking backwards while moving forwards, signifying the need to learn from the past.

The event originated in the United States, when Carter G. Woodson established African and Caribbean celebrations in 1926. In Britain, Adkyaaba Addai Sebbo is widely acknowledged as the founder of Black History Month. The inaugural event took place on 1 October 1987 during African Jubilee Year, arising from a strategic partnership between the Greater London Council, the Inner London Education Authority, and the London Strategic Policy Unit.

Black History Month has expanded with the years, and what was once unique to London is now nationwide. Its participants now encompass voluntary organizations, local authorities, museums, and the media. Events range from theatrical productions to storytelling, exhibitions, musical performances, poetry readings, and comedy shows. In line with the project's educational priorities, a number of resources have been made available (such as histories of black migrant experiences) for use in classrooms. In recent years the scope of the Month has expanded to serve as recognition of the general contribution of cultural diversity to British society, and local authorities have been proactive in hosting and organizing such events. PBP

Black and Asian Association Newsletter (Apr. 1997–Sept. 2005)

See also EMPIRE WINDRUSH; MUSEUMS

Black Man's Part in the War, The Book written by Sir Harry Johnston (1858–1927), one of the principal architects of the British Empire, and published in London in 1917. After a lifetime working in Africa, Johnston came to the conclusion that the Imperial government in London had obligations to the indigenous peoples of Africa. In *The Black Man's Part in the War* he reviewed the contribution by the non-white peoples of the Empire to the war effort, praising African soldiers for their 'pluck, gallantry and devotion' in the face of heavy gunfire. He also argued that, once the war was over, steps should be taken 'to recognize and affirm' the rights of the African as a citizen of the Empire. Johnston said that the river Zambezi should become a boundary beyond which white settlers would have no claims. In the areas north of the Zambezi it must be recognized that African lands were secure and could not be expropriated. He further argued that territories must be economically developed, education promoted, a university created for British colonial Africa, and that there must be native representatives in local legislatures. These ideas did not make Johnston a liberal on questions of race. However, his book indicates how British imperialists were beginning to think about the business of administering Empire, in terms of trusteeship rather than mere exploitation, and the future role that Africans might play in that new colonial system. DK

Johnston, Harry, *The Black Man's Part in the War* (1917)

See also FIRST WORLD WAR

Black Muslims. Evidence of a black Muslim presence in Britain dates back to Tudor and Stuart times. By 1596, so alarmed was Queen *Elizabeth I by the growing number of 'infidel' 'Blackamoors' that she unsuccessfully ordered their expulsion. While many Muslims arrived in England as merchants and traders, others were involuntary residents. In the 1620s North African corsairs operating in English waters were captured, and records testify to a number of Muslims languishing in jails in the southwest of England. However, a 1641 document suggests the presence in London of a small settled community of Muslims, and by 1725 English society had become well accustomed to their presence. During the 17th and 18th centuries black staff and servants—likely to have been Muslims—accompanied Ottoman emissaries to Britain. Many remained in Britain and Muslims came to form an important element within the 'permanent' black population. They included servants (King George I's West African servants Mustapha and Mahomet being the most prominent) as well as men and women of considerable educational, social, and cultural accomplishment. There were also occasional prominent Muslim visitors, such as *Job ben Solomon. According to a 1764 estimate, London was home to a Muslim community of about 20,000 freed slaves.

As the British Empire expanded, economic and educational opportunities attracted migrants to Britain from across the Muslim nations of Africa and the Middle East. Somali and Yemeni sailors recruited at the port of Aden, particularly after the opening of the Suez Canal in 1869, established communities in *Cardiff, *South Shields, and *Liverpool. Moroccan Muslim merchants attracted by Manchester's burgeoning textile industry established a thriving community in that city. Of the estimated 10,000 or so Muslims in Britain in 1924, a significant number were of African descent. While these communities came under violent racist attacks in 1919 and 1930, these setbacks could not prevent the continued growth of the Muslim population during the inter-war period. Their numbers were augmented by further arrivals of students, business people, and professionals from West and North Africa.

Since the Second World War, Muslims have migrated to Britain in much larger numbers. While the majority originated from South Asia, smaller Muslim communities from across Africa also settled in Britain. The Nigerian Muslim community, which has grown substantially since the 1960s in London, is now served by two mosques and a number of social and cultural establishments that organize a range of activities under the auspices of the Central Council of Nigerian Organizations. By 2001, according to the census, there were 1.6 million Muslims living in Britain, of whom 9 per cent had been born in sub-Saharan Africa. At the beginning of the 21st century the black Muslim population included 70,000 Somalis and around 5,000 African-Caribbean converts located substantially in the Brixton and Stockwell neighbourhoods of south London. While large proportions of these communities are British-born, many individuals arrived as migrants, seeking a livelihood or escaping political and religious conflict and persecution.

Black British Muslims represent a diverse and complex community. The vast majority is distributed into distinct, ethnically visible communities, primarily in industrial metropolitan conurbations such as London and Birmingham, where they uphold a range of sectarian allegiances. Sunni Muslims are predominant in Britain, but organizations representing minority Muslim traditions, such as Shia Muslims and a range of contemplative, 'mystical' Sufi orders, can also be found. For example, the Tijaniya *tariqa*, still organized along ethnic lines, is popular among Nigerian, Gambian, Ghanaian, and Senegalese Muslims of north and east London. To this list must be added groups such as the Nation of Islam, who define themselves as Muslim but are considered by many as outside the fold of Islam. Originally imported from the United States, the Nation of Islam espouses the unity of black people together with a militant, separatist, radical political and economic programme based on self-reliance within an 'Islamic' framework. Consisting of possibly 2,500 members in Britain, it has proved to be particularly influential among young urban African and African-Caribbean working-class men, endowing many who have converted to its brand of Islam with increased self-esteem and a positive sense of belonging.

Living in a society with a large non-Muslim majority, and in which non-Muslim law and government and institutions predominate, has thrown up a number of challenges for Muslims. In the late 1980s, at the peak of the protests against Salman Rushdie's controversial novel *The Satanic Verses*, they were condemned as intolerant and incapable of peaceful and rational discussion. They were deemed to be politically suspect, a fifth column, during the Gulf and Iraq wars of 1991 and 2003. They are still often seen as 'outsiders', marginal in their relationship to wider society. Thus, with wider British society largely insensitive, if not antipathetic, to their concerns, black British Muslims have had to rely on their own somewhat limited resources to build mosques, Islamic schools, community centres and facilities, and the wide range of Muslim institutions that help to cater for their needs and sustain their identities. But they have also struggled, to some degree successfully, to have their demands conceded by mainstream institutions, for instance, in education and matters of law. While there has been some social mobility into professions and businesses, a lack of skills and poor education (and, for refugees and asylum-seekers, very limited rights and opportunities) have meant that the majority of black African Muslims entered Britain at the bottom of the socio-economic ladder. Still concentrated in areas of multiple deprivation, they have continued to experience educational underachievement, high rates of unemployment, overcrowded and rundown housing, and poor health.

Black British Muslims, like other Muslims in Britain, have been affected by racism and Islamophobia (greatly exacerbated by the terrorist attacks in the United States on 11 September 2001), which makes many feel vulnerable, disillusioned, and alienated from mainstream British society. While the vast majority have sought to adjust to and accommodate existing British institutions and practices—experimenting and negotiating between actual and perceived demands, values, and norms (indeed, some of these apparently in conflict with their own) of British society—a small minority, again in line with wider trends, is attracted by radical Islamic messages, especially by their promise of martyrdom and paradise and by the enhanced sense of belonging to the greatly empowering global Muslim network—the *umma*—that legitimizes revolutionary and violent actions as global jihad.

It is this ideology, which portrays the West as morally corrupt and rejects its political system as 'un-Islamic', combined with a sense of alienation from wider British society, that has driven a tiny minority of young black British Muslims to perpetrate such terrorist acts as the London bombings on 7 and 21 July 2005. They are frustrated and angered by what they perceive as the worldwide onslaught of the West on Islam. For converts such as Jermaine Lindsay, the Jamaican-born London suicide bomber, as well as other

British-born young black Muslims, there appears no other alternative but to offer the sacrifice of their lives to resist such oppression, acts of suicide that lead to the murder and maiming of hundreds of innocent people. KHA

Fryer, Peter, *Staying Power: The History of Black People in Britain* (1984)

Black Panther Party. Formed in California in 1966, the Black Panther Party was a black revolutionary group whose original purpose was to patrol black ghettoes to protect residents from acts of police brutality. The Party was influential in shaping black radicalism in Britain.

Following the separatist black nationalist agenda pioneered by *Malcolm X, the Panthers developed into an international Marxist revolutionary group. Among the demands contained within its ten-point plan was the armed mobilization of Blacks; a radical redistribution of social and economic institutions within black communities; and reparations to Blacks for centuries of exploitation. Membership peaked around 2,000 in the late 1960s, when the Party's activities and influence were such that in 1968 it was declared by the FBI 'the greatest threat to the internal security of the United States.' Several shoot-outs in the late 1960s and early 1970s led to severe repression from the police and the FBI. Party membership had eroded by the late 1970s, but its activities diversified, including the provision of social services in deprived urban areas.

The Black Panthers' influence in Britain was presaged by Malcolm X's visit in 1965. Under his influence the black British activist *Michael X founded in 1965 the black nationalist group the Racial Adjustment Action Society (whose name was chosen because the acronym RAAS suggested a well-known expletive in Caribbean English). Another, more secular group, the Universal Coloured People's Association (UCPA), was also formed around this time. Neither group survived long, though before its demise the UCPA had adopted an increasingly militant Black Power ideology under the guidance of Obi Egbuna. Egbuna was an acolyte of Stokely Carmichael, the civil rights turned Black Power campaigner and 'honorary prime minister' of the Black Panthers, following the latter's 1967 visit to London.

These two organizations commanded national attention when they came together for the third *Campaign Against Racial Discrimination Conference in November 1967. The subsequent failure to establish a durable political or civic group embodying Black Power ideology is not to downplay the ideology's impact from the late 1960s. Instead it speaks to a diverse interpretation and application of the teachings of both Black Power *and* the less radical American civil rights activists at that time. After the riots and unrest of 1958 a number of small-scale civic and political organizations emerged, seeking more gradualist approaches to the question of integration. While the Black Power organizations and ideologues dominated headlines, the long-term work of gaining social justice and political empowerment for British Blacks was taken up by numerous local and regional groups.

A police raid on the Mangrove restaurant in Notting Hill in 1970, leading to nine arrests and a series of violent confrontations, is regarded as the high-water mark of Black Power in Britain. Ellis Cashmore has summarized it thus: 'Despite the martyrizing effects of the arrests and imprisonments, black power never achieved in Britain anything resembling the unity and collective purpose of its United States counterparts. There was never an ideology to knot the different organizations together, nor the network of communications necessary to maintain continuity.' JJGG

Cashmore, E. Ellis, *United Kingdom: Class, Race and Gender Since the War* (1989)

See also POLITICS

Black People's Day of Action. The largest ever demonstration of black people in Britain. Organized by the Black People's Assembly and the New Cross Massacre Action Committee, the mass mobilization of black people on Monday 2 March 1981

was a strategic element in a campaign organized by black community groups to draw attention to what they regarded as the failure of the Metropolitan Police Force to investigate fully the circumstances of the *New Cross fire, which had claimed the lives of thirteen young black people at a birthday party in January 1981. Many among the black community believed the fire to have been deliberately started by racists.

In the decade leading up to the New Cross fire, black and Asian people had endured a spate of racially motivated attacks against their persons, homes, businesses, and community centres. These attacks were believed to have been the work of the neo-fascist right-wing anti-immigration National Front party. Widespread beliefs that the police lacked the political will and commitment to address these sustained attacks against black communities were underscored by allegations of police brutality, harassment, and racism towards black people in general and black youth in particular. The alleged inability or unwillingness of the police to protect black communities from racist violence had severely undermined the community's trust in the police. Frustration increased further when, days after the fatal fire, and before the official investigation had begun, the police force dismissed witness allegations that the fire had been deliberately started by racists. Claims made by survivors and their families of hostile police treatment, and police attempts to discredit their evidence, added to the already tense state of relations between the police and black communities. The apparent apathy of the British media was further underscored when, barely a month after the tragic events at 439 New Cross Road, a fire broke out in a nightclub in Dublin, killing and injuring many people. The national expressions of sympathy extended to the Irish victims and their families contrasted greatly with perceived indifference shown towards the families of the victims of New Cross.

Meanwhile, local community groups organized to offer both practical and emotional support for the victims and their families, and campaigned to demand a full and thorough investigation into the causes of the fire. On 2 March between 15,000 and 20,000 black people and their supporters from across Britain mobilized in a show of unity. While the demonstration's explicit aim was to draw attention to police mishandling of the investigation and wider indifference to the plight of black communities, the demonstration also provided an outlet for black and Asian peoples to express collectively their anger and frustration at decades of political, social, and economic disempowerment as a consequence of systematic and systemic racism, discrimination, disadvantage, and poverty. Carrying placards bearing pictures and the names of the dead, and chanting 'Thirteen dead and nothing said', the demonstrators set off from the Pagnell Street Community Centre (formerly known as the Moonshot Club), gathering more supporters as the crowd wound its way through the streets of New Cross, Peckham, Camberwell, Elephant and Castle, and across Blackfriars Bridge (where a scuffle broke out as police attempted to stop demonstrators going further), before continuing into Fleet Street, then regarded as the bastion of the British media, where they were met with heckles and jeers from some journalists. When the crowd finally reached Hyde Park, a mass rally was held. Letters of protest against racism were also delivered to the Fleet Street editors, the Prime Minister, and the Police Commissioner at Scotland Yard. The Black People's Day of Action is remembered as a historic occasion that brought together in unity for the first time thousands of black people to demand racial justice. Support groups were formed and funds were collected for the victims and their families, black community organizations and self-help groups were set up, but in its demonstration of the power of black collective action, the march showed British society that black people were no longer prepared to silently accept racism. CJ

La Rose, John, *The New Cross Massacre Story* (1984)

See also LA ROSE, JOHN; RACISM

Blackman, Peter (1909–1993). Pan-African Marxist and scholar. Blackman was born in Barbados and won a scholarship to the University of Durham, where he studied theology. He was ordained in the Anglican Church and went to the Gambia as a missionary priest, where he clashed with his bishop over differences of pay for white and black clergy. Having resigned from the Church, Blackman returned to Barbados, but then, in 1938, he settled in London. He joined the leftist *Negro Welfare Association, of which he became chairman, and also the League Against Imperialism, being a major speaker on both their platforms. He also became a member of the Executive Committee of the more liberally inclined *League of Coloured Peoples, and in 1938–9 editor of its then occasional journal *The Keys*, writing critically on colonial policy; he also gave evidence to the Royal Commission on the West Indies. In November 1938 Blackman helped to establish the Committee for West Indian Affairs, becoming its secretary and convenor. The body acted as a clearing house of information on West Indian matters for members who represented black lobbies, trade unions, and also members of Parliament. At some time Blackman became a Marxist and a member of the Communist Party of Great Britain. During the war he assembled Wellington bombers in an aircraft factory, and he later worked as a railway fitter. He was an aide to Paul *Robeson, accompanying him on his visit to eastern Europe in 1949. A scholar, poet, and radical opponent of colonialism, Blackman remained a Marxist, although breaking with the Communist Party in the late 1950s. DK

Adi, Hakim, Holledge, Julie, and Sherwood, Marika, *Pan-African History: Political Figures from Africa and the Diaspora Since 1787* (2003)

See also CHRISTIANITY; COMMUNISM; POLITICS

Blake, William (1757–1827). London-born poet, printer, visionary, and 'prophet against empire'. Over the course of his lifetime Blake confronted the horrors of slavery through his literary and pictorial art. He was able both to counter pro-slavery propaganda and to complicate typical abolitionist verse and sentiment with a profound and unique exploration of the effects of enslavement and the varied processes of empire.

Blake's poem 'The Little Black Boy' from *Songs of Innocence* (1789) examines the 'mind forg'd manacles' of racial constructions in the minds of individuals, both in the poem itself, in the form of the black child and his white counterpart, and also in the minds of those involved in the political dispute over abolition. Seeming to explain a desire for racial acceptance and spiritual purity through assimilation into white British society, and seeming also to be endorsing conventional assumptions of white racial superiority, the poem actually realizes the oppressive nature of preoccupations with racial classification. According to Marcus Wood, the black boy has internalized the stereotypical symbolism of European Christianity and has therefore accepted the resulting reading of black and white in absolute moral and spiritual terms. The poem deflates the very rhetoric of racism itself, however, as, for Blake, all constructions and symbols of colour occlude true vision—'When I from black and he from white cloud free'. While assisting the agitations of the abolitionist cause, Blake's poem also subverts the sanctimonious nature of abolition racial agendas that focused primarily on Christian indoctrination.

Similarly, *Visions of the Daughters of Albion* (1793) explores the psychologically damaging effects of enslavement upon its victims and also caricatures the political debate over abolition in Britain. The triangular relationship between Oothoon the female slave, Bromion the slave-driver, and Theotormon the jealous but inhibited former lover, depicts the sufferings of those subjugated by the trade itself and mimics the position of the pro-slavery, vested-interest lobby and that of wavering abolitionists who seem to deplore the trade but cannot bring themselves to condemn it openly. The poem, with its attention to 'the voice of slaves beneath the sun', was, according to David Erdman, directing the light of the French Revolution upon the most vulnerable flaw in the British constitution, and the engravings surrounding Blake's verse illuminate conditions on the plantations in the Caribbean.

At the time Blake was producing *Visions of the Daughters of Albion*, he was also working on at least sixteen engravings for Captain J. G. Stedman's *Narrative, of a Five Years' Expedition, Against the Revolted Negroes of Surinam* (1793). Blake's engravings portray a series of slave figures suffering brutal torture on the plantation, among them *A Negro hung alive by the Ribs to a Gallows*, *The Execution of Breaking on the Rack*, and *Flagellation of a Female Samboe Slave*. These engravings are undoubtedly compassionate as they lend the victims of the torture a power and dignity largely absent in the accompanying accounts by Stedman (a Theotormon figure for Blake). Indeed, the first of these engravings has been construed as an explicit attack on the slave trade. Blake depicts the skulls of the murdered slaves looking out over the sea to a slave ship in the distance while the most recent victim of plantation cruelty swings on the gallows in the foreground. The images of the female slave in Blake's engraving have been seen as more problematic, however. It has been argued that there is a fanciful and voyeuristic element that makes the artist, and perhaps the viewer, complicit in the suffering of the enslaved. Giving Blake the benefit of the doubt, Wood argued that it is possible to see the image as one that 'teeters on the edge of pornography in order to confront us with our own corruptibility'.

Superseding sensibility, sympathy, and religious devotion, the sincerity of Blake's anti-slavery and anti-colonial philosophy lies in the fact that it is deeply embedded within his antipathy to the processes and systems of what he termed 'Universal Empire'. This exploitative network of production and consumption, facilitated by political, economic, and military might, exceeds even the realities of the British Empire, which becomes situated within its compass. Blake's total opposition to this imperial 'world-system' of retrograde capitalist modernization allows him to connect the plight of the enslaved in the Caribbean with the urban poor and millworkers of Britain's cities, not for the purposes of articulating competitive comparisons on the scales of suffering, but rather to extol the potential and the power of extra-parliamentary resistance. Indeed, Blake was among the few British writers who actively advocated slave rebellion and believed that it was at the edges of empire that true revolutions would occur.

CMC

Erdman, David V., *Blake: Prophet Against Empire* (1977)

Makdisi, Saree, *Romantic Imperialism: Universal Empire and the Culture of Modernity* (1998)

Wood, Marcus, *Blind Memory: Visual Representations of Slavery in England and America 1780–1865* (2000)

See also ABOLITION; SLAVE TRADE; SLAVERY

Blyden, Edward Wilmot (1832–1912). Scholar, lifelong champion of African rights, and Liberia's first accredited diplomat to the Court of St James, London. Edward Blyden was born in August 1832 in Charlotte-Amalie, the capital of the island of St Thomas in the Danish West Indies. The third child of free parents—his father was a tailor and his mother a teacher—Blyden enjoyed a tranquil early childhood of personal tuition from his mother, combined with attendance at the local primary school. In 1842 the family moved to Porto Bello in Venezuela, where Blyden's linguistic talents first came to prominence. By the age of 12 he was fluent in Spanish, while at later stages in his life he would also master Latin, Hebrew, and Arabic. On returning to St Thomas two years later, Blyden continued his schooling in the mornings while serving out a five-year apprenticeship as a tailor in the afternoons.

In 1845 the Revd John P. Knox, a white American, arrived in St Thomas, an event that was to have a dramatic impact upon Blyden's future. As pastor of the local

Dutch Reformed Church, Knox was greatly impressed by the teenage Blyden, who now expressed a wish to become a clergyman. In May 1850 they travelled to the United States together, with the aim of enrolling Blyden in theological college. However, despite Knox's patronage, Blyden was refused entry into three such establishments on racial grounds, including Rutgers Theological College, where Knox had trained. Deeply distressed by his experience of racial discrimination, Blyden swiftly accepted an offer from the New York Colonization Society of a free passage to Liberia. He sailed from Baltimore aboard the packet *Liberia* on 21 December 1850 and, despite a stormy and difficult journey, arrived safely in Monrovia on 26 January 1851.

Once settled in Liberia, Blyden discovered that there was no possibility of working in his tailoring trade, because all clothing was imported ready-made. So, at the age of 19, he decided to return once more to education. In August 1851 he began to study theology, classics, geography, and mathematics at the Alexander High School, a newly founded Presbyterian institute. Blyden made rapid progress, and by 1854 was employed as a tutor at that school, as well as serving briefly as acting principal. In 1858 and still only 26 years old, Blyden was ordained as a Presbyterian minister, and also appointed principal of the Alexander High School. Just four years later he was appointed Professor of Classics at Liberia College, a position he continued to hold until 1871. In addition to his role as educator, Blyden served in a number of ministerial roles, including the position of Secretary of State for Liberia between 1864 and 1866.

Although he was a brilliant scholar and, in Lynch's words, the 'most learned and articulate champion of Africa . . . of his time', Blyden was also a highly controversial figure, particularly in his attitudes towards 'Mulattos'. Ironically, in December 1856 Blyden had married a 'mulatto' woman, Sarah Yates, who was the niece of the Vice-President of Liberia. The marriage was an unhappy one, and when one of their three children was born retarded, Blyden felt he was being punished for marrying 'outside' his race. As his outspoken hatred of 'Mulattos' grew, his popularity among the populace of Liberia declined, and in May 1871 he was attacked by a mob and dragged through the streets with a rope around his neck. Only the timely intervention of a colleague, D. B. Warner, saved him from certain death and, as a result, Blyden fled from Liberia to Sierra Leone.

For the next two years Blyden lived in Freetown, where he founded and edited the *Negro* newspaper. He returned to Liberia in 1874, where he again held a variety of academic and ministerial posts, including that of Ambassador to the Court of St James, London, from 1877 to 1878 and again in 1892. Although he failed as a diplomatic negotiator with the British government, Blyden was a great social success in London and met many influential figures. This included an audience with Queen Victoria in 1892, to whom he presented a copy of his book *Christianity, Islam and the Negro Race* (1887).

In 1885 Blyden was defeated as a presidential candidate in Liberia, and from then onwards divided his time between Liberia, Sierra Leone, and Lagos. He continued to write and edit for a number of nationalist newspapers, and between 1901 and 1906 worked as Director of Mohammedan Education in Freetown. Towards the end of his life Blyden found himself in ill health and applied to the British government for financial assistance. He was granted a small pension in 1909 and subsequently died in Freetown on 7 February 1912.

Despite his lengthy career as a politician and academic, it is for his writing that Blyden is now chiefly remembered. Throughout his life he published numerous articles, pamphlets, and books on African culture and the 'Negro' race, many of which were highly controversial in nature. His scholarly reputation was largely established by a collection of four articles that first appeared in *Fraser's Magazine* between 1871 and 1876. In these he argued that Christianity had served as a negative force in the lives of black people, while Islam had been 'a healthy amalgamation, and not absorption or an undue repression'. He subsequently published other important works, including *From West Africa to Palestine* (1873), *The Jewish Question* (1898), *West Africa Before Europe* (1905), and *African Life and Customs* (1908). Blyden received several awards for his work, including two doctorates from Lincoln University, honorary membership of the Athenaeum and St George's in 1878, and the Coronation Medal of King Edward VII and Queen Alexander. After his death a bust was erected in Water Street, Freetown, to commemorate his life and works.

DD

Blyden, Edward W., 'Mohammedanism and the Negro Race', *Fraser's Magazine*, 12 (1875)

Lynch, Hollis R., *Edward Wilmot Blyden: Pan-Negro Patriot 1832–1912* (1967)

Bonetta, Sarah Forbes (*c.*1843–1880). Orphan from Dahomey (now Benin) reputed to be of royal lineage, who was brought as a slave to England, where she became Queen Victoria's protégée. Sarah was named, ignominiously, after the ship *Bonetta* on which she was transported to England. Ironically, she was given to Captain Frederick Forbes by King Gezo of Dahomey in a conciliatory gesture following Forbes's unsuccessful attempt to persuade the King to give up trading in slaves. Forbes, in his account of his travels *Dahomey and the Dahomans* (1851), used Sarah as an example of the potential for progress in the intellect of the African at a time when pseudo-scientific enlightenment theories of race were rampant: as Forbes noted, 'it being generally and erroneously supposed that after a certain age the intellect [of the African] becomes impaired and the pursuit of knowledge impossible'.

Sarah was presented to Queen Victoria and thereafter raised under her protection. The Queen, impressed by Sarah's intelligence and command of English, and moved by her story—as a child Sarah had witnessed the massacre of her parents by enemy warriors—assumed financial responsibility for her and had her sent for schooling in Sierra Leone. She returned to England in the late 1850s and was sent to Brighton to complete her introduction to society. Sarah had become an accomplished pianist and linguist. It was in Brighton that she was introduced to an African merchant, James Davies, who proposed marriage. The marriage in 1862, attended by a number of mixed-race couples, was widely reported in the newspapers, including the *Anti-Slavery Reporter*. In 1863 Sarah gave birth to a girl, whom she named Victoria in honour of her royal patron. Queen Victoria became the child's godmother, gave her an annuity, and remained in close and regular contact with her throughout her life. James's business dealings were mostly unsuccessful, and the various court hearings following from his commercial activities took their toll on Sarah's health and she died in 1880.

JPo

Bressy, Caroline, 'Of Africa's Brightest Ornaments: A Short Biography of Sarah Forbes Bonetta', *Social and Cultural Geography*, 6/2 (2005)

Myers, Walter, *At Her Majesty's Request: An African Princess in Victorian England* (1999)

See also GEORGIAN AND VICTORIAN BRITAIN

Bridgetower, George Augustus Polgreen (1778–1860). Black violinist who performed extensively in Britain. Bridgetower was born in Biała, Poland, the son of John Frederick Bridgetower, who might have come from the Caribbean, and his wife, Marie Ann, a Polish woman who died when their son was young. Bridgetower was said to have been a child prodigy, having made his debut as a soloist in April 1789 in Paris. The environment in which he was brought up was a significant factor in the development of his talent. His father was employed by Prince Nicholas Esterhazy, and John and his son lived at the back of the opera house with the court's musicians. Haydn was also an employee of the Prince, and it is possible that the young Bridgetower studied under him. A few years later, in England, Bridgetower would play the violin in Haydn's symphonies at concerts commissioned by Johann Peter Solomon, where Haydn was also conducting.

In the autumn of 1789 Bridgetower left for England, where he performed for British royalty at Windsor Castle and the Pump Rooms at Bath. He first played in London on 19 February 1790 at Drury Lane Theatre. This performance was succeeded by a string of concerts at the Hanover Square rooms. Of particular note is his appearance as the concerto soloist at the rooms in the season of 1790. By 1794 he was performing in Covent Garden, and in 1795 he was employed by the Prince of Wales, remaining in his service until 1809.

In 1802 Bridgetower took leave from the Prince's service and visited Europe, where in 1803 he met Beethoven. The two musicians were initially inspired by one another, but they soon fell out. Beethoven's Sonata for Violin and Piano No. 9 in A minor, Op. 47, was originally written for Bridgetower, but after their disagreement he dedicated the piece to Rodolphe Kreutzer. The tuning fork that Beethoven presented to Bridgetower prior to their dispute is now held by the British Library.

When Bridgetower returned to London, he once again played at Hanover Square, but this time his brother played alongside him. Apart from playing the violin, Bridgetower also taught the piano and contributed to the educational material of the instrument. He was one of the earliest members of the Royal Philharmonic Society and in 1811 received a BM degree from the University of Cambridge. Bridgetower lived in various European cities such as Paris and Rome before finally settling down in London. He was buried in Kensal Green cemetery. DD/SS

Grove, George, 'Bridgetower, George Polgreen' in *The New Grove Dictionary of Music and Musicians* (ed. Stanley Sadie, 1980)

ODNB

Bristol. City in the south-west of England whose importance to black history is firmly established by its long-term involvement in the transatlantic slave economy, by its subsequent links to the North American anti-slavery movement, and by the developments affecting its relatively small black population since the 1960s.

1. Bristol and the transatlantic slave economy
2. The black presence in the era of slavery
3. African-Americans in Bristol in the 19th century
4. Black people in 20th-century Bristol

1. Bristol and the transatlantic slave economy 'Brize-yo', literally 'children of Bristol', was reportedly the name first given to the English by the Neyo people of what is now the Ivory Coast because of their early trading links with Bristol ships. Indeed, Bristol's trade with West Africa goes back at least into the late 1400s, when Bristol merchants in Seville first invested in the 'African trade'. By 1556 William Towerson, in search of African gold, had brought his ships safely back to Bristol from 'Guinea', and by 1593 Bristol ships were officially allowed to visit West Africa.

Involved in the early colonization of the Caribbean and North America, Bristol was Britain's second city for much of the 18th century, briefly eclipsing even *London and *Liverpool as a slave-trading entrepôt during the 1720s and 1730s and transporting nearly half a million enslaved Africans to America around 1698–1807. Although slave trading per se constituted a relatively minor part of its export trade, Bristol's involvement in the wider Atlantic slave economy—as a processor, servicer, and importer of slave-produced goods—dominated the city's economy well into the 1800s.

2. The black presence in the era of slavery Sometime between 1560 and 1595 the city's first African resident, an unnamed 'blackamore', served as gardener at the 'great house' of the prominent Bristol merchant Sir John Young. Bristol's close trading relations with Spain and Portugal and their slave colonies in the Atlantic led to the establishment by 1618 of the first sugar refinery in the city. More evidence of black residents (mainly enslaved servants) also begin to surface in the local records by this time.

The most famous of these black servants were Scipio *Africanus (1702–20), whose tombstone in Henbury churchyard in the city survives today, and Pero (1740–1818), personal servant to John Pinney, an important Bristol merchant, after serving on Pinney's plantation in Nevis. (A new footbridge was named in Pero's honour by the City Council in 1999). Recent research reveals a number of servants of African or 'mulatto' background employed at various times in Pinney's Bristol household.

Not all black people in Bristol in this era were servants. Black sailors from both West Africa and the Caribbean served aboard Bristol ships (including slavers). West African trading partners of British slave merchants occasionally sent their sons to England to learn English and bookkeeping, and at least one came to 'to take shipping at Bristol' in 1759. The mixed-race children of wealthy Caribbean planters were also sometimes sent to be schooled in Bristol.

In 1774 two young kinsmen of an important Ifik slave trader, Ephraim Robin John of Old Calabar (now in Nigeria), escaped as stowaways to Bristol, having previously been tricked into slavery and taken to Virginia. They were assisted there by one of their kinsmen's Bristol trading partners (the slave trader Thomas Jones) and received hospitality and religious instruction from Charles and John *Wesley and other local Methodists before returning to Calabar. Some 20 to 30 of the French prisoners of war kept in Stapleton prison near Bristol between 1792 and 1815 were black sailors from the Caribbean.

The black presence in the city, consisting in the late 1700s of perhaps as many as several hundred people, declined rapidly by the early 19th century, mirroring the collapse of the slave economy. Some Bristol firms and missionaries retained links with the Caribbean long afterwards, up until the 20th century. In lieu of slaves, the palm oil trade with West Africa became increasingly important to the port.

3. **African-Americans in Bristol in the 19th century** Bristol was host to a number of visiting African-Americans in the 19th century, some of international renown including Ira *Aldridge, Moses Roper (who married a local Bristol woman), Frederick *Douglass, and Booker T. *Washington. Henry Parker, an escaped slave, also settled in Bristol, married, and became a preacher of local note. Black American musicians influenced the cultural tastes of Victorian Bristol, with local musicians being particularly inspired by the Bohee Brothers, two virtuoso banjo players who played to a rapturous audience in Bristol's Theatre Royal in 1888.

4. **Black people in 20th-century Bristol** By the early 20th century, if not before, colonial links ensured that a small number of visiting students and dignitaries from West Africa made their way to Bristol. But very few black people lived as permanent residents there before the *Second World War. The next major inflow of black people to Bristol came in 1942, when African-American GIs were billeted on the city, segregated from their white fellow soldiers and often kept under restrictive conditions to minimize fraternization with local white women, many of whom did not share the Jim Crow sentiments prevailing in the US Army. On 15 July 1943 a riot between some 400 black and white servicemen broke out near the city centre and 120 military policemen were brought in to suppress it, leaving one black GI dead and an undetermined number wounded.

In 1947 immigration from the Caribbean began, mainly via London, with some young men first coming as stowaways on the banana boats steaming into Avonmouth (Bristol's modern port). By the 1960s immigration, mainly from Jamaica but also from Barbados, Antigua, and other islands, was well established. The highly visible but still small enclave of 'West Indians', servicing the city's hospitals and factories but concentrated in the blighted St Paul's area of the city, suffered from endemic and open discrimination. In 1963 a group of local Jamaicans, such as Owen Henry, Guy Bailey, and Roy Hackett, along with Paul Stephenson, a trained youth worker of West African and English descent, organized what was probably the first black-led campaign against racial discrimination in Britain when they challenged the openly racialist hiring policies of the Bristol Omnibus Company. Their efforts attracted international attention and arguably helped to set the scene for subsequent legislation banning discrimination in employment. The St Paul's Carnival began to flourish in the late 1960s, but racist practices and disadvantage still continued, as a second generation of African-Caribbeans grew to maturity. In 1980 an anti-police riot in St Paul's again brought Bristol's race relations under global scrutiny. Since then black Bristolians, including such artists as Tricky and Roni Size, have made their mark on the British music scene, as did Massive Attack, a group whose mixed origins are emblematic of evolving ethnic identities in the city. But economic progress and urban regeneration were partly stymied by the penetration of crack cocaine into the area in the early 1990s, and significant numbers of the more socially mobile black residents have since moved to neighbouring wards.

According to the 2001 census, over half of the 10,000 Bristolians classified as 'black' (out of a total population of 485,000) were of African-Caribbean origin, and most of these would have claimed Jamaican roots. Just over a fifth were termed 'Black Africans', a substantial proportion of whom were Yoruban (from Nigeria). Both populations were probably seriously under-reported in the census. Nonetheless, these startlingly small numbers of black Bristolians were made more visible by their relative concentration in the city's most deprived central wards. In the last few years, in addition to a new influx of Jamaican migrants, a substantial Somali community (estimated at 4,000–10,000) has also taken up residence in the inner-city area, a development which in future will challenge any notion of an unproblematically unified 'black' history of the city. MJD

Champion, Sarah, *The Diary of Sarah Champion* (ed. Madge Dresser, 2003)

Douglass, Frederick, 'Monarchies and Freedom, Republics and Slavery: An Address Delivered in Bristol, England, April 1, 1847', *Bristol Mercury and Western Counties Advertiser*, (3 Apr. 1847)

Dresser, Madge, *Slavery Obscured: The Social History of the Slave Trade in an English Provincial Port* (2001)

Smith, Graham, *When Jim Crow Met John Bull: Black American Soldiers in World War II Britain* (1987)

See also LASCARS AND BLACK SEAMEN; MUSIC 2: EARLY POPULAR MUSIC

British Empire Exhibition. Exhibition to celebrate the achievements of a global empire recently expanded by the inclusion of territories acquired as a result of the First World War, to encourage Imperial trade, to promote pride in the Empire, and 'the almost illimitable possibilities of the Dominions, Colonies, and Dependencies overseas'. The Exhibition, staged on a 216-acre site in Wembley, north London, was opened on St George's Day (23 April) 1924 by King George V with a radio broadcast.

Besides the pavilions provided by each Dominion and the exhibits of the different colonies, there were also a 'Pageant of Empire', military tattoos, an Imperial Boy Scout Jamboree, and re-enactments of First World War battles. Visitors could also see indigenous people, or 'races in residence' as they were called, demonstrating local crafts and skills. Special postage stamps were also issued. Of great importance for many people was the construction of the Wembley Stadium, a multi-purpose athletic and entertainment centre, which was ready for the Football Association Cup Final in 1923. Over 27 million visitors attended the Exhibition, but it lost money and was extended into 1925 in order to try to balance the books.

It is difficult to gauge the impact of the Exhibition on public perceptions of Empire. It may have been considerable given that 'nearly half-a-million post cards were sold in five months', of the Gold Coast exhibits alone. Exposure to a range of Imperial products and activities helped to widen public knowledge of many aspects of Empire. DK

British Empire Exhibition, *British Empire Exhibition, 1924, Official Guide* (1924)
Gold Coast Government, *Gold Coast Participation in the British Empire Exhibition, 1924* (1925)
Judd, Denis, *Empire: The British Imperial Experience from 1765 to the Present* (1996)

See also COLONIAL AND INDIAN EXHIBITION

British Honduran forestry workers. About 900 men from British Honduras (now Belize) were brought to Britain in 1941 and 1942 by the ministries of Supply and Labour to meet the expanding demand for civilian forestry workers. While the recruitment was based on a perceived labour shortage in Britain, it was also thought to help alleviate the growing unemployment, starvation, and suffering in British Honduras. The men were effectively indentured labourers who signed a contract with the British government. Among other conditions, their contracts provided for free transport to and from the forestry camps in Britain, free medical services, and a three-year term of engagement, after which they would be immediately returned home. The workers who comprised what was known as the British Honduran Forestry Unit were based in three camps in the north and south of Scotland.

While a welfare officer was assigned to look after the men, they faced a range of adverse treatments such as inadequate heating and hot-water services, no warm underwear, and too few sleeping huts. This made their acclimatization to an unfamiliar landscape and climate even more difficult. In addition to problems of inadequate clothing, problems over food, and medical ailments, there was a great deal of concern about the high incidence of venereal disease among the men. This created a moral panic about the possibility of 'loose' relations between black British Honduran workers and local white women. In some cases men with venereal disease would be sent home before their contracts expired. In addition, although the men were skilled, the Ministry of Supply classified them as unskilled to justify paying them minimum wages. When the men contested these conditions, they were seen as lazy and in need of discipline. Underlying these adverse conditions and poor management was a racist attitude institutionalized by the Ministry of Supply and the surrounding local communities that sought to contain the perceived threat of a 'coloured' presence. The fluctuating strengths of administration in different camps dictated the quality of life for these men.

The *League of Coloured Peoples, however, visited, scrutinized, and protested about the living and working conditions in the camps. The League raised the issue of the unequal working conditions between white and black civilian forestry workers. The plight of the workers was also eased somewhat by the inspection and subsequent recommendations of the Colonial Office's welfare officers, who arranged for the men to receive musical instruments and sports equipment. The men formed a jazz band, which provided entertainment inside the camps as well as at dances in the local communities. They also had their own football team and played against teams in the communities. Despite their efforts to improve conditions of life in the camps and build bridges with the local communities, 130 forestry workers were repatriated to British Honduras in 1943. In addition to the venereal disease panic, the Ministry of Supply made various claims that the men were lazy and incapable of being productive. While some workers did eventually return home voluntarily, some remained in Britain and found employment with the railways, British Aluminium, and the Scottish Motor Transport Company. ASW

Ford, Amos, *Telling the Truth: The Life and Times of the British Honduran Forestry Unit in Scotland (1941–44)* (1985)
Sherwood, Marika, *Many Struggles: West Indian Workers and Service Personnel in Britain (1939–45)* (1985)

See also SECOND WORLD WAR

British West Indies Regiment. In the *First World War 15,204 West Indians were recruited to fight for Britain and the British Empire.

1. The First World War
2. Recruitment and war experiences
3. Mutiny and social unrest

1. The First World War The expiry of the British ultimatum to Germany in August 1914 inevitably meant that the West Indian colonies, like the rest of the Empire, became embroiled in war. These colonies had no right of neutrality, but their display of loyalty had more to do with the informal than the formal ties they had with Britain. The majority of the inhabitants of the British West Indies had been conditioned as faithful patriots, and social progress was, in part, measured locally by the extent to which the subjects of each colony exhibited British ideals and customs. Not surprisingly, then, in spite of limited opposition, there was overwhelming support for Britain from the West Indian population.

Gifts valued at several thousand pounds and including sugar, rum, oil, lime, cotton, rice, clothing, logwood, planes, and ambulances were quickly forwarded to England to support the war effort. Added to these gifts were cash contributions of over £2 million. These donations were made despite severe hardships caused by major increases in the cost of living throughout the region as a result of the declaration of war.

Though British hegemony was pervasive, there were elements in West Indian society who on nationalistic, racial, and other grounds were opposed to providing any support for the British and their allies. In several colonies, including Trinidad, Grenada, Jamaica, and British Honduras, a number of Blacks adopted the position that it was a war among Europeans (a white man's war) and therefore black people should not become involved, but these people were severely criticized by the press, and some were punished by the local officials. At the same time West Indian middle-class Blacks were aware of the relevance of the war in their struggle for political and constitutional change, and thus couched beneath their protestations of patriotism was a clear linkage between their support for the war effort and the prospect of Britain granting them the reforms they desired for greater self-rule following the cessation of hostilities.

The feeling of loyalty soon translated into determination on the part of the colonies to send men to serve overseas as soldiers, but British Colonial Office and War Office officials were not keen on having Blacks serve on the Western Front until devastating losses suffered by the Allies forced the British government to approve the formation of West Indian contingents to serve overseas.

2. Recruitment and war experiences During the recruitment process a number of incentives and tactics were used to encourage men to volunteer to serve abroad. They were repeatedly told by recruiters of the 'very distinct' advantages of enlisting, including the prospect of gaining medals, glory, discipline, exercise, and free land at the end of the war, and those regarded as loafers and vagabonds were informed that military service would make them better men and citizens. The economic advantages of enlisting also constituted a central recruitment theme. In the prevailing conditions of high unemployment, the spiralling cost of living, and depressed wages, many working-class unemployed in the towns, plantation workers, and artisans were susceptible to the economic incentives to enlist, though issues of loyalty, patriotism, and duty were of less immediate importance to them. The recruitment process was, however, fraught with problems, including infestation with parasites such as hookworms, the high prevalence of venereal diseases, and racial posturing which resulted in many local Whites and other 'coloured' persons categorically refusing to join the black West Indian contingents, preferring to have their own contingents, or insisting that they be made officers in the British West Indies Regiment (BWIR). Eventually approximately 15,204 men were recruited and sent overseas as part of the BWIR, while many other Whites joined various British regiments.

By late 1916 the recruitment process began to come under severe pressure as the spectacle of returning invalids had a sobering effect on potential recruits. It was, however, the catastrophic journey of the third contingent of recruits from Jamaica that dramatically illustrated the possible dangers that awaited them. On 6 March 1916 the third Jamaica contingent, comprising 25 officers and 1,115 other ranks, departed for England on board the ship *Verdala*. Owing to enemy submarine activity in the region the Admiralty ordered the ship to make a diversion to Halifax, but before it could reach its destination it encountered a blizzard. Since the *Verdala* was not adequately heated and the black soldiers had not been properly equipped with warm clothing, substantial casualties resulted. Approximately 600 men suffered from exposure and frostbite and there were five immediate deaths.

The Halifax incident seriously damaged the recruitment campaign, which had to be temporarily suspended. The recruiters subsequently adopted a more vigorous strategy of house-to-house visits. Greater effort was also made, particularly after America's entry into the war in 1917, to obtain more volunteers from Panama, and it was to a large extent the recruiting of these Jamaican and other migrants in Panama that allowed further Jamaican contingents to be formed. Conscription measures were eventually passed in Jamaica and other colonies in order to get more men, especially those of quality, to enlist, but these measures were never enforced. The men who arrived overseas from the region to serve in the BWIR were therefore all volunteers, even though, as elsewhere in the Empire, some joined because of economic, legal, and private pressure.

Like other soldiers and non-combatants who served in the war, the BWIR battalions experienced conditions that were arduous and often very dangerous. They were subjected to enemy artillery bombardment, sniper fire, exploding ammunition dumps, and aerial attacks. In France life was also made uncomfortable by the prevalence of fleas, lice, and rats, while in Egypt there were problems with scorpions, lizards, snakes, and especially flies. Nevertheless, in every theatre the West Indians consistently displayed courage and discipline, and as result many won decorations. Their invaluable service and the bravery with which they performed under dangerous conditions were highly commended by senior commanding officers. However, the West Indian soldiers suffered severely from a combination of poor and irregular diet, insanitary and overcrowded conditions, neglect and inadequate medical care, and the harsh climatic conditions, which led to a high incidence of diseases like measles, scabies, diarrhoea, pneumonia, dysentery, influenza, malaria, and typhoid.

The devastating impact of disease on the 15,204 men who served in the BWIR is revealed by the fact that of total casualties, 185, or 1.22 per cent, were killed or died from wounds; 697, or 4.58 per cent, were wounded; while 1,071, or 7.04 per cent, died from disease. Additionally, even though there was a high degree of standardization and regularization in the disciplinary code structure of the Army, inequalities in attitudes towards and treatment of the different races, classes, and ethnic groups did exist. Major problems of discrimination were to be found in the practical application of army regulations in an environment in which stereotypes of race and class were prevalent.

3. **Mutiny and social unrest** By the end of 1917 there was a marked decline in morale among the soldiers of the BWIR. This discontent was further intensified by a pay dispute, which, although eventually settled in favour of the soldiers, served to generate even greater animosity among the men. More importantly, during the pay dispute the BWIR soldiers from the various islands displayed an unprecedented level of solidarity, which was a reflection of an intensification and development of

their West Indian conciousness and identity. This solidarity was again demonstrated during a mutiny at Taranto, Italy.

After Armistice Day the eight BWIR battalions in France and Italy were concentrated at Taranto to prepare for demobilization. They were subsequently joined by the three battalions from Egypt and the men from Mesopotamia. As a result of severe labour shortages at Taranto the West Indians had to assist with loading and unloading ships and do labour fatigues. This led to much resentment, and on 6 December 1918 the men of the 9th battalion revolted and attacked their officers. On the same day 180 sergeants forwarded a petition to the Secretary of State complaining about the pay issue, the failure to increase their separation allowance, and the fact that they had been discriminated against in the area of promotions.

During the mutiny, which lasted about four days, a black non-commissioned officer (NCO) shot and killed one of the mutineers in self-defence. Approximately 60 soldiers were later tried for mutiny, and those convicted received sentences ranging from three to five years, but one man got 20 years, while another was executed by a firing squad from the Worcestershire Regiment. Although the mutiny was crushed, the bitterness persisted, and on 17 December 1918 about 60 NCOs held a meeting to discuss the question of black rights, self-determination, and closer union in the West Indies. An organization called the Caribbean League was formed at the gathering to further these objectives. The headquarters for the Caribbean League was to be in Kingston, Jamaica, with sub-offices in the other colonies.

Meanwhile, the cessation of hostilities quickly led to a profound change in white attitudes to the presence of Blacks in the United Kingdom. As white seamen and soldiers were demobilized and the competition for jobs intensified, so too did the level of race and class antagonism, especially in London and the port cities. The more serious aspect of this intensification of race and class conflict was the numerous riots that erupted and the assaults on Blacks in the United Kingdom. The riots were extensive and involved thousands of Whites, who unleashed a series of attacks on non-white groups in many cities including *Cardiff, *Glasgow, Hull, *Liverpool, *London, and Newport in South Wales. Because of the large-scale onslaughts on Blacks, and in an attempt to appease the British public, the government decided to repatriate as many Blacks as they could, and by the middle of September 1919 about 600 had been repatriated.

Even more alarming to the authorities, especially those in the West Indies, was the fact that between 1916 and 1919 a number of colonies, including St Lucia, Grenada, Barbados, Antigua, Trinidad, Jamaica, and British Guiana, experienced a series of strikes in which, in the case of Antigua, Jamaica, and Trinidad, several strikers were shot and killed. When the disgruntled soldiers began arriving back in the West Indies, they quickly joined a wave of workers' protests resulting from the severe economic crisis produced by the war and the influence of black nationalist ideology articulated by the black nationalist leader Marcus *Garvey and others. Disenchanted soldiers and angry workers unleashed a series of protest actions and riots in a number of territories, including Jamaica, Grenada, and especially in British Honduras.

West Indian participation in the war was a significant event in the still-ongoing process of identity formation in the post-emancipation era of West Indian history. The war stimulated profound socio-economic, political, and psychological change, and greatly facilitated protest against the oppressive conditions in the colonies and against colonial rule by giving a boost to the adoption of the nationalist ideologies of Marcus Garvey and others throughout the region. By establishing the conditions for the contestation of Imperial ideologies, the war laid the foundation for the nationalist upheavals of the 1930s, in which veterans were to play a significant role. GH

Elkins, W. F., 'A Source of Black Nationalism in the Caribbean: The Revolt of the British West Indies Regiment at Taranto, Italy', *Science and Society*, 33/2 (1970)
Horner, A. E., *From the Islands of the Sea: Glimpses of a West Indian Battalion in France* (1919)
Howe, Glenford, *Race War and Nationalism: A Social History of West Indians in the First World War* (2002)
Ramson, J., *Carry On; or, Pages from the Life of a West Indian Padre in the Field* (1918)

See also FIRST WORLD WAR; SECOND WORLD WAR

Brixton. South *London suburb that has been home, since the 1940s, to thousands of African-Caribbean immigrants, whose presence has contributed to the making of an energetic and multicultural melting pot in the United Kingdom. Like one of its main roads, Electric Avenue (so named because it was the first street in Britain to be lit by electric lights in 1888 and immortalized in the chart-topping hit song by the singer Eddie Grant), Brixton pulses with a carnivalesque energy. Yet, beneath the vitality and easygoing tolerance for which the area is known, a troubled history lies, always, it seems, threatening to break through the veneer of new-found respectability.

1. Brixton since the Victorian era
2. African-Caribbean influences
3. Social, political, and economic problems
4. Regenerating and reinventing Brixton

1. Brixton since the Victorian era The Brixton to which the **Empire Windrush* generation of Caribbean immigrants arrived was for the most part a dreary, war-torn area with little to recommend it—a far cry from its optimistic emergence as a sought-after middle-class residential enclave at the end of the 19th century. By the 1930s the population had undergone significant demographic changes, as large numbers of working-class people moved into the area. Many of these newcomers were actors, artistes, and performers, attracted to the area because of its proximity to central London's theatreland, and because of the suburb's burgeoning entertainment industry. Cheap housing, theatres, cinemas, good cross-country transport links, and a bustling shopping centre added to the area's popularity. The Second World War, however, halted Brixton's progress. Bomb damage to housing and local amenities devastated much of the area, and the thousands of black immigrants who arrived in the following decades in search of the mythical streets paved with gold found instead a bomb-scarred and dilapidated suburb, abandoned by all but those unable to afford to move to greener surrounding suburbs.

2. African-Caribbean influences The availability of cheap housing, however, encouraged the settlement of thousands of Caribbean, Asian, and African immigrants, who settled in the area and together created the Brixton of today. Brixton market, with its jumble of stalls selling plantains, Jamaican patties, yams, green bananas, and an array of Caribbean foodstuffs, rapidly became an important focal point for the new arrivals, many of whom made their homes in the adjacent environs of Atlantic Road, Electric Avenue, Coldharbour Lane, and Railton Road. By the late 1960s much of this area had become one of the largest and most important sites of Caribbean settlement in the United Kingdom, and word of Brixton's reputation as 'the spiritual home of Caribbeans in Britain' spread 'back home', encouraging new generations of Caribbean settlers.

3. Social, political, and economic problems For all its colourful, busy, and tolerant façade, however, serious problems simmered under the surface, making it perhaps inevitable that Brixton would witness some of the most serious riots of the 1980s. Years of under-investment meant that by the late 1970s Brixton had become synonymous with urban decline and deprivation, sub-standard housing stock, few social amenities, high levels of unemployment—especially among young black people—and one of the highest crime rates in London. Systematic racial discrimination and disadvantage, and 'hard-tactics' policing measures such as the aggressive stop and search operations, embittered many African-Caribbeans. Relations between Brixton's black communities and the local police had been seriously strained for some time, and tensions were exacerbated further when, in 1981, local police launched Swamp 81, a crime-busting operation that disproportionately targeted black youth. The riots (or uprisings, as they came to be called) that erupted in the spring and summer months of that year were the outward expressions of the pent-up anger and frustration of Brixton's black communities. The riots erupted in and centred around Frontline, an area of Railton Road and Atlantic Avenue inhabited primarily by African-Caribbeans. When the riots were finally quelled, after three days in which the police struggled to maintain authority on the streets, hundreds of people had been injured and millions of pounds' worth of damage to property caused. In the rebuilding programme that came in the aftermath of the riots, the local authority invested heavily in development and regeneration programmes, building new homes and improving existing housing stock, providing social amenities, encouraging new businesses, and sponsoring job creation programmes.

4. Regenerating and reinventing Brixton The years since the riots saw Brixton successfully reinvent and rebrand itself. Investment in the area fuelled its extraordinary transformation from a run-down, deprived inner-city area to a gentrified centre of bohemian chic, aided by an influx of young middle-class professionals, and locals proudly claimed Brixton to be one of the most multicultural areas in Britain. Recent years have seen the presence of new immigrants from Africa, South America, Portugal, Sudan, Australia, and New Zealand, and this meeting of cultures is attested to by the jumble of shops, market stalls, restaurants, and wine bars that reflect the diversity of Brixton's new population; halal meat shops nestle alongside Spanish tapas bars and African restaurants. An increasingly strong Latin American presence is also making itself felt, and Peruvian, Ecuadorian, Colombian, and Cuban restaurants compete for customers. Market stalls sell fresh food and produce from seemingly every corner of the globe, while music stalls blast out world music from Algeria to Zambia, and mosques vie with Catholic and Anglican churches for congregations. Between them, Brixton's population speak over 130 languages and dialects. Once considered a no-go area, Brixton's lively mix of clubs, theatres, concert halls, bars, and restaurants now attracts visitors from across the United Kingdom and abroad, bringing jobs and much-needed revenue to the area. A 1996 visit by Nelson Mandela confirmed Brixton's image as one of the United Kingdom's most racially integrated and culturally diverse areas, and though numerous economic, political, and social problems remain, Brixtonians retain a strong sense of optimism for their area's ever-changing future. CJ

Patterson, Sheila, *Dark Strangers* (1964)
Piper, Alan, *A History of Brixton* (1996)
Scarman, Lord, *The Scarman Report: The Brixton Disorders 10–12 April 1981* (1981)

See also DENNISTON, OSWALD; IMMIGRATION; SCARMAN REPORT

Broadhurst, Robert (1859/60–1948). Pan-Africanist leader in Britain in the early 1900s. Born in Sierra Leone, in 1869 he was sent to Cheshire to be educated and started working for the family firm, Broadhurst and Sons, in Manchester in 1905. By 1936 he is known to have been a cocoa merchant in the Gold Coast. He was heavily involved in the realm of Pan-Africanist politics in Britain, becoming a founder member of the *African Progress Union between 1911 and 1925. He became secretary of the Union in his sixties and continued as a member of the executive committee until its end. He worked with other leading supporters such as Duse Mohamed *Ali, Edmund Fitzgerald Fredericks, and 'the Black doctor of Paddington' John *Alcindor. The Union organized around issues related to the welfare of 'Africans and Afro-Peoples' worldwide and vociferously advocated self-determination. This involved, for example, protests about the lack of police protection during anti-black riots in *Liverpool in 1919.

Broadhurst was also a member of the *West African Students' Union, one of the strongest anti-colonial unions in Britain. He was also actively involved in the *International African Service Bureau from its inception in 1937, and was president of the first Pan-African Federation. Broadhurst collaborated and worked with other important Pan-Africanists such as George *Padmore. Through the African Progress Union he networked with and provided support to international colleagues such as the National Congress of British West Africa, especially promoting nationalist interests. ASW

Fryer, Peter, *Staying Power: Black People in Britain Since 1504* (1984)
ODNB

See also PAN-AFRICANISM

Broadwater Farm riots. Notorious riots that took place on a housing estate in Tottenham, north London, in 1985.

1. The catalyst
2. The riots
3. Police and community relations before the riots
4. Broadwater Farm estate: pre-riot problems
5. Rebuilding the Broadwater community

1. The catalyst On 5 October 1985 police officers stopped and questioned 24-year-old Floyd Jarrett. Later that day police raided and searched Jarrett's home near the Broadwater Farm estate. In the course of the search, Floyd's mother, Cynthia Jarrett, who suffered from heart problems, collapsed and subsequently died. Mrs Jarrett's death was to be the catalyst for serious riots by young local Blacks. She was the second black mother to have sustained injury following a police raid on her house within the space of a week: days earlier Cherry Groce, a Brixton mother, was accidentally shot and seriously injured after armed police raided her home in search of her son. Cherry Groce was left paralysed below the waist. Following her shooting, crowds of black people, already angry about what was considered over-zealous policing tactics of the black community, staged a demonstration outside Brixton police station. Tensions spilled over and a riot ensued.

2. The riots Coming only days after Cherry Groce's shooting, the death of Cynthia Jarrett inflamed anger among Haringey's African-Caribbean community. The following day a crowd gathered outside Muswell Hill police station to protest at her death. Stones were thrown, and two police officers were injured by flying bricks. Local community leaders attempted to dampen down the tension, but the violence escalated and several more police and residents were injured. Soon a full-scale riot erupted, lasting for two days. Property was damaged, scores of people were hurt, and in the midst of the disturbances, Police Constable Keith Blakelock was stabbed to death.

Local youths, Winston Silcott, Mark Braithwaite, and Engin Raghip (known as the Tottenham Three), were subsequently arrested and convicted of PC Blakelock's murder in 1987. A sustained campaign saw the Court of Appeal overturn all three of the convictions in 1991. Silcott received £50,000 compensation for wrongful conviction. PC Blakelock's killer has yet to be identified.

3. Police and community relations before the riots The disturbances that occurred on Broadwater Farm estate took place against the backdrop of sustained police harassment of black communities over a period of years. Between 1981 and up to the time of the Broadwater disturbances, riots had broken out across British cities. Though to some extent triggered by the poor state of police–black community relations, wider social and economic problems were also contributory factors. Young black people suffered from under-education, disproportionately high rates of unemployment, imprisonment, homelessness, incarceration in mental health facilities, and a general feeling of exclusion from mainstream society.

4. **Broadwater Farm estate: pre-riot problems** Broadwater Farm was widely recognized as an estate with serious problems. Built in the 1970s, it was originally hailed as a model of modern living. It was among the first of a new generation of concrete estates replicated across Europe as a means of post-war slum clearance, but also as an inexpensive way to provide modern homes for large numbers of socially deprived people. Initially, Broadwater Farm proved popular with residents. The flats were spacious and the indoor bathrooms and central heating were welcome innovations for the tenants.

But the failings of such huge concrete estates quickly became apparent. Huge numbers of working-class Whites and African-Caribbean peoples had been housed on estates that were mostly managed from distant council offices, and, in the absence of caretakers and cleaners, quickly became dilapidated. At Broadwater Farm services to tenants were poor. The long concrete walkways turned it into a rabbit warren, providing safe-holes for criminals while leaving residents isolated. The estate's environment deteriorated and it soon turned into a hard-to-let ghetto and a 'dumping ground' for those with social problems. Residents, nearly half of whom were African-Caribbean, complained of fear of going out, high levels of crime, muggings, and high suicide rates, but neither the police nor the local council appeared able to address the estate's problems. When the riots erupted in 1985, Broadwater Farm and its attendant social problems was thrust into the national spotlight.

5. **Rebuilding the Broadwater community** Many residents claim that the estate had started to turn around by the time of the riot. Haringey Council had begun to devolve the management to the estate, acceding to the demands of the strong residents' association. Local black youths not only had established a club for the estate's youngsters, but also had helped create a lunch club for the estate's mostly white pensioners, which at the time was regarded as highly unusual. A visit by the Princess of Wales before the riots signalled the optimism of the residents.

A 1986 inquiry into the disturbances by Lord Gifford identified the estate's economic and social problems as the underlying cause of the rioting, and made some specific recommendations for alleviating them. Several changes in police tactics and equipment were introduced, and efforts were made to re-engage with the community; many residents now believe that there has been a positive change in police–community relations. The local council invested considerable resources into the estate, with about £33 million spent on redesigning its layout, giving each block a unique identity. A huge mural painted on the side of one of the council blocks features Martin Luther King, M. K. *Gandhi, Bob Marley, and John Lennon—four apostles of peace looking down on what many consider to be a transformed Broadwater Farm.

Not only does the estate look and feel different; the previous ethnic mix of the predominately white working class and Afro-Caribbean population has changed and the estate now boasts a vibrant community of 39 different nationalities with the arrival of Turkish Kurds, Ghanaians, and Somalis, among many others. At the beginning of the 21st century Broadwater Farm was regarded by many as a beacon of racial harmony. However, despite this encouraging progress, there were still signs of concern over issues relating to policing methods. CJ

Gifford, Lord, *The Broadwater Farm Inquiry: Report of the Independent Inquiry into Disturbances of October 1985 at the Broadwater Farm Estate, Tottenham* (1986)

See also CRIMINAL JUSTICE SYSTEM; HOUSING; RACISM; 'SUS LAW'

Brown, Henry 'Box' (b. *c.*1815). Prominent 19th-century African-American abolitionist who escaped to England. Brown was born into slavery on a plantation in Richmond, Virginia. After having been forcibly separated from his wife and children, Brown and a white friend, Samuel A. Smith, conceived an ingenious plan for his escape from slavery. In March 1848 Brown hid in a wooden crate supposedly containing dry goods, and had himself shipped via the Adams Express Company to William H. Johnson, an abolitionist sympathizer. Having arrived in Philadelphia, Pennsylvania, a free state, Brown claimed his freedom and thereafter took the name 'Box' as his own. With the help of anti-slavery friends, he became an abolitionist lecturer and author. In 1849 Charles Stearns wrote and published 'Box' Brown's narrative of his daring escape. A year later, however, with the passage of the Fugitive Slave Act of 1850, fearing possible capture and return to slavery, Brown fled instead to Liverpool, where he began to lecture regularly on the abolitionist lecture circuit. When, in 1851, an edited version of his *Narrative of the Life of Henry Box Brown, Written by Himself* was published, it received popular acclaim, and a new edition soon followed. Despite his widely publicized amazing escape from slavery, Henry 'Box' Brown sank into obscurity and died in anonymity. ARF

Brown, Henry Box, *Narrative of the Life of Henry Box Brown, Written by Himself* (1851)

See also BROWN, WILLIAM WELLS; DOUGLASS, FREDERICK; UNITED STATES OF AMERICA, BRITAIN, AND ABOLITION

Brown, James. Previously known as Cato, or James Cato (b. 1750), black crewman on Nelson's flagship, the *Victory*. Brown was originally known as Cato, following the common practice of slave owners of giving slaves Roman or Greek names. Brown is thought to have been a black *Loyalist, a slave siding with the British during the American War of Independence. Living in Nova Scotia, he was of mixed parentage, his mother reputed to be a member of the prominent Liverpool merchant Gough family.

Cato left Nova Scotia, running away to sea while still a child, ironically serving on ships involved in the slave trade, and assuming the name James Cato. He later joined the Royal Navy and changed his name again, to James Brown, serving on one of the most famous ships of all time, Nelson's flagship *Victory* at the Battle of Trafalgar in 1805. When he left the Navy, James, a very large man (20 stone in weight), worked in Liverpool as a foundry worker, marrying three times to local women. His two sons were John Gough Brown, a temperance advocate born in the early 19th century, and James Brown, Jr. (1815–81), who became involved in the Chartist cause in the Isle of Man. One of the younger James's sons was James William Ross Brown (b. 1858), who became a lawyer on the northern circuit at the age of 30 in 1888, rising to become a deputy judge. RHC

Faragher, M., 'The Browns of the *Times*: An Instance of Black Social Mobility in the 19th Century Black Presence in the North West', *North West Labour History*, no. 20 (1995–6)
ODNB

See also LASCARS AND BLACK SEAMEN

Brown, William Wells (*c.*1814–1884). African-American abolitionist and fugitive slave who toured Britain. Brown was born on a plantation in Kentucky, the son of a slave woman and a white man. After 20 years of enslavement, he escaped on New Year's Day 1834. His personal experience of slavery compelled an active fight against the system in the United States, which eventually led to his journey to Europe. In August 1849 he travelled to Paris as the American Peace Society's delegate to the International Peace Congress. Subsequently Brown began a lecture tour of Britain, enjoying the relative freedom which he lacked in the racially tense United States. Using England as his base, he ventured to the rest of Europe, speaking passionately about the cruelties of slavery. In London he chaired a meeting of fugitive American slaves and drafted, for the meeting, an 'Appeal to the People of Great Britain and the World'. His thoughts and experiences of slavery were recorded in *Narrative of William W. Brown, an American Slave, Written by Himself* (1849), which sold 12,000 copies in Britain. In 1853 his novel

Clotel; or, The President's Daughter: A Narrative of Slave Life in the United States was published in London. Because of the fortification of the 1793 Fugitive Slave Law in the United States in 1850, it became dangerous for Brown to travel back home. He thus remained in Britain, all the while touring and lecturing, for the next four years. In that time he addressed over 1,000 meetings, travelling nearly 12,000 miles throughout the country. DD/SS

Brown, W. W., *Narrative of William W. Brown, an American Slave, Written by Himself* (1849)

Farrison, W. E., *William Wells Brown, Author and Reformer* (1969)

See also UNITED STATES OF AMERICA, BRITAIN, AND ABOLITION

'Brown babies'. Children born out of wedlock to white mothers and black fathers, mostly American GIs during and immediately after the *Second World War. From 1942 onwards a total of 130,000 black GIs, part of a racially segregated US Army, were stationed in various parts of Britain, the largest presence of black men in the country's history. The US forces introduced their 'Jim Crow' policies into Britain, and for diplomatic reasons the British government permitted this. The British authorities also often ignored these practices when the Americans extended them off their military bases. Black GIs socializing with white women resulted in increased racial tension. Between 1943 and 1947 some 700–1,000 'brown babies' were born to white British women, most of whom were unmarried, although some had husbands serving in the forces. Marriage to a black man and settlement in the United States was not an option. Many mothers reluctantly surrendered their children to voluntary care homes; colour prejudice made it difficult to find adoptive or foster homes.

The 'problem' of illegitimate mixed-race children exercised both the British and the American authorities, although action was largely in the hands of black individuals and organizations on both sides of the Atlantic. The future of 'brown babies' was briefly discussed at the Pan-African Congress in 1945. How to raise funds, care for unwanted children, and arrange adoptions became a contentious issue between black-led groups. In Liverpool, Pastor Daniels *Ekarte had well-intentioned but illusory schemes for care homes; also in Liverpool the Negro Welfare Centre attempted to raise money from the United States. Meanwhile the elite-led *League of Coloured Peoples pursued plans that seemed more practical but ultimately delivered less than was promised. Children's homes sponsored by both organizations soon closed for lack of proper care. A few children were adopted by families in Britain, but most were probably brought up in care homes run by local authorities and voluntary agencies. DK

Rose, Sonya O., 'Girls and GIs: Race, Sex, and Diplomacy in Second World War Britain', *International History Review*, 19 (1997)

Sherwood, Marika, *Pastor Daniels Ekarte and the African Churches Mission* (1994)

Smith, Graham, *When Jim Crow Met John Bull: Black American Soldiers in World War II Britain* (1987)

See also MISCEGENATION

Bruce, Esther (1912–1994). Black Londoner whose life as a working-class seamstress was documented in *Aunt Esther's Story* (1991), published by Hammersmith and Fulham's Ethnic Communities Oral History Project, and co-authored with her nephew Stephen Bourne. *Aunt Esther's Story* provides a first-hand account of Bruce's life as a black Briton in the pre-**Empire Windrush* years. Her father, Joseph (1880–1941), arrived in London from British Guiana (now Guyana) in the early 1900s and settled in a tight-knit working-class community in Fulham. He worked as a builder's labourer. When Bruce was a young child, Joseph instilled in his daughter a sense of pride in being black. After leaving school, she worked as a seamstress, and in the 1930s she made dresses for the popular African-American stage star Elisabeth Welch. She also befriended another black citizen of Fulham: the Jamaican nationalist Marcus *Garvey. She told Bourne, 'he was a nice chap who wasn't treated with respect like I was. He was middle-class and the costers wouldn't speak to him. He told me the English are no good but I said there are *some* good people in this world.' She remembered the community spirit that existed during the Blitz and described the experiences of her cousin Leon and his family after they arrived in Britain on 'a ship and a prayer' from British Guiana in 1959. Friendly and outgoing, Bruce integrated easily into the multicultural Britain of the post-war years. The success of *Aunt Esther's Story* gave her a sense of pride and achievement towards the end of her life.

SB

Bourne, Stephen, *Speak of Me As I Am: The Black Presence in Southwark Since 1600* (2005)

—— and Bruce, Esther, *Aunt Esther's Story* (2nd edn., 1996)

ODNB

Businesses. As black communities across Britain expand and develop, the demand for an alternative 'ethnic' market to serve the consumer needs of the black British population has increased. However, the acculturation of the younger generations has limited the expansion of a Black British market as the mainstream market has to some extent become a sufficient provider to consumer requirements. The older generations have retained distinctive aspects of their culture and therefore have a higher demand for products provided by the 'ethnic' market. Indeed, various factors contribute towards the shape of this market, namely the age, sex, and socio-economic status of the consumers as well as the areas of concentration of the black population. For example, the highest number of West Indians in the United Kingdom is to be found in inner cities, and therefore the quantity of West Indian shops is high. Mike McLeod states that 'the ethnic market is an inner-city phenomenon by virtue of the residential concentration of the West Indian population'. The report made by the National Consumer Council in 1982 on Asian and West Indian shoppers in Bradford states that West Indians predominantly shop at places within ten minutes of home, buy from both 'ethnic' and English shops, and show little 'ethnic' loyalty to service their shopping needs. Therefore, West Indian shops are not the sole source of West Indian consumption.

Furthermore, well-established white and Asian businesses are involved in the importation of Caribbean products for both mainstream and 'ethnic' markets, thereby creating competition for West Indian-owned businesses. This is so because Caribbean goods that require little merchandising can be sold by any retailer once a local need has been recognized. The main 'ethnic' product importers are large mainstream companies as well as independent English and Jewish companies. West Indian involvement in the importation of Caribbean goods is relatively low. Asian-owned firms are also increasingly importing products from the Caribbean, thereby making it unnecessary for the existence of exclusively West Indian shops. The West Indian 'ethnic' market, therefore, is not a West Indian monopoly. Even consumers of this market are not ethnically homogenous. The 'crossover' of the 'ethnic' market into the mainstream market suggests that non-West Indians as well are consuming West Indian products. Foods like mangoes and pawpaws as well as music such as *hip hop and *reggae circulate in the mainstream market. In the clothing industry, African fabrics are sold in street markets in Camden and Brixton.

Travel is an important industry in the West Indian 'ethnic' market. It involves both West Indian and English consumers, especially with the escalation of tourism. The frequent travel of West Indians from the United Kingdom to the Caribbean in order to visit relatives or, in the case of the older generation of West Indians residing in the United Kingdom, to retire and settle down, has prompted travel agencies and airline companies such as British Airways to provide 'ethnically' for their customers. British Airways, for example, offers special food and in-flight services for their West Indian customers. The shipping needs of West Indian consumers who send items from the United Kingdom back to the Caribbean are provided for by freight-forwarding companies who deal extensively with West Indian communities.

The growth of multiple chain industries in post-war British retailing has impeded the development of independent businesses. The Asian distribution network, which wholesales not merely for the Asian community but for other 'ethnic' minorities as well, has interfered with the expansion of West Indian-owned businesses. Thus, West Indian industries are mainly micro-enterprises such as 'convenience' and 'corner' shops and market stalls. They are mainly located in densely populated West Indian areas. In less concentrated West Indian districts, they are challenged with competition from Asian and English retailers. The immensity of the Asian distribution network also means that even if West Indian entrepreneurs seek to enter into wholesaling, they will lack the resources, experience, and level of integration already achieved by the Asian retailers.

West Indian businesses, however, flourish in areas requiring a specific craft where individual skill is of prime importance. Such areas include car maintenance, tailoring, travel, entertainment, and hairdressing. Esme's Beauty Salon in Birmingham, for example, was started in order to cater specifically for West Indian women. Aunt Mary's Travel was set up in the same city to deal with the travel and shipping needs of exclusively West Indian consumers. It is important to note that there are sizeable and successful black businesses, for example, publishing companies such as Hansib and Nu Vox. They began as reporters of community events such as weddings, carnivals, and parties, and eventually extended their publishing horizons. Social events are an integral part of West Indian community life and they provide opportunities for photographers and caterers to expand their businesses. Beauty pageants are also popular among West Indians. Thus, modelling agencies, hairdressers, and fashion designers are given an occasion to advance their industries. Sponsors of these pageants promote their products, thereby gaining more visibility among potential West Indian consumers.

Although British-based West Indian entrepreneurs have shown interest in developing direct business linkages with the Caribbean, these are scarce owing to information and knowledge constraints as well as financial and bureaucratic complications. Some West Indian firms do import raw materials and finished goods from the Caribbean, but there are not a significant number. Caribbean exporters endeavouring to penetrate UK markets are often relegated to the 'ethnic' market and fail to reach the mainstream market. Therefore, these exporters are unable to expand the distribution of their products. Altogether, then, trade between British-based West Indian enterprises and the West Indies is small compared to the trade conducted with the region (e.g. in sugar, bauxite, telecommunications, and tourism) by 'white' British companies. SS

McLeod, Mike, *Trading with the Inner Cities: Ethnic Minorities and the Development of Caribbean Trade* (1991)

Wilson, Peter E. B., *Black Business Enterprise in Britain: A Survey of Afro-Caribbean and Asian Small Businesses in Brent* (1983)

See also PICTON, CESAR; WELLS, NATHANIEL

Buxton, Sir Thomas Fowell (1786–1845). Social reformer and active fighter for the abolition of slavery. Thomas Fowell Buxton was born at Castle Hedingham, Essex, to an Anglican family. Despite this, his mother was a member of the religious Society of Friends, and Buxton soon became acquainted with Quakerism. Through the Society of Friends he became closely connected to the Gurney family, who were Quakers, and later married one of the Gurney daughters, Hannah. The Quakers were renowned for their social reformation campaigns, and Buxton became heavily involved in many of these movements, most notably with one of the Gurney daughters, Elizabeth Fry, to whom he provided financial support for her prison reform work. In 1818 he was elected member of Parliament for Weymouth and worked, within the House of Commons, for the abolition of the slave trade. He helped William *Wilberforce with the founding of the Society for the Mitigation and Gradual Abolition of Slavery in 1823 (later the *Anti-Slavery Society) and, subsequent to Wilberforce's retirement in 1825, Buxton became the leader of the campaign in the House of Commons for the fight against slavery. He published *The African Slave Trade and Its Remedy* in 1839, which promoted mediation with African nations to end the slave trade. Correspondingly, the British government sent a mission to the Niger delta in 1841, but the expedition was a failure because of the numerous deaths from disease within the party. Buxton was made a baronet in 1840, and there is a monument to him in Westminster Abbey as well as one dedicated to him and the abolition struggle in Victoria Tower Gardens, near the Houses of Parliament.

DD/SS

Barclay, Oliver, *Thomas Fowell Buxton and the Liberation of Slaves* (2001)

Carey, Brycchan, *British Abolitionism and the Rhetoric of Sensibility: Writing, Sentiment and Slavery, 1760–1807* (2005)

See also CHRISTIANITY

C

Cadbury Brothers. In 1847 the brothers John and Benjamin Cadbury established a cocoa and chocolate firm, Cadbury Brothers of Birmingham (Cadburys). After their partnership was dissolved in 1860, John's sons Richard and George ran the business. They were the founders of the Bournville works in Birmingham. Strongly influenced by Quakerism, they were very aware of the social conditions of their workers. In Bournville they were able not only to expand their industry but also to improve employment conditions and create a housing estate model. After Richard's death in 1899, George became the chairman of Cadburys. He became involved in many social activities and was a pacifist. In 1901 he acquired a controlling interest in the *Daily News* in order to give a voice to the Liberal Party and to oppose the Boer War.

In that same year Cadburys learnt that its cocoa beans, acquired from Portuguese-owned plantations on the island of São Tomé, off West Africa, were produced by slave labour. The *London Standard* accused Cadburys of hypocrisy for using slave-grown cocoa. Cadburys sued, and the ensuing court case revealed issues of business ethics and corporate responsibility. Although Cadburys won, the jury awarded the company damages of a mere farthing. Cadburys was forced to move to the Gold Coast (now Ghana) but continued to use slave-produced cocoa beans until 1909.

In the Gold Coast small to medium-sized farmers, encouraged by members of the Basel Mission (an important German-speaking Protestant missionary society founded in 1815), had been growing cocoa, which would soon turn the country into one of the most important producers in the world. In 1910 Cadburys started to buy cocoa from the Gold Coast at market price, and by 2001, 90 per cent of its cocoa came from that country. In 2001 Cadburys issued an appeal for international resolve to end child slavery in African cocoa plantations after a ship bound for the Ivory Coast was found to contain some 250 slave children. Allegations in the press that up to 40 per cent of chocolate eaten in Britain was probably linked to conditions of slavery encouraged companies like Cadburys to examine their commercial practices.

ARF

Satre, Lowell, *Chocolate on Trial: Slavery, Politics and the Ethics of Business* (2005)

See also AFRICA AND BRITISH COLONIALISM; SLAVERY

Campaign Against Racial Discrimination. Group set up in 1965 to campaign against racism in Britain. Britain had entered a testing phase in the immediate post-Second World War period: the black population had increased enormously, and was far greater than at any time in the long history of the black presence. By the mid-1960s it was estimated that 1 million 'black' (non-white) migrants had settled in Britain, comprising three main groups: West Indians, Indians, and Pakistanis. They had come to better themselves and, in the main, they occupied the lower end of the employment hierarchy, largely in semi-skilled and manual jobs, which worked well for the British economy.

In the years that followed, the migrants' settlement was marked by a number of grievances, including racial discrimination in a number of key areas including employment, *housing, and welfare. Predictably, many who protested monitored events in the United States, and not surprisingly the visit of the symbol of the American Civil Rights Movement, Dr Martin Luther King, Jr., to London in 1964, en route to receive the Nobel Peace Prize in Stockholm, was significant. Marion Glean, a West Indian-born activist, took the opportunity of inviting him to a meeting of various interested groups, at which he spoke on race relations. The next day he warned of Britain's racial problems becoming much worse if organized direct action was not undertaken. A few years later Glean said that the sole purpose for calling together a group of migrants to meet Dr King was 'to discuss with him one thing—being powerless'. The aim was to break the 'circle of dependency' within which migrants were entrapped. It was a hopeful time, of which Ms Glean said,

> I remember those first few weeks after King's visit when ordinary immigrants, some hardly literate, wrote to ask simply to help. I recall their excitement and their hopes. I recall too the people and organizations who were not immigrant but whose philosophy had led me vainly to hope that they would at least understand. I was to learn during those weeks how very few of them could accept immigrants as people, who like all other people could speak for themselves and out of their own culture and experience. (*Race Today*, 1973)

Encouraged by King's visit, the various Commonwealth migrant groups agreed to form an 'organization of organizations' to speak on behalf of all 'coloured' people in Britain. The organizations represented were the Campaign For Nuclear Disarmament, the Indian Workers' Association (Southall), the Standing Conference of West Indian Organizations (London Region), the *West Indian Students' Union, the British Caribbean Association, the Anti-Apartheid Movement, the National Federation of Pakistani Associations, and the Council of African Organizations.

At a meeting held on 10 January 1965 the name the Campaign Against Racial Discrimination (CARD) was officially adopted, and a few weeks later the body declared its opposition to all forms of racial discrimination and called for legislation as one means of fighting it. Predictably, there were many doctrinal battles as tensions between Executive Committee members revealed two main factions: the effective working majority and the dissidents. At least to begin with, both factions were committed to change the Race Relations Bill, but the personal rivalry and attitudes of the factions persisted, causing continued disunity and powerlessness.

Following its Founding Convention in July 1965, CARD made further representations against the Labour government's White Paper on Immigration from the Commonwealth. In particular it was concerned with the introduction of new powers of detention and deportation and with the government's dangerous and arbitrary authority. Unfortunately, it was riven with disagreement and tension as new dissidents and new alliances emerged.

The hope of unity was soon dashed when, in February 1966, the Standing Conference of West Indian Organizations disaffiliated from CARD. Moreover, CARD's efforts to coordinate the work of the Indian and Pakistani groups in Britain were, in effect, no more successful than its attempts to attract West Indians. The Indian Workers' Association (IWA) was never formally affiliated to CARD, while the National Federation of Pakistani Associations was barely functioning in 1967. Both organizations (especially the IWA) were complex and problematic, and characterized by factional divisions.

Apart from its relations with the Southhall IWA, CARD's contacts with local Indian associations were rare and weak, in spite of some branches' being in touch intermittently with their local CARD groups. Nonetheless, it was evident by spring 1967 that CARD was far removed from its community base, and internal division did not help. While some of the Executive Committee members were hoping for the passage of an extended anti-discrimination law that summer, a different group were laying plans for the future: their immediate goal was not to press for legislation, but to attempt a takeover of CARD.

Ironically, at this time a new mood of militancy was stirring race relations in Britain. On 26 July 1967 the Home Secretary, Roy Jenkins, had announced the government's intention to extend the Race Relations Act of 1965 to housing, employment, and insurance and credit facilities. The ban on entry to Britain of the American Black Power leader Stokely Carmichael, and the arrest of *Michael X on charges of violating the public order provisions of the Race Relations Act 1965, aroused resentment among black people.

In the brief period since Dr King had met migrant leaders in London in 1964 and served as the catalyst for a new organization, migrants were still without power. CARD as a potentially united front for all migrants had split and finally collapsed in the late 1960s. The enigma of how to develop political consciousness among migrants in Britain, and how to secure their active participation in an organization to oppose racial discrimination, had eluded CARD officials throughout its existence. RR

Desai, R., *Indian Immigrants in Britain* (1963)

Peach, Ceri, *West Indian Migration to Britain: A Social Geography* (1968)

See also IMMIGRATION; RACISM

Campbell, Robert (1829–1884). Pan-Africanist and African traveller. Born in Kingston, Jamaica, of black and white parents, Campbell began his working life as a printer's apprentice but gained some formal education and became a teacher. In the 1850s he emigrated to the United States, via Central America, where he worked as a teacher at an African-American institute in Philadelphia. Campbell, ambitious for further education, was largely self-taught.

In 1858 Martin R. *Delany invited him to become a member of the Niger Valley Exploring Party, to find a site in southern Nigeria for an African-American farm colony. 'Return to Africa' was controversial and divided African-American opinion; many argued that, even with its pervasive racism, America was their home and not Africa; a further problem was that black emigration was supported by the white African Civilization Society. Campbell came to Britain in 1859 and, although he failed to gain the support of missionary and philanthropic societies, the expedition was endorsed by abolitionists and cotton manufacturers. In West Africa, Campbell joined up with Delany and, with the help of Samuel Ajayi *Crowther, they secured a treaty with Egba chiefs. Both men came to Britain in 1860, soliciting funds and support, which came from the newly formed African Aid Society, the first British Pan-African organization.

Campbell and Delany both wrote accounts of their West African expedition, Campbell's being a travelogue that also denounced racist ideas current in many British books. In 1861 they presented their findings to the Royal Geographical Society in London. Campbell returned to Lagos and for the rest of his life played an active role in the colony's economic, social, and cultural life, as an editor of a weekly newspaper, *The Anglo-African* (1863–5), an educator, and an entrepreneur. He firmly believed in the value of Britain's civilizing influence, which he thought best served the 'advancement' of Africa. DK

Campbell, Robert, *A Pilgrimage to My Motherland: An Account of a Journey Among the Egbas and Yorubas of Central Africa, in 1859–1860* (1861)

See also PAN-AFRICANISM

Cardiff (*Welsh* **Caerdydd).** Capital city of Wales and home to one of the oldest black communities in Europe. The first black settlers were seamen from Africa, the West Indies, and America, and arrived in Cardiff around the middle of the 19th century. This was at a time when the city was enjoying a period of economic growth, having started on the road to becoming the major coal port by the late 19th century. Attracted by the prospect of employment, many seamen stayed and made the docklands area of Butetown (disparagingly known as Tiger Bay) their home. Many, too, married or befriended local white women and raised families. Indeed, such was the multiracial population of Butetown that it was popularly said you could see the world in 1 square mile.

Cardiff's economic growth was relatively short-lived, however, and went into a steep decline soon after the *First World War. When returning Welsh servicemen found themselves competing for jobs and women with black seamen, tensions soon erupted into what was considered to be one of the most vicious outbreaks of racial violence on British soil, an event that was to shape race relations in the city for many years to come. In 1925 the introduction of The Alien (Coloured Seamen) Order forced foreign sailors to register as aliens whether they were British subjects or dependants or not. Intended to limit the number of foreign seamen entering British ports, the Order effectively stripped many seamen of African descent of their status as British subjects. This later made it impossible for them to find employment on ships subsidized by the British government.

There can be little doubt that the deep segregation and discrimination of the inter-war years cast a long shadow over Cardiff's black community. The geographical segregation of Butetown, bounded on all sides by canals, railway tracks, and the sea, combined with its racial composition, rendered it effectively a ghetto, hampering any attempts at wider integration and participation in Cardiff city life. The vices associated with any port such as brothels, illegal drinking, and gambling dens were readily conferred onto the black community simply by virtue of its proximity to this underbelly of seafaring life. The official solution to the city's 'colour problem' was repatriation, but as many of the seamen in Butetown had wives and families, few took up the offer. These mixed-race relationships were roundly condemned and considered one of the evils of the time. Muriel E. Fletcher's social investigation recommended 'reducing the number of unions between coloured men and white women' given the problem of 'half-caste' children. In his 1929 Report to the Watch Committee, the Chief Constable of the time described how 'They [coloured seamen] come into contact with the female sex of the white race and their progeny are half-caste, with the vicious hereditary taint of their parents'.

Yet, despite appalling poverty and prejudice, a picture of the richness of black Cardiff and the influence of specific black individuals comes from accounts of resistance in this period. Aaron Mossell (1863–1951) was an American lawyer and leading Pan-Africanist who moved to Cardiff in 1926. Mossell understood that, in order to improve their situation, the black community of Butetown would need to work together. He was instrumental in uniting the many black organizations in Cardiff into the United Committee of Coloured and Colonial Organizations. Formed in Cardiff in 1931, the Coloured Seamen's Union played an important role along with the *League of Coloured Peoples in securing the restoration of British citizenship to seamen of African descent in 1936. By this time the League of Coloured Peoples, considered the first effective black pressure group in Britain, had a membership of 262, of which 178 were in Cardiff. These accounts locate Cardiff as a significant centre of black political life in Britain and beyond, through links to *Pan-Africanism.

The demand for labour brought about by the *Second World War led to a gradual but positive change of attitude towards the black community of Butetown. The *South Wales Echo* ironically recorded in 1942 that 'coloured men are Britain's finest gentlemen, bringing in the food we so much enjoyed for supper'. Yet other evidence suggests that these changes were only cosmetic and born out of economic necessity. As late as 1957 the South African External Affairs Minister Eric Louw was able to cite Butetown as an example of British hypocrisy in their condemnation of apartheid, suggesting that Butetown was a ghetto worse than any to be found in Cape Town.

Post-war reconstruction of Butetown during the 1960s had a considerable impact on the lives of the black community.

Neighbourhoods were broken up as homes were demolished and replaced with high-rise flats and maisonettes. Although some residents were resettled in the area, others were displaced, and Butetown as a stronghold of social and political organization for black people lost much of its former glory.

Today a revamped Cardiff Bay boasts Wales's Millennium Centre, the National Assembly, and expensive dockside apartments. Yet, on its doorstep Butetown has been largely excluded from all this capital spending and from most of the jobs it has generated. It remains the most deprived area of Cardiff, subject to high unemployment and new tensions between ethnic groups to parallel some of those of the 1920s. Today, as then, the highest proportion and the highest absolute numbers of black people in Cardiff are still resident in the docklands area of the city. CFW

Evans, N., 'Regulating the Reserve Army: Arabs, Blacks and the Local State in Cardiff 1919–1945' in K. Lunn, *Race and Labour in Twentieth Century Britain* (1985)

Fletcher, Muriel E., *Report on an Investigation into the Colour Problem in Liverpool and Other Ports* (1930)

Sinclair, N. M. C., *The Tiger Bay Story* (2003)

See also LASCARS AND BLACK SEAMEN; 'RACE' RIOTS, 1919; WALES

Caribbean, British colonies in the. 'Our hammock slung between the Americas' is how Derek Walcott described the Caribbean, and inspection of a map of the region provides visual evidence for his words. To the west, the large islands of Cuba, Jamaica, Hispaniola, and Puerto Rico extend from the American mainland. To the east, northward from Venezuela we find Trinidad and Tobago; Barbados, a sedimentary deposit; Grenada, St Vincent, St Lucia, Dominica, Montserrat, Nevis, and St Kitts (British), Martinique and Guadeloupe (French), forming the volcanic rim of the eastern Caribbean Sea; and further north, islands such as Anguilla, Barbuda, and Antigua cast leeward into the Atlantic. The map's lower-right base is anchored in the massive territories of Guyana (British), Suriname (Dutch), and French Guiana, themselves dwarfed by Brazil.

1. Early contact
2. Entry of the British
3. The Anglo-Dutch Wars
4. 'King Sugar'
5. Capitalism and slavery
6. 'The Williams thesis'
7. Problems of slave societies
8. Inching towards independence
9. Decolonization
10. What may the future hold?

1. Early contact The region has experienced two genocides: the partial extermination of the Amerindians by Spanish pioneers, and the murder of Africans by governing European powers from the 16th to the 20th centuries. Spain, given the rights to settle the whole of the Western world by the Catholic Church in 1493 (Portugal was granted the East, but later negotiated Brazil), forced the indigenous Carib and Arawak peoples into mines, massacred them, infected them with diseases, and deported them to Mexico. When the labour supply ran out, they began to import slaves from Africa to work as cowboys on the ranches supplying western Europe with hides and tallow. The trade in slaves for Spain, the Asiento, became a prized diplomatic jewel, vied for by Britain, France, and the Netherlands.

2. Entry of the British The Bristol privateer John *Hawkins brought three boatloads of slaves to the Spanish colonies from Guinea in the years 1562–8, making profits so lucrative that, knighted, he would show an African in chains on his coat of arms. *Elizabeth I was a shareholder in the second two voyages, having provided ships. The third voyage ended in disaster when, anchored at San Juan de Ulloa for revictualling in September 1568, Hawkins's fleet was betrayed and attacked at night by troops of Spain's new Viceroy of Mexico. Only two ships escaped: the *Minion*, with Hawkins aboard, which scraped home in January 1569 with fifteen survivors; and the *Judith*, commanded by a young Francis Drake, who in

1570, 1571, and 1572–3 would return to the Caribbean Sea, attack mainland Spanish garrisons and mule trains in alliance with escaped slaves known as the Cimarrones, and, in 1573, carry off £40,000 in treasure, almost a sixth of the English Crown's annual revenue. A seaman of genius, noted throughout successive voyages for his kindness towards Blacks and Amerindians, Drake would end Spanish mastery of the western seas, circumnavigating the globe in the *Golden Hind* in 1577–80, capturing the Caribbean capital, Hispaniola, on New Year's Day 1586, and Cartagena a month later—a severe financial setback for Spain as King Philip prepared to attempt an invasion of England—and as Vice-Admiral repulsing the Spanish Armada in 1588. Both Drake and Hawkins died in the Caribbean, during the siege of San Juan in 1595.

The first British settlements were pioneered on St Kitts in 1623 (by Thomas Warner) and then Barbados (by John Powell) in 1627, and from there colonizers spread up through the Lesser Antilles, though some settlements, such as that on St Lucia (1638–41), collapsed because of attacks by warlike Caribs. The windward colonies during these early years became overcrowded with white indentured servants—some voluntary, some 'Barbadosed', or kidnapped, and later some Quakers and prisoners of war from Cromwell's campaigns in Ireland and Scotland. Tobacco and cotton were grown, the Caribs were massacred, and the colonists, divided into political factions, relied on Dutch shipping and commerce for economic security. In the 1650s the western Caribbean became subject to expansionist Puritan designs. Warner's patron, the Earl of Carlisle, had secured the title Lord Proprietor of the Caribbee Islands in 1629; his successor, Lord Willoughby, a royalist, was stripped of the office by the Commonwealth government in 1652 after refusing to end Barbadian trading with the Netherlands (he resumed the title after the Restoration to become the first significant advocate of the West Indies as a colonial interest). In 1655 Cromwell's protectorate funded and organized an expedition from Barbados, which resulted, after an abortive raid on Hispaniola, in the invasion of Jamaica, where Admiral Penn made alliance with black runaways—their name Anglicized to 'Maroons'—to steal the island from the Spanish.

3. The Anglo-Dutch Wars With Spanish influence in the region waning, Britain, the Netherlands, and France, at war in Europe, fought among themselves for Caribbean possessions. The Second Dutch War (1665–7) saw violent fighting between English and French, with the Treaty of Breda confirming respective ownership of the Leeward Islands and the Dutch West India Company crippled as a commercial force. During the Nine Years' War (1688–97) and the War of the Spanish Succession (1702–14), British and French troops attacked each other's territories, looting and sacking plantations, even on large islands such as Guadeloupe and Jamaica. In 1689 Irish Catholics briefly rebelled against the constitutional revolution of King William II on Nevis, Antigua, and Montserrat; the French were chased from St Kitts, formerly shared, in 1702. During the period naval commanders turned to mercenaries for support, so that the Bahamas, Jamaica, Hispaniola, and Tortuga became the fiefdoms of notorious pirates such as Henry Morgan, Jean Le Vasseur, and Edward Teach (Daniel Defoe's Blackbeard), with multinational buccaneer fleets playing a decisive role in victories up to the sack of Cartagena in 1697. The Treaty of Utrecht established peace in 1713, winning the Spanish Asiento for British traders, with the first governor of the Bahamas, the former pirate Woodes Rogers, ending the reign of the buccaneers.

4. 'King Sugar' After the settlement of Virginia resulted in tobacco prices falling in the 1640s, Barbados had turned to sugar production, whose profitable nature was evident from Dutch plantations in Brazil. Labour-intensive and degrading to the soil, sugar plantations counted for 93 per cent of Barbadian exports by 1770, and 97 per cent of that of the Leewards'—these islands themselves surpassed during the 18th century by larger-scale growing operations in the Greater Antilles, where first Jamaica and then Saint-Domingue (the French end of Hispaniola, now Haiti) inherited the sugar crown. This fuelled a staggering growth in northern European sugar consumption: in 1700 the average Briton used 4 pounds of sugar per year to sweeten food and drink; by 1800 this figure had risen to 18 pounds; and by the 1960s consumption would reach 110 pounds, or a third of a pound per day. The West Indian 'sugar lords' became a powerful parliamentary interest group, their lands the focus of campaigns during a further series of international wars lasting from 1744 to 1783, their wealth, frivolity, and selfishness caricatured in literature. Despite earlier having advocated free trade in the face of restrictive 17th-century monopolies on shipping and trading, now that new markets such as India and Brazil were opening up, the planters demanded that the Empire adhere to the favourable strictures of the mercantilist system, rather than embrace expansionist, 'laissez-faire' capitalism.

When the Seven Years' War ended with the Treaty of Paris in 1763, Jamaican planters controversially urged Britain to hand back the valuable trophies of Cuba, St Lucia, Martinique, and Guadeloupe to Spain and France in exchange for Florida and snowy Canada, rather than damage their interests by allowing new sugar-growing participants to enter the protected British imperial markets. In Adam Smith's *Wealth of Nations* (written in 1776, the same year as the Declaration of Independence in America, itself provoked partly by Britain's attempting to force its American colonies to import expensive molasses from the British islands), the sugar and slave trades were condemned as a drain on British resources. Yet when, during the American War of Independence (1776–83), France conquered the majority of British sugar islands, it was imperative for Admiral Rodney to win them back by defeating the French fleet of de Grasse at the 1782 Battle of the Saints. Only in the 19th century, when the Great Reform Act of 1832 put industrial magnates such as Richard Cobden, John Bright, and Samuel Garbett (spokesmen respectively for Yorkshire wool, Manchester cotton, and Birmingham iron) into Parliament were the West Indian factions of Bristol and Liverpool defeated.

5. **Capitalism and slavery** There were exceptions to this pattern: cotton and coffee remained lucrative Caribbean crops, especially during the long trade embargo with France occasioned by the Napoleonic Wars; in British Honduras timber was the main export, and the smaller Windward Islands grew a variety of crops: ginger, nutmeg, citrus, pimento, cacao. Common to all American colonies, however, was that African slavery became the motor of production. The Spanish, finding Amerindians to be of little use in their gold and silver mines, had instigated the buying of slaves from merchants in Africa—many from England and Scotland; indeed, it has been argued that the 1707 Act of Union was necessitated largely by Scotland's attempt to set up its own Africa Company. One slave was reckoned to be worth the manpower of four Indians, at a third the cost of a white indentured servant. Hence some 12 million Africans were taken across the Atlantic in slave ships; by the 18th century the supply lines were dominated by the British. By the 1750s nine out of ten people in the Caribbean were slaves (nineteen out of twenty in the Leeward Islands), engaged in gangs on the repetitive and strenuous tasks necessary for the mass production of sugar: clearing, digging, planting and weeding the land, cutting, crushing and boiling the cane, before distilling the molasses into rum and shipping the coarse brown muscovado to refineries in Europe.

6. **'The Williams thesis'** Eric *Williams, later to become the Prime Minister of independent Trinidad and Tobago, argued in his influential history *Capitalism and Slavery* (1944) that the 'Triangular Trade' helped to fund the Industrial Revolution.

Just as Spanish gold and silver from the Americas had contributed to the use of coin in western Europe, the mercantilist system of selling slaves to the Caribbean, slave-produced commodities to the metropolis, and goods needed for this process to the slavers, all protected by monopolies to keep profits within the Empire, now ensured the development of capitalist industrial society and its bourgeois beneficiaries. The rise of the great seaports of *Bristol, *Liverpool, and *Glasgow was due to slavery, sugar, and tobacco. Bristol, represented in Parliament by West Indians throughout the 18th century, moved to sugar-refining after Liverpool (in 1565 a town of 138 householders) cornered the slave trade. Meanwhile, vital British industries such as shipping and the related trades (ropeworking, forestry, etc.), insurance (witness the rise of Lloyd's), banking, wool (slave owners were legally obliged to clothe and bury their human property in British wool), chains, and gun-making (the price of a slave was, proverbially, one Birmingham gun) flourished during the period; their profits in turn to be invested in steampower, railways, and mining. Ironically, it was industrialists, the 'children of the slave trade', who in their greed for global free markets would end protectionist policies towards the West Indies and thus hasten the abolition of slavery in the 19th century.

7. **Problems of slave societies** In the Caribbean's predominantly black societies, where a rigid social hierarchy of minority white rule was upheld with great cruelty, it was inevitable that black rebellions occurred. Most famous are those of the Jamaican Maroons, runaways who established communities in remote 'cockpits' of the island and conducted two guerrilla wars against the English. The first, lasting from the 1720s to 1740, saw first the Leeward group under Cudjoe and then the Windward group, led by the 'obeah woman' Nanny, negotiate peace treaties, including the right to self-government; in the second (1795–6), Trelawney Town in the Leeward area rose up alone in protest against white rule, and was defeated. Similar groups evolved in Guyana, Suriname, and Dominica, while 'black Caribs' intermarried with the protected indigenous population on St Vincent; the descendants of these communities retain an independent ethnic identity to the present day, with Maroon towns that were established after the 1739 treaties still existing in Jamaica.

Slave rebellions of varying sizes occurred on all islands throughout the era of slavery, the greatest number also on Jamaica. Most famous of the slave leaders are Tacky in Jamaica (1760), Cuffy in Guyana (1763), and Bussa in Barbados (1816), each of whom led thousands of slaves in violent revolt. Notably, guerrilla battalions of independent Maroons were used to put down Jamaican slave rebellions—they ambushed and killed Tacky—and after a spell in Nova Scotia the deported Trelawney Town Maroons were sent to crush uprisings of free black settlers in Sierra Leone (1800–2), before settling in Freetown. Black history on the French colony of Saint-Domingue also impacted on Britain, when in 1789 the ex-slave Toussaint L'Ouverture successfully led a Jacobin rebellion (setting back somewhat the abolitionist cause). Robespierre's agent in the Caribbean, Victor Hugues, sought to destabilize British interests by making alliance with Maroons on Jamaica, St Vincent, and Grenada; and following Napoleon's betrayal of Toussaint and the ethnic war that followed (Whites and Coloureds were massacred by Blacks), the King of Haiti, Henri Christophe, would write cordial letters to England's George III, suggesting an alliance between their proud island nations.

8. **Inching towards independence** The British abolition of slavery in 1834 followed an uprising of 60,000 Jamaican slaves under the Baptist deacon Sam Sharpe during Christmas 1831. Black emancipation came as sugar prices plummeted, with world production increasing by 700 per cent from the 1840s to 1890s, and in 1846 the British government

equalized the duties on West Indian and foreign sugar, effectively abandoning its newly emancipated colonies to slow economic decline, apart from Barbados (where planters converted the entire island to sugar production, forcing Blacks to work for imported food) and Guyana and Trinidad (where many thousands of indentured labourers were shipped from India to sustain the plantation system between 1838 and 1917). Following the 1865 *Morant Bay rebellion in Jamaica, the local assemblies, now dominated by white and coloured planters, were closed down in favour of a method of British appointments (pioneered in the newly acquired Trinidad and St Lucia in 1810) known as 'Crown colony' government, because it bypassed the electoral system. Exceptions were Barbados and the Bahamas, which remained constitutional democracies (albeit with greatly restricted franchises), and Guyana, merged from Dutch territories gained during the Napoleonic Wars, where a system of courts was retained. This, then, was the history of the Caribbean as its states moved into the 20th century: diverse and multiracial, but scarred by exploitation and waning economically.

9. Decolonization Nationalist labour leaders such as Alexander Bustamante and Norman Manley (Jamaica), Arthur Cipriani (Trinidad), Grantley Adams (Barbados), and Vere Bird (Antigua) came into confrontation with the island legislatures. In the 1930s oil began to be used instead of coal to power the British Navy, and harsh conditions on the Trinidadian oilfields prompted civil unrest; the oilworkers' unions that formed under the leadership of Adrian Cola Rienzi and Tubal Uriah (Buzz) Butler in 1937 are a much-studied aspect to the further wave of protest that shook the region. The Moyne Commission's report of 1939, advocating self-government for the British Caribbean, as well as key innovations such as trade agreements to protect the primary growers of sugar, bananas, citrus fruit, and other crops, funds for welfare state implementation, and the creation of institutions such as the University of the West Indies, had to be suppressed by the Colonial Office during the Second World War, but in the early 1950s several constitutions were adopted bringing representative government to the larger islands. An old idea of federation—dating back to the 1670s and piloted in the Leewards in 1871—was revived, largely through the collaborative ethos of regional labour leaders, at the Montego Bay conference of 1947, the aim being to protect the small islands of the eastern Caribbean economically. This suited Britain, and after two further conferences in London, elections were held in 1958 for a federal government based in Trinidad, with states such as St Kitts-Nevis, Antigua, Barbuda, Montserrat, and the British Virgin Islands separated out, allowing them to join.

The experiment was short-lived: Guyana and British Honduras (now Belize) refused to participate, and Manley (with Williams and Adams the driving federalist force) was defeated in Jamaican elections. Jamaica, advancing quickly in developmental terms and distrustful of the indigent eastern states, left the federation after three years (in 1961), after which it was dissolved. In 1962 Jamaica and Trinidad and Tobago were granted independence, Barbados following under Errol Barrow in 1966, and the Bahamas in 1973. The small eastern islands, which achieved independence between 1974 and 1983, formed an organization for economic and military cooperation. Guyana, like Trinidad, is divided among Africans and 'East' Indians (239,000 were indentured there during 1838–1917), and murderous conflict between the Indian and African political parties of Cheddi Jagan and Forbes Burnham in the early 1960s occasioned armed intervention by Britain on two occasions before independence in 1966, the CIA collaborating to block the Communist Jagan from power. The late 1960s and early 1970s saw Black Power riots, notoriously in Trinidad in 1970, and in 1980 the murder of the Guyanese intellectual Walter *Rodney by agents of

President Burnham shocked the world. The Soviet Union, through Cuba, supported left-wing governments in the region, such as that of Michael Manley on Jamaica. Maurice Bishop, a Marxist who seized power on Grenada in 1979 from the corrupt Eric Gairy, was assassinated in 1983, with US troops intervening to restore stability. Black Muslims attempted a coup in Trinidad in 1990, and in 2005 a Jamaican Muslim was one of the suicide bombers in the London Tube attack.

10. What may the future hold? At the dawn of the 21st century, ravaged by pollution and deforestation, oil-drilling and bauxite-mining, natural disasters, poverty, gun violence, and AIDS, the nations of the Anglophone Caribbean figure largely in global political discourse as a burden on the Western world, and a shipment point for the American drugs trade. Great inequalities in wealth exist between elites and the underclass, often exacerbated rather than alleviated by the new economic mainstay of the region, tourism; the ideological tensions existing between the pro-US and left-wing factions in South America divide the region politically. Yet the contributions of reggae and calypso musicians to global culture must also be noted, the world-renowned poets and novelists of the region, and the generation of West Indian immigrants to Britain who changed the face of metropolitan society by colonizing it 'in reverse' in the 1950s. CARICOM, a Caribbean-wide trading association which grew out of earlier efforts in 1973, continues to expand—since the 1990s it has included Haiti and Suriname, and in early 2006 it launched the Caribbean Single Market and Economy, which includes measures such as the relaxation of work permit restrictions, collective representation to the Free Trade Association of the Americas and the European Union, and the possibility of including the Netherlands Antilles on their dissolution in 2007, plus the remaining French and British overseas territories—showing improved prospects for unity in the region. JM

Gilmore, John, *Faces of the Caribbean* (2000)

Hart, Richard, *From Occupation to Independence: A Short History of the Peoples of the English-Speaking Caribbean* (1998)

Parry, J. H., Sherlock, Philip, and Maingot, Anthony, *A Short History of the West Indies* (4th edn., 1987)

Rodney, Walter, *How Europe Underdeveloped Africa* (rev. edn., 1988)

See also SLAVE TRADE; SLAVERY; SOUTH SEA COMPANY

Caribbean art, British responses to. The Caribbean region is more often stereotyped and dismissed in Britain than taken seriously as a location for art production, and has only ever reached small audiences, despite some significant exhibitions and critical attention.

1. Images and objects collected from the Caribbean during the colonial period
2. Migration of artists during the 20th century
3. Art reception in the 1960s and 1970s
4. Exhibitions of the 1980s and 1990s
5. Curatorial selection and its consequences

There is little consensus on what defines a coherent category of 'Caribbean art', in terms of its geographical boundaries and cultural character, and given its growing diaspora. The region's Anglophone countries have contributed the most to art exhibitions staged in the United Kingdom, the consequence of a shared colonial history and of migration. Throughout the post-Second World War period, many artists from the Caribbean, engaged in struggles for acceptance within the history of art, or for belonging and nationality in Britain, have been expressly concerned about the terms of their reception. In common with the contemporary art of Africa and Asia, British curators and critics have subjected the Caribbean region to expectations for the 'naive' and the 'authentic', which have worked to the detriment of its wider reception. As compared to other countries, which held significant shows during the 1990s (including Japan, France, Germany, the United States, and Spain), Britain had its last major exhibition of art from the Caribbean in 1986.

1. Images and objects collected from the Caribbean during the colonial period Caribbean landscapes viewed in Britain, whether by the English artist George Robertson (1748–88) in Jamaica (1773), or the later Paris-trained Michel-Jean Cazabon (1813–88), born in Trinidad of Martiniquan parents, would set a precedent by conveying their 'sublime' pleasures of the West Indies to English viewers through painting and engravings of lush and generally unpeopled plantation lands and tropical flora. These images formed part of a larger 'regime of representation' in which the Caribbean landscape was imagined and ordered by a colonial gaze, its people categorized with a view to controlling and circumscribing them, and its products—whether sugar, cocoa, tobacco, medicine, or fruit, etc.—made into commodities for metropolitan, domestic consumers. At the same time, items produced by unnamed, colonized, or pre-Columbian people would be collected as artefacts, such as Arawak (Taino) and Carib anthropomorphic sculptures and 'Bush Negro' or Maroon wood carving from Suriname. As materials that might readily have been considered objects of high aesthetic interest during the period of modernist 'primitivism', within British museum collections they represent an 'authentic' art of the Caribbean, ostensibly untouched by 'Western' contact.

2. Migration of artists during the 20th century The popularity of these two forms—the fetishized Caribbean landscape, and the fetish object—has helped to shape the conditions of reception in Britain for 20th-century art from the Caribbean, but more so the tourist projection of brilliant colours and a palm-fringed paradise. So too has a reluctance by art critics and the public to grant it equal value with the art of Whites, who comprise the modern mainstream. Some examples of success in overcoming such a disparity in patronage and art historiography include the Jamaican Ronald *Moody (1900–84). Another is the Guyanese Denis Williams (1923–98), who trained at London's Camberwell School of Art from 1946 to 1948 before working as a painter and fine-art teacher from 1950 at the Slade and the Central School of Art (now Central St Martin's). He received support from the painter and writer Wyndham Lewis, who wrote admiringly about his work ('A Negro Artist', *The Listener*, 7 December 1950), and in 1955 won second prize after Lucien Freud at a *Daily Express* Young Artists' Exhibition. The painter Frank Bowling (b. 1936), also born in British Guiana, moved to London in 1950 to complete his schooling before joining art classes at several institutions. Along with David Hockney, he attended the Royal College of Art (RCA) in 1959, and the Slade School, graduating from the RCA with a silver medal for painting. A friend of Francis Bacon, in the ten years that followed, examples of his work were bought by a major purchasing award and shown at the Tate Gallery and the Commonwealth Institute, and he was awarded several prizes as well as a Guggenheim Fellowship. Aubrey *Williams, who arrived in Britain in 1952, also met with an encouraging initial response.

3. Art reception in the 1960s and 1970s These artists were nonetheless dogged by the parochialism of British viewers of the 1950s and 1960s, unwilling to embrace their art without prejudging its significance. Bowling began to disappear from survey exhibitions of post-war British art, and from 1966 he based himself in New York for the next ten years. Some debate during the *Caribbean Artists' Movement (1966–72), of which Moody was a member, surrounded the issue of artistic 'sources'. Aubrey Williams experienced critics' attempts to categorize his paintings in terms of 'connections' to either a 'Caribbean' or a 'European' heritage, and insisted on its 'primitive urgency' (Eric Newton, *The Guardian*, 3 January 1963), evidenced in the 'tropical forests and primeval ritual dances' ostensibly there in his canvases. Even so, this first generation of artists offered a consistent struggle to overcome such structures of 'othering' posed within a climate of decolonization and often unwelcome inward migration.

4. Exhibitions of the 1980s and 1990s Frequently grouping together during the 1980s with artists of the South Asian, Middle Eastern, and other diasporas, artists of Caribbean descent led explicit demands for visibility and resources, though this second generation were more likely to identify themselves as black or African than Caribbean. In 1989 the Pakistan-born artist and activist Rasheed Araeen assembled the largest of such groupings, 'The Other Story: Afro-Asian Artists in Post-War Britain', an exhibition at London's Hayward Gallery. Alongside artists of a wider range of ethnicities, a quarter of those involved were Caribbean or of the second generation. Despite the keen attention to questioning its curatorial rationale across the print media, Caribbean artists of the older generation were generally praised, while the largely polemical work on display by the younger artists often became the focus of discomfort. Supporting the show, Richard Cork summarized why a traditional lack of awareness among critics of its artists would result in the exhibition's being so misunderstood ('Buried Treasures: An Art World that Makes You Feel an Outsider', *The Listener*, December 1989, 8).

For all its detractors, 'The Other Story' succeeded in being much written about and visited, largely because of its central location and size. Exhibitions of the art of the Caribbean and its diaspora tend to be shown in less mainstream galleries, and hence have attracted little or no critical attention. The impressive, purpose-built art gallery of the Commonwealth Institute in London, opened in 1962, has hosted by far the greatest number of group and individual exhibitions of work by Caribbean artists. Yet 'Caribbean Art Now' (1986)—proudly promoted as 'Europe's first exhibition of contemporary Caribbean art'—was the gallery's only Caribbean show to be widely and seriously reviewed. This, with 'Jamaican Intuitives' (1986) at the same gallery, and, at the Hayward Gallery and touring, 'The Other Story' and 'New World Imagery: Jamaican Art' (1996), were exceptionally well-researched and -presented Caribbean-related shows. But most Caribbean art shows at the Commonwealth Institute Art Gallery were virtually ignored by the critics: from Aubrey Williams's major series of paintings *Shostakovich* (1981) and *The Olmec Maya and Now* (1985), to the exhibition 'Trinidad and Tobago Through the Eye of the Artist: From Cazabon to the New Millennium, 1813–2000' (1997–8).

Smaller London galleries such as the 198 Gallery (Steve Ouditt, 2000; Petrona Morrison, 2004; Mario Lewis, 2005) and the October Gallery (showing Aubrey Williams six times to date since 1984; Trinidad and Tobago painting, 1992; Jamaican artists, 1994) have tended to be overlooked in the art press, perhaps because of their focus on 'non-Western' art. Limited funding has meant that Islington Arts Factory, London, since 1995, has mostly reached only local Caribbean diaspora audiences with their 'Caribbean Connections' series (1995, 1996, 2003, and 2004). Significant, if belated, recognition of Frank Bowling came in 2005 with his election to the Royal Academy. If, as Stuart Hall has suggested, Caribbean artists have been 'quietly written out of the record; not British enough for the Tate, not international enough for Bankside' (Maya Jaggi, 'Prophet at the Margins: Interview with Stuart Hall', *The Guardian*, 8 July 2000), then the Institute of International Visual Arts, London, has staged exhibitions and events ('Aubrey Williams', 1998; 'Steve Ouditt: Creole Processing Zone', 2000), frequently extensively documented, intended to change this situation.

5. Curatorial selection and its consequences Despite their influence, British responses to art of the Caribbean continue to employ typologies that have historically worked against artists' own declared interests. In 1985 Liz Waugh indicated two streams of Jamaican art, distinguishing between trained and untrained artists, 'cosmopolitans and intuitives', rehearsing a controversial hierarchy of value energetically promoted in Jamaica since 1979. A review in the *New Statesman* of *The Elders* (the South London Gallery, 1999), which placed Stanley Greaves (b. 1934, British Guiana; based in Barbados since 1987) with Brother Everald Brown (b. 1917, Jamaica, d. 2002), sought to overcome such a preoccupation about these artists' contrasting access to education by styling both men 'metaphysical artists'. The same practice was elaborated in explicitly racial terms by the curators of 'Back to Black: Art, Cinema and the Racial Imaginary' (the Whitechapel Gallery, London, and the New Art Gallery, Walsall, 2005), which alleged the shared 'blackness' of artists from Jamaica, Trinidad, Guyana, and St Lucia, regardless of how these individuals identified themselves. It convinced Sukhdev Sandhu, writing in *Modern Painters* (2005), of how centrally this art became 'formative to the black Atlantic experience'. The 2006 'Amazon to Caribbean: Early Peoples of the Rainforest' at the Horniman Museum, London, sought to enlarge a public sense of the Caribbean's cultural geography and Guyana's continental destiny. Yet placing the wood sculpture of Oswald Hussein and painting by Aubrey Williams within an ethnographic institution appears to revisit some abiding curatorial tendencies. If art from the Caribbean continues to be assigned an all-encompassing 'cultural difference'—whether of the black nationalist, exclusionist, or the ethnographic kind—it has yet to be understood for its diversity and modernity, and its place in Britain assured. LW

Araeen, Rasheed (ed.), *The Other Story: Afro-Asian Artists in Post-War Britain* (1989)

Walmsley, Anne, *The Caribbean Artists' Movement 1966–1972: A Literary and Cultural History* (1992)

See also AFRICAN ART, BRITISH RESPONSES TO; VISUAL ARTS 2: ARTISTS

Caribbean Artists' Movement. Movement formed by West Indian writers and artists in London in 1966. Its membership, programme of events, and publications from 1967 to 1972 reflected a time of crossroads in the Caribbean and for West Indians in Britain. It made a significant contribution to new directions in Caribbean arts, and to the transition from West Indian to black British arts.

1. Membership
2. Events and publications
3. Concerns and contribution
4. Central features

1. Membership The founders of the Caribbean Artists' Movement (CAM) were writers. The poet Kamau (then Edward) Brathwaite, born in Barbados, was a Cambridge graduate who had worked in Ghana, St Lucia, and Jamaica, and was in London from 1966 to 1968 with Doris, his wife, while completing his doctorate at Sussex University. The poet John *La Rose, born in Trinidad, had worked there and in Venezuela before arriving as a political exile in Britain in 1961; fluent in French and Spanish and widely read in Caribbean literature, he founded New Beacon Books in 1966 with Sarah White, his partner. Andrew *Salkey, born in Jamaica, had come to Britain in 1952 to study at London University, and was a widely published writer of adult and children's fiction alongside freelance work, mainly for BBC radio. CAM members and participants included the published novelists Wilson Harris and Orlando Patterson; the not-yet-published poets James Berry, Faustin Charles, Sebastian Clarke (now Amon Saba Saakana), Linton Kwesi Johnson, and Marc Matthews; the poet and film scriptwriter and, later, novelist Evan Jones. Artists were alongside writers in CAM from the start: Althea McNish, Ronald *Moody, and Aubrey *Williams, well established respectively as textile artist, sculptor, and painter, and younger artists such as Karl (Jerry) Craig, Paul Dash, and Errol Lloyd. Theatre people ranged from the actors Ram John Holder, Marina Maxwell, and Lloyd Reckord to the agent Pearl *Connor and the director Frank Thomasson. Practising artists were flanked by the leading intellectuals and academics C. L. R *James and Elsa Goveia, Louis James, Kenneth Ramchand, and

Gordon Rohlehr. CAM's treasurer was Oliver Clarke, later managing director of the Jamaica Gleaner Company.

2. **Events and publications** The CAM programme of meetings, or 'sessions', enabled members to become closely acquainted with each other's work, and introduced Caribbean arts to a wide audience. Most public sessions were held at the West Indian Students' Centre, Earls Court, and took the form of talks and symposiums, art exhibitions, and poetry readings. Similar sessions continued at CAM's conferences: residential at the University of Kent at Canterbury in 1967 and 1968, non-residential at the West Indian Students' Centre in 1969. Later public sessions took place in London at the Keskidee Centre, Islington, and the Co-op Hall, Seven Sisters. A feature of all such sessions was the stall of books published or sold by New Beacon Books. Art exhibitions were mounted at a wide spread of venues: from the Theatre Royal, Stratford, to the Houses of Parliament. Private sessions, advertised and open to members, interspersed public sessions; or followed them, more informally, at one of the core CAM members' homes.

Most public and many private sessions were tape-recorded. Transcripts were regularly carried in the CAM Newsletter, along with news items of interest to CAM members. *Savacou*, the journal of the Caribbean Artists' Movement, followed, edited mainly in Jamaica by Brathwaite. Numbers 9–10 (1974), edited by La Rose and Salkey, were subtitled *Away from Home*: one of the first publications to reflect early black British culture.

3. **Concerns and contribution** The concerns of CAM were a response to the historic moment in which it was active. Independence had recently been granted to former British colonies of the Caribbean, while leaders of a socialist revolution had seized power in Cuba. CAM members believed in a central role for the arts in their new West Indian nations, and, after centuries of European cultural domination, of new forms and directions. A true Caribbean aesthetic should, they considered, draw on the cultural traditions of the 'folk'. The emphasis within CAM was on African traditions, long suppressed, alongside recognition of the continuing Amerindian presence. Literature was predominant, followed by the visual arts. Music featured only tangentially; it had not yet become the leading popular cultural expression of the West Indies. But poetry in CAM pioneered features of music. Brathwaite's *Rights of Passage* at the Jeanetta Cochrane Theatre, 1967, was more performance than conventional reading. He had already urged the recognition of *jazz elements in Caribbean literature and popular music—their inclusion in a Caribbean aesthetic. Then Gordon Rohlehr challenged West Indian writers to emulate the use of the everyday rhythms of West Indian speech in the lyrics of the calypsonian Sparrow. Meanwhile, Wilson Harris expounded the 'radical new art of fiction' in which he was engaged, which recognized 'archetypal traditions running underground in the region' and was in a tradition very different from the 19th-century European novel. Ronald Moody and Aubrey Williams, through their words and their work, opened CAM audiences to the rich possibilities of art made by Caribbean people. Moody spoke of his influences coming from the art of Egypt, India, and Africa, rather than of Europe. Williams defended his use of abstraction in painting, his concern with expressing the Amerindian culture and primeval beauty of his homeland of Guyana.

Anti-immigration legislation in Britain in the late 1960s and early 1970s stemmed the flow of would-be West Indian residents, while political rhetoric fanned latent racism in the British public. Within CAM, Stuart Hall expressed awareness that the West Indian community would soon be predominantly British-born, and share more with non-white descendants of people from other ex-colonies than with West Indians. Black solidarity was also strengthened by the US Black Power movement, in particular, by Stokely

Carmichael's visit to Britain in 1967, and by Calvin Hernton's participation in CAM events. With the return to the West Indies, in late 1968, of several leading CAM figures, especially of Kamau and Doris Brathwaite, and the involvement of La Rose and Salkey in more pressing commitments within the black community, the movement's leadership passed to Donald Hinds and James Berry. Their initial status as 'ordinary immigrants' and achievements as published writers signalled CAM's transition to black British.

4. **Central features** CAM believed from the start in creative dialogue with its audience. It also provided a forum for interaction between leading artists and intellectuals and largely self-educated would-be writers and artists. CAM was essentially interdisciplinary, especially in bridging the visual and literary. CAM members were keenly aware of, and some actively involved in, social and political events of the time, and yet insisted on the need for art to retain its distinct autonomy. CAM was consciously a Caribbean, not a black, artists' movement, drawing on the particular history and traditions of the region, and encompassing the literature and art of the French- and Spanish-speaking Caribbean alongside the English. AW

James, Louis, 'The Caribbean Artists Movement' in Bill Schwarz (ed.), *West Indian Intellectuals in Britain* (2003)

Walmsley, Anne, *The Caribbean Artists Movement 1966–1972: A Literary and Cultural History* (1992)

See also LITERATURE 2: FICTION AND POETRY

Caribbean Studies. The study of the Caribbean as a series of academic disciplines within British universities. The second half of the 20th century has witnessed a dramatic development in Caribbean Studies in Britain, often due to the sustained efforts of individual scholars of Caribbean heritage. Although leading Caribbean intellectuals such as C. L. R. *James and Sir Arthur *Lewis had settled in Britain during the 1930s, several more decades were to pass before British universities really began to explore the possibility of offering courses that dealt specifically with the Caribbean region in its own right.

Initially, studies of the Caribbean tended to be part of some larger geographical or political grouping such as that offered at Leeds University in the early 1960s. Leeds Postcolonial Studies Centre claims that its School of English was the first university department to establish research and teaching in Commonwealth Literature, including that of the Caribbean. Its 1964 conference on Commonwealth Literature, the subsequent founding of the influential *Journal of Commonwealth Literature*, and the creation of a specialist chair of Commonwealth Literature were all key events in the early development of what was to lead to Caribbean Studies in Britain.

The founding of the *Centre for Contemporary Cultural Studies at the University of Birmingham was another landmark event that helped to bring studies of the Caribbean diaspora closer to the heart of British academia. Richard Hoggart established the Centre in 1964 and was replaced in 1969 by the Jamaican Rhodes Scholar professor Stuart Hall. During Hall's ten-year directorship the Centre made major contributions to the fields of literary, cultural, and historical theory, including those related to the construction of black British identities. Alumni include Professor Paul Gilroy (formerly of Goldsmiths College), who is renowned for his own pioneering work on the black Atlantic and was appointed the first holder of the Anthony Giddens professorship in Social Theory at the London School of Economics in June 2005.

Throughout the 1970s a number of individual British-based scholars were also to be found researching diverse aspects of the Caribbean. In 1974 Professor Colin Clark convened a conference on the Caribbean at the Institute for Latin American Studies, Liverpool University, and more than 30 colleagues with interests in the region attended the event. During the next two years, a number of meetings were then called by Professor David

Lowenthal to discuss the development of Caribbean Studies in Britain and to explore ways of bringing specialists on the region together. These meetings led to the establishment of the Society for Caribbean Studies, and an inaugural meeting was held at the University of York in 1976. The aims of the Society were primarily to encourage education and research about the Caribbean, but also to provide an opportunity for contact among those researching the region and its diasporas. Since 1977 the Society has held an annual conference with sessions on a wide range of academic disciplines that attracts participants from the Caribbean, Europe, Canada, and the United States. The Society has, therefore, been instrumental in helping to consolidate the developing interest in Caribbean Studies in Britain.

It was not until 1984 that the first dedicated Centre for Caribbean Studies was founded by Professor Alistair Hennessy at the University of Warwick. The specific aims of this Centre were to 'stimulate academic interest and research in the [Caribbean] region which in spite of its creative vitality and geopolitical importance has not received the academic recognition it deserves in its own right'. Professor Hennessy and the subsequent directors of the Centre for Caribbean Studies—Professors David Dabydeen and Gad Heuman and currently Dr Cecily Jones—have all played a pivotal role in firmly establishing Caribbean and Black British Studies as an integral part of the United Kingdom's intellectual landscape. The Centre enjoys a close relationship with the University of the West Indies and regularly offers fellowship awards to scholars from that university who are able to spend periods of research time at the Centre. In addition to its teaching and research activities the Centre has played host to a wide range of conferences, lectures, and symposiums that have attracted leading international scholars in the field of Caribbean Studies. These have included the annual Walter *Rodney Memorial Lecture, which was established in 1984 in recognition of the life and work of one of the most outstanding scholar-activists of the black diaspora in the post-Second World War era. In conjunction with Macmillan Caribbean, the Centre for Caribbean Studies has also pioneered the publication of a series of academic works that encompass much of the latest and most authoritative research in Caribbean Studies. To date over 40 volumes have been published, which aim to study the complexity and variety of a remarkable region and reflect the pan-Caribbean, interdisciplinary approach of the Centre itself.

In 1988 another Caribbean Studies Centre was founded in London Metropolitan University (formerly the University of North London). Led by Professor Jean Stubbs, this London-based Centre offers a wide range of multidisciplinary courses on the Caribbean, with particular strengths in cultural studies and history. The Centre has many students and members of staff of Caribbean origin, including Professor Clem Seecharan, the first Ph.D. candidate at Warwick's Centre for Caribbean Studies.

Of course, not all universities with an interest in the Caribbean have set up specialist Centres such as those in Warwick and London Metropolitan. As Dr Jean Besson has pointed out, Caribbean Studies have often been embedded across a range of disciplines and departments, as in the example of Goldsmiths College in the University of London. At Goldsmiths, by the year 2000, teaching on the Caribbean was included in the departments of Anthropology, Historical and Cultural Studies, Modern European Languages, Sociology, and English, which has a Caribbean Centre and Caribbean Network to interface with the local community.

Further opportunities to study the Caribbean and its diaspora are available within organizations such as the Institute of Commonwealth Studies (ICS) and the new Institute for the Study of the Americas at the University of London School of Advanced Study. Both of these Institutes act as coordinating bases for scholars researching the Caribbean, and have hosted numerous seminars, symposiums, and workshops on the region and its diaspora, and are discussing further intercollegiate collaboration among Caribbeanists. Furthermore, in February 2000 the ICS launched the Caribbean Studies, Black and Asian History project (CASBAH), which aims to identify and map national research resources relating to Caribbean Studies and the history of black and Asian people in Britain.

The opportunities for studying the Caribbean in Britain have therefore continued to widen and diversify as we move into the 21st century. Today there is a wide range of both undergraduate and postgraduate degrees available in universities throughout the British Isles that focus upon aspects of the Caribbean and its diaspora. In the space of little more than 30 years, Caribbean Studies has moved from being a highly specialized and unusual subject of research to one that features prominently at the centre of British academic life. LM

Besson, Jean, 'Reflections on Caribbean Studies in the Year 2000', Paper presented to the Society for Caribbean Studies 23rd Annual Conference, University of Birmingham, 4–5 July 2000

Hennessy, Alistair (ed.), *Intellectuals in the Twentieth Century Caribbean* (1992), ii

Caribbean Voices. Radio series broadcast by the BBC between 1943 and 1950 aimed, through creative writing, at capturing the Caribbean from as many sides as possible. In the life of the programme some 400 stories and poems, along with plays and literary criticism, were broadcast. There were some 372 contributors, of whom 71 were women. The years 1946 to 1958 comprised the high point of the programme, which coincided with the editorship of Henry Swanzy (1915–2004). In any period of six months during his years as editor some 24 programmes were broadcast. They contained around 28 short stories and sketches. Thirteen programmes of this total were devoted to poetry, and the remainder of the time was allocated to critical discussion groups, called the Critics' Circle, comprising a mix of critics from the Caribbean and Britain.

The programme helped to launch the careers of many authors, including a number who went on to achieve international fame as poets, playwrights, artists, and musicians, notably the region's two Nobel Prizewinners, the St Lucian Derek Walcott, and the Trinidad-born Sir V. S. Naipaul. Other internationally known writers who contributed to the programme in their early years include Kamau Brathwaite and George Lamming from Barbados, Wilson Harris and Ian McDonald from Guyana, Sam *Selvon from Trinidad, as well as Gloria Escoffery, John Figueroa, and Andrew *Salkey from Jamaica.

Caribbean Voices began as a request programme for West Indians during the Second World War and developed some literary leanings under Una *Marson. She named the series and produced early editions until 1945, when she returned to Jamaica. Two important innovations took place soon after she departed. In the interim, before Swanzy was appointed to the editorship in August 1946, the programme was managed by John Grenfell Williams (Head of Colonial Service Broadcasting). His first innovation was to establish a regional office in Jamaica. He appointed a literary agent, officially Mrs Gladys Lindo (though in practice her husband, Cedric Lindo, played the major role). The role of the agent was to stimulate contributions of new writing, to act as a contact point for local authors, and to disburse payments to local contributors. Prior to this innovation programmes took the form of readings from published work. After Swanzy took over in London, sufficient material was generated to send manuscripts to him twice a month from Jamaica. The second innovation was the willingness and ability of the BBC to pay for contributions that were used. These developments increased interest among potential writers and stimulated a range of local writing and criticism. By 1948 the programme's popularity increased to the extent that its length was doubled.

The period in which *Caribbean Voices* was broadcast coincided with a peak of nationalist sentiment and activity in the region. Many Caribbean islands were gaining universal suffrage, the short-lived West Indian Federation had been formed in 1958, and by the 1960s many islands had obtained politically independent status. Radio, and particularly *Caribbean Voices* as a social medium, was not immune from this live political process.

In the making of these radio programmes attempts to exercise power and influence involved argument and disagreement in four important areas. They were, firstly, debate and contention around the exercise and control over the work that was submitted. Most manuscripts went first to Cedric Lindo in Jamaica. This at times disturbed Swanzy, who saw Lindo as acting as a preliminary editor. Thus the focus of the discussion here involved editorial competition between Cedric Lindo and Swanzy around the selection of material.

This conflict spilled over into a question about reading styles, a second area of major contention. The argument centred on whose voice should be heard over the radio: should it be the more authentically West Indian-sounding or the more English-sounding reader? The politics here resulted in the ironic situation of the liberal metropolitan editor, Swanzy, against his own inclination and policy, being given more conservative encouragement from the Caribbean to utilize English voices in the reading of Caribbean material.

A third political issue extended into literary nationalism, especially in Jamaica. Contributors had to decide on the issue of whether or not to submit work to a programme beamed on short-wave radio from the heart of the Empire and, more importantly, on the legitimacy or otherwise of non-Caribbean critics to comment on the work submitted and broadcast in the programmes. Here national and liberal artistic sensibilities rubbed against each other, at times fiercely. For a number of years many Jamaican writers hesitated to submit their work to the programme.

Finally, power and influence were also occasionally negotiated between conservative elements of the audience supported by the local radio station. In Barbados, for example, conservative voices were raised against the more liberal authority in London represented by Swanzy. A point at issue was a threat from Barbados to screen out a short story by Sam Selvon identified as 'unacceptable material' broadcast from London.

On most of these points of contention the politically liberal metropolitan centre, in the form of Swanzy, took issue or negotiated with local nationalist forces or with conservative forces over the process of making and presenting programmes. At other times local liberal influences in the Caribbean, for example in the form of Frank Collymore (editor of *Bim*, the Barbados and regional magazine), supported Swanzy's liberal metropolitan instincts and challenged the more narrowly nationalist perspective of editors like Edna Manley at *Focus* in Jamaica and A. J. Seymour at *Kyk-Over-Al* in British Guiana.

For a time the liberal and metropolitan influences held sway. Led by Swanzy, they created an opportunity for Anglophone Caribbean literature to break out of what was a parochial frame and to become what it is today, a form of regional expression available to the world on a par with West Indies cricket and carnival.

Swanzy left the programme in 1954. It continued for four more years with a rotation of part-time editors, many of whom were established Caribbean authors. They included Edgar Mittelholzer, George Lamming, and V. S. Naipaul. The programme, however, had lost its impetus. Writers were migrating and settling more permanently in Britain. Those in the Caribbean were defining themselves from within that location. Caribbean-origin writing was shifting to become black British writing. PNa

Ramchand, K., *The West Indian Novel and Its Background* (1970)

See also LITERATURE 2: FICTION AND POETRY; MARSON, UNA; RADIO

Carlyle, Thomas (1795–1881). British writer best known for his books *The French Revolution* (1837) and *Frederick the Great* (1858–65). Born in Scotland, and settling permanently in London in 1834, Carlyle was the author of many other works, including essays and articles in periodicals. Among these was his 'Occasional Discourse on the Negro Question', originally published in *Fraser's Magazine* (London) in December 1849, and later rewritten and republished as a pamphlet called *Occasional Discourse on the Nigger Question* (1853) and in some of the collected editions of the author's *Latter-Day Pamphlets* (first published 1850).

In form, the *Occasional Discourse* is an imaginary report of a speech by a fictional orator, and it would be unwise to assume that everything in the speech should be regarded as identical with the personal opinions of Carlyle, who may have deliberately exaggerated some elements for effect. The speaker argues that contemporary social policies in Britain and Ireland are the result of the same philosophy that emancipated the slaves in the British Caribbean colonies and left them (so he claims, in a notorious passage) 'Sitting yonder with their beautiful muzzles up to the ears in pumpkins . . . while the sugar-crops rot around them uncut, because labour cannot be hired, so cheap are the pumpkins . . .' Traditional fantasies of bountiful tropical climates combined with racial prejudice to allow the speaker (and, it would seem, Carlyle himself) to assert that black ex-slaves who worked hard to support their families by subsistence agriculture were idle because they refused to work on the plantations for whatever wages a predominantly white planter class wished to offer them. The speaker claimed to have no wish to return the ex-slaves to a state of slavery, but the suggestion that they would have to be servants, perhaps 'hired for life', to the Whites he alleged were their natural masters seems little different.

Whatever allowance is made for rhetorical exaggeration, it is clear from Carlyle's other works that he would have been in agreement with the general thrust of the *Occasional Discourse*: that it was inevitable that some people should have to work for others, and that it was in the best interest of all concerned that they should be made to do so if they were unwilling. For Carlyle and others, the question of who should be master and who should be servant was one that could easily be answered by recourse to racist ideas about superior and inferior races. Not everybody agreed; there was a hostile reaction to the *Occasional Discourse*, and the economist and philosopher John Stuart Mill (1806–73) composed a protest, published first as an anonymous letter to the editor of *Fraser's Magazine* in 1850, which specifically addressed the misstatements about the Caribbean. Nevertheless, the *Discourse* illustrates a reaction by no means confined to Carlyle himself, but more widespread in Victorian Britain, against what he denounced as the 'rosepink Sentimentalism' which had seen a wide section of the British public concerned with the condition of the slaves in British colonies and help to secure their *emancipation. Nearly 20 years later Carlyle took an active part in the controversy that followed the *Morant Bay rebellion, as one of the most prominent supporters of Governor Eyre. JG

Carlyle, Thomas, *Latter-Day Pamphlets* (1858)
ODNB

Carter, Sir John (1919–2005). Guyanese lawyer, politician, and diplomat who was appointed travelling secretary of the *League of Coloured Peoples (LCP) during the *Second World War. Carter was born in the British colony of British Guiana. He attended Queen's College, Georgetown, and came to London University in 1939 to read law, qualifying as a barrister at the Middle Temple in 1942. During the war years the LCP grew in members and significance, and so did its concern for the welfare of the many military and labour volunteers from the colonies. Another concern was for the large numbers of African-American soldiers in Britain from 1942 onwards. Carter became general and travelling secretary of the LCP in early 1942, using his legal skills to deal with numerous instances of racial discrimination, and also the case of an African-American soldier sentenced to death for rape by a US military court. Carter returned home to British Guiana in 1945, where he led the branch of the LCP in the colony, and established a law practice in Georgetown. He became a member of the legislative council in 1952, and later the first chairman of Forbes Burnham's ruling People's National Congress in 1966. He was appointed a QC in 1962, and knighted when Guyana became independent in 1966. Carter served as Guyana's representative to the United States and Canada (1966–70), the United Nations (1967–9), Britain (1970), where he spent much time involved in race relations work, China, and finally Jamaica. In 1983 he retired and went to live in the United States, where he died. DK

Fraser, Peter, 'Obituary: Sir John Carter', *The Guardian*, 4 June 2005
LCP Newsletter (1942–5)

See also POLITICS

Centre for Contemporary Cultural Studies Postgraduate research centre at the University of Birmingham whose staff and students researched and published in the field of cultural studies, which it was instrumental in inaugurating.

1. Inception
2. Inspirations
3. Methodologies
4. Richard Hoggart and the aims and aspirations of the Centre for Contemporary Cultural Studies
5. Stuart Hall's directorship
6. The demise of the Centre

1. Inception The Centre was founded in 1964 under the directorship of the 'New Left' Marxist Richard Hoggart, then Professor of Modern English Literature at Birmingham. Its principal aims were to instigate research into the relationship between culture and society. Its research was a determined break with orthodox sociology, which had historically underprivileged the role of culture and cultural forms and practices in its understanding of society and social change. Its innovative critical analyses of mass media, subculture, deviance, and youth broke new ground in relating sociology to what Raymond Williams termed 'ordinary culture'.

The Centre's research interests were consolidated into the academic discipline of Cultural Studies, whose currency exploded during Stuart Hall's tenure as Centre director during the 1970s. At its peak in the late 1970s, it consisted of three staff members, two research fellows working on funded projects, and over 40 postgraduate research students. Its work was published in a journal and a series of stencilled working papers, and culminated eventually in a series of collectively written books. There have been three directors of the Centre: Richard Hoggart, Stuart Hall, and Richard Johnson.

2. Inspirations The Centre's origins in the intellectual tradition of English literature are important to an understanding of its theoretical innovations and methodologies. It had non-sociological origins, and significantly took an oppositional stand to sociology from its inception. Its inspirations were drawn from three totemic figures on the British New Left: E. P. Thompson, Raymond Williams, and Richard Hoggart. Its originating moments are best understood in terms of the texts that became the inaugural curriculum of the Cultural Studies field. Hoggart's seminal intervention *The Uses of Literacy* (1957), Williams's *Culture and Society* (1958) and *The Long Revolution* (1961), and Thompson's *The Making of the English Working Class* (1963) were all foundational to the transformation from Marxist literary criticism to Cultural Studies.

3. Methodologies Methodologically, the Centre turned away from quantitative sociology and was orientated towards qualitative approaches. Its members were concerned with producing 'thick descriptions' that demonstrated a rich understanding of the meanings within 'ordinary' culture. Their qualitative methods engaged with structuralist and post-structuralist approaches to language and meaning, as well as affiliations to American sociology and forms of social history, anthropology, and linguistics.

4. **Richard Hoggart and the aims and aspirations of the Centre for Contemporary Cultural Studies** The aims and aspirations of the Centre derive from the emergence of Cultural Studies from literary inspirations and in opposition to sociology. Hoggart and the founding members of the Centre recognized that culture was critically neglected in sociology, while conceptual divisions between mass and popular culture plagued literary criticism. Crucial to their project was a focus on the lived relations of contemporary culture, which was made through an investment in the study of popular and working-class cultures.

The Uses of Literacy sought to demonstrate the class-based nature of 'culture' in British society. Hoggart famously described Britain as 'a society marked with the fine elaborate lines of class distinction'. Like his contemporary Raymond Williams, Hoggart attacked the elitism of the F. R. Leavis-inspired Oxbridge school of culture, which sought to maintain distinctions between 'high' and 'low' culture. Hoggart felt that a new understanding of culture was needed, and wanted to use the Centre to develop that idea. The Centre was intended to be a home for Cultural Studies, within the framework of higher education and principally devoted to postgraduate research. In 1968 Hoggart left to become an assistant director-general at UNESCO, and Stuart Hall became the Centre's director between 1968 and 1979.

5. **Stuart Hall's directorship** Stuart Hall's tenure as director was a crucial catalyst for the success of the Centre and the standing of Cultural Studies as an academic discipline. Like Hoggart, he had read English Literature as an undergraduate. His contributions to the establishment of Cultural Studies as a distinct area of study have been profound, and positioned the Centre at the heart of Cultural Studies' evolution. If the Centre had been founded in confrontation with sociology, Hall further radicalized its research agenda in the face of what he perceived as attacks from the mainstream of British sociology, and the Centre even became blacklisted by the British Sociological Association in the late 1960s.

As a kind of academic 'subculture' in itself, the Centre's Cultural Studies went on to focus its research on subjects traditionally marginalized or neglected by orthodox sociology. It is particularly famed for its work on deviance, youth, and broadcasting. Hall's own work moved on to analyses of the ideological control of the media, and in particular of the way that media practitioners internalized the values of the dominant culture. He was also instrumental in debunking the generic category of the audience, and exploring, in a British context, how culture could be both a tool for domination (through the media) and a resource for resistance. The Centre became part of what Hall has referred to as the 'cultural and linguistic turn in social theory'.

6. **The demise of the Centre** The Centre and its Cultural Studies programmes were merged with Sociology during the 1980s as part of larger restructuring at the University of Birmingham. Because of that restructuring its profile as an exclusively postgraduate department was transformed by a large influx of undergraduate students. Its research also expanded into more diverse areas, such as technology and citizenship. The Centre was controversially closed in 2002, amid much academic protest, with Sociology courses absorbed into the Social Policy and Social Work Department and its Cultural Studies programmes housed in the Institute of Applied Social Science. PBP

Hall, Stuart (ed.), *Culture, Media, Language: Working Papers in Cultural Studies, 1972–79* (1980)

—— et al., *Policing the Crisis: Mugging, the State, and Law and Order* (1978)

Hoggart, Richard, *The Uses of Literacy: Aspects of Working Class Life with Special Reference to Publications and Entertainments* (1957)

Christian, George (1872–1924). Black merchant in Africa. He was one of six

Liverpool-born children of Octavia Caulfield and Antigua-born Jacob Christian. George and his brother Arthur worked for the merchant John Holt in Nigeria, and George then established his own import–export business in German Cameroon. The Germans expelled him in 1904 (his compensation claim led to correspondence with Britain's ambassador in Berlin). His youngest sister, Rubena Laura Patterson, and her husband, Oscar, and three children migrated to Saskatchewan, Canada, in 1906. His eldest sister, Julia Waldren Rogers, a widow, took her six children to Saskatchewan in 1910.

By 1910 Christian had opened four branches of his import–export business in Nigeria, and Alexander (another brother) ran the Liverpool head office, incorporated as G. W. Christian & Co. Ltd in 1911, the year he married a Liverpool nurse, Isabella Stanbury. The Nigerian enterprise flourished. Three children were born in England and a substantial home was purchased in Wallasey, Cheshire, probably using money following the sale of the company in 1919. George Christian later returned to Cameroon, where he owned a cocoa plantation at Idenau. He died there in 1924. Isabella returned to Wallasey and the children, and sold the plantation by the 1930s. Christian's nephew, Sir Herbert Gladstone McDavid, son of his sister Octavia, was the managing director of the United Glen and Blue Funnel shipping lines. JPG

Green, J., 'George William Christian (1872–1924): Liverpool Merchant' in Rainer E. Lotz and Ian Pegg (eds.), *Under the Imperial Carpet: Essays in Black History 1780–1950* (1986)
ODNB

See also BUSINESSES; PICTON, CESAR

Christianity. Many of the black people who came to Britain in the 17th–19th centuries were or became Christians. However, a specific black Christianity does not become significant until after 1950, when larger numbers of Caribbean and African peoples, often from Christian communities, entered the country. They often found that they were not welcome and that Britain was not the Christian society they had imagined. Black people did join British churches but they also created new separate black *churches with different forms of worship, liturgy, and music. Many of these were Pentecostal. Some African immigrants, increasing in number after the 1970s, also joined black churches and in certain cases planted branches of African indigenous churches in Britain.

In many American colonies both colonists and slave owners often attempted to keep slaves from Christian ideas for fear that such knowledge would make them rebellious. In slave societies, accepting that slaves could be Christians was to acknowledge their humanity. When slaves embraced Christianity, colonists then argued that they should accept their divinely ordained servile status, a position they tried to support from biblical texts. By the late 18th century many slaves in the Caribbean and North America had become Christians. Black people brought to Britain as slaves or servants were baptized, and they can often be identified from the one-line entries in English parish registers, for example: All Saints, Evesham: '2 March 1664: Martha, a Negro, aged about 17 years', and Wytham, Oxfordshire, 1766: 'William Roberts, a black boy belonging to ye Earl of Abingdon was baptised, Aug. 31st'. Most were probably young people, and the rite of baptism indicated that they now belonged to a Christian society. This did not affect their status, although some slaves falsely believed that baptism in England made them free. Some became active Christians, for example the late 18th-century black British writers Ukawsaw *Gronniosaw, Olaudah *Equiano, and Ottobah *Cugoano, whose writings contain accounts of their conversion experience.

Equiano and Cugoano were closely associated with the British Christians who campaigned to end the slave trade. Cugoano's *Thoughts and Sentiments on the Evil of Slavery* (1787) denounced both the slave trade and slavery, from biblical texts. At the same time apologists for the transatlantic slave trade argued that transporting Africans to the New World made it possible for slaves to hear the Christian gospel. The campaign to abolish the slave trade and to emancipate slaves was largely led by Christians, and it occurred at the same time as the origins and growth of the modern missionary movement. Thus there were powerful influences at work to encourage the conversion of Africans and black people, both slave and free, in the British Caribbean colonies and in the United States.

During the 19th century some elite families on the west coast of Africa sent their children to Britain for education in Christian schools. Many of the schools established in the West Indian colonies and in Africa were run by Christian missions, often with black teachers and clergy. Equiano unsuccessfully applied to the Bishop of London to be ordained. Only two black men are known to have been ordained into the Church of England in the 18th century, Philip *Quaque, who returned home to work in the Gold Coast, and the Revd Bryan Mackey (d. 1847), son a black mother and a white father, who was rector of Coates in Gloucestershire. During the 19th century ordained black Anglicans were mostly missionary clergy. There were black clergy in dissenting churches; again a good number trained in Britain primarily for missionary work in Africa, e.g. Thomas Lewis *Johnson, John *Newby, and Salim *Wilson. However, a few led British churches with white congregations, e.g. John Piper (d. 1880s) and Peter *Stanford (1860–1909). The *Fisk Jubilee Singers, who toured Britain in the 1870s to raise funds for their African-American college in the United States, were composed of Christians. They sang to both church and secular audiences and injected a new musical vibrancy into the evangelistic meetings. South African Christian choirs in the 1890s also tried to raise money in Britain but with little success.

Many of the people involved in the early expressions of black nationalism and *Pan-Africanism were Christians. The black delegates from South Africa who came to Britain in 1909 to protest at the new Union government were aided by fellow Christians from the Brotherhood Movement (a Christian organization that argued for racial harmony). When Sol *Plaatje and others came to London in 1914 to denounce the Lands Bill, they made immediate contact with the Brotherhood and spent much of their time speaking on that organization's platforms. Harold *Moody, who founded the *League of Coloured Peoples in 1931, was a committed Christian. He regarded the League primarily as a Christian organization with a Christian agenda to end racial discrimination. DK

Edwards, Joel, and Killingray, David (eds.), *Black British Christian Voices: An Anthology* (2007)

Killingray, David, 'Black Baptists in Britain 1640–1950', *Baptist Quarterly*, 40/2 (2003)

—— 'Black Evangelicals in Darkest Britain 1760s–1930s' in Mark Smith (ed.), *Evangelicals in Britain*, ii: *History and Sociology* (2007)

See also CHURCHES; MISSIONARY SOCIETIES

Churches. According to recent research, black Christianity in Britain is on the rise. A natural outcome of this surge in numbers has been the growth and proliferation of black churches.

1. Origins of black churches in Britain
2. What is a black church?
3. Comparing black churches in Britain and the United States
4. Black-majority denominational churches
5. White-majority churches and black people
6. Independent or Neo-Pentecostal black churches

1. Origins of black churches in Britain The birth of black churches in Britain largely dates from the mass migration of West Indians to Britain in the post-war era, which commenced with the arrival of 492 Jamaicans at Tilbury docks on the **Empire Windrush*, on 22 June 1948. The post-war presence of black people within inner cities in Britain, and the concomitant evolution of black churches to be found there, is a phenomenon that has been described by many sociologists and historians.

Black Christian faith in Britain can be traced to the struggles of black slaves in the 17th and 18th centuries in their fight for emancipation. The struggles of these black slaves speak to the corruption and the biased self-serving nature of English Christianity at that time. The pioneering work of such luminaries as Ignatius *Sancho and Mary *Prince was a valiant attempt to remind the English Establishment of the basic tenets of Christianity, which they had exported to their Empire throughout the colonial epoch.

2. **What is a black church?** Perhaps one of the thorniest problems when discussing the black church is the question of definition. What do we mean by the term 'the black church'? The question is somewhat easier to answer within the US context than it is in Britain. In the United States the notion of the black church is an ingrained historical, theological, sociological, and experiential reality for many African-Americans. 'The black church' has an automatic efficacy that finds expression in myriad forms of discourses and academic courses.

The black church has been perceived by many scholars as the key social, political, educational, and organizational entity in the collective and communitarian experience of diasporan people of African descent. In Britain the black church is often seen as the key location for intimations of black selfhood and collective solidarity. Within the United States the black church is a normative context out of which the black religious experience has arisen.

3. **Comparing black churches in Britain and the United States** The term 'black church', when used in the United States, is a generic one used in order to denote and describe particular faith communities in which black leadership, culture, traditions, experience, and spirituality represent the norm, and from which white Euro-American traditions and expressions are absent. These churches are termed 'generic' because, unlike in Britain, they are not perceived as belonging to any one denominational or theological slant. These churches cut across the whole spectrum of church affiliation and the multiplicity of settings in which black life is experienced. The development of the 'black church' in the United States grew out of the racism of the established churches of white, European origin.

Black churches in Britain are not confined to any one denomination. Just like their counterparts in the United States, black churches can be divided into three broad categories. The first, and by far the most visible, are black-led Pentecostal churches. These churches owe their origins to black migrants travelling from the Caribbean in the post-war migrations of the last century. The first churches were offshoots of predominantly white Pentecostal denominations in the United States. The largest and most established of these churches are the New Testament Church of God and the Church of God of Prophecy. The second strand consists of black-majority churches in historically white denominations. These churches are demographically determined, as their black-majority membership has grown out of black migrants moving into inner-city urban contexts, coupled with the white flight of the middle class. The final strand is that of independent black-majority Pentecostal churches or Neo-Pentecostal churches. This group is in many respects a dynamic development of those in the first category. These churches tend to be 'stand-alone' entities that operate as independent communities of faith outside any established national denominational structure. One of the most significant differences between the first and third categories is that, while the first was almost exclusively black Caribbean in complexion, those in category three are a mixture of black Caribbean and black African, with the latter the more expressive and growing constituent.

Within the literature of black religious studies particular emphasis is placed on the role of the black church as the major (in some respects, the only) institution that has affirmed and conferred dignity upon the inhibited and assaulted personhood of black people. To put it quite simply, black folk in the African diaspora might not have survived up to this point had it not been for their creation of safe ecclesiastical spaces in which they could seek refuge from the ravages of racism and white supremacy.

4. Black-majority denominational churches The origins of these churches in Britain date back to the mass post-war immigration of predominantly black people from the Caribbean. While some of these people came as communicant members of historically white denominations, many individuals arrived as members of established Pentecostal denominations in the Caribbean. For many, their arrival in the United Kingdom was born of an intense missionary desire to plant and establish their own churches in this new cultural and social context. A detailed history of this largely untold narrative can be found in the work of black British scholars such as Joe Aldred, Mark Sturge, and Doreen McCalla. This new narrative is challenging and dismantling the old discourse, which asserted that black Pentecostalism was a historical accident, born of English racism that forced black people to leave white historic denominations to found their own churches. This narrative at best was always a half-truth.

The churches in this category have often been perceived as being the natural equivalents of the black church tradition in the United States owing to their origins and development, which have emerged from within a black experience. What complicates this particular perspective, however, is the fact that many of these churches, although emerging from within a black experience, were founded by conservative white Americans in the United States and then planted by means of missionary work in the Caribbean. The historical developments of these churches are linked to a form of US white ecclesiastical exclusivism from which black people in the United States had to separate in order to create a version of Christianity that did not oppress them.

For many years these churches have been defined using the term 'black-led'. This term (often used by white commentators and not by the adherents themselves) has been highly contested for many years. Black theological scholars have challenged the use of this term to name predominantly black British Pentecostal churches on the grounds that defining a church on purely ethnic grounds does not cohere with the self-understanding of the churches and the members themselves.

One of the defining characteristics of black Pentecostal churches is their style of worship, which draws upon a range of black diasporan and continental African traditions, some of which are African-American in style. The invocation of the spirit within black Pentecostal worship, for example, is fused with an expressive, informal liturgy (the formal study of worship within the Christian tradition) and has been one of the defining hallmarks of black religiosity. Robert Beckford offers a carefully constructed black British Pentecostal perspective on this creative dynamic in which participation and movement is an important means by which the liberative impulse of black life is expressed.

5. White-majority churches and black people The second broad typology is that of black churches in white-majority historic churches in Britain. These churches are often identified with such denominations as the Catholic, Church of England (Anglican), Methodist, Baptist, and United Reformed churches. For many years it has been assumed that black members of these white-majority churches were not part of a black church tradition. The black experience was seen to reside within black-majority Pentecostalism.

The majority of the black members in historically white-majority churches in Britain can trace their roots to Africa and the Caribbean. The majority of these church adherents attend black-majority churches in predominantly inner-city urban contexts. These churches operate, in effect, as black enclaves within the overall white-majority structure and membership of the church as a whole. Among the most significant churches in this category are Walworth Road Methodist church (in south London) and Holy Trinity Birchfield Church of England (Birmingham).

The development of black-majority churches within these historically white-majority bodies has emerged out of demographic changes in inner-city areas within the larger cities and towns in Britain, and not through a self-conscious separation along the lines of 'race', as has been the case in the United States. The majority of black Christians in Britain belong to historically white-majority churches, by a factor of almost 2 to 1.

The place and role of black churches in predominantly white-majority historic denominations remains a deeply contentious issue. David Isiorho, a black Anglican priest, has written on the dominant images of 'whiteness' and 'Englishness' (the latter often taken as a synonym for the former) in the Church of England, which fails to acknowledge the plural and multi-ethnic nature of the Church. Writing about the seemingly inextricable link between the overarching construct of whiteness and Englishness and that of the Church of England, Isiorho argues that these twin seminal building blocks in the Established Church's self-understanding combine so as to exclude black people. This combination of whiteness being associated with Englishness (and the Established Church being the 'Church of England') means that it becomes structurally and symbolically difficult for black people to feel a representative part of this white-dominated edifice.

6. Independent or Neo-Pentecostal black churches The third category or typology for black churches in Britain emerges from within what is the comparatively newer movement of Neo-Pentecostalism in Britain. There are a good many similarities between churches in these contexts and those found in category one. Both are based upon an explicit rendering of black religious cultural expression in terms of music, preaching, and liturgy; in which the practice of 'being church' is reflective of the experiences of the black people who attend these ecclesiastical bodies.

In short, being in the worship services of one of these churches is to find oneself located in a cultural setting that is at once removed from the normative, mainstream expression of white Christianity, particularly as it is expressed in most white-majority historic churches of European origin. Charismatic worship and a strong emphasis upon the outworking of the Holy Spirit (Pneumatology), coupled with African and Caribbean musicology, characterize the distinctive contribution to British Christianity of many of these churches.

There are a number of differentiations one can deduce between churches in the first and third categories, two of which are briefly highlighted here. The first, already alluded to, is namely that, while retaining an overwhelmingly black constituency, these churches tend to have a greater proportion of members who are Africans as opposed to Caribbeans, which was largely the case for those in the first group. Secondly, these churches are much younger in provenance than those in the first. While many of the older black-majority Pentecostal churches are now approaching or have passed the half-century mark in terms of longevity, some of the newer Neo-Pentecostal churches are between 10 and 20 years old. Among the most well-known exponents of these churches (in the third category) are the Kingsway International Christian Centre, Glory House, and Ruach Ministries.

Historically, black churches of whatever denomination or theological perspective have suffered from one particular flaw. A tendency to spiritualize the central tenets of the Christian gospel has often led, as a corollary, to a disengagement from sociopolitical matters as they affected black people in Britain. The excellent work of such projects as The Black Boys Can of the Church of God of Prophecy or the ecumenical initiative against gun crime and violence, named Bringing Hope, has tempered this age-old tendency. AR

Aldred, Joe D., *Respect: A Caribbean British Theology* (2005)

Beckford, Robert, *Dread and Pentecostal: A Political Theology for the Black Church in Britain* (2000)

Isiorho, David, 'Black Theology in Urban Shadow: Combating Racism in the Church of England', *Black Theology: An International Journal*, 1/1 (2002)

McCalla, Doreen, 'Black Churches and Voluntary Action: Their Social Engagement with the Wider Society', *Black Theology: An International Journal*, 3/2 (2004)

Sturge, Mark, *Look What the Lord Has Done! An Exploration of Black Christian Faith in Britain* (2005)

See also CHRISTIANITY; ISLAM

Clare, John (1793–1864). Northamptonshire poet and labourer whose support for the Anti-Slavery Movement was consistent with his consideration for the plight of the disfranchised within society. He corresponded with the literary editor and publisher Thomas Pringle, secretary of the *Anti-Slavery Society, on the subject of the colonial trade in trafficking humans—'I have a feeling on the broad principle of common humanity that slavery is not only impiety but disgraceful to a country professing religion'—and there is evidence to suggest that Clare considered contributing to poetic anthologies on the subject. He later utilized the language of abolition to describe his own wretched state in the asylum, which he termed a 'slave ship from Africa'. While Clare expresses little condemnation for the machinery of imperialism as a system in the Blakean sense, his account of meeting a black beggar outside St Paul's Cathedral, London, and his resolve to return with 'recruited pocket' the following day, illustrates sincere compassion for those affected by enslavement. CMC

Bate, Jonathan, *John Clare: A Biography* (2003)

Clare, John, *A Champion for the Poor: Political Verse and Prose* (ed. P. M. S. Dawson, Eric Robinson, and David Powell, 2000)

See also BLAKE, WILLIAM; COWPER, WILLIAM; DAY, THOMAS; SOUTHEY, ROBERT; WORDSWORTH, WILLIAM

Clarke, Cecil Belfield (1894–1970). Medical doctor and Pan-Africanist.

Born in Barbados, Clarke won an island scholarship and came to London in 1914 to study medicine. He graduated from Cambridge in 1918 and qualified as a surgeon two years later. He set up a medical practice in Southwark, south-east London, where he worked until 1965.

Clarke was a founder member of the *League of Coloured Peoples (LCP) in 1931 and active in encouraging and also providing generous financial support for various Pan-African causes. Clarke was non-partisan and enjoyed good relations with the left and right Pan-African factions in the 1930s–1940s, and this enabled him to act as a mediator in planning for the Conference on the African Peoples, Democracy, and World Peace held in London in July 1939. Many Caribbean and African visitors to Britain stayed at Clarke's home in Barnet, which was also used for some LCP social functions, for example the reception for the Gold Coast delegation in 1934. In 1945 W. E. B. DuBois stayed with Clarke before and after the 1945 Manchester Pan-African Congress, which both men attended.

Clarke was doctor for many black people in London; he attended George *Padmore in his final illness. From 1954 to 1967 he served on the Council of the British Medical Association, and also as an adviser to the Ghanaian government in the training of doctors. In March 1957 Clarke, with George Padmore and Arthur *Lewis, attended the Ghana independence celebrations. He died on 28 November 1970. DK

Patton, Adell, *Physicians, Colonial Racism and Diaspora in West Africa* (1996)

See also DOCTORS; MEDICINE; PAN-AFRICANISM

Clarkson, Thomas (1760–1846). Campaigner against the slave trade and slavery. Clarkson was educated at the University of Cambridge, where he graduated BA in 1783, but remained to continue his studies in preparation for becoming an Anglican clergyman. In 1785 he decided to enter a university contest for a Latin essay. His aim was simply academic prestige, but the topic, set by the university's Vice-Chancellor, Peter *Peckard, was *Anne liceat invitos in servitutem dare?* ['Is it lawful to make men slaves against their will?']. Clarkson won the prize, but he was so disturbed by what he learnt in preparing his essay that he decided to devote his life to the anti-slavery cause. A revised and enlarged version of his essay was published in English in 1786 under the title *An Essay on the Slavery and Commerce of the Human Species, Particularly the African*, and this went through several editions. Clarkson dismissed all the traditional justifications of slavery and stated bluntly that 'Human liberty can neither be bought nor sold.' The *Essay* enjoyed wide circulation and helped to win William *Wilberforce to the cause.

By 1786 Clarkson had given up the idea of a career in the Church, although he was already in deacon's orders, and the fact that he had a small private fortune enabled him to be a full-time activist. He was a member of the Committee for the Abolition of the Slave Trade, established in 1787, and for a period of seven years travelled throughout England, covering some 35,000 miles on horseback, to promote the cause and to seek out information about the slave trade which could be used in propaganda in favour of *abolition. One of his most important discoveries was the high mortality rate among seamen engaged in the trade, a point which gave the lie to the often repeated argument that the slave trade was of value to the country in providing a reservoir of sailors that could be drawn on by the Royal Navy in time of war.

Exhaustion, the fact that he had spent a great deal of his own money on his travels, and the fact that his known sympathy for the French Revolution was felt to damage the abolitionist cause led Clarkson to retire from an active role in 1794. However, he returned to the struggle again in 1804–7, in the period when abolition was finally achieved. From the time he wrote his *Essay*, he had always been opposed to slavery itself, not just the slave trade, and he gave active support to the *Anti-Slavery Society, formed in 1823. He also campaigned against slavery and the slave trade outside British territory, and was a supporter of the anti-slavery movement in the United States. His many publications on slavery included a two-volume *History of the Rise, Progress, and Accomplishment of the Abolition of the African Slave-Trade by the British Parliament* (1808), which remains of value to modern historians. JG

Hurwitz, Edith F., *Politics and the Public Conscience: Slave Emancipation and the Abolitionist Movement in Britain* (1973)

ODNB

See also UNITED STATES OF AMERICA, BRITAIN, AND ABOLITION

Cochrane, Kelso (d. 1959). West Indian carpenter murdered in Notting Hill by white youths. Britain was particularly racially tense in the late 1950s, when the white working classes felt culturally and economically threatened by the presence of Blacks. Two active political groups in the Notting Hill area were the White Defence League and the National Labour Party, one claiming to be a Nazi group, the other a racial nationalist one. The culmination of the situation were the 'race' riots in 1958 in Notting Hill. The following year saw the murder of Cochrane, an Antiguan who was on his way back from the hospital after having had his broken thumb bandaged. He was stabbed with a knife on 17 May 1959 by six white youths who were never caught. Following Cochrane's murder, the black activist Claudia Jones campaigned for the black community and helped to organize strategies for approaching the government. The riots and Cochrane's murder incited awareness in both black and white communities about the dangers of racism. Gradually, as the 1960s approached, black liberation was becoming a more fortified notion, especially with the birth of the Black Power movement. However, institutions (the police, the media, and national and local authorities) were still discriminatory against Blacks, and they were to face innumerable tribulations in their fight for justice and respect. Cochrane's murder has been seen as the forerunner to the more recent murder of Stephen *Lawrence in 1993. DD/SS

Sherwood, Marika, *Claudia Jones: A Life in Exile* (2000)

See also MACPHERSON REPORT; NOTTING HILL RIOTS; SCARMAN REPORT

Coleridge, Samuel Taylor (1772–1834). English poet who wrote and lectured against slavery. Coleridge's first major poem was a Greek ode against the slave trade, which won him the Browne Gold Medal at Cambridge University. He was to write, 'my Greek ode is, I think, my *chef d'œuvre* in poetical composition'. Coleridge was inspired by the anti-slavery writings of Thomas *Clarkson, and in the 1790s, along with his friend and fellow poet Robert *Southey, began campaigning against the slave trade. During this period Coleridge actively lectured around England, particularly in the West Country and in *Bristol, where he received his first audience. When Coleridge and Southey lived at Upper College Street, Bristol, in 1795, they were surrounded by neighbours who had either had significant seafaring careers or had been captains of slave ships. One of them, for instance, was the captain of a ship that was bound for the Jamaican sugar plantations but was seized before it left the Niger delta. Coleridge would have had first-hand information on the conditions of the ships as well as the intricacies and the mechanism of the trade. His anti-slavery lectures were included in *Lectures, 1795: On Politics and Religion*. Besides those lectures, his poetical writings such as 'Ode to the Departing Year' (1797) and 'Fears in Solitude' (1798) also included attacks on slavery. Although his famous poem 'Rime of the Ancient Mariner' (1798) does not directly deal with slavery, it insinuates it in its depiction of the ill-fated ship, which resembles a vessel of the Middle Passage. Yet, though sympathetic to the plight of slaves, Coleridge denied that Othello could be a veritable negro, thinking a relationship between Desdemona and a black man to be repugnant. DD/SS

Coleridge, S. T., *Lectures, 1795: On Politics and Religion* (ed. Lewis Patton and Peter Mann, 1971)
Dabydeen, D. (ed.), *The Black Presence in English Literature* (1985)

See also BLAKE, WILLIAM; CLARE, JOHN; COWPER, WILLIAM; DAY, THOMAS; WORDSWORTH, WILLIAM

Coleridge-Taylor, Samuel (1875–1912). Celebrated black British composer of international standing. Coleridge-Taylor was born in London in August 1875. His father, Dr Daniel Taylor, came from Sierra Leone to England to study, returning home after qualifying as a doctor without seeing his son. His mother, Alice Hare Martin, raised her illegitimate son in Croydon, Surrey. Later she married George Evans, and by the 1890s they had three children.

Coleridge-Taylor was encouraged to take violin lessons for six years from a local teacher named Joseph Beckwith. He sang in a choir, and participated in concerts organized by Beckwith. It was Colonel Herbert Walters who spotted the boy's gift for music and supported his development. By 1890 he was studying violin with Henry Holmes at the Royal College of Music, as well as having five anthems accepted for publication by Novello at the age of 16.

In 1892 he became a composition student of the renowned Charles Villiers Stanford, continuing with violin and piano lessons and briefly taking organ lessons. His shyness was acute, and he was sensitive to comments about his ethnic origins. He responded to a challenge from Stanford by writing a chamber work using forces that Brahms would use, but eliminating the influences of Brahms. This was the *Clarinet Quintet* (1895), influenced by Dvořák, whom he admired. Stanford praised it, and took the work to Berlin, where his friend Joseph Joachim (1831–1907), the famous violinist, also commended it. Growing recognition for Coleridge-Taylor's achievements were announced in the London newspapers.

On leaving college, he settled in Croydon, beginning life as a professional musician, conducting, performing recitals, and teaching, while being near his mother and the rest of the family.

In the summer of 1896 Coleridge-Taylor met the African-American poet Paul Dunbar in London, intending to read his romantic and dialectic poems. He was the first African-American artist to have an influence on Coleridge-Taylor's aesthetic outlook. With the support of the US Ambassador, John Hay, they collaborated over works for a concert, and Coleridge-Taylor set Dunbar's poems, resulting in *Seven African Romances* (1897), a collection of songs.

Dunbar introduced Coleridge-Taylor to a society of musicians, writers, and artists who were to incubate his nationalistic view of music in the African diaspora. In December 1898 a one-act opera called *The Dream Lovers* was composed by Coleridge-Taylor, Dunbar having written the libretto. It was premiered in Croydon, at a concert by local amateur musicians. The opera was set in Madagascar, with four main roles, for a mulatto prince, Torado, his friend, a quadroon lady, and her sister. This was an extraordinary collaboration for two black artists of the 19th century.

Nevertheless, Coleridge-Taylor was to attain even greater celebrity in the autumn of 1898, when Elgar helped Coleridge-Taylor to receive a commission. He composed the Ballade in A Minor for the Gloucester Three Choirs Festival (1898). The London newspapers related his success. Furthermore, a repeat performance of this work was given on 5 November 1898 at the Crystal Palace, along with music by Elgar, Mozart, Stanford, and Liszt.

It was a week later when, on 11 November 1898, his newly composed work *Hiawatha's Wedding Feast* was premiered at the Royal College of Music, with Stanford conducting, which made Coleridge-Taylor a national celebrity with huge media coverage. This composition is a setting of verses from *The Song of Hiawatha* by the American poet Henry Wadsworth Longfellow.

In 1899 Coleridge-Taylor married Jessie Walmisley, a contralto and pianist and one of his classmates at the Royal College of Music. In the same year, owing to the recent successes of the Ballade and *Hiawatha*, he was commissioned to write new music. He added *The Death of Minnehaha* to the cantata, in a commission for the North Staffordshire Musical Festival in Hanley, premiered in October 1899. The Royal Choral Society commissioned him, so an overture was added, based on the spiritual 'Nobody Knows the Trouble I See' (which he had heard in programmes sung by the *Fisk Jubilee Singers who had toured in the 1870s), and premiered in March 1900 with a choir and orchestra totalling a thousand. A performance of the complete trilogy in 1900 at the Birmingham Festival received a rapturous standing ovation, whereas the first performance of Elgar's *Dream of Gerontius* had a cool reception.

Such was Coleridge-Taylor's celebrity that he was to be invited to tour the United States on three separate occasions, the first in 1904, presenting his *24 Negro Melodies Op. 59, for piano*, and performing *Hiawatha* with a specially established Coleridge-Taylor Choral Society in Washington; there he met the violinist Clarence Cameron White and Booker T. *Washington, and was invited to meet President Roosevelt in the White House. In 1906 he toured extensively, presenting new works such as *The Atonement* (1903), *The Quadroon Girl*, and *Hiawatha*. His last tour of the United States was in 1910, where he was hailed as a role model for black composers and deemed to be 'the black Mahler'.

Success should have enabled a comfortable living for Coleridge-Taylor, but Novello paid him a one-off sum of 15 guineas for the cantata, while earning the largest fortune since Mendelssohn's *Elijah* from the vast number of performances of this work internationally. Instead, Coleridge-Taylor scraped together a living by taking a professorship at Trinity College of Music (1903) and at the Guildhall School of Music (1910), and by private teaching, orchestral and choral conducting, and composing populist parlour music. His premature death from exhaustion and pneumonia, in September 1912, at the age of 37, came about because he had had to undertake several jobs. The Performing Rights Society was formed as a direct result, to defend the rights of composers, as Novello refused to give his distraught widow a just royalty. Henry *Downing, an African-American living in London, pressed Parliament and King George V to provide a Civil List pension for the composer's widow and mother in recognition of the national contribution Coleridge-Taylor had made to music. PAH

Green, Jeffrey, '"The Foremost Musician of His Race": Samuel Coleridge-Taylor of England, 1875–1912', *Black Music Research Journal*, 10/2 (1990)

ODNB

Sayers, W. C. Berwick, *Samuel Coleridge-Taylor Musician: His Life and Letters* (1927)

See also MUSIC 1: CLASSICAL MUSIC

Colonial and Indian Exhibition. Royally commissioned exhibition run between 4 May and 10 November 1886 in South Kensington, London, showcasing India and the colonies of the British Empire. Over 5 million people attended the Exhibition.

The tone of the Exhibition was one of British patriotism, evidenced by a performance of 'Rule Britannia' and a commemorative diploma given to participants depicting female figures representing the colonies paying tribute to Britannia on her throne. A map showing the reach of the British Empire was also displayed in the main hall, as were stereotypical colonial landscapes and trading ships.

Although the objective of the Exhibition was industrial development, exhibits celebrating the natural wealth of the colonies were favoured over those highlighting technological advancements. In addition to an explanation of each display, official Exhibition catalogues contained a list of all the races of the Empire.

The Indian and Ceylonese section was the primary focus and consumed a third of the Exhibition space. Displays were designed to showcase the natural wealth of India and included exhibits of arts, fabrics, tea and coffee, and a geographical and military collection. A replica palace represented Indian royalty, while a facsimile bazaar and native shops complete with Indian artisans plying their trade represented village life. Additional displays included those from Africa, Australia, New Zealand, Canada, and the West Indies. EDS

Hoffenberg, Peter, *An Empire on Display: English, Indian and Australian Exhibitions from the Crystal Palace to the Great War* (2001)

See also GREAT EXHIBITION

Colonial People's Defence Association. Established in October 1950 to foster unity and protect the collective interests of people of the 'coloured race', the Colonial People's Defence Association (CPDA) was concerned with the elimination of all forms of social discrimination. The Association also sought to create a climate of 'understanding' between the 'Negro and other races' in *Liverpool. But, unlike its predecessor, the Colonial Defence Committee, which was led by a racially mixed group, the Association had an all-black leadership. It waged protests against the Colonial Office in opposition to the recommended repatriation of black seamen after the war. A wider objective of its activism was the increased employment opportunities for Blacks in the public sector and the elimination of racist practices in the workplace.

The Association collaborated with and influenced many of the decisions of the Labour councillors on the City Council as well as the Trades Council, especially in terms of monitoring employment practices. In addition to cooperating with the Labour Party, it established links with the Communist Party (*see* COMMUNISM) and trade unions, since many of the members were also trade unionists. Working with the Merseyside West Indian Association, the CPDA waged protests against the closure of the Liverpool branch of the Colonial Office. The Association also helped to find employment and provide legal advice to members of the black community. While the Executive Committee was male-oriented, many of the social workers were women. This imbalance was somewhat rectified by the formation of the General Council of Women within the CPDA, which gave black women greater access to decision-making. ASW

Ramdin, Ron, *The Making of the Black Working Class in Britain* (1987)

See also LASCARS AND BLACK SEAMEN; POLITICS

Colston, Edward (1636–1721). Controversial philanthropist and merchant involved in the *slave trade. He was the Bristol-born son of a *Bristol merchant who spent his early life in London, but it is in Bristol that he is most famous. A staunch Anglican and Tory, he was briefly MP for the city in 1710. His huge donations to church renovation and school building projects, mainly but not exclusively in Bristol, ensured his reputation as the city's greatest benefactor, as his major statue in the centre and his fine tomb by Michael Rysbrack attest. Several Bristol streets, schools, buildings, and venerable local charities still bear his name, and his birthday is still honoured in civic celebrations.

Colston's relevance to black history lies in the fact that he was involved in the British slave trade and in the trade of slave-produced goods. By the 1670s he was a City of London merchant, trading with Spain, Portugal, Italy, and West Africa, and soon after became a member of the *Royal African Company and subsequently served on its management board. He also developed extensive links with the sugar colony of St Kitts. Some argue that his trading activities ranged so widely that he cannot be fairly characterized on the surviving evidence as a major slave trader, but as his role in the Royal African Company has become more widely known, along with his partnership in an early Bristol sugar refinery and his employment of a personal servant who was almost certainly an enslaved African, his reputation has become the subject of divisive debate in the city of his birth. MJD

Dresser, Madge, *Slavery Obscured: The Social History of the Slave Trade in an English Provincial Port* (2001)

ODNB

See also SLAVE TRADE; SLAVERY

Commission for Racial Equality. Statutory body established to combat racial discrimination, and to promote equality of opportunity and good race relations. The Commission for Racial Equality (CRE) was set up under the Race Relations Act 1976 and started its work in June 1977. However, it was in 1965 that the first Race Relations Act in Britain was passed as a first step towards eliminating racial discrimination.

The Race Relations Board, set up under the 1965 Act, coordinated the work of nine regional conciliation committees established to deal with complaints of racial discrimination. The Act dealt only with discrimination in places of public resort, but the majority of complaints received were about employment, housing, and the police. As a result, the second Race Relations Act of 1968 made racial discrimination in employment, housing, and the provision of goods, facilities, and services, including education, unlawful. The Race Relations Board was given powers to investigate complaints and secure redress for the victims of racial discrimination.

The 1968 Act also set up another organization, the Community Relations Commission, to promote good community relations and to deal with the local Community Relations Councils. However, all the research by the mid-1970s showed that the 1968 Act needed strengthening, and therefore the 1976 Act was passed. The scope of the legislation remained similar to the 1968 Act but, in addition to direct discrimination, the concept of indirect discrimination was introduced. According to the Act, direct racial discrimination takes place when a person treats another less favourably on racial grounds. Indirect discrimination occurs when all persons are apparently treated equally, but when a requirement or condition is applied with which a considerably smaller proportion of one racial group can comply as compared with another racial group; when a failure to comply is a detriment; and when the requirement or condition cannot be shown to be justifiable. Under the 1976 Act the CRE was brought into being and the Race Relations Board and the Community Relations Commission were amalgamated into this new organization.

The duties of the CRE under the Act are:

1. to work towards the elimination of discrimination;
2. to promote equality of opportunity and good race relations between persons of different racial groups; and
3. to keep under review the Race Relations Act and to recommend amendments when necessary.

The CRE was given a wider strategic role to identify and deal with discriminatory practices by employers and other organizations. The formal investigation is the main instrument for the exercise of the CRE's strategic role. Any organizations or individuals suspected of discrimination could be instructed to supply information required by the investigation, and a report would be published by the CRE with the results of its deliberations. If discrimination had taken place, the offender would be served with a non-discrimination notice with recommendations how to get rid of discriminatory practices. With direct discrimination against individuals, the victims have access to industrial tribunals for employment cases and county courts for other cases. The CRE also has the power to take action in cases alleging pressure or instructions to discriminate on racial grounds and in cases involving discriminatory advertisements.

In addition to the law enforcement part of the CRE's duties, it also uses other methods to bring about change, and for helping to tackle discrimination and provide equality of opportunity under the 1976 Act. These include codes of practice in employment, housing, and education; ethnic monitoring; and the effective use of research for law enforcement and for policy. The CRE also funds projects of more than 100 Racial Equality Councils under Section 44 of the Race Relations Act (under its Getting Results programme). Since European Union legislation and actions regarding race equality are also becoming important, the CRE is part of the UK Race and Europe Network, working with other European equality bodies.

It was in accordance with its duties under the Act and its experience of using the legislation that in 1985 and 1992 the CRE made recommendations to the Home Secretary for changes to the Act. It argued that the need for effective legislation to promote racial equality is, if anything, greater than it was in 1976. The facts relating to racial disadvantage were known. The degree to which the disadvantage was compounded by discrimination on racial grounds was increasingly well established. However, no action was taken at that time. It was after the publication of the Stephen *Lawrence Inquiry Report in 1999 and following one of its recommendations that the Labour government passed the Race Relations (Amendment) Act 2000, which strengthened and extended the scope of the 1976 Act. This first major reform of the Act extends protection against racial discrimination by public authorities and places a new, enforceable positive duty on bodies such as hospitals, schools, police, local councils, and government ministries. It is hoped that the standards expected of public bodies should influence practice in the private sector. The Home Secretary can add or delete authorities by order, and the CRE expects that a number of authorities will be added to the list over time after Home Office consultation.

The CRE has up to fifteen commissioners including a chairman and two deputy chairmen, all appointed by the Home Secretary. It has a budget of £20 million and has just over 200 staff. In addition to its headquarters in London, it has regional offices in Birmingham, Manchester, Edinburgh, and Cardiff. The CRE produces an annual report which summarizes its activities and is submitted to the Home Secretary. Looking to the future, in May 2004 the government published a White Paper, *Fairness for All*, outlining its proposals to create a single Commission for Equality and Human Rights to replace the existing race, sex, and disability commissions, but the CRE has been given an assurance by the government that it will not join the new Commission at the outset but remain independent until 2009. MA

Commission for Racial Equality, *Reviews of the Race Relations Act* (1985, 1992)

Her Majesty's Stationery Office, *Race Relations Act 1976* (1976)

—— *Race Relations (Amendment) Act 2000* (2000)

See also RACISM

Committee of African Organizations. The most prominent African organization in Britain during the 1960s. The Committee of African Organizations (CAO) was established in London in March 1958 as a result of the desire of Africans in Britain to have a unified organization and because many African organizations had united to oppose the racist legislation that was being introduced into Nyasaland and Rhodesia. The CAO was a union of thirteen constituent organizations, some of them student associations, representing all parts of the African continent. In later years African liberation organizations such as the African National Congress (ANC) also joined, so the CAO may have been the most representative of all British-based African organizations. It was certainly an organization with clear Pan-African aims.

The effort to unite African organizations was led by Alao Aka-Bashorun, a Nigerian student who was the president of both the *West African Students' Union (WASU) and the Nigeria Union. Aka-Bashorun became the first chairman of the CAO. The latter was initially based at the WASU's fourth hostel at Warrington Crescent in south London, but it soon moved its offices to Gower Street in central London, where it shared premises with the surgery of the future Labour peer Dr David *Pitt.

The CAO worked tirelessly to support the anti-colonial struggles that were breaking out in many African countries, and particularly in southern Africa. It held joint meetings with other organizations such as the Movement for Colonial Freedom and the Union of Democratic Control, and with sympathetic MPs, and it organized press conferences and other meetings for visiting African politicians such as Julius Nyerere. It also campaigned for nuclear disarmament and soon became the leading African organization in the country. In 1961 it launched its own publication, *The United Africa.*

The CAO, and Aka-Bashorun in particular, also played a leading role during the aftermath of the infamous *Notting Hill riots and the racist murder of Kelso *Cochrane in 1959. The CAO wrote a letter of protest to the Prime Minister on behalf of all the 'coloured people in the UK', sent a deputation to the Home Secretary, and helped to organize the funeral and a memorial meeting for Cochrane.

The CAO also took the lead in organizing what later became the *Anti-Apartheid Movement in Britain. In June 1959 it responded to a call by the ANC and other South African organizations for an international economic boycott of South African goods. The CAO's boycott subcommittee organized pickets of shops and South Africa House, gained the support of trade unions, and eventually forced even the Labour Party to join the boycott. The subcommittee was subsequently renamed several times. In 1960 it became the Boycott Movement Committee, with over 160 branches, and eventually the Anti-Apartheid Movement. With financial support from Kwame Nkrumah and the government of Ghana the CAO opened its own centre, Africa Unity House, in London in 1960, which soon became an important centre for African politics. In 1960 the CAO held its first All-African Students' Conference, and in 1962 established the All-African Students' Union in Europe, a body that in subsequent years held regular conferences throughout Europe and made plans for a Pan-African Youth Movement.

In 1964 the CAO became the Council of African Organizations. In 1965, at the time of its first congress, which was addressed by *Malcolm X just a few weeks before his assassination, it had a membership of over 30 organizations and claimed to represent over 40,000 Africans. But little is known about the CAO after 1966.

HA

Adi, H., *West Africans in Britain: Nationalism, Pan-Africanism and Communism* (1998)

See also POLITICS

Communism. The body of ideas associated with Marx and later Lenin concerning the need for the revolutionary transformation of existing capitalist society exerted a strong influence on many black people in Britain, especially during the early 20th century. The international communist movement's vocal and persistent opposition to colonialism and racism as well as the movement's struggle for a new socialist world attracted African and Caribbean members and supporters to the Communist Party of Great Britain (CPGB), particularly from the 1920s to the 1970s. From the late 1920s until the Second World War, the CPGB established links with black students and workers in Britain, and through them with their compatriots in Africa and the Caribbean. During the 1930s these links were maintained through the activities of a variety of organizations connected with the CPGB and the international communist movement, such as the League Against Imperialism and its affiliate the *Negro Welfare Association.

Evidence suggests that the first black member of the Party was probably the Cardiff-based leader of the Somali Youth League, Mohamed Tuallah Mohamed, who may have joined the CPGB in 1923. In 1928 the CPGB's work among black seamen and African and Caribbean students was extended by the foundation, under the auspices of the Red International of Labour Unions (Profintern), of the International Trade Union Committee of Negro Workers (ITUCNW). The ITUCNW published the influential *Negro Worker*, containing contributions from activists from Britain and British colonies in Africa and the Caribbean, including Isaac Wallace-Johnson, Jomo Kenyatta, Hubert Critchlow, Arnold Ward, and George *Padmore. Some Africans, including Wallace-Johnson and Kenyatta, were educated in Moscow during the 1920s and 1930s at the Comintern's University of the Toilers of the East. Kenyatta arrived in Britain in 1929 and under CPGB auspices travelled to Moscow. He subsequently wrote for *Labour Monthly* and other CPGB publications. The Sierra Leonean activist Isaac Wallace-Johnson probably came into contact with the British CPGB as a result of its work with black seamen. George Padmore, a Trinidadian, was educated in the United States, where he joined the Communist Party. He was an influential figure among black communists until his expulsion from the movement in 1934. During the early 1930s Padmore was the editor of *Negro Worker* and maintained close contact with black communists in Britain.

The Barbadian Arnold Ward became secretary of the Negro Welfare Association (NWA), formed under the leadership of the CPGB in 1931. The NWA became the main organization of black communists during the 1930s and included among its membership those who were actively organizing black seamen such as Chris Jones in London and Harry O'Connell in Cardiff. During the late 1930s, under the leadership of Peter *Blackman, Desmond Buckle, and others, it established stronger links with anti-colonial organizations in Africa and the Caribbean and exerted an influence on the main black organizations in Britain.

During the Second World War the NWA ceased its activities, but after the war many more black people became involved with the CPGB and the international communist movement, often through the activity of organizations such as the International Union of Students, the World Federation of Democratic Youth, and the World Federation of Trade Unions. In post-war London the CPGB established close links with such organizations as Kwame Nkrumah's West African National Secretariat. In the late 1940s Emile Burns, a leading Party propagandist, was holding classes on Marxism for over 40 West African students. In 1950 alone, over 150 Nigerians joined the Party in London, and special 'Robeson branches', named after the African-American singer and activist Paul *Robeson, were organized to accommodate these new members. Robeson had been closely connected with the CPGB from the 1930s. In 1953 a Nigerian branch was formed as part of efforts to stimulate the formation of a Communist Party in Nigeria. Subsequently a West African Party branch was also established in the capital.

The CPGB also had active links with black people in Liverpool, Manchester, Cardiff, and Birmingham. In post-war Manchester the well-known black boxer Len Johnson was a leading communist who stood in elections for the local council and formed the New International Society, which in both Manchester and Liverpool campaigned against racism in Britain and the United States and in support of anti-colonial struggles in Africa. In Liverpool one of the main communist activists was Ludwig Hesse, a seaman from the Gold Coast. Apparently, attempts were made to form a West African branch of the CPGB in Liverpool, but permission to do so was refused by the CPGB's leadership.

By the early 1950s the CPGB had established a West Indies Committee to coordinate policy on the Caribbean and also organized regular meetings of its West Indian membership. Leading communists of Caribbean origin included Trevor Carter, Chris La Maitre, and Billy Strachan, a former RAF pilot, secretary of the British branch of the Caribbean Labour Congress who edited *Caribbean News* during the post-war period. The Caribbean Labour Congress established branches in Birmingham and Leeds, and on Merseyside. The most well-known black communist in this period was the Trinidadian Claudia *Jones, a member of the Communist Party in the United States who was deported to Britain in 1955 and who was among the most important black activists in Britain until her premature death in 1964.

However, criticism of the CPGB's leadership and politics was rife. There was particular opposition to the CPGB's new programme *The British Road to Socialism*, first introduced in 1951, and its lack of clarity on such issues as racism and the anti-colonial struggle. African members in London resigned membership, leading to the creation of factions and other groupings within and outside the Party. Further disaffection and defections was caused by changes and divisions in the international communist movement in the late 1950s and early 1960s, which even resulted in some expulsions of black members from the CPGB. Since the 1970s communism has no longer commanded as many adherents, but remains an influential doctrine in radical black circles globally. HA

Adi, H., 'West Africans and the Communist Party in the 1950s' in Geoff Andrews, Nina Fishman, and Kevin Morgan (eds.), *Opening the Books: Essays on the Social and Cultural History of British Communism* (1995)

Carter, T., *Shattering Illusions: West Indians in British Politics* (1986)

See also LASCARS AND BLACK SEAMEN

Connor, Edric (1913–1968). Trinidadian actor and singer who settled in Britain in 1944. Two weeks after his arrival he made his debut on BBC radio in *Calling the West Indies*. Connor's appealing voice and charming personality endeared him to the British public, and he became a major television and radio personality. Connor saw himself as an ambassador for Trinidad and promoted Caribbean folk music and dance wherever he could. He married Pearl Nunez (also from Trinidad) in London in 1948.

For almost two decades Connor played featured roles in a number of British and American films, including *Cry, the Beloved Country* (1952) and *Moby Dick* (1956). In 1958, when Paul *Robeson turned down the role of Gower in Shakespeare's *Pericles* for the Stratford Memorial Theatre, he recommended Connor for it. Connor thus became the first black actor to appear in a

Shakespeare season at Stratford upon Avon. He also wanted to become a television producer and director at a time when no black person was employed behind the camera except as a scene shifter, but, even with his credentials, there were no openings. As a Caribbean performer in Britain he was a trailblazer. His wife recalled, 'he died much too young. He hadn't achieved everything he wanted to do. But he moved into this country and took every opportunity he had here . . . to make a lasting mark so that those who came after him would know that it was possible.' SB

Bourne, Stephen, *Black in the British Frame: The Black Experience in British Film and Television* (2nd edn., 2001)

ODNB

See also FILM AND TELEVISION 1: REPRESENTATIONS OF BLACKS; FILM AND TELEVISION 2: FILM-MAKERS AND ACTORS; RADIO

Connor, Pearl (1924–2005). Trinidad-born theatrical agent who settled in Britain in 1948. For nearly half a century this dynamic, outspoken campaigner worked for the recognition and promotion of African and Caribbean arts. In London, in 1948, Pearl Nunez married the Trinidadian folk singer and actor Edric *Connor, and in 1956 they founded the first agency to represent black and other ethnic-minority actors, writers, and film-makers in the 'mother country'. In the early 1960s the Connors were instrumental in setting up the Negro Theatre Workshop, one of Britain's first black theatre companies. The company was best known for productions of Wole Soyinka's *The Road* (1965), first staged for the Commonwealth Arts Festival, and *The Dark Disciples* (1966), a black-cast version of the St Luke Passion, which was chosen to represent Britain at the first World Festival of Black and African Arts in Senegal.

Widowed in 1968, Connor married, in 1971, Joseph Mogotsi, the South African lead singer of the Manhattan Brothers. Together they planned and organized tours throughout the world for black South African singers, dancers, musicians, and actors. Occasionally Connor was called upon to contribute to television and radio documentaries including the BBC's *Black and White in Colour* (1992). Another contributor to that programme, the actress Carmen Munroe, described Connor as 'the mother of us all'. She said, 'Pearl made things happen for us. She took chances. She took risks. She pushed, and we learnt a lot from her, and from the way she handled situations. She stuck her neck out.' SB

Bourne, Stephen, *Black in the British Frame: The Black Experience in British Film and Television* (2nd edn., 2001)

ODNB

See also LITERATURE 3: DRAMA

Constantine, Sir Learie (1901–1971). Cricketer, politician, and broadcaster born into a middle-class family in Trinidad. When he left school, he became a clerk in a local company, a post he held for the next ten years until 1927, the year he married Norma Cox. His father was a good cricketer and Constantine also became an excellent fielder. He played for his school and as a member of the Trinidad team in inter-colonial matches; he was selected for the West Indies team to tour England in 1923, and again in 1928. During that tour Constantine's distinguishing moment came in the match against Middlesex in June 1928 when his skills as bowler, fielder, and scorer enabled the West Indies to defeat their opponents by three wickets. C. L. R. *James wrote of him, 'he took 100 wickets, made 1,000 runs and laid claim to being the finest fieldsman ever'. Constantine was asked by Nelson, a prominent Lancashire League team, if he would become their professional player. He agreed and played for Nelson until 1937. Constantine made his home in Nelson until 1949 and a number of black visitors stayed with him, including his fellow countryman James, who helped him to write his first book, *Cricket and I* (1933). In the 1930s Constantine was among the best-paid sportsmen in Britain. Until 1945 he played in test matches for the West Indies, touring Australia in 1930–1 and also India. He also played cricket for the *League of Coloured Peoples (LCP) team, and for several years organized cricket matches to raise money for the League.

Constantine and his wife experienced racial hostility when they went to live in Nelson. However, their easy manner and graciousness earned them local friends and to some extent his cricketing fame protected them from the kind of abuse that many black people suffered on a daily basis. Early in the *Second World War, while Constantine was working in a solicitor's office in order to be articled, he was asked to serve as a welfare officer for the Ministry of Labour and National Service looking after the interests of West Indian munitions workers and West African seamen in the *Liverpool area. Part of this work involved negotiating with trade unions and employers who refused to accept black people as members or employees. Constantine wrote that older unions, such as the Boilermakers', opposed black workers entering the industry, whereas the electrical unions were more cooperative and black members served their union committees. When 'some firms either refused to take on coloured men, or put endless delays in their way hoping to make them seek work elsewhere', wrote Constantine, 'I used to get the Ministry to press those firms for most urgent delivery of orders, and then they found that they must take some coloured workers or get none of any kind. With urgent work to be done, they were forced to give way.'

In mid-1943 Constantine and his family were involved in an incident of gross racial abuse that made the national headlines. Given special leave to go to London so that he could captain the visiting West Indies team, Constantine booked accommodation and paid a deposit to the Imperial Hotel, and, 'having had unhappy experiences in the past', he also checked that the hotel would accept 'coloured people'. On arrival at the hotel in Russell Square he was told in insulting terms by the woman manager that 'we will not have niggers in the hotel because of the Americans. If they stay tonight, their luggage will be put out tomorrow and the doors locked.' The interests of racially prejudiced white customers were then commonly used as an excuse to exclude non-white people from hotels, restaurants, and dances. Constantine and his family went to another hotel, but he sued the Imperial for breach of contract. The case was heard in June 1944 and Constantine was awarded damages. The incident publicized, but did not bring to an end, racial discrimination in places that served the public, although the LCP and other bodies unsuccessfully demanded legislation to outlaw such behaviour. Constantine's book *Colour Bar* (1954) provides his rather bitter account of prevailing racial prejudice and discrimination in Britain and in the British Empire several years after the end of a war fought partly over racism.

In 1945 Constantine was the only black member of a Dominions team that played against England, but thereafter he ceased to play first-class cricket and worked at an alternative career as a broadcaster, particularly on cricket, and studied to become a lawyer. Awarded the MBE in 1946, he qualified as a barrister and was called to the Bar in 1954. By 1945–6 Constantine was more closely associated with the LCP, for which, over several years, he had raised considerable sums of money through sponsored cricket matches. In 1947, following Harold *Moody's death, he became president of the LCP, but it was not a happy period owing to rival factions and infighting among members. Constantine was asked but refused to stand as the Liberal candidate for Shipley in the general election of 1950. This was not because he was not political; James's judgement was that Constantine's deep convictions meant that he 'had always been political'. Those interests found expression in Trinidad, when he returned to live in his home island in 1954. Constantine became chairman of the People's National Movement, was elected to the legislative council, and in 1956 made Minister for Communications, Works, and Utilities in Eric Williams's administration. Williams was a difficult man to work with, and Constantine was pleased to be appointed as Trinidad and Tobago's first High Commissioner to London in 1961. Even in that post he encountered some problems: Williams was not happy when he accepted a knighthood in 1962; and with many Caribbean migrants coming to Britain, Constantine probably exceeded his diplomatic role when he intervened in a case of racial discrimination in a Bristol bus dispute. Having resigned as High Commissioner, Constantine remained in Britain and was flattered to become a member of Sir Dingle Foot's legal chambers. He continued to broadcast on the BBC and became a governor of the Corporation in 1968. Earlier he had become a member of the Sports Council (1965) and the newly created Race Relations Board (1966); he was elected Rector of St Andrews University in 1967. In 1969 he became a peer as Lord Constantine of Maraval and Nelson, the first member of the House of Lords of African descent. DK

Howat, G., *Learie Constantine* (1975)
James, C. L. R., *Beyond a Boundary* (1963)
ODNB

See also POLITICS; SPORT

Coree the Saldanian (d. 1627). Reluctant early 17th-century Khoikhoi immigrant to Britain, tragically manipulated by the East India Company. Coree was taken from the area around the Cape of Good Hope (then known as Saldania) in southern Africa, and unwillingly brought to Britain. He and a companion both suffered the misfortune of being captured after boarding Gabriel Towerson's East India Company ship *Hector*, but of the two, only Coree survived the voyage. The cause of his fellow captive's death was recorded, unconvincingly, as being due to 'extreme sullenness'. On his arrival in Britain, Coree was placed in the household of a merchant and then governor of the East India Company, Sir Thomas Smith. It was hoped that Coree would provide the company with useful information about his homeland and, as a result, he was relatively well treated with accommodation, food, fine vestments, and even a suit of armour. However, according to Peter Fryer, upon learning the English language, the miserable Coree did little more than express his desperate desire to return home, frequently imploring 'Cooree home goe, Souldania goe, home goe'. On his repatriation, despite immediately tearing off his European clothing, Coree did subsequently negotiate with his Khoikhoi compatriots on behalf of British trading interests. This act of exclusive loyalty resulted in the harshest of responses from the Dutch, who, frustrated by his refusal to trade with them, executed Coree in 1627. CMC

Debrunner, H. W., *Presence and Prestige* (1978)
Fryer, Peter, *Staying Power: The History of Black People in Britain* (1984)

Country houses. In the 18th century 'West Indians' were among the great patrons of art and architecture. 'West Indians' is an 18th-century term for wealthy absentee Caribbean sugar planters and merchants who, unlike mainland American plantation owners, chose to live in Britain. They were predominantly, but not uniquely, of white British origin, as fathers of mixed-race children would sometimes send them to live with British relatives or to boarding school in England. Nathaniel *Wells, mixed-race heir to several plantations in St Kitts and owner of Piercefield Park in Monmouthshire, was one such person, described by a contemporary as 'a West Indian of large fortune, a man of very gentlemanly manners, but so much a man of colour as to be little removed from a Negro'.

West Indians were notorious in 18th-century Britain for their conspicuous wealth, coarse, flamboyant manners, and love of turtle soup. Sir Peter Pepperpot, the hero of *The Patron*, a comedy written by Samuel Foote in 1764, is introduced by the play's narrator as 'a West Indian of overgrown fortune. He saves me the trouble of a portrait' (Act I scene i). Of course, the caricature of the West Indian concealed the complexities of the Caribbean sugar business. While some absentees came from established colonial families of several generations on the islands, a sojourn in the West Indies was an alternative to the East India Company as a means for a young British man to make a fortune. And, following the Seven Years War (1756–63), a sugar plantation was seen as a profitable, if risky, part of an investment portfolio for the banking families of the nascent British Empire.

In *Capitalism and Slavery* (1944) Eric *Williams argued that Britain's Industrial Revolution was funded from the proceeds of Caribbean sugar plantations and the slave trade. However, more recent scholarship has shown that during the period 1700–1836, when West Indian influence in Britain was at its height, slave-generated capital was invested into colonial enterprises and into British country estates rather than manufacturing industry.

As befitting their position as 'gentleman landowners', wealthy West Indians were prominent patrons of British art, architecture, and landscape design. Several of the architect Robert Adam's patrons had Caribbean connections, including Edwin Lascelles, William Pultney, and the Jamaican plantation owner William *Beckford. Many of J. M. W. Turner's early watercolour paintings were for West Indians, including William Beckford, Jr. (*see* WILLIAM THOMAS BECKFORD), John Boyd, Edward Lascelles, and the Jamaican absentee Rose Fuller.

But it was in the area of landscape gardening that West Indian wealth had most effect upon British culture. Absentees were instrumental in the introduction of new ornamental species from the colonies into Britain. For example, William Beckford established an 'American garden' in his estate at Fonthill. But it was not just the introduction of 'exotic' species that marked West Indian patronage. Edwin Lascelles at Harewood in Yorkshire, heir to plantations in Barbados, was an early patron of Lancelot 'Capability' Brown and his fashionable 'natural' style of landscape gardening. Other West Indians, such as John Boyd of Danson in Bexleyheath and William Young of Delafield in Buckinghamshire, also created a similar parkland style of landscape—grassland dotted with clumps of trees—on their own estates. Indeed, the mid-18th-century craze for the extravagant transformation of British farmland into 'lawns' of 70 or more acres of low-intensity—and thus low-income—grazing may well have signified that the owner had an alternative income source from colonial trade or investments.

West Indian investment was also instrumental in establishing 'tourism' in the west of Britain. The Antiguan absentee Valentine Morris created the cliff walks at Piercefield near Chepstow, just across the Severn from the Atlantic port of *Bristol, in the early 1750s. Regarded by fashionable visitors from *London, Bath, and Bristol as a model of Edmund Burke's ideas of the 'Sublime' they were to become one of the most visited and influential gardens of 18th-century Britain. By the end of the century a boat trip down the river Wye to see Piercefield's cliffs and the nearby ruins of Tintern Abbey was a popular 'tourist' route and the subject of William *Wordsworth's well-known poem 'Lines composed a few miles above Tintern Abbey' (1798).

John Pennant, the son of a Liverpool merchant and heir to Jamaican estates, encouraged tourism in the mountains of North Wales by the construction of several roads through his estate at Penrhyn near Anglesey. Many West Indians invested in new turnpike roads, indeed frequently providing the capital required for the necessary Turnpike Acts in Parliament. It is clear that Pennant's original interest in road-building was to improve communication to his quarries and to ports dealing with Irish trade, but that he quickly realized the potential for tourism, building hotels and new sections of road to allow access to Mount Snowdon itself.

Pennant and Morris were not the only West Indian plantation owners to invest in the Wye Valley and North Wales. Indeed, given the propensity of Caribbean estate owners and merchants to invest in land near the major 'West Indian' ports of London, Bristol, *Liverpool, *Whitehaven, and *Glasgow, their financial abilities to absorb agriculturally unproductive British land, and their propensity for road-building, it can be argued that some of the most 'scenic' areas of Britain, including the Wye Valley, Snowdonia, the Lake District, and the Highlands, owe their status as tourist destinations to Caribbean investment. While slavery's profits may not have provided the fuel for Britain's Industrial Revolution, they helped to transform Britain's upland landscapes and the way they were seen and appreciated. VJP

Morgan, K., *Slavery, Atlantic Trade and the British Economy 1660–1800* (2000)

Whateley, Thomas, *Observations on Modern Gardening* (1770)

Williams, Eric, *Capitalism and Slavery* (1944)

See also BEAUTY, CONCEPTS OF; CARIBBEAN, BRITISH COLONIES IN THE; WEST INDIA INTEREST

Cowper, William (1731–1800). English poet who lent his pen to the anti-slavery cause. Cowper was a supporter of international commerce, which he saw, idealistically, as the means by which mankind could share in God's bounty. In his poem *Charity* (1782), trade is described as 'the golden girdle of the globe', and Cowper writes of the 'genial intercourse' between nations effected by 18th-century mercantile activity. The slave trader, however, betrays the principle of mutuality underpinning international commerce and brings shame to a Christian nation such as Great Britain ('Canst thou, and honour'd with a Christian name | Buy what is woman-born, and feel no shame?'). Religion apart, the slave trader also betrays the spirit of the age, its growing championing of liberty. To Cowper, the existence of slavery calls into question the very nature of humanity:

> Then what is man? And what man, seeing this
> And having human feelings, does not blush
> And hang his head in shame, to think himself a man?
>
> (*The Task*, 1784)

It was such insistence on the humanity of Africans that characterized the Anti-Slavery Movement in the 1780s and created the iconic medallion of 1787, manufactured by Josiah *Wedgwood, with its powerful question 'Am I not a man and a brother?' To popularize his message Cowper, at the suggestion of his friend the Revd John *Newton (once a slave ship captain before becoming an evangelical minister) composed anti-slavery lyrics that could be set to the tune of popular songs and sung in taverns or on the streets. These anti-slavery ballads differ from the more formal and elitist verse produced by anti-slavery poets, with its limited readership. In the simplicity of their language and emotional appeal, Cowper's ballads constitute an important effort to spread anti-slavery sentiment among the common people. DD

Newton, John, *Thoughts Upon the African Slave Trade* (1788)

See also ABOLITION; BLAKE, WILLIAM; CLARE, JOHN; COLERIDGE, SAMUEL TAYLOR; DAY, THOMAS; SOUTHEY, ROBERT; WORDSWORTH, WILLIAM

Craft, Ellen (1826–1891)**, and Craft, William** (1824–1900). Enslaved married abolitionists whose self-liberation from *slavery in Georgia to freedom in England represents one of the most daring escapes from American enslavement. In 1848 light-skinned Ellen conceived a plan to escape by cutting her hair, donning male clothing, and 'passing' as a southern white male slaveholder travelling to the North for medical treatment, while her darker-skinned husband William posed as a faithful slave valet. After a dangerous journey through the South, the couple reached Boston, where their story of escape made them causes célèbres in abolitionist circles. With the fugitive slave William Wells *Brown, the Crafts gave a series of anti-slavery lectures throughout New England. Their freedom was threatened, however, by the passing of the 1850 Fugitive Slave Law, which provided for the return of fugitive slaves to their masters in the South, and also mandated the assistance of northerners in the fugitives' capture. In November 1850 the couple evaded attempts by agents of their former master to recapture them and fled to England. Settling in London, the Crafts continued working with anti-slavery organizations, and toured England and Scotland to denounce American slavery. In June 1851 they staged a demonstration against slavery at the *Great Exhibition, and in 1860 published *Running a Thousand Miles for Freedom*, the narrative of their daring escape. In 1868, following the American Civil War, the Crafts returned to the United States.

CJ

Craft, William, and Craft, Ellen, *Running a Thousand Miles for Freedom* (1860)

ODNB

Sterling, Dorothy, *Black Foremothers: Three Lives* (1998)

See also SLAVERY

Crime and black people (*c*.1700–*c*.1800). Most work done on black people and the law in the 18th century concentrates on the handful of cases in which the question of the legality of slavery in England and Wales was brought to court, most notably the *Somerset* case, which led to the landmark Mansfield judgment. Black people were, however, involved in cases in lower courts, both criminal and civil.

Before the systematic collection of statistics in the 20th century it is impossible to know how many black people were involved in criminal trials or civil hearings because colour and ethnic origin were rarely recorded in the court papers. These factors had no legal significance.

1. Trials at the Old Bailey
2. Defendants
3. Prosecutors
4. Other information from trial reports

1. Trials at the Old Bailey There is, however, a unique source of information about the involvement of black people as defendants, prosecutors, and witnesses in criminal trials in the London area, where the black population was largest. Transcripts of proceedings at the Old Bailey, where various courts, notably the Crown Court for Middlesex and the Crown Court for the City of London, sat, were published between the middle of the 17th century and 1834, when it became the Central Criminal Court. Outside London the black population was much smaller and, though there are occasional references in newspaper accounts to the appearance of black individuals in trials, the numbers here are so small that no valid conclusions about their treatment by provincial courts can be drawn.

At least 120 black people, both of African origin and from the Indian subcontinent, appeared at the Old Bailey before the 19th century. It is not always possible to distinguish between the races because descriptions of colour or ethnic origin are often imprecise and the word 'black' was regularly used to describe any dark-skinned person, including people of British and European origin. In some cases no mention of colour or ethnic origin was made in the *Proceedings* but can be recovered from other sources, like prison records or newspaper reports, or deduced from witnesses' evidence. Nevertheless, the total number of black participants and their ethnicity remain uncertain.

2. Defendants The most common crime with which black people were charged was theft, sometimes aggravated by assault. None was indicted for any crime resulting from cultural practices like scarification of children, polygamy, or female circumcision.

Even allowing for their smaller numbers in the country and the generally fewer numbers of female criminals, black women seem to have been exceptionally law-abiding: only nine were charged with a crime. This number is too small to make any conclusions about their treatment valid.

Over the whole period of the 18th century black men were apparently more likely to be found guilty of the crime with which they were charged and not to have the charge reduced or to be acquitted. Since it is probable that not all have been identified, this conclusion is tentative. Such apparent discrimination may reflect the lack of an influential support network in this country as sentences passed on the general population depended on factors like testimony from character witnesses or the willingness of respectable citizens to take responsibility for a malefactor's future conduct. The percentage of black people on whom the death penalty was passed and carried out is apparently the same as for the rest of the population.

3. **Prosecutors** Black prosecutors displayed confidence in using the courts. There were procedures in lower courts to go through before reaching the Old Bailey, which suggests that there were sources of support and advice for those not familiar with the system. Crimes committed against black prosecutors were overwhelmingly simple theft. None apparently was the victim of burglary, suggesting a lack of householders among the black population.

Verdicts on those who committed crimes against black people seem to have been broadly the same as the verdicts passed in cases involving only the indigenous population, but again the difficulty of identifying all black people in the records makes this a tentative conclusion.

4. **Other information from trial reports** Of great interest are the glimpses into the lives of black people that emerge from the evidence. Although people from the Indian subcontinent used translators, no one of African origin seems to have been offered one: this may reflect the difficulty of finding a translator for the many African languages, or the fact that those who came to court had an adequate grasp of English. Foreigners were also entitled to a jury consisting of half their countrymen. Again this was not offered to, or demanded by, any of the black defendants at the Old Bailey. At least one swore on the Koran rather than the Bible.

In only one case is slavery mentioned. That man had been a slave in the West Indies but had come to England as a seaman and the court regarded him as free. Most seem to have been servants. From evidence given it seems that a number had moved from one employer to another, or were between posts. The next largest number were mariners in the Royal Navy or on merchant ships. Besides servants and mariners, there were soldiers and musicians as well as a number carrying out semi-skilled jobs or general labour. There was even at least one black man involved in the administration of the law: in 1746 the parish constable of St James Clerkenwell was described as a 'negro'. The few women who came into contact with the court seem to have been servants or prostitutes. However, the occupations of many, both male and female, are unknown.

In evidence from white witnesses transcribed in the *Proceedings*, there seems to be no evidence of stereotyping. Nor did contemporary newspaper reports of court cases involving black people in either London or the provinces contain any editorial comment that might suggest that the general population viewed them as more or less law-abiding than the average person.

KAC

Myers, Norma, 'Thief, Victim, Witness, Transportee: The Black Presence Through Criminal Records' in Myers, *Reconstructing the Black Past: Blacks in Britain, 1780–1830* (1996)

Proceedings of the Old Bailey <http://www.oldbaileyonline.org.>

See also CRIMINAL JUSTICE SYSTEM

Criminal justice system. As with other aspects of British society, black people have had a long and sometimes difficult and contentious relationship with the criminal justice system.

1. Historical background
2. The *Empire Windrush* and after

1. **Historical background** There has been a notable black presence in Britain since the 16th century, but it is difficult to chart the interactions of black people in any collective sense since black immigrants were dispersed throughout the country and there were no established or distinct black communities. The number of black people in Britain increased alongside the expansion of British involvement with the slave trade. One important result was that a number of major legal cases involving black people focused on issues relating to the slave trade.

Blacks present in Britain throughout the 17th and 18th centuries were something of a legal enigma and as the slave trade intensified, they came to be viewed as legal anomalies. The **Somerset* case of 1772 had established that black slaves in Britain could not be forcibly removed from the country, but this was a theoretical victory since in reality black slaves could only hope to access rights at the whim of their owners. Even 'free' Blacks could not expect to enjoy recourse to justice in the manner it was afforded to white people. Nevertheless, the *Somerset* case did highlight a shift in attitudes and hinted at increasing recognition of the need to legislate in a manner that acknowledged the place of Blacks in society.

The legal status of Blacks in Britain remained uncertain prior to the Abolition of the Slave Trade Act 1807, when slave-trading in the British Isles became illegal. This was followed many years later by the 1833 Abolition Act, which came into force in 1834.

In the latter part of the 20th century, and in contrast to an era when Blacks in Britain remained on the fringes of the legal system, mass immigration meant that they had now become an integral part of British society and therefore of its criminal justice system. Today black people have a range of interactions with the criminal justice system, which sees them upholding, enforcing, shaping, challenging, and falling foul of the law.

2. The *Empire Windrush* and after The history of the black presence in Britain provides the context within which to explore the developments of the 20th century. There is undoubtedly some correlation between the establishment of black communities in Britain and legislative changes. This can be partly illustrated by consideration of what has been called the *Windrush* era.

The arrival in 1948 of the SS **Empire Windrush* at Tilbury docks in Kent heralded the start of a mass migration of black Caribbeans that would continue over the next fifteen years. On reaching Britain, the new immigrants soon found that access to employment, housing, and good-quality education was not to be taken for granted, and this period of displacement and the subsequent struggles set the scene for later tensions between state institutions and black people. Research at the beginning of the 21st century highlighted unemployment as the key factor influencing individual decisions to offend. Other primary factors such as poverty, poor education, and accommodation have also been cited.

In 1958 race riots took place in Notting Hill, London, and the city of Nottingham. Although the violence and disorder carried out by the minority group was largely regarded as being a reaction to their circumstances, these events inflamed fear and hostility among the indigenous majority. By the 1970s the American term 'mugging' was adopted by media and was used by the prominent MP Enoch *Powell to refer to a form of robbery of which black men were considered the main perpetrators. In the 1980s more riots occurred, in *Bristol (1980), *Brixton and *Liverpool (1981), and *Birmingham (1985). Unlike the previous riots, these were not focused on racists within the community but were largely initiated by increasing hostility between young Blacks and the police. The former blamed the police for misusing their powers under Section 4 of the Vagrancy Act 1824, colloquially known as the *'Sus Law', to stop and search black youths deemed to be acting in a suspicious manner.

By the end of the 20th century black people had made positive contributions to the criminal justice system in the form of lawyers, magistrates, and offender managers (formerly called probation officers), among others. Nevertheless, the overriding concern remained the over-representation of Blacks as offenders and their under-representation as prominent law-enforcers.

While the relationship between black people and the criminal justice system has been fraught with difficulties, there have been triumphs in the form of measures taken to redress perceived injustices. One example is the implementation of the Race Relations (Amendment) Act 2000, which imposed a duty on institutions within the system to promote racial equality. In addition, a new code was prepared to accompany the Police and Court Evidence Act 1984, supported by the Stop and Search Action Team, in order to ensure that police powers of stop and search were used in a fair and effective manner.

Concerns remained over the disproportionate use of custodial sentencing for black offenders compared with their white counterparts. This was most apparent within the female prison population—a result partly of foreign women being recruited as drug couriers. Much attention was also focused on the drug and gun crime culture in urban black communities, many of the key offenders being Jamaican nationals. Consequently, leaders from black minority ethnic communities were invited to join strategy groups such as Trident in order to address these issues. Recognition of the international nature of modern crime prompted transnational initiatives such as the reciprocal recruitment of policing personnel between Britain and Jamaica.

These new legislative and policy measures suggest that the criminal justice system was becoming more aware of its impact on black people, and that there was now a commitment to forging more positive relationships between law enforcers and black communities. AS

Chigwada-Bailey, R., *Black Women's Experiences of Criminal Justice: Race, Gender and Class: A Discourse of Disadvantage* (2003)

Hood, R., *Race and Sentencing* (1992)

See also NEW CROSS FIRE; SCARMAN REPORT

Crowther, Samuel Ajayi (*c.*1807–1891). The first African bishop of the Church of England in West Africa. An Egba, he was born in Yorubuland and enslaved as a teenager, but rescued by a British ship and landed at the British settlement of Freetown. He was the first liberated African to be formally educated at the Church Missionary Society (CMS) grammar school, Freetown. Crowther became a Christian and was baptized in 1825, taking the name of an English clergyman. From 1825 to 1827 he was in London studying at the Islington parish school.

On his return to West Africa, Crowther trained at the Fourah Bay Institute, Freetown, and became a schoolteacher. His linguistic abilities and reputation for a devout life led the CMS to suggest he join the British Niger expedition in 1841 as an interpreter. The expedition failed to achieve its purpose of planting an agricultural settlement of liberated slaves, promoting trade, and combating the slave trade, but Crowther's written account of the expedition so impressed the CMS that they invited him to Britain to study for the Christian ministry. He was ordained in 1843 and returned to Freetown as a missionary. In 1845 he went to southern Nigeria as a member of a mission party to evangelize Yorubuland. In the course of this mission Crowther met and baptized his elderly mother.

Crowther was a good linguist and was largely responsible for translating the Bible into Yoruba. During a visit to Britain in 1851 he was promoted by the CMS as a model African leader for a self-governing, self-supporting, and self-propagating church in Africa. This was demonstrated in the new mission that he opened in Nigeria in 1857, which was staffed entirely by Africans, and in Crowther's ordination in Canterbury Cathedral in 1864 as 'Bishop of the countries of Western Africa beyond the Queen's dominions'. He extended missionary activity and translation work in southern Nigeria, but in the 1880s his diocesan authority and his African clergy were increasingly criticized by a new group of evangelical British missionaries imbued with ideas of racial superiority. Crowther's authority and integrity was questioned and his diocese dismantled; he died of a stroke and was succeeded by a white bishop. DK

Ajayi, J. F. A., *Christian Missions in Nigeria 1841–1891: The Making of a New Elite* (1965)

—— *A Patriot to the Core: Samuel Ajayi Crowther* (1992)

ODNB

See also CHRISTIANITY; CHURCHES; MISSIONARY SOCIETIES

Cuffay, William (1788–1870). Journeyman tailor and prominent leader of the Chartist movement. Cuffay was born in Chatham, Kent. His father, originally from St Kitts, had come to Britain on a British warship. Cuffay became a journeyman tailor in his teens, but involvement in the strike by the Grand National Consolidated Trades Union in 1834 resulted in the loss of his job. Angered by this, he joined the movement in support of the People's Charter, advocating universal suffrage. He was militant in his left-wing views, and in 1839 contributed to the founding of the Metropolitan Tailors' Charter Association. He also became a member of the Masters and Servants Bill Demonstration Committee, which opposed the power given to magistrates to imprison employees for two months based solely on the employer's statements. His involvement in the Chartist movement grew, and in 1842 he was elected the president of the London Chartists. He was one of three London delegates to the National Chartists' Convention in 1848, which sought to organize a march in London to present a Chartists' petition to the House of Commons. The march was called off, much to Cuffay's dismay. Later that year he was accused by government spies of planning to set fire to buildings to signal an uprising. He was convicted and sentenced to 21 years in Tasmania (then Van Diemen's Land). Although he was pardoned three years later, Cuffay chose to remain in Tasmania, involving himself in trade unions and radical politics. He died in poverty in 1870. DD/SS

Fryer, Peter, *Staying Power: The History of Black People in Britain* (1984)

Goodway, David, *London Chartism 1838–1848* (1982)

ODNB

Cuffee, Paul (1759–1817). Mixed-race American sea captain who, as a champion of the abolition movement, journeyed to Britain in 1811 to meet sympathetic friends from the *African Institution. Cuffee (also spelt Cuff, Cuffe, Cuffey) was born in Massachusetts to a manumitted slave, Cuffee Slocum, and a Native American, Ruth Moses. A committed Quaker, Cuffee was impassioned about the redemption of Africa: he aligned himself with the Colonization Society of America and the idea of a return to Africa of free African-Americans. To this end, as a means of cutting off the slave trade at its source, Cuffee made two trips to Sierra Leone (*see* SIERRA LEONE SETTLERS). To discuss his views on abolition and colonization with friends from the African Institution, Cuffee sailed to Britain, docking in Liverpool in 1811. Here and in London he met fellow abolitionists, including the Duke of Gloucester, who was president of the African Institution, as well as slave traders and ex-slave traders. Cuffee presented the Duke of Gloucester with African artefacts, 'to show that the Africans were capable of mental endowments and so forth', he wrote in his journals. He sailed on from England to Sierra Leone, arriving in November 1811, to spend three months there before sailing home. He returned in 1815 to Sierra Leone with 38 African-American colonists. His early death at 58 prevented him from fully realizing his mission. JPo

Cobb Wiggins, Rosalind, *Captain Paul Cuffee's Logs and Letters, 1808–1817: A Black Quaker's 'Voice from Within the Veil'* (1996)

Sherwood, Henry Noble, 'Paul Cuffe', *Journal of Negro History*, 8/2 (1923)

See also CHRISTIANITY; GARVEY, MARCUS

Cugoano, Quobna Ottobah (b. 1757). Writer, denunciator of slavery, and leader of Africans in Britain. Cugoano was born in the Fanti Country of the Gold Coast, which today is part of Ghana. He was kidnapped and enslaved as a child through 'some treachery' by 'several great ruffians', and shipped to Grenada, where he began his work as a slave. After some time in the West Indies, he was taken to England by his master and freed. In order to avoid future enslavement, Cugoano converted to Christianity and took the name John Stewart. In the 1780s he became friendly with the political leader, writer, and abolitionist Olaudah *Equiano, and together they joined the abolitionist group Sons of Africa, in which they contributed to the fight against slavery. Cugoano became acquainted with the abolitionist Granville *Sharp and collaborated with him in the struggle to rescue black people in Britain from being kidnapped and sold into slavery in the Americas.

In 1787 Cugoano wrote and published a powerful condemnation against the practice of slavery, *Thoughts and Sentiments on the Evil and Wicked Traffic of the Slavery and Commerce of the Human Species*. In the book Cugoano uses Christian logic to challenge the justification of slavery by Europeans. A simple yet strong argument put forward by him concerns the value of Christian virtues such as loving one's neighbour, empathy, and humanity amidst the horrors of slavery. Furthermore, supposedly civilized nations that were rich in culture, science, and the arts were the perpetrators of the fate of 'the poor unfortunate Black People'. It becomes useless to boast of the 'advantages of light, learning, knowledge, and civilisation', he wrote, if in contradiction barbarities were carried out. He also denounced apologists of slavery who exploited Christian doctrines to validate the practice of slavery.

Thoughts and Sentiments is written in intimate and rhetorical tones that produce varying effects throughout the text, and as a consequence some have disputed the idea that Cugoano wrote the entire manuscript. Bearing in mind his education, and his political and economic awareness, it is likely that he would have possessed the intellectual capacity to produce arguments of the sort that appear in the book, but it has been suggested that *Thoughts and Sentiments* was written with the help of Equiano. This is more than likely as the two men experienced similar struggles, inclinations, and ambitions, namely the abolition of slavery. Both aimed to dispel the notion of African compliance with their predicament, and Cugoano equated the perpetrators of the African slave trade to robbers who had stolen not only men but the right of freedom from Africans. Additionally, he disputed the belief that African slaves were more advantaged than the most disadvantaged in Europe, stressing that slavery was one of the greatest acts of villainy and accusing slave owners of being unfit to be Christians. Their final judgement, he wrote, would be in the hands of God. Nations that engaged in the practice of slavery would also receive the anger and punishment of God. Although Cugoano believed that God would be the ultimate purveyor of truth and justice, he argued that slaves should not be the passive victims of theft and cruelty. Instead they should react and rebel against their predicament because it was their right to do so.

Cugoano focused on the role and duties of Britain in, firstly, the propagation of slavery and, secondly, its obligation to abolish it. As a nation that advocated virtues such as liberty, justice, morality, humanity, and equality, there was no justification for its involvement in barbarous practices that contradicted such virtues. Britain had to reclaim its prior possession of morality and Christian conduct. Cugoano suggested a plan that might aid the freedom of enslaved Africans. While this plan was open to whichever nation was fit to put it into practice, he anticipated Britain's leading role in its initiation. The plan demonstrates a sharp economic awareness in its support for the notion of free labour, not merely on humane grounds but on financial ones as well. In line with Adam Smith's famous argument that free labour was cheaper than slave labour, Cugoano stated that employers of free labourers would not have to contribute to the welfare of their workers. Moreover, production levels would be higher as Africans would be in a position to enjoy the benefits of their labour.

While he praised British efforts to establish a free colony in Sierra Leone, he questioned the viability of such a project in view of Britain's involvement in the slave trade in other African regions. What he demanded from the perpetrators of slavery and its trade was loyalty to Christian philosophy, which, supposedly, formed the basis of their religious lives. He attacked them for their hypocrisy but extolled those who condemned slavery. One of the first few sentiments in his book is congratulatory. He lauds 'several learned gentlemen of distinguished abilities, as well as eminent for their great humanity, liberality and candour, [for having] written various essays against that infamous traffic of the African Slave Trade'.

In 1788 Cugoano's book was translated into French, and in 1791 a shorter version of *Thoughts and Sentiments* was published. In the latter text, Cugoano proposed the establishment of a school for Blacks who wanted a Christian education. Nothing, however, is known of Cugoano or his efforts beyond this point. It has been stated that he married an Englishwoman, but there is no substantial record of this. He remains a figure of historical significance in the fight to abolish slavery, being the first African denunciator of slavery to be published and one of the first to demand the abolition of slavery. DD/SS

Carey, Brycchan, *British Abolitionism and the Rhetoric of Sensibility: Writing, Sentiment and Slavery, 1760–1807* (2005)

ODNB

Ogude, S. E., *Genius in Bondage* (1983)

Woodward, H., *African British Writings in the Eighteenth Century* (1999)

See also LITERATURE 2: FICTION AND POETRY

Cunard, Nancy (1896–1965). Journalist and activist born to wealthy parents, against whom she rebelled. Cunard became well-known in the London modernist movement, and throughout the busiest period in her career, the 1930s, was a controversial advocate of black emancipation in the United States and Africa.

At 855 pages long, weighing nearly 8 pounds, with 150 contributors, the *NEGRO* anthology of 1934 was Cunard's most ambitious publication: a collection of essays, polemics, and poetry from France, Britain, and America designed to highlight the vibrancy of the black world and to lobby for black freedom. Writers of interest include the future African presidents Jomo Kenyatta and Nnamdi Azikiwe, the Pan-Africanists George *Padmore and W. E. B. DuBois, the black modernist novelist Zora Neale Hurston, and the poets Nicolás Guillen, Langston Hughes, Sterling Brown, Countee Cullen, Alain Locke, William Carlos Williams, Ezra Pound (who confessed he 'should have more respect for the Afro-American intelligentzia and for the Negro millionaires, etc., that are rumoured to flourish in Harlem if they had shown more alacrity in hearing of' Leo Frobenius, 'an author who has shown their race its true character of nobility'), and Edgell Rickword (who provided a digest of Anti-Slavery Movement papers). There is also a Communist manifesto signed by French surrealists, including André Breton. Most striking are Samuel Beckett's vigorous translations from the French of music journalism and poems on Louis Armstrong. Though dated, it will be seen that *NEGRO* marked a significant coming together of modernist intellectuals on behalf of Africans in the diaspora. Most of the 1,000 copies printed were destroyed during the Blitz.

The impetus for the book was provided by Cunard's lover the African-American jazz pianist Henry Crowder, whom she met in Paris in the mid-1920s. In 1928 he moved to England to work at her publishing company, the Hours Press (later publishing his musical scores to poems by Beckett and Richard Aldington), prompting a row with Lady Maud Cunard which resulted in Nancy being disinherited. The socialite's revenge was to publish a pamphlet, 'Black Man and White Ladyship', portraying her mother as a racist, in 1931.

The same year the couple travelled to America to make contact with black intellectuals such as Locke. *NEGRO* was under way, though the relationship with Henry had become strained and difficult. During a second research trip, undertaken alone in 1932, Cunard was vilified widely in the US press for 'amatory relations with Negroes'. The £1,500 she gained in out-of-court legal settlements funded the publication of *NEGRO* by Wishart and Company.

Much of Cunard's ensuing work during the period shows a concern for black and left-wing causes. She reported from Geneva on the League of Nations debates on Abyssinia, and in the late 1930s she worked in Spain, covering the Civil War for the Associated Negro Press, the *Manchester Guardian*, and Sylvia Pankhurst's **New Times and Ethiopian News*. A trip to the Caribbean in 1938 led to her internment on Ellis Island. Her wartime activities included a spell in London, translating for the Free French and co-writing *The White Man's Duty* with Padmore. Cunard died in 1965. JM

Cunard, Nancy, *NEGRO* (abridged, ed. Hugh Ford, 1970)

Davey, Kevin, *English Imaginaries: Anglo-British Approaches to Modernity* (1998)

North, Michael, *The Dialect of Modernism: Race, Language and Twentieth-Century Literature* (1994)

See also PUBLISHING

Cunningham, Laurie (1956–1989). Footballer born on 8 March 1956 in London. A winger, Cunningham played for Haringey Schools and South-East Counties Schools before joining Leyton Orient in July 1974. His delicate skills and lightning change of space soon attracted football's elite. In 1977 he signed for West Bromwich Albion, joining fellow black players Brendan Batson and Cyrille Regis. The team became known for their flamboyant and exciting football, while Cunningham, Regis, and Batson were labelled by the manager Ron Atkinson football's Three Degrees, after the US soul group.

In April 1977 Cunningham played for the England under-21 team against Scotland, the first black footballer to do so (but not the first player of colour to wear an England shirt). He graduated to the full England team, and between May 1979 and October 1980 he won six caps. During this period he was transferred to Real Madrid, the giants of European football, for £995,000. Unfortunately, his form never replicated the consistent excellence shown at West Bromwich Albion. He joined Manchester United on loan in 1983 before playing for Leicester City, Marseille (France), Sporting Gijon (Spain), and Charleroi (Belgium). He finally returned to England with Wimbledon in 1987–8, coming on as substitute in the 1988 FA Cup final win over Liverpool. He later signed for Rayo Vallecano in Spain.

Tragically, at the age of 33, Cunningham was killed in a car crash. His West Bromwich Albion colleague Cyrille Regis has said that the shock of his close friend's premature death led him to re-evaluate his life and return to practising his Christian beliefs. PV

Back, Les, Crabbe, Tim, and Solomos, John, *The Changing Face of Football* (2001)

ODNB

See also SPORT

D

Daggers, William (1795–1886). Early Liverpudlian solicitor. He was born in Kingston, Jamaica, the son of a wealthy white member of the plantocracy and his mixed-race mother, Hannah Woodcock. On his father's death, William and his sisters were brought back to *Liverpool by their uncle, John Daggers, a prominent and respected gentleman. William's family connections and his social class apparently helped to ease his entry into Liverpudlian society because he appears to have been accepted into the highest social circles.

William Daggers was a contemporary of Joshua Lace, founder of the Liverpool Law Society, set up in 1824. Daggers followed Lace into the legal profession, and in 1819 gained his certificate as a solicitor. Though he seldom appeared in court, he was widely sought after and consulted for his brilliant knowledge of equity and conveyancing. He acquired a reputation with the Council for his work on issues affecting the Corporation. For twelve years he held the position of Sergeant at Mace to the Lord Mayor of Liverpool, a ceremonial title usually given to a very senior lawyer who carries the regalia before the Lord Mayor during processions. His authority locally was said to be almost equivalent to that of the Sheriff of the county. He died in Liverpool in 1886 at the age of 91.

RHC

Liverpool Courier, 1 Mar. 1886

Register of Sasines, National Archives of Scotland, R53/445, fos. 238–240^{v}

See also GEORGIAN AND VICTORIAN BRITAIN

Davidson, William (1781–1820). Renowned figure in the British radical movement during the Regency. He was born in Jamaica to the island's Attorney-General and a local black woman. At 14 he was sent to Glasgow to study law, and later became apprenticed to a lawyer in Liverpool.

Davidson's radical inclinations were formed quite early on in his life and, while still in Scotland, he joined in the public demand for parliamentary reform. After failing to continue his studies, he set up a cabinet-making business in Birmingham, and taught in a Wesleyan Sunday school. The Peterloo massacre in 1819 incited anger in him and he resumed his radical politics, joining the Marylebone Union Reading Society, which was formed as a result of the massacre. He was introduced to George Edwards, a police spy pretending to be a radical, who recruited Davidson to fellow radical Arthur Thistlewood's groups, the Committee of Thirteen and the Executive of Five. They were plotting the deaths of major members of the government and had plans to blow up the House of Commons. Their most significant plan, which became known as the Cato Street conspiracy, was to murder all the members of the Cabinet as they dined at Grosvenor Square in the home of Lord Harrowby. Unfortunately for them, as they discussed their tactics at a hayloft on Cato Street, George Edwards was already planning their arrest. Davidson along with four other, white colleagues were charged with high treason and sentenced to death. They were hanged and then decapitated on 1 May 1820 in England's last public decapitation.

DD/SS

Fryer, Peter, *Staying Power: The History of Black People in Britain* (1984)

Lang, Sean, *Parliamentary Reform, 1785–1928* (1998)

ODNB

See also POLITICS

Day, Thomas (1748–1789). English poet, philanthropist, and early voice of the abolition movement. Day was born in London and educated at Oxford, where he became influenced by the philosophy of Jean-Jacques Rousseau. In 1773 he came across a newspaper account of the death of a slave who had committed suicide to save himself from a return to plantation labour. The story inspired Day and his friend John Bicknell to produce *The Dying Negro* (1773).

This long poem is written as a slave's suicide note to his future wife and can be read as a response to the previous year's Mansfield decision, which declared that no slave could be legally forced to return to labour against his or her wishes. *The Dying Negro* oscillates between a first-hand account of slavery and comment on the slavery system. The poem was a popular early vehicle for the abolition movement and was expanded, revised, and paired with an anti-slavery essay dedicated to Rousseau in two reprints.

Day was keen to spread his anti-slavery message to a wide audience and made the abolition campaign a feature of *The History of Sandford and Merton* (1783), argued to be the first novel written specifically for older children and Day's most popular work. He also provided the abolition movement with further texts in the form of numerous poems similar to *The Dying Negro*, and political essays. EDS

Rowland, Peter, 'The Life and Times of Thomas Day, 1748–1789', *Studies in British History*, 39 (1996)

See also ABOLITION; SLAVERY

Delany, Martin Robison (1812–1885). African-American physician, abolitionist, soldier, and black nationalist who fought for the emancipation and self-reliance of Blacks. Delany was born in Charleston, Virginia, to a free mother and a slave father. Due to his mother's free status, he was deemed free as well. All his life Delany insisted on the need for black people to recognize and absorb their African heritage and culture. As such, he anticipated the rise of *Pan-Africanism. He rejected notions about the inferiority of Blacks, promoting instead the values of self-sufficiency and entrepreneurial effort. He advocated emigration rather than subjection to racial harassment at home. In July 1859 he sailed to West Africa and signed a treaty with the local rulers on 27 December 1859 that permitted Blacks linked with Delany to settle in vacant tribal lands. In 1860 he arrived in Britain seeking financial assistance for his project. In London he successfully persuaded cotton dealers that Christian African colonies were as competent in cotton production as those in the American South. In Britain he was also the delegate to the Fourth International Statistical Congress. He spent eight months in Britain giving anti-slavery talks and contributing to the founding of the African Aid Society. The Society agreed to partially fund Delany's African project, but the American Civil War meant the project had to be terminated. DD/SS

Fryer, Peter, *Staying Power: The History of Black People in Britain* (1984)

See also ABOLITION; SLAVERY

Denniston, Oswald (1913–2000). Passenger on the **Empire Windrush* (1948) and key figure in London's growing immigrant community. Oswald 'Columbus' Denniston was the first African-Caribbean trader in *Brixton market, London, where he became central to a vibrant community. Born in St James, Montego Bay, Jamaica, Denniston left school at 14 to work on a sugar plantation. He then trained to become a signwriter and decorator and, by the time he left on a one-way ticket bound for England, had established his own business. Arriving in Britain, he publicly thanked government officials for assisting in the resettlement of the Caribbean migrants. Almost straight away he was offered work as a signwriter in Balham, London. In the first few weeks he met his future wife, Margaret, at a church tea party. He became a founder member of the Association of Jamaicans and the Lambeth Community Relations Council and was active in a number of Lambeth Caribbean community groups.

During the 1950s he opened a jukebox coffee bar, the Sugar Cane, in Brixton. His main market stall became a hub for locals to meet and discuss current affairs. He numbered among his clients and friends key figures from the black community, including Sir Herman Ouseley (former chairman of the Commission for Racial Equality), Darcus Howe (radical social commentator and writer), and the dub poet Linton Kwesi Johnson. Denniston was part of the *Windrush* anniversary celebrations in 1998. JPo

Phillips, Mike, 'Oswald Denniston', *The Guardian*, 17 Feb. 2000

—— and Phillips, Trevor, *Windrush: The Irresistible Rise of Multi-Racial Britain* (1999)

Despard, Edward Marcus (1751–1803), **and Despard, Catherine** (*fl.* 1785–1803). British colonel turned revolutionary, and his African-Caribbean wife (also described as African-American in origin). In 1790, when Colonel Despard arrived in London after nearly twenty years of British military service in the Caribbean, he brought with him his wife, Catherine, and their young son James. Catherine's background remains unclear: by some accounts she was the daughter of a Jamaican preacher, by others an educated Spanish Creole. The couple had married some time between 1786 and 1789, while Edward was Superintendent of the newly created British enclave of Belize. The Despards' mixed-race marriage was perhaps the only such example in Britain at the time.

In London the Despards, turning their backs on respectable society, threw themselves into radical politics, Catherine focusing her energies on abolitionism and prisoners' rights. Edward's political views fell under government suspicion, and Catherine took an increasingly public role in defending him against charges of treason and sedition. When he was imprisoned without trial from 1798 to 1801, she enlisted the radical MP Sir Francis Burdett to campaign on his behalf. Her letter protesting against her husband's treatment was read to the House of Commons in 1799. She visited him frequently in Newgate prison and smuggled out his writings in her clothing.

In 1803 Edward was convicted, on scanty evidence, of high treason, and became the last man sentenced to be hanged, drawn, and quartered. Catherine persuaded his former comrade in arms Lord Nelson to intercede with the Prime Minister, Henry Addington, and the sentence was commuted to public beheading. After Edward's execution Catherine was disowned by the Despard family but supported by a pension from Sir Francis Burdett. MJ

Jay, Mike, *The Unfortunate Colonel Despard* (2004)

Linebaugh, Peter, and Rediker, Marcus, *The Many-Headed Hydra* (2000)

Diplomats and embassies, African (*c.*1500–1936). From the 16th century onwards African states sent occasional diplomatic representatives to certain European states including England. Most of these embassies were from North Africa. From the 18th century the number of African diplomats coming to Britain increased, but it was not until the 19th century that the number of African diplomats making their way to London grew in significance (e.g. Madagascar 1836, Zanzibar 1838 and 1842, Egypt 1846, Morocco 1850). A proposed Asante embassy to London in 1820 failed because the British would not provide a ship to convey the ambassadors. However, in the face of British official hindrance, an embassy led by John Owusu Ansa arrived in London in 1895, but it failed to secure Asante independence from British imperial ambitions. Also in 1895 three southern African chiefs from what is now Botswana travelled to London to try to persuade Queen Victoria to protect their lands from Cecil Rhodes. There were similar African deputations to London from the Swazi and Zulu (1882), from Buganda (1881), and even from the Comoro Islands, most aiming to protect their interests from Imperial expansion. African deputations also visited London to protest against the policies of local colonial governments, for example, from the Eastern Cape in 1836; from the Gold

Coast in 1865, 1898, and 1912; by nationalists from South Africa in 1909, 1913, and 1919–20; and by the National Congress of British West Africa in 1920. Other African official representatives came to London for Queen Victoria's Golden and Diamond Jubilees and for the coronations in 1902 and 1911. The first Haitian representative in London was Prince Sanders, or Saunders, in 1816. Liberia was recognized by Britain in the mid-19th century and its most distinguished ambassador in London was Edward *Blyden (1877–8). Emperor Menelik gained British recognition for Ethiopia in the late 1890s. During the Italian invasion of 1935–6 the Ethiopian minister in London was Dr Charles *Martin, who had been brought up in India, where he studied medicine. DK

Mukasa, Ham, *Uganda's Katikiro in England, with Notes and an Introduction by Simon Gikandi* (Manchester, 1998)

Parsons, Neil, *King Khama, Emperor Joe, and the Great White Queen: Victorian Britain Through African Eyes* (1998)

Wilks, Ivor, *Asante in the Nineteenth Century: The Structure and Evolution of a Political Order* (1975)

See also POLITICS

Dobbs, Bobby (1858–1930). Boxer and ex-slave from Tennessee, United States, who made a number of trips to England to fight. Dobbs was born into slavery in Knoxville, Tennessee, and picked cotton until he was 15. A slight man, standing 5 feet $8\frac{1}{2}$ inches and weighing just 9 stone 9 pounds, he trained as a lightweight and welterweight. During his illustrious career he fought over 1,000 matches, not retiring until he was 60. In 1898 he made his first trip to England, where, in an infamous fight with Dick Burge, he was offered a bribe by a bookmaker of £100—a huge sum in those days—to lose the fight. He agreed to the deal and was provided with laxatives before the match, but switched with a friend, who bore some resemblance to him and who was willing to take the medication. Dobbs won the match. On the same trip he knocked out two reputable boxers, Pat MacDonald and Jerry Driscoll. Dobbs returned to Britain in 1902 to continue his fighting career and remained for the next eight years. He won over half of the 42 prizefights in which he competed. In England he toured with Professor Bill Moore's booth, where he became well known as 'a total abstainer, non-smoker, diet expert, and fresh air fanatic'. He travelled to Berlin and Budapest and established boxing schools there. On his return to the United States he became a trainer in Philadelphia and Charleston. JPo

Fryer, Peter, *Staying Power: The History of Black People in Britain* (1984)

See also SPORT

Doctors (*c.*1800–*c.*2000). For much of the 19th century medical practice in Britain did not enjoy high status, although by 1860 the old system of training through apprenticeship was in decline. An Act of 1858 established the General Medical Council, which began to police practitioners but did not make unqualified practice illegal. Nevertheless, in the next 20 years medical training had become more professional, more scientifically based, and the practice of medicine more highly esteemed. Training lasted several years and was costly. Increased numbers of qualified doctors made for an overcrowded profession. There was little scientific education in colonial secondary schools, and full medical training was not available in the British West Indies or in the African colonies, although in the mid-19th century Fourah Bay College, Freetown, Sierra Leone, provided some basic pre-medical instruction; the Yaba Medical Training College in Nigeria was not opened until 1930, and then only to award diplomas. Only in the late 1940s and early 1950s were medical schools established in the African and West Indian colonies.

Thus black men from the colonies wishing to study medicine had to go to Britain (a few West Indians studied in the United States and Canada), while some also gained the higher MD degree from Brussels. A number of African-Americans, fugitives from slavery or denied a place in white medical schools in the United

States, studied in Britain, for example Ewing Glasgow and Robert Johnson, who both graduated from Edinburgh in 1858.

Women were excluded from British and North American medical schools until the late 19th century; the one known black woman to have qualified as a doctor was Sarah *Remond, who trained and practised in Italy. By the beginning of the 20th century black women from overseas colonies were arriving to train as nurses in British hospitals. As potential members of a much less valued profession they encountered institutional racial discrimination, some being refused admission at a hospital by matrons who until their arrival had been unaware that they were black.

Perhaps the first African to study medicine in Britain was Ajai *Crowther's son, who failed to qualify at King's College London. He was followed by three young men from Fourah Bay, Freetown, sent to King's College London in order to train as army surgeons for service in West Africa. They included James Africanus *Horton, who wrote books about West African diseases, and William Davies. A small stream of men, mainly from elite families in Sierra Leone, and later from the Gold Coast, Nigeria, and Mauritius, studied medicine in British universities. Most returned to work in West Africa in private practice or government service. Some West Indian doctors who trained in Britain also worked in Africa for colonial governments (e.g. D. H. R. Waldron and J. Numa Rat), a few as medical missionaries (e.g. Theophilus *Scholes). George Rice (1848–1935), from Trinidad, studied in London and had a distinguished medical career in south-east London and Surrey. Three black doctors from Edinburgh, John *Alcindor, W. C. B. Meyer, and Agnes Savage, attended the Pan-African Conference in London in 1900. The racially discriminatory West African Medical Service, founded in 1901, reduced the pay and status of African doctors and brought a protest from 35 African and West Indian medical students in Britain in March 1902.

The number of Africans and West Indians arriving in Britain to study medicine increased in the early decades of the 20th century. This included a number of women, for example Agnes Savage, who graduated from the University of Edinburgh. Black medical students experienced discrimination from fellow students and when qualified, sometimes with high honours, were denied employment in British hospitals. During the First World War, black doctors such as Albert Meyer were refused commissions but offered a lower rank in the Royal Army Medical Corps as King's Regulations stated that officers had to be of 'pure European parentage'. Official and institutional discrimination meant that most doctors who remained in Britain in the years 1905–40 established private practices, often in inner-city areas: for example, John Alcindor, 'the Black doctor of Paddington', Harold *Moody in south London, James Jackson Brown in Acton, Cecil Belfield *Clarke in Southwark (all from the Caribbean), Robert Wellesley Cole in Liverpool and Newcastle (from Sierra Leone), and Hastings Banda, the future dictator of Malawi, in London. Albert Kaggwa, originally from Uganda, trained in Britain and practised in London's East End. Medical doctors played a prominent role in Pan-African political organizations in Britain; John Alcindor was president of the *African Progress Union (he also chaired the second Pan-African Congress in London in 1921); the *West African Students' Union had medical members, while Harold Moody, with the support of Belfield Clarke, founded the *League of Coloured Peoples (LCP) in 1931. In 1939–40 the LCP successfully campaigned for black officers in the Army and those admitted included doctors and dentists; among doctors who served were Moody's elder daughter, Christine, and his eldest son. David *Pitt, who graduated from Edinburgh in 1938, returned to the West Indies to practise but came back to Britain in the 1950s as a family doctor and also to enter politics.

After the 1940s, although new medical schools were being opened in the colonies, there was a steady flow of black students coming to train in medicine in

Britain, some at graduate level in the schools of tropical medicine in London and Liverpool. Most were from the West African and Caribbean colonies; the first East African students studied in Wolverhampton in 1948–9. As in the inter-war years, the majority returned home to staff the expanding medical services and the new universities. A few returned to Britain, the most eminent being David Pitt (later Lord Pitt). Children born of immigrants who had arrived in Britain after 1948 supplied a further small number of black doctors. Most were employed within the National Health Service (NHS). They were joined after 1960 by a steadily growing number of doctors, particularly from African states, who came to Britain either as political refugees or as economic migrants in search of a better life. This included men and women trained in non-British medical schools and from states that had not been British colonies. By 2000, according to a report in *The Observer*, black doctors formed 3.4 per cent of the NHS medical workforce (8 per cent of nurses were black), but they were more widely represented in the Cinderella services of psychiatry and geriatrics, where they held a high number of consultancies. They were less likely to be promoted to consultancies in other branches of medicine. Few senior NHS management positions were held by black people. DK

Green, Jeffrey, 'Dr J. J. Brown of Hackney (1882–1953)' in Rainer E. Lotz and Ian Pegg (eds.), *Under the Imperial Carpet: Essays in Black History 1780–1950* (1986)

Patton, Adell, Jr., *Physicians, Colonial Racism and Diaspora in West Africa* (1996)

Witherspoon, Ian, 'The British Empire and International Students at the University of Edinburgh 1880–1914', Ph.D. thesis (University of Edinburgh, 2002)

See also MEDICINE

Douglass, Frederick (1818–1895). African-American leader of the abolitionist movement in the United States who toured and lectured in the British Isles. Douglass was born a slave in February 1818 on Holmes Hill Farm on Maryland's eastern shore in the United States. All his life, Douglass was renowned for his oratorical skills. He travelled to Great Britain in 1845 because the widespread publicity of his autobiography, *Narrative of the Life of Frederick Douglass, an American Slave*, meant that his former owner in America would be able to track him down and reclaim his 'property'. His friends thus encouraged him to go on tour in Britain. He set sail on the *Cambria* for Liverpool on 16 August 1845 and arrived in Ireland, where he lectured to crowds who were spellbound by his rhetoric. Douglass was known to have verbal stamina and could speak for up to three hours at a time. His main venues for lecturing were Protestant churches. He also called himself a Chartist and worked closely with the Chartist leader Henry Vincent. Douglass spent three months in Scotland, where he managed to incite anger in the members of the Free Church of Scotland because he overtly criticized them for accepting money from slaveholders in the southern states. They retaliated by demonstrating against him with signs that read 'Send back the nigger'. Despite this hostile event, Douglass, like many other African-Americans, enjoyed a relatively prejudice-free stay in Britain between 1845 and 1847. He returned to America in 1847, where he became a nationally renowned spokesman for black freedom and an adviser to Abraham Lincoln. DD/SS

Lampe, G. P., *Frederick Douglass: Freedom's Voice, 1818–1845* (1998)

See also BROWN, WILLIAM WELLS

Downing, Henry Francis (*c.*1841–1928). African-American playwright and journalist in London. Downing enjoyed a varied career. In his youth he was a sailor, and later worked for the United States foreign service in Angola. He also managed a New York press agency representing prominent black leaders including Booker T. *Washington, Frederick *Douglass, and Ida B. Wells. Around 1895 Downing and his reputedly white American wife, Margarita (*c.*1873–*c.*1950), arrived in England and settled in Chiswick, west London.

A fortuitous meeting with the African-American poet Paul Dunbar in London resulted in Downing's management of Dunbar's 1897 successful reading tour throughout England. As Dunbar's manager, Downing played an instrumental role in bringing together two of the most famous and talented black artistes of the 19th century. Impressed by his stewardship of Dunbar's tour, Samuel *Coleridge-Taylor contacted the pair, and thus began a series of collaborations between the two artistes, including the song collection *Seven African Romances* (1897). The Downings enjoyed a close friendship with Coleridge-Taylor, and shared with the composer a deep commitment to *Pan-Africanism. All three attended and served on the committee of the 1900 Pan-African Congress held in London.

Downing's own career and reputation as a playwright was consolidated during this period. By 1913 he had written at least eight plays, including *The Exiles* and *The Arabian Lovers*, and collaborated with his wife on a further two scripts. He counted among his friends in Britain many of the leading black performers and musicians of the day, including Amanda *Aldridge. He also maintained a lively correspondence with his American contacts, and when W. E. B. DuBois sent his daughter to school in England the Downings befriended Mrs DuBois, who had moved to London.

After his return to America, around 1916, Downing was commissioned by a New York monthly paper to write brief recollections of his composer friend Coleridge-Taylor, who had died in 1912.

JPG

Lotz, Rainer E., and Pegg, Ian (eds.), *Under the Imperial Carpet: Essays in Black History 1780–1950* (1986)

See also LITERATURE 3: DRAMA

Dub music. Electronically manipulated and extended music, usually remixes of existing reggae recordings. Dub was pioneered in Jamaica in the late 1960s, widely acknowledged to have been created by King Tubby. The first dub 'versions' were popular reggae songs with vocals removed to emphasize the drum and bass, to which a DJ could add vocals, a form of commentary known as 'toasting', making much use of alliteration and rhyme. These were specifically intended to be played by DJs on sound systems at dances and other social events. Advances in sound engineering facilitated experimentation and the ability to remix the music in numerous ways, increasing the popularity of dub versions, so much so that it became common for a dub version to be issued as the B side to a '45' single record. The evolution of 16- and 24-track recording led to further developments as sound engineers sought to enhance or clarify the meaning of a song by selectively dubbing in key words and phrases from the original lyrics. By the mid-1970s lyrical elements were disappearing and dub was predominantly rhythms, melodies, and sounds that carried expressive qualities without being linguistically comprehensible. Key dub artists at this time included Lee Perry, King Tubby, Errol Thompson, Prince Jammy, Keith Hudson, and Augustus Pablo.

Jamaican migration to Britain in the 1950s and 1960s guaranteed a market for Jamaican music, and much dub was imported. Although British Jamaicans started producing their own music early on, it was not until 1974 that the first British dub album, *Pick a Dub*, by Keith Hudson appeared. From the 1980s Britain became a key centre for dub, heavily influenced by Mad Professor (Neil Fraser), one of the leading producers, whose trademark is the use of electronic sounds. Dub's transition into the digital age was aided by his *Dub Me Crazy* albums, some of his many releases. He also created remixes for artists such as Pato Banton and Sade. Another key figure in British dub is Adrian Sherwood of the On-U Sound record label. He is highly experimental in his production and has worked with many dub and other artists.

Dubhead Records was established in 1995 and has played an important role in contemporary dub, promoting the underground dub scene and releasing albums by artists who would have struggled to do so otherwise. Dub artists at the forefront of the early 21st-century dub scene include Alpha & Omega, Dub Judah, the Disciples, and the Vibronics.

Another element of dub is *dub poetry, a poetic style fusing reggae music with the spoken word. This seems to have been born out of confrontation and rejection of British ideals, and is expressed through the use of reggae, Rastafarian imagery, and the employment of Jamaican patois. Well-known British exponents of this style include Linton Kwesi Johnson and Benjamin Zephaniah. SM

Jones, Simon, *Black Culture, White Youth: The Reggae Tradition from JA to UK* (1988)

Katz, David, *People Funny Boy: The Genius of Lee 'Scratch' Perry* (2000)

Potash, C. (ed.), *Reggae, Rasta, Revolution: Jamaican Music from Ska to Dub* (1997)

See also BLACK BRITISH ENGLISH; REGGAE

Dub poetry. A genre popularized in the 1970s, the seminal texts of which are 'Dis poem' by Mutabaruka, 'The mad woman's poem' by Jean 'Binta' Breeze, 'Roots' and 'Mi cyaan believe it' by Mikey Smith, and the 1970s and 1980s output, textual and musical, of Linton Kwesi Johnson.

Dub poetry was largely associated with Jamaican writers and had its antecedents in the dialect poems of Claude *McKay and Louise Bennett, its theoretical logic in Kamau Brathwaite's assertion in *Nation Language* (1984) that 'the hurricane does not roar in pentameters'. Johnson originally coined the term to describe Jamaican 'toasting', where poems are performed to the accompaniment of reggae music; Mervyn Morris was central in promoting the genre, editing the collections of Breeze and Smith.

Its Caribbean roots sprouted when the Guyanese academic Walter *Rodney was forbidden to return to Jamaica, where he taught at Mona campus, in 1968, following attendance at a Canadian conference. Students, academics, and poets protested against the Jamaica Labour Party government, taking to the streets in support of Rodney's campaign to bring education to the public 'yard'. The publication of journals followed, notably *Savacou* 3/4 in 1970, in which dub poets were represented alongside oral forms and Creole dialect writers.

In Britain poets such as Benjamin Zephaniah and Lemn Sissay have achieved wide cultural recognition for their oral work. In 2002 Johnson became the second living poet to be included in the Penguin Modern Classics series, with the publication of a collection of selected works, *Mi Revalueshanary Fren*. Among the more accomplished of the contemporary practitioners are Dreadlock Alien (Richard Grant) and Diké Omeje; such poets often compete at 'slam contests', where a 'slam champion' is elected according to the effect their work has on an audience. The movement is widespread in regional cities such as Birmingham, Nottingham, Manchester, and Leeds, as well as London.

Much Caribbean poetry is written at some point along a continuum between the written and the oral, and it is therefore difficult to differentiate entirely dub poetry from the more textual work of poets like Mbala (Michael Bailey), 'Shake' *Keane (Ellsworth McGranahan Keane), Dennis Scott, Amryl *Johnson, and John Agard. Not all dub poets write consistently in a dub style, and Paula Burnett's anthology of Caribbean verse contains an oral poetry section, including lyrics by Bob Marley as well as the poems of Mutabaruka, Delano Abdul Malik de Coteau, Oku Onuora, Bongo Jerry, and others.

Caribbeanist literary critics such as Gordon Rohlehr and Stewart Brown have been cautious in discussing the merits of dub; the danger of confusing the poetic craft with 'mouthing off in front of a microphone' has been raised. Carolyn Cooper characterizes the live aspect, epitomized by Smith's screech of 'Laaaawwwwwwwwd' in 'Mi cyaan believe it', as 'a privileged reading of the text, voiced by the poet', but rejects a wider definition of 'performance poetry' suggested by Morris, where 'dub' applies only to poetry that uses reggae rhythms or backing, as being unfaithful to the ideology of working-class revolution, which has inspired many Caribbean poets. She argues for a concept of 'oraliteracy' specific to Jamaican English, which yokes together, through the medium of dialect poetry, a peasant tradition of song and event with the English poetic idiom.

In live readings the rhythm can be altered through pauses and by speeding up or slowing down syllables, as in rap music and song lyrics, or supplemented by gesture and voice, meaning that the performance metric may be heavily contrived and impossible for another reader to emulate. Clichés, banalities, and even elementary errors in spelling and grammar are harder to spot, with the result that performance poets may undervalue the ability to redraft and improve work to a publishable standard. Conversely, more complex philosophical or existential ideas, daring imagery, and intricate patterning are unlikely to translate successfully into the live format. Simple, unwrought, first-person narrative becomes the norm.

In the contested and crowded arena of Caribbean identities, this allowed interesting possibilities; for the many British amateur poets taking the microphone in the many small bars inviting people to 'come along and perform your poems in a friendly atmosphere', it is less fruitful. The results are all too often facile musings on love, sex, and grief, with a disregard for metre, poetic forms, and literary inheritance that is abhorrent to the serious writer.

Performance poetry thus represents the muzzling of a Jamaican art form that once stood comparison with the jazz poetics of Eliot or Auden and the sonorous blank verse of Milton, all of whom can be read in performance, and all of whom likewise developed a new voice in response to specific historical circumstances. The criterion for excellence must be that the writer has something new to say, and the poems with lasting appeal will be those that survive on the printed page. In this context, the work of Dorothea Smartt, and of younger Jamaican-origin practitioners such as Kim Trusty and Kei Miller, who use dub performance as one technique within a wider range of poetic registers, is worthy of note.

JM

Breeze, Jean Binta, *Riddym Ravings and Other Poems* (ed. Mervyn Morris, 1988)
Burnett, Paula (ed.), *The Penguin Book of Caribbean Verse in English* (1986)
Cooper, Carolyn, 'The Performance Poetry of Jean "Binta" Breeze and Mikey Smith' in Anna Rutherford (ed.), *From Commonwealth to Post-Colonial* (1992)
Miller, Kei, *Kingdom of Empty Bellies* (2006)
Sissay, Lemn (ed.), *The Fire People: A Collection of Contemporary Black British Poetry* (1998)
Smith, Michael, *It a Come* (ed. Mervyn Morris, 1986)
Trusty, Kim, *Darker than Blue* (2002)

See also BLACK BRITISH ENGLISH; LITERATURE 2: FICTION AND POETRY; REGGAE

Dunbar, Rudolph (1899–1988). Classical musician and war correspondent born in British Guiana (now Guyana). Dunbar began his musical career with the British Guiana militia band. He moved to New York at the age of 20, where he studied music at Columbia University. In 1925 he moved to Paris, where he studied music, journalism, and philosophy. By 1931 he had settled in London and founded the Rudolph Dunbar School of Clarinet Playing. The same year *Melody Maker* invited him to contribute a series of articles on the clarinet. These were successful enough for him to publish in 1939 *A Treatise on the Clarinet (Boehm System)*. Dunbar was a successful conductor, especially in the 1940s, when he became the first black man to conduct an orchestra in many of the major cities of Europe, including, in 1942, the London Philharmonic at the Albert Hall, to an audience of 7,000 people; the Berlin Philharmonic (1945); and in 1948 at the Hollywood Bowl.

Dunbar was also a journalist. In 1932 he became London correspondent of the Associated Negro Press, reporting for them on the debates in the House of Commons in 1936 on the Italian invasion of *Ethiopia. He served as a war correspondent with the American 8th Army, and crossed the Channel on D-Day. He distinguished himself by warning the US 969th battalion of an ambush near Marchin during the Battle of the Bulge.

Despite appearances on the BBC in 1940 and 1941, his post-war musical career declined. He continued to teach and encourage younger musicians, but he grew introspective, believing that his racial origins thwarted his progress. Dunbar died, unmarried, of cancer in 1988. MK

Dunbar, Rudolph, *Treatise on the Clarinet (Boehm System)* (1939)
ODNB

See also MUSIC 1: CLASSICAL MUSIC

E

Edmonstone, John (b. *c.*1800). Freed black slave from British Guiana (now Guyana) who taught the evolutionist Charles Darwin taxidermy. Edmonstone was taken to Glasgow by his slave owner, Charles Edmonstone, probably in 1817. He was taught taxidermy by the explorer, naturalist, and conservationist Charles Waterton, who had travelled extensively in South and North America. Edmonstone moved to Edinburgh in 1823, where he still resided in 1833. He was hired by Darwin, author of *The Origin of Species* (1859), to teach him taxidermy while Darwin was studying medicine at Edinburgh University. From 1824 to 1825 Edmonstone lived at 37 Lothian Street, in close proximity to the university and to Darwin's residence. Darwin was an outspoken critic of slavery, and had long conversations with Edmonstone about the latter's experiences as a slave and his life in British Guiana. These conversations probably helped to shape Darwin's views on the slave trade. On his voyage on the *Beagle* to Tierra del Fuego, Darwin met three Fuegians. Recalling Edmonstone, his autobiography records, 'I was incessantly struck, whilst living with the Fuegians on board the *Beagle*, with the many little traits of character, shewing how similar their minds were to ours; and so it was with a full-blooded negro with whom I happened once to be intimate.' JPo

Browne, Janet, *Charles Darwin: Voyaging* (2003)
Freeman, R. B., 'Darwin's Negro Bird-Stuffer', *Notes and Records of the Royal Society of London*, 33/1 (1978)

Education. While there are cases in earlier periods where we have some evidence about the education of individual black people (such as that of Francis *Barber) or members of particular professions (e.g. *doctors), a more general picture only begins to emerge with the growing black presence from the middle of the 20th century. This entry focuses on the history of black people and education since *c.*1950.

1. Introduction
2. The assimilationist approach (late 1950s–1960s)
3. Integration (late 1960s to late 1970s)
4. Multicultural education (1970s and early 1980s)
5. Anti-racist education (from the mid-1980s)
6. African-Caribbean boys
7. Conclusion

1. Introduction Education serves many fundamental purposes, but crucially it is the site where children acquire the qualifications and skills needed to compete on equal terms in the job market. Initiatives to redress inequalities of social class, gender, and race within the education system have been at the centre of political discourse and policy since the immediate post-war era. Arguably, however, it is around the issue of race inequalities in education, especially as it relates to the education of children of Caribbean heritage, that the debate has been most controversial.

Although the vast majority of Caribbean immigrants arrived during the 1950s and the early 1960s, their children became a significant presence in the school system only in the 1960s and beyond. Within a short space of time, serious concerns were emerging about Caribbean children's experiences of the school system. It became clear that children were the subject of discriminatory practices, being labelled unresponsive, dull, disruptive, poor learners, and low achievers, and were being relegated to the lowest academically performing streams within schools. Large numbers of children were leaving school with few qualifications, leaving them unable to compete successfully in a competitive labour market. Concerned about their children's futures, black parents mobilized to draw public attention to these problems, to demand government action to redress the inequalities, and to organize support schooling for their children.

Despite various policy initiatives implemented since the 1960s, concerns continue to surround the educational performance of black children. Among scholars and researchers the major focus of concern has been to understand why black British children of African-Caribbean heritage achieve less well academically than pupils of all other ethnic groups and are subject to disproportionate exclusion from schools. This continuing problem stands in marked contrast to improvements in the educational attainments of children of other minority ethnic groups. Various theories have attempted to explain the persistent low levels of attainment and the failure of strategies and policies to redress the problem. These theories range from the low intelligence of black children, especially dominant in the light of IQ tests in the 1960–1970s, which purported to 'prove' the innate intellectual inferiority of black peoples, to the pathological nature of the black family, poor self-esteem, racism within society and the school system, or poor-quality and poorly resourced schools. While many theorists concluded that racism was an overriding factor, few authorities accepted this explanation, insisting instead that the underachievement of Caribbean pupils was directly related to their home environment.

It is pertinent at this point to explore the different responses by government and educationists to the education of black children. These different approaches were shaped by wider frameworks for addressing the problem of race in British society. The struggles around the education of Caribbean children in Britain have to be placed against the backdrop of race politics as they played out in Britain from the late 1950s onwards. Hence, policy responses to the poor educational experiences of African-Caribbean children reflect governmental responses to the wider problem of race relations.

2. The assimilationist approach (late 1950s–1960s) As white hostility to the black presence grew, tensions spilled over, leading to disturbances throughout British cities. The response of the government to the 'colour problem' was to introduce controls to limit black immigration, while encouraging the reduction of race tensions by promoting a policy of assimilation. The assimiliationist model was conceived as a panacea for the social ills of a racially divided Britain. Underpinning this policy was the notion that immigrants—and the wider society—would prosper most by their absorption into wider society. In essence, this meant that immigrants were encouraged to downplay their cultural differences and adopt instead 'British' cultural norms, mores and values. The expectation was that the nation would eventually become homogenized and, as cultural differences were eroded, social stability would be reached. Indeed, African-Caribbean schoolchildren were viewed as the conduits through which the cultural values of the dominant majority might be passed onto their parents.

By their very presence in schools, black children also threatened to undermine the education of white children, as teachers were forced to divert essential time, skills, and resources away from white children to meet the linguistic and cultural needs of black children. Hence, black children's race and cultural difference came to be defined as *the* problem, rather than the shortcomings of a system unprepared and unable to respond positively to their needs and aspirations.

Funds were made available under Section 11 of the Local Government Act 1966 to enable teachers to provide black children with the skills that would facilitate their 'successful' assimilation into British society. Two dominant strategies emerged; firstly, a focus on teaching the standard English language (so that children could learn English quickly and then be placed in neighbourhood primary schools); and, secondly, 'bussing', a policy of dispersing immigrant children to prevent too many from attending the same neighbourhood school. This latter policy left black children vulnerable to racist bullying, harassment, and attacks. In the assimilationist model there is no recognition of the necessity for modifications to the traditional ethnocentric school curriculum, no indication that syllabuses should be changed to incorporate the cultural and experiential learning needs of immigrant children, no undermining of assumptions of white superiority.

By the late 1960s the failure of assimiliationist policy within and outside education was becoming apparent. Even those Blacks who attempted to assimilate found their prospects blocked by white hostility to immigrants and institutionalized racism within *housing and labour markets. In the arena of education, there was increasing evidence that African-Caribbeans, South Asians, and some other ethnic minorities were achieving substantially poorer results at school than white children.

3. Integration (late 1960s to late 1970s) The retreat from a full-scale policy of assimilationism was signalled by the Home Secretary Roy Jenkins's encouragement towards integration, which did not entail the absolute erasure of ethnic difference, but stressed instead an acceptance of cultural diversity and mutual tolerance, accompanied by the promotion of equal opportunity to enable black children to achieve their potential. Interestingly, though this model retained its focus on Blacks as the problem, it did lead the way to the introduction of multiculturalist teaching. Schools were encouraged to revise their curriculum to include knowledge of other cultures, to take into account the different cultural heritages of non-white children.

However, these changes were not accompanied by changes in the school culture, and neither did they entail challenging the assumed superiority of the majority culture. As in the wider society, the integrationist model did little to transform the fortunes and experiences of black children, and was met with criticism from black educationists and parents as little more than assimilation with a new name. Certainly, it did not result in improved educational outcomes for African-Caribbean children, or transform their experiences within schools. Teachers' assumptions about the lower intellectual ability of black children led many children, especially boys, to be labelled as 'educationally subnormal' and subsequently dumped in educationally subnormal (ESN) schools, where pupils were denied the educational opportunities that would equip them with the qualifications they needed to take their place in the labour market.

In 1971 Bernard Coard's book *How the West Indian Child Is Made Educationally Sub-Normal in the British School System* documented the deepening crisis facing African-Caribbean children within the schooling system, and exposed the institutional racism that was 'dis-educating' West Indian children through labelling them as educationally subnormal and sending disproportionate numbers to ESN units. Coard's research revealed that by 1970, in 'normal' London schools, 17 per cent of pupils were from ethnic minorities, but in ESN schools that figure was 34 per cent. He argued that schools were failing to recognize the effects of culture shock experienced by many newly arrived pupils from the Caribbean, and suggested that their poor performance was also exacerbated by culturally biased assessments, such as IQ tests, for which they were ill-prepared.

Coard's critique of the institutionalized

racism and its impact on black pupils turned previous orthodoxy about black children on its head, and instigated a row over the education of black children that has raged ever since. It made grim reading for everyone concerned with the education of black children, not least for black parents, who organized campaigns to secure improvements in their children's education. They pressured governments to introduce changes in the school curriculum and closer scrutiny of standards and values, and for the upgrading of educational facilities, especially in under-resourced inner-city schools where black children were concentrated. Alongside these campaigns, black parents and educationists took matters into their own hands, establishing supplementary and Saturday schools to raise the educational achievements of their children. In these informal settings black children were taught formal curriculum subjects alongside courses in Black History, in efforts to raise their self-esteem.

4. Multicultural education (1970s and early 1980s) The failure of previous approaches to schooling in a multiracial society that were based initially on assimilation and subsequently on integration was evident by the 1970s. However, some important changes, given impetus by Coard's critique, were on the horizon. Between 1973 and 1982 black parents and educationists exerted pressure on the government to produce national policies and funding to tackle the underachievement of 'ethnic-minority' children. In 1975 the Bullock Report was published, which looked at standards in English reading, writing, and speaking. More importantly, this report recognized the multicultural nature of British society, and recommended that this be taken into account within the school curriculum. The government had by now accepted that it needed to reform the law, 'to address the continuing unequal status of Britain's racial minorities', especially in the wake of a renewed surge of racism in the 1970s, which resulted in some success in local elections for extremist political parties such as the anti-immigration, anti-black National Front. Frustration at discriminatory treatment, exclusion from political participation, and over-zealous policing of black communities led to serious clashes between the police and disaffected black youth at the *Notting Hill riots in August 1976. That year saw the passage of the Race Relations Act 1976, along with the establishment of the *Commission for Racial Equality, the body charged with implementation of the Act. The Act outlawed discrimination in public services, and placed a special duty on educational authorities to take action to promote race equality and to ensure the elimination of race discrimination.

By the late 1970s, educational policy began to be formulated within the framework of multiculturalism, heralded by the 1977 Green Paper *Education and Schools*, which stated that, since 'our society is a multicultural, multiracial one . . . the curriculum should reflect a sympathetic understanding of different cultures and races'. The House of Commons Select Committee on Race Relations and Immigration urged the government to initiate an inquiry into the causes of the underachievement of children of African-Caribbean origin in education, and to propose remedial action. In 1979 a committee of inquiry into the education of children from ethnic-minority groups was set up, chaired by Anthony Rampton. In 1981 an interim report, the Rampton Report, was published, which looked at the educational needs and attainments of children from all ethnic-minority backgrounds with particular emphasis on African-Caribbean children. The Report highlighted their underachievement, showing, for instance, that 3 per cent of African-Caribbean pupils obtained five or more GCSEs at O level, compared with 18 per cent of Asians and 16 per cent of other groups. The Report, however, found 'no single cause' for the poor experiences of black children in schools but cited a variety of contributory factors; racism within schools and society; inadequate pre-school provision; language issues; and teachers' low expectations of Caribbean children.

Rampton proposed several important recommendations, which served to strengthen the multicultural education model; among these proposals were that the curriculum in all schools should reflect Britain's multiracial and cultural diversity; teachers should play a leading role in seeking to bring about a change in attitudes on the part of society as a whole towards ethnic-minority groups; and West Indian and ethnic-minority teachers should be recruited to ensure equal opportunities at all levels in the education service.

Multicultural education was viewed as a progressive pedagogical strategy for improving the performance of Caribbean children. Teaching black children about their own cultures, while equipping them with improved self-esteem, was seen to be critical to raising their performance levels, while the celebration of cultural diversity would also foster white children's appreciation of the important contribution of black and minority ethnic peoples to the building of Britain. It would also allay the concerns of black parents about their children's poor educational experiences and performance, and would ultimately lead to improved race relations as different communities learnt more of, and came to respect, each other's cultures and histories.

Yet many parents and educationists opposed the content of the multiracial curriculum, arguing that the introduction of African drumming, steel pans, and the 'four Cs' (costume, calypso, carnival, and cricket) into the school curriculum not only trivialized black history and culture, but had little overall effect on raising performance levels. It attracted much negative attention from some sections of the media, who routinely ran stories such as those of white parents complaining about their children 'coming home talking Indian'. Such fears among white parents that multicultural education was undermining their children's education were made manifest when, in 1987, parents at a school in Dewsbury, Yorkshire, refused to send their children to a school where Asian pupils represented 85 per cent of the intake, and demanded separate education. Many in the Conservative Party and on the political right viewed multicultural education as an attack on British values and forecast a loss of British identity.

In 1985 another landmark publication on educational policy appeared. This was the Swann Report, *Education for All*, which outlined the need for the aspirations and concerns of majority and minority communities to be reconciled if further fragmentation and hostility were to be avoided. The Report reaffirmed many points in the Rampton Report. As in the Rampton Report, data from the Department of Education and Science School Leavers Survey were used which showed that African-Caribbean children performed less well in examinations than white children. It looked at underachievement solely on ethnic lines, based on comparison between Asian, African-Caribbean, and mainly white school leavers. Asian children achieved the same level as white children except in English. The Report suggested that much of the difference in average IQ scores between African-Caribbean and white children was related to differences in their socio-economic backgrounds and status, which was in turn aggravated by prejudice and discrimination. As Rampton had concluded, there was no single cause of underachievement, and therefore no single solution. What was required instead was positive action from schools to counter the underachievement of black children, and the prejudice of white children and teachers towards black children. Among some of Swann's recommendations were that all local education authorities (LEAs) should declare their commitment to the principles of *Education for All*, to the development of a pluralist approach to the curriculum, and to countering the influence of racism; every LEA should have at least one adviser and perhaps a senior officer with responsibility to promote the policies put forward, to act as a catalyst to encourage teachers and other advisers to adopt a pluralist perspective in their work; all LEAs should expect their schools to produce clear policy statements on *Education for All* and monitor this practical implementation; all schools, whether multiracial or white, should review their work in the same light of the principles put forward; all schools should adopt clear policies to combat racism.

5. Anti-racist education (from the mid-1980s) The Swann Report was an important factor in pushing forward multicultural and anti-racist education. While many LEAs embraced multicultural education, the inherent assumptions on which it rested were criticized by its detractors. From the mid-1980s multicultural education came to be supplanted by, or in many instances supplemented with, anti-racist education, a critical pedagogical model inspired by Marxist politics. Anti-racist educationists regarded education as having a key role to play in the elimination of structural racial inequalities, and criticized multiculturalism's superficial focus on and celebration of cultural difference, arguing that it did little to dismantle institutional racism and subverted resistance, and hence functioned to maintain power inequalities. Such a direct and politicized critique of power relations inevitably attracted criticism. In 1987 the Prime Minister, Margaret Thatcher, identified anti-racism with left-wing extremism, decrying the fact that 'Children who need to be able to count and multiply are learning anti-racist mathematics, whatever that is.'

Many commentators have argued that, laudable as the goals of anti-racist education are, it is not without problems. Critics suggest that anti-racist education policies may be counter-productive in that there is a tendency to regard all black people as victims and white people as natural racists, and reductivist in its homogenizing tendencies. Moreover, parents still complain that schools continue to expect and demand less of their children, and point to the continuing underperformance of Caribbean boys in particular.

6. African-Caribbean boys A 285-page study by the Department for Education and Skills published in 2005 highlighted the chronic underperformance of African-Caribbean boys at school. In national examinations African-Caribbean boys were the lowest achieving group at practically every key stage for the previous four years. Only 33.3 per cent of black Caribbean boys achieved five or more grades A*–C at GCSE and equivalent, compared with 49.4 per cent of girls—a difference of 16.1 percentage points compared with a difference nationally of 10.1 percentage points. The reason for this disparity is a matter of controversy. The research showed that African-Caribbean boys started their schooling at broadly the same level as other pupils, but began to fall behind by the end of Key Stage 2 (age 11). As they continued their schooling, progress continued to decline, so that by the end of Key Stage 3 (age 16) only about 38 per cent achieved five A*–C GCSEs (the national average is 52 per cent). Underperformance in the secondary-school system frequently defines the future for Caribbean males. Unsurprisingly, the 2001 census indicated that African-Caribbean men were the least likely of all men to have a degree or equivalent qualification. In 2005 there were twice as many black men in prison as there were at university. British black men formed 12 per cent of the prison population despite representing just 1 per cent of the population as a whole.

The disproportionate exclusion of African-Caribbean boys from schools is also of major concern. The rate at which black Caribbean pupils are excluded from school has declined over the past few years, owing, to considerable degree, to the campaigns by black parents and educationists. But, as the figures for exclusions for 2001–2 demonstrate, they were over four times more likely to be excluded from school than all pupils nationally. With only 15 per cent of permanently excluded young people reintegrated into mainstream school, their successful transition into adulthood, employment, and independence is unlikely, spurring Trevor Phillips, chair of the Commission for Racial Equality, to raise the prospect of a permanent underclass of black males.

Initiatives to redress the continuing underperformance of African-Caribbean children abound, from proposals for mentoring schemes that will provide good role models to young black males, intensive tuition to overcome particular barriers such as low self-esteem, and, in 2005, a controversial proposal by Trevor Phillips for segregated education. Efforts to increase the number of black teachers within the school system are also seen as key to achieving improvement. Although the number of ethnic-minority teachers had increased from 1,009 in 2000 to 2,637 in 2002, there is still a shortfall in the number of black male teachers, and proposals have been tabled to offer black males financial incentives in efforts to encourage them into the teaching profession.

7. Conclusion The publication in 1971 of Bernard Coard's *How the West Indian Child Is Made Educationally Sub-Normal in the British School System* sparked a furore among black parents and educationists when he revealed the depths of the crisis facing Caribbean schoolchildren. Coard's exposure was to instigate many long-lasting and far-reaching changes within the school system, but at the beginning of the 21st century the British education system is still faced with the reality of underachievement among black children. CJ

Arora, Ranjit, *Race and Ethnicity in Education* (2005)

Coard, Bernard, *How the West Indian Child Is Made Educationally Sub-Normal in the British School System* (1971)

Department for Education and Skills, *Ethnicity and Education: The Evidence on Minority Ethnic Pupils* (2005)

Education for All: A Brief Guide to the Main Issues of the Report, Swann Report, Cmnd. 9453 (1985)

Gillborn, D., and Mirza, H., *Educational Inequality: Mapping Race, Class and Gender* (2000)

West Indian Children in Our Schools, Rampton Report, Cmnd. 8273 (1981)

See also MULTICULTURALISM; RACISM

Edwards, Samuel Jules Celestine (1857–1894). Campaigning Christian evangelist, author, journalist, and Pan-Africanist born in Dominica but educated in the neighbouring West Indian island of Antigua. An influential friend in Antigua was the Revd Henry Mason Joseph, later president of the African Association in London in 1897. In 1870 Edwards stowed away on a ship and over the next few years he travelled the world as a seaman visiting North and South America and Europe. He landed in Sunderland and thereafter lived briefly in Edinburgh and Newcastle, and worked with a group of black entertainers. At some point he was converted to Christianity, and as a Primitive Methodist worked as a temperance evangelist in Lancashire and Cheshire. He had ambitions to go to Africa as a missionary but gravitated to east London, where he ran a weekly Bible class for men and regularly preached in Victoria Park. Some referred to him as 'the Black Champion of Christianity'. Edwards studied theology at King's College London and enrolled at the London Hospital. He was a frequent speaker at large meetings in London and in other towns and cities. At some of these he condemned racial discrimination and harsh British Imperial policies in Africa.

In 1892 Edwards became editor of *Lux*, the weekly journal of the Christian Evidence Society (CES). From this new platform and at public meetings up and down the country he served as a prominent apologist for Christianity, arguing against atheism, the drink trade, and racial discrimination. In 1893 Catherine Impey invited Edwards to edit **Fraternity*, a role he combined with his work for the CES. Edwards also wrote books and pamphlets and was known to prominent people in London: 'Everybody seemed to know him, and to everybody he was homely, gentle, and dignified.' As a proponent of black rights, he helped prepare the way for the first Pan-African gathering in London in 1900, but he did not live to see the event. Suffering from ill health, Edwards battled on, giving lectures and writing. He eventually went back to Dominica to recuperate but died there in July 1894. DK

Fraternity (Sept. and Nov. 1894)
ODNB

See also CHRISTIANITY; CHURCHES

Ekarte, Daniels (1896/7–1964). Pastor, community activist, and black leader in *Liverpool. Born George Daniel, Daniels Ekarte worked as an errand boy with the Free Church of Scotland in Calabar, Nigeria. Inspired to become a missionary in England, he left as a galley-hand on board a ship bound for Liverpool in 1915. There, instead of encountering a charitable Christian people, Ekarte met with strong racist attitudes and felt deceived by the missionaries in Nigeria. After a period of disenchantment, he began worshipping with Africans, holding prayer services both in private spaces and in the street. With sponsorship from the Church of Scotland, Pastor Ekarte opened the *African Churches Mission in Liverpool in 1931. The Mission was primarily aimed at providing a space of worship and socializing for Blacks in Liverpool.

As a community activist and leader, Pastor Ekarte also had a keen interest in the education and welfare of black children. He tried his best to ensure that children would not go hungry, or homeless people go unsheltered. Under him, the Mission became a sanctuary for those in need. As an air-raid warden during the *First World War, he also provided space for families who had lost their homes. He helped stowaways and black seamen, providing food and sometimes shelter. One of Pastor Ekarte's major accomplishments was the use of the Mission as a home for 'coloured illegitimate children', although his efforts to raise funds for a permanent home failed. The breadth of his charity and mission was dictated by the degree of poverty in Liverpool. Intimately connected to his charitable activities was a political concern about race and poverty in British society and the wider Pan-African world. ASW

Sherwood, Marika, *Pastor Daniels Ekarte and the African Churches Mission* (1994)

See also CHRISTIANITY; CHURCHES

Elaw, Zilpha (*c*.1790–*c*.1850). African-American Primitive Methodist evangelist who preached in Britain. Elaw was born near Philadelphia, the child of free parents. Employed as a servant in a Quaker family, she was converted to Christianity and became a Methodist. In 1810 she married a fuller and they settled in New Jersey, where she had a daughter. Revival 'camp meetings' in 1817 and 1819 gave Elaw's life a new direction. She was convinced that her life should be devoted to preaching. Being an itinerant and self-supporting preacher to both black and white congregations placed strains on her marriage, but she was widowed in 1823. In her memoirs (published in London in 1846) she records preaching during the 1830s in the slave-holding states, at great personal risk, and throughout New England. In 1840 she came to Britain convinced that God had directed her to do so. In five years she claimed to have preached over 1,000 sermons in various parts of Britain, although this was condemned by some who opposed women preaching. The final pages of Elaw's memoirs briefly describe her evangelistic work in Britain, for example, in the North-East, where 'in heat and cold, through wet and dry weather, by night and day, I laboured in that part of God's vineyard, preaching the gospel of Christ incessantly, wherever opportunity was afforded me'. It would appear from the memoirs that her intention was to return to the United States, but her life after 1846 is unknown. DK

Andrews, Willam L. (ed.), *Sisters of the Spirit: Three Black Women's Autobiographies of the Nineteenth Century* (1986)
Elaw, Zilpha, *Memoirs of the Life, Religious Experience, Ministerial Travels and Labours of Mrs. Zilpha Elaw, an American Female of Colour* (1846)

See also CHRISTIANITY; CHURCHES; MISSIONARY SOCIETIES

Elizabeth I (1533–1603). Queen of England and patron of slave-trading ventures.

1. Genesis of the British slave trade
2. Africans in Elizabethan England

3. Scapegoating 'Blackamoors'
4. Attempts to expel Blacks

1. Genesis of the British slave trade The historical narrative of England's involvement in the transatlantic *slave trade is generally related to the enterprising ventures of 16th-century male English merchant traders who, recognizing the vast wealth to be made from the exploitation of Africa, attempted to plunder that continent systematically of its natural and human resources. Large-scale British involvement in the trade of humans, however, stemmed from the ambitious desires of one woman, Queen Elizabeth I.

In 1562, three years after ascending to the throne, Elizabeth was approached by John *Hawkins, an English navigator and privateer adventurer. Hawkins had recently returned from a lucrative, though illegal, slave-trafficking voyage from Africa to the Spanish West Indies, where he sold a human cargo of 300 enslaved Africans for a healthy profit. Back at home Hawkins persuaded his Queen to sanction a further slave-trading venture, arguing that bringing the heathenistic and savage Africans from a 'wild and barren country' would be a beneficial, civilizing act. Elizabeth's initial response to English involvement with the transatlantic trade in humans was cautious, however, and indeed she warned Hawkins that slavery was 'detestable' and would 'call down vengeance from heaven upon the undertakers'. Mindful of Elizabeth's ambitions to acquire substantial wealth to foster a cultural renaissance in England, and to amass wealth and power through the expansion of empire, Hawkins drew his Queen's attention to the enormous profits to be generated through the slave trade. His cogent arguments overcame the Queen's moral qualms, and in 1564 Elizabeth agreed to sponsor Hawkins's second slave-trading expedition, though not before expressing the hope that Africans would not be enslaved without first giving their free consent. With the Queen's blessing, Hawkins became the first privateer to gain official royal support for the transatlantic trading of Africans, a cataclysmic event that would reshape the historical fortunes of England and Africans across the Atlantic world.

Elizabeth's investments and financial support significantly helped to legitimize and facilitate English participation in the African slave trade. Along with Hawkins, Elizabeth further sanctioned privateering ventures by Sir Francis Drake, and both men were pivotal agents in England's rise as a maritime power, and as a major operator in the transatlantic slave trade. Between 1562 and 1569 Hawkins and Drake made five slave-trading ventures to Guinea and Sierra Leone and enslaved an estimated 3,000 Africans. After this date, ongoing conflict with Spain disrupted England's ambitions for maritime dominance, and it was not until after the Restoration that England fully realized its aims to control the transatlantic slave trade.

2. Africans in Elizabethan England The majority of enslaved Africans were transported to plantations throughout the Americas, but many others were brought to England by merchants and traders. London became home to the majority of these displaced Africans. Valued for their 'exotic appearance', wealthy English purchased Africans as outward symbols of their social status. Enslaved African women, men, and children served in the homes of aristocratic families as domestic servants and footmen, and numerous others served as courtesans and entertainers to the Elizabethan Court. Elizabeth herself enjoyed the entertainment of a troupe of 'Blackamoors', and in 1577 purchased a 'Garcon coate of white Taffeta, cut and lined with tincel, striped down with gold and silver . . . pointed with pynts and ribands', for a favourite 'lytle Blackamore'.

Not all Africans in England were enslaved; some free Africans served as maidservants and apprentices, gaining skills in trades that enabled their economic survival. Surviving records suggest that a few acquired some wealth, though most Blacks, like the white poor they lived among, existed in dire poverty.

3. Scapegoating 'Blackamoors' Evidence suggests that most 16th-century English people viewed Blacks with a degree of tolerance. However, a series of social and economic problems—unemployment, famine, and growing urban vagrancy—prompted fears among the wealthy of growing social disorder. Elizabeth's government responded to the crisis by passing a series of Poor Laws, but limited resources proved insufficient to tackle the social problems. It was perhaps inevitable that Elizabeth and her government would cast about for a scapegoat on which to lay the blame for the country's economic and social problems. Deploying a nascent discourse of racial and religious difference, she identified black people as a major source of England's social ills.

4. Attempts to expel Blacks In 1596 the Queen commissioned a merchant to transport all Blacks from England. In an open letter to the Lord Mayor of London, Elizabeth justified her actions:

> Her Majestie, understanding that there are divers Blackamoors brought into this realm, of which kinde of people there are already here too manie, considering how God has blessed this land with great increase of people of our own nation . . . whereas manie for wante of service and means to set them on work fall on idleness and to great extremity. Her majesty's pleasure is that those kinde of people should be sent forth of the land.

A group of slaves were rounded up and dispatched from England, but this attempt to expel Blacks from Britain proved ineffective, for few masters or owners of slaves were prepared to give up their slaves and servants without compensation. The limited success of Elizabeth's plans to deport Africans is borne out from the size of London's black community, estimated in 1601 at 15,000–20,000. The same year Elizabeth issued another order for the deportation of these 'aliens', 'fostered and relieved here to the great annoyance of [the Queen's] own . . . people, that want the relief, which those [black] people consume'. In drawing attention to the dependence of many Blacks on the limited poor relief, and in highlighting their religious difference, Elizabeth sought to justify their deportation. Yet, this second attempt also failed, for as the historian James Walvin argued, 'Blacks had become too securely lodged at various social levels of English society to be displaced and repatriated.' CJ

Hazelwood, Nick, *The Queen's Slave Trader: John Hawkyns, Elizabeth I, and the Trafficking in Human Souls* (2004)

Walvin, James, *Black Ivory: Slavery in the British Empire* (1994)

See also REPATRIATION; SLAVERY

Emancipation. Term used to refer to the act or process by which slaves were freed, individually or collectively. This entry describes the political processes in the early 19th century that led to all slaves in the British colonies becoming free in law over the period 1834–8.

1. The movement towards emancipation
2. Christianity
3. Slave revolts
4. The final push

1. The movement towards emancipation The aim of abolishing the slave trade in 1807 had been simple. Planters, now no longer able to buy fresh Africans, would henceforth have to treat their slaves better, and thus encourage the slave population to increase from natural growth. This, in some unspecified way, would lead to the natural decay of slavery itself. It was thus important to devise a system to monitor abolition.

The immediate mood after *abolition in 1807 was one of wait and see. No one really knew what the end of the slave trade would bring. As the wars with France finally drew to a close in 1814–15, Europe tried to put itself back together after a generation of warfare. Before the wars, the Atlantic slave trade had been a relatively unquestioned feature of European maritime trade and prosperity. Now the British, the senior partner among the victors, had renounced their slave trade, and were not about to allow the defeated French to revive their own trade. Thomas *Clarkson, the leading abolitionist, lobbied European statesmen at the peace negotiations, pressing for an *international* abolition of the slave trade. Faced with the prospect of a renewal of French slave-trading, British abolitionism was revived in 1814–15, and something like 1.5 million people (from a population of 12 million) signed the new abolition petitions. Talleyrand, the chief French negotiator at the Congress of Vienna, thought that British abolitionism had become 'a passion carried to fanaticism, and one which the Ministry is no longer at liberty to check'. As peace settled on Europe in 1815, the British were determined to prevent others from doing what they had perfected in the last century. They (and the abolitionist Americans) were not, however, completely successful, for over the next half-century, until the 1860s, when the Atlantic slave trade was effectively brought to an end, more than 2 million Africans were shipped to the Americas.

Abolitionists were worried about news from the West Indies. There, Nonconformist missionaries were attracting and converting ever more slaves by the year, despite the planters' strenuous efforts to obstruct and confuse. And as more slaves became Christian, they seemed to offer more and more strenuous resistance. Between the end of the war (1815) and 1831 slave uprisings, each one more violent than the last, each one repressed with a plantocractic and colonial violence that appalled British onlookers, seemed to confirm that West Indian slavery was a system that could only be kept in place by violence on a medieval scale. Throughout, of course, the West Indies lobby, its power on the wane in London, objected and obstructed.

Equally troublesome for abolitionists was the realization that cutting off the supply of imported Africans would not, in itself, bring slavery in the Americas to an end. This was particularly clear when abolitionists looked at the United States. Although North America had been in the vanguard of abolition in the revolutionary years, and had ended its own slave trade in the 1808, by the 1820s it had a thriving internal slave system in the cotton fields of the South, with enormous beneficial consequences for the material well-being of the United States in general. Cutting off supplies of Africans had clearly *not* brought slavery to an end there.

But the main British concern was the Caribbean. There were, of course, many people in Britain who knew the islands very well indeed. In addition, a number of prominent churches and sects had dispatched missionaries to work in the islands to win over the slaves to Christianity, and consequently information about slave life was readily available in Britain. But it required editing and dissemination. The government also began its own information-gathering (via slave registration) about slave society, beginning in Trinidad in 1812. This 'registration' of the slave population—a census—was the only accurate means of assessing the real impact of the abolition of the slave trade. In the bitter parliamentary struggle about extending registration to all West Indian slaves, planters and their backers inevitably resisted the idea of *any* form of government or colonial interference between them and their slaves. But eventually, in 1819, an Act was passed authorizing the registration of all slaves from 1820 onwards. Though the data were slow to accumulate, after 1820 indisputable demographic evidence began to emerge about the exact impact of abolition.

Abolitionists now had access to raw demographic data, which they could use to promote slave emancipation. In the process a marked change came over the campaign for slave emancipation. Like the initial evidence about the slave trade, the use of slave registration data by the abolitionists shifted the arguments about slavery from the impressionistic and hearsay to the specific and indisputable. Whatever flaws existed about those data, they were minor when set against the powerful evidence they made available to the abolitionist camp.

Planters, of course, had been bitterly opposed to slave registration. They hated the abolitionist movement, and resisted any attempt to make them accountable for their day-to-day management of plantations and slaves. Above all slave owners continued to worry about slave unrest. Haiti had, after all, become an independent black nation as recently as 1804, and the shadow of the *Haitian Revolution continued to trouble planters throughout the Americas. Planters accused abolitionists and their friends of encouraging slave unrest and of elevating slave expectations. Then, in 1816, the Bussa rebellion erupted in Barbados.

Violence and resistance were part of the broader story of African slavery in the Americas (though less strikingly so in North America.) Slave revolts in the British Caribbean were widespread, common, and unpredictable. Planters and colonial authorities feared them, planned how best to head them off or crush them, and never fully trusted the slaves (who greatly outnumbered them.) Yet Barbados seemed an unlikely place for a slave revolt. Its slave population was overwhelmingly local-born, and imported Africans no longer played a major economic or social role as they did in so many of the other islands. But local planters had made a rod for their own back. They denounced slave registration, and their careless and indiscreet table talk helped to persuade slaves that planters were denying them the freedom already granted by London. Bussa's rebellion of 1816 was crushed: 120 slaves killed, 144 executed, 132 deported; but relieved Barbadian planters were in no doubt that slave unrest continued to simmer, fanned by the debate about emancipation.

Above all, planters feared the slaves, with their simple but persistent demand for freedom; secondly, they feared British abolitionists demanding positive action and change in the slaves' condition; thirdly, they feared missionaries, who were industrious in luring armies of slaves to their church or chapel. Lastly, and not least, planters had to contend with the British government, which seemed always eager to criticize planters on behalf of the slaves.

Slaves everywhere had traditionally resisted their bondage, in Africa, on the slave ships, and on the plantations, though their resistance was not always violent or threatening. Foot-dragging, feigning ignorance, acting stupid, misunderstanding orders, running away—all and more formed a leitmotif of slavery throughout the Atlantic slave empires. But violence was rarely far away.

Violence was at its most obvious in the raw, brutal realities of slave life (on the slave ships and on the plantations). The growing awareness of the violence at the heart of slavery helped to swing British opinion against slavery. The abolitionist campaigns made clever and effective use of slave sufferings to create a public mood that was resolutely opposed first to the slave trade, and later to slavery itself. In fact the inhuman realities of slavery had begun to dawn on the British reading public even *before* the abolitionist campaign was launched in 1787. Slave cases in English courts, notably the **Somerset* case of 1772, the words of a small number of black writers and activists living in London in the 1770s and 1780s, and some powerful visual images helped to reveal the truth about Atlantic slavery. Black writers, for example, provided the public with first-hand accounts of slave life, and of black experiences in Britain itself.

For all their differences, black writers returned, each in their own distinctive way, to common themes: to the inhumanity of slavery, to the ungodly acts of Christian Britons, and to the attainments of industrious, independent black people (i.e. the authors) when allowed to flourish outside slavery. These were the very issues promoted by the abolitionists in order to establish the simple point that blacks were indeed men and women, brothers and sisters.

In this protracted campaign against slavery, the full horror of what was being revealed sometimes overwhelmed even the staunchest of abolitionists, never more graphically than in the **Zong* massacre of 1781. Yet no one was brought to account for that mass murder. Despite its unique, unspeakable horror, the *Zong* case was in keeping with the fate of slave rebels and resistant slaves on other ships and on the plantations. Slave disputes, plots, outbursts, violence, and individual truculence, all and more were greeted by white brutality on an astonishing scale, and all doled out by sailors, soldiers, planters, and colonial officials. Violence was the essential lubricant of the slave system: in the management of slave ships, and in the daily conduct of plantation life. Slaves inevitably responded with violence of their own, though it merely provoked further white brutality against them and a tightening of the local slave laws. Slave violence further hardened the heart of the whites against slaves in general. Haiti provided the slave lobby with the ultimate proof of their view that slaves were untrustworthy, and that it was madness to tamper with the slave system.

The details of slave life in the Caribbean were, then, basic to the ebb and flow of British political argument between 1787 and 1838. After the return of peace in 1815 there was a greatly heightened interest in Britain about slaves and slavery. In this the slaves played their own role, notably via the revolts, beginning with Bussa's rebellion in 1816. By then, the planters had found that slavery was being undermined from a number of different directions. The slaves' own stratagems of resistance gnawed away at slavery. Missionaries were also digging away, often unconsciously, at its foundations. At a grander, strategic level, debates about the slave trade made headlines wherever European diplomats gathered after the war. All this, taken together, gave slavery an unprecedented political importance. Moreover, the slaves themselves were acutely aware of the debate in Britain. Planters, merchants, and traders, sailors and visitors to the islands, all and more discussed and argued, chatted and gossiped, about the way slavery was being handled in London. Information about the emancipation debate quickly passed from the great house to the slave cabins. The Atlantic world had always been characterized by information networks, as hard news and gossip passed from one corner of that system to another: via slave ships and seamen, via slaves and their masters, from merchants to planters. Slaves knew they had friends in Britain, and they also knew that their Caribbean owners were resistant to whatever beneficial changes were being planned.

2. Christianity It was also clear that the work of missionaries was having a profoundly disruptive effect on slavery. Though British churches laid down strict rules about missionary work, ordering their representatives in the slave colonies not to upset the delicate social balance in the slave colonies, it proved an impossible task. The missionaries' very presence among the slaves was deeply unsettling. So too was their message, however much it might be couched in theological terms. The established Anglican Church had long failed to minister to the slaves (or to the planters for that matter). But that changed, from the 1780s, when a string of Nonconformist missionaries began to make major inroads into the slave communities. Baptists and Methodists, following where German Moravians had begun in the mid-century, set sail for the islands with strict warnings ringing in their ears. 'Remember that the object is not to teach the principles and the laws of an earthly kingdom . . . but the principles and laws of the Kingdom of Christ.'

It was not quite that easy, and there was an inevitable slippage from the theological to the secular. Much of what the missionaries said to the slaves seemed (at least to the slaves) to speak directly to their worldly condition. More telling still, the Christian message quickly passed into the hands of local black preachers. Local chapels, mastery of the Bible, the hymns, and home-grown slave preachers, all served to place a potent weapon in the hands of the slaves.

Many Anglicans, including prominent evangelicals, felt uneasy about the work of the missionaries to the slave islands, though everyone agreed that Christianity was the first step towards 'civilizing' the slaves. Christianity was both a means and an end—the way forward in winning over the benighted peoples of the world to a civilized form of society. It was hard to see how they could proceed down that road without causing unpredictable social consequences among the slaves themselves.

The Christianization of slaves was, then, a vital part of the aspirations of all abolitionists. In his 'Sketch of a Negro Code' (1792) Edmund Burke specified that 'A competent minister of some Christian church or congregation shall be provided for the full instruction of the Negroes . . . '. Christian churches would provide slaves with the armoury of personal and social skills to enable them to survive as free people. If slaves could gradually adopt the social skills acquired by Christian conversion, the task of emancipation would be so much easier. What no one realized or predicted was that this drive into the slave quarters would have remarkable consequences.

It created, for example, a growing band of British supporters of black freedom. The very groups actively converting the slaves, especially the Baptists and Methodists, were also expanding rapidly in Britain. British Nonconformists naturally felt a bond of sympathy for their Caribbean co-religionists, even though they were slaves. There were, for example, more than a quarter of a million British Methodists by the 1820s, and perhaps 100,000 British Baptists twenty years later. By then there were almost 15,000 dissenting places of worship across Britain. Nonconformity had clearly become a major force in Britain, and this was to have a major impact on the campaign against slavery. Moreover, British Nonconformity was increasing most rapidly in new, industrializing areas of rapid population growth. It was as if the people of this 'new Britain' (the Britain we normally associate with industrial change) were the very people who lent their numbers and gave voice to demands for an end to slavery. Nonconformity could muster growing numbers of British people, and it spoke with great eloquence in the British campaign for slave emancipation in the 1820s and 1830s. Equally importantly, Nonconformist Christianity transformed slave life itself.

3. Slave revolts Before 1807 planters had been able to replenish their enslaved labour force by purchasing Africans from the slave ships. Some islands, notably Barbados (like North America), had been able to dispense with the Atlantic slave trade and rely on their own local-born slaves. Other slave colonies, notably the 'new' colonies acquired in the recent wars (such as Trinidad) and recently established frontier societies (such as Demerara, from 1831 part of British Guiana), continued to need new Africans—or other forms of labour. Now, after 1807, planters everywhere had to rethink their slave management systems: they had to plan for a world without imported Africans. For their part, abolitionists, government officials, and other outsiders looked at the islands with very great suspicion. The planters had long since shown their true colours: always hostile to the abolition of the slave trade, they continued to resist *any* outside interference with the slave system in the islands, and were permanently reluctant partners in any scheme emanating from London. It was clear to all concerned, on both sides of the Atlantic, that planters (and the slave lobby as a whole) would drag their feet in any change demanded of them.

The most obvious and immediate consequence of the end of the slave trade in 1807 was a short-term decline in the slave population. With fewer slaves at their disposal, planters increased their demands on their labour force. They began to reorganize their labour force, switching slaves around, demanding more of all of them, and generally interfering with work systems and labour conventions on the plantations which slaves had long been accustomed to. Planters also began to shuffle slaves around from one property to another: 'rationalizing' their labour force to suit their broader interests. Such changes often caused great inconvenience and distress to the slaves. Women and children found themselves undertaking tasks previously reserved for males. Privileged, skilled, or elite slaves might now find themselves thrust into rougher, more physically demanding work. Slaves who had long been accustomed to better working conditions now found themselves toiling in the fields. While all this made economic sense to planters, it angered and confused the slaves themselves.

These changes are easily illustrated. There were, for example, now more women working in the sugar fields. Similarly, there were more 'coloured' slaves in the fields. Stated crudely, fairer-skinned children could no longer expect the preferential treatment normally accorded to the offspring of black and white. On top of all this it was clear enough that slaves were *not* becoming more docile. It was as if the expectations of the abolitionists were being dashed at the very time that the fears of the planters were confirmed. The truth was altogether simpler, however. The events of 1807 had been a leap in the dark, and no one knew exactly what would happen when the transatlantic flow of Africans stopped.

Planters hoped that as the older generation of Africans died naturally, a new population of Creole slaves, born into Caribbean slavery and never having known freedom or Africa (except via slave folklore), would become more manageable and biddable. Yet the very contrary seemed to be happening, and planters assumed that the slaves' truculence was heightened by outside interference: by a critical and inquisitive British government and its colonial officers, and by the swarm of missionaries luring slaves to the chapels and prayer meetings. What happened after 1807 confirmed their greatest fears.

First there was Bussa's rebellion in Barbados. But worse was to follow. The newly developed slave lands in Demerara attracted a new breed of aggressive investors and planters, including John *Gladstone, father of the future Prime Minister. These planters managed their slaves by a draconian system that flew in the face of abolitionist (and government) expectations. Missionaries dispatched to that unforgiving climate were shocked by what they found.

The exploitation of slaves, though commonplace in the story of Atlantic slavery, was often at its worst in the early days of settlement and expansion, in societies that were frontier communities. Demerara's plantocratic crudeness may be explained by its early state of development: it was perhaps comparable to 17th-century Barbados and Jamaica. But times and sensibilities had changed. What had gone unnoticed and uncriticized two centuries earlier was unacceptable to an ever more inquisitive British society of the early 19th century. The planters, however, seemed *not* to have changed, though now, in the 1820s, and unlike the earlier days of settlement, their every move was scrutinized by missionaries on the spot. Reports of plantocratic wrongdoings sped back to British congregations.

Slaves in Demerara, heavily concentrated on the coastal regions and along the rivers, had long been notable for their resistance and for running away, and barbaric punishment was commonplace. When John Smith arrived as a missionary in 1817, slaves in Demerara flocked to his new congregations. Six years later, in 1823, local slaves rose in revolt, to be swiftly suppressed by colonial and plantocratic forces. The subsequent summary and legal punishments were excessive and gory. In response to the killing of three white people some 250 slaves were killed. Smith, too, was tried in a protracted hearing made all the more dramatic by his own decline into consumption. He died in jail in February 1824, shortly before his royal pardon was received.

Smith's death provoked an outcry in Britain, and succeeded in focusing attention on slavery, instantly reviving the flagging British abolition cause. The revolt naturally sent shock waves through the other slave islands, but its most important impact was in Britain, where it was now abundantly clear that West Indian slavery stood condemned by the actions of its principal proponents and beneficiaries.

Humanitarians seized on Smith's death to goad a hesitant government to move towards slave manumission. Ever more people wanted to wash their hands of the entire slave system and there was a mood of profound disgust, and a feeling that slavery must brought to an end.

The practical problem remained: what to do? In the 1820s slave registration returns showed that the slave population was in decline, and would continue to decline until a new generation of slaves entered their child-bearing years. The labour regime controlling the slaves was tighter than ever, and everywhere Christian missionaries were winning over more and more slaves. The open hostility of planters towards these missionaries and towards Christian slaves merely confirmed the need to bring down the system. At the precise moment when religious disabilities (notably against Roman Catholics) were being removed in Britain, it was ironic to see newly converted slaves harassed and obstructed in their Christian worship in the West Indies. Casting a shadow over the whole region was the violence that seemed to be the hallmark both of plantocratic management and even of colonial administration.

By the mid-1820s the slave islands seemed like survivors from a lost epoch. The death of John Smith and the legions of slaves slaughtered at the same time dispelled any remaining optimism that the slave islands could be expected to improve themselves. In 1823 it was time, once again, to rally the abolitionist troops.

4. The final push The new abolitionist campaign really began with the idea that slavery could be undermined by an attack on sugar duties. Without the help of these duties, British Caribbean islands could not compete with sugar grown in other parts of the world. The abolitionists' new idea was simple: expose slave-grown sugar to free competition and it would simply collapse from its own inefficiencies. Some of the earliest abolitionist arguments (in the 1770s and 1780s, for example) had embraced an economic critique of slavery, though rarely as a pivotal objection. By the 1820s, however, other, cheaper sugars were readily available on the world market. The economic point that free and open competition for sugar would undermine West Indian slavery, originally advanced by Quakers with interests in the East Indies in the early 1820s, had become widely accepted by the end of the decade.

James Cropper, a Quaker with East Indies interests, was especially prominent in addressing the economics of slave-grown sugar, and he and other abolitionists were convinced that they needed public opinion on their side: what they needed was a reprise of the campaign against the slave trade.

With this in mind the Society for the Amelioration and Gradual Abolition of Slavery was founded late in January 1823. Within a year Thomas Clarkson (the durable survivor from the 1780s) had galvanized the creation of 250 societies across Britain. Over the next decade these local societies, whose membership was largely female, provided the impetus for the campaign. A central London committee orchestrated the campaign, with the country divided into organizational districts, and all were encouraged to rally support and petitions for black freedom. It was instantly a national and influential pressure group, made all the more influential by the energy and activities of female abolitionists, many working through their own associations.

The ideological core of the campaign was, however, different from that of its forebears. The economics of anti-slavery had now shifted to the centre of the argument, though always aligned with the older moral and religious objections. Thus, for the first time, slavery found itself under attack from a powerful combination of economic and moral objections. The argument that slavery was both wrong and uneconomic appealed to huge numbers of British people, and the West Indies lobby found itself facing an impossible task: of trying to support both the morality *and* the economic utility of the slave system. Yet on both counts they were outflanked by events, and by abolitionist arguments. What possible justification could be offered for the recent treatment of slaves in Demerara, or for the persecution of black Christians in the islands? And why should British consumers pay more for their sugar just to keep the slave system in place?

By the mid-1820s planters were clearly on the defensive, and were facing massive well-organized, articulate ranks of British people who were now wedded to demands for black freedom—sooner rather than later. Abolition had in effect captured the high ground of both morality and economics.

Early in 1823 the Commons, under this pressure, established a key principle, by resolving to press for *gradual* slave emancipation. The indefatigable Clarkson found support from all corners of the country, from all political quarters, and, critically, from most churches. Despite resistance in the Lords, black freedom no longer divided the British but had, instead, become an issue that united them as no other. Abolitionists were confident that they could create outraged public opinion, which would make emancipation inevitable: Parliament would be unable to resist demands for black freedom.

After 1823 the campaign for emancipation was characterized by petitions, publications, and lectures to packed audiences, often (to modern eyes) of incredible length. Overspill audiences, people locked out, hundreds defying bad weather to get to a lecture—all and more bore testimony to the staggering popularity of the abolitionist campaign. Through all this, female abolitionists and their own, discrete organizations were vital; these women were at the heart of the campaign, as organizers, lecturers, and audiences. Female abolition was important in itself, but also as part of the much broader and more deep-seated shift towards female political activism. Abolitionist publications fluttered down in profusion on an increasingly literate people. Between 1823 and 1831 the Anti-Slavery Society issued more than 3 million tracts, about half a million in 1831 alone. This was in addition to the publications from local abolition groups and abolitionist material in the local and London newspapers.

Nonetheless, abolition in Parliament languished. Wilberforce was old and weary, handing over the parliamentary leadership to Thomas Fowell *Buxton. But by 1830 little headway had been made in Parliament, despite public feeling. Of course emancipation was only one of a number of reforming issues confronting Parliament. Dominating everything was the reform of Parliament. Younger abolitionists began to tire of their leaders' apparently endless patience in asking for black freedom, and in 1832 the Agency Committee was founded by George Stephen and Emmanuel and James Cropper (both Quakers) to press for *immediate* emancipation. However, the British political scene was overwhelmed by the national panic caused by the terrible cholera epidemic of 1832, which killed 32,000 people. Many thought that the disaster was divine punishment for a national sin: and what sin could have been greater than slavery? And, as if to confirm this judgement of the Almighty's wrath, Jamaican slaves revolted in 1831–2.

The Jamaican revolt was quite unlike those in Barbados in 1816 or Demerara in 1823. It was a massive upheaval involving 60,000 slaves; it caused the death of fourteen Whites and saw the killing of 540 slaves. Led by the inspirational preacher Sam Sharpe, the revolt raced out of control through western Jamaica, with estates torched and Baptist slaves at the forefront. There was something new about this revolt. Sharpe, though still a slave, personified the power of black Christianity and the disruptive message inherent in biblical imagery.

News of the Jamaican revolt, and of its violent repression, caused an outcry in

Britain. On the eve of the debate for parliamentary reform, missionaries returning from Jamaica roused British audiences with all the latest news from the island. Their messages added an emotive element to the wider debate both for black freedom and for the Reform Bill. When a parliamentary election was called in August 1832, using the new reformed franchise, abolitionists seized their chance to force parliamentary candidates to declare their views on emancipation. Something like 200 MPs declared themselves for black freedom. The reform of Parliament in 1832 thus paved the way for the ending of slavery.

Earl Grey's new government resolved to end slavery—but the Lords, again, remained doggedly supportive of the planters. Now, however, the arguments in Parliament were about when, and under precisely what conditions, slaves would be freed. Finally, the Abolition of Slavery Bill of August 1833 initiated black freedom in August 1834. It was a limited form of freedom. All slaves under the age of 6 were freed immediately, and the rest became 'apprentices' for up to six years, working most of their time (for free) for their ex-owners. Bermuda and Antigua opted for immediate emancipation.

Parliament also allocated a staggering £20 million to be distributed on a per capita basis, not to the slaves, but to the slave owners. Lord Harewood, for example, already fabulously wealthy from his family's sugar trading and West Indian plantations, received more than £26,000 for the 1,277 slaves still in his possession. Abolitionists asked the obvious questions: why not compensate the slaves instead?

The apprenticeship scheme, monitored by a new breed of magistrates dispatched to the islands, was clearly a temporary sop to the planters' demand for labour, but evidence of the scheme's failings was abundant, and was used by abolitionists to continue their demands for full freedom. They kept up the pressure using the old tactics. They spoke for a 'new' Britain, of urban, industrial, and dissenting British life. Slavery tended to find support in small-town, rural Britain—and the Lords. However, there was little the slave lobby could do to save slavery, and on 1 August 1838 apprenticeship was brought to an early end, and full manumission was granted.

Convinced that ex-slaves would remember the long litany of personal and collective grievances, planters feared an understandable revenge. In the event, three-quarters of a million ex-slaves celebrated their newly won freedom in the most peaceable fashion: large numbers simply went to church. Across the Caribbean, 1 August 1838 was celebrated peacefully. Freed slaves made their way to celebrate freedom in parades, public meetings, but above all in crowded churches. It was a staggering turn of events. Here after all was a system which for almost three centuries had defined relations between black and white in the Americas, and which had been rooted in violence. At every point of the compass—from Africa, in mid-Atlantic, or on the American plantations—slavery had throughout been characterized by violence. Although slavery had been ended in Haiti by the volcanic slave revolt in the 1790s and, although slavery in the United States was to end in the bloodshed of the Civil War, the British system ended peacefully. And both the slave trade and slavery itself had been ended by Acts of Parliament. JW

Ferguson, Moira, *Subject to Others: British Women Writers and Colonial Slavery, 1670–1834* (1992)

Green, William A., *British Slave Emancipation: The Sugar Colonies and the Great Experiment, 1830–1865* (1976)

Jennings, Judith, *The Business of Abolishing the British Slave Trade, 1783–1807* (1997)

Midgley, Clare, *Women Against Slavery: The British Campaigns, 1780–1870* (1992)

Turner, Mary, *Slaves and Missionaries: The Disintegration of Jamaican Slave Society, 1787–1834* (1982)

Wood, Marcus, *Blind Memory: Visual Representations of Slavery in England and America 1780–1865* (2000)

See also SLAVE TRADE; SLAVERY

Emidy, Joseph Antonio (*c*.1775–1835). Violinist and composer, celebrated and admired as a remarkable musician in Cornish society after his humble beginnings as a slave. Emidy, was born in Guinea, West Africa, sold into slavery in 1787 by Portuguese traders, and then taken to Brazil. He came to Lisbon with his new owner, who recognized his interest in music and provided him with a violin and a tutor. He progressed musically, and by 1795 was a second violinist in the orchestra of the Opera House in Lisbon.

However, in 1795, when Sir Edward Pellow brought his ship the *Indefatigable* into the river Tagus in Lisbon for repairs, he and other officers attended the Lisbon opera. After seeing Emidy perform in the orchestra, they kidnapped him, forcing him to come aboard their ship as their fiddler to perform dances (which he loathed) to entertain the sailors and raise their morale as they sailed.

After four years he was released in Falmouth in February 1799. To earn a living he taught music in Cornwall: the piano, violoncello, and clarinet. He conducted an orchestra of a local harmonic society and composed symphonies for orchestra, quartets, and quintets that were received enthusiastically throughout Cornwall. Through his marriage to Jenefer Hutchins in 1802, six children were born and he was warmly welcomed into Cornish social circles. Attempts to raise his profile in London with sponsors such as Johann Peter Salomon (1745–1815) failed, owing to fears concerning prejudice against his race. Emidy died in Truro in 1835. PAH

Buckingham, James Silk, 'Emidy, a Negro Musician' in Buckingham, *The Black Perspective in Music* (1973)

Wright, Josephine, 'Early African Musicians in Britain' in Rainer E. Lotz and Ian Pegg (eds.), *Under the Imperial Carpet: Essays in Black History 1780–1950* (1986)

See also MUSIC 1: CLASSICAL MUSIC

Empire Windrush. Ship that brought the first large group of Caribbean immigrants to the United Kingdom in 1948. The *Empire Windrush* actually started life in 1931 as a German liner, the *Monte Rosa*. During the Second World War she was commandeered by the Third Reich and in 1947 was transferred to the British as one of the spoils of war. Renamed the *Empire Windrush* in March of that year, she then served as troopship, carrying servicemen to and from parts of the British Empire. In both 1947 and 1948 she voyaged to the Caribbean and on that latter trip stopped over in Jamaica. An advertisement was placed in the *Daily Gleaner* newspaper to say that 300 passage berths to England would be available for the sum of £28 10s. each. Because of the depressed economic situation that existed in Jamaica at that time, there was great competition for these very limited places. Thus when the *Empire Windrush* sailed on 24 May, there were 492 passengers (and six stowaways) on board.

Most of the passengers were young adult men, including a number of ex-servicemen, a small group of boxers, and the Trinidadian calypsonian Lord *Kitchener (Aldwyn Roberts). Most of them viewed the journey to England as an opportunity to learn a new trade, and thus only intended to stay in the country for a limited period of time.

In Britain itself the imminent arrival of these immigrants sent the Civil Service into a panic over who had authorized them to come to the country. The Minister of Labour, George Isaacs, was quick to sound warnings that, rather than opportunities, these men should expect to encounter difficulty and disappointment. Nevertheless, when the *Empire Windrush* docked at Tilbury on 22 June, the passengers were greeted with some degree of civility and a great many were housed in shelters in Clapham South until they were able to find work. Most of this initial group subsequently found employment within a month, and gradually were able to establish themselves within the community at large.

Today the arrival of the *Empire Windrush* is viewed as a turning point in the recent history of Britain, and has come to symbolize the many ways in which Caribbean people have contributed to and transformed aspects of British life. She was, however, just one of a whole series of ships that would subsequently bring Caribbean immigrants to Britain over the next thirteen years. Despite popular misconceptions, until 1951 the numbers arriving from the region were quite small and never exceeded 1,000 a year. The bulk of Caribbean migration took place between 1955 and 1961, peaking at 66,000 in that latter year as the final rush took place to beat the new Commonwealth Immigrants Bill, which was announced in October 1961 and became law in July 1962. The *Empire Windrush* herself played no further role in this movement of people from the Caribbean, and was sadly lost at sea after a massive fire in her engine room in March 1954. LM

Phillips, Mike, and Phillips, Trevor, *Windrush: The Irresistible Rise of Multi-Racial Britain* (1998)

Seybold, W. N., *The Loss of the Troopship Empire Windrush* (1998)

See also REFUGEES AND ASYLUM-SEEKERS

England, Carmen (1909–1991). Pioneering black businesswoman and one of the founders of the *Notting Hill Carnival. Born Carmen Maingot in Port of Spain, Trinidad, she came to England in 1931 to attend the Royal Academy of Music, studying piano and violin. Among her friends in England were C. L. R. *James and Eric *Williams. She stayed in England, pursuing her musical career, until 1938, when she returned to Trinidad, playing the piano in public concerts, teaching music, and starting a hairdressing business. She returned to England in 1946, travelling with one of her pupils, Winifred *Atwell.

She met and married the impresario Paul England, but unlike Atwell decided not to continue her career in music. Instead she continued hairdressing, setting up a salon in a Forces club managed by her husband and beginning to produce hair products for her black customers—an example imitated by Atwell in the 1950s. When the club closed, she opened a salon, Carmen Colonial Hairdressers, in South Kensington. She opened a social club in the basement, which had murals painted by the Trinidad artist Althea McNish. Carmen England worked for television and film, did broadcasts on the BBC Overseas Service, and trained many women from Africa, the Caribbean, as well as Europe, in hairdressing. The initial meetings for the Notting Hill Carnival, started by Claudia *Jones, were held in her home, and England coached contestants for the Carnival Queen competition, which she supervised. By 1971 she had opened a new salon in Piccadilly Arcade, but her last years were plagued by ill health and a long legal battle with the Bristol-Myers Corporation over the use of the name Carmen. PF

Oliver, Paul, *Black Music in Britain: Essays on the Afro-Asian Contribution to Popular Music* (1990)

See also BUSINESSES

Equiano, Olaudah (1745?–1797). The most important and one of the most widely published authors of African descent in the English-speaking world of the 18th century. Equiano helped to found the genre of the slave narrative when he published *The Interesting Narrative of the Life of Olaudah Equiano, or Gustavus Vassa, the African: Written by Himself* in London in March 1789. The *Interesting Narrative* is a spiritual autobiography, captivity narrative, travel book, adventure tale, slavery narrative, economic treatise, apologia, and argument against the transatlantic slave trade and slavery. From its first appearance the *Interesting Narrative* has also been recognized as the classic description of an African society before contact with Europeans, as well as of the forced transatlantic transportation of enslaved Africans known since the 18th century as the Middle Passage.

By his own account, Equiano was born in 1745 in 'Eboe', in the kingdom of Benin, in what is now south-eastern Nigeria. He says that he was the youngest of six sons of one of the 'elders or chiefs . . . styled Embrenché', and named '*Olaudah*, which, in our language, signifies vicissitude, or fortunate also; one favoured, and having a loud voice and well spoken'. When he was about 11 years old, he tells us, he and his only sister were kidnapped by other Africans and eventually separated and sold to European slave traders, who took him to Barbados. After a few days in the West Indies, he writes, he was taken to Virginia, where he was sold to a local planter. Michael Henry Pascal, a lieutenant in the British Royal Navy, soon bought him from the planter, ironically renamed him Gustavus Vassa after the 16th-century Swedish liberator of his oppressed countrymen, and took him to London in 1757. Equiano served under Pascal in the Seven Years War (1756–63), but, refusing to free him, Pascal sold him into West Indian slavery at the end of 1762. He purchased his own freedom in 1766.

Equiano remained in the employ of his former master, the Quaker Robert King, for a year, making several trading trips to Georgia and Pennsylvania. Between 1767 and 1773, now based in London, he worked on commercial vessels sailing to the Mediterranean and the West Indies, and commented on all the versions of slavery, white and black, he observed. After joining an expedition to the Arctic seeking a Northeast Passage in 1773, he returned to London, where he embraced Methodism. Soon growing restless again, in 1775–6 he helped his friend and former employer Dr Charles Irving in a short-lived attempt to establish a plantation in Central America, with Equiano acting as buyer and driver (overseer) of the black slaves. He returned to London in 1777, and published hostile newspaper reviews of pro-slavery books and argued for racial intermarriage (he married an Englishwoman, Susanna Cullen, in 1792). He became increasingly involved with Thomas *Clarkson, Quobna Ottobah *Cugoano, James *Ramsay, Granville *Sharp, and others in efforts to help his fellow Blacks, with the project to resettle the black poor in Sierra Leone (*see* SIERRA LEONE SETTLERS), and with the drive to abolish the African slave trade.

Equiano's *Interesting Narrative* was immediately recognized as a remarkable achievement, earning the praise of Mary Wollstonecraft and other reviewers. His pre-publication advertisements for the book and supervision of the publication and distribution of nine British editions between 1789 and 1794 make him an important figure in the history of book publishing. During his lifetime unauthorized editions and translations appeared in the Netherlands (1790), New York (1791), Germany (1792), and Russia (1794). Part of the book's great popularity can be attributed to the timing of its initial publication at the height of the movement in Britain to abolish the slave trade. The *Narrative* offered the only account by a former slave of slavery in Africa, on the Middle Passage, as well as in the West Indies, North America, the Mediterranean, the Middle East, and Britain. His first reviewers quickly acknowledged the significance of the first-hand perspective of the *Narrative*, which greatly influenced the development of the 19th-century African-American slave narrative. Equiano's will demonstrates that when he died on 31 March 1797 he was the wealthiest black man in the English-speaking world, having achieved the economic and social status he had sought throughout his life.

Unfortunately, Equiano did not live to see the abolition of the slave trade he had done so much to accomplish. The political triumph of the abolitionist cause in 1807 came ten years too late for him to celebrate. It might not have come as soon as that, however, had he not contributed to the cause by so skilfully and creatively fashioning the story of his life 'to put a speedy end to a traffic both cruel and unjust'. He gave the abolitionist cause the African voice it needed. The role he played in the last mission of his life earned him the right to claim an African name that 'signifies vicissitude, or fortunate also; one favoured, and having a loud voice and well spoken'. That role also entitled him to accept the name of a European liberator of his people ironically given him in slavery.

Recent biographical discoveries, however, cast doubt on Equiano's story of his birth and early years. Baptismal and naval records suggest that he was born in South Carolina around 1747 and thus that he may have invented his African heritage and his much quoted account of the

Middle Passage on a slave ship for rhetorical purposes. Other recently discovered evidence proves that he first reached England in December 1754, making him significantly younger when he came under Pascal's control than he claims. On the other hand, all surviving archival and published records from the period after 1757 attest to Equiano's astoundingly accurate memory of his life once he arrived in England.

Equiano's autobiography has become a true classic of world literature, as well as a primary historical document. He has far more readers today in Africa, Europe, and America than he had during his lifetime, despite the great popularity of the *Interesting Narrative* in his own day. Whether authentic or not, his description of the Middle Passage from Africa to America remains the most frequently quoted account of that experience. His African-British autobiography became the model for writers of 19th-century African-American slave narratives, as well as for later authors of fictional representations of slave life in the Americas. VC

Carretta, Vincent, *Equiano the African* (2005)

Edwards, Paul (ed.), *The Life of Olaudah Equiano* (1969)

—— and Walvin, James, *Black Personalities in the Era of the Slave Trade* (1983)

See also GRONNIOSAW, JAMES ALBERT UKAWSAW; SANCHO, IGNATIUS; WHEATLEY, PHYLLIS

Ethiopia, Italian invasion of. Fascist Italy's unprovoked invasion of Ethiopia in 1935, then better known abroad as Abyssinia, was one of the most important international events between the two world wars. Carried out in defiance of the League of Nations, it produced worldwide indignation, notably in Britain and among African nationalists.

Italy's interest in Ethiopia dated back to the late 19th century, when the Italian government established the colonies of Eritrea and Somalia, to the north and south of the country respectively. The Italians had tried to establish a protectorate over Ethiopia in 1889, but this was foiled by the Ethiopian emperor Menelik II's victory at Adowa in 1896. This was remembered in Italy: the Italian dictator Mussolini sought to 'revenge Adowa', and obtain a 'place in the sun' for Italy's supposed 'surplus population'.

Mussolini's decision to invade was taken in 1933. Road, port, and airport facilities in Eritrea were thereupon rapidly expanded. Mussolini's pretext for war was the Wal Wal incident of 5 December 1934, when Ethiopian soldiers clashed with Italian irregulars 60 miles into Ethiopia's semi-desert Ogaden province. Emperor *Haile Selassie proposed arbitration, but Mussolini rejected it and intensified his military preparations.

Faced with imminent war, the British and French governments, whose colonial territories surrounded Ethiopia, adopted a policy of 'neutrality', by denying military equipment to both sides. This scarcely affected Italy, which produced its own armaments, but left Ethiopia, which had to import them, with few modern weapons.

The invasion, launched from both Eritrea and Somalia, began without any declaration of war on 3 October 1935. The League of Nations branded Italy the aggressor, on 11 October, and imposed economic sanctions, which were, however, too mild to halt the invaders. They had overwhelming military superiority, and complete control of the skies—from which they dropped mustard gas and tons of bombs. The Emperor, defeated in March–April 1936, fled the country at the beginning of May. Ethiopian patriots, however, continued their resistance throughout the occupation, which continued until 1941.

The invasion provoked excitement throughout the continent, and generated growing Pan-African awareness. Jomo Kenyatta, of Kenya, and other Africans in Britain formed the International African Friends of Abyssinia, whose members later propagated Pan-African ideas. Interest in Ethiopia—and its resistance to the Italians—was strong among politically conscious Africans, notably in Nigeria and the Gold Coast (now Ghana), and among peoples of African descent in America and the West Indies. Sylvia Pankhurst's pro-Ethiopian weekly the *New Times and Ethiopian News* was widely read, and quoted in African publications, while the *Voice of Ethiopia*, run by Dr Melaku Beyen, an Ethiopian refugee in the United States, activated black Americans. Awareness of Ethiopia's 'heroic struggle', and of the Emperor's defence of his country, did much to encourage *Rastafarianism and the foundation of the Ethiopian World Federation, which still exists. RKPP

Makonnen, Ras, *Pan-Africanism from Within* (1973)
Mockler, Anthony, *Haile Selassie's War* (1984)
Pankhurst, Richard, *Sylvia Pankhurst, Counsel for Ethiopia* (2003)
Waley, Daniel, *British Public Opinion and the Ethiopian War* (1976)

See also SECOND WORLD WAR

Eugenics. The science of selective breeding for the health of a race, considered to have directly contributed to racist theorizing.

1. Galton, eugenics, and racial superiority
2. Eugenics and the health of the nation

1. Galton, eugenics, and racial superiority The term 'eugenics' was introduced to Britain by Sir Francis *Galton, a cousin of Charles Darwin, in his *Inquiries into the Human Faculty* (1883). Galton defined eugenics as 'the study of agencies under social control that may improve or impair the racial qualities of future generations either physically or mentally'. In *Natural Inheritance* (1889), Galton concluded that genius was inherited and passed on through blood relations.

Eugenics may be characterized as the coming together of the scientific, the statistical, and the social. This synergy is exemplified in the work of Karl Pearson, a student of Galton. Pearson, a Fellow of the Royal Society and a professor at London University, eventually disagreed with some eugenicists over what he saw as its moral conservatism. He argued against rigid racial typologies, positing that the alleged purity of races was hard to believe in since Europe was itself comprised of hybridized nations. A man with contradictory views who accused the Eugenics Society of being unscientific, Pearson believed black people to be of genetically inferior origin, arguing, 'History shows . . . one way, and one way only, in which a high state of civilisation has been produced, namely, the struggle of race with race, and the survival of the physically and mentally fitter race.' In Pearson's view, those races deemed inferior and exterminated by conquering powers were no more than the 'stepping-stones' that had brought superior races to their higher intellectual state.

Developed at a time when there was an increased demand for administrative, technical, and scientific government agents to manage the sprawling British Empire, the 'science' of eugenics provided a justification for the actions of the new imperial bureaucrats and professionals, who believed that their 'racial' superiority suitably bred them for the imperial roles. Eugenics discourses were thus deployed to justify and legitimize European imperial dominance of the peoples and societies of Africa, Asia, the Caribbean, and other colonies. These populations were viewed as lacking moral character, intellectual ability, and civilized instincts. The need to impose a moral and physical order on colonial subjects was seen as the duty of the Christian, civilized nation.

2. Eugenics and the health of the nation Towards the end of the 19th century, establishing and maintaining racial and social hierarchies was not a task exclusively for colonial administrators. The social and economic disorder in Britain also needed addressing. At this time, the health of the British nation was linked to social and sexual propriety. Promiscuity and prostitution were seen as evidence of the degeneracy of British working people. Terminology rooted in medical metaphors such as 'infection', 'scourge', 'diseased', 'plague' is extensive in eugenicist literature of this period. For eugenicists, intellectual, physical, and moral attributes were determined by hereditary factors. This is important because it meant that social ills could not be addressed effectively by social policy since, if degeneracy is innate, it cannot be mitigated through social engineering.

Pearson's 'The Problem of Alien Immigration into Great Britain, Illustrated by an Examination of Russian and Polish Jewish Children' appeared in 1925 in the journal he founded, the *Annals of Eugenics*. The study brought together statistics, science, and social planning. Pearson feared that the intellectual class was not producing offspring at a quick enough rate compared to those of 'inferior stock'. He advocated a national programme to breed intelligence—in other words, a population control programme aimed specifically at limiting the reproductive capacities of the intellectually inferior working classes, whom he viewed as the source of Britain's degeneracy.

Eugenics was not a marginal set of ideas taken up only by the socially conservative: in the early part of the 20th century it gained favour in various forms in mainstream British life. Among the prominent intellectual supporters from Britain were H. G. Wells, Julian Huxley, George Bernard Shaw, and Marie Stopes. In 1905 an international society that subsequently linked organizations such as the German Society for Race Hygiene, the British Eugenics Education Society (established in 1908), and the North American Eugenics Record Office (established in 1910) was formed to promote eugenicist theories and practices. The Eugenics Record Office was established, and in 1911 the Galton Eugenics professorship was set up at University College London.

The theory and practice of selective breeding for the health of the nation was adopted with devastating effect by German Nazism. In 1935 a Law for the Preservation from Hereditarily Diseased Posterity established a programme of sterilization in Germany. Arguing that racial hygiene programmes were 'indispensable to all civilised countries', Wilhelm Frick, the architect of the law, wrote into the legislation that anyone with an addiction problem or who was physically or mentally disabled, or even those whose looks caused offence, were to be sterilized. Between 1934 and 1937, 225,000 people were sterilized in Germany, and many people in the United States and in Britain supported what they viewed as a necessary act to preserve or enhance mental and physical health.

The idea of eliminating undesirable elements from the population through sterilization was not confined to Nazi Germany. In the United States between 1905 and 1972 approximately 70,000 Americans were deemed suitable for sterilization on the grounds that they were feeble-minded, mentally retarded, or otherwise socially inadequate.

Although eugenics is associated with the late 19th and early 20th centuries, the debate about the health of nations continues. The controversies surrounding 'designer babies', euthanasia of disabled children, and birth control in developing countries may all be described as part of continuing political and public concern with the future health of society.

LY

Barkan, Elazar, *The Retreat of Scientific Racism: Changing Concepts of Race in Britain and the United States Between the World Wars* (1996)

Gould, Stephen Jay, *The Mismeasure of Man* (1981)

Hannaford, Ivan, *Race: The History of an Idea in the West* (1996)

See also MISCEGENATION; RACISM; SKIN COLOUR AND RACE, THEORIES OF

Exeter. City with a low black population, but a good example of the historical presence of Blacks in areas outside the major port cities, an indication of how omnipresent they were in Britain from the 17th century onwards.

Parish registers provide examples such as the burial on 4 February 1631 at St Mary Major of 'Thomas, sonne of a Blackamore'; the baptisms on 16 February 1689 at St Stephen's of 'Mary Negro, black', on 9 April 1735 of 'Charles English, negro', and on 4 December 1778 of 'Thomas Walker, a black boy'; and the burial on 8 May 1791 of 'Robert Hill, black, a servant at the Devon and Exeter Hospital'.

A contemporary broadsheet in November 1668 gives details of '200 blacks brought from the plantations of the Netherlands in America', part of the procession led by William of Orange on his way to claim the throne in London. On 22 March 1792 Exeter's newspaper the *Flying Post* carried details of a runaway apprentice who seems to have been of African descent.

There was interest in both sides of the movement for the *abolition of the *slave trade and *slavery. Numerous meetings were held throughout Devon's towns and cities in support of abolition. The end of slavery itself in 1834 brought compensation to slave owners in Devon, though not to the slaves of African descent themselves. Among those compensated were the Bishop of Exeter, the Right Revd Henry Philpotts, and his three partners, who received £12,729 4*s*. 4*d*.

In 1812 Tom *Molineaux, the famous black boxer, was beaten at a wrestling match in St Thomas, across the river from Exeter.

Reports in an Exeter newspaper in 1854 identify a 93-year-old African woman, born in Senegal, ending her days in the union workhouse after life as a slave in the West Indies and in service in Exeter.

Local history everywhere links with national and world history. In the *Second World War black people from British colonies and the United States contributed to the fight against fascism. This included black American GIs and British service personnel who came to Devon. Some of their descendants remain there. The writing of Exeter's black history is at its beginning, but the overview of evidence given here suggests the wealth of material that awaits discovery by researchers. LMacK

MacKeith, Lucy, *Local Black History: A Beginning in Devon* (2003)

See also 'BROWN BABIES'; GEORGIAN AND VICTORIAN BRITAIN

Exhibits, black people as. From as early as the 16th century, black people were employed in Britain as musicians and performers, and there was often an element of display in the employment of black servants, whose exotic appearance served to advertise their masters' wealth, colonial connections, or both.

Rather different was the way in which, particularly in the 18th and 19th centuries, there were cases of black people being displayed as exhibits to appeal to the curiosity of white viewers, especially if they were in some way out of the ordinary. Sometimes the curiosity was allegedly scientific, as with the 'white boy' (an albino child of African parents, born in Virginia in 1755) who was brought to Britain and 'shewn before the Royal Society' in London in January 1765. More often it was the result of the same sort of attitude that attracted paying customers to exhibitions of white people who were seen as being in some way physically abnormal, such as dwarfs, the very tall, such as the 'Irish Giant' (a name used to advertise both Patrick Cotter, alias Patrick O'Brien, *c.*1760–1806, and Charles Byrne, 1761–83), or someone like Daniel Lambert (1770–1809), whose fame was based on the probably well-founded claim that he was the fattest man in England.

In the same sort of category would appear to be the black albino woman variously known as Amelia Lewsam or Newsham, or Amelia Harlequin. She was born in Kingston, Jamaica, about 1748, and brought to London as a child, when she 'was purchased by and resided with John Burnet a person who kept a Bird and Beast Shop . . . as a Shew or Exhibition'. She was exhibited from at least the early 1760s until at least 1798. She seems to have travelled about in different parts of the country to be exhibited, but it is not clear what relationship she had with whoever managed the show, or if she received any of the money people paid to see her. She was reportedly seen by members of the royal family, 'who expressed great Satisfaction at the Sight', and in 1795 a halfpenny token was produced with a portrait of 'Mrs. Newsham the white Negress', which was described as 'To be had at the Curiosity House City Road near Finsbury Square London'.

A child called George Alexander

Gratton, born on the Caribbean island of St Vincent in 1808, had a brief career in England as 'the wonderful spotted boy . . . the progeny of Negroes . . . being beautifully covered over with a diversity of spots' before his early death in 1813. He was exhibited by a well-known showman called John Richardson (1766–1836), who was reportedly genuinely fond of the boy and in his will asked to be buried in the same grave with him.

Mrs Newsham and George Gratton would seem to have attracted attention because they were albinos and not because they were black. However, the case of Sarah *Baartman shows that there were black people who were exhibited in a manner that was both racialized (that is, focused on physical features that were different only in the sense that they were not those of white people) and racist, in that it was intended to demonstrate the alleged inferiority of blacks. The same was also true of the way in which groups of supposedly 'primitive' peoples were put on display at the Colonial and International exhibitions and World's Fairs that were popular in Europe and North America from the mid-19th century to the mid-20th, and of much early *photography of black people by white photographers.

Nevertheless, there were also black people who were not exhibited by others, but performers on their own account. The modern historian Peter Fryer has drawn attention to an 18th-century black fencing master called George Turner, and a 'surprising Negro, or African Prince' who performed as a fire-eater and contortionist in London in 1751–2, both of whom would appear to fit into this category. William Darby (1796–1871) was a black circus performer who was particularly known for his feats on horseback. For 30 years he owned a circus of his own, with which he travelled all over the country, especially in the north of England. Millions who know nothing of Darby are nevertheless familiar with the performing name he adopted, Pablo Fanque, as it appears in the Beatles' song 'Being for the Benefit of Mr. Kite!' on the *Sgt. Pepper* album. JG

Edwards, Paul, and Walvin, James, *Black Personalities in the Era of the Slave Trade* (1983)

Fryer, Peter, *Staying Power: The History of Black People in Britain* (1984)

Parsons, James, 'An Account of the White Negro Shewn Before the Royal Society', *Philosophical Transactions of the Royal Society of London* (1765)

Schlicke, Paul, 'John Richardson (1766–1836), showman', *ODNB*

Turner, John M., 'Pablo Fanque', *ODNB*

Willis, Deborah, and Williams, Carla, *The Black Female Body in Photography* (2002)

See also RACISM

F

Fadipe, Nathaniel Akinremi (1893–1944). Writer and one of the lesser known Pan-Africanist leaders born in Nigeria, the son of a Baptist mission preacher. Fadipe was brought up in the church missionary school. He became the personal secretary to the manager of Barclays Bank, Lagos. He travelled to Britain and earned a BA degree at the London School of Economics in 1929. He was subsequently awarded fellowships to study at Woodbrooke College in Birmingham and then for his MA at Columbia University, New York. His dissertation entitled 'A Yoruba Town: A Sociological Study of Abeokuta', was the first study of its kind by an African academic on Nigeria. Fadipe subsequently took up a teaching post at Achimota College in the Gold Coast but returned to London after his contract was not renewed.

Once again at the London School of Economics in 1934, Fadipe pursued a Ph.D., working on the first major sociological study of the Yoruba. His publications on topics such as South Africa and the Italian invasion of *Ethiopia in British journals aimed to educate the public about the unfair conditions of colonial rule in Africa. This brought him into close working relationship with organizations such as the *West African Students' Union and the *League of Coloured Peoples, as well as with anti-imperialists and Pan-Africanists such as George *Padmore and Jomo Kenyatta. He wrote and protested on issues concerning the welfare and economic conditions of Blacks in Britain, especially racial discrimination and employment. Fadipe himself was a victim of such discrimination and had to eke out a living working as a clerk, examiner, and translator. He succumbed to a brain haemorrhage in 1944, but remains an important activist figure in the anti-colonialist struggle in Britain and Africa. ASW

ODNB

See also PAN-AFRICANISM

Families. While there is a growing African presence among Britain's black communities, sociological research on black families in Britain has tended to concentrate on families of Caribbean origin, and this is the focus of this entry.

1. Theorizing the black Caribbean family
2. Social policy implications for the black Caribbean family
3. Reconstituting the Caribbean family in the United Kingdom
4. The Caribbean family: leading the way to a postmodern family?

1. Theorizing the black Caribbean family The general typology of black families captured in representations of family and community life in Britain and the Caribbean is that of the lone mother who, alongside her roles of rearing, nurturing, and providing models of adult life for the child, also bears primary financial responsibility for their material security and welfare. Scholars in the Caribbean have variously suggested that this family type may be properly described as matrifocal, because the family and household are composed of adult females and dependent children, with men having a relationship with the younger women on a visiting basis. While marriage and the nuclear family unit are desirable, they tend to come well after child-rearing has commenced, and can be quite late in the parents' relationship. Thus, for example, according to the 1991 UK census, 51 per cent of African-Caribbean mothers were lone parents as compared to 14 per cent of mothers in the population as a whole, and less than 10 per cent in the Asian communities. Some writers have argued that the living arrangements in these circumstances may be more complex than the notion of a matrifocal home suggests.

2. Social policy implications for the black Caribbean family In both Britain and the Caribbean the depiction of the black matrifocal family has long been a politically contested matter, with important implications for social policy. Three examples may be in order here.

Firstly, the matrifocal family has come to be regarded as a pathological family form, a deviation from the Western nuclear model. This 'deviant' form of familial organization has been identified as the source of many social ills within the black communities. A major problem identified by social commentators is seen to be the poor levels of parenting of black children within lone-mother households, resulting from the assumed marginality of black fathers within the family unit.

There is, however, no question about the dedication of mothers to their offspring; indeed, in interviews about family life respondents tend to see their mothers in highly positive terms because of the care, love, and guidance they provided. Fathers too tended to express a sense of care about their children, and did not necessarily regard residential absence from the home of the mother and child as being always indicative of an absence of responsibility for the child. Moreover, the marginal familial role of many black fathers is not to assume the absence of black males from black family life. Indeed, the role of the biological father may be adopted by other males, such as uncles, grandfathers, and older siblings. Rising concerns about the detrimental impact of male marginality within black families—most especially high levels of male educational underachievement, and rising juvenile crime rates—has prompted the emergence of groups of black males to provide positive role models to children, particularly boys.

Secondly, black families of Caribbean backgrounds in Britain have faced the problem of an absence of the extended family, the household, and kinship networks they would have relied upon in the Caribbean. This may be due to two factors: firstly, the migration patterns from the region; and, secondly, the tendency of older black people to return home. In the first instance, many migrants who came to Britain between the late 1940s and the early 1960s ended their working lives in the 1980s and 1990s. Many opted to realize their long-held dream of returning to the Caribbean. While there may have been frequent visits in both directions across the Atlantic, the absence of grandparents means that families may now be in much the same position as they were during the early years of immigration, with an absence of the extended members to provide guidance and practical help for black Caribbean mothers who—more so than mothers in other communities—are likely to be employed, and most often in full-time labour.

This leads to a third problematic issue: it may be hypothesized that black families of Caribbean backgrounds in Britain are not sites or agencies for the accumulation of resources that support upward social mobility. In nearly all social indices that measure social upward mobility, such as employment, residence, and education, Caribbeans are situated at the lower ends, with many offspring doing less well than their parents and their grandparents, the original migrants. When combined with such factors as high levels of violence in the communities, high levels of mental breakdown, and over-representation in prisons, it becomes clear that the family is both a crucial location for the individual as well as being an institution that cannot reasonably cope with the pressures brought to its doorstep.

3. Reconstituting the Caribbean family in the United Kingdom With regard to the wider national British community, two general features of Caribbean families appear striking. While the social capital that has been described as 'bonding'—between all members of a group, between spouses, between fathers and offspring, etc.—may be seen as comparatively loose and fluid in black families, the kind of social capital that theorists describe as 'linking' is very strong. Black people have made links and built bridges across racial and ethnic boundaries, particularly into the majority ethnic communities. While friendships, membership of community and sporting organizations, and so forth, are important in this, of far greater significance has been the creation of families across these boundaries. Marriage, or perhaps more properly 'partnering', tends to be highly exogamous rather than endogamous, unlike most other communities. This, of course, raises tantalizing questions about the Caribbean family in Britain, such as whether it is adequately described as simply black.

4. **The Caribbean family: leading the way to a postmodern family?** Finally, these features combine to give black Caribbean families in Britain the appearance of being precursors of some family types that are characteristic of late modernity. These include such features as single-parent, mother-centred, or mother-led families; the looseness of the family structure and relationships; the porous boundaries emerging between family members across racial and ethnic identities; and, perhaps most significantly, the growing tendency towards individualistic choice and autonomy. These features of late modernity involved serious risks along gender (men and women) and generational (children and the elderly) lines as traditional feelings of obligations and trust are presumed to erode. One lesson to be learnt from the Caribbean family model is that, while these risks remain, and while they raise questions about the specific nature of state provision for family members, they also show that care and obligations can be maintained. HG

Goulbourne, H., and Chamberlain, M. (eds.), *Caribbean Families in Britain and the Trans-Atlantic World* (2001)

Reynolds, Tracey, *Caribbean Mothering: Identity and Experience in the UK* (2005)

See also RETURNEES

Feminism. Black British feminism as a theoretical and intellectual movement had its genesis in the 1940s and 1950s, in the activism and struggles of black women migrants from the Caribbean, Africa, and the Indian sub-continent. Official statistics and texts documenting the main period of migration often overlook the female contribution to the post-Second World War period of migration. However, stories of black women's participation and experiences have been kept alive by black women writers who challenge their negation from history, disrupting the often neat telling of those times: for example, the black women soldiers in the Second World War; Una *Marson, who campaigned for the *League of Coloured Peoples in the 1940s; the political activist Claudia *Jones in the 1950s; the grass-roots activist Olive *Morris in the 1970s; and the trade unionist Jayaben Desai.

With its simultaneous interrogation of the racial and gendered subtext of Britishness, black British feminism challenges the meaning of British national identity and its unspoken assumption of whiteness. In this sense black British feminism as a body of scholarship occupies a destabilizing position of 'unlocation', which has been referred to as a 'third space'. From this position black women reveal other ways of knowing that challenge the normative discourse of white privileged patriarchal values. For black feminists the 'third space' overlaps the margins of the race, gender, and class discourse.

Although there are many different voices among black feminists, they speak of black feminism, not black feminism(s), as the political project has a single purpose: to excavate the silences and reveal the pathological appearances of a collectivity of women assigned as the 'black other' as they are produced in a gendered, sexualized, and racialized discourse. However, the concept of 'black' has not been without its tensions, as the call to African–Asian unity by the *Organization of Women of African and Asian Descent (OWAAD) demonstrates. In the 1960s and 1970s black British feminism evolved as a political project. In *The Heart of the Race: Black Women's Lives in Britain* (1985) Beverley Bryan, Stella Dadzie, and Suzanne Scafe show how in 1978 the grass-roots black women's movement became a landmark in terms of an emerging black British feminist consciousness. Their struggles reveal the political agency of black women of different languages, religions, cultures, and classes who consciously constructed a politically based identity in response to the exclusion of women's experiences of racism from the anti-racist movement. While African–Asian unity appeared a strategic political goal at the time, OWAAD folded under pressure from within to assert heterogeneous identities. Other black women's groups such as the *Southall Black Sisters and Women Against Fundamentalism, who have campaigned for African and Asian women's rights since the 1970s, still survive and demonstrate the value of heterogeneity as a dynamic for expanding democratic practices within feminist organizations.

In the 1970s and 1980s the insidious erosion of rights in the workplace emphasized Asian, African, and Caribbean women's shared social and material conditions in a highly structured, gendered, and racialized labour market. While Asian women were largely located in the private sector in factory and production, Caribbean and African women were situated in the public service and caring industries. Black women in large numbers compared to the white female population were (and are) disproportionately employed in low-paid, low-status work. The pervasive image of the invisible or passive black woman was interrupted by the labour struggles that exploded in the 1970s, exposing the existence of British sweatshops. Amrit Wilson, in *Finding a Voice: Asian Women in Britain* (1978), gave a first-person account of the conditions and struggles for social and economic justice among Asian women workers on the picket line in the Grunwick dispute.

In the 1980s black British feminism as a critical theoretical project was concerned with revealing the mechanisms that promote, contest, and resist racist thinking and practices in the everyday lives of the collectively constituted 'black woman'. One such effort was the struggle of black women to claim a space within the modernist feminist discourse. The criticism levelled against white feminists was that they claimed universal womanhood in theory but in reality practised exclusion. White women, it was argued, consciously or unconsciously tended to represent their own cultural experiences as universal.

Throughout the 1980s black feminists in Britain responded, and resisted what they deemed to be the overarching imperial mission of white feminism by refusing to be defined by others. They challenged stereotypical images of black women as passive victims through studies, research, and writing that revealed the hidden world of migrant black British women. They wrote of Asian and African-Caribbean girls' resistance to racism in schools and at work; they revealed black women's struggle against domestic violence, unfair immigration controls that kept black families apart, and overzealous policing of black communities. They engaged in black lesbian activism.

Black British feminism, though positioned 'on the margins', can no longer be considered marginal scholarship. Black feminist scholars now explore issues as diverse as 'mixed-race' identity, lone motherhood, and representations in popular culture and the media. They challenge theories of racism and nationalism, rethink definitions of 'blackness', and redefine black female sexuality. Revealing their world through a variety of methodologies such as the oral traditions of storytelling, life histories, and autobiography, and reworking sociological and psychological theory, black British feminists demonstrate the critical creativity engendered by the 'marginal' space they occupy. HSM

Amos, V., and Parmar, P., 'Challenging Imperial Feminism', *Feminist Review*, Special Issue, 17 (1984)

Carby, H., 'White Woman Listen! Black Feminism and the Boundaries of Sisterhood' in Centre for Contemporary Cultural Studies, *The Empire Strikes Back: Race and Racism in 70s Britain* (1982)

Feminist Review, Special Issue, 22 (1986)

Mirza, H. S. (ed.), *Black British Feminism: A Reader* (1997)

See also RACISM

Ferguson, George Ekem (1864–1897). Fante surveyor and colonial agent born on the Gold Coast and educated in Freetown, Sierra Leone. He became a teacher and then a civil servant. As an employee of the Gold Coast colony he accompanied the Governor on a mission inland, producing a map that showed the ethnic divisions of the colony. He was entrusted with a further mission to the interior that resulted in Akwamu becoming part of the British protectorate. Ferguson's surveying skills were developed by his work with the British–German Boundary Commission of 1886. In 1887 he came to London and studied mining and surveying at the School of Mines, graduating with a first-class certificate. During the 1890s Ferguson led important political missions to Asante and to the northern hinterland of what is now modern Ghana. By 1894 he had signed eighteen treaties of trade and friendship with northern rulers. Ferguson's reports and precise maps of the region contained detailed information of topography, flora and fauna, peoples, languages, and cultures. This was recognized by the Royal Geographical Society in 1894 when they awarded him their Gill Memorial Grant and a gold watch for his services to exploration.

In 1897 Ferguson was a member of a British military expedition to the north-west interior in order to show the flag in an area then threatened by the freebooting armies of Samori Touré. The expedition was attacked, and during the retreat Ferguson was wounded and then killed. His British companion Lieutenant F. B. Henderson wrote of the 'irreparable loss the Colony has sustained by the death of Mr. George Ferguson . . . I have lost a valued friend and the Colony an invaluable servant'. Governor Maxwell of the Gold Coast praised Ferguson's 'scrupulous fidelity' and wrote that his 'work both as an explorer and as a political agent proved to be of the highest value'. Indeed, the boundaries of modern Ghana are largely due to the work of Ferguson. DK

Arhin, Kwame (ed.), *The Papers of George Ekem Ferguson: A Fanti Official of the Government of the Gold Coast, 1890–1897* (1974)

See also DIPLOMATS AND EMBASSIES, AFRICAN

Film and television 1: Representations of Blacks. Black people have a long history of appearing on British film and television screens: as long as the history of the media themselves. Most black people feel that neither dramatic nor documentary representations capture the diversity of contemporary or historical black British experiences. Comparisons are frequently made with what is often viewed as a more favourable media context for black media practitioners in the United States.

1. Race and the analysis of moving images
2. Pre-Second World War British film and television
3. Post-Second World War British film and television

1. Race and the analysis of moving images Before cinema became a popular medium in Britain, *photography was used to illustrate evolutionary explanations of human development. It became a key factor because the photographic image was considered to be an objective representation of reality, presenting the viewer with a transparent window onto a previously unknown world. Thus, in the late 19th century seeing was linked not only to 'believing' but also to 'knowing'. By the beginning of the 20th century white Europeans thought that they had accumulated full and complete knowledge about Africa and Africans. This 'knowledge' had been gained through the representations and stereotypes constructed by, and sustained in, myths, ancient travellers' narratives, and later in literature and popular fiction, anthropology, photography, and cinema. The beginnings of cinema coincided with the peak of colonial expansion towards the end of the 19th and the first decades of the 20th centuries.

A great deal of criticism has been levelled at films and television programmes that fail to reflect accurately the reality of black people's experiences. Issues relating to the representation of black people are important because such images can help to shape and inform how white people view them and how black people see themselves. This is a difficult and complex subject that involves a discussion of positive and negative images, stereotypical imagery, and the role of the moving-image media. The desire for 'authentic' representations that depict life 'as it really is' is strong, and it is encouraged by those forms of realism that claim to be able to present a 'window on the world'.

Theories of ideology, representation, reality, and the diversity of black experiences were not addressed in most of the early critical works on race and representation. These works were mainly concerned with the truthfulness of images of black people and did not attempt to analyse the complex interrelationship between text, representation, reality, and viewers that more recent developments in theories of cultural reproduction have indicated.

Discussions of stereotypes and positive and negative images of blackness have examined a wide range of television programmes and films, although there are so few examples of leading roles for black people in British films other than as gangsters and prostitutes that long, detailed studies are few compared to the output from the United States.

It has been argued that simply to label particular images as representing 'Uncle Toms' or 'whores' without examining the historical and cultural context in which they have been produced is a superficial exercise. Another interesting question is the extent to which the North American experience of racial representations is applicable to Britain. For example, the African-American film historian Donald Bogle's seminal analysis *Toms, Coons, Mammies, Mulattoes and Bucks* (1991) examines many stereotypes of blackness that have arisen from a specifically North American set of experiences of slavery and its consequences. Although there are many similarities, it is important to remember that British experiences were dissimilar in important respects, and colonialism and imperial conquest have operated quite differently here than in the United States. For example, the class system in Britain has developed differently: it is far more institutionalized than it is in the United States, and closely connected to notions of community and national identity. Also, historically, the way in which social and sexual relations and hierarchies under slavery were organized differed in significant ways. Nonetheless, comparison with images from the United States is inevitable given the substantial number of television programmes and films imported and distributed in this country.

The construction of analytical categories has proved an expedient way of examining how black people have been represented in the moving image, for example, organizing films and television programmes under headings such as: (1) colonial-based dramas: films set in the colonies that serve to reinforce notions of white and/or British cultural superiority (*Sanders of the River*, 1935, is an example of this type of British film); or (2) 'race-based' dramas: films that seek to address a specific 'race problem' and were mainly made in the 1950s and 1960s (for example, *Flame in the Streets*, 1961). However, a drawback of this type of analysis is its concentration on surface content for the purposes of categorization.

In early North American cinema it was not unusual for white actors to portray black characters in films such as *The Birth of a Nation* (1915), a controversial drama whose 'black' protagonist rapes a white woman. White people 'blacking up' had its roots in vaudeville and music hall traditions in the United States and Britain respectively. This practice was not confined to the United States or to early television programmes. A notorious example of it was the BBC's long-running popular entertainment *The Black and White Minstrel Show*: it was only in 1978, after continuing protests, that the show was axed. By adopting the title *The Black and White Media Show* this BBC television critique of racism on television linked the outmoded *Black and White Minstrel Show* to documentaries, drama, news, and situation comedies.

Whether it is possible to produce 'real' or 'authentic' black representation is a contentious issue, especially if it is claimed that such a representation is possible from a single, unified 'black perspective'. The underlying assumption is that it is possible to lay claim to a mandate to be able to speak with an 'authentic voice' about 'the black experience'. The notion of 'positive' and 'negative' images can also be problematic. Ideas about what is positive and what is negative may change over time and vary from one person to another. Since it is still very difficult for black programme- and film-makers to get their products made and aired, a burden of expectation is placed on those that do appear. There is evidence to suggest that many black people still crave positive images and are disappointed with white and black film-makers who do not accommodate such ideas.

2. Pre-Second World War British film and television Much of the literature of the late 19th century contains examples of 'knowledge' about the character of Africans based on white attitudes informed by the sense of their own superiority. The literary texts of the period are of note because several important films of the 1930s such as *King Solomon's Mines* (1937), *The Four Feathers* (1939), and *Sanders of the River* (1935) were based on these novels. In these films the notion of British colonialism as a global civilizing mission is explicit. African colonial subjects are depicted as cowardly, childlike, primitive. In *Sanders of the River*, for example, a British functionary is able to rule the life of a village single-handed.

Films such as *The Song of Freedom* (1936) and *Men of Two Worlds* (1946) slide between portraying black African subjects as an ignorant, primitive, undifferentiated mass and an assumption that specific individuals may be redeemed by being appropriately schooled in the moral and cultural values of western Europe. Both films show the black protagonists living and working in England, and it is possible to see their interaction with white English people in terms of class as well as 'race'. Nonetheless, in the scenes that take place in Africa, the primitivism that besets the main black protagonists' African brethren is displayed by the ignorant, evil witch doctors.

In spite of the limited roles available to black actors in early British cinema history, several stars from the field of music and light entertainment made it onto British television. The BBC's first regular television broadcast in November 1936 featured the African-American song and dance duo Buck and Bubbles starring in a variety show. They were followed by Paul *Robeson's co-star from the film *Song of Freedom*, Elisabeth Welch, who had already starred in her own radio series in 1934.

3. Post-Second World War British film and television The term 'racial problem', previously associated with the racial traumas of South Africa and the United States, took on a whole new dimension in the 1950s, when black people started to settle across Britain. Significant numbers of settlers from Africa, South Asia, and the Caribbean came to Britain after the Second World War, and it was to these groups that film-makers who wished to explore racial difference turned in the latter part of the 1950s. The well-known television dramatist Ted Willis wrote a play about racial prejudice, *Hot Summer Night*, which was screened in 1959. This later became the film *Flame in the Streets*.

During the 1960s and 1970s there were few black people on British television, one of whom was the singer, actor, and guitar player Cy Grant. Grant performed a calypso version of a top news story on the magazine news programme *Tonight*. From the mid-1960s there was a dramatic increase in programmes that dealt with racial issues, but it was white people's views that were sought, their expressions of rage and resentment encouraged. Documentaries in the *Man Alive* (1967–82) strand and other similar series often dealt with the reactions of white people to black immigration in general, along with specific issues such as 'mixed' marriages, and were specifically couched in terms of 'racial problems' brought about by the presence of black peoples.

The 1960s hospital soap drama *Emergency Ward 10* featured a storyline in which a black female doctor seemed about to embark on a love affair with a white male doctor. Her character was written out after a controversial episode in which they chastely kissed. Hospital dramas such as *General Hospital* (1972–9), *Angels* (1980–2), *Casualty* (1985–), and *Holby City* (1999–), along with other fiction series focusing on the police such as *Z Cars* (1960s), *The Bill* (1984–), and *Waking the Dead* (2000–) and popular soap operas such as *Family Affairs* (1997–), *Coronation Street* (1960–), and *East Enders* (1985–), have all featured black characters and storylines to some extent.

There were other flashpoints in television regarding race. One notable example is the play *Fable* (in which Rudolph Walker made his television debut). *Fable* (1965) told the story of a Britain in which an apartheid-like regime had been established—only it was black people ruling over white in this dystopia. It was created at a time of heightened tension, when race and anti-immigration were under the spotlight during the general election and a subsequent by-election. Questions were asked about the play in the House of Commons, and there was a temporary broadcast ban.

Not every television drama featuring black people provoked such controversy. In 1967 the BBC's *Rainbow City*, a six-part drama series starring Errol John as a Jamaican lawyer, contained a variety of storylines that gave voice to a range of black British experiences. More than ten years later the first black-focused television drama series to be written by a black person was screened. In 1978 *Empire Road* seemed to represent a breakthrough, but the hoped-for momentum did not materialize, and programmes made by, for, and about black people continued to appear only spasmodically. In retrospect, although recurrent figures such as the petty criminal, the black man lusting after white women, and the 'good negro' to some extent transferred from the cinema to the television screen, some of the dramas produced in the 1960s and 1970s offered a more complex picture than a simple assemblage of stereotypes.

Situation comedy is a genre that deals almost exclusively in caricature and stereotypes. Several of these in the 1970s and early 1980s had black characters with varying degrees of visibility and/or made racist jokes. Indeed the main white protagonists often promoted racist views themselves through their words or actions, and the black characters present served as a counterpoint to illustrate white racism. Programmes such as *Mind Your Language* (1977–9), *Till Death Us Do Part* (1965–75), and *Love Thy Neighbour* (1972–6), while all in their own ways claiming to debunk racial myths, perpetuated stereotypes of 'foreigners' in general and black people in particular.

In the 1980s dramas such as *Wolcott* (1981), *Black Silk* (1985), and *South of the Border* (1988) seemed self-consciously to promote positive images of the key black protagonists. At the same time comedies focused on black people attempted to portray a lighter side of black life in Britain. For example, *No Problem* (1983) and *Desmond's* (1989–94) tried to reflect the specifics of black British experiences in the situation comedy format in distinction to the earlier *The Fosters* (1976–7), which was essentially a refashioning of a US import.

Black film-makers such as Horace Ové experienced difficulties in raising funds for their work, which was viewed as too 'black' and controversial. *Pressure* (1975) was the first feature-length film by a black person in Britain, and the first film directed by a black person to be funded by the British Film Institute: it was also Ové's first feature-length film. With the advent of Channel 4 in 1982, expectations were raised that the new, radical—by the standards of the time—television channel would provide hitherto unimagined access for black film- and programme-makers, writers, and performers. Some of this promise was fulfilled: the film workshop agreement instituted by Channel 4 meant that black film organizations formed and potentially had the opportunity to pitch for work. In their different ways, both the Ceddo Film and Video Workshop and the Black Audio Film Collective challenged conventional television documentary orthodoxies through their consciously subjective, partial accounts of civil disturbances in London (*The People's Account*, 1985) and Birmingham (**Handsworth Songs*, 1986). The British-based film workshop Sankofa overturned traditional aesthetics, which privileged white people's faces and bodies as the epitome of (heterosexual) desire, with films such as *Looking for Langston* (1989), *Dreaming Rivers* (1988), and *The Passion of Remembrance* (1986).

Recently a handful of contemporary black actors have enjoyed some success with Oscar and other nominations and awards. Marianne Jean-Baptiste (*Secrets and Lies*, 1995; *Spy Game*, 2001), Sophie Okonedo (*Hotel Rwanda*, 2004; *Doctor Who*, BBC, 2005), Adrian Lester (*Primary Colours*, 1998; *Hustle*, BBC, 2004–), and Chiwetel Ejifor (*Kinky Boots*, 2005; *Four Brothers*, 2005) are examples of leading black British actors who have won a wider variety of more challenging, high-profile roles in the United States than is currently possible in the United Kingdom. LY

Bourne, Stephen, *Black in the British Frame: Black People in British Film and Television 1896–1996* (1998)

Malik, Sarita, *Representing Black Britain: A History of Black and Asian Images on Television* (2001)

Pines, Jim (ed.), *Black and White in Colour: Black People in British Television Since 1936* (1992)

Young, Lola, *Fear of the Dark: 'Race', Gender and Sexuality in the Cinema* (1996)

See also FILM AND TELEVISION 2: FILM-MAKERS AND ACTORS

Film and television 2: Film-makers and actors. Definitions of black films and black television programmes have varied over time. In the 1980s the issue was to conquer media space for distinctly black representations, and cultural critics like Stuart Hall and Kobena Mercer demanded a clear political message, taking the blackness of the film-makers and actors for granted. More recent critics like Jim Pines, Sarita Malik, Barbara Korte, and Claudia Sternberg, responding to the fact that black productions have moved to the mainstream, take a broader view. They consider a culturally specific black perspective in themes, characters, and storyline sufficient characteristics, even if not all production team members are of the same ethnic background.

1. Developments in black British film
2. Blacks in television formats
3. Performers

1. Developments in black British film Black people figured in British films all through the 20th century: in the 1910s and 1920s as natives of Africa in travel and adventure films; from the 1930s to the 1950s as individuals living among white communities in Britain. The perspective then was always a white one, even if the issue was a critique of racism. This changed in the 1960s, when black film-makers were first given the chance to present their own views. A realist tradition developed to portray black life in Britain from black perspectives. A number of documentaries were produced and some trendsetting shorts. *Jemima and Johnny* (1964), directed by the South African Lionel Ngakane, features the hope-inspiring friendship of a black girl and a white boy against the backdrop of racial tension, while *Ten Bob in Winter* (1963), made by the Jamaican Lloyd Reckord and the first film with an entirely black cast, deals with a black student's shame about his poverty. The first feature-length films, *Pressure* (1975) by the Trinidadian Horace Ové (b. 1939) and *Burning an Illusion* (1981) by Menelik Shabazz (born in Barbados in 1954), continued in the realist style, focusing on the political awakening of young protagonists from the second generation. Ové, who had already made some documentaries such as *Reggae* (1970) and *King Carnival* (1973), connects contrasting milieux in black British life through the experiences of a young hero: the school leaver Tony is torn between his mother's wish for integration, reflected in her choice of furniture, clothes, and food, and his brother's black politics, which in the end he follows after bitter disappointments in his search for work and shocking encounters with the police. *Burning an Illusion* foregrounds a young woman's experiences following her development from a conventionally bourgeois lifestyle to political activism as a member of a black women's group, mirrored in her changing appearance and surroundings.

In the 1980s black British film-making received a boost, paradoxically as an indirect consequence of intensifying racial conflicts under Margaret Thatcher. Worried about the growing tension, in 1981 representatives of various cultural and political organizations—the British Film Institute (BFI), the Regional Arts Association, the Independent Film and Video Association, and the Association of Cinematographic, Television, and Allied Technicians—signed the Workshop Declaration, an agreement to subsidize non-commercial film-making by black and Asian British artists in order to create more opportunities for expressing black perspectives. Channel 4, founded in 1982 with a remit to promote multicultural representations, joined the ranks of black film promoters and has been one of the strongest supporters of black film ever since. Five workshops were set up and financed for five years, in and around which a lively theoretical debate on black aesthetics emerged. The most productive were the Sankofa Film and Video Collective, the Black Audio Film Collective, and the Ceddo Film and Video Workshop. Young artists such as Isaac Julien (b. 1960), John Akomfrah (b. 1957), Maureen Blackwood (b. 1960), and Martine Attile (b. 1959), all born in Britain and graduates of British art or film schools, rejected the realist approach as inadequate to reflect a complex reality. They developed an experimental style collaging documentary footage and narrative in a manner that connected the present to history, experience to theory.

Outstanding productions were Akomfrah's **Handsworth Songs* (1986) and Blackwood and Julien's *Passion of Remembrance* (1986), in which the realistic portrayal of a young black woman's personal life is intersected with documentary footage presenting important moments of black British history and symbolist scenes in which gender roles are discussed. A more intimate female perspective is presented by Attile's *Dreaming Rivers* (1988). On her deathbed a simple old woman who had immigrated with her husband decades before reviews the past in dreamlike scenes and discussions with her estranged children. Julien's *Looking for Langston* (1989), by contrast, pays homage to a famous figure of black cultural history, the American poet Langston Hughes. The Harlem Renaissance of the 1920s, black creativity, male black beauty, and homosexual love are celebrated in elegant, skilfully stylized black-and-white images. These highly artistic films were sometimes criticized for suffering from 'the burden of representation' (Kobena Mercer's term), i.e. for being too heavily charged with meaning to be entertaining or even representative of contemporary black life in Britain.

When subsidies were seriously reduced in about 1990, most black film-makers were forced to turn to the market and majority tastes. Combining popular narrative with a political perspective proved difficult, and black film-makers were less successful at the box office than some of their Asian-British colleagues. An early attempt at a humorous approach was Horace Ové's *Playing Away* (1986). It connects a white rural and a black urban community in playful competition, the 'national' game of cricket functioning as their symbolic battleground—an idea that may have inspired the internationally successful Indian film *Lagaan*, nominated for an Oscar in 2001, in which a peasant team beats the colonizers. Most commercial black films, however, address the biggest group of cinema-goers, the young, and celebrate the greatest black contribution to British culture, music.

An early example is Isaac Julien's *Young Soul Rebels* (1991). Julien takes up the realist formula again, yet the film breaks new ground in that it no longer focuses exclusively on racial tensions, but also stresses black creativity transcending the traditional binary oppositions of race and gender. Two young DJs broadcasting *soul music from a pirate station—one mixed-race and straight, the other black and gay—get involved in a murder case, lose their studio through racist arson, but undauntedly continue with their music. Julian Henriques's film *Babymother* (1998), a celebration of dance hall music, has been criticized for being too light and thus conformist. It is true that the film eclipses all racial friction, but it addresses another social problem: the difficult conditions for female creativity. Anita, a young woman, tries hard and against the wishes of her husband, a popular DJ, to realize her own aspiration of becoming a DJ while embracing her role as a mother at the same time. Newton Aduaka's *Rage* (1999), also set in the music scene—this time *hip hop—is less optimistic in tone: the heroes, three friends from different racial backgrounds, do not manage to achieve their common aim of cutting a record. *Bullet Boy* (2004), by the white director Saul Dibb, presents social drama unrelieved by musical talent, depicting the lives of black boys growing up on a council estate where sliding into crime is almost inevitable.

Financial support for black films was never entirely stopped, and commissions from the BBC and Channel 4 allowed directors like Akomfrah and Julien to continue with their experimental work in some shorts, feature films, and, above all, numerous documentaries, in which documentary material, interviews, and fictional scenes are mixed to unusual effect. While some focus on social problems, such as Akomfrah's *Riot* (1999) and *Prostitutes* (2001), most present aspects and figures of worldwide black culture. Films on cultural movements are, for instance, Julien's *The Darker Side of Black* (1994), which explores the connection between music and violence in Jamaica, his *Baadassss Cinema* (2003), dedicated to the history of American blaxploitation film, and Akomfrah's *A Touch of the Tar Brush* (first broadcast 1991), which presents a little-known community of mixed-race descendants of black immigrants to Liverpool 200 years ago. Films that approach outstanding cultural figures are, for example, Julien's *Frantz Fanon: Black Skin, White Mask* (1996), Akomfrah's *Martin Luther King—Days of Hope* (1997), *The Wonderful World of Louis Armstrong* (1999), and *Who Needs A Heart?* (1992), which explores the impact of Michael de Freitas, alias Michael Abdul Malik, alias *Michael X, an impostor, but nevertheless an influential figure in the British Black Power movement. Julien has also moved into video art and become highly acclaimed for his gallery installations, often operating with multiple screens. Examples are *The Long Road to Mazatlán* (1999), a homage to homosexual love, *Vagabondia* (2000), dealing with the colonial approach to history and nominated for the Turner Prize, and *Paradise Omeros* (2005).

One recent documentary, less artistically ambitious but a piece of straightforward reporting, caused a scandal as it exposed gross cases of continuing institutional racism. Ken Fero and Tariq Mehmood's film *Injustice* (2001) presents several dubious cases of death in custody and documents the families' fight for a proper investigation. The findings were considered so explosive by Channel 4 that they refused to broadcast the work they had commissioned.

The BFI—like the television channels—has also continued to promote black film. In a strategy paper, *Towards Visibility* (2000), they pledged to promote films reflecting black and Asian British life and to employ more staff from these population groups. Special campaigns were started, the most recent being Blackworld 2005, a six-month nationwide programme comprising events such as film viewings, workshops, and debates, plus the release of important older films on DVD.

An important independent black initiative was the foundation of the bimonthly *Black Filmmaker Magazine* (*bfm*) by Menelik Shabazz in 1997, which reports on black films, music, and media worldwide and also organizes a yearly festival, the *bfm International Film Festival*.

2. **Blacks in television formats** Apart from sponsoring films, television companies have produced their own formats reflecting the black presence. In the 1950s and 1960s a few 'social responsibility programmes'—interview shows and social dramas—addressed racism as a community problem, while other programmes ambiguously flourished on racist undertones, for instance the sitcom *Till Death Us Do Part* (BBC, 1965–75), figuring the racist hero Alf Garnett, and *The Black and White Minstrel Show* (BBC, 1958–78), a musical variety show in which white entertainers blackened their faces. The 1970s brought a qualitative change, with the first shows presenting a black perspective and addressing a black audience. *The Fosters* (ITV, 1976–7) was the first comedy series with an all-black cast, pursuing the exploits of an ordinary working-class family in south London. In 1978 the first black soap, *Empire Road* (BBC, 1978–9), followed, picturing the not-so-easy lives of West Indians in Birmingham. In the 1980s and 1990s a string of magazine shows discussed issues of black community concern addressing a black audience: *Ebony* (BBC, 1982), *Black on Black* (1982–5, produced by Trevor Phillips), *The Bandung File* replaced by *Black Bag* in 1991 (all Channel 4), and *Black Britain* (BBC, 1996). From 1989 the BBC established special production units to take care of black and Asian British interests, which also produced educational programmes.

Meanwhile, black entertainment shows increasingly attracted mainstream audiences. Especially successful in that respect was Channel 4's sitcom *Desmond's* (1989–94). Written by the West Indian Trix Worrel and directed by white Charlie Hanson, the show presented the loving family of a barber's shop owner in south-east London in a light-hearted manner that had a broad appeal. The BBC's comic sketch show *The Real McCoy* (1991) had similar success. Some later programmes, such as *All Black* (BBC, 1993) and *Doing It With You . . . Is Taboo* (Channel 4, 1995), were criticized for exploiting the attraction of sex and crime stories dealing with phenomena like single mothers or rent boys, but others responded to a growing serious interest in black history. The fiftieth anniversary of the arrival of the **Empire Windrush* was celebrated in a variety of programmes, an outstanding one being the four-part series *Windrush* (BBC 2, 1998), written and produced by Trevor and Michael Phillips, and turned into a book. Well-made drama series like *The Final Passage* (Channel 4, 1996) and *White Teeth* (Channel 4, 2002), based on novels by Caryl Phillips and Zadie Smith, explored family histories of black Britons. Lighter entertainment shows also increasingly cater for a mixed audience. Examples are the three-part thriller *Blood Rights* (BBC 2, 1990), figuring a black private eye, based on a novel by Mike Phillips, and the popular sitcom *Babyfather* (BBC 2, 2001–2), based on a novel by Patrick Augustus. In this series four young black men pursue their pleasure-oriented private lives. Recently, in the nation's most popular shows, such as *Coronation Street* and *East Enders*, more and more black characters have been included.

Among the policies launched to promote black participation in television the most important was probably the foundation in 2000 of the Cultural Diversity Network by all the leading television companies. Strategies include special job offers and training schemes, fellowships, audience research, and programme planning. There are, however, mysterious lapses; for example, in 2005 the BBC suddenly failed to screen the events of *Black History Month as it had in the years before.

3. **Performers** Among black actors men have been more successful than women, partly perhaps because women are also under-represented as directors, producers, and scriptwriters. Two actors who have achieved great popularity are Norman Beaton, who died in 1994, and Lenny Henry. Beaton played leading roles in the series *The Fosters*, *Desmond's*, and *Empire Road* (1978–9) and starred as the captain of the victorious black cricket team in Ové's *Playing Away*. Henry was so successful in several comedy shows that the BBC gave him his own shows, *The Lenny Henry Show* (1984–8, 1995, 2004), *Lenny Henry Tonite* (1986), and *Lenny Henry in Pieces* (2001–2). Thomas Baptiste also made an impressive career, appearing in 25 films such as *Jemima and Johnny* (1966) and figuring in various television shows, including the mainstream *Coronation Street* and *East Enders*. Among the actresses of an older generation Corinne Skinner-Carter, starring in *Burning an Illusion*, *Dreaming Rivers*, and *Babymother*, and Carmen Munroe, appearing in several television series including *The Fosters* and *Desmond's* and in films such as Ové's *A Hole in Babylon* (1979), have been able to make a living in Britain. The younger Marianne Jean-Baptiste, however, who received an Oscar nomination for her performance in Mike Leigh's *Secrets and Lies* (1996), the story of the reunion of a white mother with her mixed-race daughter once given up for adoption, left for the United States in search of employment. None of the many talented young actors figuring in recent films and shows have yet made it to stardom.

In the news and politics section some black presenters such as Sir Trevor McDonald, working for ITN since 1973 and knighted in 1999, and the young Gillian Joseph of News 24 have made impressive inroads into a still predominantly white domain. MacDonald worked as news, sports, and diplomatic correspondent before he became a newscaster for ITN, presenting *News at Ten*. For Trevor Phillips the road led from journalism to politics. From 1980 he worked for London Weekend Television, and later Channel 4 and Thames Television, producing several political programmes and shows, *Black on Black* being the most popular. In 2000 he was elected chairman of the Greater London Assembly and, three years later, was appointed chairman of the *Commission for Racial Equality. IvR

Korte, Barbara, and Sternberg, Claudia, *Bidding for the Mainstream? Black and Asian British Film Since the 1990s* (2004)

Malik, Sarita, *Representing Black Britain: Black and Asian Images on Television* (2002)

Pines, Jim (ed.), *Black and White in Colour: Black People in British Television Since 1936* (1992)

Ross, Karen, *Black and White Media: Black Images in Popular Film and Television* (1996)

See also RADIO

First World War (1914–1918). The First World War highlighted the shortcomings of British Imperial rule and politicized many colonial subjects who took part in the war effort. This precipitated a rise in nationalist sentiment and anti-colonial movements throughout the Empire. But equally significant was the impact of the war on race relations and racialized identities in the British Isles. In many ways, the articulation of racial difference, from 1914 until demobilization in 1919, foreshadowed that more commonly associated with mass migration to Britain in the decades after the Second World War.

The outbreak of hostilities in 1914 was widely seen as an opportunity for Imperial subjects to support the Empire with the expectation of post-war political, economic, and social progress. The Universal Negro Improvement Association, founded on the eve of the war in Jamaica by Marcus *Garvey, issued a declaration of loyalty to the King and Empire, pledging the support of black people throughout the globe against German aggression and barbarism.

In Britain itself members of the black population presented themselves as volunteers at army recruiting offices. They were joined by black people from across the Empire, who travelled either at considerable personal expense or as stowaways. Despite the desire of the government to present the image of a united Empire, their services were routinely rejected. While the British Nationality and Status of Aliens Act 1914 defined subjects throughout the Empire as 'natural born British subjects', military law effectively contradicted this claim on citizenship by classing non-white subjects as aliens whose recruitment to home forces was to be strictly regulated. Furthermore, black soldiers were barred from becoming commissioned officers. Black volunteers were accepted or rejected according to the prejudices or legal knowledge of individual recruiting officers.

During the war the black population in Britain, numbering about 10,000 at the outset, became more visible. Aside from the arrival of black volunteers, many black merchant seaman were stranded without employment, as hostilities affected the movement of shipping. Wartime industries, such as munitions and engineering, provided alternative livelihoods to seafaring, resulting in migration away from the port cities, such as *London, *Cardiff, and *Liverpool, where black communities had previously been concentrated. These industries also attracted a small number of new migrants from West Africa and the Caribbean.

The visibility of the black population increased as the idealized image of rational and stoical white masculinity began to be seriously undermined. Thousands of British soldiers were not able to cope, physically and mentally, with the demands of modern warfare. The numbers of traumatized, 'shell-shocked' men in the military hospitals increased dramatically after the Somme offensive in the summer of 1916. There was also considerable public anxiety that the British nation would not recover from the loss of its fittest young men on the Western Front, and increasing concern that the Army was struggling to find sufficient able-bodied recruits among the industrial working class.

In these circumstances, the presence of black soldiers and war workers proved disconcerting, especially as they often provided more inspiring visions of masculinity than the war-weary Tommy. When the West Indian war contingents paraded at the Lord Mayor's Show in November 1915, they were described in the press as 'huge and mighty men of valour'. But such favourable coverage rapidly turned to hostility. Increasingly, black men were represented as a menace to local women and moral standards—a 'Black Peril' threatening to breach the sexual and racial boundaries of Empire. The Salvation Army was so concerned about mixed-race relationships that it commissioned a study into what it termed 'the coloured invasion' in Manchester. Some newspaper correspondents suggested that legislation on segregation, along the lines of laws already in place in South Africa, should be introduced to prevent black men and white women from forming relationships. Other newspaper articles were less overtly hostile, but suggested that, while the rest of the population endured wartime hardship at home or on the front line, the sight of apparently well-paid and well-dressed black men proved an irresistible attraction to impressionable young women.

From the autumn of 1916 the trade union movement outlined proposals to oppose further black migration. This marked a hardening in attitude. The National Sailors' and Firemen's Union, for example, although opposed to the use of cheap Chinese labour in the maritime industry, had previously been fairly sympathetic to black workers. The Cardiff branch of the Union even took up the cause of unemployed black sailors who were rejected for military service. But in December 1916 the Miners' Federation, the National Union of Railwaymen, and the National Transport Workers' Federation passed a joint resolution opposing 'the sinister movement to import coloured labour into this country'.

Black men, both industrial workers and servicemen, responded angrily to both negative press coverage and official hostility. Some wrote letters of protest to the newspapers, while others sent clippings of hostile articles back home to warn other potential volunteers and war workers of the reception they were likely to face in Britain.

In July 1917 disturbances occurred in the maritime district of Canning Town, home to the largest black community in London. Several black seamen were attacked in their lodging houses or on the street. Two male and three female assailants were subsequently found guilty of assault and damage to property. A black seaman was fined for discharging an unlicensed firearm in an attempt to disperse the mob. Local newspapers reported the case under the headline 'Baiting Black Men: Girls Infatuation Leads to Trouble'. The wartime climate of sexualized racial anxiety would eventually culminate in sustained racial attacks against black communities in seaport towns and cities throughout much of 1919. Many black people in Britain were forcibly or voluntarily repatriated as a result. Nevertheless, those who remained in the inter-war years formed a kernel of pioneering communities—an advance guard for the mass migrations after the Second World War. RS

Sandhu, Sukhdev, *London Calling: How Black and Asian Writers Imagined a City* (2003)

Smith, Richard, *Jamaican Volunteers in the First World War: Race, Masculinity and the Development of National Consciousness* (2004)

Tabili, Laura, *'We Ask for British Justice': Workers and Racial Difference in Late Imperial Britain* (1994)

See also LASCARS AND BLACK SEAMEN; MISCEGENATION; 'RACE' RIOTS, 1919; SECOND WORLD WAR

Fisk Jubilee Singers Negro vocal ensemble renowned for introducing to the concert platform a body of slave songs and spirituals. Fisk University was founded in 1866 in Nashville, Tennessee, to educate former slaves. A financial crisis was generated as a result of dilapidated accommodation that needed to be restored and developed. In response to this, during 1871, George L. White (music teacher and bursar) formed the Fisk Jubilee Singers, to tour and fundraise. They planned to sing ballads, arias, and popular religious choral works, showing how cultured former slaves could be; but audiences preferred their authentic slave songs and spirituals, expressing Christian themes of compensation in heaven for the injustices and trials endured on earth. Aptly, their name came from Old Testament history, when at every fiftieth Pentecost a year of Jubilee followed, and when by Hebrew law slaves were freed.

Between 1871 and 1878 they toured extensively, receiving critical acclaim for their performances, in England, Scotland, Ireland, and Wales; going into Europe, to Belgium, the Netherlands, France, Switzerland, Italy, and Spain. In England they were warmly received by the Earl of Shaftesbury, the Prime Minister William Gladstone, Queen Victoria, and the Duke and Duchess of Argyll, while the public applauded their vision and high educational aspirations for Fisk University. In addition, they were admired for bringing new repertoire to the concert platform, with polished delivery, bringing them international acclaim and funds totalling over $150,000 for Fisk University. They returned to the United States in 1878, when the President of the university, the Revd Cravath, advised the Jubilee Singers to disband. PAH

Pickering, Michael, '"A Jet Ornament to Society": Black Music in Nineteenth-Century Britain' in Paul Oliver (ed.), *Black Music in Britain: Essays on the Afro-Asian Contribution to Popular Music* (1990)

Seroff, Doug, 'The Fisk Jubilee Singers in Britain' in Rainer E. Lotz and Ian Pegg (eds.), *Under the Imperial Carpet: Essays in Black History 1780–1950* (1986)

See also GOSPEL MUSIC; MUSIC 2: EARLY POPULAR MUSIC

Fraternity. Monthly newspaper, costing 1*d*., founded in 1893 by the Quaker activist Catherine Impey as a successor to an earlier journal, *Anti-Caste*. Published in Street, Somerset, it ran until July 1896. The journal was the monthly organ of the Society for the Recognition of the Brotherhood of Man, which had been founded by Impey in the mid-1880s. *Fraternity*'s masthead showed clasped black and white hands. From an initial subscription of 3,000, by October 1893 it claimed 7,000 readers. The first editor was S. J. Celestine *Edwards. The newspaper campaigned to raise public awareness of the number of lynchings of African-Americans in the United States. Impey was a close friend of Frederick *Douglass, and she actively supported Ida B. Wells (1862–1931) in her campaign to raise international condemnation of lynching in the United States during two speaking tours of Britain in 1893 and 1894. *Fraternity* maintained a steady flow of information, supplied by Wells and drawn from the US press, on lynching. Under Edwards's brief editorship it denounced racial discrimination in Britain and the brutalities of British imperialism in Africa, in particular the military action against the Ndebele in central Africa (e.g. 15 December 1893, and 15 January 1894). The newspaper also drew attention to the condition of African labour in the South African mines (1 July 1896). The newspaper is a useful source of information on the activities of black people in Britain. It includes references to people such as T. L. *Johnson, Theophilus *Scholes, and Peter *Stanford, and contains a substantial sketch of Edwards's life (September, November–December 1894). DK

Fraternity (1893–6), British Newspaper Library, Colindale, London (1895 not available)

See also NEW TIMES AND ETHIOPIAN NEWS

Freeman, Thomas Birch (1809–1890). Black British Wesleyan missionary and traveller in West Africa. Freeman was born in Hampshire, the child of a black father and a white mother. Little is known of his early years, but he was employed as a gardener in Suffolk and became a Christian, joining the Wesleyan Methodists. In 1838 Freeman went as a missionary to the Gold Coast, an area of West Africa where he was to spend most of his life. He built Methodist churches at Cape Coast and Accra, promoted education, and trained local men for the ministry. He established a mission station in Kumase, the Asante capital, and visited towns in southern Nigeria and also the kingdom of Dahomey, where he urged King Gezo to stop the slave trade. On furlough in Britain in 1843 Freeman actively promoted missionary work and also the anti-slavery cause, both helped by publication of his travel accounts. In 1847 and 1848 he accompanied the Governor of the Gold Coast on official visits to Dahomey and Kumase. He married four times; his first two, white British, wives died shortly after arriving in West Africa; thereafter he married two local women, which gave him close links to coastal society, although his inability to speak Fante limited his mission work. Freeman was an ardent missionary but not a competent financial manager. Owing to misunderstandings with the Wesleyan Mission, he separated himself from that body and worked for the colonial government. He rejoined the Mission in 1873 and, with his son, promoted Methodist work in the southern Gold Coast. DK

Birtwhistle, Allen, *Thomas Birch Freeman: West African Pioneer* (1950)
ODNB

See also BLACK CHURCHES, CHRISTIANITY

Froude, James Anthony (1818–1894). English writer on historical subjects. Froude was widely admired for his literary skill, but frequently criticized for his inaccuracies, which did not stop him eventually being appointed Regius Professor of Modern History at Oxford in 1892. He was a staunch advocate of British imperialism, which he saw as the justifiable expansion of a superior 'Anglo-Saxon race'. His superficial travel book *The English in the West Indies* (1888) defended Crown Colony government in the Caribbean in the aftermath of the *Morant Bay rebellion, and alleged that African-Caribbean people were not fitted for self-government. His inaccuracies and racist arguments were vigorously rebutted by John Jacob *Thomas. Froude was a friend of Thomas *Carlyle and wrote a biography of him (1882). JG

Froude, J. A., *The English in the West Indies; or, The Bow of Ulysses* (1888)

Thomas, J. J., *Froudacity: West Indian Fables by James Anthony Froude, Explained by J. J. Thomas* (1889, 1969)

Fuller, Joseph Jackson (1825–1908). Jamaican missionary and public speaker born the son of an enslaved woman and Alexander Jackson, a member of the Spanish Town Baptist mission. In the aftermath of *emancipation (1838), some freed Jamaicans returned to Africa to assist in the anti-slavery cause, aided by Jamaican Baptists, who proposed the establishment of a mission to West Africa. As well as spreading the Christian gospel, the mission would provide a stimulus for the repatriation of African-Caribbeans to Africa. Among the Jamaican missionaries were Alexander Fuller and his son Joseph, who were recruited to assist the establishment of a Baptist mission in Fernando Po, an island off the Gulf of Guinea. Joseph arrived in 1844.

Despite early optimism, the Fernando Po mission did not thrive, and the Baptist Missionary Society (BMS) relocated to Cameroon in 1846. Fuller served out a five-year apprenticeship with the Cameroon BMS before becoming a full member. He married Elizabeth Johnson (reputedly a Sierra Leonean and mother of his son Alexander), but was widowed in 1859. His second wife, Charlotte, whom he married in 1861, was the daughter of missionaries, and Charlotte herself played an active role at the mission.

Fuller played a key role in the development of the BMS Cameroonian mission, operating the mission's printing press, building schools, training teachers, and supervising the work of the deacons. He was instrumental in securing African converts to Christianity, helping to eradicate local indigenous practices that he considered antithetical to Christianity and to African development. His brilliant negotiating skills led him to play a pivotal role as a peace arbitrator between the missionaries and local tribal peoples. On furlough to Jamaica in 1872, Fuller spoke at large public meetings about the African mission, and successfully raised funds for a BMS chapel in Cameroon.

In 1881 Fuller completed a translation into Duala of Bunyan's *Pilgrim's Progress*. Between 1884 and 1888 he also supervised the transfer of the mission to the Basel Mission Society, after Bismarck's annexation of Cameroon made it difficult for the BMS to maintain its activities there. His significant contributions have, however, been ignored by historians, who attributed much of his achievements to Alfred Dekar, the senior missionary in command. Fuller served the BMS for many years until 1888, old age forcing his retirement to London, where he died in 1908. JPG

Newman, Las, 'A West Indian Contribution to Christian Mission in Africa: The Career of Joseph Jackson Fuller (1845–1888)', *Transformation*, 18/4 (2001)

ODNB

See also CHRISTIANITY; MISSIONARY SOCIETIES

Funk. Music essentially defined by the strong rhythmic pulse and percussive attack that James Brown brought to rhythm and blues in the mid-1960s. The lively London club scene of the late 1960s that revolved around venues such as the Cricketers, Upstairs at Ronnie Scott's, and Bumbles is largely credited as the birthplace of black British funk. Funk's marriage with local music in Africa and South America has produced distinctive results. In Britain, the multicultural mix also put an individual spin on the beat.

Cymande, a pan-Caribbean combo who graduated from the London scene, were arguably the key exponent of black British funk. Their West Indian roots were clear in their music and lyrics. *Rastafarianism and 'nyabinghi' drumming styles blended with the influence of *jazz icons such as Miles Davis and the funk overlord James Brown to produce unique songs like 'Pon De Dungle'.

Other groups such as the Equals,

Gonzalez, Matata, and Kokomo also reflected the multicultural character of the British funk scene. These artistes would inspire another wave of bands comprised of Londoners of both Caribbean and European descent in the late 1970s. Incognito, Light of the World, Hi-Tension, Linx, and Freez spearheaded a movement termed 'Brit funk'.

Despite the commercial success of some of the aforementioned, the momentum of the scene was lost in the mid-1980s. Generally speaking, the 1980s groups had a glossier, less gritty sound than their predecessors. Then again, *soul music and funk had become glossier and less gritty in America too.

By the end of the decade DJs had returned to the source of all things funk-a-delicious—James Brown—and a new term, 'rare groove', was coined to describe obscure 1970s records that captured the imagination of dancers. Things came full circle as British groups like Cymande and the Equals were rediscovered alongside JB, War, Mandrill, and Curtis Mayfield.

All of this old music inspired new British acts such as Young Disciples and Brand New Heavies to make funk with 'traditional' instruments like drums, bass, and horns. This ran counter to the 'sampling' that had become prevalent since the advent of *hip hop in the early 1980s. This new crop of 1990s artists was loosely categorized as 'acid jazz' but leaned predominantly towards funk and soul. Other artists who creatively blended funk, soul, hip hop, and dub *reggae were Soul II Soul, Caron Wheeler, Opaz, Mica Paris, and Omar. If black British funk owed a debt to James Brown, then these musicians stumped up some payback. They exerted a major influence on American 'neo-soul' stars such as Erykah Badu, D'Angelo, and Maxwell a few years later.

By the end of the 1990s the black British music scene had become so multifaceted that there was no funk movement per se but a wide range of musicians who brought funk into collision with anything from ragga and techno to soul and house.

One of the most original producers and writers working in the United Kingdom today, IG Culture, a Londoner of Jamaican descent, has been at the forefront of a subgenre called 'broken beat'. This music has jittery, staccato grooves set to complex drum patterns. It is insidiously funky. Bugz in the Attic, Dego, Kaidi Tatham, and Mark De Clive-Lowe have, like IG, also taken their lead from American jazz–funk pioneers such as Roy Ayers, but they've pushed their rhythms in a new direction. Theirs is a sound made in Britain. KLG

Thompson, D., *Funk* (2001)

Vincent, Rickey, *Funk: The Music, the People and the Rhythm of the One* (1996)

See also MUSIC 2: EARLY POPULAR MUSIC

G

Galton, Sir Francis (1822–1911). Eugenicist and statistician. A cousin of Charles Darwin, Galton's interests in statistics (he founded the science of biostatistics) and genetics led him to the idea that selective breeding to improve the human race would lead to the development of 'a galaxy of genius'. He first set out these thoughts in an article published in 1865 but at the same time demonstrated that his views on the differences between 'races' was conventional: to him Africans were lazy, stupid, and cruel. The basic theory that underlay his political eugenics programme was that, heredity being more important than environment, selective breeding was the only way to improve humanity.

His lasting legacies were his use of statistics and his research into heredity, but he is best known for his eugenics programme. Though his own interpretation of eugenics tended to be fairly benign, focusing on research into hereditary disease or supporting the intelligent to have large families, the consequences of eugenicist ideas in other hands were disastrous. In liberal Sweden sterilization was used, as it was, along with the killing of the unfit, in Nazi Germany. In the United States supporters of eugenics were able to dabble in inhumane experiments that involved both white and black Americans. The racialization of eugenics was implicit in its origins: Galton's emphasis on heredity deflected attention from social and economic change, and his ideas about races justified the separation and subsequent maltreatment of different population groups. The actions of his followers, rather than Galton's own, condemned a project flawed from its beginnings. PF

Black, Edwin, *War Against the Weak: Eugenics and America's Campaign to Create a Master Race* (2003)
Kuke, Stephan, *The Nazi Connection: Eugenics, American Racism and German National Socialism* (1994)
ODNB

See also RACISM; SKIN COLOUR AND RACE, THEORIES OF

Gandhi, Mohandas Karamchand. Religious title Mahatma Gandhi (1869–1948), political leader and social reformer often regarded as the 'father' of modern India and one of the most influential figures of the 20th century. The series of non-violent civil disobedience campaigns he led against British colonial rule between 1919 and 1942 brought him to worldwide prominence. Although never holding high political office, the aura of spiritual authority he projected is frequently seen as having enabled Gandhi to transform India's nationalist struggle from an elitist political campaign into a mass moral crusade. As a result, he had a considerable impact on Britain too. From 1919 onwards, every British Cabinet had to contend with the Mahatma; his erosion of the moral credibility of colonial power in India was pivotal to Britain's reassessment of its role as an imperial nation.

Gandhi was born in India in the town of Porbandar on the south-west coast of Gujarat. His family was middle-class and middle-caste, but by 1885 their social and financial position had slipped. The young Gandhi was chosen to revive the family's fortunes by going to London to train as a barrister in 1888. He returned three years later ready to establish himself as a lawyer. His career stalled, however, until in 1893 he was invited to go to South Africa to represent a Porbandar-based firm in a legal dispute. The 21 years he subsequently spent there were decisive in his political development. It was in South Africa that he first witnessed racism and colonial abuse to an extent he had not known in either London or Gujarat. Believing Indians to have been granted legal equality as British subjects within the Empire, he was shocked to discover the institutionalized discrimination they were exposed to. The proposed new Asiatic Law Amendment Ordinance, which further entrenched the second-class status of Indians, led to Gandhi's first 'passive resistance' campaign of 1907–9. He adopted the term 'satyagraha' to define his particular concept of non-violent power as a means of effecting political change. By the time he left South Africa in 1914, he had pressured the government into introducing the Indians' Relief Bill, which helped to improve (though it by no means secured) Indian rights.

Despite returning to his native country with the reputation of a saint after his work in South Africa, Gandhi was not at first seen as central to its independence struggle; indeed, he was somewhat out of touch with political and social conditions in India. He thus embarked on a long tour of the country, which led to an increased identification with India's peasantry. This was to form the basis of his political philosophy: Gandhi regarded village society, with its supposed self-sufficiency and mutual cooperation, as the antidote to corrupt industrial society; his promotion of local labour was integral to his later national policy of boycotting foreign goods as a means of wresting economic control from the British. As support for Gandhi among the peasantry grew following his intervention in a number of disputes (Champaran in 1917; Kheda in 1918), he sought to broaden his campaign. The repressive Rowlatt bills of 1919 offered him a specific issue around which to mount a coordinated nationwide satyagraha.

By now Gandhi's ability to mobilize the people was clear, and it won him greater influence in the Indian National Congress. He was thus able to have the party support the Non-Cooperation and Civil Disobedience Movement (1920–2). Through this and other subsequent protests (in particular, the Salt March in 1930 and his various fasts), he helped to challenge the legitimacy of British rule while bringing India's anti-colonial struggle to worldwide attention. With the rise of younger leaders such as Nehru, the nationalist movement grew in strength. In 1942 Gandhi launched the Quit India movement, his last nationwide satyagraha. Independence came in 1947, but was marred by the bloody partition of the country. Disappointed, Gandhi tried hard to promote Hindu–Muslim unity, though his efforts made him many enemies among Hindu nationalists. In January 1948 he was assassinated by a Hindu extremist.

Gandhi's time in Britain had a substantial impact on his own development, while his actions contributed to significant shifts in British opinion as regards empire. A number of scholars have highlighted his early experiences as a student in London as formative. James D. Hunt argues that it was here that Gandhi 'began his intellectual awakening, his moral maturation, and the opening of his mind to spiritual questions'. Indeed, while in London, he joined the Vegetarian Society, which not only enabled him to acquire familiarity with public speaking and organizational activity, but also introduced him to the ideal of a simple, moral life. He also encountered the Theosophists, whose influence has been accredited with awakening his interest in Hinduism.

Gandhi visited Britain in 1906, 1909, and 1914. His most important subsequent visit, however, was in 1931, when he attended the Round Table Conference in London to discuss India's future constitution. Although the Conference itself was not a success for Gandhi, his visit to the textile towns of Lancashire, where he demonstrated support for striking millworkers, made him something of a popular hero. The powerful impression he made on Britain, particularly in terms of the perceived moral righteousness behind his actions, helped to bring to attention issues of imperial oppression and to alter both public and political opinion. Indeed, on the death of Nehru in 1964, the Labour politician Tony Benn commented, 'Gandhi and Nehru liberated us. By winning their freedom, they freed us from the ignorance and prejudice that lay behind the myth of Britain's imperial destiny.'

While Gandhi's fame is indisputable, there have been arguments over the efficacy and success of his ideas and actions. Some have seen his saintly image as a cultivated illusion, one that stifled criticism of the specifics of his policies. And although he did mobilize mass support, it has been observed that not only did he virtually ignore the industrial working class, but Gandhi's non-violence often empowered only those already secure in the social hierarchy for whom it conveniently bypassed more threatening forms of revolutionary upheaval. Poorer peasants in revolt against Indian landlords were frequently told to forgo such violent class struggle and simply practise a more moral lifestyle. However, the undoubted recognition Gandhi achieved on the world stage, alongside the impact he had on British opinion, means he remains one of the most significant figures in terms of promoting the anti-imperial struggle and transforming people's perceptions of race and the status of empire. MGN

Arnold, David, *Gandhi* (2001)

Gandhi, M. K., *An Autobiography; or, The Story of My Experiments with Truth* (1949)

Horsburgh, H. J. N., *Non-Violence an Aggression: A Study of Gandhi's Moral Equivalent of War* (1968)

Hunt, James D., *Gandhi in London* (1993)

See also NAOROJI, DADABHAI; POLITICS

Garvey, Amy Ashwood (1897–1969). Co-founder with Marcus *Garvey (whose wife she was) of the Universal Negro Improvement Association (UNIA) and member of the London-based Pan-African movement. Ashwood was not only a political activist, but also a journalist, music producer, playwright, lecturer, and businesswoman. In 1914 she met Garvey at a debate in Kingston and helped to organize the inaugural meeting of the UNIA. The same year, aged just 17, she became UNIA's first secretary and a member of its management board, and co-founded its Ladies' Auxiliary Wing. Ashwood married Garvey in New York in 1919, where the couple established the American headquarters of UNIA. Her role as Garvey's chief aide and general secretary helped to build UNIA into an international Pan-African organization.

After the collapse of her marriage in 1922, Ashwood travelled worldwide, lecturing on black self-determination, *Pan-Africanism, and women's rights. In England she found her intellectual home among the circle of leading Pan-Africanists, working with C. L. R. *James and George *Padmore. In 1924 she co-founded the Nigerian Progress Union, and between 1935 and 1938 managed a restaurant, which became a meeting place for Pan-Africanists in London. She was a founder member of the *International African Service Bureau, and helped to organize the Fifth Pan-African Congress in Manchester in 1945, at which she delivered the sole paper on women's rights. A talented artist, Ashwood worked with the feminist activist Claudia *Jones to promote the London *Notting Hill Carnival. In her last years she resided intermittently in Africa. She died in poverty in Jamaica in 1969. CJ

Martin, Tony, *Amy Ashwood Garvey: Pan African, Feminist and Wife No. 1* (2001)

ODNB

See also POLITICS

Garvey, Marcus Mosiah (1887–1940). Jamaican-born champion of black solidarity and founder of the Universal Negro Improvement Association (UNIA) who lectured and later lived in Britain. Garvey was born on 17 August 1887 in St Ann's Bay, Jamaica. His father was a mason and a deacon of the Methodist Church, and his mother was a pious Christian who devoted much of her time to the young Garvey. He attended infant and subsequently elementary school at St Ann's Bay Methodist school, where he was deemed a bright and astute student. When he was 14 he became a printer's apprentice under his godfather and five years later worked at the government's printing office in Kingston. His experience in the field of printing would later aid the establishment and development of his numerous newspapers and journals.

Garvey was passionate about racial and class issues from a young age. A possible catalyst for his belief in the importance of black pride was the fact that at school children were taught British culture rather than African or Caribbean subjects. When he was older, he became acquainted with the anti-colonial struggles of George William Gordon, Paul Bogle, Alexander Bedward, and Dr Robert Love. As a result, his sense of 'race' consciousness was heightened, as well as his belief that culture was a means of promoting racial liberation and pride. In 1910 he started a newspaper, *The Watchman*, which sought to encourage black self-confidence. Although the publication was short-lived, it was followed by a string of various journals with a similar agenda. Of particular note are *Negro World* (1918–33) and the *Blackman* (1929–31). His newspapers were banned in most British colonies for their seditious content. In New York in 1923, for example, the British Consul-General upheld a pro-British magazine, the *British West Indian Review*, as counter-propaganda material to Garvey's UNIA publications. This, however, did not impede the publication or distribution of the newspapers.

Garvey first arrived in England in 1912. While in London, he worked on the newspaper the **African Times and Orient Review*, which was published by the Egyptian journalist Duse Mohamed *Ali and was widely regarded as a primary Pan-African journal. It did not merely focus on black liberation issues, but incorporated various anti-colonial struggles across the globe. Garvey declared that his first trip to England, which lasted two years, was crucial to the formation of his ideas. He not only met and worked alongside black seamen and students but also learnt about the mechanism of British democracy which allowed representation for the working classes. Ideas that were shaped by his English experiences influenced the impetus behind the formation of the UNIA in June 1919. The Association aimed to represent all black people, whether in the diaspora or in Africa, and provide them with an outlet for asserting pride in their 'race'. In effect, the UNIA, which endorsed economic self-reliance, ran various businesses such as the Negroes' Factories Corporation, Universal Laundries, a Universal millinery store, several Universal restaurants and grocery stores, a hotel, and a doll factory, as well as a printing press. A particularly ambitious business was the Black Star Line, which began in 1919. It sought to provide passages aboard vessels exclusively for black people. Although the venture was not entirely successful, it was a milestone in the effort to provide Blacks with mobility and freedom and to encourage them to visit Africa.

Garvey was attracted to the ideals of the British Labour Party, especially the welfare socialism that it promoted. He imagined that the Party would be sympathetic to the black struggle. When Labour's Ramsay MacDonald became Prime Minister in 1923, Garvey sent him a telegram informing him that he viewed the Labour Party as allies in the black fight for justice. The UNIA was particularly grateful to the Party for assisting unemployed Blacks in finding work in London. Seven years later, during the British general election, Garvey spoke at Hyde Park on behalf of the Labour Party, addressing the issue of Britain's relationship with its colonies in the West Indies, Africa, and India. Large demonstrations in Britain by the working class and the unemployed due to the world capitalist crisis were significant sources of inspiration for Garvey in his own fight for black liberty. His speeches directed at the British public were imbued with notions of self-determination for the oppressed, particularly the black 'race'. On 6 June 1928, at the Royal Albert Hall in London, he highlighted Britain's function in the slave and colonial system: 'cotton mills of Lancashire, the great shipping port of Liverpool, tell the tale of what we have done as black men for the British Empire . . . Upon that cotton your industry has prospered and you have been able to build the great British Empire of today.' He viewed Africa as the only place where black redemption could be sought, and from where Blacks could claim equality with the rest of the world. Hence, he advocated the return of pioneers to Africa, to aid its development and create an environment in which all Blacks could prosper. He also urged black people to visit independent African countries like Ethiopia and Liberia. In London, Garvey worked with numerous young black activists who would later become influential leaders in organizations such as the *West African Students' Union and the *International African Service Bureau.

Although he was often regarded as a separatist, deeply antithetical to intergrationists such as W. E. B. DuBois, Garvey believed in the solidarity of the oppressed and the colonized. He was a supporter, for instance, of M. K. *Gandhi's anti-colonial efforts in India, and in 1931 he was the guest of honour at the Indian Club in London. Furthermore, the *Blackman* had a regular column in the mid-1930s called 'The Truth About the Indian Situation'. He was, however, most passionate about the emancipation of his 'race' and was perpetually forming ways to further his struggle. In 1929, for instance, he had formed the People's Political Party, Jamaica's first modern political party, and campaigned for a seat in the legislative council. He was jailed for three months for contempt by British judges after he claimed that he would reform the bench should he be elected. This, however, was not the first time that Garvey had faced a jail sentence. In 1925 he had been sentenced to a five-year term at the Atlanta federal prison on a charge of mail fraud.

In 1935 Garvey shifted UNIA's base of operations from America to England. He continued to actively address large crowds, especially at Speakers' Corner in Hyde Park, and kept closely in touch with events in Africa and the West Indies. He maintained work on the *Blackman*, and in 1938 set up a School of African Philosophy to train future leaders of the UNIA. He died in London in June 1940. DD/SS

Lewis, Rupert, *Marcus Garvey: Anti-Colonial Champion* (1987)

Martin, Tony, *Race First: The Ideological and Organizational Struggles of Marcus Garvey and the Universal Negro Improvement Association* (1976)

See also JAMES, C. L. R.; MORANT BAY REBELLION; PADMORE, GEORGE; POLITICS; RASTAFARIANISM

Georgian and Victorian Britain. The nearly 200 years (1714–1901) that comprise the Georgian and Victorian periods in England were also the most formative and important in the history of Blacks in Britain.

1. The arrival and settlement of Blacks in Britain
2. The legal position of Blacks in Georgian Britain
3. Prominent Blacks in Georgian and Victorian Britain
4. A picture of black identity in Georgian and Victorian Britain

1. The arrival and settlement of Blacks in Britain Although Blacks began to enter Britain in the 16th century, the burgeoning slave trade and increasing trade with Africa saw their numbers increase steadily throughout the Georgian period. They entered in a variety of ways, as slaves and servants to American and West Indian planters; as students from Africa and the Caribbean; as sailors and musicians. It has been assumed that with end of the slave trade in 1807 and the end of slavery in 1833, the numbers of black British declined, but recent studies have shown a steady population throughout the Victorian period, less recognized because they assimilated into the general population through intermarriage, or were no longer tallied by abolitionists. Areas of *Liverpool, for instance, can trace a continuous black presence dating back to the Georgian period, when that city was a flourishing point of departure for ships involved in the slave trade. Estimates of the black 18th-century population range from 10,000 to 20,000; no reliable figures exist for the black British population in the 19th century.

Already accustomed to representations of Blacks in popular stage productions, the 18th-century British increasingly encountered actual people on the streets of London, in *country houses, and in the audiences of theatres. By the mid-18th century young black boys and men had become highly desirable as 'fashion accessories', outfitted in elaborate livery, carrying the purchases and pets of society women, and waiting at table. They also worked less visibly below stairs, in the kitchens of the upper classes and the growing middle classes, often those made wealthy by the slave trade. No Londoner could pass through the streets of that city without frequently encountering black people; one estimate puts the number of black Londoners as high as 1 in 30 during the late part of the century. They were not all servants, however, nor did they only live in the metropolis. Throughout the century, the kings of Africa also sent their sons to be educated in England and Scotland, where they could learn English and the fundamentals of business. Girls too were sent to be educated, some of them the daughters of white planters and their slaves. Among the servant class the overwhelming majority were male, many of them marrying into the white servant class. Such marriages were entirely legal.

2. The legal position of Blacks in Georgian Britain The courts struggled for decades to define the legal position of British slaves. On the one hand, they were viewed as property, a position that was increasingly challenged as numbers increased and Blacks sought recourse to enslavement in the courts. On the other hand, while slavery itself was condoned both within and outside Britain, legal challenges to slavery on British soil and to the forced removal to slave plantations of slaves were frequent. For nearly 100 years the courts walked a tentative line between individual legal rights of slaves and the collective economic rights of slaveholders, who brought great wealth to the nation.

From the middle of the 18th century, residence in Britain conferred a quasi-legal freedom, although more in the self-congratulatory myth than in the practice. Blacks themselves mounted legal challenges, often with the assistance of white abolitionists. For instance, John and Mary *Hylas were married, with their masters' consent, in 1758. John became free, but when Mary's master sold her back into West Indian slavery in 1766, John sued for the recovery of his wife and damages. Two years later the courts ordered her return, but this case did not set a precedent for the abolition of slavery. Even the famous **Somerset* case of 1772 ruled only that a slave could not be forced out of the country, rather than banning English slavery, as is so commonly believed. Ironically, the judge in this case, Lord Mansfield, was the doting great-uncle of a black woman who lived in his house, Dido Elizabeth *Lindsay.

3. Prominent Blacks in Georgian and Victorian Britain The 18th century saw a number of important writings by black authors. Ignatius *Sancho, who with his wife ran a small shop in London, composed music and corresponded with influential English figures; his letters form an important window onto the lives of black Britons. Corresponding with a white friend, he expressed his mixed feelings about England: 'I love [England]—for its freedom, and for the many blessings I enjoy in it.' At the same time, 'your country's conduct has been uniformly wicked in the East—West Indies—and even on the coast of Guinea'. Other important narratives and treatises were written by James Albert Ukawsaw *Gronniosaw and Quobna Ottobah *Cugoano (John Stewart), the latter of whom was one of the 'Sons of Africa' who kept the anti-slavery issue before the public in the English newspapers.

Undoubtedly the best known of these public figures was Olaudah *Equiano, or Gustavus Vassa, who made England his home after purchasing his freedom in 1766. His youthful experiences included baptism and education in Britain in the home of three white women, before resuming his work as a seaman. His ground-breaking narrative went into multiple editions in his lifetime, and brought the Middle Passage, slavery in Africa and the Americas, and black life in Britain to a wide and general public. As a sailor he travelled much of the known world, repeatedly seeing warfare at first hand, and sailing as far as the Near East, Russia, and the Arctic Circle, as well as experiencing slavery in the West Indies and the southern American states. Readers learnt not only the extent to which Blacks had participated in the wider world, but read of the insults, pain, and depredations inflicted upon Africans. As a literate and well-travelled man, and a Christian with a white wife, he was able through his extensive lecturing tours to bring alive the horrors of slavery and racism to audiences all over the British Isles. His influence in England was so great that he was selected to outfit and accompany the 'black poor' to the new colony at Sierra Leone (*see* SIERRA LEONE SETTLERS); however, his uncovering of embezzlement and corruption caused those implicated to insult him publicly, and he was dismissed from the post. Still, he died in 1797 a well-off man, known and admired by thousands. Many view him today as perhaps the most important black man ever to have lived in Britain.

With the end of slavery in the early Victorian period, Blacks in Britain continued to express themselves in a variety of professions and public acts. Queen Victoria had an 'adopted' black daughter, Sarah *Bonetta. William Darby, using the stage name of Pablo Fanque, was a black British-born circus owner and proprietor known throughout Britain and Ireland, and thrilled audiences with his trick horseback riding, re-enacting such stories as 'Uncle Tom's Cabin'. Samuel *Coleridge-Taylor, born to a white mother and African father, was a respected musical composer whose work *Hiawatha* played to popular acclaim.

It is Mary *Seacole, however, who comes down as the best-known black person in Victorian Britain, rivalling in her time the nursing exploits of Florence Nightingale. Trained as a nurse, and armed with her own provisions and skills, she set up what became known as her 'British Hotel', ministering to soldiers during the Crimean War from 1855 to 1857. In 1856 the grateful country launched a four-day fundraiser at the Royal Surrey Gardens in her honour, publicized through the *Illustrated News* and *Punch*, at which thousands cheered her. She settled in England, and was awarded the Crimean Medal by Queen Victoria. Her book *The Wonderful Adventures of Mrs. Seacole in Many Lands* was published in 1857, and enjoyed great popularity. Dr James Africanus *Horton was the first black graduate of a British university. William *Cuffay's participation in the Chartist movement led to his banishment to Tasmania in 1849.

4. A picture of black identity in Georgian and Victorian Britain Although these people and others achieved fame in Britain, it is important to remember that thousands of other black British people lived more obscure lives. For every Equiano or Sancho there were hundreds of others dispersed throughout the countryside, toiling in lonely houses, supporting families, and forming social clubs. In the 18th century they did so against a growing public representation of blackness, fuelled on the one hand by those determined to end the slave trade and slavery, and on the other by those equally determined to preserve the wealth that slavery engendered. In street signs, comic drawings, serious paintings, literature, and the stage, the white British offered portraits of their black countrymen that either romanticized or denigrated them. As the Georgian period moved into the Victorian, and the *'Scramble for Africa' saw European countries carving up the African continent for their own economic gain, black Britons struggled to maintain their dual British and African identities in a land that continued to view them as outsiders, even though they had lived there for many generations. Their situation was far better than that of black Americans, who marvelled at the freedoms Britain afforded them. Visitors such as Frederick *Douglass and Ida B. Wells found some of the greatest support for their abolitionist and anti-lynching causes in Britain, as well as the ability to socialize and travel without segregation. But for every Douglass or Wells there were thousands of readers who found the caricatures of Blacks presented in books like Thackeray's **Vanity Fair* amusing, or found Thomas *Carlyle's racist essays convincing. It was at this time that modern notions of racialism solidified around their presence at home and abroad, through the advent of 'scientific racism', and events surrounding the American Civil War.

In the late Victorian era, these representations found new venues. Black-face minstrelsy found an eager audience in British music halls, and such acts continued into 20th-century radio and television as wholesome family entertainment. Black performers did in fact appear on stage—among the most famous was the Shakespearean actor Ira *Aldridge—and in the extravagant exhibitions held throughout Britain at Alexandra Palace, Earls Court, in Sheffield, and elsewhere. These exhibitions purported to show actual life from countries all over the world, and inevitably included portrayals of African villages. As difficulties arose in finding actual Africans to remain throughout the long, cold runs of these exhibitions, black actors from London took on the roles without their audiences' knowledge that they were, in fact, their neighbours. In one frightening episode a fire at one of the exhibitions forced the actors to flee in costume, having to scale a fence and cross a railway line. One of the first films to feature black actors, Louis Lumière's *The Wandering Negro Minstrels*, was shot in London's Leicester Square in 1896. As the 20th century dawned, the black population lived a largely unnoticed life among their fellow Britons. However, the anti-Imperialist Pan-African Conference held in London in 1900 ushered in a new period of black activism.

In recent years genealogists and historians have begun to piece together a more complete picture of black Georgians and Victorians. Their methods include looking at all the public records, including tax, marriage, housing, police, and school documents. Family records held in private hands tell the bigger story, and only slowly have they, along with photographs, come sufficiently to light to show just how large and varied the black Victorian population was. Victorian magazines, particularly those for children, often featured stories about actual people, but for the most part the Victorians looked to Africa and the United States for information on black people, little acknowledging those living in their midst for hundreds of years, and indeed little recognizing that they had been there for so long. Samuel Coleridge-Taylor's gravestone speaks for centuries of Blacks living in Britain when it refers to his 'happy courage in an alien world'. What it ignores is that, as a native-born Englishman, it was very much his own world as well. GG

Gerzina, Gretchen, *Black England: Life Before Emancipation* (1995)

—— (ed.), *Black Victorians/Black Victoriana* (2003)

See also SLAVE TRADE; SLAVERY

Gilroy, Beryl (1924–2001). African-Caribbean British teacher, writer, and novelist. Born in Springlands, Berbice, British Guiana (now Guyana), she trained as a teacher in Georgetown and moved to England in 1951. Once in England, she became friends with other Caribbean migrant writers such as E. R. Braithwaite and Andrew *Salkey. Her initial experiences in England were education-related. In 1968 she became deputy head of Beckford primary school, and later its head. She was London's first black headteacher. Her experiences as a teacher are recorded in her 1976 publication *Black Teacher*. Gilroy joined London University's Institute of Education as well as the Inner London Education Authority's Centre for Multicultural Education. She was involved in educating and aiding immigrant children and children with birth defects.

Apart from teaching, she also obtained a doctorate in counselling psychology. She began writing fiction in the 1980s and her first novel, *Frangipani House*, was published in 1986. Subsequently, she focused progressively on Caribbean and African diasporic history and found in it inspiration for her writing. Her 1996 novel *Stedman and Joanna*, for instance, is set in the age of slavery. Gilroy was honoured for her achievements by the Institute of Education, which made her a Fellow, and the University of North London, which awarded her an honorary doctorate. She died of a heart attack at the age of 76. DD/SS

Gilroy, B., *Black Teacher* (1976)
ODNB

See also EDUCATION

Gladstone, John (1764–1851). Slave owner, instigator of the 'coolie trade', and father of the British prime minister William Ewart Gladstone (1809–98). Sir John Gladstone was a leading member of the West Indian Association of Liverpool, a group of plantation owners and merchants trading with the West Indies in slave-produced commodities. He owned sugar estates in Jamaica and British Guiana and was a passionate opponent of *abolition. In 1830, in a series of last-ditch attempts to persuade the government not to end West Indian slavery, Gladstone (then a member of Parliament and spokesman for the *West India interest) argued that slavery was normal in primitive societies, and that West Indian Blacks had peculiar constitutions, enabling them to work easily under a tropical sun. He held up the dreadful prospect of freed slaves slaughtering the smaller white populations.

In 1833 Gladstone was deputed by Liverpool's West Indian interest to devise a scheme for compensation, in preparation for the legal emancipation of slaves. He proposed that planters be paid £20 million, with £4 million going to British Guiana (which had an estimated 69,500 slaves). He also proposed a gradual, phased end to slavery. All slaves over the age of 16 should be registered as apprentices for twelve years from the date of emancipation, guaranteeing their labour to a particular plantation. Those under 16 should be apprenticed until the age of 24 (for men) and 20 (for women). Apprentices should work a 60-hour week.

Gladstone, realizing that his proposals to the British government would not find favour, embarked on a scheme to save his own plantation interests. Not trusting in the stability and dependability of his freed slaves, in 1836 he contacted Gillander, Arbuthnott, a firm of agents in Calcutta, with a view to recruiting Indians ('coolies') as indentured labourers. In May 1838 the first two ships in the 'coolie trade' docked in British Guiana. Between 1838 and 1917, when the system of indentureship ended, more than 238,000 'coolies' had been shipped to British Guiana, in excess of 40 per cent of the total number of indentured Indians taken to the region. His son William Gladstone (who in 1835 was given the post of Under-Secretary of State for the Colonies) was uneasy about his father's involvement in slavery and indentureship, his strong religious convictions making him worry over issues of justice and morality. Nevertheless, he repeatedly defended his father, in private correspondence and in Parliament, against charges of the cruel treatment of slaves and high Indian mortality rates in the Guiana estates. DD

Checkland, S. G., *The Gladstones* (1971)
Dabydeen, David, *The Counting House* (1996)

See also ABOLITION; SLAVERY

Glasgow. One of Britain's leading trading ports between the 17th and 20th centuries. Links between Glasgow and the black world originated through trade. In the late 17th century the merchant guilds of Glasgow added to its flourishing trade with the colonial tobacco plantations in mainland North America by forging trading connections with the West Indies. The Glasgow West India Association was founded in 1807. The Association spent many of its early years defending the slave trade interest. Glasgow was involved in the slave trade, but to a much smaller degree in comparison to the major slaving ports of *Bristol, *London, and *Liverpool. Trade connections and the slave trade led to the creation of a permanent black presence in Glasgow by the late 18th century as black people arrived, settled, and married. One early black Glaswegian was David Cunningham, 'lawfully' born to Anthony, a black labourer, and a white mother, Margaret Pollok, in 1782 (Glasgow Public Record of Baptisms, 12 October 1782, Mitchell Library, Glasgow).

The Glasgow merchants' main interest was the tobacco trade. This was chiefly conducted with North America, but also with the West Indies, where sugar and rum were also traded. Trade with Africa remained negligible until Britain began to extend its African empire in the latter half of the 19th century. Glasgow's tobacco trade was severely disrupted in the 1860s by the outbreak of the American Civil War. Hence the conditions were ripe to look to Africa for fresh markets. By the early 1870s Glasgow had forged trade links with West Africa. This commerce was expanded later in the century to include trade with Egypt and South Africa. By the end of the 19th century Glasgow's volume of trade with Africa was only bettered by the ports of London and Liverpool.

Glasgow's substantial colonial trade may well have facilitated the arrival of Andrew *Watson in the city. Watson was born in Georgetown, British Guiana (now Guyana), in 1857. He was expensively educated at Halifax grammar school and Rugby, and went to Glasgow in the 1870s to complete his education at Glasgow College. An impressive school rugby player and athlete, Watson made a name for himself as an excellent amateur footballer, playing for various Glasgow clubs before winning international honours while at the leading amateur Scottish club Queen's Park. According to the census of 1881, the year of his international football debut, Watson was employed in Glasgow as a warehouseman. He was married to a local woman, Jessie Maxwell, and had one son, Rupert. Watson won the first of his three caps in March 1881 in a match for Scotland against England, held at the Oval in London. Scotland won the match 6–1. In playing his part in this handsome victory Watson became the first recorded black international footballer.

By the beginning of the 20th century Glasgow's black population was well established and included families, students, professionals, skilled workers, and sailors. In 1919 Glasgow had its own black political organization, the African Races Association of Glasgow, and a black social club. Those employed as entertainers of one sort or another were found among other black people resident or passing through the city. One such short-term inhabitant was the black journalist, actor, and newspaper proprietor Duse Mohamed *Ali. In his 1937 reminiscences printed in the Nigerian newspaper *The Comet*, Ali recalled some time spent touring in Glasgow in the 1890s in a play entitled *The Jew's Revenge*, which he also produced. The play was staged at the Empire, Glasgow. Ali also gave some local recitals to help pay his costs. Other black entertainers who found their way to Glasgow around this time included 'E.E.', a West Indian music hall performer who had stowed away on a ship to get to Britain in August 1906. E.E. was admitted to the Glasgow poorhouse suffering from bronchitis. He stayed for sixteen days before leaving at his own request. Meanwhile, recalling Glasgow's black population in the early 20th century, one long-time local Clydeside resident noted that, aside from sailors, the only other black person he knew was a 'show man' called Jasper.

In 1919 Glasgow witnessed the first in a spate of riots that affected nine ports in Britain and involved attacks by sections of the white working class, principally merchant sailors, against black sailors, who were viewed as unfair economic competitors. The Glasgow riot of January 1919 began on the dockside as black and white British sailors attempted to sign on for a ship then in port. Serious violence erupted as a large crowd of both white British and foreign sailors armed with knives and sticks chased a group of black sailors out of the harbour yard. The black sailors were pursued to their nearby boarding house. The boarding house was then laid siege to by the white crowd, which had been swelled by white locals, until the black sailors were taken and removed to safety by 50 police officers. The cornered black sailors offered no resistance to the police intervention. Three sailors, one black and two white, received serious injuries as a result of the violence.

To quell the Glasgow riot the police took the black sailors into 'protective' custody and charged them with rioting and shooting offences. Of the 30 black sailors arrested (all British West Africans from Sierra Leone), the cases against 27 were subsequently dropped through lack of evidence. The remaining three were convicted on a much reduced charge of breach of the peace. One white man was arrested and later convicted of assaulting a police officer. No white people were arrested or prosecuted for attacks on the black sailors.

In the wake of the rioting, black sailors were offered financial incentives to quit Glasgow for good and return to the colony of their birth under a nationwide government repatriation scheme. For those who refused the offer, life in Glasgow, and elsewhere in Britain during the inter-war years, remained a constant struggle against unemployment, poor housing, and racist attitudes. JLMJ

Jenkinson, Jacqueline, 'The Glasgow Race Disturbances of 1919' in K. Lunn (ed.), *Race and Labour in Twentieth Century Britain* (1985)

Smout, T. C., *A History of the Scottish People 1450–1830* (1998)

Thompson, W., 'Glasgow and Africa: Connexions and Attitudes, 1870–1900', Ph.D. thesis (University of Strathclyde, 1970)

See also 'RACE' RIOTS, 1919; SCOTLAND; SPORT

Golliwog. A black-faced, shock-haired, fat red-lipped, and goggled-eyed character in brightly coloured clothes introduced to Britain in 1895 with the publication of Bertha and Florence Kate Upton's *The Adventures of Two Dutch Dolls*. Such was the popularity of the central Golliwog's character that the Uptons produced twelve sequels until 1909, which were reprinted many times until the late 1970s. The character was brave, courteous, and lovable, 'the prince of golliwogs', based on a black-faced minstrel doll Upton had had as a child in America. During the First World War she put the original manuscripts and toys up for auction, raising £472 10s., which purchased an ambulance called the Golliwog for the Red Cross. The buyer presented the items to the Prime Minister, and they lived at Chequers for some 90 years before being recently moved to the Museum of Childhood in Bethnal Green.

As neither the Uptons nor Helen Bannerman, creator of Little Black Sambo, filed for copyright, British manufacturers, writers, and artists were free to adopt the character as their own. The earliest golliwog doll was sold at Gamages department store in 1902. Golliwogs were to be found everywhere, from postcards to the sixth movement of Claude Debussy's *Children's Corner*, entitled 'Golliwog's Cakewalk'.

In 1910 James Robertson & Sons, the British jam manufacturer, adopted a golliwog named Golly as their mascot, featuring him on their packaging with the slogan 'Golly it's Good!' In the 1920s they began producing Golly badges, which could be obtained by collecting tokens.

The popularity of golliwogs began to decline after the Second World War as other toys and games flooded the market. By 1981 only 2,500 were being sold a year. They were also affected by the growth of 'political correctness', and what was once seen as a harmless, jolly toy became a controversial political item. In the early 1980s revised editions of Enid Blyton's *Noddy* books replaced Mr Golly, the golliwog proprietor of the Toytown garage, with a teddy bear. In 1983 the Greater London Council boycotted Robertson products as offensive. In 1988 the character ceased to be used in television advertising. In August 2001 the company replaced Golly entirely with Roald Dahl characters.

However, in September 2001 Richard Eddy, deputy leader of Bristol's Tory councillors, was forced to resign following a scandal involving the erection of a foot-high golliwog on top of a filing cabinet in Bristol Town Hall, in what he called a stand against political correctness. In May 2005 George Wood, a senior Scottish lawyer, was fined £1,500 for telling a joke about golliwogs at a dinner in Falkirk.

Despite this, golliwogs are still being produced by the British manufacturers Merrythought, who estimate sales of 10,000 a year. In 2006 they stocked twelve different golliwog products, ranging in price from £27.99 to £139.95. Golliwogs have also become desirable collectors' items, the rarest of Robertson's Golly badges selling for more than £1,000. MK

Derricks, Clinton, *Buy Golly! The History of the Golliwog* (2005)

See also RACISM

Gospel music. Protestant vocal music celebrating Christian doctrine in emotive, sometimes dramatic, ways. Gospel music is used to express personal testimony, encouraging thought about personal needs and experience, warning of the consequences of sin, and promising spiritual release. Gospel is performed by vocal soloists, and by groups and choirs of varying sizes. Some groups utilize close harmony technique with a lead vocalist who improvises, employing their wide vocal range, often heavily ornamenting the melodies. Others utilize the African call and response style, the leader improvising above the group, who provide the responses en masse. Gospel music's roots lie in late 19th- and early 20th-century America in the 'Holiness' movement churches, but today it has moved beyond these churches and is commonplace in other Christian churches, on dedicated gospel radio programmes, and in concert venues.

Until the 1950s the British experience of gospel was limited to visiting American groups such as the *Fisk Jubilee Singers and soloists such as Mahalia Jackson, whose 1952 visit launched gospel as a musical experience outside church. The mass of West Indians arriving in Britain from 1948 to the 1960s led to the development of independent black *churches where gospel was nurtured, including the Church of God in Christ, which had a choir established in the mid-1950s. Key figures in the late 1950s were Philip Mohabir, who founded the umbrella organization now known as the African Caribbean Evangelical Alliance, and the evangelist Ken McCarthy, who aired the first known gospel radio show on Radio Caroline, and managed a number of groups including the Soul Seekers.

Gospel's first major British exposure was the 1962 staging of a Broadway show, *Black Nativity*, featuring the American gospel artists Marion Williams and Alex Bradford. A number of groups emerged in the 1960s: the Singing Stewarts, a Caribbean-born sibling group, were among the first British gospel groups to enjoy recording success. The Golden Chords were exponents of the unaccompanied style of gospel little heard today, focusing on harmony and balance between the voices. The Harmonisers were one of the first electronic gospel groups and paved the way for the style of gospel popular from the 1980s; a brief alliance with the renowned gospel singer Lavine Hudson in 1978 resulted in a recording contract and many live performances.

The arrival of American recordings of artists such as the highly influential Andrae Crouch in the early 1970s inspired young British gospel performers. This influence waned in the 1980s, since when more British artists have recorded their music, some setting up their own companies to record, distribute, and sell their music to counteract the lack of opportunities with major labels. Further development was stimulated by the introduction of publicly staged concerts by local church-based promoters, such as Ken Johnson of Miracle Music Promotions, Ralph Weekes of Pure Gospel Promotions, and Roy Francis of Roy Francis Productions, the first gospel television producer to capture on film the key British gospel artists of the 1980s in the TV South–London Weekend Television series *People Get Ready*. In the late 1970s Juliet Fletcher started Oasis Promotions, and today manages Gospel Grand Summit, the annual UK gospel industry event.

Groups from the 1980s included Kainos, featuring Carl Booth and Bazil Meade, the Doyley Brothers, and Paradise. Bridging the gap between secular and gospel, Paradise, with Paul Johnson as lead vocalist, enjoyed short-lived success with a record in the UK pop charts. Youth choirs had been formed in many churches since the 1960s, leading to the establishment of groups such as the Challengers, the Merrybells Gospel Choir, the Majestics, and the Highgate Choir. The Inspirational Choir of the Pentecostal First Born Church of the Living God backed the pop group Madness on a hit that reached number 2 in the British pop charts in the early 1980s. This led to further records in their own right, and also to controversy in the church community about their role in the secular music scene. This trend continued into the 1990s, and fewer British gospel groups and choirs were formed as disillusion set in, with many singers striving for commercial success, notably the vocalist Bryan Powell and the mixed quartet Nu Colours, featuring Lawrence Johnson (who now manages many gospel singers operating in mainstream music).

A major figure in black British gospel since the 1970s is the Revd Bazil Meade, best known as the leader of the London Community Gospel Choir. Strongly influenced by American evangelists, he first moved away from the traditional style of church singing in the late 1960s and, drawing on the membership of local Pentecostal churches, formed the Choir in 1982, which by 1984 numbered over 100 musicians and singers. Meade decided to take gospel music out of church buildings, and toured soul clubs and discos in London, Manchester, and Liverpool, promoting *Fill My Cup*, the choir's first release. The choir is highly successful, with an international concert diary and numerous recordings, and has received many awards. Other highly successful choirs originating in the 1980s are Re:mission, the Wood Green Gospel Choir, and the London Adventist Chorale (the 1994 Sainsbury Choir of the Year), which have also toured, released recordings, and appeared on television and radio.

'Praise and Worship' is the biggest-selling form of gospel singing in Britain since the mid-1990s. Its leaders are the 'new stars' of the music, notably Noel Robinson with his vocal ensemble Nu Image; the songwriter Mark Beswick and his Power Praise singers and band; the gospel singer David Daniel, leading his People Fellowship Choir; and the Christian radio personality Muyiwa, a Nigerian male vocalist who has inspired a generation of African-British gospel artists.

In the 21st century British gospel is entering a defining new phase with a developing network of radio and club DJs, a flourishing gospel circuit, inclusion in arts programmes, a boom in community and school-based choirs, plans for an official UK gospel chart, and the acknowledgement of artistes' achievements through dedicated awards such as the Gospel Entertainment Music Awards. Leading the scene are British-born artists including Freddie Kofi, Cie, Siani, Blessed Voices, Four Kornerz, Natalie Phillips, Dee Moore, Sam Moore, Witness, and IDMC; and leading 'urban gospel' is Raymond & Co., a five-piece group excelling in the American tradition of strong, harmonious gospels.

The Gospel Music Heritage Foundation was launched in 2005 with the express purpose of documenting the history and development of British gospel, providing an extensive source of information.

SM

Broughton, Viv, *Black Gospel: An Illustrated History of the Gospel Sound* (1985)

Darden, Robert, *People Get Ready! A New History of Gospel Music* (2005)

Schwerin, Jules, *Got to Tell It: Mahalia Jackson, Queen of Gospel* (1993)

See also GRAMOPHONE RECORDINGS; MUSIC 2: EARLY POPULAR MUSIC

Gramophone recordings. By 1900 records and inexpensive gramophones had become part of Britain's entertainment industry. The Canada-born black banjoists George and James Douglass

Bohee had recorded wax cylinders in 1890, their instrument being ideally suited to the primitive recording techniques of the period as was the music of Seth Weeks (born in Illinois) in 1900–2, who recorded twenty sides. Another theatrical entertainer, Chicago-born Belle Davis, recorded 'The Honeysuckle and the Bee' in 1902.

The highly successful *In Dahomey* show, in London from May to December 1903 and then touring, brought 40 black Americans to Britain, including Pete Hampton (born in Kentucky), who was based in London until 1914. Hampton recorded 120 sides for several London companies, singing and playing the banjo, often with his partner Laura Bowman (born in Illinois). Another *In Dahomey* veteran, Norris Smith, made recordings until 1930. He was a member of the Four Black Diamonds stage act, and also reported on black affairs in Britain for the *Chicago Defender*. The stars of *In Dahomey*, Bert Williams (from Nassau, Bahamas, educated in California) and George Walker (from Kansas), recorded in London in 1903 but, as with the Bohees, there are no surviving copies. Bert Williams's songs were also recorded by others.

In 1905 the six pygmies from eastern Congo who were literally on show at the London Hippodrome made five recordings, one in Swahili and the others in Batwa. This was the first commercial recording of Africans in Britain, though anthropologists and travellers had made recordings before.

The first African-Caribbeans to have their British recordings released were George Carlisle (possibly from Trinidad) and Harry Welmon (who had been in America after leaving Bermuda), who recorded piano duets and their cross-talk humour act in 1912. Jamaican musicians in Britain included the *Native Choir (1906–8), numbering ten to fifteen men and women, of whom several were active in British entertainment into the 1920s; unfortunately, no recordings of them have been found. The choir recruited Liverpool-born William Masters, who did record (in Paris in 1923) before settling in Argentina.

The pianist and bandleader Daniel Kildare was born in Jamaica and settled in New York before moving to London, where in 1916–17 he made nearly 30 sides as Ciro's Club Coon Orchestra ('coon' was widely used even by black people: 'coon shouts' were up-tempo black-style vocalizations). With other players in 1918–19 he recorded as Dan and Harvey's Jazz Band. Harvey White (born in New York) was the drummer.

Will Marion Cook (born in Washington DC) had directed the orchestra for *In Dahomey* and returned to London in 1919 with the *Southern Syncopated Orchestra. This group appeared all over Britain into 1921, recruiting instrumentalists and singers of British, Caribbean, and African birth to replace Americans who found other opportunities in Britain, but they never recorded. Cook requested assistance from Edmund *Jenkins (a graduate of the Royal Academy of Music born South Carolina), but he was leading a successful dance-jazz group in London. Jenkins made several recordings in 1921. His friends the Versatile Four, active in Britain from 1913, started their British recording career in 1916, continued into 1923, and returned to America in 1926. Tony Tuck, Charlie Mills, Gus Haston, and Charlie Johnson played standard popular songs including 'After You've Gone', written by John Turner Layton and Henry Creamer. The Washington-born pianist Layton formed a partnership with the singer Clarence 'Tandy' Johnstone that was tremendously popular in Britain from 1924 to 1935. Hundreds of thousands of their records were sold. Their picture appeared on sheet music covers, as did that of the Grenada-born pianist–singer Leslie 'Hutch' *Hutchinson, whose 30-year British recording career started in 1927.

That year the British Parlophone company issued New York recordings of Caribbean music, borrowing the masters from America, but sales were slow. The Trinidadian singer, bandleader, and entertainer Sam Manning was featured on seven of these discs, working in London from 1934 and recording for export in 1934 and 1935.

British record companies issued American *jazz recordings, notably the Parlophone Rhythm Series, but there were black Americans who recorded in the jazz style in England, in particular the orchestras that accompanied song-and-dance shows such as the *Blackbirds* shows, from 1923. The recordings of the songwriter Noble Sissle (born in Indiana) in 1929–31 included the trumpeter Arthur Briggs (presumably born in the West Indies, but raised in Charleston) and the clarinettist Sidney Bechet (born in New Orleans). Both had been with Cook's orchestra in 1919. The London bandleader Spike Hughes employed the Jamaican-born multi-instrumentalist Leslie Thompson in his 1931 recordings; Thompson later recorded with Louis Armstrong in Paris, and helped to form the group that became Ken *Johnson's West Indian Dance Orchestra, employing British-born musicians including Joe Deniz on guitar and the drummer Al Craig. Johnson's band made a dozen recordings and many broadcasts in the late 1930s.

There were recordings of spirituals and African songs by the concert singers Roland *Hayes and Paul *Robeson in the 1920s, and more Robeson in the 1930s. The Washingtonian Duke Ellington's orchestra gave concerts in 1933 and recorded 'Hyde Park'. It was at that time that Benny Carter (born in New York) directed dance music for BBC radio; he made several recordings in London, including accompaniments for Elisabeth Welch, the cabaret artist and actress also born in New York who made London her home from 1933. Other American visitors including Thomas 'Fats' Waller made records; the Barbados-born trumpeter Dave *Wilkins of the Ken Johnson band played on them, along with the London-born drummer Ray Ellington. Una Mae Carlisle (born in Ohio) had worked with Waller in the United States, and employed Wilkins on her 1938 Jam Band recordings in London. The singer Adelaide *Hall (born in New York) settled in Britain in 1938, working and recording with the Nigerian Fela *Sowande. The Academy-trained Londoner Evelyn Dove recorded 'Somewhere, Over the Rainbow' and other ballads.

With imported and local talent, the issuing of American archive materials, and the demand for live bands in dance halls and for radio, there was a wealth of black musical activity in the 1930s. The London recordings of the Mills Brothers, a vocal group imitating the sounds of a jazz band, sold well; and so did the Royal Choral Society's abridged version of the choral masterpiece *Hiawatha* by the London born Samuel *Coleridge-Taylor. The revenue from that boxed set saved the veteran Society from bankruptcy. JPG/REL

Brooks, Tim, *Lost Sounds: Blacks and the Birth of the Recording Industry 1890–1919* (2004)

Green, Jeffrey, *Black Edwardians: Black People in Britain 1901–1914* (1998)

Lotz, Rainer E., *Black People: Entertainers of African Descent in Europe and Germany* (1997)

Walker, Edward, *English Ragtime: A Discography* (2000)

See also MUSIC 2: EARLY POPULAR MUSIC

Grant, Bernie. Nickname of Bernard Alexander Montgomery Grant (1944–2000), Labour Party politician. Grant was born in Georgetown, British Guiana (now Guyana), the second of five children. He won a scholarship to St Stanislaus College, a Jesuit boys' secondary school in Georgetown, but although he passed several GCEs at O Level, he left school a year later, and went to work for two years as a laboratory analyst before leaving to join his family in England.

Grant's first job on arrival in London was that of railway clerk, after which he went on to study at Tottenham Technical College in north London from 1965 to 1967. After leaving college, he went to study for a degree in mining engineering at Heriot-Watt University in Edinburgh. He left the university in 1969 without completing his degree as a protest at the discriminatory treatment of black students who were unable to participate in work experience in apartheid South Africa.

For the next nine years Grant worked as an international telephonist, becoming a shop steward in the Union of Post Office Workers, and an advocate for the rights of fellow workers. By 1978 he had become a full-time Area Officer for what was then the National Union of Public Employees, responsible for its local authority and health workers. He subsequently founded the Black Trade Unionists' Solidarity Movement, and worked for the organization full-time between 1981 and 1984.

Grant joined the Tottenham Labour Party in 1973, and was elected a councillor for the London borough of Haringey in 1978. He helped to found a national organization for black and Asian councillors, and was a prime mover in the fight for black sections in the Labour Party, arguing, against internal Labour Party opposition, that black sections were necessary because the Party was not listening to its black members. He also argued that the Party was not promoting enough black people to positions of responsibility.

In the early to mid-1980s England was unsettled by civil unrest across the country. Young people took to the streets in several major cities including *Liverpool, *Birmingham, and *London. Although there were frequently described as 'race riots', the people involved were often from those black and white communities who felt that their voices were not being heard by politicians and officials. Violent disturbances took place on the Haringey Council's *Broadwater Farm housing estate in 1985 after police raided the home of Cynthia Jarrett, who collapsed and died in their presence. During the unrest, a policeman was murdered and Grant quickly rose to national prominence when he stated that the youths on the estate felt that they had given the police 'a bloody good hiding'.

Grant's remarks about the riots were consistently misrepresented in newspapers, and the British tabloid press in particular singled him out as a figure of hate, publishing crudely racist stereotypical images and referring to him as 'Barmy Bernie'. In spite of this, he ousted Norman Atkinson, who had been the constituency MP for twenty years, and the Tottenham electorate voted him into Parliament in 1987 as one of the first black MPs in modern times. He was keenly aware of the importance of history and heritage and, publicly acknowledging his African ancestry, he entered his first State Opening of Parliament in African clothing.

A founder member and chair of the Parliamentary Black Caucus, which was established in 1988, Grant brokered links between black people in Britain and people of African descent around the world. Another important initiative to which he was deeply committed was the Africa Reparations Movement. As chair of the Movement he supported the Organization for African Unity in its efforts to secure compensation for the slave trade and the consequences of colonization.

In 1990 Grant accompanied the African-American former presidential candidate the Revd Jesse Jackson to South Africa, greeting Nelson Mandela on the day of his release.

Grant spoke on institutionalized racism in health, sport, housing, education, and immigration policy, and argued for greater resources for inner-city areas. With the advent of the Labour government in 1997 he became chair of the All Party Group on Race and Community, and of the British Caribbean Group. In addition, he was appointed a member of the Select Committee on International Development, continuing to argue for the elimination of overseas debt for poor nations, and for the recognition of the ongoing consequences of the past injustices of colonialism and slavery.

For many years Grant's high-profile political activism meant that he was in the forefront of debates about race relations and racism, but he was popular with constituents from a wide range of ethnic backgrounds. In his later political life, although he still had many critics within and outside the Labour Party, he became a widely respected politician.

Grant had lived with diabetes for many

years, and it eventually impaired his sight and his mobility. After he underwent major heart surgery in 1998, his kidneys failed. In spite of these setbacks to his health, he continued working until his death on 8 April 2000. Building on his desire to develop pride in local communities through area regeneration, his last big project was to work towards establishing a dedicated black arts and cultural facility in his Tottenham constituency. LY

Lusane, Clarence, 'Hands Across the Atlantic: Comparison of Black American and Black British Electoral Politics' in James Jennings (ed.), *Race and Politics: New Challenges and Responses for Black Activism* (1997)

ODNB

Phillips, Mike, 'Bernie Grant: Obituary', *The Guardian*, 10 Apr. 2000

Young, Lola, *Guide to the Bernie Grant Archive* (2004)

See also LAWRENCE, STEPHEN; PITT, DAVID THOMAS; POLITICS; SCARMAN REPORT; TRADE UNIONISM

Great Exhibition. International industrial exhibition held in London's Hyde Park between 1 May and 15 October 1851. The Great Exhibition was the first gathering of its kind to showcase foreign industry alongside British products. Commissioned by Prince Albert and the Royal Society of the Arts, it was inspired by new theories of free trade and designed to increase peace and understanding between England, her colonies, and the rest of the world.

Britain's colonies played a dominant role in the Exhibition's 15,000 displays. The largest personal contributor was the Indian Ranjit Singh, former ruler of the Sikh kingdom, whose estate was donated to Queen Victoria by the East Indian Company. Jewels from the estate were immediately named the Crown Jewels. The substantial Indian section also contained displays on the manufacturing of opium, embroidered shawls, wood and ivory carvings, musical instruments, agricultural tools, armour, silks, and carpets, and was a personal favourite of the Queen. The West Indies were represented by sugar samples, as well as tropical flowers, vegetables, and fruits. Tapestries, dried fruit, perfume, and metalwork from Tunis were arranged in mock bazaars to represent Africa.

The Exhibition attracted both international exhibitors and audience: in addition to Britain's colonies, countries such as France, Greece, Russia, and China were represented, and it is estimated that one-third of the Exhibition's 6 million visitors came from outside Britain. EDS

Fay, C. R., *Palace of Industry, 1851: A Study of the Great Exhibition and Its Fruits* (1951)

See also BAARTMAN, SARAH; GEORGIAN AND VICTORIAN BRITAIN

Greater London Council. Local government administrative organization for Greater London. The body was formed in 1965 and lasted until 1986, after which it was replaced by the Greater London Authority. The Greater London Council (GLC) took over from the London County Council, which covered a smaller area. Regions covered by the GLC included London, certain sections of Surrey, Essex, Kent, Middlesex, and Hertfordshire, as well as the county boroughs of Croydon, East Ham, and West Ham.

The GLC was culturally, politically, and socially involved in matters concerning ethnic-minority communities. Of particular note was the campaigning done by the GLC's Police Committee division for police accountability during the racially tense period in the 1980s. The GLC also provided opportunities for ethnic-minority groups to develop skills and talents. Practical training schemes were created, such as the one inaugurated in April 1985 to train black and other ethnic minorities in the field of arts administration. The Public Relations section organized numerous conferences, among them one on 'Women, Racism and Health' on 27 July 1985, which dealt with the way in which racism affected the mental health of ethnic-minority women. On a cultural level, the GLC hosted various events such as its literature competition, in which many now prominent black British writers such as Caryl Phillips and Beryl *Gilroy won prizes. SS

Flynn, Norman, Leach, Steve, and Vielba, Carol A., *Abolition or Reform? Greater London Council and the Metropolitan County Councils*, Local Government Briefings (1985)

See also EDUCATION; POLITICS

Green, Joe (*fl.* 18th century). Coachman painted by Sir Joshua Reynolds. His portrait hangs in the home of Sir John Quicke just outside Newton St Cyres near Exeter, Devon. The oil painting on board shows a smiling African wearing a greeny-brown velvet jacket, a white cravat, and a black trimmed hat with gold braid over a conventional wig of that time. The handwritten paper label on the back of the portrait reads: 'Joe Green, Black Coachman for many years to Mrs Quicke. Painted by Sir Joshua Reynolds'.

Records on the Quickes are scarce. In 1739 Mrs Quicke inherited £40,000 from her father, Thomas Coster, a merchant in *Bristol with interests in the slave trade who was a mayor of that city and an MP. John Quicke was Jane's second husband and we know that she lived in Bath as a widow.

As to Joe Green, searches so far have not revealed any records of baptism, marriage, or burial, nor any wife or children in Devon or Bath. The Reynolds portrait is a typical example of the tiny glimpse we get of black history in Britain and of the detailed work needed to uncover more of that history. LMacK

MacKeith, Lucy, *Local Black History: A Beginning in Devon* (2003)

See also VISUAL ARTS 1: REPRESENTATIONS OF BLACKS

Greenfield, Elizabeth Taylor (1817–1876). African-American singer celebrated in Great Britain. She was born in Natchez, Missouri, as a slave, and taken to Philadelphia, Pennsylvania, as a child by her mistress, Mrs Greenfield. When Mrs Greenfield joined the Quakers, advocating a just society for all people in the United States, she freed her slaves. Nevertheless, Elizabeth was loyal and stayed with Mrs Greenfield, who advised her to cultivate her gift for singing. She took her advice by continuing her study of music, and in 1851 she made her debut as a public performer in Buffalo, New York. This was followed by a tour of several cities.

In March 1853, following a concert in Buffalo, friends raised funds to enable Elizabeth to go to Europe for further study. Unfortunately, her agent in Britain reneged on an agreement to devise a British tour. To get out of this disastrous situation she sought the support of Lord Shaftesbury, Harriet Beecher Stowe (the American anti-slavery activist), and the Duchess of Sutherland.

She performed for the first time in London in May 1853, covering various cities in Britain and Ireland. The public received her warmly, and admired her vocal ability, known for its resonance and enormous range, nicknaming her 'the Black Swan'. In 1854 she was commanded to give a performance for Queen Victoria at Buckingham Palace. In the same year insufficient funds for vocal studies forced her to return to the Philadelphia to teach and perform. She died in March 1876. PAH

Pickering, Michael, '"A Jet Ornament to Society": Black Music in Nineteenth Century Britain' in Paul Oliver (ed.), *Black Music in Britain: Essays on Afro-Asian Contribution to Popular Music* (1990)

See also MUSIC 1: CLASSICAL MUSIC; MUSIC 2: EARLY POPULAR MUSIC

Gronniosaw, James Albert Ukawsaw (b. 1710×14, d. after 1772). African slave who lived in England and recorded his experiences in a narrative. His *Narrative of the Most Remarkable Particulars in the Life of James Albert Ukawsaw Gronniosaw, an African Prince, as Related by Himself* (1772) was published when he was 60 years old. It was written down by a young Christian woman from the town of Leominster, who was initially interested in Gronniosaw's story for personal reasons, but eventually published the narrative to expose the realities of his life, as well as to aid Gronniosaw and his family financially. The profits from the sales of the narrative were entirely received by him.

Gronniosaw was born in Bournou, Nigeria, of a royal family. His mother was the eldest daughter of the King of Bournou, and he enjoyed a happy childhood—his grandfather doted on him. A deeply curious child, Gronniosaw was perplexed by spiritual, divine, and religious matters from an early age. In his *Narrative* he attributes his departure from home at the age of 15 to this inclination, being unable to cope with his inner struggle and unhappiness. He left his family to join a merchant who was on his way to the Gold Coast, but ended up being sold into slavery and shipped to Barbados, from where he was soon taken to North America. He became a domestic slave in New Jersey, in the family of Theodorus Jacobus Frelinghuysen, a clergyman of the Dutch Reformed Church. They were kind to Gronniosaw and sent him to school, where he learnt how to read. However, the personal torment of his earlier years returned to challenge him. His belief in his own corruption and wickedness nearly led him to commit suicide. A divine revelation soon after this incident secured his Christian faith and he became a deeply committed Christian. Soon after this, in 1747 or 1748, Frelinghuysen died, leaving Gronniosaw his freedom in his will. Gronniosaw worked for members of the Frelinghuysen family for some years, and then served in campaigns in the Caribbean, in the crew of a privateer, and later as a soldier in the 28th Regiment.

In 1762 Gronniosaw arrived in England, an event that he describes as a dream fulfilled. He had always been convinced, through contact with his master's English friends and through his own reading, that English people were holy. Upon arrival in Portsmouth, however, he was gravely disappointed by the crudity and dishonesty that he encountered. The woman who put him up in her public house, for instance, cheated him of his money. He declared England to be 'worse than Sodom' and became increasingly saddened by the absence of any Christian friends. Consequently, he left Portsmouth for London, where he met the famous Methodist preacher George Whitefield, whom he had known in North America, and who paid for his lodgings in Petticoat Lane. It was during this time that Gronniosaw met his future wife, Betty, a poor white widow. He then worked for a Dr Gifford, who baptized him, and Gronniosaw took the Christian names of James Albert. Throughout his life, he was plagued by poverty and relied on the good nature of others, among them wealthy Quakers for whom he worked in various parts of the country such as Colchester and Norwich. However, nothing is known about his life after the publication of his narrative. Although relatively short, Gronniosaw's narrative contains much interesting detail. It is the earliest of the now famous 18th-century slave narratives, and introduces several themes also found in later examples of the genre. DD/SS

Gronniosaw, James Albert Ukawsaw, *A Narrative of the Most Remarkable Particulars in the Life of James Albert Ukawsaw Gronniosaw, an African Prince, as Related by Himself* (1772)

ODNB

Potkay, Adam, and Burr, Sandra (eds.), *Black Atlantic Writers of the Eighteenth Century: Living the New Exodus in England and the Americas* (1995)

See also CUGOANO, QUOBNA OTTOBAH; EQUIANO, OLAUDAH; PRINCE, MARY; SANCHO, IGNATIUS; WHEATLEY, PHILLIS

H

Haile Selassie (1892–1975). Emperor of Ethiopia, 1930–74, and exile in Britain, 1936–40. Born in Harar province, eastern Ethiopia, in 1892, he was the son of Ras Makonnen, Emperor Menelik's governor of the region, and until his accession to the imperial throne was called Tafari Makonnen. Educated by French Catholic missionaries, and at Ethiopia's first modern school, the Menelik, he succeeded his father as Harar's governor in 1910.

Menelik's young grandson and successor Lij Iyasu adopted a pro-Muslim attitude, and favoured the Germans and Turks in the First World War. This alienated the Ethiopian Orthodox Church, the nobility, and the local representatives of the Allied Powers, Britain, France, and Italy. Iyasu was overthrown by a *coup d'état* in 1916, whereupon Menelik's daughter Zawditu was appointed Empress, while Tafari became heir to the throne and regent. He was responsible for foreign affairs, while Zawditu presided over court cermonial.

Tafari emerged as a reformer. Having curtailed the slave trade in 1922, he gained Ethiopia's entry into the League of Nations in 1923, and in 1924 undertook a visit to several European countries. In 1923 he founded a printing press and a reformist newspaper called *Berhanena Selam* ['Light and Peace']. He opened Addis Ababa's first modern hospital in 1924, and a modern school in 1925, as well as a number of provincial schools and hospitals. He also improved the country's road network, dispatched students for study abroad, and purchased Ethiopia's first aeroplane in 1929.

On Zawditu's death in 1930 Tafari, who had already been proclaimed King two years earlier, acceded to the imperial throne. He adopted the name Haile Selassie, literally 'Power of the Trinity', and staged an impressive coronation. Accelerating his reform programme, he established Ethiopia's first Constitution in 1931. He set up the country's first Parliament, established a wireless station, strengthened anti-slavery legislation, and nationalized the formerly private Bank of Abyssinia, thereby creating a national Bank of Ethiopia. He also modernized the administration, erected ministry buildings, and established legations abroad. His consort, Empress Menen, founded the first girls' school.

Such reforms ended with Fascist Italy's unprovoked invasion on 3 October 1935. The Italians attacked from their colonies of Eritrea to the north and Somalia to the south. The Emperor travelled north to resist the main attack, but was defeated, in March–April 1936, by the invaders' overwhelming military superiority, mastery of the air, and use of mustard gas. He retreated to Addis Ababa, and on 2 May left for exile in Britain, travelling by train to Djibouti, then sailing to Palestine to pray in Jerusalem. He then sailed on through the Mediterranean (for safety, on a British warship, which was, however, withdrawn when he reached Gibraltar). Throughout the journey, and on arrival in England, the British government avoided giving him official recognition, but on his arrival at Waterloo Station, in London, he was welcomed by many British admirers and several Africans resident in Britain. He later took up residence in the city of Bath.

On 30 June 1936 he travelled to Geneva to address the Assembly of the League of Nations. Noisy Fascist journalists tried to prevent him from speaking, but the Romanian chairman, Titulescu, ordered them from the chamber. Haile Selassie then delivered his most famous address. He demanded justice for his people, and asked, 'What reply shall I take back to my people?' His appeal was largely ignored. Though Ethiopian patriots continued to resist the invader, most foreign countries recognized Italy's 'conquest' of Ethiopia: however, the United States, USSR, and Mexico refused to do so. Haile Selassie spent virtually his entire exile in Britain, keeping the flag of Ethiopia's independence aloft.

The entry of Italy into the *Second World War on 10 June 1940 changed the fortunes of Ethiopia and its Emperor. Britain, anxious to remove the Italians from East Africa, where they threatened her route to India, needed Haile Selassie's help. They flew him to Sudan on 23 June. Several British officials, including Sir Stuart Symes, Governor of the Anglo-Egyptian Sudan, and Sir Philip Mitchell, former Governor of Kenya, opposed Ethiopian independence. They favoured a virtual British protectorate, or Ethiopia's partition to benefit neighbouring British territories. Haile Selassie rejected such proposals, and returned to his capital, with British help, on 5 May 1941, the fifth anniversary of its occupation by Fascist Italy in 1936.

Haile Selassie rapidly re-established his government, and resumed his programme of modernization, centralization, and reform. Turning increasingly to the United States, but maintaining close relations with Tito's Yugoslavia (a fellow victim of Italian Fascist aggression), in 1942 he established a State Bank; in 1945 a new currency; and in 1946 a national airline, Ethiopian Airlines, and a Highway Authority. Again he sent numerous students for study abroad, and opened hospitals, schools, and colleges. In 1961 the latter were brought together as Haile Selassie I University. He sent troops to participate in the UN's Korean War, and also supported African independence struggles. He granted scholarships to students from colonial Africa, trained freedom fighters, and participated in UN peacekeeping in the Congo. Achieving the federation of Eritrea with Ethiopia in 1952, he established a new Constitution in 1955, and played a major role in founding the Organization of African Unity in 1963. This, like the UN Economic Commission for Africa, has its headquarters in Addis Ababa.

Though then regarded as a 'grand old man' of Africa, Haile Selassie's latter years witnessed increasing discontent: hostile student demonstrations; an abortive *coup d'état* in December 1960; famine in the late 1960s and early 1970s; and the February Revolution of 1974, which ended his long reign. He was deposed on 12 September, and died in detention eleven months later, probably murdered. RKPP

Lockot, Hans, *The Mission: The Life, Reign and Character of Haile Selassie I* (1989)

Marcus, Harold, *Haile Selassie I: The Formative Years* (1987)

See also ETHIOPIA, ITALIAN INVASION OF

Haiti, British relations with. British relations with Haiti commence with the ill-fated 1793 invasion of Saint-Domingue, when Britain tried—but failed miserably—to wrest the richest colony in the world from French control during the upheavals of its revolutionary war (1791–1803). When Haitian independence was finally proclaimed in 1804, the British government (along with all of the other major powers) refused to recognize the second republic in the Western hemisphere, largely because it was also the first to constitutionally abolish slavery. Haiti's revolutionary foundation initiated a long-running debate throughout the Atlantic world over how to react to the existence of a black republic at the core of the transatlantic system of slavery that drove the world economy.

In the northern Kingdom of Haiti, Henri Christophe (President, 1806–11, King, 1811–20) wished to establish friendly relations with Britain partly as protection against French reconquest. He modelled his government on Britain's liberal monarchy, applauded British anti-slavery philanthropy, and assiduously avoided any appearance of supporting slave revolts in the British colonies. He encouraged English schoolteachers to settle in Haiti to help organize the educational system (including the abolitionist Thomas *Clarkson, with whom the King had a lengthy correspondence). King Henry, as he spelled his name, also published a French translation of the Anglican Book of Common Prayer, and stated that he wished to make English the official language of Haiti. Despite these efforts, suspicion of Haiti ran high within neighbouring slave colonies, which continued to treat it as a pariah state.

The recognition of the Central and South American republics by Britain and the United States in 1823 was especially galling to the Haitians since Alexandre Pétion (President, 1807–18) had aided Simón Bolívar. The British government expressly forbade by law any civil or commercial intercourse between Jamaica and Haiti (6 Geo. IV, c. 114, s. 48), yet runaway slaves were known to seek refuge there because Haiti welcomed all people of African descent as citizens. Investigations into a Jamaican conspiracy in 1824 charged that Haitian aliens had kept up an improper connection with Haiti ever since the Revolution. Two leading activists in the movement for 'free coloured' rights, Lewis Celeste and John Escoffery, who were of Haitian ancestry, were accused of fomenting a 'Haitian plot' and were exiled. The Haitian government denied any knowledge of the two.

Jean-Pierre Boyer (President, 1818–43) unified the entire island and signed a controversial indemnification treaty with France in 1825. In return for French recognition, the Haitian government agreed to pay 150 million francs over five years to compensate losses by French colonists. This paved the way for diplomatic recognition and Haitian ports were opened to foreign trade. Only at this point did the British government establish official relations with Haiti, preparing the way for a British mercantile presence and attempts to found Protestant missions. Haiti was also viewed as a crucial experiment in slave emancipation, and the British Consul Charles Mackenzie (a 'free man of colour') was instructed by the Foreign Office in 1826 to investigate how agricultural labour was maintained without slavery. Mackenzie judged Haiti a danger to British colonial stability and described the Haitian people as 'young Barbarians'.

Britain's abolition of slavery in 1834 and ending of the apprenticeship system in 1838 brightened prospects for improved relations with Haiti. Haitians warmly welcomed and celebrated British Emancipation Day (1 August) as a festive occasion. Britain finally removed restrictions on trade with Haiti in 1843, just as Boyer's regime was falling. In the mid-19th century there were strong links between Haitian politics and the development of a racially conscious and democratic public culture among people of colour in the British West Indies. Haiti served as a beacon of hope for African liberation, black self-governance, and emerging ideas of racial unity. The possibility of intra-regional trade was an important aspect of a developing African-Caribbean identity and sense of distinct interests counter to metropolitan needs. The intermingling of Haitians, African-Americans, and West Indians of colour in Haiti is thought to have helped to create a diasporic black sensibility.

However, ongoing political unrest in Haiti also fuelled racist depictions of the failure of black government, exemplified by Thomas *Carlyle's vitriolic rant against emancipation in his 1850 essay 'The Nigger Question'. The infamous 1889 memoirs of Sir Spenser St John, British Consul in Port au Prince, also popularized the image of Haitians as savages. It was not only a revolutionary past and African heathenism (particularly 'voodoo') that inspired fear and ridicule of Haiti, but also its continuing anti-slavery and anti-colonial stance. In Jamaica there were crucial connections between black activists in the 1865 political movement that preceded the *Morant Bay rebellion and certain Haitian exiles attempting to overthrow President Geffrard (President, 1859–67) in Haiti. The Jamaican Governor Edward Eyre ordered all of the Haitian exiles to be arrested, and they were ordered to leave the island. Even if they were not directly involved in the Jamaican rebellion, evidence suggests that they were supporting Sylvain Salnave's attempt to overthrow Geffrard, who was receiving British military assistance at the time.

Various Haitian leaders sought to gain British support by offering concessions of suzerainty over portions of their territory. Britain was also involved in internal coups in Haiti such as encouraging a group of exiles led by Boyer Bazelin to invade Haiti from Jamaica in 1883. Like the other Great Powers, Britain occasionally used 'gunboat diplomacy' to protect the interests of its merchants who operated in Haiti, including Syrians who were British citizens and importers of English manufactured goods. Yet by the early 20th century, US and German naval and mercantile power in the Caribbean far outweighed British interests, and Anglo-Haitian relations were largely about neutralizing potential rivals and avoiding outright conflict. Many British subjects in Haiti who were black or 'brown' could not prove their British citizenship, and a naturalization treaty signed with Haiti in 1906 allowed Britain to largely abandon the English-speaking West Indian population in Haiti.

In the 20th century Haiti played a crucial role in black British identity formation, particularly in relation to the memorializing of the Haitian Revolution and the emergence of *Pan-Africanism, black nationalism, and Caribbean anticolonialism. For many British West Indians, Haiti became a powerful symbol of black freedom and progress, demonstrating the capacity for black military success, self-liberation, and self-government, as well as some of the pitfalls of revolutionary politics. British West Indian efforts to recast the meaning of Haiti from a self-consciously 'black' perspective represent both a symbolic recuperation and an attempt to challenge the racist social structures of white colonial societies. C. L. R. *James's classic ground-breaking study of the Haitian Revolution *The Black Jacobins* (1938) exemplifies the extensive influence of Haiti on shaping black British politics, identity, and self-understanding in the 20th century. Later this connection would be solidified by intellectuals who frequented John *La Rose's New Beacon Books (founded in 1966) and read the publications of Bogle-L'Ouverture Press (founded in 1991), whose name commemorates the intimate yet often invisible connections between the Jamaican and Haitian revolutionary traditions. MSh

Nicholls, David, *From Dessalines to Duvalier* (1996)
Sheller, Mimi, *Democracy After Slavery: Black Publics and Peasant Radicalism in Haiti and Jamaica* (2000)

See also HAITIAN REVOLUTION

Haitian Revolution. Upheaval in Haiti in 1791, when thousands of slaves rose in revolt against their masters and the slave system in the French colony of Saint-Domingue. After a twelve-year revolutionary struggle, and despite a series of invasions from British, Spanish, and Napoleonic imperial armies, all of whom were eager to lay their hands on what had been the most profitable colony in the 18th-century Atlantic world, Haiti became the first independent black republic outside Africa on 1 January 1804.

Historians have traditionally located the start of the Revolution in a vodun ceremony led by the slave and houngan (vodun priest) Boukman in August 1791, during which it is thought that a plan for a colony-wide insurrection was laid. Eight days after what has become known as the Bois Caïman meeting a massive slave insurrection began that quickly enveloped nearly all of the colony. The circumstances of the outbreak of the Revolution highlight one of its most contested issues: the extent to which the Revolution may be justly regarded as having been motivated by the ideals of the French Revolution or if in fact the Revolution was a slave revolution shaped by local conditions and informed by non-European, non-Enlightenment ideologies. The paucity of the historical archive does little to confirm or deny these opposed claims.

The narrative of the Revolution itself is highly complex, at the heart of which resides a three-way racial conflict between the colony's Whites, Mulattos, and Blacks. The colony was also divided by class conflict between rich white planters (*grands blancs*) and poorer Whites (*petits blancs*), free Blacks, Mulattos, and slaves, as well as conflicts between advocates of independence, those who remained loyal to France, and those who formed alliances with Britain or Spain. The diplomatic history of the Haitian Revolution was intimately affected by the course of the French Revolution, and, with the changes of direction and tragic reversals in France, various classes and parties changed their allegiances many times over the course of the conflict. Agitation for independence was first expressed by the *grands blancs*, who resented the mercantile restrictions imposed on the colony's foreign trade by France. The majority of the *grands blancs* realigned themselves with the royalists and the British within a few years of the outbreak of the revolution. The *affranchis* (free coloureds) had been actively appealing to France for full civil equality with Whites since 1780 and, in 1792, a decree awarded full rights of citizenship to Mulattos and free Blacks.

The most significant individual to rise to prominence in the course of the Revolution was Toussaint L'Ouverture, a former black domestic slave who had learned to read and write and who is now recognized as the Revolution's great architect and tactician. Along with other black leaders of the Revolution, L'Ouverture initially aligned himself with the Spanish, who governed the neighbouring colony of Santo Domingo, in their military campaign against the French. However, in a much celebrated move of diplomatic cunning, after the abolition of slavery in Saint-Domingue in 1793, L'Ouverture declared himself for the French Republic. Under his political and military leadership the slaves proceeded to restore most of the territory of Saint-Domingue to France, but L'Ouverture effectively ruled the colony independently. In 1801 he proclaimed a new Constitution for Saint-Domingue, in which the acknowledgement of French sovereignty was merely nominal. He also made himself governor for life of Saint-Domingue. In response, having observed the colony's steady progression to independence, Napoleon Bonaparte dispatched an expedition of approximately 17,000 French soldiers to the island to restore French rule and slavery. Divided loyalties were by now creating new factions within the black revolutionary leadership; L'Ouverture regarded this new war as a disaster from the start and was eager to come to terms with General Leclerc, the commander of the invading French forces. He wrote to Napoleon offering the French a way out of what had become a costly military disaster in the hope that negotiations on the status of the colony could begin. However, he was deceived into a meeting at which he was arrested and shortly thereafter deported for France, where he died imprisoned at the Fort de Joux on 7 April 1803.

After the return of the colony to Napoleonic rule Saint-Domingue was briefly peaceful, but, with the restoration of the *ancien régime*'s discriminatory policies against Mulattos in October 1802, the remaining former revolutionary leaders rebelled once again. Leclerc, who had died of yellow fever like much of his army, had been succeeded by General Rochambeau, who fought a brutal war of extermination against the Blacks, bringing man-eating dogs from Cuba. The atrocities committed in this final military phase of the Revolution helped to rally many former French loyalists to the black revolutionary cause. Eventually, under the leadership of the ex-slave Jean-Jacques Dessalines, independence was achieved after the French forces were finally defeated at the Battle of Vertières in 1803.

However, independence arrived at a huge cost: years of war had weakened the economy, and in 1806 Haiti descended into civil war. Diplomatic relations were refused to the independent Haiti, and in 1825 the Haitian government agreed to pay an indemnity to France, undertaking a debt whose disastrous consequences for the Haitian economy have endured ever since.

Perhaps unsurprisingly, the Haitian Revolution has long held a fascination for writers, artists, and intellectuals. In Britain the public debates on race and slavery were deeply affected by the events of the Haitian Revolution, with many choosing to emphasize the savage barbarity of the slave insurgents and their black magic 'voodoo', while abolitionists also used the example of Haiti to advance their cause. In the wake of the Revolution a vast range of literary works was produced by writers including William *Wordsworth, Victor Hugo, Heinrich von Kleist, Alphonse de Lamartine, Harriet Martineau, and John Greenleaf Whittier. Moreover, the Revolution has become an iconic moment in black history, and the events have had a persistent afterlife, inspiring imaginative writings by some of the principal figures associated with the *négritude* movement and the Harlem Renaissance, as well as writers from across the Americas, including the Haitian Jacques Stephen Alexis, the Trinidadian C. L. R. *James, the Martinican Edouard Glissant, and the Cuban Alejo Carpentier. PK

Césaire, Aimé, *Toussaint L'Ouverture* (1981)
Dubois, Laurent, *Avengers of the New World: The Story of the Haitian Revolution* (2004)
Trouillot, Michel-Rolph, *Silencing the Past: Power and the Production of History* (1995)

See also HAITI, BRITISH RELATIONS WITH

Hall, Adelaide (1901–1993). African-American jazz vocalist and vaudeville star. Born on 20 October 1901 in Brooklyn, New York, Hall made her debut with the 1921 Broadway musical *Shuffle Along*. She went on to perform at Harlem's famous Cotton Club, alongside great bandleaders and musicians including Duke Ellington, Fats Waller, and Cab Calloway, and introduced her signature wordless phrase on the recording of 'Creole Love Call' in 1927.

From 1928 to 1929 Hall starred in the musical *Blackbirds*, the show that featured her notable hits 'I Can't Give You Anything But Love, Baby' and 'I Must Have That Man'. Her solo concert tour brought her to London in 1931, and she visited again in 1938, appearing in *The Sun Never Sets* at the Theatre Royal, Drury Lane, and this time settling in Britain.

Hall hosted her own radio series, making her the first black star to be given a long-term contract with the BBC. She recorded over 70 discs for Decca Records, and during 1941 was reported to be the highest-paid entertainer in Britain. She performed regularly at the Florida club in Mayfair, which she co-owned with her husband, Bert Hicks, and made frequent radio and, later, television appearances.

Hall's career declined in the 1960s and 1970s, but saw a renaissance in the 1980s with the release of Francis Coppola's film *The Cotton Club* (1984). In March 1992 she performed two concerts at Carnegie Hall. She died on 7 November 1993 at the Charing Cross Hospital in Hammersmith. LFK

ODNB
Williams, Iain Cameron, *Underneath a Harlem Moon: The Harlem to Paris Years of Adelaide Hall* (2002)

See also JAZZ; RADIO

Hammon, Briton (*fl.* 1747–1760). African-American seaman, probably a slave, who was injured and treated in London while fighting the French in the Napoleonic Wars. The years of Hammon's birth and death are unknown. Hammon published a narrative of his life, *Narrative of the Uncommon Sufferings and Suprizing Deliverance of Briton Hammon, a Negro Man*, in 1760. Nothing is known of his life apart from what is recorded in the narrative.

The question of whether he was a slave or not is not entirely known, although he was the servant of a General John Winslow of Marshfield, Massachusetts. He was separated from his master in 1747 and became a captive of the Spanish on his many sea travels. He travelled for almost thirteen years, enduring various hardships such as imprisonment and enslavement. During his travels Hammon held various jobs. Notably, he worked as a cook aboard a slaver that was bound for Africa and as a dockworker in London. His tale bears the influences of an Indian captivity narrative, but with features of a slave narrative. Hammon served in the King's Navy at a time when America was still a British colony. In 1759, while fighting the French in the Seven Years War, he was injured and treated at the Greenwich naval hospital. His hospitalization lasted six weeks and left him in financially dire circumstances. After his discharge, Hammon worked on various ships. His narrative ends with his reunion with his 'good Master' in London. There are disputes over whether Hammon actually wrote the narrative or whether it was composed by a white editor or writer. DD/SS

Hammon, Briton, *Narrative of the Uncommon Sufferings and Suprizing Deliverance of Briton Hammon, a Negro Man* (1760)

ODNB

See also CUGOANO, QUOBNA OTTOBAH; EQUIANO, OLAUDAH; GRONNIOWSAW, JAMES ALBERT UKAWSAW; SANCHO, IGNATIUS

Handsworth Songs. The first documentary by the Black Audio Film Collective, directed by John Akomfrah (1986). This film was designed to give an alternative, black perspective on the state of race relations in Britain, which had been in the forefront of mass media coverage throughout most of 1985. This was the year that saw both the uprisings in the Handsworth district of Birmingham and the *Broadwater Farm riots, which took place in October, following the death of Cynthia Jarrett during a police raid on her home in Tottenham.

Handsworth Songs is now recognized as a landmark film for its visual representation of alleged police oppression and the politics of resistance within the black community. Along with its (then) controversial content, the film's innovative form also broke with the conventions of documentary realism. It contrasted interviews with members of the black community against shots of bewildered politicians, and juxtaposed monochrome archive material of black historiography with contemporary colour footage of the riots. It also utilized an eclectic range of music from 'Jerusalem' to reggae, and assailed the viewer with recurrent images whose impact was heightened by a variety of poetic voice-overs. In place of a linear, subjective narrative that traditionally positioned Blacks as aliens at the margins of British society, this film provided a radically different viewpoint that placed them firmly in the dramatic centre. LM

Bhabha, Homi, *The Location of Culture* (1994)

Mercer, Kobena, *Welcome to the Jungle: Positions in Black Cultural Studies* (1994)

See also FILM AND TELEVISION 1: REPRESENTATIONS OF BLACKS; FILM AND TELEVISION 2: FILM-MAKERS AND ACTORS

Hargrave, Francis (*c*.1741–1821). British barrister who came to prominence in the **Somerset* case. Hargrave was born in London, and entered Lincoln's Inn as a student in 1760. Having written to the abolitionist Granville *Sharp offering his services, Hargrave was the most prominent of the five lawyers who appeared on behalf of James Somerset, a slave who was brought from Boston, Massachusetts, then a British colony, to England in 1769. Somerset escaped, but was recaptured and imprisoned on a ship bound for Jamaica, also a British colony. At Sharp's intervention, hearings began in February 1772.

In this, Hargrave's first appearance in court, he argued that, while colonial law might permit slavery, those laws did not apply in England and, further, that English law did not allow for any person to enslave himself by contract. Somerset was freed, and Hargrave's argument was decisive in Lord Mansfield's ruling that slaves could not be taken by force to be sold abroad, although it fell short of declaring slavery illegal in England.

Soon after the *Somerset* case, Hargrave was appointed King's Counsel. In 1797 he was made Recorder of Liverpool, and for many years was Treasurer of Lincoln's

Inn, and a leading parliamentary lawyer, publishing many works of legal history.

In 1813 Hargrave became ill, probably with Alzheimer's disease, and the government purchased his valuable collection of legal books and manuscripts, depositing it in the British Library. Hargrave died on 16 August 1821, and was buried in the chapel of Lincoln's Inn. LFK

Wise, S., *Though the Heavens May Fall: The Landmark Trial that Led to the End of Slavery* (2005)

See also HYLAS, JOHN, AND HYLAS, MARY; KNIGHT V. WEDDERBURN

Hawkins, Sir John (1532–1595). The first Englishman to transport African slaves across the Atlantic. The son of a sea merchant and Mayor of Plymouth, Hawkins inherited the family sea business after his father's death. After early voyages to the Canary Islands, he moved to London in 1560 to seek support for voyages to the West Indian colonies, then under tight Spanish control.

Hawkins's first slave trading voyage departed for the west coast of Africa in October 1562. Upon arrival in Upper Guinea, Hawkins raided Portuguese ships for African slaves and other merchandise. Three hundred slaves were brought to Hispaniola, where he illegally sold them. The financial gains of the expedition were so extensive that Queen *Elizabeth I supported an equally profitable second voyage in 1564, which moved over 400 slaves from Sierra Leone. A third slaving voyage in 1567, also supported by the Queen, was not as successful. After transporting 500 West Africans to the Caribbean, Spanish ships attacked Hawkins's fleet while in port in Veracruz, Mexico. Only a handful of his crew survived.

Hawkins continued to fuel tension between Spain and England by foiling a Spanish plot to assassinate the Queen in 1570 and was rewarded with a seat in Parliament and made Treasurer to the Royal Navy. Reforms made to the Navy under his direction were instrumental in the British victory over the Spanish Armada, for which he was knighted in 1588. EDS

Kesley, Harry, *Sir John Hawkins: Queen Elizabeth's Slave Trader* (2003)

See also ELIZABETH I; SLAVERY; TUDOR BRITAIN

Hayes, Roland (1887–1977). African-American international tenor born in Georgia, United States, in June 1887, the son of ex-slaves. When his father died in 1898, Hayes had limited schooling as he had to work to support the family. His mother ensured that he regularly attended church. Here he sang in the choir and founded the Silver-Toned Quartet. He was inspired to sing by hearing Caruso's recordings, and received vocal tuition from Arthur Calhoun, a local choral director. In 1905 he went to study at Fisk University, and then on to Boston, but, despite success with his continuing vocal studies, recitals, and producing his own recordings, he was unable to get the support of an agent.

On his arrival in London in 1920 Amanda *Aldridge helped Hayes to settle and to find representation, along with coaching from George Henschel and Victor Beigel. He went on to give a critically acclaimed recital at the Wigmore Hall, and to perform at Buckingham Palace for King George V in April 1921. Glowing reviews appeared in *The Times* and the *Daily Telegraph*.

Hayes received adulation touring Europe, singing well-balanced programmes including songs by Schubert, Schumann, Brahms, Debussy, Fauré, and Montague Ring, and Negro spirituals. He also performed with a number of high-profile orchestras in London, Paris, and Amsterdam. His fine interpretations of song were superior, possessing a sensitive range of tonal nuances. He was welcomed warmly in the United States in 1923, and continued to enjoy a remarkable career, also supporting emerging black singers. In 1977 he died in Boston of pneumonia. PAH

Hughes, Langston, 'Roland Hayes' in Hughes, *Famous Negro Music Makers* (1955)

Abdul, Raoul, 'The Art of Roland Hayes' in Abdul, *Blacks in Classical Music: A Personal History* (1977)

Heart of Darkness. Novel by Joseph Conrad, first serialized in *Blackwood's*

Magazine in 1899 and published in book form in 1902. It indicts Belgian colonialism in the Congo, where a quest upriver into the steamy 'horror' of Africa reveals the descent into savagery of civilized man. The novel is modelled on Conrad's own experience of captaining a sternwheeler, the *Roi des Belges*, up the Congo in 1890. Before departing for the interior, he stayed for three weeks at Matadi Station with Roger Casement, the British consular official who exposed the savage behaviour of the Belgian colonizers, and who was later to be executed for treason during the First World War. Casement had the soul, Conrad wrote, of Bartholomé de las Casas, the Spanish emancipator of Amerindians: 'I would help him but it is not in me. I am only a wretched novelist inventing wretched stories.'

For Chinua Achebe, spearheading the decolonization of literature in the 1970s, Conrad was notoriously a 'bloody racist' ('bloody' was amended to 'thoroughgoing' in subsequent reprints of his essay 'An Image of Africa'). Achebe drew attention to Conrad's depictions of Africans in the novel, where they appear only as corpses, savages, and whirling shadows on the riverbank, arguing that, despite condemning imperialism, Conrad was unable to free his mind of the racist world-view on which empire 'sharpened its iron tooth'. The novel's central concern was the degeneration of Kurtz into savagery, and Africa was merely the place where this could happen. This Eurocentrism was inverted by the early generation of post-colonial African novelists: Chinua Achebe, Wole Soyinka, Ngugi wa Thiong'o, Tayeb Salih, Ama Ata Aidoo, and others have variously satirized the bigotry of the Marlow character, refashioned him as a Europeanized African returning to the continent, or sent black explorers into Europe. Conrad has also been Caribbeanized, most notably in the work of the Guyanese novelists Wilson Harris and David Dabydeen, where river voyages into Amerindian territory result in the commingling of protagonists' identities, suggesting the possibility of moving beyond the grand narratives of imperialism. JM

Achebe, Chinua, 'An Image of Africa: Racism in Conrad's *Heart of Darkness*' in Robert Kimbrough (ed.), *Heart of Darkness* (3rd edn., 1988)

See also MODERNISM; POST-COLONIAL THEORY.

Heart of the Race, The. Seminal socio-historical study exploring, for the first time, the diverse, though frequently overlooked, realities of black women in Britain after the Second World War. Written by Beverley Bryan, Stella Dadzie, and Suzanne Scafe, black feminist activists in the 1980s, and published in 1985, the book uses the voices of 'ordinary' women and historical texts to document, describe, and celebrate the contributions of black women to the making of the British nation. *The Heart of the Race*, subtitled *Black Women's Lives in Britain*, accomplishes two important goals. First, it acts as a corrective to mainstream women's history, which, for the most part, excludes the significant contributions of black women as historical actors, and, secondly, disrupts the tendency to narrate the post-war experiences of black peoples from a masculine perspective.

The Heart of the Race is at once a sobering and uplifting book, which places black women's experiences to the fore, hence revealing black women's historical agency, manifested in their long traditions of resistance to enslavement. It is this tradition of resistance that forges the link between the past and the present. The authors describe women's critical roles in production and reproduction within the plantation economy, and outline women's resistance to the iniquitous institution. It is this same spirit that serves them as they later responded to Britain's urgent call for labour in the post-war era. Thousands of women from across the Caribbean came to join small, long-established black communities, drawn to the 'mother country' by the promise of a new life for themselves and their families. Indeed, a survey of 1961 immigration patterns revealed that the number of black women who immigrated was equal to the number of men, and almost three-quarters were single. Like their menfolk, black women also experienced disillusion as they endured racism, prejudice, discrimination, and hostility from the white population. Yet, at a time when the government actively sought to push white women back into the domestic sphere after the war, black women's participation in the labour market was a significant component of Britain's post-war economic revival.

Without government assistance, these women relied on friends, relatives, and their own resources to settle, find employment, and provide childcare and the spiritual sustenance needed to survive in a hostile environment. They confronted the matrix of sexism, racism, and class oppression, while at the same time taking leading roles in protecting and nurturing their families and communities. Black women worked in multiple jobs to support their families, and protested against the impoverished education their children were receiving within an education system that placed little value on black children, their culture, or their aspirations. They organized to protect their communities from police harassment and brutality, while demanding greater protection from racists. They set up housing cooperatives, fought for better housing and other public services, and managed 'pardners' (informal credit unions). They played leading roles within the social and religious life of their churches, and joined trade unions to secure improved labour conditions. They protested against unwanted intrusions by the state (most often in the form of social services) into their family lives; rejected damaging stereotypical representations of sexuality; campaigned against the prescribing of carcinogenic birth control measures such as Depo-Provera (which was first trialled among black and working-class women); and, critically, were instrumental in perpetuating and passing on to their children their cultural heritage. CJ

Bryan, Beverley, Dadzie, Stella, and Scafe, Suzanne, *The Heart of the Race: Black Women's Lives in Britain* (1985)

See also IMMIGRATION; MORRIS, OLIVE; ORGANIZATION OF WOMEN OF AFRICAN AND ASIAN DESCENT

Hercules, Felix Eugene Michael (1888–1930s). Pan-Africanist and journalist born in Trinidad who became a schoolteacher. During the First World War he arrived in Britain and studied at London University. In 1918 John Eldred Taylor asked him to become the editor of a new newspaper in London, the **African Telegraph*. Hercules also became general secretary of the Society of Peoples of African Origin and associate secretary of the *African Progress Union. In this capacity he spoke at a protest meeting at Hyde Park Corner condemning the race riots in *Liverpool, also writing to the Colonial Secretary demanding that black people should be protected from white violence. In particular he fiercely condemned in the *African Telegraph* the assault by hundreds of white soldiers on black soldiers who were patients at the Belmont Hospital in Liverpool. When it was announced that black soldiers would not participate in the victory celebrations in London in July 1919, Hercules, in an *African Telegraph* editorial, denounced this insult to men who had 'fought with the white man to save the white man's home. . . . Black men all the world over are asking to-day: What have we got?' In late July 1919 Hercules began a tour of the West Indies, visiting Jamaica, Trinidad, and British Guiana; the authorities closely monitored his speeches and actions. In Britain the *African Telegraph* ran into financial difficulties and closed in December 1919 following a libel case, while Hercules moved to New York and disappeared from the scene. DK

Elkins, W. F., 'Hercules and the Society of Peoples of African Origin', *Caribbean Studies*, 1/4 (1972)

See also PUBLISHING

Hip hop. Novel form of party music created by the Bronx-based DJ Kool Herc, becoming a multi-million-dollar worldwide industry. Attempts by British artists to create a distinctive localized form of hip hop music have never met with a great deal of commercial success or media attention. Exactly why home-grown British hip hop, combining rhythmical rhyming (or rapping) with sampled beats and instrumental breaks has not left a greater mark on the British musical landscape is a largely neglected question. There have been several examinations of isolated hip hop scenes within the United Kingdom, notably Andy Bennett's excellent ethnographic survey of the localization of hip hop in Newcastle upon Tyne. But there are surprisingly few studies of just how the British version of hip hop has evolved.

The best attempt to address the creative lag experienced by UK rappers remains David Hesmondhalgh and Caspar Melville's survey of 'Urban Breakbeat Culture' (2001). Drawing upon Paul Gilroy's idea of a 'black Atlantic', where a complex network of exchange across black diasporic cultures results in a productive syncretism that creates new forms of music, Hesmondhalgh and Melville argue that the greatest legacy of hip hop's arrival into the United Kingdom has been the development of myriad distinctive new musical forms including drum 'n bass and trip hop. British artists such as Tricky, Grooverider, and Asian Dub Foundation have melded hip hop with other influences, including dance hall reggae, dub, and techno, to turn hip hop into something altogether new.

One could argue that this trend towards diversification has continued with the popularity of grime, a more lyrically focused offshoot of the UK 2-Step garage scene. However, some critics would argue that grime, and other generic offshoots such as eski and sublow, are so heavily influenced by hip hop that they occupy part of the British rap scene.

Although its popularity may be questioned, there is no denying that a uniquely British form of hip hop has evolved organically. Initial development was slow; for years imported rap music had to compete with the likes of soul, soca, and ska at groove clubs in London, Manchester, Leeds, and Nottingham, or at sound system parties in Notting Hill or Bristol. Each of the four core elements of hip hop culture—MCing, DJing, break dancing, and graffiti—all enjoyed cult appeal in British cities. But rappers and DJs were slow to develop their own sounds.

Nonetheless, the developing hip hop scene was a firmly multiracial project. One of the most popular groups of breakers on the Manchester scene in the early 1980s were the Rochdale-based Dizzy Footwurk. By the early 1990s they had reformed as the Kaliphz and were spearheading a new wave of British-Asian rap, along with groups like Fun-Da-Mental and Hustlers HC.

Many people credit the first authentically 'British' hip hop tune as the 1984 underground electro anthem 'London Bridge Is Falling Down' by DJ Newtrament and Krew. This innovative track was one of the first British tunes to make references to the land of its origins, such as tangling with the 'boys in blue'.

It took several years for a uniquely British style of rapping to develop. Newtrament rapped in a cod American accent and this style was copied by the likes of Derek B and Monie Love, the first British-born rappers to make an impact on the UK charts. Yet vocal styles copied from across the Atlantic soon became unfashionable. This was in part due to the confident vocal style of the influential London Posse, whose unique style of cockney rap combined London slang with dance hall style toasting.

Nowadays nothing marks a British MC as unworthy quite like the casual use of Americanisms. Rappers such as Braintax from Leeds and MC Pitman from Nottingham take a lot of pride in rapping in their regional accents and using local slang like 'twocking' and 'ginnel'. Although there is much debate over whether hip hop should be seen primarily as a form of emancipatory creative expression shaped by African-American street culture, or as a product of a complex dialogue between diverse diasporic cultures, there is no doubt that many of British rap's sensibilities stem from its reaction to trends in US hip hop.

While American rappers may celebrate their wealth and their ability to diversify their business interests and earn money. British rappers are more likely to relate stories of debt and poverty, such as Blak Twang's 'Red Letters' or Sway's 'Flo Fashion'. While American rappers and producers tend to use sampling to develop their sound, British producers have often created their own beats from scratch, unable to rely on record labels to license expensive samples.

Some critics of UK hip hop have argued that British rappers have done much to marginalize themselves by complaining of a lack of respect from the mainstream. Yet the lack of support from commercial radio remains a problem to this day, despite the efforts of DJs like Tim Westwood, Mike Allen, and Shortee Blitz. Mainstream record labels have also been reluctant to take on British rappers, and the most influential British hip hop labels have struggled for recognition and profits, like Greg Wilson's influential Street Sounds, the now defunct Music of Life, or the productive but underrated Low Life Records. As a result, British hip hop frequently celebrates the cult of the 'bedroom rapper', who toils thanklessly without the support of the industry, reduced even to distributing his own mix tapes. This notion of 'keeping it real' can be traced back to hard-core British rap groups like Gunshot and Son of Noise, whose songs 'No Sell Out' (1991) and 'Poor but Hardcore' (1992) celebrated the integrity of rappers who remained true to their humble roots.

Yet despite a series of creative lulls and financial hiccups, UK rap seems poised to at last break free from the underground. In 2005 Sway beat the hottest names in US hip hop to win the Best Rap category at the MOBO Awards. Although the British hip hop scene has long been an exclusively male preserve, a new breed of female rappers such as Lady Sovereign, Shystie, Estelle, and C-Mone is beginning to emulate the early success of Monie Love, the Cookie Crew, and the She Rockers. Through the emergent popularity of the British urban music broadcaster Channel U, which prioritizes content from home-grown artistes, and Internet portals like myspace.com, British hip hop can at last get the exposure it has long been denied.

DL

Bennett, A., *Popular Music and Youth Culture: Music Identity and Place* (2000)
Gilroy, Paul, *The Black Atlantic: Modernity and Double Consciousness* (1993)
Hesmondhalgh, David, and Melville, Caspar, 'Urban Breakbeat Culture' in T. Mitchell (ed.), *Global Noise: Rap and Hip-Hop Outside the USA* (2001)
Krims, A., *Rap Music and the Poetics of Identity* (2000)
Ogg, Alex, *The Hip Hop Years* (1999)

See also JAZZ; MUSIC 2: EARLY POPULAR MUSIC

Hirson, Baruch (1921–1999). Historian, editor, and political activist born on 10 December 1921 near Johannesburg, the child of Latvian Jews. Hirson was educated at Hebrew school in Johannesburg, and studied mathematics at the University of Witwatersrand, where he later worked as a physicist. In 1940 he joined the left-wing Hashomer Hatzair, subsequently becoming a member of various Trotskyist groups. Between 1944 and 1946 he was a political organizer for the Workers' International League.

Hirson participated in setting up black trade unions, in extremely difficult conditions created by the Suppression of Communism Act. He became involved in the Non-European Unity Movement, and in the late 1950s joined the Congress of Democrats, the white arm of the ANC-led Congress Alliance.

After the Sharpeville massacre in 1960 Hirson and his colleagues, highly critical of the Congress Alliance's leadership and policies, organized the National Committee for Liberation, which advocated sabotage as a substitute for peaceful action. In 1964 he was arrested and sentenced to nine years' imprisonment. Upon his release in 1973, he was presented with a banning order, and fled with his family to Britain.

Hirson began lecturing in physics, first at Bradford University, and later moving to

Middlesex University, where he enrolled for a doctorate in history in 1986. He edited *Searchlight*, a left-wing journal of South African history and politics, between 1988 and 1995. Hirson published five books on South African revolutionary history, and a great many articles. He died, after a long illness, on 3 October 1999. LFK

Hirson, Baruch, *Revolutions in My Life* (1995)

See also ANTI-APARTHEID MOVEMENT; COMMUNISM

Hogarth, William (1697–1764). The most prolific painter and engraver of Blacks in 18th-century British art. They figure in each of his major satirical series, from *A Harlot's Progress* of 1732 to the *Election* pictures of the 1750s. They are depicted as prostitutes, lovers, fairground entertainers, strolling actresses, household pets, thieves, and servants, the variety of their occupations suggesting the ubiquity of the black presence in 18th-century Britain.

The black figure is a detail pregnant with meaning in Hogarth's work, an intricate part of its elaborate narrative structure. Blacks are used to expose the sexual, cultural, and economic corruption of upper-class life. In pictures like *The Four Stages of Cruelty* (1750–1), the brutishness of English society is gauged by references to the 'savage' practices of Africans (and American-Indians). Hogarth consciously employs myths about Blacks relating to their sexuality, paganism, and simian ancestry so as to comment on the morality of the English aristocratic and mercantile classes. The Black is used as a yardstick, as well as a stick with which to beat the Whites. To use such myths at all, however satirically or ironically, was to risk giving them validity, especially since most viewers would not have appreciated the various levels at which his satire and irony operated. Hogarth himself complained of people's superficial appreciation of his art.

Perilous as his flirtation with racist myths was, it is equally clear that he reveals in *A Harlot's Progress* a deep sense of the communalism of suffering and pleasure between lower-class Whites and the black slave-servant. Hogarth's sympathy for the 'nobodies', that is, the lower classes, extends to a sympathy for black people. The black woman beating hemp in the prison scene of *A Harlot's Progress* is the earliest example of anti-slavery sentiment in English painting, if not in British art, anticipating by several decades the more detailed images of William *Blake, J. M. W. Turner, and others. Hogarth's views on slavery are peripheral and implicit, but it is well to remember that there was, at the time, no orchestrated public opinion against the inhumanity of the slave trade, merely sporadic voices that went largely unheeded. *A Harlot's Progress* makes seminal connections between race, class, and gender; Hogarth gropes towards an understanding of the female (black and white) experience of subjugation, he senses a solidarity between Blacks and lower-class Whites that overrides racial division, a solidarity of peoples victimized by an economic system controlled by the moneyed class.

It is significant that Hogarth uses the metaphor of slavery in describing his own condition as an artist. He describes the way artists are 'kept Day and Night at Work at miserable Prices whilst the overgrown Shopkeeper has the main Profit of their Labour'. The situation amounts to a 'Scene of Slavery in a Country that boasts of the Liberty of even the meanest of its Inhabitants'. DD

Dabydeen, David, *Hogarth's Blacks: Images of Blacks in Eighteenth Century English Art* (1985)

Wood, Marcus, *Blind Memory: Visual Representations of Slavery in England and America 1780–1865* (2000)

See also BEAUTY, CONCEPTS OF; VISUAL ARTS 1: REPRESENTATIONS OF BLACKS

Horton, James Africanus Beale (1835–1883). West African medical doctor, army officer, and political writer born in Freetown, Sierra Leone, the son of a liberated slave. He went to school and studied at Fourah Bay Institute with a view to entering the Christian ministry. However, along with two other men, he was selected in 1853 to study medicine in Britain with a view to returning to West Africa as an army medical officer. Horton studied first at King's College London and graduated from Edinburgh in 1859. He was very conscious that he was an African and adopted the name 'Africanus'. Commissioned into the Army, he returned to West Africa, where he spent twenty years practising as a military doctor and occasionally serving as an administrator. He retired as a lieutenant-colonel in 1880. Early in his career many of his white fellow doctors resented his role and they persuaded the War Office not to appoint further African officers.

Horton wrote three medical books (in 1867, 1868, and 1874), but his best-known work, written while he was on leave in London in 1866–8, was *West African Countries and Peoples* (1868). In this book he contested theories of white racial superiority and argued that Africans were capable of creating modern self-governing independent nations that could develop into a united West Africa. These Pan-African ideas were put into practice when Horton returned to West Africa and supported the attempts by African chiefs and businessmen on the Gold Coast to form a Fanti Confederation. Horton saw this as a step towards African self-government, but the British colonial authorities refused to recognize the Fanti Constitution. Horton's response was to write a series of letters to the Colonial Office, which was published as *Letters on the Political Condition of the Gold Coast* (1870). The Fanti Confederation fell apart in the face of African squabbles, and thereafter Horton turned to writing and to commercial activities. DK

Adi, Hakim, and Sherwood, Marika, *Pan-African History: Political Figures from Africa and the Diaspora Since 1787* (2003)

Fyfe, Christopher, *Africanus Horton: West African Scientist and Patriot* (1972)

Geiss, I., *The Pan-African Movement* (1974)

Nicol, Davidson, *Africanus Horton: The Dawn of Nationalism in Modern Africa* (1969)

ODNB

See also DOCTORS; MEDICINE

Housing.

1. Post-First World War settlement
2. The *Windrush* era
3. Discrimination in social housing
4. Comparisons with South Asians
5. African migrants and housing

1. Post-First World War settlement There has been an African presence in Britain since Roman times, but it was not until the early 20th century that sizeable concentrations of Blacks appeared in Britain's towns and cities. Mainly of Caribbean origin, a majority of the early migrants were merchant seaman or had seen naval service in the *First World War, so, not surprisingly, there were settlements in towns with major ports, most notably *Liverpool, *Bristol, and *Cardiff.

It was shortly after the First World War that their presence became a focal point for considerable urban unrest. The conflict in Liverpool in 1919 was rooted in the high level of segregation between white and black communities compounded by sexual, housing, and labour market competition. The ongoing influence of the *eugenics movement fuelled white anger around miscegenation, more specifically the accusation that 'they' (black men) were stealing 'our' (white) women. The International Division of Labour had generated a situation in which black sailors were in direct competition with returning (white) war veterans if they had signed on in the United Kingdom, and were seen as undercutting white rates if they had been recruited overseas. They were also in competition over housing resources. Additionally, the fact that they were segregated from Whites was interpreted as providing the context for likely sedition—in other words, they constituted a direct threat (echoing the familiar characterization of the black male as both physically powerful and dangerous). Ironically, they were being blamed for a segregation that had to a large extent been forced upon them.

2. The *Windrush* era It is important to recognize this historical background, because it demonstrates the sheer longevity of the African-origin population in the United Kingdom. Although there had also been a long-term South Asian presence, it was small in comparison. It is now well documented that, following the Second World War, Britain turned to eastern and southern Europe for replacement labour (in preference to the New Commonwealth), as Conservative governments in the 1950s were concerned about the potential dangers posed by black migrants. Only when this source had begun to dry up did the government renew its commitment to recruiting black labour. The initial phase of migration was represented symbolically by the arrival in 1948 of the SS **Empire Windrush*.

Many, if not most, migrants came to Britain harbouring the idea that they were returning 'home', i.e. to the mother country. They therefore felt that work (and decent housing) would be plentiful, and they expected to be welcomed. As in the case of earlier migrants, however, there was little evidence of a cordial welcome from their 'hosts'. The housing discrimination faced by early post-war migrants was vividly recalled in Mike and Trevor Phillips's book, *Windrush* (1998), published to mark the fiftieth anniversary of the post-war West Indian presence. A formal investigation by the *Commission for Racial Equality showed that blatantly discriminatory practices had yet to be eradicated, despite a quarter of a century of anti-discrimination legislation. Published in 1990 and entitled *Sorry It's Gone*, this featured paired (white–black) applicants responding to lettings advertisements. Black applicants were invariably told that the house or apartment had already been let. When white applicants visited properties that had 'already been let', however, they were in most cases offered a viewing.

Lack of funds prevented all but a handful of Caribbean migrants from purchasing property, not least because the majority came to look for work in major cities, and in particular London. In the latter case, even with the creative use of the 'pardner system', owning was simply not an option. Given the rigid application of residence requirements, the social housing sector was also difficult to access. The end result was a heavy reliance on private rented property, which, quite apart from the access problems already noted, was notorious for being extremely poor in quality. The desperation faced by early Caribbean migrants often led them into the clutches of unscrupulous landlords. This became such a major issue in the 1960s that the phenomenon was enshrined in the concept of Rachmanism (named after one of the most infamous exponents of this form of exploitation).

Much of the focus for discussion was London because then (as now) this is where the majority of post-war Caribbean migrants settled. A classic study of Birmingham in the 1960s by John Rex and Robert Moore, however, revealed similar problems, but also introduced a new concept, pariah landlordism. This name was applied to those whom the authors described as having been 'forced to buy'. Desperate at not being able to access social housing and being discriminated against by high street banks and building societies, these were people who resorted to short-term, high-interest loans from the fringe banking sector to buy up larger pre-1919 terraced properties to sublet. Those to whom they let rooms in these lodging houses were usually of a similar ethnic heritage to themselves. Landlords were accorded pariah status, but were effectively compelled to charge high rents to sustain their outgoings.

3. Discrimination in social housing Social housing became a more realistic proposition after migrants had lived in the United Kingdom for at least five years. From the 1960s onwards the amount of council and housing association accommodation increased sharply. The expectation was that the large-scale shift from the private to the public sector would automatically lead to an improvement in the average quality of dwellings let to Caribbean migrants. There is, however, much evidence to suggest that this was very often not the case. Research showed that they tended to be housed in hard-to-let properties on sink estates and in unpopular deck-access maisonettes. Assessment of 'housekeeping standards' (by housing officers) was used to disqualify Caribbean families from the better-quality properties and more desirable areas. In other words, black applicants were given the properties they 'deserved', on the basis of highly questionable, culturally biased, and prejudiced comments about the way 'these people live'. There were allegations about 'unconventional' lifestyles and flamboyant decor, specifically the use of 'garish colour schemes'. The end result of allocation processes was invariably a degree of segregation from the 'deserving' (i.e. white) poor.

At this point reference should be made to the distinctive nature of Caribbean migration (as compared with that involving South Asians). Among the latter, early migrants were overwhelmingly male. In contrast, many of the primary migrants from the Caribbean were female. Women had been a particular target of recruitment campaigns (in the Caribbean) by the National Health Service, on the grounds that nurses were in very short supply in Britain. (Doctors, on the other hand, were recruited from the Indian subcontinent.) It was especially ironic that the Health Minister responsible for the early campaigns was none other than Enoch *Powell, someone not normally associated with support for black immigration. The gender issue is crucial because it played a dominant role in more recent housing debates.

4. Comparisons with South Asians Following the arrival of increasing numbers of South Asian migrants, social commentators confronted the issue of why it was that their housing, and particularly tenure, patterns differed so radically from those of the Caribbean population. South Asian groups (with the sole exception of Bangladeshi migrants in the early years of settlement) exhibited extremely high levels of owner occupation (higher indeed than those for Whites). Caribbean households in contrast displayed a much higher than average presence in the social housing sector. Out of this grew a highly popular theory, one that has acquired almost paradigmatic status. This is that South Asians are peculiarly (culturally) predisposed to buy property, whereas social renting is the overwhelming preference of Caribbeans. This is an important issue, not least because it drives the policies and practices of exchange professionals in the housing market.

It is a seductive theory because it so obviously resonates with the 'facts'. But it is also false, except in a highly qualified form. Where one is placed in the housing market is not an unambiguous guide to choices, and certainly not to cultural propensities. Research in the 1990s began to question the relationship between ethnicity and housing market position. Although the arguments are complex and convoluted, the key point is that, if one investigates social class and household structure, most of the differences between South Asian and African-Caribbean households evaporate. Essentially, the latter population contains higher proportions of working-class and female-headed households. They are also much more likely to be living in London, where property prices are extremely high. Comparing like with like suggests that housing market position is much more likely to be linked to these factors than to be explainable within a deterministic culturalist model.

5. African migrants and housing Migration from sub-Saharan Africa began in earnest after the Caribbean population was already well established. Data from the 2001 census of population suggests that this 'Black African' group is even more highly concentrated in London than the Caribbeans: 78 as against 61 per cent. Even larger proportions live in social housing: 50 per cent as against 40 per cent. Home ownership rates remain well below the national average for both groups, at 48 per cent for 'Black-Caribbeans' and 25 per cent for 'Black-Africans'. The new African migrants tended to be very different from earlier black immigrant groups in terms of class background, large numbers entering Britain as students (often the children of relatively affluent parents). Marked differences (or, at times, perceived differences) in wealth and status, especially when viewed in the context of the historical relationship between West Africa and the Caribbean, have led to strained relations, and even hostility, between the groups in recent years. This is made all the more likely given that the two groups (or, more accurately, 'collectivities'—given their internal heterogeneity) tend to live in relatively close proximity to one another.

According to Peach and Rossiter, by the 1990s there was some evidence of residential concentrations in the metropolis based around (Caribbean) island of origin. In general, however, black groups, irrespective of precise heritage, are by no means as highly segregated as are most South Asian groups. There is also evidence of increasing social mobility on the part of both African and African-Caribbean groups and a degree of out-migration from the urban cores to the suburbs, and even to the countryside.

PR

Peach, Ceri, and Byron, Margaret, 'Caribbean Tenants in Council Housing', *New Community*, 19/3 (1993)

—— and Rossiter, D., 'Level and Nature of Spatial Concentration and Segregation of Minority Ethnic Population in Great Britain, 1991' in Peter Ratcliffe (ed.), *Social Geography and Ethnicity in Britain: Geographical Spread, Spatial Concentration and Internal Migration*, vol. iii of *Ethnicity in the 1991 Census* (1996)

Phillips, Mike, and Phillips, Trevor, *Windrush: The Irresistible Rise of Multi-Racial Britain* (1998)

Ratcliffe, Peter, *Racism and Reaction: A Profile of Handsworth* (1981)

Rex, John, and Moore, Robert, *Race, Community and Conflict: A Study of Sparkbrook* (1967)

See also IMMIGRATION

Hutchinson, Leslie 'Hutch' (1900–1968). Entertainer and recording artiste. Leslie Arthur Julien Hutchinson was born in Grenada, West Indies. Clever, handsome, and ambitious, he soon travelled to America, pretending to his sponsors that he wanted to qualify as a doctor. He left for Harlem, learned stride piano, accompanied blues shouters on recordings, and made a name for himself, especially with white punters like the Vanderbilts. After witnessing a violent attack in Florida by the Ku Klux Klan, he set off to seek his fortune in Europe. He taught the Charleston to the royal family in Madrid, created his own band in Paris, and played in Venice for Cole Porter; and he became the favourite exponent of Cole Porter's songs in Paris nightclubs.

The impresario Charles Cochran was tipped off by Edwina Mountbatten, the royal socialite millionairess, to invite Hutchinson to London in 1924 to play in his revues—it was to be his home for the rest of his life. Hutchinson made over 450 recordings and can fairly be acclaimed the father of English cabaret owing to a capable combination of timing, pianistic skills, light tuneful voice and depth of repertoire, an enormous powerful acquaintance, wide popularity, and charisma and charm. He became as adept at holding small smart audiences in cabaret as the thousands who applauded him in vast variety halls, and appeared in seven films and often on radio and TV. For a decade he earned more than any other UK performer.

After success on the home front through the war in the forces entertainment service, ENSA, his star waned in the 1950s and he battled with drink problems. His career revived again briefly, especially in the former colonies of India, Kenya, Hong Kong, and Australia, before his penurious death in 1968. He left many children, who are mostly musical, but did not know their father. His music is still current and published annually. CB

Breese, Charlotte, *Hutch* (1999)

ODNB

See also GRAMOPHONE RECORDINGS; MUSIC 2: EARLY POPULAR MUSIC

Hylas, John, and Hylas, Mary (*fl.* 1754–1768). Former slaves whose kidnapping case was fought by the 18th-century abolitionist Granville *Sharp. John Hylas and his wife, Mary, were both born in Barbados. In the year 1754 they were each brought to England—John by his mistress, Judith Aleyne, and Mary by her master and mistress, Mr and Mrs Newton. They met in England, and married with the consent of their owners in 1758. After their marriage John Hylas was set free, and the couple lived happily together until, in 1766, Mary was kidnapped by her former owners and sent to the West Indies to be sold as a slave.

Having heard of Granville Sharp's fight for the liberty of *Jonathan Strong, in 1768 John Hylas approached Sharp, who prepared a memorandum enabling him to begin an action against Newton.

The court found in favour of Hylas, who was awarded 1*s*. nominal damages, and Newton was ordered to bring Mary back to England. Sharp charged that Hylas was 'as much entitled to £500 damages, at the least . . . as the first lawyer of the kingdom would be, if he should lose his wife in the same manner'. The court, however, was not convinced that the Habeas Corpus Act applied to black people. The case did not decide the legal status of Blacks in England: it decided only that, since Hylas had been freed, he and his wife were entitled to their liberty.

LFK

Shyllon, F. O., *Black Slaves in Britain* (1974)

See also KNIGHT V. WEDDERBURN; SOMERSET CASE

I

Immigration

1. History and demography
2. Political responses to immigration
3. White reactions to immigration
4. Current immigration trends and debates

1. History and demography Small settlements of Blacks in port cities such as *Cardiff, *Liverpool, *London's East End, and Manchester were mainly established by colonial seamen, especially after the *First World War. These communities were swollen in later decades by the presence of several thousand black soldiers and seamen who had participated in the *Second World War but, on demobilization, had remained in Britain. From 1948 onwards substantial migration from the Caribbean region began as Caribbean workers and their families heeded Britain's call for labourers to assist in its economic rebuilding programme.

Prior to the Second World War the migration of Blacks to Britain had consisted almost entirely of middle- and upper-class individuals, but war service brought working-class Blacks into the country. For example, 7,000 West Indians enlisted for the Royal Air Force and were stationed in Britain; the presence of thousands of African-American GIs also substantially increased the black wartime presence. The war was thus an important catalyst of black post-war migration. However, other factors also contributed, including an overseas volunteers' scheme supervised by the Ministry of Labour, which encouraged subsequent immigration to Britain from the West Indies; for example, 245 West Indian skilled craftsmen were recruited during the war to work in factories on Merseyside. The *Annual Report on Jamaica* for the year 1946 gave a depressing account of the unemployment situation there, revealing the particular difficulties encountered by ex-servicemen returning after the war.

In previous years the economic difficulties experienced by many Caribbean islands had been somewhat alleviated by opportunities for agricultural labourers in the United States and Canada. However, after the war and the passing of the 1952 McCarran-Walter Act, migration from Jamaica to the United States was restricted to a mere hundred workers per year. The great demand in Britain for unskilled labourers to rebuild the post-war economy therefore represented the only hope for West Indian migrants.

The British Nationality Act 1948 created a single category of citizenship (that of 'British subject: citizen of the United Kingdom and Colonies') for persons belonging not just to the United Kingdom itself, but also to any place which was still a British colony on 1 January 1949. This had the effect of ensuring that people from British colonies in the Caribbean (and elsewhere) had a legal right to come to the United Kingdom to live and work.

The start of mass immigration of black people in the post-war era was the arrival at Tilbury docks in Kent of the SS **Empire Windrush* in June 1948. On board were 492 immigrants from Jamaica, most of whom had worked in Britain during the war, and had returned to the West Indies. The *Empire Windrush* was followed by two more passenger ships, the SS *Orbita* and SS *Georgia*.

From 1951 immigration from the West Indies was encouraged by the Conservative government elected that year, though some concern began to be voiced about the numbers of 'coloured' immigrants arriving in Britain. As pressure for immigration control grew, the Conservative Party changed its policy of free personal movement and migration for all Commonwealth citizens to a policy of immigration control, and published a bill on 1 November 1961 to restrict immigration. However, increasingly voluble debates on immigration control motivated thousands of West Indians to migrate to Britain to beat the impending restrictions. Between the beginning of 1961 and the middle of 1962, when the Commonwealth Immigrants Act 1962 came into force, 98,000 people migrated to Britain from the West Indies.

Migration from the West Indies was initially very small: until 1951 it was on average under 1,000 a year. It is estimated that in 1951 the total number of immigrants in Britain from the West Indies and West Africa was 20,900, which was numerically not very significant. In 1953 the estimated number of black immigrants was 24,200. However, by 1960 the situation had changed and the number of arrivals from the West Indies between 1955 and 1960 reached 161,450. The prospects of an impending ban also contributed to increased migration, as a large number also came in 1961 and 1962.

Those who entered Britain before the 1962 Act were predominantly economically active persons, and a high proportion of them were women, who were especially required to meet the labour need of the nascent National Health Service. A voucher system introduced under the Act enabled those black migrants who were already in Britain to arrange jobs for friends and relatives wanting to join them. It thus developed into chain migration. In addition, the dependants of those already in Britain were allowed to come without vouchers. As a result the balance shifted between black workers and black dependants entering Britain. For example, between 1962 and 1967 far fewer West Indians with vouchers, 1,550, entered Britain compared to 55,310 dependants for the same period. In addition, 11,050 dependants from West Africa entered Britain during this period compared with 3,220 voucher holders.

The numerical predominance of dependants arriving in this period represented a drastic decline in the number of black immigrants coming to Britain as workers. The 1966 census estimated the two main groups of Blacks in Britain to be as follows: West Indians 454,100 and West Africans 50,700. These figures include those children born in Britain to parents from those regions.

It would seem, then, that the 1962 Act had a decisive effect on the pattern of migration. It turned a movement of workers, many of whom were probably only interested in staying temporarily, into a relatively permanent immigration of families. In addition, the voucher system reinforced the kinship and friendship bonds, and therefore reinforced the pattern of settlement. Ongoing debates about the number of non-white immigrants and immigration controls forced migrants to bring over their wives and children before losing their right of entry. It appears that the controls were mainly to prevent or slow down the entry of Blacks and other non-white people.

The decrease in immigration figures since 1971 clearly shows that large-scale immigration of Blacks is now over, and that the main source of a small-scale immigration is the unification of divided families. However, the number of Blacks in this period has grown significantly, including those born in Britain. The 1991 British census included, for the first time, an ethnic question instead of 'birth place of the head of the household' as was used in the 1981 census. The census showed that 30 per cent of the 3 million ethnic-minority population were black (0.89 million). The 2001 census also showed that the black population had increased to 1.14 million, but migration from other countries was not the main reason for this increase. In fact, the Home Office Immigration Statistics show that in 2001 only 18,690 people from Africa and very few from the West

Indies were accepted for settlement in Britain.

The migrants from the 1940s onwards settled mainly in those areas where labour shortages were acute such as London, *Birmingham, and Manchester. After 40 years, this pattern of settlement was still continuing, as was evident in the 2001 census, which showed that 78 per cent of black Africans and 61 per cent of black Caribbeans lived in London. In addition to 1.1 million black Caribbeans, black Africans, and black 'other', there were 0.7 million mixed-race people in Britain, the majority of whom had black–white parents. It is clear that Blacks are now an integral part of the British population.

The majority of Blacks are now British-born. Therefore, the balance between the first-generation migrants and the second- and third-generation British-born Blacks has shifted in terms of numbers. With this, their expectations and behaviour have also changed. For example, young Blacks are more assertive as British citizens compared to their migrant parents.

A few demographic characteristics of Blacks in the 1960s that are relevant to the immigration process are worth noting. In 1966, 38 per cent of all West Indians were under 15 years of age compared to 23 per cent of Whites in the total population. Also in 1966 the number of households without children for West Indians was 36 per cent and for West Africans it was 69 per cent. This shows that West Africans were mainly single people at that time. There was overcrowding among West Indian households. In 1966 in London, Jamaicans were living 1.07 people per room and those from West Africa 1.1 people per room, compared with 0.57 for Whites. A similar pattern was found in the West Midlands conurbation. Similarly, the household size of Blacks in the early period of immigration was larger (3.57 people) than Whites (2.72 people). In 1966 over 70 per cent of black households were 'sharing households' compared with just over 30 per cent of white households in this situation. As a result almost half of the Blacks in London were sharing a bath and WC compared with about 15 per cent of Whites. In the 1960s very few Blacks were owner-occupiers compared with Whites, and therefore the majority of Blacks lived in rented accommodation. However, the 2001 census shows that there is a significant improvement in the *housing conditions of Blacks and the gap between Blacks and Whites has narrowed.

2. Political reponses to immigration The political and public reactions to the immigration of black and other ethnic minorities started after the arrival of the *Empire Windrush* in 1948. There was some interest shown in the House of Commons in the form of MPs questioning relevant ministers, and the government set up an interdepartmental working party to look into the issue of non-white immigration. This working party and another interdepartmental committee in 1950 recommended ways and means of keeping colonial immigrants out of Britain. In its Cabinet meetings, the Labour government discussed the immigration of non-white immigrants in May and June 1950. It concluded that no decision should be taken: the numbers were too small and legislation to control immigration could be controversial. Between 1951 and 1955 the immigration issue was raised again by MPs in the House of Commons: a few discussions took place in Cabinet meetings, and in November 1955 a Committee of Ministers was set up. No action was taken but the Committee felt that non-white immigration was a problem and that it should be kept under review.

The turning point came with the race riots in Nottingham and Notting Hill (*see* NOTTING HILL RIOTS) in London in August and September 1958, which made the headlines in the national newspapers and broadcasting media: the issue of immigration control was discussed widely and became the subject of opinion polls. The Labour Party condemned the riots and issued a statement on racial discrimination, opposing both it and immigration control. The discussion on this issue continued, and at the 1964 general election

Labour accused the Conservatives of using immigration as an excuse for their poor performance in education and housing. In Smethwick, Peter Griffiths of the Conservative Party, who ran an anti-immigration campaign, defeated Patrick Gordon Walker, Labour Shadow Foreign Secretary. It appeared that in some other areas anti-immigration candidates had also benefited. The Labour government passed the second Commonwealth Immigrants Act in 1968 restricting the entry of Kenyan Asians with British passports. Enoch *Powell MP, who was writing in newspapers and making speeches against large-scale New Commonwealth immigration in 1967, made his now infamous 'Rivers of Blood' speech on 20 April 1968. Edward Heath, the Conservative leader, declared Powell's speech to be racialist in tone and dropped him from his Shadow Cabinet. However, this did not stop Powell getting some public support and making non-white immigrants a topic for his speeches in the following period. Mr Heath's government, elected at the 1970 general election, passed the Immigration Act 1971.

3. White reactions to immigration The issue of non-white immigration also led to the formation of several active anti-immigrant organizations. The first two to oppose immigration in 1960 were the Birmingham Immigration Control Association and the Southall Residents' Association. The National Front was founded in 1966 and started contesting elections, particularly in the 1970s, on an anti-immigrant platform. Another anti-immigrant organization was the British Campaign to Stop Immigration, which contested the 1972 parliamentary by-election in Rochdale followed by local elections in Rochdale and Bradford. The right-wing Monday Club started a Halt Immigration Now campaign in 1972. On the whole the British public reaction to immigration of non-white people has been harsh compared to previous migrations of Whites to Britain. Signs such as 'ALL BLACKS GO HOME' and 'SEND THEM BACK' were everyday occurrences. 'Paki-bashing' and other anti-immigrant activities conducted through leaflets, speeches, and demonstrations were common. There is evidence of racism even now in the thousands of racial attacks and racial harassment cases and in the acts of racial discrimination many Blacks and other ethnic minorities face.

4. Current immigration trends and debates If the objective of the immigration controls was to stem the net inflow into Britain, this does not seem to stand examination. Immigration statistics showed that almost every year since the war, and certainly until 1983, more people left Britain to settle abroad than have become residents in Britain. Analysis of immigration debates over the years shows that the real objective was to control black and other non-white immigration from the New Commonwealth countries. This was and still is partly based on the argument that good community relations in Britain depend on strict immigration control. Another argument was that the tolerance of white people could not continue unless there was an end to non-white immigration. The fact, however, is that political responses in the form of immigration legislation and strict control policies were reactions to racist attitudes in society and that a certain amount of discrimination had taken place on the basis of colour in the immigration legislation and controls. MA

Anwar, Muhammad, *Race and Politics* (1986)

Layton-Henry, Zig, *The Politics of Immigration* (1992)

See also POLITICS

Indian Mutiny. Name commonly given to a series of uprisings against British rule in India, now often referred to (particularly in India) as the First War of Independence, or the War of Independence of 1857. In the years prior to the Mutiny there had been a steady decline in relations between the British officers and the Indian ranks of the East India Company's (EIC) Bengal Army. The political ambitions of the EIC had caused disquiet among both

Hindus and Muslims, and many of those feelings were shared by the sepoys of the Bengal Army. Both discipline and command were considered inferior to that of the Company's two other armies, with Indian soldiers openly expressing dissatisfaction with pay and certain regulations. This situation deteriorated still further when the Pattern 1853 Enfield Rifle was introduced. On 22 January 1857 a labourer was reputed to have told a high-caste sepoy at the Dum-Dum musketry depot near Calcutta that the British deliberately greased the new Enfield cartridges with pig and cow fat, offensive to both Muslims and Hindus alike. In February 1857 the 19th Infantry refused to use these cartridges and were summarily dismissed. Their actions, however, led to a series of events throughout northern and central India that we now identify as the Indian Mutiny.

On 10 May 1857 a telegraph arrived from Meerut, 30 miles north-east of Delhi, about some 'excitement' over men of the 3rd Light Cavalry who had also refused to use these new cartridges. Eighty-five sepoys had been given sentences of between five and ten years for this refusal and had appeared shackled in irons at morning parade on 9 May. The 'excitement' mentioned in the telegraph was no less than a mutiny by their Indian comrades, who rescued the captives and then marched on Delhi. With the murder of all its British officers, Delhi swiftly fell to the rebels on 11 May 1857. News of this uprising spread rapidly, and a series of other mutinies subsequently took place involving all ten Bengal Light Cavalry regiments and most of the seventy-four Bengal Native Infantry regiments. Cawnpore fell to the mutineers on 27 June 1857 and more than 200 British women and children were killed by the rebels. The Residency at Lucknow was under siege from 4 July 1857 and, despite the slaughter of almost 2,000 Indians in retaliation for Cawnpore, the British did not manage to recapture the city until 16 March 1858. On 20 September 1857 Delhi was stormed by the British, but it was not until the following June that the Mutiny was finally ended with the decisive British victory at Gwalior.

After Gwalior all mutineers and those suspected, often incorrectly, of aiding them were dealt the most severe penalties by the British authorities. The EIC was then abolished by an Act of Parliament and the government of India was transferred to the Crown. As a further precaution the Indian Army was reorganized, with the sepoys relegated to a subordinate position and only issued with inferior weapons to their British counterparts.

In Britain itself all blame for the many acts of violence perpetrated during the Mutiny was placed firmly at the door of the sepoy. *The Times* expressed some concern that the British authorities might have been excessively severe in their reprisals, but, in Chamberlain's words, 'they were over-shadowed by the well-publicised crimes of the mutineers, especially the massacre of the women and children at Cawnpore'. The *London Gazette* had actually gone so far as to publish a list of all the victims in May 1858 (subsequently known as the 'Gazette of Blood'), with the express wish that it should become 'a pillow in the bivouac and a watchword in the battlefield'. The Indian soldiers were thus effectively demonized as 'the incarnation of every passion that blackens and enslaves hell', while the atrocities committed by the British troops were swiftly and summarily forgotten.

LM

Chamberlain, Muriel E., *'Pax Britannica'? British Foreign Policy 1789–1914* (1988)

Chaudhuri, S. B., *English Historical Writings on the Indian Mutiny 1857–1859* (1979)

See also MORANT BAY REBELLION

Inkle and Yarico. One of the most popular themes in 18th-century British (and European) literature, the story of Inkle and Yarico became part of the growth of feeling opposed to the *slave trade and *slavery in the later part of the century.

In his *True & Exact History of the Island of Barbadoes* (1657), Richard Ligon (*c.*1590–1662) described meeting there an Amerindian woman called Yarico. He reported how she was originally from the coast of South America, where she had rescued a young Englishman who was in danger from her compatriots, and how in return the young man had taken her to Barbados and sold her as a slave. Ligon's story may have been based on fact, but in 1711 the well-known Irish writer Richard Steele (1672–1729) published a version that added many fanciful details, giving the young man the name of Thomas Inkle, and making him the father of Yarico's child, saying that when she begged him not to sell her because she was pregnant by him, 'he only made use of that information, to rise in his demands upon the purchaser'.

Numerous versions of the story, based on Steele, but often increasingly fanciful, appeared in English and in every major European language. It was adapted in prose and verse, and as drama, ballet, and pantomime, while there are also a number of visual representations of the story. Both the geographical setting and the racial identity of the unfortunate heroine were often changed or became vague. The originally Amerindian Yarico was sometimes explicitly described as an African, or referred to in terms that left it unclear whether she was meant to be African or Amerindian, while some versions tried to make her both at once.

Invariably the reader was invited to sympathize with Yarico's plight, but the story was usually rendered as one of male ingratitude to women. As in *Oroonoko*, the reader's sympathy for an individual seen as unjustly enslaved did not require condemnation of slavery as an institution. However, some later 18th-century versions, including the very popular *Inkle and Yarico: An Opera* by the English playwright George Colman the Younger (1762–1836), which was first produced in 1787 and then performed with some frequency over the next 50 years in Britain and further afield, did interpret the story so as to offer criticism of slavery as such.

JG

Carrington, Sean, Fraser, Henry, Gilmore, John, and Forde, Addinton, *A–Z of Barbados Heritage* (2003)

Felsenstein, Frank (ed.), *English Trader, Indian Maid: Representing Gender, Race and Slavery in the New World. An Inkle and Yarico Reader* (1999)

Price, Lawrence Marsden (ed.), *Inkle and Yarico Album* (1937)

See also LITERATURE 1: REPRESENTATIONS OF BLACKS; NOBLE SAVAGE; SLAVERY

Institute of Race Relations. Body set up in 1958 to monitor race relations in Britain. If 'race relations' was central to the formation of the Institute of Race Relations, so was politics. In 1952 it was felt that the Department of Race Relations, which was part of Chatham House (the Royal Institute of International Affairs), needed to serve a wider constituency.

The end of empire and the emergence of the British Commonwealth also saw increasing attention being paid to the Department. By April 1958 it was relocated to Jermyn Street, London, and renamed the Institute of Race Relations. For some observers, the new Institute's independence as an agent for much-needed change was paramount.

Importantly, from the outset the Department of Race Relations had declared that it would not commit itself to 'any particular race or group' and it was 'precluded by the Memorandum and Articles of its incorporation from expressing an opinion on any aspect of the relations between races'. All this was clear enough. But given the diverse and emotive views in society on 'race relations', any limiting constraints were likely to be potentially contentious. All the more because it was crucial that the Department's research and findings should address the problems of black people and not see them as the 'problem'.

Against this background, the Department pursued its goals, but in doing so, its industrial financiers and consultants were vigilant. Thus, the surveys and studies of post-empire race relations were regarded by many as being 'biased' in favour of the vested groups and therefore came under increasing scrutiny.

The 'immigration question' had kept 'race relations' in the headlines but prior to 1958 the Department had only a limited range of literature on immigration and race relations in Britain. To add to what already existed, and to fill a gap, the survey *Colour and Citizenship* by what was now the Institute of Race Relations was published in 1969. In his foreword, Philip Mason stated that the book was the result of events that had begun in 1962, when the Institute 'decided to sponsor a wide and penetrating survey of the existing state of race relations in Britain'. Although the *Notting Hill riots revealed 'how dangerous the situation had become . . . it was still fluid', he wrote. Therefore, a 'searching analysis at this juncture might throw light on the whole scene and mould opinion'. He identified the pioneering work of Michael Banton, Kenneth Little, and Anthony Richmond, and expressed his sense of the Institute's 'good fortune' in finding the authors of the work, especially E. J. B. Rose and Nicholas Deakin. But, while this work met with the approval of some, largely policy-makers, it was for others a clear case of 'ruling-class bias'. Consequently, Robin Jenkins, a researcher at the Institute, amidst growing dissatisfaction and tension among many on the staff, broke the silence. After delivering his critique, Jenkins was targeted by the Institute's Council.

Increasingly, the gap between the policy-makers and staff became apparent. The problem for those who were deeply dissatisfied was how to express their views and bring about a change in direction. Earlier in December 1968 a new editor of the Institute's *Newsletter* was appointed and change did come. The *Newsletter* was renamed *Race Today*, a journal that covered a range of views including those of members of staff of the Institute. This was unprecedented, and when the editor resigned more change was to come. In March 1970, when Alexander Kirby became editor, he used the journal's editorial to 'speak his mind'. This 'opinionated' position was a clear shift from the 'impartiality' that the Institute's Council had expected. Thus, confrontation was inevitable.

On Mason's retirement, Professor Hugh Tinker from the School of Oriental and African Studies became the new director. But the widening division between the Council, on the one hand, and the position of Robin Jenkins and members of the staff, on the other, came to a head at an extraordinary general meeting of Institute members on 18 April 1972, at which the Council was defeated and resigned.

By 1972 a new Council was formed, and it was decided to relocate the Institute and also to establish a political group that would use *Race Today* to express a range of views including those of black people, on whose behalf so much of the Institute's work was claimed to be based. In March 1972 the Institute moved to the Pentonville area of central London and 'Towards Racial Justice' became its political wing. This major shift, both physical and intellectual, brought new hope among the Institute's members generally. But who were the members of the new Council? In large part, they were academics and community workers for whom direction and perspective were paramount.

The departure of Kirby as editor of *Race Today* and his replacement by a black political activist was another indication of positive change, and further emphasized the direction that the Institute had taken towards addressing the problems and issues that faced black people abroad and in Britain.

By 1974 both Kirby and Ambalavaner Sivanandan, the Librarian and later Director of the Institute, felt the need to set the record straight and published their views on the Institute's shortcomings. In his account Kirby said that those interested in the 'race relations industry' could do worse than 'study the chain of events which came to a head in early 1972 at the Institute. . . . for that hitherto respectable pillar of the Establishment was racked by a struggle between two groups portrayed by the Press as liberal, on the one hand, and, on the other as radical'. Thus Kirby confirmed the divisions and the impulse for change, while Sivanandan in a fuller account (*Race and Resistance*, 1974) wrote about the 'task' of the Institute, which was primarily to reveal how Third World countries were economically and politically dominated and exploited; and proposed a 'catchment area' in London for the Third World intelligentsia and activists. Holding seminars and meetings as a regular feature of the Institute would bring thinkers and writers into a forum that would be served by the Institute's library, its journal, and other publications. The objective was to 'infiltrate the cloisters of academe and generate an insurgent sociology and an insurgent politics' that would help us to better 'understand and change reality'. That 'task' has, in essence, been integral to the hopes of the Institute of Race Relations as it evolved from the mid-1970s to the present. RR

Ramdin, Ron, *The Making of the Black Working Class in Britain* (1987)

Rose, Eliot Joseph Benn, *et al.*, *Colour and Citizenship* (1969)

Sivanandan, A., *Race and Resistance: The IRR Story* (1974)

See also IMMIGRATION; RACISM

International African Opinion. Journal first published in London in July 1938. The successor to **Africa and the World* and the *African Sentinel*, it served as the media organ for the *International African Service Bureau (IASB). When Wallace-Johnson, editor of the previous two IASB journals, returned to Sierra Leone, the Trinidadian historian, theorist, and activist C. L. R. *James assumed control of the new, monthly publication. Fellow IASB founder member Ras *Makonnen was equally influential, securing publishing offices and managing to have printing costs defrayed.

Under James, the journal sought to be more radical than previous black writing from London. It called on black intellectuals to identify with the struggle of the masses around the world and no longer to rely on the supposed charity of the imperialist powers. With its motto, 'Educate, Cooperate, Emancipate. Neutral in nothing affecting the African people', the journal was aimed at activists and was not to be a literary paper dispensing detached advice. It also wished not to supersede other black organizations, but to coordinate their activities. Indeed, as James stated in his first editorial, 'Problems differ from country to country, but there is a common bond of oppression, and as the Ethiopian struggle has shown, all Negroes everywhere are beginning to see the necessity for international organization.' The magazine covered a wide range of events and exhibited a campaigning yet well-grounded style, being one of the first to attack the biased official report into the Trinidad Oilfield riots of 1937, for example. The outbreak of the *Second World War, however, disrupted publication and forced the closure of the journal.

MGN

Fryer, Peter, *Staying Power: The History of Black People in Britain* (1984)

See also PUBLISHING; INTERNATIONAL BOOK FAIR OF RADICAL BLACK AND THIRD WORLD BOOKS

International African Service Bureau. Black-led organization founded in 1937 to campaign for black social progress. George *Padmore, a young West Indian Marxist intellectual, arrived in England in 1935, where he met his friend and fellow Trinidadian C. L. R. *James, and Ras *Makonnen, I. T. A. Wallace-Johnson, and Jomo Kenyatta. Together they founded the International African Service Bureau (IASB), which denounced the Italian invasion of *Ethiopia and campaigned for educational and economic assistance for people of African descent worldwide. The IASB's motto was 'Educate, Cooperate, Emancipate. Neutral in nothing affecting the African people'.

The IASB worked closely with the *League of Coloured Peoples and other black organizations on major matters like the making of representations to the West India Royal Commission appointed in 1938 (the Moyne Commission) to inquire into social conditions in Britain's Caribbean colonies following a series of labour disturbances in the region.

There were important disagreements among the membership over the role of black people in the preparations for war with Germany. In his book *Pan-Africanism from Within* (1973) Makonnen declared that 'there is only one war we will fight. It is the [anti-colonial] war against Britain. So don't tell us about Hitler. We are not interested. We are only concerned about the man who is on our shoulders now.' Others were more inclined towards coming to the assistance of the 'mother country'. Padmore merged the activities of the IASB with the Pan-African Federation and worked tirelessly for the historic fifth Pan-African Conference held in Manchester in 1945. RR

International African Opinion, 1/1 (1938)

See also RACISM

International Book Fair of Radical Black and Third World Books. Publishers' fair and literary festival organized by three black presses in London, New Beacon Books, Bogle-L'Ouverture, and Race Today Publications, to promote black literature and politics in the context of anti-colonial movements in the Third World. The Book Fair ran annually from 1982 to 1991, and again in 1993 and 1995, its venue from 1985 the Camden Centre near King's Cross. In 1985 regional events were started in Manchester and West Yorkshire (Leeds or Bradford), and also in Glasgow in 1993 and 1995. In 2005 a commemorative volume was published by New Beacon Books in association with the George Padmore Institute, containing reproductions of the brochures and programmes for the twelve festivals, as well as a historical synopsis and participants' memoirs.

Founded by John *La Rose and Jessica Huntley following the *New Cross fire and the *Black People's Day of Action in 1981, the Book Fair was a momentous expression of literature as well as politics, and a call to arms against the perceived racism of the Thatcher government. Writers from the Caribbean, Africa, India, and the Muslim world, as well as black Britain, France, and Germany, were invited. Common cause was made with other opponents of the Thatcher regime, such as the National Union of Coalminers, who regularly sent delegates to participate in the panel discussions. Supported throughout its life by the Oilfields Workers' Trade Union of Trinidad (itself instrumental in setting the climate for Caribbean independence before the Second World War), in 1987 the Book Fair aided the inception of a sister event in Trinidad, the Caribbean Peoples International Book Fair and Book Fair Festival, which ran for two years.

The first London Book Fair, held at Islington Town Hall on 1–3 April 1982, was opened by the Marxist philosopher C. L. R. *James, then 81 years old and emblematic, for many participants, of black intellectual achievement in the 20th century. Aside from Huntley and La Rose, key members of the organizing committee were Linton Kwesi Johnson and Sarah White, and in later years Darcus Howe, Gus John, and Leila Hassan. Issues of urgency for discussion included a campaign of hate by the National Front in which black bookshops had been graffitied and threatened. Panel discussions on similar topics would be a feature of the Book Fairs over the following decade.

In 1984 the festival brochure commemorated the coup against Maurice Bishop, President of Grenada, the previous October, in which he and his Cabinet were executed before the United States intervened. The 20th anniversary of the death of *Malcolm X in 1985, the 20th anniversary of the coup against Kwame Nkrumah in 1986, the freeing of Nelson Mandela in 1989, the tenth anniversary of the New Cross fire in 1991, were all marked in programmes and keynote speeches. In 1989 the fatwa against Salman Rushdie, called by the Ayatollah Khomeini following the publication of *The Satanic Verses*, was condemned, with Farrukh Dhondy (and La Rose in Bradford) speaking out on behalf of Rushdie and the novel.

Significant writers appearing at the Book Fair, either to speak on panels or to perform at the International Poetry

Evenings, included Édouard Glissant, Nancy Moréjon, Ngugi wa Thiong'o, Okot p'Bitek, Maryse Condé, Tariq Ali, Earl Lovelace, John Agard, James Berry, Valerie Bloom, Oku Onuora, Odia Ofeimun, Jean 'Binta' Breeze, Caryl Phillips, Ama Ata Aidoo, Amiri Baraka, Ben Okri, Mervyn Morris, Paul Gilroy, Henry Louis Gates, Jan Shinebourne, Jackie Kay, Wangui wa Goro, Lemn Sissay, Roy Heath, John Hendrickse, the Mighty Chalkdust, Jayne Cortez, and scores of others.

The Jamaican dub poet Mikey Smith read at the first International Poetry Evening in 1982, recorded and later released by New Beacon Books. He was stoned to death in 1983 in Jamaica.

The Malawian poet and linguistics scholar Jack Mapanje, one of Anglophone Africa's foremost writers, read at the same event. By 1989 the brochure carried reports on his 1987 arrest and imprisonment by Hastings Banda, for writing satirical praise poems comparing the dictator and his wife to hyenas. Mapanje was jailed for three years, his wife and children were evicted from their university residence, and he now lives in Britain.

May Ayim, the African-German poet and academic who founded the Initiativ Schwarze Deutsche, introducing a new mode of black expression into German literature, appeared at the Book Fair in London in 1993 and Leeds in 1995. In 1996 Ayim's suicide, achieved by leaping from the thirteenth floor of a building, provoked a haunting elegy by Linton Kwesi Johnson, 'Reggae fi May Ayim'.

The last Book Fair ran in 1995. Its committee having steadfastly refused to apply for grant funding for political reasons, the onus on delegates and organizers to support the institution had become burdensome, and independent small presses increasingly lacked the resources to send representatives. Over the years hundreds of publishers, both small and large, had been involved, and the fusion of the literary and the politically engaged remains striking. Memoirs of the Book Fair stress its warmth and friendliness, illustrating how it fostered black achievement in an atmosphere of solidarity and alertness. JM

Johnson, Linton Kwesi, 'John La Rose', *The Guardian*, 4 Mar. 2006

White, Sarah, Harris, Roxy, and Beezmohun, Sharmilla, *A Meeting of the Continents* (2005)

See also LITERATURE 2: FICTION AND POETRY; LITERATURE 3: DRAMA

Ireland. From 1172 until 1922 Ireland was governed by England and considered by the English a part of Britain. It is not surprising, therefore, that during the 18th century its history is implicated in *slavery and the *slave trade and other colonial enterprises. Nevertheless, the historical 'black presence' in Ireland was almost completely ignored until 2002, when W. A. Hart published his seminal article 'Africans in Eighteenth Century Ireland'. In the absence of further historical research, however, we can only offer glimpses of the black presence in Ireland over the past three centuries.

Many Irishmen owned estates in the Caribbean and brought slaves to serve them from the Caribbean to Ireland. Eighteenth-century newspapers in Ireland carried advertisements offering rewards for runaway slaves. Thus, in 1766 the *Belfast Newsletter* displayed a notice offering a reward of 3 guineas for 'a young negro manservant' named John More, described as 'straight and well made'. A 1768 issue of the *Dublin Mercury* carried the following advertisement: 'A most beautiful black negro girl, just brought from Carolina, aged eleven or twelve years, who understands and speaks English, very fit to wait on a lady, to be disposed of. Applications to be made to James Carolan, Carrickmacross, or to Mr Gavan in Bridge Street, Dublin.'

If the existence of a slave community in Ireland has been ignored by Irish historians, so too has the presence of free black men and women. One catches just a hint of that presence in a letter written by the Irish radical William Drennan in 1790, where he describes a procession led by fellow nationalists, and notes, 'in particular I distinguish a negro boy well-dressed and holding on high the Cap of Liberty'. As in England, status was conferred by the possession of a black servant, and in 1783 the *Dublin Journal* condemns the 'preposterous Predeliction for Exotics' displayed by those who prefer black foreigners to native Irish servants. But the newspapers also carry apparently unbiased descriptions of marriages between black male servants and white Irishwomen. The regimental drummers for the Irish 29th Regiment were all black men. Mr Cudjoe, a black servant to Lord Halifax, Lord Lieutenant of Ireland, was appointed to be one of Ireland's state trumpeters. A black actor played the part of Mungo in Dibdin's comic opera *The Padlock* in Dublin in 1773. The actor and playwright John O'Keeffe refers in his autobiography to the singer Rachael Baptist, described as an African and 'a native of Ireland', who led a successful career as a singer in Ireland and England for over 25 years. O'Keeffe remembers her as an outstanding singer who 'was heard by the applauding company with great delight, without remarks upon her sables'.

Hart estimates that between 1750 and 1800 the number of black people who entered Ireland may have been between 2,000 and 3,000, mostly found on the east coast and in Dublin, Cork, and Belfast. Additionally, abolitionists in Ireland sponsored numerous tours by black speakers between 1780 and 1865. Olaudah *Equiano toured Ireland for eight months in 1791, publishing in Dublin the ninth edition of his *Narrative*, and commented that Ireland was where he was most warmly received. Later tours by Frederick *Douglass and Charles and Sarah Parker *Remond were an enormous success, and many of them, like Equiano, comment on the exceptional hospitality they received in Ireland. Samuel Ringgold *Ward, who visited Ireland in 1854 and 1855, devoted a whole chapter of his *Autobiography of a Fugitive Negro* (1855) to that visit, and hoped that his findings might ameliorate the bitter anti-Negro sentiment expressed by American-Irish.

The warm reception encountered by such black speakers may have encouraged William Allen to tour Ireland and settle there for some time. Allen, a Professor of Classics, had fled to England in 1852 after being threatened by a lynch mob in New York State following his marriage to one of his white students. His keynote speech at the Irish Cogler Anti-Slavery Society in June 1855 produced a huge crowd and enthusiastic reviews. He moved to Dublin in 1856, where he made a rather meagre living teaching elocution, giving private tuition, and lecturing. Three of his children were born in Dublin, where he published his autobiography, *A Short Personal Narrative* (1860). He later returned to London, where he became head of a school in Islington.

The 19th century also saw tours by black singers and minstrel groups. William Fay, one of the founders of Ireland's Abbey Theatre, records how he spent a year in the early 1890s touring Ireland with a black company staging *Uncle Tom's Cabin*, and learned step dancing from this group. The manager, George Lewis, was an ex-slave from Virginia, and died rescuing members of his cast from a fire in Fermoy. Fay says of Lewis, 'He was a good actor, a beautiful singer and a kind manager to his company. May he rest in peace in Irish soil.'

During the 20th century Irish involvement in African missionary schools encouraged a constant flow of African students to Ireland. African scholars also spent time in Ireland. One of these was the anthropologist and poet Dr Raphael Armattoe (1913–53), exiled from Ghana because of his opposition to Nkrumah. Armattoe lectured and wrote widely on African civilization and history, and racial changes in Britain and Ireland, and was a founder in the early 1940s of the Lomeshie Research Centre for Anthropology and Race Biology in Londonderry. Nominated by a group of Irish members of Parliament for the Nobel Peace Prize in 1949, Armattoe published two volumes of poetry, *Between the Forest and the Sea* (1950) and *Deep Down the Blackman's Mind* (1954).

In the second half of the 20th century Africans came to Ireland mainly as students, clerics, nurses, doctors, and refugees. Black musicians have also made an impact in Ireland: the African-Brazilian–Irish rock musician Phil Lynott (1949–86) is now commemorated by a statue in Dublin's city centre, and the African-Irish music group De Jimbe became popular in the 1990s. The 2002 census recorded over 20,000 people of African birth living in Ireland. CLI

Fay, William, *The Fays of the Abbey Theatre* (1935)
Hart, William A., 'Africans in Eighteenth Century Ireland', *Irish Historical Studies*, 33/129 (2002)
O'Keefe, John, *Recollections* (1826)
Rolston, Bill, and Shannon, Michael, *Encounters: How Racism Came to Ireland* (2002)

See also MUSIC 2: EARLY POPULAR MUSIC

Islam. Britons had knowledge of Islam almost from its inception in the 7th century, primarily because of the major Muslim incursions into Europe, which brought Arabs as close to England as Poitiers in France in 732. References to the religion of the Saracens date from the Anglo-Saxon period. The English acquired knowledge of Islam from contacts with Muslim Spain or pilgrimage to Jerusalem. Scholars in medieval England were, thus, familiar with the works of Islamic scholars such as Razi, Avicenna (Ibn Sina), and Averroes (Ibn Rushd).

1. Building an Islamic presence in Britain
2. Consolidating Islam in Britain
3. Islam in post-Second World War Britain
4. Globalization and Islam

1. Building an Islamic presence in Britain British knowledge of the Muslim world increased during the early modern period, in large part derived from the dominance of Muslim naval power in the Mediterranean. Queen *Elizabeth I, for instance, referred to the Ottoman sultan Murad III, as 'a fellow monotheist' in 1588. In 1636 a chair of Arabic was established at Oxford University, and Charles I corresponded with Morocco's Muslim rulers. In 1649 the first English translation of the Koran was printed and widely circulated. Oliver Cromwell, in his letter to the ruler of Algiers in 1656, displayed familiarity with an essential Islamic tenet: 'loving righteousness, hating wrong, & observing faithfulnesse in covenant'.

Muslims settling in Britain in the 19th century retained many of their religious values, although, for the poorer among them, their approach to religion was often pragmatic. It was different for Muslims of more substantial means: Moroccan merchants, for example, created a separate enclave in Manchester in which they retained key features of their religion—congregating for Friday prayers and the provision of halal meat. With the expansion of the British Empire, however, Islam was increasingly identified as a religion that regarded the 'killing and plunder of infidels' as being 'as much an act of worship as prayer'. William Gladstone, among others, gave full vent to his deeply rooted suspicions of Islam, referring to the Koran as 'that accursed book'.

2. Consolidating Islam in Britain By the late 19th century, however, Islam had acquired a more textured presence. In the 1890s W. H. Quilliam, a convert to Islam, initiated a Muslim congregation, the Liverpool Mosque and Institute, in Liverpool. Alongside orthodox Islamic practice, Quilliam attempted to found an indigenous tradition with which potential converts were familiar: Jesus was honoured and Christmas celebrated; morning and evening services were organized on Sundays, where hymns were sung, many of them adapted from the Christian tradition. With the demise of the Liverpool Mosque and Institute on Quilliam's departure for Turkey in 1908, another important Islamic initiative began to take shape, this time centred around London's Muslim, largely South Asian, population. In 1889 the first purpose-built mosque in Britain, in Woking, Surrey, was constructed with substantial financial help from the female ruler of the Indian princely state of Bhopal. The mosque subsequently fell into disuse until 1912, when Khwaja Kamaluddin, a barrister from

Lahore, took it over and established the non-sectarian Woking Muslim Mission there. Much effort was devoted to demonstrating similarities between Islamic and Christian beliefs and values. At weekly lectures conducted at the mosque and later at the Prayer House established in London, and in its journal, the *Islamic Review*, the Mission's leading lights delicately elaborated their views on issues that aroused controversy or seemed at variance with Christian practice, always adopting rational approaches to the discussions. It was joined in its efforts by the British Muslim Society, set up in December 1914 by an influential convert, Lord Headley. While the Woking mosque remained the hub of Muslim activity during the 1920s and 1930s, efforts were made to establish a central mosque in London itself. Eventually, the east London mosque was inaugurated in 1941, and the Islamic Cultural Centre, the precursor of the central London mosque in Regent's Park (opened in 1977), in 1947.

Meanwhile, other groups of Muslims, largely comprising Yemeni, Somali, and West African seamen, reproduced more traditional, albeit ethnically distinctive, forms of Islamic practice. Lacking purpose-built mosques, collective worship was regularly performed in boarding houses. Between 1936 and 1951, under the leadership of Abdullah Al-Hakimi, *zawiyas* (centres of religious activity) were founded to give an organized shape to these communities' social and religious life. Here Muslim marriage ceremonies were conducted, newly converted wives and their offspring were given religious instruction, and circumcision rituals were celebrated.

3. Islam in post-Second World War Britain From the end of the Second World War, Britain's increasing Muslim population, made up largely of people from rural backgrounds, settled and reproduced religio-cultural practices drawn from elsewhere. The more Muslim communities became rooted in Britain, the more their members put structures in place to practise their particular forms of Islam, reflecting the diversities present within British Islam. The coexistence of different Muslim cultures in Britain has facilitated exchange of ideas across sectarian lines. The freedom of thought and expression available in Britain means that living here has opened up opportunities for Muslims to (re)assess beliefs, traditions, and practices. While some have become more secular, others have become firmer and less compromising in their religious convictions. Critical of the 'Islam of their forefathers', regarded as increasingly irrelevant to the British context, younger Muslims in particular have sought 'true' Islam through their own interpretation of religious sources. Often feeling devalued, humiliated, and stigmatized by mainstream society, they explore strategies designed to resist the onslaught of what they perceive as hegemonic ideology and political culture. Their reading of religious texts has led them to seek solutions in what might be regarded as 'religious extremism'. Disaffected and disfranchised perhaps, they have been drawn to the appeal of jihad, which they interpret, as often as not, as violent action to realize Islam globally, and to Islamist ideology more broadly, which offers a credible challenge to Western politico-cultural hegemony.

4. Globalization and Islam Undoubtedly, Islam in Britain has become affected by globalization trends. As well as integrating British Muslims with the worldwide Islamic community, the Internet has helped to increase the availability of the diversity of (many critical) Islamic perspectives and of disparate Muslim voices. Thus, British Muslims are critiquing not only the West, but also aspects of Islam itself. In this process they are seeking to create a kind of Islam that is better able to address the dilemmas of British life in a rapidly globalizing context. Diasporic living has compelled British Muslims to encounter alternative interpretations and generate innovative critical thinking that command the potential for producing a new theology more responsive to the pressures and assumptions of a relativizing postmodern and sceptical world.

KHA

Ansari, Humayun, *'The Infidel Within': Muslims in Britain Since 1800* (2004)
Matar, Nabil, *Islam in Britain* (1998)

See also BLACK MUSLIMS

J

Jacobs, Harriet (1813?–1897). The first female African-American author of a fugitive slave narrative, *Incidents in the Life of a Slave Girl* (1861). Born in North Carolina to an enslaved mother, who died when Jacobs was aged 6, she then lived with her grandmother and her mistress, from whom she learnt to read and write. Following her mistress's death, Jacobs was sent to Dr James Norcom, who subjected her to prolonged physical, sexual, and emotional abuse. To avoid Norcom's unwanted sexual attentions, Jacobs began a relationship with a white attorney, with whom she had two children.

Hoping that by running away she might persuade Norcom to sell her children to their father, in 1835 Jacobs concealed herself above a storeroom in her grandmother's house, before escaping to the North in 1842. She joined a circle of abolitionists who worked for the *North Star*, Frederick *Douglass's newspaper. In 1853 her employer purchased her freedom from Norcom's family. Encouraged to publish her story, she penned her narratives, travelling to England in 1858 seeking a publisher. *Incidents* was published to popular acclaim in 1861, under the pseudonym Linda Brent. Jacobs's stark depictions of enslaved women's sexual oppression shocked American and British readers. After the Civil War she campaigned against racial and social injustice, returning in 1868 to England to raise funds for the needy. A renowned social crusader, prolific letter writer, noted speaker, and peer of many prominent abolitionists, Jacobs died in 1897. CJ

Jacobs, Harriet, *Incidents in the Life of a Slave Girl* (1861)

Yellin, Jean Fagan, *Harriet Jacobs: A Life* (1987)

See also CRAFT, ELLEN, AND CRAFT, WILLIAM; REMOND, SARAH PARKER

James, C. L. R. (1901–1989). Trinidadian historian, novelist, philosopher, and cricket fan credited with extending Marxist philosophy to black politics. Cyril Lionel Robert James was born in Tunapuna, Trinidad, to Robert, a rural schoolteacher and son of a sugar plantation worker, and Bessie, an avid reader. James won an exhibition to Trinidad's Queen's Royal College at the age of 9 and taught history at the College after graduation. Teaching was coupled with a semi-professional cricket career and the publication of two early short stories, 'La Divina Pastora' (1927) and 'Triumph' (1929).

At the age of 31 James immigrated to England to pursue a career as a novelist. The Trinidadian cricketer Learie *Constantine, with whom James lived in Lancashire after a short stay in London, aided his move. James's bond with Constantine was encouraged by a mutual interest in West Indian independence, which climaxed in the publication of *The Case for West Indian Self-Government* (1932), much of which was drafted before James left Trinidad. An abridged version of the book was published in Leonard Woolf's pamphlet series in 1933. The two collaborated again on *The Colour Bar* (1954), a study of racial discrimination in Britain. The close relationship with Constantine also encouraged James's love of cricket; his first stints as a cricket reporter were for the *Manchester Guardian* from 1933 to 1935 and the *Glasgow Herald* the following year.

James's exposure to the working class of Lancashire fostered an increasing interest in political theory, and it was during this time that he began to read the work of Marx, Engels, Lenin, and Trotsky. His attempt to fit his colonial upbringing and interest in black politics to Marxist theory brought a new approach to the European revolutionary tradition, and James soon began to see Caribbean slaves as the world's first proletariat group. His revolutionary thinking, largely inspired by Trotskyism, turned to African politics through involvement with the African Service Bureau and the publication of *Abyssinia and the Imperialists* (1936). *World Revolution* (1937), a history of the Communist International, was published shortly after.

Interest in the African struggle for freedom of colonial rule peaked with James's study of the *Haitian Revolution and its hero Toussaint L'Ouverture. *The Black Jacobins: Toussaint L'Ouverture and the San Domingo Revolution* (1938) was published to much acclaim and is regarded as a key text in the study of the African diaspora. A play derived from the manuscript of the book entitled *Toussaint L'Ouverture* was staged at London's Westminster Theatre in 1936 and starred Paul *Robeson. It was designed to agitate debates surrounding the Ethiopian crisis occurring at the time.

Publication of *The Black Jacobins* solidified James's position as a leading Marxist philosopher and member of the Trotskyist movement. In 1938 the Socialist Workers' Party invited him to tour the United States and speak about the pre-war political situation in Europe and his Trotskyist ideas on black politics. Ignoring the limitations of his visa, he remained in America to form the Johnson Forest Tendency with Raya Dunayevskaya, Trotsky's former secretary. Results of his collaboration with Dunayevskaya were published in the lengthy essay *Dialectical Materialism and the Fate of Humanity* (1947) and the Marxist study *The Class Struggle* (1950).

James also used his time in the United States to familiarize himself with American politics and culture. Much of his work with the Johnson Forest Tendency was applied to American social and racial problems, the results of which were published in *The Revolutionary Answer to the Negro Problem in the USA* (1948). Recovery from an ulcer in 1942 fostered James's love of American popular culture, particularly Hollywood cinema. *American Civilization* (1949) contained lengthy discussion of American popular arts, including soap opera and film, as well as critical readings of the work of Walt Whitman and Herman Melville. James also wrote *Mariners, Renegades and Castaways*, an extended essay on Melville's *Moby-Dick* that reads the novel as an allegory for modern America, while in detention on Ellis Island in 1952 for overstaying his visa.

Inspired by the struggle for Trinidadian independence, James returned to the Caribbean in 1958 after an absence of 28 years. Eric *Williams, leader of Trinidad's People's National Movement (PNM), invited James to edit the party's newspaper, *The Nation*. Believing independence would lead to increased cooperation among West Indian countries, James used his editorial space to establish himself as a leading philosopher of West Indian federation. He also published his support of West Indian federation in the appendix to a new edition of *The Black Jacobins* (1962), entitled *From Toussaint L'Ouverture to Fidel Castro*. Disappointed by the failure of federation and disagreeing strongly with Williams's nationalistic politics, James left Trinidad weeks before it was granted independence in 1962. The autobiographical book *Beyond a Boundary* was published a year later (1963).

Tensions between James and Williams peaked in 1965 when James returned to Trinidad to establish the Workers' and Farmers' Party and edit and launch the party newspaper, *We, The People*. James's party won barely 3 per cent of the national vote, while Williams's PNM won 68 of the 100 seats in Parliament. James returned to London after the election but remained active in Trinidadian politics by providing advice to rebels inspired by the American Black Power Movement. Williams banned James's books in Trinidad.

James continued to develop his interest in African politics while living in Trinidad, introducing Caribbean readers to the continent with *The People of the Ivory Coast* (1960). Inspired by the Ghana revolution, James became involved with *Pan-Africanism and published *The Rise and Fall of Nkrumah* (1966) after leaving Trinidad. He returned to the United States in 1968 to teach at the University of the District of Columbia. C. L. R. James spent the last years of his life in Brixton, London, making occasional media appearances in the company of black radicals like Darcus Howe. EDS

Grimshaw, Anna (ed.), *The C. L. R. James Reader* (1992)
ODNB

See also COMMUNISM

Jazz. The visit in 1919 of the white Original Dixieland Jazz Band is often credited as the starting point of jazz in Britain, but the British jazz scene had solid roots in the ragtime and minstrel music of African-American visitors of the Edwardian era, such as the mandolinist Seth Weeks and the singer Pete Hampton, both of whom recorded in London. The band that the pianist Joe Jordan brought to London in 1905 was described as the first modern jazz band ever heard on a New York stage.

From 1913, when the Versatile Four began a long residency at Murray's Club, African-American string bands were popular with West End society. In 1914 Victor Joyner's Imperial Four played at the Lotus Club and the drummer Louis Mitchell's Beaux Arts Orchestra at Prince's Restaurant. Mitchell, who later claimed to be the first man to bring jazz to Britain, returned in 1915 with the pianist Dan Kildare's Clef Club Orchestra to appear at Ciro's Club. He toured widely in 1915–17, and his 1917 tour with his Seven Spades was especially influential in exposing African-American musical developments to a wider audience. This era's music was recorded much more extensively in Britain than in the United States.

In June 1919 the *Southern Syncopated Orchestra (SSO) brought the first of the New Orleans 'jazz greats' to reach Britain, the clarinettist Sidney Bechet. Jazz was only a small part of the orchestra's repertoire, but as the original American personnel dropped out to play in London dance clubs and were replaced by non-American members of the African diaspora or even by white musicians, the SSO spawned a two-pronged educational drive in the new music. Among future participants in the London jazz scene who were members of later versions of the SSO were the Trinidadian Blake brothers, Cyril, first a vocalist, later a trumpeter, and George, a drummer known professionally as Happy Blake. Billy Taylor, born in Manchester in 1898, progressed from playing bones with the SSO to working and recording with the pianist Freddy Johnson in 1930s Paris.

Among those who played with the jazz groups spawned by the SSO were the Ghanaian pianist Mope Desmond, born Caleb Quaye, a member of the Five Musical Dragons with the African-American trumpeter Arthur Briggs. Two other African-American SSO members, the trumpeter Milford 'Horns-In-F' Warren, and the drummer Al Young, with the trombonist Ellis Jackson, who had been in Britain since 1907, recorded with Victor Vorzanger's Broadway Band, a racially mixed band in an era when this was anathema in the United States. Among the few others from this era to leave a recorded legacy was the drummer Gordon Stretton, born in Liverpool of mixed Jamaican and Irish ancestry in 1887, who entered show business as a Lancashire clog-dancer before gravitating to jazz.

African-American visitors of the 1920s included James P. Johnson's Orchestra with the 1923 show *The Rainbow*, Will Vodery's Plantation Orchestra, first in 1923 and then with the *Blackbirds* orchestra in 1926, and the pianist Eubie Blake in 1926 with the singer Noble Sissle. Sissle returned in 1929–30 leading a jazz orchestra including such major players as Tommy Ladnier, Buster Bailey, and Rudy Jackson. The 1920s also brought a commercial version of blues to Britain with visits from Edith Wilson, Alberta Hunter, who would be a regular visitor throughout the 1930s, and Ethel Waters.

By 1930 union pressure was further

limiting visits by African-Americans, creating opportunities for non-American players. Ellis Jackson led the band of black British nationals that replaced Sissle's at Ciro's. He was poached by the bandleader Billy Cotton and long featured by Cotton as a trombonist and tap-dancer. The Guyanese clarinettist Rudolph *Dunbar, who had played with the *Blackbirds* orchestra in 1927, is found with Cyril Blake at the Deauville Restaurant in 1930 in a band led by the African-American violinist Leon Abbey. Dunbar established a teaching practice in London in 1931 and from 1932 to 1935 led his Coloured Orchestra in London clubs and on tour. Though highly regarded by the jazz cognoscenti, it made only one record, accompanying an English vocalist.

Visits by African-American name bands did continue, with Louis Armstrong (1932, 1933–4), Duke Ellington (1933), and Cab Calloway (1934). In 1934 Armstrong formed a band of European-based black musicians, which recorded in Paris; British recruits were Jamaican trumpeter Leslie *Thompson and saxophonist Harry Tyree from Manchester, whose father came from Virginia. Coleman Hawkins toured as a featured soloist with Jack Hylton in 1934, but in March 1935 the Musicians' Union succeeded in getting American musicians barred from Britain. Benny Carter was able to work as arranger for Henry Hall's BBC Dance Orchestra, but officially played only on record. Fats Waller and the trumpeter Valaida Snow toured in variety and recorded with local musicians. Valaida's British records enabled her to create the only significant body of surviving work by a female jazz horn player of the era. Shows also came, including the Cotton Club Revue (1937), whose band, led by Teddy Hill, included the trombonist Dickie Wells and trumpeter Dizzy Gillespie.

As a result of the exclusion policy, demand for 'authentic' black jazz far exceeded supply. In 1936 Leslie Thompson and the Guyanese dancer Ken 'Snakehips' *Johnson formed the Emperors of Jazz, featuring also the trumpeter Leslie 'Jiver' Hutchinson, saxophonists Louis Stephenson and Bertie King, and pianist Yorke De Sousa, all of Jamaican ancestry, along with Cyril Blake, Harry Tyree, and the guitarist Joe Deniz, Welsh-born of Cape Verdean ancestry. After becoming sole leader, Johnson imported players from the Caribbean, notably the trumpeters Wally Bowen (from Trinidad) and Dave *Wilkins (from Barbados), and reedmen Carl Barriteau and Dave Williams (both Trinidadian).

Johnson's orchestra remained a major force on the London jazz scene and broadcast extensively until Johnson and Dave Williams were killed when the Café de Paris was bombed on 8 March 1941. Most black musicians worked in London clubs; the period's ambience was captured by live recordings of Cyril Blake's band at Jig's Club in December 1941, featuring the Trinidadian guitarist Lauderic Caton.

HR

Chilton, John, *Who's Who of British Jazz* (1997)

Rye, Howard, 'Fearsome Means of Discord: Early Encounters with Jazz' in Paul Oliver (ed.), *Black Music in Britain: Essays on the Afro-Asian Contribution to Popular Music* (1990)

See also MUSIC 2: EARLY POPULAR MUSIC; SOUL MUSIC

Jea, John (1773–1816). African preacher who travelled around England and Ireland sermonizing. Jea was born in Old Calabar (now Calabar, Nigeria) and at the age of about three was taken, along with his family, to North America, where they became the slaves of Oliver and Angelika Triebuen. They were ill-treated and not properly clothed and fed. Working hours were long and intense, as Jea records in his narrative *The Life, History, and Unparalleled Sufferings of John Jea, the African Preacher* (1815).

The text captures his life as a slave, his rebellion against Christian hypocrisy, the finding of his faith, his travels, and the significance of his sermonizing. Laden with quotations from the Bible, it is itself a piece of Jea's preaching, often questioning the virtues and beliefs of his readers. Following his discovery of Christianity at the age of 15 (when, as he writes, 'the Lord was pleased to remove gross darkness, superstition, and idolatry, from my heart . . . and renewed a right spirit within me'), the shift from his initial perception of his master as God, to God as an idea beyond bondage to his owner, occurs. Consequently, he travelled around parts of North America with the intention of preaching and converting people to Christianity. The desire to do so sprang from a strong sense of divine duty.

Soon enough he felt the importance of crossing the Atlantic in order to spread the word of God, and travelled on a ship called *The Superb of Boston*, which stopped in Amsterdam for three weeks before landing in Liverpool. Contrary to some of his experiences in North America, Jea felt welcomed in England. He gained success and earned a creditable reputation in London as a preacher. Before long he was sent to the country to deliver his sermons there. Jea also visited Manchester and towns in Yorkshire, where he records he 'had greater success than at any place I ever had preached in before; for I was permitted to preach in every place of worship, in the Methodist, Baptist, Calvinist, Presbyterian, and every other place, excepting the Church of England'. Conversion of souls seems to have been the main purpose of his preaching, and success was measured according to the number of listeners transformed.

Predictably, Jea's accomplishments in England meant that he also faced enmity from English preachers, who probably felt the burden of having to compete with a black man. Jea, however, was a popular figure among his audience and returned to England twice after his first trip. He also managed to travel to Ireland, where he arrived in Limerick and was well received. His fame escalated and he began preaching in country villages around Ireland. Jea married an Irishwoman called Mary Jea and they eventually settled down in Portsmouth, Hampshire.

DD/SS

Dabydeen, David, and Sandhu, Sukhdev (eds.), *Slavery, Abolition and Emancipation: Writings in the British Romantic Period*, i: *Black Writers* (1999)

See also ABOLITION; CHRISTIANITY

Jekyll, Joseph (1753?–1837). Biographer of Ignatius *Sancho, the African writer whose letters were published in England in 1782. Jekyll was the only son of Edward Jekyll, a captain in the Royal Navy. Details concerning his place of birth are uncertain. He studied at Christ Church, Oxford, left for France upon completion of his studies in 1774, and was called to the Bar at Lincoln's Inn in 1788.

Jekyll may have met Sancho during this period, but there is no confirmation of this. In fact, information regarding their relationship is scarce and is left to much speculation. However, one piece of evidence affirms that Jekyll and Sancho did indeed meet and had some form of connection that extended beyond the purely professional. A letter written around 1803 by Sancho's son William to Jekyll, suggests that Jekyll was generous to the Sancho family:

> To Joseph Jekyll Esq. M.P. From the publisher As a most humble testimony of Gratitude of his great Liberality in Affording His Aid in so handsome a manner & rendering the Life Still more interesting by his corrections.—As a Tribute which by Reason of my Infancy I was unable to acknowledge when he stood forth so very much the Friend of myself & Family.—In very grateful Remembrance of these & other obligations I beg leave to subscribe myself, Sir Your most Humble Srvt. Wm. Sancho.

In 1782 Jekyll's biography of Sancho, *The Life of Ignatius Sancho*, was published. He was never an active abolitionist but the publication of the biography may have aided Jekyll's political ambitions, allowing Jekyll's name to become more widely known. In 1787 he was returned to Parliament, and in 1805 he was made Solicitor-General.

DD/SS

Carey, Brycchan, *British Abolitionism and the Rhetoric of Sensibility: Writing, Sentiment and Slavery 1760–1807* (2005)

See also ABOLITION

Jenkins, Edmund Thornton (1894–1926). African-American composer born in Charleston, South Carolina, where his father had recently founded an orphanage where vocational training included music. Jenkins abandoned his studies in

Atlanta to play the clarinet with a band appearing at the Anglo-American Exhibition in London in 1914. The band's performance was a success, and Jenkins decided to remain in England after the band's return to the United States. He then enrolled as a student at the Royal Academy of Music. His studies included composition with Frederick Corder, a Wagner enthusiast. He taught the clarinet, and graduated in 1921. With Caribbean students in the Coterie of Friends, Jenkins mounted a concert in 1919 with himself conducting; four instrumentalists were from the *Southern Syncopated Orchestra, an American group in Britain until 1921. They played his *Charlestonia*, an orchestral work with three black melodies, and works by Samuel *Coleridge-Taylor.

John *Alcindor, who had been a friend of Coleridge-Taylor, encouraged Jenkins to serve on the committee of the *African Progress Union, and he attended the Pan-African Congress in 1923. Visits to America (1920, 1923–4) shattered his dreams for a market for music merging African-American traditions and European concert styles, and, disillusioned, Jenkins left America and settled in France, where he died. JPG

Green, Jeffrey, *Edmund Thornton Jenkins: The Life and Times of an American Black Composer, 1894–1926* (1982)

See also MUSIC 1: CLASSICAL MUSIC

Jenkins, Edward (1838–1910). English lawyer and Victorian novelist whose examination of Indian indentured labourers influenced post-abolition politics. The son of a Wesleyan missionary, Jenkins was born in Bangalore, India. He was educated in Canada before moving to Britain in the 1860s and qualifying as a barrister in 1864.

Jenkins became involved with the National Association for the Promotion of Social Science after starting his law practice. His involvement with the Association nurtured the link between domestic public health and international social policy that would dominate his later political writing. In 1870 the Aborigines Protection Society and the *Anti-Slavery Society commissioned Jenkins to travel to British Guiana and investigate injustices within the indentureship system. His criticism of the plantocracy focused on the medical, legal, and labour mistreatment of Indian and Chinese indentured workers and was documented in *The Coolie: His Rights and Wrongs* (1871). Half travelogue and half legal report, the 446-page document was written to appeal to lawmakers and the general public, and remains the most complete account of indentureship in the 19th-century. It was followed by *Discussions on Colonial Questions* (1872), which linked the plight of English agricultural workers with indentured workers, African slaves, and child labourers in South Africa and Polynesia. *Lutchmee and Dilloo: A Study of West Indian Life*, a novel inspired by his experience in British Guiana, was published in 1877. EDS

Jenkins, Edward, *The Coolie: His Rights and Wrongs* (1871)

—— *Lutchmee and Dilloo: A Study of West Indian Life* (ed. David Dabydeen, 2003)

Job ben Solomon. Also known as Ayuba Suleiman Diallo (*c*.1702–1773?), one of the very few victims of the transatlantic slave trade to survive and get back home. Son of an important Muslim cleric from Bondou in what is now the Gambia. In 1731, while on a journey down the river Gambia to trade and sell slaves, Job was himself kidnapped and sold as a slave, together with his servant and companion Loumein Yoai. The two were shipped across the Atlantic and sold, separately, in Maryland.

Job soon ran away. Although he was speedily recaptured, he was allowed to write a letter, in Arabic, to his father, asking him to try and arrange for his ransom. This was sent to London for transmission to the Gambia, and a copy came to the attention of James Oglethorpe (1696–1785), the founder of Georgia, who was then deputy governor of the *Royal African Company. Oglethorpe arranged for Job's letter to be translated and was so impressed by the contents that he decided to organize his redemption.

Job arrived in London in April 1733. On

board ship he had been befriended by Thomas Bluett, an Anglican clergyman, who taught him some English. Bluett also helped to organize a subscription for the purchase of Job's freedom, which was officially conveyed to him on 27 December 1733 by the Royal African Company, which had become his legal owner. Bluett was also responsible for an account of Job published in 1734.

In June 1734 Job left London on a ship belonging to the Royal African Company, reaching the Gambia on 7 August. He eventually returned safely to Bondou in July 1735. He subsequently had a narrow escape from being enslaved once more, this time by the French, but he continued to be in communication with friends he had made in England, and with the Royal African Company, until at least 1744. Thanks to Job's requests, and with money from his patron, the Duke of *Montagu, his companion Loumein Yoai was redeemed from slavery in Maryland in 1737 and returned to the Gambia the following year.

While in England, Job attracted the attention and sympathy of many prominent people, including the Duke of Montagu and Sir Hans Sloane (1660–1753), creator of the collections that formed the nucleus of the British Museum. Sloane arranged for Job to be formally presented at Court to King George II and Queen Caroline (who gave him a gold watch). He was elected a member of the Gentlemen's Society of Spalding (in Lincolnshire, but with many distinguished members from other parts of the country); the Society's minute book eventually noted his date of death as 1773, though on what evidence we do not know. He was a devout member of a monotheistic religion and, even though he was not a Christian, this counted for a great deal. He was also learned: he wrote out three copies of the Koran from memory while in England and helped Sloane with translations of the inscriptions on some of his Arabic coins. Finally, he was a person of some consequence in his own country, and it is clear that the Royal African Company hoped that helping his safe return would be of significant benefit to their trading ventures in that part of Africa, including the trade in slaves. All this meant that many British people found it possible, indeed desirable, to sympathize with and give help to Job because he could be seen as unjustly enslaved, without this having much effect on their acceptance of slavery as an institution, or leading them to extend their sympathy to other slaves who did not have the characteristics they found admirable in Job.

Job himself helped to secure the freedom of Loumein Yoai because he was a fellow Muslim, and he persuaded the Royal African Company to make arrangements for the redemption of any enslaved Muslims who fell into their hands in the future, but it is clear that he had no objections to slavery as such. He himself had sold slaves, and the redemptions were to be effected in exchange for two other slaves for each Muslim slave redeemed.

JG

Grant, Douglas, *The Fortunate Slave: An Illustration of African Slavery in the Early Eighteenth Century* (1968)

See also BLACK MUSLIMS; ISLAM; SLAVERY

Johnson, Amryl (1944–2001). Poet of Trinidadian origin. Johnson migrated to Britain when she was 11. According to the critic Stewart Brown, for much of her career she was primarily concerned with 'exploring, understanding and writing through her consciousness of operating in that liminal space between two cultures known but never fully claimed'.

Johnson was educated at secondary school in London, then studied British, African, and Caribbean literature at the University of Kent, before taking up a part-time teaching position at the University of Warwick. From the 1980s onwards and up to her death Johnson gave creative writing classes in schools, colleges, and universities. She was a regular fixture in the black poetry reading circuit in Britain, and her work took her to Belgium, Germany, Sweden, and America. She was particularly regarded in Spain, and was a regular visitor to the universities of Barcelona, Seville, Córdoba, and Huelva.

Her poetry, addressing British and European audiences, gave voice to the anger and frustration of Britain's black communities, but she was also passionately interested in female identity. Her 1992 anthology *Gorgons* analysed the situation of contemporary women in light of the Greek myth of Medusa. Like Derek Walcott, Wilson Harris, and other Caribbean writers, she was fascinated by classical mythology and its applicability to black British and Caribbean life.

Her return visits to the region were uncomfortable, in terms of her difficulty of coming to terms with the people and landscape she had left as a child. Her complex relationship to 'home' was poignantly explored in her collection of poetry *Long Road to Nowhere* (1985). DD

Brown, Stewart, 'Amryl Johnson', *The Guardian*, 29 Mar. 2001

Dowson, J., and Entwistle, A., *A History of Twentieth-Century British Women's Poetry* (2005)

See also LITERATURE 2: FICTION AND POETRY

Johnson, Frank. Nickname of Francis Johnson (1792–1844), African-American bandleader, bugler, and composer. Johnson, a free Black from Philadelphia, first achieved local eminence as a fiddler while still in his youth. Around 1815 he was noted for introducing the keyed bugle to the United States. During the 1820s Johnson published compositions, and worked with Philadelphia militia units including the First Troop Philadelphia City Cavalry and the Washington Grays. In 1824 he received two major commissions, one to compose the music for the return to Philadelphia of the revolutionary hero the Marquis de Lafayette, and another to score the musical *The Cataract of the Ganges*.

Johnson and his band toured Britain from 1837 to 1838, with a repertoire ranging from Mozart and Rossini to American popular songs. They are considered to be the first black American musicians to visit Europe, and the first to play for Queen Victoria, who presented him with a silver bugle before his return to America.

In March 1841 he conducted a 50-piece orchestra and a 150-voice chorus in a performance of Haydn's *Creation*. His 1843–4 promenade performances were the first integrated concerts in the United States. One of the most prolific early American composers, with well over 200 published pieces, Johnson was the first black person to publish sheet music. He died on 6 April 1844 in Philadelphia. LFK

Appiah, Kwame Anthony, and Gates, Henry Louis, Jr. (eds.), *Africana: The Encyclopaedia of the African and African American Experience* (1999)

See also MUSIC 1: CLASSICAL MUSIC

Johnson, Joseph (*fl.* 1815). Black beggar and performer in 19th-century London known as 'Black Joe'. The details of Johnson's birth are unknown, but he is immortalized in a drawing, first published in 1815, which is featured in John Thomas Smith's *Vagabondiana; or, Anecdotes of Mendicant Wanderers Through the Streets of London* (1817).

Johnson had served in the merchant navy until he retired following an accident. Not being entitled to any relief payments because of his foreign birth, he was obliged to earn a living by begging. In order to avoid confrontation with the local beadles, he first started on Tower Hill, where he amused passers-by by singing George Alexander Stevens's 'Storm', and later ventured into the public streets, becoming a so-called 'Regular Chaunter'. Johnson built a model of the ship *Nelson* and fixed it to his hat, so that by bowing his head, he was able to simulate the motion of the sea. With the help of sympathetic wagoners, he was able to perform in marketplaces in Staines, Romford, and St Albans, singing shanties such as 'The British Seaman's Praise' or Green's more popular song 'The Wooden Walls of Old England'.

The drawing of Johnson is often evoked, in recent years, as a potent symbol for 'black Atlantic' and 'black British' identity alike, illustrative as it is of a characteristic act of appropriation of European artefact, which reflects, with both pathos and humour, the complexity of a black historical identity attached to more than one place, and informed by a life at sea. LFK

Gilroy, Paul, *The Black Atlantic: Modernity and Double Consciousness* (1993)

See also WATERS, BILLY

Johnson, Ken 'Snakehips' (1914–1941). Bandleader who for a brief period early in the *Second World War was one of the best known in Britain and definitely the best-known black one. Born in Georgetown, British Guiana (now Guyana), he learnt the violin but his father discouraged his early interest in dancing. He attended the leading secondary school, Queen's College, and was sent to England for further education. Johnson soon abandoned the study of law for a career as a dancer, studying with the American Clarence 'Buddy' Bradley, who had a dance school in London. His professional career took off and in 1934–5 he toured the West Indies and the United States. At this stage, still primarily a dancer, he was encouraged by the popularity of jazz bands to form one with Leslie *Thompson, a much superior musician from Jamaica. Though popular, the band fell apart in 1937 and Johnson formed his own band, eventually known as the West Indian Dance Orchestra. Elegant and handsome and conducting with great showmanship, he and the Orchestra even appeared in an early television broadcast. Just after the outbreak of war they obtained an engagement at the Café de Paris in London. He continued to broadcast with his band and was acknowledged as the first British band to 'swing' in the American style. A pioneer and a model for subsequent black musicians in Britain (his main vocalist was the Cardiff-born Don Johnson) he was killed when, in March 1941, the Café de Paris was bombed. PF

The Guinness Encyclopaedia of Popular Music (ed. Colin Larkin, 1992)

ODNB

Thompson, Leslie, *An Autobiography* (1985)

See also DANCE; MUSIC 2: EARLY POPULAR MUSIC

Johnson, Samuel (1709–1784). English writer born at Lichfield in Staffordshire. After an unsettled and somewhat aimless youth, which included a period of just over a year (1728–9) at the University of Oxford, he made his home in London in 1737. In the capital he slowly established himself as a man of letters, and the appearance in 1755 of his *Dictionary of the English Language* gave him widespread recognition. This, and the astonishing variety of literary work that he continued to produce until his death, made him probably the best-known British writer of the later 18th century.

Unlike many of his contemporaries—and unlike his rather younger friend and biographer James Boswell (1740–95)—Johnson was a staunch opponent of slavery and the slave trade. Johnson had taken this stance long before it became fashionable; for example, his review of his friend James Grainger's *The Sugar-Cane: A Poem* (1764) complained about Grainger's versified advice on buying slaves, saying that 'The poet talks of this ungenerous commerce without the least appearance of detestation; but proceeds to direct these purchasers of their fellow-creatures with the same indifference that a groom would give instructions for chusing a horse.'

A shocked Boswell noted how 'Upon one occasion, when in company with some very grave men at Oxford, his toast was, "Here's to the next insurrection of the slaves in the West Indies."' Johnson took an interest in the case of **Knight v. Wedderburn*, and Boswell records a legal and philosophical argument that Johnson dictated in favour of Joseph Knight's claim to freedom. Johnson was also a friend of Hannah *More. Francis *Barber was Johnson's servant for more than 30 years, and Johnson left him a portion of his estate.

JG

Boswell, James, *Life of Johnson* (ed. R. W. Chambers, introd. Pat Rogers, Oxford, 1980)

Gilmore, John, *The Poetics of Empire: A Study of James Grainger's 'The Sugar-Cane'* (2000)

ODNB

Johnson, Thomas Lewis (1836–1921). American missionary, author, and evangelist. He had been a house slave in Virginia, but reached England in 1876, where he and his brother-in-law studied at Spurgeon's College. He became a Baptist missionary in Cameroon in 1878–9, but ill health forced him out. He then promoted self-help ideas among American Blacks, travelling widely in the United States. He gathered sufficient support in Britain and Ireland to send Dr T. E. S. *Scholes and a carpenter named Ricketts (both from Jamaica) to the Congo. In Britain he associated with the evangelist Henry Gratton Guinness, the *Anti-Slavery Society, the Pan-Africanist Henry Sylvester *Williams, and the choirmaster Frederick Jeremiah Loudin. In 1900 Johnson became a British citizen. He now lived in Bournemouth, where he was a well-respected individual who would talk of American slavery, tropical Africa (where his first wife, Henrietta, had died), and the Christian message.

First published in London in 1882, his expanded autobiography *Twenty-Eight Years a Slave: The Story of My Life on Three Continents* was printed in Bournemouth in 1909. A volume of 21 hymns was published in Belfast. He spoke at gatherings all over Britain, a living reminder of slavery and of the obligation to help others. His second wife, Sara, was from Chicago, and she may have returned there after his burial in Bournemouth. Their daughter Ruth died aged 6 in 1892. JPG

Green, J., 'Thomas Lewis Johnson (1836–1921): The Bournemouth Evangelist' in Rainer E. Lotz and Ian Pegg (eds.), *Under the Imperial Carpet: Essays in Black History 1780–1950* (1986)
ODNB

Jones, Claudia Vera (1915–1964). Political activist, journalist, black nationalist, community leader, and feminist. Born in 1915 in Port of Spain, Trinidad, Jones moved to New York with her parents and three sisters at the age of 8. Her formal education was ended prematurely by tuberculosis, which damaged her lungs and permanently affected her health. She became actively involved with the Young Communist League of the American Communist Party, and was a vociferous advocate of human and civil rights. She was the editor of Negro Affairs for the Party's paper the *Daily Worker*, and in 1948 was elected to the Party's National Committee.

After being arrested four times for her involvement in campaigns for a socialist revolution, Jones was deported from the United States and given asylum in England. In exile she worked closely with London's African-Caribbean community and founded and edited the *West Indian Gazette*, which was vital to her fight for equal opportunities for black people. Her campaigns heightened during the race riots in 1958 in London, and from that point she became a key black leader in Britain. She was also a member of the British Communist Party.

In 1959 Jones helped to launch the *Notting Hill Carnival as a showcase of Caribbean talent that would hopefully act as a bridge between cultural differences. She died of a stroke in 1964 and is buried in Highgate cemetery next to Karl Marx. She was clearly one of the leading figures in the equal rights struggle in the 20th century. ASW

Cobham, P. J., 'Caribbean Hall of Fame—Claudia Jones', *Precious Magazine*, 31 Jan. 2006; <http://www.preciousonline.co.uk/arts/june02/Claudia.htm>
ODNB
Sherwood, Marika, *Claudia Jones: A Life in Exile* (2000)

See also COMMUNISM; POLITICS

Jordon, Edward (1800–1869). Newspaper editor, statesman, and Mayor of Kingston, Jamaica. Jordon was born a freeman on 6 December 1800. He founded the *Watchman and Jamaica Free Press* in Kingston, which printed an editorial in 1832 calling to 'knock off the fetters, and let the oppressed go free'. Jordon was tried for sedition—a crime that carried the death penalty—but was eventually acquitted.

He campaigned vigorously against slavery and, having won the Kingston seat in the House of Assembly in 1835, saw complete *abolition in Jamaica in August 1838. He then founded the *Morning Journal*, became manager of Kingston Savings Bank, and director of the Planters' Bank.

Jordon was the first appointment to the

Executive Committee under Sir Henry Barkly's governorship, and in 1854 the first man to be appointed both Mayor of Kingston and Custos. In 1860 Queen Victoria made him a Companion of the Bath, the first time this honour was bestowed upon a black man. From 1861 to 1864 he was Speaker in the House of Assembly, and was finally appointed Colonial Secretary.

Jordon's moderate stance left him powerless in the face of Governor Eyre's brutal handling of the *Morant Bay rebellion in 1865. When Jamaica was designated a Crown Colony in 1866, the office of Colonial Secretary became the privilege of an Englishman, but Jordon held the post until his death on 8 February 1869. A memorial statue to him was unveiled in Kingston in 1875. LFK

Roberts, W. A., *Six Great Jamaicans* (1951)

See also PUBLISHING

K

Keane, 'Shake'. Nickname of Ellsworth McGranahan Keane (1927–1997), internationally established jazz flugelhorn player born into a family of musicians in St Vincent. His nickname derived from his great love of Shakespeare and literature in general. He established a reputation locally as a trumpeter but it was after he emigrated to England in 1952 that he began to consider himself as a *jazz musician. In the 1960s he became one of a select band of musicians who, because of the clarity and quality of his playing, was rarely out of work. He played with the Joe Harriott Quintet, the Michael Garrick Quintet, and later, in a move to Germany, with bands led by Kurt Edel Hagen, Francy Boland, and Kenny Clarke.

But poetry was equally his passion. *L'Oubli*, his first collection, was published in 1950 when he was 23 years old, followed by *Ixion* in 1952. He went on to publish three more collections, *One a Week with Water: Rhymes and Notes*, which won the prestigious Casa de las Americas Prize in 1979; *The Volcano Suite* (1979); and *Palm and Octopus* (1994). In 2005 his collection *The Angel Horn: Collected Poems* was published posthumously.

In 1972 Keane returned to St Vincent to become Director of the National Department of Culture. This position lasted for only two years. In 1981 he again emigrated, this time to live in New York, where he made his home until his death at the start of a tour to Norway in 1997. A large and gregarious man with a sharp sense of humour, he was more at home with the informality of jazz and poetry than in formal and bureaucratic worlds.

PNa

ODNB

Oliver, Paul (ed.), *Black Music in Britain: Essays on the Afro-Asian Contribution to Popular Music* (1990)

See also MUSIC 2: EARLY POPULAR MUSIC

Kendrick, Massa (1798–1844). Boxer born in St Kitts on 11 May 1798. Kendrick moved to London around 1811, trained under Bill *Richmond, and boxed for public entertainment between the years 1819 and 1826. He was described as tall, bony, and athletic, weighing around 13 stone, and ever seeking a fight. On one occasion, when he criticized the methods of Bill Richmond, he and the American started a fist fight in the street. Later he baited Tom *Molineaux, and, on another occasion, stood at the door of the Fives Court during a benefit, threatening 'to mill all the "big ones"'.

Kendrick's most impressive performance arose when he presented himself, uninvited, at a private sporting dinner in Westminster, on 11 May 1819, offering to fight any of the heroes present. The dining table was cleared away, and a purse of 25 guineas was put up for the fight between Kendrick and George Cooper. Despite Cooper's confidence, the fight lasted for 69 rounds before Kendrick admitted defeat. A purse of £50 was offered for Kendrick and Cooper to have a ring fight, but Cooper declined it, observing that 'defeating Kendrick would not add to his reputation'.

Kendrick's worst defeat saw him almost killed in thirteen rounds against the well-known English boxer Henry Sutton. His refusal to train properly cost him any greater success he might have achieved, and he retired in 1826. He died at the age of 46, after a prolonged illness.

LFK

Miles, Henry Downes, *Pugilistica* (1880–1)

See also SPORT

Kitchener, Lord. Alias of Aldwyn Roberts (1922–2000), calypsonian born in Arima, Trinidad and Tobago. He was already a successful performer in his native island when, while on a tour of Jamaica, he decided to join his fellow calypsonians Lord Beginner (Egbert Moore, 1904–80) and Harold Phillips (1928–2000) in taking a passage to England on the *Empire Windrush*.

Kitchener provided two of the most iconic images of post-war Caribbean migration to Britain. The Pathé newsreel that recorded the arrival of the *Windrush* in 1948 featured a still youthful Kitchener singing 'London Is the Place for Me', which he had written on the ship, and later recorded on disc in 1951. And it was Kitchener who led the invasion of the pitch when the West Indies cricket team won at Lord's in June 1950, though it was Lord Beginner who celebrated 'those little pals of mine, | Ramadhin and Valentine' in his 'Victory Test Match'.

Although Kitchener's early attempts to woo British audiences appear to have met with hostility or incomprehension, after a few months he began to be better received. He was encouraged by the BBC radio presenter Denis Preston, who introduced him to Cyril Blake (d. 1951), a guitarist and bandleader who had come to Britain from the Caribbean after the *First World War. Kitchener recorded 'The Underground Train' with Blake and his Calypso Serenaders in 1950, and made several successful recordings with other groups during his years in Britain, mainly with the Parlophone and Melodisc labels. The initial optimism of 'London Is the Place for Me' gave way to a frank recognition of the problems of immigrant life in songs like 'My Landlady' (1952) with its 'And every Monday, Mister give me my rent' and 'the convenience is terrible . . . and she has the audacity to tell me I living in luxury'. Kitchener's 'If You're Not White You're Black' (1953) offers a more complex and significantly less rosy view of race relations than Lord Beginner's 'Mix-Up Matrimony' (1952). 'Sweet Jamaica' (October 1952?) expressed the immigrant's frustration with the British climate, post-war rationing, and difficulties in finding employment: 'Many West Indians are sorry now | They left their country and don't know how.' From a later perspective, there is also a certain irony in listening to the very Trinidadian-sounding Kitchener singing 'I regret the day I left sweet Jamaica' as, by the end of the 1950s, it was music of Jamaican origin that was beginning to take over, both as the popular sound among black British audiences and as white listeners' idea of what Caribbean music was all about. 'During that decade', as Richard Noblett puts it, it was certainly Trinidadian calypso that was the 'soundtrack of Black Britain', and Kitchener was perhaps its leading exponent during this period. Nor was it all social commentary—for sheer *joie de vivre* it would be hard to rival that hilarious antithesis of the staid conventions of 1950s Britain, the non-stop double entendres of Kitchener's 'Saxophone No. 2' (September 1953?).

Kitchener moved from London to Manchester in 1953. He owned a nightclub for some time, and continued to record. He returned to Trinidad in 1962, and remained there for the rest of his life. He became one of the country's most celebrated calypsonians, enormously popular in Trinidad and throughout the Caribbean, and continued to perform almost until his death. JG

London Is the Place for Me, i: *Trinidadian Calypso in London, 1950–1956* (selected by Mark Ainley and Richard Noblett, annotated by Richard Noblett, Honest Jon's compact disc HJRCDZ, 2002)
ODNB

See also GRAMOPHONE RECORDINGS; MUSIC 2: EARLY POPULAR MUSIC

***Knight* v. *Wedderburn*.** Scottish court case in 1778 that decided that no one could be held as a slave in Scotland.

1. Background
2. Litigants
3. Facts

4. Progress
5. Argument
6. Effect

1. **Background** This was the third case directly addressing the status in Scotland of black men and women who had been held as slaves in the colonies. While there were few such individuals in Scotland, the issue was important because of Scottish investment in the West Indies and the Chesapeake. The earlier cases, *Sheddan* v. *Montgomery* (1754) and *Dalrymple* v. *Spence* (1770), were inconclusive because of the death in one instance of the alleged slave and in the other of the alleged master.

2. **Litigants** Around 1766 Joseph Knight had been bought by John Wedderburn in Jamaica as a 13-year-old slave freshly arrived from West Africa. He was employed as Wedderburn's personal servant. The son of Sir John Wedderburn of Blackness, a baronet executed and forfeited after the Jacobite rebellion of 1745, Wedderburn had also participated as a young man in the rebellion, fleeing, after the Battle of Culloden, to Jamaica, where some of his brothers joined him. There he worked hard to restore his family's fortunes, initially as a physician, before acquiring plantations.

Knight became a favourite of Wedderburn's, and when the latter finally returned to Scotland in 1768, he took Knight with him. Knight learned to read and write, and was instructed in Christianity, before being baptized in the Church of Scotland. In 1769 Wedderburn married Margaret, daughter of the Jacobite Earl of Airlie (in whose regiment, known as Lord Ogilvy's, he had served in the rebellion) and purchased the estate of Ballindean, Perthshire, near Dundee.

3. **Facts** At Ballindean, Knight and Ann Thomson, a chambermaid, conceived a child. Wedderburn gave Knight money to support Thomson at Dundee during the pregnancy and birth, but dismissed her from his service. After the death of the child Wedderburn refused any further assistance, hoping Knight would desert Thomson. Instead, they were married by David Johnston, minister of North Leith, in Edinburgh on 9 March 1773. Knight, confident of Wedderburn's affection, wanted him to re-engage Thomson and give them a house on the estate. Wedderburn refused. Knight had read of the decision in the *Somerset* case in the *Edinburgh Advertiser* (3 July 1772), which he claimed he understood as meaning he was now free, though employed in Wedderburn's service. Knight decided to leave Wedderburn to seek employment in Dundee, where his wife lived.

4. **Progress** On discovering Knight's intention to leave his service, on 13 November 1773 Wedderburn sought a warrant from the Justices of the Peace of Perthshire to have Knight detained as his slave. The warrant granted, the Justices convened at Ballindean on 15 November to investigate. Present were George Oliphant Kinloch of Kinloch, James Smyth of Balharry, and Sir John Ogilvy of Inverquharity. Kinloch and Smyth were related to each other and to Wedderburn by marriage, and the first employed James Wedderburn, John's brother, as overseer of his plantation in Jamaica. Ogilvy's father-in-law had made his wealth in the West Indies. It is no surprise that this group found in favour of Wedderburn.

Knight managed to take the case before the Sheriff Court at Perth on 22 December 1773, allegedly influenced by his knowledge that the Sheriff-Depute, John Swinton of Swinton, would be sympathetic. The Sheriff-Substitute, however, William Mercer, dismissed the action on 5 January 1774 because of the proceedings before the Justices. Knight challenged this, and the Substitute referred the case to Swinton. On 20 May Swinton found 'That the State of Slavery is not recognised by the Laws of this Kingdom and is inconsistent with the principles thereof and Found that the Regulations in Jamaica concerning slaves do not extend to this Kingdom and repelled the Defender's Claim to perpetual Service'.

By the end of May, Wedderburn had

started the procedure to get the case reconsidered by the Court of Session, the central civil court. On 7 February 1775 the parties argued before Lord Kennet that the case should be advocated to the Court of Session. Kennet ordered production of written memorials, on the basis of which, at a hearing on 7 March, he decided to take the matter before the whole Court. Both parties were required to prepare printed 'informations', which repeated the arguments of the memorials. The cause was argued before the Lords of Session over several days in February 1776, with distinguished counsel on both sides. The Lords wished to consider further the arguments raised, and required the parties to give additional information. The case resumed early in 1768, with the Lords delivering their opinions on 15 January.

5. Argument Before the Sheriff, Knight's argument had been based on natural liberty, countered by Wedderburn's that, although slavery might be repugnant to natural liberty, it was accepted by the law of nations, while Knight must owe labour to Wedderburn for the cost of his upbringing and education. To defeat arguments based on contemporary theories of the law of nature and nations (which accepted slavery or, at least, perpetual servitude for life), Knight's lawyers thereafter emphasized the circumstances of African *slavery and the *slave trade, showing how the reality did not correspond with the theories of the natural lawyers. This meant there could be no legitimacy in Knight's original enslavement, even if the arguments of Wedderburn were accepted.

Relying on an Act of 1701 prohibiting the transportation of an individual out of Scotland without either judicial decree or consent before a judge, the judges, one apparently disagreeing, generally denied that Wedderburn could send Knight back to Jamaica against his will. Otherwise, the twelve opinions recorded were very varied. Three thought he remained a perpetual servant for no wages; the others were for greater freedom. Some were convinced that slavery might be valid, but Knight could not have become a slave validly, and so was free in Scotland. Lord Auchinleck, James Boswell's father, emphasized that slavery was unchristian and inhumane: Knight was 'our brother; and he is a man, although not our colour'. He should be allowed to remain in 'a land of liberty'. The vote of the majority led to acceptance of Swinton's judgment in its entirety, although his strong ruling probably did not reflect their common opinion.

6. Effect If Somerset's case left the simple issue of freedom unclear, this did not: a slave on entering Scotland became free. The *Caledonian Mercury* of 17 January 1778 recognized the significance of this, commenting: 'it must give a very high satisfaction to the inhabitants of this part of the United Kingdom, that the freedom of negroes has obtained its first *general determination* in the Supreme Civil Court of Scotland'. Knight, Thomson, and their children thereafter vanish from the records. JC

Cairns, J. W., 'Stoicism, Slavery, and Law: Grotian Jurisprudence and Its Reception' in H. W. Blom and L. C. Winkel (eds.), *Grotius and the Stoa* (2004)

Karras, A. R., *Sojourners in the Sun: Scottish Migrants in Jamaica and the Chesapeake, 1740–1800* (1992)

L

La Rose, John (1927–2006). Poet, essayist, publisher, film-maker, trade unionist, and cultural and political activist. La Rose was born in Arima, Trinidad, where his father was a cocoa trader and his mother a teacher. At 9 he won a scholarship to St Mary's College, Port of Spain, where he later taught before becoming an insurance executive. He later also taught in Venezuela. Culture, politics, and trade unionism were central to his vision of change. He was an executive member of the Youth Council in Trinidad and produced their fortnightly radio programme *Noise of Youth* for Radio Trinidad. In the mid-1950s he co-authored, with the calypsonian Raymond Quevedo ('Atilla the Hun'), a pioneering study of calypso entitled *Kaiso: A Review* (republished in 1983 as *Atilla's Kaiso*).

One of La Rose's favourite sayings was 'We didn't come alive in Britain', an allusion to the struggles that had been waged by Caribbean peoples in the Caribbean against colonialism and for workers' and people's power. In the 1940s in Trinidad he helped to found the Workers' Freedom Movement and edited its journal, *Freedom*. He was an executive member of the Federated Workers' Trade Union, later merged into the National Union of Government and Federated Workers. He became the General Secretary of the West Indian Independence Party and contested a seat in the 1956 Trinidad general election after being banned from other West Indian islands by the British colonial authorities. He was also involved in the internal struggle of the Oilfield Workers' Trade Union, siding with the rebel faction, which wanted a more radical and democratic union. The rebels prevailed in the 1962 union election and La Rose became their European representative, a position he held until his death.

Soon after he arrived in Britain in 1961, he was again engaged in activism. In 1966 he founded New Beacon Books, the first Caribbean publishing house, bookshop, and international book service in Britain. In that same year, together with the Jamaican writer and broadcaster Andrew *Salkey and the Barbadian poet and historian Kamau Brathwaite, he co-founded the *Caribbean Artists' Movement. In 1972–3 he was chairman of the *Institute of Race Relations and Towards Racial Justice, which published the radical campaigning journal **Race Today*, edited by Darcus Howe.

La Rose was also involved in the Black Education Movement in the 1960s, particularly in the struggle against banding, and the placing of West Indian children in schools for the educationally subnormal. He founded the George *Padmore Supplementary School for West Indian children in 1969 and was one of the founders of the Caribbean Education and Community Workers' Association. That organization published Bernard Coard's ground-breaking *How the West Indian Child Is Made Educationally Sub-Normal in the British School System* (1971). He was also instrumental in the founding of the National Association of Supplementary Schools in the 1980s and was its chairman for two years.

In 1975, after a black schoolboy was assaulted outside his school by police in the London borough of Haringey, La Rose, together with concerned parents, founded the Black Parents' Movement to combat the alleged criminalization of young

Blacks, and to agitate for youth and parent power and decent education. By then the *Race Today* journal had severed links with the Institute of Race Relations and was now the journal of the Race Today Collective. The Black Parents' Movement allied with them and with the Black Youth Movement.

This alliance became the most powerful cultural and political movement organized by Blacks in Britain, winning many campaigns for justice against police racism, agitating for better state education, and supporting black working-class struggle. It was the alliance that formed the New Cross Massacre Action Committee in response to an arson attack that resulted in the deaths of thirteen young Blacks in 1981, and mobilized 20,000 people in protest. La Rose was the chairman of the Action Committee and gave support to the bereaved families.

In 1982 La Rose was instrumental in the founding of Africa Solidarity, in support of those struggling against dictatorial governments in Africa. That year he also became chairman of the Committee for the Release of Political Prisoners in Kenya, whose founder members included the Kenyan novelist and critic Ngugi wa Thiong'o. In response to the rise in fascism and xenophobia, he helped to found European Action for Racial Equality and Social Justice, bringing together anti-racists and anti-fascists from Belgium, Italy, France, and Germany. He made a short film on the black Church (*see* CHURCHES) in Britain for a special Caribbean edition of *Full House*, which he produced for BBC2 in 1973, and co-produced and scripted Franco Rosso's documentary film *Mangrove Nine*, about the resistance of the black community to police attacks in the popular Mangrove restaurant in London.

One of La Rose's greatest achievements was the *International Book Fair of Radical Black and Third World Books (1982–95), organized jointly with Bogle-L'Ouverture Books and Race Today Publications. He was joint director with Jessica Huntley of the Book Fair. In the call to the first Book Fair, he wrote: 'This first international book fair of radical black and Third World books is intended to mark the new and expanding phase in the growth of the radical ideas and concepts and their expression in literature, politics, music, art and social life.' The Book Fair was, indeed, 'a meeting of the continents for writers, publishers, distributors, booksellers, artists, musicians, filmmakers, and people who inspire and consume their creative productions'.

The George Padmore Institute, a library and educational research centre housing materials relating to the black community of Caribbean, African, and Asian descent in Britain and continental Europe, was established in 1991 and chaired by La Rose. He was also the editor at New Beacon Books and of their journal *New Beacon Review*, and published two volumes of his own poetry, *Foundations* (1966) and *Eyelets of Truth Within Me* (1992). LKJ

Johnson, Linton Kwesi, 'John La Rose', *The Guardian*, 4 Mar. 2006

See also EDUCATION; POLITICS; PUBLISHING

Lancaster. Small port on the north-west coast of England, favourably located to participate in the 18th-century African slave trade, with clearances at their most prolific between 1750 and 1775. The port's direct trade with the Americas, meanwhile, largely accounts for Lancaster's historical black presence; above all, the result of slaves accompanying masters returning home from the West Indies.

1. The slave trade
2. The black presence

1. The slave trade Lancaster, a few miles up the river Lune from Morecambe Bay, ranks as Britain's fourth slave-trading port albeit not in the same league as *Liverpool, *Bristol, or *London. Lancaster merchants outfitted around 180 slaving voyages to West Africa between 1736 and 1807, which resulted in the transportation of over 30,000 slaves to the island and mainland plantations of the Americas. The majority of these vessels departed directly from Lancaster's St George's Quay, although it wasn't unknown for some of the port's slavers to clear via Liverpool, 50 miles to the south, where additional cargo or crew might be taken on board. Local investors, small ships, and carefully selected destinations in both Africa and the Americas were some of the hallmarks of Lancaster's triangular trade.

Early Lancaster slaving partnerships typically featured newcomers to colonial commerce, men eager to improve their wealth and status. On the one hand, these were young men with some capital to invest, such as William and John Watson, the sons of a country vicar; and, on the other, established tradesmen, such as the Lancaster apothecaries William and Thomas Butterfield. Their captains were the younger sons of farmers, mariners, and shopkeepers from across the region, who, where successful, progressed to become land-based investors themselves, employing a new generation of captains and adding first-hand knowledge to the management of the trade. This continuity and growing local expertise set Lancaster above many of the other smaller ports venturing into the slave trade.

Navigation of the river Lune required small ships (typically 70–100 tons), but these enabled quick turnarounds and ready access to the rivers of the Gambia, Sierra Leone, and the Windward Coast. Lancaster entries in a Liverpool bead book testify to the importance of these regions, where all manner of decorated beads were bartered for slaves. African cargoes generally came from manufacturing areas south of Lancaster. Certain exports originated closer to home, however, among them Guinea kettles from the Furness ironworks across Morecambe Bay. Moreover, evidence suggests that, once at sea, some Lancaster slavers supplemented their cargoes with duty-free goods (legitimate until 1765) warehoused on the Isle of Man.

Slaves from the Gambia and surrounding regions were especially popular with the rice planters of South Carolina, making Charleston a popular market for Lancaster ships. The 100-ton *Cato*, for example, traded 288 slaves there in 1758. Its subsequent cargoes of 360 slaves to Jamaica and 560 to Guadeloupe, meanwhile, show not only instances of tight packing on the Middle Passage but also the importance of Caribbean destinations. Selling in Guadeloupe, moreover, exemplifies Lancaster's opportunistic adoption of new markets acquired through war. Across the islands, resident merchants with close ties to the home port, such as Thomas Millerson in Barbados and Richard Hetherington in Tortola, provided a valuable network for both selling slaves and purchasing return cargoes. Lancaster merchants capitalized on a local demand for mahogany, in addition to more usual imports of sugar, on account of the city's well-known cabinet-making firm Gillows.

Individual involvement in the slave trade could be substantial; Thomas Hinde's near 50-year commitment, first as a captain then a merchant, constitutes a noteworthy example. Miles Barber, meanwhile, not only invested in slave ships but also established slave factories to supply vessels trading on the African coast. It is instructive to note that both men would, over time, transfer more of their operations to Liverpool, where larger ships could be accommodated and the trade was increasingly centred, making it harder for lesser ports to compete. Even so, their partnerships continued to reveal strong ties with Lancaster, and the port's involvement was to continue right up to the slave trade's *abolition in 1807, despite regulatory legislation in 1799 ruling that all slaving vessels must clear from Liverpool, London, or Bristol. Accordingly, Lancaster's last slaver, the *Johns*, made five consecutive African voyages from Liverpool before returning to its home port in 1808. In choosing the vibrant new slave markets of Suriname and Trinidad, its owners were every bit as opportunistic as the port's earlier traders.

2. The black presence Although it is impossible to provide accurate numbers or much detail on Blacks living in and around 18th-century Lancaster, local records, notably parish registers, do paint a partial picture and attest to over 50 living locally. Their presence was a consequence of the Atlantic slave trade and American slavery. While a few may have been brought directly from Africa, sold on arrival to the profit of slave ship captains, most would have come by way of the Americas, entering, typically, as enslaved domestics to merchants or captains returning from the West Indies.

Probably the earliest church record tells of Thomas, a black servant to Captain Peter Woodhouse of Lancaster, baptized in nearby Heysham in 1738. Such entries continue to pepper local registers, the last before civil registration (1837) being the burial of John Hodges, a 47-year-old Black from the West Indies, long resident in Lancaster. Thomas presumably served his master on board ship while others, such as Frances Johnson, who accompanied the newly-wed John Satterthwaite on his return from St Kitts in 1777, lived and worked in the houses of some of Lancaster's more prosperous merchants. John Chance exemplifies the status Blacks could bring. He was servant to William Lindow in his brand new residence in fashionable Queen Square. Not all local Blacks would have been in service, however. As in other ports, some were paid mariners. William York, a black sailor, married in 1775, and shortly afterwards a West-Indiaman crew list named Robert Gibson, a 51-year-old grey-haired boatswain of black complexion.

Young men dominate black entries in the parish registers, but references to females, adolescent boys, and men of riper years add to the profile. The most poignant reminder of the area's historic black presence is *Sambo's windswept grave at the mouth of the Lune. More recent is Lancaster's quayside memorial, *Captured Africans* (2005), to the Blacks carried aboard its slave ships. AME

Elder, M., *The Slave Trade and the Economic Development of 18th-Century Lancaster* (1992)
Schofield, M. M., 'The Slave Trade from Lancashire and Cheshire Ports Outside Liverpool, *c.*1750–*c.*1790' in R. Anstey and P. E. H. Hair (eds.), *Liverpool, the African Slave Trade, and Abolition* (enlarged edn., 1989)

See also SLAVE TRADE; SLAVERY

Lane, William Henry (1825–1852). The first African-American dancer to perform in Britain. Lane was born in Rhode Island and began performing at a young age, mainly at the dance halls and saloons in the Five Points neighbourhood in Manhattan. Lane first danced in Britain in 1848, where he performed in various minstrel shows in London's Vauxhall Gardens and later in Liverpool. Also known as 'Master Juba', he impressed his audiences with his moves, which were unusual to British crowds. His style was phenomenal owing to his flexibility, and contemporary accounts of Lane's performances describe his movements as unique. Various American and British writers commented on his style and labelled him as the greatest dancer ever known. Charles Dickens wrote about him in his *American Notes* (1842), describing him as 'a lively young negro, who is the wit of the assembly, and the greatest dancer known. He never leaves off making queer faces, and is the delight of all the rest, who grin from ear to ear incessantly.' He also competed in various dance competitions, always excelling. Perhaps his biggest success was defeating the Irish dancer Jack Diamond, who was regarded as the best white dancer. Lane went on to perform in Europe before settling in London, where he danced with an English dance company. He also opened his own dance studio. Lane is regarded as the founder of tap-dancing, and the 'Juba dance' is named after him. SS

Lott, Eric, *Love and Theft: Blackface Minstrelsy and the American Working Class* (1993)
Magriel, Paul (ed.), *Chronicles of the American Dance* (1948)

See also BLACK DANCE

Lascars and black seamen. Indian and Caribbean workers employed in British shipping from the early 19th century.

1. Who were the Lascars?
2. Pay and conditions
3. Black seamen in British ships

4. Racial and gender divisions in maritime labour
5. Lascars, black seamen, and the National Union of Seamen
6. Significance

1. Who were the Lascars? Originating with the East India Company in 1823, 'Asiatic' or 'Lascar' labour contracts began and terminated in India or other colonial ports. Gangs of labourers recruited by a headman, or *serang*, most Lascars came from India, but by the 20th century similar conditions were imposed on seafarers from Malaya, East and West Africa, Trinidad, Port Said, Goa, the Red Sea ports, China, and West Africa, effectively racializing contract labour by identifying it with colonized subjects possessing little recourse. Having coerced most colonized seafarers into contract labour, British officials increasingly applied the term 'Lascar' to any such man in Britain, implying illicit entry through breach of contract, since if British subjects their presence was perfectly legal.

2. Pay and conditions 'Asiatic' articles of agreement offered a fraction of the European wage and inferior working, living, and contractual conditions. While British seamen's historically squalid working conditions improved gradually owing to unionization, Lascars' wages stagnated from the early 19th century to the Second World War, amounting to one-third or less of union-mandated wages. Asiatic articles permitted unregulated hours of work, cramped living space, and inferior or adulterated rations, while limiting men's freedom to bargain or quit. Consequently, Lascar seamen suffered disproportionately from tuberculosis, pneumonia, 'heat apoplexy', beriberi, heatstroke, heart failure, dementia, suicide, and other conditions attributable to malnutrition and overwork. In India and, allegedly, Britain, Lascars endured underemployment and corrupt recruitment practices in which employers connived. Employers justified these arrangements with the unassailable assertion that the colonial standard of living was lower, and indeed relations between colonized and British-based maritime labour increasingly reproduced inequalities of well-being between colonizers and colonized in the British Empire at large. Lascars protested, mutinied, struck, and 'voted with their feet' by travelling to Europe to obtain work on European terms. Such men most often found work in the poorest-paid sector of the industry with the least reliable employment, tramp shipping, concentrated in *Cardiff and *South Shields, and then usually as firemen, shovelling coal into a steamship's boilers.

3. Black seamen in British ships Black men from the Caribbean and elsewhere worked on similar contractual terms to white sailors from at least the 17th century. With men from Britain's newly acquired possessions in Africa and elsewhere, their relative situation deteriorated from the late 19th century. Segregation, discrimination, and grandfathered 'customary' practices relegated black sailors to menial and unpleasant jobs while denying them union-mandated protections such as overtime pay.

4. Racial and gender divisions in maritime labour The late 19th-century racialization of colonized status articulated with the industrial restructuring of maritime labour. The introduction of steamships created industrial divisions of labour and status aboard ship. Employers manipulated these to divide and intimidate mariners by race, language, gender, and class, mirroring colonial hierarchies and divisions of labour. By the 20th century colonized seamen filled the worst jobs and earned less, relieving white seamen of the most menial labour. To black sailors fell heavy, hot, dirty, and often lethal stoking, and the low-status 'women's work' of the stewards and catering staff, while white men more often comprised deck crews, performing less unpleasant and imputedly more skilled work. Defending discrimination, shipowners used Orientalist (*see* ORIENTALISM) rhetoric, feminizing black seafarers to justify their assignment to 'women's work', while bestializing, infantilizing, and exoticizing them to justify their consignment to 'unskilled' stoking. Re-creating Imperial race, class, and gender relations aboard ship proved economically rational for employers: 'dividing and conquering' their workforce minimized labour costs for black and white seafarers alike while maximizing labour control and flexibility. Employers further fomented racial divisions by threatening militant white and black seamen with replacement by contract labour. Between 1901 and 1938 Lascars increased as a proportion of British crews, from 18.5 to 26 per cent, or 37,392 to 50,700.

5. Lascars, black seamen, and the National Union of Seamen The National Union of Seamen colluded in and benefited from contract labour at the expense of their members, black and white, as well as Lascars themselves. The union focused on the few thousand colonized seafarers in the 'free' labour market, deflecting attention from their failure to organize all sectors of the workforce. They refused assistance to Indian and other colonized seamen's unions for most of the 20th century.

6. Significance Even more than sailors on union-sanctioned contracts, super-exploited contract workers and other under-remunerated black seafarers subsidized Britain's moribund industry into the middle of the 20th century. While the pejorative term 'Lascar' was abolished in 1947, racial subordination originating in the world's largest mercantile marine persists in the global maritime workforce, while racial divisions continue to weaken the working-class movement. LET

Balachandran, G., 'Searching for the *Sardar*: The State, Pre-Capitalist Institutions and Human Agency in the Maritime Labour Market, Calcutta, 1880–1935' in Burton Stein and Sanjay Subrahmanyam (eds.), *Institutions and Economic Change in South Asia* (1996)

Broeze, F. J. A., 'The Muscles of Empire: Indian Seamen and the Raj, 1919–1939', *Indian Economic and Social History Review*, 18/1 (Jan.–Mar. 1981)

Tabili, L., *'We Ask for British Justice': Work and Racial Difference in Late Imperial Britain* (1994)

See also CARIBBEAN, BRITISH COLONIES IN THE; IMMIGRATION; RACISM

Lashley, Joe (*fl.* 1791). The first recorded black boxer in Britain. Lashley fought Tom Treadaway, the brother of a celebrated fighter, Bill Treadaway, at Marylebone Fields on 13 June 1791. The match lasted 35 minutes and ended when Treadaway was knocked unconscious; he never recovered from his injuries. In match commentaries Lashley was praised for agility, power, and skill in the ring. Records of two other Lashley fights exist, also in 1791. A fight against Stewey the Breakman also left Lashley's opponent with lasting injuries, indicating that he was a fighter of great strength. NAA

Egan, Pierce, *Boxiana, or; Sketches of Ancient and Modern Pugilism* (1812)

Fleischer, Nat, *Black Dynamite: The Story of the Negro in the Prize Ring from 1782–1938* (1938)

See also SPORT

Latimer, Lewis (1848–1928). African-American scientist and inventor who worked in Britain. Lewis Latimer's parents were Rebecca and George Latimer, fugitive slaves from Virginia who gained their liberty in the free state of Massachusetts, where Lewis was born. Lewis served in the American Civil War (1861–5), after which he worked as an office boy in a patent law firm. His employers soon recognized his talent for drawing and made him head draughtsman. He married Mary Wilson (1848–1937) in 1873 and wrote a poem for his wedding, which he later published in his collection *Poems of Love and Life*.

When he was 25, Lewis invented an improved toilet for railway carriages, and in 1876 Alexander Graham Bell hired him to produce the drawings he needed to patent the telephone. Lewis was later head-hunted by the US Electric Lighting Company, and in 1882 was awarded a patent for a new type of light bulb filament that enabled the production of better light bulbs than Thomas Edison's. He then moved to London to oversee the installation of electric lighting throughout the city. During this period Lewis also began work on an improved design for lifts. The new design was never patented, despite his attempts to interest several US corporations. He remained in London for less than a year, complaining that he found the 'relations of English bosses and employees to say the least peculiar'. He went on to supervise the installation of electric lighting in a number of major cities in the United States and Canada. In 2003 his house in Lewisham, south-east London, was nominated for a blue plaque to commemorate his stay. IJ

Fouche, Rayvon, *Black Inventors in the Age of Segregation* (2003)

Norman, Winifred Latimer, *Lewis Latimer* (1994)

See also DOCTORS; EDMONSTONE, JOHN; MEDICINE

Lawrence, Stephen. On 22 April 1993, 18-year-old Stephen Lawrence was murdered at a bus stop in Eltham, south-east London. Though police investigations failed to secure the convictions of his killers, Stephen's murder was the catalyst to some of the most important changes to the operation of the criminal justice system and to race equality legislation in the United Kingdom since the passing of the 1976 Race Relations Act.

1. The murder of Stephen Lawrence
2. The police investigations
3. The Lawrence family campaigns for justice
4. The MacPherson Inquiry and Report

1. The murder of Stephen Lawrence Stephen Lawrence was a GCSE A Level student preparing for a career as an architect. On the day of his murder he and his friend Duwayne Brooks were returning from a visit to a relative. As Stephen and Duwayne were waiting for a bus home at 10.30 that evening, they were set upon by a group of five or six white youths. Duwayne managed to escape, but Stephen received fatal stab wounds to his chest. Stephen managed to run over 100 yards with Duwayne before collapsing, and died soon after.

2. The police investigations Within hours of his death informants provided the names of five suspects known to belong to a local racist gang to the police, but the police failed to follow up evidence from several key witnesses, and it was some weeks before police eventually arrested the suspects. Two were identified by Stephen's friend Duwayne. A case was brought by the Crown Prosecution Service against the two suspects, but in July 1993 the case was dropped on the grounds of insufficient evidence.

The aftermath of Stephen's murder and the failure to identify and convict the suspects marked a low point in relations between black communities and the police. Stephen was by no means the first black youth to have been murdered at the hands of racists in this area. Indeed, his killing marked the third time in two years that a racist stabbing had occurred in south-east London. This time, however, pent-up anger and frustration at police inability properly to investigate previous racist murders, the revelations that police had failed to offer first aid to Stephen as he lay dying, that they failed to treat his killing as a racially motivated murder, their insensitive and patronizing treatment of his parents, and their failure to prove the guilt of the suspects in Stephen's killing, unleashed a national debate on racism in British society and bolstered a groundswell of public support for the family. Determined to secure justice for their son, Doreen and Neville Lawrence formed one of the most important national campaigns of the 1990s, a campaign that would culminate in some of the most far-reaching transformations of the criminal justice system and other public bodies.

3. The Lawrence family campaigns for justice Angered by what they saw as police incompetence in the handling of the investigation into their son's death in 1994, Mr and Mrs Lawrence launched a private prosecution against three other suspects. This civil case also collapsed in 1996 when the three suspects were acquitted after the judge ruled Duwayne Brooks's evidential identification unreliable. When an inquest was held into Stephen's death in 1997, the suspects refused to answer any questions. The inquest ruled that Stephen had been 'unlawfully killed in a completely unprovoked racist attack by five white youths'. This verdict left the Lawrences with some hope that the case was not closed. In February of that year a national newspaper, the *Daily Mail*, published pictures and names of the suspects, publicly labelling them 'murderers', and challenging them to sue for libel. To date they have not done so, though they continue to protest their innocence. Later that year the results of an inquiry into the Metropolitan Police Force's handling of the investigation of Stephen's death by the Kent Police on behalf of the Police Complaints Authority criticized many aspects of the Metropolitan Police Force investigation.

4. The MacPherson Inquiry and Report The Lawrence family's campaign for justice finally bore fruit when, at the request of Mr and Mrs Lawrence, the Rt. Hon. Jack Straw MP, the new Home Secretary, ordered a new public inquiry into the police investigations of Stephen's murder. The Inquiry Commission was appointed on 31 July 1997, under the chairmanship of Sir William MacPherson, a former High Court judge. In 1999 the Inquiry's findings were published in the *MacPherson Report (sometimes referred to as the Lawrence Report or the Stephen Lawrence Report). In his Report, MacPherson criticized the Metropolitan Police Force's investigation into Stephen's death. The Inquiry concluded that 'Stephen Lawrence's murder was simply, solely and unequivocally motivated by racism,' vindicating Mr and Mrs Lawrence's assertions that Stephen's death was racially motivated. It also found that police racism was a key factor in the mishandled investigation. Further, the Report significantly concluded that 'The [police] investigation was marred by a combination of professional incompetence, institutional racism and a failure of leadership by senior officers.' In identifying the existence of institutional racism, the Report went further than any previous inquiry into race relations in the United Kingdom, publicly confirming for the first time the long-held beliefs of minority ethnic communities. The Inquiry's Report made 70 recommendations and had an enormous impact on the race relations debate, from criminal justice through to the role of the public authorities. The degree to which the Report has achieved the elimination of racism within the police force and improvements in police procedures in handling racially motivated attacks has been criticized by many. However, perhaps one indication of the changes in police handling of racially motivated attacks is the rapidity with which the Merseyside police acknowledged racism as the prime factor in the brutal murder of another young black male, 18-year-old Anthony Walker, in Liverpool in July 2005. Within days of Anthony's killing, Merseyside police had arrested and charged the main suspects.

The persistence and courage of the Lawrence family in the face of tragedy and bitter disillusionment and disappointment were outstanding. Mr and Mrs Lawrence remained steadfast in their determination to secure justice for their son and one day to see their son's killers convicted. Influenced by their campaign, the government has declared its intention to scrap the rule of double jeopardy in English law, which prohibits suspects from being tried twice for the same crime. The Lawrences worked hard to ensure that disadvantaged young people are not denied the same opportunities of which their son dreamed. In 1998 the family and their supporters established the Stephen Lawrence Charitable Trust, an organization that supports the entry of disadvantaged young people into architecture, planning, and associated professions, and there were also plans to establish a Stephen Lawrence Academy. In 2002 Mr and Mrs Lawrence were made OBEs for services to community relations. In 2006, nine years after the murder, the Metropolitan Police Force finally apologized to Duwayne Brooks for treating him dismissively at the scene of the crime and in its aftermath. CJ

The Stephen Lawrence Inquiry: Report of an Inquiry by Sir William MacPherson, Cm. 4262-I (1999)

See also CRIMINAL JUSTICE SYSTEM; 'SUS LAW'

League of Coloured Peoples. Political organization founded in 1931 by Harold *Moody. Moody's passionate involvement and belief in the good of Christianity provided the fuel for his energy, compassion, and broad-mindedness in the struggle for better social conditions for black people.

Moody had lived in London from 1904, and would have been familiar with all the student and civic organizations that came into being before and after the First World War. He would have known of Duse Mohamed *Ali, Henry Sylvester *Williams, Casely Hayford, Ladipo *Solanke, and Claude *McKay. He was an admirer of James E. K. *Aggrey, among other activists, and acted as a mediator between West Indians and continental Africans over the former's contempt for and arrogance towards the latter.

Moody's journal *The Keys* felt compelled to report on this collision after a meeting was called at Aggrey House to discuss the issue: 'It is in our view impossible to exaggerate the necessity for West Indians to make an effort to break through the anti-African propaganda with which their educational system is saturated, and to try to re-establish contact with the civilisations in which they have their roots.'

In spite of this collision, there were undoubtedly many collaborations between committed Africanists from the Caribbean and Africa. Moody's organization the League of Coloured Peoples (LCP) had several Africans on its Executive Committee: for example, Stephen Thomas of West Africa was secretary of the LCP during the 1933–4 period, while his sister Stella Thomas was the librarian; Alex H. Koi, also of West Africa, was the vice-president, while Lewis Mbanefo of Nigeria (who later became a judge in Nigeria) was on the Executive Committee. Moody dealt with this question cleverly, since he himself had suffered from a disdain for Africans.

But this was merely a phase in the psychological development of the colonized, and Moody was no different from many educated Africans who fell victim both to propaganda and to the complex of colonial-produced inferiority. That Moody moved steadfastly to deal with the problem publicly and within the structure of his own organization speaks well for him.

The Keys was the mouthpiece of the LCP: it was campaigning, it was critical not only on social issues but on cultural ones, and it recorded the various developments and events that took place in Britain and other parts of the world. The LCP's policies can be best described as civic, for example, it was concerned primarily with social injustice and interracial harmony, as the title of its journal implied, derived from Aggrey's dictum 'You can play a tune of sorts on the white keys, and you can play a tune of sorts on the black keys, but for harmony you must use both the black and white keys.'

Through Moody's Christian connections, members of his organization were warmly welcomed at Christian Endeavour guest houses, and the journal reported on these events as well as on racial discrimination. In one issue a report disclosed that the Port of London Authority refused to hire any more African men, while its union carried out disciplinary action against men who refused to work with Africans. The LCP also held concerts at the Indian hostel where John Payne, the African-American singer, performed along with the Guyanese pianist Bruce Wendell and the clarinettist Rudolph *Dunbar, while Stella Thomas and Una *Marson, respectively the organizer and compère, gave two recitations each. In the same issue it was reported that Marson's play *At What a Price* was successfully staged at the YWCA Central Hall Club, London, on 23 November 1933. Moody also held an annual garden party, which members of his organization and influential English people attended. The purpose, it seemed, was to keep close to those who could be called upon to help with events that affected people of colour. Moody was well connected, exchanged letters with the Colonial Office, and was familiar with government officials and prominent members of society.

Three key issues stand out in the LCP's political development: its concern for high levels of unemployment among black seamen (and the notorious Nationality Acts); its questioning of racial discrimination against black commissioned officers during the Second World War; and its exposure of the killing of civilians during the Italian invasion of *Ethiopia. These events played a major role in undermining black people's belief in British justice and fair play, but what prevented Moody and the LCP from moving to a more aggressive position in terms of political engagement was his fundamental Christian orientation. Thus, the LCP remained a conservative organization within the Pan-African spectrum, and came to an end soon after Moody himself died in 1947. ASS

Vaughan, David A., *Negro Victory: The Life Story of Dr Harold Moody* (1950)

See also PAN-AFRICANISM

Leo. Nom de plume of Egbert Martin (1861?–1890), one of the earliest West Indian poets to be published in Britain. Martin, described by his contemporaries as a 'mulatto', was born and educated in Georgetown, British Guiana (now Guyana). An invalid from an early age, he died aged around 29 of phthisis (pulmonary tuberculosis). His death certificate listed his 'rank or profession' as 'nil'.

Nil he was not, being the first West Indian of colour to publish more than two books (*Poetical Works*, 1883; *Leo's Local Lyrics*, 1886; *Scriptology*, 1888). His poetry ranges from meditations on sickness and loss to 'Negro' village life. Melancholia and sentimentality permeate most of his writings. His descriptions of the Guianese landscape are generalized. There is little attempt to name flora and fauna, Martin eulogizing 'a humble daisy in a dell' rather than the local frangipani or passion flower.

Martin achieved prominence in 1887, in a blaze of Empire glory. In Queen Victoria's Jubilee year an Empire-wide competition to add verses to the British national anthem was held by the London *Standard*. Martin won first prize, the princely sum of £50. His two additional versus reveal patriotic commitment to the 'mother country':

> And, like a bird at rest
> In her own ample nest,
> Let Britain close
> Far-reaching wings and strong
> O'er her colonial throng,
> Guard, keep and shield them long
> From all their foes.
>
> While o'er the Empire's bound
> The Sun shall skirt his round,
> Shining serene
> On one broad amity
> Holding from sea to sea
> Free rule and subjects free:
> God save the Queen.

Lord Tennyson, the Poet Laureate, was said to be impressed by Martin's poetry, according to *The Argosy* and the *Guiana Herald* (local newspapers), thinking Martin's *Poetical Works* 'worthy of an autograph acknowledgement'. DD

Cameron, N. E. (ed.), *Guyanese Poetry* (1931)
Seymour, A. J., 'The Poetry of Egbert Martin', *Kyk-Over-Al*, 1/3 (1946)

See also LITERATURE 2: FICTION AND POETRY

Leslie, Jack (1901–1988). Left-winger for Plymouth Argyle Football Club and one of the first prominent black footballers in the English League, rumoured to have been recommended to England selectors. Leslie's football career began at his local club, Barking Football Club. He was 20 years old when he was spotted and signed by Plymouth Argyle's manager Robert Jack. In his first season at Argyle between 1921 and 1922 he played in nine games. During the 1924–5 season he became a regular player, missing only two League fixtures and scoring 40 goals. His partnership with Sam Black from 1924 onwards proved a huge success. His last match for Argyle came in 1934, after an Argyle career that spanned 400 League and FA appearances and 134 goals. Leslie and Black were famous nationwide for being one of the country's finest left-flanking partnerships. However, only one of the two left-wingers was eligible for England selection. Although Robert Jack informed the press that Leslie was being considered for England, no call-up came for him, and Black was selected. It was widely rumoured that Leslie was not chosen owing to fears that English supporters would react unfavourably to the selection of a black player for the national side. After the end of his football career Leslie managed a pub in Cornwall before moving to east London as a boilermaker. After retirement and in his seventies he returned to football as a part-time bootboy for West Ham United. He died in London in 1988. NAA

Vasili, Phil, *Colouring Over the White Line: The History of Black Footballers in Britain* (2000)

See also SPORT

Lewis, Sir Arthur (1915–1991). Distinguished public intellectual, one of the founding figures of the field of development economics, which came to prominence after the Second World War. For his pioneering work in this field, he was awarded the Nobel Prize in 1979.

1. Lifetime of achievements
2. Academic career
3. Lewis's theory of economic development
4. Lewis and African and Caribbean nationalists

1. Lifetime of achievements In addition to his many academic achievements, including a long list of pioneering publications in economics, Sir William Arthur Lewis consulted regularly for the British Colonial Office during and immediately after the Second World War, was involved in the decolonization of British Africa, serving as Ghana's chief economic adviser during the country's first two years of independence, and was the Vice-Chancellor of the University of the West Indies when it became an independent, self-governing university in 1962. In recognition of his leadership of the university, Queen Elizabeth II knighted him in 1963, just prior to his accepting a professorship in Political Economy at the Woodrow Wilson School of Public and International Affairs of Princeton University.

2. Academic career Born on the small island of St Lucia in the British West Indies in 1915, Lewis won a government scholarship to study in Great Britain in 1933, electing to matriculate as a BA student in Commerce at the London School of Economics (LSE). His original intention was to return to the West Indies in government service or with a business organization, but his luminous talents in the field of economics led him to pursue a Ph.D. at the LSE and to enter an academic career in Great Britain. His appointment as a lecturer at the LSE in 1938 marked the first time that that institution had had a person of African descent on the faculty. Lewis went on to shatter many other racial barriers in his profession. He became the first person of African descent to hold a professorship in a British university when he became the Stanley Jevons Professor of Political Economy at the University of Manchester in 1948, the first black professor at Princeton University when he joined the faculty there in 1963, and the first person of African descent to receive a Nobel Prize in any field other than literature and peace.

3. Lewis's theory of economic development In his teaching and research Lewis was increasingly drawn to the problems of economic development that faced the less developed countries in Asia, Africa, and the Caribbean as they were emerging from colonial rule after the Second World War. He introduced the LSE's first course in what was then called colonial economics, a field that was soon referred to as development economics. He also began to publish in this field, insisting that the problems that faced less developed economies required different approaches from those that worked in highly developed and industrialized countries. A large number of publications quickly ensued, most of which appeared while Lewis was teaching at the University of Manchester, where he built a strong programme in development economics.

Lewis's single most influential and widely cited work was an article published in the journal *Manchester Studies* in 1954 under the title 'Economic Development with Unlimited Supplies of Labour'. Here he described the way in which Britain and other European countries had initiated economic growth at the turn of the 19th century. He argued that similar processes could be employed in the developing parts of the world. Specifically, he claimed that less developed societies were characterized by two radically different economic sectors: a small but modern and highly productive sector, usually urban and industrial, and a large and backward traditional sector, usually rural and agrarian. Lewis believed that labourers could be extracted from the traditional sector and enter the modern sector without any decline in productivity because workers here were 'surplus' labourers, who contributed little or nothing to traditional-sector productivity. Surplus and cheap labour moving from the traditional sector to the modern sector would be the engine of economic growth, spurring industrialization.

Lewis followed this article by writing a general book on economic development, *The Theory of Economic Growth*, published in 1955. This book became the most widely used primer on economic development. It was assigned in college courses and read by government officials in newly established agencies responsible for planning economic development in less developed countries.

4. Lewis and African and Caribbean nationalists Lewis's appeal to the leaders of newly independent countries in the 1950s and 1960s was enormous. Not only was he recognized as an expert on questions of economic change, but his background as a person of colour who had grown up in the West Indies made him appealing. In 1952 the young nationalists in the British colony of the Gold Coast were already asking him to advise them on how best to promote industrial development as the country was moving towards independence. His report *Industrialization and the Gold Coast Economy*, published in 1953, was a masterful overview of the possibilities and limitations of this economy in the lead-up to political independence. It was hardly surprising, then, that these same leaders asked Lewis to return and serve as the chief economic adviser to the country, which became independent as Ghana in 1957. He complied, but became increasingly frustrated with the Ghanaian leadership and especially its dynamic Prime Minister, Kwame Nkrumah, who wanted economic change to move forward more rapidly than Lewis thought possible. A falling-out led Lewis to resign and to return to the West Indies.

In 1959 Lewis became Principal of the University College of the West Indies, and in 1963 the first Vice-Chancellor of the University of the West Indies. Here, too, he fell foul of nationalist politicians. Believing that the West Indies could only succeed politically and economically through a political federation, he threw all of his political energies into rescuing plans for the political federation of the British West Indies, which were being promoted in the early 1960s. This scheme failed, largely because the political leaders of the larger islands—Jamaica and Trinidad and Tobago—wished to pursue their own national agendas and subverted plans for federation. By the time that this situation had become clear, Lewis had worn himself out physically and emotionally and decided to return to a full-time academic position, accepting the offer from Princeton University to join its faculty.

Lewis remained on the faculty at Princeton University until he retired in 1983. He returned to scholarship with renewed vigour. His most notable publications were *The Evolution of the International Economic Order* (1977) and *Growth and Fluctuations, 1870–1913* (1978), both of which the Nobel Prize committee cited in its recognition of his most important publications. He remained active in scholarship right up to his death in 1991 at the age of 76. RLT

ODNB
Tignor, Robert L., *W. Arthur Lewis and the Birth of Development Economics* (2005)

See also EDUCATION

Lewis, Sir Samuel (1843–1903). Lawyer and leading public figure among the Krio (then called 'Creole') people of Sierra Leone. His father was a wealthy businessman who sent him to London to study law. Called to the Bar in 1871, on his return home he built up a substantial legal practice. Quiet-mannered, a dedicated Methodist, unobtrusive in appearance, he owed his success to his well-grounded legal knowledge, not to histrionic display. Although he occasionally acted for the government, he preferred the independence and financial rewards of private practice.

From 1882 Lewis was a member of the Legislative Council. There, though he was ready to oppose the government, sometimes with great tenacity, in general he supported its measures, even to earning widespread hostility when he went against public feeling. When Freetown became a municipality in 1895 he was elected Mayor, and in 1896 was awarded the first African knighthood.

When the Protectorate was proclaimed in 1895, Lewis raised legal objections to some of the proposed arrangements, rousing the bitter antagonism of the Governor, Sir Frederic Cardew, who, when the 1898 Hut Tax War broke out, blamed the Krio community, including Lewis, for having incited it (a ridiculous charge). By the time Cardew left, Lewis was suffering from cancer. He also suffered financially when the extensive agricultural plantations on which he had long vainly lavished money failed. He went to London for medical treatment but died there on 9 July 1903. CF

Hargreaves, J. D., *A Life of Sir Samuel Lewis* (1958)

See also SIERRA LEONE SETTLERS

Lindsay, Dido Elizabeth (Belle) (b. 1763). Reputed daughter of Sir John Lindsay, then in the Royal Navy, on duty in the West Indies about 1760–5. Sir John discovered Dido's mother, a slave, on board a captured Spanish ship. She was brought to England, where it was speculated that a brief relationship between them resulted in Dido's birth. Soon after her birth, and for reasons unknown, Dido (also known as Belle) was taken to Kenwood House to be brought up with her 'cousin' Lady Elizabeth Murray by Lord and Lady Mansfield, Sir John Lindsay's uncle. Lord Mansfield was the Lord Chief Justice who would later be responsible for the landmark ruling of 1772 that freed the runaway slave James Somerset (*see* SOMERSET CASE). Sir John Lindsay died in 1788, when Dido was 25, leaving £1,000 in his will to share between Dido and a mysterious 'brother'.

Dido lived at Kenwood for 30 years, and was described by visitors both as a slave and as a companion to her cousin Elizabeth. The two of them were famously captured in a painting (*c.*1779, attributed to Johann Zoffany) showing them in the grounds of Kenwood. Dido left Kenwood after Lord Mansfield's death in 1793, when she inherited £500 and an annuity of £100. At this time slavery was still legal, and Lord Mansfield took the precaution of confirming in his will Dido's guaranteed freedom. His concern for her was recorded by Thomas Hutchinson, an American living in London in 1779, who remarked, on visiting Kenwood, 'that a Black came in after dinner and sat with the ladies . . . she was taken care of by Lord M., and has been educated by his family. He calls her Dido . . . he knows he has been reproached for showing fondness for her—I dare say not criminal.'

After her departure from Kenwood records show that Dido's surname changed to Davinier. Her income and family background may have afforded her the opportunity to marry well. However, no further information exists with regard to Mr Davinier (who may have been a clergyman) and no documentation has come to light about their future. LP

Gerzina, Gretchen, *Black England: Life Before Emancipation* (1995)
Greater London Council, *A History of the Black Presence in London* (1986)

Hutchinson, Peter Orlando, *The Diary and Letters of His Excellency Thomas Hutchinson, Esq.* (1886)
ODNB

See also ZONG

Literature 1: Representations of Blacks (*c.*1700–*c.*1900) As much recent literary criticism produced within the broad field of post-colonial studies has emphasized, literature is not independent from politics and society, but rather deeply implicated within it on an ideological level. Hence, the politics of race and empire that have long been overlooked in the study of British literature are vitally important to a fuller understanding of Britain's Imperial history, of its involvement in the slave trade and the abolitionist movement, as well as of the formation of certain racist stereotypes that have shaped contemporary society. Representations of 'blackness' in literature are inextricably bound to constructions of 'whiteness' as an artificial pure identity that allays anxieties produced by contacts with other peoples.

1. The racialization of 'black' and 'white'
2. The 'noble savage'
3. Slavery
4. The myth of the 'dark' continent

1. The racialization of 'black' and 'white' From the 1550s onwards, at the time when Britain's involvement in African trade and colonial travel was increasing, the pre-existing binarism of black and white became more visibly racialized, as references to skin colour, to Africa, and foreign wealth abounded. Indeed, 'blackness' and 'whiteness' are recurring tropes in Renaissance literature, as for instance in the sonnet cycle *Astrophel and Stella* (first published in 1591) by Sir Philip Sidney. In this widespread metaphoric system employed to represent white characters, 'blackness' is constructed as undesirable and counteracted by a desire for 'whiteness' and 'whitening'. These tropes are often gendered, as the 'white' and 'fair' woman becomes the symbolic repository for 'white' English culture. The polarizing evocations of 'blackness'–'darkness' and 'fairness'–'whiteness' have often been read exclusively as originating in the European aesthetic tradition, rather than as participating in a discourse on racial difference that supports an exploitative ideology serving British interests in African trade. This de-historicizing approach has been challenged by recent scholarship, which has emphasized the fact that the aristocratic class that shaped the discourses of 'whiteness' had vested interests in the trading voyages into Africa. Renaissance conceptions of beauty were thus shaped by contact with black peoples in the context of colonial exploitation.

2. The 'noble savage' A widespread stereotypical representation of Blacks that gained in currency from the late 17th century onwards is the primitivist figure of the 'noble Negro', often a royal African reduced to slavery and one of the many incarnations of the 'noble savage'. The 'noble Negro' appeared under various guises in novels, poems, and plays throughout the 18th and the beginning of the 19th centuries. **Oroonoko* (1688), the immensely successful novel by Aphra Behn, may be said to have inaugurated this tradition. It was transformed into a play by Thomas Southerne (1696) and later revised by John Hawkesworth (1759). The popularity of the stage versions ensured that the legend sustained and fuelled primitivist representations of Blacks. Similarly, Richard Steele's '*Inkle and Yarico' (1711), which was dramatized by George Colman in 1787, contributed to the popularization of this stereotype, albeit in a female incarnation.

In the primitivist imagination, the 'noble African', who refuses to submit to slavery, rebels, delivers impassioned speeches, and dies, is constructed to contrast with European greed and corruption, essentially acting as a foil against which European vices become visible. It is telling to note that, since the 'noble Negro' is only one particular embodiment of the 'noble savage', this stereotypical representation often conflated ethnic differences between Africans, Indians, and American 'Indians'. Furthermore, the 'noble Negro' was Europeanized, often on a physical as well as a cultural level, thus partially erasing cultural and ethnic difference in order to make him more palatable to the European readership and transforming him into a projection of European ideals.

The 'noble savage' tradition therefore cannot be said to correlate to any real interest in other cultures. Furthermore, despite featuring black protagonists, the texts belonging to the primitivist tradition are not necessarily abolitionist in nature as their interest often did not lie in the defence of human rights. Indeed, *Oroonoko* does not betoken the author's sympathy with the oppressed, nor any active engagement on their behalf; instead, the novel stresses the difference between the princely African and the 'ordinary' Africans, and the protagonist himself is not on principle opposed to the enslavement of those 'who were by Nature Slaves'. In contradistinction to the figure of the 'noble Negro', another popularized representation of Blacks during the 18th century was that of the suffering slave, which exacted a sentimental response from the reader and was employed by most abolitionist literature.

3. **Slavery** The 18th century was shaped by the British expansion of commerce and empire, and the great financial importance of the *slave trade for Britain's economy. Discussions of *slavery therefore feature in many works of prose and poetry. Daniel Defoe's **Robinson Crusoe* (1719) reflects the contemporary ideology of the supposed economic necessity of the slave trade. The protagonist, Crusoe, does not morally object to slavery and callously sells his devoted friend Xury into slavery. His relationship to his docile servant Friday, a Carib 'noble savage', may justifiably be read as a disavowed reference to slavery. Friday's slave-like position is 'justified' by the fact that Crusoe had saved him from his fellow cannibals, echoing contemporary arguments that slavery was benevolent. In their celebration of commerce, poets like Cornelius Arnold and John Dyer equally shift the blame for slavery onto the 'barbarous' Africans enslaving each other, while the poet Edward Young praises commerce's, and hence slavery's, civilizing effect on '*Afric's* black lascivious slothful breed' (*The Merchant*, 1741), reinforcing the widely held belief in the innate inferiority of black peoples. Attempting to justify slavery through aesthetics, *The Sugar-Cane* (1764) by James Grainger, a slave-owning emigrant living in the West Indies, minimizes the brutality of slavery through picturesque descriptions of slaves at work.

The topic of slavery was particularly attractive to the writers of sentimental novels who, rather than directly challenging the institution of slavery, employed the theme of the oppressed slave to cater for sentimental taste. Sentimentalism posited a universal equality of feeling unprejudiced by skin colour, but failed to move beyond quietist representations towards a critique of the system of exploitation on which British prosperity was based. Interestingly, recent criticism has pointed to the potential influence of the African writer Ignatius *Sancho on Laurence Sterne, who included discussions of slavery in *Tristram Shandy* (1759–67), the prototypical novel of sensibility, and *A Sentimental Journey* (1768). Sancho had suggested the theme of slavery to Sterne in a letter, declaring his belief in the awareness-raising potential of the sentimental novel. Other examples of popular sentimental novels that contain passages that deal with the issue of slavery include Sarah Scott's *The History of Sir George Ellison* (1766) and Henry Mackenzie's *Julia de Robigné* (1777). Both feature white protagonists who epitomize the qualities of sensibility and virtue expressed in their concern for slaves, and the latter also employs the trope of the royal slave; yet both novels argue for mitigating the conditions of slavery rather than abolishing it as an institution.

Pro-abolitionist poetry, spurred on by and contributing to the abolitionist movement during the second half of the 18th century, again patronizingly depicted Africans as noble and uncorrupted by

European civilization, and employed images of the suffering slave for sentimental effect. Thomas *Day's primitivist and sentimental poem 'The Dying Negro' (1773) may serve as an example. Most of the poets associated with Romanticism (1770–1830), including William *Cowper, Samuel Taylor *Coleridge, Anna Laetitia Barbauld, William *Wordsworth, Robert *Southey and William *Blake, wrote anti-slavery poetry. Examples of these include Blake's 'Little Black Boy' (1789) and Southey's 'The Sailor Who Had Served in the Slave Trade' (1799). Romantic anti-slavery verse was characterized by a disjunction in the representations of Blacks, employing the stereotype of the 'noble Negro', as well as depicting docilely suffering slaves. There were of course important ideological differences between the various Romantic poets; Blake, for instance, was a strong critic of colonialist ideology, whereas Wordsworth was reluctant to join the abolitionist cause, receiving benefits from relatives participating in the slave trade. In his sonnet 'To Toussaint L'Ouverture' (1802) Wordsworth consequently depoliticizes the slaves' insurrectionist demands by translating them into Romanticism's claims for the inconquerability of the human mind. Yet even in the works of explicitly pro-abolitionist writers, the basic assumption of the superiority of European civilization remained largely unchallenged, helping to prepare the way for 19th-century British imperialism in Africa on an ideological plane. Cowper's 'On Slavery' (1788) and Hannah *More's 'The Sorrows of Yamba' (*c*.1795), for instance, praise the civilizing effects of the British Empire and Christianity.

It is instructive to compare these representations with the ones offered by autobiographical narratives of 18th-century writers like Olaudah *Equiano, Quobna Ottobah *Cugoano, and Ukawsaw *Gronniosaw. These African writers were ex-slaves living and publishing in England. In their texts they adopt multiple identities as both African and English. Captivity is not a metaphor in their writing, as their narratives recount actual experiences of enslavement and transportation and are thus very explicit in their political denunciation of slavery and their demands for emancipation. Their texts were aimed at a large audience to propagate the abolitionist cause, whereas Romantic poetry was directed at a relatively small audience. The anti-slavery productions of the Romantics did not necessarily stem from a deep personal involvement in the *abolition movement, since the evocation of slavery often merely constituted routine exercises exploited for commercial success, as the suffering slave had become a popular literary trope.

4. The myth of the 'dark' continent During the 19th century representations of Africa as innocent paradise uncorrupted by European greed shifted to the myth of Africa as the 'dark' continent, the centre of evil and 'ignoble savagery', which European civilization would exorcise. The blame for the evil of slavery was again increasingly shifted onto the Africans themselves, who were seen as 'savages', and the British began to view themselves as the potential saviours of Africa. Racist ideologies of the supposed lower status of the African and African civilization were lent pseudo-scientific credibility by social Darwinism and evolutionary *anthropology. In imperialist literature 'primitive' peoples are represented as belonging to an earlier stage in the progressive history of humanity than the more 'advanced' European civilizations. Travel narratives by explorers such as David Livingstone and Sir Henry Morton Stanley, which portrayed the European explorer as a bearer of light in a place of darkness, also exerted an immense influence on British culture and contributed to the formation of 19th-century imperialist ideology. The shift in representation is visible even in novels that are not centred on Africa. In *Bleak House* (1852–3) by Charles Dickens the African location of the Borriobola-Gha project indicates the futility of Mrs Jellyby's charitable enterprises.

Victorian literary discourse about Africa

mainly took the form of the 'tale of adventure', which imitated the narratives of the explorers (some of whom also published novels). The writers of the tales of adventure include H. Rider Haggard, Mayne Reid, G. A. Henty, W. H. G. Kingston, and R. M. Ballantyne. Haggard's *King Solomon's Mines* (1885), written towards the beginning of the imperialist *Scramble for Africa, juxtaposes (African) 'savagery' and (European) 'civilization', thus stressing the need to eliminate the former as 'white' heroes penetrate into the 'darkness'. In his much discussed novel **Heart of Darkness* (serialized in *Blackwood's Magazine* in 1899), Joseph Conrad self-consciously employs these racist dichotomies and, while not able to imagine or portray Africans in any other way than that of his predecessors, partially subverts the Manichaean binaries; Europe and its 'civilizing' mission become the centre of 'darkness'. However, racist assumptions about social evolution and a hierarchy of the races are carried over into the 20th century by novels such as John Buchan's *Prester John* (1910). KDO

Brantlinger, Patrick, *Rule of Darkness: British Literature and Imperialism, 1830–1914* (1988)

Hall, Kim F., *Things of Darkness: Economies of Race and Gender in Early Modern England* (1995)

Sypher, Wylie, *Guinea's Captive Kings: British Anti-Slavery Literature of the XVIIIth Century* (1942)

Thomas, Helen Sarah, *Romanticism and Slave Narratives: Transatlantic Testimonies* (2000)

See also LITERATURE 2: FICTION AND POETRY; LITERATURE 3: DRAMA

Literature 2: Fiction and poetry. It is now conventional to trace black British writing back to the 18th and 19th centuries, and the autobiographical narratives of Ukawsaw *Gronniosaw (1772), Ignatius *Sancho (1782), Olaudah *Equiano (1789), and Mary *Seacole (1857). However, the more distinct genres of black British *fiction* and *poetry* do not fully emerge until the early decades of the 20th century. Two towering figures of the 1920s and 1930s deserve special mention in this context: Claude *McKay and Una *Marson.

1. McKay and Marson
2. 'Pioneer fictions'
3. The Caribbean Artists' Movement
4. The 1980s and after

1. McKay and Marson McKay lived in England between 1919 and 1921, during which time he published numerous poems in the *Workers' Dreadnought*, the revolutionary newspaper of Sylvia Pankhurst. Although he found it a cold, unsympathetic place, England exercised McKay's poetic imagination from the early Jamaican dialect poem 'Old England' (1912), to his later sonnet in the 'Cities' series, 'London' (*c.*1934). While these poems deserve further critical attention in their own right, they also share significant resonances with the work of now well-established post-war black British writers such as Louise Bennett, Sam *Selvon, and George Lamming. The Creolization of England's monumental spaces in McKay's 'Old England', like the symbolic figuration of the fog in 'London', invites the reader to establish a series of echoes and connections beyond and before the so-called **Empire Windrush* tradition.

These connections are even more compelling in the work of Una Marson, who travelled from Jamaica to England in 1932, and whose poem 'Quashie Comes to London' (1937) constitutes an illuminating intertext for Selvon's short story 'Finding Piccadilly Circus' (1950). Marson was a journalist and poet who worked for the BBC during the Second World War. While at the BBC she organized an overseas broadcast, *Calling the West Indies*, which allowed servicemen from the West Indies to keep in touch with friends and family at home. Under Marson's influence this programme developed into a literary feature which, after the Second World War, became **Caribbean Voices*, the now famous radio programme credited with the establishment of a nascent 'black British' literary community. Broadcasting around 400 short stories and poems between 1945 and 1958, *Caribbean Voices* brought together the work of figures such as V. S. Naipaul, Sam Selvon, George Lamming, Kamau Brathwaite, Wilson Harris, and Andrew *Salkey.

2. 'Pioneer fictions' George Lamming was one of the first to recognize the collective significance of this early post-war writing when he connected the international rise of West Indian literature with the 'phenomenon of the Caribbean novelist'. Between 1950 and the late 1960s at least 150 novels by Caribbean writers were published, the majority of them in London. The city represented the publishing capital for this first generation of writers, but it was also a symbolic centre for a body of literature that was subsequently labelled 'black British', and which included Sam Selvon's *The Lonely Londoners* (1956), Andrew Salkey's *Escape to an Autumn Pavement* (1960), and George Lamming's *The Emigrants* (1954).

3. The Caribbean Artists' Movement These so-called 'pioneer fictions' were later augmented by the *Caribbean Artists' Movement. Active in Britain between 1966 and 1972, the Movement was conceived by John *La Rose, Edward Brathwaite, and Andrew Salkey as a forum through which to reinvigorate the flagging black arts scene following the earlier explosion of fiction in the 1950s. Linton Kwesi Johnson, who would emerge as one of the key poets of the next generation, has subsequently spoken of the formative influence the Movement had on his own artistic career. Johnson himself came to embody the new wave of black British writing during the late 1970s and early 1980s, which was largely poetry-based, vernacular, and often overtly political. The work of this generation was gathered in anthologies such as James Berry's *Bluefoot Traveller* (1976) and **News for Babylon* (1984). Much of it was indebted to Brathwaite's influential call for a new aesthetics of poetry that abandoned the rigidity of the iambic pentameter in favour of 'nation language'. (This at a time when black Britons were being encouraged to speak 'standard' English in order to resolve the racial tensions that had emerged during the time of the *Brixton riots of 1981.)

4. The 1980s and after The year of the Brixton riots also saw the publication of *Midnight's Children*, Salman Rushdie's 'Booker of Bookers'. Although this celebrated literary event may appear a remote, even isolated, moment within the larger context of an embattled and marginal black literary history, in many ways it does anticipate the unprecedented rise of the black British *novel* during (and since) the 1980s, as well as the emergence of an increasingly visible British Asian literature. Writers like David Dabydeen seemed to embody this crossover in writings that shifted confidently between poetry (*Slave Song*, 1984) and fiction (*The Intended*, 1991), between a 'black British' (*Disappearance*, 1993) and Asian diasporic (*Coolie Odyssey*, 1988) imagination. Along with artists like Rukshana Ahmad, Caryl Phillips, Fred D'Aguiar, Hanif Kureishi, and Ben Okri, Dabydeen contributed to the emergence of an increasingly experimental, self-conscious literature in the late 1980s and 1990s. These writers shifted their emphasis away from the realist documentation of an immediate 'black British' community in order to articulate a broader diaspora experience composed of transnational movements and migrations. Meanwhile, writers like Hanif Kureishi worked to foreground black and Asian experience as an everyday, rather than an ex-centric, aspect of British life. Novels like *The Buddha of Suburbia* (1990) refuse any easy sense of ethnicity as 'other' or marginal; on the contrary, they expose Englishness as an ethnicity while articulating a new sense of being at ease in England.

The *Windrush* anniversary of 1998 saw the documentation and celebration of 50 years of mass migration from the West Indies to Britain, and a renewed attention to the historicity of black British experience in fiction and poetry. Zadie Smith's *White Teeth* (2000), Monica Ali's *Brick Lane* (2003), the novels-in-verse of Bernadine Evaristo (1997, 2001), and most recently Andrea Levy's *Small Island* (2004), all turn to the past—whether it is the 1980s, the early post-war decades, or the years of the Roman occupation—in ways that inform their various visions of the black British present. The conspicuous success of all these writers suggests that in some respects black fiction and poetry has moved from the margins to the mainstream.

However, it remains to be seen whether these developments are more than skin deep. The persistence of institutional racism in the police force, the election at the beginning of the 21st century of British National Party councillors in the north of England, and popular hostility towards *refugees and asylum-seekers are also important, contradictory contexts against which the celebrated fictions of Smith and Levy need to be read. Partly in response to this lived contradiction, a number of black British novelists have fictionalized the experience of asylum, including Abdulrazak Gurnah in *By the Sea* (2002) and Caryl Phillips in *A Distant Shore* (2004). Meanwhile, Phillips has commented that, given the conspicuous success of contemporary black British writing in recent years, 'the lack of any reciprocal imagining on the part of white British writers is puzzling'. His comments appear in an article entitled 'Kingdom of the Blind' (2004), which points to the presence of a multicultural blind spot in the white literary imagination since the 1950s. Within this context, the black subjects of Colin MacInnes's London novels (*City of Spades*, 1957; *Absolute Beginners*, 1959; *Mr Love and Justice*, 1960), Shelagh Delany's play *A Taste of Honey* (1958), or, more recently, the work of Alan Hollinghurst in *The Swimming-Pool Library* (1988) and *The Line of Beauty* (2004), or Paul Bailey in *Sugar Cane* (1993), represent notable exceptions to the rule. JRP

Dabydeen, David (ed.), *The Windrush Commemorative Issue: West Indians in Britain 1948–1998*, *Kunapipi*, 20 (1998)

Innes, C. L., *A History of Black and Asian Writing in Britain 1700–2000* (2002)

Lee, A. Robert, *Other Britain, Other British: Contemporary Multicultural Fiction* (1995)

Procter, James (ed.), *Writing Black Britain 1948–1998: An Interdisciplinary Anthology* (2000)

Stein, Mark, *Black British Literature: Novels of Transformation* (2004)

Wambu, Onyekachi, *Empire Windrush: Fifty Years of Black Writing About Britain* (1998)

See also LITERATURE 1: REPRESENTATIONS OF BLACKS; LITERATURE 3: DRAMA

Literature 3: Drama. Plays by immigrants from Africa and the West Indies but mostly, from the 1980s, by second- and third-generation black writers whose cultural experience, although solely British, is predicated on race.

1. Introduction
2. The 1950s
3. The 1970s
4. The years 1980–2004

1. Introduction Black drama is by definition culturally and racially specific and has been concerned primarily with the bicultural nature of black people's experience in Britain, affected either by the West Indian diaspora, or, in the case of those brought up in Britain, the individual's sense of identity. Although many deal with interracial issues, some explore concerns specific to the urban black community, such as Mustapha Matura's *Welcome Home Jacko* (1979), which portrays alienated black youth, and Kwame Kwei-Armah's *Elmina's Kitchen* (2003), which highlights endemic black-on-black violence. In *Leave Taking* (1987) Winsome Pinnock explores the conflict between immigrants and their children, and in *A Rock in the Water* (1989) focuses on recent black British history by celebrating the life of Claudia *Jones, who ran the first black newspaper in Britain and inspired the *Notting Hill Carnival. Maria Oshodi's *Blood, Sweat and Fears* (1989) is specifically relevant to the black Caribbean community in that it focuses on hereditary sickle-cell anaemia, which is confined to that racial group.

These themes are explored through the interaction, in a realistic context, of a variety of culturally representative characters. These reveal the dreams, disillusionment, and dislocation of those who desire to migrate from the West Indies to Britain, immigrants attempting to establish a place for themselves in a hostile society or pining to return home, and parents who feel alienated from their children born in Britain. In addition, the characters of second-generation drama are often alienated young people attempting to establish their status within both the black and white culture and defining what it means to be black and British. Black dramatists have utilized the realism employed by white dramatists since the 1950s. However, their plays often contain the distinctive rhythms and dialect of West Indian patois and black urban street talk, introduced by Mustapha Matura during the 1970s, that locate the characters within a specific cultural environment

2. The 1950s The significant presence of black drama in Britain began in 1957 with the Trinidadian immigrant Errol John's *Moon on a Rainbow Shawl*, set in a back yard in Trinidad. The play had already won the *Observer* play competition in 1950. It portrayed a man's struggle to escape from a Port of Spain slum. Its production in 1958 by the Royal Court, the cradle of the new British theatre, reflected the increased black immigrant presence in British society and brought to the attention of white audiences aspects of Caribbean history and culture. This awareness was extended by the Royal Court's productions of Barry Reckord's *Flesh and a Tiger* (1958), about residents of a Jamaican slum trying to emancipate themselves without falling under white domination, and *You in Your Small Corner* (1960), about a black family that apes white bourgeois values. Reckord's play *Skyvers* (1963), dealing with violence among schoolboys resulting from frustration and limited choices, was deprived of its black identity by being performed by an all-white cast because, it was claimed, there were not enough black actors available to fill the roles. After this promising beginning there was, however, a lull in the production of black British drama until the beginning of the 1970s with the appearance of Mustapha Matura.

3. The 1970s Mustapha Matura emigrated from Trinidad to Britain in 1961. He was inspired to write by the 1960s black consciousness movement in America, and supported by the new British experimental theatre movement in the form of Ed Berman's Open Space theatre, which produced his first short plays, *Black Pieces*, about young male Trinidadian immigrants. The focus in his first full-length play, *As Time Goes By* (1971), is also on the Trinidadian immigrant experience. The Trinidadian-Asian Ram exploits his racial difference, posing as a holy man to make money and establish an identity. His wife, Batee, desires to return home. The topics explored in Matura's subsequent plays centred, however, on the diaspora and post-colonialism in Trinidad. *Play Mas* (1974), *Independence* (1979), *Meetings* (1982), and *The Coup* (1991) portray the post-colonial political and social situation in Trinidad. The latter was the first play by a black dramatist to be commissioned by Britain's National Theatre. In 1973 Michael Abbsenett's *Sweet Talk* also portrayed the diasporic displacement experienced by an African-Caribbean immigrant in a cold and alien England who fantasizes about returning to the Caribbean to escape his nightmarish life, and fails to do so. Matura's *Welcome Home Jacko* (1979) is also set in England. In it unemployed West Indian youths who pass their time in a community youth centre are revealed to be searching for identity and meaning in their lives. It prefigures concerns that second-generation black dramatists considered to be relevant to their own experience.

4. The years 1980–2004 Although the effects of the diaspora are also dealt with by such second-generation dramatists as Winsome Pinnock in *Leave Taking* (1987) and Roy Williams in *The Gift* (2000), the focus of black British drama is now on living and establishing an identity in post-colonial England. Themes include gang, gun, and drug culture, gender relationships in a macho male environment, and what it means to be British.

As the comprehensive inclusion of black and white characters in Roy Williams's plays suggests, what it means to be British is now a question applicable not only to the immigrant community but to the British population as a whole. Indeed his *Sing Yer Heart Out for the Lads* (2004), produced at the National Theatre, includes more white characters than black. It explores what it means to be English or British through the responses of a variety of characters to the televised World Cup Match against Germany in 2000. Black drama has not only appeared at the National Theatre. In 2005 Kwame Kwei-Armah's *Elmina's Kitchen* (2003) transferred from there to the West End and was broadcast on national television. Black drama has now tentatively begun to make its presence felt in the mainstream and commercial British theatre. DKP

Gilroy, Paul, *There Ain't No Black in the Union Jack* (1987)

Hall, Stuart, 'New Ethnicities' in James Donald and Ali Rattansi (eds.), *'Race', Culture and Difference* (1992)

See also LITERATURE 2: FICTION AND POETRY

Liverpool. City in north-western England which, by the end of the 18th century, had become one of Europe's greatest ports because of its involvement in the *slave trade.

1. 18th-century settlers
2. The 1919 riots
3. Black seamen
4. Social and economic disadvantage

1. 18th-century settlers The Liverpool black community is distinguished by its continuity, some black Liverpudlians being able to trace their roots in the city for as many as ten generations. This community pre-dates even the American War of Independence, which caused numbers of free black *Loyalists to settle in London and the growing township of Liverpool. Early settlers ranged from freed slaves and black servants to the student sons and daughters of African rulers, who had visited the port from at least the 1730s. Thus, by no means all of the black settlers in Liverpool were slaves or servants.

Liverpool's black community has its origins in trade and education, but both were by-products of the slave trade. During the 18th century Britain's African trade formed part of the Atlantic network linking her with the Americas and West African coast, dealing in ivory, gold, wax, dye-woods, and slaves. Early coastal forts such as Anomabu, Cape Coast Castle, and other British settlements carried out the day-to-day trade and soon found the coastal peoples of West Africa to be not at all the naive aboriginals they had possibly hoped for. Soon the coastal peoples were acting as middlemen between European traders and the various African nations of the African hinterland.

Notions of the inferiority of Blacks put forward to justify slavery and colonization led to a reduction in the popular image of all black people, irrespective of rank. Poor Blacks at the end of the 18th century by and large included slaves, ex-slaves employed as servants, and discharged sailors and soldiers from the American war. On the other side of the coin were those African children and young adults whose prosperous parents desired an education deemed useful for European trade.

There was a good deal to be gained politically by the British encouraging overseas scholarships. Other European powers, such as France, were deeply involved in trade rivalries, and it was thought that by offering educational opportunities in Britain, the sons of chiefs would receive an indoctrination favourable to the British viewpoint, strengthening the political bonds between the two countries. The children of African rulers sent to Britain to be educated in Britain, both as groups and individually, were usually under the guardianship of traders or ship's captains and were frequently reared alongside their patrons' own children.

In the Parish of St James alone some 34 black adults were christened between April 1801 and September 1808. Their social class is difficult to ascertain from these entries, but some possible clues are to be found in the fact of groups or batches of young adults being baptized simultaneously and such occasional references as:

> 1801 April 12th William Thomas, a native of Africa aged 17 years
> Now resident at Mr. Davies in Rodney Street.

This entry is not conclusive evidence of slave or servant status, but may be an indication of social status. This teenage boy living in Rodney Street (still at the beginning of the 21st century an upmarket, partly residential street in Liverpool city centre) might well have been the son of an African ruler rather than a servant: during the last half of the 18th century there were quite a number of children with this background to be found in Liverpool and the surrounding area.

Black people were being born in Liverpool by at least the latter part of the 18th century. Resident at Old Dock, now Canning Place, in the dockland area around Liverpool's first dock, George, the son of Mercurius Stevens from Antigua, was baptised on 6 August 1795 in St James's Church, along with Thomas, the son of Jack Brown, described as 'a native of Savannah'. In spite of their Anglophone names, we know that they are black, as at the beginning of the first volume of St James's baptismal records of 1775 to 1807 black people are to be found segregated on a separate page.

Another black American, Charles Williams, was baptized with his wife, Margaret, and son Charles on 21 September 1797. Black Loyalists were shipped out of America to Britain in the late 1780s from the American port of Savannah after the British surrender to the American rebels. Both Williams and Brown are common names among the black Loyalists, suggesting that they may have belonged to slave owners of that name.

During the period between the *abolition of the slave trade and the colonial period there was always a black population in Liverpool. This community seems to have been continually augmented from its inception, as newer black settlers and visitors, each with their own language, culture, and religion, have contributed to the making of the present-day black community.

2. The 1919 riots The almost simultaneous explosion of race riots in a number of British cities in 1919 (*see* 'RACE' RIOTS, 1919), including Liverpool, *Cardiff, and *London, seemed like some form of spontaneous combustion, but historical racism and common economic causes were nearer the truth. At the end of the First World War there were something in the region of 20,000 black people in Britain, the Liverpool black community by then swollen to 5,000. The better pay that had come with the changes after the war soon ended, and by 1919 there was competition once again between Blacks and poor Whites and a growing disillusionment when promises of better conditions, 'homes fit for heroes', after the war were slow in their fulfilment. In May 1919 severe riots broke out, in which white rioters attacked individual Blacks in the streets and homes, mobs reportedly as large as 10,000 rampaging in the areas of black settlement. Buildings such as the Elder Dempster Shipping Line's hostel for black seamen and the David Lewis Hostel were sacked and many houses in the Stanhope Street area burned in the orgy of violence. The scenes might have prefigured the infamous *Kristallnacht* in Germany in 1938, when Jewish premises had their windows broken, and many were set on fire. In a climate of widespread unemployment, feelings ran high against black people who, wrongly in the case of the majority of Liverpool Blacks, were considered newcomers to these shores.

3. Black seamen Life became no easier for black people living in Liverpool during the period between the two world wars. The British shipping industry was, like the rest of the world, passing through a troubled time, resulting in less freight and diminishing profits. This affected migration in search of other forms of labour, limiting the aspirations of both black and white alike. Black seamen had been cheaper to employ as stokers and firemen since the national seamen's strike of 1911. Black Liverpudlians, though born or resident in the port, received no advantage from this, and were treated no differently than black 'aliens' (frequently from British colonial countries, in fact, and not strictly foreigners). Black Liverpudlian seamen fell between two stools as they were still regarded by poor Whites as an alien force competing for jobs and not part of the same working class.

Where there were jobs, white foreign seamen were employed rather than the recently demobilized indigenous Blacks, but complaints of the increasing numbers of alien labourers in the industry and the displacement of 'British' (meaning white) crews by colonial crews led to a change in the Seamen's Union's policy of lower wages for black and brown seamen, the Union now pressing instead for higher wages for white seamen, to be secured by forcing black seamen out of the employment market altogether. This movement resulted in the Aliens Order of 1920 and the Special Restriction (Coloured Seamen) Order of 1925, one of the worst moments in the history of the old black community. The new regulations meant that many black Liverpudlians and men from other older black communities such as Cardiff were, like all black seamen in British ports, required to carry documentary proof of identity, despite the fact that their family had been British for generations, and to register with the police as aliens, on colour grounds alone. West Indians and other British blacks were told that it was really foreign Arabs that the Act was aimed at. Those found to be without their 'pass books' were imprisoned in the local 'bridewells' (police cells). Local British Blacks were encouraged by local policemen to register for passes that, strictly speaking, they did not need, as British citizens of many generations, on the grounds that it would prevent mistakes being made by officers who did not know them. This in itself was an admission that the use of the word 'British' was regarded by the majority of the public as meaning 'white'.

4. Social and economic disadvantage The elegant terraced side streets and the grand façades of Toxteth's main streets fell into a state of disrepair between the two world wars. As was happening in most English industrial cities, Liverpool City Council implemented a slum clearance plan, including rehousing and redeveloping the South Dock area, in which the predominantly poor immigrant population lived. However, black residents often rejected relocation to more predominantly white working-class areas because of fears of racial harassment. While the outward migration of the white middle class from the Granby area, later one of the main areas of black settlement, was being completed, black residents and immigrants who could not afford better accommodation moved into multiple-occupancy bedsit apartments. The black population seemed to accept this situation for quite a time, preferring the relative safety of Toxteth, and local government was happy to let sleeping dogs lie, but the period after 1945 was one of simmering resentment, culminating in an unprecedented outpouring of anger in the form of the infamous Toxteth riots of 1981. It seemed as though all the repression of the past two centuries had culminated in a few days of total anarchy.

The Liverpool black community has never been a true ghetto, as throughout the 19th century white immigrants from Ireland and parts of Europe found homes within the existing black settlement, frequently intermarrying with Blacks. Poor Whites from the area, however, are still able to achieve a greater degree of social mobility than their black counterparts, who continue to suffer social and economic difficulties that are distinctly their own. RHC

Costello, R., *Black Liverpool: The Early History of Britain's Oldest Black Community 1730–1918* (2001)

Law, I., and Henfrey, J. (eds.), *A History of Race and Racism in Liverpool 1660–1950* (1981)

Little, Kenneth, *Negroes in Britain: A Study of Race Relations in English Society* (1947)

Lorimer, Douglas A., *Colour, Class and the Victorians: English Attitudes to the Negro in the Mid-Nineteenth Century* (1978)

See also LASCARS AND BLACK SEAMEN

Locke, Alain Leroy (1886–1954). One of the most influential figures in promoting the intellectual and artistic life of the black diaspora during the first half of the 20th century. He was especially interested in the visual arts but also encouraged black dramatists.

Locke was born in Philadelphia, graduated from Harvard University in 1907, and then attended Oxford University from 1907 to 1910 as the first black Rhodes Scholar. He then did advanced work in philosophy in Berlin before returning to the United States. He joined Howard University in 1912, only leaving to do his doctorate at Harvard. He then stayed at Howard until his retirement in 1952. He was the chief ideologue of the Harlem Renaissance and edited the influential anthology *The New Negro* (1925), in which he tried to lay out a cultural programme that would provide for African-Americans a cultural and artistic life comparable to that of other American ethnic groups.

On the whole Locke remained, like W. E. B. DuBois, a believer in the elite, believing that the 'only safeguard for mass relations in the future must be provided in the carefully maintained contacts of the enlightened minorities of both [black and white] race groups'. He also remained committed to the belief that the 'Negro mind reaches out as yet to nothing but American events'. He repudiated the black separatism of Marcus *Garvey and his followers. Yet he did see the future of the black intellectuals and writers as being connected to the black masses, who 'No sane observer would contend . . . are articulate as yet'. Conservative politically, as the Harlem Renaissance faltered, he despaired of the influence of communists and the failure of various artistes such as Paul *Robeson and Roland *Hayes to live up to his ideas, but remained convinced that 'Eventually there must be true Negroes—really free Negroes.'

In some ways his interest in and support for the visual arts and artists saved him—African visual arts had been made respectable by Picasso and other Cubists; by focusing on the African roots of black art, Locke lent support and prestige to this position within the African-American community. The rigour of his thinking and his wide cultural knowledge ensured the wider acceptance of these ideas, which had become current with the effect of the Garvey movement. Unlike the narrow world-view he had noted among African-Americans, his own range of cultural and intellectual contacts was impressive: in England he had met Theophilus *Scholes before the First World War; in the 1930s he encouraged Eric *Williams to go to Howard to teach, and published his first book, *The Negro in the Caribbean* (1942), in his Bronze Booklets series. He delivered lectures on the arts in Haiti. He also encouraged a production of C. L. R. *James's play about the Haitian Revolution at Howard and corresponded with George *Padmore and Una *Marson. At Howard he formed part of a distinguished group of African-American scholars who promoted the study of the African diaspora before it became fashionable to the mainstream. PF

Lewis, David Levering, *When Harlem Was in Vogue* (1981)

Locke, Kath (1928–1992). Community leader and political activist in Manchester. Kath Locke was born to an English mother and a Nigerian father. A high achiever at school, her mixed-race background led her to experience racism from an early age in school and in employment. Her experiences motivated her to campaign for social justice and racial and gender equality throughout her life.

She qualified as an adult teacher and trainer and participated in community politics in Manchester's deprived Moss Side estate, establishing numerous support organizations, including George Jackson House for homeless children in 1973. She campaigned against the poll tax and educational material that stereotyped black people. She contributed significantly to efforts to increase awareness of black history in Manchester, including the successful campaign for a plaque commemorating the 1945 Pan-African Congress. A committed socialist, she was nevertheless critical of the excesses of culturalism and black nationalism, always emphasizing the importance of direct political engagement. She established a women's centre and was active in the promotion of educational and cultural activities, including the formation of Moss Side's celebrated women's dance group, Asabindi, in 1980. In 1991 she retired from her position as development officer for the North West District Workers' Association's educational project. The women's centre founded by Locke was renamed the Kath Locke Centre after her death. The Centre has played a key role in the regeneration of the Moss Side estate, and received a Best Practice Award from the British Urban Regeneration Association in 1999. NAA

Randall, S., 'Obituary: Kath Locke', *North West Labour History*, 17 (1992–3)

London. Capital of the United Kingdom and a historic centre of black political and cultural organization and development.

1. The black population in 2005
2. From Roman to Elizabethan London
3. London and the slave trade
4. Georgian and Victorian London
5. Black organizations

1. The black population in 2005 In 2005, while 1.1 per cent of people in England and Wales were classified as black Caribbean, with a further 0.9 per cent as black African (another 0.2 per cent recorded themselves as 'other black'), people of African origin formed more than 20 per cent of the population of the London boroughs of Lewisham, Lambeth, Brent, and Hackney. More than 10 per cent of Southwark and Newham were black African, with those describing themselves as 'other black' comprising 2 per cent of the populations of Hackney, Lambeth, and Lewisham. London has the largest black population of any city in Britain. In 2005 over 40 per cent of Britain's black population lived there, making it the most significant black cultural centre not only in the country but in Europe.

2. From Roman to Elizabethan London The story of the black presence in the British Isles is intimately connected with the history of Britain's capital. Whether as a financial hub, a port city, a magnet for political organization, or a destination for voluntary and involuntary black settlers, London has remained the central focus in the creation and development of black society in Britain.

The earliest records hint at the arrival of African people during the period of Roman colonization as both slaves and soldiers. Debate (at various levels) continues over the ethnicity of the Emperor Septimius Severus, who died in Britain in 211, although the fact of his birth as an indigenous inhabitant of Leptis Magna (Libya) is beyond dispute.

More reliable records appear from the early 16th century. In November 1501 Catherine of Aragon arrived at the Royal Dockyard in Deptford on her way to marry Henry VII's son Prince Arthur. In her retinue were a number of African slaves. Black people were present as servants or entertainers in all the Tudor courts. Both Henry VII and Henry VIII employed a black trumpeter by the name of John Blanke, and Henry VIII engaged an unknown African diver to search for the wreck of his flagship the *Mary Rose*.

In 1555 the merchant John Lok brought four men from what is now Ghana to London to be trained as interpreters. They were described as 'taule and stronge men' who could 'well agree with our meates and drynkes' but the 'colde and moyst aire doth somewhat offend them'. In 1562 the Royal Dockyard at Deptford played a central role in the foundation of the British slave trade when Captain John *Hawkins, with the backing of several London merchants, sailed for Africa and captured 300 people from what is now Sierra Leone to be sold as slaves in the Caribbean. The profit he made from that voyage allowed him to obtain financial backing and approval from *Elizabeth I for further slave-trading ventures. His second and third voyages were made in the 700-ton *Jesus of Lubeck*. For the third voyage the monarch herself supplied two ships.

3. London and the slave trade The financial involvement of the royal family and the country's aristocracy was central to the growth of the first London-based slave-trading companies. The Royal Adventurers into Africa (1660) counted seven knights of the realm, four barons, five earls, a marquess, two dukes, and King Charles II and his Queen among its backers. A later corporation, the *Royal African Company, made London the only English city that would benefit from the slave trade until 1698. *Bristol and *Liverpool were soon to overtake London's position as the leading slave-trading ports, but the City of London had already grown very rich indeed, and its links with slavery ran longer and deeper than anywhere else. By this time London had profited from the capture and sale of more than 100,000 Africans and the importation of over 30,000 tons of sugar from the Caribbean plantations.

The stranglehold of the slave traders and plantation owners over the City of London was very powerful. No less than fifteen Lord Mayors of London, 25 sheriffs, and 38 aldermen of the City of London were shareholders in the Royal African Company between 1660 and 1690. The Bank of England itself also featured in the slave trade. For almost two centuries the interests and fortunes of the Bank and the West India lobby were largely coextensive. An illustration of this connection was Sir Richard Neave, who, as the director of the bank for 48 years, was also the chairman of the Society of West India Merchants. Richard Neave's son-in-law Beeston Long became governor of the Bank of England, and, like his father-in-law, was the chairman of the Society of West India Merchants.

As a result of their financial and parliamentary power, it soon became very easy for the slave traders and plantation owners to influence Parliament directly. A writer for the *Gentleman's Magazine* in 1766 estimated: 'there are now in parliament upwards of forty members who are either West India planters themselves, descended from such or have concerns there that entitle them to this pre-eminence.'

It was only a matter of time before such concentrated political and economic power produced another phenomenon in British society: William *Beckford, the first millionaire. As the owner of more than 22,000 acres in Jamaica, Beckford sat as a London MP for sixteen years and was twice elected Lord Mayor. Families such as the Beckfords could now use their money and influence to buy seats in Parliament, to corrupt the course of justice, and to try to sway public opinion in favour of the slave trade.

Although few reliable statistics exist for London's black population in the 16th century, it is interesting to note the response of Elizabeth I, who on two occasions (1596 and 1601) issued proclamations calling for the arrest and expulsion of the 'great numbers of negars and Blackamoors which . . . are crept into this realm . . . who are fostered and relieved here to the great annoyance of her own liege people'. These pronouncements set the template for a form of 'repatriation rhetoric' that exists to the present day in discourse on ethnicity and resource allocation.

4. **Georgian and Victorian London** London in the 18th century was home to a large and diverse black population. Estimates vary as to its size. A figure of 20,000, mentioned in a 1764 edition of the *Gentleman's Magazine*, is often cited. This is widely considered to be an exaggeration. However, even those authorities who accept more conservative figures between 5,000 and 10,000 concede that black Londoners formed a significant and very visible minority during this period. They have left an abundance of trails in the parish records of the capital's eastern, waterside, and central parishes—Wapping, Deptford, and Covent Garden, in particular.

Despite the majority appearing to have been either in some form of service, runaways, or seafarers, a small but significant black business class makes an appearance with instances of black publicans, grocers, hairdressers, and merchants, among whom the best known are Ignatius *Sancho and Francis *Williams.

The moneyed, mixed-heritage sons and daughters of West Indian merchants and planters (of whom Nathaniel *Wells, with his extraordinary inheritance and his Pall Mall apartment, is the ultimate exemplar) formed an even smaller, though much commented upon, set.

Black London in the 18th century is still considered to have been a largely male world, but recent research in the boroughs of Lambeth and Tower Hamlets, where consistently high numbers of black women have been discovered, is prompting a reappraisal of this assumption.

London, the heart of Britain's empire, paradoxically provided the platform for the earliest black political organizations in Britain. With its free press and comparative freedom of association, the city had become a magnet for people from all parts of the African diaspora. In 1773 the young slave Phillis *Wheatley had her first collection of poetry published by a Whitechapel printer. A spectrum of black voices from Ignatius Sancho to Ottobah *Cugoano and Olaudah *Equiano would appear in print before the turn of the century. The latter two authors were prominent among the black lobbyists who collectively signed as 'the Sons of Africa'.

Just as London-based black activists and writers were a key feature in the development of the abolitionist movement, they were also present during the growth of organized labour in the form of William *Davidson (the Cato Street conspirator), Robert *Wedderburn (whose synthesis of black Jamaican and British evangelical religion, republicanism, and traditions of slave resistance and rebellion forged links between hitherto unaligned struggles), and William *Cuffay (the elected leader of the capital's Chartists).

5. **Black organizations** Assimilation and an end to immigration led to a decline in London's black population during the Victorian and Edwardian periods. There was, however, an increase in the number of scholars, writers, and radicals who chose to settle and study in the capital. Their energies centred around the Pan-African philosophies that were taking root throughout the African diaspora. Much of the Pan-African writing of Theophilus *Scholes, James *Horton, and Celestine *Edwards was published in London. The African Association was founded by and for people of African origin in 1897. The first Pan-African Conference was held at Westminster Town Hall in the summer of 1900. In 1906 Henry Sylvester *Williams and John Richard *Archer were elected as London councillors in Marylebone and Battersea respectively. By 1912 the **African Times and Orient Review* was being published to an Empire-wide readership from a Fleet Street address. The following year would see John Archer elected as Britain's first black mayor in Battersea. In common with many of Britain's port cities, London experienced a summer of racist attacks on non-white settlers in 1919. The violence was confined to east London, with the worst outbreaks occurring around Cable Street, where a 3,000-strong crowd attacked a café frequented by black and Arab sailors.

Between the wars London hosted a number of black organizations including the *League of Coloured Peoples, the *Negro Welfare Association, and the *West African Students' Union. The arrival of the **Empire Windrush* at Tilbury docks in 1948 and the dispersal of the majority of its 492 Jamaican passengers throughout the city led to the formation of new areas of black settlement in south-east (*Brixton) and north-west (Ladbroke Grove) London. A marked rise in racial assaults occurred, the most serious of which was an attack on a group of black seamen at a hostel near Deptford Broadway in April 1949. Nine years later the *Notting Hill riots were more focused and sustained, and featured an element of organization and provocation by right-wing groups. The template was thus set for decades of sporadic inter-ethnic friction as well as a more sustained and systematic conflict between young black people and the police which would erupt most violently in Brixton in 1981 and in the *Broadwater Farm riots in 1985. An unforeseen outcome of the riots in 1958 was the establishment of the *Notting Hill Carnival, which attracts up to 2 million revellers onto the streets of West London every year. SIM

Fryer, Peter, *Staying Power: The History of Black People in Britain* (1984)

Gerzina, Gretchen (ed.), *Black Victorians/Black Victoriana* (2003)

Green, Jeffrey, *Black Edwardians: Black People in Britain 1901–1914* (1998)

See also BUSINESSES; 'RACE' RIOTS, 1919; ROMAN BRITAIN; SELVON, SAMUEL; TUDOR BRITAIN

London Transport. Government-funded organization employing over 7,000 Caribbean immigrants between 1956 and 1970. During this period the population of immigrant employees within London Transport far outweighed the national average of 3 to 10 per cent, with some divisions registering as many as 41 per cent Caribbean workers. Most of this staff was recruited in a joint venture between London Transport and the Barbadian government, resulting in the immigration of approximately 400 employees per year between 1956 and 1965.

The tradition of black workers within the London Transport system dates back to Joe Clough, a Jamaican immigrant employed by the London General Omnibus Company in 1908. However, mass employment of Caribbean immigrants did not begin until the years following the Second World War. Eager to return to a male-majority staff and to replace female workers employed during the war, London Transport began looking outside the United Kingdom for bus conductors, underground workers, and canteen assistants when a shortage of male staff made it difficult to fill lower-paying jobs. An obvious place to recruit from was the British Caribbean, which was experiencing a population increase and a corresponding rise in unemployment.

In 1956 London Transport and the Barbadian government established a recruitment scheme to employ Caribbean men and women within the organization. This scheme was extended to Jamaica and Trinidad in 1966. Most of the employees recruited by London Transport were skilled working- or middle-class labourers, trained as carpenters, mechanics, clerks, or policemen. Many immigrated to England to travel and experience the 'mother country', while others took jobs with London Transport to escape unemployment or join friends and relatives already living in the United Kingdom. Between 1956 and 1965 nearly 4,000 Barbadians were recruited by London Transport—a substantial fraction of the 21,000 sponsored migrants who left Barbados during this period under similar recruitment schemes, including those by British Rail and the *National Health Service.

To aid immigration, the Barbadian government loaned London Transport employees the travel fare to England, which was paid back over the following two years. The Barbados Migrants' Liaison Service found accommodation for recruits.

To qualify for employment with London Transport, Caribbean recruits had to be between the ages of 20 and 35. Candidates who passed a simple arithmetic test were educated about spoken and written English and life in London in evening classes provided by the Barbadian Ministry of Education. Differences between the Caribbean and England were stressed, including the weather, increased time spent indoors, confined living conditions, and the necessity for warm clothing and substantial shoes. In addition, the *Information Booklet for Intending Emigrants to Britain* was provided to each recruit. London Transport was aware of unrealistic perceptions of London and the 'mother country' held by many recruits, and warned that, while new employees may initially regret the move, feelings would change after a short time in the city. A public relations film about London life and the transport system shown during evening classes promoted idealized visions of British life, leading to disappointment when new immigrants were faced with racial hostility, poor living conditions, and overcrowded housing.

While black London Transport employees reported racial prejudice from the British public, a surprisingly small amount of discrimination was experienced at work. Initial resentment towards Caribbean immigrants resulted from fears that the introduction of an immigrant workforce would lower wages and conditions of English workers. English workers also questioned the loyalty of black workers. However, reports suggest that the introduction of the immigrant workforce was less controversial than the employment of female bus conductors during the Second World War. Trade unions were unsuccessful in their attempt to place a quota on recruited workers, and strike action due to racial hostility was only threatened in one or two garages of the Central Buses division during the early stages of the recruitment scheme. The London bus strike of 1958 marked an important strengthening in relationships between immigrant and English workers when black workers stood unified with their white peers. Rapport between black and white workers grew to be so strong that London Transport benefited from the discriminatory practices of other employers, attracting the applications of black workers who otherwise would not have considered work in buses and trains.

Immigrant workers signed a one-year contract with London Transport, though the majority remained employed by the organization for much longer. High UK unemployment levels, comparable wages and conditions, a reasonable degree of job security, and the value placed on London Transport jobs (which many workers compared to the high-status occupations of policemen, firemen, and postmen) encouraged black workers to remain. Loyalty was also supported by extensive social and sports activities organized by London Transport, of which immigrant employees partook in greater numbers than English workers.

The Barbados recruitment scheme slowed significantly after the publication of the White Paper on Immigration from the Commonwealth in 1965, which greatly restricted immigrant employment. In 1966 London Transport recruited only 138 employees from Barbados, while only 200 were recruited between 1968 and 1970. The employment of black workers was also greatly diminished by privatization and technological advances, which decreased the number of workers required on buses and underground trains. (London Transport employed 87,000 staff in 1958; today its successor employs fewer than 35,000.) EDS

Brooks, Dennis, *Race and Labour in London Transport* (1975)

See also COMMISSION FOR RACIAL EQUALITY; SELVON, SAMUEL

Long, Edward (1734–1813). Historian of Jamaica and writer on slavery. Long was born in England, a member of a family that had long been settled in Jamaica and owned plantations there. Long himself spent only twelve years (1757–69) in Jamaica, where he was a judge, a member of the House of Assembly, and (for a very brief period) its Speaker, but he always identified himself with the interests of the Jamaican plantocracy, that is, the group of white landowners whose prosperity depended on the ownership of sugar plantations worked by slaves.

Long's major work was *The History of Jamaica* (1774). This contains an enormous amount of information on all aspects of the island, and is still an essential source for historians of the Caribbean. However, the work is strongly marked by his partisan support for the plantocracy, which leads him not only to emphasize Jamaica's importance to Britain, but to assert the plantocracy's right to rule Jamaica in their own interest, and to defend the institution of slavery in the aftermath of the **Somerset* case. Long took racist justifications of slavery to new extremes by manipulating contemporary scientific developments to claim that black people differed 'from other men not in *kind*, but in *species*'. Any evidence that appeared to contradict his argument that black people were naturally inferior to Whites (such as the career of Francis *Williams) Long did his best to explain away. Even in his own time there were those who found him deeply offensive, and his claims were rejected by writers such as James *Ramsay. Nevertheless, *The History of Jamaica* was widely read, and had considerable influence on the development of racist ideologies well into the 19th century. JG

Howard, Robert Mowbray, *Records and Letters of the Family of the Longs of Longville, Jamaica, and Hampton Lodge, Surrey* (2 vols., 1925)

Johnson, Howard, 'Edward Long, Historian of Jamaica', introd. to Edward Long, *The History of Jamaica* (facs. repr., 2002)

[Long, Edward], *The History of Jamaica* (3 vols., 1774)

See also RACISM

Loyalists in the American War of Independence. Escaped slaves and their families who sought protection under the British and who fought for the Loyalist cause during the American War of Independence. (Some white Loyalists also came to Britain after the end of the conflict, but theirs is a different story.) At the outbreak of the war in 1775 British commanders immediately looked for allies, recruits, and reinforcements among the estimated 500,000 slaves held in the colonies. Despite some initial resistance, Lord Dunmore, the Governor of Virginia, declared in November 1775 that 'every person capable of bearing arms' should 'resort to his Majesty's standard'. In this instance 'indented servants, negroes, or others free' were included in the call to arms. During the week following this proclamation over 300 slaves had fled to join the 'Ethiopian Regiment' whose motto, 'Liberty to Slaves', was stitched across their uniforms. This regiment would serve with distinction at the battles of Kemp's Landing and Great Bridge. Freedom was the spur that drove tens of thousands of black people from bondage. According to Thomas Jefferson, over 30,000 fled from Virginia alone. It is believed that as many as 100,000, or a fifth of all slaves in North America, made their way on foot, by sea, or otherwise, often with their families, to British lines. Inevitably, large numbers of slaves captured by the British were directly pressed into service.

The black Loyalists, initially, were part of an enormous recruitment drive by the British colonial army that drew in local Indian tribes, pardoned criminals, and foreign mercenaries. Their wartime duties ranged from dam-building and catering to active combat and service at sea. Despite the promises of freedom, many black Loyalists found themselves equally enslaved (and liable to be sold) at the hands of the British. The 3,000 who escaped with the evacuating armies to Nova Scotia (free black men, women, and children) were 10 per cent of all Loyalist evacuees to Canada. Many thousands more departed for Florida, the Bahamas, St Vincent, Bermuda, Dominica, and Dublin. Between 400 and 1,000 travelled to London. They were the lucky ones. Towards the end of the war slave masters were travelling up from Virginia and North Carolina to hunt down their runaway slaves in the streets of New York.

The majority of the black Loyalists in London were unskilled and illiterate, and those who did not have a white person to intercede on their behalf usually forfeited the pensions that were their due. Records from the Commissioners for American Claims show that 47 Blacks applied for compensation compared to 5,000 Whites. They were swiftly absorbed into the city's pre-existent 'black poor' community, and many turned to mendicancy or to funds from the Committee for the Relief of the Black Poor. In 1786 this group, with government support, initiated the ill-fated Sierra Leone Scheme, which would see over 350 black Londoners set sail for West Africa on 9 April 1787. Only 60 of the original settlers were still alive in 1791.

This was also the year that Thomas Peters, a representative of the ill-served and largely landless black Loyalist communities in Canada, travelled to London to present a petition for their promised land rights to the Secretary of State. Through the agency of the Sierra Leone Company, the philanthropist Granville *Sharp proposed free passage to Sierra

Leone for all black people wishing to leave Canada. John Clarkson, who accompanied Thomas Peters back to Canada, declared that the inhabitants of Birchtown, then the largest free black community outside Africa, were 'unanimous in the desire for embarking for Africa, telling me their labour was lost upon the land in this country and their utmost efforts would barely keep them in existence—being now sunk to the lowest wretchedness they had made up their minds for quitting this country'. In all, 1,190 (almost one half of Birchtown's residents) sailed to Sierra Leone from Halifax in 1792. Personal accounts of the history and extraordinary experiences of this unique set of pioneers in North America, Great Britain, and Africa were recorded by the black Loyalist writers David George, Boston King, and John *Marrant, among others.

SIM

Carretta, Vincent (ed.), *Unchained Voices: An Anthology of Black Authors in the English-Speaking World of the Eighteenth Century* (1997)

Marrant, John, *A Narrative of the Lord's Wonderful Dealings with John Marrant, a Black (Now Going to Preach the Gospel in Nova Scotia)* (1785)

Pulis, John W. (ed.), *Moving On: Black Loyalists in the Afro-Atlantic World* (1999)

See also BRITISH WEST INDIES REGIMENT; FIRST WORLD WAR; SECOND WORLD WAR; SIERRA LEONE SETTLERS

M

Macaulay, Herbert Samuel Heelas (1864–1946). Influential political activist and founder member of the Nigerian National Democratic Party. The son of distinguished African missionaries, Macaulay was educated at the Church Missionary Society grammar school founded by his father. After completing his education in 1881, he entered the civil service. In 1890 he travelled to England, where he became the first Nigerian to qualify as a civil engineer. On his return to Lagos, he was appointed as a surveyor but soon became dissatisfied with the system, which discriminated against African civil servants. In 1898 he left the civil service to go into private practice as a licensed surveyor and architect, but his business never proved to be a success. In financial difficulties, Macaulay misappropriated funds and was sentenced to two years' imprisonment, effectively barring him from public office. Nevertheless, he grew to be an influential figure in Nigerian politics through his staunch editorials for the newspaper he co-owned, the *Lagos Daily News*. He also travelled to England as an adviser in two significant court cases defending indigenous rights. In both cases the Privy Council found in his favour. In 1923 he founded the Nigerian National Democratic Party, one of the first organized political parties in West Africa. From the 1930s onwards he focused his energies on campaigning for a united coalition of political groups against colonial rule. He died in 1946, aged 82, after suffering a rheumatic attack on a national tour to promote the anti-colonial cause.

NAA

Tamuno, T., *Herbert Macaulay: Nigerian Patriot* (1975)

See also PUBLISHING

Macaulay, Zachary (1768–1838). Philanthropist instrumental in the founding of the *Anti-Slavery Society. The eldest of twelve children of a Scottish minister, at 14 Macaulay was placed in a merchant's office in *Glasgow. In 1784 he was sent to Jamaica, where he eventually became the manager of a plantation. His experiences during the eight years he spent in the West Indies caused him to dislike and eventually oppose the system of slavery. In 1796 he was appointed Governor of the Sierra Leone colony for freed slaves, which had been established by Granville *Sharp and Henry *Thornton in 1791. He resigned from the post in 1799, returning to England to attempt to end the institution of slavery and with 40 African children who were to be educated in Clapham.

Macaulay married Selina Mills in 1799 and was father to nine children, including the distinguished historian Thomas Babington Macaulay. He was a prominent member of the Clapham Sect, a group of evangelical Anglicans who shared political views on abolition and penal reform. From 1802 to 1816 he edited the sect's journal, the *Christian Observer*. From 1807 to 1812 he also held the post of secretary to the *African Institution. In 1823 he helped to found the Anti-Slavery Society, and in 1825 he founded the *Anti-Slavery Reporter*. Macaulay owned a modest but prosperous West African trading business. Due to incompetent management the business faced bankruptcy in the mid-1820s, ruining him despite the best efforts of his son Henry. Macaulay died in London in 1838, aged 70.

NAA

Booth, Charles, *Zachary Macaulay: His Part in the Movement for the Abolition of the Slave Trade and of Slavery. An Appreciation* (1934)

Carey, Brycchan, *British Abolitionism and the Rhetoric of Sensibility: Writing, Sentiment and Slavery, 1760–1807* (2005)
ODNB

See also ABOLITION; SIERRA LEONE SETTLERS

McCoy, Millie-Christine (1851–1912). Conjoined African-American twins who became successful performers. Born into slavery in North Carolina, Millie-Christine, as the girls were known, were often referred to as one person, and, indeed, often referred to themselves as such. While still in their infancy they were stolen from their parents, sold three times, kidnapped, and displayed as curiosities at fairs and shows across America. Their 'owner', the showman J. P. Smith, first exhibited Millie-Christine as a 'freak of nature' to an American public avid for glimpses of this biological phenomenon. At each new venue the girls were forcibly and humiliatingly stripped and examined by physicians to prove to sceptics that the 'two-headed girl' was no fraud.

A rival show owner stole Millie-Christine and for two years he too toured America exhibiting them. Fearing that they were about to be 'recaptured' from him, their new 'owner' fled with them to Britian, where they were publicly exhibited throughout Scotland and England.

Accompanied by Momoenia, the girls' mother, Smith arrived in England to retrieve his property, but a court case determined that, since slavery was banned in England, he had no legal claim over Millie-Christine, and the girls were placed into their mother's custody. The girls enjoyed a brief period of celebrity, even being summoned to meet Queen Victoria. Homesick for their family, Millie-Christine voluntarily decided to return with Smith to enslavement in America. Once the 6-year-olds had returned to North Carolina in 1857, the apparently benevolent Smith and his wife educated them—an illegal act at the time—and managed their budding show business career. Millie-Christine eventually became among the most renowned performers of their day. Fluent in five languages, accomplished singers, pianists, and dancers, they toured Europe, performing as 'the Two Headed Nightingale', and entertaining European monarchs. In England they appeared four times before Queen Victoria and the royal family, and went on to enjoy a successful career with the Barnum circus. They were variously known as 'the Two-Headed Lady', 'the Eighth Wonder of the World', and 'the Puzzle of Science', among other names. In 1912 Millie-Christine died on the same plantation on which they had been born—only by then, *they* owned the land. Their great-grandnephew eulogized them thus: 'She was more than just a circus freak. She was a talented, generous black woman who was one of the greatest black women of her time. She said that when God made her, he gave her two heads and two brains because her responsibility was so great.' CJ

Martell, Joanne, *Fearfully and Wonderfully Made* (2000)

See also EXHIBITS, BLACK PEOPLE AS

McKay, Claude (1889–1948). Jamaican poet and novelist who travelled extensively in the United States, Europe, and North Africa, but retained an abiding love for his native Jamaica, shown in his early poems and stories, and in his novel *Banana Bottom* (1933). A prominent figure in the Harlem Renaissance, McKay's novels included *Home to Harlem* (1928), a celebration of African-American life, and *Banjo: A Story Without a Plot* (1929), set among the cosmopolitan drifters of the Marseilles waterfront, including black people from Africa, the Caribbean, and North America.

McKay was strongly critical of British colonialism as he had experienced it in Jamaica (to which he never returned after he left for the United States in 1912), though he was grateful to Walter Jekyll, an aristocratic Englishman living on the island who had befriended him and encouraged his early writing. McKay lived in England from the end of 1919 to the beginning of 1921 and, although he had been looking forward to it, was far from enjoying the experience. He disliked the climate, and found that 'the English as a whole were a strangely unsympathetic people, as coldly chilling as their English fog'. He had an introduction from the writer and editor Frank Harris (1856?–1931), whom he had known in New York, to the Irish playwright George Bernard Shaw (1856–1950), who was then at the height of his fame. Shaw entertained McKay one evening at his house, but made the stereotypical comment that, as a black man, McKay might have been better off choosing boxing rather than poetry as a profession. Shaw did help McKay to get a reader's ticket for the British Museum, for which McKay was grateful as it was not an easy thing for 'a stranger in London' to acquire, but he declined to write a preface for McKay's collection of poems, *Spring in New Hampshire*, which was published in London in 1920.

McKay survived what he called 'the ordeal of more than a year's residence' in London mainly through three things. He was a member of two clubs, the membership of which was 'overwhelmingly foreign', and it was this that provided him with a social life. He had time to read, and 'London was not wholly Hell, for it was possible . . . to compose poetry some of the time.' Finally, he got a job on the radical weekly newspaper the *Workers' Dreadnought*, edited by Sylvia Pankhurst (1882–1960). McKay seems to have enjoyed his involvement with the radical side of British politics, but Pankhurst was arrested and subsequently imprisoned as a result of an article carried in the *Dreadnought* in September 1920, and this formed part of a government crackdown on radical political activity that appears to have decided McKay to return to New York.

McKay's autobiography, *A Long Way from Home* (1937), includes some interesting descriptions of his experiences in London, and both *Home to Harlem* and *Banjo* mention anti-black riots in Britain. JG

James, Winston, *A Fierce Hatred of Injustice: Claude McKay's Jamaica and His Poetry of Rebellion* (2000)

See also LITERATURE 2: FICTION AND POETRY; PUBLISHING

McKenzie, Ernest (*c.*1898–1949). Trinidadian writer and political campaigner active in British politics. McKenzie trained as a teacher in Trinidad and emigrated to Britain in 1927 in the hope of studying journalism. Unable to pursue journalism or teaching, he undertook a series of jobs, including the running of two restaurants, while persevering with writing articles, plays, and poetry. His only available publication is an article in *The Keys*, the journal of the *League of Coloured Peoples. McKenzie was known as an effective public speaker and attended the 1945 Manchester Pan-African Congress as the representative of the Antigua Trades and Labour Union. After the war he opened the Caribbean Bureau in London, which was a press agency, information bureau, and importer of Caribbean products. After the death of his first wife in Trinidad, he married Elsie Hartz, the daughter of Russian Jewish emigrants to Britain. He travelled to Trinidad several times, in part to visit his remaining family, which included his children by his first wife. During one of these trips he decided to add the African name Mavinga to McKenzie. Due to his unstable income, regular trips around England and to Trinidad, and the lack of support the couple received from Elsie's disapproving family, the couple's first three children were placed in care. In 1990 he was made the subject of a book, *In Search of Mr McKenzie*, by his daughters Isha McKenzie-Mavinga and Thelma Perkins. The book charted the sisters' attempts to trace their parents and their genealogy. NAA

McKenzie-Mavinga, Isha, and Perkins, Thelma, *In Search of Mr McKenzie* (1990)

See also PUBLISHING

Mackenzie, Lambert (*fl.*1852–1864). First black West Indian ordained into the Church of England. Educated at Queen's College school in Demerara, British Guiana (now Guyana), Mackenzie travelled to England in 1852 to attend St Augustine's Missionary College, Canterbury, where he gained the Hebrew Prize. He was recommended for the priesthood by the Society for the Propagation of the Gospel and was admitted into the ministry of the Church in Demerara in 1855. He was ordained into the order of deacons in Lagos by Bishop Samuel Ajayi *Crowther in 1864. NAA

Ajavi, J. F. Ade, *A Patriot to the Core: Bishop Ajayi Crowther* (2001)

Lorimer, Douglas A., *Colour, Class and the Victorians: English Attitudes to the Negro in the Mid-Nineteenth Century* (1978)

See also CHRISTIANITY; MISSIONARY SOCIETIES

MacPherson Report. Report of the public inquiry into the police investigation of the murder of the black teenager Stephen *Lawrence in south-east London on 22 April 1993. The Report, published on 24 February 1999, was to have a profound impact on the *criminal justice system in Britain, and on other government agencies, including the *National Health Service, local authorities, and the state education system. The Lawrence Inquiry put the police and British justice as a whole on public trial. It raised allegations of systematic corruption and institutionalized racism.

Although there was widespread dismay over the police handling of the case, as well as more general concerns regarding previous police investigations of racist murders, the Home Secretary at the time considered that it was not necessary to commission a public inquiry. However, the Lawrence family and their supporters campaigned vigorously for a major public inquiry, and, following the election of a Labour government in May 1997, the new Home Secretary, Jack Straw, agreed that a public inquiry was essential to establish why the Metropolitan Police had initially failed to investigate fully the murder of Stephen Lawrence.

Sir William MacPherson, a former High Court judge, was assisted by, among others, the Revd John Sentamu (later consecrated the first black Archbishop of York in 2005). He presided over an exhaustive public inquiry, hearing evidence from dozens of witnesses, including several key suspects. Following the completion of the inquiry, MacPherson published a comprehensive report in which he set out in distressing detail the collective and individual failure of the Metropolitan Police Service and its officers to investigate the murder thoroughly and to treat the victim's family with the due degree of sensitivity or respect.

MacPherson found that police incompetence allowed suspects, some of whom were identified by local people within hours of the killing, to destroy evidence and arrange alibis. Five young white men were eventually arrested and charged only after inexplicable delays. One senior police officer with 30 years' experience appeared unsure of his powers of arrest. Other officers refused to acknowledge the murder as racially motivated, and some of the first officers at the scene failed to give first aid, and assumed that Stephen Lawrence, and his friend Duwayne Brooks, who survived the attack, must have been involved in drug-dealing. MacPherson drew particular attention to the insensitive treatment by police officers of Duwayne Brooks in the immediate aftermath of the murder, and of the victim's parents, Doreen and Neville Lawrence, throughout the initial police investigation. In 2006 the Metropolitan Police publicly apologized to Brooks and offered him financial compensation.

A councillor for the London borough of Greenwich, where the murder took place, told the public inquiry he believed that, if the victim had been white and the assailants black, the police investigation would have been handled very differently. For many in the black community this observation had the ring of truth, and MacPherson himself sympathized with the sense of frustration and anger that informed this view.

A second police investigation was led by a new team of detectives, who conducted, in MacPherson's words, 'a more imaginative' investigation, which led to the arrest of the five key suspects and the removal from the community of the father of one of them, who was suspected of intimidating potential witnesses. However, the initial delays in gathering evidence meant that the Crown Prosecution Service took a deeply controversial decision not to prosecute the suspects owing to lack of evidence. The Lawrence family were then forced to mount a rare private prosecution against the five, which also failed for lack of evidence.

One of the Report's most crucial findings was that the Metropolitan Police—and by implication other criminal justice agencies—was institutionally racist, and this had informed their treatment of all the victims—Stephen and Duwayne at the scene of the murder, and their parents and family—and had also played a major role in the subsequent failed investigation. Macpherson's recognition of the existence of widespread institutional racism vindicated the long-held assertions of black communities, who had experienced and complained of racism in the service provision of public sector agencies. His finding was accepted—albeit reluctantly in some quarters—and MacPherson's definition of institutional racism became the standard definition for use in the public sector: 'The collective failure of an organisation to provide an appropriate and professional service to people because of their colour, culture or ethnic origin. It can be seen or detected in processes, attitudes and behaviour which amount to discrimination through unwitting prejudice, ignorance, thoughtlessness and racist stereotyping which disadvantage minority ethnic people.'

A commitment to stamp out institutional racism thus defined has become a core feature of the mission statement of every self-respecting local authority and central government agency, and it is expected that the private sector will follow suit. For example, the Home Office defines its 'mandate' in the following terms: 'to build a safe, just and tolerant society for everyone in the UK, regardless of their race, religion, gender, sexual orientation, disability or age.'

MacPherson's 70 recommendations led to new legislation defining a range of 'racially aggravated' offences for which the penalties were to be more severe than for the 'normal' version of the offence. These offences included criminal damage (racist graffiti, desecration of cemeteries, and similar acts), racist verbal abuse, and racially motivated assault. This legislation perhaps predictably led to a rash of arrests by police officers of members of minority ethnic groups accused of racially aggravated offences against other minority ethnic—and white—victims. This was not what MacPherson had intended.

However, one positive consequence of the MacPherson Report was the Race Relations (Amendment) Act 2000, which goes further than previous legislation in placing a statutory duty on the police and other public sector agencies to put in place policies and procedures to combat institutional racism, discrimination, and disadvantage. CJ/IJ

The Stephen Lawrence Inquiry: Report of an Inquiry by Sir William MacPherson, Cm. 4262-I (1999)

See also CRIMINAL JUSTICE SYSTEM

Magdala Ethiopian treasures. Treasures looted by British troops from Emperor Tewodros of Ethiopia's mountain capital of Magdala (now Amba Mariam) on 13 April 1868. Most came from Tewodros's palace and the nearby church of Medhane Alem. The loot was transported, on fifteen elephants and 200 mules, to a nearby site, where a two-day auction raised 'prize money' for the troops. Most of the booty was purchased by the British Museum's representative Sir Richard Holmes, who also secretly acquired an icon for himself. Over 400 manuscripts went to the British Museum (later British Library), while the finest were given to the Royal Library in Windsor Castle. The Victoria and Albert Museum received two crowns, one of solid gold, and the Museum of Mankind, two embroidered tents.

Tewodros's successor Emperor Yohannes IV in 1872 requested the return of the icon, and a manuscript on the Queen of Sheba. The Museum, which had two copies, returned the inferior, but the icon, though in Holmes's possession, was not traced. Later, during the visit to Britain in 1924 of Ras Tafari (later Emperor *Haile Selassie), the British government returned the inferior of the two crowns. Later again, in 1965, Queen Elizabeth repatriated Tewodros's imperial seal.

Such piecemeal restoration is condemned by the Association for the Return of the Magdala Ethiopian Treasures, founded in 1998, with branches in Ethiopia and Britain. It demands the restitution of all Magdala loot. One of its first successes was the repatriation of the amulet Tewodros wore at the time of his suicide. RKPP

Marcus, H. G., *A History of Ethiopia* (2002)

Makonnen, Ras. Adopted name of George T. N. Griffith (*c*.1900–1983), Pan-Africanist born in Buxton, British Guiana (now Guyana). His background provides an insight into his later political development. His paternal grandfather was reported to have been born in Tigre, Ethiopia, and taken by a Scottish miner to British Guiana. In the village of Buxton many of the African descendants owned their own plot of land, and the tradition of co-operative work existed, which enabled families to plant and harvest together. His maternal grandmother was one of the founders of a village (possibly Buxton itself), and wielded tremendous power in its social and cultural organization. She shared a husband with two or three other women. Makonnen commented that 'nobody cared much about this sort of thing', and that their marriage had survived slavery intact. His father was a gold and diamond miner. It was perhaps from his father that he inherited his entrepreneurial gifts, for at an early age he and his cousin sought out ways to mine minerals.

While in British Guiana, Makonnen was exposed to Marcus *Garvey's *Negro World*, and *The Crisis*, the magazine of the National Association for the Advancement of Colored People in the United States. He later travelled to the United States in the early 1930s with the intention of studying mineralogy at San Saba, Texas, but ended up in Texas working for the YMCA. He then attended Cornell University between 1932 and 1934, studying agriculture and animal husbandry. During his stay with the YMCA he travelled though different states conducting various courses linked with the institution. This afforded him a variety of contacts, including Ethiopians and other members of the African community. He also met Ethiopian students while a student at Cornell. Makonnen's contacts at Cornell proved useful in bringing him to the Danish Royal Agricultural College in Copenhagen, in 1935. He spent about eighteen months in the country, touring the cities and travelling to Sweden and Norway. While in Denmark he published an article in the press claiming that the country was producing the mustard gas used to kill civilians in the Italian invasion of *Ethiopia. He was swiftly deported, and settled in Britain in 1937. He studied history at Manchester University and set up a chain of restaurants in the city which acted as venues for black British activists as well as black American troops stationed nearby. His business helped to fund court cases involving black people as well as the 1945 Manchester Pan-African Congress, in which he played a major part as co-organizer. Makonnen emigrated to Ghana in 1957, then to Kenya, where he died in 1983.

ASS

Adi, H., and Sherwood, M., *Pan-African History: Political Figures from Africa and the Diaspora Since 1787* (2003)

King, Kenneth (ed.), *Ras Makonnen: Pan-Africanism from Within* (1973)

ODNB

See also BUSINESSES; PADMORE, GEORGE

Malcolm X. Adopted name of Malcolm Little, also known by his Muslim name, el-Hajj Malik el-Shabazz (1925–1965), influential black nationalist. Raised in a Baptist family but bereaved of both parents at an early age, Malcolm's troubled childhood and adolescence is vividly retold in the posthumous best-selling *Autobiography* (1965). It was during his imprisonment for burglary (1946–52) that Malcolm discovered the Islamic faith which was to become the driving force in his life. For the next eleven years he dedicated himself to the cause of race pride and black nationalism, spreading the teachings of Elijah Muhammad and the influence of his organization, the Black Muslim sect (later to become the Nation of Islam). In 1964 Malcolm left the organization and formed his own group, the Organization of Afro-American Unity. It was in the following years of antipathy between Malcolm and his former leader and followers that he visited Britain twice as a part of a worldwide tour.

Malcolm X's most important visit to Britain came just a matter of days before his assassination in Manhattan on 21 February 1965. Though brief (and left out of Spike Lee's famous 1992 film of his life, *Malcolm X*), the visit was part of a tour that pointed to a more internationalist political vision for Malcom's US-based black nationalist group. It also served as an important catalyst for the politicization of black communities and the organization of black nationalist initiatives in Britain. He gave an address to the Oxford Union, and three months later, in early February 1965, he gave talks at the London School of Economics. He vociferously argued that the revolt of African-Americans should build solidarity with Africans the world over, instigating a 'global rebellion . . . of the exploited against the exploiter'.

More famously, on 12 February Malcolm visited Smethwick, an industrial town in the West Midlands. Smethwick was a town that had recently come to symbolize racism, specifically, institutionalized racism, in Britain. During the general election campaign a few months previously the Tory candidate, Peter Griffiths, had won the Smethwick seat with the slogan 'If you want a nigger for a neighbour, vote Labour'. His campaign led to the defeat of the Labour candidate, Patrick Gordon Walker, who had been expected to win easily and become Foreign Secretary in the new administration. With the media in tow, Malcolm strolled down the then notorious Marshall Street, where white residents had persuaded the Tory-run local council to buy all available houses in order to sell them on exclusively to white families. The visit was intentionally inflammatory: 'I have heard they are being treated as the Jews under Hitler,' he told the press. 'I would not wait for the fascist element in Smethwick to erect gas ovens.'

The influence of Malcolm's London talks and the Smethwick publicity stunt quickly gained substance. At that time the still ghettoized **Empire Windrush* generation was fertile ground for Malcolm's black nationalist sentiments. During his stay he met the young Trinidadian Michael de Freitas. With a similar eye for the media de Freitas rapidly became *Michael X, or Michael Abdul Malik, and with comrades formed the Racial Adjustment Action Society (RAAS) in February 1965. A controversial figure, Michael gained much media attention but was by no means universally popular among black communities. As Stuart Hall has commented, 'if he had fully remade himself, he could have been . . . possibly the sort of person in a Malcolm X relation to British Black Politics', but 'he never had the support of ordinary, respectable, black working people'.

Despite the collapse of the RAAS in the late 1960s and Michael X's subsequent flight to Trinidad, the legacy of Malcolm X in Britain has lived on in the varied thinkers, writers, and movements for whom religion, politics, and the fight against racism were to become central, if not always reconcilable, tenets, the Rastafarian movement of the 1970s being but one example. JJGG

Bruce, Perry (ed.), *Malcolm X: The Last Speeches* (1989)
Malcolm X and Haley, Alex, *The Autobiography of Malcolm X* (1965)
Phillips, Mike, and Phillips, Trevor, *Windrush: The Irresistible Rise of Multi-Racial Britain* (1998)

See also BLACK PANTHER PARTY; POLITICS; RASTAFARIANISM

Manning, Eddie Nickname of Edgar McManning or Manning (1889–1931), Jamaican criminal. Living in London by 1916 and working in an armaments factory,

Manning achieved notoriety through widespread newspaper reports. Their misrepresentations have since fuelled memoirs, biographies, and histories. He shot three men in 1920 and was sent to prison for sixteen months. In 1922 he was alleged to be dealing in cocaine. *The Times* described him as an 'important drug trafficker': he pleaded guilty to being in possession. A year later he was again found with drugs, and again pleaded guilty. Newspapers linked him with a young woman's death through heroin, and with prostitution, but without evidence.

Cocaine use was expanding in London and the amended Dangerous Drugs Act changed the maximum sentence for possession from six months to ten years. Manning was the first to be convicted under these rules, and went to prison for three years. He returned to London and ran a seedy restaurant-club in Soho. Petty-criminal activities—harbouring prostitutes, obstructing the police, and, in 1929, theft—again brought his name into the newspapers. He was sentenced to three years. He died in Parkhurst prison in 1931.

JPG

Fabian, Robert, *London After Dark* (1954)

Kohn, Marek, *Dope Girls: The Birth of the British Drug Underground* (1992)

ODNB

Streatfeild, D., *Cocaine: An Unauthorised Biography* (2001)

Mansfield Park. Novel by Jane Austen in which the wealth and status of the Bertram family is underpinned by oblique references to their ownership of a slave plantation in Antigua. *Mansfield Park* (1814) is set in a large country estate in Nottinghamshire. Its narrative revolves around Sir Thomas Bertram, the owner of Mansfield Park, and his extended family. Bertram is characterized by an over-reliance upon a value system of order and emotional distancing that falls apart, with disastrous consequences, when challenged. The Bertram household consists of his wife and four children, his sister-in-law Mrs Norris, and one of his nieces, Fanny Price. Fanny has been taken in by the Bertrams owing to her family's poverty and, in contrast to Sir Thomas, she embodies compassion, warm emotions, and sensibility. Although he is central to the plot, Sir Thomas is largely absent from Mansfield Park owing to his growing concerns about 'recent losses on his West India estate'. During his prolonged absence in Antigua, in which he has to deal with 'unfavourable circumstances . . . and great uncertainty', the moral standards and orderly nature of his household decline rapidly. The untimely arrival of the frivolous Mary and Henry Crawford lead to inappropriate relationships with his own children, and matters finally erupt when Sir Thomas eventually returns to find them all engaged in an undesirable theatrical project. While Sir Thomas ostensibly appears to restore order to Mansfield Park, the scandalous failure of his daughter Maria's marriage and the dissipation of his elder son, Tom, leave both him and the family reputation in tatters. It is left to his niece Fanny, finally betrothed to his younger son, Edmund, to show that the only way to re-establish moral sensibilities is through a warm and compassionate attitude towards others.

Until the publication of Edward Said's *Culture and Imperialism* in 1993, Austen's references to the Bertram's Antiguan estate had been largely overlooked by critics. However, with *Mansfield Park* featuring so strongly in Said's arguments about the necessity for colonial possessions to support the kind of lifestyle enjoyed by Austen's fictional Bertrams, that kind of critical oversight is no longer tenable. Instead, as Said has written, we have to acknowledge that 'The Bertrams could not have been possible without the slave trade, sugar and the colonial planter class.' Suddenly Austen's limited mentions of Sir Thomas's estate in Antigua can be seen as revealing the author's belief in 'the importance of an empire to the situation at home'. While there are clearly no explicit references in *Mansfield Park* to the exact nature of the 'problems' faced by Sir Thomas as an absentee plantation owner, or to the true nature of the property itself, we must now acknowledge that it can only have been a sugar plantation and therefore maintained by slave labour. By linking Sir Thomas so closely to the fortunes of his Caribbean property, Austen is reinforcing the notion that colonial expansion and exploitation are an integral part of that system of imperialist 'morality' for which he and his family stand. *Mansfield Park* thus provides us with a microcosm of 19th-century domestic imperialist culture and highlights the collective denial about its slave-owning past. LM

See also LITERATURE 1: REPRESENTATIONS OF BLACKS

Marechera, Dambudzo (1952–1987). *Enfant terrible* of Zimbabwean literature, he was born in Rusape, Southern Rhodesia (now Zimbabwe), and grew up with all the hardships experienced by the son of a poor black township family in colonial Southern Rhodesia. The irreverent and dynamic experimentation of his fiction, poetry, and drama arose from the dual experience of poverty and racial oppression, on the one hand, and a prodigal intelligence both nurtured and frustrated by a colonial education, on the other. He won scholarships to St Augustine's Secondary School, to the University of Rhodesia, and to New College, Oxford. He was expelled from all three institutions for speaking out against colonial syllabuses and protesting against institutionalized racism.

Having made a solo protest march against the Rhodesian premier Ian Smith, Marechera fled to Botswana and then to England, where he gained political asylum. He studied at New College, Oxford, from 1974 to 1976 before being sent down for his antisocial behaviour. He lived and worked in London until his return to Zimbabwe in 1982. His first novella and short story collection, *The House of Hunger*, written while at Oxford and was published in 1978 to great acclaim, winning the *Guardian* Fiction Prize in 1979. Marechera's less well-received second novel, *The Black Insider* (1980), typifies his developing style: surrealist, nihilistic, and caustic towards all forms of authority. His third book, *Mindblast*, was published in 1984. Marechera died of an AIDS-related illness in Zimbabwe in 1987. *Cemetery of the Mind*, the first comprehensive collection of his poems, appeared in 1994 along with *Scrapiron Blues*, a miscellany of all the genres in which he wrote. JJGG

Veit-Wild, Flora, *Dambudzo Marechera: A Sourcebook on His Life and Work* (2002)

See also LITERATURE 2: FICTION AND POETRY

Marrant, John (1755–1791). African-American preacher born a free man in the colony of New York. He had an itinerant childhood, during which he worked with a carpenter and learned to play the French horn and violin. He was converted to Christianity at one of George Whitefield's services in 1769 or 1770, and he then spent two years evangelizing, including a period of captivity, among Native American peoples. Sometime during 1775–6 he was impressed into the Royal Navy. He took part in the siege of Charleston in 1780, saw action in British waters, was wounded, and then was discharged in Plymouth in 1782. He went to London, and preached in Spa Fields chapel, which belonged to the Countess of Huntingdon's Connection, into which body he was ordained at Bath in May 1785. At about that time he told his story to William Aldridge, a Methodist minister and friend of the Countess, who wrote it down and had it published as *The Narrative of the Lord's Wonderful Dealings with John Marrant (A Black)* (1785). Marrant then sailed to Nova Scotia, where in 1785–7 he preached to black *Loyalists but experienced considerable poverty and opposition from Methodists, who disapproved of his Calvinist doctrines. He moved to New York, where he continued preaching and was also involved in freemasonry. Never far from controversy, he returned to England in 1790, where he died in April 1791. Marrant was buried in Islington, London. His *Narrative* went into many editions, being published repeatedly between 1785 and 1850. DK

Carretta, Vincent (ed.), *Unchained Voices: An Anthology of Black Authors in the English-Speaking World of the Eighteenth Century* (1996)

Potkay, Adam, and Burr, Sandra (eds.), *Black Atlantic Writers of the Eighteenth Century: Living the New Exodus in England and the Americas* (1995)

See also CHRISTIANITY; MISSIONARY SOCIETIES

Marshall, Malcolm Denzil (1958–1999). Barbadian and English county cricketer. Marshall was born and grew up in Barbados, where he first developed his love for cricket at St Giles' Boys' School. He later described how, as a boy, he would go along to Sunday School with his Bible in one hand and a cricket ball in the other. He first played competitively at the under-15s level at Parkinson School, and later played for the Texaco Club, for the famous local club Spartan, and for Banks' Brewery.

His appearance for Barbados against Jamaica in 1978, when he took six wickets for 77 runs, marked the beginning of nineteen years of first-class cricket, cut short only by the illness that was to kill him at a tragically early age. He first appeared for the West Indies in their tour of India in 1978, and he was also to play for the English county side Hampshire (where he played and coached for a total of fourteen seasons) and for Natal in South Africa. In 1995 he played five matches for Scotland in the Benson and Hedges Cup. Writing Marshall's obituary in *The Times*, the English sports journalist Christopher Martin-Jenkins commented that in 408 first-class matches Marshall had dismissed 1,651 batsmen at an average of nineteen runs each: 'In Test cricket his victims cost only 20 runs each and his rate of striking proclaims him to have been the most incisive of all the outstanding fast bowlers of his time.' Statistics are not everything, however, and Marshall was especially admired for his style, and for his quickness at sizing up the weaknesses of a batsman and making the most of them. The great West Indian player Wes Hall commented that Marshall was the smartest and 'the greatest fast bowler in history'. He was also well known as, in the words of the distinguished Barbadian cricketing commentator Tony Cozier, 'a perceptive and generous coach'. He was held in high esteem at home and abroad, and the 3,000 mourners who attended his funeral at the Garfield Sobers Complex in Barbados included distinguished Barbadians from all walks of life, as well as outstanding cricketers from all over the Caribbean and from England. JG

Carrington, Sean, Fraser, Henry, Gilmore, John, and Forde, Addinton, *A–Z of Barbados Heritage* (2003)

See also SPORT

Marson, Una (1905–1965). Jamaican poet, playwright, and journalist born in the county parish of St Elizabeth. As the daughter of a middle-class Baptist minister, Marson's intellectual development took place within the context of a religious home and the conservative and colonial Hampton high school, where she had won a scholarship place. When Marson left school in 1922, she directed her studies to commerce and secretarial work, and her decision to work with the Salvation Army and the YMCA in Kingston was an early indication of her commitment to ideas of social justice. Her interests in journalism were also evident, and in 1928 she founded and edited her own monthly journal, *The Cosmopolitan: A Monthly Magazine for the Business Youth of Jamaica and the Official Organ of the Stenographers' Association.* The editorial statement of this bold and defiantly 'modern' publication with a strong emphasis on women's issues proclaimed: 'This is the age of woman: what man has done, women may do.' Marson herself certainly lived up to this axiom, and by the time she left Kingston for London in 1932 she had also established her literary credentials, having published two volumes of poetry (*Tropic Reveries* in 1930; *Heights and Depths*, 1931) and staged her first play, *At What a Price*, to public acclaim.

Although Marson's arrival in London in 1932 coincided historically with that of C. L. R. *James, her cultural and intellectual ideas set her apart from both the 'angry young men' who came in the 1930s and the later generation of emigrants. As her journalism and her creative works had already demonstrated, Marson was always concerned to represent issues of gender and women's liberation alongside those of racial equality and cultural nationalism. In London she lodged at the Peckham home of fellow Jamaican Dr Ronald *Moody, and soon became involved with the *League of Coloured Peoples, an organization founded by Moody in 1931 to address issues of racial division and prejudice. As editor of the League's journal, *The Keys*, Marson was easily networked into black British circles and had opportunities to meet many of the key figures in the emergent nationalist and anti-colonial movements. Her interest in *Pan-Africanism developed during this period, and in 1934 she met the King of Ghana, Ofori Atta. However, her interest in women's rights continued to be equally strong and in the same year she gave a speech at the Women's International League Conference in London. In 1935 her internationalism and conviction on issues of women's rights meant that she was the first Jamaican invited to speak at the International Alliance of Women for Suffrage and Equal Citizenship Conference in Istanbul and, in the same year, the first black woman invited to attend the League of Nations at Geneva, where a meeting with the Ethiopian delegation at the conference further raised her awareness of the urgent struggle against colonialism. Provoked and outraged by the Italian invasion of *Ethiopia in 1935, Marson immediately offered her help to Dr Charles *Martin, the Ethiopian Minister. She went on to work as personal secretary to HIM *Haile Selassie, but by September of 1936 she was severely depressed and unable to continue.

Marson returned home to Jamaica during a period of intense social and political unrest, but the sense of social ferment and the anticipation of certain change appear to have restored her public voice and her commitment to politics. By 1937 she had a regular column in *Public Opinion*, the weekly paper of the People's National Party led by Norman Manley, and published a series of strident articles, including one entitled 'Feminism'. It was also in September of this year that she published her third volume of poetry, *The Moth and the Star*, with many poems clearly and purposefully addressed to issues of gender and race politics that also animated her play *Pocomania*, staged in January 1938. Retaining her early practical commitment to social justice, Marson worked hard to raise money for a Jamaica Save the Children Association (Jamsave) while also reporting for the *Jamaican Standard*.

In 1938 Marson returned to London in order to report on and give evidence to the Moyne Commission (a British government commission investigating the riots and unrest that had swept across the Caribbean region) and to fundraise for Jamsave. After the declaration of war in 1939 she witnessed changes in the black community in Britain, as fewer students made the journey and many of those based in London moved north. Although she wrote about the unofficial 'colour bar' operating in the workplace that had disadvantaged her along with others, Marson's own fortunes improved when she took freelance work with the BBC and in 1941 was appointed full-time programme assistant for the radio programme *Calling the West Indies*, which had developed by 1943 into the now famous **Caribbean Voices* literary showcase. Despite fragile health, in 1945 Marson published another volume of poetry, *Towards the Stars*, mostly from collected works, before returning to Jamaica. It is a mark of her prominence at that time that on her arrival she was met by huge crowds, and a lunch organized in her honour by the Poetry League of Jamaica was attended by Edna Manley, a prominent sculptor and wife of the future prime minister Norman Manley. Marson worked for some years for the nationalist Pioneer Press, the book-publishing arm of *The Gleaner*. In 1960 she moved to the United States, but after a failed marriage, returned to Jamaica, where she died in 1965 of a heart attack. It was only in the 1990s that her pioneering work as a writer, journalist, and intellectual found sustained acknowledgement in both Caribbean and black British histories.

AJD

DeCaires Narain, Denise, *Contemporary Caribbean Women's Poetry: Making Style* (2002)
Donnell, Alison, 'Una Marson: Feminism, Anti-Colonialism and a Forgotten Fight for Freedom' in Bill Schwarz (ed.), *West Indian Intellectuals in Britain* (2003)
Jarrett-Macauley, Delia, *The Life of Una Marson, 1905–65* (1998)
ODNB

See also LITERATURE 2: FICTION AND POETRY; PUBLISHING; RADIO

Martin, Charles. Alias of Azaj Warqnah Ishete (1865–1952), Ethiopia's first modern-trained physician and Ethiopian Minister to London at the time of the Italian invasion of *Ethiopia in 1935. Born in Gondar, at the age of 3 Ishete was abandoned by his family during the capture of the fortress of Magdala in 1868. Two British officers took him to India, assumed responsibility for his education, and christened him Charles Martin. Martin graduated from Lahore Medical College in 1882, becoming a medical officer in Burma in 1891. He was reunited with his family and his Ethiopian name on his visit to Addis Ababa in 1899. On another trip in 1908 as temporary medical officer in the British legation he treated the ailing Emperor Menelik. In 1919 he returned to Ethiopia to settle, practising medicine and undertaking various forms of development work including the founding of girls' schools and the running of mineral springs, farms, and flour mills. Martin was appointed Governor of Charchar in 1930. With Italian invasion imminent, in 1935 Haile Selassie appointed him Ethiopian Minister to the Court of St James. During his time in London he made considerable efforts to communicate Ethiopia's position to Britain and the world, garnering wide sympathy and support. He spent the later years of the Italian occupation in India but returned as an elder statesman to Ethiopia after its liberation in 1941, where he lived in retirement until his death in 1952. NAA

O'Brien, H. R., 'Dr. Warqnah Charles Martin of Ethiopia', *Journal of Medical Education* 41/1 (1996)
Ofosu-Appiah, L. H. (ed.), *Dictionary of African Biography* (1977)

See also DOCTORS; MEDICINE

Masques. Pre-dramatic pageant entertainments, increasing in popularity through the Tudor period, which the poet Ben Jonson developed during the reign of King James I into courtly plays. The masques for Queen Anne's annual festivities cost James up to £3,000 each and lasted for several hours, utilizing the lavish costumes and Italian mechanical stages of Inigo Jones. Traditionally, the masque's transition was from discord to order, though Jonson brought a more complex literary sensibility to his, including many of them in his published *Works* of 1619, together with notes on the staging. Disagreement with Jones over the relative importance of staging and literary effect would eventually sour relations between the two men.

Their first collaboration, *The Masque of Blackness*, was performed on Twelfth Night 1605. Jonson would not develop his innovation of the 'anti-masque'—chaotic, digressive, and grotesque—until later in his career; instead, *Blackness* seems to have been an attempt at staging a metaphysical poetic sequence. The Queen had requested that she and her ladies were to black up for the non-speaking parts, and a courtier, Dudley Carleton, gave an eyewitness account of the frivolity: 'their Faces, and Arms up to the Elbows, were painted black . . . you cannot imagine a more ugly Sight, than a Troop of lean-cheek'd Moors.' The Queen was so heavily blacked up that she nearly stained the lips of the Spanish ambassador.

Jonson used this decadent framework to give a startling deconstruction of racial prejudice. Oceanus and the river Niger—one blue, grey-bearded, and robed in sea-green, the other 'in form and colour of an Ethiop, his hair and beard curled, shadowed with a blue and bright mantle'—were accompanied by the twelve masquers, 'nymphs, Negroes and the daughters of Niger' riding in an illuminated, rocking shell, jewelled with 'the most choice and orient pearl, best setting off from the black'. In the opening song it was emphatically stated that black people could be beautiful:

> bright
> And full of life and light
> To prove that beauty best
> Which not the colour but the feature
> Assures unto the creature.

The idea that beauty depended only on fashion was developed throughout the masque.

Jonson radically reworks the biblical myth of Ham, twice. Niger says that his daughters, the 'first formed dames of earth', were blackened by the sun's attraction, which proves their beauty, since he is the best judge of this: 'shows | That in their black the perfect'st beauty grows'. However, envious, 'brainsick' poets have sung of other empires' 'painted beauties', insinuating that Phaethon, who lost control of the chariot of the sun in Graeco-Roman myth, burned the nymphs, changing them from 'fair as other dames' to 'black with black despair'. Like the differing interpretations of the sun, black's metaphorical connotations come after the fact, and are due to slander, which is mocked as a pagan archaism. The nymphs are so upset by the human reading of their colour that Niger overflows with tears.

The moon—Aethiopia—instructs them to seek a land ending in *-tania*, and after travelling northwards through 'black Mauretania', 'swarth Lusitania', and 'rich Aquitania', they arrive in England: unified with Scotland under James to form Britannia. Here the sun will refine them to beauty again, through his temperance 'blanch' and 'salve' them—presumably a metaphor for the tolerance of 'Britain men'. They go to live in the sea, on each full moon being summoned to bathe their limbs in sea foam, and once a year entitled to enjoy the English sunshine. Given that Jonson was a fierce classicist—his sources of information about the Niger were Pliny, Solinus, Ptolemy, and 'Leo the African'—and that the sun is described as emitting a 'light sciental', this can be taken as a gentle exhortation to James, who had only been on the throne a year, to be an enlightened, 'temperate' ruler; and as subverting the discourse of imperial expansion, in the conceit of Sir Philip Sidney's *Apology for Poetry*, inciting virtue by delivering a 'golden' ideal.

It was three years before Jonson was commissioned to write another masque. He printed Queen Anne's command that he should 'answer the former, still keeping them the same persons, the daughters of Niger, but their beauties varied according to promise [i.e. made white], and their time of absence excused, with four more added to their number'—then opened *The Masque of Beauty* with 'Boreas, one of the winds, as my fittest messenger, presenting him thus: In a robe of russet and white mixed, full and bagged, his hair and beard rough and horrid, his wings grey and full of snow and icicles, his mantle borne from him in wires, and in several puffs, his feet ending in serpents' tails, and in his hand a leafless branch laden with icicles'. No chillier picture could be given of the dawning 1608. Night, annoyed at the moon's presumption and 'mad to see an Ethiop washèd white', though not wanting to demean her own colour, has trapped the Nigerian nymphs under the sea. *Beauty*'s resolution, in which the nymphs are rescued, leaving their blackness in the waves, betrays the idealism of *Blackness*—'Nor shall this veil the sun hath cast | Above your blood more summers last'—where the colour black was merely the objective correlative for its negative association, ugliness. It necessitates another mythical invention, turning them to stars, into which Jonson once more encodes his own covert support of the black nymphs:

> Yield then, night, to the light,
> As blackness hath to beauty,
> Which is but the same duty.

The two masques show us a world of delicate censorship and a rationalist intellectual's subtle protest at the hardening of the Jacobean regime from promise to intolerance. JM

Jonson, Ben, *The Complete Masques* (ed. Stephen Orgel, 1969)

Mickel, Lesley, *Ben Jonson's Anti-Masques: A History of Growth and Decline* (1999)

See also BEAUTY, CONCEPTS OF; LITERATURE 1: REPRESENTATIONS OF BLACKS; RENAISSANCE DRAMA

Medicine. In the 1850s the Medical Register was established in Britain. It listed those who were entitled to practise. Nurses and dentists had yet to be treated in this manner. Communities continued to trust individuals who attended mothers in childbed, herbalists, and those who could set broken bones. There were charlatans, the makers of dubious remedies, fairground fakers, and abortionists. Black people had a part in all of this, with gullible patients seeing extra powers in their very appearance.

James McClune Smith, a New Yorker who qualified in medicine at Glasgow University in the 1830s, returned to practise in New York. Active in the anti-slavery movement, Smith's British experience is known through his recollections of the actor Ira *Aldridge. Less public medical personnel are more difficult to identify.

Sierra Leonean Africans were the first to qualify under the 1858 legislation. William Davies and James Africanus *Horton qualified in London that year, then studied in Scotland. As medical training facilities were absent from the tropical Empire, would-be doctors had to study in Britain, Ireland, or Canada. Robert Smith and Thomas Spilsbury qualified in 1865, and Daniel Taylor, also Sierra Leonean, in 1874; he is best known as the father of the composer Samuel *Coleridge-Taylor. John Easmon (1879), William Renner (1880), Smith's brother Joseph, and Sylvester Cole (1883) are others. Easmon and Renner had many descendants who were doctors.

Nathaniel King (1874) encouraged modern sanitation in Lagos; Obadiah Johnson (1884) wrote *The Therapeutics of West Africa*; John Randel (1888) wrote on worm infestations and cancer; Oguntola Sapara (1895) led the campaign to destroy smallpox worship; Benjamin Quartey-Papafio (1886), also of Ghana, wrote his thesis on malaria.

African-Caribbean doctors such as Derwent Waldron (1879; a graduate of Edinburgh University, called to the Bar in 1893, and Fellow of the Royal Meteorological Society) from Jamaica worked in Africa, although a proportion settled in Britain. These young men were often educated privately in Britain, and a significant part of their lives had been spent with the British. Their training had them walk the wards of Britain's hospitals. A career in the colonial medical service had significant disadvantages, for less qualified Whites were promoted over Blacks.

Among Barbados-born doctors were Athelstan Stoute, whose surgery was in Hammersmith (west London), Elkin Cumberbatch (central London), and Belfield Clarke (south London). Clarke was a guest at Ghana's independence celebrations in 1957. Risien Russell had a surgery in Wimpole Street and a fine reputation as a nerve specialist as early as 1913; John *Alcindor from Trinidad (Edinburgh, 1899) worked in Paddington (west London); James Brown from Jamaica (1914) in Hackney (south London) after studies in Montreal. Philip Harry, who returned to Jamaica after qualifying at Edinburgh (1904), had an architect son who lived in London. The Jamaicans Harold and Ludlow Moody qualified in London; Harold *Moody settled there.

Frederick Kerry from British Guiana studied in London in the 1920s; the Trinidadians Ferdinand Leekam qualified in 1921, his brother Felix in 1923. George Alfred Busby worked in east London before migrating to Ghana to work among the poor; Robert Munro practised in Epsom. For some, like John Henry Pierre, there was employment at a colonial hospital or, like E. J. de Verteuil, work as a medical officer, also in Trinidad. Raymond Dolly studied at St Bartholomew's Hospital in London; Cumberbatch practised in central London. They and H. E. Bond, who was deeply interested in tropical lunacy but was frustrated when working in Kingston and so returned to London, were friends of Brown. Their fellow Jamaican Theophilus *Scholes (1884) worked independently in Africa and wrote several books in London in the first decade of the 20th century.

Harold Moody's *League of Coloured Peoples was aware of discrimination faced by Caribbean nurses seeking training in Britain, but there had been African student nurses such as C. Amado Taylor (a midwife) in 1919. The most famous nurse was the Jamaican Mary *Seacole, who had tended to soldiers in the Crimean War and died in London in 1881.

Experiences were mixed. One Jamaican wrote enthusiastically to his brother in New York in 1938, explaining how unprejudiced his Kensington patients were. Dr Rice, an American who had experienced slavery, rose in local government medical work and left a reputation in 1930s Sutton (Surrey) that survived 70 years. Brown and Alcindor were rejected by the Royal Army Medical Corps since doctors were automatically officers but army regulations prohibited Blacks from becoming officers. The rule was not always effective, for the England-born son of a Barbados father, Walter *Tull, was an infantry lieutenant in 1917. His brother Edward Tull-Warnock was a dentist in Aberdeen and Glasgow from 1912. Another dentist was the Guianese, A. A. Dummett, who returned to Georgetown. Wartime flying in the Royal Air Force took Ronald Hall from British Guiana to qualify as a dentist; his surgery was in Tulse Hill, south-east London.

Harold Piper was the first African-Trinidadian to qualify as a pharmacist (London, 1919); his friend James Fletcher worked as a doctor in Islington and Bayswater for over half a century. Peter Milliard, a Guianese doctor in Manchester, was active in the 1945 Pan-African Congress; attending it were black Red Cross nurses from the US forces. By 1950 most cities in Britain had seen black medical personnel—Robert Wellesley Cole in Newcastle, Edric Donaldson in Hale, Easmon in Huntingdon, an alleged abortionist from Trinidad in Brighton. Identification has been difficult without veterans' assistance.

African names included Thomas Lambo from Nigeria, who pioneered psychiatric medicine in Lagos, then headed the university at Ibadan, and Geoffrey Dove, who worked in Africa before settling in London. Hastings Banda became the President of Malawi after decades of work in London. The British-born children of doctor settlers who followed their father's profession included Brown's son Leslie, the Goffes of Jamaica, and the Barbadian Colin Franklin's daughter.

There were opticians, surgeons, nurses, and, as the *National Health Service replaced charity, municipal, and private medical services, cleaners, catering staff, drivers, and administrators.

'My patients need a doctor; they seldom see my colour' was one recollection of the 1980s. The black contribution to British medicine has not been fully described, but it is clear that many of these men and women were remarkable people. JPG

Patton, Adell, *Physicians, Colonial Racism, and Diaspora in West Africa* (1996)

See also DOCTORS

Memoirs and Opinions of Mr. Blenfield. An anonymous novel published in 1790 expressing anti-slavery sentiments. The narrator, the Mr Blenfield of the title, is a young man from a wealthy and genteel background who describes how he meets and is impressed by various young ladies, and eventually marries one of them. At the same time he offers the reader his views on a very miscellaneous range of subjects. The novel is not remarkable for strength of either characterization or plot. However, one of Mr Blenfield's friends is 'Shirna Cambo, by birth an African', who is recognizably based on Ignatius *Sancho, and described in a very favourable manner: 'his philanthropy and integrity were the examples and admiration of his neighbourhood; sensibility was a distinguished feature of his character; his imagination was pure, but unlimited; his conceptions nervous; and his conversation animated and engaging.' He is credited with making Mr Blenfield an opponent of slavery, but this is not a major theme of the novel, although, in an unrelated incident, there is a short description of a visit by two of the other characters to Jamaica, and some reflections on the cruelty of slave owners. While Cambo plays only a relatively minor part in this indifferent novel, he is perhaps the first realistic black British person to feature as a character in prose fiction, as distinct from purely background figures such as the two black servants who play the French horn in Tobias Smollett's novel *Humphry Clinker* (1771), or 'noble savages' like *Oroonoko. Particularly noticeable is the fact that Cambo's presence in the genteel circles in which Mr Blenfield moves is felt by the author to require no explanation—the black British friend is simply a fact of life. JG

Memoirs and Opinions of Mr. Blenfield (2 vols., 1790)

See also LITERATURE 1: REPRESENTATIONS OF BLACKS

Memorial Gates. Monument marking the contributions of Africans, Indians, and Caribbeans to British efforts in the two world wars (contributions 'nothing short of a miracle', in the words of Winston Churchill), inaugurated on 8 November 2002 on Constitution Hill, near Hyde Park Corner in London. The home countries of colonial servicemen are carved, and where they fought, with the motto 'When you go home, tell them of us, and say: For your tomorrow we gave our today'.

Baroness Flather of Windsor and Maidenhead in the Royal County of Berkshire, a British Indian Conservative life peer in the Lords, spearheaded the parliamentary campaign to fund and erect the monument. Her grandfather had served during both wars, along with 1.5 million and 2.5 million other Indians respectively.

In the First World War 15,600 Blacks served in the British West India Regiment, a third from Jamaica; they were segregated from white West Indians in the Merchants and Planters Contingent. In the Second World War 16,000 served as army volunteers, and there was a significant West Indian presence in the Royal Air Force and the Royal Navy.

During the First World War 55,000 Africans were deployed to capture the German colonies of Togo, Cameroon, Namibia, and German East Africa. During the Second World War 375,000 Africans were used when both the Royal West Africa Frontier Force and, from East Africa, the King's African Rifles fought in North Africa, Italy, and the Middle East. The 81st and 82nd West Africa divisions of the 14th Army, composed of troops from the Gambia, Nigeria, Sierra Leone, and Ghana, fought the Japanese in Burma. JM

Smith, Richard, *Jamaican Volunteers in the First World War: Race, Masculinity and the Development of National Consciousness* (2004)

Somerville, Christopher, *Our War: How the British Commonwealth Fought the Second World War* (1998)

See also FIRST WORLD WAR; SECOND WORLD WAR

Mental health. The provision of mental health services to black people in Britain has been a major concern among both the black community and mental health professionals.

1. Introduction
2. Mental health and the African-Caribbean experience in Britain
3. The media
4. The criminal justice system
5. Diagnosis and assessment of mental ill health
6. Treatment services

1. Introduction A growing body of research supports anecdotal evidence that black people are over-represented in psychiatric institutions. A study in south *London found that black populations had a rate of admission to medium-secure mental health institutions seven times higher than their white counterparts: 28 as compared to 4 per 100,000 population for white people. Research by Deryck Browne carried out at two psychiatric hospitals found that black people were over-represented among compulsorily detained patients compared with their numbers in the local population. Of the 224 patients admitted to one hospital, 106 (51 per cent) were black, 16 (8 per cent) Asian, and 86 (41 per cent) white. Census data from 1991 showed that 71 per cent of the population of the area studied was white (including the 5.2 per cent who were Irish), 17.2 per cent black, and 9.2 per cent Asian;

2.7 per cent classified themselves as 'other'.

More than any other minority group, black people are more likely to be diagnosed with schizophrenia; more likely to be treated with higher dosages of medication; and more likely (together with Irish-born people) to be detained in locked psychiatric wards. One explanation of this pattern is that the *racism and disadvantage experienced by black people has a deleterious impact on their mental health. A second explanation rests on institutional racism of the mental health system together with a lack of understanding of cultural differences. Moreover, studies suggest that the quality of aftercare provision for black mental health service users is poorer than that offered to their white counterparts.

2. Mental health and the African-Caribbean experience in Britain Frantz Fanon, the renowned black psychiatrist, argued that 'the psychological effect of colonialism is one of the enduring disabling legacies bequeathed to "natives" by their colonial masters'. Fanon's belief was that black people's experiences in the modern world cannot be separated from their histories as colonial subjects. The colonial relationship between Britain and the Caribbean fundamentally shaped the beliefs and behaviours of African-Caribbean people, and contributed to feelings of inferiority that are difficult to 'throw off' living in the 'mother country'. Hence, not only do black immigrants to Britain experience culture shock, alienation, and racism, but they may also be subject to unmet social and cultural needs, thereby increasing the likelihood of mental distress. Moreover, gender functions as a key determinant of the quality of mental health care offered and experienced. Gender stereotyping serves to produce qualitatively different experiences for black male and female users of mental health services. Black women face sexism and class disadvantage, factors aggravated by the negative racial stereotypings of black women by health professionals as difficult and aggressive, or alternatively as strong and able to withstand trauma and stress. A report by Cochrane found that African-Caribbean men have 4.3 times, and women 3.9 times, the rate for white people for first admission with a diagnosis of schizophrenia. The psychiatrist Suman Fernando argued in 1991 that young African-Caribbean men were up to ten times more likely to be given this diagnosis than their white counterparts. In a study by Wilson and Francis of over 100 African-Caribbean and African users of mental health services in Britain, it was found that almost half had been given a diagnosis of schizophrenia.

Age represents another crucial factor influencing the response of mental health professionals to black service users. Research has shown that black people who migrated to Britain in the 1950s and 1960s are now, as elderly people, often suffering from isolation and comparatively poor health. As an example, many elderly black people are misdiagnosed as suffering from Alzheimer's disease because it is often not recognized that diagnostic tests are culture-specific and therefore are not appropriate to all cultures. Other issues relate to reversion to a first language as dementia develops. Many elderly black people face a deterioration in physical and mental health with the prospect of lower standards of care than that available to elderly Whites.

3. The media Race and mental health are controversial issues that have become closely intertwined in recent years. The two issues combined contain extremely negative connotations in the public imagination, fuelled by a mass media that often exploits the image of 'black and dangerous'. As a result Francis argued that in the late 20th century 'madness has become synonymous with blackness'. Nazroo's 1997 survey of black patients' views found that 26 per cent of respondents felt that the media bore some responsibility for the discrimination they experience. A further 17 per cent cited public fears about black people as a cause of discrimination. In 1998 Sarah Neal analysed media coverage of the murder in 1992 of Jonathan Zito, a white man, by Christopher Clunis, a black mental health patient. Neal showed how the victim was largely ignored by the media, which instead focused attention on his widow, Jayne Zito. In article after article photographs of Jayne Zito were juxtaposed with those of Christopher Clunis to highlight the contrast between Mrs Zito, frequently described as 'blonde and tanned', 'courageous', and 'beautiful', and Clunis as 'knifeman' and 'deranged killer'.

4. **The criminal justice system** Section 136 of the 1983 Mental Health Act allows the police to detain anyone appearing to be mentally ill and take them to a 'place of safety', generally a psychiatric hospital. Sixty per cent of black people enter psychiatric hospitals via Section 136 compared to 10–15 per cent generally. However, following Christopher Clunis's conviction for the murder of Jonathan Zito, a public inquiry into the quality of care offered to Clunis equivocated over the issue of whether there had been any racial discrimination in his diagnosis and treatment. The inquiry found evidence of a lack of continuity of care and poor coordination between the various agencies involved, but also concluded that there was evidence that some professionals were reluctant to diagnose schizophrenia or to label Clunis as violent or dangerous. Instead he was regularly misdiagnosed as having drug-induced psychosis, itself a racially stereotyped diagnosis for a young black man. No attempt was made to involve his family or his general practitioner in his care, indicative of an assumption that he would not have a support network. The reluctance to label Clunis as a paranoid schizophrenic can be interpreted as ill-conceived anti-racist practice, for he clearly did have a severe mental illness requiring high standards of diagnosis and care.

The inquiry into Christopher Clunis's contact with mental health services revealed that in 1989, when the police attempted to remove him from a hostel from which he had been evicted, officers were reluctant to arrest him, or to use their powers under Section 136, despite evidence that he had threatened them with a knife. The police response to Roger Sylvester ten years later was very different. Sylvester was a 30-year-old black man who worked at a mental health drop-in centre. He had suffered from depression but had been well for two years when, on 11 January 1999, police were called to his home, where they found him naked in his own front garden. He was wrestled to the ground by eight officers, restrained, and handcuffed.

Sylvester was detained under Section 136 and taken to hospital 'for his own safety'. Officers continued to restrain him en route to the hospital and during medical examination. He then collapsed and was in a coma until his life support machine was switched off a week later. Police officers initially confirmed that Sylvester had not been at all violent or threatening, but after his death the investigation focused on his mental health history rather than on the actions of the police officers involved in his death. The psychiatrist Dr Aggrey Burke, a specialist in deprivation and mental illness in ethnic-minority families, has said psychiatrists pigeonhole black people as difficult and therefore in need of restraint not healing.

5. **Diagnosis and assessment of mental ill health** Behaviour that may be considered 'mad' in one culture may not considered the same way in another society. There is evidence that many mental health professionals lack the awareness of cultural values and norms necessary to discharge their duties effectively when dealing with black people. Recent research suggests that although more black Caribbean people are treated for psychosis, this may not indicate that they are more likely to have such illness. Rather, it could be that the manner in which they express their symptoms is interpreted in such a way that they are more likely than others to

be prescribed treatment for these symptoms. It is this failure to incorporate an understanding of the significance of race and culture into a systematic professional response that makes the diagnosis of black mental ill health unreliable and highly stressful.

6. Treatment services Poor experiences of mental health services have resulted in many black service users exhibiting suspicion, mistrust, and antipathy towards psychiatric health services. Some studies have indicated that black communities receive an inferior or discriminatory service where stereotyping is common. The Mental Health Act Commission in its fourth Biennial Report commented on the fact 'that many professionals seemed to lack basic knowledge about the different needs of minority ethnic communities and have little real understanding of institutional racism and the effect of cultural differences on the nature of mental disorder'. There are also indications that service users, as well as carers and workers in mental health from the black community, believe that institutional racism is endemic and remains a key barrier to progress.

Despite the over-representation of black people in the mental health system, a recent study found that people of Caribbean origin with psychosis spend more time in remission and are less likely to have a continuous psychotic illness in the early course of their illness than their white peers. Allegations have often been made of the overuse of cheaper coercive treatments such as electro-convulsive therapy and drugs, especially major tranquillizers, rather than more expensive non-physical, preventative treatments or counselling, psychotherapy, or group therapy. Moreover, most users are likely to receive medication as their main treatment.

Complementary and support services such as culturally sensitive counselling and self-help groups are provided by black-run organizations. The effectiveness of these agencies, many of them operating with few resources, has been highlighted and documented. They are largely responsible for innovative developments that more closely meet the mental health needs of black and other minority ethnic communities. While black people are over-represented in the mental health system, they are under-represented in the psychiatric profession. According to the Royal College of Psychiatrists, 24 per cent of its 9,000 members describe themselves as non-white. However, unofficial estimates indicate that there are fewer than a dozen African-Caribbean psychiatrists and around 50 who are African. The National Service Framework for Mental Health recognizes that having more black and minority ethnic individuals and organizations directly involved in the planning and delivery of mental health services would do much to eradicate institutional racism and poor standards of diagnosis and care for black service users. IJ/CJ

Browne, Deryck, *Black People and Sectioning* (1997)

Burke, Aggrey, interviewed by Sonia Goodchild, 'Blacks Failed by Our "Racist" System of Care for Mentally Ill', *Independent Digital*, 28 Sept. 2003

Cochrane, R., and Sashideran, S., *Mental Health and Ethnic Minorities. A Review of the Literature and Implications for Services*, Report available from Professor Cochrane, School of Psychology, University of Birmingham (n.d.)

Fanon, Frantz, *Black Skins, White Masks* (1967)

Fernando, Suman, *Black People and the Psychiatric System* (1989)

—— *Mental Health, Race and Culture* (1991)

—— Ndegwa, David and Wilson, Melba, *Forensic Psychiatry, Race and Culture* (1998)

Francis, E., 'Psychiatric Racism and Social Police: Black People and the Psychiatric Service' in W. Harris and C. James (eds.), *Inside Babylon: The Caribbean Diaspora in Britain* (1993)

Guite, H., *et al.*, 'Diversion from Courts and Prisons to Psychiatric Inpatient Care in a District', unpub. report, Department of Health and Epidemiology, King's College London (1996)

INQUEST, *Report on the Death in Police Custody of Roger Sylvester* (2000), <http://inquest.gn.apc.org/briefings/sylvester.html>

Nazroo, James, *Ethnicity and Mental Health: Findings from a National Community Survey* (1997)

—— and King, M., 'Psychosis: Symptoms and Estimated Rates' in K. Sproston and J. Nazroo (eds.), *Ethnic Minority Psychiatric Illness Rates in the Community (Empiric)* (2002)

Neal, Sarah, 'Embodying Black Madness, Embodying White Femininity: Populist (Re)Presentations and Public Policy—The Case of Christopher Clunis and Jayne Zito', *Sociological Research Online*, 3/4 (1998), <http://www.socresonline.org.uk/3/4/contents.html>

Wilson, M., and Francis, J., *Raised Voices* (1997)

See also CRIMINAL JUSTICE SYSTEM; DEATHS IN POLICE CUSTODY; MEDICINE; NATIONAL HEALTH SERVICE

Mercer, Mabel Alice (1900–1984). Legendary cabaret singer. Mercer was born in Staffordshire, the daughter of Mabel LaBlanche, a white English–Welsh music hall performer, and a black American jazz musician whom she never knew. After leaving convent school at the age of 14, she joined her aunt Rhoda King's vaudeville act, appearing also in several *minstrelsy shows, including all-black shows, such as *Spades and Diamonds*, *Colored Society*, and *The Chocolate Kiddies*. For a short time she also performed as a male impersonator, including one as an orchestra conductor.

Mercer and her aunt toured throughout Britain (in *London, in 1927, she won a small part in *Show Boat*, alongside the young Paul *Robeson), and, after the Armistice, travelled throughout Europe, including Belgium, where she saw her first black American band. It was in Paris, a mecca for black musicians and artistes, that she found her metier as a cabaret singer, and career success soon followed. By the 1930s she was the toast of Paris, and counted among her admirers luminaries such as Josephine Baker, the Prince of Wales, Ernest Hemingway, Gertrude Stein, F. Scott Fitzgerald, and Cole Porter.

With the outbreak of the *Second World War, the threat of Nazism forced Mercer to leave Paris, and she moved to America, where she performed at some of New York's finest venues, enjoying brilliant concert triumphs and record-breaking appearances across the United States.

Mercer returned to Britain in 1977, after an absence of 41 years. So great was the public acclaim on her return to London that the BBC filmed three evenings of extraordinary footage of her earlier performances, and later devoted an entire week to a series of late-night half-hour television broadcasts—an honour never before bestowed upon an entertainer. Throughout her illustrious career she was the recipient of many prestigious awards, prizes, and honorary doctorates. In 1983, at a White House ceremony, President Ronald Reagan presented her with the Presidential Medal of Freedom, America's highest civilian honour. Her original recordings and numerous reissues are, today, highly prized collector's items. CJ

Cheney, Margaret, *Midnight at Mabel's* (2000)

Haskins, James, *Mabel Mercer* (2000)

See also MUSIC 2: EARLY POPULAR MUSIC

Merriman-Labor, Augustus (*c.*1870s–1920s). Sierra Leonean journalist and novelist born in Freetown, where he was employed in the Colonial Secretary's office. During the Hut Tax rebellion in 1898 he wrote, and had published in Liverpool, an anonymous pamphlet, *The Last Military Expedition in Sierra Leone*. This claimed to have been written by an Englishman twenty years in Africa. Merriman-Labor also wrote the *Handbooks of Sierra Leone*, which went into two editions in 1901–2 and 1904–5. In 1904 he came to Britain with the hope that he might be the 'Mark Twain of West Africa'. He found work as a clerk, taught Sunday school at the Railway Orphanage in south London, and eventually studied law at Lincoln's Inn. In 1907 Merriman-Labor, with other Blacks, formed a committee to commemorate the anniversary of the abolition of the slave trade, and they laid wreaths on abolitionists' memorials in Westminster Abbey. His novel *Britons Through Negro Spectacles* was published in London in 1909. This had first been serialized in a Freetown newspaper, and aimed to dispel the inflated and romantic ideas that his fellow Creoles had of Britain. He commented on abuse and insults hurled at him in the street, the racial discrimination practised by some landladies, and sensational and distorted reporting in newspapers. He was still in London in 1913 as he attended the Conference for Africans, but thereafter nothing is known of his life. DK

Green, Jeffrey, *Black Edwardians: Black People in Britain 1901–1914* (1998)
Jones, Eldred, 'Turning Back the Pages (No. 1)', *Bulletin of the Association for African Literature in English*, 2 (1965)

See also LITERATURE 2: FICTION AND POETRY; PUBLISHING

Michael X. Adopted name of Michael de Freitas (1933–1975), black revolutionary and civil rights activist in London. Michael X was born in Trinidad to a Portuguese father and Barbadian mother. He immigrated to London in 1957 and lived in the Notting Hill area. Before converting to Islam, Michael X, who was also known by the name of Michael Abdul Malik, was a pimp and a hustler, similar to his idol *Malcolm X. He founded the Racial Adjustment Action Society and in 1967 became the first person to be imprisoned under England's Race Relations Act. Michael X's impulsive nature resulted in several convictions, among them an eighteen-month jail sentence for advocating the shooting of black women who were seen in the company of white men. He argued for the congregation of Blacks in social communes. In 1969 he was given money to start a commune in Islington but it did not succeed. He became the self-appointed leader of a Black Power commune in north London and later, in 1971, when he and four others were charged with extortion, he started an agricultural commune in Trinidad, which stressed black resurgence. In 1975 he was convicted of the murder of Joseph Skerrit, a member of the Black Liberation Army, because he refused to attack a local police station. He was hanged in the Royal Gaol, Port of Spain, Trinidad. Michael X also managed to write a book entitled *From Michael de Freitas to Michael X* (1968) under the name of Michael Abdul Malik. His life story is also the basis of V. S. Naipaul's long essay *The Return of Eva Peron with The Killings in Trinidad* (1980). DD/SS

Humphry, Derek, *False Messiah: The Story of Michael X* (1977)
Malik, Michael Abdul, *From Michael de Freitas to Michael X* (1968)

See also BLACK PANTHER PARTY; POLITICS

Middleton, Charles (1726–1813). First Baron Barham, British naval administrator, and politician active in the campaign to abolish slavery. Middleton entered the Royal Navy in 1741, passing his lieutenant's examination in 1745. He was appointed to the illustrious position of Comptroller of the Navy in 1778, despite a lack of experience of naval administration. He proved to be adept at his role, creating numerous structural and administrative reforms to increase the efficiency of the Navy, for example, the introduction of lemon juice into navy victuals to prevent scurvy, and the introduction of the carronade cannon. His attention to strategic details at ship level contributed significantly to the victory at Trafalgar. His achievements as naval Comptroller were publicly recognized when he was created a baronet in 1781. Middleton and his wife held profoundly evangelical Anglican beliefs. During the 1780s, and through the influence of the clergyman James *Ramsay, a former navy surgeon, the Middletons assumed a position of leadership in the abolitionist movement, recruiting, bringing together, and encouraging the campaign's leading adherents, including Thomas *Clarkson and William *Wilberforce. His home, Barham Court, served as the pre-eminent centre of the crusade against the slave trade. In 1784 he was elected MP for Rochester. In 1790 he served alongside Wilberforce on the Committee of the Whole House to Consider Further of the Circumstances of the Slave Trade. In 1805 he was rewarded with a peerage, becoming Baron Barham of Teston. NAA

Carey, Brycchan, *British Abolitionism and the Rhetoric of Sensibility: Writing, Sentiment and Slavery, 1760–1807* (2005)
ODNB

See also ABOLITION; CHRISTIANITY

Miller, William (1890–1970). Labour activist and Plymouth city councillor, among those early black representatives elected to local government bodies in England. The son of a Sierra Leonean father and a white British mother, Miller was born in Stonehouse, Devon. He attended local schools, worked in the building industry, and during the *First World War served in the Royal Flying Corps. Working as an electrician in Devonport dockyard, he was an active trade unionist and also a member of the Labour Party. In 1925 he was elected to Plymouth City Council, a position in which he served with various interruptions for most of his life. In 1938, concerned about the safety of people in the city in event of war, Miller became a civil defence warden. When the city was heavily bombed in 1941, he unofficially organized the evacuation of many women and children. For this he was arrested and reprimanded. However, vindication came within a few days when the government ordered just such an evacuation. In the Labour electoral victories of 1945 Miller was returned to the City Council, now under Labour control, and, as chairman of the Housing Committee (1945–50, 1953–9), oversaw the post-war rebuilding and planning of Plymouth. His vision was not only for new houses but for new communities that would help to mould the lives of future citizens. Miller gained a national reputation for his leadership in civic *housing. He became Deputy Lord Mayor of Plymouth in 1962. His son Claude (b. 1915) was also a member of the City Council, becoming Lord Mayor in 2004. DK

Wood, Jonathan, *Bill Miller, Black Labour Party Activist in Plymouth* (2006)

See also POLITICS

Milliard, Peter (1882–*c*.1953). Pan-Africanist campaigner born in the colony of British Guiana and educated at Queen's College, Georgetown. He graduated from the medical school of Howard University, Washington DC, in 1910, and then went to work in the Panama Canal Zone. Shortly after the First World War, he came to Britain and secured a medical qualification from the University of Edinburgh in 1923. Milliard settled in Manchester in the early 1930s, practised as a doctor, and also began to promote the interests and welfare of the small black population of the city. In 1935 he helped to found the International African Friends of Abyssinia and spoke at open-air meetings, where he denounced the Italian invasion of *Ethiopia and colonial policies. In 1943 Milliard founded the Negro Association, which held monthly meetings. Its membership, which rarely exceeded 80 people during the next ten years, was composed of students, black service personnel, and people from the local black communities; Jomo Kenyatta was briefly a member while living in Manchester in 1945. In 1944 Milliard took the initiative in promoting a Pan-African united front movement by bringing together many of the separate black organizations to form the loosely organized Pan-African Federation, of which he was the first president. As such he played a central role in bringing about the fifth Pan-African Congress held in Manchester in 1945. George *Padmore, who knew Milliard well, wrote that he was 'a man of considerable charm and striking presence . . . widely read . . . a passionate internationalist . . . a life-long democrat and socialist' who 'served human beings regardless of race or colour as best he could'. DK

Adi, Hakim, and Sherwood, Marika (eds.), *The 1945 Manchester Pan-African Congress Revisited* (1995)

Padmore, George, *Pan-Africanism or Communism?* (1956)

See also DOCTORS; MEDICINE; POLITICS

Minstrelsy. Musical and humorous entertainment style popular from about 1850 to 1970. The entertainers blacked up, a grotesque parody of black Americans in the Southern slave states. When African-descent entertainers participated, they too wore burnt-cork make-up. Minstrel shows were musical, vibrant, amusing, and capable of swiftly adapting to new circumstances.

Most societies have entertainers who use masks and gaudy clothes, speak with false accents, dance in exaggerated ways, and play musical instruments with visible enthusiasm. The minstrel show did all these. A minstrel show was a self-contained entertainment.

Minstrelsy originated in the United States, where it once showed both the evils of slavery and the allegedly happy plantation slave. The best-selling anti-slavery novel *Uncle Tom's Cabin* added dramatic elements; then Negro spirituals, brought to England by the *Fisk Jubilee Singers from 1871, added songs including 'Go Down, Moses' and 'Steal Away to Jesus'. Costumes ranged from ragged hand-me-downs to primary-coloured broad-striped fashions, dinner jackets, and the 18th-century styles favoured by 'court minstrels'.

Minstrelsy encouraged audience interaction. Opening with the entire company in a semicircle, with individual acts including dialect songs and dances, the cast would join in the chorus. In the centre was the pompous interlocutor, or master of ceremonies, personifying dignity. The endmen had comic roles, making jokes often about the interlocutor. The audience joined in their mockery. With malapropisms and vulgar dialect the endmen—Brudder Tambo and Brudder Bones—were in turn mocked by the interlocutor. He directed the action on stage, swiftly responding to the audience: another reason why minstrel shows were very successful.

The show would include handsome tenors singing emotional songs. This sharply contrasted to Tambo and Bones, who made puns, contorted their bodies, and wore the most flamboyant costumes. The second act could include a range of entertainers, providing time for the closing act's set to be put up behind the curtains. Almost any style of act might be seen, but the main attraction was a stump speech. An ill-educated, verbose, overserious speaker would include the latest political and local news in this act, which usually ended when he fell off his soapbox. Local dignitaries and leaders of society were parodied. This was the heritage of the jester.

The age of minstrelsy was in an era when music publishing, the manufacture of inexpensive musical instruments, and easy movement afforded by railways led to composers and performers of popular melodies achieving fame and fortune. Minstrel shows led to so-called dialect songs reaching most parts of Britain. Audiences enjoyed minstrels' singing of 'Away Down in de Kentuck [Kentucky] Brake', 'Dixie', and 'Dar Is a Place Call'd Loozyann [Louisiana]'. The sentimental sighed when they heard 'Old Mass Was de Best ob [*sic*] Men'.

Men and women purchased banjos—and mandolins and guitars—and played the songs at home. Groups played together; singers performed to the piano in domestic music-making. Amateur groups were widespread: the squire's in rural Oxfordshire in the 1880s is recalled in Flora Thompson's *Lark Rise to Candleford* memoirs.

Professional groups reached every urban centre of Britain. Several groups named the Christy Minstrels, notably that run by George 'Pony' Moore, had continuing success. St James Hall in Piccadilly, London, a 550-seat basement beneath a grander hall, became the centre for minstrel shows until it was demolished in 1904. The Moore Minstrels set the standard for four decades.

Although Tambo and Bones and the interlocutor retained vital roles, the scope had widened. Though plantation and Southern state theme songs remained, there were Irish songs, comic songs, and dramatic ballads, sometimes presented by operatic singers.

Following emancipation in the United States many black Americans played in Britain. Sam Hague publicized his Georgia Minstrel Troupe of 26 freed slaves, whose tour opened in Liverpool in July 1866. In time experienced white performers replaced many of them. Aaron Banks was the longest-surviving original member working in Britain.

Other black American minstrels in Britain included the composer James Bland ('Carry Me Back to Old Virginny', 'Oh dem Golden Slippers') and the comedian Billy Kersands. By 1903, when Bert Williams was starring in *In Dahomey* in London (his acting impressed the dramatist George Bernard Shaw), with burnt cork and exaggerated white lips, he had attained black support in America for his amusing dialect talk. Normally he spoke standard American (he had been brought up in California). English comments on *In Dahomey* noted problems with the accents, nevertheless. The cardsharp, the pompous speechmaker, the enthusiastic dancers, and the humour made *In Dahomey* a semi-minstrel show on the West End stage.

Theatres and halls lost their monopoly as the cinema gained popularity, but minstrels (and genuine Blacks) continued to entertain at seaside resorts in the summer, the burnt cork often the sole survivor of the tradition. When Ken *Johnson's West Indian dance orchestra was playing in an exclusive West End club around 1938, a customer was heard to ask the debonair leader (a Guyanese doctor's son) if he played the bones, such was the legacy of minstrelsy.

Minstrelsy's success was due to its being a family show, with choral and solo singing, instrumental selections, humour, topicality, sentimentality, and joy. African-descent performers were often first-class, as with the Bohee Brothers, Canada-born banjoists. Will Garland, an American based in London, kept minstrel elements in his black shows into the 1930s.

Burnt cork was just one of minstrelsy's negative images of Blacks. The entry of a watermelon cart would lead to the entire cast breaking away to munch the sweet fruit; scenes set in a bar would involve poker players cheating, and threatening each other with razors. The cast would stop to dance at the slightest opportunity.

When *The Black and White Minstrel Show* appeared on British television in the 1960s, many welcomed it, but protests eventually led to its being terminated in 1978. An era was over. JPG

Nathan, Hans, *Dan Emmett and the Rise of Early Negro Minstrelsy* (1962)

Reynolds, Harry, *Minstrel Memories: The Story of Burnt Cork Minstrelsy in Great Britain from 1836 to 1927* (1928)

Toll, Robert, *Blacking Up: The Minstrel Show in Nineteenth-Century America* (1974)

See also BLACK DANCE; MUSIC 2: EARLY POPULAR MUSIC

Miscegenation. Term used to refer to sexual relations between different races resulting in 'mixed' offspring. It comes from the combination of two Latin words: *miscere* (to mix) and *genus* (race). Across the centuries miscegenation has been the subject of heated discourse and debates about the desirability, or otherwise, of cross-racial sexual unions, especially when referring to sexual relationships between peoples of black African and white European descent.

1. Britain and miscegenation
2. The legal apparatus and miscegenation in the United States

1. Britain and miscegenation The belief among 18th-century racial theorists of the existence of discrete and biologically distinctive races led them to the conclusion that the progeny of sexual unions between black and white people would be sterile. The term 'mulatto' originates from this belief, deriving as it does from 'mule', the hybrid infertile offspring of a donkey and a horse. Theorists of white racial superiority therefore opposed cross-racial sexual unions, fearing that such relations would ultimately lead to the degeneracy of the superior white race. Many staunchly argued that the consequence of miscegenation would be the descent of society into a 'raceless' chaos and disorder. Among such theorists was Edward *Long, a Jamaican historian and planter, who articulated his horrific distaste of 'race-mixing' in his three-volume *History of Jamaica* (1774). Long especially vilified 'the lower class of [white] women'—a group always morally and sexually suspect within elite white English imaginations—for their fondness for 'lascivious' black males, fearing that the offspring of sexual unions between these two categories of people would eventually contaminate the white society. Undoubtedly, much of the unease about white female transgression was rooted in anxieties about the possibilities of sexual relations between poor white women and black men, and the consequences that interracial unions posed for white racial purity and superiority. Moreover, anxiety over interracial sex was directed not towards the sexual behaviour of white men, but towards the sexual freedom of white women.

Disputes over whether humans developed from one species (monogenesis) or many (polygenesis) are key to the analysis of the development of race theories in the 19th century. Notions of hybridity and miscegenation are important because they form part of 19th-century anthropologists' and scientists' understanding of human difference. It was believed by many that interracial relationships would lead to the social, moral, and physiological decay of whiteness and of society.

Unlike the United States, Britain has never enacted anti-miscegenation laws, though during the first two decades of the 20th century the presence of black seamen in British ports and their sexual relationships with white women represented serious cause for concern among many quarters. After the First World War significant numbers of black sailors in *Liverpool, in the north-west of England, were subjected to racist attacks, as opposition to their relationships with white women grew. Newspaper articles of the time reported that, although it had to be admitted that some black men were good husbands to their white wives, these relationships were viewed with aversion by most white people.

Black people were not the sole targets of this kind of scrutiny: sometimes Jewish, Maltese, and Chinese people were regarded in a similar manner. For example, in the 1920s the Eugenics Society supported an investigation into interracial sexual relations in Liverpool that focused on children born to parents of Chinese and English origins.

In 1927 the Chief Constable of Cardiff, James Wilson, argued for legislation to prohibit interracial sexual intercourse similar to the recently enacted Immorality Act in South Africa. In 1929 the *Daily Herald*, using the language of *eugenics, reported that 'hundreds of half-caste children with vicious tendencies' were growing up in Cardiff as a result of 'black men mating with white women', while numerous 'dockland cafes run by coloured men of a debased and degenerate type are rendezvous for immoral purposes'.

During the Second World War the presence of thousands of African-American soldiers precipitated further anxieties about miscegenation in Britain. Regional police headquarters were asked to monitor the troops' behaviour. Although US Amy troops were meant to be policed by their own personnel, in the areas where black soldiers were concentrated, local police were required to make reports to Home Intelligence, the Foreign Office's North American Department, and the Ministry of Information about their sexual activities.

The need to monitor and control sexual relations between black men and white women was foregrounded again in the 1950s as more migrants from the Caribbean and Africa settled in Britain. Much of the anthropological and sociological scholarship about black migrants from the late 1940s contained at least one section dealing with the controversial issue of interracial sexual relationships.

Official and unofficial scrutiny of the sexual activities of black men in particular has been a consistent feature of reactions to the presence of black people of African descent in Britain. A glimpse of the intensity of feeling on the subject is illustrated by the experience of the Revd Clifford Hill, who carried out a poll among Whites in north London, asking 'Would you approve of your sister or your daughter marrying a coloured man?' Of those who responded 91 per cent replied that they would not approve. The Revd Hill had appeared on a radio programme and had himself been posed this question regarding his own daughter. Hill's response that he would have no objections to such a marriage earned him many threats to his life, a burning cross in his front garden, and numerous abusive letters from Britain and overseas. It was this sordid experience that prompted him to conduct his extensive sociological survey.

In spite of its earlier history, continued racism, and racially motivated attacks, Britain nevertheless has one of the highest rates of interracial marriages globally. The number of dual-heritage or mixed-raced people in Britain grew by more than 75 per cent during the 1990s to around 415,000, representing 10 per cent of the total population of ethnic minorities.

2. The legal apparatus and miscegenation in the United States Laws prohibiting interracial sexual relations were enacted in the United States as early as 1661, although the term 'miscegenation' was not used until 1864. In that year the Democratic Party newspaper the *New York Globe* published a pamphlet intended to bring into disrepute the Lincoln administration and the abolitionist movement. The pamphlet, entitled *Miscegenation: The Theory of the Blending of the Races, Applied to the American White Man and Negro*, claimed that the Republican Party wanted Americans of European and African descent to produce children together until the races were indistinguishable from each other. In the context of a divided society still caught in a civil war, fought—to some extent—for the emancipation of enslaved African-Americans, this was an inflammatory statement to those opposed to black freedom.

In reality, opponents of interracial unions need not have worried, for there was already in place a vigorous legal framework—supported by moral and social proscriptions—to discourage sexual relationships between black men and white women. This body of legislation pre-dated the Lincoln administration by centuries. For example, as early as 1662 Virginian legislators, concerned by increasing social problems arising from troubling levels of fornication, illegitimate births, and illicit sex, took the decisive lead in enacting statutes that explicitly prohibited and criminalized marriages between Whites and Blacks. In 1691 Virginia reinforced the undesirability of interracial sexual unions by requiring that white women who gave birth to bi-racial children either had to pay a fine or had to become an indentured servant for five years. The children of such women who transgressed racial–sexual boundaries would also face 30 years in this condition of servitude.

Scholars have suggested that New World slavery was as much a system of sexual control as it was a system of economic exploitation of Africans. The ruling-class white male plantocracy insisted on the rights to regulate and control the sexual freedoms of every individual enmeshed within the social relations of slavery. Though prohibiting by custom, taboo, and law sexual relations between white women and black men, they nevertheless insisted on retaining unrestricted rights to access the bodies of black women. By the 18th century many colonial societies witnessed the emergence of a community of 'coloured' or bi-racial people, many of whom were the consequences of white male rape of enslaved black women.

That white males could freely access black women's bodies without fear of punishment or racial contamination was facilitated by a matrilineal inheritance principle that tied the legal status of children to the legal identity of their mother. Hence, white males could freely sexually abuse and exploit enslaved women in the knowledge that any children born to the woman would also inherit its mother's status, incidentally adding to the plantation's enslaved population. On virtually every plantation could be found numbers of children of mixed parentage. At the start of the American Civil War the 1860 federal census classified over half a million persons as 'mulattos'. For children who were very light-skinned there was the option of disguising their racial identity and 'passing' as a white person. Some white fathers accepted limited responsibility for their bi-racial children, but the majority of such children born to enslaved women were treated like other slaves, although there is evidence to suggest that lighter-skinned slaves were more likely to be within the plantation household than in the more physically arduous field work.

Between 1850 and 1860 the notion of 'hypodescent', the practice of determining the lineage of a child of mixed-race ancestry by assigning the child the race of his or her more socially subordinate parent, gained ascendancy within American society. This principle helped to sustain the racial hierarchy by ensuring that bi-racial children and their descendants would remain enslaved. In its most extreme form, hypodescent came to be a 'one-drop rule', meaning that an individual having one drop of black blood was considered to be black. An example was Virginia's 1924 Act for the 'Preservation of Racial Integrity', which defined as white a person with 'no trace whatsoever of any blood other than Caucasian'. To a large extent, the principle of hypodescent undermined the formation of people of mixed race as distinctive ethnic groups. The varying terms used to indicate the proportion of African to European heritage—most notably, 'mulatto', 'quadroon', 'octoroon'—became for the most part meaningless when anyone with a black ancestor, no matter how far distant, was now defined as black.

The term 'mulatto' is still used in some places today, although it is considered offensive by many, owing to its associations with animal husbandry. Usage of 'half-caste' has also fallen into disrepute over the years. Today, if it is thought appropriate to identify an individual with a diverse racial heritage, the terms most frequently used are 'dual heritage', 'bi-racial', or 'mixed-race'. Each of these terms is predicated on the presence of immutable differences between national and ethnic groups and is thus a part of 'race discourse'.

During the 1860s the stereotype of black men's unbounded sexual appetites for white women was prevalent, and interracial sexual relations were demonized by white Americans. Draconian laws were introduced that automatically voided all marriages between black and white people. If a couple left their home state and married, then sought to return, they could still be prosecuted and subject to stiff penalties, including imprisonment.

Until the 1950s almost half of the states in the United States had anti-miscegenation laws. For instance, only a day after the Supreme Court unanimously outlawed legally imposed racial segregation in public schools in *Brown* v. *Board of Education* on 17 May 1954, the *Jackson Daily News* in Mississippi—the state that would soon be referred to as the South's 'citadel' of racial segregation, oppression, and injustice—editorialized: 'White and Negro children in the same school will lead to miscegenation. Miscegenation leads to mixed marriages and mixed marriages lead to mongrelization of the human race.' Anti-miscegenation laws covered Asians and Native Americans as well as people of African descent. The 1967 case of *Loving* v. *Commonwealth of Virginia* produced a landmark ruling. Perry Loving, a white man, and his African-American–Native American wife, Mildred Jeter, married in Washington DC as the law forbade such marriages in their home state, Virginia. The couple returned to Virginia and were promptly jailed. Eventually such laws were deemed contrary to citizens' rights under the American Constitution, though it was not until the 1998 mid-term election year that South Carolina voters finally did away with their 1895 constitutional prohibition of 'marriage of a white person with a Negro or mulatto or a person who shall have one-eighth or more of Negro blood'.

The United States was not alone in having anti-miscegenation laws or prohibitions. Apartheid South Africa's Immorality Act of 1949 banned mixed marriages and, a year later, prohibited all sexual relations between Blacks and Whites. These Acts created offences analogous to those under Virginia's Racial Integrity Act (1924). A central tenet of apartheid rule in South Africa was that sexual relations between the statutorily designated racial groups were undesirable. Marriage between 'races' was therefore forbidden as miscegenation was seen as a threat to the racial integrity and superiority of the white race, on which apartheid South Africa was based.

In Australia a different approach to the problem of miscegenation was pursued. Marriage between Aborigines and white Australians was discouraged, but during the late 1920s and early 1930s there was mounting concern about the numbers of Aboriginal people with white antecedents. As a result, a number of government officials with eugenicist leanings took the view that women of dual heritage should marry white men. A Dr Cook was particularly enthusiastic about promoting this policy and is said to have brokered over 50 such relationships between women from the Darwin 'half-caste home' and European men during the 1930s. The intention was to 'breed out' the colour of Aboriginal people.

The language of miscegenation carries within it an acceptance of the concept of separate, biologically differentiated races. Although anti-miscegenation is most often associated with anti-black racism, many black people have themselves argued against interracial sexual relations. Marcus *Garvey and the Universal Negro Improvement Association were opposed to miscegenation and sought complete segregation from white people. Garvey and other anti-miscegenation Blacks opposed miscegenation on the grounds that it would eventually lead to 'racial suicide'. Yet, despite its opponents, and the sustained efforts by various governments to legislate against interracial sexual unions, such relationships have been, and continue to be, a fact of modernity, and, judging by the global increase in such marriages, look set to become commonplace in the future. LY

Brah, Avtar, and Coombes, Annie E. (eds.), *Hybridity and Its Discontents: Politics, Science, Culture* (2000)

Rich, Paul B., *Race and Empire in British Politics* (1986)

Young, Lola, *Fear of the Dark: 'Race', Gender and Sexuality in the Cinema* (1996)

Young, Robert, *Colonial Desire: Hybridity in Theory, Culture and Race* (1995)

See also MIXED-RACE IDENTITY, THEORIES OF; SKIN COLOUR AND RACE, THEORIES OF

Missionary societies. Christian missionary societies were founded in Europe, principally in Britain, Germany, and France, and also in North America, in the late 18th and early 19th centuries largely as a result of the Protestant evangelical revival. Protestant missions employed many lay people, whereas the Roman Catholic Church, which only later developed modern mission work, relied largely on ordained priests. Thus Protestant missions were first in the field, and among their mission workers and clergy were a good number of black people from the diaspora as well as African converts.

From the late 18th century onwards there was a strong idea among many black Christians in the diaspora that they should help to 'redeem their own people'. Some even argued that the slave trade, in bringing Africans to the Americas and to an awareness of Christianity, was of 'providential design' in order to bring about 'race redemption'. Thus black Christians attracted to overseas mission tended to look to Africa, and to some extent the Caribbean, as the logical fields for service. (There were a few exceptions, for instance, Jellorum Harrison, a West African from Sierra Leone who accompanied Henry Brunton to the north Caucasus, 1802–13.) Olaudah *Equiano, for example, unsuccessfully applied to the Bishop of London for ordination in 1779 so that he might go to Africa as a missionary, and this was nearly two decades before the first missionary societies were founded. Black churches in North America and the Caribbean from the 1820s onwards established their own missionary societies, and mission training colleges, that sent black workers to Africa. Thus black missionaries to Africa, and also the Caribbean, came from two sources: from the black diaspora in the Americas, and to a far lesser extent from Britain; and also from the small but strongly mission-orientated West African church formed from liberated slaves and new converts.

In the middle of the 19th century the idea of employing Africans as missionaries and catechists in Africa was promoted by

Henry Venn, the secretary of the Church Missionary Society (CMS), whose ambition was to develop an African-led church. The idea of the 'native agency', as it was called, was reinforced by the failure of the 1841 Niger expedition and the high white mortality rate. It was argued that black people had a higher resistance to African diseases, that culturally they were better suited to evangelize Africa, and that they were also cheaper to employ than white missionaries. Thomas *Buxton, the British abolitionist, argued for 'the deliverance of Africa by calling forth her own resources'. A number of Africans also saw missionary work throughout the continent as having a Pan-African purpose. James 'Holy' Johnson, from Sierra Leone, wrote to the CMS secretary in 1875 that 'he was following the fortunes of the [CMS] East African Mission with patriotic interest. I say "patriotic" because I feel that whatever concerns Africa, it matters not in whatever part of the vast Continent, concerns, or should concern, me.'

Until the 1840s only the CMS and the Wesleyan Methodists had institutions in Britain for the formal training of missionaries. Their colleges trained both white and black missionaries, many of the latter coming from West Africa but also from the Americas. Most of these black missionaries were then employed by white-controlled missions. The first Church of England college, founded in the early years of the 19th century, was the Church Missionary Society Training Institution in Islington, which Samuel *Crowther and other West Africans attended. Some years later, in 1845, St Augustine's College at Canterbury was opened to serve the more High Church part of the Church of England, training non-graduate clergy for the colonies of the British Empire. Lambert *Mackenzie from British Guiana studied there in 1853–5, the first black West Indian ordained as an Anglican. So also did Jeremiah, the son of the King of the Sotho, who died during his course in the 1860s; several other fellow South Africans who returned home to work for the Anglican Church in the Eastern Cape; and, in the 1880s, Cecil Majaliwa, from East Africa. Another Church of England institution was the Dorchester Missionary College, founded in 1878. John Cala Salfey from Ethiopia, who as a child was rescued from an Arab slave ship and brought to England, studied at Dorchester, was ordained, and went as a missionary priest to the diocese of Lebombo (modern Mozambique) in the 1890s, where he was involved in translation work.

Not all black missionaries went through a programme of formal training. Thomas Birch *Freeman satisfied the Methodist Conference that he was suitable for mission work in the Gold Coast at an interview and by preaching two 'trial' sermons. Alexander Crummell arrived to study at Cambridge in 1850, already an ordained minister of the American Episcopalian Church; after graduating he went out to Liberia as an Episcopal missionary. Tiyo *Soga studied at Glasgow University, and as the first South African ordained minister of the United Presbyterian Church returned to South Africa as a missionary clergyman in 1857. Dr Archibald Hewans, a Jamaican graduate of the Royal College of Surgeons, was employed at the Scottish mission in Calabar on the strength of his medical qualifications. And a black Scot, Thomas Jenkins, originally from West Africa, who was brought up in Hawick, studied at Edinburgh and went to Mauritius as a missionary teacher on behalf of the Society for Promoting Christian Knowledge.

In the early years of the 19th century the Methodists educated young West Africans at various schools in Britain in the hope that some would return home as Christian agents. From the 1840s Methodist clergy and missionaries, both white and black, were trained at colleges in Didsbury (Manchester) and Richmond, Surrey. Salim *Wilson, in the 1880s, went to the non-denominational Cliff Hulme College in Derbyshire, but then worked for the CMS. James *Newby studied at the Grattan Guinness's East London Institute for Home and Foreign Mission, and also worked for the CMS in West Africa. For the Baptists, Pastors' (later Spurgeon's)

College in London trained men for the Baptist home ministry and for overseas mission work with the Baptist Missionary Society (BMS). Thomas *Johnson and Calvin Richardson, both African-Americans, studied there and went as BMS missionaries to West Africa in the late 1870s, while a later graduate, William Forde from Barbados, served the Jamaican BMS for 50 years in Costa Rica. Many of these training institutions continued to function into the 20th century and to train black students from Africa and elsewhere for missionary work, as did Roman Catholic seminaries, but mainly to produce priests. One interdenominational, and mainly postgraduate, institution training missionaries today is All Nations Christian College in Hertfordshire, established in 1947 in Thomas Buxton's former home, which had a Zambian principal in 2006.

One late 19th-century development in the training of Africans in Britain for missionary work in Africa was William Hughes's Colwyn Bay Institute, established in 1887. By the time it closed in 1911 over 80 black students, many from Africa, had been trained at what was then known as the *African Training Institute in North Wales. Black missionaries such as Thomas Johnson and Dr Theophilus *Scholes, and African clergy, visited the Institute and commended its work.

Many black missionaries and assistants serving in Africa came to Britain to assist with translation work, to attend conferences, and on deputation work to help promote the work of mission. Diligent work by Brian Joyce in local newspapers has revealed that in the lower Medway region of Kent, during the late 19th and early 20th centuries, visiting black missionaries and clergy regularly spoke in the churches of Chatham and Rochester. Their visits helped to inform British people about African mission and also collected funds for the work. In the 1860s the most prominent African in mission circles was undoubtedly Bishop Crowther, respected for his linguistic knowledge and for his gentle piety. When Harold *Moody came to London to study medicine in 1904, he came armed with letters from representatives of the London Missionary Society (LMS) in Jamaica. Throughout his life in Britain, Moody supported the work of the Congregational LMS, sitting on its committees, speaking publicly on its behalf, and in 1943 becoming its chairman.

British missions were run by white bureaucrats in the metropolis, while in the field the superintendents were invariably Europeans. It was not until the 1870s–1880s that positive steps were taken to involve Africans and other black Christians in overseas mission in Africa and the Caribbean. Thereafter, in a period when scientific racism was allied to increasing imperialism, race and colour intruded in the business of missions and the role of black missionaries was often disparaged. For example, Freeman, although a black Briton, was discriminated against by home committees because of his colour. Black missionaries active on the mission field often had lower status and levels of pay, and did not receive the same degree of respect accorded to their white companions when it came to leave and provision for the education of children. Intermarriage between black and white was increasingly frowned upon by white mission officials. By the early 20th century colonial governments in Africa viewed black missionaries with suspicion and sought to exclude them, suspecting that they encouraged independent churches, Ethiopianism, and black nationalism. This was a prejudice often shared by white mission societies. The result was that by the 1920s there were relatively few foreign black missionaries in Africa.

A small number of black missionaries who trained in Britain and then served in Africa returned to Europe to work as evangelists, or, one might say, as black missionaries to darkest Britain. Salim Wilson was briefly a missionary in West and North Africa but spent most of his life preaching in northern England. Thomas Lewis *Johnson had a similar career as an itinerant evangelist. Isaac Dickerson left the *Fisk Jubilee Singers to study theology at Glasgow University and then served as a missionary in France; he died in south London in 1900. And a few black missionaries retired to live in Britain, for example, the Jamaican John Pinnock, a BMS worker in the Congo, who ended his days as an active member of a Baptist church in north London. By the late 20th century the business of mission had been partly reversed, with many Africans coming to Britain as clergy, as missionaries, for example with the London city mission, and to establish churches and to evangelize. Black-run British churches, a result of post-Second World War immigration from the Caribbean and Africa, were also supporting and sending candidates to work in home and overseas mission. DK

Birtwhistle, Allen, *Thomas Birch Freeman: West African Pioneer* (1950)

Edwards, Joel, and Killingray, David (eds.), *Black British Christian Voices 1770–2000: An Anthology* (2007)

Hughes, W., *Dark Africa and the Way Out* (1892)

Johnson, Thomas Lewis, *Twenty-Eight Years a Slave; or, The Story of My Life in Three Continents* (1909)

See also CHRISTIANITY; CHURCHES

Mittelholzer, Edgar Austin (1909–1965). Novelist and short-story writer born in New Amsterdam, British Guiana (now Guyana). From a schoolboy, his ambition was to be a writer, and he never wavered from this, persisting through repeated publishers' rejections. In 1941 the British firm of Eyre and Spottiswoode published his novel *Corentyne Thunder*, only for most copies to be destroyed soon afterwards as a result of wartime bombing of a warehouse. Mittelholzer moved to London in 1948 and worked with the British Council. His second novel, *A Morning at the Office*, was published in 1950 and was a critical success, which established him as a writer. He lived in Barbados from 1953 to 1956, but then returned to England, where he lived until his death.

As the title of his autobiography put it, Mittelholzer was 'a swarthy boy', a person of mixed race whose family were reluctant to acknowledge their African ancestry. The Caribbean (and, particularly, Guianese) history that had created this situation were one of Mittelholzer's major themes. His *Kaywana Trilogy* of historical novels—*Children of Kaywana* (1952), *The Harrowing of Hubertus* (1954; later reissued as *Kaywana Stock*), and *Kaywana Blood* (1958)—based on the history of British Guiana and that of his own family, became international best-sellers, though he also wrote novels with English settings that had no Caribbean characters. His works were translated into at least nine languages. In later life, however, he adopted views on political and social issues that others often considered extreme, and he once more found that it was difficult to get his work published. Like the main character in his last novel, *The Jilkington Drama*, which appeared a few weeks after his death, Mittelholzer died as a result of setting himself on fire.

Mittelholzer published over twenty books and many shorter pieces. By the beginning of the 21st century not a single one of his titles remained in print, though some of his work (particularly *A Morning at the Office* and *My Bones and My Flute*, a ghost story set in the Guianese jungle and published in 1955) continues to be esteemed by Caribbean critics. His most enduring legacy is perhaps the fact that, as the earliest of the post-war group of Caribbean writers in Britain who did so much to change the face of literature in English, he provided, by both example and personal encouragement, an important stimulus to the careers of others. JG

Collymore, Frank A., 'Edgar Mittelholzer: A Biographical Sketch', *Bim*, 41 (June–Dec. 1965)

Mittelholzer, Edgar, *A Swarthy Boy* (1963)

ODNB

See also LITERATURE 2: FICTION AND POETRY

Mixed-race identity, theories of. Theories of 'mixed race'—also referred to as 'mixed parentage', 'mixed ethnicity', 'multiracialism', and the pejorative 'half-caste'—apply to descendants of two or more 'racially' or ethnically classified groups.

1. Global variations
2. Terminology
3. Concept and background
4. Psychological theories

5. Theories of identity formation
6. Theories of government influence
7. Conclusion

1. Global variations The notion of a 'mixed-race' identity is varied and depends on social context. How 'mixed-race' identity is formed and expressed differs among individuals and countries. Experiences of growing up 'mixed' in a 'race'-sensitive society and historical factors shaping 'mixed-race' status have been noted as affecting one's identity. Major differences in the political status of 'mixed-race' populations throughout the world have demonstrated the potency of these global variations.

Within the British framework, 'mixed-race' refers primarily, though not exclusively, to black–white parentage and to the set of historical events that have led to 'mixed' populations. It also includes discussions of public attitudes towards 'race-mixing' and 'mixed-race' people, and the personal experiences of 'mixed' Britons today.

2. Terminology Associated with colonial notions of 'race', the terminology used to describe 'mixed-race' has been fiercely debated. In Britain especially, 'race' has been generally replaced with 'ethnicity'. However, 'mixed' individuals are often discussed in 'racial' (black–white) rather than 'ethnic' terms ('Scottish–Irish' or 'Jamaican–Nigerian'). The preferred US term 'multiracial' has been rejected in the United Kingdom for its association with the racist belief of innate biological division. However, 'multiracial' and 'mixed' have both been criticized for supporting the idea of 'racial purity'. It is suggested that since all 'mixed-race' terminology is based on a 'race' concept widely regarded as imperfect, it is difficult to select a neutral yet descriptive term that avoids racist undertones.

3. Concept and background The concept of 'racial mixing' relies on the acceptance that there are distinct 'race' groups that can be 'mixed'. This concept is rooted in 19th-century pseudo-scientific attempts to establish the existence of 'races' as biologically discrete groups 'naturally' ranging from superior to inferior. Each group's position along the scale of humanity was thought to show in its physical and cultural characteristics. Hence, there is an implicit hierarchy of 'races'. Although differences among 'race' groups were obsessively noted, differences in personality and appearance among individuals were not recognized. The presumed innate intellectual and cultural superiority of white people justified their conquest and domination of these foreign, and often 'non-white', lands. Their control over the 'lesser races' extended even to the sexual dominance, exploitation, and abuse of the sexuality of 'non-white' women and men. Yet, 'interracial' unions threatened to disrupt white hegemony and the assumed purity of whiteness. Hence, though in many colonial sites patriarchal, white ruling-class males enacted legislative measures to ensure the socio-sexual control of 'their' white women by limiting the possibilities for interracial sexual unions between white women and black men, they retained for themselves the masterly prerogatives of unrestrained access to black women. Sexual exploitation and abuse of black women was common, especially in slave societies. While 'interracial' unions between white male colonists and black women frequently occurred in the colonies, in Britain the majority of single-'race' fathers were black sailors, and the mothers white women from port towns. In all cases, 'mixed' children signalled their parents' 'immorality' and the nation's sexual and moral decline. The 'mixed' population came to represent 'racial' impurity, and was regarded as socially and physically degenerate. The intention to prevent further 'mixing' has at times provoked anti-black riots in the streets and anti-immigrant initiatives in the government. It was assumed that removing the element of blackness would guarantee that whites would propagate with other whites only.

From this legacy, three major areas of scholarship have emerged regarding 'mixed-race' identity: (1) the psychological impact of living in a single-'race' world, (2) identity formation among 'mixed' individuals, and (3) the government's role in influencing self-identification.

4. Psychological theories Until the 1980s the first theories of the 'mixed' person's psychological profile proposed that 'mixed' people are emotionally unstable and exist on the outskirts of society. The widely accepted belief that 'mixed' individuals suffer a split identity has since been acknowledged to reflect society's confusion over 'mixed' people's 'racial' status, rather than 'mixed' people's own disorientation. The scholarship that developed in the United States as part of a 'multiracial movement' seeking government recognition explores the psychological impact of being 'mixed-race' in a single-'race' world. Pressures include being classified by others as single-'race', i.e. most often as black, being treated as confused or emotionally damaged, and being seen as an exotic curiosity. Studies indicate that 'mixed' individuals often face unwanted attention from single-'race' communities, attention often triggered by the 'mixed' person's appearance. 'Mixed' people have reported experiencing hostile rejection from one or more single-'race' groups, invasive questioning about their background, intense interest in their physical characteristics, and demands to choose a single-'race' identity.

5. Theories of identity formation The second cluster of 'mixed-race' theories to emerge centres on the process of identity formation. Again, outcomes vary across national, regional, cultural, and personal lines. How a 'mixed' subject relates to each single-'race' heritage group depends upon family relationships, neighbourhood, the political climate, and individual personality. While pinpointing a single 'mixed-race' profile is difficult, numerous studies and interviews have demonstrated some common factors in the formation of a 'mixed' identity.

It has been proposed that the 'mixed-race' identity is a complex and evolving process that allows for layered self-understandings. An individual's self-label might differ from one circumstance to another, such as identifying as 'mixed-race' in the home and 'black British' in public. It may be a compound identity: 'I'm African *and* "mixed".' Multiple generations of 'mixing' in the family can also influence an individual's self-chosen identity and level of comfort while in social groupings that are mainly single-'race'. Based on their experiences, some 'mixed' individuals build a single-'race' identity and reject the label 'mixed'.

Geographic location has also been noted to affect how identity is formed. It has been suggested that individuals are more likely to identify as 'mixed' in urban centres with denser 'mixed' populations and more ethnic diversity. In other parts of the United Kingdom mixed people are more likely to be seen by themselves and others as a single-'race' 'black' or type of 'black'.

In probing identity development, scholars have explored how 'mixed' children and youth may self-identify in response to parental guidance or pressure from either parent. They may also reassess their identity in later years and change their identity from one label (e.g. black British) to another (e.g. Caribbean and English). Outside pressure and perceptions, such as hostility from an intolerant family member or discrimination in the local community, might cause the 'mixed' individual to feel alienated from one or both 'parent' groups. Conversely, the presence of a 'mixed' peer has been suggested to strengthen 'mixed-race' identity by providing psychological support for 'mixed' individuals who feel isolated in hostile environments.

6. Theories of government influence The third theory cluster explores the role of government in influencing 'mixed-race' identity. Studies have looked at the census as a tool for determining how 'mixed' populations count in their society, including the group's official name and how the 'mixed' category is represented on the census form. In the British census, 'mixed' identity is influenced, even limited, by the identity options provided by the census. Identity options that are not shown on the form do not officially exist, and individuals must modify their selection according to the options listed.

This tacit requirement for 'mixed' individuals to conform their identity to government standards has been seen as coercive. The government's influence has been argued to reverse the practice of an individual identifying his or her 'ethnic' self on the form. In situations where identity options are limited, 'mixed' individuals must place themselves within a pre-selected category regardless of whether they consider their selection accurate.

More generally, the census and similar 'race' classification projects have been criticized for reinforcing 'race' thinking. It is argued that the practice of listing the 'race' or ethnic categories that 'officially' matter implies the importance of continuing to classify people by 'race' or 'ethnic' group.

While naming the 'mixed' group advantageously indicates political recognition, government documents that selectively list 'mixed-race' sub-groups frequently misinform. For example, the listing of one sub-group but not another may overemphasize the listed sub-group's size or importance while suggesting that any unlisted group is non-existent or insignificant.

7. Conclusion Scholarly theories of 'mixed-race' identity have offered concepts for understanding the current 'mixed-race' landscape in Britain and in countries with similar backgrounds. In Britain these theories on the psychological stress generated from single-'race' individuals and institutions, the many factors in identity formation, and the government influence in shaping or limiting self-identity continue to question the relationship between the identity of 'mixed' individuals and the societies in which they live. JYD

Ifekwunigwe, Jayne O., *Scattered Belongings: Cultural Paradoxes of 'Race', Nation and Gender* (1999)
Parker, David, and Song, Miri (eds.), *Rethinking 'Mixed Race'* (2001)
Song, Miri, *Choosing Ethnic Identity* (2003)
Tizard, Barbara, and Phoenix, Anne, *Black, White, or Mixed Race?* (1993)

See also MISCEGENATION; MULTICULTURALISM; RACISM

Modernism. There is little comparable in British modernism with the primitivism of Matisse, Picasso, and Stravinsky, or the revolutionary black expression of the Harlem Renaissance. Nancy *Cunard's *NEGRO* anthology linked the two, but contains few artistic works by British figures. Wyndham Lewis, the 'fascist modernist', produced primitivist drawings for some of his books, but the extent of his literary engagement with the non-European world—which included *Filibusters in Barbary*, a 1931 travel book set in Morocco, and a 1929 collection of essays, *Paleface*, on race relations in America—has not been catalogued and discussed.

Blacks are a strong presence in the corpus of T. S. Eliot, from youthful stories set in the South Pacific to the 'dead Negroes' carried away by the 'brown god' Mississippi (presumably a childhood memory) in 'The Dry Salvages' (1941). Eliot's savages are often juxtaposed with images of civilized culture, which Robert Crawford links to Eliot's interest in anthropology—as editor of *The Criterion*, he reviewed numerous works of anthropological theory, and his essays on culture drew on this (a famous example, 'Marie Lloyd and Music Hall', from 1922, compared Londoners to the Melanesian tribesfolk W. H. R. Rivers argued were dying of boredom because they couldn't go headhunting). Throughout Eliot's poetry and criticism, tribal drumming is equated firstly with the revolutionary urge to remake the literary canon and also with the process of artistic creation, in which the individual personality disappears into tradition.

At the same time Eliot wrote lewd poems concerning 'King Bolo and his big black Qween' to friends, and exchanged letters with Ezra Pound in African-American dialect. Most significantly, his jazz play *Sweeney Agonistes* (1925) borrows from music hall and *minstrelsy: it casts two black-face musicians called Swarts and Snow, as well as deploying exoticist imagery of 'Gauguin maids', banyan and bamboo, missionaries and cannibalism, rendered in percussive rhythms, to reveal a savage void at the heart of 1920s city life. Michael North claims that Eliot, along with Cunard, Gertrude Stein, and others, brought the minstrel show to Britain, shoring up stereotyped fragments of black expression against the ruined, enervated centre of modernist identity.

D. H. Lawrence toured Ceylon, Australia, and the South Pacific in 1922, staying in Mexico for three years, which resulted in the novels *Kangaroo* (1923), *St. Mawr* (1924), *The Woman Who Rode Away* (1924), and *The Plumed Serpent* (1925), as well as numerous journalistic articles, published in America, on Indian festivals such as 'the Dance of the Sprouting Corn' and 'the Hopi Snake Dance'. However, a full investigation into his use of the primitive, which generally involved the intense surge of being in a moment of bestial immediacy, with sensationalist accoutrements of bloodlust, sacrificial knives, obsidian eyes, etc., has yet to be conducted. At present Lawrence criticism either downplays the Eurocentrism and exoticism of his work or ignores it entirely (though one work of contemporary criticism on the 'Oriental Lawrence' argues that, despite his not having read the Vedas and Upanishads, nor the Yogic and Buddhist texts, 'systematically', he can be understood in terms of his 'radically non-western ontology', and seen as a practitioner of tantric sex). After a near-fatal illness in 1925 Lawrence turned against Mexico and went home: 'Altogether I think of Mexico with a sort of nausea . . . really I feel I never want to see an Indian or an "aboriginee" or anything in the savage line again.'

In the visual arts in Britain the absence of modernist representations of Blacks is also striking. Stanley Spencer's 1934 painting *Love Among the Nations*, held at the Fitzwilliam Museum, Cambridge, in which Blacks are presented in a stylized manner, voluptuously fingering the clothes of Whites, is a rare example. JM

Chaudhuri, Amit, *D. H. Lawrence and 'Difference'* (2003)

Crawford, Robert, *The Savage and the City in the Work of T. S. Eliot* (1987)

Doherty, Gerald, *Oriental Lawrence: The Quest for the Secrets of Sex* (2001)

See also HEART OF DARKNESS

Molineaux, Tom (1784–1821). African-American boxer who gained a significant reputation in England. Molineaux was born in Virginia and was the slave to a wealthy playboy who frequently used him in fights against other slaves. In one particular event Molineaux's master bet $100,000 that he would defeat another slave in a match and promised to grant him his freedom should he win. Molineaux won and left for England in 1803, where he met and subsequently trained under Bill *Richmond, another African-American boxer of consequence. Molineaux's first match in England was against Tom Blake, whom he knocked out in the eighth round. Richmond prepared Molineaux for his important fight against Tom Cribb, an opponent whom Richmond had never managed to defeat. In December 1810 the match between Cribb and Molineaux took place at Copthorne, near East Grinstead, and after 39 rounds Molineaux lost. The fight was an especially trying one as the weather was severe and Cribb's supporters became rowdy following Molineaux's impending triumph. They entered the boxing ring, attacking Molineaux and consequently breaking his finger. Despite this, he persevered and knocked Cribb out in the 28th round. Cribb's seconds, however, claimed that Molineaux had lead bullets in his fists, causing more riotous behaviour from Cribb's supporters. By sheer accident, Molineaux, despite his skilled performance, slipped and hit his head on a ring post and lost. He requested a return fight for the next year, which was held on 28 September 1811 in Leicestershire, where 15,000 people attended the match. Luck was not favourable to Molineaux yet again as he broke his jaw in the sixth round and was knocked out by the eleventh. He continued fighting until 1815. Whatever money he earned during his boxing career was spent on alcohol and womanizing. He died in poverty in 1821. DD/SS

Fleischer, N., *Black Dynamite: The Story of the Negro in the Prize Ring from 1782 to 1938* (1938)

Fryer, Peter, *Staying Power: The History of Black People in Britain* (1984)

ODNB

See also SPORT

Montagu, John, second Duke of Montagu (1690–1749). Patron of Blacks, John succeeded his father as duke in 1709. A wealthy and learned man, if not scholarly in any systematic way, Montagu was regarded as a whimsical eccentric who dabbled in many different things. In 1722 he obtained a royal grant of the Caribbean islands of St Lucia and St Vincent, and made an unsuccessful attempt to have these colonized on his behalf, which reportedly lost him a great deal of money.

Montagu was the patron of at least two black people who became well known in the British society of his time. In 1734 he entertained *Job ben Solomon on several occasions, gave him presents, and organized the redemption of Job's former companion Loumein Yoai from slavery in Maryland. At a later date Montagu befriended the young Ignatius *Sancho and gave him books. Subsequently, after the duke's death, Sancho was employed by other members of the Montagu family at different times.

According to Edward *Long, Montagu paid for the education of Francis *Williams at the University of Cambridge. However, there is no other evidence for this, and it is certain that Williams was never matriculated as a member of the university. JG

Grant, Douglas, *The Fortunate Slave: An Illustration of African Slavery in the Early Eighteenth Century* (1968)

ODNB

Sancho, Ignatius, *Letters of the Late Ignatius Sancho, an African* (ed. Vincent Carretta, 1998)

Monuments and memorials. One way to understand how a nation lives with its past and present is by locating monuments and memorials—markers and places that commemorate historic events, celebrate achievements of individuals, help the bereaved remember and mourn the dead, give meaning to the past, and locate the presence of groups who have contributed to the nation's history.

1. Roman Britain
2. 18th- and 19th-century burials
3. Other sites of memory
4. Modern memorials
5. War memorials

The black African is no stranger to the long history of Britain, from the Roman invasion to the present day. Yet, only a few national monuments and memorials recognize black Africans (mostly of West Indian lineage) whose long-term residence in Britain and pivotal role in the making of Britain's history, culture, and heritage can be documented.

1. Roman Britain The memorial to the earliest documented African presence in Britain is an inscription carved in an altar stone found in Beaumont, 2 miles east of Burgh by Sands, near Hadrian's Wall in Cumbria. Archaeological and historical evidence locates this as a place where black Roman soldiers, military officers, and slaves were stationed between the 2nd and 4th centuries AD.

2. 18th- and 19th-century burials Marking Britain's lucrative trade in African captives are several 18th- and 19th-century burials of Blacks, which have become national memorials where people leave flowers, messages, and photographs. Such places of pilgrimage are the gravestone just outside Bristol of Scipio *Africanus (d. December 1720); *Sambo's grave (*c.*1736) at Sunderland Point in Lancashire; the gravestone of an Ethiopian slave in Cumbria; the 1787 memorial tablet and human remains of Nestor, which are maintained by the Church of Sts Peter and Paul, Teston, Kent; the graves of George John Scipio Africanus (1763?–

24 May 1834), who is buried in Nottingham; of Ned (d. 1778), who is buried in the Quakers Friars churchyard in Bristol; and of Philip Scipio (d. 1784) at Werrington, then in Devon. Although not a burial, Pero's Bridge, also in Bristol, commemorates the 1790s enslaved labourer of the Pinney merchants. Similarly, a small board with his picture and some biographical notes mark the former grave in Westminster of Ignatius *Sancho (1729–80). In Kenwyn churchyard, Cornwall, the nation's very first black composer, Joseph Antonio *Emidy (*c.*1775–1835), is buried, and a dedicatory plaque to him hangs in Falmouth parish church. Categorically worlds apart from their servant contemporaries are Nathaniel *Wells (1779–1852) and George Augustus Polgreen *Bridgetower (1778–1860). The latter, the famed composer who introduced Bach into British culture, is buried in Kensal Green cemetery, London. For Nathaniel Wells, son of a wealthy St Kitts planter from Cardiff, a memorial plaque was unveiled in St Arvan's parish in the Wye Valley.

Burial sites are as much local monuments as they are national sites for remembering Britain's involvement in the scattering of African peoples throughout the Atlantic basin. On the British Isles and in Scotland the memory of ambiguously described black servants or slaves is inscribed on tombstones. Samuel Ally (d. 1822) is buried in Douglas, capital of the Isle of Man. In Scotland the inscriptions on the tombstones of Robert Story and Felicity Oglevie tell us their story. In central Edinburgh the remains of Malvina Wells (1805–82), 'a faithful servant to the Maclean Family for over 70 years, from the West Indies', are in Old Calton cemetery.

3. Other sites of memory Deeply located in local history and in critical discussions of the national politics of remembrance are former sites of shipwrecks, auction blocks, and racially motivated killings. At Rapparee Cove, near Ilfracombe on the North Devon coast, there is a memorial plaque to approximately 150 Africans who died when the slave ship *London* was wrecked in 1796. Though only historical documentation remains, at Newgate prison the memory of the beheading in 1820 of William Davidson, enemy of the state, is fused to this place. In Liverpool the very waters of the Merseyside docks mirror clear images of Liverpool slaving vessels, as well as scenes of racial violence. Memories of Africans for sale and the mob murder of Charles Wooton, a black seaman who was attacked with stones in 1919 at Queen's Dock, are geographically fixed to these docks. Although now defunct, Charles Wooton College in Toxteth was a short-lived attempt at a permanent memorial to the seaman. On the other hand, an entire gallery on Merseyside is devoted to 'Transatlantic Slavery: Against Human Dignity'; and facing the two oldest dry docks is a plaque that reads, 'If These Stones Could Speak', to mark this as the place where slave ships were repaired.

4. Modern memorials Throughout Great Britain global and historic issues are being claimed both locally and nationally, as two local memorials bear out. In Manchester a plaque in Peace Gardens, St Peter's Square, reads, 'In memory and remembrance of the victims of slavery who were forcefully displaced from their homeland for profit. May their souls rest in perfect peace. Established 1 August 2001.' In the same vein is the Soweto Memorial of the African Woman and Child in central Edinburgh, by the Aberdeen sculptor Ann Davidson.

Among the oldest of memorials in the country are the blue, red, green, and black plaques on residences of renowned individuals, or on buildings of architectural importance or associated with historic events. English Heritage annually erects blue plaques to commemorate nationally selected individuals. A brief inscription denotes the person's importance to science, medicine, the arts and media, literature, business, or politics. Other than the composer Samuel *Coleridge-Taylor and the civil rights activist and recipient of many medical awards Dr Harold *Moody, very few British-born Blacks are remembered with blue plaques. Cognizant of its record, English Heritage has approved the installation of blue plaques for Ottobah *Cugoano, Mary *Prince, Olaudah *Equiano, and Ignatius *Sancho. While discussions continue around the relocation of Mary *Seacole's blue plaque to 14 Soho Square, Westminster City Council has unveiled its green plaque to her at 147 George Street. Moreover, Seacole's burial, in St Mary's Catholic cemetery in Kensal Green, numerous buildings and schools in her name, as well as portraits and statues of her throughout the country, equally serve as memorials to her dedication to soldiers in the Crimean War.

Several city councils and local history and related societies promote the coloured-plaque schemes, as well as exhibits and portraits. Westminster City Council awards green plaques to its historically noteworthy—and nominated—residents. A green plaque at 73 Riding Street commemorates the place where Equiano wrote his autobiography, *The Interesting Narrative of the Life of Olaudah Equiano, or Gustavus Vassa, the African*, in 1789, and the burial sites of Equiano's wife and daughters sustain the memory of his major role in British abolitionism. The London borough of Southwark has awarded blue plaques to its local icons, living and dead: Rio Ferdinand, the star footballer from Friary Estate in Peckham; the actress Marianne Jean-Baptiste of Camberwell; and the Jamaican-born Una *Marson, feminist and the first black woman in the BBC, who lived in Nunhead and Peckham Rye. Like Seacole's, Marcus *Garvey's memory is of local and national significance, and is honoured by a memorial park in the London borough of Hammersmith and Fulham, and an English Heritage blue plaque. In the London borough of Haringey plaques commemorate Cynthia Jarrett, and mark the 50th anniversary of the arrival at Tilbury of the **Empire Windrush*. In the Town Hall of his birthplace, Liverpool, a portrait hangs of John Richard *Archer, the first black Mayor of Battersea, in south London, elected in 1913 and 1919; there has been an exhibition dedicated to Archer at Wandsworth Museum; and his grave is in Morden cemetery. The Town Hall in Leamington, Warwickshire, salutes the memory of the boxing champion Randolph *Turpin with a plaque.

The city and University of Manchester have also adopted coloured-plaque schemes. Two red plaques on the old Chorlton-on-Medlock Town Hall in Manchester commemorate the Pan-African Congress of 1945; a rectangular one lists those who attended the conference. At the University of Manchester a blue plaque at the entrance to the Economics Department recognizes Sir Frank Worrell, a graduate in 1959, who was knighted for his achievements in cricket.

Besides plaques, renamed streets and buildings and more tombstones honour the spirit of individuals who deserve national recognition. For example, in Doncaster, Yorkshire, a memorial stone now rests on the grave of Arthur *Wharton, Britain's first black professional footballer. A monument to Lieutenant Walter *Tull, the first black officer in the British Army and second black professional footballer, stands outside Northampton football ground. In Liverpool a renamed street and a plaque honour James Clarke, the Guianese-born swimmer who prevented countless children from drowning in the Leeds–Liverpool canal. In Bristol, Owen Henry Close commemorates a West Indian advocate for first-generation *Windrush* immigrants. Also in Bristol a bust of the playwright Alfred Fagon (1937–86) can be found in St Paul's. In Buckinghamshire the Sir William Borlase Grammar School has installed a commemorative plaque to Ken 'Snakehips' *Johnson. The name of the Kath *Locke Centre, in Hulme, Manchester, honours the community health-care activist who founded it.

More common locally, however, are conventional utilitarian monuments and memorials to a few African diasporans whose iconic international status, occasional visits, or short-term residence have lasting merit. In addition to Marcus Garvey, C. L. R. *James, Paul *Robeson, and Jomo Kenyatta—who all have English Heritage blue plaques—this group includes Harriet Tubman, Frederick *Douglass, and Nelson Mandela, who is honoured in various boroughs and counties with over 80 memorials. College buildings nationwide commemorate Steve Biko, Mandela, Albert Luthuli, or Julius Nyerere. Relatedly, the University of Edinburgh recognizes its own African graduates with a memorial plaque to James Beale Africanus *Horton, its first African graduate student, and a millennial plaque to Nyerere, the first President of Tanzania.

5. **War memorials** Lastly, monuments to Great Britain's war dead pay tribute to collective memories, and rarely identify individual heroes. Examples of two war memorials to unidentified black figures among others are the American Civil War Memorial in Edinburgh and Nelson's Column. Explicit recognition of a black veteran is shown by the rectangular stone statue in London to Thomas Allen (1777–1838), Nelson's devoted sailor and 'faithful servant' of seven years; Allen is buried in the old Greenwich cemetery. In November 2002 the *Memorial Gates in Hyde Park were inaugurated to 'remember the peoples of the Indian sub-continent, Africa and the Caribbean who fought in both World Wars. No longer will they be forgotten by history'. AML

Bourne, Stephen, *Speak of Me As I Am: The Black Presence in Southwark Since 1600* (2005)
Eickelmann, Christine, and David Small, *Pero: The Life of a Slave in Eighteenth-Century Bristol* (2004)
Martin, Steve, *Britain's Slave Trade* (1999)
Myers, Norma, *Reconstructing the Black Past: Blacks in Britain, 1780–1830* (1996)

See also ROMAN BRITAIN

Moody, Harold (1882–1947). Black doctor and activist. Harold Moody was born in Kingston, Jamaica, in 1882 and arrived in London in 1904 to study medicine. His mother, a dark woman, was aware of the liability of black skin in colonial Jamaica for she advised her son to make friends with those fairer than himself. Moody's father worked on the Panama Canal and returned with enough money to open a pharmacy. Moody was sent to a prestigious school in Kingston run by Sir William Morrison, and was then transferred to Woolmer's Free School until 1899. His scholarship was sound, and upon graduation he opened his own school, where he taught for some time. From his very early beginnings Moody was a devout Christian, becoming secretary of the Christian Endeavour Society at the age of 19. He also was a preacher at two churches in Kingston.

As early as 1912 Moody was elected president of the Young People's Branch of the Colonial Missionary Society and in the same year was appointed a member of the board of directors. In 1921 he was elected chairman of the board of directors of the Society (although he was unable to commit the Society to the issue of race), and in 1931 he became president of the London Christian Endeavour Federation. In 1936 he became president of the Christian Endeavour Union of Great Britain and Ireland, and in 1937 he was elected a member of the Executive Committee of the British and Foreign Bible Society.

Moody founded the *League of Coloured Peoples in 1931. He built it into a respectable organization, fostered Establishment and political relations with the Conservative and Labour parties, and geared the League's work within the context of anti-racism and civil equality. ASS

Moody, Harold, *The Colour Bar* (1945)
ODNB

See also CHRISTIANITY; MEDICINE; MISSIONARY SOCIETIES

Moody, Ronald (1900–1984). Jamaican sculptor working in Britain. Ronald Moody was born on 20 August 1900 in Kingston, Jamaica, the youngest of six children. He attended Calabar College in Jamaica, and, following the aspirations of his family, he chose to study dentistry. He duly arrived in Britain in 1923 and attended King's College London, where he graduated in 1930 and found employment in London as a dentist. His initial fascination with sculpture was expressed through experiments with plasticine; he then graduated to clay, then wood and bronze. His first sculpture in wood was the piece *Wohin*, expressing his interest in European classical composers. His first public exhibition was at the New Burlington Galleries in a group show in 1935. His primary patron was the Italian film-director Alberto Cavalcanti, whose contacts with Paris led him to his first solo exhibition at the Galerie Billiet-Vorms in 1937. The impact was electric among French critics and this boosted Moody's confidence.

Interestingly, English galleries were more interested in Moody's portraits while the French were keen on his sculptural figures. Moody's interest was initially ignited by his first and subsequent frequent visits to the British Museum, where he discovered the artefacts of Egyptian civilization. Of his Ancient Egyptian figures *Seated Sarong Figure* (1938) is a version of the scribe in meditation; the nude *Annie* (1938) is a version of the nude Ancient Egyptian female figures that abound in its sculpture; while *Harpy* (1960) is a well-known version of the Ancient Egyptian divinity Hor (Greek: Horus) in his form as Harpocrates. Moody's engagement with diverse cultures and philosophies (man as moral being, as ascension) is the spark that fuels his sculptural world, and he has also acknowledged Indian, Chinese, and African art.

Since Moody's death in 1984 his work has been shown in the Netherlands, the United States, Scotland, and France. His work is in the collections of the Tate Gallery, the National Portrait Gallery, and the National Gallery of Jamaica, and in many private collections. He was awarded the Musgrave and the Jamaica Institute Centenary Medals. His artistic estate is in the hands of his niece, the retired film-maker Cynthia Moody. ASS

Araeen, Rasheed, *The Other Story: Afro-Asian Artists in Post-War Britain* (1989)

Beauchamp-Byrd, M. J., *Transforming the Crown: African, Asian and Caribbean Artists in Britain 1966–1996* (1997)

See also VISUAL ARTS 2: ARTISTS

Morant Bay rebellion. On 11 October 1865 a crowd of several hundred people attacked the court house in the town of Morant Bay in the parish of St Thomas in the East, Jamaica, where a meeting of the vestry (the official body responsible for local government at the parish level) was taking place. Officials had been expecting trouble, and members of the local volunteer militia were present to protect the meeting. After the crowd had begun to throw missiles and attack the volunteers, they opened fire, killing seven members of the crowd and wounding others. The crowd resumed their attack, eventually setting fire to the court house and killing eighteen officials and members of the militia and wounding 31 others. Over the next few days other places in the parish, mainly plantations, were attacked, and there were two further deaths.

Opinion has been divided among both contemporaries and modern historians about the nature of these events, with some seeing them as essentially a relatively small-scale riot in protest against economic and social conditions, and others interpreting them as an abortive attempt at an island-wide rebellion that aimed at the overthrow of British colonial rule in Jamaica.

The response of the authorities was swift and devastating. The island's colonial Governor, Edward John Eyre, proclaimed martial law, and a combination of British soldiers and sailors, local militia, and maroons swept through the affected areas. Several hundred local people were shot in confrontations with the troops, in many cases simply because they were running away, and not because they were engaged in any active resistance. Several hundred more were subsequently executed after trials that were often a travesty of justice. In addition, there were hundreds of floggings, and about 1,000 homes were burnt by the troops in revenge for the outbreak.

Attitudes to race inevitably affected responses to the rebellion. Most (though not all) of those killed by the rebels were white, while the rebels themselves and the victims of the official repression were black. Governor Eyre claimed that he had acted swiftly to prevent what would otherwise have been a wholesale massacre of the island's white population by the rebels and a recurrence of the *Haitian Revolution, while the more recent events of the *Indian Mutiny were widely seen as offering another parallel.

When the news reached Britain, government and public opinion initially favoured Eyre, but as details of the campaign of repression became better known, many people began to feel that it was at least excessive, and perhaps actually criminal. Particular attention was paid to the fate of George William Gordon, a mixed-race, middle-class radical politician who was arrested on the direct instructions of Eyre and sent from Kingston (where martial law did not apply) to Morant Bay (where it did), and then tried and hanged. Although Gordon was an associate of Paul Bogle, who had led the attack on the Morant Bay court house, the evidence that Gordon himself was in any way responsible for the rebellion was at best extremely tenuous, and his death was essentially because Eyre and his supporters regarded him as a troublemaker.

The British government sent a Royal Commission to Jamaica to investigate, and their report (published June 1866) praised Eyre for his prompt action, but declared that the scale of the repression had been excessive. As a result, Eyre was dismissed as governor, and returned to England in August. Many people greeted him as a hero, while others denounced him as a murderer. A Jamaica Committee had been formed, which sought to have Eyre charged with murder, while a Governor Eyre Defence Committee provided him with financial and other support. Legal proceedings continued until 1868, but the Jamaica Committee's attempts to have Eyre and (separately) two officers prosecuted for their actions during the rebellion and its aftermath ultimately failed in the law courts.

British society was divided on the issue, with many public figures taking a stand on one side or the other. Supporters of Eyre included Thomas *Carlyle, Charles Dickens, Alfred Tennyson, John Ruskin, and Charles Kingsley, while the Jamaica Committee and its supporters included John Stuart Mill, Charles Darwin, T. H. Huxley, and Charles Lyell. The controversy was far from being solely about what had happened in Jamaica, as a major question was that of the legality of martial law. Those who were radicals in British politics feared that if Eyre were exonerated, this might pave the way for martial law to be applied in Ireland, or even against popular protest in Britain itself, where the 1860s were a decade of political upheaval. The Jamaica Committee enjoyed widespread working-class support, but also faced the hostility of many middle-class voters who resented the extension of the franchise in Britain (which in 1867 gave the vote to most working men) and who believed that any sort of political upheaval should be firmly dealt with. Nevertheless, the collapse of the case against Eyre was essentially a victory for those who claimed that British rulers were indeed entitled to act in the colonies in ways that they would not in Britain itself, and who often justified this on explicitly racist grounds. Coming after the atrocities that marked the suppression of the Indian Mutiny, the Morant Bay rebellion set a precedent for later abuses of power in many other parts of Britain's colonial empire. JG

Heuman, Gad, *'The Killing Time': The Morant Bay Rebellion in Jamaica* (1994)

Semmel, Bernard, *The Governor Eyre Controversy* (1962)

See also CARIBBEAN, BRITISH COLONIES IN THE

More, Hannah (1745–1833). Writer and anti-slavery campaigner. Hannah More first became widely known as a dramatist, with her play *Percy* proving a great success in 1777. She later turned to writing on social and religious topics, and had a particular interest in the education of women. She was a long-term resident of *Bristol, and the extensive acquaintance that her literary work brought her included John *Newton, Beilby *Porteus, and William

*Wilberforce. In 1788 she published *Slavery, a Poem*, which, while including traditional Eurocentric assumptions about Africans, insisted on their humanity and right to freedom:

> Tho' dark and savage, ignorant and blind,
> They claim the common privilege of kind;
> Let Malice strip them of each other plea,
> They still are men, and men shou'd still be free.

The slave trader was denounced as a 'White Savage', and More called on Britain to free her slaves: 'O let the nations know | The liberty she loves she will bestow.' The fact that More was already well known, and that the poem appeared with her name on the title page (in an age when many publications, especially those penned by women, were anonymous), helped to make *Slavery* an influential contribution to the burgeoning anti-slavery movement. Henry Thompson, an early biographer of More, noted that 'It was . . . highly commended by the bishops and influential clergy; and it was widely circulated and eminently popular.'

More was also responsible for the *Cheap Repository Tracts* (1795–8), written by herself and collaborators. Distributed in the millions, these were intended (in the wake of the French Revolution) to encourage the English working classes to prefer the acceptance of their lot, as advocated by Evangelical Christianity, to the attractions of radical politics. This essentially conservative outlook did not prevent the inclusion of several anti-slavery titles. Quantities of the *Tracts* were distributed among slaves in the Caribbean by missionaries of the Conversion Society founded by Porteus. JG

Gilmore, J. T., 'Episcopacy, Emancipation and Evangelization: Aspects of the History of the Church of England in the British West Indies', Ph.D. thesis (University of Cambridge, 1985)

Richardson, Alan (ed.), *Slavery, Abolition and Emancipation: Writings in the British Romantic Period*, iv: *Verse* (1999)

Thompson, Henry, *The Life of Hannah More: With Notices of Her Sisters* (1838)

See also WHEATLEY, PHILLIS

Morris, Olive (1952–1979). Activist and community leader. In 1969, after intervening in an incident involving police harassment, Morris was herself arrested and brutally assaulted. This incident ignited her lifelong struggles against racism and injustice. In *Brixton she became active in organizing black and community groups, helping to establish the first black bookshop in south London, and was instrumental in launching black women's groups, including the *Organization of Women of African and Asian Descent. A passionate supporter of the homeless, she successfully campaigned to defend squatters' rights before Lambeth Council agreed, in 1973, to purchase some abandoned flats on behalf of squatters. In 1975 she began a degree in Manchester, combining her studies with activism in Moss Side. She campaigned with black parents for better education for their children, and helped to establish a supplementary school. Membership of the *Black Panther Party helped to develop her anti-racist and anti-imperialist political ideology, and inspired a visit to China in 1978, which strengthened her belief in self-help and self-reliance for black people. The same year she completed her studies and returned to Brixton, where she resumed her work with black, community, and black women's groups. Aged 26, Morris died tragically of cancer, but during her brief lifetime her remarkable courage and spirit proved inspirational to many. Her contributions to her community were recognized by Lambeth Council, which in 1986—ironically perhaps—named the local housing benefits office Olive Morris House in her memory. CJ

Bryan, Beverley, Dadzie, Stella, and Scafe, Suzanne, *Heart of the Race: Black Women's Lives in Britain* (1985)

See also FEMINISM; HOUSING

Mosley, Sir Oswald Ernald (1896–1980). Best known for his attempt in the 1930s to develop a fascist mass movement in Britain, Mosley ended his political career in the late 1950s and 1960s by attacking West Indian and other non-white immigrants to Britain. He served on the Western Front in the *First World War. This experience shaped his outlook: he tried to avoid war, to build a society fit for heroes, and used the military as his template for solving social problems. He was elected to Parliament as a Unionist candidate in December 1918 but rebelled against the violence of the pro-Unionist irregulars (the Black and Tans). He left his party in 1920 and eventually joined the Labour Party in 1924, attempting to outline new economic policies. In the 1929 election, which brought Labour to power again, he became Chancellor of the Duchy of Lancaster but felt that only a new political movement could meet contemporary economic and social challenges. He was expelled from the Labour Party, formed his New Party, which acquired a private army but no parliamentary seats. In 1932 he formed the British Union of Fascists with its strong anti-Jewish programme. His support for fascism led to his internment in 1940 until 1943. After the war he formed a pro-united Europe movement but began to attack non-white immigration. Besides causing trouble and amusement it did little: he lost his deposit in 1959 and again in 1966. PF

Mosley, Nicholas, *Beyond the Pale* (1983)
—— *Rules of the Game* (1982)
ODNB

See also IMMIGRATION; RACISM

Multiculturalism. A controversial policy approach for managing cultural diversity in multi-ethnic societies. Multiculturalism stresses mutual respect and tolerance for cultural differences within a society.

1. Introduction
2. Origins and definitions
3. Early 21st-century views
4. Race equality

1. Introduction Britain represents one of the most culturally diverse societies in the developed world. Since the 1960s at least, the concept of multiculturalism has been a primary political strategy for the management of 'race relations' between the many 'races' and ethnic groups that make up UK society. However, the concept of multiculturalism has come under increasing attack. To understand why, it helps to explore its historical development and how it is defined, and, secondly, to appreciate the current political context.

2. Origins and definitions According to Vipin Chauhan, the response to people of colour in Britain has been based on four different models, the last three of which can work in unison.

1. The assimilationist, or 'colourblind', approach, prevalent until the late 1960s and based on the view that we should treat everyone the same *regardless* of colour and promoted by Patrick West and colleagues from the highly controversial Civitas Report 2005, *The Poverty of Multiculturalism*. ('I'm no socialist, but I do believe that the best way to achieve a more just world is not to celebrate difference, but to ignore difference.')
2. The multicultural approach, which theoretically is based on the view that different cultures can be appreciated and live harmoniously together in one society.
3. The anti-racist approach, which challenges individual, group, or systemic racism to enable equality as a basis for a democratic and fair society.
4. The black empowerment approach, which takes the view that black communities are denied rights and equality and are disfranchised and kept on the margins of society by racism. The politics of difference is asserted—'we should treat people appropriately and differently according to need'—in full recognition of their historical and cultural background.

For black activists and organizations multiculturalism, while important, is only one of the ways of working for an equal society. This is partly because multiculturalism has been defined and used for different purposes, swayed by different political drivers at different times. So, for example, in the 1970s in particular, multiculturalism was, for some, a well-meaning attempt to challenge the politics of assimilation to enable a celebration of difference and promote 'tolerance'. However, this was exemplified in a voyeuristic conception of the exotic nature of different cultures and came to be signified by the 'steel band and samosas' syndrome.

To celebrate difference in this way was often an excuse to avoid discussing the political recognition of racism or the effects of power. In fact power differentials were reinforced by such terms as 'tolerance', which implied the largesse of the majority towards something inherently inferior.

By the 1980s the anti-racist movement was at its height and demanded attention to structural inequality. Multiculturalism was posited variously as: pluralism, where cultures coexist but there is little integration; or assimilation: the 'when in Rome do as the Romans do' model, in which ethnic particularities survive but are subsumed within the mainstream ethnic society.

By the 1990s and into the 21st century the emphasis on individual and institutional racism did not engender much debate about multiculturalism in itself. The primary preoccupation of the anti-racist movement and black political organizations such as the National Black Caucus, the 1990 Trust, Operation Black Vote, and the National Assembly Against Racism was the disfranchisement of black people in political and economic terms and the historic denial of racism in Britain. Black communities' revolt at this denial was at last crystallized by the Stephen *Lawrence Inquiry and the *MacPherson Report (1999), which was instrumental in that the establishment itself recognized institutional racism and legislated to remove it with the Race Relations (Amendment) Act 2000. However, as if all of this was too much to bear for the beast of racism, and even before the 11 September 2001 terrorist attacks and 7 July 2005 bombings in New York and London, respectively, several commentators, including David Blunkett, the Home Secretary at the time, questioned the concept of multiculturalism. The terrorist bombings were a gift to this agenda, and multiculturalism became the scapegoat for the failure to deliver race equality.

The early conceptions of multiculturalism may have been flawed, but they at least signalled the acceptance of a diverse Britain. Today multiculturalism is being redefined as interculturalism. That is, different ethnicities must be recognized (within a legislative framework for all), not just in relation to external features of dress, language, and food, but also in relation to historical and political background. As Urmee Khan writes,

> Multiculturalism has defended the rights of minorities to preserve their culture, while also seeking to ensure they become fully participatory citizens—that is, integrating without assimilating. Different communities have been allowed to engage in a political discourse without having to give up their cultural and religious identity. Recent debates about scrapping multiculturalism therefore threaten to destabilise the efforts towards coexistence of the diverse community groups which make up the UK. Instead, multiculturalism enables unity to happen because it allows different cultures to feel a parity of esteem. And, as an incidental by-product, it invites cross-community participation.

3. Early 21st-century views At the beginning of the 21st century a set of ideas, under the labels of integration, cohesion, and citizenship, conspired to question multiculturalism, and threatened to set the framework for present and future discourse on race in Britain. Critics were wary of allowing these ideas to crystallize into a residual ideology for race as they are rooted in a pathologizing discourse of 'blaming the victim'.

The discourse (in reaction to the civil unrest in Burnley, Oldham, and Bradford in 2001, and to the 11 September 2001 terrorist attacks and 7 July 2005 bombings) suggested that integration was failing *because of multiculturalism*, that there had been too much emphasis on the value of different cultures and not enough on sharing British values.

The denial of multiculturalism was imbued with the poison of Islamophobia. It suggested that the responsibility for Islamist terrorism and extremism lay with the entire Muslim community and the multiculturalism that had enabled that community to live peaceably in Britain. This argument was demonstrated by the 2005 report by Civitas entitled *The Poverty of Multiculturalism*:

The fruits of 30 years of state-endorsed multiculturalism have increased inter-racial tension and inter-racial sectarianism . . . The fact that the London suicide bombers of 7 July and the would-be bombers of 21 July 2005 were born and bred in Britain—and encouraged by the state to be different—illustrates that Hard Multiculturalism has the capacity to be not only divisive but decidedly lethal.

Others argued the opposite, that it was the onslaught on multiculturalism that was fuelling racism. Lee Jasper writes:

How this manifests itself—concretely—is an onslaught on British Muslims, using the religion of Islam as a battering ram. Islam is promoted as uniquely evil, or uniquely backward. The most explicit example is the British National Party, which issued thousands of anti-Muslim leaflets after the London bombings with a graphic illustration of the devastated No 30 bus. According to the BNP, multiculturalism was to blame. The BNP is feeding on the mainstream onslaught against the Muslim communities and multiculturalism.

There was a sad irony in this. The United Kingdom has arguably a better track record on social integration than the rest of Europe and some parts of the United States. The facts of economic and structural inequality remain, and it is this inequality which, arguably, segments Britain, not issues of cultural difference. The Annual Report (2004) of the Ethnic Minority Employment Task Force stressed that black communities were more likely to live in poverty. An estimated 34 per cent of all ethnic minorities resided in low-income households compared with 16 per cent of the white population, and unemployment rates among these groups far exceeded that of the white population. There was also continuing under-representation within the formal political sphere.

4. **Race equality** One of the keys to delivering race equality is a change in the language and conception of multiracial Britain. Discussions on integration, cohesion, citizenship, and multiculturalism perpetuate a narrative of 'us and them'. And it is this discourse that arguably underpins the cultural maintenance of racism at individual, group, and structural levels. Lee Jasper states:

The celebration of diversity is what won us the Olympic games. This model values difference and requires strong commitment and political leadership. It helped to build the kind of unified response we had in the aftermath of the London bombings. This is what we put at risk when we lightly dismiss multiculturalism—a model that actually works.

For Jasper, the whole emphasis of the 'cohesion' agenda needs to be changed and decoupled from the delivery of race equality. Multiculturalism or interculturalism needs to be reasserted as the fundamental premiss for a prosperous Britain and for the well-being and equality of all of its citizens. This must sit alongside a much greater emphasis on economic development, revival of local democracy, anti-poverty strategies, and eradicating institutional, cultural, and individual racism, with more attention paid to the power divide that marginalizes black communities.

KJC

Chauhan, Vipin, *Beyond Steel Bands 'n' Samosas* (1989)

Jasper, Lee, 'Trevor Phillips Is in Danger of Giving Succour to Racists', 14 Oct. 2005, <http://www.blink.org.uk>

Khan, Urmee, 'In Defence of Multiculturalism', 16 Nov. 2005, <http:/www.blink.org.uk>

West, Patrick, *The Poverty of Multiculturalism*, Civitas Report (2005)

See also IMMIGRATION; RACISM

Mungo. Black character in the comic opera *The Padlock*, written by Isaac Bickerstaff (1733–1808?), with music by Charles Dibdin (1745–1814). *The Padlock*, first performed in 1768, was not an opera in the modern sense, but a play interspersed with songs.

In a plot adapted from a novel by the Spanish writer Miguel de Cervantes (1547–1616), Mungo helps Leander, a student, to woo the beautiful young Leonora, even though she is kept locked up by her old guardian, Mungo's master, Diego, who plans to marry her himself. Even more than Ursula, the elderly white woman employed by Diego to guard Leonora, Mungo is the type of servant who is expected to be loyal in spite of being overworked, beaten, and generally mistreated by his master. At the end of the play Diego reconciles himself to the marriage of Leander and Leonora (to whom he gives a handsome dowry), and Ursula is sent away with a large sum of money, but Mungo is promised only more blows.

The Padlock was enormously successful; the first production ran for fifty-three nights, and Mungo's lines about what was expected of a servant,

> what a terrible life I am led! . . .
> Whate'er's to be done,
> Poor black must run;
> Mungo here, Mungo dere,
> Mungo everywhere,

became a catchphrase. It was Bickerstaff's most popular play, often revived in the 18th century, adapted into other European languages, and reprinted in a collection of standard plays (Dolby's British Theatre) as late as 1823.

In the first production Mungo was played by Dibdin himself, a popular (white) actor of the day, and this was the first appearance of a black-face comic character on the English stage. It was also the first attempt at dramatic representation of *Black British English, and marked a departure from the stereotyped 'noble Africans' seen in stage adaptations of **Oroonoko* and other plays. In spite of the Spanish setting and the comic treatment of the character, Mungo must have provoked comparison with the lives of the domestic servants who made up a large proportion of the 18th-century black British population. Bickerstaff seems to have been opposed to slavery; his earlier play *Love in the City* (1767) gives an unfavourable picture of the character Priscilla Tomboy, a white Creole accustomed to mistreating her slaves. Thomas *Clarkson indicates that at least some later 18th-century productions gave *The Padlock* a more explicitly anti-slavery tone. JG

Bickerstaff, Isaac, *The Padlock, a Comic Opera, in Two Acts* (1823)
Gänzl, Kurt, 'Isaac Bickerstaff', *ODNB*
Sypher, Wylie, *Guinea's Captive Kings: British Anti-Slavery Literature of the XVIIIth Century* (1942)

See also LITERATURE 1: REPRESENTATIONS OF BLACKS

Museums. Black British history was apparently little considered by British museums until pioneering campaigners in the 1970s and 1980s raised the subject, and it was not until the accession of the New Labour government in 1997, with its concerns about social inclusion, that museums embraced black history to any significant extent. Although important progress has been made in incorporating black British history in British museums, the enterprise is still in its infancy and vulnerable to the ebb and flow of government funding.

1. Black history in British museums before the 1997 general election
2. The consolidation of black history in British museums
3. Contemporary developments and debates

1. Black history in British museums before the 1997 general election An important milestone in this progress was the founding of the Black Cultural Archive in *Brixton, south London, by Samuel Walker and Len Garrison in 1981. This was the very year of the Brixton riots, and their aim to collect and store artefacts and documents relating to black history in Britain and on the Continent was motivated by a wish to redress the invisibility of black history in schools and museums. Their pioneering act threw down the gauntlet for a future, more inclusive, museum collections policy.

The existence of a black historical presence in Britain had been substantiated beyond doubt by Peter Fryer's paperback history *Staying Power* (1984), which built on the earlier scholarship of Fọlarin Shyllon and James Walvin. It was further buttressed by a new edition that same year of the *Wonderful Adventures of Mrs. Seacole in Many Lands* (whose editors, Ziggi Alexander and Audrey Dewjee, had, five years before, organized a small travelling exhibition on black history). Important, too, were David Dabydeen's revelatory *Hogarth's Blacks*, which documented the black presence in 18th-century English art, and Beverley Bryan, Stella Dadzie, and Suzanne Scafe's *The *Heart of the*

Race (both published in 1985). These developments came at a time of increased anxiety about the educational underachievement of black children in the British schools system and the growing recognition of the need, as detailed by the 1985 Swann Report, for a more ethnically and culturally inclusive school curriculum.

A subsidiary factor affecting the development of black history in museums had to do with the estimated 378 'ethnographic' (and largely non-European) collections held in British museums. Many of the items in these collections, which were first gathered (and in some cases plundered) during Britain's imperial heyday, were woefully under-exhibited and poorly provenanced. This was due partly to underfunding and partly to an ethnocentric misunderstanding of their wider significance. This combination of triumphalism, condescension, and neglect was perhaps first criticized by the Ghanian film-maker Kwate Nee-Owoo in his 1973 film *You Hide Me*, which lambasted the way priceless Benin bronzes were left to languish in the basement of the British Museum. By the 1980s the growing popular interest in African history, as evidenced by the growth of *Rastafarianism among black British youth, and by BBC programmes by Basil Davidson and Ali Mazrui, also helped to subvert traditional attitudes.

The ethnocentricity of British museums began to be further challenged as increasing racial tensions, the conflict over Northern Ireland, and the campaigns for Welsh and Scottish devolution raised questions about the very nature of British identity. As postmodernist and postcolonial theory also began to impact on debates around museum practice, a more reflective and self-critical approach began to take root. Around this time, too, feminist activists, some of whom were teachers and librarians, began to address the issues of racism in schools and museums. Bruce Castle Museum, the local history museum for Tottenham in London, was near the scene of the 1985 *Broadwater Farm riots, and in 1986 staff there, inspired by Sylvia Collicott's publication *Connections: Haringey–Local–National–World Links*, staged a multiracial history exhibition on the local area and subsequently held a conference on racism and museums. In 1986, the year after the Handsworth riots there, Birmingham's City Museum and Art Gallery launched its 'Gallery 33' project, which tried to reinterrogate its ethnographic collections in the light of consultation with the city's ethnic-minority communities. In 1987 the Geffrye Museum, on the advice of Rehana Minhas of the Inner London Education Authority, commissioned the historians Peter Fryer and Rozina Visram to devise a multicultural interpretation of the British room interiors that made up that museum. That year also saw the largely white Women, Heritage, and Museums group (WHAM!) organize the first-ever fringe meeting on racism at a Museums Association conference.

One of the most important grass-roots initiatives that helped to raise consciousness in this regard was the institution in 1987 of *Black History Month. The very concept had been an adaptation of an idea first promoted in 1926 by the African-American historian and publisher Carter Godwin Woodson and amplified by black nationalists in the United States in the 1970s. With 1987 the centenary of Marcus *Garvey's birth, Adkyaaba Addai Sebbo, then a Greater London Council (GLC) employee, promoted, with the help of the GLC, Britain's first Black History Month event in London that year. The idea quickly spread to other cities, providing a focus for an increasingly wide range of history-related activities, a growing number of which became organized by museums, archives, and libraries. Its popularity was further boosted by an independent inquiry headed by Lord Gifford and funded by Liverpool City Council, which in 1989 published a preliminary report into race relations in *Liverpool in the wake of the unrest in the Toxteth area of the city. Pointedly entitled *Loosening the Shackles*, the Report criticized the

Liverpool Maritime Museums' 1984 exhibition on the Port of Liverpool for glossing over the city's role in the slave trade, and concluded that Liverpool's museums and public institutions, when they present Liverpool's history, should give a full and honest account of the involvement of black people in the city.

Five years later, in 1989, a one-day conference at Exeter Museum seems to have been the only museum-based event to celebrate the bi-centenary of the publication of *An Interesting Narrative*, Olaudah *Equiano's historic anti-slavery tract.

By 1991 a group of academics and activists connected with the Institute of Commonwealth Studies, including Marika Sherwood and Hakim Adi, formed the Association for the Study of African, Caribbean, and Asian Culture and History in Britain (renamed the Black and Asian Studies Association in 1997). This Association lobbied ceaselessly through newsletters, conferences, deputations, and letters to promote the development of black history in schools, archives, libraries, and museums.

By the early 1990s temporary exhibitions on the black presence in various British cities were funded in Liverpool, Nottingham, and *London. Liverpool's 1991 exhibition, entitled 'Staying Power' in homage to Peter Fryer's book, grew out of collaboration between museums, the City Council, and a grass-roots anti-racist group. The Museum of London's major exhibition 'The Peopling of London', in 1993–4, also recontextualized the city's history in the light of its ethnic minorities and included significant sections on the black presence.

The year 1994 also saw the historic opening of the 'Transatlantic Slavery: Against Human Dignity' exhibition at the Merseyside Maritime Museum. This was the first permanent exhibition to seek to examine transatlantic slavery and its impact on the modern African diaspora, but it would not have happened without the proactive financial support of a private philanthropist, Peter Moores. Despite its real efforts to show enslaved Africans as active agents with individual identities, the use of older museum practices such as dioramas was seen by some as 'essentializing', rendering the Africans thus portrayed as objects rather than subjects. It was criticized, too, for its relatively small size and basement location, as well as for its depiction of the Middle Passage. Yet the exhibition was successful in many ways, not the least of which was the often stormy consultation process, spanning community groups and academic advisers, first initiated by Alison Taubman and continued by the exhibition's curator, Tony Tibbles. The exhibition would later utilize the offices of the Museum's outreach officer, Gary Morris, one of the first black Britons to hold such a post in the United Kingdom.

In 1996 Bristol City Museum, under its new director, Stephen Price, began, in response to local grass-roots pressure, a strategy to include a discussion of the slave trade and its legacy in the city. This included a small exhibition about the slave-owning activities of the Pinney family, whose *Bristol residence had become the city's Georgian House Museum, and a Bristol slavery trail leaflet noting slavery-related sites in the city. There were plans, too, for a larger exhibition the following year, and the consultation procedures initiated in Liverpool were adopted in Bristol.

In the meantime, three other, smaller exhibitions were staged around this time, two in Scotland and one in London. These were of note because they featured not slavery but rather the experience of individuals and/or families of African descent. The Scottish exhibitions (both held at Edinburgh's City Arts Centre in 1996 and 1997 respectively) focused on those of African-Scots heritage. The first, 'A Celebration of Cultural Diversity', at Edinburgh's City Art Centre, was a joint project by the Workers' Educational Association and the People's Story Museum utilizing oral history interviews, photographic recording, and textile work by members of the city's African-Caribbean and African residents. The second, 'Roots, the African Inheritance in Scotland', made innovative use of three family archives, covering over a century of Scots-African heritage. The third, 'Ignatius Sancho', was held at the National Portrait Gallery in London from January to May 1997 and brought together new material about both Sancho and his social circle in Georgian England.

In January 1997 David Anderson's report to the Department of Culture, Media, and Sport, *Common Wealth: Museums in the Learning Age*, stressed the potential of digital museums and the importance of the wider educational role of museums.

2. The consolidation of black history in British museums By May 1997 Labour's landslide victory in the general election ensured that the pressure for change gathered pace. By December the Prime Minister, Tony Blair, had set up the Social Exclusion Unit, designed to promote social inclusion of previously marginalized groups. In 1997, too, the Black Cultural Archive joined with Middlesex University in a Lottery-funded project aimed at developing current collections of documents, artefacts, videos, audio tapes, and other materials and at devising policies for making them accessible to the wider public.

Over the next few years the government increasingly urged museum professionals to see museums as instruments of social regeneration. The pressure gathered force in 1998 when the 50th anniversary of the voyage of the SS **Empire Windrush* focused attention on post-war Caribbean migration to Britain and research for the Museum and Galleries Commission documented how poorly British museums had catered for their ethnic-minority populations. That same year pronouncements by the Chancellor, Gordon Brown, and guidelines published by the Heritage Lottery Fund made clear that funding would be awarded to museums sensitive to the agenda of social inclusivity. That year also saw the Diversity Project set up at Leicester University to provide bursaries to increase the number of ethnic-minority curators. The rise of Holocaust museums in the 1980s and 1990s in America and Europe appears to have stimulated rather than suppressed institutional interest in ethnic-minority history in Britain more generally, and a project on the hidden histories of Asian, black, and Jewish immigrants to Britain initiated by the Jewish Council for Racial Equality, the Asian–Black–Jewish Forum, and Southampton University, which began in 1998, resulted in the Connections web site and travelling exhibition for schools.

Such developments overrode the significant if muted opposition to the opening of Bristol City Museum and Art Gallery's temporary exhibition 'A Respectable Trade? Bristol and Transatlantic Slavery in 1999', which, though it came too early to benefit from central funding, proved unprecedentedly popular, attracting 120,000 visitors in six months. (A third of the original exhibition was later transferred to Bristol's Industrial Museum on a more permanent basis.) The National Maritime Museum in London also included slavery and the experience of black sailors in its new permanent Trade and Empire Gallery, which opened in May 1999.

The following year saw continuing government emphasis on social inclusion and the promotion of ethnic diversity in the museum world. The 2000 Race Relations (Amendment) Act, which grew out of the Stephen *Lawrence Inquiry, specified the responsibility of public bodies such as museums to combat racial discrimination. An Arts Council symposium, Whose Heritage?, funded in part by the Heritage Lottery Fund, the Museums Association, and the Museums and Galleries Commission, again problematized the Eurocentric assumptions of traditional museum practice and underlined the rarity of black curators in the museum service. A handful of new bursaries was set up in the Department of Museum Studies at Leicester University in response to this problem.

3. Contemporary developments and debates That year 2,000 museums, libraries, and archival services in Britain came under the guidance of a single strategic body, the Museums, Libraries, and

Archives Council. This stimulated communication between these separate services and, as diversity was one of the Council's stated aims, also encouraged more ethnically sensitive attitudes towards cataloguing and collecting. This in turn made possible further discoveries in black history. Linked to this development was the institution of the Caribbean Studies, Black and Asian History project (1999–2002), a pilot project that aimed to identify and map sources relating to Caribbean Studies and the history of black and Asian people in Britain which complemented the work already begun by the Archive Museum of Black Heritage project.

The Internet, too, further blurred the boundaries between museums, libraries, and archives and the outside world. In 2001 the 'Discovering Bristol' digitization project, financed by Lottery money through its New Opportunity Funding programme, put online a virtually expanded version of Bristol's 1999 exhibition 'A Respectable Trade?' This was soon incorporated into the wider Port Cities web site, whose London and Liverpool sections also include material on transatlantic slavery and black history. The BBC and Channel 4 web sites also spawned pages on black history, and the Victoria County History project of the Institute of Historical Research financed the digitization of an enhanced version of the Bristol Slavery Trail, based on the trail commissioned by Bristol City Museum and Art Gallery four years before.

In 2003 the Moving Here web site, covering the history of Britons of Caribbean, Irish, Jewish, and South Asian origin from 1850, made available over 150,000 digitized sources from 30 museums, libraries, and archives in England for the first time. A related Lottery-financed initiative, the Black Presence, an online exhibition dealing with black British history between 1500 and 1800, was produced by the National Archive in collaboration with the Black and Asian Studies Association. The Birmingham Black History web site is another substantive site developed in partnership with the Birmingham Museum and Art Gallery. Related to this development are other educational materials stimulated by the confluence of artists, archivists, and curators, as exemplified by the *What in the World* comic book about black and Asian history published by Manchester City Council and the Manchester Museum and Art Gallery (2002) and the CD-ROM and related materials that make up the Understanding Slavery initiative (2004), financed by the Department of Education and Science and produced by a consortium including the National Maritime Museum, the British Empire and Commonwealth Museum, National Museums Liverpool, and the city museum services in Bristol, London, and Hull.

Although libraries and community groups have led the way with collecting oral testimony from ethnic-minority and dual-heritage Britons, museums too have begun to exploit its potential, the extensive oral history collections at the British Empire and Commonwealth Museum constituting a particularly valuable resource. The Northampton Council for Racial Equality secured Lottery funding for an oral history project involving the city's museum and library. More recently Glenn Jordan's long-standing oral history work at Butetown History and Arts Centre was featured in a Black History Month event at the Welsh National Museum in Cardiff in 2003, while the British Museum has taped reactions from African and African-Caribbean Londoners to augment its labelling of African artefacts in its Africa'05 events. Grass-roots groups continue to use Black History Month as a way of getting museums to engage with black history seriously, the work of the Glasgow Anti-Racist Alliance in Scotland since 2000 being a prime example.

In recent years Black History Month itself has come under increasing fire for encouraging the 'ghettoization' of black history. Critics rightly point to the confinement of most temporary events and exhibitions on black history to October of each year. Yet Black History Month has undeniably provided a crucial impetus for new and creative exhibitions and events that have helped museums to leapfrog over the traditional curatorial boundaries between the arts, history, and ethnography. Such boundaries, as Lucy MacKeith has observed, often impede the development of black history in museums. A vibrantly wide-ranging series of events and temporary exhibitions between 2000 and 2005 included 'Black Looks—A Century of Black and Asian Footballers' at Leicester's New Walk Museum (2000), 'The Colourful Face of Brighton' (2003) at Brighton's Regency Town House, and the Victoria and Albert Museum's exhibition on 50 years of 'Black British Style' (2004), while the 'Black Poppies' film series at the Imperial War Museum (2005) focused on the contribution of black soldiers in the two world wars. The Science Museum's 'Unsung Heroes Day' examined the contribution of black doctors and nurses, inventors, and surgeons through drama and workshops (2005).

At times the events of Black History Month seem to have less to do with historical rigour than with a celebration of contemporary culture. But, properly strategized, this can prove to be a fruitful approach. The British Empire and Commonwealth Museum's Commonwealth FM Radio Station, which ran on three successive Octobers from 2002 to 2004, was not particularly historically oriented, but it attracted new black constituencies to the museum and thereby provided the contacts and ideas for new developments in black history projects there.

But there is likewise a danger that black history in museums might become profoundly uncritical in a bid either to avoid controversy or to court popularity. Authored exhibitions and more coordinated liaison with universities researching in the field would go some way to making black history in museums more accountable to the public.

Equally importantly, black history has begun to become integrated into representations of 'mainstream' British culture, as the 2003 'Below Stairs' exhibition about servants at the National Portrait Gallery, and the installation of the 'West Indian Front Room' by Michael McMillan in the Geffrye Museum (2005), variously attest. MJD

Black and Asian Association Newsletter, 17–45 (Apr. 1997–Sept. 2005)

Dresser, M., and Giles, S. (eds.), *Bristol and Transatlantic Slavery: A Catalogue of the Exhibition 'A Respectable Trade? Bristol and Transatlantic Slavery'* (2000)

Garrison, L., 'The Black Historical Past in British Education' in P. Stone and R. MacKenzie (eds.), *The Excluded Past: Archaeology in Education* (1990)

Gilroy, Paul, *Picturing Blackness in British Art 1700s–1990s*, Tate Gallery, 28 Nov. 1995–10 Mar. 1996 (1995)

MacKeith, Lucy, *Local Black History: A Beginning in Devon* (2003)

See also VISUAL ARTS 1: REPRESENTATIONS OF BLACKS; VISUAL ARTS 2: ARTISTS

Music 1: Classical music. Black composers and musicians have made valuable contributions to classical music in Britain over the centuries, and, in order to do this, they have had to grapple with the social constraints of the period in which they lived.

1. 18th-century music and musicians
2. 19th-century African-Americans
3. The survival of the classical tradition

1. 18th-century music and musicians Earliest records of black composers and musicians involved in classical music in Britain stem from the 18th century, when the black communities in this country were an estimated 20,000. It was a time when the slave trade was flourishing.

Wealthy Whites in this period considered the ownership of black people as servants and slaves a symbol of their social status. Many of the aristocracy and landed gentry dressed their black servants in fine court livery. These servants were generally regarded as curiosities and often treated rather like pampered household pets. It was in this situation that musicians from the servant classes benefited from tuition in music from their aristocratic employers and owners, who wished to cultivate a culturally appreciative workforce in their households. Beneficiaries from such support include Olaudah *Equiano, who took up the French horn in 1767. Julius *Soubise, the son of a Jamaican slave and protégé of the Duchess of Queensberry, was an enthusiastic violinist and composed songs, which were Italian in style. Moyse, a servant to General Charles O'Hara, learned to play the oboe before being appointed to a command on foreign service. Nevertheless, it was Ignatius *Sancho, of this servant class, who as an amateur musician under the patronage of the Duke of Montagu, developed to the point where his musical compositions were acknowledged by European standards as being sufficiently refined and tasteful. Among his publications are a *Theory of Music*, *A Collection of New Songs*, two books of dances and minuets written for various instrumental ensembles, and *Twelve Country Dances* (1779) for harpsichord. His musical style is in keeping with early classical music, but he was most comfortable composing with small musical forms, rather than using the larger musical structures of the classical era. He had a special gift for setting words to music; in particular the poetry of Shakespeare and David Garrick. He became one of the earliest black composers remembered for his achievements as an amateur in classical music.

Musicians from the servant classes were sometimes expected to entertain their patrons and friends, and also provided their own music at their Black Balls, attended solely by Blacks. These Balls were held at public houses, where the music was performed on violins, French horns, and other instruments, which could be heard playing instrumental music as well as supporting the dancing.

Some black musicians became sufficiently professional to be awarded regimental positions in janizary (Turkish) bands, which were very fashionable in mid-18th-century Europe. This music had a profound influence on the music of Mozart, Haydn, and Beethoven, and they adopted it into their own compositions. Janizary music referred to the campaign music of the janizaries, who were employed by Sultan Orkran (1326–59). They came into Europe at the end of the 17th century when the Turkish army had to retreat in the Balkans, and rulers captured these bands, embracing the idea of campaign music. Their instrumentation included shawms (or oboes), fifes, kettledrums, tenor drums, a bass drum, tambourines, triangles, cymbals, and the jingling johnny. The jingling johnny was a percussion instrument made from a pole, with a canopy, along with other shapes hung with bells and pieces of jingling metal. The sound was designed to make a warrior wild and strike terror into the heart of the enemy. When these ensembles first came into Poland, black musicians replaced the Turkish musicians. Likewise, British regiments such as Thomas Farrington's and the Grenadier Guards favoured the use of black musicians, for their impeccable sense of rhythm. They were famed for being able to march along, playing the jingling johnny in numerous positions, throwing drumsticks in the air and catching them, while parading in dazzling uniforms, wearing sashes, tunics, turbans, and plumes. The public in Britain loved the spectacle.

However, to break into the realms of the professional classical music establishment during the 18th century was more difficult for people of colour as there was considerable prejudice. Despite this, a number of musicians managed to integrate into British social circles and become respected for their musical abilities. One of these was the brilliant violinist George *Bridgetower, who may have received his early musical instruction from Franz Joseph Haydn, on the Esterhazy estate in Austria. He sealed his international fame through success at the Concert Spirituel in Paris, and then moved on to London under the patronage of the Prince of Wales, later George IV. From here on his rise through the ranks of the British musical establishment was meteoric. He was to tour Germany and Austria and encounter Beethoven, and premiered the 'Kreutzer' Sonata with him in Vienna in May 1803. He was later to graduate from Cambridge

University with a degree in composition, in June 1811. Bridgetower stunned his audiences when he performed in Britain, and they came to hear him in large numbers.

Le Chevalier de *Saint-Georges enjoyed similar international success, as a conductor, composer, and a brilliant violinist. He commissioned Haydn to compose the 'Paris' Symphonies and went to London to perform during 1789–90, where he was recognized as a brilliant composer and performer. He was at ease moving in royal social circles, both in France with the Duke of Orléans and with Marie-Antoinette, who was known to attend his concerts at the Loge Olympique, and in London, where he also gave fencing demonstrations for the Prince of Wales. Nevertheless, it was racial prejudice that was to prevent him from becoming the director of the Paris Opera, where several women protested to the Queen, stating their objection to taking directions from a 'mulatto'.

Another violinist who enjoyed success was Joseph *Emidy, who from slavery became a second violinist in the orchestra at the Lisbon Opera. When his time as fiddler to the sailors who had kidnapped him came to an end on the ship the *Indefatigable*, he was set free in Falmouth. However, after settling into the community and establishing himself as a composer and receiving recognition locally, racial prejudice was to be the stumbling block, preventing him from being accepted by sponsors of the London professional concert series (one of whom was Johann Salomon, 1745–1815), who were considering ways in which to raise his profile. It was considered to be too great a risk for a man of colour to undertake such enterprise.

Nevertheless, these three musicians had done much to break down racial barriers during the 18th century, within musical circles in Britain. This opened up new avenues for musicians of colour in the 19th century to develop their careers. Despite the success, it is clear that the black musicians of the servant class, the black janizary band musicians, as well as the violinists Bridgetower, Saint-Georges, and Emidy, had built their success on the accepted aesthetic standards that were set by the white musical establishment. There was a satisfaction in what was accomplished, as being familiar and tasteful. The achievements of this group of musicians were also related to the lowly status accorded to people of colour of this epoch. By their achievements these black musicians had demonstrated an intellect that was equivalent to that of white people in this sphere of artistic endeavour, and inspired a sense of awe, amazement, and sheer pleasure for those who attended concert performances. In addition, they had demonstrated the ability to be charming, refined, and cultured, which made them acceptable in white society, a far cry from what was expected of primitive slaves.

2. 19th-century African-Americans By the second quarter of the 19th century the patronage of musicians of the servant class, the bandsmen, and the exceptionally talented classical musicians was beginning to be a process of the past. Instead, visiting black performers, such as Elizabeth Taylor *Greenfield, the *Fisk Jubilee Singers, and many others, arrived on the scene from America, mostly with a new brand of popular music, or with music forced into a popular mode. Elizabeth Taylor Greenfield was welcomed to Britain in 1853, and, despite her agent in Britain failing to complete promised arrangements, she was able to find support and patronage in Lord Shaftesbury, the anti-slavery activist, Harriet Beecher Stowe, and the Duchess of Sutherland. She was then able to sing for London's elite circles, including foreign ambassadors. Despite her musical ability and the favourable reviews she received in the press from her performances around the country, in, among other towns, Brighton, Dublin, and Lincoln, climaxing in a command performance before Queen Victoria and being dubbed 'the Black Swan', she failed to secure further training for her voice as she had hoped. It was this and the depletion of her finances that caused her to return to the United States in 1854. Her voice was felt to be expressive in the ballads she chose, such as 'The Cradle Song' and 'Home Sweet Home', but audiences preferred raw talent that had not been refined by training; she was considered to be a 'genius' in the romantic sense of the word.

Another musical sensation to visit the British music scene was 'Blind Tom' *Bethune, who, in contrast to Elizabeth Taylor Greenfield, was viewed as an autistic savant. His master, James N. Bethune, financially exploited his musical gift over a period that spanned the American Civil War and beyond. Although he was able to hear and perform music he had never heard before, as well as being able to improvise, he also gave piano recitals of European classical music in the United States and in Europe. Despite his great technical ability and enormous talent, he was paraded as a vaudeville attraction, and his real genius was undermined by the fact that he was treated as a bit of curiosity who merited scientific testing. The way in which he was treated contradicted the fact that he was bright and intelligent, his blindness enabling the development of his considerable memory. There were attempts to define him as 'primitive'—fitting a racial stereotype—and operating on instinct rather than using an ability to study music. However, the testimonies of Ignaz Moscheles, Charles Hallé, and many other eminent people are evidence that he was a musician and composer of great talent and substance.

The Fisk Jubilee Singers, a troupe from Fisk University in Nashville, Tennessee, made an enormous impact on Britain in the latter part of the 19th century. They realized their dream of fundraising for the university by touring Britain twice, in April 1873–May 1874 and May 1875–October 1877, taking time to visit the Netherlands for two months. Later Frederick J. Loudin, one of the original members of the Singers, returned to Britain in 1884 and also in 1887 with another vocal ensemble. Their repertoire was such as had not been encountered by the white musical establishment, who did not know how to assess its authenticity since there were *minstrelsy groups mimicking the Negro spiritual tradition; and, in addition to the spirituals, they added sentimental songs to their programme. Their performances were enjoyed wherever they toured in Britain as they were so polished, and their visit was so popular that, in keeping with the tradition of the time, they were invited to give a command performance before Queen Victoria, which was well received. This further enhanced their marketability in Britain, Europe, the United States, and beyond as they performed to packed houses. Audiences included the aristocracy, the gentry, and the clergy, as well as local and regional dignitaries. At this point in the 19th century *Uncle Tom's Cabin* was widely read and there was considerable anti-slavery sympathy within the audiences, who understood the struggle of the Fisk Jubilee Singers, who were striving to fundraise to enable ex-slaves to have a decent education. Newspapers such as *The Standard*, the *Hull News*, the *Daily Telegraph*, and the *Birmingham Morning News* all pronounced on their excellence as they toured cities such as Derby, Sheffield, and Leicester.

The presence of musicians such as Marian *Anderson, the Fisk Jubilee Singers, Edmund Thornton *Jenkins, Roland *Hayes, and Paul *Robeson highlighted the fact that there were better opportunities to build a career in Britain than in segregated America. Fela *Sowande, Ayo *Bankole, and Samuel *Akpabot came from Nigeria, having a knowledge of European and Anglican Church Music as well as their own musical culture, and, by fusing Western with African approaches to composition, they created new worlds of sound.

3. The survival of the classical tradition Classical musicians survived alongside their popular counterparts. Black musicians in the classical music world were taking responsibility for their newfound freedom to determine the direction of their artistic futures, with opportunities they had never had in America.

Amanda *Aldridge played a seminal role in London by welcoming many African-American musicians and artists, and in turn musicians such as Roland Hayes performed her songs at their recitals.

A leading light in London was the composer Samuel *Coleridge-Taylor, who trained at the Royal College of Music. For his monumental composition *Hiawatha* he received such a meagre payment from his publisher that the Performing Rights Society was founded to protect composers' rights. Coleridge-Taylor established himself internationally as of equal importance to—and respected by—such luminaries as Edward Elgar, Arthur Sullivan, Charles Stanford, and Joseph Parry. With his connections with African-American musicians he was able to forge a musical identity that appealed to many black musicians in the African diaspora, yet connected with mainstream tastes in classical music. PAH

Floyd, Samuel A., Jr. (ed.), *Dictionary of Black Composers*, i and ii (1999)

Omojola, Bode, *Nigerian Art Music* (1995)

Wright, Josephine, 'Early African Musicians in Britain' in Rainer E. Lotz and Ian Pegg (eds.), *Under the Imperial Carpet: Essays in Black History 1780–1950* (1986)

See also MUSIC 2: EARLY POPULAR MUSIC

Music 2: Early popular music. Before the First World War British music hall circuits had a strong weekly demand for new acts, catered for by specialist booking agencies and by theatre chains, notably Moss, Stoll, and Barrasford. There were widespread performances by black groups copying the *Fisk Jubilee Singers, which had presented spirituals across Britain from the 1870s. And there were the concert and recital room creations of the London-born composer Samuel *Coleridge-Taylor, whose *Hiawatha* and instrumental works were popular into the 1950s. African-American visitors introduced vaudeville, burlesque, and song and dance to British audiences, and deeply influenced black British artists.

American black musical revues were booked for London and provincial theatres. Most started in England, then toured to continental Europe. From the 1920s tours often started in Paris; some moved to London. Although American musicians found it difficult to obtain work permits, there was a steady stream of visitors. The 1930s saw a growth in the number of black Britons, often Caribbean, in mainstream entertainment, dance, and popular music. But it was after the arrival in 1948 of the **Empire Windrush* that Caribbeans settled in great numbers, and established a musical identity as documented in calypso recordings and, later, the *Notting Hill Carnival.

1. Musical shows and revues
2. Entertainers and bandleaders
3. Composers and conductors
4. Singers

1. Musical shows and revues The all-black show *In Dahomey* took London by storm in 1903. It consisted of 40 Americans, and took Bert Williams and George Walker to stardom. Inspired by this success, Will Garland (born in Iowa) settled in London and toured with his *A Trip to Coontown* from 1906. He directed other revues and a 'coloured opera troupe' into the 1930s and in these mainly employed black Britons and long-term American residents: *Coloured Society* in 1916 and again in 1922, *All Black* in 1917, *Down South* in 1923, *Coloured Lights* in 1925, *Brownbirds* in 1927 and again in 1937; and *Down South* in 1936.

The year 1923 brought two 'Plantation' revues from New York to London: *The Rainbow* at the Empire, Leicester Square (with music provided by the band of the New Jersey-born composer, soon to be famous for the Charleston, James P. Johnson) and *Dover Street to Dixie* at the Pavilion (with music provided by the Philadelphia-born Will Vodery's orchestra). Both productions also included white segments, and both experienced racial comments in Parliament, by the Musicians' Union, and in the press. The three stars of *Dover Street to Dixie*—the song and dance artist Florence Mills, the singer Edith Wilson, and the acrobatic dancer Ulysses S. Thompson—also starred in the white promoter Lew

Leslie's *Blackbirds of 1926*, which came to the London Pavilion from Paris. Johnny Dunn's Plantation Orchestra was essential to the show, but the regular theatre orchestra remained on the payroll (as a condition of the work permits). Tennessee-born Dunn's band recorded in London. The projected transfer from Paris of Lew Leslie's *Blackbirds of 1928* never took place. An unrelated British *Blackbirds of 1928* did tour (February 1928–May 1929), with music provided by white pit orchestras. Leslie returned to Britain with *Blackbirds of 1934*, with 67 cast members, including a twelve-strong Blackbirds Orchestra directed by the Baltimore-born trumpeter Clifton 'Pike' Davis, augmented in London by eight local musicians (including the Jamaica-born trumpeter Leslie *Thompson). The star was Valaida Snow, who conducted the orchestra for 'Rhapsody in Blue', a title not included in the Tennessee trumpeter's twelve visits to recording studios.

Two different shows bore the name *Blackbirds of 1936*, a British road company, featuring Valaida's sister Lavaida Carter and the Nigerian pianist Fela *Sowande, and Lew Leslie's London production, which retained Carter and Sowande. This latter company of 36 also included the composer–pianist J. Rosamond Johnson, the singers Una Mae Carlisle and Eunice Wilson, and the tap-dancing Nicholas Brothers. Carter and the Nicholas Brothers recorded two numbers each from the show. There were other shows up to 1940, including Teddy Hill and the Cotton Club's revue *Harlem on Parade* of 1937 (first in Paris, then at the London Palladium), with the American cast from the United States except for the Memphis-born singer Alberta Hunter, who was recruited in France; and Lew Lake Jr.'s *Blackberries* (1937–8).

After the war the black music and dance revue tradition was revived. The group Les *Ballets Nègres, founded by the Jamaican dancer and choreographer Berto Pasuka, enjoyed a successful first season in 1946, featuring in, for example, the June 1946 issue of *Theatre World*. In 1948 the celebrated African-American dancer and choreographer Katherine Dunham brought her show *Caribbean Rhapsody* to London, where it ran for several months at the Prince of Wales Theatre. One review said: 'A first-night audience was bewildered, enthralled, wildly enthusiastic about a new-type musical which exhilarates with its speed and animal primitiveness.' The music included elements of ragtime, Caribbean melodies, boogie-woogie, blues, and a number of ballroom dance tempos.

2. Entertainers and bandleaders A very popular genre of entertainment, both in vaudeville and on records, were piano duets and cross-talking acts. George Carlisle (possibly from Trinidad) and Harry Welmon (who had been in America after leaving Bermuda), performed in England from 1908 to the early 1920s. John Turner Layton from Washington DC could already look back on an extremely successful career as an entertainer, lyricist, songwriter, and recording artist when he teamed up with Clarence Johnstone (an orthopaedic surgeon) and left the United States for London in 1924. As Layton & Johnstone they were among the highest-paid entertainers in Europe, and their discs sold by the million. Their pictures were also printed on sheet music. The partnership was dissolved in 1935 but Layton continued as a solo performer on stage, radio, and television; he died in 1978.

The Americans Eubie Blake and Noble Sissle arrived in 1925 and returned several times. They were so successful that about ten of their joint compositions were accepted by London publishers within a few months, and their recordings sold well. Of the American pianist Ford Lee Washington and his tap-dancing partner John Sublett it was said that their 'gagging was so good as to overshadow their music' (they visited as Buck & Bubbles in 1930 and 1936, and recorded).

Leslie 'Hutch' *Hutchinson was born in Grenada, and studied law in New York and music in Paris. He arrived in London in

1927 to perform in several revues. His velvet voice and polished piano style made him one of the United Kingdom's favourite cabaret artistes for decades in top-class restaurants and hotels. He did broadcasts, made recordings, entertained troops during the *Second World War, and was professionally active until shortly before his death.

Hutchinson's namesake the trumpeter Leslie 'Jiver' Hutchinson (1907–59) worked with Bertie King's band in his native Jamaica. In England from 1934, he worked with his fellow Jamaican multi-instrumentalist Leslie Thompson's Emperors of Jazz, and recorded with Ken 'Snakehips' *Johnson. In 1944 he was, for billing purposes, nominal leader of a swing band supported by his four business partners Bertie King, Dave Wilkins, Yorke de Souza, and Clinton Maxwell. The balance of the band included other black Caribbean musicians, some of whom had previously been with Ken Johnson (who had died in a bombing raid in 1941). Johnson, a self-taught dancer from British Guiana with no musical training, had been sent to school near London. In 1937 he assumed leadership of Thompson's group and developed it into one of the best swing orchestras in England, making British audiences aware of the contribution of black musicians to *jazz.

3. Composers and conductors Edmund Thornton *Jenkins played in bands at the Jenkins's orphanage established by his father in Charleston, South Carolina. From 1914 to 1921 he studied at the Royal Academy of Music in London. While in Europe he earned his living by playing in jazz-dance bands, some directed by him. Inspired by Samuel Coleridge-Taylor and Will Marion Cook, his aspiration was to become a conductor and composer of serious music, but racial prejudice made this impossible in the United States. In his symphonic works he attempted to fuse African-American and European music. More than 60 years after his early death in Paris his music was performed and recorded in America.

Rudolph *Dunbar from British Guiana studied music in the United States. In 1925 he went to Europe, and settled in England in 1931, where, like Jenkins, he worked as a clarinettist with jazz as well as classical groups. He recorded with his African Polyphony and led the orchestra in the 1934 stage show *Black Rhythm*. In 1942 he made his debut as the youngest and first black conductor with the London Philharmonic Orchestra. He was also the head the School of Modern Clarinet Playing in London.

Benny Carter (1907–2003), a New Yorker, came to Britain with a work permit to arrange for the BBC Dance Orchestra. He stayed for a year and provided four or five arrangements per week for broadcasting purposes. He composed new tunes, two being published by Peter Maurice, and many were recorded during his four visits to the Vocalion company studios, including 'Nightfall', 'Blue Interlude', and a vocal version by Elisabeth Welch of 'When Lights Are Low' (with words by Spencer Williams). The composer–lyricist Spencer Williams (1889–1965), born in New Orleans, was one of the most prolific writers of popular songs, with 'Basin Street Blues', 'Careless Love', 'Royal Garden Blues', and 'I've Found a New Baby' to his credit, to name but a few. From 1925 he worked in Europe, and lived near London from 1932 to the 1950s. He contributed the English words 'A Bluer Kind of Blues' to Django Reinhardt's Parisian wartime hit 'Nuages'.

Reginald Foresythe (1907–58) was born in London to a West African barrister and a German mother. He spent some time in the United States, where he wrote arrangements for Earl Hines and Paul Whiteman, and recorded in an orchestra alongside Benny Goodman, John Kirby, and Gene Krupa. In England in 1933 he formed a band, recording his own witty, avant-garde compositions with little improvisation. He made use of woodwind, including the oboe and bassoon, examples being 'Serenade for a Wealthy Widow',

'The Autocrat Before Breakfast', and 'Dodging a Divorcee'. He also wrote and recorded longer works, such as *Southern Holiday: A Phantasy of Negro Moods*.

4. **Singers** The first half of the 20th century witnessed the arrival of American singers, dancers, and actresses. Florence Mills (1896–1927), perhaps the most famous African-American entertainer of her generation, performed in two London revues (she was also in the 1926 *Blackbirds*). Alberta Hunter (1895–1984) introduced genuine blues singing to Britain, but is best remembered for starring opposite Paul *Robeson in *Show Boat* at the Drury Lane Theatre in 1929. Brooklyn-born Adelaide *Hall left Paris, where she was replaced by the black Briton Mabel *Mercer, for London in 1938, to become one of Britain's best-loved and most versatile entertainers, equally at home in nightclubs, the concert hall, radio, and variety. Elisabeth Welch (1904–2003) settled in London in 1933 to become a permanent fixture in London's West End musical theatre, and film. In London in 1929 the Pennsylvania-born blues singer and comedienne Ethel Waters (1896–1977) made her first vaudeville appearance in Europe. Other visitors of the 1930s included Nina Mae McKinney, Una Mae Carlisle, and Ada Brown. Evelyn Dove, born in London of a Sierra Leonean father, appeared in the Trinidadian Edric *Connor's music series *Serenade in Sepia* on both radio (from 1945) and television (1947). In 1948 the two appeared in the London musical *Calypso*. Sam Manning arrived in 1934 from Trinidad via New York; a year later his were the first recordings of idiomatic English-speaking Caribbean music made in Britain. During the late 1940s West Indians arrived in greater numbers: Lord Beginner, Lord Invader, Freddie Grant, Lord *Kitchener, the Lion, Mighty Terror, and Mona Baptiste are some of the performers who became well known through their recordings of calypso music.

Paul Robeson broadcast and recorded spirituals, and made films in the 1930s. The Musicians' Union still placed substantial barriers to reduce and prevent foreign musicians from working in Britain. The entertainment world changed with widespread access to television from the 1950s, and dance halls changed to present rock 'n' roll, itself a result of black American folk musicians such as William 'Big Bill' Broonzy and the duo Brownie McGhee and Sonny Terry, who visited Britain and whose recordings sold widely. Older blues records were reissued and enthusiasts copied them, and thus were born the Beatles and the Rolling Stones, whose globally popular versions of black American music changed British popular music for ever. The Trinidad-born concert pianist Winifred *Atwell made many television appearances in the 1950s, and sold thousands of discs of semi-ragtime tunes; and the Yorkshire-born Geoff Love's (1917–91) orchestral arrangements sold millions on vinyl LP, especially as Manuel and His Music of the Mountains. Neither entertainer was following the traditional route in black entertainment. Their audiences were distinct from the new teenage culture that had developed through blues and rock 'n' roll. JPG/REL

Breese, Charlotte, *Hutch* (1999)

Lotz, Rainer E., and Pegg, Ian (eds.), *Under the Imperial Carpet: Essays in Black History 1780–1950* (1986)

Oliver, Paul (ed.), *Black Music in Britain: Essays on the Afro-Asian Contribution to Popular Music* (1990)

Storyville, 1–162 (Oct. 1965–June 1995)

See also BALLETS NÈGRES, LES; BLACK DANCE; GRAMOPHONE RECORDINGS; MUSIC 1: CLASSICAL MUSIC

N

Naimbana, Henry Granville (*c*.1767–1791). Student, born the son of Bureh, regent (Nengbana) of the Koya Temne of Sierre Leone, who in 1791 granted land for a settlement to an agent of the London-based Sierra Leone Company (who mistakenly called him King Naimbana). Aged about 24, he went to England for education at the Company's expense. The directors welcomed 'the Black Prince' enthusiastically, particularly Henry *Thornton, the chairman, and Granville *Sharp, the originator of the settlement project, from whom he took new names and became Henry Granville Naimbana. They saw in him a means of fulfilling their mission to introduce 'the Blessings of Civilization and Industry' into Africa.

Described as 'easy, manly and confident' in deportment, 'pettish and implacable' in disposition, and with 'a great thirst for knowledge', he proved an excellent student. A surviving letter he wrote is lucidly expressed and well written. Thornton recorded anecdotes of his reactions to life in England: how he reacted violently against anyone who spoke ill of Africa or defended the slave trade, and how, to illustrate his strong religious feelings, when reading aloud from a book that contained what he thought was an impure idea, he dashed it in fury against the wall.

In 1793 he returned home, fell ill on board ship (his feelings were also wounded by the sailors' obscene language), and died in his mother's arms within a few hours of landing. CF

Falconbridge, Anna Maria, *Narrative* (2000)

Rydings, R. A., *Sierra Leone Studies*, new ser. (1957)

See also SIERRA LEONE SETTLERS

Naoroji, Dadabhai (1825–1917). The first Asian elected to the House of Commons. Dadabhai Naoroji was born in Bombay in 1825. The son of a Parsee priest, he was educated at Elphinstone Institute School and later became a teacher.

In 1855 Naoroji was appointed Professor of Mathematics and Natural Philosophy. He became involved in politics and in 1867 helped to establish the East India Association. He was one of the first leaders of the Indian nationalist movement, who supported independence for India. He played an important role in establishing the Indian National Congress in 1865 and in 1886 was appointed President of the Indian National Congress.

Naoroji moved to England and joined the Liberal Party, and in July 1892 was successfully elected to Parliament, where he represented Finsbury. He therefore became the first Asian to be elected to the House of Commons. Although he promised that his first duty would be to his constituents, he made no secret of the fact that he would also be representing India's interests.

Over the next few years Naoroji campaigned against the financial drain on India caused by British imperialist taxation and trade regulations. On the left wing of the party, he also advocated Irish Home Rule and extensive social reforms.

Following his defeat in the 1895 general election Naoroji concentrated on writing books such as *Poverty and Un-British Rule in India* (1901) and *The Rights of Labour* (1906). By the time of his death in 1917 he became to be known as the Grand Old Man of India. SUM

Naoroji, Dadabhai, *Essays, Speeches, Addresses and Writings* (1887)
ODNB

Narayan, Rudy. Nickname of Rahasya Rudra Narayan (1938–1998), barrister and civil rights activist. He was born in British Guiana (now Guyana), the ninth of ten children of Indo-Guyanese parents. He arrived in Britain in 1953, and after a series of menial jobs enlisted in the Royal Army Ordnance Corps, where he served until 1965, before leaving with the rank of sergeant. He then read for the Bar, at Lincoln's Inn, where he helped to found the Bar Students' Union, and later also became the Union's first president. He was called to the Bar in 1968, a year before his marriage to Dr Naseem Akbar, with whom he had two daughters.

When, in 1973, Narayan and Sighbat Kadric QC founded the Association of Commonwealth Lawyers (the predecessor to the Immigrant Lawyers' Group, which became the Society of Black Lawyers in 1981), the chairman of the Bar Council called the move divisive, unhelpful, and contrary to the traditions of the Bar. He went on to link the formation of the organization to a form of legal apartheid. But prior to 1973 only UK citizens could become solicitors, and by excluding minority lawyers on the basis of this citizenship test, the legal profession had itself been operating a form of apartheid for hundreds of years.

As a barrister Narayan quickly developed a reputation as a fluent, powerful, and persuasive speaker. At a time when the black community felt itself under siege by the *criminal justice system, he emerged as one of the foremost advocates and defenders of black civil rights. He successfully defended a series of high-profile trials involving confrontations between black people and the police, and acquired a reputation among the black community as 'a people's champion'. However, his forthright and very public criticisms of racism within the criminal justice system were to have lasting consequences for his career as a barrister. In 1974 he publicly accused his colleagues at the Bar of being racists, a charge that led to disciplinary action by the Bar Council. In 1980 he was again reprimanded by the Council for discourtesy to a judge, and in 1982 he again faced charges of professional misconduct, after issuing a press statement in which he claimed that senior law lords, including the Attorney-General and the Director of Public Prosecutions, were in collusion with the extreme right-wing National Front. On that occasion, though his accusations were adjudged to be 'scandalous and contemptuous', he was nevertheless acquitted. He was, however, temporarily suspended from the Bar after being found guilty of four other unrelated charges. His career as a barrister foundered in 1984 after his expulsion from his chambers in the Inner Temple following an assault on the chambers' head at a conference. The series of disciplinary adjudications culminated in 1994 in his disbarment for professional misconduct.

Despite his tempestuous relations with his colleagues at the Bar, Narayan achieved success in the trials arising out of the Bristol riots of 1980 and the Bradford petrol bomb case of 1982. In the same decade he helped to found *Brixton's Community Law Centre, of which he was the first chairman, and where he held regular surgeries, providing free or affordable legal advice to the Lambeth community. He also became involved in local politics, and in 1989 stood, unsuccessfully, as an independent candidate in a by-election in the south London constituency of Vauxhall, in protest at the Labour Party's 'outrageous and blatant exclusion of black candidates for a constituency made safe for Labour by black votes'. Referring to the racism of the British criminal justice system, Narayan charged that 'if the brilliant Afro-American lawyer who defended O. J. Simpson, Johnny Cochrane, had been born in England instead of the United States, his life and career would have been destroyed a long time ago by Britain's judiciary and the legal profession'. His books *Black Community on Trial*

(1976), *Black England* (1977), *Barrister for the Defence* (1985), and *When Judges Conspire* (1989) highlighted the legal system's self-assurance about racial discrimination. Such public denunciations of his profession did little to enhance his reputation among his colleagues, or the media, which systematically vilified him. In 1995 he was accused by the press, politicians, and the police of having incited a minor riot that erupted after a speech he delivered to a crowd of angry young Blacks outside Brixton police station, following the death of a black man in custody.

His first marriage having ended in divorce, he married, on 26 March 1988, Saeeda Begum Shah, though this second marriage also ended in divorce. Narayan died at King's College Hospital, Lambeth, on 28 June 1998. CJ

Narayan, Rudy, *Barrister for the Defence* (1985)
ODNB

National Health Service. The National Health Service (NHS) was established in 1948 to provide free and accessible health care for all. Labour shortages in crucial areas such as nursing led to recruitment campaigns throughout the Caribbean for workers to staff this new public service. Ironically, the recruitment drive was led by the Minister of Health, Enoch *Powell MP, who would later emerge as one of the most vociferous anti-immigration politicians. Powell's brief was to recruit nurses and other support workers from the Caribbean to help build the nascent NHS. Nurses were recruited from across the English-speaking Caribbean but primarily from Jamaica, Barbados, Trinidad, and Guyana. Doctors also came from the Caribbean.

Early studies showed that black women from the Caribbean who migrated to England in the 1950s and 1960s were channelled into ancillary and auxiliary jobs within the NHS. Even when they attempted to undertake nursing training, many were offered training opportunities within the less senior and lower-status state-enrolled nurse programmes, a pattern that continues to the present day. Indeed, recent changes in nursing training and promotion policies have weakened the position of state-enrolled nurses still further. Black nurses were also channelled into the least prestigious areas of work: psychiatric and geriatric nursing in particular.

Although the new NHS was established with the labour of black women, recent changes in the professionalization of the NHS have impacted negatively on their position within the service. Indeed, C. V. Baxter argued in 1988 that black nurses were becoming an endangered species, with discrimination operating within nursing training schools and colleges. Discrimination in training and the limited promotion opportunities have meant that fewer black women are choosing to undertake nursing training.

Although the NHS is still one of the largest employers of staff, black and minority ethnic workers are located within the lower sectors of the organization, with very few black senior managers. A King's Fund survey of non-executives of health authority and trust boards reported that only 45 out of 1,531 non-executive members of regional health authorities, NHS trusts, and special health authorities in March 1993 were from black and minority ethnic communities (3 per cent). Similarly, only four out of 534 chairs of health authorities and trusts were from black and minority ethnic communities, and only one of these was female.

Early research on the health care of black and ethnic minorities focused very much on illnesses and diseases that were seen as exotic: tuberculosis and inherited blood disorders such as sickle-cell anaemia and thalassaemia. It is only relatively recently that health research has started to focus on social and economic factors that influence the health of Caribbean communities in the United Kingdom. While there has been a dearth of research on the reproductive health of black and minority ethnic women, there has been a focus on hypertension, mental health, and inherited blood disorders. More recently research has focused on exploring the intersection of ethnicity, gender, and social class.

Early reports by the Brent Community Health Council in 1981 highlighted discrimination in service provision to black communities. These results were worrying, especially given the concentration of black nurses among NHS staff. Areas of discrimination highlighted were in access to appropriate services; diagnosis and misdiagnosis of specific conditions (particularly mental health); and poor treatment by some white NHS staff. In terms of inherited blood disorders predominant within the black community—sickle-cell anaemia and thalassaemia—screening and treatment for these conditions is still patchy. In many hospitals there is still inadequate recognition of the dietary needs of black and minority ethnic people, either in relation to the provision of hospital meals or in relation to the provision of appropriate dietary advice by dietitians, health visitors, or midwives.

Where changes in health services have been made, these have often been the result of campaigns for more appropriate health services organized by black community organizations such as the Sickle Cell Society. In 2001 the Race Relations (Amendment) Act 2000 came into force, which extended the duty to promote race equality to all public sector organizations, including the NHS. JD

Baxter, C. V., *The Black Nurse: An Endangered Species* (1988)

Beishon, S., Virdee, S., and Hagell, A., *Nursing in a Multi-Ethnic NHS* (1995)

Bryan, Beverley, Dadzie, Stella, and Scafe, Suzanne, *The Heart of the Race: Black Women's Lives in Britain* (1985)

See also FEMINISM

Native Choir from Jamaica. The Kingston Choral Union, renamed for a British tour 1906–8. Sir Alfred Jones, shipowner and merchant, employed the Kingston Choral Union to sing at the Colonial Products Exhibition in *Liverpool in early 1906. Billed as the Native Choir from Jamaica, it numbered six males and four females, including the pianist Henry Nation, the bass and comic Carlton Bryan, the prima donna Adeline McDermot, the soprano Connie Coverley, and the conductor Ellis Jackson. The press reported that they had sung 'in good English' and that the 'dusky' singers—'strangers from beyond the seas'—had presented 'our National Anthem'. The singing was praised, and concerts had to be repeated. Theatrical entrepreneurs saw an opportunity, and the choir toured Britain. 'Native costumes' were worn; otherwise formal wear dominated.

Summer seaside entertainment included concerts in Whitby and Bridlington, and two spells in Worthing. The tour reached Ireland in December 1906. Members of the choir returned to Jamaica, but most were back in Liverpool in March 1907. This time the choir numbered fifteen, including William Masters, the Liverpool-born son of a Jamaican father, recruited in Wrexham. This tour continued into 1908, with appearances in Plymouth (August) and Blackpool (September), closing in Liverpool in November. Their performances included Jamaican street songs. The tenor Louis Drysdale settled in London, where he taught singing into the 1930s; the soprano Marie Lawrence performed in London in the 1920s. JPG

Green, Jeffrey, *Black Edwardians: Black People in Britain 1901–1914* (1998)

See also GOSPEL MUSIC; MUSIC 2: EARLY POPULAR MUSIC

Negro Operetta Company. A company of singers and dancers led by Will Garland, a black theatrical entrepreneur. Garland, an African-American, was multi-talented, from a background of singing, dancing, and comedy-acting in minstrel troupes between 1899 and 1900. As an entrepreneur he carved out a career presenting 'Negro operetta'. This genre description was misleading, as operetta for him meant a song-and-dance ensemble, forming a Creole troupe. For help with dance he relied on artistes like Louis Douglas (an African-American with whom he worked in

1914), famed for his creativity in dance and choreography.

Garland developed a career in London from the 1900s to the 1930s. He presented shows such as *A Trip to Coontown* (in 1906), *A Journey in Negroland* (in 1910), *Coloured Society* (in 1917), and *Brownbirds* (in 1927). He toured England, the Netherlands, Belgium, Hungary, Austria, and Russia with these shows, employing black Americans, white song-and-dance performers, and non-American Blacks who were British subjects.

A Trip to Coontown was a farce, relating the story of a conman whose schemes fail, bringing about a happy ending. Premiered in New York in 1898 this show was a first, being written, directed, and performed by Blacks. The show, like many of this epoch, included plantation songs, *minstrelsy acrobatics, and the cakewalk, satirizing the posturing that took place at slave owners' balls. The impact of such genres helped to reinforce stereotypical images of the black performer and life on slave plantations. PAH

Lotz, Rainer E., 'Will Garland and His Negro Operetta Company' in Rainer E. Lotz and Ian Pegg (eds.), *Under the Imperial Carpet: Essays in Black History 1780–1950* (1986)

See also MUSIC 2: EARLY POPULAR MUSIC

Negro Servant, The. Story by the Revd Legh Richmond (1772–1827), unusual in that it describes a genuine relationship between a Cambridge-educated vicar and a former slave. When it was first published, probably in 1804, few British anti-slavery sympathizers would have met any Africans. They might well have shared Richmond's overview of Africa as a 'mass of gloom' inhabited by 'the degraded Hottentot and the poor benighted Negro'. Richmond, however, got to know an African slave: William, taken as a child to Jamaica, and now the freed servant of a naval family in his Isle of Wight parish. His tract records the transformation of William 'from the once dark, perverse and ignorant heathen to this now convinced, enlightened and believing Christian'. Their dialogues capture the flavour of Jamaican speech: 'Some wicked people, dat do not love Jesus Christ, call me great fool, and Negro dog, and black hypocrite—me say nothing again to them.' Richmond's attitude of patronizing benevolence developed into genuine respect: 'I leant upon his arm with the feelings of a *brother*.' Introduced into a cottage prayer group, William was overcome by their unexpected welcome. One of the labourers present said, 'I see, Sir, that though some men are white and some are black, true Christianity is all of one colour.'

This is the message of *The Negro Servant*, one of several stories about Richmond's poorer parishioners, whom he much admired. It was later included in his *Annals of the Poor* (1814), selling over 2 million copies and read by Queen Victoria and the Tsar of Russia. BW

Richmond, Legh, *Annals of the Poor* (1814)

See also CHRISTIANITY; MISSIONARY SOCIETIES

Negro Welfare Association. One of the most prominent black organizations in Britain during the 1930s. Formed in London in 1931, the Negro Welfare Association (NWA) was an affiliate of both the British section of the League Against Imperialism and the International Trade Union Committee of Negro Workers, formed in 1928. The NWA included prominent members close to the Communist Party such as Reginald Bridgeman, Hugo Rathbone, Ben Bradley, and the heiress Nancy *Cunard, who was also an early member. Its leading black activists were the Barbadians Arnold Ward and Peter *Blackman and two West Africans, Desmond Buckle and Rowland Sawyer.

The NWA stood 'for the complete liberation and independence of all Negroes who are suffering from capitalist exploitation and imperialist domination', and its membership, which included such personalities as Jomo Kenyatta and Isaac Wallace-Johnson, were mainly active in London, Liverpool, Manchester, and Cardiff. It campaigned against racism and the colour bar in Britain, as well as supporting anti-colonial struggles in African and the Caribbean. It maintained contacts with organizations and individuals in Africa, the Caribbean, and the United States. Its members were particularly active during the Scottsboro campaign in the 1930s to secure justice for nine African-American teenagers falsely accused of rape in Alabama, when it was instrumental in forming the Scottsboro Defence Committee, and in regard to the problems faced by black seamen and their families. Among its many other activities it regularly organized seaside outings for deprived children.

In 1935 the NWA produced a new constitution asserting the need for entirely 'Negro' leadership, and although it became increasingly active during the late 1930s, particularly in regard to the labour rebellions in the Caribbean and under the leadership of Peter Blackman and Desmond Buckle, its activities ceased during the Second World War. HA

Adi, Hakim, Holledge, Julie, and Sherwood, Marika, *Pan-African History: Political Figures from Africa and the Diaspora Since 1787* (2003)

See also COMMUNISM

Nelson, Edward (1874/8–1940). Lawyer in Lancashire and Cheshire born in British Guiana (now Guyana). The son of a Georgetown builder, Nelson studied at St John's College, Oxford (1898–1902), where he was an officer of the Oxford Union under Prime Minister Asquith's son Raymond. He was called to the Bar at Lincoln's Inn in 1904, and established his legal practice in Manchester and his home at Bowdon, then Hale, Cheshire. He married, had a daughter, played cricket, and was elected to Hale Council from 1913 to his death. He chaired the Council in 1937.

Nelson achieved fame following the murder of George Storrs at Stalybridge in 1909. As defence lawyer, Nelson secured the acquittal of Mark Wilde, who had been accused of the crime. The *Yorkshire Herald* called him 'the coloured barrister' (29 October 1910) but the *Stalybridge Reporter* of that date just published his photograph.

Fifteen black males on trial following riots in *Liverpool in mid-1919 were defended by Nelson, his fees paid by London's *African Progress Union. Nelson was involved in establishing the *League of Coloured Peoples in London in 1931. He kept in contact with British Guiana, had relatives visit, and was involved in the Manchester International Group, a refugee aid group whose founder recalled Nelson as a 'quiet gentleman'. JPG

Goodman, Jonathan, *The Stabbing of George Harry Storrs* (1984)
ODNB

New Cross fire. In the early hours of Sunday morning, 18 January 1981, a fire engulfed a family home at 439 New Cross Road, in south-east London, where a birthday party was being held. Thirteen African-Caribbean youths, all aged between 15 and 20, lost their lives. A further 27 people suffered injury, and a fourteenth partygoer died in 1983, following a deterioration of his mental health in the wake of the dreadful events he had witnessed.

The New Cross fire was to mark a pivotal point in race relations in England. The tragic deaths occurred at a particularly turbulent time in British race relations. Throughout the 1970s black communities across the country had been experiencing a wave of racist attacks and murders. What was widely perceived to be police indifference and failure to protect black people fuelled anger among black communities. The *'Sus Law' that was used specifically to target young Blacks further worsened relations between black communities and the police. In this state of heightened racial tension, the early dismissal by the police of surviving partygoers' claims that the fire had been deliberately started by a firebomb thrown into the house by racists, and the counter-suggestion by police that the fire had probably been started by one or more disgruntled black youths, ignited the anger of the African-Caribbean community. Frustrated by the lack of police progress in establishing the cause of the blaze, local black groups organized the *Black People's Day of Action on 2 March 1982, a historic occasion which, for the first time in Britain, mobilized over 20,000 black people to march through the streets of London to Downing Street, where they presented a petition demanding a full and proper investigation into the fire. An inquest held in April and May 1981 returned an open verdict, a finding that was subsequently challenged by the New Cross Families Committee. When riots erupted in *Brixton in the spring of 1981, it was widely believed that the police handling of the fire and the initial police reaction to it had been catalysts for the uprisings.

Sustained pressure from the New Cross Families Committee forced the Metropolitan Police to begin a new investigation in 1997, and in January 2001 the Metropolitan Police put up its biggest ever reward—£50,000—in a bid to discover those responsible for starting the blaze. The following year saw a new High Court action, which led to an order for a second inquest, which was held in 2004. This second inquest also resulted in an open verdict, though in the intervening period more information had been discovered in police files, and advances in forensic technology had helped to remove some of the uncertainty about the causes of the fire. There is now a growing acceptance that the fire was the result of an unfortunate accident; however, criticisms surrounding the initial police investigations and their indifferent treatment of the victims' families remain. CJ

La Rose, John, *The New Cross Massacre Story* (1984)

See also CRIMINAL JUSTICE SYSTEM; LA ROSE, JOHN

New Times and Ethiopian News. Newspaper established by Sylvia Pankhurst in 1936, following the Italian invasion of *Ethiopia. Pankhurst (1882–1960) was a veteran of the campaign in Britain to secure women's right to vote. She was also involved in various working-class women's organizations; as a socialist pacifist she opposed the *First World War, welcomed the Russian Revolution, and condemned Italian Fascism. Pankhurst realized that Mussolini's imperial plans would lead to war with Ethiopia. She helped to found the Abyssinian Association and wrote articles in British newspapers in support of that country's interests. After Italy invaded Ethiopia in 1935, Pankhurst founded her weekly newspaper, the *New Times and Ethiopian News*, which she edited for exactly twenty years, from 1936 to 1956. In the 1930s the newspaper sold 10,000 copies and was published in Woodford, Essex. It supported the League of Nations, opposed Fascism, contained news about Italian violence in Ethiopia, campaigned for Ethiopian interests in Britain, and protested at various aspects of British imperialism.

The Italian aggression in East Africa stimulated black nationalist feeling around the world and the *New Times and Ethiopian News* gained an international readership especially in West Africa and the West Indies. In Britain pro-Ethiopian organizations were set up, such as the International Friends of Abyssinia, which cooperated with existing black lobbies such as the *League of Coloured Peoples and the *West African Students' Union. When Ethiopia collapsed and Emperor *Haile Selassie came to Britain in exile, Pankhurst campaigned for his country to be treated as an ally in the *Second World War and for the integrity of the country's frontiers to be acknowledged. After the war the *New Times and Ethiopian News* opposed the British occupation of the Ogaden region of Ethiopia. DK

Pankhurst, Richard, *Sylvia Pankhurst: Counsel for Ethiopia* (2003)

Newby, James R. (*fl.* 1850–1884). African-American seaman, evangelist, and missionary born in the United States, the child of freed slaves. As a seaman he travelled over a large part of the world, living what he later described as the dissolute life of a prodigal. He arrived in Edinburgh sometime in the early 1870s. While living in Leith, in 1873, he entered a mission hall and was converted to Christianity. From then on he became an evangelist, first in Leith and then as an itinerant preacher with a travelling tent mission in the Scottish midlands.

Newby wanted to go to Africa as a missionary, and so he trained at the Harley

Institute in east London from 1874 to 1876. He sailed for West Africa in July 1876 to work for the Church Missionary Society in the Niger delta region. As part of his evangelistic work he went with an expedition into the Nigerian interior. He also visited Fernando Po, and within a year had joined the Baptist missionary J. J. Fuller in Cameroon. Ill health sent him back to Britain in 1879. While in London he met E. W. *Blyden and married a white wife, with whom he returned to West Africa, this time to the St Paul's River region of Liberia. Newby's wife died, and he came back to Britain a sick man. His life story is similar to many late 19th-century conversion narratives. DK

McHardie, E., and Allan, Andrew, *The Prodigal Continent and Her Prodigal Son and Missionary; or, The Adventures, Conversion and African Labours of Rev. James R. Newby* (2nd edn., 1885)

See also CHRISTIANITY; CHURCHES; MISSIONARY SOCIETIES

News for Babylon. Landmark 1984 anthology of West Indian and black British poetry. The 1980s were momentous years for black Britons in terms of the coincidence of social agitation and literary production. Riots in *Brixton and other parts of London were directed against the police, young people reacting to a perceived culture of police harassment, intimidation, and racist violence. The *Scarman Report detailed the wrongs suffered by black British people. Physical dramatization of grievance, in the form of street demonstrations, was accompanied by non-violent forms of protest and self-expression. Small black presses (Akira, Karnak House, Karia, and others) were set up to give space to new as well as established writers. These presses supplemented the work of earlier black publishing houses like New Beacon Books and Bogle L'Ouverture Publications (established in 1967 and 1969, respectively). In 1983 Karnak House issued Grace Nichols's *I Is a Long Memoried Woman*. It was a major moment in black publishing history, the collection of poems winning the 1983 Commonwealth Poetry Prize and bringing the young black writer to national prominence.

News for Babylon appeared the following year, a ground-breaking publication because its publishing house Chatto & Windus was 'mainstream' and distinguished for its international poetry list; and also because the anthology was edited by James Berry, who in 1981 made history by becoming the first poet of West Indian origin to win the Poetry Society's National Poetry Competition.

News for Babylon showcased the variety of West Indian and black British voices and subjects, ranging from the metaphysical and visionary poetry of Wilson Harris and Faustin Charles to the realist writing of Rudolph Kizerman. The fierce energy and humour of the Creole language were represented in the poetry of Valerie Bloom and John Agard. The lyricism of the West Indian character and landscape was captured by Fred D'Aguiar. A long-lost poem by Samuel *Selvon was rediscovered. E. A. Markham was given new prominence. *News for Babylon* quickly sold out, and, though never reissued, remains a standard text in educational institutions teaching colonial and post-colonial literature. DD

Donnell, Alison, and Welsh, Sarah Lawson (eds.), *The Routledge Reader in Caribbean Literature* (1996)

Guptara, P., *Black British Literature: An Annotated Bibliography* (1986)

See also BLACK BRITISH ENGLISH; LITERATURE 2: FICTION AND POETRY; PUBLISHING

Newton, John (1725–1807). Clergyman of the Church of England who led what he later considered to be a reprobate youth and worked in the *slave trade. It was while on a slaving voyage (1748–9) that he experienced a religious conversion. Nevertheless, he continued to work in the slave trade, and made three more voyages before retiring from the sea in 1754. He became widely known as an evangelical Christian, and was eventually ordained as a clergyman of the Church of England in 1764, serving first in the parish of Olney in Buckinghamshire, and later, from 1780 until his death, at St Mary Woolnoth in London.

At Olney, Newton became a close friend of the poet William *Cowper, and together they wrote the collection known as the *Olney Hymns*. Newton's own contributions include the words to some of the best-known hymns in the English language: 'Glorious things of thee are spoken', 'How sweet the name of Jesus sounds in the believer's ear', and 'Amazing Grace'. He came to regret deeply his participation in the slave trade, and in later life was an active campaigner against it, publishing his abolitionist *Thoughts Upon the African Slave Trade* in 1788. His writings on religious subjects long enjoyed a considerable influence. JG

ODNB

Noble savage. Term popularized in the 18th century denoting the uncorrupted man of nature as opposed to the degenerate man of civilization. Although the notion of the noble savage was idealized and propagated during the age of English Romanticism, its origins have been traced to the Middle Ages, when the conception of a Golden Age anticipates the formation of the pristine and virtuous 'natural man'. This 'natural man' was initially associated with the Caribs in the Americas, but as the notion expanded, the inclusion of American Indians, South Sea Islanders, and Blacks came to signify the generalization of the non-white, colonizable 'savage'.

One of the earliest travellers to glorify the primitive man was Christopher Columbus. His association of the Caribbean islands with a terrestrial paradise simultaneously fashioned their inhabitants as Edenic creatures, unfettered by the lures of materialism, progress, and civilization. Similarly, Sir Walter Ralegh's *Discovery of the Large, Rich and Beautiful Empire of Guiana* (1596), which relates the untainted existence of various tribes along the Orinoco River, typifies the noble savage as decidedly antithetical to the Western man, whose sophistication and accumulation of scholastic learning has made him a subject of tyranny and degradation.

When travel accounts became popular in the 18th century, the notion of the noble savage became more entrenched. Jean-Jacques Rousseau was the most influential 18th-century writer to propound the notion of the noble savage in works such as his *Discourse on the Origin and Basic Inequality Among Men* (1754) and *Émile; or, On Education* (1762).

Writers disillusioned with the consequences of progress created characters that displayed qualities such as physical sturdiness, generosity, innocence, sexual prowess, fearlessness, and a strong engagement with nature. One such character in English literature is Man Friday from Daniel Defoe's **Robinson Crusoe* (1719). Certain poets of the Romantic movement, namely William *Wordsworth, Robert *Southey and Samuel Taylor *Coleridge, were also affected by this 18th-century sentimentalism, and favoured the noble savage as a figure whose primitive virtues needed to be exalted in the face of rapid modernization and colonization. Southey, for instance, criticized English decorum through the character of *Omai, a Tahitian noble savage, in his poem 'To John May, June 29, 1824'.

The depiction of the black man as noble savage was often made for humanitarian and anti-slavery purposes. Instead of identifying with nature, the black slave was placed against the black savage, prior to his enslavement. Typical examples of this trait are James Montgomery's poems 'The Ocean' (1805) and 'The West Indies' (1809), in which Africa is depicted as idyllic and Africans as peace-loving, joyous people before the invasion of the colonizers. The anti-slavery campaigner William *Roscoe also represented the pre-slave African as gentle and pleasure-loving in his poem *The Wrongs of Africa* (1778). DD/SS

Fairchild, Hoxie Neale, *The Noble Savage: A Study in Romantic Naturalism* (1928)

See also LITERATURE 1: REPRESENTATIONS OF BLACKS

Notting Hill Carnival. Annual two-day street festival in London's Notting Hill celebrating Britain's West Indian community. The Notting Hill Carnival takes place on the Sunday and Monday of the August Bank Holiday weekend and is the biggest street festival in Europe, with audiences numbering over 2 million.

The five disciplines of the Carnival include: mass bands, or costumed processions and floats; calypso, political commentary set to music originating from Trinidad; soca, a fusion of *soul music and calypso; steelpan, a traditional Trinidadian instrument; and static sound systems, originally from Jamaica and most often playing *reggae music. The Notting Hill Carnival is greatly influenced by Trinidadian carnivals, which originated when slaves were permitted to dance, play musical instruments, and wear costumes impersonating their masters during traditional European carnivals held on Caribbean plantations.

Debate surrounds the founder of the Notting Hill Carnival. The local community leader Rhaune Laslett was long credited with creating the Carnival in 1966 as a means of promoting racial harmony in the Notting Hill area. The area had long been a seat of poor living conditions, drug abuse, and racial conflict, most notably in the *Notting Hill riots of 1958. Laslett's vision was to unite the many races of Notting Hill in a series of cultural activities and performances. The original Carnival was therefore not focused solely on Notting Hill's West Indian community but instead celebrated the rich ethnic diversity in the area. Performers included the London Irish Girl Pipers, the Asian Music Circle, and a Turkish-Cypriot band, while the 1967 Carnival Queen was a Norwegian woman masquerading as Marie-Antoinette. The political activist and *West Indian Gazette* editor Claudia *Jones was later credited with creating the Carnival because of her call to gather London's West Indian community in St Pancras Town Hall in response to the 1958 riots.

The Carnival did not become synonymous with Caribbean culture until the 1970s. West Indian residents of Notting Hill faced surging levels of unemployment when the economic success of the 1960s began to fade. The amicable relationship between Notting Hill's black and white residents became strained as jobs became scarce—a tension strengthened by the fear of immigration featured in the speeches of Enoch *Powell and a violent confrontation between black demonstrators and white police in 1970 outside a local restaurant. In response, Notting Hill's West Indian community claimed the Carnival as a celebration of Caribbean culture and the black struggle in Britain. The Trinidadian teacher Lesley Palmer facilitated this shift when he began to organize the Carnival in 1973. Influenced by Trinidadian carnival, Palmer encouraged local artists to design masquerade costumes according to Caribbean traditions and made steel and mass bands the focus of the Notting Hill Carnival.

Racial tension continued to increase in mid-1970s as the Carnival grew to a national scale. To attract London's booming young West Indian population Palmer introduced stationary discos, or sound systems, to the Carnival. The sound systems embraced reggae, a new Jamaican musical form popular with a second generation of West Indian immigrants frustrated by institutional racism and a lack of employment. The change greatly increased Carnival attendance, attracting a quarter of a million people for the first time. The larger audience, as well as the presence of black youths associated with petty crime and violence, resulted in a dramatic increase in police presence and complaints from Notting Hill residents concerning noise and damage to gardens and property along Carnival routes. Tension climaxed in 1976 when gangs of aggravated black youths confronted 1,500 policemen on patrol, throwing bottles and stones. In response, the leader of the local council wrote a letter to the Home Secretary asking for the Carnival to be cancelled, while suggestions were made to contain the Carnival in a nearby park or stadium. Additional 'mini-carnivals' in other areas of London designed to divert participants away from Notting Hill were also encouraged.

Unemployment trebled during the early 1980s, increasing the frustration of West Indian youths, which was heightened by a 'stop and search' policy adopted by London police unjustly targeting young black men. Carnival policing became highly specialized during this period, with as many as 13,000 policemen connected via interpersonal communication systems, helicopter radio and video contacts, and instant access to central headquarters. The 1987 Carnival was marked by the worst violence in the event's history, with 798 reported crimes (one murder), 300 arrests, and almost 100 injuries. However, the 1980s also saw the Notting Hill Carnival embraced by government and corporate sponsorship. The establishment of the Carnival and Arts Committee (CAC) resulted in Carnival participants receiving Arts Council funding for the first time, as well as public support from authorities such as Caribbean high commissioners, Scotland Yard chiefs, the Prime Minister, and Prince Charles. Additional support quickly followed government funding when the CAC presented the Carnival as an 'official' event to black corporations and began marketing the event as 'the greatest street cultural event in Europe'.

A rigid police framework introduced in 1989 that restricted activities to a well-defined route and ended celebrations at 7 p.m. eased the violence of previous Carnivals. In addition, the number of sound systems was cut by 75 per cent, helping to decrease the attendance of black youths by tens of thousands. The framework was made more lenient after complaints from Carnival participants and the appointment of a new police chief in 1990. Under the direction of the Notting Hill Carnival Enterprise Committee today's Carnival also continues the commercialization begun in the 1980s by selling official merchandise and permitting greater numbers of food, drink, and craft vendors along Carnival routes. EDS

Cohen, Abner, *Masquerade Politics: Explorations in the Structure of Urban Cultural Movements* (1993)

Lovelace, Earl, *The Dragon Can't Dance* (1979)

See also RASTAFARIANISM

Notting Hill riots. Series of race-related disturbances that took place in the 1950s and the 1970s.

1. Introduction
2. Roots of the 1958 riots
3. The murder of Kelso Cochrane and its aftermath
4. Riots in the 1970s

1. Introduction The West London suburb of Notting Hill is popularly known as the site of the annual two-day Notting Hill *Carnival, a celebration of Caribbean cultural creativity and artistic expression that takes place on August bank holiday weekend. Today, up to 2 million revellers come from far and wide to watch the parades of thousands of costumed dancers and colourfully decorated floats, dance to the rhythms of soca, calypso, and reggae music blaring out from sound systems. Carnival is the largest street festival in Europe, and its importance as an event for racial integration is widely recognized. Yet, since its inception, the Carnival's colourful history has been associated with, and at times, marred by, racial conflict.

2. Roots of the 1958 riots The Notting Hill Carnival was promoted by the political activist Claudia *Jones and the Caribbean community as a positive response to racial tension in 1950s Britain. In 1958 tension between white and black communities across England was already commonplace. Much of this tension was fuelled by the activities of fascist organizations promoting anti-black immigrant rhetoric, but the media also helped to stir antagonism towards black immigrants. Gangs of teddy boys frequently roamed the streets violently attacking young Blacks and vandalizing black homes and community centres.

Violence against black immigrants across Britain was not new; in the years leading up to 1958 several towns had witnessed fascist-led racial disturbances. Notting Hill was itself the scene of several race-related incidents throughout the summer of 1958. On the evening of 17 August a crowd of Whites smashed the windows of a house occupied by black people in nearby Shepherd's Bush, and a few days later a black man was savagely attacked by a group of white men. Over the next few days, gangs of white youth roamed the streets 'nigger-hunting', indiscriminately attacking black people. By the end of August, attacks against Blacks were a daily event. These sustained unprovoked attacks were to culminate in the first of many post-war race riots, as local fascists keen to exploit simmering racial tensions continued their campaign of anti-black violence. Following an open-air meeting of fascists on the August Bank Holiday weekend, between 300 and 400 'Keep Britain White' mobs, many of them Teddy boys armed with iron bars, butcher's knives, and weighted leather belts, roamed the streets of Notting Hill, attacking Blacks and their property. The first night left five black men lying unconscious on the pavements of Notting Hill. Black people responded by organizing to defend their community and homes, some groups making pre-emptive strikes against known fascist headquarters. Full-scale battles between young Whites and Blacks raged over the weekend as the black community attempted to defend itself.

3. The murder of Kelso Cochrane and its aftermath Anti-black violence quickly spread to surrounding areas of North Kensington, Shepherd's Bush, Paddington, and Maida Vale, and continued sporadically until they finally abated in the middle of September. When a young Antiguan carpenter, Kelso *Cochrane, was stabbed to death the following year, tensions between white and black threatened to erupt once more. The ferocity of Notting Hill 'racial riots' as the press called them at the time, shocked the sensibility of the British public into realizing that it was not above the kind of racial conflict then being played out in the American deep South. The riots were also a pivotal moment in black British political activism, for they led to the formation of black community organizations and the forging of a distinct black political identity.

In efforts to dampen down racial tension, Claudia Jones organized the first ever carnival in 1959 as an annual showcase for Caribbean talent. Claudia hoped to transplant the subversive Trinidadian tradition of carnival to Britain, to forge a collective unity between West Indians, and to reach out to white Britain. The first Carnival, organized by the *West Indian Gazette*, was a small affair, a cultural evening held in St Pancras Town Hall in London, along with a small outdoor procession in Powis Square, North Kensington.

4. Riots in the 1970s Over the years the Carnival has grown into one of the most important and ethnically diverse of European festivals, but since wide-scale 'disturbances' in the 1970s it has come to be regarded by critics as a potential focus for political confrontation. The Carnivals of 1975 and 1976, in particular, were marked by confrontation between young Blacks and the police. The failure of the police force to protect black people from racist attacks, combined with what many regarded as excessive police harassment and brutality, was a key source of tension throughout the 1970s. When, in 1975, sound systems were introduced for the first time, the numbers of young carnival revellers dramatically increased. Some minor skirmishes broke out and a few arrests were made, and, alarmed by the huge increase in carnival-goers, the police reinforced their presence to over 1,500 officers the following year. It was widely believed that this massively reinforced police presence sparked the 1976 riot that has stained the Carnival's name ever since.

As the 1976 Carnival was under way, rioting broke out between young Blacks and police. The riot started after police attempted to arrest a suspected pickpocket. Crowds of carnival-goers went to his aid, and within minutes one of the most serious disturbances of the

1970s had erupted. The riot spread over the whole Ladbroke Grove area and lasted well into the night. Many observers claimed that heavy police presence and their use of aggressive behaviour acted as the catalyst to the riot, which saw young Blacks take control of Notting Hill's streets for two days. Over 100 policemen and over 60 carnival-goers were injured, and around 66 young Blacks were arrested. In a subsequent trial seventeen young Blacks faced 79 charges, though only two were convicted of carnival-related offences after the court case.

Though at the time described as the fiercest and most protracted of street battles in mainland Britain since the 1936 Cable Street riots, the Carnival continued to grow in popularity, though continuing to be marked by tensions throughout the 1970s and 1980s. The tendency of the media to focus on the Carnival as a source of crime rather than a celebration of diversity has caused conflict between the organizers, the black community, and the police, ensuring that the Carnival remains the subject of heated political debate, even in the absence of further serious riots. CJ

Harker, Joseph, 'The Carnival Is Over: The Spirit of Notting Hill Was Lost When It Started To Be About Cross-Cultural Harmony', *The Guardian*, 26 Aug. 2000

La Rose, Michael, *The Story of Notting Hill Carnival* (2004)

Pilkington, Edward, *Beyond the Mother Country: West Indians and the Notting Hill White Riots* (1988)

Sherwood, Marika, Prescott, Colin, and Hines, Donald, *Claudia Jones: A Life in Exile* (2000)

See also CRIMINAL JUSTICE SYSTEM; 'RACE' RIOTS, 1919

O

Omai. Polynesian islander taken from the South Pacific to London as an example of a *'noble savage' in 1774. Britain invaded Otaheite (Tahiti) on 24 June 1767; Omai (Mai) later claimed to have been among the crowd of islanders sheltering on a hill above Matavai Bay, on whom Samuel Wallis fired a cannon from the *Dolphin*. During Captain Cook's second Pacific voyage the crew of Cook's companion ship the *Adventure* befriended Omai, then in his early twenties, and he travelled to England as a crew member, arriving in Portsmouth on 14 July 1774 to be greeted by Lord Sandwich, First Lord of the Admiralty.

The voyages to the 'Friendly Islands' had opened up a new world, where the primitive societies imagined in the utopian literature of Montaigne and Rousseau seemed to survive in peace and harmony, replete with breadfruit and bare-breasted women. Yet a theme in travel-writing of the period was the scepticism explorers faced from the scientific establishment in Europe. Hence Omai, placed under the charge of Cook's naturalists Joseph Banks and Daniel Solander, 'entered' society, where his politeness was remarked upon. Three days after arriving in England, he was presented to George III and Queen Charlotte at Kew, when it is said he knelt before the king saying, 'How do, King Tosh!' He was taken to the theatre and the races, and in August 1775 went on a tour of Yorkshire, where he stayed in York and Kirkleatham, shooting game on the North Yorkshire Moors.

He appears in the memoirs of Samuel Johnson, Horace Walpole, and Fanny Burney, and various portraits exist: a chalk drawing by William Hodges, made during Cook's voyage (engraved by James Caldwell, 1777); the famous full-length painting by Joshua Reynolds (*c.*1775; engraved by Johann Jacobe in 1780); and a group composition by William Parry (1775–6).

Omai returned to Otaheite with Cook in 1776, during the third Pacific voyage (which ended with Cook being killed by Hawai'ians in 1779). Cook's diary tells of Omai's arrival home: from aboard ship he managed to win the respect of King Otoo (Tu, later crowned Emperor Pomare I of the Society Islands) by sending a gift of red feathers. Provided with a wealth of English produce—port, gunpowder, muskets, bullets, a globe, tin soldiers, crockery and kitchen utensils, a hand-organ, a suit of armour, a horse, and other livestock (a drawing exists of him, in armour on the horse, attributed to the crew member John Rickman)—Omai was advised by Cook to distribute this wisely among the natives. Yet, says the diary, he 'suffered himself to be duped by every designing knave' and, left by Cook at Huahine amid emotional scenes on 2 November 1777, in a wooden house built by Spanish interlopers, he was later reported (when the *Lady Penrhyn* stopped at Otaheite after dropping convicts at the Port Jackson penal colony in 1788) to have sickened and died, with warriors from Raiatea taking his possessions.

In 1785 *OMAI; or, A Trip Round the World*, by John O'Keefe, was produced at the Theatre Royal in Covent Garden. With Otaheitean costumes provided by the set designer John Webber, the artist on Cook's third voyage, and 'special effects' by Philippe de Loutherbourg, the pantomime was a hit, with 70 performances in two years. Set among the Pacific islands, an unlikely plot saw Omai returning to win back his throne and the hand of the fair 'Londina'. JM

Fairchild, H. N., *The Noble Savage* (1928)

See also LITERATURE 1: REPRESENTATIONS OF BLACKS

Omoniyi, Bandele (1884–1913). Early Nigerian nationalist, Pan-Africanist writer, and student politician born on 6 November 1884 in Lagos, Nigeria. He first arrived in Britain in 1905 and soon commenced his political activities, eventually giving up his studies at Edinburgh University. Omoniyi sent a series of letters to the British Prime Minister, Campbell-Bannerman, and other British politicians, including the future Labour Party leader Ramsay MacDonald, demanding political representation for Africans in the colonies and opposing the military campaigns that were still being conducted in Africa.

In 1907 Omoniyi wrote a series of articles criticizing colonial rule in the *Edinburgh Magazine* and became the first African to write for the Independent Labour Party's *Labour Leader*. He also published several articles in the West African press. In 1908 his major work, *A Defence of the Ethiopian Movement*, was published in Edinburgh and dedicated 'to The Right Honourable and Honourable Members of the British Parliament'. Here he urged political reforms in the colonies, warning that without them a revolution might take place in Africa that would bring an end to British rule. As a consequence of his activities he came to the attention of the Colonial Office.

Omoniyi later moved to Brazil, where he sold gold-mining concessions, involved himself in Brazilian politics, and wrote a 'Manifesto', one of the first modern political documents produced by a Nigerian. He was subsequently arrested and imprisoned for his political activities in Brazil. In prison he contracted beriberi and died at the age of 28. HA

Adi, H., *West Africans in Britain: Nationalism, Pan-Africanism and Communism* (1998)
ODNB

See also PAN-AFRICANISM; POLITICS

Organization of Women of African and Asian Descent. Radical black women's group formed in 1978 as an important force for radical resistance to the specific social, economic, and political conditions that African, Caribbean, and Asian women confronted in Britain. OWAAD represented the first national black women's umbrella network in Britain until its demise in 1983. For many Asian, Caribbean, and African women OWAAD provided the opportunity to prioritize, unite, and mobilize against racism, sexism, and class oppression. It supported women to reaffirm cultural identities, community struggles, and feminist consciousness that were denied or subsumed by national liberation movements, the predominantly white mainstream Women's Movement, and left-wing organizations.

OWAAD inspired its members to set up local black and ethnic-minority women's groups that challenged racist and sexist subordination in education, employment, housing, and health care. It was also concerned with the issues of police brutality, state harassment, and immigration abuse. At a national level OWAAD was fundamental to the regional development and coordination of ethnic-minority and black women's organizations. It increased the political awareness of Caribbean, African, and Asian women from diverse backgrounds through non-hierarchical meetings, special project committees, day schools, the newsletter *FOWAAD*, and annual conferences. It generated campaigns around issues such as the much hated *'Sus Law', which targeted young black people, the labelling of black children as 'educationally subnormal', trials of the carcinogenic contraceptive Depo-Provera on black women, and the virginity testing of Asian women at Heathrow Airport. The significant legacy of OWAAD is evident in contemporary black and ethnic-minority women's groups, several of which are a consequence of OWAAD, and which continue to tackle power inequalities in Britain. AM

Bryan, Beverley, Dadzie, Stella, and Scafe, Suzanne, *Heart of the Race: Black Women's Lives in Britain* (1985)

See also FEMINISM; SOUTHALL BLACK SISTERS

Orientalism. In 1978 Edward W. Said (1935–2003), a Palestinian musicologist, journalist, and cultural critic living in America, published *Orientalism*, a revisionist study of the academic discipline by the same name, thereby revolutionizing how we view textual representations of other cultures and helping to shape postcolonial studies.

Said, a member of the Palestinian National Council from 1977 to 1991, was fluent in French and hence familiar with the work of Marxist cultural theorists such as Foucault and Kristeva, as well as that of the early generation of Third World historians such as Samir Amin, Anwar Abdel Malik, and C. L. R. *James. He considered knowledge and power to be inextricably linked, at the time a radical stance, and treated the subject Orientalism, until then renowned for its traditions of scholarship and breadth of learning, simply as a worldly body of discourse, exhibiting the ideological prejudices of its age, and at its most extreme a wilfully sealed, self-perpetuating 'system of references' to ancient racial stereotypes, devoid of objectivity. It should be noted that controversy surrounds Said's arguments outside postcolonial studies, with vigorous attacks on his methodology by eminent Orientalists in history, politics, and the media, and books continuing to be published propounding the nobility and relevance of Orientalist projects. Here, however, we shall focus on the main components of Said's argument, developed in *Orientalism* and subsequent books, before briefly considering its ongoing possibilities for postcolonial and black studies.

1. Historical overview
2. New directions

1. Historical overview The Orient (the term Said uses for the Middle East and the Indian subcontinent together, though he limits his discussion to British and French representations of the Middle East) is geographically and historically a rival, an ancestor, and therefore the antithesis of the 'West', which, as contact and material exchange between the two increased during the Middle Ages, was absorbed as a concept to become a fundamental part of the Western outlook, allowing the latter to 'orientate' itself. The branch of knowledge, at first a disparate collection of artistic representations of the East, that crystallized into the academic discipline of Orientalism during the 19th century Said thus dissociates from any reality of the Eastern world. It is instead a type of cultural apparatus developed to uphold this conception of a binary opposition between cultures—and therefore an imperialist ideological project, given that, at the time, Britain and France were extending their sway over the regions in question. (The United States is argued to have developed its own branch in the 20th century from Far Eastern parameters.)

The features of this discursive paradigm are that it is constructed; that it is irrelevant to any notion of the real-life Orient; that it enforces, through stereotyping and distortion, the 'pattern of relative strength' vis-à-vis West and colonized East; that it therefore tells us more about the ideological mechanics of 'European-Atlantic power over the Orient' than about the reality of the meeting of cultures; and that Orientalism, for the best part of 150 years feted as a systematic academic field built on research, should be seen as a discourse—nothing so definite as a model or impetus for action, because it is built on generalizations—shaped by socially based forms of power. This is the kernel of Said's argument, which he then expands through an elegant and sweeping series of chapters on 18th- and 19th-century classics of Orientalist scholarship.

The beginnings of Orientalism, for Said, date back to ancient Greek texts such as *The Iliad* and Aeschylus' *The Persians*; academically speaking, the eleventh canon of the Church Council of Vienne in 1312 set up chairs in Greek, Arabic, Hebrew, and Chaldaean at the great universities of Bologna, Avignon, Salamanca, Paris, and Oxford. With infidel encroachments on Christian Europe's borders from Ottoman Turkey, Moorish North Africa, and the Arab Near East, site of crusading conflict between the Christian and Muslim worlds, it was vital to learn about such cultures—through their texts—in order to limit the spread of heathen ideas. Study of the Orient being firmly linked with the oversimplified belief in things Oriental as a threat to things European, closer contact arising in the Middle Ages from religious expansionism in both directions led to what Said characterizes as 'Western ignorance [becoming] more refined and complex'. Metaphorically, the Orient is viewed as 'the stage on which the whole East is confined'—a Western projection, because Orientals are now the figures on the stage, manipulated by Western puppeteers.

For the British, India became the 'definitive Orient', while for the post-Napoleonic French, Egypt was granted this label: a situation more symptomatic of the rivalry between England and France than of any real valuation (if such a thing were possible) of the respective colonized areas. Said views French Orientalism as more imaginatively sophisticated than British, contending that not until the travel writer Richard Burton (1821–90) did Britain have a humanist writer of real intellectual distinction. Said's main area of discussion is Orientalism during the age of empire, where global expansionism, confrontation with dark-skinned peoples, a proselytizing pity for their benighted ways, and a desire for the rational classification of phenomena were key intellectual trends. In Britain projects such as 'the Baptist Missionary Society (1792), the Church Missionary Society (1799), the British and Foreign Bible Society (1804), the London Society for Promoting Christianity Among the Jews (1808) . . . the trading societies, learned societies, geographical exploration funds, translation funds, the implantation in the Orient of schools, missions, consular offices, factories' etc. were symptomatic of a politico-economic interest. Bolstering the scientific project to impose a system of order on random accruals of facts and prejudice were the texts of literary figures such as 'Goethe, Hugo, Lamartine, Chateaubriand, Kinglake, Nerval, Flaubert, Lane, Burton, Scott, Byron, Vigny, Disraeli, George Eliot, Gautier . . . Doughty, Barrès, Loti, T. E. Lawrence, Forster', in whose works the stereotypes of the Oriental are dramatized, developed, and broadcast. An important theme brought forward was that of the Orient's own pre-barbaric history, now collapsed into decadence and corruption. Orientalism's inability to adapt to new ideas was shown, Said argues, in its various bewildered encounters with national liberation movements. Indeed, to come across the real Orient would often lead to a disillusionment, for it was seldom the same as that encountered in the literature—certainly this is proved with regard to 19th-century French poets. As worldly power increased, knowledge accumulated and stood in for the subject of the encounter.

2. New directions The 20th century saw greater combat between imperial powers and an intensified rivalry for colonial possessions, as well as the dawn of the American empire. For Said, the 'coincidence between geography, knowledge and power' was completed in the global network of Britain. In academic terms, Orientalism as a field of study converged with the pseudo-scientific theories then at large—'contemporary comparative grammar, comparative anatomy, and racial theory . . . imperialism, positivism, utopianism, historicism, Darwinism, racism, Freudianism, Marxism, Spenglerism'—meaning that various pathologies of the Oriental mindset became credible within the field. Meanwhile, a closer relationship developed between Orientalism as a scholarly milieu and the Orient itself—in terms of increased political and military interventions in the Orient—to create Britain's finest contribution to the field, the colonial administrators and advisers such as

'T. E. Lawrence, Edward Henry Palmer, D. G. Hogarth, Gertrude Bell, Ronald Storrs, St. John Philby, and William Clifford Palgrave'. Orientalism was no longer the sole preserve of academics, but had become an intellectual mindset whose 'scholarly frame of reference, such as it was, was fashioned by people like William Muir, Anthony Bevan, D. S. Margoliouth, Charles Lyall, E. G. Browne, R. A. Nicholson, Guy Le Strange, E. D. Ross, and Thomas Arnold . . . [and whose] imaginative perspectives were provided principally by their illustrious contemporary Rudyard Kipling'. So ubiquitous were the structures that all new observations merely went to confirm the inferiority of the Oriental world: indeed, in an astounding inversion, the specific came to stand in for the general. It is for this phenomenon that Said reserves his most withering critiques. We see 'white Orientals', typified by Lawrence, who, though they shared its prejudices, abhorred the scholarship of Orientalism, preferring a spurious integrity of experience; they became 'Oriental prophets', living among the people and therefore coming to see their unique position between two cultures as a representation of the entire West.

It is hard to overestimate *Orientalism*'s contribution to post-colonial studies. Said's thesis is notable for his profound ability always to put himself in the place of the other, and, through contextualizing what at first seem to be no more than shoring up assumptions, to create a sense of simmering injustice at the way slants of opinion go to make up an infrastructure for oppression. Its influence can be traced in two subsequent scholarly fields: history and historiography, and literary criticism, which tends towards a more reductive usage of the theory.

With regard to Said's use of literary works, there is an assumption that all writing enacts an ideology of dominance over the topic under discussion: a 'didactic speaker . . . displays his material to the disciples'. Said plays with this idea, often effecting a vengefully deterministic process of 'orientalization' on his Orientalists (his subsequent work, *Covering Islam* (1981), on the US media's anti-Islamic hysteria following the 1979 Iranian Revolution, is subtitled, presumably for comedy's sake *How the Media and the Experts Determine How We See the Rest of the World*). But what happens, in post-Said analyses of travel-writing or foreigners in European fiction, to the reality of the human encounters that the text represents? Obviously human perception is a subjective and socially mediated construct, where no two participants in an event will perceive it in the same way. Yet, at its more uncreative, racially obsessed extremes, literary criticism seems unable to move beyond using a simplistic reading of Said to reduce all writers into propagandists for empire and oppression, and ignoring potentially liberating ironies of form and emplotment, not to mention sincere attempts at speaking out on behalf of subalterns by maverick figures within the discourse of the hegemonic world. Critics of this model exist, most notably the British Indian novelist and literary theorist Amit Chaudhuri, yet in post-colonial literary syllabuses and seminar series, the Saidian critique of the text is preferred, perhaps because contesting imperial and neocolonial hegemonies is a critical imperative. Regarding the black world, the closest parallel to *Orientalism* is probably that provided by Chinua Achebe's reading of *Heart of Darkness* (taken up by Said in his later work, *Culture and Imperialism*, 1993), where, regardless of Conrad's explicit condemnation of Belgian atrocities in the Congo, reading his representations of Africans in the novel in the light of contemporary primitivism and colonialism makes him complicit in the propaganda of empire.

Yet in *Orientalism* one feels a tug between the requirements of the anticolonial struggle and a sense of respect due to writers and scholars for the integrity of the aesthetic work. In the introduction and early chapters, for example, it is hinted again and again that Marx, who drew on India for his model of socioeconomic revolution, will be incriminated in the European colonial project—yet, after only two pages laying out the paradox between his sympathy for the underclass and his totalizing Eurocentric depictions of Indians, he is let off the hook with some brief comments about a 'censor in the vocabulary'. Such is the depth of Said's humanism that the 'other' can even extend to the bigoted others of the Western imperial past. A reprieve is thrown out to the 'compelling' H. A. R. Gibb (and Massignon in France) for their erudition and breadth of scholarship: despite the assumptions within their writing, one feels them to be modernist heroes, their fiefdoms overthrown by less worthy inheritors.

One reason Said gives for this is the power of narrative, 'the specific form taken by written history to counter the permanence of vision . . . [it] introduces an opposing point of view, perspective, consciousness to the unitary web of vision'. The devil is in the detail, and to shake up the binaries of us and them, black and white, rich and poor, requires more realistic narratives. A recognition of the divergence and density of the real-life Orient seems therefore to be the way out of the crime of empire; it overcomes the broad racist oversimplification of other cultures. Here is Said's contribution to the philosophy of history, recognizably relevant to all students of cultural exchange: it should disturb structuring myths by providing greater detail. The Subaltern Studies school of historiography both utilized and refined *Orientalism* in their calls for Indian history to be rewritten from the perspective of the peasantry. Eminent historians of the Caribbean, such as Walter Rodney and Brinsley Samaroo, dwell on the complexities and gradations of white and African societies, rather than their homogeneities. Conversely, a growing body of scholarship exists in China, debunking Chinese representations of the West in a similar manner. Said's influence stimulates research at the forefront of media studies, cultural studies, translation theory, and post-colonial history.

JM

Kabbani, Rana, *Imperial Fictions: Europe's Myths of the Orient* (1994)

Said, Edward W., *Covering Islam: How the Media and the Experts Determine How We See the Rest of the World* (1997)

—— *Orientalism: Western Conceptions of the Orient* (rev. edn., 1995)

Turner, Brian S., *Orientalism, Postmodernism and Globalism* (1994)

See also POST-COLONIAL THEORY

Oroonoko. In her novel *Oroonoko; or, The Royal Slave* (1688), the English writer Aphra Behn (*c*.1640–1689) describes how the title character, an African prince, was treacherously kidnapped by slave traders and sold as a slave in Suriname during the brief period in the 1660s when it was an English colony. Here he is reunited with his lover, Imoinda. Although Oroonoko is treated with the respect due to his royal birth, and 'suffer'd only the Name of a Slave, and had nothing of the Toil and Labour of one', fear that his child by Imoinda will be born into slavery causes him to plan and lead a slave revolt, which proves unsuccessful. Oroonoko surrenders on the promise of good treatment, but is then whipped. He later kills Imoinda to free her from slavery. He fails to commit suicide, and is tortured to death by some of the colonists, a process he endures with heroic fortitude.

The book is subtitled *A True History* and the story is told by a first-person female narrator who claims to have been present in Suriname at the time, and to have heard the details of her subject's earlier life in Africa from Oroonoko himself. It is at least possible that Behn had in fact been in Suriname, and some of those who appear as characters in the book are identifiable as real individuals. However, just as her Africa is a fantasy garnished with some authentic details that could have been taken from contemporary travel writers, so Behn's Suriname is a mixture of the realistic and the implausible. Whatever basis it may have had in fact, the story of Oroonoko as presented in Behn's book has to be regarded as a work of fiction.

Oroonoko is sometimes discussed as if it were an early anti-slavery work, but the reality is more complicated. Oroonoko himself is treated as a heroic figure, but for Behn this is achieved mainly by separating him from both other Africans in general and the other slaves in Suriname in particular. He is described as having had a French tutor, as being able to speak English and Spanish as well as French, and acquainted with European learning and culture. His physical features are described so as to seem Europeanized, 'bating his Colour': we are told that he took 'particular Care' to straighten his hair, and that his mouth was 'the finest shap'd that cou'd be seen; far from those great turn'd Lips, which are so natural to the rest of the *Negroes*'. The enslavement of Oroonoko and his subsequent ill-treatment and horrific death at the hands of the English colonists are presented as unjust and discreditable to the Europeans involved. However, it is the enslavement of a prince, rather than the enslavement of Africans more generally, that is treated as unjust. We are told that Oroonoko had himself dealt in slaves, and, after nearly all of the slaves whom he had led in revolt decide to surrender to the colonists who are pursuing them, he says 'he was asham'd of what he had done, in endeavouring to make those Free, who were by Nature *Slaves*'. That some human beings 'were by Nature *Slaves*' was an argument frequently employed by those who sought to justify slavery on racist grounds. Finally, it should be noted that some modern critics have seen the book as a coded work about contemporary British politics and the position of the Stuart dynasty, and not about slavery or Suriname at all. Certainly, at least some late 17th-century readers would have found the description of Oroonoko's death as the 'frightful Spectacles of a mangl'd King' reminiscent of the execution of Charles I in 1649.

Although Behn's novel continued to be reprinted at intervals, it was the several adaptations for the stage that did most to keep the Oroonoko story before the 18th-century British public, with those by Thomas Southerne (1695) and John Hawkesworth (1759) proving especially popular. As with the *Inkle and Yarico story, readers and audiences waxed sentimental over the sufferings of an individual without this affecting their complacency about the slave trade and slavery more generally. Only towards the end of the 18th century, when attitudes were changing, did Oroonoko come to be seen as an anti-slavery narrative, and in his *Am I not a man and a brother?* (1788) Peter *Peckard referred to 'the well known story of Oronoko [*sic*]' as if it were fact, and as an example that supported his protests against the injustice and immorality of the slave trade. In the same year, by contrast, in her *Slavery, a Poem* (1788), Hannah *More felt it necessary to reject the sentimental emphasis on 'individual griefs' by pointing out that 'millions feel what Oroonoko felt'. JG

Behn, Aphra, *Oroonoko* (ed. Joanna Lipking, 1997)
Sypher, Wylie, *Guinea's Captive Kings: British Anti-Slavery Literature of the XVIIIth Century* (1942)

See also LITERATURE 1: REPRESENTATIONS OF BLACKS; NOBLE SAVAGE; SLAVE TRADE; SLAVERY

Othello. The first recorded performance of *The Tragedy of Othello the Moor of Venice* was in 1604. Shakespeare took the bones of the story from Geraldi Cinthio's 16th-century collection *Hecatommithi*, which would have been available in its original Italian or in Gabriel Chappuys's French translation. Taking this cautionary tale of the credulousness and barbarity of Moors, where Othello's and Iago's prototypes plot to kill Desdemona, mutilating her body before they are tortured and executed, Shakespeare expands the cast, using a character of his own invention, the jealous suitor Roderigo, to useful effect, to turn it into a psychological study of the central characters: the black Venetian general Othello and his embittered 'ensign' Iago.

The play is set in an outpost of the Venetian empire, Cyprus, under attack by Turks. Othello, a Blackamoor, who once unflinchingly watched his brother's arm blown off by a cannonball, is vital to the Venetian defence, but he is distracted by Iago, who, frustrated by lack of promotion, leads him to believe that Captain

Cassio, a Florentine, is carrying on an affair with the ageing Othello's new wife, Desdemona. Othello's stories of witches and cannibals had enchanted Desdemona, causing her to fall deeply in love with him—a fact that her father, Brabantio, attributes to black magic. Yet Othello succumbs easily to Iago's insinuations, made in language of a pornographic nature, and, raving and foaming at the mouth, publicly beats his wife and eventually smothers her.

The story was an instant hit, though scholarship shows that its swear words were removed before publication in 1622. Richard Burbage first played the part of Othello, which went on to become a classic of 18th- and 19th-century theatre, depicted by Thomas Betterton, Thomas Quin, and John Kemble. In 1814 Edmund Kean made the part his own, 'browned' up in a turban and sandals, prompting a critical debate that continued into the 20th century: was Othello a sub-Saharan 'Negro' or an Arabic 'Moor'? Such were Romantic tastes that for Samuel Taylor *Coleridge, 'it would be something monstrous to conceive this beautiful Venetian girl falling in love with a veritable negro'.

When Kean collapsed onstage, playing Othello, in March 1833, the black celebrity actor Ira *Aldridge took the part, touring, Ruth Cowhig tells us, 'in every sizeable town in Britain, including Ireland, and receiving enthusiastic press notices'—except in London, where reviewers focused on Aldridge's lack of suitability to play a character of such depth, and his allegedly strange way of accenting the Shakespearean metric. Aldridge embarked on a tour of Europe, and did not return to London until 1865. The French poet Théophile Gautier praised his St Petersburg production of *Othello* as an authentic re-creation of Shakespeare, despite the fact that, while Aldridge spoke English, all the other characters used Schlegel's German translation. It was while touring *Othello* in Łódź that Aldridge died, in August 1867.

Paul *Robeson played the Moor at the Savoy Theatre in 1930, going on to participate in the famous big-budget American production of 1943, and returning to London in 1959, and it is with this actor that the play began to be understood as a text centrally concerned with the idea of race—a tradition that has continued with the embarrassing spectacle of Laurence Olivier blacking up for the part at the National Theatre in 1965 ('he fell on the text like a tiger', according to Kenneth Tynan, 'stark and harsh, with vowel-sounds subtly alien as Kwame Nkrumah's'), or the 2001 adaptation by Andrew Davies for ITV where 'John Othello', Britain's first black chief of police, became emblematic of institutional racism in the London Metropolitan Police.

White Othellos on screen have included Orson Welles (1952) and Anthony Hopkins (1981, BBC); the critical paradox that arises is to square their treatments of the play purely as a dramatic achievement and psychological case study, regardless of its protagonist's skin colour, with the question of why the theatrical profession might be unwilling or unable to cast black actors in theatre's most famous black role. In America a more politicized approach has come to be preferred: in the late 20th century there have been Asian and Native American Othellos, and black Iagos, and in 1997–8 a production at the Landsburg Theatre in Washington DC inverted the play's racial symbolism, making Patrick Stewart in the title role the only White in the cast. Productions of *Othello* faithful to the text have included Kenneth Branagh's 1995 film, with Laurence Fishburne in the title role, and the Royal Shakespeare Company's 1999 production starring Ray Fearon.

For Cowhig, blackness is, as in the court masques that preceded the play, the dramatist's tool for expressing a universal artistic message: in *Othello*'s case the power of jealousy to ruin men. We are invited, like Desdemona, to see 'Othello's visage in his mind', to foreground the rare fact of a black central character but give it little psychological and greater aesthetic value: a symbolic challenge that values the meaninglessness of race rather than its salient characteristics. Germaine

Greer, on the other hand, has likened Othello's storytelling to African-American 'panhandling', suggesting both that his personality is exaggerated to the point of exoticism, but also that this has elements of realism.

Whether *Othello* is a play about race in the modern sense has been debated, however. For C. L. R. *James, 'you could strike out every single reference to his black skin and the play would be essentially the same'. Theories have been put forward to the effect that Shakespeare's proximity to the world of black London (as suggested by the 'Dark Lady' of his Sonnets) called for a more humanistic inversion of the character Aaron in **Titus Andronicus*, but, being built on assumptions about the writer's biography, they are speculative.

The crossover between Aaron and Iago, Titus and Othello, is striking. The machiavellian schemer, in Coleridge's view a force of 'motiveless malignancy', is no longer black, but works against a black character of high rank, so honourable and Christianized that, as he stabs himself, he loudly reminds us of his crusading zeal against the infidel Turks.

Yet if Othello is viewed as a play where jealousy, the 'green-eyed monster', is the tragic flaw under the microscope, then Iago suffers from its gaze as badly as Othello. It is Iago who obsesses on the black man's sexual prowess, Iago who first believes that Othello has cuckolded him. Iago incites Brabantio to legal confrontation in deliberately racist terms, and when Othello finally lets his own doubts prey on him, saying Desdemona betrayed him ('haply for I am black'), it is a gullible echo of Iago's words a few moments earlier. The play dissects the workings of a jealous mind, which casts around to realize its fantasies and finds the colour of Othello's skin an easy target. JM

Cowhig, Ruth, 'Blacks in English Renaissance Drama' in D. Dabydeen (ed.), *The Black Presence in English Literature* (1985)

James, C. L. R., 'Othello', radio presentation (1964) in James, *Spheres of Existence* (1980)

See also ELIZABETH I; RENAISSANCE DRAMA

P

Padmore, George. Assumed name of Malcolm Nurse (1902–1959), leading black intellectual and primary advocate of black liberation and radical *Pan-Africanism in the 1940s and 1950s. Padmore was born in Trinidad. As a young man he went to school with and befriended C. L. R. *James, who would in later years also become a staunch advocate of black liberation. He also claimed to be a nephew of Henry Sylvester *Williams, another radical black leader. Enrolled in medicine, Nurse became a student activist at Fisk University, Tennessee, in the 1920s, and by 1926 he was considered an exceptional speaker on international issues and colonial debates. In part because of the deeply racist climate in Tennessee he transferred to New York University and then enrolled at Howard University's Law School.

Under the assumed name of George Padmore, Malcolm Nurse became heavily involved with the Communist Party by 1928, positioning himself as an advocate of racial consciousness and a youth leader. He also wrote articles in New York's *Daily Worker* and became involved with the Harlem Workers' Centre. As a result of increasing concern over colonial rule in Africa in the Communist Party, he began to divert his attention to Africa and in 1929 was elected as an organizational committee member at the second Congress of the League Against Imperialism in Frankfurt. He became the head of the Negro Bureau of the Communist Trade Union International and also served as Secretary of the International Trade Union Committee of Negro Workers. This was significant to the success of the first International Conference of Negro Workers in Hamburg, 1930, which supported the struggle for independence in Africa. Yet he was adamant that such struggles could not be successful if led by a black bourgeoisie. In 1931 he served as editor of the *Negro Worker* in Hamburg. However, in 1933 he defected from the Communist Party after it removed the International Trade Union Committee of Negro Workers as the Soviet Union sought to improve relations with west European powers.

After separating from the Communist Party and their colonial policies, Padmore returned to London, where he used the *West African Students' Union to unite Blacks from America, Africa, and the Caribbean. While he read and wrote for several left-wing publications such as *Controversy* and *Left*, he restricted his membership to organizations concerned mainly with African issues. His philosophy of facilitating a Pan-African brotherhood was underlined by a set of colonial grievances that were noted in his books, such as *How Britain Rules Africa* (1936), *Africa and World Peace* (1937), and his most renowned, *Pan Africanism or Communism?* (1956). His journal **International African Opinion* was quite influential in providing a space for black radical debate, and Padmore was himself a father figure to other black leaders and thinkers. He was instrumental in establishing the *International African Service Bureau, which served to network African and Caribbean intellectuals and political agents. The Bureau, under Padmore, was involved in a collaborative petitioning of the Royal Commission to investigate worsening conditions in the West Indies, resulting in the now infamous Moyne Commission Report.

Taking an anti-war stance in the No More War Movement (an Independent

Labour Party initiative), Padmore also organized meetings and protests to raise race awareness among both Blacks and Whites, advocating that the war continued to entrench the exploitation of subject peoples. At the same time he advocated a universal end to the colour bar. With support from the West African Students' Union, he became more convinced of the futility of indirect rule and the urgent need for self-government in Africa. This objective was further institutionalized by Padmore when, along with other activists such as Ras *Makonnen and Peter *Milliard, he formed the Pan-African Federation in 1944. The Federation essentially absorbed the International African Service Bureau and became a strong advocate of the unity and independence of African peoples. Under this umbrella Padmore spoke out against the increasingly fascist style of colonial rule in Nigeria, and engaged in activities that would strengthen the objective of a Pan-African brotherhood.

As the momentum of the Pan-African Federation mounted, Padmore and other activists organized the fifth Pan-African Congress, held in Manchester in 1945. The Congress was historic in bringing together the primary proponents of Pan-Africanism such as F. Kwame Nkrumah and W. E. B. DuBois. It reiterated the belief that a West African federation was crucial to the realization of solidarity in Africa. While he kept a close eye on issues confronting Blacks in Britain, Padmore's attention to West Africa took centre stage. He was responsible for linking Nkrumah and Nnamdi Azikiwe, leading freedom fighters and Pan-Africanists in Ghana and Nigeria respectively. In particular, his role in championing political nationalism and movements of independence in English-speaking Africa is especially noted in Ghana, where he had a strong friendship with and marked influence on the independence leader Nkrumah. He not only acted as a close adviser to Nkrumah but vehemently advocated that the latter provide a model for political leadership in the rest of Africa. In fact he was appointed by Nkrumah as a personal adviser on African affairs in 1957. Although his role in the story of Ghana's independence is often downplayed, he is considered by some as the 'silent hero' of Ghana. While he continued to support other nationalist initiatives in Africa, his time in Ghana had exposed many obstacles to a decolonized and united Africa. This disenchantment, coupled with deteriorating health, sent him back to London, where he succumbed to liver problems in 1959.

As an important revolutionary figure in the anti-colonial movement, Padmore argued for black people to have the power of self-determination and be free of Eurocentric ideologies. While he embraced Pan-Africanism, he maintained a Marxist critique of capitalism. His political activism and revolutionary visions set the stage for many new black states in the Caribbean and Africa to emerge, which is why he was referred to as the Father of African Emancipation by the Pan-Africanist radical C. L. R. James. ASW

Ramdin, Ron, *The Making of the Black Working Class in Britain* (1987)

See also POLITICS

Pan-Africanism. Sociopolitical movement that advocated the global solidarity of Blacks. Britain was the centre for Pan-Africanist activities owing to its escalating empire and the fact that many Blacks either moved to Britain, visited it, or were born there. It provided Blacks with a space to engage in ideas and discuss their mutual oppression under the colonial system. Before the rise of Pan-Africanism as an established form of racial expression, there were numerous figures living and working in Britain who anticipated its inception. Peter Fryer cites several 'proto-Pan-Africanists', among them Martin Robison *Delany, Edward Wilmot *Blyden, James Africanus Beale *Horton, and Samuel Jules Celestine *Edwards, who urged Africans to unite and gradually unshackle the ties of colonialism.

The first Pan-African Conference was held in London in 1900. It brought together 37 delegates from various places in Britain where there were significant communities of people of African descent. The Conference was organized by the Trinidadian Henry Sylvester *Williams, who had founded the African Association in 1897. Even before the inauguration of the Association, Williams had felt the need for Blacks around the world to come together. It has been suggested that the term 'Pan-African' was first used in 1899, but the source of its usage is not entirely known. The Pan-African Conference was the first occasion when black people gathered to voice their opinions and discuss notions concerning issues such as imperialism, colonialism, and racism. The chair was taken by Bishop Alexander Walters, head of the African Methodist Episcopal Zion Church in the United States and president of the National Afro-American Council. Others who attended the Conference were delegates from various African states. Among the papers that were presented were C. W. French's 'Conditions Favouring a High Standard of African Humanity', which insisted on the treatment of Blacks as human beings, and Benito Sylvain's 'The Necessary Concord To Be Established Between Native Races and European Colonists', which firmly attacked British colonialism.

Presentation of the papers was followed by discussions concerning the pragmatics of activating the ideas that had been offered. What materialized was the implementation of an 'Address to the Nations of the World' as well as the integration of the African Association into the Pan-African Association. The address was sent to various heads of state where Blacks were oppressed. It requested the cessation of racism and the acceptance of Blacks as human beings with rights. The aims of the new Pan-African Association were outlined and defined by the conference delegates:

1. To secure Africans throughout the world true civil and political rights.
2. To meliorate the conditions of our brothers on the continent of Africa, America and other parts of the world.
3. To promote efforts to secure effective legislation and encourage our people in educational, industrial and commercial enterprise
4. To foster the production of writing and statistics relating to our people everywhere.
5. To raise funds for forwarding these purposes.

The Conference was a general success as it managed to identify the problems, practicalities, and issues that needed urgent attention among the global black community. Major newspapers in Britain such as the *Westminster Gazette* reported the event, and this alerted the British public to the black state of affairs. Another positive feature of the Conference was the commencement of African-Asian solidarity. Dadabhai *Naoroji, a British Indian, contributed financially to the event, and this was the first recorded occasion of such Indian and African cohesion.

Following the Conference, Williams left for Jamaica, Trinidad, and the United States in order to establish branches of the Pan-African Association. During his time away the Association was dissolved by its treasurer, Dr R. J. Colenso, who claimed that the organization had run out of funds. Williams attempted to revitalize the Association, but failed. In October 1901, however, he did begin the journal *The Pan-African*, which sought to recapitulate the aims of the Pan-African Association while providing a space for discovering new Pan-Africanist ideas. The first issue declared that 'no other but a Negro can represent the Negro'. Despite the verve with which Williams launched the publication, it only survived one issue.

Pan-African congresses were also held. The first was organized by W. E. B. DuBois and took place in Paris on 19–21 February 1919. Present at the event were 57 delegates representing fifteen countries. However, since the British Caribbean had no representatives, the Congress did not manage to attain a balance of opinions. Delegates at the Congress agreed that what was necessary was an insistence that Africans be involved in the governance of their own countries. More congresses took place, with several sessions conducted in Brussels and Paris. The events in London took place at the Central Hall, Westminster, on 27 and 29 August 1921. It was attended by 113 delegates and chaired by DuBois, Dr John *Alcindor, and J. R. *Archer. The London sessions were viewed as more radical than the other congresses across Europe since representatives were more militant in their condemnation of colonial policy. The 1921 London Congress implemented the 'Declaration to the World', which criticized the unjust distribution of wealth across the world. The third London Congress was held on 7 and 8 November 1923 at Denison House, Vauxhall Bridge Road. Thirteen countries were represented on this occasion, and demands included the right of Africans to access their own land and the progress of Africa for its own people.

The most representative Pan-African Congress was held in Manchester in 1945. Ninety delegates attended the event, of which 20 represented 15 West African organizations, 6 for East Africa and South Africa, 33 for the West Indies, and 35 spoke for numerous British organizations. Many future political leaders and influential figures such as Jomo Kenyatta, Amy *Garvey, Kwame Nkrumah, and George *Padmore were gathered together amidst a climate of intense black consciousness following the Second World War. The Manchester congress differed from the earlier ones because it managed to involve the masses, a good indication of which was the impressive representation at it of various trade unions. Key issues discussed at the event were racism in Britain, imperialism in North and West Africa, the oppression of black women, and discrimination against black seamen. Nkrumah drafted the 'Declaration to the Colonial Workers, Farmers and Intellectuals', which urged intellectuals to organize the masses and to encourage workers to fight against imperialism. The Manchester congress was a sizeable success as it demonstrated the unity of various black leaders and their ability to work closely with those under their leadership. SS

Fryer, Peter, *Staying Power: The History of Black People in Britain* (1984)

Langley, J. A., *Pan-Africanism and Nationalism in West Africa 1900–1945: A Study in Ideology and Social Classes* (1973)

See also AFRICA AND BRITISH COLONIALISM; POLITICS

Peach, Blair (1946–1979). New Zealand-born teacher and anti-racist activist who was killed during an anti-fascist demonstration in Southall. Peach arrived in Britain in 1969 and taught at the Phoenix Special School in east London. He was politically active and became a member of the Socialist Workers' Party and the Anti Nazi League, and was the president of the National Union of Teachers in east London. He was involved in several trade unions and campaigned against apartheid in South Africa as well as other racist injustices. On 23 April 1979 the far-right National Front held an election meeting in the predominantly Asian area of Southall, much to its residents' disapproval. The day before the meeting took place 5,000 people marched to Ealing Town Hall protesting against the National Front. Despite this, the meeting went ahead, resulting in demonstrations that, according to Dilip Hiro and other witnesses, were handled violently by the Metropolitan Police. Peach was hit on the head by officers from the Metropolitan Police's Special Patrol Group as he was attempting to escape the troubled scene. His death, perceived by many in the black community as an act of murder, came to signify the abuse of police aggression, and the related issue of the death of black people in police custody was widely discussed in ethnic-minority newspapers, generating support and solidarity from racially oppressed groups. Peach's body remained unburied for eight weeks so as to allow people to pay their respects. He was finally buried on 13 June 1979. No public inquiry was made into his murder. A school was named in his honour, the Blair Peach School in Southall. DD/SS

Hiro, Dilip, *Black Britain, White Britain* (rev. edn., 1992)

<http://www.anl.org.uk/13-blairpeach.htm>

<http://www.dkrenton.co.uk/anl/southall.htm>

Peckard, Peter (bap. 1717, d. 1797). Clergyman of the Church of England and campaigner against the *slave trade. Peckard was educated at the University of Oxford and held various positions in the Church before becoming Master of Magdalene College, Cambridge, in 1781. He retained this office until his death, and was also Dean of Peterborough from 1792.

In 1785, as Vice-Chancellor of the University of Cambridge, Peckard set the subject for a university Latin essay competition: *Anne liceat invitos in servitutem dare?* ['Is it lawful to make men slaves against their will?'] The prize was won by Thomas *Clarkson, who entered the competition in search of academic honours but discovered his life's work in the process.

Peckard was himself an eloquent critic of the slave trade. In a 1788 sermon before the University of Cambridge, he stated that there was no validity in any of the arguments usually brought forward in defence of what he called 'this vile traffick of the British Man-Merchant'. On the contrary, the trade was inhumane and unchristian, 'radically, absolutely, and essentially Evil, loaded with all possible malignity, and totally destitute of any Real Good'. Similar arguments were made in his *Am I not a man and a brother?* (1788), which, a modern biographer suggests, 'may have launched the phrase as an anti-slavery slogan'.

Peckard was one of the subscribers to the *Interesting Narrative* of *Olaudah Equiano, and wrote a letter of introduction, which Equiano used in his promotional material. JG

Equiano, Olaudah, *The Interesting Narrative and Other Writings* (rev. edn., ed. Vincent Carretta, 2003)

ODNB

[Peckard, Peter], *Am I not a man and a brother?* (1788)

—— *Justice and Mercy Recommended, Particularly with Reference to the Slave Trade* (1788)

See also CHRISTIANITY

Pennington, James W. C. (1807–1870). African-American abolitionist, teacher, Christian preacher, temperance worker, and peace activist. Pennington was born into slavery in Maryland, where he worked as a blacksmith. He escaped, educated himself at night school, and became a teacher. Following a conversion experience, he served as a pastor of several black Congregational churches. Much of his life was devoted to self-improvement and the cause of *abolition and black civil rights. As a prominent African-American spokesman he was a delegate to the second World Anti-Slavery Convention, and also the Peace Congress, both held in London in 1843. Pennington believed that US slavery and racialism could best be challenged by mobilizing international opinion. To this end he preached and spoke all over Britain. He frequently compared his treatment in Britain to that which he received in America, where 'If I meet my white brother minister in the street, he blushes to own me; meet him in our deliberative body, he gives me the go-by; meet him at the communion table, and he looks at me sideways'. Pennington visited Britain again in 1849–50, speaking for the Free Produce Association, which opposed importing goods produced by slave labour. The University of Heidelberg awarded him an honorary doctorate.

In the vivid story of his life, *The Fugitive Blacksmith* (1850), Pennington spelt out for British readers the brutal realities of chattel slavery and that, as a runaway, he was liable to be re-enslaved under the terms of the Fugitive Slave Act of 1850. Scottish supporters bought his freedom. Although he raised financial support in Britain for the abolitionist cause, back in the United States Pennington's career was dogged by questions about his integrity and competence and his alcoholism. He was a diminished figure when he visited Britain for a third time in 1861. He made few speeches and in 1862 was imprisoned in Liverpool for one month for theft. Pennington's final years were spent as a poorly paid itinerant minister to black churches in the United States. DK

Armistead, Wilson, *A Tribute to the Negro* (1848)

Blackett, R. J. M., *Beating Against the Barriers: The Lives of Six Nineteenth-Century Afro-Americans* (1986)

See also SLAVERY

Perry, John (*fl.* 1845–1849). Black boxer who fought and lived in Britain. Perry was born in Annapolis, Nova Scotia. He initially served on a British man-of-war for four years and, after being discharged, turned to a career in boxing. His time on the man-of-war earned him the nickname John 'the Black Sailor' Perry. He arrived in London in 1845 after walking from Birmingham, having hoped to find a patron for his prizefighting along his journey. In London he met Johnny Broome, a former British lightweight champion. Broome trained Perry, and in the following year he faced his first professional opponent, Bill Burton. Perry was an entertaining fighter not simply because he was physically impressive (he was handsome, 6 feet 1½ inches tall, and weighed 212 pounds), but also because he moved with skill and poise. His style of milling was particularly striking, where he would move around his opponent while balanced on his toes until finally delivering clean punches. Burton was a resilient fighter but Perry was the more gifted boxer and eventually knocked the former out. A few months after the fight Perry was transported for life to New South Wales after being arrested for being an accomplice to a group of American forgers. His boxing career in Britain thus ended. He did, however, recommence prizefighting in Australia, where he won the Australian heavyweight championship in 1849. He remained in the country and went on to train young boxers. SS

Fryer, Peter, *Staying Power: The History of Black People in Britain* (1984)

See also MOLINEAUX, TOM; RICHMOND, BILL

Peters, Samuel (d. 1861). Haitian soldier who served in the 71st (Highland Light Infantry) Regiment. He enlisted in Cork in January 1815. The reasons behind his arrival and stay in Ireland are unknown. The 71st left for the Low Countries in 1815 after Napoleon escaped from his prison on Elba and sent his men to Belgium. Following the battle at Waterloo, over 200 out of the 800 men in the Regiment were dead, wounded, or missing. Peters survived and remained in Belgium for the next two years. He was part of the Army of Occupation and was awarded the Waterloo Medal for his bravery and efforts during the battle. In 1820 he transferred to the 2nd West India Regiment after serving for five years in the 71st in England and Ireland. In the 2nd West India Regiment he served in the Gold Coast campaign of 1823–4. During his service he reached the rank of corporal and was discharged with a pension in May 1841. He died on 16 November 1861. The Army offered black men like Peters and his fellow soldier George Rose an opportunity to earn equal pay with white men. In this respect, it was an attractive option for black men, and therefore the significant number of black soldiers in various British regiments in the 18th and 19th centuries is not surprising. Most black soldiers showed high levels of racial solidarity and usually enlisted in groups. In the same way, if circumstances induced black soldiers to desert, they usually did so together. SS

Ellis, J., 'Distinguished in Action . . . The Black Soldiers of the 4th Dragoons 1715–1842', *Journal of the Queen's Royal Hussars Historical Society* (2003)

—— 'Drummers for the Devil? The Black Soldiers of the 29th (Worcestershire) Regiment of Foot 1759–1843', *Journal of Army Historical Research*, 80/323 (2002)

See also FIRST WORLD WAR; SECOND WORLD WAR

Photography. The first substantial body of photographic images of the black presence in Britain date back to the years and decades immediately following the end of the Second World War.

1. Documenting success: 1940s–1970s
2. Vanley Burke
3. Armet Francis
4. Horace Ové
5. The 1980s onwards

1. Documenting success: 1940s–1970s The bulk of these photographic images consists of documentary and journalistic photographs of newly arrived Caribbean immigrants, either disembarking into seaport arrival halls, or waiting to be collected from boat-train transit terminals such as London's Victoria Station. Almost without exception, these photographs show people dressed in their finest clothes. Such pictures speak of an age when people wore their best clothes to travel, and similarly dressed to arrive. We see dapper-suited young men and equally well-dressed young women, nearly all of whom are wearing hats, without which they would have considered themselvely to be incompletely dressed. The message conveyed by these photographs is remarkably clear: these immigrants respect themselves, have full confidence in their own abilities to make good lives for themselves in 'the mother country', and have a corresponding confidence in the hospitality which they expect to receive. The photographs, dating from the mid–late 1940s to the early 1960s, give a very good indication of the contemporary styles not only of the travellers themselves, but of the communities they left behind in the Caribbean. Perhaps the most celebrated photograph of newly arriving Caribbean immigrants is that of the **Empire Windrush* arriving at Tilbury docks in June 1948, bringing with her nearly 500 Jamaican immigrants. This group were the first of a significant number of Caribbean immigrants seeking to start a new life in Britain. As such, the iconic photograph of the crowded bow of the *Empire Windrush* has become a graphic symbol of post-war immigration from the Caribbean and other parts of the Commonwealth.

The next body of photographs that act as benchmarks of the post-war presence of Caribbean immigrants are studio portraits. These portraits, primarily dating from the 1960s and 1970s, were produced by numerous high street photographers who drew much of their patronage from the immigrant communities. The portraits invariably consisted of individuals or small groups of family members, again dressed in their finest clothes, or their professional uniforms, against a variety of studio backdrops. Caribbean immigrants and their families in effect commissioned portraits that indicated a real or imagined sense of career development and individual prosperity. Sitters were frequently photographed wearing the uniforms of their professions, such as transport or nursing. At a time when very few Caribbean immigrants could afford to have telephones in their homes, many were photographed speaking into telephones. These images were frequently sent back to family and friends back 'home'. High street photographs provided an invaluable service to their patrons, who could ill-afford their own cameras. Various factors contributed to the demise of the high street photographer, and by the late 1970s such studios had become a rarity, though, correspondingly perhaps, a sense of black British photography had begun to emerge and develop.

2. Vanley Burke One of the first British-based black people to distinguish themselves in the field of photography was Vanley Burke. Born in Jamaica in 1951, Burke came to England in 1965, having received his first camera as a present for his tenth birthday a few years earlier. For him, 'Photography started to develop as a means of looking at people and how they lived.' To this end, he became responsible for producing many highly engaging photographs of Birmingham's Caribbean communities, through the course of the later decades of the 20th century. These photographs—depicting black people at work, at play, at church, on the streets, and in their homes—have come to be regarded as key documents chronicling the lives of black people in the country's second largest city. Through these images we can chart the development, importance, and growing confidence of black Britain. In Burke's photographs we see elderly black men playing dominoes in a local pub, groups of young people hanging out in the park, baptisms, weddings, and burials. We see also confrontations between the police and young Blacks, people dancing, portraits of college graduates, and many other things illustrative of a vibrant, confident, and multifaceted community of black British people. Unfortunately,

Burke's pictures suffer from a lack of referencing, so viewers are invariably left to calculate for themselves the approximate date of his documentary photographs. This lack of definitive reference points mars what would otherwise be an extraordinarily important document of the growth and coming of age of black Britain.

3. **Armet Francis** Another important practitioner who must be regarded as a pioneer of black British photography is Armet Francis. Born in Jamaica in 1945, by the early 1970s Francis had become an important chronicler not only of black people in Britain but of people of African origin throughout the world. His most celebrated work was *The Black Triangle*, a seminal exhibition and publishing project of the mid-1980s. The book comprised three pictorial sections, each consisting of photographs taken by Francis on his travels through Africa (Kenya, Nigeria, Senegal, and Zimbabwe), the Caribbean (Barbados and Jamaica), and Britain and the United States. Taken between 1969 and 1981, these photographs offer an invaluable insight into aspects of the late 20th-century African diaspora. In Francis's photographs we can chart the dynamic rise of *Rastafarianism and the attendant 'dread' culture, as it developed among communities in Jamaica and the United Kingdom. We see dancers and performers in Lagos, in London, in New York. We also see portraits of what we might call ordinary people, proud, confident, self-assured witnesses to the post-independence years of hope and optimism that typified continental and diasporic African identities during the 1960s and 1970s. Celebrated, too, within Francis's photographs is the new independence of Zimbabwe.

4. **Horace Ové** Horace Ové must also be considered a pioneering figure of black British photography. He was born in Trinidad and Tobago in 1939 and came to London as a young man. Over the course of the 1970s he became known as one of a small number of the leading black independent film-makers to emerge in Britain. He is widely respected for his pioneering and ground-breaking work as a director of films such as *Pressure*. Made in 1975, the film tackles the issues that came to shape and influence the lives of a new generation of black Britons. A timely, engaging, and deeply empathetic work, *Pressure* was, and remains, a gritty and dynamic study of a generation in crisis.

Equally important is Ové's work as a photographer. During his time in London in the politically and culturally heady days of the 1960s and 1970s, he became responsible for some of the most remarkable and candid photographs reflecting the emergence of black Britain. He photographed important black literary, political, and cultural figures of the period, both British, such as C. L. R. *James and Darcus Howe, and American, such as James Baldwin. He also captured a rare spectacle—Stokely Carmichael, Allen Ginsberg, and *Michael X at an early Black Power gathering in London in 1967.

Ové was responsible for the most compelling documentation of the development of a uniquely British element of African diasporic cultural identity. He photographed Samuel *Selvon, Andrew *Salkey and John *La Rose, the founding members of the *Caribbean Artists' Movement. He also photographed the birth and development of the *Notting Hill Carnival and the growing importance of *reggae music to British youth. Like others before and alongside him, we see in Ové's work copious and fascinating evidence of the clothing styles of black Britain from the 1960s onwards.

Perhaps his most remarkable photographs are his studies of the self-styled firebrand Michael X. The historical significance and importance of the photographic body of work produced by Ové cannot be overstated.

5. **The 1980s onwards** Since the mid-1980s new generations of black British photographers have emerged. By and large these are British-born, art-school-trained practitioners, keen to work with the medium of photography in a marked range and variety of ways. This new generation includes

photographers such as Faisal Abdu'Allah, Ajamu, Rotimi Fani-Kayode, Joy Gregory, Sunil Gupta, Mumtaz Karimjee, Roshini Kempadoo, Dave Lewis, Ingrid Pollard, and Franklyn Rodgers. The practice of these artists reflects the ways in which photography has become a compelling and indelible element of a wider fine art practice. As such, the work of these photographers has been exhibited at art galleries across the United Kingdom and further afield. Complementing this group of photographers are those fine artists whose practice incorporates elements of photography. The practice of such artists (for example, Keith Piper and Yinka Shonibare) focuses, to varying degrees, on what we might refer to as narratives of 'race' and 'representation'. It might perhaps be more accurate to describe these artists as using photography, rather than being photographers. They employ the photographic medium as a means of animating and graphically illustrating potent debates about culture, history, and identity, and the ways in which such concerns are reflective of the black experience and African diasporic sensibilities and aesthetics.

Mention should also be made of Autograph, the Association of Black Photographers. Formed in London in the late 1980s, Autograph ABP is a photographic arts agency with a brief to support and promote the work of black British photographers 'and to advocate their inclusion in all areas of exhibition, publishing, education and commerce in the visual arts'.

ECh

Bailey, S., and Hall, S. (eds.), *The Critical Decade: Black British Photography in the 1980s* (1992)

Burke, Vanley, *A Retrospective* (1993)

Francis, Armet, *The Black Triangle: The People of the African Diaspora* (1985)

Hall, S., and Sealy, M., *Different: A Historical Content. Contemporary Photographs and Black Identity* (2001)

Picton, Cesar (1755–1836). African servant who worked in England and later became a successful businessman. Picton was brought to Kingston, Surrey, from Senegal at the age of 6 as a gift to Sir John Philipps of Norbiton from Captain Parr, a British army officer. He was most probably born a Muslim but was baptized into the Christian faith on 4 December 1761. It was then that he was christened Cesar. Details of his Senegalese name are not known. He developed a close bond with the Philipps family. They, being strongly in favour of education and Christian missionary work, encouraged the young Cesar. When Sir John died in 1764, Cesar gained his independence and rented a coach house and stables from the money that he had inherited from Sir John. It was during this time that he gave himself the surname of Picton. Subsequently, he set up as a coal merchant, and by 1795 he was a lucrative businessman and able to purchase various pieces of property. He eventually moved out of Kingston in order to rent his property there, and settled in Thames Ditton, where he lived for twenty years. He inherited money from the Philipps children following their deaths, and used it to invest further in property and other valuable assets. He died in 1836 at the age of 81. Picton is buried in All Saints' Church, Kingston. Every year the Kingston Racial Equality Council and Kingston University organize a Cesar Picton Lecture in commemoration of the contribution of Blacks to Kingston's and British history.

DD/SS

Myers, Norma, *Reconstructing the Black Past: Blacks in Britain, 1780–1830* (1996)

See also BUSINESSES

Pitt, David Thomas (1913–1994). Lord Pitt of Hampstead, general practitioner and politician born in St David's, Grenada, the son of Cyril S. L. Pitt. A prominent figure in Caribbean politics in the 1940s, Pitt later became involved with the Labour Party in Britain. He provided active support to a number of charity organizations and social campaigns throughout his career, playing a significant role in the *Anti-Apartheid Movement (AAM). His medical career was equally distinguished, and in 1985 he was elected president of the British Medical Association. Always keen to ensure that the political establishment remained relevant and accessible to the public, Pitt became well known as a spokesperson for those who felt marginalized by the system and for encouraging their participation in electoral politics and other institutional bodies. The Lord Pitt Foundation was established in 1983 to mark his seventieth birthday. After his death the Race Equality Unity launched the annual Lord Pitt memorial lecture, its aim to address the issues of racial equality Pitt had done so much to promote.

Educated at St David's Roman Catholic School, Grenada, and the Grenada Boys' Secondary School, Pitt won the Grenada scholarship in 1932, enabling him to study abroad. He went to Edinburgh University to pursue medicine, graduating in 1938. Later he would maintain that it was his experience of the depression years in Scotland that made him a socialist. But his experience was also typical of many Caribbean intellectuals of that generation: the early years of colonial tutelage followed by exposure to the harsh realities of the 'mother country' acting as a catalyst for an anti-imperial political stance (albeit one very much shaped by the ideological legacy of the former colonial power).

It was in this context that Pitt returned to the Caribbean, aiming to involve himself in the region's politics. He believed strongly in independence for individual colonies. However, like many at the time, he regarded this as attainable only within the framework of a larger, more secure Caribbean federation. Having moved first to St Vincent to work as a district medical officer, Pitt went to Trinidad in 1940, where he was employed as house physician at San Fernando Hospital. The following year he established his own general practice in the area. In the same period he became a member of the Town Council, on which he served until 1947 (also becoming Deputy Mayor from 1946 to 1947). In 1943 he helped to found, and was elected president of, the West Indian National Party, the primary objectives of which were to push for a Caribbean federation and Trinidadian independence.

In 1947 Pitt travelled to England to lobby the government for changes in Trinidad's constitutional position. He was accompanied by his wife, Dorothy Elaine Alleyne (whom he had married in 1943), and their three children. After two unsuccessful years of campaigning, Pitt became disillusioned with his project. Sensing that federation was unlikely now, he decided to remain in England. He settled in London and opened a surgery in North Gower Street, close to where a large number of immigrants had established themselves around Euston and Camden Town. He soon became a highly recognizable and sought-after figure: as the only African-Caribbean doctor available he was in constant demand by black people seeking help and advice on health and social issues. He became an informal spokesman for the black British community. By 1953 Pitt had been drawn back into a more formal political role, becoming involved in the Labour Party through the Campaign for Nuclear Disarmament. Four years later he was selected as the Labour Party candidate for Hampstead, although he failed to win his seat in 1959 following a racist campaign against him in the general election. By then, however, as a result of his part in the response to the *Notting Hill riots of 1958 and his support for the Anti-Apartheid Movement, he had assumed a prominent position in the struggle for racial equality; so much so, in fact, that in 1961 his surgery, which served as the headquarters for the AAM, was targeted by arsonists. Undeterred, he helped to establish the *Campaign Against Racial Discrimination in 1964 and acted as its first chairman. Meanwhile, he had been elected to the London County Council in 1961 as the member for Hackney; when it was absorbed by the Greater London Council in 1964, he retained his position, serving until 1977 (in 1974 he became its first black chairman, a post he held until the following year). The year 1970 saw him run once more for Parliament, this time in Clapham South. He lost and never stood for office again. In 1975, however, he was made a life peer as Baron Pitt of Hampstead.

Throughout the 1970s and 1980s Pitt continued both to maintain his general practice and to take an active role in social and political projects. Alongside regularly attending the House of Lords, he became chairman of the Community Relations Commission in 1977 and in 1978 chaired an investigation into recent riots in Bermuda, his findings helping to instigate moves towards greater racial equality there. As chairman of the charity Shelter (1979–90; vice-president 1990–4), he was actively involved in the campaign to end homelessness and bad *housing in Britain. Two years after attaining what he considered his most prestigious honour, the presidency of the British Medical Association, he became chairman of the newly created Race Equality Unit, a position he held until his death from prostate cancer on 18 December 1994.

On Pitt's death, Robert Hughes, writing in *The Independent*, commented that there 'is still a long way to go until we can say that racism is extinct in Britain, but Pitt's charm, tolerance and passionate advocacy helped immensely to change the climate in society'. In his medical career as in his political career Pitt not only achieved a great deal but was also often a pioneer. As Mike Phillips observes, Pitt's emphasis on an engagement in electoral politics during the 1960s appeared too restrained for some more radical black activists; by the time of his death, however, it 'had become clear that when Pitt urged young migrants to join the police forces, the civil service, or the political parties, he had simply been ahead of his time in pursuing full integration'. Indeed, Pitt played a vital role in securing institutional recognition for minority groups in Britain, as well as contributing to the wider global struggle for racial equality. MGN

ODNB

See also DOCTORS; MEDICINE

Plaatje, Sol (1876–1932). Journalist, linguist, author, and early member of the African National Congress in South Africa. After school in South Africa Solomon Tshekisho Plaatje (Sol) became a government clerk and an interpreter; he spoke several vernacular languages and also English, Dutch, Afrikaans, and German. During the South African War (1899–1902) he worked for the British, and his vivid diary of the siege of Mafeking, written in a school exercise book, was discovered many years after his death. He founded several newspapers that defended African rights against white rule.

A founder member of the South African Native National Congress (SANNC; later the African National Congress), Plaatje was a member of a delegation to London to protest at the South African Land Bill. From 1914 to 1917 he lived in London, speaking wherever he could against the Land Bill, and also writing a book, *Native Life in South Africa* (1916), which appealed for British help against South African government policies. In Britain he was closely involved with the Brotherhood Movement, a Christian organization that argued for racial harmony. Back in South Africa in 1917, he promoted Brotherhood in Kimberley. In 1919 he was a member of an SANNC delegation to London that failed to get African interests discussed at the Versailles Peace Conference. During 1919–21 he travelled in North America speaking on South African issues.

Plaatje wrote poetry and translated several Shakespeare plays into Tswana. He also wrote *Mhudi* (1930), one of the first novels to be written by an African. DK

Plaatje, Sol, *The Boer War Diary of Sol T. Plaatje, an African at Mafeking* (ed. John L. Comaroff, 1973)
—— *Mhudi: An Epic of Native Life 100 Years Ago* (1930)
—— *Native Life in South Africa* (1916)
Willan, Brian, *Select Writings* (ed. Brian Willan, 1996)
—— *Sol Plaatje, South African Nationalist, 1876–1932* (1984)

See also CHRISTIANITY; CHURCHES; MISSIONARY SOCIETIES

Plymouth. One of the many ports on Devon's two coasts through which black people passed in and out of all parts of the country. The city has long-term connections with the history of people of African descent, most of the earlier connections being because of the transatlantic *slave trade. The now famous print of the *Brookes* slave ship used in the abolition campaign was originally produced for the Plymouth Committee for Abolition. The initiator of the British slave trade, Sir John *Hawkins, was born in Plymouth, where he has been long recognized as a significant figure. However, the part that Africans and their descendants played in the city's history, directly and indirectly, has not been sufficiently acknowledged.

Early records of the black presence in Plymouth include references to Sir James Bagg, who in 1628, ordered that his newly arrived 'negrowe' should be 'handsomely clothed', and the baptism of 'Elizabeth, daughter of Angell, a Blackmoore' at St Andrew's Church in 1633. In 1780 there was a riot at Plymouth dock when a large crowd took sides in a quarrel between two black bandsmen from the Somerset militia and some white soldiers from the Brecknock militia. There have been black sailors on English ships at least since the 18th century, and many of them would have passed through Plymouth. One record from the 19th century is in the parish register of East Stonehouse, which lists the baptism on 13 February 1835 of an African ship's boy from the HMS *Africa*, Thomas Scott MacLean, who was taken in infancy from the coast of Mozambique.

Prisoners, white and black, from the Anglo-French conflicts in the Antilles and from the American War of Independence were kept in six hulks off Plymouth before the opening of Dartmoor prison in 1809. Peter Courlon, a black servant to General Rochambeau, returned to France at the end of hostilities via Plymouth in May 1811 but returned later to his wife, Suzanne (née Parker), and family in Moretonhampstead. Olaudah *Equiano, working as the commissary for supplies for the expedition to Sierra Leone, resigned in Plymouth in disgust at the behaviour of others working on the project.

The black presence in Plymouth in the 20th century is similarly under-recorded. William Miller was a black councillor and alderman from 1925 to 1970, but he never became Mayor. However, his son Claude Miller, after many years as a councillor, became Lord Mayor of Plymouth in 2005.

Plymouth deserves a more complete history of the city, which will only be revealed by further research into the black people who have made their contributions in the past and continue to do so today. LMacK

Collicott, Sylvia L., *Connections: Haringey Local-National-World Links* (1986)
Devon Black History trail, <http://www.exeter.gov.uk/media/pdf/i/c/Devon_Trail.pdf>
Tattersfield, Nigel, *Forgotten Trade* (1998)

Politics. The struggle for social, political, and economic justice has been central to the history of black peoples in Britain. This struggle has continued unabated since at least the 18th century, a period that ushered in the beginnings of the establishment of permanent black communities. Over the centuries black women and men such as Olaudah *Equiano in the 1780s, Claudia *Jones in the 1950s, and Bernie *Grant in the 1980s have worked tirelessly for the achievement of freedom, equality, and justice. The commitments of such activists and political campaigners to tackle racism and all forms of social injustice have left a lasting legacy for British society.

1. Introduction
2. Origins of radical black politics
3. Organizing for representation in the 20th century
4. The Labour Party and the struggle for representation

1. Introduction Charting the evolution of the political struggles of black activists reveals the legacy that has given black and other minority ethnic peoples in Britain a level of political participation and representation unrivalled in Europe. Furthermore, because of their endeavours, Britain has a strong anti-racist discourse, backed by legislative powers—the 1976 Race Relations Act and the 2000 Race Relations (Amendment) Act—that are the envy of many countries. Lastly, it is a legacy that continues to inspire today's political activists.

2. Origins of radical black politics One of the most eloquent articulations of the dehumanization and suffering of slavery was that of the former slave Equiano. William *Wilberforce, Thomas *Clarkson, and Granville *Sharp were key protagonists in the abolition of slavery, but it was also Equiano's writing and political activism that gave meaning to the unacceptability of *slavery. Equiano skilfully utilized the language and Christian sensibilities of his oppressors to make the human and political case for *abolition.

Equiano's masterpiece was his best-selling autobiography *The Interesting Narrative of the Life of Olaudah Equiano . . . the African* (1789), in which he chronicled his life as a slave and his degrading experiences at the hands of cruel masters and overseers. His narrative exposed to the British public the full horror and brutality of slavery, and the human costs of the *slave trade, which henceforth could no longer be regarded merely as an economic enterprise.

Equiano was far more than an abolitionist: his vision was for a society based on justice for all. It is no surprise, therefore, that Britain's first black political activist of note was also one of the founder members of the London Corresponding Society, an organization set up by Thomas Hardy to campaign for political suffrage for working men.

3. Organizing for representation in the 20th century The late 19th and early 20th centuries witnessed an unprecedented form of black political participation. Although slavery had been abolished some 50 years before, *racism and social injustice were still endemic throughout Britain and its widespread empire, and a new generation of black British activists responded accordingly. The struggle for complete emancipation now took on a global dynamic, with solidarity between black people from Africa, Asia, and the Americas. The composer and activist Samuel *Coleridge-Taylor, the first Asian MP, Dadabhai *Naoroji, John *Archer of Battersea, and Henry Sylvester *Williams were all key in their own right, but were also instrumental in organizing and participating in the world's first Pan-African Conference.

The period from the 1920s marked a significant phase in the development of black political life in Britain. In the aftermath of the First World War competition for scarce economic and social resources created tensions between white workers and the black community, many of whom were demobilized servicemen who had fought for the British in the conflict. Racism and discrimination was rife, and it was perhaps not surprising that the frustrations of both Blacks and Whites should culminate in 1919, in a series of 'race' riots throughout the country. Though the government embarked on a programme of repatriation, those Blacks who remained began to organize to demand black rights, while at the same time promoting black self-help and self-reliance. Throughout the 1920s many black-led groups emerged, many of them building on earlier Pan-Africanist philosophies. The liberal humanitarian *League of Coloured Peoples was founded in 1931 by Harold *Moody, a Jamaican-born physician. It was London-based and functioned alternately as a social club, housing bureau, employment agency, and political pressure group.

However, it was not until after the large-scale black immigration of the **Empire Windrush* era that black people began to make major headway in terms of their participation within the British political system. Once again, it was another tragedy, this time the *Notting Hill riots of 1958 and the murder of the Antiguan-born Kelso *Cochrane, that drove individuals such as Claudia *Jones to organize and mobilize a black political force to protect the civil rights of their communities.

The seeds for mass protest, organization, and political activity had already been sown in 1945 at the fifth Pan-African Conference. Staged in Manchester, the Conference brought together some of the greatest minds of the black world: George *Padmore, W. E. B. DuBois, Kwame

Nkrumah, and Jomo Kenyatta. At its core were the teachings of black self-determination extolled by Marcus *Garvey. In 1959 a committee was organized in response to Cochrane's murder to lobby Parliament about his untimely death and to demand recognition of, and action to address, the racism and discrimination endured by Britain's black population. This committee was convened under the chairmanship of Amy Ashwood *Garvey (wife of Marcus Garvey), with Dr David *Pitt, later to become Lord Pitt of Hampstead, centrally involved.

While activists organized and lobbied, angry black people took to the streets and fought running battles with the police and Teddy boys in what became known as the Notting Hill riots. Out of the ashes of struggle, a number of black political organizations and individuals emerged that would reshape British politics and British society.

The West London community activist Claudia Jones's response to the 1958 riots was to set up a 'Carnival of Unity'. Her idea was to bring all the communities, black and white, together to begin the healing process. Little was she to know that her 'Carnival of Unity' was to become the largest cultural celebration in Europe: the *Notting Hill Carnival.

4. **The Labour Party and the struggle for representation** Dr David Pitt became a significant figure during this period. He launched the ground-breaking organization the *Campaign Against Racial Discrimination (CARD). With lawyers and prominent activists, CARD pressured the government to introduce the Community Relations Act in 1968, the precursor of the Race Relations Act of 1976. In contrast to many CARD members, Pitt believed that the black community's interests were best served by working with the Labour government of that time. It was these conflicts about how strongly affiliated CARD should be with Labour that would eventually tear the organization apart. Pitt himself went on to break further political ground by becoming the first black Deputy Chair of the London County Council and first black Chair of the *Greater London Council.

During the 1970s and 1980s the Labour Party commanded the allegiance, support, and vote of the majority of black voters. Yet, many felt dissatisfied with Labour's commitment to redressing racialized inequalities. The defining question for many black Labour activists was therefore *how* they could work effectively within the Labour Party—how the Party could be made to work for black Britons. The solution appeared in the shape of proposals for the establishment of a black caucus, or Labour Party black sections (LPBS). Black sections would form part of the constitution, with rights to send resolutions to the constituency Labour parties, and delegates to the Party's General Management Committee, to nominate parliamentary candidates, and ultimately to have black representation on Labour's National Executive Committee. The proposal, supported by Bernie Grant and other black activists, was put forward as a pivotal means of involving black people within the Party's structures.

The ideological thinking of Grant and other key black activists at the time—Paul Boateng, Diane Abbott, Marc Wadsworth, and Kingsley Abrahams—was very much rooted in black self-determination. All were involved in the South African *Anti-Apartheid Movement, and they shared a belief that it was the right political moment to put collective pressure on the Labour Party for black representation within the Party. The result in 1983 was the formation of the LPBS. Grant argued that, 'although black people solidly voted Labour for decades this was not reflected in party policies, priorities or in its hierarchy'.

The Labour Party under Neil Kinnock and Roy Hattersley vociferously resisted incorporating the LPBS. Many LPBS activists were aligned with what was seen as the radical left wing of the Party, and the Labour leadership was attempting to 'modernize' by bringing it closer to the political centre. Nevertheless, despite the problems the LPBS had before and after the 1987 election, its main victory was nothing short of outstanding. From having no black politicians at Westminster for five decades, the LPBS can take much credit for delivering in 1987 four black MPs who would all go on to give substantial service at Westminster. Two would become ministers, including Paul Boateng, the nation's first black Cabinet minister. Once elected, the black parliamentarians found themselves constrained by Kinnock's leadership. The LPBS remained outside the Party until it was transformed to the Black Socialist Society in 1991, but by this time the firebrand group of MPs had grown apart and their earlier collective power had dissipated. SW

Ali, R., and O'Cinneide, C., *Our House? Race and Representation in British Politics* (2002)

Anwar, M., 'The Participation of Ethnic Minorities in British Politics', *Journal of Ethnic and Migration Studies*, 27/3 (2001)

Saggar, S., *Race and Representation* (2000)

See also MULTICULTURALISM; PAN-AFRICANISM; RACISM

Poor black children (*c.*1700–*c.*1800). Poor black children rarely appear within historical records. Several thousand African children were brought to England to labour as unpaid servants in the households of the wealthy. Many were abused, ran away, and grew up alongside the poor white population. Those born outside the country had no legal status, and hence, no access to parochial relief or education. Many worked as crossing-sweepers, street hawkers, or ballad singers, others made a living at fairs as puppeteers, acrobats, rope-dancers, and musicians, and some became beggars. As the century progressed, more black children were born in England, but specific references to poor black children in parish records are rare. Several were admitted to the London Foundling Hospital, and others to parish workhouses. Young boys served in the Navy and the Marine Society, and others enlisted in the Army. The records of the criminal justice system reveal the suffering of poor black children as well as their involvement in crime. As the black population grew, its offspring were seen as a serious social problem and some were sent to the disastrous Sierra Leone colony created in 1787. By the end of the century, baptismal records indicate a growing number of children of interracial relationships. DEP

Fryer, Peter, *Staying Power: The History of Black People in Britain* (1984)

Gerzina, Gretchen, *Black London: Life Before Emancipation* (1995)

Shyllon, Fọlarin, *Black People in Britain 1555–1833* (1977)

See also CRIME AND BLACK PEOPLE; PROSTITUTION; SIERRA LEONE SETTLERS

Poor Laws. Before the Reformation the poor and sick were largely cared for by the Roman Catholic Church through monasteries and hospitals. After the dissolution of the monasteries in 1538, responsibility for supporting the poor, unemployed, and sick passed to individual Church of England parishes. In the following centuries laws were passed to define which parish or, from the later 19th century, local authority would have responsibility for an individual and his or her children. The key issue, established in 1662, was in which parish a person had 'settlement', and there were initially two ways to gain it: by being born in a parish or by receiving wages for working there for a year for a master who had settlement. These were the ones that impacted on the majority of black people in England. Later Acts gave settlement to those who had completed a full apprenticeship, served as a parish official, or rented a house worth over a certain amount, and a smaller number of black people fell within these categories.

Legally the authorities could remove people back to the last place where they had gained settlement, but this was not done in the case of those black people born overseas, presumably on the grounds of expense. Officials were not generally much concerned with young, able-bodied men who were capable of finding work or who were the servants of rich people. As these formed the largest section of the black population, they rarely appear in the documents produced by investigations into settlement status or by expenditure on paupers' care. In the case of those who could not support themselves, attempts were usually made to find someone, such as an ex-master, who could reimburse the parish for their upkeep. On occasions, however, individual black people in need entered the workhouse or were given financial relief even though not legally settled.

One effect of these laws was the way in which black people were entered in parish registers of baptism and burial. Clerks recorded an individual's colour, ethnic origin, or place of birth as well as relevant occupations such as servant, apprentice, sailor, or soldier to make their status under the Poor Laws clear should this later become legally important. This also applied to the white population and to members of other minority communities, such as the Huguenots.

These significant factors are rarely recorded in marriage entries, because marriage had no implications under the Poor Laws. Nor are they usually mentioned in burial entries if a individual had gained settlement since baptism. This means that many black people seem to disappear, even if they remained in the parish, married, and raised a family, which a number did. The effect is to under-record the number of black people in England and Wales, especially women. A woman took her husband's settlement status on marriage so that her origin became irrelevant and was not entered in the register. Children also took their father's status if their parents were married. KAC

Chater, K., 'Hidden from History: Black People in Parish Records', *Genealogists' Magazine*, 26 (2000)

See also 'SUS LAW'

Porteus, Beilby (1731–1809). Clergyman of the Church of England and campaigner against the *slave trade. Porteus was an acquaintance of James *Ramsay, whom he encouraged to publish his influential *Essay on the Treatment and Conversion of African Slaves in the British Sugar Colonies* (1784).

As Bishop of Chester (1776–87), Porteus preached a sermon in 1783 before the Society for the Propagation of the Gospel in which he urged them to take steps to ensure the Christianization of the slaves the Society owned on its plantations in Barbados, a plea that fell on deaf ears. As Bishop of London from 1787 until his death, Porteus took an active interest in the Anglican Church in the British West Indian colonies, at that date considered part of his diocese, but difficulties of communication and the fact that the Bishop possessed little in the way of legal powers over his clergy in the colonies limited his capacity for active intervention. However, he consistently pressed for greater efforts to Christianize the slave population, and in 1793 secured a Royal Charter for the Society for Conversion and Religious Instruction and Education of the Negro Slaves in the British West India Islands, which sent a few missionaries to the Caribbean, although only very modest results were achieved in Porteus's lifetime. He spoke against the slave trade in the House of Lords, but, even after the *abolition of the trade in 1807, did not envisage that *emancipation could take place until the slaves had been prepared for it by a process of education and religious instruction, which he expected would only be complete 'at some very distant Period'.

According to his biographer Robert Hodgson, Porteus was one of the 'earliest promoters and most strenuous advocates' of the abolition of the slave trade, and he was a friend of Hannah *More, William *Wilberforce, and many others involved in the cause. JG

Gilmore, J. T., 'Episcopacy, Emancipation and Evangelization: Aspects of the History of the Church of England in the British West Indies', Ph.D. thesis (University of Cambridge, 1985)

Hodgson, Robert, *The Life of the Right Reverend Beilby Porteus, D.D. Late Bishop of London* (1811)

See also CHRISTIANITY

Post-colonial theory. Form of analysis derived from and applied to the writing, culture, and history of peoples from formerly colonized countries.

1. The history and evolution of post-colonial theory
2. Edward Said and post-colonial critics
3. Post-colonial writers

1. The history and evolution of post-colonial theory It emerged in the academic field in the late 1970s. Prior to this, much scholarly work had of course been done on the impact of colonial expansion and on the nature and development of post-colonial societies. However, it was only in the changed political and economic context of the late 20th century that the theory could take shape in the way that it did. Appearing first within the field of literary studies before being taken up in departments of cultural studies, history, sociology, and anthropology, post-colonial criticism was closely connected to post-structuralist theory (in particular its critique of dominant narrative modes), as well as to elements of Marxist social analysis.

Central to the critical strategy of post-colonial theory is an interrogation of Eurocentric analysis. Although European thought developed out of specific cultural traditions, these were obscured by false notions of 'universality'; it was assumed that many values and the frameworks that defined them—philosophical, linguistic, social, and psychological models—could (and should) be applied across time and space. Such thinking not only failed to deal adequately with the particular complexities of alternative traditions, but also silenced this 'Other'—just as colonialism physically constrained the native 'Other'. Post-colonial theory set out to contest such repressive universalism. It decentred the traditional (European) perspective and opened a space from where the Empire could 'write back' to, and challenge, the imperial centre. The result has been a transformation in, for example, the literary canon and the way in which literature and history are taught.

Before its institutionalization as a theoretical tool, the term 'post-colonial' did have a specific temporal meaning. It referred to the period immediately after decolonization, when those who had gained power at independence took control of, and sought to transform, the colonial sociopolitical structures they had inherited. The subsequent emergence of the term as an ideological concept, one that aims to critique particular social and intellectual formations over different times and spaces, can be attributed to several factors. The variety of possible 'post-colonial' moments (for example, the collapse of the Spanish Empire in Latin America in the 19th century), as well as the continued existence of some forms of colonial control, immediately complicate the idea of a clear period 'after' colonialism. What really marked the appearance of post-colonial criticism as such, however, was a shift in the world economic system in conjunction with growing problems in those regimes spawned by the decolonization movement.

On the one hand, the 1970s saw the reassertion of new forms of imperial dominance, partly because of the increasingly global reach of capital and its concentration in the hands of certain more technologically advanced countries (in particular, the United States). On the other, the attempt made by this new economic order to contain the challenge from now independent Third World states reinforced the failure of the newly elected governments in many such nations. Central to this failure was a propensity to replicate not only the socio-economic structures of the imperial order they had once fought against, but also the silencing tendencies of 'official' discourse, no matter that it was now in the hands of the 'post-colonized'. Hence, it became clear that representation by certain classes or social groups symptomatically disfranchised the very people it was supposed to represent. It was against this background that post-colonial theory took shape, recognizing that popular consciousness—the practices and beliefs of the people—had to be recuperated from beneath the 'official' or elite narratives of the nation (which itself led many scholars to focus upon the suitability of the nation state as a means to organize the community). Thus, post-colonial criticism could be said to have emerged in response to this gap between the people and the institutional frameworks through which they are represented. The discipline entered the academy alongside a number of other 'minority' research programmes (such as feminist and gay studies), all of which aimed to investigate how dominant systems of knowledge had silenced and oppressed marginalized cultural traditions.

2. **Edward Said and post-colonial critics** If one wished to attach a date to the 'birth' of post-colonial theory, then the publication in 1978 of Edward Said's landmark study **Orientalism* is perhaps the most obvious reference point. *Orientalism* analysed the way in which the Orient had been 'constructed' through its misrepresentation in colonialist discourse. Although Said never denied that there was a 'real' Orient (a source of debate between critics), his book revealed the consistency and power of these (mis)representations—their ability to manage and even constitute the world they described. In turn, this was shown to produce the colonized native as 'Other', a dark, unknowable, silent presence confined to the margins and against which Europe defined itself as the light of civilization, with European nations regarded as the centre and their colonies as peripheral adjuncts. Not only did post-colonial theory reveal the constructed nature of this relationship; it also showed how the colonial power's projection of itself as civilized was constituted upon its antithetical conception of the 'Other'.

This awareness transferred to canonical literary texts, such as *The *Tempest* and **Robinson Crusoe*, which were shown to duplicate the same ideology, frequently marginalizing the alternative cultural tradition even as the latter was revealed to be integral to the dominant power's construction of itself as central. The relationship in *The Tempest* between Caliban and Prospero, with the former representative of the oppressed native whose island home has been usurped by the latter, became a paradigm for the colonial condition, one taken up by numerous writers seeking to analyse or renarrate this history. Post-colonial theory helped to clear a space in which 'Caliban' could speak. The perspective it provided on all kinds of texts enabled the dominant narrative—history as defined by the colonizers—to be interrogated and dismantled to release the eclipsed, diverse histories of the oppressed. It also constituted a mode of reading to be utilized with literary works by 'post-colonial' authors, one that was attentive to the way in which these writers contested the power of imposed value systems and sought to recentre their own cultural traditions, or to articulate the new social formations born out of the colonial past.

Post-colonial theory cannot be thought of as a unified or homogeneous concept. There have been as many different approaches to the post-colonial condition as there have been colonial systems and forms of resistance. Alongside Said, Homi Bhabha and Gayatri Spivak are perhaps the most commonly cited names in the field. Bhabha approached the colonizer–colonized relationship from a psychoanalytical standpoint, exploring the impact of factors such as desire, mimicry, and hybridization upon the construction of power and identity. Spivak was associated with the Subaltern Studies group, which sought to uncover the hidden stories and consciousness of those spoken for and about in elite representation; her particular position, however, was captured in her famous assertion that 'The subaltern cannot speak.' The position of the lower class, specifically female, 'subject' is such, argued Spivak, that in fact she is never a subject, only an object of discourse. The subaltern can neither access the means of representation nor be represented since to be 'read' as subaltern is to be immediately constrained and distorted—made over into something else—by the already existent frameworks of knowledge.

Another key figure to have influenced theoretical approaches to post-colonial issues is Frantz Fanon. His seminal books

Black Skin, White Masks (1952) and *The Wretched of the Earth* (1961) analysed, respectively, the psychological effect on the colonized of colonial control and the struggle for national liberation. They became touchstones for scholars, who incorporated their critical insights. (In an indication of how post-colonial theory can impose a new orthodoxy, however, the 'post-colonial reading' of Fanon has at times been guilty of obscuring other interpretations of his work, such as those that would stress his position as a Third World activist.) Other important reference points within the field include: the analysis of cosmopolitanism, migration, diaspora, and globalization; the study of language and Creolization (how the colonizer's language supplanted indigenous forms, but also how the former has been reappropriated by those forced to use it); cultural hybridity (see in particular the work of writers such as Wilson Harris, Kamau Brathwaite, and Edouard Glissant from the Caribbean, where historical circumstances have led to an emphasis on cultural contact); and the analysis of land rights and the environment.

3. **Post-colonial writers** As the brief survey offered above suggests, post-colonial theory is an expansive, and expanding, scholarly field. Since its emergence within academia, numerous critical books, readers, and journals have appeared dedicated to the topic. The decentring of the literary canon has had a noticeable effect outside the university too. Since the mid-1980s, the Nobel Prize for Literature has been won by a variety of 'post-colonial' writers, including the Africans Wole Soyinka (1986), Naguib Mahfouz (1988), Nadine Gordimer (1991), and J. M. Coetzee (2003); Derek Walcott (1992) and V. S. Naipaul (2001) from the Caribbean; and the African-American Toni Morrison (1993). A list of past winners of the Booker Prize in Britain is likewise testimony to the impact of authors from, or associated with, the former colonial world. Salman Rushdie (*Midnight's Children*, 1981), Keri Hulme (*The Bone People*, 1985), Ben Okri (*The Famished Road*, 1991), and Arundhati Roy (*The God of Small Things*, 1997) are just some of those whose novels have triumphed.

The increasing emphasis on once marginalized voices and the light they shed on the culture both of the former colonizer and of the former colonized has also influenced how literature and history are taught in schools. That pupils should be made aware of the impact of the British Empire, and in particular local responses to its policies, has become a subject of debate among education specialists. There have been calls for events such as the Mau Mau rebellion in Kenya in the 1950s to be read in addition to the common focus on, for example, the Second World War. Similarly, the influence of post-colonial writers on language and fiction is such that any taught course on post-1945 literature written in English must now incorporate their work. Thus, the 2006 GCSE English Literature course administered by the AQA examination board included as a set text the Trinidadian Michael Anthony's *Green Days by the River*, while an optional module, 'Poems from Different Cultures', takes as its key text an anthology containing works by writers such as the Nigerian Chinua Achebe, the Anglo-Pakistani Monica Alvi, and the Guyanese Grace Nichols.

The critical insights that post-colonial theory provides into colonial history and the practices, traditions, and art of those from the former colonial world have contributed to a shift in the understanding of culture. The emergence of once suppressed, alternative voices means that any approach to world literature and history must take into consideration the post-colonial perspective if it is to offer a fully comprehensive account. Similarly, the decentring of Eurocentric thinking has thrown new light on many of the assumptions that underpin certain intellectual and social models. Debate continues among scholars over the efficacy of different post-colonial theoretical approaches, and in particular over whether some do not silence the 'Other' all over again. There remains the fundamental issue of the gap between the academy—the site from which post-colonial theory emanates—and the situation of those it theorizes. Nevertheless, in its emphasis upon minority discourse and the impact of cultural contact, post-colonial theory has helped to establish a critical lens through which to appreciate better the complex legacies that shape both the global order and multiracial societies such as Britain. MGN

Ashcroft, Bill, Griffiths, Gareth, and Tiffen, Helen, *The Empire Writes Back* (1989)
Bhabha, Homi, *The Location of Culture* (1994)
Nelson, Cary, and Grossberg, Lawrence (eds.), *Marxism and the Interpretation of Culture* (1988)
Said, Edward, *Orientalism* (1978)

See also ORIENTALISM

Powell, Enoch (1912–1998). Right-wing Conservative politician whose inflammatory speeches increased popular support for anti-immigration policies and led to his sacking from the Shadow Cabinet.

Despite his later prominence, John Enoch Powell was a relative latecomer to race and immigration politics in the United Kingdom. The trailblazers for controls on 'coloured' immigration were active from 1954 onwards, led in Parliament by Cyril Osbourne, the MP for Louth, Lincolnshire—a region that in his day had virtually no black immigrants. Though active in Parliament from 1950, Powell made no grand pronouncements in support of immigration restrictions until 1964.

Following on from his careers as Professor of Greek at Sydney University and, during the Second World War, a brigadier in the British Army in India, Powell entered politics after the war in the role of staunch defender of the British Empire. Seeking a position in the Conservative Party's research department he described himself as 'an imperialist and a Tory'.

On winning election to Parliament for the West Midlands constituency of Wolverhampton South West in 1950, Powell's pro-imperial politics were revealed in a quixotic defence of the Queen's title as Head of the Commonwealth, and of the presence of British troops in the Suez Canal Zone. His conviction that Britain's aspirations for world governance were, or should be, liberal and humane was shown in an attack he launched in the Commons in July 1959 against the role of the UK authorities in the killing of eleven pro-independence detainees in the Hola camp in Kenya. He also served in Macmillan's government as Minister of Health for a three-year period, during which time his ministry was actively involved in the recruitment of nursing staff from the Caribbean.

Powell revised his thinking on imperialism, and after 1960 his political focus switched from the maintenance of Empire to strident advocacy of free-market economics. To support a nation run on robust, laissez-faire principles a 'new patriotism' was needed, and in an anonymous article published in *The Times* in April 1964 he argued that the institutions of the UK state were too precious to be shared with newly independent Commonwealth countries who appeared to despise them.

During the following years the logic of this new position was followed scrupulously. The politician who had once proclaimed that 'I have set and always will set my face like flint against making any difference between one citizen of this country and another on grounds of his origin,' became by stages the leading advocate of the view that 'The West Indian or Indian does not, by being born in England, become an Englishman. In law he becomes a United Kingdom citizen by birth; in fact he is a West Indian or Asian still.'

A member of Edward Heath's Shadow Cabinet, Powell had tested relations with his leader throughout 1967 with a series of speeches and newspaper articles in which he set out the 'threat' to Britain from the growth of its black population, arising from both the immigration of dependants and the birth rate in the United Kingdom. An infamous speech delivered in Walsall in April 1968, in which Powell predicted 'rivers of blood' as the consequence of the presence of black people in Britain, marked the breaking point with the Tory mainstream.

Sacked from the Shadow Cabinet, Powell moved outside the ranks of mainstream Conservatism altogether, resigning from both the Party and Parliament in 1974, in protest against the leadership's support of the Common Market. 'Powellism', now proclaimed by elements as diverse as east London dockworkers, anti-EEC xenophobes, and, in even more virulent form, by the National Front, continued, even if without the official endorsement of its progenitor.

Later Powell pursued a strange revival of his parliamentary career as an MP for the Northern Irish constituency of North Down, believing that Protestant Unionism might form the model for the British nationalist renaissance he was seeking. By then the baton of anti-immigration campaigning had passed to others. DF

Foot, Paul, *The Rise of Enoch Powell* (1969)

Humphry, Derek, and Ward, Michael, *Passports and Politics* (1974)

Layton-Henry, Zig, *The Politics of Immigration* (1992)

See also IMMIGRATION; REPATRIATION

Prince, Mary (b. *c.*1788). The first black woman in Britain to be the subject of a biographical narrative. Prince was born into slavery in Bermuda, and lived as a slave there, in the Turks and Caicos Islands (probably in Grand Turk), and in Antigua. Around Christmas 1826, while she was living in Antigua, she married in the Moravian Church a free black man called Daniel James, an action that greatly annoyed her owners, a local merchant called John Wood and his wife.

In 1828 she went to England with the Woods, and worked for them (without wages) in the house they occupied in London. Continued ill treatment led her to quarrel with the Woods, who threatened to turn her out of the house. They appear to have felt that, as she knew no one in Britain and would wish to return to her husband in Antigua, she would eventually be forced to come back to them of her own accord and cooperate with their demands. Believing that she was free in Britain, Prince left the Woods' house. She was helped for a while by a working-class couple called Mash (the husband cleaned shoes and knives for a living, while the wife worked as a laundress), who allowed her to live with them 'a good many months'. She subsequently found work as a domestic servant, first with a Mrs Forsyth, and later (from December 1829) in the household of Thomas Pringle, secretary of the *Anti-Slavery Society, and his wife.

Prince had earlier sought the help of the Anti-Slavery Society, who had obtained a lawyer's opinion that, while she was free in Britain, this would not affect her legal status as a slave if she were to return to Antigua. While she wished to be reunited with her husband, she was naturally reluctant to risk a return to slavery, particularly as she had ample reason to fear the vindictiveness and ill will of the Woods. Repeated efforts were made by Pringle and the Anti-Slavery Society to persuade John Wood to agree to sell Prince her freedom, but he persisted in his refusals. In 1829 Pringle also organized the submission of a petition from Prince to the British Parliament in an attempt to have her declared free, but this likewise had no result.

Partly to put pressure on Wood, partly to raise money for Prince's benefit, and partly because her account of her life gave a vivid picture of the cruelties to which slaves were subjected in Bermuda and the Caribbean, and therefore would serve as useful propaganda for the purposes of the Anti-Slavery Society, in 1831 Pringle arranged for the publication of a pamphlet called *The History of Mary Prince, a West Indian Slave*, which went through three editions in the year of publication. This was described on the title page as 'related by herself'. While Prince was at least to some extent literate, she had told her story to a friend of the Pringles called Susanna Strickland, who wrote it down, and it was then edited by Thomas Pringle before publication. While the *History* appears to have been the first biographical account of a black woman to be published as a separate work in Britain, the circumstances of its creation make it difficult to categorize it as autobiographical as we cannot be certain of the extent to which Strickland and Pringle altered Prince's account. There is no reason to doubt the general outline of Prince's life as it is given in the *History*, or what she says of her own sufferings as a slave and of those of other slaves. However, while Pringle's preface seeks to minimize the extent of the alterations, claiming that the *History* was 'essentially her [Prince's] own, without any material alteration further than was requisite to exclude redundancies and gross grammatical errors, so as to render it clearly intelligible', it is clear that the narrative was considerably rewritten, if only in order to present it in a form of language that is almost entirely a standardized British English, with only occasional words or turns of phrase that are Caribbean. On at least one occasion Strickland referred to herself as the 'Biographer' of Prince. The *History*'s modern editors, Moira Ferguson and Sarah Salih, suggest that Pringle was also responsible for playing down references to sexual matters, partly to avoid offending the intended readership and partly to make Prince appear more of a passive victim. Nevertheless, there are certainly passages where what appears to be Prince's personal voice comes through, as, for example, where she says, 'I have been a slave myself—I know what slaves feel . . . The man that says slaves be quite happy in slavery—that they don't want to be free—that man is either ignorant or a lying person. I never heard a slave say so.'

The publication of the *History* did nothing to persuade Wood to change his mind and, instead, involved Pringle in two lawsuits with Wood's supporters. Prince gave evidence at the court cases, in February and March 1833; she was then still living with and working for the Pringles, but no evidence has yet been discovered about her life after this. She was in poor health while in England, and a postscript by Pringle to the second edition (March 1831) of the *History* stated that she was affected by an eye disease that threatened her sight.

The *History* remains a compelling account of slavery in the Caribbean. It also offers a clear example of how, before *emancipation, the life of a black person regarded as free in Britain was still restricted by the continued existence of slavery in the colonies. JG

ODNB

Prince, Mary, *The History of Mary Prince, a West Indian Slave, as Related by Herself* (ed. Moira Ferguson, rev. edn., 1997)

—— *The History of Mary Prince, a West Indian Slave* (ed. Sarah Salih, 2000)

See also SOMERSET CASE

Prostitution (*c*.1700–*c*.1800). A number of black women worked as prostitutes in 18th-century London, and some of them became sufficiently well known for details of their lives to be recorded in contemporary documents and memoirs. One of the most famous was Black Harriot, a West Indian slave working as a prostitute in London in the 1770s, her clients said to include 20 members of the House of Lords and 50 members of the House of Commons. A contemporary handbook on the sex trade (*Nocturnal Revels; or, The History of King's-Place, and Other Modern Nunneries*, 1779) informs us that Harriot was purchased as a slave on the coast of Guinea, taken to Jamaica, and sold to an English planter. The planter became enamoured of Harriot's character: she was 'a lively genius', her mental abilities 'far superior to the common run of Europeans'. Harriot was taught to read and write and to do accountancy. She was appointed 'superintendent of the other females negroes'. She bore two children with her master, who took her to England, where she remained faithful to him and ran his household of white servants with economic rigour. She created a stir among her master's friends.

> Her person . . . was very alluring; she was tall, well-made, and genteel; and since her arrival in England, she had given her mind to reading, and at her master's recommendation, had pursued several useful and entertaining books, calculated for women; whereby she had considerably improved her understanding, and had attained a degree of politeness, scarce to be paralleled in an African female.

She was 'a proper companion to the Prince de Soubise' (*see* SOUBISE, JULIUS).

Prostitution beckoned as the only mode of survival when Harriot's master died of smallpox, leaving her with next to nothing ('a scanty pittance'). She decided to make the most of 'her jetty charms' and exploit her exotic status. The wealthy made their way to her door in frenzied numbers, excited by 'the novelty' of bedding 'this black beauty' and 'new face, in every sense of the word, upon the Town'. She charged huge sums (£20 and more, today's equivalent of more than £1,500) for her favours, 'vending her charms as dear as possible [for] she found that the caprice of mankind was so great, that novelty could command almost any price'. According to *Nocturnal Revels*, she fell in love with an impoverished white soldier, who proved to be a drain on her finances. She took proprietorship of a brothel, but the venture was a failure, for the prostitutes she employed ran up debts in neighbourhood shops, or purloined her valuable possessions. Unwilling to seek legal remedy, she ended her days in a debtor's prison, the King's Bench.

Other well-known and well-patronized West Indian women included Mrs Lowes, working at Upper Charlotte Street, Rathbone Place, London, in 1788. Lowes is described in the 1788 *Harris's List of Covent-Garden Ladies* (a catalogue of available prostitutes, with their names, addresses, and fees) as 'of sweet chearful disposition, fine dark hair, and eyes of the same friendly hew; fine teeth, is short and plump . . . she expects three guineas for a whole night [today's equivalent of around £250], but if you make a short visit, one pound one shilling is the least'.

In 1793 *Harris's List* describes 'Miss Wilson, No. 27, Litchfield street, Soho' as Jamaican-born, 'a wanton Cyprian female . . . [with] a brilliant tell-tale love sparkling eye . . . a girl of considerable taste and fashion'. A frequenter of Covent Garden Theatre, Miss Wilson had costumes of her own for her client's delectation. Her many other talents included singing and dancing, which justified the large fee she charged. The contemporary description of her dwells longingly on her exotic appearance: 'an elegant set of teeth (which for whiteness stands unrivalled in the whole Cyprian corps) and dark brown tresses which flow in careless ringlets across a pair of tempting rising promontories'.

Harriot, Lowes, and Wilson were three among many 18th-century black women (overwhelmingly anonymous) who worked in the sex trade. The ubiquity of black prostitution can be gauged by the appearance of black harlots in William *Hogarth's *A Harlot's Progress* (1732) and *A Rake's Progress* (1735). James Boswell reported on a black brothel in London in 1774, patronized by titled clients. Black prostitution continued until the 19th century: Peter Fryer has discovered a black girl called Ebony Bet working around 1830 in the flagellation brothel of one Mrs Theresa Barkley of 28 Charlotte Street, Portland Place, London. Such women were paid, 'free' to capitalize on their bodies. The records do not reveal how many black slaves (male and female) in British households were subject to sexual abuse. DD

Dabydeen, D., *A Harlot's Progress* (1999)
Fryer, P., *Staying Power: The History of Black People in Britain* (1984)

Publishing. Black book publishing includes books produced by black-owned companies and black-led organizations for black authors, books produced by black-owned companies for culturally diverse authors, and books produced by companies predominantly by and about black people.

1. Community publishing
2. Women publishers
3. Other black publishers

Black publishing companies in Britain often have a dual purpose; to serve as a focal point in the black community for social gatherings and information centres, as well as publishing material of specific interest to their target audience.

The earliest book publishing company of note were New Beacon Books, established in 1966 by John La Rose and Sarah White. They published the former's poetry collection *Foundations: A Book of Poems*, under the name Anthony La Rose, in the same year, and started a specialist bookselling operation in 1967, opening a bookshop in north London in 1973. It remains the primary bookshop in the United Kingdom selling books written by and about people of African and Asian descent. They also house the George Padmore Institute, which holds in its archives New Beacon titles and other significant reports and pamphlets about the black British community.

Eric and Jessica Huntley established Bogle-L'Ouverture Publications in 1969 with their first book, *The Groundings with My Brothers* by Walter *Rodney. Bogle-L'Ouverture went on to publish Rodney's seminal title *How Europe Underdeveloped Africa*. They collaborated with New Beacon and Race Today Publications in setting up the *International Book Fair of Radical Black and Third World Books in 1982, and they too opened a bookstore in their local community of west London, the Walter Rodney Bookshop, but ceased business in 1991. They continue a limited publishing operation with their history being recorded in the Eric and Jessica Huntley Collections, housed at the London Metropolitan Archives in 2006.

Britain's youngest and first black woman publisher, Margaret Busby, met Clive Allison at Cambridge University in 1965. Their company, Allison and Busby, published authors including C. L. R. *James, Buchi Emecheta, Roy Heath, and Rosa Guy. Busby and Huntley joined forces in the 1980s with white women publishers who published selected titles by black women, to campaign for more black personnel in the UK publishing workforce. Through an Arts Council initiative, their Greater Access to Publishing campaign successfully placed a handful of black and Asian female interns in mainstream publishing houses.

Publishing in racially tense Britain in the late 1960s and early 1970s meant that bookstores, as the public face of black publishing houses, were attractive targets for racially directed attacks, especially as they were also meeting places for campaign organization.

Bogle-L'Ouverture arose from this discontent, as did other publishers such as Blackbird Books recorded as publishing as early as 1968, and other black bookshops cum advice centres in the early 1970s that produced pamphlets, newsletters, and literary magazines that can be seen as forerunners of the poetry and novels published later. *Portrait of a People*, for example, published by the Free University for Black Studies in 1973, includes a foreword by the publisher Arif Ali, who started Hansib Publications in 1970.

Ali started out with the monthly magazine *West Indian Digest*. Although he went on to publish a suite of newspapers and periodicals, he sold them to focus on book publishing, starting with the yearbook *West Indians in Britain* in 1973, and then what he termed 'conscious books' in the 1980s. He has since published over 100 titles specializing in books covering African, Afro-Caribbean, Indo-Caribbean, Asian, and other ethnic-minority issues and subjects. Although Ali had no shopfront, his activism in the black community is well documented.

In Naseem Khan's study commissioned by the Arts Council *The Arts Britain Ignores*, published by the *Commission for Racial Equality in 1976, New Beacon and Bogle-L'Ouverture were recognized as publishers cum bookshops that filled a gap in the black community, producing booklets on black issues and children's books that featured black children. She advised that they and similar firms to emerge should be given funding for their research and publication undertakings.

Black publishing companies multiplied in the 1980s, many financially aided by the Greater London Council. These included Black Star Publications and First Class Publications. Others that continue limited production are Akira Press, founded in 1983, which published predominantly poetry by Caribbean writers who had moved to the United Kingdom. A ten-book poetry series was launched in 1985 with names recognizable in various black art spheres today, such as Martin Glynn, J. D. Douglas, Frederick Williams, and Maud Sulter. Their next series encompassed nine titles in various genres including books by the playwright Michael McMillan and the novelist Mike Phillips. There was a nineteen-year gap and then, in 2003, they published *PUCKO [Peoples United Cause for Knowledge and Overstanding] Poetry* by Desmond Johnson, who founded the press. Similar to Akira, Karia Press was established by Buzz Johnson in 1985 and continues to publish sporadically. It described itself as an information agency, with Karia as the general publishers and One Caribbean Publishers as the specialist in booklets on Caribbean literature. The Intef Institute was formed as a cultural organization in 1975 by African-Caribbean artists. From this evolved Karnak House, founded by Saba Sakaana in 1985, specializing in the publication of books on global African philosophies and civilizations.

1. Community publishing Community publishing initiatives focus on local or regional publishing, with the emphasis on writing by the working class, and a management infrastructure usually based on a not-for-profit status.

A wealth of community and self-publishing emerged in the mid-1970s. A leading entity was Centreprise Publications, established by the African-American Glen Thomson in 1975. It documented the lives and history of Hackney's East End community, including individual biographies, sometimes in poetic form. The first book, a poetry collection by 12-year-old Vivian Usherwood, is still commented on today.

Such initiatives came together under the membership of the Federation of Worker Writers and Community Publishers, which started in February 1976, when representatives of eight groups engaged in local publishing met at Centreprise. These founding members recognized the need for a national organization to encourage and support local working-class writing groups and publishers. The Federation continues to operate with an international membership.

Glen Thompson eventually went on to establish the commercially viable Writers and Readers in the early 1980s, with London and New York offices. It included three imprints: the Beginner's Series, Harlem River Press, and Black Butterfly.

Yet the community publishing that Thompson had played such a major role in faced major difficulties once the net book agreement was abolished in 1997. It meant that booksellers could heavily discount books, devastating for a publisher already selling books at little above the unit cost.

Centreprise Publications ceased in the early 1990s after publishing *Word Up! from the Women's Café*. Significantly, it featured the black women poets Patience Agbabi and Valerie Mason John, who moved on to have their own books published, as did the co-editor Dorothea Smartt.

In the early 1980s the Peckham Publishing Project, based at the Bookplace bookshop, captured the lives of West Indian migrants in books such as *Captain Blackbeard's Beef Creole*, and the Trinity Arts Association in Birmingham published a mixture of poetry, autobiography, and a novel, *Bad Friday* by Norman Smith, set in Birmingham, one of the earliest novels termed as black British literature.

Commonword was started in Manchester in 1977, and established in 1986 a centre for Asian, African, Caribbean, and Chinese creative writing in the north-west of England. Under these auspices, they started to publish. *Black and Priceless* came out in 1988 under Crocus Books, but Crocus's published programme only had room for an anthology by writers of African and Asian descent every other year. Peter Kalu, Cultureword's literature development worker, decided to address this by forming Mongrel Press in 1996 to publish and promote UK black writing. He and his co-founders, John Siddique and Tang Lin, published their own poetry collections, and then, in 1998, a series of poetry CDs featuring black poets based in the

North-West. But once Lin and Siddique had moved out of the region, the press ceased. In 2004 Kalu secured a funding partnership to set up the publishing arm of the novelists' biennial competition Shorelines, which focuses on anthologies for writers in the North-West.

Kadija Sesay (Kadija George) set up the Black Literature Development Project at Centreprise in 1995. In 1996 she launched SAKS Publications with Saffiatu George and Stella Oni, and published two anthologies by writers of African descent, *Burning Words, Flaming Images*, then *Playing Sidney Poitier and Other Stories* in 1998. In 2000 they published the first issue of *Sable*, an international magazine publishing new work by writers of colour and promoting books published by independent black publishers.

Despite difficulties such as distribution and discounting, black publishing companies continue to be started up, particularly by women. The aim of the Black Inc. project, launched by Brent Library Service in 2000 and coordinated by Andrea Enisuoh, was to develop new black writers and readers. It has published two anthologies of short fiction, *Ridin and Risin* in 2001 and *Turf* in 2004. In 2005 Monsoon Press was set up by two young Asian women aiming to give a voice to black, Asian, and white working-class writers.

2. Women publishers In 2003 a symposium entitled 'Black Women Publishers: Writing and Publishing Our Future' was organized by the African Writers Abroad (PEN) Centre, to highlight the fact that the history of black publishing in Britain has been fortified by the presence of women publishers.

Tamarind, a multicultural children's book publisher, was set up in 1987 by Verna Annette Wilkins. She is the author of 30 picture books and biographies, which aim to offer children a positive profile of black people. An award-winning publisher, Tamarind has expanded its remit to produce a series of books for BBC Television's Science Challenge series.

Mango Publishing was established in 1995 by Joan Anim-Addo, the director of the Caribbean Centre at Goldsmiths College, London, where it is based. Its remit is to focus on publishing and promoting literary works by writers from British, Caribbean, and Latin American literary traditions, including translations. It started by publishing the journal *Mango Season* in collaboration with the Caribbean Women Writers' Alliance, but now concentrates on books.

Angela Royal set up ARP in 1994. She had previously been an editor with Penguin for fifteen years, so her entry into this market was heralded as a major input into black publishing. Her intention was to 'publish writers and books from around the world which challenge the cultural climate'. ARP joined forces with the literature promoters the Write Thing, but the partnership folded within six months with a backlist that included two, now acclaimed, black British women writers, Bernardine Evaristo and Leone Ross.

Rosemarie Hudson's BlackAmber launched its first title early in 1998 with the aim of adding 'another dimension in different accents to the recorded British experience'. Initially she published writers of African and Asian descent, which she expanded to include new second- and third-generation black British and European writers in all genres apart from poetry.

Vastiana Belfon, who worked as an editor for Writers and Readers, established Brown Skin Books in 1992 to publish erotic fiction by women of colour, and Becky Clarke, who worked for Heinemann's *African Writers Series for twelve years, set up in 2003 the Ayebia Clarke Literary Agency and Publishing to publish works by writers of African descent.

3. Other black publishers The journalists Steve Pope and Dotun Adebayo left *The Voice* newspaper in 1991 to establish X Press in 1992, scoring an instant success with their first publication, *Yardie* by Victor Headley. Since then, they have achieved further success by selling broadcast rights for some of their popular titles, such as *Baby Father*. They diversified into other imprints, Black Classics, 20/20, and Nia, as the X Press name became synonymous with populism. Although much criticized for this, X Press remains a groundbreaking imprint for new authors who would not traditionally have considered themselves writers.

Canongate Books created the imprint Payback Press, dedicated to black literature and culture, leading with the classic *Blues People* by Amiri Baraka in 1995, but incorporated the books into their main list in 2001. They published *The Fire People* in 1998, the last collection of contemporary black British poets to have been published.

Flipped Eye Publishing was formed in Ghana by a group of friends in a bid to start a literature revival in the country. The first book published in 1999 was *eyes of a boy, lips of a man* by Nii Ayikwei Parkes, also one of the shareholders. Six months later Parkes bought out his partners, and set up the company in the United Kingdom in 2001 with the aim of publishing all genres with a focus on poetry and a mission to raise the profile of performance and oral literature via live and printed means.

Independent publishers with strong backlists have been bought out or brought in by larger publishers. In 2005 BlackAmber was sold to Arcadia Books. Hudson maintains the list as commissioning editor. Although independents, particularly poetry publishers, secured regular funding through the Arts Council, the only publisher of black books to have been granted this has been Peepal Tree Press (who also print their own books). Established in 1985, they have become one of the largest publishers of Caribbean literature. They began to publish an increasing number of black British writers, starting with Bernardine Evaristo's *Island of Abraham* (1995).

A meeting of black publishers took place in 2005, attended by Tamarind, X Press, and Ayebia Publishing, and the Independent Black Publishers' Association was set up. Its objectives include collaborating on initiatives and planning ways of advancing black publishing.

As producing books has become easier with technological advances, independent publishers have taken advantage of this to promote and produce works via the Web, or in CD form. The new technologies have increased the number of self-published books and CDs with black performance poets at the forefront of this development. KS

Sesay, Kadija (ed.), *Write Black, Write British: From Post Colonial to Black British* (2005)

Sidney, Carol, 'Jessica Huntley: A Lifetime of Publishing', *Sable*, 6 (2004)

White, Sara, Harris, Roxy, and Beezmohun, Sharmilla (eds.), *A Meeting of the Continents: History, Memories, Organisation, and Programmes 1982–1995* (2005)

Q

Quaque, Philip. Also known as Kweku (1741–1816), the first African clergyman of the Church of England. Quaque was a Fante, born at Cape Coast in what is now Ghana. He was the only survivor of three Fante boys sent to England in 1754 by a missionary of the Society for the Propagation of the Gospel (SPG) in order that they might be educated. Baptized as Philip in 1759, he was ordained in 1765, the first African to become a priest of the Church of England.

He returned to Cape Coast in 1766, and spent most of the rest of his life there, combining the position of chaplain at Cape Coast Castle, a trading fort maintained by the African Company (successor to the *Royal African Company), who paid him a salary for his work in this capacity, with that of a missionary employed by the SPG. Many of the Company's employees were hostile, but Quaque kept a small school at the fort, and some of his pupils became clerks in the Company's service. As a missionary, Quaque made no converts at all, a failure that may well be attributed to the fact that he appears to have become thoroughly Europeanized during his long stay in England, and had lost his fluency in his native Fante. He died and was buried at Cape Coast Castle. The African Company's main business was the slave trade, and there is no indication that Quaque ever took any public stance against this. JG

ODNB

See also CHRISTIANITY; MISSIONARY SOCIETIES

R

'Race' riots, 1919. The so-called 'race' riots of 1919, which broke out in *Glasgow, *South Shields, Salford, Hull, *London, *Liverpool, and the South Wales ports of *Cardiff, Newport, and Barry, were some of the most serious and sustained incidents of public disorder in 20th-century Britain. During the 1919 riots, white working-class crowds targeted black sailors, their families, and black-owned businesses and property in these substantial British ports. Other black people, including military personnel and skilled workers, also came under attack from white crowds. One of the chief sources of violent confrontation arose due to a colour bar in hiring procedures favoured by the sailors' trade unions representing (white) workers in the merchant shipping industry. This was seen as a way of keeping up wage rates and employment levels for white British sailors. Since the mid-19th century British shipping employers had used black British, Arab, Asian, and foreign sailors of various ethnicities to undercut white British sailors' rates of pay. Wages for most sailors had been equalized after a successful national sailors' strike in 1911, but divisions among sailors remained and reduced the possibility of any seamen's trade union bringing all sailors together.

During the eight months of rioting five people (two black and three white) were killed, dozens more were injured, and hundreds arrested. The police forces of nine large towns and cities were kept occupied for weeks with the riots and their fallout. The courts likewise were engaged for many months in determining the perpetrators of the violence. The riots involved crowds of white people (often several thousand strong) and dozens of black (and also Arab and Asian) men and women. In almost all cases, members of ethnic-minority groups were attacked by white Britons, although black people often defended themselves with ferocity. Tens of thousands of pounds' worth of property was damaged during the riots. At government level an interdepartmental committee was set up—while the rioting was still taking place—in order to find a way out of the widespread unrest.

The 1919 port riots were a dramatic manifestation of the massive social and economic dislocation that affected Britain during and following the *First World War. Many immediate and interlocking causes contributed to the outbreak of the riots. The rapid demobilization of over 6 million service personnel led to social upheaval, complications in the employment market, and pressure on housing. For many months after the war's end frustrated troops were held in camps pending demobilization and, for some, repatriation overseas. In Britain's ports demobilized Royal Navy personnel sought to move back into their previous employment in the merchant navy. Meanwhile, shipowners had looked elsewhere for wartime labour. This included hiring large numbers of black and South Asian British sailors. The 1919 rioting in the ports was caused by severe post-war competition for jobs, especially in the merchant navy; and also by *housing shortages. The housing shortage across Britain by the end of the war was estimated at 600,000. This shortfall allowed anti-alien sentiment in Britain free rein as minority groups, including Chinese and Russian as well as many black people, were turned out and burned out of their homes.

For the British working class, war service was part of a bargain struck with the state. When the promised benefits (i.e. better housing, job opportunities) of this heightened level of citizenship were not forthcoming in the post-war period, there was widespread public protest. An extreme form of protest was to riot. Rioting was common around Britain during the war and throughout 1919. The influence of successful wartime riots, such as the anti-German riots, which speeded up the government's internment policy, provided a useful example for those who resorted to direct action.

There is strong evidence of wider economic and social reasons for the port rioting that occurred in the months after the end of the First World War. Even so, racist behaviour and motivations were often evident in the actions of the white rioters. Moreover, official responses to the riots were often blatantly racist. Black people in Britain were blamed for the riots. The local police forces were often biased in their arrest policy during the rioting, the courts rather less so. The main government response was the decision of the interdepartmental committee to pursue an active repatriation programme to clear black Britons from Britain itself and disperse them around the Empire. Around 2,000 black Britons (some with their British-born dependants) were given a small financial inducement and shipped back to their places of birth. Many arrived back 'home' with burning resentment against their treatment by the 'mother country'. Some became involved in local protests and riots against white authority; others joined black political movements that helped to draw attention to the severe post-war economic difficulties in Britain's colonies, particularly in the Caribbean. The port riots and their consequences posed a challenge to the nature of Britain's imperial rule and raised questions about the status of colonial peoples both in the heart of the Empire and in the colonies.

In the two years following 1919 there were further riots and violent unrest in Britain's ports. The economic difficulties in the merchant shipping industry evident in 1919 continued as the slump spread across British industry. The ranks of unemployed black sailors did not disappear. Faced with an increasingly rigid colour bar, often at the instigation of white ex-service organizations, as well as continued opposition from sailors' union officials, many black sailors and their families were left destitute. For those who remained out of work for long periods, there was no entitlement to state unemployment relief. Some black people used a variety of self-help mechanisms to tide them over, others relied on charities; the stark alternative was often the workhouse. Although the British government continued its repatriation scheme of June 1919 into 1921, the numbers involved were greatly reduced since those who turned down offers in 1919 were no longer eligible for the scheme. In the longer term the government solution to the 'problem' of unemployed black people came with the introduction of special measures in 1925. These regulations reclassified thousands of black British sailors as 'alien' workers on whom 'special restrictions' could be placed in terms of both job opportunities and freedom to move around the country in search of work. JLMJ

Jenkinson, Jacqueline, 'The 1919 Riots' in P. Panayi (ed.), *Racial Violence in Britain in the Nineteenth and Twentieth Centuries* (1996)

—— 'The 1919 Race Riots in Britain: A Survey' in Rainer E. Lotz and Ian Pegg (eds.), *Under the Imperial Carpet: Essays in Black History 1780–1950* (1987)

Race Today. Journal first published by the *Institute of Race Relations in London in May 1969. Its aim was to draw attention to the position of minority groups both in Britain and across the globe; it sought to cover political events anywhere in the world with a significant black population, adopting a Marxist-internationalist perspective. The magazine ran for 29 years until 1988, during which time it gave vocal support to numerous civil rights campaigns and workers' strikes within Britain, while also promoting black and Asian art and culture.

As part of the Institute of Race Relations, a non-political organization established in 1958, *Race Today* began as a means to publicize the issues and policies put forward by the Institute. It soon became noted for its campaigns against police harassment, in particular its coverage of the trial of the Mangrove Nine in the early 1970s. However, the Institute's governing Council began to feel that the increasingly committed stance of its affiliates was compromising its 'non-political' status. Things came to a head in March 1972 when the Council tried to close down *Race Today* following its coverage of the Rhodesian settlement and Race Laws. In what looked to be its penultimate issue the journal defended its position, stating in an editorial that if 'the Institute wishes to deal solely in dispassionate data *about* black people, no doubt it will add lustre to many an academic career . . . But that sort of Institute will neither listen to black people nor speak to any but a tiny minority of white, unless it is prepared, as we have tried to be, to let black people speak for themselves' (4/4, April 1972). The Council was ultimately defeated and *Race Today* continued, although it was now published by the independent subsidiary Towards Racial Justice. Indeed, the journal went through a number of changes. In 1974 the former *Black Panthers member Darcus Howe became editor, declaring that the 'new' *Race Today* would 'respond to new developments within the black community itself'; criticizing the liberal tendency to see black people merely as victims, Howe stressed that 'our task is to record and recognise the struggles of the emerging forces as manifestations of the revolutionary potential of the black population' (6/1, January 1974).

The combination of militant protest and advocacy of the creative achievements of the black community defined the journal throughout the 1970s and into the 1980s. In May 1974 it instigated a national campaign in support of the three-month strike by the predominantly Asian workforce at the Imperial Typewriter Company factory in Leicester. As regards the arts, *Race Today* provided a space for the publication of poetry, drama, and short stories by black writers such as Martin Carter, Andrew *Salkey, and Linton Kwesi Johnson (whose first poetry collection was published there in 1974). Indeed, by the 1980s the magazine had launched an annual subsidiary publication, the *Race Today Review*, dedicated to the arts and edited by Howe and Johnson. The main magazine continued, meanwhile, until its final issue in 1988.

MGN

Race Today (1969–88)

See also INTERNATIONAL BOOK FAIR OF RADICAL BLACK AND THIRD WORLD BOOKS; PUBLISHING

Racism. Racism is a long-standing feature of human societies, but it has taken many different forms and been interpreted in many different ways in the course of history.

1. Theorizing race and racism
2. Early British racisms
3. Colonialism and domestic racism in the colonial era
4. Racializing non-whiteness
5. The situation at the start of the 21st century

1. Theorizing race and racism Theories of the origins and nature of 'race' and racism abound, as do theories of how racism may be remedied. An inherent difficulty lies within the very definitions of the concepts of race and racism. Scholars agree that colonialism and imperialism led to the reification of 'race' as a principal organizing feature of modern societies, but there is less consensus on how race or racism is to be theoretically conceptualized. John Solomos and Les Back have acknowledged that efforts to theorize race and racism necessarily involve a difficult walk across shifting and constantly contested terrain. Scholars have pointed to the transhistorical and unfixed nature of racial meanings, and thus the multiplicity of forms in which ideas about race appear. From the 19th century, for instance, race was discursively constructed as a natural, biological, and transhistorical category, a classification based on hereditary traits (skin colour, stature, hair colour, etc.). Most contemporary theorists, however, define race as a social construction that serves a particular ideological function and is produced in the process of human social and political relations.

The social constructedness of 'race', then, means that any definition of racism has to be located within specific social, historical, cultural, and political contexts. Historically, 'race' has signified radically different things, and racism has had many manifestations. As the concept of race is polysemous, so too is the concept of racism. Since the magnitude of what we know to be the whole gamut of racisms—racist thoughts, ideas, and behaviours as well as racist outcomes (both nationally and internationally)—is so overwhelming, it is understandable that these definitions are constantly developing, being honed and sharpened. What is widely accepted is that there exists a multiplicity of racisms.

The word 'racism', in its usual sense, actually designates two very different things. On the one hand, it is a matter of behaviour, usually a manifestation of hatred or contempt for individuals who have well-defined physical characteristics different from our own; on the other hand, it is a matter of ideology, a doctrine concerning human races. The two are not necessarily linked. The racist is not a theoretician justifying his (or her) behaviour with 'scientific' arguments. Conversely, the ideologue of race is not necessarily a 'racist'. His (or her) theoretical views may have no influence whatsoever on his acts. Anti-black racism (racial stereotyping, prejudice, and discrimination) may have had its origins in Europe with the trade in enslaved Africans, but there is evidence to suggest that, until the early to mid-19th century, attitudes in Britain towards black peoples were ambivalent. While many Britons benefited from the trade, it is also possible that the majority knew little of the racist justifications for enslavement.

Even explanations of racism are contested. Scholars propose two causes of racism in western Europe. One has its genesis in colonialism and the building of nation states, and the other is derived from current processes of social, economic, and political change. The neo-Marxist view is that 'race' conflict was unknown among the ancients, and racism has only arisen in modern times as a phenomenon of capitalist exploitation of peoples and its complementary social attitudes. Analyses of race relations, it is argued, must be linked to issues of class as well as other social processes, thus emphasizing the economic imperative underlying racism.

2. Early British racisms As early as the 11th century, when the Crusades began, racism against Jews and Muslims had acquired an eschatological character: their elimination was warranted to clear the historical decks for the second coming of Christ. Already, the infidels of the East were being allotted a role within a Western drama, linked to a notion of historical progress. The East was demonized as a monstrous realm needing to be captured by Christendom and transformed according to a God-given mandate. It was a belief whose form would be preserved in the later models of interaction with these nations, in the colonial and post-colonial era. In 1290 Edward I responded to a mood of growing anti-Semitism by expelling all Jews from England. He had earlier ordered all Jews to wear a yellow badge of identification. In the Middle Ages the fear and hatred of Europe's Islamic enemy had racial resonances. Although Islam was a multiracial civilization, it was homogenized within the European mind, and came to be associated primarily with Moors and Black Africans (the 'Blackamoors'). In 1596 Elizabeth I ordered the arrest and deportation of Blackamoors from the country. She had also sought the expulsion of Gypsies (the Roma) with the 1562 Egyptian Act. Still, many theorists argue that British racism did not fully emerge until the era of colonial slavery, when racialized discourses of white superiority and black inferiority were used to justify the capture, transportation, and enslavement of millions of Africans to labour on white-owned plantations throughout the Americas.

3. Colonialism and domestic racism in the colonial era In the second half of the 19th century the working classes of the British Isles were increasingly made conscious of their differences from those of different ethnicities and nationalities. The population was obsessively catalogued at this time in order to measure the racial 'health' of the nation. For example, John Beddoes in *The Races of Man* compiled an index of 'nigrescence' of the inhabitants of the British Isles, which he found to be increasing in the lower classes owing to the presence of, and intermarriage with, Irish immigrants, whom he described as 'Africanoid'.

The imperialist mission had a galvanizing effect on Britain as all classes were seen as superior to the inferior races who were being colonized. The cohesiveness of Britain was enhanced through a collective sense of racial belonging. The full force of this can only be understood through reference to the level of class fracture and working-class oppression. Rather than uniting with the oppressed peoples of the colonies, the workers of imperialist nations began to perceive their welfare as being tied up with the economic strength of the nation, which in turn was dependent upon a strong empire.

Reforms for the British working classes in education and health were premissed upon the need to breed and preserve 'an imperial race'. Reforming groups such as the Fabian Society relied upon the notion of this imperial race to justify government intervention to uplift the working classes. The dilution of this race through immigration became a cause for paranoia. Sidney Webb, in 1907, was worried that England was threatened by 'race deterioration, if not race suicide'. There was a threat in his mind of 'this country gradually falling to the Irish and the Jews'. The government must intervene in 'the production of healthy, moral and intelligent citizens', argued Webb. The conflation of physical or regional racial type with characteristics is present throughout—other races are unhealthy, immoral, and unintelligent.

The meanings of colonialism and imperialism for the British can be summed up in the words of Winston Churchill:

> The West Indies, two hundred years ago, bulked very largely in the minds of all people who were making Britain and making the British Empire. Our possessions of the West Indies, like that of India—the colonial plantation and development, as they were then called—gave us the strength, the support, but especially the capital, the wealth, at a time when no other European nation possessed such a reserve, which enabled us to come through the great struggle of the Napoleonic Wars, the keen competition of the commerce of the 18th and 19th centuries, and enabled us not only to acquire this worldwide appendage of possessions we have, but also to lay the foundation of that commercial and financial leadership which, when the world was young, when everything outside Europe was undeveloped, enabled us to make our great position in the world.

The injustice of contemporary racism is the continuing non-recognition of the significant role of colonized 'others' in creating the British nation. Black Caribbean and Asian peoples in Britain are still considered to be 'burdensome' on the state, takers rather than givers, peoples to be tolerated rather than communities who have a right to be here.

4. Racializing non-whiteness One way in which racism perpetuates itself is through the persistent representations of black and non-white peoples as 'raced', and white people as being neutrally 'raced', or not 'raced'. This is demonstrated on a daily basis in media reporting, with newspaper and television reports, for instance, persistently naming the 'race' or ethnicity of non-white alleged offenders, while remaining silent on the 'race' or ethnic status of white alleged offenders. The effect of this has been to reproduce traditions of knowledge that problematize blackness, while taking whiteness as an unproblematic, naturally given, category. Richard Dyer highlights what he refers to as the 'non-racing' of white people, which has the effect of constituting white people as 'just people', whereas other people are 'something else', always subjected to and identified through perceived racial definitions. As an illustration, Dyer points to the naming of racialized identities, (e.g. the black drag queen, the black actor, the black lesbian) in texts while white images go unraced. By not naming white images, whiteness remains unchallenged as the normative criteria for humanity.

5. The situation at the start of the 21st century There remains some way to go before most black people in western Europe can be fully integrated into the political processes of their societies. Disaffection with their exclusion from the political processes has led young black and Muslim citizens of western Europe to take more direct action, as seen clearly in the riots of summer 2001 (England) and in autumn 2005 (France). It is indicative of governments' indifference to their plight that they are still referred to as second-, third-, and fourth-generation Pakistanis, Bangladeshis, and North and West African immigrants, rather than British or French youth. The racism directed towards black males is reflected in their over-representation as inmates of mental health and prison institutions. The number of young Blacks incarcerated within the penal system far exceeds that of their presence on university campuses in Britain.

Black and minority ethnic peoples in the United Kingdom have behind them a long tradition of self-organization. Black political activists have argued for equal rights, in the fullest sense of the word, and have fought, alongside white anti-racists, against state oppression. Those usually opposing this fight have come from the political right, including extremist groups such as the British National Party. While the political left may have been uncomfortable with aspects of black struggles for equality, justice, and respect, they have broadly given their support for these demands. This 'new' political agenda, however, with its emphasis on community cohesion through integration, adoption of 'the British way of life', and allegiance to 'Britishness', can be traced back to the political agenda of the Fabians.

There appears to be a new paradigm in transglobal politics, the effects of which are not yet fully apparent. The events of 11 September 2001 changed the way in which 'terrorism' was handled and defined. Traditional methods of evidence-based prosecution were no longer deemed appropriate. Actions taken by the British and American governments against black, Middle Eastern, South Asian, and Muslim communities began to have the hallmarks of racism. These actions arguably transgressed international laws and standards, and yet they were ongoing and regarded as acceptable by the governments of several nations and large sections of their populations. There is little doubt among anti-racist and human rights communities that these actions would not have been committed against a group of people, no matter how large or threatening, who were white. Different standards still apply, and examination of the various forms of racism will need to include the added factor of religion.

In addition, there remain many causes to be fought within Britain. Health (including mental health), housing, education, the criminalization of communities, Islamophobia, lack of adequate representation in politics and the media, racist violence, and many other issues continue to demand attention. There have been significant advances at some levels. Following the *MacPherson Report on the death of Stephen *Lawrence, there was a notable change in people's perceptions of the racism endured by black citizens. MacPherson's identification of pervasive institutional racism within the police, criminal justice system, and other public bodies merely verified at last what many black people had long known was the reality. TL

Dyer, Richard, *White* (1997)

Hall, Stuart, *Race as a Floating Signifier*, Sage Anniversary Lecture, Goldsmiths College (1996)

Miles, Robert, *Racism* (1989)

Solomos, John, and Back, Les, *Racism and Society* (1996)

See also SKIN COLOUR AND RACE, THEORIES OF

Radio. Among the earliest contributions by Blacks to British radio, before the arrival of the **Empire Windrush* in Britain in 1948, was the BBC's **Caribbean Voices* programme, founded by the Jamaican Una *Marson in 1943. Marson was the first black female programme creator at the BBC, and *Caribbean Voices* was intended to promote the writings of Caribbean authors in Britain. It was broadcast on Sundays from London to the Anglophone Caribbean and continued to run until 1958, after Marson's departure from the BBC in 1945. The programme certainly provided Caribbean writers with a showcase for their work, but exposure of black creativity was not limited to exclusively black programmes like *Caribbean Voices* for black musicians, actors, and writers were performing on various radio shows. Indeed, a significant number who were regular features on *Caribbean Voices* went on to do more readings or dramatic adaptations for the BBC. Among them were Andrew *Salkey, George Lamming, Sam *Selvon, and John Figueroa. In 1965 Figueroa and Lamming read their poems on the programme *Many Islands, Many Voices*, and in the same year Selvon's drama *A House for Teena* was aired. Selvon went on to write more plays for the BBC such as *Highway in the Sun* (1967), *You Right in the Smoke* (1968), and *Milk in the Coffee* (1975).

Black artistes also made appearances on popular shows like *Desert Island Discs*. In 1952 the Trinidadian pianist Winifred *Atwell appeared on the programme. A year later another Caribbean musician, Leslie 'Hutch' *Hutchinson, was a guest, as was the Trinidadian folksinger Edric *Connor in 1959, proving the popularity of black artistes among the British audience. The proliferation of radio dramas involving either black actors or black themes indicates both the extent of black productivity as well as its favourable reception. From 1955 the production on radio of numerous plays such as *Cry, the Beloved Country* (1955, an adaptation of Alan Paton's novel of the same name), *The Green Pastures* (1956, an adaptation of Marc Connelly's stage play), *Cindy-Ella* (1957, a retelling of Cinderella with a black cast), and *Christophe* (1958, written by James Forsyth) sought both to inform the British public of black culture and to affirm it for the black population. A notable production in 1998 was the dramatization of C. L. R. *James's novel *Minty Alley*.

An important contribution to the promotion of black British culture was Alex Pascall's *Black Londoners*, the first daily black radio programme, which began broadcasting in 1974. It provided an outlet for black people to reflect on themselves and their history, culture, lifestyle, and future. Pascall's intention was to combat and reform negative black stereotypes through the use of radio. Additionally, he wanted to politicize the black figure as one who was very much a part of the British makeup. The inception and production of *Black Londoners* was historically significant, not simply because it was the first of its kind, but because it was broadcast during a time when the media was culturally hostile towards Blacks, which strengthened Pascall's determination to address the issue of the black presence in British society.

Following Pascall's revolutionary work, there have been other BBC programmes dedicated to black British matters. On BBC Scotland, for example, a series called *Scotland's Black History* ran from 14 September to 19 October 2003. It was produced by Billy Kay and featured six programmes: *The Invisible Man*, *Will Ye Go Tae the Indies?*, *The Virginia Slave's Lament*, *The Mission*, *Black Blood, White Skin*, and *Bringing It All Back Home*. In them Kay dealt with Scotland's involvement with Africa and people of African origin from Roman times to the slave trade, and discussed the contribution of Blacks to Scottish culture. The BBC's *Woman's Hour* has also featured black themes. On 10 February 2004 it ran a special feature on the Jamaican nurse Mary *Seacole to reassess her role in the

Crimean War, which has often been overshadowed by Florence Nightingale's work. More recently, on 5 October 2005, *Woman's Hour* broadcast a programme on black British style in conjunction with an exhibition at the Victoria and Albert Museum.

Black British radio stations have also been established, such as BBC 1Xtra (which plays urban and black music), Choice FM (*hip hop and rhythm and blues), Jazz FM 102.2 (which provides over 200 *jazz programmes presented by the United Kingdom's leading jazz specialists), Jazz 100.4 FM, and KISS FM. Most of these stations aim to play and promote black British music. Besides this, certain stations, such as Choice FM, provide a space on their web site for news updates on the black community as well as current events.

Apart from programmes run specifically for the British public, the BBC World Service broadcasts to listeners across the world. It transmits in 33 languages to about 150 million people. About 66 million people tune into the service in Africa and the Middle East. The English-language service broadcasts 24 hours a day and is funded by the British government through the Foreign and Commonwealth Office. Programmes cover a wide range of cultural, political, and social issues in Africa, Asia-Pacific, Europe, the Middle East, South Asia, the Americas, and the United Kingdom.

The representation of Blacks on British radio remains, however, subject to two criticisms: firstly, that racial stereotypes are still being perpetuated; and, secondly, that black historical issues are still not given sufficient coverage. Nevertheless, since the fiftieth anniversary of the arrival of the *Windrush* to Britain, the BBC has made more resources available for programme-making on black subjects.

SS

Jarrett-Macauley, Delia, *The Life of Una Marson 1905–65* (1998)

Ramsay, James (1733–1789). Clergyman of the Church of England and critic of Caribbean slavery born in Scotland. Originally trained as a surgeon, he spent six years in the Royal Navy in that capacity. On one occasion during this period he visited a slave ship where there was an epidemic on board in order to provide treatment to the victims. Ramsay eventually decided to leave the Navy because of an accident that had left him lame. In 1762 he was ordained by the Bishop of London, and returned to the Caribbean island of St Kitts (St Christopher), which he had previously visited while in the Navy. He spent most of the next nineteen years in St Kitts, as rector of two parishes there, and married the daughter of a local planter.

Ramsay's attempts to preach Christianity to the slaves, and his involvement in local political issues, made him unpopular with his white parishioners in St Kitts. Worn down by their hostility, he left the island in 1781 and went to England, where he became vicar of Teston and rector of Nettlestead, neighbouring parishes in Kent. Here he became acquainted with Beilby *Porteus, then rector of the nearby parish of Hunton as well as Bishop of Chester. It was Porteus who persuaded Ramsay to write what was published in 1784 as *An Essay on the Treatment and Conversion of African Slaves in the British Sugar Colonies*.

Although others, such as Granville *Sharp, had criticized slavery before, Ramsay's *Essay* was the first extended treatment of the subject by someone who had lived in the Caribbean and been in a position to observe the workings of plantation slavery at close hand for a protracted period. Ramsay did not call for the slaves to be freed. He argued only that they should be better treated, and that this would prepare the way for their freedom at 'a distant period'. Indeed, so moderate was his tone that some contemporary readers wondered if he was not actually in favour of slavery and the slave trade, something he then felt obliged to deny explicitly. While he did mention examples of slaves deliberately maimed or killed, the picture he gave of plantation slavery was essentially one of widespread, routine brutality, of a system that ground down its victims by overwork, insufficient food, and generally poor conditions.

The *Essay*, and its author, were immediately attacked by pro-slavery writers, involving Ramsay in a pamphlet controversy that lasted until his death. The resulting publicity stimulated the discussion, which was increasing in Britain in the 1780s, about the slave trade and slavery, and Ramsay's *Essay* was a significant influence on Thomas *Clarkson, William *Wilberforce, and others. JG

Gilmore, J. T., 'Episcopacy, Emancipation and Evangelization: Aspects of the History of the Church of England in the British West Indies', Ph.D. thesis (University of Cambridge, 1985)

Ramsay, James, *An Essay on the Treatment and Conversion of African Slaves in the British Sugar Colonies* (1784)

Shyllon, Fọlarin, *James Ramsay: The Unknown Abolitionist* (1977)

See also ABOLITION

Rastafarianism. Religious movement in the Caribbean and Britain, mainly among people of Jamaican origin.

1. Background
2. The Bible
3. Religious traits and practices

1. Background Since the 1960 report by social scientists of the University of the West Indies much has happened to the image and reception of Rastafari not only in Jamaica but worldwide. Very little, however, is known of the history and philosophy of Rastafari itself (two Amarynya words contracted into one). The significance of the Bible is fundamental to an understanding of Rastafari as well as its historical context of slavery. Slave masters and colonialists forbade literacy and education to slaves, but missionary activity led to black people becoming acquainted with the Bible. Although the Bible is replete with examples of brutality and savagery, it also expresses graphically the condition of servitude, captivity, and rebellion in several instances. The readings of the Bible by people who desired transformation of their condition led to identification with characters in the Bible. The Bible became a weapon of rebellion and redemption.

Marcus *Garvey's Universal Negro Improvement Association in the early 1920s, with its organizational and colourful impact in the United States, also had reverberations around the African world: the entire Caribbean, despite distinct colonial tongues, Central America, and Africa itself. Garvey's use of the Bible as a tool for radical preaching, coupled with a political understanding of colonialism, precipitated the genesis of Rastafari itself. Garvey himself declared,

> Since the white people have seen their God, through white spectacles, we have only now started out (late though it may be) to see our God, through our own spectacles. The God of Isaac and the God of Jacob, let him exist for the race that believes in this God of Isaac and the God of Jacob. We Negroes believe in the God of Ethiopia, the everlasting God . . . That is the God in whom we believe, but we shall worship him through the spectacles of Ethiopia.

In 1930, upon the coronation of Haile Selassie as King of Ethiopia, many black Christians believed that biblical prophecy of Isaiah 9: 6 had been fulfilled: they identified Haile Selassie as the Prince of Peace, the new King: 'For unto us a child is born, unto us a son is given; and the government will be upon his shoulder; and his name shall be called Wonderful Counsellor, Mighty God, Everlasting Father, Prince of Peace.' This led to the deification by some Jamaican Rastafarians of Haile Selassie as God and by others as the Son of God. The identification that he was an African appears to have been confirmed by Daniel 9: 7: 'and the hair of his head like the pure wool', while Psalms 87: 4 identifies the country: 'behold Philistia, and Tyre, with Ethiopia; this man was born there'.

None of these identifications was historically alien to African belief systems. The African Egyptian pharaoh Akhenaten promoted himself as the sole representative of God on earth, and every pharaoh before and after him proclaimed himself the Son of God. Traditional African kingdoms acknowledged the king as divine, for example, the Yoruba, whose mythology, like that of the Asante, had their kings descended from God himself. Thus Rastafari was, in this instance, recalling the models of African history. The radical rejection of the middle-class standards of dress, behaviour, and speech by Rastafarians, and the open condemnation of king and country, marked them out as a lunatic and threatening fringe in Jamaica, and they were projected as such in the popular press. The Rastafarians experienced attacks and persecution from colonial and post-colonial governments.

2. **The Bible** Rastafari was informed by interpretations of the Bible:

- Psalms 87: 4 is taken to confirm the birth of humankind in Ethiopia.
- John 1: 14: 'God pronounced the Word and it was made flesh' (humankind).
- Revelation 14: 4 identifies Haile Selassie as the Lamb.
- Leviticus 11: 3 and 7 dictate prohibition on certain foods.
- Leviticus 6: 5 and 19: 27 are seen as the law determining dreadlocks.
- Isaiah 43: 5–7 inspires appeals for repatriation.
- Revelation 22: 2 is interpreted as the sanctioning of marijuana: 'In the midst of the street of it, and on either side of the river, was there the tree of life, which bare twelve manner of fruits, and yielded her fruit every month: and the leaves of the tree were for the healing of the nations.' Reference is also made in Psalms 104: 14: 'He causeth the grass to grow for the cattle, and herb for the service of man: that he may bring forth food out of the earth.'

3. **Religious traits and practices** In most traditional African societies dreadlocks were seen as priestly or representing wisdom. Thus Rastafarians referring to dreadlocks as 'the crown' were simultaneously expressing a most ancient interpretation: the African pharaohs adorned their heads with a uraeus, a serpent that rested on the forehead symbolizing the significance of the brain. Similarly, the Yoruba word for head is *ori*, which has special significance and prohibition for initiates, who shy away from anyone touching or daring to wash their heads because the head is the source of wisdom and spirituality (when one is initiated head-washing is pivotal to the ceremony). The pig was purificationally avoided by some African royal families (including the ancient pharaohs) as an unclean animal, so too with the Rastafarians. Fundamental Rastafari also impose strict vegetarianism and in some instances veganism.

Critical to Rastafari is the use of the holy herb (marijuana). The herb is both a sacramental object of communion, not only with God but also among brethren and sistren, and also a source of income. Trance states or shifts in consciousness through the use of hallucinogenic substances are integral to most ancient religions: Brahman priests or sadhus of India, shamans of South America and the Caribbean, a number of Nonconformist Christian churches, as well as in traditional Africa. In modern societies, including Britain, the use of marijuana was seen as an illegal act but because of the recent change in the law in 2005, it can now be consumed legally but restricted to certain quantities.

Rastafarians have historically been shorn of their locks when imprisoned, whether in Jamaica or in Britain. In the early formation in the 1970s of organizational structures and the illegal squatting of buildings in Britain, Rastafarians were often subjected to heavy-handed arrest and imprisonment. This has now stopped in Britain as the prison system recognizes Rastafari as a religion, and persecution because of hairstyle is prohibited. Also, the popular trend of non-Rastafari people to wear locks in public offices—banks, institutions of state, the commercial sector—has now rendered persecution ridiculous.

One of the most significant tenets of Rastafari is not only repatriation to Africa but also financial compensation characterized as *reparations. Although Rastafarians are certainly not the first to prosecute this subject, they have been the most vociferous and consistent for over 70 years. Rastafari representatives had already been given an audience with UN officials on the subject of reparations in the 1960s, as Douglas Mack detailed in his book *From Babylon to Rastafari* (1999).

Rastafarians have always accepted that financial security can only be generated by work, and preferably by self-employment. The founding fathers of Rastafari, in keeping with the African tradition of co-operative economics, have occupied lands communally in Jamaica. Many Rastafari brethren and sistren are involved in agricultural work in the Caribbean and in Africa.

Since the first Rastafarian mission to Africa in 1961, several other missions have been successfully mounted, financed by successive African governments in terms of accommodation, meals, and transportation. The emissaries of Rastafari met with prime ministers and presidents, and prosecuted their repatriation appeal with such conviction that they were ethusiastically welcomed in the respective countries of visitation. Leaders such as Jomo Kenyatta of Kenya and Kwame Nkrumah of Ghana were formerly ardent followers of Marcus Garvey; hence the cordial reception given to Rastafarians. Today Rastafarians productively occupy lands in Ethiopia and Ghana and are concretely contributing to the local economy.

One of the earliest Rastafarians in Britain was Brother Zorro, who in 1940 joined the Royal Air Force, returned to Jamaica after the war, and remigrated to London in the late 1950s. Other Rastafarians migrated to Britain, fleeing colonial repression, seeking new ground, or as a staging point for the trek to Ethiopia. In the 1960s there was no organized Rastafarian body, but today there are several organizations, such as the Ethiopian World Federation (established in 1972 in Portobello Road, London); the formation of local tabernacles in Kennington in 1968, where the Twelve Tribes of Israel also set up their headquarters in 1974; and across the country groups that observe several important dates in the Rastafari calendar: the birthdays of Haile Selassie (23 July) and Marcus Garvey (17 August); 11 September as the New Year; and the celebration of the Ethiopian Orthodox Church's Christ's birthday on 7 January. These and other celebratory events have served as points of coalescence and unity for Rastafari, maintaining the drive of the movement and the sharing of beliefs.

ASS

Ahkell, Jah, *Emperor Haile Selassie and the Rastafarians* (1997)

Augier, Roy, Nettleford, Rex, and Smith, M. G., *The Rastafari Movement in Kingston, Jamaica* (1960)

Chevannes, Barry, *Rastafari: Roots and Ideology* (1994)

Garvey, Marcus, *The Philosophy and Opinions of Marcus Garvey* (ed. Tony Martin, 1982)

Zips, Werner (ed.), *Rastafari in the Third Millennium* (2006)

See also CHRISTIANITY; CHURCHES; ETHIOPIA, ITALIAN INVASION OF

Refugees and asylum-seekers. A refugee is a person fleeing persecution or suffering, under the entitlements of international law. The largest proportion of the world's refugees live in poverty-stricken countries of the Third World, to which they move from neighbouring areas afflicted by war, dictatorship, famine, drought, or other natural disasters. The term 'asylum-seeker' is specific to Britain, denoting applicants who may be granted official refugee status, humanitarian protection, or discretionary leave to remain. Those rejected during the asylum process are, in effect, illegal immigrants attempting to enter the country by false means: they are returned to their home countries or moved to a third state (either one they have passed through to reach Britain or a further point of stoppage). Since the accession of the east European states to the European Union in 2004, debates on illegal immigration have become applicable almost exclusively to non-white immigrants.

Until the late 19th century there were no immigration controls in Britain; various Aliens Acts were passed, some aimed at Jews throughout the late Middle Ages and Renaissance, others in the wake of the French revolutions in 1789 and 1848, but they deported unwelcome foreigners rather than limiting entry. The arrival of 120,000 Jews fleeing persecution in eastern Europe between 1875 and 1914 triggered a debate on the need for border controls, but no law was passed. From Huguenots escaping the 16th-century wars of religion in France, to the 130,000 Poles who fled Europe during the Second World War and the Vietnamese 'boat people' in the

1980s, conflict has generally been accepted as an impetus for coming to Britain.

Some commentators on British immigration laws argue that border controls distinguishing refugees from asylum-seekers are simply a means to limit all immigration by categorizing its motives as legal or illegal. Economic liberalization has meant the opening up of global trade, with the result that wealth is free to move across national borders, in general from the producer nations of the Third World to the consumers of the developed areas. Immigration controls are arguably designed to stop people following that wealth.

As Hugh Gaitskell, the Labour Opposition leader at the time of the 1962 Commonwealth Immigrants Act, pointed out, economic migration generally occurs to states with high employment. If there were no opportunities for work in the target countries, there would be no immigration, a process more beneficial to the developed world than to the workers' original countries: in the Second World War 13,500 Caribbeans were recruited by the Royal Air Force to work as ground crew, 1,000 technicians were brought to the Merseyside munitions factories, and 1,200 Hondurans felled trees in Scotland. After the war *London Transport, the British Hotels and Restaurants Association, and the Ministry of Health recruited from the Caribbean; Enoch *Powell, as Health Minister, continued to bring Caribbean, Indian, and Pakistani workers into the National Health Service in the 1960s, and the policy continues today. Given the ageing population of early 21st-century Britain, many political commentators have argued the need to welcome further immigrants, 80 per cent of whom are aged 15–35. An anomaly in the current situation is that while asylum-seekers' cases are decided through a complex system of assessments and appeals, they are fed and housed at state expense but cannot work or be taxed: 66,705 received government support in 2004.

The 1962 Act introduced a work voucher system to assess prospective immigrants according to their level of skilled labour. Rab Butler, the Conservative Home Secretary, told his Cabinet colleagues that 'Although the scheme purports to relate solely to employment and to be non-discriminatory, the aim is primarily social and its restrictive effect is intended to, and would in fact, operate on coloured people almost exclusively.' When Kenya, in 1967, and Uganda, in 1971, embarked on ethnic Africanization policies, their Indian middle classes were exiled: 10,000 Kenyans, holding British passports, came to Britain in February 1968. The Labour government passed a second Commonwealth Immigrants Act, making ownership of a British passport subject to immigration controls and restricting the number of Kenyans allowed in per year. Edward Heath's government, elected in 1970, though it doubled the annual quota to 3,000 and accepted 29,000 Ugandans, passed a further Act abolishing the distinction between Commonwealth and foreign citizens in 1971.

In more recent years the debate has changed: rather than focusing on economic productivity or ethics, the asylum issue is discussed in largely emotional terms: sensationalist stories proliferate of millionaire Central African princes claiming benefits, or of starving Kosovars barbecuing swans in the wastelands of Newham and Brent. In the supposedly more reasoned arguments of government, problems of 'assimilation' are evoked to justify the measures employed in limiting the number of immigrants. Differences of language and cultural traditions are portrayed as being alien to integration—the assumption being that immigration will dilute British culture and identity, whatever that might be. In the popular imagination asylum is consistently linked with criminal activities—drug-smuggling, passport and identity theft, people-trafficking and prostitution, benefit and housing fraud, illegal labour, and most recently international terrorism. A major justification for the identity card measures under debate since 2001—using technologies such as iris-scanning and DNA sampling, uncomfortably resonant with discredited eugenicist debates—is that society has been criminalized by such acts, which are linked with non-white immigration.

From the late 1990s to the time of writing there have been increased asylum applications from the Middle East and Africa. In 2004 the highest numbers were from Iran, Somalia, China, Zimbabwe, Pakistan, Iraq, the Democratic Republic of Congo, India, Afghanistan, and Sudan. Following a limiting campaign by the Home Office—including tighter visa requirements for 43 Third World countries, the introduction of new technologies to search freight at continental ports, and a system of 'fast-tracking' applications at the Harmondsworth and Oakington detention centres, which resulted in 100 per cent of applicants failing the initial assessment—there was a 32 per cent fall in applications from 2003. Of the 40,625 applicants, 24 per cent were granted leave to remain. Countries certified 'safe' by the Secretary of State, automatically disqualifying their nationals from asylum, included Albania, Jamaica, Bangladesh, and South Africa.

At the beginning of the 21st century some of the British government's attempts to reduce the numbers of incoming refugees (already low by the standards of several other EU countries) appeared to risk contravening international law. Under the 1999 Asylum and Immigration Act failed asylum-seekers under exceptional circumstances, for instance Iraqis and Zimbabweans unable to return home for reasons of safety, become entitled to a reduced amount of support from the National Asylum Support Service. The 2004 Act, noting more people using this loophole, added that it requires them to perform community service; in other words, the procedures for restricting immigration revived, in the opinion of some, a type of slavery. Accusations of arbitrary arrest and detention were commonly made against officials, causing civil rights organizations to criticize the government for compromising Britain's human rights record. JM

Field, Frank, and Haikin, Patricia, *Black Britons* (1971)

Hayter, Teresa, *Open Borders: The Case Against Immigration Controls* (2nd edn., 2004)

See also IMMIGRATION

Reggae. Musical form dominant in black British culture. The large-scale migration of Afro-Caribbean people to Britain during the period after the Second World War saw the readjustment of black social, cultural, and leisure institutions. Faced with racism at most entertainment venues, they created private venues to host exclusively black parties, such as 'shebeens' or 'blues parties', where music was a predominant feature. Music was seen not merely as a form of entertainment, but it also functioned as a vehicle for social and political aspirations. Reggae music, which originated among the working classes in Jamaica in the late 1960s, was a mode of expressing the collective struggles of the black poor. Recurrent themes in reggae lyrics include that of protest against waged labour as well as criticism of capitalist law, poverty, and colonialism. The mass conversion of reggae artistes in the late 1960s and early 1970s to *Rastafarianism augmented the political and spiritual dimensions of reggae music. The commodification and internationalization of reggae in the 1970s shifted its concentration from a purely Jamaican working-class audience to involve African-Caribbeans living in places such as Britain.

In its initial stages the British reggae market was dependent on the Jamaican one. The political situation in Jamaica, which was reflected in the reggae tradition, had special significance for the black community in Britain. Simon Jones wrote that 'the 1970s as a whole were characterised by an extraordinary degree of synchronisation between the political ideologies expounded in Jamaican popular music and the conditions of race and class oppression experienced by Blacks in Britain'. Music by the Wailers affected the black British community, especially with their first two albums, *Catch a Fire* (1973) and *Burnin'* (1973). In them subjects concerning anti-imperialism and racial solidarity were raised, thereby creating a sense of race and class consciousness. The Wailers toured Britain in the early 1970s and influenced thousands of young Blacks with their Rastafarian ideology. Other reggae artistes who popularized Rastafarianism and made an impact on the black community include Gregory Isaacs, Burning Spear, and Black Uhuru.

The popularization of reggae in the mainstream market owes something to the punk movement. The ideological foundations of both genres were similar in that they were grounded in anti-establishment affirmations. In the late 1970s punk and reggae groups formed an alliance for the Rock Against Racism concerts, which managed to bring together black and white youths in a musical and political environment. This incited an interest in reggae among white listeners, thereby expanding the black British reggae market. Groups such as Misty and Aswad were able to sign with major companies. When musicians like Bob Marley signed and recorded with the large company Island Records, reggae reached the mass music market. Consequently, when Marley toured Britain in 1975, he played to large, mixed audiences in Manchester, Birmingham, and London. Young Whites found in reggae, and especially in Marley's songs, the political verve and subversive quality needed for their self-expression. However, rivalry did exist between young Whites and Blacks, particularly in the late 1970s, when organizations such as the National Front were advocating far-right racism. They targeted young Whites, propelling them to fight the 'race war' against Blacks. Publications like *Bulldog* and *Young Nationalist* were inverting reggae discourse to implement racial hostility against young Blacks. Slogans from Marley's songs such as 'stand up for your rights' were used to encourage Whites to stick together.

In the mid-1970s a type of reggae indigenous to black British culture emerged. While the first generation of reggae musicians and listeners were inspired by the Wailers and the Rastafari movement, the second and third generations were gradually dissociating their creative, artistic, and political fervour from the Jamaican context. Furthermore, when Jamaica underwent its economic recession in the 1980s, the production and dissemination of reggae suffered, thus transferring the reggae torch as it were to Britain. Black British reggae groups such as Steel Pulse, Matumbi, and Black Slate emerged, and Britain developed its own unique brand of reggae, characterized by a merging of soft soul and reggae. The Lovers' Rock movement, which began in the mid-1970s, was the first indication of black British reggae. It showcased black British female reggae vocalists who were reacting against the heavy, masculine rhythms of Jamaican 'roots' reggae. The very existence of the movement indicated the improvement of black British female autonomy. All-female groups such as Brown Sugar, Black Harmony, and Sister Love inspired both male and female reggae enthusiasts in the late 1970s. Those who succeeded in the Lovers' Rock market went on to make their mark in all fields of the reggae industry. They became musicians, vocalists, DJs, producers, label owners, and sound system operators.

In the 1980s reggae increasingly became a mode for black self-expression amidst the racial hostility in the political and social arenas. As xenophobia became more prevalent in British society, black reggae musicians found inspiration in subverting the racially antagonistic political and social climate. They sought to define 'black Britishness' in order to establish themselves as a distinct community. Reggae music in Britain was thus developing its own distinctive flavour with songs such as 'Cockney Translation' fusing standard English, black British Creole derivative of the Jamaican version, and English working-class accents.

Reggae audiences in Britain have declined over the years, especially following the death of Bob Marley in 1981. Many black British youths have turned towards *hip hop, possibly because their attachment to their Caribbean roots has weakened owing to acculturation and the prevalence of American culture. In more recent years there has been a 'crossover' of reggae to hip hop, an occurrence unique to Britain. SS

Jones, Simon, *Black Culture, White Youth: The Reggae Tradition from JA to UK* (1988)

Oliver, Paul (ed.), *Black Music in Britain: Essays on the Afro-Asian Contribution to Popular Music* (1990)

See also JAZZ; MUSIC 2: EARLY POPULAR MUSIC; SOUL MUSIC

Reid, Vincent Albert (1935–2001). West Indian passenger on board the **Empire Windrush*. In 1948 Vincent Reid arrived in England on the *Empire Windrush*, the youngest West Indian to do so. Consequently, he became the first member of the post-war West Indian migration to experience the school system at first hand. Born in Kingston, Jamaica, he was brought up by adoptive parents, who decided to seek work in England. He was placed in a secondary modern school in London, where he was the only black child, being put in the lowest-ability class. He soon moved to the top form but encountered a teacher who laughed at his accent. In his own words, he 'basically stopped going to school, because he felt angry and ashamed'. Having left school without qualifications and unhappy at home, he joined the Royal Air Force, serving in Malaya at the time of the Emergency. A boxer, he was passionate about football and especially West Indian cricket. A variety of jobs followed until he went to Sussex University, where he read African History. After graduation he attended the School of Oriental and African Studies for his MA and took a teaching diploma. He joined Brixton College in 1974, retiring in 1995 as a senior lecturer. Teaching was clearly his true vocation. The *Windrush* celebrations of 1998 allowed many to hear him lecture on his experiences. He was passionately opposed to racism in its many forms; equally passionate about the politics of the West Indies and Africa. PF

Fraser, Peter, 'Vincent Albert Reid', *The Guardian*, 24 May 2001

Phillips, Mike, and Phillips, Trevor, *Windrush: The Irresistible Rise of Multi-Racial Britain* (1998)

See also EDUCATION

Remond, Sarah Parker (1826–1894). African-American abolitionist and women's rights campaigner born in Salem, Massachusetts, to John and Nancy Lenox Remond, free middle-class Blacks. Despite her family's wealth, racial discrimination within the northern segregated school system meant that she received a limited education and she was primarily self-educated. Raised in a family that included many abolitionists, Remond learned from childhood of the horrors of slavery and witnessed many incidents involving the Underground Railroad. Her parents played host to many of the movement's leaders, including William Lloyd Garrison and Wendell Phillips, and to more than one fugitive slave.

At the age of 16 Remond began to join her brother Charles Lenox Remond, the leading abolitionist of his day, on anti-slavery lecture circuits across northern states. A vociferous opponent of both slavery and of the racial segregation that existed in the 'free' North, in 1853 she successfully won a case for damages for injuries sustained when she was forcibly ejected from an operatic performance at the Boston Athenaeum for refusing to sit in the segregated seats reserved for black people. She was a close associate and friend of many leading abolitionists of the day, and in 1856, at the age of 30, went to work for the American Anti-Slavery Society, quickly becoming one of the Society's most persuasive and powerful lecturers. She proved to be such a good speaker and fundraiser that she was invited to take the anti-slavery message to Britain.

In 1859 Remond arrived in Britain, where she gave over 40 anti-slavery lectures throughout England, Scotland, and Wales. Her eloquent and moving lectures drew huge crowds, and many were published by the media. She spoke out against northern segregation and southern slavery, and often stressed the sexual exploitation of enslaved black women. During one lecture she appealed to the sympathies of white English women, telling them that if they 'knew the unspeakable horrors to which their sex was exposed on southern plantations', they would 'demand for black women the protection and rights enjoyed by white women'. She also supported the emancipated Blacks in the Caribbean, and in 1865 published a letter in the *Daily News* protesting attacks on black people in the London press after an insurrection in Jamaica. Her commitment to the cause of race equality won her many influential supporters within and beyond Parliament.

Despite a heavy lecture programme Remond realized her ambition to acquire the education denied to her in America. She attended Bedford Ladies' College in London (later incorporated into the University of London), where she studied a range of subjects including Latin and French. At the outbreak of the American Civil War, she remained in England, using her substantial influence to build British support for the Union cause. When the war ended, she turned her attention to lecturing and fundraising on behalf of the freed men and women. One lecture that she delivered in London, 'The Freeman or the Emancipated Negro of the Southern States of the United States', was published in *The Freedman* (London) in 1867. She played active roles within the London Emancipation Society and the Freedmen's Aid Association, two organizations that solicited funds and clothing for the emancipated slaves. In 1866 she left England for Florence, and at the age of 42 entered medical school. She became a doctor, married an Italian, and died in self-imposed exile in Rome. CJ

Clark Hine, Darlene (ed.), *Black Women in America: An Historical Encyclopaedia*, ii: M–Z (1993)

Sterling, Dorothy (ed.), *We Are Your Sisters: Black Women in the Nineteenth Century* (1997)

See also ABOLITION; CRAFT, ELLEN, AND CRAFT, WILLIAM; JACOBS, HARRIET

Renaissance Britain.

1. The arrival of Blacks in Britain
2. Legal status: servant or slave?
3. Evidence for the black presence
4. Black slave mothers
5. Free Blacks
6. Renaissance culture and black people
7. Deportation

1. The arrival of Blacks in Britain Blacks arrived in Britain in a variety of ways from a variety of countries during the 15th, 16th, and 17th centuries, only some of which were related to the Renaissance voyages of 'discovery'. Initially, Africans transported to Portugal as part of the *slave trade from the coast of West Africa, beginning in the 1440s, were then sold on and brought to England by Europeans, mainly from Portugal and Spain, but also from Italy and the Netherlands. Some Blacks from both East and West Africa continued to arrive in southern Europe via North Africa. The first Africans transported directly from West Africa to England during this period arrived in 1555, and by the 1580s black slaves who had originally been transported to the West Indies were also on occasion subsequently brought to England (for example, an indeterminate number of black slaves were landed in Portsmouth after Sir Francis Drake's voyage to Santo Domingo and Cartagena in 1585–6). Sir John *Hawkins has the unfortunate distinction of being England's first slave trader, and in 1565 a written blazon explained that his new crest—a half-length bust of a bound Moor wearing gold earrings—had been chosen on account of his victory against them. The coat of arms of the early Portuguese slave trader Fernão Gomes, who had been ennobled in 1474, likewise contained three Moors' heads, all with gold necklaces, earrings, and noserings. The crest of Sir Thomas More also contained a Moor's head, but in this case it was a pun on the name of the bearer, whereas there does not seem to be a similar rationale for the inclusion of this particular representation in the coats of arms of other English families. The lives of Africans, both in their places of origin and elsewhere, prior to their arrival in Britain have not yet received attention, yet they must have had considerable bearing upon their subsequent trajectories.

2. Legal status: servant or slave? The most pressing question is what the exact legal status of these Blacks was—whether slavery was legal in Renaissance Britain—but although at the moment it seems likely that it was not legal, there is no absolutely secure answer. However, for practical purposes it may have been almost irrelevant. Given that Blacks arriving in England would either have come via Portuguese- or Spanish-speaking countries where slavery was part of the social fabric and enshrined both in royal and local statutes and in Roman law, or have come directly from Africa in chains, and they would not have understood English, let alone English law, it is safe to assume that they would have believed themselves to be slaves on arrival, a belief shared by their 'owners'. There is only one piece of evidence that could indicate that a sub-Saharan African was aware that English law might support his case for choosing his own master, seen in Portuguese and Roman law as the defining feature of a free man. In 1587 the Portuguese Hector Nuñez paid £4 10*s*. to an English sailor for an 'Ethiopian' (this was a generic word for African), and was astonished first of all when the 'Ethiopian' refused point blank to be his slave, and even more when he subsequently discovered that he had no recourse under common law. Nuñez was compelled to apply to the Court of Requests to try to recoup his investment. Converted Portuguese Jews (so-called 'New Christians') such as Nuñez and Jeronimo Lopez brought Iberian slave-owning mentalities with them when they relocated to England, and their households in London, like other New Christian households across Europe, for example in Venice, included black slaves. As they were no longer classified as Jews, they were able to circumvent the canon law restriction on Jews employing Christian servants or slaves.

However, while it is true that virtually all sources in Renaissance Britain describe Blacks as servants rather than slaves, some Blacks in England not only were labelled as slaves but were treated as such. The Venetian Pier Paolo Corsi put his black slave, the expert diver Jacopo Francesco, up for sale in Southampton in 1548, but no buyer claimed him. Other examples of slaves being hired out in England for their labour, and being paid a wage that was then given to their master, show that this continental European practice was also common in England. In 1620 John Anthony, the black slave of Sir Henry Mainwaring, successfully petitioned the Crown for payment of wages owed for services on board the *Silver Falcon*.

3. Evidence for the black presence No attempt can be made to quantify the numbers of Blacks in Renaissance Britain, although baptismal and burial records in London and Plymouth, where the Navy was based, are suggestive. The terminology used to indicate black skin clusters around two main words and their variations: 'blackamore' and 'negar'/'negro'. More promising as a line of enquiry is an analysis of the various names by which Africans were known in Renaissance England. These range from African names such as Easfanyyo and Cassangoe, to Portuguese and Spanish names such as Domyngo and Francisco, to supposedly comic names such as 'John Come Quicke' and Christian White, to auspicious names in both English and Latin such as Fortunatus, Charity, or Reasonable. Occasionally names give a clue to previous place of residence, as in Symon Valencia; and, very occasionally, place of origin is recorded, as in a baptism of 1610, where it was stated that Walter Nosser had been born in the kingdom of Dungala in Africa (Dūnķūla in Sudan). Street names are often a tell-tale indication of former residents, and there are references to two Blackman streets in London in 1639 and 1640, one in Newington and the other in St George's, Southwark.

4. Black slave mothers Black female slaves in England constantly ran the risk of pregnancy, through either forced or consensual sex. Baptismal records of the children that resulted from these encounters indicate once again that these Blacks were considered slaves, because slaves were not allowed to marry, and virtually all of these women were unmarried and identified according to their master. In Plymouth many of the black slave mothers alleged that the fathers were white Europeans—Dutch, Flemish, or Portuguese—whereas in London the putative fathers were white men in boarding houses, for example. The legal and social position of these mixed-race children has not been investigated, but in continental Europe 'mulattos', if acknowledged by a wealthy or patrician father, were often at a considerable advantage in relation to Blacks. However, in two instances black 'couples' are recorded. In 1630 a son was born to two Blacks, Grace and James Diego, who both were or recently had been 'servants' of Mr Bromfield of Limehouse. And a family of free Blacks, headed by a silkweaver, lived in a Southwark parish in London in the 1580s and 1590s.

5. Free Blacks Free and freed Blacks, while certainly rare, did exist in Renaissance Britain. As slavery may have been contrary to law, it is not surprising that so far no instances of testamentary manumission in Renaissance Britain have come to light, although there are instances of testamentary bequests being made to Blacks. On the other hand, the sons or relatives of African rulers came to southern Europe in order to learn European languages and mores or to be schooled in Christianity, and one can even be found in England. In 1611 Dedery Jaquoah, the son of Caddi-biah, king of a kingdom near the river Cess on the Pepper Coast in Guinea (now in Liberia), was baptized John at St Mildred Poultry in London. According to the entry in the baptismal register, he had been sent to England on an English ship specifically to be baptized; it is more likely that he had been sent by his father to learn about English trading habits, and was baptized as a side issue. It is also probable that Anthony Vause, the trumpeter whose 'black-more' wife, Anne, died in London in 1618, was free or freed, and possible that he too was black, because many Blacks—e.g. John Blanke, the black trumpeter of Henry VII and Henry VIII—were employed as musicians at courts across Europe. There is pictorial evidence (a painting from *c.*1575 attributed to Marcus Gheeraerts the Elder) that *Elizabeth I and documentary evidence that James I also employed black musicians, minstrels, and dancers.

6. Renaissance culture and black people Another fundamental question concerns the extent to which the Renaissance (which only arrived in England in the 16th century) had an impact on Blacks and their representation. If the Renaissance is understood both as a period and as a cultural movement, the period initiated the European voyages of 'discovery' down the west coast of Africa, pioneered in the 15th century by Portugal and taken up only after the mid-16th century by England. In terms of movement, a major tenet of Renaissance life was the centrality of high culture, and real and imagined Blacks, and representations of them, featured at the English Court, as they did at all the major and most of the minor European courts. Elizabeth I had other black members of her household and entertainers, in addition to musicians: for example, she ordered and paid for the most extravagant costume in white taffeta with gold and silver stripes, lace, ribbons, and buttons for her black pageboy.

In literary terms, the Court was also central for imagined Blacks because James I's queen Anne commissioned the playwright Ben Jonson to write a court masque in which she and her ladies could appear disguised as 'Blackamoors'. *The Masque of Blackness* was first performed in 1605, followed by its companion piece, *The Masque of Beauty*, in 1608. There was a long tradition in continental Europe of Whites dressing up as Blacks in courtly, republican, and guild entertainments and entries, increasingly frequent occurrences during the Renaissance. William

Shakespeare's plays, in particular *Othello*, and to a lesser extent *Titus Andronicus* and *The Tempest*, showed very clearly the practical and psychological difficulties and prejudices encountered by black characters. After the introduction of the motif of the black page as an attendant on a white woman in Italy in the first half of the 16th century, and soon afterwards in Portugal, painters in England (such as Paul van Somer, Daniel Mytens, Anton van Dyck, and Sir Peter Lely) followed suit in the 17th century, and the fashionable genre was extended to include a black page with a white man or a white couple with children. This was clearly a reflection of reality, as members of the royal family, and of the aristocracy and gentry, kept black pages in their households.

7. Deportation Elizabeth I is also known for her attempts to order the deportation of Blacks from England in 1596 and 1601. The evidence from 1596 is contained in drafts of an open letter and an open warrant (which she may not have seen), whereas in 1601 this was hardened into a royal proclamation. The reasons adduced in the three documents change, from economic (an increase in population and drain on resources), to nationalistic, to (in the final document) a forceful combination of economic, nationalistic, practical, and religious. A merchant from Lübeck, Caspar van Senden, had procured the release of 89 English people held in Spain and Portugal and had transported them to England. He needed 'bodies' to take in the opposite direction to offer in exchange, and the idea of using Blacks, superfluous people who were taking livelihoods from Englishmen and who were mainly not Christian, was mooted. Its outcome is unknown. KJPL

Earle, T. F., and Lowe, K. J. P. (eds.), *Black Africans in Renaissance Europe* (2005)

Hall, Kim F., *Things of Darkness: Economies of Race and Gender in Early Modern England* (1995)

Knutson, Roslyn L., 'A Caliban in St. Mildred Poultry' in Tetsuo Kishi, Roger Pringle, and Stanley Wells (eds.), *Shakespeare and Cultural Traditions: The Selected Proceedings of the International Shakespeare Association World Congress, Tokyo, 1991* (1994)

Walvin, James, *Black and White: The Negro and English Society, 1555–1945* (1973)

See also MASQUES; TUDOR BRITAIN; VISUAL ARTS 1: REPRESENTATIONS OF BLACKS

Renaissance drama. Elizabethan and Jacobean drama saw the proliferation of African images, contexts, and characters. Contact between Britain and Africa, which began as early as the 14th century, became more prevalent in the 16th century and led to an interest in travel, discovery, and the dramatic representations of 'Moors'. Before the publication of contemporary travel accounts by sailors and travellers, writers often used Scripture and philosophy to construct ideas of Africa and its people. In the 13th century Roger Bacon utilized this blend to fashion geographical knowledge of Africa. Similarly, Geoffrey Chaucer's interpretation of African contexts was an amalgamation of fact and fantasy. Writers of the 16th century, besides deriving knowledge from travellers' accounts, maintained travel tales of the ancients as one of their prime sources of notions about Africa.

In the second half of the 16th century numerous publications on Africa, which ranged from histories to travelogues, contributed to the escalating dramatic fascination with Blacks. Sources of information became more reliable, and publications such as Wyllyam Prat's *Description of the Country of Affrique* (1554), William Waterman's *The Fardle of Facions* (1555), Peter Martyr's *The Decades of the New World* (1555), and John Leo Africanus' *History and Description of Africa* (1600) provided dramatists with more profound and realistic descriptions of Africa. *Mandeville's Travels* (1371) was an important publication for its contribution to concepts such as the relationship between heat in Africa and skin colour, as well as for introducing the legend of Prester John, a fabulously wealthy Christian king living in a land full of precious stones. The growing publication of serious books on Africa allowed dramatists such as Ben Jonson and Christopher Marlowe to use high levels of erudition in their plays. Such scholarship is evident in

Marlowe's *Tamburlaine* (1587) and Jonson's *Masque of Blacknesse* (1605).

Representations of African figures in English culture ranged from *masques, 'Morisce' or 'Morisco' dancing, and the mystery plays of the medieval period, to pageants and plays of the Elizabethan, Jacobean, and even Caroline eras. What is notable about this scale of depictions is the emphasis on blackness, both literally and symbolically. Grades of colour were never stated with the exception of Robert Peele's *The Battle of Alcazar* (1594) and William Shakespeare's **Titus Andronicus* (1594) and *The Merchant of Venice* (1600), where clear distinctions are made between black and white 'Moors'. The colour division also denotes a distinction in morality. In Peele's play, for example, the black Moor Muly Hamet is the villain and 'subtle plotter', while his uncle Abdilmelec, the white Moor, is noble and righteous. The black Moor stereotype of the devilish, insidious villain was often utilized by Elizabethan dramatists as a deliberate contrast to white, incorruptible characters. In John Fletcher's *The Knight of Malta* (1647) the degradation of Mountferrat, the respectable knight, occurs when he moves from the white Oriana to the lustful and forthright black maid Zanthia. Similar depictions of black characters are made in *Lust's Dominion* (anon., 1657) and John Marston's *Wonder of Women: The Tragedy of Sophonisba* (1606), in which black men are presented as villainous, barbarous, and treacherous, and the women are seductive, charming, and impious.

The culmination of the representations of Blacks in Renaissance drama is perhaps Shakespeare's **Othello* where a blend of adherence to and deviation from the black stereotype creates a more human than racial character. Shakespeare used John Leo Africanus' information on black Moors, as well as his life story, to create Othello's character. Additionally, encounters with Africans on the streets of London and elsewhere in England would have provided Shakespeare with primary experience and material for his dramatization of Blacks. According to Eldred Jones, 'In the end Othello emerges, not as another manifestation of a type, but a distinct individual who typified by his fall, not the weakness of Moors, but the weakness of human nature.' The play proved to be particularly relevant to black actors such as Ira *Aldridge and Paul *Robeson, who found it to be symbolic of the black struggle for recognition and equality.

A popular dramatic figure in the Elizabethan and Jacobean period was that of Cleopatra. Four main productions that emerged were Samuel Daniel's *The Tragedie of Cleopatra* (1594), Shakespeare's *Antony and Cleopatra* (1623), John Fletcher's *The False One* (1620), and Thomas May's *The Tragedie of Cleopatra, Queen of Egypt* (1639). Apart from Shakespeare, dramatists usually depicted Cleopatra as a Greek princess ruling in an Egypt that was foreign and removed from her, where her light skin contrasted with the swarthiness of her subjects. Shakespeare, however, boldly departs from his sources, and creates a queen who is indeed the soul and embodiment of Egypt.

The ways in which actors blackened themselves changed over time. During the medieval period soot was used, but it was impermanent and faded too quickly. By 1547 black velvet masks, stockings, and gloves were used, despite the unrealistic effects they produced; the low level of realism needed in masques, however, meant that these were suitable options. When new degrees of realism in masques were established, black paint replaced the use of cloth. To produce more accurate portrayals of characters, wigs and headgear were worn to simulate African hair. In *Titus Andronicus* Aaron's reference to 'My fleece of woolly hair that now uncurls' would have been accommodated with a wig with short, curled hair tied with a ribbon. Costumes used in masques were generally grand and elaborate rather than realistic. On the popular stage, costumes varied from Moor to Moor. Aaron, in keeping with his exiled status, would have worn a more Western costume of a long-sleeved, square-necked, skirted doublet and tight-fitting breeches to emphasize his detachment from an African context. Abdilmelec, on the other hand, would have been dressed in flowing, exotic robes to signify his association with a foreign culture.

Contact between England and Africa augmented the dramatic scope of playwrights in the Elizabethan and Jacobean era, and provided them with multiple sources for their work. Even playwrights who did not deal directly with African characters referred to the gold of Barbary or to the mythic monsters, thus suggesting the magnitude with which Africa touched the dramatic imagination of Renaissance England. DD/SS

Hill, Errol, *Shakespeare in Sable: A History of Black Shakespearean Actors* (1984)

Jones, Eldred, *Othello's Countrymen: The African in English Renaissance Drama* (1965)

See also RENAISSANCE BRITAIN; TUDOR BRITAIN

Reparations. Term used to refer to the making of amends, particularly by the payment of financial compensation, for wrongs committed. It first came into widespread use with reference to payment for damages caused in wartime, particularly the reparations imposed on Germany by the Treaty of Versailles in 1919, following the First World War. In the late 20th century, at first in the United States and then elsewhere, the term increasingly came to refer to the argument that present-day governments of countries formerly engaged in the transatlantic *slave trade have an obligation to pay financial compensation to the descendants of those who were enslaved.

1. The terms of the debate
2. Britain, slavery, and the reparations debate
3. The case for black reparations
4. Conclusions

1. The terms of the debate By the mid-20th century the institutions of *slavery and slave-trading were recognized by international law as 'crimes against humanity', a special category in a long list of human rights violations and abuses. Immediately, the principle of retroactivity called into question the legal viability of redressing the wrongs associated with the enslavement of Africans in European modernity and genocidal actions against indigenous peoples caught within Europe's colonial project. The idea that it is possible to redress legally such historic wrongs at the level of national legislatures and judiciaries has given impetus to reparations discourses throughout the Atlantic world, and has spawned what is emerging as a global reparations movement.

The enslavement of Africans in the Americas and Europe was big business. The English occupied centre stage. An estimated 15 million enslaved men, women, and children were shipped by European merchants to 'new world' colonies. The English were second only to Portugal as principal exporters. The Portuguese accounted for an estimated 40 per cent of the transatlantic trade, the English 30 per cent. The English, however, seem to have been better at it in terms of financial gain, and their slave colonies in 1807, when the trade was declared illegal, were considered the most valuable.

The French Assembly has declared colonial slavery a crime against humanity. The British Parliament has not. The Dutch and Norwegian governments have called upon citizens to engage in acts of atonement and break the silence by actions of public recognition. In 2006 the Church of England issued a statement of regret, not an apology, for its role in fostering the transatlantic African slave trade, and for owning enslaved Africans on Caribbean sugar plantations. For most of the 18th century the Church owned hundreds of enslaved persons on two sugar estates in Barbados. The British government has issued no apology. It has been suggested that this reticence relates to legal opinion that such an action is likely to precipitate an avalanche of requests for reparations by descendants of the enslaved. In 2003 the government of President Aristide in Haiti placed a formal request before the French government for $21 billion in slavery reparations to assist with education and health care for the descendants of French slaves. Within months his government was overthrown by a join French–US military invasion force. The replacement government withdrew the claim and described it as 'criminal'.

In Britain advocates of reparations have tended to locate their arguments within international law. The Permanent Court of International Justice states that the essential principle contained in the actual notion of crimes against humanity is that, when proven, reparation must, as far as possible, follow. Reparations should wipe out all consequences of the illegal act and seek to re-establish a situation that in all probability would have existed if the act had not been committed.

In addition, the United Nations Charter, in Article 55, provides that the organization shall promote universal respect for human rights and fundamental freedoms for all without distinction as to race, sex, and religion. Slavery is defined as a crime against humanity that violates human rights, against which all victims have a right to reparations as a form of redress. The claimant is required to establish before law the following: that the crime was perpetrated; that there is documentary proof of the same; that there is continued suffering in the case of descendants; that there is a direct link between ongoing suffering and the historic crime. In addition, advocates of reparations have drawn attention to bilateral and multilateral treaties and conventions signed by the British government that are enforceable within national law.

Reparation is conceived as a process of repairing the damage done, and is legally set out in three distinct stages. Firstly, a formal apology is given to the victims of the crime by perpetrators and beneficiaries; secondly, there is a statement of commitment to repair the damage; and, thirdly, a commitment is offered not to repeat the crime. The formal apology, then, is the first step in a legal procedure, and is therefore avoided by those not willing to engage in the reparation process. Non-legal responses are usually preferred to a formal apology by avoiders, such as the issue of a statement of regret.

In Western government circles there has been a tendency to avoid reparations procedures. The preference has been for the issue of statements of regret and the making of voluntary settlements. This is considered a compromise position in that it may or may not acknowledge that a crime has been committed; it admits of no responsibility for the consequences of any illegal act; no apology is considered necessary or logical, but a sum of money or other material action is directed at alleged victims with rehabilitative objectives. The German government, for example, has paid reparations to the Jewish community for crimes committed against it before and during the Second World War by the Nazi regime. The Japanese government has made a settlement with the Asian Women's Fund for the sexual enslavement of Korean women by Japanese soldiers during the Korean War. The Japanese Diet has made a financial settlement but offered no apology. The German state has done both.

2. Britain, slavery, and the reparations debate While the case for reparations continues to face stiff opposition within the United Kingdom from academic communities, public policy formulators, state officials, and a wide cross-section of professional knowledge groups, there is evidence of growing support for a settlement approach that seeks intergovernmental financial compensation to post-slavery black countries in the form of debt forgiveness and relief, and broad-based financial support for development strategies. None of these has come into effect.

There are several reasons for this tendency. Reparations generate greater passion than any other contemporary issue, largely on account of their continuing resonance among descendants of the enslaved and enslavers alike. Those who oppose them have argued that slavery was not a crime, and certainly not a crime against humanity, within the historic context of the time; furthermore, that slavery was legally established in the constitutions of colonial societies, and supported by recognized legal opinion; in addition, that canon law, emanating from the Christian Church, provided moral and theological justifications.

Colonial English laws upheld property rights in enslaved Blacks and sanctioned slave-trading as the lifeline of the Empire. Laws provided that the enslaved be declassified as humans and confirmed their status as property, chattels, and real estate with no right to life or protection under any law designed for the governance of Whites. The legal denial of the humanity of Africans is considered by reparations advocates as the strongest proof of the crime of slavery in international law. Africans were described in early English colonial laws as a brutish and barbarous species. These laws, vetted and approved by government officials in Whitehall, classified Africans with livestock and other material assets. This status, furthermore, was reserved for Blacks. A white person could not be legally enslaved in any colonial jurisdiction. Blacks were presumed enslaved unless a document was presented to prove otherwise. The racial nature of enslavement anticipated the German crimes against the Jews, who were targeted as a race irrespective of class or other considerations. The Holocaust, too, was legal in that it received the backing of the German legislature and was the official policy of government. International law, however, provides that those who commit crimes against humanity should receive no solace or protection with the claim that the activity was legal under national law. There is provision to ensure that perpetrators and beneficiaries of such crimes are not absolved under national law.

The argument that slave-owning was legal in colonial jurisdictions and customary within Britain also serves to illustrate how the force of entrepreneurial interest assisted in shaping public opinion. In Britain there was legal and moral opposition to African enslavement from the outset. A considerable body of organized legal, moral, and political opinion spoke of its criminality. The more profitable the slavery complex became, the greater the marginalization of such anti-slavery voices. At the end of the 18th century these voices rose in importance and facilitated the sweeping away of the transatlantic slave trade and colonial slavery in 1807 and 1838 respectively. The timing of this development has also been persuasively presented in terms of the evolved economic vulnerability and diminished political utility of the slave system.

The presence of thousands of enslaved Africans in England urged Lord Mansfield to rule in the seminal 1772 **Somerset* case that as far as the legality of slavery was concerned a firm distinction ought to be made between colonial and metropolitan jurisdictions. The latter, he indicated, was a legal space that could offer slave owners no comfort on account of the repugnant nature of slavery to English jurisprudence. English society, he noted, featured the recognition of human rights as a legal concept that opposed the reduction of humans to slavery. The colonial space, however, was a different matter. The English, then, acknowledged that slavery was a crime, best practised in distant lands.

The enslaved, however, did not accept that their enslavement was legal. They recognized the crime, and opposed it whenever and wherever they could. Slave narratives that capture the views of the enslaved are replete with references to the perceived criminality of enslavement. Every generation of the enslaved in the Caribbean, for example, rose up in violent rebellion in order to overthrow the slavery order and regain their freedom.

3. The case for black reparations The argument against reparations also draws sustenance from the notion that political leaders in West Africa were major partners in the slavery projects. African governments and commercial elites, it has been said, were primary beneficiaries and partners, and therefore should equally be the target for reparations claims. Critics of this view argue that when Europeans arrived in West Africa to participate in slave-trading, they had already established in law and custom that slavery would not be applied to their own, and that Blacks were the only candidates for global enslavement. They have shown that many African governments resisted the trade, and some were destroyed as a consequence. Most, however, came to recognize that silence or collaboration was necessary for survival.

All crimes against humanity of this magnitude have generally had local collaborators. At the Nuremberg trials it was revealed that at least 2,000 Jews worked for the Nazi regime, and profited from its crimes. Jews everywhere, however, were targeted by the Nazis. Europeans were the principal beneficiaries of the slavery system, in that they built massive global empires upon its trade and production aspects, and used its networks to stimulate domestic economies. The existence of collaborators serves not to undermine European responsibility for the crime but to illustrate its heinous nature. Theories of victimization show, for example, that individual and group survival strategies invariably involve a measure of self-victimization through such collaboration and silence.

For crimes against humanity the right to redress is not lost by the passage of time. Descendants of victims are entitled to justice, and there are many instances where this has been done. Yet, the descendants of enslaved Africans have met considerable resistance at every turn, even though it is generally recognized that the transatlantic slave system constitutes the greatest crime against humanity known in the modern world. In British law there is no statute of limitation in respect of crimes against humanity. For this reason it has been argued by the reparations movement that the crimes of the 18th and 19th centuries can be addressed by legal procedures. Blacks continue to carry the stigma of antisocial racist ideologies and suffer the greatest degree of institutional discrimination. A series of official UK reports documents that Blacks receive the greatest hostility from police and the criminal justice system generally. These contemporary experiences of discrimination and deprivation are linked directly to the ideology of racial supremacy embedded in English society after 400 years of black enslavement.

The World Conference Against Racism, Racial Discrimination, Xenophobia and Related Intolerance held in Durban in 2001 provided a global forum for the ventilation of an official British position on the reparations issue. The British government joined with the European Union in attempting to block any formal discussion of the subject, and lobbied for its removal from the agenda. Following the walk-out by the United States on account of the item being so placed, the nations of Europe with a record of African enslavement secured non-binding status for the discussion insisted upon by African, Caribbean, Latin American, and Asian countries. The British position was that slavery is historically remote and not recoupable within the context of reparations discussion. Why should the British government apologize now, when slavery was abolished nearly 200 years ago? In any event, it suggested, slavery was legal at the time of its practice and not considered a crime against humanity. The slave owners are long gone, it was said, and the current government had legislated against all forms of slavery. A formal apology to Blacks, then, could not be considered a logical or ethical response.

The challenge to this argument was swift and precise. Slavery provided a principal source of revenue for growth within the private sector that contributed greatly to the emergence of industrial society in Britain. Furthermore, the proceeds of slavery enabled all citizens to achieve a higher standard of living and a greater sense of national well-being. Economic historians point to a direct causal link between Britain's rise as the leading slavery nation in the mid-18th century and development as the world's leading industrial nation. Britannia ruled the waves because it was motivated to protect a slave-based empire in the Atlantic world that was supported by slave ships and slave-based plantations.

British global success facilitated a popular culture and consciousness that was fuelled by the politics of global African subordination. In response, British officials suggested that slavery practised by state and citizens today would certainly be a crime against humanity.

4. Conclusions In the United States reparations have been paid by the state to groups other than Blacks and the indigenous community. Japanese Americans who were imprisoned and their property confiscated during the Second World War received reparations. Corporations have paid reparations to the descendants of Blacks whose forebears were owned as slaves by the company. Recently PJ Morgan, a leading financial corporation whose subsidiary in the 19th century owned slaves and used them as property in mortgage contracts, paid reparations to descendants. In the United Kingdom Lloyd's of London, which insured slaves and slave ships, has not formally owned up to its engagement. The first major English slave trade corporation, the *Royal African Company, established in 1672 with the Duke of York as chairman and other members of the royal family as major shareholders, enriched the monarchy in ways that are easily demonstrable. Queen Elizabeth II has apologized on behalf of British society for crimes committed against native Australians and New Zealanders. No formal apology has been offered to the descendants of enslaved Blacks. A major consideration no doubt is fear of reparations claims against the Crown.

It has been said that the reparations movement, despite winning minor victories in Durban, continues to hamper its own efforts. Loose talk of cash handouts and litigation against individual descendants of slave-owning families, including the royal family, have served to distract from more effective efforts at institutional empowerment. A recent survey by a group of distinguished British analysts suggests that the British state would be required to pay £7.5 trillion to compensate 6 million enslaved people in the Caribbean for 300 years of unpaid labour, trauma, pain and suffering, and loss of property that was a feature of British enslavement. In Durban, Caribbean nations framed their proposals in terms of full exposure and open debate of the evidence and financial support for relevant infrastructural development. Facilities and programmes listed for support included monuments, museums, sites of memory, school curriculum and criminal justice reform, and research centres.

The reparations debate has assumed global dimensions because of the global nature of the crime, and the cycle of guilt that has entrapped communities around the world. It has certainly generated considerable amounts of scientific research, though emotional rhetoric has predominated. This is understandable, since there has been no crime against humanity of this magnitude that has remained without redress at the highest official levels. It is a debate that is likely to gain intensity as the United Kingdom and other parts of the slave-owning world continue to stand by their formal denials. HB

Bray, Tamara, and Killion, Thomas W. (eds.), *Reckoning with the Dead* (1994)

Brooks, Roy L. (ed.), *When Sorry Isn't Enough* (1999)

Daniels, Roger, Sandra C. Taylor, and Harry H. L. Kitano (eds.), *Japanese Americans: From Relocation to Redress* (rev. edn., 1991)

Jones, Adam (ed.), *Genocide, War Crimes and the West: History and Complicity* (2004)

Williams, Eric, *Capitalism and Slavery* (1944)

Williams, Patricia, *The Alchemy of Race and Right* (1991)

See also BANKING AND INSURANCE

Repatriation. The demand for the repatriation of black immigrants and their UK-born dependants emerged as a major, disruptive demand placed on government by a campaigning right-wing anti-immigrant movement during the second half of the 1960s, and remained as a prominent and discordant feature of politics throughout the following decade. At one point it seemed possible that the basic structure of British political life established over the previous half-century, of a relatively stable two-party system mobilized on broadly centre-right and centre-left principles, was capable of being shattered by the establishment of a new movement advocating authoritarian, nationalist policies drawing its support from the lower-middle and working classes.

1. Immigration after the Second World War
2. Racial tension and violence
3. Calls for repatriation

1. Immigration after the Second World War All matters to do with *immigration during the immediate post-war period were looked on with apprehension by the British government, but the arrival of 'coloured' workers from the Caribbean, all with British subject status and therefore exempt from normal controls, was viewed as particularly disturbing. But the unexpectedly booming conditions of the post-war economy, creating a huge demand for new workers in key sectors, forced the authorities to improvise migration schemes that served the needs of British employers.

The first choice of the Attlee government was for workers of European stock who, as aliens and therefore subject to immigration controls, could be recruited on contracts that directed them into the labour shortage industries. However, the scope for recruitment of such workers was more restricted than the government had hoped, and out of the 720,000 job vacancies identified as being available for migrants only 345,000 were brought in under the European Voluntary Worker Schemes.

The resulting shortages opened up scope for migration from colonial territories and Commonwealth countries, whose peoples, being British subjects, were, in principle at least, free to live and work in the United Kingdom. Among this group, workers from the Caribbean, escaping high levels of unemployment, showed a particular propensity to take advantage of migration opportunities. Colonial and Commonwealth immigration rates are estimated at up to 10,000 a year from 1948 up to the mid-1950s, increasing to over 40,000 by 1956–7, before dropping back in response to a depression invoked by government deflationary policies to below 30,000 in 1958–9. Caribbean workers demonstrated that they were a useful addition to the UK labour market.

This is not to say that they were popular with government itself. As early as 1948 an interdepartmental government committee, convened to consider migration strategies, was warned in a memorandum from the Ministry of Labour that the **Empire Windrush* passengers had been 'useless and unwilling' for agriculture, and that female Caribbean workers were unsuited for employment in the textile industries. One of the Ministry's most senior officials warned that 'any scheme for the importation of coloured colonials for permanent settlement here should [not] be embarked upon without full understanding that this means that a coloured element will be brought in for permanent absorption into our own population'.

In the following years no less than five separate government committees met to consider measures to bring colonial and Commonwealth migration into a regime of controls, but failed in each instance because of the problems inherent in dividing 'undesirable' black immigration from the movement of 'kith and kin' from the dominions. In addition, and somewhat paradoxically given the evidence of racial prejudice in British towns and cities, there was throughout the 1950s an absence of obvious popular support for such measures. Attempts had been made by a group of pro-control MPs, led by Cyril Osborne, in 1954 to limit the admission of migrants from the colonies and Commonwealth countries, but generally these positions gained no political momentum.

2. Racial tension and violence But if this racism did not engage with the issue of immigration controls, it was operative at the level of the labour and housing markets in marking out the spaces, in terms of employment sectors, skill grades, professional occupation, and the areas that immigrants might be permitted to inhabit. Though officially deplored, the 'colour bar' was allowed to operate unchallenged by the authorities, on the grounds that it was improper for government to interfere with the liberties presumed to exist in civil society that allowed employers and landlords to take on as employees or tenants whomsoever they wished, in accordance with whatever prejudice.

This toleration of a festering culture of race prejudice in civil society demonstrated dramatic negative consequences later in the decade when major outbreaks of white violence against Blacks took place in the Nottingham and *Notting Hill riots in the spring and summer of 1958. The political elites chose to configure these developments as the basis for a revival of its own long-thwarted ambitions to introduce restrictions on Commonwealth immigration, rather than the alternative of a campaign to root racism out of civil society. During the course of the next few years the forces were assembled that allowed for the passage of the first Commonwealth Immigrants Act, in 1962, which introduced measures allowing the authorities to clamp down on the types of migration typical of people coming from the Caribbean, while leaving the routes used by mainly white Commonwealth citizens largely unaffected.

Throughout the debates that led to the introduction of these new policies, the government presented its approach as being in the interests of the immigrants themselves because controls were said to create the conditions in which their integration into the mainstream of British society might take place. In this way the imposition of immigration controls had supposedly benefited race relations and promoted the best interests of black minorities.

Whatever the benefits that arose from the race relations legislation promoted by the Labour government from the mid-1960s onwards, the reduction of controversy about the immigration of Commonwealth and indeed British citizens of colour was not one of them. The breaching of the principle of unrestricted rights for Commonwealth citizens which the 1962 Act embodied created an ever more voracious appetite for further restrictions, which, in 1968, were directed against Asian British passport holders who had been made victims of the expulsion policies of President Idi Amin in Uganda. But, more than this, agitators for further controls also had in their sights the further reduction of immigration from the Caribbean, which since 1968 had continued in the form of the reunification of the family members of immigrants who had already settled in Britain.

3. Calls for repatriation But even halting new arrivals was not enough for an even more militant wing of the anti-immigration movement. They would not be satisfied until the state equipped itself with the power to reduce the size of the black population of Britain with the adoption of strictly applied repatriation policies. Always present in immigration policy throughout the post-war period, repatriation moved from being a little-commented-upon instrument allowing for the payment of passage costs of immigrants, plus a small gratuity, to those who wished to return to their homelands, to a persistent and virulent demand for something that grew successively closer to the enforced removal of black people from the United Kingdom. As commentators remarked at the time, it was as though extreme anti-immigrant sentiment had been inflamed by the control measures introduced in the 1960s, rather than reduced.

The anti-immigrant cause, until then led by minor backbench figures who had been easily castigated by the party leaderships for their unsavoury views, gained momentum with the recruitment of the austere and grimly intellectual figure of Enoch *Powell to its ranks. Previously considered neutral on the question of immigration—and indeed during his three years as Minister of Health in the Macmillan government an active promoter of migration from the Caribbean for workers seeking employment in the National Health Service—Powell emerged from 1964 onwards as one of the most outspoken and extreme advocates of the anti-immigration position.

In his new guise Powell commenced his work with a defence of the racist positions taken by the Conservative Party and its candidate Peter Griffith during a notorious by-election in Smethwick in 1964. Within the space of a year he developed his position to the point of calling for controls to be supplemented by the repatriation of settled immigrants and their dependent family members. In an anonymous article published in *The Times* in November 1965, Powell advocated a 'steady flow of voluntary repatriation for the elements which are proving unsuccessful or unassimilable'.

In the summer of 1967 'race riots' in the United States startled British public opinion and allowed the right-wing press to ask 'if it could happen here?' Duncan Sandys, a Conservative Cabinet minister, made a speech in July, warning that 'The breeding of millions of half-caste children would merely create a generation of misfits and create national tensions.' In the renewed climate of anti-immigrant media coverage, even the Conservative leader, Edward Heath, seen as a liberal voice in the Party, was moved to call for strict controls and voluntary repatriation.

Powell then took the repatriation argument even further in a speech given in Gloucester in October 1967: 'We not only have to secure no addition to the Commonwealth immigrants still coming at an annual intake of 50,000, but we have got to establish an outgoing for those not fitting in, or fitting in less well . . . They must return to the country where they belong.'

The discourse of anxiety over the emergence of a generation of British-born black people, outnumbering even the increases brought about through migration, was developed during these days, with the only remedy being a form of repatriation moving from voluntary to something much closer to coercion. Vivid invocations of the 'madness' into which Britain had descended with its acceptance of black immigrants formed the themes of speeches by extremists up and down the country, until Powell's virulent 'Rivers of Blood' speech, delivered in Walsall in April 1968, forced his sacking from the Shadow Cabinet of Edward Heath, and led to a line being drawn within the Conservative Party indicating what forms of anti-immigration politics would be tolerated. It was clear that Powell was on the wrong side of that line, and henceforth the beneficiaries of his extremist advocacy would be a batch of new ultra-right-wing parties, which until then had been beyond the pale of normal electoral politics.

Chief among these was the National Front, which had been formed from an amalgam of ultra-right splinter groups during these years in order to take advantage of the new possibilities it believed existed for interventions into the political mainstream. Taking up Powellite themes after 1968, the National Front built an electoral base, which, by the general election of 1970, saw its small clutch of candidates polling an average of nearly 4 per cent in the constituencies they contested. From this modest start the party exploited the renewed immigration controversy associated with the arrival of Kenyan Asians, holders of British passports, which developed during the course of 1972. Calling openly for compulsory repatriation of all non-white people, including black people born in the United Kingdom, the National Front claimed large-scale defections from the mainstream parties to its ranks, and saw Martin Webster, one of its leaders, polling 16.3 per cent of the vote in the West Bromwich by-election of May 1973.

The National Front retained its position as the most successful fringe party in the country for several more years. In March 1977 it won an 8.2 per cent share of the poll in a by-election in Stechford, pushing the Liberals into fourth place. Fielding 91 candidates for the 92-seat *Greater London Council in May that year, it collected 120,000 votes, including nearly 18 per cent in Tower Hamlets, 14 per cent in Hackney, and 12.5 per cent in Newham. By this time the call for repatriation had been thoroughly associated with the

National Front's brand of extreme and often violent street politics, provoking the Conservatives to pull up the gang-plank that had linked its right wing to the National Front, blocking their rival's efforts to present themselves as 'respectable' in electoral terms.

Repatriation was, by this time, a policy that belonged exclusively to the National Front, and no longer had a meaningful resonance in its older 'voluntary' form. If the challenge of the National Front could be settled, the call for repatriation would fall by the wayside.

In 1977 the anti-racist left rallied its forces with the formation of the Anti Nazi League. Committed to a populist mobilization of anti-authoritarian, multicultural youth sentiment, the League organized a series of giant marches and anti-racist festivals that finally turned the tide of the right-wing campaign. But perhaps as significant was the emergence of a new right-wing leader in the Conservative Party in the form of Margaret Thatcher, who, practising a new form of 'racecraft', managed to reunite anti-immigrant feelings (as well as other prejudices) behind the banner of her brand of radicalism, without actually mentioning the 'r' word.

Paradoxically, one of the effects of the association of the demand for repatriation with extreme right-wing politics was the end of the plans that many Caribbean immigrants had to return to their home countries after completing a period of employment in Britain. The closure of the possibility of economic migration from the islands in 1962 had transformed the temporary residence of black workers into permanent settlement, and henceforth the Caribbean population grew as the immigrants sent for their partners and children from back home. The popularity of the once uncontroversial policy of voluntary repatriation after completing a stint working in Britain was continued in black communities by the agitation of members of the Rastafarian sect, who, following the tenets of their religion, called for a return, not to the Caribbean, but to the African homeland from which their ancestors had departed during the centuries of the slave trade. The energetic leadership of the Jamaican Ras Sam Brown in the 1960s led to negotiations between branches of the sect and governments in West Africa and Ethiopia, which were backed by supporters in the United Kingdom. Though the numbers who made the journey to Africa were small, *Rastafarianism continues to use the term 'repatriation' as an expression of its hope that Africa will become a home for all those scattered in the diaspora.

But for mainstream politics in Britain, a decade of turbulence induced by populist anti-immigrant campaigning ended with most of the players back in the places they had been in in the early 1960s, before the whole quarrel had begun, with the Conservatives characteristically opposed to all immigration, and Labour presenting itself as champions of racial harmony and integration. The worst effects of a disruptive, politicized racism, splitting the mainstream parties and threatening them with a new right wing, working-class populist movement, had, for the time being, been contained essentially through the state reassuring public opinion that it could itself manage immigration in the racially discriminatory way that appeared to be popular with the masses. There was therefore no need for the distressing hullabaloo that had characterized the debate to that point. This, of course, was the place the governing elites had wanted to be in from the very earliest days of the race and immigration debate, in the distant 1950s.

Repatriation seldom figures as an explicit demand of immigration control in contemporary Britain, and even the British National Party, the heirs to the National Front's legacy, claim that it has repudiated the ambition to remove all Blacks from the country. And yet, perhaps unnoticed by many, the British state has equipped itself with the power and authority to remove modern-day 'undesirable' and 'unassimilable' migrants from the country, in the form of the deportation of failed asylum-seekers, with an efficiency that would have provoked envy on the part of the early advocates of controls. Whether it is enough to settle the matter for future generations of xenophobes and racists remains to be seen. DF

Harris, Clive, 'British Capitalism, Migration and Relative Surplus-Population', *Migration*, 1/1 (1987)
Layton-Henry, Zig, *The Politics of Immigration* (1992)
Paul, Kathleen, *Whitewashing Britain: Race and Citizenship in the Postwar Era* (1997)

See also IMMIGRATION; REFUGEES AND ASYLUM-SEEKERS

Returnees. Immigrants who have returned to resettle in their country of origin. This entry looks particularly at immigrants from the Caribbean to Britain who have subsequently 'returned', either literally or in some other, more figurative, sense of the term.

1. Introduction
2. Categories of migration
3. Experiences of return

1. Introduction In the post-Columbian era the Caribbean has been a destination for migrants from most parts of the world, a source of emigration and a point of practical return. This tradition of people moving around—both within the region and across the North Atlantic world—is of particular relevance to the Commonwealth or English-speaking Caribbean. While the world in which they move around includes Africa, Asia, and Europe, in the main much of this movement has been to and from North America and Britain. Smaller in land mass and population than the Spanish and French Caribbean, but larger than the Dutch and American Caribbean, the English-speaking Caribbean has spread its people across the world, where they have made their presence felt in many areas of social, cultural, and political life. An essential aspect of this narrative is their propensity to return to the point of their departure.

In general, Caribbean returnees have historically engendered the sense of a common Atlantic world which has consolidated or extended the notion of a black or an African Atlantic. This returnee effect is not new. It goes back at least to the returnees from the great wars in Europe during the last century: after the *First World War the returning soldiers, sailors, and others arrived in the Caribbean with a new sense of nationalism that had been reawakened in places such as Ireland, and strengthened the regional movements for more self-government that had commenced in the 1880s. The *Second World War gave greater impetus to this movement. In the inter-war years sizeable migration to the United States had provided one of the bases for possibly one of the largest mass movements in modern times, that is, the messianic Marcus *Garvey movement, with its motto 'Africa for the Africans', and a call for Africans in the diaspora to return to the continent. Garveyism also spawned *Rastafarianism, which has been a significant feature in Britain.

2. Categories of migration But the experience of migration is heterogeneous and complex. Many Caribbean migrants leave home with the intention of gaining employment, saving, collecting desirable goods, and returning eventually either to the physical area they left, or to an area where they would have aspired to live in the normal course of upward social mobility, independent of the migration experience. Many such migrants move to other countries, with Britain, Canada, and the United States being perceived as among the most attractive destinations at different historical periods. However, the importance of migration within individual Caribbean countries—nearly always a migration from country to town—should not be underestimated.

Some migrants never return to their homelands at all, while others do so on a permanent basis. Other cases can perhaps be described as a kind of partial return, such as, for example, where the migrant arrives in the United Kingdom, then moves to the United States or to Canada in order to take advantage of opportunities, or simply to join family members who went directly from the Caribbean to that traditionally preferred destination, and are also closer to home. Another type of migration which is not, strictly speaking, a return, occurs when, as part of the process of globalization, family and kinship members, friends, neighbours, and leisure seekers visit (sometimes for protracted periods) the homes of those who have previously settled in a country like the United Kingdom, and then use this as a basis for further travel around the Atlantic world. This may include seeking to make diasporic links with Africa. Finally, descendants of immigrants born in a country such as the United Kingdom, including people of dual or multiple heritage (Caribbean and others), may decide to 'return' to the Caribbean for shorter or longer periods in search of jobs, to make investments, for leisure purposes, or some combination of these. Some individuals may undergo more than one of these experiences. Nevertheless, return remains a dream for the majority of migrants and their offspring, even though they may continue to use the dream as an inspiration for poetry and prose, music and art, as well as for seeking social and political change in the countries in which they live.

3. **Experiences of return** Those who have returned to the Caribbean tended, in their adopted countries, to be successful in business or the professions, and therefore took back with them a commodity with which to negotiate their way into the society to which they had returned. The returning migrant must be patently economically successful, and this was evidently the case in the decades of the 1960s and 1970s, a period in which few migrants returned permanently. Thus, the main contingent of returnees from the late 1980s appear to have been migrants who, decades earlier, arrived in Britain as young, healthy working people, but had now arrived at retirement age. These early, older returnees had often amassed capital in the form of savings, pensions, sometimes money from the sale of their homes in a buoyant UK property market, and other funds, as well as a very favourable rate of currency exchange. Returnees, therefore, may often represent an economic asset, and this has led governments for the first time to establish units in relevant government ministries to monitor returnees and encourage their return. HG

Abenaty, F., 'The Dynamics of Return Migration to St Lucia' in H. Goulbourne and M. Chamberlain (eds.), *Caribbean Families in Britain and the Trans-Atlantic World* (2001)

Goulbourne, H., *Caribbean Transnational Experience* (2003)

Nutter, R., 'Implications of Return Migration from the United Kingdom for Urban Employment in Urban Kingston, Jamaica' in R. King (ed.), *Return Migration and Regional Economic Problems* (1986)

See also FAMILIES

Richmond, Bill (1763–1829). African-American boxer who settled in Britain and became the first black boxer of international repute. Richmond was born in Cuckold's Town near New York and was a servant to a British general based there who later became Lord Percy, the Duke of Northumberland. In 1777 Percy sent Richmond to Yorkshire to study, after which he became an apprentice to a cabinet-maker in York. He taught himself how to box and subsequently turned to prize-fighting in London.

Richmond apparently created his own style of sidestepping and dodging the bull rushes of opponents. He was a formidable fighter despite his small physical structure. In 1805 he defeated two respected fighters—the Jewish boxer Youssop, and Jack Holmes, otherwise known as 'Tom Tough'—and his reputation took off. A major fight with Tom Cribb, one of England's most feared boxers and a future national heavyweight champion, saw an ignominious defeat, and he left the boxing ring for three years. When he returned, he beat Jack Carter and earned the nickname 'Black Terror'. As could have been expected, he received acerbic remarks about his skin colour in and out of the boxing ring. When he met Tom *Molineaux, another African-American boxer, they became friends, and Richmond trained Molineaux, who would later fight Cribb as well. Richmond retired at the age of 55 and kept a public house as well as a boxing academy, among whose students was the essayist William Hazlitt. DD/SS

Fryer, Peter, *Staying Power: The History of Black People in Britain* (1984)
Miles, H. D., *Pugilistica* (1880–1)
ODNB

See also SPORT

Robeson, Paul (1898–1976). African-American actor, singer, and political activist whose career was significantly based in Britain. He was born in Princeton, New Jersey, to William Drew Robeson, an escaped slave, and Maria Louisa Bustill. He was educated at Somerville high school, New Jersey, and Rutgers College and read law at Columbia University Law School, graduating in 1923. Precocious, he was an impressive figure, endowed with many talents, including that of athlete, footballer, singer, and actor, of which the last two would ultimately mark his international celebrity. Robeson's love of the theatre flourished early in his life, and his involvement in acting came in 1920, when he played Simon in Ridgely Torrence's 1917 play *Simon the Cyrenian*. Another early role was in Mary Hoyt Wiborg's *Taboo* (1922; later renamed *Voodoo*), which took him to England for the first time on a provincial tour of the play in 1922.

In England, Robeson gradually developed a political sensibility from his identification with the labouring and working classes. The mutual plight of oppressed communities, beyond the strictures of race, struck him profoundly. He forged a close relationship with English workers, seeing in their condition of neglect a similarity with the exploited black Americans. Of particular importance to him was the hospitality of the English towards him, which bore a striking contrast to the situation in the United States. After *Voodoo* failed to be taken to London, Robeson returned to America, where he starred in Eugene O'Neill's *All God's Chillun Got Wings* (1924) and *The Emperor Jones* (1920) with the non-commercial artistic group the Provincetown Players (Eugene O'Neill had insisted from the very first performance that black actors, as opposed to blacked-up Whites, should play the lead role). When the latter play opened on Broadway in 1925, the English producer Sir Alfred Butt negotiated for a London production. Robeson returned to England with his wife, Eslanda Goode (whom he had met at Columbia University, where she was the first black woman to head its pathology laboratory and with whom they would later have a son, Paul Robeson, Jr.). The play aroused various reactions in the British public, for they were not accustomed to the idea of a black dramatic actor. What was notable to them about the production was Robeson himself: his substantial presence, and his height, build, and colour. Thus, while the play was received with tepid enthusiasm, Robeson was acclaimed as something of an individual phenomenon.

Robeson's love of England was such that he could effortlessly claim that 'in England I have found perfect freedom and peace'. His treatment in England was not common for all Blacks, but Robeson managed to gain the affection and respect of even the most steadfast of imperialists. England provided him with the space and the opportunity to meet numerous public figures of the time, notably H. G. Wells, the imperialist press magnate Lord Beaverbrook, the daughter of the great African-American Shakespearian actor Ira *Aldridge, James Joyce, and the Jamaican writer and poet Claude *McKay. When, in 1927, he performed in *Show Boat* (1927), his rendition of 'Ol' Man River' gained him special recognition as one of the foremost singers of Negro spirituals. He received continuing support from the British public, and he in turn was sensitive to this reception. His affinity with the common people deepened to the extent that he began to sing for them at prices that they were able to afford. His desire was to bring together the peoples of the world through international folk music spanning areas as disparate as Ireland, Russia, Wales, Hungary, Slovenia, China, and

America. Throughout his life he would always adhere to the precept that 'the human stem was one'.

Robeson's role as Othello in the 1930 London production of Shakespeare's play fomented hostility and excitement among the British public as he was to play the part opposite Peggy Ashcroft, a white actress. The play itself was pertinent to Robeson because it symbolized the racial struggle endured by the colonized, particularly 'the problem of my own people'. *Othello* proved to be a success, and Robeson's stature as an actor in Britain increased. Subsequently he acted in numerous British productions such as Eugene O'Neill's *The Hairy Ape* (1921) and *All God's Chillun Got Wings*, and the Korda brothers' movie *Sanders of the River* (1935), a film that propagated uncritical notions of the benevolence of the British Empire. Robeson's participation in it was criticized by some of his admirers, but his involvement was not entirely negative as he met the future Kenyan leader Jomo Kenyatta on the set of the movie (Kenyatta had a bit part as a colonial native). This furthered his aspirations for acquiring a more formidable sense of his African roots. His meetings with various other future African leaders such as Nnamdi Azikiwe and Kwame Nkrumah, as well as the Trinidadian writer and historian C. L. R. *James, propelled him towards 'discovering' Africa, while at the same time shaping his sense of being black in Britain. He acted in C. L. R. James's play on the Haitian revolutionary Toussaint L'Ouverture, *Black Majesty* (1936), as well as in two films with an African theme, *Song of Freedom* (1936) and *King Solomon's Mines* (1937). Robeson also became patron of the *West African Students' Union.

The Spanish Civil War prompted Robeson's lifelong fight against fascism. His first overtly political act was perhaps at a rally in aid of Spanish refugee children at the Albert Hall in London in 1937, when he declared that he would no longer act in commercial films. He joined the left-wing theatre group Unity Theatre, and acted in unpaid productions with coherent working-class messages such as Ben Bengal's *Plant in the Sun* (1939). Despite his star status he refused special treatment, sharing with fellow actors in menial jobs like sweeping the stage. He became more active in the British labour movement and sang at several rallies in Britain, all the while provoking suspicion among the ruling classes because of his sympathies with the Soviet Union and his insistence that there could be no Western triumph over the Russians because that would augment the colonialist spirit. Robeson was soon labelled a communist and was investigated by the FBI for his supposed association with the Communist Party. In 1952 he was prohibited from travelling outside the United States. British support for him was immense and culminated in the 1956 Let Paul Robeson Sing Again campaign, which sought revalidation of his passport. He had earned distinction as a political activist, known for the earnestness which he displayed in his battle against colonialism, imperialism, racism, and oppression of any kind, and manifested in his protest against the imprisonment of black leaders in Kenya, his remonstration against South African racist policies, his support for the plight of the Welsh miners, and his advocacy of nuclear disarmament.

Another addition to Robeson's accomplishments is his autobiographical book *Here I Stand*, which was published in 1958. In 1959 he made British history by being the first black man to sing at the lectern in St Paul's Cathedral, London. The last performance of his dramatic career was, once again, as Othello at the Shakespeare Memorial Theatre in 1959. Robeson died on 23 January 1976 and was buried in Harlem, New York. DD/SS

Duberman, Martin Bauml, *Paul Robeson* (1989)

ODNB

Ramdin, Ron, *Paul Robeson: The Man and His Mission* (1987)

See also COMMUNISM; LITERATURE 3: DRAMA

Robinson Crusoe. Archetypal colonial novel by Daniel Defoe first published in 1719. Friday, a noble savage enslaved by

Crusoe, is often read along with *The Tempest*'s Caliban as the first fictional account of a colonized person.

The Life and Strange Surprizing Adventures of Robinson Crusoe of York, Mariner is based on the true story of the shipwrecked seaman Alexander Selkirk, who related his experience to Defoe after returning to England in 1712. In Defoe's story Robinson Crusoe is a middle-class Englishman who decides to find adventure on the sea rather than obey his father's wish to study law. A trip on a merchant ship turns to disaster when Moorish pirates capture Crusoe's vessel and he is sold into slavery in North Africa. He and a young slave, Xury, escape their captors and sail to freedom along the African coast, where Crusoe eventually buys his way to Brazil by selling Xury to a Portuguese captain.

Crusoe reinvents himself as a successful plantation owner in Brazil. Sea trouble soon strikes again when he is shipwrecked on an island off the coast of Trinidad during a slave-gathering mission to the West Indies. He lives in isolation on the island and becomes extremely religious, convinced that his predicament is punishment for disobeying his father. After several years he discovers a solitary footprint on the beach that he assigns to the cannibals who live nearby. Soon after, he saves a victim of a would-be cannibalistic feast and names him Friday. After instructing Friday to call him Master, he teaches Friday some English words and converts him to Christianity. Crusoe and Friday live harmoniously on the island and are eventually joined by Friday's father and a Spanish prisoner, after further confrontations with the cannibals. An English ship finally rescues Crusoe, who later returns to his island to find it a successful colony under Spanish rule.

Several elements of *Robinson Crusoe* make it relevant to colonial studies. The first is the recurring theme of slavery in the novel. After becoming a slave himself, Crusoe sells a companion back into slavery, sets out to buy slaves for his plantation, and creates a slave of Friday. Crusoe's transformation from slave to colonial master is made complete by his dominance over the island—he names himself 'king' shortly after being washed ashore, systematically exploits the land for his livelihood, and never questions his position of authority on the island. The methods in which Crusoe enslaves Friday also link him to colonial history. A fervent Christian, Crusoe is horrified by Friday's cannibalistic practice. He conceives of the cannibals as consuming solely human flesh and ignores Friday's claim the cannibals eat only enemies captured in battle. Crusoe replaces Friday's savagery with basic concepts of Christianity, making no attempt to understand Friday's culture. Crusoe also secures Friday's obedience by teaching his slave only a few words of English relating to daily island life and Christian morals, denying Friday a voice of his own.

A second theme that makes *Robinson Crusoe* relevant to studies of colonization is that of the *noble savage, common to other colonial texts such as Aphra Behn's **Oroonoko*. Although Friday is a descendant of what Crusoe believes to be a barbaric, cannibalistic culture, Friday is clearly not like other cannibals. Crusoe describes Friday as more European than black, with olive skin and typically European features, such as straight hair, a small nose, and flat lips. Friday's attitude towards learning and servitude also sets him apart from other natives. He is the perfect servant, never questioning his master's lesson or disobeying an order. The loving relationship between Friday and his father—a relationship Crusoe misses in his own life—again strengthens Crusoe's approval. Friday's noble savagery allows Crusoe to distinguish his slave from the nearby cannibals and makes Friday a perfect mould from which to create a loyal, European-style servant. Crusoe grows attached to Friday, who is the only person he expresses love for in the novel. However, it is only Friday's distance from his savage ancestry that allows Crusoe to engage with him in this way.

In addition to being read as an archetypal text of colonial literature, *Robinson Crusoe* is important to post-colonial literature. The abolitionist activist and writer Thomas *Day used Defoe's novel as inspiration for his best-selling children's anti-slavery story *The History of Sandford and Merton* (1783). The first text to rewrite Defoe's novel through Friday's eyes was Adrian Mitchell's play *Man Friday* (1972), made into a film starring Peter O'Toole in 1974. Mitchell's Friday is surprised when a European stranger 'rescues' him from a burial ceremony he is performing with his tribe. Instead of returning to England at the end of the play, Crusoe begs to be returned to Friday's island but is refused because Friday believes his presence will corrupt native tribes. J. M. Coetzee also deconstructs Defoe's text in *Foe* (1986), in which Friday is completely silenced when slavers cut out his tongue and is only able to express himself through dance. Other modern rewrites include Michel Tournier's *Vendredi; ou, Les Limbes du Pacifique* (1972), which explores the psychological aspects of Crusoe and Friday's relationship.

Robinson Crusoe also features in Caribbean literature. Saint-John Perse wrote the sequence 'Images à Crusoé' in 1920, while the figure of the castaway is a recurring theme of Derek Walcott's poetry, appearing in *The Gulf* (1970) and *Omeros* (1990). Inspired by the isolation of Crusoe's existence and his proximity to Trinidad, Walcott draws direct connections between Defoe's protagonist and the Caribbean experience in the *Castaway* collection, most notably in 'Crusoe's Journals' (1965). In later writing Walcott turns his attention to Friday; the play *Pantomime* (1978) gives voice to Crusoe's slave through a native-born Caribbean servant and a white expatriate hotel owner who act out Defoe's story in Tobago. EDS

Defoe, Daniel, *Robinson Crusoe* (1719)

Novak, M. E., *Daniel Defoe, Master of Fiction* (2003)

See also LITERATURE 1: REPRESENTATIONS OF BLACKS; POST-COLONIAL THEORY

Rock Against Racism. Movement set up in 1976 to combat the rise of the National Front in Britain through music. The Anti Nazi League, established in 1977, was a closely connected group that sought similar objectives through political organization.

Glam rock musicians such as David Bowie and Siouxse Sioux had flirted with swastika imagery, and after Enoch *Powell's 'Rivers of Blood' speech Eric Clapton spoke in support of the politician at a Birmingham concert. The photographer Red Saunders wrote a furious reply in the *New Musical Express*: 'Half your music is black. You're rock music's biggest colonist.' This triggered the Rock Against Racism movement.

Saunders, along with Roger Huddle, David Widgery, and others, organized two carnivals in London in 1978. The first, on 30 April, saw 80,000 people march from Trafalgar Square to Victoria Park, where acts such as the Clash, Sham 69, UK Subs, Misty, Tom Robinson, and the *reggae band Steel Pulse played. The second, on 24 September, brought 100,000 people to Brockwell Park. Smaller carnivals ran in Manchester, Cardiff, Southampton, Harwich, and Edinburgh, the last in Leeds in 1981.

The Clash emblematized the movement, which transformed punk into a multicultural, anti-racist phenomenon and influenced the *Two Tone revival. Their song 'Police and Thieves' adapted a Jamaican protest tune, while 'White Riot' encouraged young Whites to side with ethnic minorities in protesting the social problems of the period.

For Ashley Dawson, Rock Against Racism's relationship with the Anti Nazi League marked a grass-roots appeal to agitation, in line with C. L. R. *James's theories of community-based revolution. For Paul Gilroy, it attempted to decolonize the mind of *white* society. JM

Dawson, Ashley, 'Love Music, Hate Racism: The Cultural Policies of the Rock Against Racism Campaigns, 1976–81', *Postmodern Culture*, 16/1 (2005), <http://muse.jhu.edu/journals/postmodern_culture/toc/pmc16.1.html>

Gilroy, Paul, *There Ain't No Black in the Union Jack* (1987)

Renton, Dave, *When We Touched the Sky: The Anti-Nazi League 1977–81* (2006)

Widgery, David, *Beating Time* (1986)

Rodney, Walter (1942–1980). Guyanese historian and revolutionary. Rodney was born in Georgetown, British Guiana (now Guyana). His father was a tailor and his mother a seamstress, and despite hailing from a working-class background, Rodney excelled academically and won various scholarships to further his education. He was awarded a Ph.D. in African history in 1966 from the School of Oriental and African Studies. His doctoral thesis, which was on slavery between 1545 and 1800 on the Upper Guinea Coast, was published in 1970. Rodney was a daring academic and challenged Western suppositions of history and historiography. His first teaching post was in Tanzania, but he soon returned to the Caribbean to advocate the strengths of the Black Power Movement. The notion of Black Liberation was one that he spread across the poor in Jamaica, disclosing his knowledge of African history to the Rastafarians. Rodney's closeness to the lower classes incited suspicion in the Jamaican government. Thus, when he attended a Black Writers' Conference in Canada in 1968, the Jamaican Labour government forbade him to re-enter the country, leading to the outbreak of what became known as the Rodney riots. When Rodney returned to Tanzania, he became more involved in the struggles of the African people and as a result wrote his second major work, *How Europe Underdeveloped Africa*, which was published in 1972. When he returned to Guyana in 1974, he founded the Working People's Alliance and became active in the fight against the dictatorial government. Rodney and seven others were arrested and charged with arson after the burning of two government offices. He was assassinated in a car bomb explosion on 13 June 1980. DD/SS

Kwayana, Eusi, *Walter Rodney* (1988)
ODNB

See also POLITICS

Roman Britain. A common misconception is that the Romans in Britain were all born in Italy, had white skin, and spoke Latin. Not so: ever since the Emperor Claudius' multi-ethnic Roman army landed at Richborough in Kent in AD 43, there has been a black African presence in Britain (Britannia). Two types of Africans came to Britain: those who were Roman citizens, from African families of the ruling classes who had embraced Romanization (the acceptance of Latin and Roman culture), and those who did not necessarily have a choice, such as slaves and soldiers mustered in one of the Roman provinces in Africa.

1. Evidence
2. High-ranking officials
3. Soldiers

1. Evidence We have evidence of Africans and African influences in Roman Britain from a variety of sources: epigraphical (inscriptions), textual (written documents), and pottery (cooking and drinking vessels).

Robin Collingwood and Richard Wright show how inscriptions are to be found all round Britain, from Hadrian's Wall to London (Londinium), on a diverse range of objects, such as altars and dedication slabs (or parts of them), devoted to gods and goddesses, or the exploits of the Roman army; tombstones for the departed; building stones and makers' stamps on *mortaria* (earthenware mortars).

Robert Ireland explains that the Notitia Dignitatum, originally written about the 4th century AD, is known from an 11th-century copy called the Codex Spirensis. This 'Register of Dignitaries' was effectively two separate documents, the first dealing with the disposition of commands in the Western Empire, the second with the situation in the East. The Notitia is the main source of written evidence of one African presence in Britain.

Pottery is not necessarily an indicator of a physical African presence so much as of African influences on Roman Britain. Paul Tyers describes how North African cylindrical two-handled amphoras (used for storing wine and olive oil) and North African red-slip ware (plates, bowls, and dishes), produced in Tunisia and widely distributed around the western

Mediterranean and across the north-west provinces from the 2nd to 5th centuries AD, have both been discovered across Britain. For instance, red-slip ware has been found in large quantities at the Romano-British settlement of Bowness-on-Solway (Maia) in Cumbria, north-west England.

Gillian Dunn has recently published research that suggests that Roman *mortaria*, originally discovered during archaeological excavations in the 1930s at Chester Roman amphitheatre, showed signs of decoration used in North African *mortaria*, which led archaeologists to consider that it might have arrived in Chester with a North African soldier who was stationed there in the 2nd century AD.

2. **High-ranking officials** Anthony Birley notes how the Emperor Septimius Severus was born in Leptis Magna (Libya) and ruled the Roman Empire from AD 193 until his death at York in 211. Severus had overseen a number of military actions in defence of Roman Britain against barbarian forces and also undertook reconstruction of Hadrian's Wall. During the reign of Severus the Roman Empire was a multicultural mix of peoples from Syria, Germany, Spain, and Africa, and this was shown in the number of African men in positions of authority, such as the African Quintus Lollius Urbicus, who, Anthony Birley notes, governed Britain in AD 138.

3. **Soldiers** We have both epigraphical and documentary evidence of a number of African soldiers, legionaries, and auxiliaries stationed in Britain. Stanley Ireland describes how some of the Roman legions in which they served often took the names of either the Emperor who formed them, such as II Augusta in honour of the Emperor Augustus, or military exploits, such as Legio XX Valeria Victrix (Valiant and Victorious). Both legions were involved in the invasion of Britain in AD 43. Pete Salway estimates that legions had upwards of 5,000 men. Frank Snowden also gives an account of a black (Ethiopian) soldier, a popular jester in the army, greeting Septimius Severus after he had visited the fort at Luguvallum, now Carlisle.

Richard Benjamin notes that African auxiliary soldiers might have been stationed at the Roman fort of Burgh-by-Sands (Aballava) on Hadrian's Wall in Cumbria. The site was occupied from about the 2nd to the 4th centuries AD, and the evidence for this auxiliary unit, the Numerus Maurorum Aurelianorum (unit of Aurelian Moors which might have numbered up to 500 men), consists of an inscription found in 1934 at the village of Beaumont, 2 miles east of Burgh-by-Sands. The Beaumont Inscription was carved into an altar stone dedicated to the god Jupiter.

Eric Birley suggests that the name Aurelianorum refers to the unit being named in honour of the Emperor Marcus Aurelius (AD 161–80). He also notes how the Notitia Dignitatum mentions the *praefectus numeri Maurorum Aurelianorum, Aballaba*, 'prefect of the *numerus* of Aurelian Moors, at Aballava'.

Slavery was also a major part of Roman society, and as such many of those who were captured in military campaigns in Africa and other parts of the Empire would have made their way to Britain. In conclusion, epigraphical, textual, and pottery evidence shows us that there were Africans present in many sectors of Romano-British society and that, for almost 400 years, Roman Britain was very much a cosmopolitan society. RPB

Benjamin, Richard Paul, 'Roman Wall: Barrier or Bond?', *British Archaeology*, no. 77 (July 2004)
Birley, Anthony, *The African Emperor: Septimius Severus* (1988)
—— *Marcus Aurelius* (2000)
Birley, Eric, 'The Beaumont Inscription, the Notitia Dignitatum, and the Garrison of Hadrian's Wall', *Transactions of the Cumberland and Westmoreland Antiquarian and Archaeological Society*, 39 (1939)
Collingwood, Richard, and Wright, Richard, *The Roman Inscriptions of Britain* (1965)
Dunn, Gillian, *Africans in Chester* (2004)
Ireland, Robert, *Notitia Dignitatum* (2000)
Ireland, Stanley, *Roman Britain* (1986)
Salway, Pete, *A History of Roman Britain* (2001)
Snowden, Frank, *Blacks in Antiquity* (1970)
Tyers, Paul, *Roman Pottery in Britain* (1996)

Roscoe, William (1753–1831). English historian, writer, and active denouncer of the African slave trade. Roscoe was born in *Liverpool and was repelled by the *slave trade and its ubiquity in his home town, where most of its wealth was derived from the trade. He became politically active in the 1790s, and in October 1806 he was elected member of Parliament for Liverpool. One of his earliest speeches called not only for parliamentary reform and peace with France, but for the *abolition of the slave trade. He was spoken of highly by William *Wilberforce. Wilberforce referred to Roscoe as 'a man who by strength of character has risen above the deep-seated prejudices of his townspeople and eventually won their respect'. Roscoe's first published work, *Mount Pleasant, a Descriptive Poem* (1777), deprecated the slave trade. In 1787 he wrote and published *The Wrongs of Africa.* The poem promoted him to the position of leader of the movement for the abolition of the slave trade in Liverpool. As a consequence of Roscoe's writings and campaigning, he not only incited the anger of slave trade merchants, but also managed to get involved in a controversy with a former Roman Catholic priest who was using the Bible to defend the slave trade. The riots organized by slave traders and merchants in reaction to Roscoe's abolitionist efforts led to the termination of his parliamentary career. DD/SS

Chandler, G., *William Roscoe of Liverpool* (1953)

ODNB

Sanderson, F. E., 'The Liverpool Abolitionists' in R. Anstey and P. E. H. Hair (eds.), *Liverpool, the African Slave Trade and Abolition* (1976)

See also BLAKE, WILLIAM; CLARE, JOHN; COLERIDGE, SAMUEL TAYLOR; COWPER, WILLIAM; DAY, THOMAS; SOUTHEY, ROBERT; WORDSWORTH, WILLIAM

Royal African Company. English slave-trading monopoly active between 1672 and 1713. The Company is credited with sending 5,000 ships to Africa carrying £500,000 of English goods, transporting over 90,000 African slaves to West Indian plantations, and importing 30,000 tons of sugar by the beginning of the 18th century.

The Royal African Company was formed on 27 September 1672 by a group of English merchants previously involved in the Company of Adventurers of London Trading into Parts of Africa. It suffered financial troubles from the start, blamed largely on the slow turnover of trade and the extensive credit granted to West Indian planters. The Company's funds were also crippled by its role in the construction and strengthening of forts on the West African coast, believed by the British Parliament to be essential to maintaining English interests in Africa.

The Company traded English textiles, metalware, and firearms to three regions of the West African coast: the north-west, specializing in goods sold in England; the Gold Coast, providing gold and slaves; and the mid-east, supplying slaves. African goods were shipped directly to England, while slaves were traded for sugar in Jamaica, Barbados, Nevis, St Christopher, Antigua, and Montserrat.

The Company's monopoly was largely criticized by English merchants eager to enter the slave trade. In 1698 African trading was opened to all on payment of a 10 per cent duty; this Act expired in 1712 and was not renewed. EDS

Davies, K. G., *The Royal African Company* (1957)

See also SLAVE TRADE; SLAVERY

Royal African visitors. During the Scramble for Africa delegations from several African countries travelled to Britain. Many were royal delegations, often well organized and well funded. Despite the preconceptions held by many Europeans of the period, many of these leaders were worldly, well connected, and often knowledgeable about the process of imperialism that they were experiencing. Many spoke several languages and, thanks to their contacts with missionaries, they tended to be Christian and literate. Such knowledge and education led some African leaders to believe that an opportunity existed for them to negotiate directly with the British Crown and government in London, thereby bypassing the often less sympathetic colonial authorities and thwarting the expansionist ambitions of Britain's men on the ground in Africa.

The most successful of the royal African delegations to travel to Britain was that of Bechuanaland, modern-day Botswana. In 1895 three paramount Bechuana chiefs, Bathoen, Sebele, and Khama, travelled to Britain. They came in an attempt to persuade Queen Victoria and the Secretary of State for the Colonies, Joseph Chamberlain, to protect their lands from Cecil Rhodes's British South Africa Company. Rhodes was planning to incorporate their kingdoms into the Crown territory that was to become Rhodesia. With the assistance of the London Missionary Society this trinity of African kings toured Britain appealing to the sentiments of the British middle classes. They were the sensation of 1895 and were successful in negotiating directly with Chamberlain. Although they lost land, they were able to keep out of Rhodesia, a development that built the foundations for the eventual creation of the independent state of Botswana.

Some royal African visits seem also to have had a large impact upon how the great mass of British people viewed empire. The African kings arrived in their finery at a time when there were perhaps only a few thousand black people in Britain. The combination of royal status and black 'otherness' was highly exotic and caused great excitement. In the case of the Bechuana delegation this excitement appears to have reached its peak when the kings toured the British provinces, taking the exoticism of the Empire out of London to parts of Britain from which Africa seemed even more distant and remote.

Very little is known about what these educated literate Africans made of high Victorian and early Edwardian Britain. The best source for their views is the journal of the Ugandan diplomat Ham Mukasa, who visited Britain in 1902 as part of a royal delegation to attend the coronation of King Edward VII. DO

Comaroff, John L., and Comaroff, Jean, 'Through the Looking Glass: Colonial Encounters of the First Kind', *Journal of Historical Sociology*, 1 (1988)

Mukasa, Ham, *Uganda's Katikiro in England: Being the Official Account of His Visit to the Coronation of His Majesty King Edward VII* (1904)

Parsons, Neil, *King Khama, Emperor Joe, and the Great White Queen: Victorian Britain Through African Eyes* (1998)

Rushton, Edward (1756–1814). Abolitionist poet. Rushton lived most of his life in Liverpool, but gained first-hand experience of the slave trade and of Jamaica when he worked as a ship's mate in the 1770s. A slave friend, Quamina, whom he had taught to read, died rescuing him when his boat capsized. During this time he contracted ophthalmia, which left him blind for most of his life. On his return, he bore witness to the brutality of slavery in his *West-Indian Eclogues* (1787), a series of four poems written in the voices of fictional slaves and presenting them as dignified and seething with righteous anger. The poems, which attracted wide public notice, including that of Thomas *Clarkson and William *Roscoe, deal explicitly with the sexual abuse and sadistic punishments inflicted on slaves, and their right to violent resistance. The notes to the *Eclogues* make a more conservative case for the economic expediency of better treatment of slaves. After the publication of this work Rushton remained a republican and radical campaigner. His 1806 collection of poems included a poem in support of Haitian independence, and a new Jamaican eclogue. In 1797 he publicly reproved George Washington for owning slaves. He also wrote an *Essay on the Causes of the Dissimilarity of Colour in the Human Species*, first published posthumously in 1824, in which he argued against biologically determinist notions of racial hierarchy. KO'B

Rushton, Edward, Jr., 'Biographical Sketch of Edward Rushton', *Belfast Magazine* (Dec. 1814)

Shepherd, W., 'Sketch of a Life of the Author' in Edward Rushton, *Poems and Other Writings* (1824)

See also COLERIDGE, SAMUEL TAYLOR; COWPER, WILLIAM; SOUTHEY, ROBERT; WORDSWORTH, WILLIAM

Rutherford, Anna (1932–2001). Publisher and Professor of Commonwealth Literature. Ceaselessly energetic in her organizational and publishing activities, Australian-born Anna Rutherford was revered in Commonwealth academic circles for her efforts to establish the study of post-colonial literature in Europe.

For 28 years, from 1968 to 1996, Rutherford directed the Commonwealth Literature Centre at the University of Aarhus, organizing symposiums, seminars, and readings involving leading British-based black scholars and writers such as Wilson Harris, Sam *Selvon, Buchi Emecheta, and Shiva Naipaul. She introduced African and West Indian courses and, in 1971, organized the first European conference on the Commonwealth novel, a project involving many future British professors including Louis James (Kent) and Paul Edwards (Edinburgh), who went on, in their own universities, to promote the research that gave the discipline of Commonwealth literature intellectual respectability.

Rutherford was the first woman chair of the Association of Commonwealth Language and Literature Studies (which draws scholars from 300 universities) and, in the 1970s, founded the Association's European branch, which became a powerful lobby for the expansion of the English literature curriculum in European academies.

Rutherford was editor of *Kunapipi*, then Europe's leading post-colonial literary journal. *Kunapipi* regularly carried prose, poems, and interviews by black British writers like Caryl Phillips, Fred D'Aguiar, Grace Nichols, and John Agard. She also owned and managed a small publishing house, the Dangaroo Press. It was her love of the finely produced book, and her disdain for the slick commercialism of the publishing industry, that attracted writers to her small press. Every year, laden with a huge rucksack of new books, she would trudge along Charing Cross Road, calling in at various bookshops to sell a copy here and there. She loved books in all their stages—from the editing of manuscripts to the supervision of printing and placement with the bookseller.

In later years the constant struggle to access small grants to subsidize her books or conferences wore Rutherford down. She began to suffer from physical ailments, and then severe depression. She resigned from Aarhus, ending up at the University of Warwick in 1998 as a visiting fellow. In 1999 she returned to the place of her birth, Newcastle, Australia, where she died in 2001. Tributes from scholars and writers from all over the Commonwealth were read out at her funeral. DD

Nelson, K., and Nelson, D., *Sweet Mothers, Sweet Maids* (1986)

See also INTERNATIONAL BOOK FAIR OF RADICAL BLACK AND THIRD WORLD BOOKS; PUBLISHING

S

Sable Venus, The. Poem written in Jamaica by the Revd Isaac Teale (d. 1764), an Anglican clergyman, at the request of his pupil Bryan Edwards (1743–1800), who was probably responsible for its appearance as a separate item printed in Kingston, Jamaica, in 1765. Edwards later printed it, in a slightly different form, first in a collection of poems published in Jamaica in 1792, and then in his *History, Civil and Commercial, of the British West Indies* (first published 1793; several later editions and reprints).

Edwards claimed that in the poem 'the character of the sable and saffron beauties of the West Indies, and the folly of their paramours, are pourtrayed with the delicacy and dexterity of wit, and the fancy and elegance of genuine poetry'. At least on the surface, *The Sable Venus* is a celebration of the beauties of black women, which are claimed to be equal or superior to those of their white counterparts, and much is made of the attractiveness of these beauties to white Jamaican men. It is possible that the poem was intended to be satirical; Edwards certainly disapproved of the custom, widespread in the Caribbean, of white men keeping black or mixed-race mistresses, calling it a 'vicious system of life, as odious in appearance, as it is baneful to society'. At the same time, he rejected interracial marriage, saying, 'the very idea is shocking'.

Teale was a competent versifier and the poem could be said to have a certain charm within the literary conventions of its time. However, it does not take much reading between the lines for the modern reader to realize that the central episode of the poem (in which the Sable Venus, on her voyage from Angola to the West Indies, in a sea-chariot drawn by winged fish, is accosted by Neptune in the form of a British naval captain) is an allegory of rape on board a slave ship, and that the poem as a whole celebrates racialized sexual exploitation, rather than black beauty as such. While Edwards was not as virulently racist as Edward *Long, his inclusion of Teale's poem in his well-known *History*, thus giving it a considerable circulation, probably contributed to the phenomenon that it exemplified, the commodification of black women as objects of curiosity or desire for white men. The way in which Sarah *Baartman's British contemporaries called her the 'Hottentot Venus', for example, appears intended to inscribe her into the same discourse.

The second edition of Edwards's *History* (1794) added an illustration of the Sable Venus, engraved by William Grainger (*fl.* 1784–94) after a painting (now untraceable) by Thomas Stothard (1755–1834), a well-known British artist of the period. Both the poem and the illustration have been extensively commented on by modern scholars of slavery and racial attitudes.

JG

Edwards, Bryan, *History, Civil and Commercial, of the British West Indies* (5th edn., 1819)

—— *et al.*, *Poems, Written Chiefly in the West-Indies* (1792)

Smith McCrea, Rosalie, 'Dis-Ordering the World in the Eighteenth Century: The Voyage of the Sable Venus. Connoisseurship and the Trivialising of Slavery' in Sandra Courtman (ed.), *Beyond the Blood, the Beach and the Banana: New Perspectives in Caribbean Studies* (2004)

[Teale, Isaac], *The Sable Venus, an Ode. Inscribed to Bryan Edwards, Esq.* (1765)

See also LITERATURE 1: REPRESENTATIONS OF BLACKS

Saint-Georges (or Saint-George), le Chevalier de. Assumed name of Joseph de Bologne (or Boulogne) (*c*.1740–1799), international composer and violinist and one of the best fencers in Europe. He was born in Guadeloupe as Joseph, the son of George de Bologne, a wealthy plantation owner. His mother, Nanon, was an African slave. He and his mother were taken to France in 1753. He received a gentleman's education at the fencing school La Boëssière's Royal Academy of Arms. Its focus was on academic study, music, dance, and languages. His fame at fencing was such that he was called le Chevalier de Saint-Georges.

François-Joseph Gossec (1734–1829) invited him to be leader of the Concerts des Amateurs orchestra in 1769, and later, its musical director. Between 1772 and 1777 he composed, premiered, and published violin concertos, some of the earliest string quartets in France, violin sonatas, and symphonies concertantes. George *Bridgetower performed the concertos in England. Saint-Georges was in demand for his virtuosity as a violinist. However, his bid to be a director of the Paris Opera failed owing to racial discrimination, and his operas were not often performed.

During 1781 he set up the Orchestra de la Loge Olympique, which performed in the Palais Royale. In 1785 he played a key role in the commission of Haydn's 'Paris' Symphonies. Employment from 1779 with the Duke of Orléans ended in 1785, on his death, so Saint-Georges gave fencing exhibitions in London for the Prince of Wales. Between 1790 and 1793 he was involved in French revolutionary activity as a colonel in the National Guard. He died in 1799, in Paris, all the French national newspapers celebrating his memory with respect and emotion. PAH

Banat, Gabriel, 'Le Chevalier de Saint-Georges, Man of Music and Gentleman-at-Arms: The Life and Times of an Eighteenth Century Prodigy', *Black Music Research Journal*, 10/2 (1990)

Floyd, Samuel A., Jr. (ed.), *Dictionary of Black Composers* (1999)

Ribbe, Claude, *Le Chevalier de Saint-Georges* (2004)

See also MUSIC 1: CLASSICAL MUSIC

Salkey, Andrew (1928–1995). Novelist, travel writer, and poet. Born in Panama, at the age of 2 Salkey left for Jamaica, the focus of much of his literary work. There, cared for by his grandmother until the arrival of his mother (his father stayed in Panama), he attended St George's College and Munro College. It was at this point that Salkey made his first connections with the London literary scene through the submission of his writing to the BBC's **Caribbean Voices*. When he migrated in 1952 to study English Literature at the University of London, he continued his artistic pursuits, and through further involvement in *Caribbean Voices*, began to build up many contacts within the arts industry.

These proved useful when, in 1966, Salkey joined forces with Edward Kamau Brathwaite and John *La Rose to create the *Caribbean Artists' Movement (CAM). However, such contacts were also invaluable to many new writers such as V. S. Naipaul, who became acquainted with his publishers André Deutsch through Salkey, and Wilson Harris, whom Salkey introduced to Faber and Faber. Alongside his work for CAM, Salkey was employed as a freelance scriptwriter, interviewer, and broadcaster for the BBC, working not only for the Caribbean Service, but for the African, Pacific, and Overseas Services too. Interestingly, through this position he was able to interview Martin Luther King on his visit to the United Kingdom in 1964.

Salkey's own literary career began with the publication of his first novel, *A Quality of Violence*, in 1959. This was followed by around 30 books, written and edited by Salkey, ranging from novels for adults and children to travel journals and poetry anthologies. Throughout, his consistent concern is with investigating the Caribbean and its relationship to its colonial past. For instance, in his novel *The Late Emancipation of Jerry Stover* (1968) social realism is used to examine the vibrant world of 1960s Kingston, in which the egotistic youth Jerry Stover and his friends reside. Throughout the novel Salkey deconstructs the seemingly affluent liberation of these characters, showing that emancipation is fictitious. Although slavery has been abolished, Jamaican society remains entrapped in indifference and an unconscious acceptance of capitalism and colonial values.

In 1976 Salkey moved to the United States, becoming a Professor of Writing at Hampshire College in Massachusetts. He died on 28 April 1995. Salkey is remembered for being a writer prepared to call out wholeheartedly for Caribbean people to discover who they are, and to understand (to quote from his poem 'Jamaica'), 'how much history | under them skin'.

CA

Dance, Daryl Cumber (ed.), *Fifty Caribbean Writers: A Bio-Bibliographical Critical Source Book* (1986)

James, Louis, *Writers from the Caribbean* (1990)

ODNB

Walmsley, Anne, *The Caribbean Artists Movement 1966–1972: A Literary and Cultural History* (1992)

Sambo (of Sunderland Point, Lancaster) (d. *c.*1736). African slave and servant buried on the north side of the Lune estuary and subject of an 18th-century elegy. Sambo had been brought to Sunderland Point around 1736, most probably as an enslaved servant to a ship's captain. Wharfs and warehouses had existed here since *c.*1720, when the Quaker merchant Robert Lawson had them built for his colonial trade, primarily with the West Indies. Disease would seem the most likely explanation for Sambo's untimely death following his transatlantic crossing, and he was buried close to the shoreline in unconsecrated ground to the west of the village.

Some 60 years later, the Revd James Watson came to hear of Sambo's fate when staying at Sunderland Point and was moved to pen a sentimental elegy wherein he represents Sambo's life as captured African turned plantation slave, dutiful to his master and convert to Christian belief. The retired chaplain and Lancaster headmaster went on to have a freestone slab, complete with commemorative brass plaque, placed over Sambo's grave, paid for by visitor donations. Ironically, the Revd Watson's two younger brothers were some of Lancaster's most committed investors in the slave trade. Interestingly, it was after both had died that he executed his tribute to Sambo in 1796.

Today, Sambo's isolated yet much visited burial site at Sunderland Point endures as a powerful evocation not just of one life tragically uprooted but of many lives transformed for ever by transatlantic slavery.

AME

Rice, A., *Radical Narratives of the Black Atlantic* (2003)

Sancho, Ignatius (1729–1780). African writer whose letters, published posthumously in 1782, became a best-seller, attracting 1,181 subscribers including the Prime Minister, Lord North.

Sancho was born on board a slave ship en route to the West Indies. His mother died soon after, of a tropical disease, and his father chose to commit suicide rather than endure slavery. Sancho was brought to England by his master, at the age of 2 or 3, and given to three maiden sisters living in Greenwich. The sisters named him Sancho, thinking he resembled Don Quixote's squire. They kept him in ignorance, not teaching him to read or write. He was rescued by the Duke of *Montagu, who lived nearby in Blackheath. The Duke, encountering the boy by accident, took a liking to his frankness of manner, and frequently took him home, where the Duchess introduced him to the world of books and of high culture. He eventually ended up working as a butler in the Montagu household.

The patronage and encouragement of the Duchess inspired Sancho's creativity. He wrote poetry, stage plays, and a theory of music, and composed songs and minuets for violin, mandolin, flute, and harpsichord. An annuity left him by the Duchess enabled Sancho to set up a grocery shop in Charles Street, Westminster, selling slave-produced goods such as tobacco, coffee, and sugar. The shop became a meeting place for artists, musicians, writers, and politicians. Charles James Fox, the Whig leader and first British Foreign Secretary, visited him there. Sancho, who had established a reputation as a connoisseur of the arts, was often sought out for his opinions. In 1779 the writer George Cumberland was so delighted to discuss literary matters with him, and so elated at the latter's high opinion of his writing, that he vowed to buy all his tea and sugar from Sancho's shop. Other friends and acquaintances included David Garrick, the Shakespearean actor; the novelist Laurence Sterne; the sculptor Joseph Nollekens; and the artist Thomas Gainsborough (who, in 1768, painted his portrait). Samuel Johnson promised to write his biography, but died before it could be undertaken.

The Letters of Ignatius Sancho, some 159 pieces of correspondence to friends and admirers, range over subjects as diverse as family life (his abiding and tender love for his black wife, Anne, and seven children), the state of the arts, political manoeuvrings, social inequalities, and the Gordon riots. Sancho was an eyewitness to the last, recording the mob violence, the nightly burnings, and devastation, in his own words, 'the worse than Negro barbarity of the populace'. The ironic description reveals his willingness to poke fun at himself and his colour. In many letters he called himself a 'coal-black, jolly African', 'a poor Blackie grocer', and 'a man of a convexity of belly exceeding Falstaff—and a black face into the bargain'.

His friendship with Laurence Sterne began in 1766, Sancho writing to express his admiration for *Tristram Shandy* and entreating Sterne to turn his literary attention to the subject of slavery. Sterne, whose own father died in 1731 from a fever after his regiment had been posted to Jamaica to quell a slave rebellion, responded immediately and with considerable excitement at receiving a letter from an African. Sterne obliged by including in the final volume of *Tristram Shandy* (which appeared in 1767), an argument about the humanity of black people. His prose style—full of digressions and strewn with dashes, asterisks, and diagrams—had a direct influence on Sancho's writing, which is similarly non-linear, disorganized, eccentric, broken. Sancho's adoption of Sterne's style allowed him to express in *literary* form the experiences of the diasporic enslaved African, which were of instability, uprootedness, and rupture.

The letters reveal Sancho's profound love of literature and the depth and breadth of his reading. He is always recommending books to the young. In 1778, for instance, he writes to Jack Wingrave, the son of a bookseller friend, recommending Oliver Goldsmith's *Roman History* and *History of England*; two volumes of sermons by Mr Williams, a dissenting minister; and poems by John Milton, Edward Young, and James Thomson, poems that 'were my summer companions for near twenty years—they have mended my heart—they improved my veneration of the Deity—and increased my love to my neighbours'. In 1780 he writes to Jack again, saying, 'I would neither give thee *Money*—nor *Territory*—*Women*—nor *Horses*—nor *Camels*—nor the height of Asiatic pride, *Elephants*;—I would give thee *Books*, fair Virtue's advocates and friends!' In his various illnesses (gout, dropsy, asthma) it is his inability to write that frustrates him. In 1780, the year of his death, he complains to friends of his 'scrawling hand—in truth my eyes fail me'. On 7 December 1780 he writes his last letter, to his friend and patron John Pink, which ends with the bleak confession that 'my poor belly is so distended, that I write with pain—I hope next week to write with more ease'. He died exactly a week later, of an illness complicated by gout and corpulence.

Sancho's letters were collected from his various friends and published in 1782, the editor declaring that her purpose was to show that an untutored African possessed abilities equal to a European, and to raise money for his family. The book reviews were enthusiastic, the *European Magazine* of 1782 declaring that the volume 'presents to us the naked effusions of a negroe's heart, and shews it glowing with the finest philanthropy, and the purest affections'. Sancho's son William turned the grocery store into a bookshop. DD

King, Reyahn, Sandhu, Sukhdev, Walvin, James, and Girdham, Jane, *Ignatius Sancho, an African Man of Letters* (1997)

ODNB
Sancho, Ignatius, *The Letters of Ignatius Sancho* (ed. Paul Edwards and Polly Rewt, 1994)

See also ABOLITION; EQUIANO, OLAUDAH; SLAVERY

Scarman Report. Following the *Brixton disorders of April 1981 the Home Secretary, William Whitelaw, appointed Lord Scarman to undertake an investigation into the causes of the disturbances. The results of the Inquiry were published in the Scarman Report, which offered a scrupulous examination of the social issues behind the violent events of Brixton and included a number of relevant recommendations.

Before considering the course and pattern of the events that occurred between 10 and 12 April, the Report presented an outline of Brixton's local environment, addressing in particular the issues of education, poor housing, discrimination, and unemployment. It identified in this complex of social, political, and economic factors the key elements that 'create a predisposition toward violent protest'.

The event that precipitated the unrest took place on Friday 10 April, when two police officers attempted to assist a young black man who was severely injured. Under the impression that he was being arrested, three other black youths jostled the police officers and encouraged the injured man to run off. He was intercepted shortly afterwards by two other officers, who administered first aid and called for an ambulance. An inquisitive crowd rapidly gathered and suddenly a group of 30 to 40 people, mainly young Blacks, surrounded the officers. The injured man was pulled away, carried off by the crowd, and then put in a private car and taken to the hospital.

In the meantime bricks and bottles were thrown at the police officers, who called for assistance. A missile broke the windscreen of a police transit van and a police officer was wounded as a result. The unrest lasted for about an hour, and by the time the incident was over six people had been arrested, six police officers injured, and four police vehicles damaged. In the light of the day's events, foot patrols in the area were increased with effect from 11 p.m. and continued throughout Friday night and into Saturday.

Rumours about the incident involving the injured youth began immediately to circulate in Brixton. It was said that the police officers had prevented the youth from going to hospital, that they had refused to call an ambulance, and that they had in fact caused the youth's injury themselves. On Friday night several community leaders were summoned to a meeting with the police to be presented with the facts of the day and to assist in dispelling the rumours and easing the tension.

On Saturday 11 April heavy police presence was noticeable in the streets of Brixton. Besides this, Swamp 81, a crime control operation employing officers in plain clothes to patrol the streets in pairs and to stop suspects, was kept in action in the area. At about 4.40 p.m. two officers engaged in the operation saw a man placing something in his socks; suspecting that he was dealing in drugs, they stopped him and searched his car. A hostile crowd rapidly gathered, and a black man was arrested for obstructing the police in the execution of their duties. It was at that point that the disorders broke out again and the situation slipped out of control.

The confrontation between crowd and police quickly escalated into chaos. A wide area of central Brixton was affected by episodes of violence, arson, and looting. Several people were assaulted in the attacks on public houses and shops, and altogether 219 police officers, 14 firemen, and 45 members of the public were reported injured. A total of 145 premises were damaged and 4 ambulances, 9 fire appliances, 61 private vehicles, and 56 police vehicles were damaged or destroyed. Although less intense, the disorders recurred on Sunday and finally ceased by 1 a.m. on Monday.

The Scarman Report found that the disorders were not premeditated, but originated spontaneously as a reaction to what was seen as police harassment. However, an element of leadership and direction did rapidly emerge and the disturbances soon developed into a riot. Despite the strong racial element in the disorders, the Report discarded the argument that they were racial riots and concluded that they were essentially an outburst of anger and resentment by black youths against the police arising from complex socio-economic circumstances.

The Report also gathered that a major cause of the hostility was loss of confidence in the police, caused by 'hard' policing methods; the collapse of the police liaison committee in 1979; distrust in the procedures for investigating complaints against the police; and racially prejudiced conduct by some police officers. Both the police and the community leaders carried some responsibility for the enduring atmosphere of distrust that lurked behind the outbreak of the disorders.

Lord Scarman advanced a number of proposals and recommendations for improving the quality of policing in modern multiracial societies. In particular, he recommended the study of methods of enhancing the recruitment of ethnic minorities into the police; the extension of the initial period of training for police recruits; and the re-examination of policing methods in sensitive areas. He also endorsed a proposal by the *Commission for Racial Equality to incorporate racially prejudiced behaviour as a specific offence in the Police Disciplinary Code and to make it punishable with dismissal.

In general, the central contention of the Report was the need to embrace social policies that effectively eradicate racial disadvantage. It explicitly advised the government to tackle inner-city problems, with particular attention to the areas of housing, education, and employment, and to create ethnic-minority opportunities in all sectors. LG

Scarman, Lord, *The Scarman Report: The Brixton Disorders 10–12 April 1981* (1981)

See also MACPHERSON REPORT; 'SUS LAW'

Scholes, Theophilus Edward Samuel (*c.*1858–*c.*1940). Doctor and writer who was born in Jamaica and grew up in Stewart Town. He studied medicine in Glasgow, later touring Scotland and Ireland to raise funds for Africans to Christianize Africa. He left for the Congo in 1886, where he ran a sanatorium. He returned to Europe in 1887 and eventually took an MD degree at Brussels in 1893; in the same year he went to the *African Training Institute at Colwyn Bay, a training school for Africans. He went to Calabar, Nigeria, for the Institute. This experience stimulated his writing, and in 1899 he published *The British Empire and Alliances: Britain's Duty to Her Colonies and Subject Races*, in which he attacked the disparagement of Africans and pointed out the similarities across societies in development. In 1903 his *Chamberlain and Chamberlainism: His Fiscal Policies and Colonial Policy* attacked the controversial Colonial Secretary Joseph Chamberlain. Two years later volume I appeared of his major work *Glimpses of the Ages; or, The 'Superior' and 'Inferior' Races, So-Called, Discussed in the Light of Science and History* (volume II was published in 1908). Here he attacked the beliefs that underpinned the colonial Empire and pointed to its inefficencies and incompetence, the propaganda that supported it, and the ways in which black people were prevented from developing.

Scholes had a wide circle of admirers, among them Pixley Seme, a founder of the African National Congress in South Africa, Alain *Locke, the African-American scholar, and Sol *Plaatje, the author of *Native Life in South Africa* (1916), who asked him to read the manuscript. In the 1930s Jomo Kenyatta and the British Guianese Ras *Makonnen, the Pan-Africanist, visited him. He apparently returned to Jamaica in the 1930s and died there. PF

Green, Jeffrey, *Black Edwardians: Black People in Britain, 1901–1914* (1998)
ODNB

See also DOCTORS; MEDICINE

Scotland. The black presence in Scotland can be traced back as early as the 16th century. However, it is not until the late 18th and 19th centuries that one finds significant groupings of African,

Caribbean, and African-American peoples in Scotland, and so more detailed records of their activities. These relate in particular to a number of black students in Scottish universities at the time. With the institutions of Oxford and Cambridge then only admitting members of the Church of England, many African and Caribbean people wishing to study in Britain went instead to London or Scotland. In 1998 the Nobel Prizewinning author Toni Morrison, invited by the University of Glasgow to give a reading from her work, is reported to have expressed her pleasure at the offer from what at one time was 'one of the few places in the world where African-Americans could gain a higher education'.

Although in the 3rd century there was a contingent of black African Roman soldiers stationed near the border town of Carlisle to protect Hadrian's Wall, the first reliable documented evidence of Blacks in Scotland pertains to a small group of Africans attached to the Court of King James IV. Probably taken from a Portuguese slave ship, there were several women among the group, one of whom was baptized and one of whom had a poem written about her by the Scottish poet William Dunbar. Dunbar records her participation in a spectacular show—the black knight and the black lady—in which the King himself played the part of the knight. In 1513 there were still two black women at the Scottish Court; and by the reign of James VI at least one African continued to live in Edinburgh: he stood in for a lion as a pageant performer in 1594 during celebrations to mark the birth of the King's eldest son.

In 1757 the black presence again surfaced within the machinery of the Scottish state as the courts came to consider the issue of slavery. A slave bought by Robert Sheddan in Virginia claimed his liberty, having been baptized in Scotland; but the slave died before the court reached a decision. In 1778, however, the **Knight* v. *Wedderburn* case—the Scottish equivalent of the **Somerset* case—found in favour of Knight, with the court asserting that black slavery was not recognized by Scots law—a more sweeping judgment than Lord Mansfield's in 1772. Interestingly, the slave-owning Wedderburn's son, conceived with a slave from Jamaica, went on to become the black revolutionary Robert *Wedderburn.

As the *Wedderburn* case suggested, some of the more radical anti-slavery opinions in Britain were to be found in Scotland. In 1833 the Glasgow and Edinburgh Emancipation Societies were formed following the abolition of slavery in the British West Indies; they called for abolition worldwide, and especially in the United States. The anti-slavery campaigner Frederick *Douglass found a receptive audience in Scotland, and spent a large part of the first six months of 1846 there, returning again in July, September, and October to deliver well-attended lectures. In addition, the 19th century saw many black students at Scottish universities. At Edinburgh the Afro-West Indian Literary Society was established, which, in 1900, sent two delegates to the Pan-African Conference in London: John *Alcindor, a Trinidadian who had graduated from Edinburgh University medical school in 1899 with first-class honours in three subjects; and William Meyer, another Trinidadian from the same institution. Also educated there were Theophilus E. Samuel *Scholes, the Jamaican author of three critical studies on British imperialism, and James Africanus *Horton, born in Sierra Leone and the author of four medical and three political books.

Other significant black students at that time included Christopher James Davis, a Barbadian who studied medicine at Aberdeen, served as house physician at St Bartholomew's Hospital, went to France during the Franco-Prussian War to help fever-stricken and starving peasants, and died of smallpox at the age of 31. Thomas Jenkins, meanwhile, reputedly the son of a king from the Guinea coast, was brought to Scotland for his education. Left stranded when his benefactor died, he educated himself until sufficiently qualified to apply for a schoolteaching post.

Rejected on this occasion because of his colour, Jenkins was later provided with his own school and stipend by the Duke of Buccleuch, before continuing his education at Edinburgh University. Abdullah Abdurahman, the future president of the South African Native and Coloured People's Organization (later known as the African People's Organization), also studied in Scotland, qualifying as a physician at Glasgow University in 1893. The black cabinet-maker and radical William *Davidson likewise received his education from various Scottish institutions.

Alongside these elite figures were lower-class Blacks who, while their numbers were not sufficient to form large communities of the kind seen in London, nevertheless had an impact on a local level. As one of Britain's leading trading ports, *Glasgow in particular was a focal point for immigration and settlement. Indeed, by the beginning of the 20th century its black population was well established. By 1919 a black social club and the African Races Association of Glasgow had been founded. However, in the same year it also experienced the first in a series of *'race' riots, which would affect nine ports in Britain and were provoked by attacks on Blacks by certain sections of the white working class. A little over 60 years later Edinburgh was the scene of race riots, this time directed against the police and part of the wave of disturbances that swept Britain following the *Brixton uprising.

Although the number of Blacks in Scotland remains relatively low compared with England, the black presence continues to exert an influence upon culture. Indeed, the question of a black Scots identity has become an issue within discussions over the construction of a 'post-colonial' Scottish identity following devolution and the establishment of the Scottish Parliament in 1999. Novels such as Irvine Welsh's *Trainspotting*, for example, have taken up the theme, with the depiction of black Scots and attitudes towards them forming part of the interrogation of national identity. MGN

Jenkinson, Jacqueline, 'The Glasgow Race Disturbances of 1919' in K. Lunn (ed.), *Race and Labour in Twentieth Century Britain* (1985)

Lorimer, Douglas A., *Colour, Class and the Victorians: English Attitudes to the Negro in the Mid-Nineteenth Century* (1978)

See also ROMAN BRITAIN; TUDOR BRITAIN

Scramble for Africa. The British presence in Africa dates back to the 16th century, but until the 19th century its territorial control was limited to a few forts and strategic enclaves. During the Napoleonic Wars, British forces briefly occupied Cape Colony (1795–1803) and Egypt (1801–4). Sustained British territorial occupation of the continent began with the acquisition of Cape Colony (1806), Sierra Leone (1808), the Gambia (1817), Lagos (1861), and the Gold Coast (1874). A mixture of mercantilism, the African *slave trade, European imperial rivalry, and later anti-slavery and Christian evangelization drove the British presence in Africa.

The pace of the British acquisition of territories quickened with the onset of the European Scramble for Africa in the 1880s. Fuelled by industrialization, the quest for raw materials and new markets, the opportunity to invest excess capital, as well as pseudo-scientific racism and imperial chauvinism, different European countries rushed to control as much African land, people, and resources as they could through dubious treaties, intimidation, and violence. British missionaries, traders, and adventurers also fuelled the imperial rush by actively campaigning for their country's military and political control of African states and societies.

Historians debate the precise events that triggered the European Scramble for territories in Africa. Some argue that three events in 1879, namely the French exploratory missions to construct a trans-Saharan railway, the appointment of Major Gustave Boignes-Desbords as commander of Upper Senegalese French troops with an expansionist mandate, and the Congo missions and treaties of Henry Stanley Morton (1841–1904) and Pierre Savorgnan de Brazza (1852–1905), set off the Scramble.

Others posit the British military occupation of Egypt after Ismail Pasha's default on his international debt and the Ahmad Urabi Revolt in 1881–2 as the main trigger.

By 1884–5 there was no doubt that the Scramble for Africa was at full speed; Britain along with twelve other European countries and the United States met in Berlin under the auspices of the German Chancellor, Otto von Bismarck (1815–98), to hammer out the rules of colonization of the continent. From 1884 to 1914 the continent was embroiled in conflict as the British and other Europeans wrested territory and power from different African states and peoples. Some African groups succumbed to British imperialism out of fear; many others resisted fiercely. In Sudan the Mahdist Movement held off British colonial forces between 1881 and 1899. Between 1898 and 1899 Bai Bureh (1840–1908) fought British expansion into the Sierra Leone hinterland. In 1900–1 Yaa Asantewa (b. 1821), Queen Mother of Ejisu, led Asante forces in a final stand against the British. Muhammad Abdullah Hassan (1856–1921) resisted British colonialism in Somaliland from 1899 to 1920.

By 1910 the European Scramble was over and African resistance largely quelled. Britain ended with seventeen colonies, encompassing over 4.07 million square miles and 61.4 million people. The colonies were Egypt, Anglo-Egyptian Sudan, Kenya, Uganda, British Somaliland, Northern Rhodesia (now Zambia), Southern Rhodesia (now Zimbabwe), Nyasaland (now Malawi), Bechuanaland (now Botswana), Basutoland (now Lesotho), Swaziland, South Africa, Sierra Leone, Nigeria, British Gold Coast (now Ghana), and the Gambia. IR

Boahen, Adu, *African Perspectives on Colonialism* (1987)

Hobson, John A., *Imperialism: A Study* (1902)

Packenham, Thomas, *The Scramble for Africa: The White Man's Conquest of the Dark Continent from 1876–1912* (1991)

See also AFRICA AND BRITISH COLONIALISM

Seacole, Mary Jane (*c.*1805–1881). Jamaican nurse, hotelier, entrepreneur, writer, and heroine of the Crimean War. She was born Mary Grant, but no official records of her birth or parentage exist; in her autobiography, *Wonderful Adventures of Mrs. Seacole in Many Lands* (1857), she stated her father to be a soldier of Scottish descent (possibly James Grant of the 60th Regiment of Foot) and her Creole mother to be the keeper of a Kingston hotel, Blundell Hall, and a well-respected 'doctress', skilled in the traditional African use of herbal remedies. Her mother's guests and patients included British army officers garrisoned in Kingston, and Grant enjoyed a close relationship with the Army all her life. She had one sister, Louisa Grant (*c.*1815–1905), and a half-brother, Edward Ambleton, who died during the 1850s.

Grant was educated by an elderly woman described in the autobiography as 'my kind patroness' (p. 2), and by her mother in cookery and medicine. During her teens, succumbing to what she called an irresistible and unladylike 'inclination to rove' (p. 2), she twice travelled to London, and in her twenties sailed to the Bahamas, Cuba, and Haiti, trading home-cooked pickles and preserves for shells and fancy goods, for which she found a ready sale in Kingston.

In 1836 Grant wed an Englishman, Edwin Horatio Hamilton Seacole (1803–44), in Kingston. She believed her husband to be a godson of Lord Nelson, but this cannot be confirmed. Together the Seacoles moved to the port of Black River, on Jamaica's south-west coast, to open a general store. Like Edwin's health, however, this venture failed to thrive and by 1843 both were back in Kingston.

Blundell Hall was consumed by the great fire of 29 August 1843; Edwin died in October 1844, and Seacole lost her mother around the same time. Temporarily cowed by this triple blow, she settled in Kingston to rebuild her livelihood. But by 1851 she was off again, choosing Panama—then the Republic of New Granada—for her next destination. Her brother Edward had already set up a hotel at Cruces, en route across the isthmus to the newly discovered California goldfields; Seacole opened her own hotel right opposite Edward's.

Seacole struggled to make the hotel pay. American clients, she complained, preferred not to patronize any establishment fronted by a black woman, and there were not enough British visitors—whom she favoured—to go round. An alternative income came from an outbreak of cholera during her stay: using her experience of treating yellow fever in Jamaica, she nursed all comers, gladly accepting payment from those with the money. She carried out a pioneering autopsy one night on an infant, the better to understand the disease and help her patients.

Seacole was back in Jamaica when she heard of the outbreak of the Crimean War in 1854. Her immediate response was to apply to British authorities as a nurse. She considered herself eminently qualified, being medically experienced, independent, strong, fiercely patriotic, and eager to do her duty. Expecting a grateful welcome, she sailed to London in the autumn of 1854. She applied to the War Office, the Quartermaster-General's Department, the Crimean Fund, and to Florence Nightingale's organization. Perhaps understandably, she was ubiquitously rejected. None had the courage to engage a stout 'yellow' woman (her word) dressed in vulgarly bright colours, at nearly 50 well past middle age, 'unprotected' (i.e. without male relations to take responsibility for her), loudly insistent, and obviously used to being in charge. Seacole was stunned: she had rarely met what she considered to be colour prejudice from the British before, and found it impossible to justify. But the setback only fuelled her desire to reach the Crimea for the sake of her 'sons', or British soldiers. Entering into a business partnership with Thomas Day, a relative of her late husband, she announced the imminent opening of a Crimean 'British hotel' and general stores, and sailed for Balaklava in February 1855.

The hotel, fondly known as Mother Seacole's Hut, soon became a Crimean institution. It was built of scrap beside a stream on Spring Hill, between Balaklava and Sevastopol. Seacole is mentioned with affectionate admiration in first-hand accounts of the war, as famous for her fine roasted bustards or rice puddings as for tending the sick and wounded with warmth and good humour. But Florence Nightingale mistrusted her, and feared her nurses associating with this unorthodox exotic. Nightingale's principal objection was that she served alcohol at her hotel, and prescribed it to her patients. Nightingale aimed to change the system; Seacole simply wanted to make her 'sons' feel better.

A hasty evacuation of troops followed the war's end in April 1856, leaving Seacole with unsettled bills and unsaleable stock. On her return to London that summer she was declared bankrupt. But a philanthropic succession of benefit festivals and subscription funds, patronized by Queen Victoria and other members of the royal family, ensured relative comfort for the rest of her life. In 1857 her autobiography—the first by an African-Caribbean woman in Britain—was published to great acclaim. The next quarter-century was punctuated by visits to Kingston, where she owned two properties; she unsuccessfully volunteered to nurse victims of the *Indian Mutiny in 1857 and the Franco-Prussian War in 1871; she enjoyed what appears to have been a remarkably close relationship with Princess Alexandra; and sometime between 1857 and 1860 she converted to Roman Catholicism.

Seacole died in London on 14 May 1881, and was buried at her own request in St Mary's Catholic cemetery at Kensal Green. She was mourned as a British heroine, then promptly forgotten, surely in part because her colour and defiant self-possession forbade her from becoming a fashionable role model for Britain's young ladies. Recently she has emerged again, thanks to a reprint of *Wonderful Adventures* edited by Ziggi Alexander and Audrey Dewjee in 1984, as a peerless model of self-belief, triumph over prejudice and preconception, and sheer strength of character. JHR

ODNB
Robinson, Jane, *Mary Seacole* (2005)

Seacole, Mary, *Wonderful Adventures of Mrs. Seacole* (ed. Sarah Salih, 2005)

See also GEORGIAN AND VICTORIAN BRITAIN

Second World War (1939–1945). After the *'race' riots, 1919, the black presence in Britain was increasingly regarded as a social problem. Black men continued to be portrayed as feckless and immoral, with a tendency to prey on white women, who in turn were depicted as either vulnerable or dissolute. Popular press coverage of the criminal trials of Jamaican-born Eddie *Manning, the so-called 'Dope King of London', provide the most notable examples. Making their appearance periodically for much of the 1920s, these reports exemplified a widespread sense of unease around race and gender identities that were destabilized during the war and Depression era.

In a less sensationalist fashion, the press kept alive fears of *miscegenation, a primary influence upon white racial violence during and after the *First World War. In the eyes of the media, children born of white women and black men served as tangible proof that the race and gender boundaries of Empire had been violated. By the 1930s the fate of these children became a central feature of discussions around race relations in Britain. 'Mixed-race' children were presented as victims, who, having inherited the black man's purported disinclination for industrious activity and tendency to irrational behaviour, would be condemned to life on the margins of society. The *League of Coloured Peoples (LCP) tried to counter this negative coverage with two reports that linked the poverty and lack of opportunity experienced by the black population to official and popular discrimination. But anxieties around miscegenation became even more pronounced during the Second World War when black service personnel began arriving in Britain from the British West Indies and, from 1942, the United States.

By the late 1930s, in the Empire at large, dissatisfaction with British rule was becoming increasingly apparent. This was most evident in the wave of industrial and political unrest throughout the British West Indies and Pan-African protests directed at the failure of the League of Nations to challenge the Italian invasion of *Ethiopia. In the United Kingdom anti-colonial sentiment was most evident in the pages of the *Negro Worker* (distributed by the Red International of Labour Unions), the *Negro Welfare Association, and the *West African Students' Union.

However, the declaration of war in September 1939 once more encouraged black people throughout the Empire to demonstrate their loyalty to Britain. Not only did many harbour renewed hope of post-war reform, but, for those committed to national liberation, a war considered as a struggle between the 'free world' and Fascism instilled a profound sense of duty. But many of the obstacles to equal black participation in the forces were still in place, including the denial of commissioned rank to black men and women. The LCP immediately began to lobby the Colonial Office to demand the removal of this obstacle, forcing the reversal of the policy, albeit for the duration of the war only. The four children of the LCP's founder, Harold *Moody, were among the small number of black British subjects from across the Empire who successfully enlisted as officers, in both the armed and medical wings of the forces.

Many black Britons also served in a civil defence capacity. The LCP's *News Letter*, which had replaced *The Keys* at the start of the war, proudly listed the names of black people in Britain who had enlisted in the war effort as air raid wardens and first-aiders, including the Jamaican boxer 'Buzz' Barton.

From 1941 the British government began to recruit service personnel and skilled workers in the West Indies for service in the United Kingdom. Over 12,000 saw active service in the Royal Air Force. A further 2,500 were employed in war factories in the North-West or as foresters in Scotland. About 600 West Indian women were recruited for service in the Auxiliary Territorial Service, arriving in Britain in the autumn of 1943. The enlistment of these volunteers was accomplished despite official misgivings and obstruction. But the arrival of the US Army in 1942, along with its segregationist regulations, contributed to the hardening of official British policy towards black Britons, contrasting with the usually less overt conventions of paternalistic Imperial racism.

The British War Cabinet tried to tread a fine line between acquiescing in US segregationist attitudes and maintaining the loyalty of black volunteers from the Empire. At first, the British urged the Americans to restrict the numbers of black troops they sent to Britain, the excuse being that any enthusiasm shown towards them by British Whites would offend US racial sensibilities.

When this failed, the British government prevaricated, until Major-General Arthur Dowler, military administrator in charge of southern Britain, circulated proposals on the conduct of relations between white British and black American troops. Although Dowler had broken War Cabinet instructions by committing his guidelines to paper, in the absence of further official advice his notes became the main authority on the issue. The memo characterized black Americans as simple-minded and spendthrift, and insisted that white service personnel, especially women, should avoid any contact with black servicemen to avoid potential racial unrest.

Increasingly, despite the loyal commitment of black troops and the wartime rhetoric of a united Empire, black Britons continued to be regarded as third-class citizens, denied access to both opportunities and services. This was illustrated most profoundly in 1943 when the cricketer Learie *Constantine, who was serving in the Ministry of Labour as a welfare officer for West Indian war workers, was refused accommodation in London's Imperial Hotel. In a landmark case, Constantine successfully sued the hotel for breach of contract, although he only received token damages.

But the Second World War is perhaps most significant in the context of the black British experience because it helped to shape the pattern of post-war migration and post-war race relations. During the war many of the ethnic and cultural groups from both the Caribbean and Asia, who would characterize mass migration to Britain, began to arrive in small numbers, either as workers or as military volunteers. Equally significant was the emerging vision of Britain as a beleaguered island race, rather than a great Imperial power, particularly after the humiliating surrender of Singapore to the Japanese in February 1942. This image would be dramatically recast after the end of the war and the onset of mass migration. Despite the eventual Allied victory, many sectors of society increasingly saw Britain as a nation engaged in a rear-guard action against the growing black presence. RS

Bousquet, Ben, and Douglas, Colin, *West Indian Women at War: British Racism in World War II* (1991)
Little, Kenneth, *Negroes in Britain: A Study of Race Relations in English Society* (1947)
Noble, E. Martin, *Jamaica Airman* (1984)
Sherwood, Marika, *Many Struggles: West Indian Workers and Service Personnel in Britain (1939–45)* (1985)
Somerville, Christopher, *Our War: How the British Commonwealth Fought the Second World War* (1998)

See also EMPIRE WINDRUSH; FIRST WORLD WAR; WEST INDIAN WOMEN AT WAR

Selvon, Samuel (1923–1994). Trinidadian writer and founding member of the Caribbean literary renaissance best known for introducing Creolized English to British literature. Selvon was born in the town of San Fernando, Trinidad, the son of a first-generation East Indian immigrant and an Anglo-Scottish mother. Though racial tension was widespread in the Caribbean at the time, Selvon spoke widely of his strictly Creolized upbringing. The theme of Creolization would later dominate his writing.

Selvon did not continue his formal education beyond high school, which he left at the age of 17. Influenced by his literature lessons at school, he began to write while working as a wireless operator for the Royal Naval Reserve during the *Second World War. Following the war he became a journalist for the *Trinidad Guardian* and later the fiction editor of the literary magazine the *Guardian Weekly*. During this time Selvon's poems, short stories, and articles appeared in Caribbean literary magazines such as the Barbadian journal *BIM*, while the BBC Overseas Service programme **Caribbean Voices* broadcast several of his radio plays. Most of this early writing is featured in his *Foreday Morning* (1989).

Inspired by the British landscape, which influenced his writing, Selvon immigrated to London in 1950 and survived his early years in England through various part-time jobs and freelance writing. His first novel, *A Brighter Sun*, was published to critical acclaim in 1952 and focuses on the development of Tiger, a young Indo-Trinidadian farmer. He decided to become a professional writer after spending time in hospital with pulmonary tuberculosis and being awarded his first Guggenheim fellowship in 1955.

Although Selvon's professional writing career was sustained by frequent part-time work, his period in England was prolific. *An Island Is a World* (1955), acknowledged by Selvon to be his most personal novel, is also set in Trinidad and marks his first exploration of the Trinidadian middle class. *Turn Again Tiger*, the sequel to *A Brighter Sun* and also set in rural Trinidad, appeared in 1958. He began what is commonly referred to as his 'London', or 'immigrant', writing with *The Lonely Londoners* in 1956. The episodic novel, narrated in Creolized, non-standard English, highlights the difficulties of a Trinidadian immigrant, Moses Alloeta, and his friends in establishing themselves in England. *Moses Ascending* (1975) and *Moses Migrating* (1983) are regarded as sequels to the earlier novel, though both feature a distinct departure from the Creolized language of *The Lonely Londoners*. Selvon's 'immigrant' writing is completed by the short-story collection *Ways of Sunlight* (1957), half of which is set in London, the other half in Trinidad.

Selvon was awarded a Trinidadian government scholarship and published *I Hear Thunder*, again set in middle-class Trinidad, in 1963. *The Housing Lark* (1965), his most comic novel, added to the theme of housing difficulties faced by black immigrants in England introduced in *The Lonely Londoners*, and employed a similar dialect in the narrative voice. After being awarded a second Guggenheim fellowship in 1968 and the Trinidadian honour, the Humming Bird Medal, in 1969, he returned to the island when commissioned by the British sugar company Tate & Lyle to write about the sugar industry. The experience resulted in *The Plains of Caroni* (1970). *Those Who Eat the Cascadura* (1972) is also set in Trinidad and focuses again on the island's rural Indian community.

In addition to novels and short stories, Selvon's career includes radio and television plays broadcast by the BBC between 1955 and 1978, adapted from his previous novels and published in *Highway in the Sun* (1991) and *Eldorado West One* (1998). The stage play *Switch* was performed in London at the Royal Court Theatre in 1977 and the screenplay *Pressure* (1978) was one of the first black feature films released in the United Kingdom. In 1978 Selvon left England and moved to Canada. He taught creative writing courses and lectured at numerous universities across North America, Britain, and the Caribbean, most notably as a long-standing writer in residence at the University of Calgary. He was the recipient of an honorary doctorate from the University of Warwick in 1988 in recognition of his work as a pioneering Indo-Caribbean writer.

Early responses to Selvon's work focus on his experimentation with form and language. In a time of political turmoil in the Caribbean, his calypso-influenced episodic form and use of Caribbean dialect in texts such as *A Brighter Sun* and *The Lonely Londoners*, among others, was read as presenting the emergence of a national consciousness. This interpretation was strengthened by his fellow Caribbean writer George Lamming's classification of Selvon as a 'peasant' or 'folk' writer reporting local stories and language and Selvon's repeated discussion of his Creolized upbringing in numerous interviews. Consequently, Selvon's work was long pigeonholed as concerned primarily with humour and pathos and as technically inferior to his fellow Indo-Trinidadian writer V. S. Naipaul.

Recent criticism of Selvon's texts is changing this opinion. Once regarded as lacking in technique, novels such as *The Lonely Londoners* and *Moses Ascending* are being reread as tightly constructed responses to the 19th-century British novels that influenced him at school. His use of dialect, originally read as a simple recording of Caribbean speech, is now seen as the creation of a modified form of Caribbean standard English, incorporating aspects of both Caribbean dialect and received standard English, that works to close the gap between Selvon's rural Caribbean and immigrant characters and his British audience. EDS

Donnell, Alison, and Welsh, Sarah Lawson (eds.), *The Routledge Reader in Caribbean Literature* (1996)

Nasta, S., *Critical Perspectives on Sam Selvon* (1998)

ODNB

Ramchand, Kenneth, *Sam Selvon* (2004)

See also LITERATURE 2: FICTION AND POETRY

Sessarakoo, William Ansah. Also known as William Ansah, Cupid, 'the Royal African' (*fl.* 1740–1750), son of the ruler of Annamaboe (now Anamabo in Ghana), known to English traders as John Corrente. There was considerable rivalry in the area between the English and the French, and the French had scored a tactical success by persuading John Corrente to allow them to take one of his sons to France. The young man was well treated, and returned to Annamaboe laden with presents and impressed by the grandeur of France. As a result, John Corrente began to give more favour to the French, but it occurred to him that it might be to his advantage to secure a similar study tour from their English rivals for one of his other sons, who was accustomed to visiting the local fort of the *Royal African Company and known to the English traders as Cupid, because of 'his sweet and amiable Temper'. He entrusted Cupid to a 'separate trader' (that is, one not connected with the Royal African Company), who, instead of taking him to England, sold him as a slave in Barbados in 1744. While Britain and France were at war during the War of the Austrian Succession (1740–8), British naval bombardments of Annamaboe in 1747 forced John Corrente to agree to expel the French traders, but in return the Royal African Company promised to find his missing son.

In Barbados the youth had, so it was later claimed, fallen 'into the Hands of a Gentleman of distinguished Character, where he was treated with much Humanity'. The Royal African Company's agent tracked him down 'without much Difficulty' and 'a valuable Consideration being given to the Gentleman who bought him, he was happily restored to Liberty, and to his former good Opinion of the Candour of the *British* Nation'. This was in 1748. He was then brought to England, where he became something of a celebrity. An anonymous account, *The Royal African*, was published, with a title echoing Behn's **Oroonoko; or, The Royal Slave*, describing the adventures of 'The Young Prince of Annamaboe' and stressing the importance to British commerce of John Corrente's friendship. While in England, the young man was baptized (30 November 1749) as William Ansah Sessarakoo, and a fine mezzotint portrait (by John Faber, Jr., 1684–1756, after Gabriel Mathias, 1719–1804) was published, showing him elegantly dressed in European style and with a caption giving some details of the sitter's history. A version of this later appeared in the *Gentleman's Magazine* (June 1750) together with a portrait of *Job ben Solomon, emphasizing the similarity of their stories. In a curious example of art imitating life imitating art, Sessarakoo was taken to see a dramatized version of *Oroonoko*, and was reportedly deeply moved by the parallel he saw with his own history. This in turn was made a prominent part of two poems by William Dodd (1729–77), which were imaginary letters from 'the African prince' to his (imaginary) lover Zara at his father's court; originally published in the *Gentleman's Magazine* in July and August

1749, these poems were reprinted in several anthologies.

Unlike the vast majority of those enslaved, Sessarakoo eventually returned safely home. As was the case with Job ben Solomon, it seems clear that his rescue from slavery owed a great deal to British self-interest. While the widespread sympathy which his misfortunes aroused would appear to have been genuine, it was sympathy for someone who was believed to be a prince unjustly enslaved, rather than sympathy for enslaved people in general. The anonymous author of *The Royal African* asserted that 'whatever some Men may think, Human Nature is the same in all *Countries*, and under all *Complexions*', but it was 'selling a *Free-Man*, and a Person of Consideration, whatever his *Complexion* may be, for a *Slave*' that aroused his wrath, not slavery as such. On the contrary, one of the main reasons for keeping John Corrente happy was precisely the fact that a large proportion (one-sixth, in the opinion of the author of *The Royal African*) of the total number of slaves sent each year from the West African coast were shipped from Annamaboe. Similarly, Dodd's Zara calls slave traders 'Barbarians of the fiercest kind', but her protest is directed against the enslavement of her lover and there is little in Dodd's poems to suggest any questioning of slavery as an institution.

JG

Anon., *The Royal African; or, The Memoirs of the Young Prince of Annamaboe* (n.d., [1749])

Dodd, William, *The African Prince, when in England, to Zara, at His Father's Court; and Zara's Answer* (2nd edn., 1755)

Grant, Douglas, *The Fortunate Slave: An Illustration of African Slavery in the Early Eighteenth Century* (1968)

Sharp, Granville (1735–1813). Writer and anti-slavery campaigner born in Durham but living mainly in London from 1750. From 1758 to 1776, when he resigned as a result of his opposition to the American War of Independence, he was a government clerk in the Ordnance Office. He subsequently lived off the support of his brothers William and James, and the money he could make from his published works, which were numerous and on a wide range of subjects. Sharp was a largely self-taught man, with what would now be called well-developed research skills.

These were put to good use when, in 1765, Sharp became interested in the fate of Jonathan *Strong, a slave who had sought help from Sharp's brother William, and who two years later became involved in an important legal case. This seems to have been when he first became involved with the anti-slavery cause, which was to occupy him for much of the rest of his life. Although he had no formal legal training, his researches on the legal status of slaves in Britain led him to publish several works on the subject, such as *A Representation of the Injustice and Dangerous Tendency of Tolerating Slavery* (1769), and also caused him to be concerned with other issues relating to political and civil liberties. He was involved in other legal cases relating to slaves in Britain, including the **Somerset* case (1772), and attempted, without success, to bring a private prosecution for murder against those responsible for throwing over 100 slaves overboard in the notorious case of the ship **Zong* (1783). He was one of the founders of the Society for the Abolition of the Slave Trade in 1787, although he was unable to persuade his colleagues that they should from the start be campaigning for the immediate *abolition of slavery as well as the slave trade. Sharp also took an active part in the establishment of the colony in Sierra Leone (*see* SIERRA LEONE SETTLERS).

JG

Davis, David Brion, *The Problem of Slavery in Western Culture* (1966)

ODNB

Shyllon, F. O., *Black Slaves in Britain* (1974)

See also EQUIANO, OLAUDAH

Sierra Leone settlers. Black Americans who liberated themselves from slavery during the American War of Independence and were settled in Sierra Leone. Preferring liberty under the flag of empire to slavery under the flag of liberty, they joined the British and were brought to Nova Scotia, where they were promised land. Land grants were delayed, so in 1791 their spokesman, Thomas Peters, who had served as a sergeant in the British Army, ventured to London to seek redress. Here he met the directors of the Sierra Leone Company, wealthy abolitionists who had founded a colony in Sierra Leone to provide an alternative to the slave trade by trading in produce instead. Primarily a commercial enterprise, their Company also aimed to introduce 'the Blessings of Industry and Civilization' into Africa. They needed settlers and were ready to accept the 'Nova Scotians', as they became known, sending a young naval lieutenant, John Clarkson, to organize their departure. Nearly 2,000 volunteered.

They were enterprising, self-reliant men and women, who had freed themselves from slavery and were ready to seek a new home in Africa. Some were skilled and literate. Their main focus of loyalty was to their churches: their pastors were their leaders. These included David George, who as a slave had founded the first black church in America. But they first demanded a promise of freedom in their new home and that their land be given them free of charge. This Clarkson promised.

On board ship they organized themselves into orderly companies and then disembarked in Freetown in January 1792 to clear the site and put up temporary accommodation. They found confusion. The Company had instituted an administration by a council whose members neglected their duties and refused to cooperate. When the heavy annual rains started, malaria and dysentery broke out and nearly 100 settlers died—though, once established, their health adjusted easily to the new environment. Clarkson eventually took charge as Governor. The settlers' experiences in America had inevitably left them tenacious of their rights as free people, and suspicious of authority. He made himself their champion, until eventually the directors in London felt he was putting settler interest before theirs and dismissed him.

Under his successors, relations between Company and settlers deteriorated steadily. The two were on different wavelengths. The directors saw themselves as sponsors of a high-minded enterprise, working for the good of Africa, in which the settlers were to play an allotted part. The settlers saw themselves as free people who had come to Africa to make a new life of freedom for themselves and their children.

In 1794 a French revolutionary naval squadron bombarded the defenceless town, and the crews looted and burnt it. When they left, the settlers rebuilt it and resumed daily life. Some farmed their land, though the mountainous terrain offered only subsistence. Others built boats and traded with their Temne neighbours for produce, including rice for Freetown's food supply, or opened retail shops. They put their profits into building houses to live in or let to white officials, thus establishing the economic base of Freetown's future prosperity: the import-export trade and investment in property.

Their rights were protected by a trial by jury and by an elected local authority, which made laws subject to approval by the Governor and his council, and their own constables. Their preachers enforced the norms of Christian conduct. Whatever their feelings against the Company, they were a peaceful, law-abiding community.

As the Franco-British war extinguished the Company's hope of commercial profit, the directors decided to raise some revenue from the land. In 1796 they proposed that the settlers pay a small annual quit-rent. But what in London seemed a perfectly reasonable charge on land where, at great expense, they had provided the settlers with homes, the settlers could only see as a breach of the promise made to them in Nova Scotia, which threatened a future of landless slavery for them and their children. The Company also raised money from the British government by agreeing to take as settlers a community of Jamaican 'Maroons' who had been deported for rebellion, along with a small garrison of soldiers to keep order.

Law-abiding though they were, the settlers would not accept quit-rent. They believed the land was theirs and not the Company's. When, in 1796, payment was demanded, their elected leaders adamantly refused to pay and began to talk of rebellion. Some left the colony and settled along the shore in a community of their own. The directors waited two years and then demanded that the tax be collected. The Governor, new and inexperienced, waited before collecting, but the people were determined never to pay. Their delegates began to demand a greater share in government. Finally, in 1800, they openly rejected Company rule and issued their own code of laws, which restricted Company jurisdiction to its own affairs. This was rebellion. The Governor gave out firearms to the constables, who went to arrest the signatories, fired on them, and wounded several people. Isaac Anderson, their leader, then assembled his followers in arms to attack the government. Only about 50 of the 300 or so householders joined him, but the threat was serious. Then a ship anchored in the harbour with the Maroons and soldiers on board. They landed and together dispersed the rebels. Anderson was eventually hanged and others were banished from the colony. They included Henry Washington, a farmer less successful in rebellion than his former farmer owner.

The Company's government struggled on. Quit-rents were forgotten, and the settlers settled down quietly side by side with the Maroons, though always remaining distinct from them. Then, in 1808, the British Crown took over and Sierra Leone became a new home for the influx of thousands of people liberated from transatlantic slavery by the British Navy. The settlers were soon far outnumbered, surviving as a tiny self-constituted elite, tenaciously protective of their own identity. A few of their descendants still live in Freetown. CF

Fyfe, Christopher, *A History of Sierre Leone* (1962)

Schama, Simon, *Rough Crossings: Britain, the Slaves and the American Revolution* (2005)

See also ABOLITION; SLAVERY

Ska. Jamaican musical form that became very popular in Britain in the 1960s. The roots of ska were in Jamaica in the late 1950s, but it was around the time of independence from Britain in 1962 that the term became widely popular as the sound was employed by musicians wishing to create a distinctive Jamaican musical identity. Ska is rhythmic and syncopated; the rhythmic emphasis of the music is reversed, with the emphasis falling between the beats (rather than on the beat), creating a choppy and lively effect. This, and the emphasis on the bass, an important factor in ska as dance music, became key elements in later Jamaican popular music. Traditionally, ska is played by groups consisting of electric guitar, bass guitar, Hammond organ, and drums, accompanied by a brass section.

Many Jamaican expatriates arrived in major British cities in the early 1960s, and one way they maintained a link with home was through their music. During the early period of settlement Jamaican music was imported and distributed by the sound systems (travelling discos) and a few individuals. As early as 1963, 15,000 records a month were being imported from Jamaica, almost all being sold to the expatriate community. Increasing demand led to the establishment of independent businesses specializing in the import and sale of Caribbean musics. The most important of the white-owned of these was Island Records, owned by Chris Blackwell, a white Jamaican, which became the main outlet for Jamaican music in Britain in the 1960s. In 1961 Melodisc Records set up the Blue Beat label to release Jamaican music (ska was also known in Britain as Blue Beat in the 1960s because many records were on this label). Lee Goptal followed in 1964, setting up B & C Records, which established outlets in areas of London where the West Indian communities lived. Clubs such as Four Aces, 007, Ram Jam, and Roaring Twenties became important venues for young Blacks keen for the latest sounds from Jamaica.

Ska emerged on the British music scene in 1964, when Prince Buster, the greatest of the Jamaican ska artists (who later inspired the British pop group Madness), appeared on the British music television programme *Ready Steady Go*. He also recorded 'Al Capone', the most definitive of ska songs. In that same year the guitarist Ernest Ranglin (a founder member of the Jamaican group the Skatalites), played on and produced Millie Small's hit 'My Boy Lollipop', which achieved international success and inspired Jamaican musicians to move to London in search of recording opportunities. Prince Buster songs such as 'Thirty Pieces of Silver' and 'Madness' were extremely popular, together with the ska style of dancing, in south London dance halls. Live London venues such as the Marquee Club and the Flamingo Club regularly held Jamaican ska sessions including artists such as Syko and the Caribs, the Exotics, Mickey Finn, Derrick Morgan, and the Skatalites. These sessions helped to raise ska's profile owing to the large black audiences they attracted. Another important figure on the 1960s music scene was Laurel Aitken, who had contributed to the establishment of the recording industry in Jamaica, and made substantial contributions to the British *reggae scene. Dandy Livingstone was also successful in Jamaica before moving to the United Kingdom, where his success continued, especially with his record 'A Message to You Rudy' with Rico Rodriguez, a trombonist who was one of the first Jamaican musicians to establish a career on the London music scene.

Black American R & B and *soul music were already popular with the young Whites who lived in the same inner-city areas as the Jamaican expatriates; thus their adoption of ska was not surprising. Artists like Desmond Dekker and the Upsetters were highly successful, becoming working-class heroes, especially to a new cult group, the skinheads, who emerged in the late 1960s. Skinheads signified their identity with shaven heads, Doc Martens footwear, and ska. Some British ska was released specifically targeting the skinhead market, such as Derrick Morgan's 'Moon Hop' and Laurel Aitken's 'Haile Selassie' and 'Pussy Price Gone Up', which were also notable for their use of the slower rhythms that were popular in Jamaica at the end of the 1960s. The association with skinheads contributed to ska losing its mainstream popularity in the early 1970s, along with the fact that a slower, subtler form, reggae, had emerged. Ska's demise can also be attributed to the fact that the BBC did not play it, or any other Caribbean music, and that the mainstream record shops did not stock it.

A ska revival in the late 1970s and early 1980s, under the guise of Two Tone, resulted from the coming together of black and white communities in inner-city areas of the West Midlands, notably in Coventry and Birmingham. The multiracial members of bands such as UB40, the Specials, the Beat, and the Selecter reflected the multiracial communities in which they had grown up. Jerry Dammers established the Two Tone record label and the Specials, as well as developing the black and white theme synonymous with Two Tone.

'White' reggae of London bands like Madness and Bad Manners attracted racists who expressed themselves through the skinhead style. With the skinhead movement and increasing National Front activity in the late 1970s, ska acted as a link on the music scene, as black, white, and Asian youths shared dance floors across the country, dancing to the Two Tone scene. An essential element of ska was the fashion (smart, snappy dressing for snappy music): black and white clothing (suits for men), Fred Perrys, Doc Martens, and pork pie hats.

Today there is an active ska scene in Britain, albeit not in the mainstream, recreating the traditional sound of ska, as well as some experimentation, fusing the music with other genres. SM

Chambers, Iain, *Urban Rhythms: Pop Music and Popular Culture* (1985)

Potash, C. (ed.), *Reggae, Rasta, Revolution: Jamaican Music from Ska to Dub* (1997)

Thompson, Dave, *Wheels Out of Gear: 2 Tone, the 'Specials' and a World in Flame* (2004)

See also MUSIC 2: EARLY POPULAR MUSIC

Skin colour and race, theories of. Racial categories are still being practised, even though most scientists agree that genetically speaking there is little or no validity for dividing groups of humans in this way. Although the creation of racial hierarchies has to a large extent fallen into disrepute, skin colour remains a powerful signifier in contemporary British society and elsewhere.

1. Introduction Although theories giving rise to racial categorization, and theories of skin colour, are not coterminous, when reference is made to race it is often implicitly assumed to be related to black/African and white/European peoples. Race has proved a pervasive conceptual framework, shaping the way in which people think about and act towards each other in societies across the world. Overarching theories of racial difference that posit the inferiority and superiority of racial groups may have retreated significantly since the horrors of the Holocaust and Nazism, but the language and discourse of race permeates everyday public and private conversation and debate, politics and policy-making, and representation and the media. The significance of racial difference owes more to political pressures and imperatives than to scientific validity.

It has been argued that until the emergence of transatlantic chattel enslavement, little thought was given to the inherent superiority or inferiority of human groups based on skin colour. Thus in antiquity the Greeks and the Romans did not view their Ethiopian slaves as inferior to slaves from elsewhere. However, the enslavement of Africans by Europeans had been steadily developing into an international trade since the 16th century and many thinkers saw black people's alleged inherent inferiority as justification for enslavement and domination. Others also thought black people were inferior—childlike and primitive—but argued that this should not deprive them of their right to liberty. Some also felt that, with the right kind of education and environment, black people could be raised to the intellectual and moral level of white people.

2. The development of scientific racism Race began to acquire the meanings associated with it today at the end of the 18th and the beginning of the 19th centuries during the period of increasing contact with the peoples of Africa, India, and the 'Orient'. Prior to that, race had resonance in literature rather than science—which was just beginning to emerge as a discourse of truth—and was simply used as a category of persons or even objects. Even in the early part of the 20th century 'race' was still being used as a synonym for humanity as a whole, or for nations, as well as referring to specific groupings, and this can cause confusion when reading literature of the period.

Historically, various reasons have been sought to explain the darker skin of black peoples. One explanation circulating during the Renaissance was the curse placed on one of Noah's sons, Ham. Ham's punishment for his sin of disobedience was to be made 'black'—and this was interpreted as a biblical explanation for African peoples' dark skin. For those English adventurers who travelled to West Africa from the 16th century, skin colour seemed to be the most obvious difference between them and these newly encountered peoples. Many different theories were advanced to explain variations in skin colour, often comprising a mix of myth, religion, and prejudice.

In Europe 19th-century speculations about the causes of skin colour cited leprosy and syphilis as the reason why black people had darker skins than white people, thus linking black people to disease and degeneration. Another explanation put forward was that of climatic determinism: African peoples' skin colour was dark because they were exposed to so much sun. This theory did not stand up to scrutiny as babies of African descent born in England were still dark-skinned. There seems to have been little curiosity among white Europeans about why they were pale-skinned; the underlying assumption was that they represented the norm.

There is a significant body of work that became increasingly influential during the late 18th and 19th centuries sometimes referred to as scientific or pseudo-scientific racism, which purported to explain racial difference and implicitly rationalized dominance and subjugation. As emerging disciplines in the 19th century, biology and *anthropology were called upon to explain physiological differences between groups of humans and to provide an explanation for social inequalities. Identifying and cataloguing the signifiers of racial difference was coupled with a denial of the humanity of people from races other than white European as these 'others' were deemed to deviate from the European 'norm'. This deviation was seen as indicating their weakness and degeneracy as a 'race'. It almost inevitably followed that the races identified were placed in a hierarchy with white Europeans at the top and black people of African descent at the bottom.

These theories of race had at their heart a belief in biological definitions of race, and described and analysed the physical, mental, and, importantly, moral and intellectual characteristics and capabilities attributed to the different peoples from around the world. The terminology of racial classification remains today, e.g., when people refer to 'Caucasians'.

Science has played a major role in developing theories of race. The work of early scientists such as the 18th-century Swedish botanist Carl von Linné—also known as Linnaeus—had a major impact. He is credited with developing one of the first taxonomies of human races. Making no distinction between subjectively assessed character traits and objectively noted physical characteristics, Linné described Africans as 'ruled by caprice' while Europeans were 'ruled by customs'. African women, he wrote, were 'Women without shame, breasts lactate profusely'. African men were lazy and 'covered themselves in grease'. Georges Cuvier, who chronicled his distaste for Sarah *Baartman (also known as 'the Hottentot Venus') in the early 19th century, was an acclaimed naturalist who referred to Africans as 'the most degraded of human races whose form approaches that of the beast and whose intelligence is nowhere great enough to arrive at regular government'.

The cultural context within which theories of racial difference developed and circulated took for granted that ranking races was necessary and desirable. Few during this period were concerned with notions of equality, freedom, and rights for black people. There were two significant schools of thought that sought to explain racial difference prior to the development of evolutionary theories in the early to mid-19th century. Monogenism held that all peoples were descended from a unitary source: Adam and Eve, and the Garden of Eden. Although within monogenism many shades of opinion coexisted, the basic premiss was that human races had degenerated from the prelapsarian ideal.

While it was acknowledged that white Europeans had fallen into moral and spiritual decline, it was held that they had done so less than other peoples. Black people were deemed to have degenerated the most: some thinkers felt that it was possible to diminish the effects of this decline; others felt that it was irreversible. Based on the belief that climate caused racial difference, opinion was divided over whether moving black people to European climates would improve them or make no difference. Samuel Stanhope Smith, President of the College of New Jersey, which was later to become Princeton, hoped that black people brought to America would at some point turn white as the climate was more suited to a European demeanour.

While those who promoted monogenism believed in a literal and symbolic Adam and Eve, the polygenecists discarded religion as an explanatory model. For them the human races represented different biological species ordered into a hierarchy with white people representing the peak of civilization and black people the nadir. Regarded as a separate species, black people were deemed not human and therefore subject to domination by a superior species—Europeans.

In the 19th century craniology—the study of skull shapes—contributed significantly to scientific racism and, by naming Caucasian skulls as the most beautiful, served to normalize the idea that racial affiliation determined what was considered beautiful. The broader significance of beauty in racial terms was that it was seen as indicative of the health and fitness of the race so that ideals of beauty were implicated in the later development of eugenics.

Unsurprisingly during a period in which Britain's Empire was spreading across the globe, these theories were part of the armoury used to justify the subjugation of peoples deemed inferior, and some of the most prominent philosophers and scientists of the age succumbed to belief in them. For example, David Hume, the renowned 18th-century philosopher, wrote: 'I am apt to suspect the negroes and in general all the other species of men . . . to be naturally inferior to the Whites. There never was a civilised nation of any other complexion than white, nor even any individual eminent either in action or speculation.'

Personal beliefs and prejudices played a significant role in the development of race theories in the 18th, 19th, and 20th centuries, and as such there are frequently contradictions, and anomalies to be observed. It had been argued that people of different species would not be able to breed successfully: they would not be able to produce fertile offspring. Particularly during African enslavement it was clear that black and white people produced children who were themselves able to reproduce, thereby undermining the argument that black and white people were from different species. Other areas of scientific enquiry concluded that black people were less intellectually capable than white people, more likely to be criminal, and suffered from mental illnesses that caused them to try and escape from enslavement.

4. **Contemporary racial theories** The notion that human beings form exclusive groups based on 'race' because it is natural to do so has been identified as a key component of what has been described in Britain as the 'new' or 'cultural' racism during the 1980s. It was said to be new because the focus shifted away from the biological aspects of racism to the cultural aspects of racial difference. Thus black people were not to be excluded or repatriated because they differed in skin colour but because their behavioural norms and cultural values are at variance with established British traditions. Nonetheless, those scientists, sociologists, and historians who promote theories designed to demonstrate the superiority of white Europeans cite hereditary factors as the cause of racial differences. It seems that white scientific racism has shifted focus from visible physical characteristics to the powerful but invisible workings of genetic determinism. Psychologists and sociobiologists periodically produce research that purports to prove innate racial differences, usually claiming to demonstrate the intellectual inferiority of black people (and often women too).

There are common threads that run through the historical and many of the contemporary theories of racial difference. There is the reference to or creation of a scientific theory or theories to justify the concept of 'race'; the perceived necessity for racial purity in order to maintain group integrity; an emphasis on the moral, intellectual, and physical superiority of 'our own' group as distinct from the 'other'; the pathologization of the other's culture. The political subtext that underpins the explanation is also often clearly observable.

The development of a body of work concerned with researching, describing, and analysing race and skin colour has more recently emerged from black thinkers and theorists as well as white. Adopted by, among others, some activists in black organizations such as the Nation of Islam, these theories also seek to explain racial difference, and to propose alternative conceptual models.

Traditionally, European and North American systems of racial categorization have been constructed by white people to demonstrate that black people are inferior: some of the Afrocentric theories of race have created theories that oppose such thought and invert the model to produce one that posits the superiority of black people and the moral and/or sexual degeneracy of white people. For example, in *The Isis Papers: The Keys to the Colors* (1991), Frances Cress-Welsing argues that white people are the result of genetic albinism. Her theory proposes that white people's behaviour arises from their alienation due to their lack of skin colour. Interestingly, she attributes white people's lack of colouring to leprosy, thereby inverting the 19th-century theorists' model cited above.

Cress-Welsing and others argue that the concentration of melanin that produces black skin confers superior intellectual and artistic powers on black people. Some of the theories developed by writers with an Afrocentrist perspective refer to melanin—the substance that determines skin pigmentation—as having almost supernatural power. Arguably, these theorists use similar strategies to 19th-century scientific racial ideologies in the ways in which they draw on scientific theory to make their point. There is an assumption that there is a biological justification for racializing difference; they articulate a desire to keep their race 'pure' and argue that their racial group is superior to others.

Both 19th-century and contemporary theories of race and skin colour underplay the significance of economic, cultural, social, and other environmental factors in shaping people's levels of attainment. Such theories often demonstrate implicitly or explicitly political imperatives for the development and promotion of these ideas.

The explanation of skin colours may well lie in human life having evolved in Africa and spread northwards. In this model dark skin is seen as a protection against persistent sunlight, but not well adapted to the loss of vitamin D that arises from the lack of sun in the northern hemisphere. In northern Europe white people are at an advantage as their skin protects against vitamin D deficiency but is a poor shield against the sun. Theories of racial hierarchies and inferences drawn from the range of human skin colouring are frequently undermined by the variety of skin tones and linguistic and cultural diversity across the world and especially in the Caribbean, Africa, and the Americas.

Melanin is present in all human races, and the variation in the amount is actually small in spite of what is perceived as vast differences in the range of human skin tones. Whatever the truth of the origins of variations in skin colour, it is in the interpretation of these signs of difference that the problem lies, especially when co-opted into a political agenda that supports racial hierarchies. LY

Alleyne, Mervyn, *The Construction and Representation of Race and Ethnicity in the Caribbean and the World* (2001)

Gould, Stephen Jay, *The Mismeasure of Man* (1981)

Stepan, N. L., *The Idea of Race in Science: Great Britain, 1800–1960* (1982)

See also BEAUTY, CONCEPTS OF; BLACK MUSLIMS; CARLYLE, THOMAS; EUGENICS; EXHIBITS, BLACK PEOPLE AS; GALTON, SIR FRANCIS; LONG, EDWARD; MISCEGENATION

Slave trade. The Atlantic slave trade was the enforced transportation of humanity between Africa and the Americas. Some 12 million Africans were loaded onto slave ships (though a much smaller number arrived at the ships' destinations). This staggering historical phenomenon is hardly diminished in scale by the global human tragedies of the 20th century.

1. Historical background
2. Slave ships

1. Historical background The Africans caught in this trade were the human pawns in a massive commercial system that was driven forward by the widely accepted belief that the slaves were things, not people: chattels, not humanity. Grotesque to the modern mind, such a view, for all its contradictions and confusions, was the necessary philosophy that underpinned the whole Atlantic business. To concede the African's humanity was to allow the slave system to unravel. And that is exactly what happened, in the late 18th century, when voices of moral and religious (and economic) dissent began to challenge the idea of the African as commodity.

The Atlantic trade in Africans was orchestrated by commercial and political interests in Europe and, later, in the Americas. At first it was a relatively simple trading structure: a flow of people, goods, and trade linking Europe, Africa, the Americas, and Europe. But it soon gave way to a remarkably complex system. The economic focus of the British trade was *London, but the centre of slave trading itself shifted from London first to *Bristol, and later to *Liverpool, while *Glasgow came to dominate the trade in slave-grown tobacco from the Chesapeake. Many other, smaller ports joined in, dispatching local vessels out to profit from the slave trade, but the British slave trade was dominated by those major ports. Throughout, the finance and insurance, the complicated flow of money, letters of credit, and insurance and trading instructions, all passed through trading houses and banking facilities primarily in London.

The bold statistics of the Atlantic slave trade are now familiar. Twelve million Africans were loaded onto the ships, 10.5 surviving to landfall in the Americas. There were something like 27,000 known slave voyages, of which about 12,000 were British or British colonial, mainly North American. About 5,000 slave voyages originated in Liverpool. Such statistical snapshots—which are likely to be revised upwards as research continues—can easily mask the human misery they are intended to capture. The majority of those African captives were male, although the sex ratio on the slave ships changed over time. By the last years of the slave trade, in the mid-19th century, when the last (illegal) slave ships heading for Brazil and Cuba were trying to outrun the British and American anti-slavery patrols, their cargoes consisted largely of very young and predominantly male Africans.

We can arrange these figures in any number of ways. But one particular formulation demonstrates the dominance of Africans in the overall human migrations westwards to the Americas. Until about 1820 the African was the typical migrant across the Atlantic. Before the 1820s some 2.5 million Europeans migrated to the Americas, but in the same period almost 8.5 million Africans had been transported in the slave ships. Of the total number of Africans landed in the Americas, fewer than 10 per cent were taken to North America. The great majority were shipped to Brazil and to the Caribbean. The explanation is simple: the great majority of all Africans were destined to work in the sugar fields of Brazil and the Caribbean. Despite the dispersal of slaves to all corners of the American economies, it was sugar that was the engine behind much of the Atlantic slave trade.

The ideal aim of the slave traders on the African coast was to fill their holds quickly with Africans and to quit the African coast as soon as possible. They were rarely able to do so. The longer they lingered on the coast, the higher the death rates among the crew (some experienced death rates of 45 per cent per month when on the coast). Yet the slave ships had to linger until they had acquired enough Africans to make the crossing economically worthwhile. Of course slaves were not the sole African export, and until about 1700 the total value of other exported African goods (led by gold) was higher than slave exports. Whatever the nature of trade, Europeans were, throughout, effectively in the hands of African coastal traders and African governing elites. In their turn, they were dependent on the flow of slaves and other goods from the African interior. Slave captains and European traders developed highly complex and ritualized negotiations with African merchants, traders, and local elites in search of human cargoes: handing over, by way of exchange, their imported cargoes from Europe or goods trans-shipped from

Asia. The early casual offerings of baubles and trinkets were soon forgotten as Africans developed specific trading demands and learned the commercial value of their human commodities. What appear to be simple negotiations on the coast were in fact only the most visible (to the Europeans) of hugely complex and geographically diverse trade systems that stretched from the African coast far into the interior. The consequences of that trade were enormous, at their most extreme helping to bring down indigenous African states, and encouraging violence and warfare in search of prisoner-slaves for onward sale to traders on the coast.

When Africans entered the slave ships, this was only the latest of the transactions that had seen them enslaved and moved onwards, mainly on foot, from their distant homelands to the coast. Most had almost certainly never seen white men before, nor had they ever seen the ocean or European sailing ships.

The Atlantic slave trade was a harsh commercial business, and all the people involved expected a profitable return on their risky investments. The slave traders' aim was to transport Africans across the Atlantic and to the American slave markets, without loss or injury. Dead or sick Africans meant a financial loss. Atlantic slave traders (for all the brutality of the system) were anxious to deliver as many Africans as possible, and in as good a condition as possible. Brutality was endemic, and death was everywhere, but the aim was *not* to damage or harm—and certainly not to kill—the Africans but to ship them for a profit. In fact, the overwhelming majority of all Africans loaded onto the ships did indeed land in the Americas, though large numbers arrived sick (a fact reflected in the death rates among newly landed slaves). A sizeable proportion did not survive the crossing.

2. Slave ships On board the slave ships Africans were packed below decks, normally divided by sex, with the young sharing the women's quarters. They were more crowded than any other comparable maritime travellers (including troops), though the *degree* of packing did not seem to affect the levels of shipboard mortality. There were huge variations in the death rates among Africans on slave ships, though the overall level decreased over time: death rates in the late 18th century were half those of the early days of the slave trade. This was true on all European ships. The critical factors seem to have been the point of departure from Africa and the length of time of the voyage. What helped to reduce the death rates was the growing experience of slave-trading itself. Traders developed an expertise in how best to ship, load, and transport large numbers of people on the African coast, and then to ship them swiftly across the Atlantic. Like other businesses, slave traders learned from experience and they simply got better at their trade, and this was true of all the nationalities involved.

Slave ships were smaller than other vessels plying the West Indian or American routes, and the size of a ship was important for Africans' survival. Through trial and error over a very long period, the smaller, swifter vessels emerged as the most suitable vessels for carrying Africans across the Atlantic. They were not, however, best for carrying American produce back to Europe, and there thus emerged a distinct and separate leg, of different ships bringing produce back to Europe. The so-called 'triangular trade' was in fact a complexity of criss-crossing sailing routes: direct to and from Africa, from Europe to the Americas direct, and back; from North America to the West Indies and back. There was a similar series of criss-crossing routes across the South Atlantic, to and from Brazil.

Of course all ships were at the mercy of the natural elements: of the oceanic dangers. Atlantic slave traders learned the maritime tricks of the Atlantic system: how best to pick up the winds and currents to get to their chosen destination, when (and when not) to leave, and when to quit the hurricane-prone Caribbean. Nevertheless, the duration of transatlantic crossings varied hugely: the average time to Brazil was one month, to the Caribbean and North America two months. Over the long span of the Atlantic slave trade crossing times got shorter, and the ships got bigger. With the exception of slave ships destined for North America (in the mid-18th century carrying 200 slaves), European slave ships carried more Africans by the end of the 18th century than they had previously: 390 for the British, 340 for the French and Portuguese—even higher, in the 400s, in the last phase of the illegal 19th-century slave trade to Brazil.

The Africans' miserable captivity did not consist solely of time spent on the ships. Most had been enslaved for months *before* they were thrust into the slave holds. Most had trekked for months to the coast from the point of their initial enslavement. Many were then held for long periods on the African coast. We do not know how many Africans died *before* reaching the slave ships, though we have a clear idea of the mortality levels on the slave ships. Some 1.5 million Africans died on board the ships, to be cast overboard, their numbers (never their names) simply struck from the ships' logs, like so much lost cargo. Even so, levels of mortality declined from about 20 per cent in the early 17th century to half that figure a century later. There were, of course, catastrophic cases, when contagious disease swept away huge numbers of Africans, quite apart from the death and destruction brought about by slave insurrection or resistance. We also know of almost 400 instances of shipboard insurrection, but current research suggests a much higher figure is likely.

Most deaths on the slave ships were from gastro-intestinal disorders, mainly the 'bloody flux'. Inevitably, untold numbers of survivors stumbled ashore suffering from the same condition; weakened, aged (often 'bunged up' by slave traders anxious to pass them off as fit), and destined for an early grave in the Americas. At this point we return, inevitably, to the issue of historical interpretation. How are we to capture, present, and discuss suffering on such an epic scale? How best can we present such personal, humiliating distress, where private functions were public, when privacy had no meaning, and where living quarters quickly descended into the squalor of a seaborne stable?

Slaves were shackled below, normally in small groups. They fed from communal supplies, they shuffled, in chains, to the necessary tubs, but, when sick, they relieved themselves where they lay, their faeces soiling and contaminating themselves and their fellow prisoners. In bad weather they were neither cleaned nor exercised, because the crew was too busy grappling with a storm-bound ship. It took a hardened surgeon, or a calloused crewman, to venture into the stinking slave holds in these conditions. Africans, on the other hand, had no choice in the matter, and were obliged to pitch their filthy way across the Atlantic in conditions that often pass belief and description. Even when weather and security permitted the crew to bring Africans on deck for exercise, they did so in small groups; sailors always feared that Africans might resort to violence or simply end their troubles by leaping overboard. The litany of such maritime horror stories, from men who had served on the slave ships, were presented to Parliament in the late 1780s, and they proved a telling factor in turning opinion against the trade itself.

Through all this, a discussion about the statistics of the slave trade may seem oddly inappropriate. Yet they are clearly vital for any historical understanding of what happened. Without them, we have mere guesswork. Nonetheless, the data can also be curiously deceptive, leading the reader down a gentle statistical path that tends to blur rather than refine the historical vision. They can also divert the human attention. When we peer into the slave hold, if we try to capture the physical reality of the slave ship, to catch a whiff of a slave ship's distinctive stink (other vessels could smell them miles downwind), we begin to get a clear sense of what the slaves actually experienced. Here after all is one of those historical topics (the Holocaust is surely another) that defies easy historical grasp and reconstruction. Perhaps there is no obvious or certain way of imagining life below decks on the slave ships.

Even when land was once again in sight and, when the Africans finally quit the holds, their torments did not end. Indeed they merely entered another phase of what must have seemed an unending horror story. They were prepared for sale by crewmen keen to present their human cargoes in the best commercial light (i.e. as fit and well as they could manage). This involved a period of cleaning, resting, and feeding the Africans in an attempt to make good the human wear and tear of the Atlantic crossing. Many Africans were beyond help and little could be done to restore them to health (and saleability). There is perhaps nothing more revealing of the whole wretched story than the fate of the 'refuse slaves', those Africans incapacitated and rendered commercially worthless by sickness, and destined to a miserable end soon after landfall in the Americas. Even among those who *were* sold, a substantial proportion entered their new American homes afflicted by the ailments and frailties acquired in the protracted period of enslavement and transportation. Large numbers died within the first years after arrival.

The patterns of physical inspection on shore were similar wherever the slave ships made landfall, repeating the Africans' initial encounters with slave traders on the African coast. Africans were scrutinized and probed, handled and inspected, in the most intimate, medical-like manner. Potential owners wanted to know their weaknesses, strengths, and imperfections: after the Atlantic crossing there were plenty to look for. In barracoons, on board ship, or in auction pens and markets, Africans were inspected by potential purchasers, by agents, planters, and merchants, all keen to acquire healthy (i.e. profitable) slaves.

Hundreds of thousands of Africans were shipped on, yet again, from their point of arrival, to other destinations. About 200,000 Africans were trans-shipped from Jamaica, mainly to Spanish and French possessions. Similarly, Africans were trans-shipped to Spanish colonies from the small Dutch island of Curaçao. Many Africans were moved onwards, to the Isthmus and to Columbia: others crossed Panama and thence to Lima. Many of the Africans landing in the Chesapeake Bay region had *already* been trans-shipped in the Caribbean, and now faced a daunting trek into the American interior.

Atlantic slave ships headed for those American regions in the full flood of local slave-based development, depositing their human cargoes where labour was most wanted. It was a pattern that changed over time. Before 1600 Spanish America and Brazil attracted most of the Africans. After 1640, and the explosive growth of the sugar islands, the bulk of African slaves were shipped to the Caribbean. The numbers gathered pace as the plantations proliferated, and as Europe devoured increasing volumes of slave-grown commodities. Between 1640 and 1700, 1.6 million Africans were landed in the Americas. In the years 1690–1807 more than 3 million Africans were shipped across the Atlantic. Despite the British and American abolition of the slave trade in 1807–8, a further 3 million Africans crossed the Atlantic as slaves in the 19th century, destined primarily for Brazil and Cuba.

The end result of these massive enforced movements of African peoples was that Africans were scattered to all corners of the Americas—and beyond—as slaves. Africans dominated the population of Brazil: they greatly outnumbered Whites in all the West Indian sugar islands, and they formed a substantial minority in the slave colonies of North America. Africans worked in towns and cities across the Americas, they toiled on boats and ships in all maritime and riverine trades, and as agricultural workers in all forms of labouring and skilled tasks.

Africans thus became ubiquitous, appearing in all corners of the Atlantic economy, from the American frontier, to the dockside communities of London and Liverpool. Black people, free and enslaved, were not only integral to the evolution and prosperity of the Atlantic world, but they were an inescapable feature of social life on both sides of that world in the 18th century. And all this had been brought into being by the Atlantic slave trade.

JW

Eltis, David, *The Rise of African Slavery in the Americas* (2000)
Klein, Herbert, *The Atlantic Slave Trade* (1999)
Walvin, James, *England, Slaves and Freedom 1776–1838* (1986)

See also EMANCIPATION; SLAVERY

Slavery. System of unfree labour in which human beings were claimed to be the absolute property of others, as distinct from, for example, systems of serfdom or indentureship, which theoretically involved claims to ownership of people's labour only, and not to ownership of the people themselves.

1. Background: Europe, Britain, Africa
2. Slavery in the United States

1. Background: Europe, Britain, Africa Slavery died out in Europe at the very time it was introduced into the Americas, primarily to cultivate export staples from the tropics and semi-tropics. With the few early exceptions of Amerindian slaves, slavery in the Americas took the form of imported Africans. In order to tap the economic potential of the Americas, Europeans perfected a new form of slavery. The millions of Africans forcibly shipped across the Atlantic formed the labour force that conquered and then developed key areas of the Americas. They also helped to enrich various European colonial powers. It was a complex process linking American land, African labour, and European prosperity.

In the years before 1807 African slaves formed the great majority of all the people crossing the Atlantic: something like 3 million Africans crossed the Atlantic in British slave ships. But in the same period only 1 million Europeans settled in the Americas. In many key respects it was the African who was the pioneer of settlement in critical regions of the Americas. Africa provided the answer to a problem Europeans had encountered from their early days of settlement: how best to tap the vast potential of land in the Americas. Though initially Europeans had barely a toehold on the continent, in time their settlements and colonies were on such a scale that white migrants (free and indentured) and handfuls of Amerindians were rarely adequate to the economic task. Africa seemed to provide the answer.

Europeans were familiar with African slaves even before they began to settle the Americas. Their early maritime and trading ventures along the West African coast had yielded African slaves, along with other items of trade. African slaves were traded to Portugal and Spain, later to the new Iberian outposts on the Atlantic islands. It was, then, a logical step for those settlers in the Americas who needed labour to turn to Africans. But it was through the development of the early sugar industry, effectively pioneered on Brazilian sugar plantations, that African slave labour emerged. Later it was transferred north, to the Caribbean islands (again for sugar cultivation). Then African slavery slipped further north to the tobacco plantations of the Chesapeake and, later still, to the rice plantations of the Carolinas. Above all, however, it was sugar that was the engine that absorbed Africans in ever growing numbers.

African slavery in the Americas differed greatly from one colony to another. Different crops dictated different structures of slave life, and very different patterns of slave work. These ranged from the large, military-like slave gangs on the big sugar plantations in Brazil and Jamaica, through the smaller work groups (black and white together) on Virginia's tobacco plantations, to the task system commonplace on the Carolina rice plantations.

African enslaved labour quickly moved into all corners of the Atlantic economy. As settler communities developed into sophisticated societies, slaves could be found everywhere: from the urban life of towns and ports, through to cowhands on the expansive frontier, from enslaved sailors in the Atlantic maritime fleets, through to skilled craftsmen and -women across the rural and urban Americas. Inevitably, it also found its way to Europe. In Britain, although its legal status remained in dispute, slavery was a fact of life by the early 18th century. Yet, from the beginning to the end, the prime purpose of slavery was to provide the brute manual labour in the Americas: in sugar, tobacco, rice, and cotton, and a string of other slave-worked commodities.

Slavery greatly enhanced the material well-being of the Western world, and African slaves were integral to the emergence of a massive Atlantic-wide economy. Europe, Africa, and the Americas were, by 1700, locked into an intimate economic and social interdependence. Goods from Europe, along with Asian goods trans-shipped through Europe (all backed by growing European financial and trading systems) were shipped to Africa to be exchanged for enslaved Africans, who were then traded throughout the American slave colonies. Slave-grown tropical staples were shipped back for processing and sale in Europe (and beyond). It was, however, a hugely complex human, geographic, and economic system (too complex to be described merely as 'triangular').

The Atlantic slave system was made possible by a remarkable maritime system. We know of at least 27,000 slave voyages, and of some 12 million Africans loaded onto the Atlantic ships. There was an inevitable consequent impact on port development on both sides of the Atlantic. There were, in addition, major economic and social ramifications throughout the broader hinterlands of the ports linked to the Atlantic slave system (again, in three continents). The millions of Africans who survived to landfall in the Americas (and many did not, of course) had endured a unique oceanic trauma *even before* being turned over to the lifetime of American slavery. Africans arrived sick, virtually naked, and with no material possessions. Yet, within a generation they had shaped a string of vibrant slave societies, which had all the basic ingredients—of family, communities, beliefs, and cultural patterns—which provided the framework for black life (enslaved and free) thereafter. Slave social life, rooted in an African past (itself varied, of course) but transformed by the specific circumstances of local life, differed from place to place. Much depended on geography and the nature of local work, and on the structure of local white society. Slave societies were very different between Brazil, the Caribbean, and North America. And even then, there were marked distinctions *among* slaves even within those broader regions—distinctions shaped in large measure by the kind of work the slaves undertook. Life was very different for a domestic slave compared to a slave working on a coffee plantation. But whatever the system or work, slaves were kept at their toil by a mix of force, incentives, and—especially in the fields—by crude violence.

In Britain itself slavery was never commercially important, and was really an accidental by-product of plantation slavery and of the Atlantic slave trade. It took root in Britain when planters, merchants, government officials, and the military returned home with slaves in tow. Slaves could be bought and sold through English newspapers, and black domestics (slave and free) were common sights in 18th-century society, from poor street life to the grand homes of aristocrats and royals. The legality of slavery in England (and Scotland) was regularly challenged, and it was not until the **Somerset* case of 1772 (decided on a narrow point of law) that the law began to move decisively against slavery.

What united slaves everywhere was the enslaved people's hostility to slavery itself. Slaves everywhere, from Elmina to Rio to London, went out of their way to resist, and to render their bondage more tolerable. From the first moment of African enslavement to final *emancipation, slave resistance was a feature of slavery throughout the Atlantic world. Resistance, however, was a complex phenomenon, ranging from running away, open resistance, and violence (which was inevitably punished by the most draconian of slave owners' brutality) through to the smallest acts of passive resistance. Slaves did what they could to change their enslavement. Yet only once, as a result of the *Haitian Revolution, was local slavery utterly destroyed by the slaves.

Despite all this, slavery in the Americas was remarkably durable, and for most of its history was able to deflect its critics. There had been, from the early Spanish settlements, notable critiques of slavery, on ethical, Christian, and even economic grounds. But the simple and pervasive economic success of slavery rendered most criticisms irrelevant. Objections were simply overwhelmed by the sounds and sights of profitable trade and business. Yet all that began to change from the mid-18th century onwards.

2. Slavery in the United States American slavery, and the Atlantic slave trade, were at their height when convergent critical forces began to attack the Atlantic system. French and Scottish Enlightenment writers (most influentially Montesquieu and Adam Smith) merged with a new theological voice, led initially by Quakers and other Dissenters, to attack the Atlantic slave trade itself. Slaves played a crucial role in this campaign to undermine slavery, notably through major Caribbean slave rebellions and the effect they had on changing European views about slavery. The Revolution in France in 1789, and its impact on the French slave islands, produced the greatest slave convulsion in the Americas: the slave revolution in Saint-Domingue and the eventual emergence of an independent Haiti (in 1804). Shock waves from Haiti travelled throughout the Americas, but, despite the fears and uncertainties, slavery elsewhere held fast—in the short term. The ending of the slave trade by Britain in 1807 and by the United States in 1808 was intended to cut off fresh supplies of Africans to the American plantations. (By then, however, North America did not need new Africans, thanks to the expansion of the local slave population.) Even so, something like 3 million Africans were shipped to the Americas *after* abolition, primarily to Brazil and Cuba. In both those countries, and in the United States, slavery enjoyed a revival on the back of new slave-grown crops. Cuba wanted labour for its tobacco plantations, Brazil for coffee and tobacco; the United States needed slaves for the cotton plantations of the South. The United States, however, had no need for Africans. There were plenty of slaves available *within* the country, mainly in the older slave states in the East. The North American slave trade after 1800 was thus an *internal* US slave trade, as coffles of slaves were moved and sold from the old slave states to the new slave–cotton frontier. Spared the agonies of seaborne migrations, this slave population was nonetheless afflicted by widespread family separation, uprooting, and relocation to distant regions of the United States.

In the 19th century slavery seemed anomalous. On the one hand, US cotton slavery illustrated, once again, the economic returns to be made from unfree labour. On the other, slavery was now a much-denounced and disliked institution. In North America the economic ramifications of cotton slavery were enormous. Cotton was the nation's largest export. Inevitably, the North was deeply involved, via banking, finance, and trade. Yet at the same time there was a growing chorus of northern religious and ethical opposition. The British on the other hand developed a new role as the world's major abolitionist power. A generation after ending their slave trade, the British ended colonial slavery, at a massive cost of £20 million compensation (paid to the slave owners, not to the slaves). Thereafter, the British embarked on a global abolitionist crusade, trying to persuade other European slaving nations, and those in the Americas (led by the United States) to see the errors of their ways and to abandon slavery. It was a remarkable volte-face: the greatest slave trader of the 18th century became the most powerful abolitionist nation in the 19th century. The power of the Royal Navy and pressure from the Foreign Office was able to impose abolition on swathes of Africa and other regions. But slavery remained stubbornly resistant, in the United States, Brazil, and Cuba, largely because of its profitability. Slaves cultivated the coffee for which Brazil became a byword, and the tobacco which made Cuba's name, and in both countries slave numbers were augmented by illicit imports of Africans until the 1860s. Slave-grown cotton poured from plantations across the US South. By 1850 the South was producing 2.5 million 400-pound bales of cotton per year. Although slavery could be found in many other states, the concentration of the enslaved population was in and around the cotton belt. The slave population had been half a million at Independence in 1776, growing to 1.4 million in 1810. On the eve of the Civil War there were almost 4 million slaves in the United States.

Slave-holding was widespread in the South: there were 400,000 slaveholders in the United States on the eve of the Civil War. Slavery had seeped throughout the country, into urban life, into the skilled crafts, domestic service, agricultural life, and the street trades. But the heart of slavery was the South, where the slave-owning class clung tenaciously to the institution that had become a way of life. Large numbers of Americans could not imagine life without slavery, whatever economic blips and downturns might come the way of cotton. There was, however, no reason to feel that slave-grown cotton was in decline or doomed. What brought it down was the violence of the Civil War and, finally, the Thirteenth Amendment in 1865. Like slavery elsewhere, those most closely involved—notably the slave owners—fought to the end for the continuation of slavery.

The 19th century was, in many respects, the classic period of US slavery—the years most commonly associated with slavery. Yet it was only the latest transformation in a form of bondage that had characterized human settlement across the Americas for centuries. Equally, and like the earlier slave systems, cotton slavery was linked to the economies of the wider world. Cotton from the South fuelled the Industrial Revolution in Britain, which, in its turn, helped to clothe the world in cheap cotton garments. Once again, key areas of economic development in the West were intimately linked to slavery in the Americas.

The British, once again, benefited from slave labour (in the form of slave-grown cotton). Yet from the 1830s they had abandoned slavery in their own possessions (though they were not opposed to the reintroduction of indentured labour). Now they were able to present themselves as virtuous abolitionists, with little mention of the British slaving past.

Africa, the source of enslaved labour throughout the Americas, was persistently damaged by this enforced drain of people. Moreover, this haemorrhage of Africans continued long after the Atlantic slave trade had ended. African slaves were moved north across the Sahara and east through East African slave ports. At the same time indigenous slave systems were consolidated in the 19th century. One result of the *external* slave trade from Africa was the strengthening of slavery *within* Africa itself. It was a great irony that abolitionists found themselves tackling the problems of slavery *inside* Africa after they had helped to undermine slavery in the Americas. But in both places, on both sides of the Atlantic, the size and strength of slavery were directly linked to earlier European (and later American) economic dependence on slave labour.

Slavery had a slow and long-drawn-out death across the Americas. It survived in Cuba until 1886, in Brazil until 1888, but by then had been ended elsewhere across the Americas. In some places slavery had simply faded away, devoid of support or friends and overtaken by new economic circumstances. Yet in two main areas where slavery had dominated the economy (in the West Indies and in the US

South) demands to end slavery had been resisted. Even in Brazil, where slavery slowly lost influence and importance, it retained a residual importance in some regions until the bitter end.

The consequences of African slavery were, at once, obvious and yet hidden. Demands for African slave labour had scattered millions of Africans and their locally born descendants across the face of the Americas. African sweat converted whole regions of the Americas into profitable cultivation. The cultures of Africa, though transformed in passing from Africa to the Americas, became a basic, and sometimes dominant, feature of American life. Slavery also bequeathed a malignant legacy to later generations (indeed to the modern world). African slavery in the Americas, quite unlike other slave systems in other societies, was a highly racialized system. To be enslaved was to be black: to be black was to be enslaved. Economic usage, legal custom, and, perhaps more important, popular convention, rendered the African an item of trade. The African as *a thing, an object*, was basic to the whole system. The ideas and values that underpinned that transformation of black humanity to the level of non-human survived long after slavery itself had vanished from memory. In all this the British had played a critical and formative role. It is a remarkable fact that the society that had brought Atlantic slavery to such levels of economic importance and social significance was also the society which, a century later, fought tenaciously to advance abolition in all corners of the globe. JW

Davis, David Brion, *The Problem of Slavery in Western Culture* (1967)

Patterson, Orlando, *Slavery and Social Death* (1982)

Walvin, James, *A Short History of Slavery and Abolition* (2006)

See also SLAVE TRADE

Soga, Tiyo (*c.*1829–1871). Missionary and first black South African ordained as a Christian minister. Soga was a Xhosa speaker born in the Eastern Cape. He received his first formal education at the Presbyterian Mission school at Lovedale. During the Xhosa–British War of 1846–7, Soga and his Christian mother became refugees. In 1848 a missionary took him to Scotland for further education, where he was also baptized; he returned to South Africa as a catechist in 1849. In the continuing conflict between the Xhosas and white settlers on the Eastern Cape frontier, Soga lived in Grahamstown and was identified with European interests. In 1851 Soga went to the Free Church Seminary in Glasgow to train for the ministry. He was ordained and returned to South Africa in 1857 with his white Scottish wife, Janet Burnside. Soga and his wife experienced considerable racial prejudice in South Africa, but moved inland to a mission station in the Eastern Cape. This was a time of great trouble just after the Xhosa cattle killing of 1857, which left many people displaced and starving. But it also provided Soga with missionary opportunities, and his congregation grew. He preached in Xhosa and English, and also wrote occasional articles that were published. He also translated Bunyan's *Pilgrim's Progress* into Xhosa in 1866, and wrote a number of hymns. Poor health led to his early death, leaving Janet with seven children. His eldest sons were educated in Scotland; William Anderson Soga was a medical missionary and John Henderson Soga a missionary and Xhosa historian. John also married a Scottish wife; they retired to Britain and were killed in a German air raid in 1941. DK

Chalmers, James A., *Tiyo Soga: A Page of South African Missionary Work* (1877)

Soga, Tiyo, *The Journal and Selected Writings of the Reverend Tiyo Soga* (ed. Donovan Williams, 1983)

Williams, Donovan, *Umfundisi: A Biography of Tiyo Soga 1829–1871* (1978)

See also CHRISTIANITY; CHURCHES; MISSIONARY SOCIETIES

Solanke, Chief Ladipo (*c.*1884–1958). Founder of the Nigerian Progress Union and the *West African Students' Union (WASU) born in Abeokuta, Nigeria. He was educated in Nigeria and Sierra Leone and in Britain, and was called to the Bar in

1926. As a student he was one of the first teachers of Yoruba at the School of Oriental and African Studies, London.

In 1924 Solanke and Amy Ashwood *Garvey formed the Nigerian Progress Union. The following year he became the joint founder and secretary-general of the WASU. Solanke was one of the main propagandists of the WASU and in 1927 published *United West Africa at the Bar of the Family of Nations*, a demand for recognition of equal political rights for Africans. Throughout his life he wrote many letters and articles demanding self-government for Britain's West African colonies, as well as on traditional Yoruba institutions and culture. He was the first person to make a radio broadcast in Yoruba, and he also made several of the first Yoruba musical recordings during the 1920s.

Solanke led the WASU's attempts to establish a hostel for West Africans in London, and between 1928 and 1932 conducted a fundraising tour throughout West Africa. On his return he became warden of the WASU hostel that opened in Camden in 1933. From 1944 to 1948 he conducted a second fundraising tour prior to the opening of the WASU's third London hostel in 1949.

During the 1950s political differences forced Solanke to form the breakaway WASU Unincorporated. He continued to run a student hostel in London until his death from cancer in 1958. HA

Adi, H., *West Africans in Britain: Nationalism, Pan-Africanism and Communism* (1998)

See also WEST AFRICAN STUDENT CHRISTIAN UNION; WEST INDIAN STUDENTS' UNION

***Somerset* case.** Slave owners from overseas colonies frequently brought slaves to Britain and a handful of cases involving such people came before the courts, including those of Dinah Black (1687), Katherine Auker (1690), an unnamed man who died during the course of the hearing (1757), Jonathan Strong (1767), John and Mary *Hylas (1768), and Thomas Lewis (1771). Abolitionists hoped to gain a definitive ruling against slavery but these cases were resolved by reference to their individual circumstances, or, in the case of the unnamed man, by his death and therefore had no wider implications. It was the case of James Somerset, or Sommersett, in 1772 that resulted in the momentous ruling known as the Mansfield judgment.

1. Somerset's background Somerset was purchased in Virginia by Charles Stewart, or Steuart, a customs officer, who brought him from Boston, Massachusetts, where slavery was legal, to England in November 1769. Somerset left him, and was baptized on 12 February 1771 in St Andrew's, Holborn, in London, perhaps in the hope that this would liberate him. It was a common belief that christening conferred freedom. Later that year, on 26 November, Stewart had Somerset captured and put on board the *Ann and Mary*, a ship bound for Jamaica. Three sympathetic witnesses, Thomas Walklin, Elizabeth Cade, and John Marlow, obtained from Lord Mansfield, the Lord Chief Justice, a writ of habeas corpus, a legal test of the right to imprison someone. This required the ship's captain, John Knowles, to produce Somerset in court, and on 7 February 1772 the case came before the Court of King's Bench, the highest court of common law in England and Wales. Scotland had, and still has, a separate legal system and the situation in relation to slaves there was finally resolved in the case of **Knight* v. *Wedderburn*.

2. The legal arguments Granville *Sharp, the abolitionist, became involved in the case. There were five counsel on Somerset's side. William Davy and John Glynn argued that slavery was a product of local laws and did not exist in England and Wales. James Mansfield (not related to the judge) and Francis *Hargreave argued that the law only permitted a man to contract to serve a master for life, not to enslave himself, and even that might be unenforceable. Alleyne argued that the cruelties suffered by slaves in America could be introduced here if slavery were found lawful.

On Stewart's side, his two counsel, William Wallace and John Dunning, relied on the legality of slavery and the slave trade in Africa, Virginia, and Jamaica as well as the inconvenience to slave owners and the wider financial implications of releasing a slave from his owner's service.

Aware of the economic and social implications of any judgment he made, Mansfield ordered several recesses, in which he unsuccessfully attempted to persuade Stewart to release Somerset or one of Somerset's supporters to purchase him. He also researched what English law had to say on the subject of slavery.

Finally, on 22 June 1772, Lord Mansfield delivered his judgment: Somerset could not be sent overseas without his consent. 'Whatever inconveniences, therefore, may follow from the decision, I cannot say this case is allowed or approved by the law of England; and therefore the black must be discharged.' Although some historians have severely criticized Mansfield for such a cautious and limited judgment, it is difficult to see how, as the law then stood, he could have come to any other conclusion.

3. Mansfield's reasons The primary reason Mansfield gave for his decision was the impossibility of making a ruling in one country based on another's laws (this holds true today), even if that country were a colony of Britain and therefore technically subordinate. Slavery, he found, no longer existed in England and Wales.

Mansfield referred to other judges' pronouncements on the subject of slaves in Britain. The most important was the opinion given in 1729 by the Attorney-General (Sir Philip Yorke) and the Solicitor-General (Charles Talbot), who said that slaves coming from the West Indies with or without their masters did not become free, baptism did not confer freedom, and their masters could compel them to return to the plantations. In 1749 Philip Yorke, by then the Lord Chancellor, reiterated that baptism did not confer freedom. Mansfield found that these were simply legal opinions and had not been delivered in circumstances that gave them the weight of law. His review of the laws relating to servants and to property found nothing pertinent. However, he confirmed that baptism did not emancipate slaves. In the course of his judgment, Mansfield also gave his opinion that the state of slavery was 'odious', and only 'positive' law, specific Acts of Parliament defining it, could support it.

4. Effects of the judgment The culmination of the case, the release of Somerset, was greeted with joy by black people and with dismay by slave owners. Both groups believed that it meant the emancipation of slaves in England and Wales, but they were mistaken. People did not distinguish a judge's views, his *obiter dicta*, from the actual legal judgment being delivered. Although Mansfield spent some time castigating slavery and said that 'if the Negro Somerset was a man—and he should conclude him one until the court should adjudge otherwise—it was impossible he could be a slave in England', these were only his opinions: his legal conclusion was simply that Somerset must be discharged and could not be sent out of the country.

In the course of the hearing Mansfield pointed out that it was not the place of the courts to decide on such a momentous issue: only the creation of legislature by Parliament could do so. The abolitionists took note and switched their fight to Parliament, even though the kidnapping and shipping of black servants back to the Caribbean colonies continued. What became of James Somerset, the focus of the case, has yet to be discovered. KAC

Fryer, Peter, *Staying Power: The History of Black People in Britain* (1984)

Howell's State Trials, vol. 20: (1816), cols. 1–6, 79–82

See also ABOLITION; EMANCIPATION; SLAVERY

Soubise, Julius (1754–1798). Equestrian and man of letters, favourite of the

Duchess of Queensberry and contemporary of Ignatius *Sancho and Olaudah *Equiano. Born on the Caribbean island of St Kitts, he was brought to England at the age of 10 and given to the Duchess of Queensberry as a gift. Under the Duchess's direction Soubise became an accomplished fencer and equestrian, serving as assistant to the Italian fencing master Dominico Angelo Malevolti Tremamondo.

Soubise is best remembered as a fop in London high society. Claiming to be an African prince, he was known for entertaining audiences in fashionable London clubs with comic songs and amateur theatre. He often escorted aristocratic women to the opera and was rumoured to be sexually engaged with the Duchess—a relationship depicted in an engraving by William Austin of the pair fencing (1773).

While Soubise regarded himself as a talented letter writer and poet of romantic sonnets, only one sample of his writing survives. In a love letter published in the anonymous *Nocturnal Revels* (1779) Soubise confesses his love for 'Miss G ——', referring to himself as her 'Negro Slave'.

In 1777 Soubise was accused of rape by one of the Duchess's maids. Continuing her habit of relieving his debt, the Duchess paid for his passage to Calcutta, where he established a fencing academy and became known as a horsebreaker. He died of head injuries in August 1798 after falling from a horse. EDS

ODNB

Sandhu, Sukhdev, *London Calling: How Black and Asian Writers Imagined a City* (2003)

See also GEORGIAN AND VICTORIAN BRITAIN

Soul music. The UK soul scene grew out of rhythm and blues (R & B), in which, in Britain, acts were copying the original compositions, style, and techniques of African-Americans. In London in the 1960s this music was centred at the Flamingo Club in Wardour Street, which was rented every Friday and Saturday night by the brothers Rick and Johnny Gunnell. An all-nighter, it featured recorded music and live bands, notably Georgie Fame & the Blue Flames, Chris Farlow & the Thunderbirds, and later, as it evolved into soul, the former African-American GI Geno Washington and the Ram Jam Band and Malcolm McGarron and the Q-Set. These two were the primary R & B and soul acts that performed regularly at the Flamingo and throughout Britain, but they never had a successful recording. The Flamingo also regularly exposed soul acts from the United States, such as Lee Dorsey, Solomon Burke, and Wilson Pickett. Performing American soul chart hits did not create the popularity or originality of British acts. With the coming of the Liverpool-based soul band the Real Thing in 1976 with the Number 1 hit 'You To Me Are Everything', the fortunes of black British soul music changed.

In London several soul bands arose, such as High Tension, with their first album (1985) of the same name, the single from which was a Top Twenty hit. Their record label, London Records, had among their senior personnel Trinidad-born Roger Aimes, who later went on to become managing director of both London Records and the Polygram Group in the United Kingdom. Island Records, which always released both African-American and British acts, released Light of the World's debut album and the single 'London Town', which reached the charts in the late 1970s.

The apotheosis of soul's success came in the form of Heatwave (1977), led by the singer Johnny Wilder and its highly successful songwriter Rod Temperton, who went on to work with Quincy Jones and several acts in the United States. Billy Ocean's 'Caribbean Queen' (a US and UK Number 1 in 1984) was an international sensation. Then came Jazzy B's Soul II Soul (1989), which synthesized soul and *reggae with strings, most notably in 'Back to Life'. Soul II Soul's production and musical technique had such an international impact that not only did they hit Number 1 in both Britain and America, but they also won a Grammy Award. These highly successful acts were followed by others, such as Incognito, Sweet Sensation, Junior, Loose End, Imagination (with several Top Ten hits in Britain and on the Continent), Sonique, M People, and many more who brought the UK soul scene to the fore, although several 'white' acts scored significantly in the US charts: Average White Band and Pete Wingfield's 1975 hit '18 With a Bullet' are examples. ASS

Oliver, Paul (ed.), *Black Music in Britain: Essays on the Afro-Asian Contribution to Popular Music* (1990)

See also DUB MUSIC; GOSPEL MUSIC; MUSIC 2: EARLY POPULAR MUSIC

South Sea Company. British company formed in 1711, granted by the Treaty of Utrecht (1713) exclusive rights to supply African slaves to the Spanish colonies in the New World. Although very little trade was done by the Company, its propaganda about potentially vast profits to be made from the New World resulted in a giddy escalation of its share price. Trading in shares peaked in August 1720, then the 'Bubble' burst, the share price tumbled, and thousands of investors who had gambled fortunes were ruined. It was the greatest economic calamity of the 18th century.

Contemporary writers described the greed of stockjobbers and gamblers as a cannibalistic frenzy. Charles Cotton in *The Compleat Gamester* (1721 edn.) satirized such gamblers as 'Anthropophagi or Man-Eaters'. The writers revealed how speculators in South Sea stock thought little or nothing upon the morality of the Company's commerce, which involved exploitation of Africans as well as indigenous Indians. J.B.'s satire *A Poem Occasion'd by the Rise and Fall of South Sea Stock* (1720) describes how 'thousand swarthy slaves do daily sweat | beneath the precious Ingots pond'rous Weight' and refers to the 'mean abject Slave with dewy brow'. One South Sea satirical illustration, appropriately on a playing card (Queen of Hearts, Pack 242, Phillips Collection, Guildhall Library, London), shows a black slave manufacturing snuff for white people, and the suffering as tobacco dust blinds him. The defrauded and exploited subscriber to the South Sea Company (and other 'Bubble' companies that sprang up in 1719–20) is related to the black slave: the blindness of the latter is compared to that of the former, and the overseer who works his black slave is compared to the Company director who 'works' his subscribers into yielding up their money. The ragged, half-starved, and crippled Indian pulling the 'Chariot of Bubbles' in Bernard Picart's engraving *A Monument Dedicated to Posterity in Commemoration of Ye Incredible Folly Transacted in the Year 1720* can be interpreted as an indication of the exploitation and destruction of native life that the system of European commerce involved. DD

Carswell, J., *The South Sea Bubble* (1961)
Dabydeen, D., *Hogarth, Walpole and Commercial Britain* (1987)

See also SLAVE TRADE; VISUAL ARTS 1: REPRESENTATIONS OF BLACKS

South Shields. Arab seamen from Yemen in south-west Arabia began visiting South Shields at the end of the 19th century. By the early 20th century some had become domiciled there and were shipping out regularly from the port, a major coal-exporting centre at that time. Arabs were engaged mainly as firemen, especially in the coal-carrying tramp trades. Their numbers grew rapidly during the First World War, when South Shields became the largest centre of Arab seamen in Britain after Cardiff. They contributed significantly to the war effort, filling the vacuum in the merchant marine created when British seamen were called up for service in the Royal Navy and the Army. Many were killed when their ships were torpedoed.

Some Arabs settled down in the town, married local women, and opened a number of seamen's boarding houses, cafés, and shops, but the majority were transients and sojourners, and after a number of years in seafaring, when they had earned a sufficient amount of money, they returned to their home villages in Yemen and were often replaced by other family members. When ashore, most Arab seamen lived in one of the Arab boarding houses run by a fellow countryman and had only limited contact with the host society.

Once the exceptional demands of the First World War were over, the Arab seamen found themselves unwanted guests and faced mounting hostility and racial prejudice at both official and popular levels. The war had dislocated the vitally important coal trade of north-east ports, and the onset of the economic depression of the inter-war years seriously affected the shipping industry, resulting in intense competition for jobs between white seamen and Arabs in an overstocked labour market. Sexual jealousy and moral outrage at the association of Arabs with white women also contributed to racial tensions that erupted in serious street violence in February 1919. There were further violent clashes in August 1930, the so-called 'Arab riot', when police intervened after a disturbance at the Shipping Federation Offices during picketing by the Communist-led Seamen's Minority Movement and those Arabs opposed to the introduction of a new rota system of registration for Arab seamen by the shipowners and the National Union of Seamen. Some of the Arabs arrested were later deported.

As Muslims, the Arabs appear to have encountered few obstacles from the local authorities in observing their religious obligations and rituals, and there is no evidence that popular hostility towards the Arabs was rooted specifically in prejudice against Islam. Rather, they were vilified as 'coloured aliens' who took jobs from 'white Britishers'. Indeed, the activities of several transnational Islamic organizations were officially encouraged to help enforce social control.

There were further heavy losses during the Second World War, especially among seamen serving in the merchant navy. After the war the decline in the port of South Shields resulted in little new immigration into the town from Yemen. Through intermarriage, the Arab community gradually 'dissolved' into the general population of the town and prejudice declined. RIL

Lawless, R. I., *From Ta'izz to Tyneside: An Arab Community in the North-East of England During the Early Twentieth Century* (1995)

See also LASCARS AND BLACK SEAMEN; 'RACE' RIOTS, 1919

Southall Black Sisters. Located in Southall, in the west London borough of Ealing, the Southall Black Sisters (SBS) was formed in 1979 as an autonomous black women's organization, bringing together a group of Asian and African-Caribbean women activists. SBS combined, from its inception, a strong campaigning strand with advocacy work, and placed great emphasis on the evolution of a vibrant cultural politics. Begun in the aftermath of neo-fascist violence in Southall in April 1979, which witnessed the death of Blair *Peach and the arrest of over 300 protesters, it campaigned, in its first year, against institutionalized racism of the state, racist immigration legislation, 'virginity' testing of would-be migrant women, and a local beauty contest; it supported the strikers at the Chix factory; it conducted women's only advisory sessions at Southall Rights; it wrote and performed a feminist play; and it affiliated to the *Organization of Women of African and Asian Descent.

SBS received Greater London Council funding in 1983 to establish a women's centre, and became well known for its campaigning work on violence against women (the Krishna Sharma Campaign in 1984; Free Kiranjit Ahluwalia Campaign 1992; agitating against forced marriages; lobbying for changes in legislation; providing training on the issue). It was at the forefront of a national momentum to develop better policies and practices on the question of violence against black and minority women. SBS continues to provide support to individual women, and to advocate on issues of women's right to a secure life, *mental health issues, child protection, *immigration, and asylum. It has won many awards and continues to be a secular black feminist organization, celebrating 25 years of its work in 2004. PM

Gupta, Rahila (ed.), *From Homebreakers to Jailbreakers: Southall Black Sisters* (2003)

See also FEMINISM

Southern Syncopated Orchestra. Thirty-five-piece African-American orchestra formed in the United States by Will Marion Cook and George Lattimore to fill an engagement at the Philharmonic Hall, London, which opened on 4 July 1919. Although its repertoire encompassed ragtime, spirituals, and light classical music as well as *jazz, its historical importance lies in bringing to Britain several major creative figures in jazz, including the clarinettist Sidney Bechet, the trumpeter Arthur Briggs, and the drummers Benton Peyton and Buddie Gilmore. In December 1919 the orchestra was reduced in size, Bechet and others moving into small jazz groups, whose performances in London dance clubs were highly influential. The orchestra toured in Scotland and the provinces with an ever-shifting personnel, which increasingly recruited members of the African diaspora of British, Caribbean, and African birth, to replace the departed Americans. These included future leaders of the London jazz scene such as Cyril Blake. There were periods when more than one version of the Orchestra was touring following disagreements between the principals, which engendered lengthy litigation in the English courts. With some lay-offs the Orchestra continued to perform through 1920 and 1921. A summer season at the Dome, Brighton, in 1921 was followed by a Glasgow engagement, after which the Orchestra sailed to Ireland on the SS *Rowan*, which sank off Corsewall Point on 9 October with the loss of eight members, including the Philadelphia-born drummer Pete Robinson. The survivors resumed the Irish tour but disbanded in November. HR

Gioia, T., *The History of Jazz* (1999)

See also MUSIC 2: EARLY POPULAR MUSIC; SOUL MUSIC

Southey, Robert (1774–1843). British Poet Laureate (appointed in 1813) whose radical literary output included poems against the slave trade. Southey, born in the slave port of *Bristol, was moved by the egalitarian principles of the French Revolution (1789), and co-wrote with Samuel Taylor *Coleridge a play celebrating revolutionary social change, *The Fall of Robespierre* (1794). With Coleridge and other friends he planned to set up a 'Pantisocracy' in New England—a communal utopian settlement of fraternity and harmony.

His poem 'To the Genius of Africa' (1797) is a passionate and revolutionary call to Africans to take up arms against slave traders ('Avenging Power awake—arise!'; 'awake! arise! avenge!'). It is a powerful denunciation of European involvement in what Southey deems to be criminal activity. It pulls no punches in exposing 'Afric's wrongs and Europe's guilt', Southey writing of black bodies whipped and wounded until they become 'stiff and hard with human gore'. Such neo-Gothic images of sadism and suffering are repeated in the six sonnets on the slave trade (1797), Southey's anger a savage counterblast to the apologists for West Indian planters and merchants. The opening lines of Sonnet I can barely contain Southey's fury: 'Hold your mad hands! for ever on your plain | Must the gorged vulture clog his beak with blood?' The graphic image of a tortured slave in Sonnet VI recalls William *Blake's illustrations to J. G. Stedman's *Narrative, of a Five Years' Expedition* (1796), *A Negro hung alive by the Ribs to a Gallows*: 'High in the air expos'd the Slave is hung | To all the birds of Heaven, their living food.' Southey indicts those who continue to take sugar in their tea and coffee ('the blood-sweetened beverage'), his call for a boycott of slave-produced goods giving a practical dimension to his moral outrage. DD

Dabydeen, D. (ed.), *The Black Presence in English Literature* (1985)

See also ABOLITION; CLARE, JOHN; COWPER, WILLIAM; LITERATURE 1: REPRESENTATIONS OF BLACKS; WORDSWORTH, WILLIAM

Sowande, Fela (1905–1987). Professor, composer, and organist, celebrated and internationally renowned as being a founding father in the development of modern Nigerian art music. He was born in Lagos in 1905, where, under

Dr Ekundayo Phillips, he was trained as a chorister and organist at Lagos Cathedral, being exposed to west European church music and Yoruba traditional musical culture. In 1934, after studying European classical music in London, he gained a Bachelor's degree in music (University of London) and Fellowship of the Royal College of Organists by private study with George Oldroyd and George Cunningham. Later he became a Fellow of Trinity College of Music.

After studying, Sowande undertook a diverse range of activities as an organist–choirmaster, composer, and jazz musician. He became music adviser to the Colonial Film Unit of the British Ministry of Information in London (1941) and head of music and research for the Nigerian Broadcasting Corporation (1950s); he held professorships at the University of Ibadan (1968), Howard University (1968–72), and the University of Pittsburgh (1972–87). He died in 1987 aged 82.

Sowande's musical output includes folk song arrangements, organ music, sacred choral music, solo songs, African-American choral music, and orchestral music. His musical style manifests eclectic influences, including hi-life and jazz idioms, 19th-century European harmony, liturgical music blending Anglican and Yoruba influences, and Yoruba traditional music. *African Suite* (1955) and *Folk Symphony* (1960) express his cultural and nationalistic style. He received many honours, including an MBE from Queen Elizabeth II, in 1965, for his distinguished services to music. PAH

Omojola, Bode, *Nigerian Art Music* (1995)

See also MUSIC 1: CLASSICAL MUSIC

Sport. Blacks' involvement in British sport dates back to the late 18th century, when black prizefighters astonished spectators with their prowess. That prowess remained a source of fascination for over 200 years, prompting explanations that were often based on, and indeed provided momentum for, racist theories.

1. After the first battle
2. A handful of coloured
3. In the blood
4. Mind and muscle

1. After the first battle It is difficult to know exactly whether Tom *Molineaux was in breach or observance of norms when he challenged the all-England champion Tom Cribb in 1810. The fight, which took place in Copthorne, about 30 miles south of London, featured a black former slave from America against the most celebrated pugilist of his day. Molineaux was assisted by Bill *Richmond, another former slave turned prizefighter. Giving Cribb such a tough and punishing fight before losing in the thirty-ninth round (the Queensberry Rules were not introduced until 1867) violated the English sense of superiority. Yet Molineaux also observed the codes of what Ella Shohat and Robert Stam, in their *Unthinking Eurocentrism*, call 'animalization'. An account of the day described Molineaux: 'The Black stripp'd, and appeared of a giant-like strength, large in bone, large in muscle and with arms a cruel length.'

It is a resonant portrayal and one that reveals Whites' curiosity about the physical characteristics of Blacks. The curiosity went beyond sport: in their attempts to make the difference between themselves and those whom they conquered appear natural rather cultural, colonial Whites associated Blacks with natural, instinctive ability rather than learned competence. The trope endured.

In the same year as the Molineaux–Cribb match, Sarah *Baartman, a South African woman known as 'the Hottentot Venus', was exhibited like a freak in England and France. Spectators would examine her body, feeling her ample buttocks should they wish. After her death in 1816 the noted anatomist Georges Cuvier dissected her body and used its parts as evidence to support his theory of fixed racial types. Like other prominent Blacks who displayed their bodies, she was an emblem of exoticism and Otherness.

The racial studies pursued by Cuvier and many others in the 19th century were, according to Audrey Smedley's *Race in North America: Origins and Evolution of a Worldview*, a reaction to the success of the anti-slavery movement. The view finds favour with Jan Nederveen Pieterse, who, in his *White on Black: Images of Africa and Blacks in Western Popular Culture*, argued that 'the science of race developed after the first battle had been won in the struggle against slavery, with the British prohibition of the slave trade in 1807'.

The appearance of black prizefighters in the aftermath of the abolition of the slave trade aroused further fascination with the sources of Blacks' physical distinctness. As the search for a justification of slavery gained pace, black sportsmen (unlike today, there were no female pugilists), like Molineaux and the several other prizefighters who followed him, were seen as much as specimens as athletes. Every time a black athlete stepped up to the scratch mark (the line from which the fighting commenced), he became an exhibit. Ex-slaves, like Bobby *Dobbs, and sons of slaves, such as Bob Travers, toured England, attracting the praise of journalists and audiences alike. They were, of course, rarities and as such became curiosities rather than the objects of disdain Blacks were to become in the 20th century. Yet they were still exhibits, shown publicly for the amusement of others or as living proof of the animalism of black people. Perhaps the most dramatic instance of this was the caging of an African youth in a Belgian zoo in the mid-19th century.

Even by 1907, when South Africa-born Andrew Jeptha became the first black boxer to hold a British title, Blacks remained objects of enthralment. Two years before, in a spectacle reminiscent of the Hottentot Venus exhibition, six Moutis from the territory we now know as the Democratic Republic of Congo appeared at the London Hippodrome. The 'children of nature', as they were called by *The Times* (4 June 1905), did not sing, dance, or perform in any way: they simply came out on stage to be peered at.

The moral horizons of the 19th century were set by religious and scientific discourses. The publication of Darwin's *On the Origin of Species* in 1859 affected both. If evolution and natural selection were the principles of natural existence, the reason why the poor remained poor and Blacks were in a position of servitude lay in their deficiencies rather than in social arrangements or historical circumstances. So it seemed reasonable to suppose that the demonstrable prowess of black sportsmen was the result of a natural surfeit of physical capacities. The same fortitude that had allowed them to survive the rigours of slavery had equipped them to excel in competition (this type of argument was to reappear in another guise in the 20th century, as we shall see).

The sporting achievements of Blacks, especially following *emancipation, would have been consistent with this worldview. So it was possible for the itinerant prizefighter Peter Jackson to draw acclaim and enjoy what we would now call a celebrity lifestyle. 'I knew him in the days of his greatness when sitting on top of the pugilistic world, fêted and lionized,' recalled the Earl of Lonsdale. As Jackson's fame waned in the 1880s, Arthur *Wharton appeared as a goalkeeper for Darlington Cricket and Football Club and distinguished himself as an exceptional all-round sportsman when he became the first man to run 100 yards in even time (10 seconds) at the Amateur Athletics Association (AAA) championships of 1886. In his *The First Black Footballer: Arthur Wharton, 1865–1930* (1998), Phil Vasili quotes from a speech given by a politician who alluded to Wharton's proficiency in Darwinian terms. The British Empire, he said, was composed of 'representatives of almost every race of men, and every stage of human progress . . . It is far from easy to understand savages.' Wharton was born in Ghana. Both he and Jackson died destitute, a fate that awaited many later black sportsmen. (Andrew *Watson is sometimes offered as the first black football player, playing briefly for the Scottish club Queens Park in the 1870s, though Wharton is conventionally credited with the distinction.)

After Wharton, the next black footballer to play for a British club was Walter *Tull, who appeared in the Tottenham Hotspur team of 1909. The sprinters Harry Edward and Jack London, both from British Guiana, were regulars on the athletics circuit in the 1920s. By this time Jeptha, who lived in London, had retired. He held his title before the British Boxing Board of Control was established. In 1929, when the Board took control of the sport, its secretary justified a new policy with a oblique acknowledgement of Blacks' natural advantage: 'It is only right that a small country such as ours should have championships restricted to boxers of white parents—otherwise we might be faced with a situation where all our British titles are held by coloured Empire boxers.'

2. A handful of coloured Boxing's rule prohibited Larry Gains, among others, from fighting for a British title. Born in Canada, Gains moved permanently to England when he was 30, having already challenged for a version of the world heavyweight title in the United States in 1928. This was a time when the 'color bar', as Americans called it, operated to prevent African-Americans and Whites from competing together. Blacks played baseball in 'Negro leagues', organized all-black basketball teams (the Harlem Globetrotters started in 1927), and staged their own professional boxing championships. Gains went two years without defeat after moving to England but was denied a challenge: 'Ninety percent of the public wanted to see me win the British title,' he told this writer during an interview in 1980. 'There wasn't prejudice amongst the public then 'cause there was only a handful of coloured here, anyway.'

Gains may have been right, at least as far as numbers were concerned, though this should not obscure the presence of moderate organizations such as the *League of Coloured Peoples, which started in 1931, or the anti-imperialist lobby, which opposed the racism practised in British colonies. George *Padmore, who moved to London in 1932, was an active organizer of the Pan-African Congress, which was committed to 'civil rights for African peoples and the total abolition of all forms of racial discrimination'. At the 1945 meeting of the Pan-African Conference, Amy Ashwood *Garvey (widow of Marcus *Garvey) chaired a session on 'the colour problem in Britain', which, according Ron Ramdin in his *The Making of the Black Working Class in Britain* (1987), meant: 'unemployment, ashore and at sea, the support of illegitimate children fathered by Black Americans and discriminatory treatment by the police'.

Some prominent sports figures were granted the kind of status that removed them from the emerging 'colour problem'. MacDonald Bailey, for example, was one of the leading athletes of his generation. Born in Trinidad, he served in the Royal Air Force during the *Second World War, then settled in Britain, accumulating a record sixteen AAA titles and a bronze medal while representing Britain at the 1952 Olympic Games. His contemporary Arthur Wint also served in the RAF, though he competed for his native Jamaica at the Olympics, winning gold in 1948. He returned to Jamaica in 1955. Another Jamaican, Lloyd 'Lindy' Delaphena, played football for Middlesbrough immediately after the war and then for Portsmouth until 1958. His playing career was free of the kind of racist enmity that was to become commonplace in the 1980s.

Welcomed as athletes, they might inadvertently have concealed deeper antipathies that surfaced only occasionally. One such occasion was in 1943, when the celebrated Trinidadian cricketer Learie *Constantine was refused accommodation at London's Imperial Hotel because the management did not want 'niggers' at the hotel. The former Test player, who was revealingly described by the cricket writer Neville Cardus as 'a sort of elemental, instinctive force', was awarded damages. Lord Constantine (as he became in 1969) had been based in England since 1929.

Sport is part of what Pieterse called the 'terrain on which Blacks have been permitted to manifest themselves' (the other part being entertainment). Out of their appropriate context, they were exactly as the hotel's manager described them. Years later the American sociologist Harry Edwards wrote: 'The only difference between the black man shining shoes in the ghetto and the champion black sprinter is that the shoe shine man is a nigger, while the sprinter is a fast nigger.'

African-American champions such as the boxer Jack Johnson and sprinter-jumper Jesse Owens were well known to the British, who looked on from afar at the de jure segregation that until 1954 effectively divided the United States into two ostensibly 'separate but equal' societies. Britain had no comparable legal segregation, though, as we have seen, discrimination was present, and boxing employed its own version of a colour bar. This was lifted in 1948 when a British-born boxer, Dick Turpin, who had been boxing professionally for eleven years, was allowed to challenge (successfully) for the British middleweight title. Turpin's father was from British Guiana, his mother from Leamington Spa.

In the same year as Turpin's triumph, the Labour government introduced a Nationality Act that facilitated access to Britain from its former colonies. A labour shortage combined with a post-war economic expansion necessitated drastic measures. Even Enoch *Powell, the politician who later prophesied racial conflict, travelled to the Caribbean to recruit nurses for the understaffed *National Health Service. (Powell was, at the time, Minister for Health: in 1968 he sparked a conflagration on British race relations with a speech in which he predicted, 'in fifteen or twenty years' time, the black man will have the whip hand over the white man'.)

As if to accentuate the importance of 1948, in June 492 Jamaicans disembarked from the SS **Empire Windrush*. While they are popularly thought to be the start of a major movement, Caribbean migrants followed only slowly at first, with just over 5,000 over the next five years. Presumably heartened by the gainful employment found by the pioneers and the absence of overt hostility towards them, others followed. Mass migration from the Caribbean picked up after 1953, so that by 1958 about 125,000 émigrés had moved to Britain.

Shortly before the migration gained impetus, a black boxer secured himself a place in history by beating the seemingly invincible Sugar Ray Robinson, a fighter who had not been beaten in 91 consecutive contests since February 1943. In 1951 Randolph *Turpin, brother of Dick, became an improbable world champion, albeit for a short period of time: 64 days later he was beaten in a rematch and, though he stayed active for the next several years, never secured a third fight with Robinson. Turpin's life followed much the same elliptical path as Peter Jackson's and Arthur Wharton's, as well as those of several great African-Americans, including Jack Johnson and Jesse Owens and the heavyweight champion Joe Louis, all of whom experienced hardship once their sporting careers were over. After ascending to a sporting peak, Turpin ran into financial difficulties and was forced to engage in humiliating boxer versus wrestler freak matches when way past his prime. Turpin's demise was tragic: in 1966 he committed suicide by shooting himself.

3. **In the blood** While the Turpin brothers were born in England, most British-based Blacks in the post-war period were from either the Caribbean or Africa, their decision to domicile themselves in Britain being a pragmatic one. Migrants headed to the bigger cities, such as London, Birmingham, and Manchester, where the jobs were abundant. Traditional textile areas in Yorkshire and Lancashire were also targeted. In a period of full employment, native white workers moved up the occupational hierarchies, leaving less desirable vacancies, which migrants filled.

Caribbeans frequently worked in low-status, often unskilled positions, despite having qualifications and experience suitable for more prestigious jobs. They were also herded informally into certain parts of the cities where rents were low and overcrowding tolerated. Before 1965 there was no law to prevent overt racial discrimination. A landlord wishing to prohibit black tenants could advertise with impunity for 'Whites only'. And yet the combination of depression and chronic unemployment in the homelands and the plentiful job opportunities in Britain was a potent one and one that motivated significant population shifts from the Caribbean.

The first wave of migrants harboured a distinct ambition: to have a temporary, profitable stay in the 'motherland', as many regarded Britain, before returning to the Caribbean. This fortifying belief helped migrants to endure the often unduly harsh conditions they initially encountered, though it soon transmuted into what some called 'the myth of return'. Many black boxers would have used their purses (as boxing pay is known) to supplement their income; others had their eye on bigger prizes.

Hogan Bassey was, in many senses, a reluctant migrant: he left Nigeria for Liverpool in 1951 purely to pursue his boxing ambitions. By 1957 he had realized them, winning the world featherweight title. He retired at the relatively young age of 27 and returned to Nigeria to become a coach. Another conspicuously successful black boxer of the period was Yolande Pompey, from Trinidad, who fought his way to contention but failed in his attempt to win the world title in London in 1956.

Turpin's biographer Jack Birtley made no mention of racism, or any other kind of bigotry or unfairness that must have habitually confronted black people, when he wrote his account in 1976. During Turpin's heyday in the late 1940s–early 1950s racism was not popularly understood as a social problem, though Fryer argued, 'prejudice against black people was widespread'. At least half of Britain's white population had never met a black person. 'They saw them as heathens who practised head-hunting, cannibalism, infanticide, polygamy, and "Black magic",' wrote Fryer. 'They believed Black men had stronger sexual urges than white men, were less inhibited, and could give greater satisfaction to their sexual partners.' While Fryer did not specify whether they were regarded as 'natural athletes', we can extrapolate from his conclusions. The point is, however, that Blacks lived in a kind of peaceful, if slightly discommodious, coexistence with Whites. All this changed in 1958.

A Midlands town best known for Robin Hood and D. H. Lawrence was an unlikely site for Britain's first significant racially motivated unrest since the war. Nottingham's industry, especially in mining and bicycle manufacture, was an enticement for migrants in the post-war period. In August 1958 a gang of Whites stormed into the St Ann's Well district, where many Blacks lived, prompting 24 arrests. In the same month a similar disturbance in London's Notting Hill went on for several days. Elsewhere the pattern repeated itself, signalling the end of peaceful coexistence and the beginning of a period of hostility. There had been earlier inchoate demonstrations—in ports such as *Cardiff and *Liverpool—but nothing so clear and emphatically racist. Mindful of the Civil Rights Movement in the United States, the British government drafted two pieces of legislation: the restrictive Commonwealth Immigrants Act 1962 and the Race Relation Act 1965.

The attraction to boxing is not hard to understand. In terms of equipment its needs are minimal. Its tradition of black champions freed it from the restrictions of many other sports. Its individualism rewarded those willing to make sacrifices in the pursuit of success—as all migrants have to do. Yet there were other prominent sports performers, notably in athletics. Roy Hollingsworth, a discus-thrower from Trinidad, and Clive Long, from Guyana, both gained international honours in the 1960s, though it was a Jamaican, Marilyn Fay Neufville, who was the outstanding athlete of her day. Neufville arrived in Britain in 1961 when she was 8, and in her teens ran for Cambridge Harriers in south-east London. There was some controversy about her decision to represent Jamaica rather than Britain at the Commonwealth Games in 1970. She won the 400 metres, setting a world record of 51 seconds in the process. Her career fizzled out prematurely as she struggled against injuries.

Neufville was not jeered or beaten, though her preference for representing Jamaica while she was resident in London angered many, especially as many black boxers sought to fight for British titles but were prevented from doing so by a rule that specified that a title contestant 'has been resident in the United Kingdom for a period of not less than ten years'. It was 1970 before a migrant boxer won a British title; that was Jamaican-born Bunny Stirling, who had moved to England in 1954.

The issue of patriotic fidelity swirled in the air. South Africa-born Basil D'Oliveira was selected to play cricket for England in 1968 and prompted an international incident when a tour of the then segregated South Africa was aborted. Clive Sullivan became the first black captain of a British national team in any sport when he led the rugby league team to a World Cup win in 1972. It was another 32 years before rugby union appointed Jason Robinson as the first black captain of England. In football Viv Anderson was the first black player to represent England in 1978. Two years later Roland Butcher played cricket for England, and eight years after that David Lawrence claimed the distinction of becoming the first British-born black cricketer to play for England. Of all Britain's many black boxing champions, none expressed their Britishness more prominently than Frank Bruno, who rarely missed an opportunity to hoist the Union Jack in the 1980s and 1990s.

There was no novelty at all in black sportsmen and -women displaying pride and commitment in representing Britain. So it came as a surprise when, in 1995, Robert Henderson wrote an article for the venerable cricket publication *Wisden* maintaining that the England cricket team should consist only of 'unequivocal Englishmen'. This specious category excluded black players and white players born outside England. Portentously entitled 'Is It in the Blood?', the article prompted legal action by the black cricketers Devon Malcolm and Phillip DeFreitas, both of whom played for England and were presumably stung by the suggestion that they might not have possessed the requisite substance. Over 8 per cent of all county cricket players were from African-Caribbean backgrounds. What made the widely reported argument more staggering was its timing: a year after Linford Christie's Olympic 100 metres triumph, following which the Jamaican-born athlete had wrapped himself in the Union flag.

4. **Mind and muscle** 'Black athletic achievement is still haunted by the Law of Compensation, which postulates an inverse relationship between mind and muscle,' wrote John Hoberman in his book *Darwin's Athletes* in 1997. The link between physical and intellectual capacity on the one hand and race on the other was not a subject that engaged the British until the 1980s. But the sudden, surprising emergence of so many black athletes in the higher echelons of the nation's most popular game, coupled with concern over the persistent underachievement of black children at school, prompted serious reflection.

The early prognosis about black schoolchildren's poor educational performance was that it would improve over time as they assimilated. Nevertheless, research suggested that it had become too consistent to be so easily dismissed. In 1980 the National Association of Head Teachers, reporting to the Rampton Committee on the education of ethnic minorities, stated: 'If there is a difficulty of cultural identity among second generation West Indians, there is also much to counter-balance that deficiency including their natural sense of rhythm, colour and athletic prowess.'

Black footballers seemed to provide clear evidence. After Delaphena's disappearance in 1958, the South African Albert Johanneson played for Leeds United in the 1960s, the Bermudan Clyde Best for West Ham United in the 1970s, and the Kittitian Cec Podd for Bradford City and other clubs in the 1970s and 1980s. These were isolated cases, about which there was no disquiet. But when, in the early 1980s, black players began to appear in numbers, the reaction was startling. The players themselves were made to endure the torment of racial chants, monkey noises, and pelting with bananas from incensed crowds. They were also the focus of a media that found headlines like 'Black Magic' irresistible. The manager of West Bromwich Albion, Ron Atkinson, patronizingly dubbed Cyrille Regis, Brendon Batson, and Laurie *Cunningham 'the Three Degrees' (after the female singing trio of the time).

In a way, the incredulity is understandable. It seemed that every week a previously unknown black player would surface. Yet fans regarded black players as contaminants, and players like John Barnes, Garth Crooks, and Garry Thompson became inured to the roar of 'Nigger, nigger, lick my boots'. Football fans' racist response became one of Britain's least creditable exports: over the next several decades fans in Spain, Italy, and east European countries systematically abused black players. The practice continued in Britain into the 21st century: in 2003 fans at Sunderland chanted racist epithets during an England–Turkey game. In reply, campaigns such as Let's Kick Racism Out of Football were aimed at combating the development.

Even the more measured responses had racist undertones. The former track hero and, later, neurologist Roger Bannister, in 1995, offered his observation, 'as a scientist', as he put it, 'Black sprinters and black athletes in general all seem to have certain anatomical advantages.' It had been possible painlessly to neglect the overachievement of Blacks in many sports, but football was Britain's perennially most popular sport, and in the 1990s black players flowed into Britain from far and wide. These included Tony Yeboah, from Ghana, Ruud Gullit from the Netherlands, and Patrick Vieira from Senegal. Several coaches, managers, and owners marvelled at the brilliance of many black players and concluded it was because of natural ability rather than the painstaking acquisition of skill, practice, and sheer hard graft associated with white players. In a similar way, Ron Noades, in 1993, when chair of Crystal Palace, detected that, while black players were effective in temperate weather, in winter 'you need a few of the maybe hard white men to carry the artistic black players through'.

The animalizing trope manifests in different ways. Abusing black athletes with apelike gestures expresses long-standing racist inclinations; explaining Blacks' prowess as the result of natural talent has much the same effect. Almost two centuries after Molineaux had excited thoughts of animalistic abilities, Blacks' sporting achievements continued to be devalued or reduced to primal impulses.

Americans had become accustomed to Blacks' pre-eminence: since Jackie Robinson's historic major league baseball debut in 1948, African-Americans had graduated to the top levels of baseball, basketball, and American football, encouraging some writers to offer explanations. Martin Kane's was the most influential. First published in 1971, his article 'An Assessment of Black Is Best' mixed physiological, psychological, and historical material to produce an argument based on racial characteristics: black people were naturally equipped to do well in sport. At the time Harry Edwards opposed the view, arguing that so many black people do well in sport because alternative paths to success were obstructed by racist practices. Sport, on the other hand, seemed free of racism and attracted an extraordinary number of highly motivated young men and women.

Kane's theory had a common-sense appeal for the British: even by 1990 black people in Britain accounted for less than 4 per cent of the total population but about 20 per cent of professional footballers—not to mention over half of all boxers and perhaps even more than half of all track and field competitors. While Bannister's views seemed to complement the theory, it was Jon Entine's book *Taboo: Why Black Athletes Dominate and Why We're Afraid to Talk About It* (2000) that lent it credibility. Being careful to avoid charges of racism when explaining Blacks' sporting achievements, Entine stressed, 'genes set parameters, but it is life experiences that "express" biological capabilities'. Still, in the last instance, nature has primacy: 'Cultural conditions exaggerate the small but meaningful differences that led to the athletic edge.'

Those 'small but meaningful differences' were the subject of research by Bengt Saltin, who observed how highly trained Swedish athletes could be easily beaten by Kenyan schoolchildren and concluded that environments contribute only 20–25 per cent to an athlete's proficiency: the rest is all natural. With this kind of evidence, Entine asked, with a sideways glance at British football's pre-eminent black players: 'Is it just cultural serendipity that Brazilians are time and again the best soccer players?'

While it was asked rhetorically, it actually invited answers. If we take 'serendipity' to mean the faculty of making happy, unexpected discoveries, a reasonable historical case might be made. Slaves and their offspring, finding themselves at an impasse in which they and their forebears had their progress in society impeded by institutional arrangements (formal or informal), learned that a 'terrain on which Blacks have been permitted to manifest themselves is sport', to repeat Pieterse. Applying themselves with unparalleled motivation and a determination to overcome adversity, they found success attainable—not easily, but attainable nonetheless. Sport provided them with an area in which they could, as David K. Wiggins put it in his *Glory Bound: Black Athletes in a White America* (1997), 'realize a certain degree of dignity'. Buoyed by this, their sons and daughters followed the same path, all the time helping to carve out a tradition of accomplishment that inspired successive generations. The specific cultural conditions for Brazilian footballers' brilliance lie in Portuguese imperialism, the remnants of the plantation economy, and the corresponding enthusiasm for football after its introduction by the Englishman Charles Miller in the early 20th century.

This is the nurture side of an argument that has tended towards nature. There are echoes of the race–IQ debate, which resists every attempt to bury it and returns in new guises to explain the different patterns of educational achievement among Blacks and their peers. Sport presents a different though not unrelated conundrum. Is Hoberman's 'Law of Compensation' actually in force? If Blacks' achievements in British sport are because of their natural advantages, is their relative lack of progress in formal education because of natural disadvantages? One possibility offers the other.

The trope of the animally endowed black athlete refuses to go down without a fight. It includes expressions and images that ostensibly celebrate black achievement, while obscuring the historical circumstances that have commissioned Blacks' progress in sport—and obstructed their progress in other areas. Paradoxically, the appearance of Blacks in sports once considered out of reach has lessened its force. As recently as 1990 those who considered Blacks equipped only for events demanding muscularity and speed would not have countenanced the prospect of black golf and tennis champions. It later became clear that the barriers blocking their progress were social rather than physical.

Somewhere between the prizefighting ex-slaves of the 19th century and today's football plutocrats, black people skipped a transition. Otherwise there would be more black promoters, owners, managers, and administrators—the people who govern and oversee sport. In the United States some Blacks have moved into positions of this kind, though in Britain conspicuous gaps remain. Black athletes continue to perform and entertain, and are well rewarded for their exhibitions. But the function of exhibitions is to entertain, amuse, or edify. Blacks' disengagement from the decision-making centres of sport suggests that, in celebrating their achievement-strewn history in sport, there is the risk of concealing an inglorious exclusion that closely reflects their experience in society generally. ECa

Birtley, Jack, *The Tragedy of Randolph Turpin* (1976)

Fryer, Peter, *Staying Power: The History of Black People in Britain* (1984)

Hoberman, John, *Darwin's Athletes: How Sport Has Damaged Black America and Preserved the Myth of Race* (1997)

Kane, Martin, 'An Assessment of Black Is Best', *Sports Illustrated*, 18 Jan. 1971, 72–83

Pieterse, Jan Nederveen, *White on Black: Images of Africa and Blacks in Western Popular Culture* (1992)

Shohat, Ella, and Stam, Robert, *Unthinking Eurocentrism* (1994)

Smedley, Audrey, *Race in North America: Origins and Evolution of a Worldview* (1993)

See also EUGENICS; SKIN COLOUR AND RACE, THEORIES OF

Stanford, Peter Thomas (1860–1909). African-American Christian minister and author known as Birmingham's 'Coloured Preacher'. He was educated, with the help of the Beecher Stowe family, and, motivated by Christian faith, committed himself to the uplift of the black race. Ordained in Hertford, Connecticut, in 1878, he ministered among the black community, moving to Ontario, Canada, in 1882, where he was also editor of the *Christian Defender*. He arrived in Britain in 1883, and spent time in Liverpool, London, and Birmingham, and published his narrative *From Bondage to Liberty* (1889). The lynching of African-Americans in the United States was of deep concern to Birmingham's Christians in the early 1890s, and in 1895 Stanford was deputed by anti-lynching campaigners to return to the United States and report on the situation. Having arrived in Boston, he founded the first African-American Congregational church, St Mark, Roxbury. His book on the origins and true extent of lynchings, *The Tragedy of the Negro in America*, was published in 1897, and in the same year he became minister of the Congregational Church, Havervill, Massachusetts. He moved to Cambridge, Massachusetts, in 1898 and established the Union Industrial and Strangers' Home, an orphanage and school for black children, where he remained until his death. PFW

Stanford, P. Thomas, *Imaginary Obstructions to True Spiritual Progress* (1898)

Walker, Paul, 'The Revd Peter Thomas Stanford (1860–1909): Birmingham's Coloured Preacher', Ph.D. thesis (Manchester University, 2004)

See also CHRISTIANITY; CHURCHES

Stephen, James (1789–1859). Christian abolitionist who worked closely with William *Wilberforce. Stephen was born in Poole, Dorset, and educated in Winchester. He became a barrister and had a law practice in the West Indies. As a consequence of viewing the horrors of *slavery and the extreme ill-treatment of slaves on the islands, he started a correspondence with the abolitionist William Wilberforce and provided him with information on the practice of slavery in the West Indies. Under Wilberforce's influence, he joined the Clapham Sect, constituted of Christians working with Wilberforce, and eventually became its leader. He wrote a number of books that attacked the *slave trade, and several significant pamphlets such as *War in Disguise, or the Frauds of the Neutral Flags* and *The Slavery of the British West India Colonies Delineated*. Stephen also offered a few proposals for the ending of the slave trade. Among them was the registration of slaves in British colonies. Stephen's suggestions and publications incited awareness in the public of the realities of slavery. His election to Parliament meant that he was able to push his ideas further and aid Wilberforce's fight for the *abolition of the slave trade. DD/SS

Barron, T. J., 'James Stephen, the "Black Race" and British Colonial Administration, 1813–47', *Journal of Imperial and Commonwealth History*, 5 (1977)

See also CHRISTIANITY

Strong, Jonathan (*c*.1748–1773). The subject of one of the earliest important legal cases relating to slavery in Britain. Strong was brought to England from Barbados, where he had been a slave and which may have been his place of birth, by his master, a Barbadian merchant and planter called David Lisle. In 1765 Granville *Sharp met Strong in London, at the house of his brother William Sharp, a surgeon who gave free medical advice and treatment to the poor. Lisle had beaten Strong about the head with a pistol and turned him out into the street, and Strong had found his way to William Sharp's house in search of help. William Sharp arranged for Strong to be treated at St Bartholomew's Hospital, but his injuries were so severe that it was more than four months before he was discharged.

The Sharp brothers then found employment for Strong with a London apothecary, where he appears to have worked happily (and been paid wages) for some two years. In 1767 Lisle saw Strong by chance in the street, looking fit and healthy once more, and decided to make something out of a person whom he still regarded as his property. He proceeded to sell him to a Jamaican planter called James Kerr for £30, the money to be paid when Strong had been put on board a ship ready to sail for the Caribbean. Strong was unaware of this until Lisle had him kidnapped and lodged in a prison until a suitable ship was ready.

Strong had been baptized and appealed for help to his godfathers, who came to the prison but were refused admittance. He then sent a letter to Granville Sharp, who received it on 12 September 1767. Sharp did not remember Strong's name, but went to the prison the next day and, in the face of denials that there was anybody called Jonathan Strong in custody there, persisted in his demands until Strong was brought to see him. Sharp then remembered their original meeting, and was so moved by what he heard about the kidnapping and the danger in which Strong was of being returned to the Caribbean as a slave, that he took the case to court, arguing that Strong's detention was unlawful, since no warrant had been issued for his arrest for any offence. The case was heard on 18 September 1767 before the Lord Mayor of London, Sir Robert Kite, who ruled that 'the lad had not stolen any thing, and was not guilty of any offence, and was therefore at liberty to go away'. The captain of the ship on which Lisle and Kerr intended to send Strong to Jamaica was present in the court, and immediately attempted to seize Strong on the grounds that he was Kerr's property. Acting on advice he had been given by Thomas Beech, the Coroner of London, Sharp warned the captain that, if he did so, he would charge him for assault. As Sharp put it, 'The Captain thereupon withdrew his hand, and all parties retired from the presence of the Lord Mayor, and Jonathan Strong departed also, in the sight of all, in full liberty, nobody daring afterwards to touch him.'

That was not the end of it. Lisle sought 'satisfaction' from Sharp, that is, he challenged him to a duel. Sharp turned down the challenge, saying that Lisle 'should want no satisfaction that the law should give him.' Kerr started a lawsuit against Sharp, claiming that he was unlawfully depriving him of his property. Although professional lawyers advised Sharp that the law was not on his side, he set to studying the law with such diligence that, when he circulated in manuscript the results of his researches, claiming that the law of England did not (as had generally been accepted) sanction slavery, he impressed many of the legal profession with the force of his arguments. As a result, Kerr's lawyers decided against pursuing the case, and Kerr had to pay treble costs. Kerr later started another suit against Sharp, but again failed to proceed with it. Sharp continued to ignore repeated attempts by Lisle to persuade him of the lawfulness of his claim to own Strong as a slave, and the matter petered out.

Jonathan Strong remained at liberty until he died in London on 17 April 1773. He was only about 25, and his death may well have been attributable to the consequences of the severe beating he had received from Lisle. While Sharp had secured Strong's freedom, the legal cases surrounding this had not resulted in any generally applicable decision. As later cases such as the *Somerset case and that of Mary *Prince were to show, the issues of whether slavery was lawful in England, and whether persons in England could be returned to a state of slavery in the Caribbean colonies, remained unsettled for many years afterwards. JG

Fryer, Peter, *Staying Power: The History of Black People in Britain* (1984)

Shyllon, F. O., *Black Slaves in Britain* (1974)

See also KNIGHT V. WEDDERBURN

Sturge, Joseph (1793–1859). Committed campaigner against slavery and post-slavery apprenticeship. Sturge, the son of a farmer in Gloucestershire, was, like many other social reformers of the day, a member of the Religious Society of Friends (Quakers). In 1823 he joined the *abolition movement in Birmingham and urged the instantaneous *emancipation of slaves in the British territories. An active member of the *Anti-Slavery Society, the Central Negro Emancipation Committee, and the British and Foreign Anti-Slavery Society, he was not satisfied with the mere abolition of slavery in 1833. He demanded that the consequent scheme of apprenticeship be abolished as well. He published (with Thomas Harvey) an account of his experiences of slavery and its consequences in *The West Indies in 1837* (1838). Sturge founded the Central Negro Emancipation Committee in 1837, gaining the support of Lord Brougham, who was himself an anti-apprenticeship advocate. Two years later he founded the British and Foreign Anti-Slavery Society, which today is known as the Anti-Slavery International. To fortify his fight, Sturge brought an apprentice from Jamaica to London to give a first-hand account of the cruelties of apprenticeship, which proved successful in gaining the attention and support of people from all levels of society. One of Sturge's achievements was his success in shortening the period of apprenticeship to two years. He also gave his support to the Chartist movement and ran for Parliament in Nottingham. In 1840 he organized the World's Anti-Slavery Convention in London. He died in Birmingham in 1859. DD/SS

Hobhouse, Stephen, *Joseph Sturge: His Life and Work* (1919)

Tyrrell, Alex, *Joseph Sturge and the Moral Radical Party in Early Victorian Britain* (1987)

See also CHRISTIANITY

'Sus Law'. First brought into force in 1824 as the Vagrancy Act, this law was resuscitated during the 1970s, when it was widely used primarily as a means of policing black youth.

1. Introduction
2. Enforcing the 'Sus Law': The Special Patrol Group

1. Introduction The policing of Britain's black communities represented one of the most potent sources of tensions shaping the nature of race relations in the 1980s, and is widely believed to be a major cause of the riots that swept across Britain between 1981 and 1985. In response to a media-induced moral panic about sharp increases in 'muggings'—a crime mostly associated with young Blacks—police forces initiated a crime-reduction strategy based on saturated policing of black communities. Young Blacks were specifically targeted. In particular, the use of stop and search procedures, known as the 'Sus Law', were vigorously enforced. First brought into force in 1824 as the Vagrancy Act, this law was originally intended as a deterrent to street begging by unemployed and impoverished soldiers and sailors returning from the Napoleonic Wars. During the 20th century the Vagrancy Act fell out of use, and was not resuscitated until the 1970s, when it was widely used primarily as a means of policing young Blacks. Under the 'Sus Law', or 'Stop and Search', 'Every person or reputed thief, frequenting or loitering about in any street highway or avenue leading thereto or any place of public resort with intent to commit an arrestable offence is guilty of that offence.' Police were empowered to stop and search citizens without burden of proof merely on the basis of suspicion ('sus') that they intended to commit a crime.

The 'Sus Law' was widely regarded among the black communities to be a form of legalized victimization: not only did it license policemen to persecute black communities with little or no evidential justification, but it created an atmosphere of alienation among young Blacks, who were made to feel like perpetual suspects in their own neighbourhoods.

2. Enforcing the 'Sus Law': The Special Patrol Group The widespread use of stop and search was a tactic of the Special Patrol Group (SPG), whose vigorous application of the 'Sus Law' first came to national prominence with the *Brixton riots. The SPG had been formed in 1961 to provide a centrally based mobile squad for combating particularly serious crime and other problems that could not be dealt with by local police divisions. By the 1980s the SPG were at the forefront of street crime prevention in inner cities. The 'success' of their tactics may be measured by the disproportionately high number of imprisoned young Blacks. By the end of 1980 black people represented 17 per cent of the prison population, and over 36 per cent of young prisoners were black. In 1981 the SPG was deployed across London in Swamp 81, an aggressive, widespread police operation intended to address rising street crime. Using the 'Sus Law', police stopped and searched thousands of young Blacks, a powerful operational strategy that inflamed the anger of black communities. When, in the spring of 1981, riots broke out across London's inner cities, the disproportionate use of the 'Sus Law' against young Blacks was cited as a direct causal factor as black communities rebelled against what they perceived to be sustained police harassment. Following public inquiries into the riots, the 'Sus Law' was repealed in 1981. The 1984 Police and Criminal Evidence Act included a clause instructing that the police had to give a reason why they had stopped someone. CJ

Hall, Stuart, *et al.*, *Policing the Crisis: Mugging, the State, and Law and Order* (1978)

See also CRIMINAL JUSTICE SYSTEM; MACPHERSON REPORT; SCARMAN REPORT

T

Taylor, Damilola (1989–2000). The murder of the schoolboy Damilola Taylor led to one of the most public police investigations in the United Kingdom since the murder in 1993 of Stephen *Lawrence, and much national soul-searching about inner-city poverty, gang culture, and youth crime.

Born in Nigeria to Gloria and Richard Taylor, Damilola moved with his family to England in August 2000. They settled in Peckham, south *London. On 27 November 2000, on his way home from a computer class, Damilola was brutally attacked by a gang of youths. He was later found, just yards from his home, in the stairwell of a run-down housing estate, bleeding from a stab wound inflicted by a broken bottle, and died on the way to hospital.

Already under pressure after their failure to secure a conviction in the Stephen Lawrence murder case, police immediately launched a massive investigation. Despite encountering what they referred to as a 'culture of fear and silence' on the estate where Damilola had died, they eventually arrested and charged four teenagers aged between 14 and 16 with his murder. The revelations that Damilola's murder was committed by children made his death even more shocking, prompting national debates about the death of childhood innocence.

In an echo of the Stephen Lawrence murder investigation, critics charge that flaws in the police and trial procedures led to the collapse of the case against all four suspects in April 2002. The Taylor family and their supporters continued to press for justice for their son. When new DNA techniques led to a re-examination of the evidence obtained at the time of the murder, three teenagers (aged 19, 17, and 16) were arrested and charged with Damilola's murder in January 2005. A second trial ended in April 2006 with the acquittal of the accused. A third trial of two of the defendants in August 2006 resulted in their conviction for the manslaughter of Damilola. CJ

<http://www.met.police.uk/damilola>

See also MACPHERSON REPORT

Telephone, The. Journal of the National Society for the Protection of the Dark Races, established in London by John Edward Quinlan in 1906. Little is known of the National Society or its membership and the only issue of the ten-page journal, edited by Quinlan and which sold for 1*d*., was published in May 1907. The aims and objects of the Society, which had offices in Bayswater, London, were to encourage friendly relations between the 'dark races' and the white inhabitants of Britain, to promote and protect the rights and interests of the 'dark races', and to 'put a stop to all punitive expeditions in the British dominions beyond the seas'. One motivation for Quinlan to form the Society may have been the harsh suppression of the Bambatha rebellion in South Africa in 1906. Quinlan came from St Lucia, where he was a commissioned land surveyor; he gave evidence to the Royal Commission on the West Indies in 1897. He was a delegate to the London Pan-African Congress in 1900, and three years later he denounced the recruitment of West Indian labour for the South African mines. The photograph of Quinlan on the sole known issue of *The Telephone* describes him as 'the popular black lecturer'. *The*

Telephone contained articles on the economic development of the tropical Empire, and on the creation of clubs and social centres where the white and black working classes could meet. Quinlan had socialist ideas on Imperial labour, which he had developed in *The Labour Problem: An Idea of a British Workers' Society* (1902), including support for Labour members of Parliament and that British workers should 'return one or two dark Colonials as members of the House of Commons'.

DK

The Telephone, 1/1 (May 1907)

See also POLITICS; PUBLISHING

Tempest, The. William Shakespeare's late romance, first produced at the Court of King James I in 1611, and performed for the wedding of the King's daughter Elizabeth with Frederick V, the Elector Palatine, in the winter of 1612.

The play is a charming tale of feud and reconciliation, set on a magical island, and conforming to the Aristotelian unities of time, place, and action. A fractious Italian royal wedding party, on its way back to Naples from Tunisia, is shipwrecked on the island fiefdom of a wizard, Prospero, who was usurped as Duke of Milan by two of the party twelve years earlier and cast out to sea. Through magic, Prospero works his revenge, causing confusion and despair among his enemies until, revealing himself, he is able to forgive them, abjure his magic, win back his dukedom, and marry his daughter to the heir of Naples.

Shakespeare modelled his island on the accounts of contemporary travellers to the New World, and the play is therefore partly an intervention into the discourse of colonialism. In September 1610 the 'Bermuda pamphlets' reached England from the Virginia Company, in which Shakespeare's patron, the Earl of Southampton, was a shareholder. The accounts of Sylvester Jourdain and William Strachey, crew members aboard the *Sea-Venture*, told of being separated from a Virginia-bound flotilla in a storm and landing on the 'Bermoothes', paradisiacal islands with fresh water, plenteous timber, and edible birds so tame they would land upon the heads and arms of the hungry sailors; their narratives are echoed closely in the details of Shakespeare's island.

The play tells us a great deal about English reactions to the emergent Empire, then being extended through conquest. We are told, for example, of English people, that though they 'will not give a doit to relieve a lame beggar, they will lay out ten to see a dead Indian'. When the Italian social order collapses into recriminations and intrigue, King Alonso's brother Sebastian accuses him in tones of racial outrage of having caused their problems by marrying his daughter to an African. At the other extreme of opinion the old counsellor Gonzalo introduces utopian theories of a 'commonwealth' without rank or prejudice, drawn from Montaigne's essay 'On Canniballes' (translated by John Florio in 1603), which discusses the *'noble savage'.

In the figure of the 'abhorred slave' Caliban, a 'freckled whelp', 'hagseed', and 'most scurvy monster', 'whom stripes may move, not kindness', we meet an indigenous American or Amerindian, and it is the encounter between Caliban and Prospero that has assured *The Tempest*'s relevance to modern post-colonial literature. Caliban argues that he was usurped by Prospero; in lyrical, alliterative language that bespeaks his affinity with nature, he contests Prospero's right to enslave him, which necessitates torture. Taught to speak English, he has learned only to curse. The inability of Prospero to resolve the conflict with Caliban is a psychologically profound rendering of historical circumstances in the slave colonies.

Prospero's daughter Miranda doesn't want to look upon Caliban (her father forces her to) because he tried to rape her (she says he was stopped in the act). For his part, Caliban is unrepentant: 'O ho, O ho! Would't had been done . . . I had peopled else | This isle with Calibans!' When she does see him, it is ingratitude she charges him with: how dare he assert his savage customs when she has taught him otherwise. In the Barbadian writer

George Lamming's analysis of the colonizing process, Caliban 'has no self which is not a reaction to circumstances imposed upon his life'.

The contrast is made all the more extreme because of the parallel with Ariel, an ethereal spirit with the power to run beneath the sea, move through the veins of the frosty earth, and, in another borrowing from the Bermuda pamphlets, flame along the masts and bowsprit of a ship, who serves Prospero swiftly and obediently, singing all the while. Ariel too is a slave—Prospero threatens it with reimprisonment inside the tree in which it was pegged by Caliban's mother, a witch—an aspect to which the Martinican poet Aimé Césaire later drew attention. His 1969 version in French made Caliban an enslaved Black and Ariel a mulatto, the inference being that the mixed-race Creoles are assimilationists, collaborating with the colonizer for short-term reward.

There is a clear classification of types in *The Tempest*. At the bottom are Caliban and Ariel, the spirits of nature, shadowed themselves by the witch Sycorax and her spouse, the 'demi-devil' Setebos. Above them are two drunkards, the mate and the cook, Stephano and Trinculo, willing to enter into a mutinous 'confederacy' with Caliban. Paul Brown likens them to the 'masterless' Irish, closer to home yet colonized at the same time as the 'savage' Bermudas. The king's courtiers Sebastian and Antonio have the pretence of good manners, yet they are hollow men plotting to usurp the king when he falls asleep. Finally, at the zenith of the scale of being, Ferdinand and Miranda are innocent, courtly lovers. At the play's end Prospero, acknowledging Caliban, 'this thing of darkness', as his own, calls into question the values at the heart of their civilization. Miranda's concluding words, 'Oh brave new world, that hath such people in 't, must be taken with a degree of cynicism.

Lamming, in his 1960 collection of essays *The Pleasures of Exile*, uses the conceit of Caliban as a colonized subject to illustrate the journey of the post-war West Indian writer from his 'native kingdom' to the 'tempestuous island' of Prospero. In this diagnosis of the colonial condition, the enslaved native is 'a child of nature . . . superfluous as the weight of the earth'. The Guyanese poet David Dabydeen hits out at the opposition between Caliban and Miranda in his poems giving voice to a black peasant Caliban, trapped in the inferiority and resentment evoked by a black skin, in order to contest assumptions of the white world. Similarly, 'Shango, Shango ho!' chants Caliban in Césaire's rewrite, where the masque of the Roman fertility goddesses Iris, Juno, and Ceres is interrupted by the bawdy West African daemon Eshu, who 'beats with his penis' [*de son pénis il frappe*]. In Césaire's version, Ariel is granted his independence, while Prospero remains on the island, to engage with Caliban in guerrilla warfare. This can be read in the light of the independence struggles taking place at the time in Mozambique, Angola, Guinea-Bissau, South Africa, and Rhodesia. JM

Brown, Paul, 'This Thing of Darkness I Acknowledge Mine: *The Tempest* and the Discourse of Colonialism' (1985) in Jonathan Dollimore and Alan Sinfield (eds.), *Political Shakespeare* (1994)

Césaire, Aimé, *Une Tempête* (1969)

Dabydeen, David, *Slave Song* (1984)

Hulme, Peter, *Colonial Encounters: Europe and the Native Caribbean 1492–1797* (1986)

Lamming, George, *The Pleasures of Exile* (1960)

See also MASQUES; OTHELLO; RENAISSANCE DRAMA; TITUS ANDRONICUS

Thomas, John Jacob (*c*.1840–1889). Linguistics scholar and polemicist born in Trinidad, the son of former slaves. Little is known of his early life, but he did well as a pupil at the Woodbrook Normal School (what would now be called a teacher training college), which was then on the outskirts of Port of Spain. In 1860 he was placed in charge of a remote rural school. He moved to another school on an increased salary in 1865, but in 1867 success in a recently introduced system of competitive examinations secured him a place in the local Civil Service. He rose through a succession of posts until he was forced by ill health to retire in 1879.

As a rural schoolmaster, Thomas came into close contact with, and made a special study of, the French Creole which was then the vernacular of most Trinidadians, while at the same time studying French and Spanish on his own. At some stage he also acquired a command of Latin and Greek. In 1869 he published *The Theory and Practice of Creole Grammar*, which was printed in Port of Spain. This was a pioneering work, which not only offered what was to remain for a century the most detailed analysis of any French Creole, but also insisted on the cultural significance and expressive resources of a language that was dismissed by many, Trinidadians as well as outsiders, as a barbarous and impoverished jargon. On a visit to Britain on leave in 1873 he read a paper on Trinidad Creole to a meeting of the Philological Society, the leading learned society in its field in the English-speaking world, and the Society subsequently elected him a member.

Thomas intended a later visit to Britain to undertake research for an expanded second edition of his *Creole Grammar*, but his journey was interrupted in Grenada by a long period of illness and recuperation. It was in Grenada that he came across *The English in the West Indies*, by James Anthony *Froude, and his initial response came in a series of articles published in a Grenada newspaper in 1888. He was able to go to England later that year, and *Froudacity: West India Fables by J. A. Froude explained by J. J. Thomas* was published in London in 1889. He died of tuberculosis in London on 20 September 1889, and the second edition of the *Creole Grammar* was never completed.

Thomas was an outstanding example of a black colonial intellectual who was largely self-taught. His rebuttal of Froude's inaccuracies about Britain's Caribbean colonies and racist dismissals of African-Caribbean political aspirations achieved some favourable reviews in British periodicals. The *Creole Grammar* was arguably a more important work, as an informed and sympathetic study of a specifically black language. The author's appreciation of the political significance of culture can be seen in many comments, such as that on the Creole proverb *Ravette pas jamain tnî raison douvant poule* [translated by Thomas as 'Cockroach never is in the right where the fowl is concerned']: 'The reign of injustice, during which the insect symbolised the Negro, and the bird, his oppressor, is slowly passing away. There is now some chance for the roach, and day by day he is vindicating his claim to a little more.' Both of Thomas's books were reprinted in 1969 by New Beacon Books, but he is still not as widely known as he deserves. JG

Thomas, J. J., *Froudacity: West Indian Fables by James Anthony Froude, Explained by J. J. Thomas* (1889; new edn., with biographical note by Donald Wood, introd. C. L. R. James, 1969)

—— *The Theory and Practice of Creole Grammar* (1869; new edn., introd. Gertrud Aub-Buscher, 1969)

See also BLACK BRITISH ENGLISH; PUBLISHING

Thompson, Leslie (1901–1987). Jamaican musician and prison worker. Born in Kingston, he attended Alpha Cottage School, where his interest in music was encouraged by West India Regiment bandsmen. He joined that regiment in 1917, and went to Kneller Hall, Twickenham, in 1919–20, where he was awarded a silver medal.

Thompson and the band worked at exhibitions in Toronto (1922) and Wembley (1924). He developed music for Kingston's cinemas, and expanded this, and hotel and theatre work, after the regiment disbanded. He played the cello in the pianist Vera Manley's quartet. In 1929 he migrated to England. *Jazz was in vogue at the time, and Britons assumed he had a natural skill at it. His abilities on trumpet, trombone, bass, and with orchestrations led to work and recordings with Spike Hughes and, on stage, in Noel Coward's *Cavalcade*. He toured with Louis Armstrong, then developed an all-black orchestra, which became Ken 'Snakehips' Johnson's West Indian Dance Orchestra; he later played with the Latin-American music master Edmundo Ros.

Wartime work as a sergeant in an anti-aircraft unit was followed by music-making in *Stars in Battledress*. Thompson also aided Caribbean migrants settling in London in the 1950s. He abandoned professional music in 1954, becoming a warden at a London hostel for foreign students. He qualified as a probation officer in 1963, remaining as a welfare officer at Pentonville prison into the 1970s, often teaching music. His Christian faith, renewed in the 1950s, was substantial and sustaining. JPG

Thompson, Leslie, *Leslie Thompson: An Autobiography* (1986)

See also MUSIC 2: EARLY POPULAR MUSIC

Thornton, Henry (1760–1815). Banker, economist, close friend of William *Wilberforce, and campaigner for the *abolition of the *slave trade. Owing to his background in financial matters, Thornton was able to be of great help to Wilberforce in terms of managing the monetary aspects of their anti-slavery campaigns besides providing practical business advice. He was one of the founders of the Clapham Sect, a group of men under the influence of Wilberforce who were devoted to evangelical Christianity and believed that, through their faith in Jesus Christ, they would fight for moral, social, and political justice. The Sect was formed by Wilberforce and Thornton after their proposal for the abolition of the slave trade was rejected in 1789. It was Thornton's idea to create a Christian commune within which those dedicated to religious and political matters could live, exchange, and activate their ideas. In 1792 he purchased Battersea Rise House, which became the head office of the Clapham Sect. Thornton often contributed financially to the Sect's anti-slavery struggles and was known for his generosity. In many instances he would donate two-thirds of his income towards the fight for moral justice. DD/SS

Tolley, Christopher, *Domestic Biography: The Legacy of Evangelicalism in Four Nineteenth-Century Families* (1997)

See also CHRISTIANITY; SLAVERY

Titus Andronicus. Early play by William Shakespeare. Authoritative dating is impossible, but it is widely thought to be among his juvenile work, perhaps adapted from an earlier text in collaboration with George Peele. The first recorded performances were in 1593.

Set in a declining Rome, the play dramatizes conflict between two families, between different forms of imperial power, and, in the central figures of Titus, an ageing soldier, and Aaron, a Moor, psychological conflict between social obedience and anarchy, expressed in images of carnivalesque horror. In the bloodthirsty manner of early contemporaries such as Christopher Marlowe and Thomas Kyd, throats are slit, hands are severed, and tongues are cut out, two rapists are baked in a pie and served to their mother, and fourteen people are murdered or executed. Revulsion at the play's atrocities provoked outrage in later audiences and it was abandoned between 1734 and 1839. It saw a revival in fortunes in the late 20th century, though critical appraisal has tended to salute the skilful recovery by directors and producers of a weak and unstructured artistic work rather than the melodrama of the play itself.

Aaron, the servant and secret lover to the Goth empress Tamora, is identifiably a stock character of Renaissance theatre, the Machiavel: a deliciously wicked villain whose twisting of the plot to his own violent ends will result in himself being entangled and discovered. Inexplicably brought into Rome with the defeated Goths, he is represented as 'this barbarous Moor, | This ravenous tiger, this accursed devil', 'inhuman dog, unhallowed slave', 'wall-eyed', 'fiendlike', an 'execrable wretch', and other such epithets. There is interplay between his creativity—which includes propping corpses by the doors of their friends with messages carved in their flesh—and that of the author, but Machiavels must be punished, and order imposed on anarchy, if redemption is to be achieved. Shakespeare's Machiavels are often marked by a grossness in their nature: the hunchbacked Richard III, the bastard Edmund. Likewise Aaron's physiognomy is equated, in a simplistic way, with abomination:

What signifies my deadly-standing eye,
My silence, and my cloudy melancholy,
My fleece of woolly hair that now uncurls
Even as an adder when she doth unroll
To do some fatal execution? . . .
Vengeance is in my heart, death in my hand,
Blood and revenge are hammering in my head.

Hate-filled, devious and almost comically evil, he is a racial stereotype as heinous as those Shakespeare created in Shylock, Caliban, or the shifting, illogical Orient of Cleopatra.

For the trickster's victims, blackness is to blame. The grieving and mutilated Andronici begin to formulate a plan of revenge through a coded utterance to the effect that the black man caused their problems, and must be removed:

TITUS: Poor harmless fly,
That, with his pretty buzzing melody
Came here to make us merry, and thou hast killed him.
MARCUS: Pardon me, sir; it was a black ill-favoured fly
Like to the empress' Moor; therefore I killed him.
TITUS: O O O!
Then pardon me for reprehending thee
For thou hast done a charitable deed.

Their ensuing challenge to Lavinia's rapists is wrapped in the Latin of Horace: 'Integer vitae, scelerisque purus, | Non eget Mauri iaculis, nec arcu' ['He who lives by order, pure of crime, needs not Moorish javelins, nor arrows']. The implication is racial: the Goths' degeneracy has been masterminded by the villainous Moor. From Bassianus'

Believe me, queen, your swarthy Cimmerian
Doth make your honour of his body's hue,
Spotted, detested, and abominable,

when he discovers Tamora and Aaron sequestered, to Titus' naive

'Oh gentle Aaron!
Did ever raven sing so like a lark . . . ?

when he is tricked into chopping off his hand, the Romans repeatedly reduce Aaron's black skin to a negative indication of character.

If *Titus* is notable for its racism, then it also inverts the tradition when Aaron defends his newborn son with passion and common sense:

What, what, ye sanguine shallow-hearted boys,
Ye white-limed walls, ye alehouse painted signs!
Coal-black is better than another hue
In that it scorns to bear another hue,
For all the water in the ocean
Can never turn the swan's black legs to white
Although she lave them hourly in the flood.

In his final confession Aaron seems to signify upon his enemies' most fantastical insecurities in order to save his son's life. And from the outset he is shown to be socially mobile:

Away with slavish weeds and servile thoughts!
I will be bright, and shine in pearl and gold
To wait upon this new-made empress.

His defining transgression, like those of Marlowe's overreaching heroes, lies in seeking to rise above his station. At the play's end this creature of farcical cruelty is not murdered on stage, like the primitively cruel Titus, the lasciviously cruel Tamora, or the decadent emperor Saturninus, but taken away, to be buried upright in earth and left to starve and 'rave'. It is as if the dramatist had qualms about his racist construct, though not strongly enough to refrain from using it as a structuring device.

Two radically different versions of *Titus* illustrate how the black Machiavel can be received in a changing historical context. One was that published in 1687 by Edward Ravenscroft, which out-Heroded the original by having Aaron eat his offspring. But in the 19th century Ira *Aldridge had it rewritten to make Aaron a suitable role model for a black actor. This adaptation, in which the 'King of the Goths' liberates Lavinia, dives into a river to rescue his son from drowning, and is poisoned by Saturninus, toured the provinces between 1849 and 1860. JM

Hillman, Richard, *Shakespearian Subversions; The Trickster and the Play-Text* (1992)
Shakespeare, William, *Titus Andronicus*, New Cambridge Shakespeare (ed. Alan Hughes, 1994)

See also OTHELLO; RENAISSANCE DRAMA; TEMPEST, THE

To Sir, With Love. Semi-autobiographical novel by Edward Ricardo (E. R.) Braithwaite about the experience of being black in post-war Britain. First published in 1959, this novel deals frankly with the problems faced by Rick Braithwaite, a well-educated young black man who is unable to find employment in Britain after demobilization from the RAF. Eventually he becomes a schoolteacher in a run-down area of east London, after realizing that he is both 'too well educated . . . and too black' to be accepted into any other kind of employment in 1950s Britain. In Greenslade Secondary School he is given charge of the most unruly senior class, which his fellow teachers have already given up on. His immediate predecessor, Hackman, has, in fact, resigned in disgust because of their disruptive behaviour. Initially he is horrified by the pupils' bad language, poor hygiene, and lack of knowledge and discipline, but gradually he comes to understand how their deprived backgrounds affect their behaviour. He then starts to win their trust through his innovative and sympathetic treatment of them as young adults. Eventually he triumphs, against all odds, by turning this class of badly behaved teenagers into responsible and thoughtful young men and women. When they eventually leave Greenslade School several months later, they are well prepared for the life ahead of them, largely thanks to Rick and his intelligent understanding of their particular educational needs.

All throughout the novel Rick encounters incidences of ignorance and racial prejudice, from his pupils expressing surprise that his colour is 'only skin deep', to being turned away from accommodation for being 'some darky' who dared to imagine he might be a suitable tenant for a white family. Yet, despite everything, Rick's stoicism and determination to combat racism are eventually rewarded on a number of fronts. His first real success is when members of his class are able to overcome collectively an ingrained mistrust of 'what people would say if they saw us going to a coloured person's home' by attending the funeral of Seales's mother (Seales is a fellow pupil with a white mother and a black father). His other major achievement is in the handling of Gillian's parents, who, despite their initial reservations about their proposed 'mixed' marriage, eventually feel able to welcome him into their family on equal terms. His final triumph is, however, symbolized by the (unspecified) gift that his thankful pupils give him at the end of term, finally recognizing the selfless care and attention that he has lavished upon them, regardless of everything he has had to contend with.

To Sir, With Love is an important novel, not so much for its literary qualities, but more because it was among the first works of fiction by a Caribbean author that attempted to articulate the disillusionment with life of an immigrant in Britain. Braithwaite had been born in British Guiana in 1920 and was among the thousands of West Indians who had volunteered to fight for Britain during the *Second World War. In common with his fictional counterpart, he had been 'smiled at, encouraged [and] welcomed by grateful civilians' throughout the war years in Britain, yet as soon as the fighting was over had been unable to find the kind of work for which he was qualified, largely because of the colour of his skin. Both Braithwaite's personal experience and that of his fictional counterpart have rarely been examined in fictional writing and, in fact, it is only recently that any serious attempt has been made to document similar incidences of racial discrimination against former West Indian servicemen and women.

In 1967 a film version of *To Sir, With Love* was released by Columbia Pictures. It had been adapted, produced, and directed by James Clavell, and featured Sidney Poitier in the main role. The cast also included Suzy Kendall, Judy Geeson, Patricia Routledge, and Lulu, the latter of whom sang the theme tune. Although the film was not particularly well reviewed at the time of release—*Sight and Sound* (Autumn 1967) referred to it as a 'priggish saga . . . that prefers thinking schmaltzy to thinking tough'—it did go on to enjoy a significant level of box-office success. A television sequel—*To Sir, With Love II*—was subsequently directed by Peter Bogdanovich and released in the United States in 1996. This remake also starred Sidney Poitier but, despite a shift in location to a multiracial high school in Chicago, its frank idealism offered limited appeal to audiences of the mid-1990s.

The 1967 film had contained a number of significant changes from the novel, not least in its alteration of the main character's name from Rick Braithwaite to Mark Thackeray. Much of the overt racism that Rick had encountered in the book had also been carefully removed from the film's narrative structure. There was no sign of the woman on the bus who refused to sit next to him because he was a Black, or the waiter who deliberately spilt his soup in a restaurant. Rick's continual rejection from employment is only *obliquely* referred to through occasional shots of application letters and rejection slips. His disillusionment and angry outburst against the 'ideal of the British Way of Life' has also been erased, as has his past as a volunteer aircrew member of the RAF during the war. Furthermore, his relationship with Gillian—a blonde Suzy Kendall in the film rather than the 'brown-voiced', black-haired woman with a 'rich olive tint' to her skin in the novel—has also been altered from an impending marriage to a platonic friendship. In fact the overall tone of the film is far more moralistic and humble than its literary counterpart, changing its portrayal of the main protagonist to a black teacher who is reluctantly *accepted* by British society rather than as an individual who made a *positive contribution* to it. LM

Braithwaite, E. R., *To Sir, With Love* (1959; repr., 1971)
Phillips, Mike, and Phillips, Trevor, *Windrush: The Irresistible Rise of Multi-Racial Britain* (1998)

See also LITERATURE 2: FICTION AND POETRY

Trade unionism. In terms of forms of colonial labour control, trade unionism can be seen as following slavery and indentureship in the Caribbean. Colonial Office advice and policy decisions were often the strongest of the many pressures to which a colonial government was subjected. Labour developments in colonial territories were a vital consideration for metropolitan investment. After the First World War, in 1919, the International Labour Organization was created and labour standards in the non-self-governing territories began to receive increasing attention. In the 1920s labour problems in the colonies also received growing attention from the Colonial Office. In September 1930 a circular advocating the passage of trade union legislation was sent to all colonial governments, and further dispatches concerned the formation of trade unions. The law in the colonies had remained several decades behind that in Britain, where acceptance of the role of trade unions was concerned. Following the labour disturbances that were widespread in the British Caribbean colonies in the later 1930s, the British government's promotion of unionism in the colonies was intended to encourage gradual, rather than revolutionary, social and economic change. A significant part of the British economy (especially in sugar) was founded on an unstable dependence on colonial exploitation, on which the standard of living of many British workers depended.

The growth after the Second World War of the migrant population in Britain (people accustomed to the ideas and practices of trade unionism in their home countries) posed problems and challenges, namely the 'colour bar' and racial discrimination, which had already resulted in 'race' riots in *Cardiff and *Liverpool in 1911, 1919, and 1945. After the riots in Nottingham and *London in 1958, politicians were increasingly concerned about the unprecedented influx of non-white people seeking work and a better life. Significantly, by the time the Commonwealth Immigrants Act of 1962 brought in immigration control, a number of colonial trade unions had been formed in the West Indies and were integral to political parties that agitated for colonial freedom. But that experience did not prepare most migrants in Britain for what was to come. Put simply, finding a job was a problem even when they were adequately qualified. Many with educational qualifications, even degrees, were relegated to manual or semi-skilled jobs, and discriminatory practices also affected job mobility, job satisfaction, and promotion. Prolonged exploitation of the migrant labour force led to inevitable reaction. The many strikes that resulted involved workers at Imperial Typewriters in Leicester (1974) and at the Grunwick film processing laboratory in Willesden, north London (1976–8), among others.

The 1980s saw rising unemployment among young Blacks, and black workers were still largely employed in menial jobs. The stereotype of them being shiftless and lazy was much in evidence, and racial tensions on the shop floor were at a constant high. In terms of TUC policy and resolutions before 1955, there was no reference, either in the reports to Congress of the General Council or during Annual Conference proceedings, to race relations, racial discrimination, or immigration. At the time the TUC deemed that the arrival of New Commonwealth immigrants (particularly West Indians) was not cause for undue concern.

The 1955 Congress was instructive, for while in principle it condemned racial discrimination or colour prejudice, it nevertheless implicitly accepted that the 'problem' was not the expression of prejudice or discriminatory practice by white employers and white workers, but was attributable to the very presence of migrants from the West Indies. And if between 1956 and 1957 there was little interest in immigration and race relations at the Congresses, during 1958, the year of race riots, immigration was still viewed as 'the problem'. By the mid-1960s the TUC General Council was in favour of immigration control. According to the 1965 Congress Report, two circumstances led to its opposition to immigration as expressed in 1961, just months before the historic Commonwealth Immigrants Act came into force. The first of these was the

> growth of the proportion of Commonwealth migrants lacking an adequate knowledge of English and of British customs. Simultaneously, the arrival of the wives and children of earlier migrants has brought the recognition that whereas many immigrants are now becoming settled with their families in sufficient numbers to require access to the full range of opportunity at every level of British life, progress towards their integration is in some respects being reversed as the numbers become large enough to constitute an extension of their previous environments and to tend towards their settlement as a series of communities, differentiated amongst themselves as well as from the main body of the population.

Thereafter, between the 1960s and the early 1980s, immigration and racial discrimination were regularly debated. However, in spite of the TUC's *Workbook on Racism* and directives, black workers felt betrayed by their respective trade unions, and felt the urgent need for autonomous organization. Thus a group of militant black trade unionists formed the Black Trade Unionists' Solidarity Movement. Many of them saw clearly the link between their struggles in the workplace and in the community, and stated their intention to organize and work within the trade union movement. In other words, they wanted white workers to recognize and act on the real day-to-day problems of racism so that together they could work effectively. This black initiative had, by the mid-1980s, met with only a marginal response, for the vast majority of trade unionists had been complacent about the situation of black workers and slow to act.

By the mid-1990s and thereafter racism in the workplace and within trade unions was more closely monitored, as evidenced by TUC initiatives in conjunction with the *Commission for Racial Equality. Nonetheless, the trend towards autonomous black groups within the trade union movement has continued, and black membership, especially in the public sector, has continued to rise. A high (if unusual) point in black achievement in the trade union movement was the election of the West Indian Bill Morris as General Secretary of the Transport and General

Workers' Union from 1991 to 2003. After the Second World War West Indians had come to work on Britain's buses and trains. The election of Bill Morris signalled how far some of them had moved from their original lowly status. RR

Foot, Paul, *Immigration and Race in British Politics* (1965)

Hiro, Dilip, *Black British White British* (1971)

Miles, R., and Phizacklea, A., *The TUC, Black Workers and New Commonwealth Immigration 1954–1973* (1977)

Ramdin, Ron, *From Chattel Slave to Wage Earner* (1982)

See also COMMUNISM; LONDON TRANSPORT; NATIONAL HEALTH SERVICE

Transracial adoption. One of the most controversial social welfare issues in Britain for more than three decades, transracial adoption usually involves the adoption of black and minority ethnic children by white families.

1. Introduction
2. The history of transracial adoption in Britain
3. Arguments against transracial adoption at the beginning of the 21st century
4. Policy at the beginning of the 21st century

1. Introduction Black children are more likely to be looked after by local authorities and are more likely to be placed for adoption than white children. Thus debate has tended to focus on the adoption of black children by white families and whether white parents make suitable adoptive parents for black children.

One of the major concerns of opponents of transracial adoption is the damaging effect it can have on the child's identity development. They argue that a crucial task in raising black children is to provide them with the skills to counter the impact of racism and discrimination and to develop a positive sense of self as a black person. They therefore believe that black children lose their racial identity when adopted by white parents, and are unable to cope with prejudice and discrimination. Without a sense of identity the child will internalize racist behaviour and attitudes, resulting in a variety of negative outcomes, including mental illness. Some black activists in the United States have dubbed transracial adoption 'transracial abduction', or even 'cultural genocide'.

Meanwhile advocates of transracial adoption reply that denying black children adoption by a white family often means abandoning them to residential care and short-term foster placements while social workers search for the 'perfect match'. According to this view, the race of the adoptive parents should be irrelevant in a 'colourblind' society, and it is in the best interests of the black child languishing in the care system to become part of a nurturing, loving family that will provide stability for the child, regardless of whether the adopting family is black or white.

2. The history of transracial adoption in Britain The adoption of black and mixed-race children by white parents has been practised in this country since the 1950s, by which time an estimated 10–20 per cent of black children in care were waiting to be placed with adoptive parents. These children were generally regarded as 'hard to place' because few black families were registered with adoption agencies. West Indian families tended to favour private fostering arrangements (known to child welfare agencies as 'boarding out'). Many of these 'hard to place' children were living in children's homes because prevailing social work practice dictated that children should be placed in families that were physiologically similar to themselves. For example, in the case of white children, social workers would try to match the child with white families having the same physical characteristics in terms of hair and eye colouring. The principle that children did best with 'their own kind' informed adoption practice throughout the 1950s and 1960s. However, few black parents met the stringent selection criteria for adoption as most were tenants rather than homeowners, and most mothers were obliged to work. Thus the policy of 'race matching' made it difficult to place black children.

From the late 1960s the number of white babies for adoption declined, largely owing to the availability of contraception, increased tolerance of illegitimacy, and the 1967 Abortion Act. The focus switched to older, 'hard to place' children, including black children. Indeed, some agencies began to encourage white families to adopt black children, and the number of transracial placements began to grow from the early 1970s. One criticism levelled at transracial adoption policy is that it was only when the supply of healthy white babies declined that black babies began to be regarded as suitable for white families.

Although black and mixed-race children were increasingly placed for adoption, there was a failure to recruit black adoptive families for black children in Britain, mainly because of adoption agencies' discriminatory practices, which made black families reluctant to submit themselves to assessment processes and bureaucracy. Thus, by the 1970s a shortage of white babies and black adopters meant that the majority of black and mixed-race children were being adopted by white families, a practice that continued more or less unchallenged until the 1980s, when black childcare professionals began to insist on same-race placements. In a 1995 survey on adoption practice in 48 local authorities, 39 reported no transracial placements.

3. Arguments against transracial adoption at the beginning of the 21st century These include criticisms based on discrimination, such as that black people have always serviced whites and transracial adoption represents another form of service by providing them with black children. Moreover, transracial adoption takes from the black community its most valuable resource, its children. Finally, the black community cannot maintain its pride and dignity if advantage is defined as being brought up by white families.

Some of these criticisms are based on the anticipated experiences of a black child in a white family. Because of the child's racial and physical characteristics the adoptive family will inevitably regard the child as in some sense 'not belonging' to the family. Similarly, differences of racial and physical characteristics mean that the child will perceive itself as 'not belonging to the family', and thus become isolated from it. Furthermore, contact with others outside the immediate adoptive family will primarily be white. Although the racial background of the child might over time become insignificant to the family, it will continue to be crucially significant outside the family. The child will be unable to relate effectively in the outside world, which in itself will lead to confusion about self-identity and low self-esteem. A particular example of this will be the child's inability to relate to members of the black community, leading to his or her rejection not only by white society, but by black society also.

4. Policy at the beginning of the 21st century Few adoption agencies would admit to imposing an outright ban on transracial adoption, but this often exists in practice. *Be My Parent*, the newsletter of the umbrella group British Agencies for Adoption and Fostering, applies strict criteria in advertisements for children seeking new families. It is expected that a child of Asian or African-Caribbean origin will be placed with a family that reflects their ancestry. A black heritage always predominates, so that a child who has at least one black grandparent, for example, must be placed in a family with at least one black adoptive parent. An adoption agency will usually specify that a transracial placement cannot be considered until all efforts to secure a same-race placement have been exhausted.

The controversy over transracial adoption has raged for 30 years, and continues to be a subject of debate within the social services system. CJ

Gaber, Ivor, and Aldridge, Jane (eds.), *Culture, Identity and Transracial Adoption: In the Best Interests of the Child* (1994)

Kirton, Derek, *'Race', Ethnicity and Adoption* (2000)

Patterson, Sheila, *Dark Strangers* (1965)

See also FAMILIES; MULTICULTURALISM; RACISM; SKIN COLOUR AND RACE, THEORIES OF

Tudor Britain. From the early years of the 16th century there were Africans at both the Tudor and the Stuart Courts. Catherine of Aragon had brought some African attendants with her when she arrived to marry Prince Arthur in 1501. One of these was the trumpeter ironically named John Blanke (*blanco*, white), who was paid 8*d*. a day for his services and was depicted twice in the Great Tournament Roll of Westminster (1511). In 1523 it is recorded that Fraunces Negro was working in the Queen's stables. At the Court of James IV of Scotland, Africans first arrived as booty from a Portuguese ship seized by the Barton brothers, and from 1500 to 1504 Peter the More served the Scottish King. Living at court at this time were a 'More taubronar', or drummer, with his wife and child and two maids known as 'blak Margaret' and 'blak Elene'. One of these 'More lassis' was baptized on 11 December 1504. In 1505–6 King James tipped a nurse 28*s*. for bringing a 'Moris barne' to see him. In 1508 the treasury paid the living expenses for two 'More freris', or friars. In June 1507 and May 1508 there was a jousting tournament: 'the justing of the wild knycht for the black lady' immortalized in William Dunbar's poem 'Ane Blak More', in which the king disguises himself as a black and wild knight, and the winner of the tournament is to receive a kiss from the black lady. Dunbar's description of the lady is not highly complimentary:

> My ladye with the mekle lippis:
> Quhou schou is tute mowitt lyk ane aep
> And lyk a gangarall onto graep,
> And quhou hir schort catt nois up skippis.
>
> [My lady with the fulsome lips:
> Whose jaw is prominent like an ape
> And who's like a toad to the touch
> Whose short cat nose up skips.]

However, he wrote equally rude verse about other courtiers, which was in keeping with the Scots tradition of 'flyting'—the art of poetic insult.

There continued to be a black presence in Scotland. In 1512 Andrew Forman, the Bishop of Moray, had a 'More' as his servant. In January 1513 James IV gave 10 French crowns to 'the twa blak ledeis' (probably Margaret and Elene) as a New Year's gift. In 1527 there is a payment to 'Helenor the black moir' (this could also be Elene). In 1549 Marion, Lady Home, wrote to Mary of Guise requesting her to be good to an unnamed 'Mour' who 'is als scharp ane man as rydis' ['is as sharp a man as rides']. Mentioned in the same breath as the Spanish mercenaries, at a time when Hume Castle was occupied by the English, this may be a reference to Sir Pedro Negro, a Spanish mercenary soldier who may have been the first African ever to receive an English knighthood. In 1546 Pedro Negro travelled into France with 'diverse other Spanish knights and gentlemen', under the command of the Spanish colonel Pedro de Gamba. They won a victory on 15 July and were all awarded lifetime annuities. Negro was awarded £75 in August and £100 that September. On 28 September 1547 he was knighted by the Duke of Somerset at Roxborough, after the taking of Leith. On 7 July 1549 he led a charge through the Scots that were besieging the strategically important castle of Haddington, to provide the castle with vital gunpowder, which allowed the English to defend themselves against the more numerous enemy. According to a Spanish chronicler, it was necessary to kill the 300 horses so as not to let the enemy take them, which he calls a 'pretty feat of war'. He died in London on 15 July 1551 of the sweating sickness. His funeral was quite a ceremony, with twelve 'stayffes', 'torches burning', 'flute playing', and the street hung with black and with his arms. The preacher was Dr Bartelet, and it was attended by the company of clerks, 'a harold of armes and mony morners' ['a herald and many mourners'].

Other Africans in England did not attain such great status. Dyego Negro was working as a servant to Thomas Bowyer in 1541. In Southampton around 1546–8 lived an

African, originally from Guinea, called Jacques Frances, the slave of a Venetian named Peter Paulo who was engaged to raise sunken vessels including the *Mary Rose*. Frances was called to testify in the High Court of Admiralty in defence of his master, who had been accused of stealing tin and lead. His testimony was admitted by the court, despite the protests of another Venetian, Anthony de Nicholao Rimero, 'that the sayd James Fraunces ys a morisco born where they are not christenyd and slave to the sayd peter paulo ym And therefore . . . no Credite nor faithe ought to be geven to his Sayenges as in other Strange Christian cuntryes hit ys to no suche slave geven.' This case brings into question the legal status of Africans in England. Jacques Frances asserted to the court that he was the *famulus* of the Italian, which meant household servant, as opposed to *servus*, the normal Latin word for slave. Slavery was not recognized under English law, as we find in the 1568 Cartwright decision, in which 'it was resolved that England was too pure an Air for slaves to breathe in'.

In 1551 Englishmen made their first voyage to Barbary, on which 'there were two Moores, being noble men, whereof one was of the Kings blood, convayed by the said Master Thomas Windam into their Countrey out of England'. In May 1553 Anthoine, an Egyptian, was buried in Gravesend. In 1554 the merchant John Lok brought five Africans to England, three of whom were named Anthonie, George, and Binnie, 'whereof some were tall and strong men, and could wel agree with our meates and drinke'. Three were returned home in 1556, to act as guides and interpreters. What happened to the other two is not recorded. This evidence may well be the tip of an unrecorded iceberg of Africans living in England at this time. Their status was varied, and though they were mostly dependants, they were not slaves. MK

Edwards, Paul, *The Early African Presence in the British Isles: An Inaugural Lecture on the Occasion of the Establishment of the Chair in English and African Literature at Edinburgh University* (1990)

Fraser, P. D., '"Slaves or Free People?" The Status of Africans in England 1550–1750' in R. Vigne and C. Littleton (eds.), *From Strangers to Citizens: The Integration of Immigrant Communities in Britain, Ireland and Colonial America, 1550–1750* (2001)

Habib, I. H., *Shakespeare and Race: Postcolonial Praxis in the Early Modern Period* (2000)

Sherwood, Marika, 'Blacks in Tudor England', *History Today*, 53 (Oct. 2003)

Tull, Walter Daniel John (1888–1918). Footballer and soldier born on 28 April 1888 in Folkestone, Kent. From 24 February 1898 he lived at the Children's Home and Orphanage in Bonner Road, Bethnal Green, London. In 1908–9 he came to public prominence playing for Clapton Football Club: 'catch of the season' (*Football Star*, 20 March 1909). The following season he made his first team debut for Tottenham Hotspur in their inaugural game in the first division: 'Tull is very good indeed' (*Daily Chronicle*, 13 September 1909).

He had 'much to contend against on account of his colour', commented one contemporary anonymous journalist. Yet, 'Tull is so clean in mind and method as to be a model for all white men who play football.' Mysteriously, at the end of the following season he was transferred to Northampton Town, playing over 110 matches before enlisting in the Footballers' Battalion, Middlesex Regiment, in December 1914. On 10 May 1917 he was appointed to a commission in the Special Reserve of Officers.

Not only was it virtually impossible for a man of colour to be commissioned an officer, the *Manual of Military Law, 1914* states that 'aliens [including Negroes must] . . . not . . . exercise any actual command or power'. Second Lieutenant Tull died at the second Battle of the Somme, 25 March 1918. Decorated with the 1914–15 Star and British War and Victory medals, he was also recommended for a Military Cross for his 'gallantry and coolness' at the Battle of Piave in Italy in January 1918. PV

ODNB

Vasili, Phil, *Colouring Over the White Line: The History of Black Footballers in Britain* (2000)

See also FIRST WORLD WAR; SPORT

Turpin, Randolph (*c*.1928–1966). The first black British boxer to win a world title. Born in Leamington Spa in the Midlands, Turpin was the last of five children. His father, Lionel, originated from British Guiana, and, after fighting in the First World War, had settled in Britain. Less than a year after Turpin's birth his father suddenly died, leaving Beatrice Turpin a widow and single mother. Struggling to survive, she later remarried and settled in Warwick, where Turpin spent his formative years.

Influenced by his brother Dick, he began boxing in the early 1940s, as did Jack, the second eldest. Although potential title contenders, the British Boxing Board of Control stated that non-Whites could not compete for championship belts. The Turpins' reputation in the boxing world later became instrumental in the lifting of this ban in January 1948. Shortly after, Dick Turpin became the first black fighter to win a British title, paving the way for his brother.

In July 1951 Randolph Turpin shocked the world by beating the revered Sugar Ray Robinson to win the middleweight title. He had become the first black Briton to win a world championship, and an overnight superstar. After a mere 64 days, he sadly lost the title back to Robinson. His new-found celebrity quickly faded, and his boxing career, although celebrated, never reached such heights again. Financial difficulties and legal prosecution plagued his later years, and his mental health was questioned following his eventual suicide in 1966. KJ

Birtley, Jack, *The Tragedy of Randolph Turpin* (1975)

See also MOLINEAUX, TOM; SPORT

Two Tone, or **2Tone.** Musical genre invented in Coventry in the late 1970s and promoted through Jerry Dammers's 2Tone record label. Appropriately for a city with a large Jamaican population, it fused a punk guitar sound with elements of *ska, *reggae, and rock steady. The main bands, the Specials, the Selecter, and (from Birmingham) the Beat, were composed of black and white musicians, the concept of 2Tone being symbolic of multiculturalism as well as of the black and white 'rude boy' suits worn by the bands.

The Specials, formed in 1978, consisted of Jerry Dammers, Neville Staples, Terry Hall, Lynval Golding, Horace Panter, John Bradbury, and Roddy Radiation. Charley Anderson, a youth worker at Coventry City Council, formed the Selecter with Pauline Black, Desmond Brown, Charles Bembridge, Arthur Hendrickson, and Neol Davies in 1977. Dammers used their first song, 'The Selecter', as the B side to the Specials' first single, 'Gangsters', in 1979. Other acts on the label included Madness and Bad Manners, and two albums by the Jamaican trombonist Rico Rodriguez were released. The label closed in 1985.

The 2Tone phenomenon is generally discussed in the context of Coventry's economic decline, following the collapse of the local automotive industry. The Specials' most famous and lasting song, 'Ghost Town', depicts violence—'too much fightin' on the dance floor'—turning the city to a land of ghosts. The traditional reggae and dub (*see* DUB MUSIC) effects of horn breaks, ghostly laughter and sudden changes in tempo evoke nostalgia for a remembered Caribbean. JM

Oliver, Paul (ed.), *Black Music in Britain: Essays on the Afro-Asian Contribution to Popular Music* (1990)

See also HIP HOP; ROCK AGAINST RACISM

U

Union of Students of African Descent. The most prominent Pan-African student organization in Britain during the early 1920s. It grew out of the earlier West African and West Indian Christian Union, founded in London in 1917, and by 1924 claimed over 120 members. The Union of Students of African Descent (USAD) also had both Indian and English associate members and drew its membership from all over Britain.

At first the USAD was dominated by West Indian members, but after 1923 and the presidency of H. A. Hayfron-Benjamin, a student from the Gold Coast, it attracted more African members and focused more attention on their concerns. The USAD organized debates and social activities, helped to find accommodation for students, but became more politically active in 1924 in response to a series of racist articles in the press relating to the West African section of the *British Empire Exhibition at Wembley.

In response to these articles the USAD, led by one of its most prominent Nigerian members, Ladipo *Solanke, mounted its own campaign of protest in the press, and eventually forced the Colonial Office to take action. Following this successful action, the USAD organized a series of meetings featuring leading politicians from West Africa. It continued to maintain a West African focus, and in 1926, together with the *African Progress Union, it lobbied the Colonial Secretary, demanding more scholarships for West African students. By the late 1920s many of its most active members had joined organizations such as the *West African Students' Union, which contributed to USAD's decline and eventual demise. HA

Adi, H., *West Africans in Britain: Nationalism, Pan-Africanism and Communism* (1998)

See also COMMITTEE OF AFRICAN ORGANIZATIONS

United States of America, Britain, and abolition. Anti-slavery, the political campaign for *abolition of the *slave trade and *emancipation of slaves, emerged in Britain in the 18th century, and achieved its greatest legal victories between 1770 and 1833. Anglo-American cooperation occurred from the onset, though Britain led the way in providing the arguments, leaders, and legal precedents which the United States would adopt. In a second period, 1833–70, the force of the movement would be directed towards the abolition of *slavery in America.

1. British political strategy 1772–1833
2. The origins of Anglo-American cooperation
3. The turn to America
4. Historical interpretations

1. British political strategy 1772–1833 In Britain emancipation of slaves did not become the main objective of anti-slavery until the 19th century. In the 18th century the legal campaign for the abolition of the slave trade was the foremost movement, inaugurated by Granville *Sharp. Sharp campaigned for a definitive legal ruling protecting escaped slaves from forcible eviction from Britain, and published the first major British work of anti-slavery in 1769, presenting substantial legal arguments against slavery.

In 1772 the case of James Somerset, an escaped slave who had been reimprisoned on a slave ship to Jamaica, brought a significant ruling from Judge William Murray, Earl of Mansfield (*see* SOMERSET

CASE). Murray declared that any slave taken into territory where slavery was prohibited became free, and no one could 'take a slave by force to be sold abroad'. Abolitionists claimed the ruling as a victory, although it failed to outlaw slavery in England or the colonies.

The case of the slave ship *Zong* in 1781, in which 133 slaves were thrown overboard alive, provoked a public outcry that facilitated Thomas *Clarkson's push for a legal re-examination of the slave trade. In February 1788 the Privy Council opened an investigation of the state of the African trade and William *Wilberforce steered the campaign through Parliament, using Clarkson's evidence of the cruelty inflicted on Africans by slave traders.

In 1792 the Abolition Bill was finally passed, but amended to 'gradual abolition' by Henry Dundas. The slave traders' lobby, the *West India interest, exploited the compromise to delay the enforcement of even gradual abolition. However, the Abolition of the Slave Trade Act finally became law in 1807, banning the slave trade throughout the British Empire with the enforcement of the Royal Navy. Despite the law, trafficking in the Caribbean continued and slaves were still held in Britain. The Act banned trade, but stopped short of emancipation, which was perceived as too threatening to the welfare of the Empire. Many seemed to hope that slavery would simply wither away of its own accord in the colonies and the United States.

On the West Indian plantations slave revolts accelerated between 1807 and 1832, as Blacks demanded the unconditional emancipation they believed they had been promised. Capitalists came to view cheap free labour as more viable than maintaining their tenuous hold over slave populations. On 26 July 1833 the Emancipation Bill was passed, abolishing slavery throughout the whole Empire and paying £20 million in compensation to plantation owners in the Caribbean.

2. The origins of Anglo-American cooperation The success of the British legal campaign for abolition might suggest that movement was strictly conducted on the national level. However, the highly visible politics of parliamentary lobbying relied on the activities of ordinary citizens. Anti-slavery exhibited a surprising diversity, bringing together Enlightenment ideals with three religious–intellectual traditions: evangelicalism, Rational Dissent (later Unitarianism), and Quakerism. It closely intersected other moral reform movements including societies against prostitution and vice, missionary and tract societies, and benevolent societies. Anti-slavery strategies, therefore, reflected the different social worlds of its participants, including boycotts of slave-grown produce and fundraising bazaars organized by women's societies, the organization of subscriptions and petitions by abolition societies such as the Society for Effecting the Abolition of the Slave Trade, and the prolific publication of pamphlets, verses, novels, and sermons intended to arouse the sympathies of the general public.

Furthermore, the ideas behind the Anti-Slavery Movement arose from a network of relationships between religious, legal, and social reformers on both sides of the Atlantic. The traffic of ideas between Britain and its former colonies followed the ties of religious and family affiliations, consisting of a flurry of correspondence and, increasingly in the 19th century, visits from leaders. As early as the late 1600s George Fox, the founder of the Religious Society of Friends, preached against slavery. Anti-slavery became a fundamental campaign of the Quakers in the United States, and in 1780s they became the first society on either side of the Atlantic wholly to abolish slavery. Anthony Benezet, a Pennsylvania Quaker who had already been publishing anti-slavery treatises in Britain and America, read Granville Sharp's 1769 publication arguing for the illegality of slavery, and opened a correspondence between him and John *Wesley, the founder of the Methodist Church. From their correspondence emerged a prolonged, if informal, campaign, in which the exchange of ideas, pamphlets, and articles between Quakers, Methodists, and legal reformers sustained abolitionist sentiments in both the United States and Britain.

The American War of Independence temporarily cut off the lines of communication between British and American anti-slavery proponents. However, Benezet and other American abolitionists pressured the Continental Congress to stop the slave trade and make provisions for gradual emancipation in the Constitution. The Americans followed what news they could acquire of the British legal campaign with alacrity, particularly the push for emancipation of slaves in the West Indies. With the end of the War of Independence, the Americans were determined to follow the British example of pursuing federal legislation against the foreign slave trade, and to fight the expansion of slavery into the new western territories.

3. **The turn to America** Far from signalling the end of struggle, 1833 marked a new phase in British anti-slavery. Britain's withdrawal from the Atlantic slave trade failed to halt traffic, and slavery flourished in the United States, threatening the British sense of moral and liberal progress. Outright slavery in the colonies was replaced by the thinly veiled substitute of 'apprenticeship'. In 1839, with the organization of the British and Foreign Anti-Slavery Society (BFASS), British anti-slavery acquired an international outlook. Joseph *Sturge, the founder of the BFASS, proclaimed dramatically, 'Sin will lie at our door again if we do not agitate, agitate, agitate.' The BFASS was dedicated to the global eradication of slave systems, targeting British India, Brazil, Cuba, and, in particular, the United States.

Unlike Britain, where internal slavery was never widespread, America had depended on the slave trade since its colonial origins. The process of abolition throughout the states was gradual and uneven. The sprawling nature of American geography made a centralized campaign such as had been waged in the smaller country of Britain less practicable. Religious groups such as the Quakers and Methodists bore much of the burden of the early campaign, supported by their London counterparts. Largely as a result of their efforts, the northern states had abolished slavery by 1830, before Britain. The South, however, persisted in strident defence of slavery, despite the efforts of African-Americans such as Sojourner Truth and Martin R. *Delany, who formed their own bands of resistance, evolving out of the black churches.

African-American activists and their writings had a profound impact on individual sympathetic white activists such as the silver-tongued propagandist William Lloyd Garrison. Garrison discovered and promoted the ex-slave Frederick *Douglass, who became one of anti-slavery's most eloquent apostles, and went on to publish the widely disseminated abolitionist newspaper the *North Star*, read on both sides of the Atlantic. However, African-American activists initially had very little visibility outside the black community, and the majority of the US population viewed abolition as a 'foreign' or British import, threatening to the stability of the country. The protection of slavery under both federal and the stronger state laws made it difficult for individual citizens to attack it directly.

For British abolitionists in the 1830s and 1840s, a primary objective became the awakening of the American conscience regarding the evils of slavery. A stream of British abolitionists including George Thompson, J. J. Gurney, John Scoble, and Joseph Sturge visited America between 1834 and 1851, seeking to arouse international cooperation. Sturge employed grass-roots methods and research similar to the earlier Thomas Clarkson, personally assailing slave dealers, slave holders, newspaper publishers, and politicians with his anti-slavery arguments. Sturge, like other British abolitionists, was particularly appalled by the assertion of the leading American religious denominations that slavery was a Christian institution, and he pressured America's churches to condemn slavery as sin. Everywhere Sturge travelled, he published manifestos and urged the free states to take control of the federal government and end slave-holding.

Harriet Martineau was a British woman abolitionist with a transatlantic impact. Like her contemporary Sturge, she travelled through America, conducting her own economic and sociological research of slavery conditions. Her visit in 1834 cemented British relations with the Transcendentalists and anti-slavery proponents in Boston. She served as the English correspondent for the American *National Anti-Slavery Standard* until the Civil War, producing a flow of anti-slavery articles. In *Society in America* (1837) she demolished the American pro-slavery arguments.

The efforts of visiting British abolitionists met with hostility from the American churches and the pro-slavery federal government, but they were aided by the Anglicizing impulse that arose in early 19th-century America, despite the tensions of the American War of Independence. The Second Great Awakening compelled American northern middle-class Protestants to become actively involved in religious and civic reform, and they took British societies as models. American abolitionists emulated the British example by organizing petitions of Congress, sponsoring itinerant lecturers, and disseminating anti-slavery materials. British influence led to the formation of abolition societies directly modelled on British counterparts, such as Lewis Tappan's American and Foreign Anti-Slavery Society (AFASS), the American counterpart to the BFASS, and the first national anti-slavery organization. The leaders of the BFASS and AFASS corresponded at great length, exchanging periodicals such as Garrison's *Liberator* and *The Reporter*, and reprinting articles borrowed from one another.

Urged by both British and American abolitionists, the British government intervened in America when it could, negotiating the Negro Seamen Acts to end the quarantine of black British seamen in southern ports, and working to protect fugitive slaves seeking asylum in the British territories of Canada and the West Indies. These actions raised consciousness of slavery on both sides of the Atlantic. British societies gave money in support of Canadian anti-slavery and the resettlement of fugitives in Canada, and sent goods to be sold in American anti-slavery bazaars.

Realizing the importance of British support at the international, political, and social level, American anti-slavery leaders began to travel there. Between 1839 and 1860 almost all the leading figures in American anti-slavery visited Britain, drawn by the two World Conventions against slavery hosted by the British. Some stayed for long periods, such as Henry C. Wright, embarking on rigorous lecture tours throughout the country.

A wave of African-American abolitionists also came to Britain with the mission to raise funds and British support. Nathaniel Paul and Moses Grandy were among the many who made lengthy tours. Like Ignatius *Sancho, Olaudah *Equiano, and Ottobah *Cugoano in the century before, they were received rapturously by white audiences fascinated by black testimony to the horrors of slavery, and were highly instrumental in solidifying Anglo-American cooperation in the 1830s–1860s.

However, many southerners and US natives continued to see American abolitionists as internal enemies who were sustained and provoked from Britain. Britain was indeed embroiled in the politics of America's western expansion, seeking to interrupt the spread of slavery through the leverage of territories such as Texas. John Scoble urged the British government to support Texan independence, but to make recognition dependent upon the condition of emancipation, thus creating an asylum for escaped slaves. The Massachusetts abolitionist Stephen Pearl Andrews argued that the British should offer economic inducement to the Texans to give up slavery. However, annexation put an end to these plans.

In the 1850s American abolitionists divided over the issue of the Constitution of the United States. Some, led by Lysander

Spooner, Gerrit Smith, and Frederick Douglass, believed that the Constitution could be employed as an anti-slavery document. The Anti-Slavery Movement splintered further over issues of women's participation and the inclusion of deists and Unitarians. Garrison, though a fiery orator and fierce proponent of anti-slavery, increasingly alienated other abolitionists through his insistence on linking anti-slavery to other 'extreme' causes, including pacifism, anticlericalism, anti-Sabbatarianism, and women's rights.

At the first World Convention, the British were drawn into the dispute, when Garrisonians refused to join delegates on the convention floor because of the exclusion of women participants. The Garrisonians sought to stoke discord among British abolitionists and succeeded in splintering off the Bristol and Clifton Ladies' Anti-Slavery Society. British abolitionists attempted to heal these breaches and instigate unified action, but they progressively succumbed to sectionalism and fragmentation. Throughout the 1850s the BFASS and other British societies suffered a decline in membership, financial contributions, and meetings, becoming nearly dormant.

In the United States the Anti-Slavery Movement underwent devolution, shifting its emphasis from national societies to autonomous state organizations, each with their own periodicals and auxiliary networks. They campaigned in their specific regions, pressuring local politicians and aiding escaped fugitives. The AFASS dwindled into little more than a correspondence society, most of its energies diverted into the organization of the Free Soil, Liberty, and Republican parties on the federal level.

However, the outbreak of civil war in 1861 renewed British interest in abolition. Lincoln's preliminary emancipation proclamation of 1862 secured ecstatic British support for the Union. Organizations such as F. W. Chesson's London Emancipation Committee sprang up throughout Britain in order to counteract pro-Confederate groups and encourage the US government to prosecute the new emancipation policy.

The abolition of slavery in 1865 was hailed as a victory by abolitionists on both sides of the Atlantic. After emancipation, abolitionists campaigned to improve the rights and conditions of freedmen. The US Civil Rights Movement would eventually emerge from their principles, and they achieved equal voting rights in 1870 with the Fifteenth Amendment to the Constitution. The subsequent cooperation of British and American ships in the suppression of slave traffic finally brought the Atlantic slave trade to an end.

4. Historical interpretations While past historians tended to 'sanctify' anti-slavery as a crusade representing the zenith of Anglo-American moral progress and liberal values, contemporary approaches have been more critical. Some regard its achievements as less the triumph of religion and humanitarianism, and more the inevitable result of the shift towards industrial capitalism in Britain, which generated a new class attracted to free labour. Eric *Williams, in *Capitalism and Slavery* (1944), famously insists on the precedence of material over moral interests as the impetus for abolition and emancipation. Another perspective suggests that British slave systems were not so much rendered unprofitable, as bypassed by the changing class and social structures in Britain, for which anti-slavery proved a crucial cultural mediator. Finally, recent research such as Patrick Brantlinger's *Rule of Darkness* (1988) uncovers links between the rhetoric of anti-slavery and British imperialism, suggesting that the discourse of white superiority and black gratitude was used to justify the 'civilizing mission' of empire in Africa. However, the perseverance of transatlantic cooperation between British and American abolitionists over two centuries remains extraordinary.

SGD

Fladeland, Betty, *Men and Brothers: Anglo-American Antislavery Cooperation* (1972)

Midgley, Clare, *Women Against Slavery: The British Campaigns 1780–1870* (1992)

Ripley, C. Peter (ed.), *The Black Abolitionist Papers* (1985)

United States of America, Britain, and the Civil Rights Movement. The movement in the 1950s and 1960s for racial equality in the United States that used non-violent protest to break the pattern of racial segregation and achieve national equal rights legislation for Blacks. In Britain the movement for civil rights was largely imitative of the United States and reached its peak during a shorter period, between 1965 and 1968. It is perhaps better understood as a campaign over time for black rights and improved race relations than as a clearly delineated movement.

1. Introduction to the United States versus Britain
2. Immigration and discrimination
3. The race riots of 1958
4. Politicians and legislation
5. Mobilizing resistance
6. The Campaign Against Racial Discrimination
7. The rise of Black Power
8. The legacy of the Black Rights Movement

1. Introduction to the United States versus Britain In the United States the Civil Rights Movement reached its height in a decade of marches and protests between 1955 and 1965. The bus boycott in Montgomery, Alabama, in 1955, initiated by the National Association for the Advancement of Colored People, acted as a catalyst. The campaign continued with the student-led sit-ins organized by Stokely Carmichael's Student Nonviolent Coordinating Committee. Civil protest climaxed in 1963, with the dramatic march on Washington of 200,000 demonstrators gathering to hear Dr Martin Luther King, Jr., proclaim his dream of racial harmony and equality. In 1964 and 1965 Congress passed the Civil Rights Act and the Voting Rights Act, securing basic civil rights for all Americans regardless of race. In Britain climactic anti-discrimination legislation did not arrive until the Race Relations Act of 1968.

This delay is characteristic of the UK rights movement, which lagged behind the United States in protest and legislation. If 19th-century American abolitionism imitated the British anti-slavery movement, borrowing its symbols, methods, and leaders, the history of the modern Civil Rights Movement is a direct reversal, with Britain dependent on the events, programmes, and ideas of the United States. Not only did British leaders adopt American leaders such as Martin Luther King, Jr., Stokely Carmichael (who adopted the name Kwame Touré—also spelt Ture—in 1978), *Malcolm X, and Angela Davis as models, British opponents of minority rights modelled themselves after American extremist groups such as the Ku Klux Klan.

2. Immigration and discrimination The most obvious divergence between the United States and Britain is that African-Americans endured slavery and segregation, whereas black British people were mostly immigrants from the West Indies, South Asia, and other former colonies, who came to Britain as free citizens in search of improved quality of life. African-Caribbeans in the United Kingdom drew parallels between their experience of race riots, racial discrimination, and socio-economic difficulties in the 1950s and 1960s and the prejudice and segregation endured by their American counterparts. However, they would never achieve the same unity of resistance that distinguished the collective demand of African-Americans for voting rights, material progress, and sociopolitical equality, nor the coalition of militant, radical, and nationalist black organizations with well-defined power bases. Their campaign was a more nebulous process, emerging from the adjustment of immigrant communities to the challenges of living and working in Britain.

The **Empire Windrush* generation of West Indians who arrived in 1948 to help resolve the labour crisis encountered racial discrimination in *housing, education, and employment. Instead of receiving dignified jobs matching their levels of skill and experience, they were given manual labour with low wages and long hours. Their search for lodging was greeted by the open hostility of the 'No Dogs, No Irish, No Coloured' signs. The immigrants eventually found housing in slum dwellings in decaying inner-city areas, such as Notting Hill. They faced colour bars in pubs and clubs, and physical abuse on the streets. Many black British schoolchildren were classified as educationally subnormal and were barred from classes that reflected their real aptitude. However, unlike African-Americans, who were able to revolt against a clearly defined structure of oppressive segregation, black British people found it difficult to resist what appeared to be an amorphous set of attitudes and prejudices, rather than a visible system of discrimination.

3. **The race riots of 1958** When immigration to Britain from the Commonwealth accelerated after the Nationality Act of 1948, the pressures of integration intensified. Sir Oswald *Mosley, the pre-war fascist leader, made speeches in deprived urban areas inciting white men to drive Blacks out of the country: 'Act now to keep Britain white' was his rallying cry. Fuelled by Mosley's fascism, white gangs of Teddy boys began prowling the streets in search of Blacks and Asians. In the summer of 1958 race riots erupted in Nottingham and Notting Hill, dominating press coverage and making racial tensions suddenly and painfully visible.

The first generation of immigrants had previously repressed their experiences of racism, looking homewards for their identity or functioning on an insular level. However, the 1958 events redirected their gaze to Britain and the need to cooperate as a community. Instead of leaving Britain, black communities mobilized for the first time, organizing escorts for late-shift workers and patrolling neighbourhoods. The *West Indian Standing Conference was organized in 1959 in direct response to the killing of Kelso *Cochrane in Notting Hill. Still, black organizations at that time were mostly cultural associations and community groups without political agendas or recognized spokespersons. Little opportunity was available for organized protest on the American model, and the British government offered no legislation protecting black rights, promoting racial integration, or conceiving of national identity in multicultural terms.

4. **Politicians and legislation** The discourse of white supremacy emerging from 19th-century imperialist ideology yoked whiteness to national belonging, and blackness to servitude. After the 1958 riots, race and immigration emerged as central issues in British politics. Many politicians and civil servants were ill at ease about the 'black presence', and callously manipulated racist sentiments to secure votes. Members of Parliament such as Enoch Powell viciously attributed the economic and social problems of post-war Britain to the presence of black 'aliens', echoing the periodic alarmist rhetoric surrounding immigration in the United States. The Conservative Party passed the Commonwealth Immigrants Act in 1962, making entry dependent on the acquisition of employment vouchers. Peter Griffiths, a Tory candidate in Smethwick, Birmingham, fought the 1964 election with the openly racist slogan 'If you want a nigger for a neighbour, vote Labour'. When re-elected to power in 1964, Labour announced its intention to introduce a Race Relations Bill, but called at the same time for further restrictions on Commonwealth immigrants.

The Race Relations Act of 1965 reflected ambivalence on the part of left-wing politicians, and compromised the trust of the black British community. While the Act finally gave official recognition to the existence of racial discrimination, it lacked provisions for enforcement. Simultaneous to passing the bill, the government reduced the number of employment vouchers granted to Commonwealth immigrants and tightened immigration controls. The legislation seemed designed to take the sting out of racial protest through containment and control. By introducing a pre-emptive bill on race, the government effectively prevented black leadership from rising up from the streets and dictating the agenda as it had in America. The 1960s seemed primed to usher in a new period of despondency.

5. Mobilizing resistance However, the experience of everyday racism and the heightened political visibility of discrimination mobilized the black British to create new social institutions, including pressure groups, black-led *churches, black-controlled credit unions, and black media. In answer to the government-established bodies of the Commonwealth Immigrants' Advisory Council (1962) and the Race Relations Board (1965), black British people set up their own vehicles for justice, including the Coloured People's Progressive Association, the Association for the Advancement of Coloured People, and the *West Indian Gazette*. In 1963 Paul Stephenson organized a boycott against the Bristol Bus Company, which refused to hire black workers, taking his inspiration from the Montgomery bus boycott.

Writing provided another crucial arena for the formation of black British identity and ideologies of resistance. While the first generation of writers such as Samuel *Selvon and George Lamming primarily reflected migrant experience, in the 1960s writers looked increasingly to the works of international revolutionary writers, including James Baldwin, Leroy Jones (later Amiri Baraka), Frantz Fanon, and Eldridge Cleaver. In 1963 Linton Kwesi Johnson organized a poetry workshop within the Brixton branch of the British *Black Panther Party. *Publishing houses were set up to foster talent and raise consciousness on a larger scale. Kamau Brathwaite, Andrew *Salkey, and John *La Rose formed the *Caribbean Artists' Movement in 1966. Jessica Huntley founded the independent publishing house and bookshop Bogle L'Ouverture and published a stream of works from Caribbean and African writers, including Salkey, Walter *Rodney, and Linton Kwesi Johnson. Black British people were inspired by the discovery that they shared West Indian backgrounds with many of the prominent leaders in the United States, such as Malcolm X and Stokely Carmichael, and that a network of ideas originating with Caribbean ideologues was driving both the anti-colonial movement and the campaign for civil rights.

6. The Campaign Against Racial Discrimination By the 1960s Britain was becoming a hotbed of political and creative activity, with writers and thinkers crossing the Atlantic to discuss civil rights issues. On 5 December 1964 Dr Martin Luther King, Jr., visited London en route to Stockholm. Marion Glean, a member of Multi-Racial Britain and the Society of Friends Race Relations Committee, organized a meeting of 30 representatives from Commonwealth immigrant institutions, including the West Indian Standing Conference, the Indian Workers' Association, and the National Federation of Pakistani Associations. Dr King urged these representatives to publicize Britain's deteriorating racial relations and employ non-violent strategies of direct action to combat discrimination. Spurred by King's exhortation, a number of West Indians already involved in race relations, including C. L. R. *James, Ranjana Ash, and David *Pitt, joined together with a group of white liberals and clergy to form the *Campaign Against Racial Discrimination (CARD).

Loosely modelled on King's Southern Christian Leadership Conference, CARD's objective was to combat racial discrimination at both the community and the legislative level. More simply, it would attempt to jump-start a mass social and political movement that did not yet exist. Bayard Rustin, the American pacifist leader and associate of Dr King, was present at the creation of CARD and helped to shape its philosophy of non-violence. From 1965 to 1967 CARD pressured the government to revise deeply flawed anti-discrimination legislation, with the result that an amended Race Relations Bill was passed in 1968, providing a new framework of laws prohibiting discrimination in employment, housing, and the sale of goods and services.

CARD was short-lived, however, fracturing owing to its lack of a clear ideological foundation or grass-roots support from the black British communities. It did spawn the creation of other race relations organizations, such as Equal Rights (1967) and the *Commission for Racial Equality (1976). However, Britain lacked a tradition of philosophically driven direct action such as existed in the southern churches of the United States, and black British people seemed to find Dr King's strategies less appealing than other models of resistance.

7. The rise of Black Power In the late 1960s in America the civil rights and student movements became increasingly militant and radicalized. Black nationalism and the Black Power Movement gained momentum. The politics across the Atlantic dictated a radical turn for the Black Rights Movement in Britain. Further restrictions on immigration in the Kenyan Asian Act of 1968, and the outbreak of 'Powellism' urging the repatriation of immigrants, had an incendiary effect on black British youth, welding together disparate Caribbean communities into a single, radicalized, racialized community. 'Blackness' offered a unifying identity to the angry second generation, who denied allegiance to either Queen or country. However, the problem remained the lack of an organized response. As Farrukh Dondy states, British Black Power leaders preached apocalyptic US rhetoric: '"When the time comes we have to organise". We thought the time had come but nobody was offering us an organisation to join.'

Malcolm X visited Britain in 1964, seeking to arouse black nationalist sentiments and political support for the African-American struggle in the United States. He urged black political activists: 'never and never let the white man immobilise you by fear'. Capitalizing on his meeting with Malcolm X, a young Trinidadian named Michael de Freitas renamed himself Michael Abdul Malik, then *Michael X, and swiftly formed the Racial Adjustment Action Society (RAAS). The scatologically titled RAAS was allegedly dedicated to revolutionary struggle to liberate black people and agitate for exclusively black issues and interests. Michael X hectored his comrades to abandon non-violent protest: 'Stop twisting and hit back . . . Our last name is Black' (*The Observer*, 4 July 1965). Captivated by Michael X's flamboyant posturing, the national press eagerly hailed him as the new leader of the British Black Power Movement. He was idolized as a martyr after he was imprisoned under the Race Relations Act of 1965 for inciting racial hatred through a speech delivered in Reading. By the end of the 1960s, however, RAAS disintegrated owing to internal conflicts and financial irregularities. Michael X fled the country for Trinidad, and was hanged there after being convicted of murder. He was subsequently viewed by other revolutionaries as a mimic and a fake, whose militant persona cynically exploited Britain's hunger for black leaders as vibrant as those in the United States.

Prior to RAAS, other small black militant groups existed, most of which preached neo-Garveyite black nationalism. A branch of the Black Panther Party was formed in 1967, consisting of a mix of West Indians and a minority of Indian and Pakistani members. Stokely Carmichael's visit to London in July 1967 launched the establishment of the Universal Coloured People's Association. Under Obi Egbuna, the Association strove to translate its more moderate approach into a fully fledged militant Black Power ideology, with a pragmatic programme aimed at 'the establishment of separate educational, political and economic institutions and the encouragement of pride in the separate ideology of the black man'. However, this organization also declined after Egbuna was charged with conspiring to murder white police officers. Once more, the deprivation of a power base or clear structures of authority and ideology caused the demise of black radical groups.

8. The legacy of the Black Rights Movement British Black Power movements yielded little political change, but they generated black consciousness necessary for the growth of later religious, social, and political black movements in the 1970s–1980s. They also accelerated the emergence of black British historical studies and interventions by artists and writers concerned with reinscribing the black presence into English cultural history. The British campaign for black rights was most clearly visible in the movement for civil rights between 1965 and 1968 and the interest in Black Power from 1968 to 1971. However, the glamorous auras of civil rights and Black Power should not distract from the real progress for black rights accomplished by volunteer groups and individual Blacks in local politics. By slowly building up a tradition based on unions and local elections, migrant councillors prepared the way for the next generation of black politicians to enter British *politics and implement new legislation. Likewise, community groups set the stage for the black parents' self-help groups and coalitions to come. SGD

Goulbourne, H., *Race Relations in Britain Since 1945* (1998)

Heineman, Benjamin W., Jr., *The Politics of the Powerless: A Study of the Campaign Against Racial Discrimination* (1972)

Phillips, Mike, and Phillips, Trevor, *Windrush: The Irresistible Rise of Multicultural Britain* (1998)

See also NOTTING HILL RIOTS

V

Vanity Fair. Novel by William Thackeray published in monthly numbers between January 1847 and June 1848. Of several black and mulatto characters represented in *Vanity Fair*, Miss Rhoda Swartz is the most fully drawn. Though often overlooked by critical commentators, Miss Swartz fulfils a key role in the first half of the novel. Her last name etymologically derives from the term 'swart', which was displaced in English by 'black', or 'swarthy'. Born in St Kitts as the daughter of a black mother and a white German-Jewish slave holder, she enters English society as a rich heiress upon her father's demise. Indeed, in the novel her presence in English upper-class society, which renders visible Britain's colonial history and the suppressed hybridity of British society, is predicated entirely upon her wealth. However, in Thackeray's representation her wealth cannot erase her cultural and ethnic difference. Despite having attended the same school as the novel's two female protagonists, she can only inadequately perform the role of the educated lady, unlike Amelia Sedley and Rebecca Sharp. As a possible alternative marital match for George Osborne, she is directly contrasted with the impoverished Amelia. For George's father and sisters as true inhabitants of Vanity Fair, merit is measured by wealth. For George, Rhoda the 'Hottentot Venus', whose 'colour' he does not like, renders Amelia more desirable despite her lack of finances. Rhoda Swartz thus acts as the foil for the construction of Amelia's 'white' English identity. KDO

DeVere Brody, Jennifer, *Impossible Purities: Blackness, Femininity, and Victorian Culture* (1998)

See also LITERATURE 1: REPRESENTATIONS OF BLACKS

Visual arts 1: Representations of Blacks. By the mid-18th century Britain was at the height of its power and wealth, profiting from its leading role in the lucrative slave trade. Some of the great patrons of the age, like William *Beckford and his son, were heavily involved in slavery, owning plantations in the West Indies. During this time black people found themselves represented mostly as servants in the households of the wealthy. Not only were they anonymous figures, but they had no control over how they were portrayed. There were of course notable exceptions, paintings in which the black sitter is afforded a measure of dignity that suggests a degree of respect and recognition as a fellow human being. The painting attributed to Joshua Reynolds (1723–92) titled *Study of a Black Man* (*c.*1770) is one such example. The picture may be a portrait of one of Reynolds's own black servants or perhaps a portrait of Francis *Barber, the Jamaican companion of Samuel Johnson. In this unfinished portrait Reynolds makes no attempt to Europeanize the physiognomy of the sitter. Rather than depict him in exotic or classical clothes that would mark him out from white Europeans, he is dressed in the garments of the day and has a defiant and proud look about his countenance. Another example is the portrait of Ignatius *Sancho (1768), by Thomas Gainsborough (1727–88), in which the human warmth and affability of the sitter are captured.

Towards the end of the 18th century anti-slavery images began to proliferate in paintings and prints, examples being William *Blake's illustrations of John Stedman's *Narrative, of a Five Years' Expedition*

Against the Revolted Negroes of Surinam (1796); and George Morland's *The Slave Trade* (1788). The most recognizable image of the black figure was on the *Wedgwood medallion of 1787, with its inscription 'Am I not a man and a brother?' Though such images were motivated by compassion for the plight of abused slaves, black people were still depicted as anonymous, passive subjects.

In the 19th century slavery continued to be a theme in British art—for example J. M. W. Turner's *Slavers Throwing Overboard the Dead and the Dying, Typhoon Coming On* (1840)—but after *emancipation artists ceased to be inspired by the subject. A rich source of imagery was to be found in travel books. In the 18th century travelogues frequently presented the African in caricatured forms, as a buffoon or as a savage, but the new discipline of ethnographic illustration led to more sympathetic (if picturesque) representations of African life, such as Samuel Daniell's depictions of 'Hottentots' (1802–4). Daniell's illustrations were heavily influenced by notions of the *'noble savage' existing in a state of natural paradise. Notions of 'noble savagery' were transformed into later *Orientalist portrayals of the black female as sensuous and sexually available, in works by David Roberts (lithographs in his *Egypt and Nubia*, 1846–9), William James Müller (*Slave Market, Cairo*, 1841), and others.

Interest in racial types and in phrenology led to many studies of black physiognomy, some more 'realistic' than others. James Ward's *Three Views of the Head of a Native* (1815) views the black face from different angles so as to investigate the dimensions of the nose, forehead, and lips.

Black people, then, were subject not only to enslavement in the New World plantations, but also to the imagination of 18th- and 19th-century British artists, who represented them variously as savages, household servants, victims of abuse, figures of exotica, and 'scientific' specimens. The overwhelming majority of images are of men, though one of the finest portraits of a black person is that of Dido Elizabeth *Lindsay, famously captured hand in hand with her cousin in the grounds of Kenwood House (*c.*1779; a painting attributed to Johann Zoffany, 1725–1810).

Although there was evidence that African-American artists like Robert Douglas (1809–97) and Robert Scott Duncanson (1817–72) visited London, none of their works have surfaced. It was not until the latter half of the 20th century that black British artists began to paint themselves and their communities, exploring issues such as ethnicity and inner-city life. Sonia Boyce's work, executed in a variety of media, includes works such as *She Ain't Holding Them Up, She's Holding On*, and *From Tarzan to Rambo*, in which she asks questions about the representation of race, colour, and the legacy of centuries of cultural stereotyping of black people. Donald Rodney (1961–98) would look at contemporary culture of the young black man as 'public enemy' and the very embodiment of danger.

Some artists would explore the representations of the black image in art by using their own image in their work, such as Maud Sulter's (b. 1960) self-portrait photograph of the artist as Calliope, which formed part of a series of portraits of the nine Muses of Greek mythology. The casting of black women in these roles made the viewer question the previously accepted conviction that such roles in west European art were solely the preserve of white Europeans.

Yet, far from turning their backs on old European traditions of black representation, British artists such as the Turner Prizewinner Chris Ofili (b. 1968) have embraced some of its more positive and sublime aspects. Reinventing the historical roots of painting, Ofili invokes religious iconography and creates a look of jewel-like encrustations in his work, while also examining themes of black identity and culture. Ofili's 'Upper Room' display, exhibited at Tate Britain (2005–6) is an arrangement of twelve canvases, supported on his now famous trademark elephant dung. They flank a larger, thirteenth canvas in a specially designed chapel-like environment, which immediately suggests Christ and his twelve Apostles. Such a deliberately designed environment alludes to the Arena Chapel in Padua housing Giotto's famous frescoes (1303–5). The repeated image of a rhesus macaque monkey in Ofili's pictures raises questions of civilization, nature, the religious, and the secular, again from a world-centric perspective rather than a Eurocentric one.

LP

Dabydeen, David, *Hogarth's Blacks: Images of Blacks in Eighteenth Century English Art* (1985)

Marsh, Jan (ed.), *Black Victorians: Black People in British Art 1800–1900* (2005)

See also VISUAL ARTS 2: ARTISTS

Visual arts 2: Artists. Black British artistic practice has, since its early beginnings, found itself manifested as a strand outside the British art scene. It is an art form that has often manifested itself as distinct from the conventional traditions of the white British mainstream and artistic production. Black British art casts its net wider than British classical traditions, taking its inspiration not only from Western and non-Western cultural influences, but also from the experiences of those black artists living in Britain and the circumstances of modernity in which they found themselves in pre-war and post-war Britain; while at the same time drawing on post-colonial, now Commonwealth, influences.

1. Ronald Moody
2. Guyanese artists
3. The new generation from the 1980s onwards
4. Film media

1. Ronald Moody The early years of black artistic practice in post-war Britain saw the rise of arguably the most important progenitor of the black arts movement in Britain. The self-trained Jamaican wood sculptor and former dentist Ronald *Moody had arrived in London by 1923. His 1937 one-man show in Paris, followed by his 1938 show in Amsterdam, had already assured his early success in the European art world. Although his success was cut short by the onset of war, he was able to resume his work after the war in his London studio. It was not long before he was able to hold a one-man show in London, in May 1946, at the Arcade Gallery, off Bond Street, with subsequent regular exhibitions following throughout the 1950s. However, it was after his death that Moody became truly recognized as one of Britain's foremost modernist sculptors when, in 2002, the Tate Gallery, London, purchased and featured his work in 'A Reputation Restored'. The 1950s saw more and more black artists arriving from the colonies to establish themselves. Such was their success in this period that the painter Francis Newton Sousa (1924–2002) was quoted as saying, 'I make more money by my painting than the Prime Minister by his politics.'

2. Guyanese artists Guyanese played a significant part in the burgeoning black British art scene. The painter Frank Bowling was born in what was British Guiana in 1936, and at the age of 14 immigrated to England, where he would complete his school education. It was shortly after graduating from the Royal College of Art in 1959 that Bowling had his first solo exhibition, in 1962, at the Grabowski Galleries entitled 'Image in Revolt'. By 1966, however, he was dissatisfied with his lack of progress in London and established himself in the then modern art capital of the world, New York. He had his first one-man exhibition in 1966 at the Terry Dintenfass Gallery. Success throughout the 1960s culminated in his highly successful 1971 exhibition at the Whitney Museum of American Art, New York. Like David Hockney, much of Bowling's success has been achieved in America, although he considers himself a British artist. Indeed, after decades of being at the cutting edge of the British art scene, Bowling's contribution to British art was formally recognized with his election to the Royal Academy in May 2005, making him the first black British artist to be elected to this establishment in its over 200-year history.

The other significant artist to come out of Guyana (arriving in Britain just two years after Bowling) was Aubrey *Williams. Born in Georgetown in 1926, Williams travelled throughout Europe before eventually settling in London in 1952, where he attended St Martin's School of Art. While still a first-year student, he held his first one-man show at a gallery in Westbourne Grove, London. After marrying Eve Lafargue, also from Guyana, he was persuaded by her to give up his day jobs in a factory and a café to take up painting full-time. His big breakthrough came after he showed his work to the South African painter and teacher Denis Bowen. Bowen was the founder of the New Vision Group, a non-profit-making arts organization primarily interested in non-figurative work, which was precisely the kind of work Williams was producing at that time. Williams's work was subsequently included in the New Vision '58 Open Exhibition of 1958, and other venues that were associated with this organization also exhibited his work across London. This extensive exposure ensured greater contact with other artists in the London and international art scene, which eventually led to invitations to show in Paris, Milan, and Chicago.

These early pioneers of black British art would eventually be recognized, post-millennium, by the mainstream art establishment for their contribution to the British art scene; however, black British artists would not again experience the heady days of the 1950s. It was becoming abundantly clear that, in the decades following, the initial success of these black artists was beginning to fade from the minds of the British art establishment. This was due in no small part to the lack of support and recognition by major established art institutions; indeed, without any recognition by these institutions of the existence and impact of these particular artists' achievements, black British art could not find its way into the canon of British art history.

3. The new generation from the 1980s onwards It was not until the emergence of a new generation of black British artists in the 1980s that the British art establishment would once again be encouraged to recognize that black British artists were still present and a potent force in the art scene. Emerging out of the fertile landscape of the 1950s and 1960s, artists such as Rasheed Araeen, Rita Keegan, Donald Rodney, Steve McQueen, and Chris Ofili would be in the vanguard of this black Renaissance.

Ironically the achievements of the artists from the previous generation would be kept alive and brought to the attention of the wider British public by an artist from this new generation, Rasheed Araeen. The pioneering exhibition 'The Other Story', organized by Araeen, opened at a major British art institution, the Hayward Gallery, London, in 1989. Araeen, who was born in Karachi in 1935, did not at first train or graduate in art. His profession was civil engineering, but he soon turned his talents to sculpture, inventing a new approach to the medium of burning an object to transform it into another form. On arrival in London in 1964, he discovered the work of the modernist British sculptor Anthony Caro, whose work was to have a profound effect on him. By 1975 Araeen had turned to writing, highlighting the inherent racism and imperialistic attitudes that still existed within the British mainstream art establishment. He founded magazines such as *Black Phoenix* (1978) and its later incarnation *Third Text* (1982), and set up multicultural projects, activities that would eventually culminate in the Hayward Gallery exhibition. In 2006 Araeen was writing an inclusive history of post-war art in Britain.

The 1980s also saw the arrival on the UK art scene of another artist who would become a crucial bridge between the old and the new generation of black British artists. Rita Keegan was born in New York in 1949 and from an early age wanted be an artist. After attending art school in New York, she travelled to Europe in 1973 before eventually moving to Brixton, London, in 1982. It is here that she became involved in the black British art scene and, with the help of a grant from Lambeth Arts Council, began to produce work in Britain. This work and the contacts that Keegan made placed her at centre of the new generation of black British artists born in the 1960s that included Donald Rodney, Keith Piper, and Sonia Boyce.

By the early 1990s some steps were being made towards redressing the imbalance of black artistic representation in British recorded literature of art history. In 1989 the historian Eddie Chambers set up the African and Asian Visual Artists Archive; he coordinated the running of this facility until 1992, when Rita Keegan become its director. Keegan's own work as an artist continued throughout this period and led to her inclusion in the New York exhibition curated by Mora J. Beauchamp-Byrd called 'Transforming the Crown: African, Asian and Caribbean Artists in Britain, 1966–1996'. In this exhibition Keegan would find herself back in her native New York, but this time as a British artist.

The 'Transforming the Crown' exhibition, held in 1997, introduced black British artists to an international audience, through the work shown, re-established the connection between the earlier generation of black British artists and this new generation. The inclusions read like a 'Who's Who' of black British artists, including Sonia Boyce, Sokari Douglas Camp, Donald Rodney, Ronald Moody, Keith Piper, Maud Sulter, Aubrey Williams, Sutapa Biswas, Lubaina Himid, and many others. In many ways this exhibition was the culmination of initiatives and exhibitions throughout the 1980s in Britain such as the establishment in 1983 of the Black-Art Gallery in north London, where Keith Piper, Maud Sulter, and Sonia Boyce presented one-person shows.

One of the new generation of black British artists included in 'Transforming the Crown' was Donald Rodney (1961–98). Born and raised in Birmingham, Rodney became synonymous among his peers with innovation and versatility. With his use of images from the mass media and text-based work he explored political and social issues around racism, masculinity, and issues based around his own body and his experience of living with sickle-cell anaemia. Rodney exhibited his work in several exhibitions of young black artists in the 1980s right up to his death from the condition in 1998.

Intimately involved with raising the profile of black British artists was the British painter Lubaina Himid. Himid was born in Zanzibar in 1954, and, after studying theatre design at Wimbledon School of Art and cultural history at the Royal College of Art, London, she successfully turned her hand to curating in 1984 with 'Into the Open' at the Mappin Art Gallery in Sheffield, followed a year later by 'The Thin Black Line'. Held at London's Institute of Contemporary Arts (ICA), it featured the work of eleven women artists, including Jennifer Comrie, Brenda Agard, and Maud Sulter. In 1998 Himid was invited to be artist in residence at Tate St Ives, where she began work on a series of large paintings based on images of empty rooms, aimed at evoking a sense of insecurity and abandonment.

The fertile landscape that was the 1950s and 1960s would also give birth to the 2004 Turner Prize nominee Yinka Shonibare (b. 1962), and arguably the current two highest-profile black artists on the British and international art scene, Steve McQueen and Chris Ofili. Steve McQueen was born in England in 1969. His studies at what was then the Chelsea School of Art and Goldsmiths College in London were supplemented by an extra year at New York University's Tisch School of the Arts. The biggest impact on McQueen's work would be his discovery, during his time at Goldsmiths College, of film as a medium for his work. His films, mostly in black and white, often tend to feature the artist himself in cameo roles. McQueen's approach is one of visual simplicity, which is in direct contrast to the controlled environment of the gallery spaces in which they are projected. One such film is his 1997 work called *Deadpan*, in which he restages a memorable moment from a Buster Keaton movie. In the scene a person stands motionless in the path of a falling façade of a house and is unscathed because he stands directly in the position occupied by a window in the façade. Other works include his 1998 sculpture *White Elephant*. Winning the 1996 ICA Futures Award and the 1999 Turner Prize placed McQueen at the pinnacle of British art and arguably beyond the confines of racial categorization.

4. **Film media** In the world of film media as inspiration for artistic expression, the British film producer and conceptual artist Isaac Julien (b. 1960) would also feature prominently. Julien graduated from St Martin's School of Art in 1984, where he studied painting and fine art film. Julien went on to found the Sankofa Film and Video Collective, which released his acclaimed film *Looking for Langston* (1989), about the African-American poet Langston Hughes. Throughout his career Julien has received numerous plaudits from his peers; from his first feature film, *Young Soul Rebels* (1991), to his three-screen installation *Paradise-Omeros*, inspired by Derek Walcott's epic poem, and eventually to a Turner Prize nomination in 2001 for his films *The Long Road to Mazatlán* (1999) and *Vagabondia* (2000), both made in collaboration with the dancer and choreographer Javier de Frutos.

Moving in the same orbit of black British artists, but with a completely different approach is Chris Ofili. Born in 1968 in Manchester, like McQueen he attended the Chelsea School of Art. After a period of study from 1988 to 1991 he attended the Royal College of Art. It is in this period that the British Council awarded Ofili a travel scholarship, which gave him the perfect opportunity to travel to Zimbabwe. Much like McQueen's epiphany with the discovery of film as a medium for his work, it was in Zimbabwe that Ofili found the inspiration that would have a profound effect on his painting. The influence of ancient Zimbabwean cave paintings with their decorative dot-rendered compositions would eventually find their way into Ofili's art in works such as his 1996 piece *Afrodizzia* and his 1997 *Blossom*. His works would also begin to incorporate his now trademark elephant dung, used variously as compositional elements and as supports to stand the works on. When asked about this unique feature of his art, he said that this is a way of—quite literally—incorporating Africa into his work, while also saying 'My project is not a PC project . . . It allows you to laugh about issues that are potentially serious.'

Ofili's work has featured in two Royal Academy exhibitions promoted by Charles Saatchi, 'Brilliant!' in 1995 and 'Sensation' in 1997. In 1998 he won the Turner Prize. Such achievements as Frank Bowling's election as a Royal Academician in 2005, Steve McQueen winning the 1999 Turner Prize, and Chris Ofili representing Britain at the Venice Biennale only serve to highlight what, until recently in British art history, has not been acknowledged: that British art history has a wider and far more diverse cultural history than it previously cared to acknowledge. LP

Araeen, Rasheed (ed.), *The Other Story: Afro-Asian Artists in Post-War Britain* (1989)

Beauchamp-Byrd, Mora J., *Transforming the Crown: African, Asian and Caribbean Artists in Britain* (1997)

Walmsley, Anne, *The Caribbean Artists Movement 1966–1972: A Literary and Cultural History* (1992)

See also CARIBBEAN ARTISTS' MOVEMENT

Visual arts 3: British neoclassical statuary. Neoclassical sculpture of the 19th century is often identifiable for its obvious appropriation of a classical vocabulary, but also for its fealty to white marble. Its medium of choice signalled not merely a refusal of colour, but the ideological preference for an abstracted whiteness which held a symbolic power intertwined with contemporary racialized ideals of beauty. The medium of white marble, an inherent part of 19th-century neoclassical sculpture, functioned to mediate the representation of the racialized body in ways that preserved a moral imperative. During the mid-19th century notable neoclassical sculptors, their patrons, and critics openly rejected the aesthetic possibilities of applied (pigment applied to a medium, usually white marble) and material (the use of various and differently coloured materials) polychromy as an overtly sensual and decorative distraction that detracted from the true intention and purpose of sculpture—purity of form. The racial politics of neoclassical sculpture must be understood in terms of an overwhelming narrative intention which Joy Kasson has defined as art for morality's sake, and also be reconciled with the prolific influence of scientific racism. The material and aesthetic processes of sculpture and its investment in the notion of the ideal body were inherently well suited to the colonial practices of the human sciences, providing representational validation (in three-dimensional solidity) of stereotypes of racial difference. Since the term 'classical' was not neutral, but a racialized term which activated the marginalization of blackness as its antithesis, neoclassicism also located the privileging of the white body as the aesthetic paradigm of beauty.

1. Race, slavery, and the black body
2. Sculptural portraits

1. Race, slavery, and the black body Neoclassical sculpture was a dominant international art movement from the mid- to late part of the 19th century, a time when American slavery was still flourishing and abolitionist sympathies were swelling. The currency of abolitionist and proslavery discourses contributed to the growing visibility of the black subject. However, this representation was not, in itself, democratizing since many white artists continued to represent abject black subjects within limited thematic, narrative, compositional, and expressive circumstances. Within the colonial logic of the 19th century, race was a critical and unavoidable term of identification. The discursive and material practices of slavery reveal the signification of blackness as an inextricable component of the identification of the slave body. And yet, the black body posed a problem for the neoclassical sculptor. When a sculptural medium is fundamentally white, how is blackness signified within a colonial visual register historically reliant upon the legibility of skin colour?

Neoclassical sculpture was a site-specific international Western art movement which involved a multi-layered cultural practice anchored by the Grand Tour. Although Florence had been the destination of choice in the early part of the century, by the mid-19th century the Roman colony, of which artists like the British John Gibson were a part, was dominantly Anglo-American in make-up and attracted throngs of cultural practitioners and tourists. In 1858 the American novelist Nathaniel Hawthorne had observed the absence of Romans among the revellers of a winter carnival, noting, 'The balconies along the Corso were entirely taken by English and Americans, or other foreigners.' Rome offered sculptors cheap and skilled manual labour, marble quarries, established European sculptors who acted as mentors and instructors, an inbuilt cultural and intellectual community, and access to patronage.

Although neoclassicism made room for Blacks as subjects of representation, the production itself, as with all other forms of Western art, was almost exclusively a white male enterprise. Two well-known British sculptors who participated in this style were John Gibson and John Bell. While John Gibson's *Tinted Venus* (*c.*1851–6) did not represent a black subject, the critical outcry against his tinting of the white marble, which evoked a 'real' body through the representation of skin colour, indicates the extent to which neoclassical whiteness disavowed race at the level of complexion and saw its ultimate antithesis as the black body marked through skin colour as opposed solely to physiognomy, costume, context, or props. Like their American counterparts, British neoclassical sculptors were fascinated by what was broadly defined as the social problem of the black subject, one permutation of which was *miscegenation. John Bell's *Octoroon* (*c.*1868), whose main marker of blackness is her wavy hair and dramatic, ineffectual shackles (which are also an eroticizing gesture), took up the sentimental theme of the 'tragic mulatto' which was often strategically deployed by abolitionists to elicit sympathetic responses from white audiences. The lack of narrative context or *raison d'être* to justify the female's nudity is indicative of the heightened sexual potential of the black female subject. A fitting comparison is the American Hiram Powers's famous *Greek Slave* (1848), which had an elaborate narrative to justify the nudity of the white female subject whose fidelity, purity, and spirituality were bolstered by the presence of a locket (a symbol that she is somebody's beloved) and cross (referencing her Christianity) on the pillar beside her. The narrative situated her as a Greek prisoner in the Greek War of Independence (1821–30) between the Turks and Greeks and implied that she had been stripped against her will by villainous brown Turkish men. Bell's earlier *A Daughter of Eva* (1853) represents another shackled black female slave, this time with facial features and hair texture that would have been read as a 'full-blooded Negro' type. Interestingly, the woman's downcast eyes and solemn countenance express a feeling of introspection and humility that contradicts the contemporaneous colonial idea of black female sexual excess. Her muscled torso reveals a labouring body, diametrically opposed to the comparatively less chiselled white female bodies, which signified leisure and wealth.

2. Sculptural portraits Whereas ideal works (allegorical, mythological, biblical, fancy pieces) were the main concern of most ambitious sculptors, portraits were often their financial mainstay. For the subject, the commissioning of sculptural portraits confirmed their direct contact with the artists through the process of sittings that resulted in sculpture that bore the memory of the sitter's body and the site and process of production. However, the wealth and privilege associated with portraiture largely excluded Blacks from the role of patron. Victor Ferdinand Franz Gleichen's *Mrs. Seacole, the Celebrated Crimean Heroine* (1871) is a rather rare example of a portrait bust of a known black subject celebrated for their accomplishments in a colonial Western society.

In terms of ideal examples, Sir Richard Westmacott's *Monument to Charles James Fox* (1810–23) includes the crouched figure of a black male slave gazing sorrowfully up at Fox's reclining figure, who dies in the arms of Liberty with Peace weeping at his feet. The kneeling pose, prayerful hands, and profile position link it explicitly to the abolitionist emblem 'Am I not a man and a brother?' (*c.*1787), which was mass-produced by Josiah *Wedgwood. The black male is not an individual; rather, occupying the lowest register of the sculpture, he acts as a symbol of his grateful race. His facial features and tightly curled hair signal his blackness, and his largely exposed, muscled physique recalls the labouring body of a slave. William Theed's *Africa* (1864–72), one of the four allegorical continents anchoring the Albert Memorial, exemplifies the West's conflation of race and geography into hierarchies valued in terms of their proximity to whiteness. The central, regal female figure seated on a camel is Egyptian and therefore closer to white and supposedly more 'civilized' than the standing, partially unclothed Nubian male. This 'Nubian' type was also embraced in Henry Hugh Armstead's contemplative female *Africa* (1875), an architectural sculpture which fittingly graced the Colonial Office in Whitehall, and represented a female continent with thick, dreadlock-type hair and 'full' facial features. Africa's blackness was also conveyed through her proximity to tropical foliage, a hippopotamus and the broken shackle in her extended left hand.

Africa and the plight or 'problem' of the black diaspora preoccupied the minds of neoclassical sculptors and their contemporaries. The colonization of Africa and the enslavement of its people provided compelling and topical subject matter for neoclassical sculptors of pro- and anti-slavery sympathies. The issues of colour concern the materiality of this style as well as the degrees of blackness that artists struggled to represent. The representation of blackness in white marble was a challenge that pushed sculptors to find other means of signifying race, beyond skin colour. CN

Marsh, Jan, *Black Victorians: Black People in British Art 1800–1900* (2005)

Nelson, Charmaine, 'Narrating Blackness: Studies in Feminism, Sexuality and Race in European and American Art of the Nineteenth Century', Ph.D. thesis (University of Manchester, 2001)

Whinney, M., *Sculpture in Britain 1530–1830* (1964)

See also VISUAL ARTS 1: REPRESENTATIONS OF BLACKS

W

Wales (*Welsh* **Cymru**). The smallest though arguably the most ethnically distinct of the four nations of the United Kingdom. With a population of almost 3 million, Wales has its own language (Welsh) spoken by just over 20 per cent of the population.

There is evidence to suggest that the first Africans to visit Wales did so as part of the Roman occupation of Britain. However, the earliest black settlers in Wales arrived as a result of Wales's association with the slave trade and the fashion among the aristocracy for keeping black pageboys, maids, and servants. Parish records all across Wales tell the stories of these isolated individuals, the earliest record being that of Joseph Potiphar, a black servant baptized on 30 May 1687 at St John's Church, Cardiff. Perhaps the most well known was Jac Ystumllyn (1737–68), known locally as Black Jac. Brought to Wales at the age of 8, Jac worked as a gardener on the Ystumllyn estate. He learned to speak both Welsh and English and eventually married a local woman and produced five children. But not all the early black residents of Wales lived a lowly life. The story of Nathaniel *Wells of Chepstow (1780–1852), the illegitimate son of a Welshman and slave woman from St Kitts and himself an ex-slave, is a story of black wealth and advantage. Wells lived a very privileged lifestyle in Wales on the back of profits from the three plantations he owned in St Kitts. A highly respected member of the community, Wells was appointed Sheriff of Monmouthshire in 1818.

Welsh missionary activity also served to secure a presence for some black people in Wales, particularly during the latter half of the 19th century. The activities of William Hughes (1856–1924), a Welsh Baptist minister, identify Colwyn Bay in North Wales as an important centre of *Pan-Africanism. Hughes established the *African Training Institute (originally named the Congo Institute) in Colwyn Bay in 1887 with the aim of educating and training young Africans in missionary work and equipping them with a useful trade and skills so that they could return to their own countries and preach the gospel and be useful craftsmen. In its relatively short life the Institute enjoyed no small success and more than 100 boys from many parts of Africa passed through it. Distinguished visiting speakers included the leading Pan-Africanist Mojola Agbebi (1860–1917).

It was during the mid-19th century that the first black communities in Wales began to be established. Black sailors arriving in *Cardiff and other parts of South Wales from Africa, the West Indies, and America stayed to take advantage of jobs created as a result of the boom in the coal industry and merchant shipping. By 1914 it was estimated that there were 700 seamen of African descent living in the dock area of Cardiff alone, as well as an unknown but much smaller number in the other seaport towns of South Wales. There were substantial increases in numbers of black sailors in the *First World War.

The early flush of black immigrants to Wales slowed to a trickle during the Great Depression, which followed the First World War. By the mid-1930s the number of black seamen living in Cardiff had risen to around 2,000, many of whom were born in Wales and were British citizens.

In the second half of the 20th century

Wales was never subject to immigration from black Commonwealth countries on the scale that characterized other parts of the United Kingdom. West Indian immigrants of the **Empire Windrush* era, for example, tended to bypass Wales and head instead for other parts of the United Kingdom where the prospects of employment were greater. The picture is therefore one of a relatively settled, established black community, bolstered only very slightly since the middle of the 20th century by economic migrants and refugees. By the year 2000 there were estimated to be about 8,600 people of black Caribbean and mixed white and black Caribbean origin and about 6,000 people of black African and African and white mixed origin. The higher rate of mixed-race individuals in Wales than in all other countries of the United Kingdom confirms this pattern of long settlement.

Though relatively small in number, the black population of Wales has produced more than its share of stars of stage, field, and track, few more revered possibly than the Wigan rugby league star Billy Boston, who in 1954 became the first black player to represent the British Lions on their tour of Australia. Perhaps the best known among today's celebrities are the singer Shirley Bassey, the footballers Ryan Giggs and Rob Earnshaw, the athlete Colin Jackson, and the rugby player and athlete Nigel Walker. The significant toil of ordinary men and women has only barely been recognized or rewarded. It is a sad fact that by far the greater number of black people in Wales today still live in the poorest areas of Cardiff. Unemployment rates among the black population in Wales are still higher than for any other ethnic group.

In the historical encounter between the native Welsh and black settlers to the country there is evidence of both amicable race relations and trenchant ethnic conflict, and yet a predominant myth of Welsh national identity portrays Wales as a tolerant nation, particularly compared with its nearest neighbour, England. In any reading of black Welsh history it will be clear that the fate of the Welsh themselves as an ethnic minority within the wider context of the British Isles is a significant mediating factor in Welsh race relations. CFW

Llwyd, A., *Cymru Ddu/Black Wales: A History of Black Welsh People* (2005)

Williams, Charlotte, Evans, Neil, and O'Leary, Paul (eds.), *A Tolerant Nation? Exploring Ethnic Diversity in Wales* (2003)

Ward, Samuel Ringgold (1817–1866). African-American abolitionist who lectured in England. Ward was born a slave but managed to escape with his parents to New York State, where he was educated and later taught in black schools. He became an agent of the American Anti-Slavery Society and the Anti-Slavery Society of Canada. It was through the latter that he travelled to England on a fund-raising mission in 1853. He remained in England for two years, lecturing around the country and finally publishing the story of his life, *Autobiography of a Fugitive Negro*, in 1855. British anti-slavery gatherings often featured celebrated American abolitionist figures, such as Ward.

On 16 May 1853 Ward gave a speech alongside the American novelist Harriet Beecher Stowe at Exeter Hall, London, as part of the annual meeting of the British and Foreign Anti-Slavery Society. Thousands were packed into the hall and Ward was well received. He spoke about the hypocrisy adopted in justifying slavery through Christianity. On another occasion, this time at the Freemasons' Hall in London on 21 June 1853, he lectured on the issue of fugitive slaves in Canada and the solace that slaves found in the idea of attaining freedom once they touched British soil. This notion, he said, was integral to the education of slaves as it provided them with facts that would then allow them a practical approach to liberating themselves. Ward finally settled in Kingston, Jamaica, where he continued lecturing until his death in 1866. DD/SS

Ward, Samuel Ringgold, *Autobiography of a Fugitive Negro* (1855)

See also BROWN, WILLIAM WELLS; ELAW, ZILPHA; EQUIANO, OLAUDAH

Washington, Booker T. (1856–1915). Advocate of black self-improvement through industrial education. Born in Virginia to a slave mother and unknown white father, he founded the Tuskegee Institute in 1888. He made two visits to Britain, the first in early summer 1899 as part of a European vacation and speaking tour. He was impressed by technical and agricultural education in Britain, but shocked by social conditions in London's East End. During his visit he also gained greater insight into the effects of European rule in Africa, concluding that repatriation to Africa would not improve the lot of black Americans. His recollections of the trip also underline his conservatism, evident in an appreciation of British class deference and social order.

Washington's second visit, in 1910, was made as part of his mission to study the condition of the poor in Europe. He was accompanied by his secretary, the sociologist Robert Ezra Park, and toured London with the working-class MP John Burns. Their joint findings were published in *The Man Farthest Down* (1912). Washington's public pronouncements in Britain confirmed his gradualist approach to raising the status of African-Americans, drawing strong criticism from more radical black leaders such as W. E. B. DuBois and progressive white Republicans such as John Elmer Milholland. RS

Washington, Booker T., *The Man Farthest Down* (1912)

—— 'The Story of My Life and Work' in *Booker T. Washington Papers* (ed. Louis R. Harlan, 1972)

—— *Up from Slavery* (1986)

See also POLITICS

Waters, Billy (d. 1823). Actor, fiddler, and beggar who acted and busked around London in the 1780s. Waters was a common sight outside the Adelphi Theatre in the Strand. Apart from busking, he also acted, appearing as himself in a dramatized version of Pierce Egan's *Life in London* (1821) at the Adelphi and at the Caledonian Theatre in Edinburgh in 1822. He would also play his fiddle, becoming a street musician outside the Drury Lane Theatre. His wooden leg as well as his outfit, which resembled that of a military uniform, made him a unique and distinct character. The well-known cartoonist George Cruikshank caricatured him. Waters ended up penniless on the streets of London in the St Giles area, where the black poor congregated. In 1823 he became ill and died at St Giles's workhouse. Just before his death he was elected 'King of the Beggars' by fellow beggars, black and white. In recent years he has been resurrected as an archetypal beggar and symbol of the predicament of 18th-century Britain's black poor in fiction by Steve Martin and David Dabydeen (two black British writers of Caribbean descent). DD/SS

Dabydeen, David, *A Harlot's Progress* (1999)

Martin, Steve, *Incomparable World* (1996)

Shyllon, F., *Black People in Britain 1555–1833* (1977)

See also GEORGIAN AND VICTORIAN BRITAIN

Watson, Andrew (1857–*c.*1902). Britain's first black international footballer. Watson was a renowned amateur football player, playing full-back for *Glasgow amateur clubs Maxwell Football Club and Parkgrove in 1878–9, before winning international honours. He appeared for Scotland against England and Wales in 1881–2 while playing for the leading amateur Scottish club Queen's Park.

Watson was born in Georgetown, British Guiana (now Guyana), in 1857. His surname suggests Scottish parentage or descent although no firm information has been found on his ancestry. He had a privileged educational upbringing, being educated at Halifax Grammar School and Rugby before completing his education at Glasgow College in the 1870s. His capabilities stretched beyond the football pitch as he became match secretary and organizer of the amateur club Parkgrove. Yet, according to the census of 1881, the year of his international football debut, Watson was apparently rather humbly employed as a 'warehouseman'. He married a Glasgow woman, Jessie Maxwell, and they had one son, Rupert.

Watson won the first of his three caps in March 1881 in a match for Scotland against

England, held at the Oval in London. Scotland won the match 6–1. This appearance ensured that he became the first recorded black international footballer. After a move to London in 1882, he played for London Swifts and the famous Corinthians select side in 1884–5. He also played for the Liverpool side Bootle while working in the area in the engineering industry. He later returned to Glasgow to play once more for Queen's Park. Watson was last recorded as living in Bombay (Mumbai), India, in 1902. JLMJ

'Modern Athletic Celebrities', *Scottish Athletic Journal*, 15 Dec. 1885

See also SPORT; WHARTON, ARTHUR

Wedderburn, Robert (*c*.1762–1835?). Black working-class radical and advocate of freedom of speech. Wedderburn was born in Jamaica to James Wedderburn, a Scottish doctor and sugar plantation owner, and Rosanna, a slave. His father abandoned Wedderburn when he sold Rosanna to another estate when she was five months pregnant, stipulating that the child she bore should be free from birth. A series of resales permanently separated Rosanna from her son when still an infant, leaving him to be raised by his grandmother, a Kingston merchant and smuggler known as 'Talky Amy'. Exposure to the injustice of West Indian slavery marked Wedderburn early, most notably when his 70-year-old grandmother was flogged nearly to death when accused of bewitching a white man's ship.

Wedderburn arrived in England in 1778 after a brief stint with the Royal Navy, where he is thought to have trained as an on-board tailor. In 1785 he travelled to Edinburgh for a disastrous reunion with his father, who refused to see him and threatened him with imprisonment if he returned. Settling in London, he quickly established himself with the city's subculture of 'blackbirds'—impoverished musicians, entertainers, labourers, and petty thieves living in the St Giles area.

A Wesleyan preacher speaking at Seven Dials in 1786 capitalized on Wedderburn's lifelong fascination with the supernatural by promising salvation to all those who repented their sins. Wedderburn immediately converted to Methodism, which he was most likely attracted to because of John *Wesley's persistent criticism of slavery, and became licensed as a Unitarian preacher. He demonstrated his comfort in questioning the Church around 1790, when he penned the pamphlet *Truth, Self-Supported; or, A Refutation of Certain Doctrinal Errors, Generally Adopted in the Christian Church*. His new-found faith did little to reform his lifestyle, however; he was jailed for theft at Coldbath prison in 1813 and dodged prosecution for stealing from a government-contracted tailoring job in 1817.

Wedderburn's religious faith did not become politicized until the age of 51 or 52, when he met John Spence. Spence, a poor Newcastle schoolmaster, promoted a form of radical socialism that sought religious tolerance, abolition of slavery, and the redistribution of private land. Wedderburn became an active member of the Society of Spencean Philanthropists, a group of working-class labourers who gathered to debate issues of freedom and human rights in some of London's roughest taverns, helping to devise topics for debate and collect membership fees.

Wedderburn rose to the forefront of the Spencean movement when the leader, Thomas Evans, and Evans's 20-year-old son were jailed for high treason in 1817. In the same year Wedderburn launched his first periodical, *Forlorn Hope*, designed to promote freedom of speech. A second magazine titled *The Axe Laid to the Root* was founded shortly after. Wedderburn used his influence to increase the Spencean response to slavery, devoting two issues of this second publication to outlining his utopian vision for a post-revolution West Indies. Suggested changes included universal suffrage, the annual election of an assembly of delegates excluding Whites and those worth more than £500, the establishment of primogeniture, equal land distribution, a total ban on lawyers and clergymen, the abolishment of prisons and capital punishment, and a requirement that all individuals over 18 remain armed and ready to defend the state at all times.

Wedderburn and Evans worked together for a short time after the latter's release from prison in the spring of 1818, sharing a dissenting chapel in Haymarket and founding a group called the Christian Philanthropists, or Enquirers After Truth, which met three times a week. However, Wedderburn soon tired of the stark atmosphere of the chapel and took its benches and members to a new chapel on Hopkins Street in Soho in April 1819. The split marked the end of his relationship with Evans; Evans attempted to charge him with felony, while he accused Evans of breaking and entering.

The Hopkins Street chapel, a dilapidated hayloft reached by a stepladder, regularly filled to capacity and specialized in seditious and increasingly anti-Christian speeches that terrified the government spies frequently in attendance. Wedderburn's inflammatory and often scatological language attracted a rough crowd that shouted down any speaker who dared to read from a book. During this time he remained an avid pamphleteer, including writing an essay addressed to Jamaican slaves urging them to strike for one hour each day and take control of the land. This pamphlet is credited with being the first piece of revolutionary propaganda sent to the West Indies from Britain. Chapel discussion also focused on slavery, most notably in the questioning of whether a slave has a right to kill a master, which saw Wedderburn prosecuted for sedition and blasphemy.

Wedderburn stood trial for blasphemous libel in late 1819 (the sedition charge was dropped). The parish constable William Plush, who testified to overhearing him refer to Moses as a liar and make pejorative connections between religion and working-class oppression, presented evidence of Wedderburn's crime. Although Wedderburn rebutted with an impressive defence, in which he questioned the crime in communicating his opinion and reaffirmed his faith by identifying Christ as a symbol of working-class resistance, he was sentenced to two years' imprisonment in Dorchester prison. While serving his sentence, he received a sympathetic visit from the abolitionist William *Wilberforce.

Upon his release, Wedderburn printed the autobiographical *The Horrors of Slavery* (1824) and became involved in pornography through work with the publisher William Dugdale. He opened another Spencean chapel in White's Alley in 1828, and presented himself as the founder of the Christian Diabolists, or Devil Worshippers. But meetings were poorly attended and he was forced to close the chapel after only two months. A stint operating illegal brothels in Featherbed Lane was also short-lived; he was sentenced to two years' hard labour in Newgate in 1831 for his involvement. Little is known of his life after Newgate; it is thought that he lived in impoverishment and obscurity until his death, probably in 1835. EDS

McCalman, Iain, *Radical Underworld: Prophets, Revolutionaries and Pornographers in London, 1795–1840* (1988)

See also PUBLISHING

Wedgwood, Josiah (1730–1795). Potter and active participant in the fight for the abolition of *slavery. Wedgwood was born in Burslem, Stoke-on-Trent, the youngest son of Thomas Wedgwood, a potter. From 1787 until his death in 1795, Wedgwood sought to highlight the injustices of slavery and the *slave trade. He was politically and socially conscious and was interested in the consequences of the American War of Independence and the French Revolution. His awareness concerning slavery was probably evoked through his friendship with Thomas Bentley, a *Liverpool merchant who remained hostile to the trade and refused to welcome slavers back to the port. Another close connection of Wedgwood's was Thomas *Clarkson, who set up the Sierra Leone Company, which sought to provide a habitable colony for freed slaves. Wedgwood eventually became a shareholder of the company.

Wedgwood's most significant contribution to the abolitionist cause was the production of a medallion created for the purpose of publicizing the realities of slavery to the general public. It shows a kneeling and chained African, his hands raised to heaven, and its inscription reads 'Am I not a man and a brother?' In 1787 he made a jasper copy of the emblem of the Society for the Abolition of the Slave Trade. The design was reproduced in a cameo, and hundreds of these were donated to the Society. Women wore them on hatpins, brooches, and other fashion accessories. Clarkson commented on the pertinence of linking profound issues such as the suffering and exploitation of slaves with an area such as fashion, which was commonly associated with trivialities. In 1788 Wedgwood sent some medallions to Benjamin Franklin, who was then the president of the Abolition Society in America. Wedgwood continued to use his popularity and social standing to influence others, on both sides of the Atlantic, to agitate for the end of slavery. DD/SS

Thomas, Hugh, *The Slave Trade* (1997)

Wells, Nathaniel (1779–1852). Son of a slave and a wealthy planter on St Kitts, Wells became a major landowner in Monmouthshire, South Wales, and Britain's first black sheriff. He was probably the wealthiest black person in the country at the time.

His father, William Wells (1730–94), left Cardiff with his brother Nathaniel for St Kitts to make his fortune in the sugar and slave trade in about 1749. He married a wealthy widow in 1753, Elizabeth Taylor *née* Fenton. She bore William two children, who died in infancy, before she herself died in 1759. Subsequently William fathered at least six children with various slaves, one of whom, Nathaniel, was born on 10 September 1779, the son of Juggy, his African house slave. He was baptized on 3 March 1783 at Trinity Church, Palmetto Point. By the age of 9 Wells was living in London with his uncle Nathaniel and attending school in Newington, being groomed to become his father's heir. William intended him for Oxford University, but he did not go. In 1792 his uncle died, and two years later his father. William's will granted freedom and bequests to his five women and to his three natural daughters. The rest of his estate, including three plantations and an estimated £120,000, was left to his 'dear son Nathaniel'. Guardianship was entrusted to the executors, including his surviving brother, the Revd Robert Wells of Penmaen, Glamorgan. When Wells came of age in 1800, his uncle Robert contested the will and, to avoid the expense of going to law, was paid £10,000. In June 1801 he married Harriet Este (1780–1820), the only daughter of the Revd Charles Este, at St George's, Hanover Square. Later that year Wells helped to buy a property for his mother in Basseterre for £1,200. Juggy, then calling herself Joardine Wells, made her will in 1802, bequeathing her house and two female slaves to her sister's children. Wells was one of her executors. She died in 1811, probably never having seen her son again.

In 1802 Wells purchased Piercefield, near Chepstow, for £90,000. This large estate, situated below Tintern Abbey in the Wye Valley, was famous for the walks with spectacular viewpoints laid out in the 1750s by Valentine Morris, an Antiguan planter and later Governor of St Vincent. Other 18th-century owners had employed the noted architects John Soane and Joseph Bonomi to create a country house that matched the splendours of its surroundings. Much visited, Piercefield's owner could not fail to be mentioned in the many diaries and guidebooks written. Joseph Farington, the landscape artist, described Wells as 'a West Indian of large fortune, a man of very gentlemanly manners, but so much a man of colour as to be little removed from a Negro'. Farington also mentions Wells's half-sister Ann (1781–1842), daughter of William's slave Sue Wells, who was living in Britain by 1803 with a personal fortune of about £7,500.

Wells played a prominent part in public life. From 1804 he was churchwarden at St

Arvan's for 40 years. In 1806 he was appointed a Justice of the Peace, in 1818 Sheriff of Monmouthshire, and later Deputy Lieutenant of the county. In 1820 he was appointed Lieutenant of the Chepstow Troop, Loyal Monmouthshire Yeomanry Cavalry. Like other country gentlemen he hunted and was on the committee of the Chepstow Hunt. He was able to lead a life in Britain that would have been impossible in St Kitts.

Wells's first wife bore him ten children before she died in 1820. He married again in 1823, Esther, daughter of the late Revd John Henry Owen, who had eleven children. Of his children Nathaniel Armstrong Wells (1806–46) became an author; John Tighe Wells (1808–69) became the incumbent of the new Catholic Apostolic Church in Newman Street, London, one of his grandsons, John Bayford Wells (1881–1952), becoming a brigadier-general.

Wells leased his plantations in St Kitts before eventually selling them. He moved to Bath in about 1844, died on 13 May 1852, and is buried there in Walcot cemetery.

JAHE/AFRR

Evans, J. A. H., 'Nathaniel Wells of Piercefield and St Kitts: From Slave to Sheriff', *Monmouthshire Antiquary*, 18 (2002)

ODNB

Wesley, John (1703–1791). English evangelist, co-founder of Methodism, and celebrated preacher against slavery and the slave trade. Wesley was born in Epworth, Lincolnshire, and was an enduring challenger of slavery. He was inspired by the Philadelphia Quaker Anthony Benezet's *Some Historical Account of Guinea* (1771), which also influenced abolitionists such as Thomas *Clarkson and Granville *Sharp. In consequence, Wesley produced a pamphlet entitled *Thoughts Upon Slavery* (1774), which dealt with the dynamics of the slave trade and the viciousness of slavery, especially in terms of life on the plantations. But even before Benezet and the publication of Wesley's pamphlet, Wesley had opposed the slave system on moral, human, and religious grounds. His sermons often evoked questions directed towards the slave traders. The main issues raised involved matters of compassion, sympathy, and empathy for fellow human beings. He was also an avid reader of slave accounts and books bearing relevance to the slave trade and the quest for moral justice. He read Thomas Southerne's **Oroonoko* (1696) and was reading Olaudah *Equiano's *An Interesting Narrative* (1789) just days before his death. In 1788, at the height of the abolition campaign, Wesley gave a sermon in *Bristol, one of the most important slave ports of the time, and encountered some disorder during his session. But he risked the possible danger of preaching at such a time, and remained a passionate believer in the importance of Christian virtues for humankind. Accordingly, he actively fought against slavery until his death.

DD/SS

Collins, Kenneth J., *A Real Christian: The Life of John Wesley* (1999)

Fryer, Peter, *Staying Power: The History of Black People in Britain* (1984)

See also CHRISTIANITY

West African Student Christian Union. In 1914 the London University Club refused to admit black students, some of whom also had difficulty in finding suitable lodgings. It was estimated at the end of the *First World War that 50–60 West Indian students were in Britain, mostly in London and Scotland, and 60–70 students from West Africa. Many were active Christians or from Christian backgrounds and belonged to the Student Christian Movement (SCM). In March 1916 Robert Wilder, of the SCM, invited 30–5 West African students to meet at the home of Lady Victoria Buxton in west London. Wilder spoke on the work of the SCM, and following this nine students 'met in an adjoining room to consider the possibility of forming a West African Christian Union'. The first secretary was Oladipo Lahanmi of King's College London (who had studied at the Colwyn Bay Institute). The West African Student Christian Union (WASCU) was affiliated to the SCM, whose basis for membership was that 'I declare my faith in Jesus Christ as my Saviour, my

Lord, and my God', and its central activity was Bible study. By 1919 the WASCU had become the West Indian and West African Christian Union, and its secretary was Audrey Jeffers of Trinidad; two years later its secretary was A. J. Agard, who lived in Finchley. Individual members of the WASCU, for example Jeffers, also belonged to the *African Progress Union. In 1917 the SCM opened a hostel in London for black students. That year a broader and secular African Students' Union of Great Britain and Ireland was formed, later renamed the *Union of Students of African Descent. DK

Green, Jeffrey, and Lockhart, Randall, '"A brown alien in a white city": Black Students in London, 1917–1920' in Rainer E. Lotz and Ian Pegg (eds.), *Under the Imperial Carpet: Essays in Black History 1780–1950* (1986)

Student Christian Movement MSS, Birmingham University Library

See also CHRISTIANITY; CHURCHES

West African Students' Union. One of the most important and long-lasting black organizations of the 20th century. Formed in London in 1925, its origins can be found in previous organizations such as the *Union of Students of African Descent and the Nigerian Progress Union. The founding of the West African Students' Union (WASU) was due to the encouragement of H. R. Bankole-Bright, a member of the Legislative Council of Sierra Leone, who visited London in 1925. He urged the students to forge a unity in Britain that would mirror that established by the newly formed National Congress of British West Africa (NCBWA). Led by a Nigerian law student, Ladipo *Solanke, it was decided that an organization would be formed to allow West African students in Britain and Ireland to discuss all matters affecting West Africa and cooperate with the NCBWA. Under the leadership of Solanke the Union established itself as the main cultural and political focus for West Africans in Britain for the next 35 years. It also served as a training ground for many future political leaders, such as Kwame Nkrumah, and played an important role agitating for an end to colonial rule.

Following the formation of the WASU, the Union launched its own journal called *WASU; the journal of the West African Students' Union of Great Britain* in March 1926. The journal set out to explain the concerns of West Africans to the world at large, especially the need for progress and development. Over the years the *WASU* played a major role in championing the concerns of West Africans in Britain, not least in their demands for independence from colonial rule. In the early years it was much concerned with the concept of West African nationhood and 'the equality of the races', but it took many forms for over twenty years, and at times was published monthly. In the early 1950s the *WASU* was superseded by the *Wasu News Service*.

In its early years the WASU, and especially Solanke, were greatly influenced by Marcus *Garvey, who even donated his house as the Union's meeting place. The Union also had contacts in the United States, the Caribbean, South Africa, the Belgian Congo, and Brazil. It soon attempted to establish a student hostel, which had long been sought after by Africans in London, and made direct appeals in West Africa for funds. In 1929 Solanke was dispatched on a fundraising mission to West Africa. When he returned in 1932, the WASU opened its first hostel in Camden, north London. This was the first of four hostels opened by the WASU from the 1930s to 1950s. These hostels became important meeting places, not just for West Africans but for all black people in London and those visiting from abroad. However, when the Colonial Office opened its own hostel, Aggrey House, the WASU and its supporters, such as the Negro Welfare Association, the National Council for Civil Liberties, and the League Against Imperialism, launched a lengthy campaign opposing it as an attempt to monitor and control their activities. The WASU even produced its own propaganda pamphlet, *The Truth About Aggrey House*.

During the 1930s the WASU engaged in a range of political activities. Working with other organizations it opposed the Italian invasion of *Ethiopia, the proposed transfer of African colonies to Germany, and the continuing problem of racism and the colour bar in Britain. Solanke's trip to West Africa had strengthened the WASU's links with the growing anti-colonial movements, and throughout the colonial period it was able to act as the spokesperson and supporter of West African anti-colonialism in Britain. It aided visiting West African politicians and campaigned against attempts to introduce repressive laws into the African colonies.

During the Second World War the Union's role became even more important, and it was courted by leading British politicians, including Clement Attlee, the future Prime Minister. The WASU submitted its own demands to the Colonial Office and was the first West African organization to demand self-government for the West African colonies. In 1942 it established its own parliamentary committee, which included Labour MPs such as the future Colonial Secretary Arthur Creech-Jones, to lobby for West African interests.

In the period after 1945 the WASU suffered from some internal divisions, partly caused by developments in Nigerian politics. At the same time its members became more radical, and many of them became influenced by *communism. In the post-war period the WASU established links with the World Federation of Democratic Youth and the International Union of Students, and even sent delegates to the Congress of the British Communist Party. In 1945 the WASU, and particularly its vice-president, Kwame Nkrumah, played an important part in the Manchester Pan-African Congress and in the various activities organized in support of the Nigerian general strike.

It was also during this period that Nkrumah organized the West African National Secretariat, in order to plan for the independence of a united West Africa, and started 'the Circle' among members of the WASU. The Circle was a small revolutionary cell organized like a secret society in order to form a vanguard group within the WASU, who would take the lead in political activities. The long-term aim of the Circle appears to have been to prepare its members to transform West Africa into a 'Union of African Socialist Republics'.

Some of the members of the WASU, including Solanke, were wary of such radicalism, but during the 1950s it was the younger members who led the organization, and Solanke was increasingly sidelined. He died in 1958. Student radicalism was also of concern to the Colonial Office, which continued with its efforts to monitor the Union's activities and to include the students on its Consultative Committee on the Welfare of Colonial Students. In 1958 the WASU reorganized itself, and subsequently led the founding of the Committee of African Organizations, a coalition of all the main African organizations in Britain. HA

Adi, H., *West Africans in Britain: Nationalism, Pan-Africanism and Communism* (1998)

See also WEST AFRICAN STUDENT CHRISTIAN UNION; WEST INDIAN STUDENTS' UNION

West India interest. In the 18th and early 19th centuries the British colonies in the Caribbean were of considerable value to Britain as a result of the wealth created from slave-grown sugar and other tropical produce, and from the profits of the 'African trade', which supplied the Caribbean plantations with their slaves. This wealth made it possible for those with financial interests in the Caribbean colonies, either as owners of land and slaves (whether residents in the colonies or absentee owners living in Britain), or as merchants in Britain trading in colonial produce, to influence the political process in Britain in various ways. The effect of all this, and the individuals involved, were collectively referred to as the 'West India interest'.

From the late 17th century the various colonies in the Caribbean began to appoint what were called 'colonial agents' in Britain, a system that continued until the middle of the 19th century. The colonial agents were paid lobbyists acting on behalf of the local legislatures of their respective colonies, legislatures that largely consisted of, and represented the interests of, members of the plantation-owning class. The agents' function was to keep the British government, and people of influence in Britain, mindful of the importance of the sugar colonies, and to ensure that any British legislation that affected them did so in a manner that was as favourable to the plantation owners as possible. The agents were often members of the British Parliament. This was made possible, as was the presence of significant numbers of other MPs at Westminster with Caribbean connections, by the structure of British politics in the 18th century. While members of the House of Commons were in theory the elected representatives of the people, the right to vote was severely limited by property qualifications, and in most constituencies only a small proportion of adult males enjoyed the right to vote. For historical reasons, there were a number of constituencies with very few or even no voters at all, and these so-called 'pocket boroughs', or 'rotten boroughs', were effectively the property of the most influential local landowners (who were thus in a position to nominate the MPs), or could be bought and sold. Even in constituencies with a wider franchise, a sufficiently wealthy candidate could normally secure election by bribing the voters. Once in Parliament, the MP was in a position to trade his vote for influence on issues that interested him, or for the fruits of government patronage. It was a system that openly acknowledged the power of money to buy political influence, and in the 18th century some of the richest men in Britain (like William *Beckford and his son) were 'West Indians', a term which in the period normally referred, not to the black slave, but to the white owner of slave-cultivated plantations in Britain's Caribbean colonies. In 1764, at what was probably the high point of their influence, a contemporary (the agent for Massachusetts) estimated that there were between 50 and 60 West Indian members of the House of Commons, who were able to swing any vote whichever way they pleased. Their wealth, and the political power this gave them, allowed the West Indians to marry into the established British aristocracy, so that there also came to be members of the House of Lords who either owned Caribbean plantations themselves, or were closely related to those who did.

The interests of those with property in different Caribbean colonies were not necessarily identical. The same was true of the interests of those who owned plantations and the interests of the 'West India merchants' (the people in Britain who bought sugar and other plantation produce from the planters and made money by re-exporting it, or by selling it to others such as sugar refiners, through whom it ultimately reached the British consumer). For example, the fact that merchants normally supplied planters with what they needed for their Caribbean estates on credit, to be repaid out of the proceeds of the sugar or other produce that was consigned to them, was a constant source of disputes. In 1775, however, the growing conflict between Britain and its North American colonies, which was soon to break out into the American War of Independence, clearly posed a threat to anyone, whether planter or merchant, with financial interests in the Caribbean colonies, which were closely linked to the North American ones and depended on them for important supplies of various kinds (including several basic items of food for their slaves). The result was the formation of the West India Committee, a body that still exists, though now with a very altered outlook and objectives.

In the late 18th century the West India Committee was a group that brought together planters and merchants with interests in the Caribbean colonies. A powerful influence on British politics, it was essentially a London body, though it kept in contact with similar West Indian organizations in other British ports. After the end of the American War of Independence the main function of the West India Committee was to lobby against all parliamentary moves towards the *abolition of the slave trade, and, later, against *emancipation of the slaves in the Caribbean colonies. In these efforts it was ultimately unsuccessful, though it almost certainly contributed very largely to the length of time the entire process took. The major achievement of the West India Committee in particular, and of the West India interest more generally, in the early 19th century was in securing the payment by the British government of £20 million in compensation to the slave owners in return for their acceptance of emancipation, as opposed to the £15 million that the government had originally offered as a loan only. This in effect accepted the argument of the West India interest that their ownership of slaves was a form of property that was legally valid and had long been accepted as such by the British government and legal system.

Changes in the British political system, in particular the Great Reform Bill, which became law in 1832, sweeping away the pocket boroughs and greatly increasing the number and importance of middle-class voters, reduced the strength of the West India interest and eased the passage of the Emancipation Act in 1833. As the Caribbean declined in economic importance in the course of the 19th century, the West India interest dwindled into political insignificance. JG

Hall, Douglas, *A Brief History of the West India Committee* (1971)

See also CARIBBEAN, BRITISH COLONIES IN THE; COUNTRY HOUSES

West Indian Co-ordinating Committee. Umbrella organization operating in the Moss Side area of Manchester to promote social events, which also concerned itself with educational and commercial activities. The Co-ordinating Committee for Caribbean Organizations was set up in September 1965 and later renamed the West Indian Co-ordinating Committee.

The Committee's first two years of existence were a time of relative calm, vis-à-vis the racial situation in Manchester, where multicultural organizations had established themselves. However, conflict with the police led to growing tension between the Committee and the forces of law and order, and police raids and black working-class social activities in the Moss Side area engendered a new mood of hostility towards the host society. The migrants' perception of rejection, compounded by police harassment, resulted in bitterness towards white people. The new militant mood within the Committee was commissioned by two external imperatives: the emergence of Black Power in the United States and Enoch *Powell's inflammatory speeches on immigration.

The Committee evolved into today's West Indian Organizations Co-ordinating Committee, organizing youth projects, Saturday schools, training seminars, and cultural activities showcasing Manchester's black community. RR

Foot, Paul, *Immigration and Race in British Politics* (1965)

Kinder, C., 'West Indians in Moss Side: The Effectiveness of Voluntary Organizations in Integrating West Indians', B. Litt. thesis (Oxford University, 1966)

Maxwell, Neville, *The Power of Negro Action* (1965)

See also BLACK PANTHER PARTY; IMMIGRATION; WEST INDIAN STANDING CONFERENCE; WEST INDIAN STUDENTS' UNION

West Indian Standing Conference. Umbrella organization formed in 1958 to promote the interests of the African-Caribbean community in Britain. The *Notting Hill riots of 1958 revealed the parlous state of race relations in Britain and the fact that colour prejudice and discrimination were widespread. The High Commission of the newly federated government of the West Indies saw the need for an organization to act on behalf of the large and growing post-war West Indian population in Britain. The leaders of the various social, religious, and cultural organizations formed the West Indian Standing Conference (WISC).

The aims and objectives as stated in its constitution were that the WISC was established to communicate between the different West Indian organizations in London and the provinces and the High Commission, to provide leadership within the West Indian community, and to work towards better relations with other 'races'. Gradually the WISC's leadership strove for greater independence from the High Commission, and in 1962 there was a shift in its position. Firstly, there was the break-up of the West Indian Federation (which made redundant the High Commission and its subordinate bodies), and, secondly, the passage of the first Commonwealth Immigrants Act. These events gave added impetus to the drive for independence. Increasingly, as more and more research on West Indian migrants was conducted, suspicion and distrust were aroused. The WISC fought shy of researchers such as those working on the *Institute of Race Relations' Survey of Race Relations.

The freedom from the High Commission and the antipathy to research formed the background for approaching the subject of integration into British society differently. After the Notting Hill riots, the 'tea and bun' approach was no longer viable. Interracial gatherings were no substitute for action to create equal opportunities for black people in employment, housing, and other social sectors. The WISC became more militant in its call for social action on the part of the British authorities. 'Integration' meant full and equal access to the resources and opportunities for the society. A high point in its history was its involvement in the 1966 publication of Joseph Hunte's *Nigger-Hunting in England?*, dealing with allegations of police brutality.

The debate within WISC was whether West Indians should campaign for equality in cooperation with British organizations, or whether they should assert themselves independently. This debate split the ranks and leadership of the WISC. Although it survived, its effectiveness as a campaigning organization was diminished. By the time of the *Brixton riots in 1981 the WISC was seen by many radical Blacks as a powerless force. RR

Heineman, Benjamin W., Jr., *The Politics of the Powerless: A Study of the Campaign Against Racial Discrimination* (1972)

Patterson, Sheila, *Dark Strangers* (1963)

See also CAMPAIGN AGAINST RACIAL DISCRIMINATION

West Indian Students' Union. Formed in London in 1946 to promote the interests of West Indian students in Britain who were deeply immersed in matters relating to colonial freedom. In 1959 there were an estimated 2,400 West Indian students, including nurses, in Britain. The aims of the West Indian Students' Union (WISU) were to promote fellowship between West Indian students but also to agitate for the development of the West Indies, politically and economically, so that the region could be prepared for independence from Britain. The WISU was active too in organizing cultural events including dances, steel band performances, and theatre productions.

There was a separation between the students and working-class migrants. The majority of students belonged to a higher social group, and their stay in Britain was not only more limited but more comfortable and hopeful. In short, West Indian students posed no immediate threat to British society, though gradually they became more visible. In 1964 the organizers of the first mass meeting concerning race relations in Britain recognized WISU as one of the representative West Indian groups, and by 1967 it was one of the fifteen organizations affiliated to the *West Indian Standing Conference. A few West Indians aspired to and held office in the National Union of Students, and over the years many WISU members went on to become distinguished persons both in Britain and the Commonwealth (including L. F. S. Burnham, the future dictatorial President of Guyana; Michael Manley, the future Prime Minister of Jamaica; and Lee Llewellyn Moore, the future Prime Minister of St Kitts and Nevis). RR

Glass, R., and Pollins, H., *Newcomers* (1960)

See also EDUCATION

West Indian women at war. In October 1943 a group of 30 women from across the Caribbean arrived in Britain, determined to contribute to the Allied war effort. This group constituted the vanguard of a total of 70 West Indian women recruited to the Auxiliary Territorial Service (ATS). Motivated by loyalty to the 'mother country', these women sacrificed the relative safety of their island homes for the dangers of wartime Britain. The proud, smiling faces of the women as they paraded in their newly issued ATS uniforms, however, concealed the myriad struggles they had had to wage before they were enlisted by a racist and sexist War Office, determined to exclude Blacks from the British women's military services. Their arrival in Britain therefore represented a major victory over a discriminatory policy that sought to preserve the ATS as solely white.

1. The struggle to join the ATS
2. Other forms of wartime service

An unknown number of black women made a significant contribution to the Allied war effort, even though their offers of assistance were often met with derision and rejection. Some, such as the veteran Lilian Bader, served in the women's uniformed services such as the ATS or the Women's Auxiliary Air Force (WAAF), while thousands of others worked in vital wartime industries such as agriculture and munitions factories. Nursing was another crucial service where black women made a contribution. Still others protected their communities as air raid wardens and firefighters, as did the black Londoner Esther *Bruce.

The West Indian women who struggled to join the ATS in 1943, and the thousands of others who worked in fields and factories, were not the first such women to come to the aid of the 'mother country' in her time of need. During the First World War a number of West Indian women had also come to Britain to work as nurses, but their history remains unwritten.

1. The struggle to join the ATS In 1943 white Caribbean women were recruited by the Washington office of the British ATS, though the existence of a colour bar in the United States, and the reluctance of the British War Office to challenge American racism, served to exclude black West Indian women from the Washington-based arm of the ATS. Nevertheless, many black women still wished to join the British military services, motivated by a strong sense of patriotism. They also recognized that the future of the Caribbean was intimately tied to the outcome of the conflict. Anti-colonial feelings had erupted throughout the region during the 1930s, but no one wanted a Nazi victory. Hence, Caribbean women and men regarded Britain's fight against the Axis Powers as a fight to defend themselves from Fascist occupation. As the Second World War escalated, Britain turned to the colonies as a source of military personnel, and thousands of West Indian men came to Britain to enlist in the armed forces. An estimated 10,000 West Indian men and women volunteered for service, of whom over half served with the Royal Air Force. Thousands more were employed in the merchant navy, transporting food and other vital supplies across the Atlantic, and in key industries such as munitions and aircraft production.

Caribbean women could ill afford to ignore a war largely waged in Europe and the Pacific, for the British colonies in the region faced the threat of attack from German U-boats hunting for ships carrying oil and other supplies to Britain—and later to the United States. And it was largely women who had to cope with the shortages that resulted from the German blockade. Many, having lost fathers, brothers, or husbands to the war, saw war service as a way of honouring the sacrifice made by their menfolk.

Some black women joined Caribbean-based women's war service organizations, performing mainly administrative roles. Others performed essential war work in agriculture, where their labour proved vital in sustaining food supplies. A great number also enlisted with the overseas services, such as those who joined the ATS.

For those who joined the ATS and other military organizations, most had first to challenge and overcome existing race, gender, and class prejudices. At the outbreak of the conflict in 1939 many black British women and those from the Caribbean applied to join the women's military services but were rejected. In post-war interviews some recalled the scorn with which their attempts to enlist were met. Lilian Bader, interviewed at the age of 86, was one of three generations of her family to serve in the British armed forces. She became an aircraft instrument repairer in the WAAF, but only after sustained struggles against a racist recruitment policy that refused to admit black volunteers.

From the outset the War Office had wrestled with the question of whether the West Indies could play a valid role in the war, and, if so, how many West Indians might be recruited. Prior to 1939 an official colour bar precluded black people from joining the British armed forces, but as the war progressed it became clear that victory depended on Britain's ability to mobilize its citizens from across the Commonwealth, and thousands of West Indian men were permitted to enlist. Yet, the War Office had clearly not considered the contribution that West Indian women might also make to the war effort. Officials were aware that West Indian women—white and black—had demanded the opportunity to serve, and the idea of recruiting them into a special women's unit was considered but rejected. At the end of 1941, with the exception of nursing and the ATS, the War Office was still refusing to recognize the contributions of colonial women's organizations. However, it stopped short of actively discouraging women who wanted to organize in support of the war effort, though impressing on colonial governments that the War Office would not bear any financial responsibility for such activities.

The ATS itself remained a British-based organization, and, initially at least, its ranks were filled by white British women. It was official policy to discourage the recruitment of West Indian women to the ranks of the ATS. One manifestation of this was the stipulation that West Indian women wishing to join the ATS in Britain had to pay their return passage themselves.

Although Churchill's government denounced the Nazis for their attitude towards Blacks, British officials made every effort to keep black women out of the forces, while eventually conceding to the recruitment of white Caribbean women to the ATS. When the issue of black women's enlistment was pushed, the War Office at first attempted to renege on its commitment to permit the recruitment of white Caribbean women. This approach might well have been maintained had it not been for the overwhelming need for additional womanpower to support the flagging war effort. The War Office then drew up a scheme for the recruitment of white Caribbean women into the ATS, but this was rejected by the Colonial Office, which insisted on a non-discriminatory recruitment policy. Dismissing the War Office claim that the British climate and culture would limit the effectiveness of 'coloured' women, the Colonial Office pressed the point that to deny black women the opportunity to serve in the British ATS would generate widespread resentment in the Caribbean at the very moment when Britain needed the support of the colonies. In 1943, therefore, the Colonial Office finally managed to convince the War Office of the advantages that the recruitment of black women would lend to imperial relations. And so the first group of 30 racially diverse West Indian women was recruited to the ATS in October of that year. Even so, class prejudice remained, for the War Office insisted that only educated middle-class women should be recruited. Hence, those first Caribbean women recruited to the ATS were probably more able than their white British counterparts. That first group of 30 recruits arrived in England in October 1943, and were followed shortly afterwards by another 70 West Indian women. Hundreds more black women joined the Caribbean arm of the ATS when the War Office finally agreed to its establishment.

Achieving permission to enlist in the ATS represented only the first stage of the struggle, for few black women had ever travelled outside the Caribbean. Many experienced homesickness as a result of the alien culture and the harsh winter climate, but most adjusted quickly to life in wartime Britain. After training they were mainly assigned to administrative posts. Most of the black women were welcomed with tolerance, and indeed with kindness and acts of generosity, by the British, though many later reported shock and dismay at the pervasive race and colour prejudice of the British. Still, the women discharged their duties conscientiously—and indeed courageously in face of frequent bombing raids.

Black women in the ATS and other service organizations in Britain later reported mixed experiences of race discrimination, primarily from other service personnel. For instance, although they were initially assigned to administrative and support functions, it was not uncommon for British officers to attempt to reallocate them to more menial and domestic roles. Yet, black service women performed their roles with integrity and professionalism, and many reported rather warmer relations with the British, and a sense of camaraderie. Moreover, the media frequently praised the devotion of colonial subjects to the 'mother country'. At the war's end, however, gratitude gave way to a reassertion of pre-war prejudice, as many West Indian ex-servicewomen later reported.

2. Other forms of wartime service Black women of all classes and professions gave their unselfish and unstinting support to the Allied war effort. Female artistes such as the African-American jazz singer and Broadway star Adelaide *Hall boosted morale by performing nightly to packed audiences, even during air raids. On one occasion, while starring at Lewisham's Hippodrome Theatre, the air raid siren sounded in the middle of her act. Hall asked the audience if anyone wanted her to end the show. The crowd responded with a resounding 'no', and for the next four hours, as bombs dropped all around the theatre, she continued her performance, singing over 50 songs, until the all-clear sounded. As well as her regular stage performances, Hall frequently starred in the Florida Club's late-night revues. In 1940 the club was struck by a bomb and entirely demolished. Hall then moved to Surrey, where she spent much of her free time working on a farm. During the war she performed at every major venue in Britain, and in 1943 she joined the Forces entertainment service, ENSA, and after D-Day in June 1944 she made several trips to Europe to perform for front-line troops, often in aircraft hangars or on makeshift stages.

Adelaide Hall was only one among many black entertainers, male and female, who used their artistic talents to maintain morale among British civilians and service personnel. Another was Una *Marson from Jamaica. She was the first black woman programme-maker at the BBC. When Prime Minister Churchill made his appeal to Britain's colonies to join the fight against Nazism, Marson joined the BBC. She was appointed to the West Indian broadcasting section of the Empire Service. *West Indies Calling* was her maiden programme in her five years of working for the BBC from 1940 to 1945. This programme enabled Caribbean servicemen and women to stay in touch with their families throughout the war. Marson also opened her home to West Indian and black British servicemen and women, providing a much needed domestic respite from the stresses of war. In March 1943 she produced her own programme, **Caribbean Voices*, which was broadcast on Sundays to eager listeners throughout the Anglophone Caribbean. She invited literary figures onto the programme to discuss the works of West Indian writers. However, the fact that the BBC's overseas services were used to harness colonial labour and resources for the war effort while stifling nationalist activism was something that Marson could never stomach, and in 1945 she resigned from the BBC. As one of her biographers remarked, 'The boldness of this move in wartime London, especially for a dependent black woman, was remarkable.'

Black women in the Caribbean and Britain have a long history of resistance to oppression. They have been hardened in their struggle against slavery, and in the aftermath of slavery, in their resistance to colonial policies that sought to maintain their political, social, economic, and cultural subjugation. Yet, when the liberty of the colonizing power was itself threatened by Fascism, its colonial subjects, women and men, gave unstinting aid. In diverse ways, black women both in the Caribbean and in Britain played significant roles in the war against Fascism, yet theirs is a narrative that remains marginalized within the historiography of the Second World War, and their valiant contribution to the Allied war effort is only now beginning to be recognized. CJ

Bousquet, Ben, and Douglas, Colin, *West Indian Women at War: British Racism in World War II* (1991)

Jarrett-Macauley, Delia, 'Putting the Black Women in the Frame: Una Marson and the West Indian Challenge to British National Identity' in C. Gledhill and G. Swanson (eds.), *Nationalising Femininity: Culture, Sexuality and British Cinema in the Second World War* (1996)

See also FEMINISM; FIRST WORLD WAR; SECOND WORLD WAR

Wharton, Arthur (1865–1930). The first black British footballer in the Football League. Wharton was born in Jamestown, Accra, Gold Coast (present-day Ghana), to a half-Grenadian and half-Scottish father and a Ghanaian mother. Always a gifted sportsman, he set the first world record in 1886 for the 100-yards dash during the Amateur Athletics Association sprint. Apart from football, he was also involved in other sports such as cricket and cycling. Wharton signed up with Preston North End in 1886 as goalkeeper after being spotted while playing for Darlington. While at Preston North End, he played in the FA Cup semi-finals, one of the high points of his career. Subsequently, he played professionally for various football clubs such as Rotherham Town, Sheffield United, Stalybridge Celtic, and Ashton North End. At Sheffield United he played three games for the club's first team. Despite his strength as a goalkeeper, he could not maintain his position as United simultaneously signed a hefty 19-year-old called William 'Fatty' Foulke (also known as Foulkes), whose might surpassed that of Wharton's. Consequently, he only played three games, against Leicester Fosse, Linfield of Belfast, and Sunderland. He retired from football in 1902.

Wharton became a working-class hero for the communities in which he lived, despite hailing from a middle-class background. He was known to be a confrontational figure when faced with racial prejudice of any kind. He died in poverty after spending most of his money on alcohol, and was buried in an unmarked grave. The 1997 Sheffield United project Football Unites, Racism Divides managed to raise money to place a gravestone on his plot.

DD/SS

ODNB

Vasili, Phil, *The First Black Footballer: Arthur Wharton (1865–1930). An Absence of Memory* (1998)

See also SPORT; TULL, WALTER; WATSON, ANDREW

Wheatley, Phillis (1753–1784). African-American poet whose first collection of poems was also the first book to be published by a black woman in Britain. Wheatley was transported from Africa to America in 1761 at the age of 8 and purchased in Boston by Susanna Wheatley, the wife of an affluent tailor, John Wheatley. The Wheatleys were considerate in their treatment of their young servant and afforded her a life removed from that of the average slave. She was thus tutored at home in Latin, Greek, English, ancient history, and the Bible, proving herself to be precocious in her ability to read and understand the poetry of Pope and Milton.

Wheatley began to write poetry around the age of 13 and published her first poem, 'On Messrs. Hussey and Coffin', in 1767. It was the publication of her eulogy on the English evangelist the Revd George Whitefield in 1770 that made her well known. The poem was also published in London, thus extending her reputation not merely as a poet, but as a black female poet of significant talent. Despite the poem's success, her volume of 28 poems was rejected by Boston publishers. Consequently, she wrote to the Countess of Huntingdon in London, sending her a poem along with a covering letter proposing the publication of her poems in England. Two years later she wrote to Lord Dartmouth with the same intention.

In 1773 Wheatley sailed to London with Nathaniel Wheatley, her master's son, on account of her poor health. In London she was treated well and met numerous influential and celebrated figures such as the Countess of Huntingdon, Benjamin Franklin, Lord Dartmouth, the Lord Mayor of London, and the abolitionist Granville *Sharp, who in the summer of 1773 gave her a personal tour of London sights. In September of the same year her collection *Poems on Various Subjects, Religious and Moral* was published by Arch Bell, Aldgate, in London, but, owing to her mistress's ill health, Wheatley returned to Boston and was not present for its publication. The collection received considerable notice and was reviewed by several British magazines.

In Boston, Wheatley was granted her freedom by Susanna Wheatley, three months before Susanna's death in 1774. Subsequently, she made a living hawking her book from door to door and reading selections to potential lady customers. Her life became burdened by poverty and ill health. In 1774 she married a free black grocer, John Peters, who sent her and their three children to a Negro boarding house. Life there proved to be equally detrimental to Wheatley and her children's well-being. Following the death of two of her children, Wheatley died in 1784, at the young age of 31.

Throughout her life and after, Wheatley's position as a poet of consequence has been bound up with consideration of her race. Long treated by her contemporaries as an object of fascination and socio-anthropological interest, she was seen as a rarity among Blacks, and a challenge to Enlightenment notions of white supremacy. Thus, in order to ascertain the authenticity of a sheaf of poems apparently written by a young African girl (Wheatley), a gathering of eighteen of Boston's most prominent citizens was held to test her and confirm the authorship of the poems. After sufficient response from her, they signed an attestation as proof that the young Wheatley was indeed the author of the poems, and the attestation prefaced her book, where verifications such as 'We whose Names are under-written, do assure the World, that the Poems specified in the following Page, were (as we verily believe) written by Phillis, a young Negro Girl, who was but a few Years since, brought an uncultivated Barbarian from *Africa*' were deemed necessary for validation of publication. Wheatley did, after all, live in an age when questions were being asked, both in Europe and in America, about whether Blacks were even part of the human species. Such sensibilities, steeped in Enlightenment bigotry, were the burdens against which she battled. A review by the *London Magazine*, for example, commented that 'these poems display no astonishing power of genius; but when we consider them as the production of a young untutored African . . . we cannot suppress our admiration of talents so vigorous and lively'.

In London, Wheatley was exposed to the anti-slavery movement, which would have instigated feelings of hope for the freedom of her race, although such feelings are rarely expressed in her poems. What is predominant in her verse is Christian virtues such as patience, devotion, and humility. This apparent dissociation from the plight of her race has caused many black scholars to dismiss her as one who sold her blackness for a pottage of white acceptability. But her thoughts on the barbarity of slavery and the predicament of enslaved Africans are more evident in her letters.

Wheatley's poems have been assessed largely on the grounds of her gender, race, and youth, and the neoclassical style of her verse has been criticized as too derivative of Alexander Pope. Still, although the critic John C. Shields can claim that she is not a great poet but she is a good one, her value lies in the force of her talent, which managed to challenge her circumstances as a slave and as a black woman. Her historical significance as the author of the first book ever to be published by a black woman in Britain remains an important detail in the cultural and historical development of black Britain. DD/SS

Fryer, Peter, *Staying Power: The History of Black People in Britain* (1984)

Robinson, W. H. (ed.), *Critical Essays on Phillis Wheatley* (1982)

Wheatley, Phillis, *The Collected Works of Phillis Wheatley* (ed. J. C. Shields, 1988)

See also ASA-ASA, LOUIS; CUGOANO, QUOBNA OTTOBAH; EQUIANO, OLAUDAH; GEORGIAN AND VICTORIAN BRITAIN; GRONNIOWSAW, JAMES ALBERT UKAWSAW; SANCHO, IGNATIUS; WILLIAMS, FRANCIS

Whitehaven. Town in the county of Cumberland (modern Cumbria) developed as a port in the late 17th century by Sir John Lowther, second baronet (bap. 1642, d. 1706) to serve as an outlet for the Cumberland coal industry, which was (like Whitehaven itself) long dominated by the Lowther family. Local merchants also became involved in trading with Virginia, including both shipping local people to the American colonies as indentured servants, and importing slave-grown tobacco from Virginia, and in the 18th century Whitehaven was also trading with the Caribbean colonies, importing sugar and rum. A sugar refinery was established in the town in 1712.

Colonial trade was closely linked to the slave trade, and records show ships clearing Whitehaven for slaving voyages to Africa and the Americas between at least 1711 and 1767. A glass goblet made in Newcastle upon Tyne in 1763 by William Beilby and now in the Beacon Museum in Whitehaven is decorated with the royal arms on one side and a picture of a sailing ship on the other, and the legend 'Success to the African Trade of Whitehaven'. It was made to commemorate the maiden voyage of the slave ship *King George*, whose third mate was John Paul Jones (1747–92), later the naval hero of the American War of Independence, who subsequently expressed his aversion to the slave trade.

The ending of Whitehaven's involvement in the slave trade in the third quarter of the 18th century appears to have been as much a result of the competing demands made on the port by the coal trade, together with the fact that larger ports such as *Bristol and *Liverpool offered facilities better suited to the requirements of slaving vessels, as of any change in outlook on the part of the town's mercantile community. However, the history of Whitehaven's role as a slave port remains a striking example of how slavery and the slave trade made connections into the local economies of some of the most remote parts of Britain in the 18th century. In 2006 Copeland Council, the local council for the borough of which Whitehaven forms part, decided to issue a formal apology for slavery, in preparation for the bicentenary of *abolition. JG

Tattersfield, Nigel, *The Forgotten Trade: Comprising the Log of the Daniel and Henry of 1700 and Accounts of the Slave Trade from the Minor Ports of England, 1698–1725* (1991; rev. edn., 1998)

Wilberforce, William (1759–1833). Politician and campaigner against the *slave trade and *slavery born into a wealthy merchant family in Hull. His fortune freed him from the need to earn a living and enabled him to enter politics. He became MP for Hull in September 1780, when he was only just of legal age, and he remained in the House of Commons for some 45 years (MP for Hull, 1780–4; for Yorkshire, 1784–1812; for Bramber in Sussex, 1812–25). Wilberforce was a personal friend of William Pitt the Younger (1759–1806; Prime Minister 1783–1801, 1804–6) and of many other leading politicians, but he never sought office and maintained an independent stance. In 1785 Wilberforce had an evangelical conversion experience and, following advice he sought from John *Newton and others, determined to devote his life and political career to the service of God. It was only in 1787, however, that he came to the conclusion that, as he wrote in his journal, 'God Almighty has set before me two great objects, the suppression of the slave trade and the reformation of manners.' From then on he was the leading spokesman in Parliament for *abolition until success was finally achieved in 1807. Thereafter he continued his interest in the condition of slaves in the British Caribbean colonies, campaigned to keep the British government committed to using diplomacy to persuade other countries to end their participation in the slave trade, and in 1823 published an influential *Appeal to the Religion, Justice and Humanity of the Inhabitants of the British Empire on Behalf of the Negro Slaves in the West Indies*, in which he argued that *emancipation of the slaves was the Christian duty of the British people.

In his own time, for both supporters and opponents, Wilberforce was an important symbolic figurehead of the anti-slave trade and anti-slavery causes, and was widely known as such among the enslaved populations of the British Caribbean. His sons Robert and Samuel published a life of him in 1838, which caused Thomas *Clarkson to complain that their praise of their father undervalued his own contribution. A tendency to overstate Wilberforce's role continued until well into the 20th century, so that the suggestion made by Eric *Williams that economic factors had been crucial in both abolition and emancipation was at first regarded as truly shocking. Undeniably, many others contributed to the cause, including the many thousands of slaves in the Caribbean who participated in armed rebellions or other acts of resistance, and the many thousands of ordinary people in Britain who signed petitions to Parliament, gave up the consumption of slave-grown sugar, or campaigned in other ways for what was the first mass-based political pressure movement in British history. Nevertheless, Wilberforce's oratorical skills, his influential connections, and his contribution in Parliament, sustained over many years, were of real significance in the successes that eventually came. Cynics may be inclined to feel that, if Wilberforce's family wealth had come from Liverpool's African trade, rather than Hull's trade with the Baltic, his outlook might have been different, but we should not downplay the importance of his religious convictions in shaping his attitude to slavery. Nor does it detract from the significance of their contributions to allow that Wilberforce and other evangelicals sought abolition and emancipation as necessary preconditions for the Christianization of the slaves as much as for motives of abstract humanitarianism. JG

Brown, Ford K., *Fathers of the Victorians: The Age of Wilberforce* (1961)
ODNB

See also CHRISTIANITY

Wilkins, Dave (1914–1990). Jazz trumpeter born in Barbados. He studied the cornet with the Salvation Army and music theory by correspondence, and was influenced by *jazz recordings on disc and radio broadcasts from America. He soon abandoned demeaning work as an errand boy in Bridgetown, and moved to St Vincent and then Martinique, reaching Trinidad in 1934, where he continued to play dance music; and eventually joined the police band.

By 1938 Wilkins was in Britain, recruited by Ken 'Snakehips' *Johnson for his West Indian Dance Orchestra and recording with them and with Thomas 'Fats' Waller. The Johnson band toured widely and made numerous broadcasts, and many Britons enjoyed the singing and playing of Wilkins. He survived the bomb at the Café de Paris, London, in 1941, which killed Johnson and tenor-sax player Dave Williams. He made more recordings and broadcasts, notably with Harry Parry, whose guitar players included the Cardiff-born African-descent Deniz brothers and the Trinidadian Lauderic Caton.

Wilkins worked with other black musicians and starred with Ted Heath's orchestra (which was immensely popular from the late 1940s). Touring brought severe strain and hospitalization, and his professional career ended in 1971. Wilkins's playing still stands out: he was ahead of British contemporaries, and fully understood the jazz idiom. JPG

ODNB

Oliver, Paul (ed.), *Black Music in Britain: Essays on the Afro-Asian Contribution to Popular Music* (1990)

See also BLACK DANCE; MUSIC 2: EARLY POPULAR MUSIC

Williams, Aubrey (1926–1990). Artist born in British Guiana (now Guyana) who contributed to post-war British modernism and the anti-colonial cultural politics of British Guiana, and helped to foster a Caribbean creative community in the United Kingdom.

Williams arrived in Britain in 1952, one of a number of individuals from the West Indies who anticipated a land of opportunity and limitless creative freedom. However, like the sculptor Ronald *Moody, who came to Britain from Jamaica, and the painters Denis Williams and Frank Bowling from British Guiana, he met with a somewhat mixed reception. Nevertheless, Williams is historically important given the movement of his art between various parts of (post-)Empire, and his legacy of distinguished visual work, which has enjoyed increasing recognition since his posthumous retrospective at London's Whitechapel Gallery in 1998.

Williams was educated in Georgetown, British Guiana, where he took part in a four-year agricultural apprenticeship scheme affiliated to University College London, and was appointed an agricultural field officer in 1944. He studied at the Working People's Art Class, and travelled to Britain to become a painter. In October 1954 he took part in his first group show at the little-known Archer Gallery in Westbourne Grove, London, under the direction of Dr Mary Morris, but waited a further five years for a major exhibition, which led to invitations to exhibit in Paris, Milan, and Chicago. His first serious accolade was the only prize at the First Commonwealth Biennale of Abstract Art in 1963. Such initial success had much to do with Denis Bowen, a South African painter and teacher, founder in 1951 of the New Vision Group. Unusual in its inclusive attitude to artists from outside Britain, and for the range of spaces where they displayed, Williams's work would frequently be shown at the centrally located New Vision Centre Gallery, and multi-use spaces around West London.

When Williams began to attract the attention of art critics, reviews were typically focused on emphasizing his origins outside Britain, and stressed an exotic character. This preoccupation among the art establishment contributed to the marginalization of Caribbean artists from the mainstream of British art. By the time the *Caribbean Artists' Movement (CAM) was founded in 1966, by artists as well as the writers and critics John *La Rose, Kamau (then L. Edward) Brathwaite, and Andrew *Salkey, Williams had started to feel terribly isolated, physically and intellectually. From 1966 onwards he would spend more and more time working in the Caribbean, and finally in Florida. Nonetheless, throughout his life he continually resisted attempts to define his paintings in terms of their being either 'Caribbean' or 'European', struggling to free his art from simple connections to any particular visual heritage.

Such a critical outlook formed the basis for the Arts Council-supported exhibition 'The Other Story: Afro-Asian Artists in Post-War Britain' (Hayward Gallery, London, 1989, and touring to Wolverhampton and Manchester). It re-established Williams as a major innovator of post-war modernism, through the display of significant pieces spanning his career. These included the product of his long fascination with the chamber and orchestral music of Shostakovich: a series of 30 paintings from 1969–1981, which provoked the tragic excitement that Guy Brett has celebrated as a signature of his abstract expressionist style. Williams also explored South American Carib, Warrau, and Arawak petroglyphs and mythologies, in paintings and in murals, materializing a connection he had established with Amerindian communities in Guyana during a two-year posting in the remote north-west of the country's interior. Their formative influence on his *The Olmec Maya and Now* series (1981–5) offered a borrowed iconography that was granted new meaning within a painted and gallery-based genre. A development on both approaches was his *Cosmos* series from 1985, which took an extra-terrestrial setting as the basis for his characteristically large canvases. During each phase of his work Williams continued to produce figurative paintings, such as his series showing finely plumed tropical birds, both celebration of the global environment and protest against its destruction.

Williams would also use his base in Britain as a vantage point onto cultural and political developments in the Caribbean. One example is his painting of 1960 entitled *Revolt*, which references the rebellion of 1763 in Berbice (now a county of Guyana) when the slave leaders Cuffy, Accara, and Atta launched a revolt against their Dutch plantation owners that ended in failure. Produced in Britain, and given by the artist as a gift to the Guianese people, *Revolt* caused controversy when the Royal Agricultural and Commercial Society in Georgetown, which housed the Guyana Museum, refused to exhibit the piece in 1961, and without any public statement on its grounds for the refusal. *Revolt* was not allowed a showing until 1970 (after Guyana had gained its political independence from Britain) at the Guyana Museum at the 'Retrospective Exhibition of Guyanese Artists' organized by an art subcommittee chaired by Williams, where not without irony it was hung prominently. The painting is now in the Guyana National Gallery at Castellani House, Georgetown.

Given his migratory biography and the fact that much of his art was conceived from an imperial centre, Williams has often been linked to a history of visual imaging in the era of decolonization. His presence in Britain would contribute to debates on art within CAM, as well as those on art and identity among the second generation of Caribbean artists, particularly during the 1980s. Nonetheless, he stood apart from the often militant attitude of that 'critical decade', as he made clear at a Brixton seminar organized by Creation for Liberation in 1987, by addressing the differences between the experiences of the younger generation and that of his own.

The growing value assigned to Williams's art rests heavily on the vision he shared with many of the CAM group of the need, in relation to subsequent generations of West Indians in Britain, 'to help them see, clarify, speak, understand and name the process that they're going through', as Stuart Hall expressed it at one of their meetings in 1968. His extensively documented, posthumous retrospective in 1998 was viewed by a wide audience, as have been the ongoing exhibitions of his work at the October Gallery, London. Yet Williams's paintings are also proving to be significant in diverse curatorial contexts—such as 'Back to Black' (2005, Whitechapel Gallery) and 'Amazon to Caribbean' at the Horniman Museum (2005–6)—to reveal his growing importance for a history of art focused beyond national borders. LW

Dempsey, Andrew, Tawadros, Gilane, and Williams, Maridowa (eds.), *Aubrey Williams* (1998)

ODNB

Wainwright, Leon, 'Francis Newton Souza and Aubrey Williams: Entwined Art Histories at the End of Empire' in Simon Faulkner and Anandi Ramamurthy (eds.), *Visual Culture and Decolonisation in Britain* (2006)

Walmsley, Anne, *The Caribbean Artists Movement 1966–1972: A Literary and Cultural History* (1992)

—— (ed.), *Guyana Dreaming: The Art of Aubrey Williams* (1990)

See also VISUAL ARTS 1: REPRESENTATIONS OF BLACKS; VISUAL ARTS 2: ARTISTS

Williams, Eric Eustace (1911–1981). Historian and politician born in Port of Spain, Trinidad. In 1931 he won a government scholarship, which took him the following year to the University of Oxford, where, after his first degree, he completed a doctorate in history. His *Inward Hunger* (1969) includes an interesting description of his experiences as a colonial student at Oxford and the prejudices he encountered. From 1939 to 1948 he lived mainly in the United States, where he taught at Howard University and worked for the Anglo-American Caribbean Commission (both in Washington DC). He returned to live in Port of Spain in 1948, but continued to work for the Caribbean Commission until his resignation in 1955.

In 1956 Williams became a full-time politician, founding the People's National Movement. Electoral success later the same year meant that he led the government of Trinidad and Tobago, successively as Chief Minister, Premier, and Prime Minister, from 1956 until his death in office in 1981, and he took the country into independence from Britain in 1962.

As a historian, Williams's main work was *Capitalism and Slavery* (1944), a revision of his doctoral thesis. This put forward three main arguments: firstly, that economic reasons caused the transition from the use of European indentured labour to the use of the labour of enslaved Africans on Caribbean plantations in the 17th century; secondly, that the profits from the African slave trade and slave-grown Caribbean sugar provided the capital that enabled the Industrial Revolution in Britain; and, thirdly, that both the *abolition of the British slave trade and *emancipation of the slaves in Britain's Caribbean colonies took place for economic rather than humanitarian reasons. All three have been challenged by later historians, who have, for example, drawn attention to the way in which the development of the slave trade was facilitated by previously existing European prejudices relating to black people, or have stressed the importance of both slave rebellions in the Caribbean and the growth of a widespread political pressure movement in favour of abolition (and, later, emancipation) in Britain itself, in influencing the British government's eventual acceptance of these measures. Nevertheless, Williams's claims have been enormously influential, and *Capitalism and Slavery* continues to be essential reading in any discussion of these major aspects of Caribbean history and of Britain's role in both African and Caribbean history. JG

ODNB

Williams, Eric, *Inward Hunger: The Education of a Prime Minister* (1969)

See also BANKING, INSURANCE, AND THE COLONIAL TRADE; CARIBBEAN, BRITISH COLONIES IN THE

Williams, Francis (bap. 1697, d. 1762). Poet born in Jamaica, the son of John and Dorothy Williams, who were free black people. John Williams was a former slave who had been freed by the will of his master, Colonel John Bourden (a prominent local figure who died in 1697), and who subsequently became a successful merchant, whose activities included money-lending on an extensive scale, and trade between Jamaica and Britain.

As a young man, Francis Williams lived in Britain, possibly for several years, and may have been entrusted with the British end of his father's business concerns. On 8 August 1721 he was admitted as a member of Lincoln's Inn; while there is no evidence to suggest that he was ever called to the Bar or practised as a lawyer, the Inns of Court often functioned in this period as a sort of finishing school for young men of gentlemanly status who did not necessarily have any intention of pursuing a legal career. Little else can be said with certainty about Williams's education. He himself was to state 'Insula me genuit, celebres aluere *Britanni*' ['The island bore me, the famous Britons nourished me'], by which he appears to have meant that he was born in Jamaica but educated in Britain. In the account of Williams which he wrote in his *History of Jamaica* (published in 1774, a dozen years after Williams's death), Edward *Long claimed that the *Duke of Montagu had been responsible for Williams's education at an English grammar school, and subsequently at the University of Cambridge. However, there is no evidence to support this statement, and Williams does not appear in the university's matriculation records.

Francis Williams returned to Jamaica not long after his father's death in July 1723, and he appears to have spent the rest of his life in the island. Long claimed that the Duke of Montagu tried to get Williams a seat on the Governor's Council, although this was prevented by the Governor's objections, and that for several years Williams kept a school in the island's capital, Spanish Town, where he taught reading, writing, Latin, and mathematics. This is partly substantiated by the Revd John Lindsay (Rector of St Catherine's, Jamaica, the parish in which Spanish Town is situated, 1773–88), who wrote of Williams, 'I knew him in his latter days, when reduced to keeping of a Negroe School.'

Williams inherited a large part of his father's estate, and more property came to him on the death of other members of the family. However, surviving records show him selling pieces of land and the occasional slave from time to time, but not making new purchases. At the time of his death he was living in a leased house in Spanish Town, and the inventory of his estate suggests that his fortunes had declined. Whatever his abilities as a businessman, Williams appears to have been capable of making a vigorous defence of what he saw as his rights. In 1730, following the outbreak of the first Maroon War (an armed conflict with escaped slaves and their descendants which lasted for eight years before it was finally settled by a treaty with the Maroons), the Jamaican legislature passed an Act 'for the better regulating slaves', which also imposed a number of restrictions on free Blacks and Coloureds. Williams successfully complained to the authorities in Britain that this was an infringement of privileges conferred on himself and other members of his family by earlier Jamaican Acts, and the Act was eventually disallowed by the King in Council.

However, it was as a writer that Williams, as Long put it, 'made a conspicuous figure' in Jamaica, 'and even attracted the notice of many in England'. He appears to be the earliest black writer known in the British Empire, his career pre-dating that of figures such as Olaudah *Equiano, Ignatius *Sancho, and Phillis *Wheatley. The only surviving literary work that can definitely be ascribed to him is a poem of 46 lines addressed to George Haldane on his assuming the governorship of Jamaica in 1759, and preserved in Long's *History of Jamaica*. Long suggested that Williams may also have written the words to the song 'Welcome, welcome, brother debtor', which was popular in the 18th century, but there are other claimants. The poem to Haldane was in Latin; Long said that Williams 'was fond of this species of composition in Latin, and usually addressed one to every new governor'.

The ability to write Latin verses was a gentlemanly accomplishment highly regarded at the time, and Williams's poem to Haldane is a specimen of conventional flattery of a type found in many Latin poems written in Britain during the 18th century (including some by authors from the Caribbean). However, it is good of its kind, and it is noteworthy for passages that can be interpreted as asserting both a specifically Jamaican identity and the poet's sense of his own worth as a black man and a black writer. In particular, says Williams:

Ipsa coloris egens virtus, prudentia; honesto
Nullus inest animo, nullus in arte color.

[Worth itself and understanding have no colour; there is no colour in an honest mind, or in art.]

In other words, Williams claims, there is no distinction of 'race' in artistic capacity.

Williams was an embarrassment to Long's theories of white superiority, and Long did his best to belittle Williams and his poetry. Nevertheless, other late 18th- and early 19th-century writers, such as James *Ramsay, easily detected the prejudice in Long's account. Some, including Henri Grégoire in his influential *De la littérature des nègres* (1808), referred to Williams's literary abilities as demonstrating the humanity and equality of all black people, and thus forming an argument against slavery. The most forceful expression of this point of view was given by Robert Boucher Nickolls, the Barbadian-born Dean of Middleham in Yorkshire. In the 1788 edition of his *Letter to the Treasurer of the Society Instituted for the Purpose of Effecting the Abolition of the Slave Trade* (first published the previous year), Nickolls, clearly alluding to Long, referred to 'the friends of slavery' who 'represent the negroes as little removed above the monkey, or the oran-outang, with regard to intellects'. Nickolls went on to mention Phillis Wheatley and Francis Williams by name, and commented: 'I never heard of poems by a monkey, or of Latin odes by an oran-outang.'

There is some irony in the posthumous role thus given to Williams, who was himself a slave owner, but it is clear that in his own lifetime his very existence as a rich, free black man who wrote Latin verses was a challenge to the theories of white supremacy on which plantation societies in the Americas were based.

There is a portrait of Williams, now in the Victoria and Albert Museum, London, which has been widely reproduced, and has attracted divergent opinions. Some have viewed it as a racist caricature, with the Nigerian writer Chinua Achebe calling it 'clearly an exercise in mockery', while others have interpreted it as probably commissioned by the subject himself as a prestige item, with its failings being those of a naive artist rather than the result of malice. JG

Gilmore, John, 'The British Empire and the Neo-Latin Tradition: The Case of Francis Williams' in Barbara Goff (ed.), *Classics and Colonialism* (2005)
ODNB

See also BUSINESSES

Williams, Henry Sylvester (1869–1911). Founder of the African Association, which held the first major Pan-African Conference in 1900. Born in Arouca in Trinidad, Williams qualified as a teacher and taught until 1890, when he left for North America. Little is known of his time there but he arrived in England in 1896, studied law, and married an Englishwoman, Agnes Powell. He lectured for the Temperance Society and on colonial topics. He formed the African Association, mainly with fellow West Indians, and organized the Conference in London in July 1900. Its aims were to secure 'the full rights and promote [the] business interests' of all Africans. Encouraged initially by Booker T. *Washington, it was attended by W. E. B. DuBois, Washington's rival. DuBois was to call the second conference at the end of the *First World War. His hand can be seen in its final declaration that the problem of the 20th century was the 'problem of the colour line'. Williams visited the West Indies to publicize its aims, and founded a monthly journal, *The Pan-African*, but this and the Association were both dead by 1903. Called to the Bar in 1902, he left for South Africa, being admitted to the Cape Town Bar, and argued vigorously for equal rights. He returned to England in 1905, continued his campaigning, and in 1906 was elected to Marylebone Council. By 1908 he had left with his wife and children for Trinidad, where he practised law, but ill health curbed his political activities and he died in March 1911. PF

Hooker, J. R., *Henry Sylvester Williams* (1975)
Mathurin, O. C., *Henry Sylvester Williams* (1976)
ODNB

See also PAN-AFRICANISM; POLITICS

Wilson, Salim Charles (*c*.1865–1946). Sudanese slave who reversed the missionary process by becoming an African evangelist in England. Born Atobhil Macar Kathiec among the Gok Dinka of Sudan, he was captured by slavers, freed by the Egyptian army, and subsequently employed by the missionary Charles Wilson. Educated, baptized, and confirmed in England, Wilson joined abortive missions to the Congo and Tripoli in 1887–8 and 1893, but most of his missionary efforts were undertaken with the Methodists in England, where he become known as 'the Black Evangelist of the North'. Settling in Scunthorpe, Lincolnshire, he married his landlady in 1913, an event filmed by the local cinema. He was a popular figure in the town, where he lived until his death.

Wilson produced three books about his life and the Dinka. He wrote positively about Dinka religiosity, and traced his own awareness of God to the beliefs and prayers of his people. His acceptance of Jesus as his personal saviour paralleled, in many ways, the Dinka appropriation of personal divinities. DHJ

Johnson, Douglas H., 'Divinity Abroad: Dinka Missionaries in Foreign Lands' in Wendy James and Douglas H. Johnson (eds.), *Vernacular Christianity* (1988)

Kathish, Hatashil Masha, *Jehovah-Nissi: The Life Story of Hatashil-Masha-Kathish of the Dinka Tribe, Soudan* (1901)

Wilson, Salim Charles, *I Was a Slave* (c.1939)

See also CHRISTIANITY; MISSIONARY SOCIETIES

Windrush. *See* EMPIRE WINDRUSH.

Wordsworth, William (1770–1850). English Romantic poet whose interest in the issue of *slavery resulted in the writing of several poems on the theme of slavery. Of particular note is Wordsworth's sonnet written in 1807 and addressed to the Haitian revolutionary leader Toussaint L'Ouverture entitled 'To Toussaint L'Ouverture'. The poem focuses on the plight of L'Ouverture following his arrest and deportation to France in 1802. Control of Haiti had been contested by the French, who claimed the colony, and the British, who were planning the reintroduction of slavery to Saint-Domingue, as the island was referred to then. L'Ouverture led the revolution against the British, succeeding when they surrendered in 1798. However, when the Peace of Amiens declared the colony to be semi-independent, Napoleon Bonaparte reinstated slavery, and a second active resistance ensued, led again by L'Ouverture.

The inspiration for Wordsworth's sonnet is a complicated fusion of disillusionment with the French Revolution, a celebration of Englishness, and an elevation of the sublime. The poem upholds a dichotomy between French tyranny and English liberty, and places L'Ouverture on the side of English virtue. Wordsworth's representation of the revolutionary leader is a reflection of the time in which he was writing. Despite sympathizing with L'Ouverture, he advises him to take comfort in nature rather than perpetuate a struggle for his people, a notion that sublimates history, slavery, and the toils of the oppressed. Other poems of Wordsworth's that deal directly with slavery are the sonnet 'To Thomas Clarkson. On the Final Passing of the Bill for the Abolition of the Slave Trade' and several passages from Book X of *The Prelude*.

DD/SS

Wordsworth, William, *The Poetical Works of William Wordsworth* (ed. Paul D. Sheats, 1982)

See also BLAKE, WILLIAM; COWPER, WILLIAM; HAITI, BRITISH RELATIONS WITH; SOUTHEY, ROBERT

Y

Yearsley, Ann (bap. 1753, d. 1806). Poet and writer. Born Ann Cromartie, Yearsley was a milkwoman from Clifton, a suburb of Bristol, and represents one of the few women of the poorer classes of her day to acquire a reputation for her poetry. Her local reputation as a poet attracted the attention of Hannah *More, who secured a very long list of subscribers for the publication of Yearsley's *Poems, on Several Occasions*, in 1785, though the two subsequently quarrelled. 'Lactilla, or the Bristol Milkmaid', as Mrs Yearsley was called, wished to receive the capital from her subscriptions, but Hannah More prevaricated until the trust was handed over to a Bristol merchant and eventually to the poet.

Like More, Yearsley was drawn to the controversy about slavery, and in 1788 she published *A Poem on the Inhumanity of the Slave-Trade*. Her vivid description of the sufferings and death of an imaginary slave loses something from her calling him 'Indian Luco', even though he is a victim of what is clearly intended to be the transatlantic slave trade. Such confusion between exotic locations is not, however, uncommon in 18th-century British writing. Yearsley invites British slave traders to imagine members of their own families seized and sold into slavery, and denounces the hypocrisy of British culture and the legal system that was prepared to hang the man who stole a small sum of money out of hunger and desperation, but protected the slave trader who stole the lives and bodies of human beings.

JG

Richardson, Alan (ed.), *Slavery, Abolition and Emancipation: Writings in the British Romantic Period*, iv: *Verse* (1999)

See also ABOLITION; WHEATLEY, PHILLIS

Z

Zong. British slave ship carrying 132 African slaves thrown overboard for insurance money in an incident that generated support for the early *abolition movement. The *Zong* sailed from the island of St Thomas off the west coast of Africa for Jamaica on 6 September 1781. Under the command of Captain Luke Collingwood, the *Zong* carried approximately seventeen white crew members and 470 slaves.

By 29 November 60 slaves and seven Whites had died, with many of the remaining slaves ill and not expected to live long. Owing to the frequent deaths of slaves during transportation, a direct result of poor nutrition and conditions on board ship, insurance claims at the time did not cover slaves who died of natural causes such as disease or sickness. However, insurance could be claimed on slaves dying of unnatural causes, including drowning to prevent rebellion or to ensure the safety of the ship and crew, accident, or suicide.

Determined to limit financial loss to the shipowners (and also to himself—his contract granted him commission on the sale of the slaves in Jamaica), Collingwood decided to throw the sick slaves overboard and claim the insurance money upon return to England. The chief mate, James Kelsal, who initially protested against the captain's plan, was ordered to throw 123 slaves overboard over the course of three days, many of whom were shackled to prevent resistance. The total number of slaves killed was 132: ten slaves jumped willingly to their deaths while one managed to climb back on board. Slaves aboard the *Zong* were insured for £30 each.

The shipowners, a powerful Liverpool firm owned by William, John, and James Gregson, Edward Wilson, and James Aspinall, filed for full insurance when the *Zong* returned to London. They claimed that the 'unnatural death' of the slaves was necessary to ensure the safety of the crew, who were suffering from a lack of water. The *Zong*'s underwriters disagreed with the claim, arguing that none of the ship's crew had been on water rations by 29 November, the day the first 54 slaves were thrown overboard. Kelsal aided the insurers' defence, stating that the ship had experienced heavy rainfall that lasted for several days and produced six casks of water, sufficient for eleven days at full water allowance or 23 days at half-allowance, on 1 December, the day the second group of slaves was killed. The insurers also pointed to the fact that the *Zong* arrived in Jamaica on 22 December with 420 gallons of water to spare.

The insurance trial of *Gregson* v. *Gilbert* was heard at the Guildhall, London, on 6 March 1783. The jury, recognizing the African slaves as the property of the ship lost to the perils of the sea, sided with the shipowners and ordered the insurers to pay the £30 per slave stipulated by the insurance deal. The underwriters appealed the decision and applied to Lord Mansfield in the Court of King's Bench for a second trial on 21–2 May 1783. Lord Mansfield ruled for a new trial that would question whether Collingwood's treatment of the slaves was an act of jettison or insurance fraud. No record exists of this second trial, suggesting either that the trial did not take place or that the result did not concern a point of law and was decided on fact. Luke Collingwood, whom court testimony described as being in a state of delirium when he gave the order to throw the slaves overboard, died before the case was heard.

The *Zong* insurance case quickly sparked response from London's abolitionists. An anonymous article to the *Morning Chronicle and London Advertiser* on 18 March 1783 describing the horrors of the case caught the eye of Olaudah *Equiano, who brought it to the attention of Granville *Sharp. Sharp immediately launched an aggressive letter campaign by writing to the Oxford lawyer Dr Bever to ask for the prosecution of the captain and crew of the *Zong* on 132 counts of murder. Subsequent letters, informed by Sharp's attendance at the appeal hearings, called for a mass homicide trial and the abolition of the slave trade and were sent to the Bishops of Chester and Peterborough, the Admiralty Court, the Lords Commissioners of the Admiralty, and the Prime Minister. Depositions, vouchers, and a manuscript titled 'Account of the Murder of One Hundred and Thirty-Two Slaves on Board the Ship Zong' accompanied each letter. Sharp was not the only abolitionist to react to the *Zong* case; other critics included Thomas *Clarkson, John *Newton (*Thoughts Upon the African Slave Trade*, 1788), James *Ramsay (*An Essay on the Treatment and Conversion of African Slaves in the British Sugar Colonies*, 1784), and Ottobah *Cugoano (*Thoughts and Sentiments on the Evil of Slavery*, 1787).

Although a mass homicide trial never occurred, extensive newspaper coverage and the abolitionist reaction to the *Zong* insurance case did much to promote public awareness of their cause and organize the anti-slavery movement. The Quakers presented a petition for the abolition of slavery in 1783, the year of the trial, while four years later Sharp, Clarkson, William *Wilberforce, and others joined to form the Anti-Slavery Society.

Reaction to the *Zong* case was also seen from the government. Public outcry over the insurance trial is thought to have encouraged the Prime Minister, William Pitt, to call Parliament to consider the circumstances of the slave trade on 9 May 1788. In response a group of MPs toured a slave ship docked in the Thames. Horrified by the conditions on board, the MP for Oxford University, Sir William Dolben, proposed a bill regulating the transportation of African slaves by British ships. The bill prohibited the insurance of slaves under any circumstances other than piracy, natural disaster, insurrection, barratry, or fire, and made all contrary contracts null and void. Although MPs from slave ports protested against the bill, Dolben's Slave Carrying Bill was made law on 10 July 1788. An important revision in 1794 to Dolben's Law, as it became known, made it impossible to recover insurance on slaves thrown overboard, whatever the reason.

The *Zong* slaves were later commemorated in the famous painting by J. M. W. Turner entitled *Slavers Throwing Overboard the Dead and Dying, Typhoon Coming On* (1840). EDS

Shyllon, F. O., *Black Slaves in Britain* (1974)

See also BANKING, INSURANCE, AND THE COLONIAL TRADE

Chronology

43	Beginning of Roman rule in Britain
*c.*100–*c.*400	African auxiliary unit in the Roman army, the Numerus Maurorum Aurelianorum, stationed on Hadrian's Wall during part of this period
138	Quintus Lollius Urbicus, an African, governor of the Roman province of Britannia
211	Septimius Severus, African-born Roman emperor, dies at York
409	End of Roman rule in Britain
late 14th century	*Mandeville's Travels* popularizes the legend of Prester John in Europe
1501	Catherine of Aragon brings African attendants (including the trumpeter John Blanke) when she travels to England to marry Prince Arthur
1508	William Dunbar's poem 'Ane Blak More' records black presence at the court of the Scottish king James IV
1547	Pedro Negro knighted, perhaps the first African to receive an English knighthood
1562	First slaving voyage by John Hawkins marks beginning of British involvement in the transatlantic slave trade
1594	Shakespeare writes *Titus Andronicus*
1596	Queen Elizabeth I orders expulsion of Africans from England
	Sir Walter Ralegh publishes *Discovery of the Large, Rich and Beautiful Empire of Guiana*
1601	Queen Elizabeth I again orders expulsion of Africans from England
1604	First recorded performance of Shakespeare's *Othello*
1611	First recorded performance of Shakespeare's *The Tempest*
1623	English settlement in St Kitts, the earliest British colony in the Caribbean
1627	Coree the Saldanian killed in South Africa after his return from Britain
1636	Edward Colston born
1655	English expedition captures Jamaica from the Spanish
1657	Richard Ligon publishes *True & Exact History of the Island of Barbadoes*
1688	Aphra Behn's novel *Oroonoko* published
1690	John Montagu (later second Duke of Montagu) born
1695	Thomas Southerne adapts Aphra Behn's novel *Oroonoko* for the stage
1702	Scipio Africanus born
1703	John Wesley born
1707	Act of Union between England and Scotland, allowing Scots equal rights in previously English colonies; trade with North American and Caribbean colonies contributes significantly to development of Glasgow
1711	Richard Steele publishes story of Inkle and Yarico in *The Spectator*
1713	Treaty of Utrecht gives South Sea Company right to supply slaves to Spanish American colonies
1714	Accession of King George I
1719	Daniel Defoe publishes *Robinson Crusoe*
1720	Scipio Africanus dies
	South Sea Bubble
1721	Edward Colston dies
	Francis Williams admitted to Lincoln's Inn
1725	John Newton born
1726	Charles Middleton (later first Baron Barham) born
1729	Ignatius Sancho born on a slave ship
	Yorke–Talbot opinion supports the legality of slavery in Britain
1730	Josiah Wedgwood born
1731	Beilby Porteus born

1733	James Ramsay born
1733–4	Job ben Solomon in England
1735	Granville Sharp born
c.1736	Sambo dies and is buried at Sunderland Point, Lancaster
1741	Philip Quaque born at Cape Coast, West Africa
1745?	Olaudah Equiano born, according to his own account, somewhere in what is now south-eastern Nigeria
1748	William Ansah Sessarakoo, 'the Royal African', brought to Britain
1749	John Montagu (second Duke of Montagu) dies
1752?	Francis Barber enters the service of Samuel Johnson
1753	William Roscoe born
1754	Olaudah Equiano's first arrival in Britain
	Philip Quaque sent to Britain
	Julius Soubise born on St Kitts
1755	John Marrant born in New York
	Cesar Picton (original name unknown) born in West Africa
1756	Edward Rushton born
1759	William Wilberforce born
	John Hawkesworth writes new stage version of Aphra Behn's novel *Oroonoko*
	Francis Williams writes Latin ode addressed to the Governor of Jamaica
	Paul Cuffee born
1760	Briton Hammon publishes *Narrative of the Uncommon Sufferings and Suprizing Deliverance of Briton Hammon, a Negro Man*
	'Tacky's Revolt' (slave rebellion in Jamaica)
1761	Cesar Picton baptized in England
1762	Francis Williams dies in Jamaica
1763	Bill Richmond born in New York
1764	John Gladstone born
1765	Isaac Teale's poem *The Sable Venus* first published
	Philip Quaque becomes the first African priest of the Church of England (returns to Cape Coast the following year)
1766	John Hylas sues for return of his wife, Mary, sold back into slavery (wins his case in 1768)
1767	Legal case involving Jonathan Strong
1768	Zachary Macaulay born
	Isaac Bickerstaff's *The Padlock* first performed; the play's character Mungo is the first appearance of a black-face comic character on the English stage
	Thomas Gainsborough paints portrait of Ignatius Sancho
1769	Granville Sharp publishes *A Representation of the Injustice and Dangerous Tendency of Tolerating Slavery*
1772	Lord Mansfield delivers judgment in the case of James Somerset
1773	Jonathan Strong dies
	Case of *Knight* v. *Wedderburn* comes before the Scottish courts (finally decided 1778)
	Phillis Wheatley, African-American poet, visits Britain
	Phillis Wheatley's *Poems on Various Subjects* published in London; first book by a black woman to be published in Britain
	Thomas Day and John Bicknell publish poem *The Dying Negro*
1774	John Wesley publishes *Thoughts Upon Slavery*
	Edward Long publishes *The History of Jamaica*
1775	West India Committee founded
1779?	Painting of Dido Elizabeth Lindsay and her cousin Lady Elizabeth Murray, attributed to Johann Zoffany
1780	Ignatius Sancho dies
	William Wilberforce first elected to Parliament; continues as MP until 1825
1781	One hundred and thirty-two slaves thrown overboard from the ship *Zong* and drowned
1782	David Cunningham, one of the earliest known black Glaswegians, baptized

The Letters of the Late Ignatius Sancho, an African

1783 Court case relating to the ship *Zong* and insurance; attempt to prosecute those responsible for the deaths of the 132 slaves fails
Committee on the Slave Trade established by Quaker Meeting for Sufferings
Thomas Day publishes *The History of Sandford and Merton*, children's novel with anti-slavery theme

1784 Tom Molineaux born in Virginia
Samuel Johnson dies, leaving Francis Barber his residuary legatee
James Ramsay publishes *Essay on the Treatment and Conversion of African Slaves in the British Sugar Colonies*

1785 William Aldridge publishes *The Narrative of the Lord's Wonderful Dealings with John Marrant (A Black)*
Thomas Clarkson's Latin essay on slavery wins Cambridge University prize

1786 Thomas Fowell Buxton born

1787 Society (or Committee) for the Abolition of the Slave Trade established
Quobna Ottobah Cugoano publishes *Thoughts and Sentiments on the Evil . . . of Slavery*
Inkle and Yarico: An Opera, by George Colman the Younger, first produced
Edward Rushton publishes *West-Indian Eclogues*
William Roscoe publishes poem *The Wrongs of Africa*

1788 Peter Peckard publishes *Am I not a man and a brother?*
Hannah More publishes *Slavery, a Poem*
Ann Yearsley publishes *A Poem on the Inhumanity of the Slave-Trade*
John Newton publishes *Thoughts Upon the African Slave Trade*
African Association founded

1789 James Stephen born
James Ramsay dies
Olaudah Equiano publishes first edition of *Interesting Narrative*
William Blake publishes poem 'The Little Black Boy' in *Songs of Innocence*
French Revolution begins

1789–90 The Chevalier de Saint-Georges, black violinist, performs in London

1790 Anonymous novel *Memoirs and Opinions of Mr. Blenfield* published; possible first appearance of black British character in prose fiction

1791 John Marrant dies in London
John Wesley dies
Slave revolt in French Caribbean colony of Saint-Domingue; leads to colony's independence as the new nation of Haiti in 1804
Establishment of colony for freed slaves in Sierra Leone

1793 Joseph Sturge born
France declares war on Britain; British involvement in French revolutionary and Napoleonic wars (almost continuous until 1815) stimulates reactionary conservatism in domestic politics, which delays ending of the slave trade and colonial slavery

1795 William Daggers born in Jamaica
Josiah Wedgwood dies

1796 J. G. Stedman publishes *Narrative, of a Five Years' Expedition, Against the Revolted Negroes of Surinam*, including engravings by William Blake critical of slavery

1797 Olaudah Equiano dies
Robert Southey publishes anti-slave trade poems

1798 Julius Soubise dies

1799 Joseph Emidy, African-born violinist, released in Falmouth after a period of forced service on a British ship; works in Cornwall as a performer and composer until his death

1801 Francis Barber dies

1803 Edward Despard executed for treason; his widow, Catherine, is supported by a pension from the radical MP Sir Francis Burdett
Tom Molineaux, African-American boxer, migrates to Britain, where he continues his boxing career until 1815

1804	Independence of Haiti
1804?	Legh Richmond's *The Negro Servant* first published
1805	The boxer Bill Richmond's first major fights
1807	John Newton dies
	Britain abolishes its slave trade, with effect from 1 Jan. 1808
	William Wordsworth writes poem 'To Toussaint L'Ouverture'
1809	Thomas Birch Freeman born
	Beilby Porteus dies
1810	Sarah Baartman brought to Britain
	Tom Molineaux's famous fight against All-England champion Tom Cribb
1811	Paul Cuffee, African-American sea captain, visits Britain
	George Bridgetower, the black violinist, receives a degree from Cambridge University
1813	Charles Middleton (Baron Barham) dies
	Granville Sharp dies
1814	Edward Rushton dies
	Jane Austen publishes *Mansfield Park*
	Legh Richmond's *Annals of the Poor* first published (includes 'The Negro Servant')
1815	Napoleonic Wars end
	John Jea publishes *The Life, History, and Unparalleled Sufferings of John Jea, the African Preacher*, including descriptions of preaching tours in England and Ireland
1815/16	Sarah Baartman dies in Paris
1816	Philip Quaque dies at Cape Coast Castle
	Slave rebellion in Barbados
1817	Paul Cuffee dies
1818	Nathaniel Wells appointed Sheriff of Monmouthshire; first black person appointed to such a post
1819	William Daggers qualifies as solicitor in Liverpool
1820	William Davidson and others executed after failure of Cato Street Conspiracy
1821	Tom Molineaux dies
	Billy Waters appears as himself in Pierce Egan's *Life in London* at the Adelphi Theatre, London
1822	Billy Waters appears in *Life in London* at the Caledonian Theatre, Edinburgh
1823	Dadabhai Naoroji born in India
	Billy Waters dies in London
	Society for the Mitigation and Gradual Abolition of Slavery throughout the British Dominions (Anti-Slavery Society) established
	British government announces policies for 'amelioration' of the condition of the slaves in the Caribbean colonies
	Slave rebellion in Demerara
1825	Thomas Fowell Buxton becomes the leader in the House of Commons of the campaign against slavery
	Zachary Macaulay founds the *Anti-Slavery Reporter*
1826	Sarah Parker Remond born in the United States
1829	Bill Richmond dies
1831	William Roscoe dies
	Agency Committee of the Anti-Slavery Society formed
	The History of Mary Prince, a West Indian Slave published
	'Narrative of Louis Asa-Asa, a Captured African' published
1831–2	Slave rebellion in Jamaica
1832	Great Reform Bill becomes law; reduces strength of West Indian interest in Parliament
1833	William Wilberforce dies
	Emancipation Act passed: all slaves in British colonies formally free from 1 August 1834, though most remain subject to the apprenticeship system
	Ira Aldridge becomes first black actor to play Othello on the British stage
1834	Emancipation in British colonies, 1 Aug.
1835	Joseph Emidy dies in Truro

1835	James Africanus Horton born in Sierra Leone
1836	Cesar Picton dies
1837	Accession of Queen Victoria
1838	Zachary Macaulay dies
	Thomas Birch Freeman goes to the Gold Coast as a missionary
	First indentured immigrants brought to British Caribbean colonies from India
	End of apprenticeship system in British colonies, 1 Aug.
1839	British and Foreign Anti-Slavery Society (now Anti-Slavery International) established
	Thomas Fowell Buxton publishes *The African Slave Trade and Its Remedy*
1840	Zilpha Elaw, African-American evangelist, travels to Britain; claims to have preached over 1,000 sermons in different parts of Britain over the next five years
1842	William Cuffay elected president of the London Chartists
1843	Samuel Lewis born in Sierra Leone
	Second World Anti-Slavery Convention held in London
*c.*1843	Sarah Forbes Bonetta born in Dahomey
1845	Thomas Fowell Buxton dies
	Frederick Douglass, African-American abolitionist, tours Britain and Ireland (until 1847)
1847–8	William Thackeray's novel *Vanity Fair* receives serial publication
1848	William Cuffay sentenced to transportation to Van Diemen's Land
1849	William Wells Brown, African-American abolitionist, arrives in Britain; addresses over 1,000 meetings over the next four years
	Thomas Carlyle publishes 'Occasional Discourse on the Negro Question'
1850	Henry 'Box' Brown, African-American abolitionist, escapes to Liverpool and lectures in Britain
	James Pennington, African-American abolitionist, publishes *The Fugitive Blacksmith* in Britain
1850–68	African-American escaped slaves and anti-slavery activists William and Ellen Craft settle in Britain
1851	John Gladstone dies
	Great Exhibition held in London's Hyde Park
1853–4	Elizabeth Taylor Greenfield, African-American singer, tours Britain
1853–5	Samuel Ringgold Ward, African-American abolitionist, tours Britain
1854	Britain becomes involved in the Crimean War
1855	Mary Seacole goes to provide comforts for British troops in the Crimean War
	Samuel Ringgold Ward publishes *Autobiography of a Fugitive Negro*
1856	Crimean War ends
1857	*Wonderful Adventures of Mrs. Seacole* published
1857–8	Indian Mutiny
1858	Harriet Jacobs, African-American author, travels to Britain to seek a publisher
1859	James Africanus Horton graduates in medicine from the University of Edinburgh
	James Stephen dies
	Joseph Sturge dies
	Sarah Parker Remond, African-American abolitionist, arrives in Britain, where she lives until 1866, giving anti-slavery lectures and furthering her education
1860	Martin Delany, African-American abolitionist, visits Britain
	William Allen publishes *A Short Personal Narrative* in Dublin
	William and Ellen Craft publish *Running a Thousand Miles for Freedom*
1861	Dajazmach Alamayahu born
	Harriet Jacobs publishes *Incidents in the Life of a Slave Girl*
	American Civil War begins
1863	John Richard Archer born
1864	Samuel Ajayi Crowther consecrated as first African bishop of the Church of England
1865	Arthur Wharton born in the Gold Coast
	Charles Martin (Azaj Warqnah Ishete) born in Ethiopia
	Francis Galton first publishes his ideas on eugenics

1865	American Civil War ends
	Morant Bay rebellion in Jamaica
1866	Amanda Ira Aldridge born
	Thomas Wiggins ('Blind Tom' Bethune), African-American pianist, tours Britain
1868	James Africanus Horton publishes *West African Countries and Peoples*
1869	Henry Sylvester Williams born in Trinidad
	John Jacob Thomas publishes *The Theory and Practice of Creole Grammar* in Trinidad
1870	William Cuffay dies
1871	Samuel Lewis called to the Bar after studying in London; returns to Sierra Leone
	Edward Jenkins publishes *The Coolie: His Rights and Wrongs*
1871–8	Fisk Jubilee Singers tour Britain and Europe
1873	John Jacob Thomas reads a paper on Trinidad Creole before the Philological Society in London
1875	Samuel Coleridge-Taylor born
1876	Solomon Plaatje born in South Africa
1877	Edward Jenkins publishes *Lutchmee and Dilloo: A Study of West Indian Life*
1879	Dajazmach Alamayahu dies
1880	Sarah Forbes Bonetta dies
1881	Mary Seacole dies in London
	Andrew Watson (Scotland) becomes first recorded black international footballer
1883	James Africanus Horton dies
	Peter Thomas Stanford, African-American preacher, arrives in Britain, where he ministers until 1895
1884	Bandele Omoniyi born in Lagos
1886	William Daggers dies
	Colonial and Indian Exhibition held in London
	Arthur Wharton sets first world record for 100 yards dash; signs for Preston North End, becoming first black British footballer in the Football League
1887	Marcus Garvey born in Jamaica
	Colwyn Bay Institute (later the African Training Institute) established in Wales (closed 1911)
	British Guianan writer Leo (Egbert Martin) wins Empire-wide competition to add verses to 'God Save the Queen'
1888	Walter Tull born
	M. K. Gandhi arrives in London to train as a barrister; remains for three years
	J. A. Froude publishes *The English in the West Indies*
	Booker T. Washington founds Tuskegee Institute in the United States
1889	Claude McKay born in Jamaica
	John Jacob Thomas dies in London
	Froudacity: West India Fables by J. A. Froude, Explained by J. J. Thomas published in London
1890	William Miller born
	Thomas Birch Freeman dies
1891	Samuel Ajayi Crowther dies
1892	Dadabhai Naoroji elected MP for Finsbury, becoming first Asian member of the House of Commons
	Celestine Edwards becomes editor of *Lux*
1893	Nathaniel Fadipe born in Nigeria
	Newspaper *Fraternity* first published, with Celestine Edwards as editor; ceases publication 1896
1894	Celestine Edwards dies in Dominica
	Sarah Parker Remond dies in Italy
1895	Visit to Britain of three Bechuana chiefs persuades government to prevent their territory from being absorbed into Rhodesia, thus securing eventual creation of an independent Botswana
1896	Samuel Lewis becomes first African to receive a British knighthood
	Oswald Mosley born

1896	Henry Sylvester Williams arrives in Britain
	The Wandering Negro Minstrels (director: Louis Lumière) shot in London; one of the earliest films to feature black actors
1897	Marian Anderson born in the United States
	Paul Dunbar, African-American poet's reading tour in Britain
	British Museum acquires large collection of works of art from Benin City
1898	Paul Robeson born in the United States
	Samuel Coleridge-Taylor premieres his most famous work, *Hiawatha's Wedding Feast*
	Bobby Dobbs, African-American boxer, makes first visit to Britain
1899	Booker T. Washington's first visit to Britain
	Joseph Conrad's *Heart of Darkness* serialized in *Blackwood's Magazine*
1900	Leslie Hutchinson born in Grenada
	Ronald Moody born in Jamaica
	First Pan-African Conference, London
1901	Queen Victoria dies
	Jack Leslie born
	Learie Constantine born in Trinidad
	C. L. R. James born in Trinidad
	Leslie Thompson born in Jamaica
	Adelaide Hall born in New York
	Royal African Society founded
1902	Malcolm Nurse (later known as George Padmore) born in Trinidad
	Ham Mukasa, Ugandan diplomat, visits Britain for Edward VII's coronation; publishes his journal in 1904
	Bobby Dobbs returns to Britain and remains for eight years, competing in 42 prize fights
1903	Samuel Lewis dies in Sierra Leone
	Musical show *In Dahomey*, with African-American cast, a success in London
1904	Edward Nelson called to the Bar
1905	Una Marson born in Jamaica
	Fela Sowande born in Nigeria
	Bandele Omoniyi arrives in Britain
1906	Henry Sylvester Williams elected to Marylebone Council
1906–8	The Kingston Choral Union tours Britain and Ireland as the Native Choir from Jamaica
1907	Only issue of *The Telephone* published
	Andrew Jeptha becomes the first black boxer to hold a British title
1908	Bandele Omoniyi publishes *A Defence of the Ethiopian Movement*
1908–9	Walter Tull plays for Clapton Football Club
1909	Peter Blackman born in Barbados
	Carmen Maingot (later Carmen England) born in Trinidad
	Augustus Merriman-Labor publishes *Britons Through Negro Spectacles*
	Walter Tull plays for Tottenham Hotspur
1910	Booker T. Washington's second visit to Britain
	Walter Tull transferred to Northampton Town Football Club, where he plays until the outbreak of the First World War
1911	Henry Sylvester Williams dies
1912	Esther Bruce born
	Enoch Powell born
	Samuel Coleridge-Taylor dies
	Booker T. Washington publishes *The Man Farthest Down*
1912–14	Marcus Garvey's first visit to Britain
1913	Oswald Denniston born in Jamaica
	David Pitt (later Lord Pitt of Hampstead) born in Grenada
	Bandele Omoniyi dies in Brazil
	John Richard Archer elected Mayor of Battersea, Britain's first black mayor
	Edward Nelson first elected to the local council, Hale, Cheshire

1913	African-American string band the Versatile Four starts residency at Murray's Club, London; beginnings of vogue for jazz in Britain
1914	Cecil Belfield Clarke arrives in London from Barbados
	Winifred Atwell born in Trinidad
	Ken 'Snakehips' Johnson born in British Guiana
	Dave Wilkins born in Barbados
	First World War starts; many black troops from Britain's African and Caribbean colonies involved
1914–17	Solomon Plaatje lives in London
1915	Claudia Jones born in Trinidad
1916	West African Student Christian Union founded
	Solomon Plaatje publishes *Native Life in South Africa*
1917	Dadabhai Naoroji dies
	Sir Harry Johnson publishes *The Black Man's Part in the War*
	Attacks on black people in Canning Town, London
	Walter Tull becomes a second lieutenant; first Black to receive an officer's commission in a British Army infantry regiment
	System of indentured immigration from India to British Caribbean colonies ends
1918	Walter Tull killed in action in France
	First World War ends
1919	John Carter born in British Guiana
	'Race' riots in several British cities direct violent attacks against black people
	Claude McKay arrives in Britain, where he lives and works until 1921
	Southern Syncopated Orchestra first performs in London; tours Britain and Ireland until 1921
	Marcus Garvey establishes Universal Negro Improvement Association in New York
	Gandhi begins campaign against British rule in India
1920	British government issues Aliens Order
	Roger Fry writes influential essay 'Negro Sculpture'
1920–1	Roland Hayes, African-American singer, performs in Britain
1921	Jack Leslie starts career at Plymouth Argyle Football Club (continues until 1934)
1922	Paul Robeson's first visit to Britain
1923	Sam Selvon born in Trinidad
	Ronald Moody migrates to Britain, where he develops his career as a sculptor
	Learie Constantine first tours England with West Indies cricket team
1924	Beryl Gilroy born in British Guiana
	Leslie Hutchinson, performer and cabaret artiste, settles in London
1924–5	British Empire Exhibition
1925	Malcolm Little (later Malcolm X) born in the United States
	British government issues Special Restriction (Coloured Seamen) Order
	William Miller first elected to Plymouth City Council
	West African Students' Union founded
	Marian Anderson moves to London at the beginning of a ten-year period establishing her musical career in Europe
	International African Institute founded
1926	Aubrey Williams born in British Guiana
1927	'Shake' Keane born in St Vincent
	John La Rose born in Trinidad
1928	Kath Locke born
	Andrew Salkey born in Panama
1929	Leslie Thompson migrates to Britain, where he pursues a career as a jazz musician until 1954
	British Boxing Board of Control established; restricts championships 'to boxers of white parents'
1930	Arthur Wharton dies
	'Arab riot' in South Shields

1930 Paul Robeson first plays Othello in a British production
Coronation of Haile Selassie as Emperor of Ethiopia

1931 Coloured Seamen's Union formed in Cardiff
League of Coloured Peoples founded
Negro Welfare Association founded (active until the Second World War)
Adelaide Hall, African-American vocalist, makes first visit to Britain
African Churches Mission founded in Liverpool (closed 1949)
Carmen Maingot (later Carmen England) first comes to Britain to pursue her musical career

1932 Anna Rutherford born in Australia
C. L. R. James moves to Britain
Una Marson first moves to Britain
John Richard Archer dies
Oswald Mosley forms the British Union of Fascists

1933 Michael de Freitas (later Michael X) born in Trinidad

1934 Nancy Cunard publishes influential anthology *NEGRO*

1935 Vincent Albert Reid born in Jamaica
Marcus Garvey moves to Britain and runs Universal Negro Improvement Association from London
Amy Ashwood Garvey manages a restaurant in London (until 1938) which becomes a meeting place for Pan-Africanists
Italian invasion of Ethiopia

1936 Haile Selassie, Emperor of Ethiopia, living in exile in Bath (until 1941); Una Marson works for a short period as his secretary
C. L. R. James's play *Black Majesty* staged in London, with Paul Robeson as Toussaint L'Ouverture
New Times and Ethiopian News founded; continues publication until 1956

1937 Ken 'Snakehips' Johnson forms band which becomes known as the West Indian Dance Orchestra
International African Service Bureau established (later merged with Pan-African Federation)

1938 C. L. R. James publishes *The Black Jacobins*
International African Opinion first published (closed following the outbreak of the Second World War)
Adelaide Hall, African-American vocalist, settles in London; becomes first black star to secure long-term contract with the BBC

1939 Second World War starts; many African and Caribbean people arrive in Britain to help with the war effort; later arrivals of US armed forces include many black troops

1940 Marcus Garvey dies in London
Edward Nelson dies

1941 Musicians Ken 'Snakehips' Johnson and Dave Williams killed by bombing of Café de Paris during air raid
British government begins recruiting service personnel and skilled workers from the Caribbean to help war effort
Una Marson appointed programme assistant for BBC's *Calling the West Indies* (until 1945, when she returns to Jamaica)

1942 United States troops (including many African-Americans) begin to arrive in Britain; attempts to maintain segregationist policies by both US military authorities and British officials cause conflict
Rudolph Dunbar appears as first black conductor of the London Philharmonic Orchestra

1943 Learie Constantine and his family refused accommodation at the Imperial Hotel, London, on racist grounds
Peter Milliard founds Negro Association (Manchester)
Riots between black and white American servicemen in Bristol
BBC's *Caribbean Voices* programme starts (broadcast until 1958)

1944	Amryl Johnson born in Trinidad Bernie Grant born in British Guiana Nathaniel Fadipe dies Pan-African Federation formed Eric Williams publishes *Capitalism and Slavery* MacDonald Bailey arrives in Britain to serve in the Royal Air Force, and soon makes his mark as a champion athlete
1945	Second World War ends Pan-African Congress (Manchester); Amy Ashwood Garvey delivers paper on women's rights
1946	Winifred Atwell arrives in London to study at the Royal Academy of Music Salim Charles Wilson dies West Indian Students' Union formed First performance by black dance group Les Ballets Nègres (operates until 1953) Ronald Moody's first one-man show in London
1947	David Pitt settles in London Independence of India and Pakistan marks beginning of dismantling of Britain's colonial empire
1948	Claude McKay dies in Chicago British Nationality Act *Empire Windrush* arrives at Tilbury docks, Kent (youngest West Indian passenger is Vincent Albert Reid) Ban on black title challengers in British boxing ends; Dick Turpin successfully challenges for the British middleweight title Gandhi assassinated in India
1950	Sam Selvon migrates to Britain, where he lives until 1978 Winifred Atwell signs recording contract with Decca
1951	Randolph Turpin becomes first black British boxer to win a world title, beating Sugar Ray Robinson
1952	Olive Morris born Andrew Salkey migrates to Britain, where he lives until 1976 Dambudzo Marechera born in Southern Rhodesia Charles Martin (Azaj Warqnah Ishete) dies in Ethiopia Africa Social and Technical Society established (Liverpool) Sam Selvon publishes his first novel, *A Brighter Sun* 'Shake' Keane migrates to Britain, where he lives for the next twenty years and becomes famous as a jazz musician Visit by African-American singer Mahalia Jackson introduces gospel music inside British churches MacDonald Bailey wins a bronze medal for Britain in the 100 metres at the Olympic Games in Helsinki Aubrey Williams settles in London and develops his career as an artist
1954	Billy Boston becomes first black rugby player to represent the British Lions on tour of Australia
1955	Montgomery bus boycott in the United States
1956	Laurie Cunningham born Amanda Ira Aldridge dies London Transport starts actively recruiting in Barbados Sam Selvon publishes *The Lonely Londoners* George Padmore publishes *Pan Africanism or Communism?* Pearl and Edric Connor found first theatrical agency to represent black actors, writers, and film-makers in Britain
1957	Michael de Freitas (later Michael X) migrates to Britain, where he lives until 1971 Gold Coast becomes independent, taking the name Ghana; first African colony to become independent from Britain
1958	Institute of Race Relations established

1958	Riots in Nottingham and Notting Hill
	Errol John's play *Moon on a Rainbow Shawl* produced at the Royal Court Theatre, London; first major British production of a play by a black writer
	Kelso Cochran murdered
1959	George Padmore dies in London
	Launch of campaign in Britain for boycott of South African goods; later becomes Anti-Apartheid Movement
	Beginnings of Notting Hill Carnival as indoor event at St Pancras Town Hall; becomes street festival in 1960s
	Andrew Salkey publishes his first novel, *A Quality of Violence*
	Paul Robeson once again plays Othello in a British production
1960	Sharpeville massacre in South Africa
1961	John La Rose migrates to Britain
	David Pitt elected to London County Council
	Hayter Report leads to establishment of centres of African Studies in British universities
1962	Learie Constantine knighted
	Commonwealth Immigrants Act
	Visit of Broadway show *Black Nativity* is first major exposure of British audiences to gospel music
	Jamaica and (later) Trinidad and Tobago become the first of Britain's Caribbean colonies to gain independence
1963	Bristol bus boycott
	Ten Bob in Winter (director: Lloyd Reckord); first British film with entirely black cast
	Arrest of Nelson Mandela and other ANC leaders in South Africa
	Civil rights march on Washington in the United States
1964	Claudia Jones dies in London
	Martin Luther King visits Britain
	Ska emerges on the British music scene
	Centre for Contemporary Cultural Studies established at the University of Birmingham (closed 2002)
1965	Una Marson dies in Jamaica
	Race Relations Act
	Malcolm X makes significant visit to Britain, shortly before his assassination in New York
	Campaign Against Racial Discrimination (CARD) established
	Government of Ian Smith issues Unilateral Declaration of Independence in Southern Rhodesia
1966	Randolph Turpin dies
	London Transport extends recruitment scheme to Jamaica and Trinidad
	Caribbean Artists' Movement established (continues until 1972)
	New Beacon Books established
	Black Panther Party formed in the United States
1968	Leslie Hutchinson dies
	Edric Connor dies
	Commonwealth Immigrants Act
	Race Relations Act
	Enoch Powell's 'Rivers of Blood' speech at Walsall
1968–96	Anna Rutherford directs the Commonwealth Literature Centre at the University of Aarhus
1969	David Oluwale becomes the first black person to die in police custody
	Amy Ashwood Garvey dies in Jamaica
	Learie Constantine becomes the first black member of the House of Lords
	Police assault on Olive Morris starts her career as an activist
	Bogle-L'Ouverture Publications established
	Newsletter of the Institute of Race Relations renamed *Race Today*

1970 Cecil Belfield Clarke dies
William Miller dies
Hansib Publications established
1971 Immigration Act
Bernard Coard publishes *How the West Indian Child Is Made Educationally Sub-Normal in the British School System*
1972 Walter Rodney publishes *How Europe Underdeveloped Africa*
Ethiopian World Federation established in London
Clive Sullivan becomes first black captain of a British national team in any sport; leads rugby league team to a World Cup win
1973 Kath Locke establishes George Jackson House for homeless children (Manchester)
Trevor McDonald begins working for ITN (knighted 1999; retires 2005)
1974 Dambudzo Marechera granted political asylum in Britain; remains until his return to Zimbabwe in 1982
David Pitt becomes first black chairman of the Greater London Council
Darcus Howe becomes editor of *Race Today*
First British dub album appears (Keith Hudson, *Pick a Dub*)
Twelve Tribes of Israel headquarters established in London
1975 Michael X (Michael de Freitas) hanged in Trinidad
David Pitt created a life peer as Baron Pitt of Hampstead
Centreprise Publications established
Pressure (director: Horace Ové); first feature-length black British film
1976 Paul Robeson dies in the United States
Commission for Racial Equality established
Society for Caribbean Studies established
The Fosters, first British television comedy series with all-black cast (ITV; runs until 1978)
Beryl Gilroy publishes *Black Teacher*
Soweto rising in South Africa
1977 Commonword established
Kokuma Dance Company founded (Birmingham; functions until 2004)
Laurie Cunningham becomes first black footballer to play for England in the under-21 team
1978 Organization of Women of African and Asian Descent formed (continues until 1983)
Empire Road, first black British television soap (BBC; runs until 1979)
Edward Said, Arab-American scholar, publishes *Orientalism*
Viv Anderson becomes first black player to represent England at football
1979 Blair Peach killed during anti-fascist demonstration in Southall
Olive Morris dies
Dambudzo Marechera's *The House of Hunger* wins the *Guardian* Fiction Prize
1980 Oswald Mosley dies
Riots in St Paul's district of Bristol
Handsworth Cultural Centre founded
Daley Thompson wins a gold medal in the decathlon at the Moscow Olympics
1981 Scarman Report
Brixton and Toxteth riots
New Cross fire
Barbados-born Roland Butcher becomes first black cricketer to play for England
1982 International Book Fair of Radical Black and Third World Books founded (continues until 1995)
London Community Gospel Choir founded
1983 Winifred Atwell dies
Akira Press founded
1984 Visit of South African Prime Minister P. W. Botha to Britain leads to massive demonstrations in London organized by the Anti-Apartheid Movement
Centre for Caribbean Studies established at the University of Warwick
News for Babylon (major anthology of Caribbean and black British poetry) published

1984 DJ Newtrament and Krew bring out 'London Bridge Is Falling Down', widely regarded as first authentically British hip hop tune
Los Angeles Olympics: Daley Thompson wins gold medal in the decathlon for the second time; Tessa Sanderson wins gold in the javelin event, to become first black British woman to win Olympic gold

1985 Lord Pitt of Hampstead elected president of the British Medical Association
Karia Press founded; Karnak House founded
Amryl Johnson publishes *Long Road to Nowhere*
Community and Village Entertainment Arts Centre founded (Birmingham)
Wilfred Wood becomes Bishop of Croydon, the first black Anglican bishop in England (retires 2002)

1986 *Handsworth Songs* (director: John Akomfrah), documentary by Black Audio Film Collective
Black Dance Development Trust founded (Birmingham)
Beryl Gilroy publishes her first novel, *Frangipani House*

1987 Leslie Thompson dies
Dambudzo Marechera dies in Zimbabwe
Fela Sowande dies
General election sees Diane Abbott, Paul Boateng, Bernie Grant, and Keith Vaz elected as Labour MPs
Black History Month first observed in Britain

1988 Jack Leslie dies
Centre for Caribbean Studies established at London Metropolitan University
Race Today ceases publication
David Lawrence becomes first British-born black cricketer to play for England

1989 C. L. R. James dies in London
Laurie Cunningham dies
'Art from South Africa' exhibition, Museum of Modern Art, Oxford
Desmond's, sitcom (Channel 4; runs until 1995)

1990 Aubrey Williams dies
Dave Wilkins dies
Nelson Mandela released from prison in South Africa

1991 Carmen England dies
Mustapha Matura's *The Coup* is first play by a black dramatist to be commissioned by Britain's National Theatre
Ben Okri wins the Booker Prize for *The Famished Road*
Isaac Julien's first feature film, *Young Soul Rebels*
Stephen Bourne and Esther Bruce publish *Aunt Esther's Story*

1992 X Press founded
Amryl Johnson publishes *Gorgons*
Kath Locke dies

1993 Stephen Lawrence murdered
Peter Blackman dies
Adelaide Hall dies
Marian Anderson dies in the United States

1994 Esther Bruce dies
Lord Pitt of Hampstead (David Pitt) dies
Sam Selvon dies
Official end of apartheid in South Africa; Nelson Mandela becomes the country's first democratically elected president

1995 Andrew Salkey dies
'Africa: The Art of a Continent' exhibition in London
africa95 arts festival in London

1998 Enoch Powell dies
Commemoration of 50th anniversary of the arrival of the *Empire Windrush*
Chris Ofili wins the Turner Prize

1999	MacPherson Report
	Steve McQueen wins the Turner Prize
2000	Oswald Denniston dies
	Bernie Grant dies
	Institute of Commonwealth Studies launches Caribbean Studies, Black and Asian History project (CASBAH)
	Damilola Taylor murdered
2001	Amryl Johnson dies
	Vincent Albert Reid dies
	Anna Rutherford dies
	British Museum opens new Africa gallery
	Major terrorist attacks in the United States on 11 September
2002	Paul Boateng appointed Chief Secretary to the Treasury, becoming first black Cabinet minister
	Inauguration of Memorial Gates, Constitution Hill, London
	France returns remains of Sarah Baartman to South Africa, where she is given an official funeral
2003	Baroness Amos becomes first black woman to be a Cabinet minister
2004	'Black Style' show, Victoria and Albert Museum, London
	Jason Robinson becomes first black captain of the England rugby union team
2005	John Carter dies
	Pearl Connor dies
	Adam Afriyie becomes first black Conservative MP in the general election
	Suicide bombings in London on 7 July
	Report of the Commission for Africa, chaired by Tony Blair
	Captured Africans (memorial to victims of the slave trade) erected in Lancaster
	Frank Bowling becomes first black British artist elected to the Royal Academy
	'Africa Remix' show, Hayward Gallery, London
	Independent Black Publishers Association established
	John Sentamu becomes first black Archbishop of York
2006	John La Rose dies

Select Bibliography

ADI, HAKIM, *West Africans in Britain: Nationalism, Pan-Africanism and Communism* (1998).

—— and SHERWOOD, MARIKA (eds.), *The 1945 Manchester Pan-African Congress Revisited* (1995).

—— —— *Pan-African History: Political Figures from Africa and the Diaspora Since 1787* (2003).

AJAYI, J. F. A., *Christian Missions in Nigeria 1841–1891: The Making of a New Elite* (1965).

ALI, R., and O'CINNEIDE, C., *Our House? Race and Representation in British Politics* (2002).

ALIBHAI-BROWN, YASMIN, *Mixed Feelings* (2001).

AMOS, V., and PARMAR, P., 'Challenging Imperial Feminism', *Feminist Review*, Special Issue, 17 (1984).

ANDERSON, GERALD H., *et al.* (eds.), *Mission Legacies* (1994).

ANSARI, HUMAYUN, *'The Infidel Within': Muslims in Britain Since 1800* (2004).

ANSTEY, R., and HAIR, P. E. H. (eds.), *Liverpool, the African Slave Trade, and Abolition* (1989).

ANWAR, M., *The Myth of Return* (1979).

—— 'The Participation of Ethnic Minorities in British Politics', *Journal of Ethnic and Migration Studies*, 27/3 (2001).

ARAEEN, RASHEED (ed.), *The Other Story: Afro-Asian Artists in Post-War Britain* (1989).

ARHIN, KWAME (ed.), *The Papers of George Ekem Ferguson: A Fanti Official of the Government of the Gold Coast, 1890–1897* (1974).

ARNOLD, DAVID, *Gandhi* (2001).

BAILEY, S., and HALL, S. (eds.), *The Critical Decade: Black British Photography in the 1980s* (1992).

BARKAN, ELAZAR, *The Retreat of Scientific Racism: Changing Concepts of Race in Britain and the United States Between the World Wars* (1996).

BARRETT, M., and MCINTOSH, M., 'Ethnocentrism and Socialist Feminist Theory', *Feminist Review*, 20 (1985).

BASSANI, E., and FAGG, W. B., *Africa and the Renaissance: Art in Ivory* (1988).

BATES, DARRELL, *The Abyssinian Difficulty* (1979).

BELL, HOWARD H., *Search for a Place: Black Separatism and Africa, 1860* (1971).

BENNETT, A., *Popular Music and Youth Culture: Music Identity and Place* (2000).

BHABHA, HOMI, *The Location of Culture* (1994).

BHAVNANI, K. and COULSON, M., 'Transforming Socialist Feminism: The Challenge of Racism', *Feminist Review*, 23 (1986).

BIRLEY, ANTHONY, *The African Emperor: Septimius Severus* (1988).

BIRTLEY, JACK, *The Tragedy of Randolph Turpin* (1975).

BIRTWHISTLE, ALLEN, *Thomas Birch Freeman: West African Pioneer* (1950).

Black and Asian Studies Association Newsletter (1991–).

BLACKETT, R. J. M., *Beating Against the Barriers: The Lives of Six Nineteenth-Century Afro-Americans* (1986).

BOURNE, STEPHEN, *Black in the British Frame: The Black Experience in British Film and Television 1896–1996* (2001).

—— *Speak of Me As I Am: The Black Presence in Southwark Since 1600* (2005).

—— and BRUCE, ESTHER, *Aunt Esther's Story* (1996).

BOUSQUET, BEN, and DOUGLAS, COLIN, *West Indian Women at War: British Racism in World War II* (1991).

BRAH, AVTAR, and COOMBES, ANNIE (eds.), *Hybridity and Its Discontents: Politics, Science, Culture* (2000).

BRANTLINGER, PATRICK, *Rule of Darkness: British Literature and Imperialism, 1830–1914* (1988).

BREESE, CHARLOTTE, *Hutch* (1999).

BRESSEY, CAROLINE, 'Of Africa's Brightest Ornaments: A Short Biography of Sarah Forbes Bonetta', *Social and Cultural Geography*, 6/2 (2005).

BROEZE, F. J. A., 'The Muscles of Empire: Indian Seamen and the Raj, 1919–1939', *Indian Economic and Social History Review*, 18/1 (Jan.–Mar. 1981).

BROOKS, DENNIS, *Race and Labour in London Transport* (1975).

BROOKS, TIM, *Lost Sounds: Blacks and the Birth of the Recording Industry 1890–1919* (2004).

BROUGHTON, VIV, *Black Gospel: An Illustrated History of the Gospel Sound* (1985).

BROWN, STEWART, 'Amryl Johnson', *The Guardian*, 29 Mar. 2001.

BRYAN, BEVERLEY, DADZIE, STELLA, and SCAFE, SUZANNE, *The Heart of the Race: Black Women's Lives in Britain* (1985).

CAIRNS, J. W., 'Stoicism, Slavery, and Law: Grotian Jurisprudence and Its Reception' in H. W. Blom and L. C. Winkel (eds.), *Grotius and the Stoa* (2004).

CAMERON, N. E. (ed.), *Guyanese Poetry* (1931).

CAREY, BRYCCHAN, *British Abolitionism and the Rhetoric of Sensibility: Writing, Sentiment and Slavery, 1760–1807* (2005).

CARRETTA, VINCENT, *Equiano the African* (2005).

—— (ed.), *Unchained Voices: An Anthology of Black Authors in the English-Speaking World of the Eighteenth Century* (1996).

CARSWELL, J., *The South Sea Bubble* (1961).

CARTER, BOB, HARRIS, CLIVE, and JOSHI, SHIRLEY, 'The 1951–55 Conservative Government and the Racialisation of Black Immigration', *Immigrants and Minorities*, 6/3 (1987).

CARTER, T., *Shattering Illusions: West Indians in British Politics* (1986).

CASHMORE, E. ELLIS., *United Kingdom: Class, Race and Gender Since the War* (1989).

CENTRE FOR CONTEMPORARY CULTURAL STUDIES, *The Empire Strikes Back: Race and Racism in 70s Britain* (1982).

CHAUDHURI, S. B., *English Historical Writings on the Indian Mutiny 1857–1859* (1979).

CHIGWADA-BAILEY, R., *Black Women's Experiences of Criminal Justice: Race, Gender and Class: A Discourse of Disadvantage* (2003).

CHILTON, JOHN, *Who's Who of British Jazz* (1997).

COHEN, ABNER, *Masquerade Politics: Explorations in the Structure of Urban Cultural Movements* (1993).

COLLEY, LINDA, *Captives, Britain, Empire and the World 1600–1850* (2002).

COLLINGWOOD, ROBIN GEORGE, and WRIGHT, RICHARD PEARSON, *The Roman Inscriptions of Britain: Inscriptions on Stone* (1965).

CONSTANTINE, LEARIE, *Cricket and I* (1933).

COSTELLO, R., *Black Liverpool: The Early History of Britain's Oldest Black Community 1730–1918* (2001).

COURTMAN, SANDRA, '"Blacks in Ivory Towers Can't Write About Ghettos": West Indian Worker Writers in 1970's Britain' in Kadija Sesay (ed.), *Write Black, Write British: From Post Colonial to Black British* (2005).

DABYDEEN, D., *Hogarth's Blacks: Images of Blacks in Eighteenth Century English Art* (1985).

—— (ed.), *The Black Presence in English Literature* (1985).

—— (ed.), *The Windrush Commemorative Issue: West Indians in Britain 1948–1998, Kunapipi*, 20 (1998).

—— and SANDHU, SUKHDEV (eds.), *Slavery, Abolition and Emancipation: Writings in the British Romantic Period*, i: *Black Writers* (1999).

DANCE, DARYL CUMBER (ed.), *Fifty Caribbean Writers: A Bio-Bibliographical Critical Source Book* (1986).

DARDEN, ROBERT, *People Get Ready! A New History of Gospel Music* (2005).

DAVEY, KEVIN, *English Imaginaries: Anglo-British Approaches to Modernity* (1998).

DAVIDSON, BASIL, *Africa in History: Themes and Outlines* (2nd edn., 1974).

DAVIES, K. G., *The Royal African Company* (1957).

DAVIS, ROBERT C., *Christian Slaves, Muslim Masters: White Slavery in the Mediterranean, the Barbary Coast, and Italy, 1500–1800* (2004).

DEBRUNNER, H. W., *Presence and Prestige* (1978).

DENCH, G., *The Place of Men in Changing Family Cultures* (1996).

DEVERE BRODY, JENNIFER, *Impossible Purities: Blackness, Femininity, and Victorian Culture* (1998).

DONNELL, ALISON, and WELSH, SARAH LAWSON (eds.), *The Routledge Reader in Caribbean Literature* (1996).

DOWSON, J., and ENTWISTLE, A., *A History of Twentieth-Century British Women's Poetry* (2005).

DRESSER, MADGE, *Slavery Obscured: The Social History of the Slave Trade in an English Provincial Port* (2001).

DUBERMAN, MARTIN BAUML, *Paul Robeson* (1989).

DUFFIELD, IAN, 'Dusé Mohamed Ali: His Purpose and His Public' in Alastair Niven (ed.), *The Commonwealth Writer Overseas* (1976).

DUNN, GILLIAN, *Africans in Chester* (2004).

EARLE, T. F., and LOWE, K. J. P. (eds.), *Black Africans in Renaissance Europe* (2005).

EDWARDS, JOEL, and KILLINGRAY, DAVID (eds.), *Black British Christian Voices 1770–2000: An Anthology* (2007).

EDWARDS, PAUL (ed.), *The Life of Olaudah Equiano* (1969).

—— and WALVIN, JAMES, *Black Personalities in the Era of the Slave Trade* (1983).

EICKELMANN, CHRISTINE, and SMALL, DAVID, *Pero: The Life of a Slave in Eighteenth-Century Bristol* (2004).

ELDER, M., *The Slave Trade and the Economic Development of Eighteenth Century Lancaster* (1992).

ELKINS, W. F., 'Hercules and the Society of Peoples of African Origin', *Caribbean Studies*, 1/4 (1972).

ERDMAN, DAVID V., *Blake: Prophet Against Empire* (1977).

FABIAN, ROBERT, *London After Dark* (1954).

FAULKNER, SIMON, and RAMAMURTHY, ANANDI (eds.), *Visual Culture and Decolonisation in Britain* (2006).

FERGUSON, NIALL, *Empire: How Britain Made the Modern World* (2003).

FICK, CAROLYN E., *The Making of Haiti: The Saint Domingue Revolution from Below* (1990).

FLETCHER, MURIEL E., *Report on an Investigation into the Colour Problem in Liverpool and Other Ports* (1930).

FLOYD, SAMUEL A., JR. (ed.), *Dictionary of Black Composers* (1999).

FONER, NANCY, 'The Jamaicans: Cultural and Social Change Among Migrants in Britain' in J. L. Watson (ed.), *Between Two Cultures: Migrants and Minorities in Britain* (1977).

FORD, AMOS, *Telling the Truth: The Life and Times of the British Honduran Forestry Unit in Scotland (1941–44)* (1985).

FRANCIS, ARMET, *The Black Triangle: The People of the African Diaspora* (1985).

FREEMAN, R. B., 'Darwin's Negro Bird-Stuffer', *Notes and Records of the Royal Society of London*, 33/1 (1978).

FRYER, PETER, *Staying Power: The History of Black People in Britain* (1984).

FULLER, SOPHIE, *The Pandora Guide to Women Composers: Britain and the United States, 1629–Present* (1994).

FYFE, CHRISTOPHER, *Africanus Horton, West African Scientist and Patriot* (1972).

—— *A History of Sierra Leone* (1962).

GEISS, I., *The Pan-African Movement* (1974).

GERZINA, GRETCHEN, *Black England: Life Before Emancipation* (1995).

—— (ed.), *Black Victorians/Black Victoriana* (2003).

GILMORE, JOHN, *Faces of the Caribbean* (2000).

—— *The Poetics of Empire: A Study of James Grainger's 'The Sugar-Cane'* (2000).

GILROY, PAUL, *The Black Atlantic: Modernity and Double Consciousness* (1993).

—— *There Ain't No Black in the Union Jack* (1987).

GOODY, JACK, *The Expansive Moment: The Rise of Social Anthropology in Britain and Africa 1918–1970* (1995).

GOULBOURNE, H., *Race Relations in Britain Since 1945* (1998).

—— and CHAMBERLAIN, M. (eds.), *Caribbean Families in Britain and the Trans-Atlantic World* (2001).

GOULD, STEPHEN JAY, *The Mismeasure of Man* (1981).

GRANT, DOUGLAS, *The Fortunate Slave: An Illustration of African Slavery in the Early Eighteenth Century* (1968).

GREEN, JEFFREY, 'Afro-American Symphony' in Paul Oliver (ed.), *Black Music in Britain: Essays on the Afro-Asian Contribution to Popular Music* (1990).

—— *Black Edwardians: Black People in Britain 1901–1914* (1998).

—— 'West Indian Doctors in London', *Journal of Caribbean History*, 20/1 (1986).

GREWAL, S., KAY, J., LANDOR, L., LEWIS, G., and PARMAR, P., *Charting the Journey: Writings by Black and Third World Women* (1988).

GRIFFITH, C. E., *The African Dream: Martin R. Delany and the Emergence of Pan-African Thought* (1975).

GRIMSHAW, ANNA (ed.), *The C. L. R. James Reader* (1992).

GUNDARA, JAGDISH S., and DUFFIELD, IAN (eds.), *Essays on the History of Blacks in Britain* (1992).

GUPTA, R. (ed.), *From Homemakers to Jailbreakers: Southall Black Sisters* (2003).

HALL, KIM F., *Things of Darkness: Economies of Race and Gender in Early Modern England* (1995).

HALL, STUART, *Policing the Crisis: Mugging, the State, and Law and Order* (1978).

—— (ed.), *Culture, Media, Language: Working Papers in Cultural Studies, 1972–79* (1980).

—— and SEALY, MARK, *Different: A Historical Content. Contemporary Photographs and Black Identity* (2001).

HANNAFORD, IVAN, *Race: The History of an Idea in the West* (1996).

HARDY, PHIL, *The Faber Companion to Twentieth Century Popular Music* (2001).

HART, RICHARD, *From Occupation to Independence: A Short History of the Peoples of the English-Speaking Caribbean* (1998).

HAZELWOOD, NICK, *The Queen's Slave Trader: John Hawkyns, Elizabeth I, and the Trafficking in Human Souls* (2004).

HEINEMAN, BENJAMIN W., JR., *The Politics of the Powerless: A Study of the Campaign Against Racial Discrimination* (1972).

HENNESSY, ALISTAIR (ed.), *Intellectuals in the Twentieth Century Caribbean* (1992).

HERBERT, M., *Never Counted Out: The Story of Len Johnson, Manchester's Black Boxing Hero and Communist* (1992).

HEUMAN, GAD, *'The Killing Time': The Morant Bay Rebellion in Jamaica* (1994).

HOFFENBERG, PETER, *An Empire on Display: English, Indian and Australian Exhibitions from the Crystal Palace to the Great War* (2001).

HOGGART, RICHARD, *The Uses of Literacy: Aspects of Working Class Life with Special Reference to Publications and Entertainments* (1957).

HOOD, R., *Race and Sentencing* (1992).

HOWAT, G., *Learie Constantine* (1975).

HUNT, JAMES D., *Gandhi in London* (1993).

IFEKWUNIGWE, JAYNE O., *Scattered Belongings: Cultural Paradoxes of 'Race', Nation and Gender* (1999).
ILIFFE, JOHN, *East African Doctors: A History of the Modern Medical Profession* (1998).
INNES, C. L., *A History of Black and Asian Writing in Britain 1700–2000* (2002).
IRELAND, STANLEY, *Roman Britain* (1986).

JAMES, C. L. R., *Beyond a Boundary* (1963).
—— *The Black Jacobins: Toussaint L'Ouverture and the San Domingo Revolution* (1989).
JAMES, LOUIS, *Writers from the Caribbean* (1990).
JAY, MIKE, *The Unfortunate Colonel Despard* (2004).
JONES, ELDRED, *Othello's Countrymen: The African in English Renaissance Drama* (1965).
JONES, SIMON, *Black Culture, White Youth: The Reggae Tradition from JA to UK* (1988).
JUDD, DENIS, *Empire: The British Imperial Experience from 1765 to the Present* (1996).

KABBANI, RANA, *Imperial Fictions: Europe's Myths of the Orient* (1994).
KARRAS, A. R., *Sojourners in the Sun: Scottish Migrants in Jamaica and the Chesapeake, 1740–1800* (1992).
KATHISH, HATASHIL MASHA, *The Ethiopian Valley: The Story of the People Called the Dinkas* (1905).
KENYATTA, JOMO, *Facing Mount Kenya: The Tribal Life of the Gikuyu* (1938).
KESLEY, HARRY, *Sir John Hawkins: Queen Elizabeth's Slave Trader* (2003).
KILLINGRAY, DAVID, 'Beneath the Wilberforce Oak', *International Bulletin of Missionary Research*, 21/3 (1997).
—— 'The Black Atlantic Missionary Movement and Africa, 1780s–1920s', *Journal of Religion in Africa*, 33/1 (2002).
KING, REYAHN, SANDHU, SUKHDEV, WALVIN, JAMES, and GIRDHAM, JANE, *Ignatius Sancho, an African Man of Letters* (1997).
KNIGHT, FRANKLIN W., *The Caribbean: Genesis of a Fragmented Nationalism* (1990).
KOHN, MAREK, *Dope Girls: The Birth of the British Drug Underground* (1992).
KORTE, BARBARA, and STERNBERG, CLAUDIA, *Bidding for the Mainstream? Black and Asian British Film Since the 1990s* (2004).
KUPER, ADAM, *Anthropologists and Anthropology: The British School 1922–1972* (1973).

LAMMING, GEORGE, *The Pleasures of Exile* (1960).
LARKIN, COLIN (ed.), *The Guinness Encyclopaedia of Popular Music*, i (1992).
LAW, I., and HENFREY, J. (eds.), *A History of Race and Racism in Liverpool 1660–1950* (1981).
LAWLESS, R. I., *From Ta'izz to Tyneside: An Arab Community in the North-East of England During the Early Twentieth Century* (1995).
LAYTON-HENRY, ZIG, *The Politics of Immigration* (1992).
LEE, A. ROBERT, *Other Britain, Other British: Contemporary Multicultural Fiction* (1995).
LITTLE, KENNETH, *Negroes in Britain: A Study of Race Relations in English Society* (1947).
LLWYD, A., *Cymru Ddu/Black Wales: A History of Black Welsh People* (2005).
LORIMER, DOUGLAS A., *Colour, Class and the Victorians: English Attitudes to the Negro in the Mid-Nineteenth Century* (1978).
LOTZ, RAINER E., *Black People: Entertainers of African Descent in Europe and Germany* (1997).
—— and PEGG, IAN (eds.), *Under the Imperial Carpet: Essays in Black History 1780–1950* (1986).
LYNCH, HOLLIS R., *Edward Wilmot Blyden: Pan-Negro Patriot 1832–1912* (1967).

MCCALMAN, IAIN, *Radical Underworld: Prophets, Revolutionaries and Pornographers in London, 1795–1840* (1988).
MACKEITH, LUCY, *Local Black History: A Beginning in Devon* (2003).
MCLAUGHLIN, TIMOTHY GLEN, *Appeal to the Empire: African Appeals to Great Britain, 1881–1914* (1984).
MACPHERSON, WILLIAM, *The Stephen Lawrence Inquiry: Report of an Inquiry by Sir William MacPherson, Presented to Parliament by the Secretary of State for the Home Department by Command of Her Majesty, February 1999* (1999).
MAKDISI, SAREE, *Romantic Imperialism: Universal Empire and the Culture of Modernity* (1998).
MAKONNEN, RAS, *Pan-Africanism from Within* (1973).
MALIK, SARITA, *Representing Black Britain: A History of Black and Asian Images on Television* (2001).
MARSH, JAN (ed.) *Black Victorians: Black People in British Art 1800–1900* (2005).
MARTIN, STEVE, *Britain's Slave Trade* (1999).
MARTIN, TONY, *Amy Ashwood Garvey: Pan African, Feminist and Wife No. 1* (2001).
MATAR, NABIL, *Islam in Britain* (1998).
MAY, ROY, and COHEN, ROBIN, 'The Interaction Between Race and Colonialism: The Liverpool Race Riots of 1919', *Race and Class*, 16/2 (1974).
MERCER, KOBENA, *Welcome to the Jungle: Positions in Black Cultural Studies* (1994).
MIRZA, H. S. (ed.), *Black British Feminism: A Reader* (1997).
MITCHELL, HAROLD, *Europe in the Caribbean: The Policies of Great Britain, France and the Netherlands Towards Their West Indian Territories in the Twentieth Century* (1963).
MOCKLER, ANTHONY, *Haile Selassie's War* (1984).

MORGAN, K., *Edward Colston and Bristol* (1999).
—— *Slavery, Atlantic Trade and the British Economy 1660–1800* (2000).
MUKASA, HAM, *Uganda's Katikiro in England* (1998).
MYERS, NORMA, *Reconstructing the Black Past: Blacks in Britain, 1780–1830* (1996).
MYERS, WALTER DEAN, *At Her Majesty's Request: An African Princess in Victorian England* (1999).

NASTA, S., *Critical Perspectives on Sam Selvon* (1998).
NATHAN, HANS, *Dan Emmett and the Rise of Early Negro Minstrelsy* (1962).
NELSON, CARY, and GROSSBERG, LAWRENCE (eds.), *Marxism and the Interpretation of Culture* (1988).
NICOL, DAVIDSON, *Africanus Horton: The Dawn of Nationalism in Modern Africa* (1969).
NJAMI, S. (ed.), *Africa Remix: Contemporary Art of a Continent* (2005).
NOBLE, E. MARTIN, *Jamaica Airman* (1984).
NORTH, MICHAEL, *The Dialect of Modernism: Race, Language and Twentieth-Century Literature* (1994).

OGG, ALEX, *The Hip Hop Years* (1999).
OGUIBE, O., and ENWEZOR, O. (eds.), *Reading the Contemporary: African Art from Theory to the Marketplace* (2000).
OLIVER, PAUL (ed.), *Black Music in Britain: Essays on the Afro-Asian Contribution to Popular Music* (1990).

PADMORE, GEORGE, *Pan-Africanism or Communism?* (1956).
PANAYI, P. (ed.), *Racial Violence in Britain in the Nineteenth and Twentieth Centuries* (1996).
PANKHURST, RICHARD, *Sylvia Pankhurst, Counsel for Ethiopia* (2003).
PARKER, DAVID, and SONG, MIRI (eds.), *Rethinking 'Mixed Race'* (2001).
PARSONS, NEIL, *King Khama, Emperor Joe, and the Great White Queen: Victorian Britain Through African Eyes* (1998).
PATTON, ADELL, JR., *Physicians, Colonial Racism and Diaspora in West Africa* (1996).
PERRY, BRUCE (ed.), *Malcolm X: The Last Speeches* (1989).
PHILLIPS, MIKE, and PHILLIPS, TREVOR, *Windrush: The Irresistible Rise of Multi-Racial Britain* (1998).
PHILLIPS, TOM (ed.), *Africa: The Art of a Continent* (1995).
PICTON, J. (ed.), *Image and Form in Africa: Prints Drawings and Sculpture from Southern Africa and Nigeria* (1997).
—— *et al.*, *The Art of African Textiles: Technology, Tradition and Lurex* (1995).
PILKINGTON, E., *Beyond the Mother Country: West Indians and the Notting Hill White Riots* (1998).
PINES, JIM (ed.), *Black and White in Colour: Black People in British Television Since 1936* (1992).
PLAATJE, SOL, *The Boer War Diary of Sol T. Plaatje, an African at Mafeking* (ed. John L. Comaroff, 1973).
—— *Native Life in South Africa* (1916).
PORTER, BERNARD, *Critics of Empire: British Radical Attitudes to Colonialism in Africa 1895–1914* (1968).
POTASH, C. (ed.), *Reggae, Rasta, Revolution: Jamaican Music from Ska to Dub* (1997).
POTKAY, ADAM, and BURR, SANDRA (eds.), *Black Atlantic Writers of the Eighteenth Century: Living the New Exodus in England and the Americas* (1995).
PRINCE, MARY, *The History of Mary Prince, a West Indian Slave, as Related by Herself* (ed. Moira Ferguson, 1987, rev. edn., 1997).
PROCTER, JAMES, *Dwelling Places: Postwar Black British Writing* (2003).
—— (ed.), *Writing Black Britain 1948–1998: An Interdisciplinary Anthology* (2000).
PULIS, JOHN W. (ed.), *Moving On: Black Loyalists in the Afro-Atlantic World* (1999).

RAMCHAND, K., *Sam Selvon* (2004).
RAMDIN, RON, *The Making of the Black Working Class in Britain* (1987).
RAMPTON, BEN, *Crossing: Language and Ethnicity Among Adolescents* (1995).
RATCLIFFE, PETER, *Racism and Reaction: A Profile of Handsworth* (1981).
—— (ed.), *The Politics of Social Science Research: 'Race', Ethnicity and Social Change* (2001).
REYNOLDS, HARRY, *Minstrel Memories: The Story of Burnt Cork Minstrelsy in Great Britain from 1836 to 1927* (1928).
REYNOLDS, TRACEY, *Caribbean Mothering: Identity and Experience in the UK* (2005).
RICE, A., *Radical Narratives of the Black Atlantic* (2003).
RICH, PAUL B., *Race and Empire in British Politics* (1986; 2nd edn., 1990).
RICHARDSON, ALAN (ed.), *Slavery, Abolition and Emancipation: Writings in the British Romantic Period*, iv: *Verse* (1999).
ROBINSON, JANE, *Mary Seacole* (2005).
RODNEY, WALTER, *How Europe Underdeveloped Africa* (1972; rev. edn., 1988).
ROGOZINSKI, JAN, *A Brief History of the Caribbean: From the Arawak and Carib to the Present* (1999).
ROSE, ELIOT JOSEPH BENN, *et al.*, *Colour and Citizenship* (1969).
ROSE, SONYA O., 'Girls and GIs: Race, Sex, and Diplomacy in Second World War Britain', *International History Review*, 19 (1997).
ROSS, KAREN, *Black and White Media: Black Images in Popular Film and Television* (1996).

SAGGAR, S., *Race and Representation* (2000).

SAID, EDWARD, *Covering Islam: How the Media and the Experts Determine How We See the Rest of the World* (1997).

—— *Culture and Imperialism* (1993).

—— *Orientalism: Western Conceptions of the Orient* (rev. edn., 1995).

SALKEY, ANDREW, *Jamaica* (1973).

SAMANTRAI, R., *AlterNatives: Black Feminism in the Postimperial Nation* (2002).

SANCHO, IGNATIUS, *The Letters of Ignatius Sancho* (ed. Paul Edwards and Polly Rewt, 1994).

SANDERS, RONALD, *Crumbled Small: The Commonwealth Caribbean in World Politics* (2005).

SANDHU, SUKHDEV, *London Calling: How Black and Asian Writers Imagined a City* (2003).

SCARMAN, LORD, *The Scarman Report: The Brixton Disorders 10–12 April 1981* (1981).

SCHAMA, SIMON, *Rough Crossings: Britain, the Slaves and the American Revolution* (2005).

SEACOLE, MARY, *Wonderful Adventures of Mrs. Seacole in Many Lands* (ed. Sara Salih, 2005).

SEALEY, MARK (ed.), *Vanley Burke: A Retrospective* (1993).

SEBBA, MARK, *London Jamaican: Language Systems in Interaction* (1993).

SEMMEL, BERNARD, *The Governor Eyre Controversy* (1962).

SESAY, KADIJA (ed.), *Write Black, Write British: From Post Colonial to Black British* (2005).

SEYBOLD, W. N., *The Loss of the Troopship Empire Windrush* (1998).

SEYMOUR, A. J., 'The Poetry of Egbert Martin', *Kyk-Over-Al*, 1/3 (1946).

SHEPPERSON, G., 'Notes on Negro American References and the Emergence of African Nationalism', *Journal of African History*, 1/5 (1960).

SHERWOOD, MARIKA, *Many Struggles: West Indian Workers and Service Personnel in Britain (1939–45)* (1985).

—— *Pastor Daniels Ekarte and the African Churches Mission* (1994).

—— PRESCOTT, COLIN, and HINES, DONALD, *Claudia Jones: A Life in Exile* (2000).

SHUKRA, K., *The Changing Pattern of Black Politics in Britain* (1998).

SHYLLON, F. O., *Black People in Britain 1555–1833* (1977).

—— *Black Slaves in Britain* (1974).

—— *James Ramsay: The Unknown Abolitionist* (1977).

SIMPSON, ALAN, *Stacking the Decks: A Study of Race, Inequality and Council Housing in Nottingham* (1981).

SINCLAIR, N. M. C., *The Tiger Bay Story* (2003).

SMITH, GRAHAM, *When Jim Crow Met John Bull: Black American Soldiers in World War II Britain* (1987).

SMITH, RICHARD, *Jamaican Volunteers in the First World War: Race, Masculinity and the Development of National Consciousness* (2004).

SMITH MCCREA, ROSALIE, 'Dis-Ordering the World in the Eighteenth Century: The Voyage of the *Sable Venus*. Connoisseurship and the Trivialising of Slavery' in Sandra Courtman (ed.), *Beyond the Blood, the Beach and the Banana: New Perspectives in Caribbean Studies* (2004).

SNOWDEN, FRANK, *Blacks in Antiquity* (1970).

SOGA, TIYO, *The Journal and Selected Writings of the Reverend Tiyo Soga* (ed. Donovan Williams, 1983).

SOLOMOS, JOHN, *Race and Racism in Britain* (2003).

SOMERVILLE, CHRISTOPHER, *Our War: How the British Commonwealth Fought the Second World War* (1998).

SONG, MIRI, *Choosing Ethnic Identity* (2003).

SOUTHERN, EILEEN, *Biographical Dictionary of Afro-American and African Musicians* (1982).

STEIN, MARK, *Black British Literature: Novels of Transformation* (2004).

STERLING, DOROTHY, *Black Foremothers: Three Lives* (1998).

STREATFEILD, D., *Cocaine: An Unauthorised Biography* (2001).

SUDBURY, J., *'Other Kinds of Dreams': Black Women's Organisations and the Politics of Transformation* (1998).

SUTCLIFFE, DAVID, *British Black English* (1982).

SYPHER, WYLIE, *Guinea's Captive Kings: British Anti-Slavery Literature of the XVIIIth Century* (1942).

TABILI, L., *'We Ask for British Justice': Workers and Racial Difference in Late Imperial Britain* (1994).

THOMAS, HELEN SARAH, *Romanticism and Slave Narratives: Transatlantic Testimonies* (2000).

THOMAS, J. J., *Froudacity: West Indian Fables by James Anthony Froude, Explained by J. J. Thomas* (1889), with biographical note by Donald Wood, introd. C. L. R. James (1969).

—— *The Theory and Practice of Creole Grammar* (1869), introd. Gertrud Aub-Buscher (1969).

TIZARD, BARBARA, and PHOENIX, ANNE, *Black, White, or Mixed Race?* (1993).

TULLOCH, C. (ed.), *Black Style* (2004).

TURNER, BRIAN S., *Orientalism, Postmodernism and Globalism* (1994).

VASILI, PHIL, *Colouring Over the White Line: The History of Black Footballers in Britain* (2000).

—— *The First Black Footballer: Arthur Wharton (1865–1930). An Absence of Memory* (1998).

VEHANEN, KOSH, *Marian Anderson: A Portrait* (1941).

VEIT-WILD, FLORA, *Dambudzo Marechera: A Sourcebook on His Life and Work* (2002).
VINCENT, RICKEY, *Funk: The Music, the People and the Rhythm of the One* (1996).
VISRAM, R., *Ayahs, Lascars, and Princes: Indians in Britain 1700–1947* (1986).

WADE, MICHAEL, *Peter Abrahams* (1971).
WALEY, DANIEL, *British Public Opinion and the Ethiopian War* (1976).
WALKER, EDWARD, *English Ragtime: A Discography* (2000).
WALMSLEY, ANNE, *The Caribbean Artists Movement 1966–1972: A Literary and Cultural History* (1992).
—— (ed.), *Guyana Dreaming: The Art of Aubrey Williams* (1990).
WALVIN, JAMES, *An African's Life: The Life and Times of Olaudah Equiano 1745–1797* (1998).
—— *Black and White: The Negro and English Society, 1555–1945* (1973).
—— *Black Ivory: Slavery in the British Empire* (1994).
WAMBU, ONYEKACHI, *Empire Windrush: Fifty Years of Black Writing About Britain* (1998).
WHITE, SARAH, HARRIS, ROXY, and BEEZMOHUN, SHARMILLA (eds.), *A Meeting of the Continents: History, Memories, Organisation, and Programmes 1982–1995* (2005).
WILLAN, BRIAN, *Sol Plaatje, South African Nationalist, 1876–1932* (1984).
WILLIAMS, CHARLOTTE, EVANS, NEIL, and O'LEARY, PAUL (eds.), *A Tolerant Nation? Exploring Ethnic Diversity in Wales* (2003).
WILLIAMS, ERIC, *Capitalism and Slavery* (1944).
WILSON, A. *Finding a Voice: Asian Women in Britain* (1978).
WOOD, MARCUS, *Blind Memory: Visual Representations of Slavery in England and America 1780–1865* (2000).

X, MALCOLM, and HALEY, ALEX, *The Autobiography of Malcolm X* (1965).

YELLIN, JEAN FAGAN, *Harriet Jacobs: A Life* (1987).
YOUNG, LOLA, *Fear of the Dark: 'Race', Gender and Sexuality in the Cinema* (1996).
—— *Guide to the Bernie Grant Archive* (2004).
YOUNG, ROBERT C., *Colonial Desire: Hybridity in Theory, Culture and Race* (1995).

Select Index